The
Renaissance
New
Testament

Randolph O. Yeager

VOLUME FIVE

John 5:1—6:71
Mark 2:23—9:8
Luke 6:1—9:36

PELICAN PUBLISHING COMPANY

GRETNA 1980

Library of Congress Cataloging in Publication Data

The Renaissance New Testament.
Volumes 1-4 originally published in 1976-1978 by
Renaissance Press, Bowling Green, Ky.
    1. Bible. N.T.—Concordances, Greek. 2. Greek
language, Biblical. I. Title.
BS2302.Y4 1981   225.4'8'0321   79-28652
ISBN 0-88289-257-6 (v. 5)

Manufactured in the United States of America

Published by Pelican Publishing Company, Inc.
1101 Monroe Street, Gretna, Louisiana 70053

To

Gaylen, Linda, Lyn and Bret

my son, daughter-in-law, granddaughter and grandson

Preface

WHY MINISTERS SHOULD USE THE GREEK NEW TESTAMENT

By Julius Robert Mantey

With the marvelous gospel we have to preach, we ministers should do everything possible to equip ourselves to do the maximum in order to preach it worthily. The discipline and development, alone, received in mastering Greek will add increased power and efficiency to the student. Without this knowledge the deeper things and the underlying currents of truths in the New Testament will be just beyond his reach. It is an unspeakable thrill and asset to know that you know a thing, expecially to have firsthand knowledge of a word or a statement that came from the pen of the inspired writer. We see the gospel truth in new settings and with fuller meaning. Every paragraph and often every verse suggests thoughts that otherwise would elude us. Knowledge of the Greek helps us to know accurately the will of the Lord, to sense and catch the spirit and zeal of the inspired writer, and to declare the matchless gospel with authority and power.

Hundreds of passages, when read in the Greek, become illumined and take on new meanings and furnish fresh, vital sermon material. For example, the fact that the main verbs in Matthew 16:19 are future perfect passive in form gives us just the opposite translation from what we find in our regular versions. "Whatsoever ye shall bind on earth shall have been bound in heaven, and whatsoever ye shall loose on earth shall have been loosed in heaven." Dr. C.B.Williams, in his modern speech *New Testament* so translates these verses.

Matthew 18:18 should be translated the same way, for the same verbs, but in the plural number, occur there; also, John 20:23, because the verbs *forgive* and *retain* are in the perfect tense, when translated literally, reads, "Whosoever sins ye forgive, they have been forgiven; whosoever sins ye retain, they have been retained." All three passages teach that man is to ratify and concur in what God has done. And the inference is that only regenerate people should be allowed to become church members. These passages are quoted in the Catholic Encyclopedia as the Scripture basis for their claim that the pope and priests can forgive sins, and that God concurs in that forgiveness. Of course, the whole trend of the New Testament is against such a conception, as well as is a correct translation of these verses.

Knowledge of Greek also helps us with the error of the claims made by perfectionists who say they have been sanctified and never sin any more. The command in Eph.5:18 implies frequent or continued filling and not just one act, for the present tense is used - "Be filled (time after time) with the Spirit." This agrees with the frequent fillings recorded in Acts. I John 3:8,9, properly translated, reads, "He that continues sinning is of the devil . . . He that is born of God does not continue sinning, because the seed of God abides in him and he is not able to continue sinning." The verbs for *sin* are in the present tense and imply action going on, not a single act as the perfectionists interpret these verses."

-Dr. Mantey is author with H.E.Dana of *A Manual Grammar of the Greek New Testament,* and with E.C.Colwell of *A Hellenistic Greek Reader with Vocabulary."* He is Professor Emeritus of New Testament Interpretation of Northern Baptist Theological Seminary and he lives in active retirement in New Port Richey, Florida.

Introduction

THE MAN WITH THE HOE

Written After Seeing the Painting by Millet

God made man in His own image, in the image of God made He him.

-Genesis

Bowed by the weight of centuries he leans
Upon his hoe and gazes on the ground,
The emptiness of ages in his face,
And on his back the burden of the world.
Who made him dead to rapture and despair,
A thing that grieves not and that never hopes,
Stolid and stunned, a brother to the ox?
Who loosened and let down this brutal jaw?
Whose was the hand that slanted back this brow?
Whose breath blew out the light within this brain?

Is this the Thing the Lord God made and gave
To have dominion over sea and land,
To trace the stars and search the heavens for power,
To feel the passion of Eternity?
Is this the Dream He dreamed who shaped the suns
And pillared the blue firmament with light?
Down all the stretch of hell to its last gulf
There is no shape more terrible than this-
More tongued with censure of the world's blind greed-
More filled with signs and portents for the soul-
More fraught with menace to the universe.

What gulfs between him and the seraphim!
Slaves of the wheel of labor, what to him
Are Plato and the swing of Pleiades?
What the long reaches of the peaks of song,
The rift of dawn, the reddening of the rose?
Through this dread shape the suffering ages look;
Time's tragedy is in that aching stoop;
Through this dread shape humanity betrayed,
Plundered, profaned, and disinherited,
Cried protest to the Judges of the World,
A protest that is also prophecy.

O masters, lords, and rulers in all lands,
Is this the handiwork you give to God,
This monstrous thing distorted and soul-quenched?
How will you ever straighten up this shape,
Touch it again with immortality;
Give back the upward looking and the light;
Rebuild in it the music and the dream;
Make right the immemorial infamies,
Perfidious wrongs, immedicable woes?

O masters, lords, and rulers in all lands,
How will the Future reckon with this Man?
How answer his brute question in that hour
When whirlwinds of rebellion shake the world?
How will it be with kingdoms and with kings-
With those who shaped him to the thing he is-
When this dumb Terror shall reply to God,
After the silence of the centuries?

Edwin Markham

The Man With the Hoe, the subject of Millet's painting and of Markham's poem, was a victim of the economic and social exploitation imposed upon him by the feudal lords and therefore a culturally deprived victim of the injustice of the Middle Ages.

Our world, in the last quarter of the twentieth century, also produces the man with the hoe, despite the fact that we have advanced far beyond Medieval standards in terms of political and economic development. He is still "bowed by the weight of centuries" and he also leans, not upon his hoe, but upon whatever happens to be near and "gazes on the ground" with "the emptiness of ages in his face and on his back the burden of the world." A part of this burden is his own unbelief and the superficiality which accompanies it.

Somebody has made him "dead to rapture and despair." We call it apathy or malaise. He is "a thing that grieves not and that never hopes." If it be objected that we ought not to call him a "thing" it can be conceded that according to a biology textbook he is a person, not a thing, but when we measure him against the standard of "the Lord God (who) made (him) and gave to have dominion over sea and land, to trace the stars and search the heavens for power, to feel the passion of eternity," we can conclude that he is indeed only a "thing." He certainly is no seraph. He seldom grieves; he never hopes; he is "stolid and stunned, a brother to the ox."

Whom shall we blame? Who should bear the moral responsibility for this unfortunate product of "man's day?" (I Cor.4:3). Timothy Leary, the high priest of drug addiction comes to mind. The education professor who misinterpreted John Dewey at the expense of academic standards with the result that Johnny can neither read writing nor write reading. Do not forget B.F.Skinner whose fear of the environment suggested that the only safety could be found in a box. Karl Marx, who thought that the man with the hoe was only a thing and therefore taught, with considerable logic that he could only react to an impersonal environment until his world crashes in chaos about him. The Church also must be indicted since she has produced a litter of preachers who do not believe the Bible and have substituted a diet of unitarian deism for the Reformed theology.

It has always been fashionable to blame something or somebody for our plight. Casca, plotting to murder Caesar, whom he regarded as a tyrant, was not a determinist. He believed that he had some control over events:

> "Men at some time are masters of their fates:
> The fault, dear Brutus, is not in our stars,
> But in ourselves, that we are underlings."

> —Julius Caesar, Acts I, Scene I, 139-141

Brutus, Skinner, Marx and all other environmental determinists have a way to escape moral responsibility for what happens. Astrologers ask you the precise time of your birth, consult a horoscope and then tell you whether or not it is worthwhile to get out of bed in the morning. Brutus also laid it all on the stars. If this is valid then this is the "age of Aquarius" and we ought all to take off our clothes and dance.

Marx said that all of the trouble could be laid at the doorstep of the capitalist mode of production. The profit motive was the culprit. Skinner thinks that it is sociology. Flip Wilson says that the devil made him do it. Democrats and Republicans blame each other.

Who is the real enemy?

We meet him every day. He is with us constantly. We have lunch with him. We sleep with him. We play golf with him. We know him very well indeed. Pogo knows. "We have met the enemy and *he is us*." Of course Pogo did not go to the Teachers' College. Instead he read his Bible and that is the reason why the modern man with the hoe pays no more attention to him than he would any other 'possum in the swamp.

The modern man with the hoe sits in the seat of the scornful. He says that he knows enough to know that he knows utterly nothing. Total agnosticism is the hallmark of this pseudointellectual who fancies himself a social aristocrat, though his banker knows what a pauper he is. He can be found anywhere - in the college classroom, on the board of deacons and even on occasion in the pulpit. Most theological seminary student bodies can provide a sample or two.

He has lost the art of entertaining himself. The inner springs of creativity cast up only mire, sludge and dirt. Beset with intolerable ennui he turns with resignation to the greatest source of boredom which our culture has yet produced. There is some justification for calling it "the boob tube." He sits in its holy presence, looks at and listens to seven minute segments of sex, violence and dialogue, both vapid and vacuous, interspersed with an exasperating stream of commercials, recorded at a volume level that destroys his auditory anatomy, and seeking to sell him hair tonic, tootn paste, peanut butter, Time magazine, the latest reducing formula and American Express travellers' checks.

Occasionally he may go to church. Society demands it on Easter Sunday, Christmas Eve, when the boss dies or his mother comes to visit. There, if he is fortunate enough to have been the object of divine guidance, he will find a true man of God - a hard working student of the Greek New Testament, with a love for the message of God's grace and a sincere desire to point him to the cross.

But if directed, not by God, but by society, he will find another man with the hoe.

Pulpit hoemen come in two types so all of the customers can be served. There is a model who thinks that he has outgrown the Word of God and cannot therefore waste his time in examining its message. He does not wish to get involved in exegesis. The reason he gives is not the real one. It is hard work and calls for a sophistication of which he is incapable. So he damns it with faint praise by alluding to some remote passage and forthwith departs from it to deliver a quasi-socio-psycho-economico-politico-religious lecture upon some theme with which he is currently fascinated.

Any text will do, since he plans to disregard it anyhow. For hoeman type one we suggest the observation of Jacob to his mother in Genesis 27:11 - "Behold, Esau my brother is a hairy man, and I am a smooth man." With a little ingenuity that text can relate to most anything that the preacher has in mind - for example what would happen if the Russians dropped a hydrogen bomb on New York City. The conclusion would follow that Congress ought to abolish the Department of Defense or, failing that, Christians ought to refuse to pay their income tax.

Pulpit hoeman type two occupies the other end of the continuum. This type went to the Bible Institute a year or two, or, better yet, he bought a Doctor of Divinity degree for fifty dollars. He has mastered the message of the Bible so thoroughly that there is nothing more in its pages to be revealed that he does not know. Can we expect an expository sermon? Far from it. He is a textual or a topical homiletician. Why else would he have "Handfuls on Purpose" in his library? So the Word of God is robbed of its opportunity to fall with the impact of a ton of bricks upon an audience. The sermon will have an introduction, followed by three points, preferably alliterative, and a poem, after which the congregation will rise and sing "Just As I Am."

Whether then we are speaking of the deistic existentialist or the bigoted fundamentalist, the result is the same. The former ignores while the latter neglects the Greek New Testament. Both the contempt for the Bible that stems from unbelief and the intellectual sloth that is the rotten fruit of a moribund fundamentalism contributes to the same sad result. The Greek New Testament is becoming a neglected and all but forgotten book and its supernatural message is being widely ignored.

It is customary for preachers to say something religious during a church service. So what comes from the pulpit, whether occupied by a skeptical modernist or a dogmatic fundamentalist is a soporific seepage of inconsequential verbiage, garnished with periodic Vesuvian eruptions of turgid oratory. If the auditors are thinking of anything except suppressed profanity, they are reminded of the Time magazine commercial. However in this case the phone call isn't free!

Pulpit oratory like this, devoid of perspicuity, perspicacity, force and elegance has replaced the earnest exposition of the Word of God as it was practised by the Apostles. It does nothing to call the elect for whom Christ died and whom the Holy Spirit is seeking, to repentance and faith. It does nothing to encourage Christians to behave themselves in keeping with the ethics of Jesus Christ.

The Bible itself has told us of this development which is to characterize the closing days of the church age. Amos wrote, "Behold, the days come, saith the Lord God, that I will send a famine in the land, not a famine of bread, nor a thirst of water, but of hearing the words of the Lord" (Amos 8:11). The sad result of this dearth of Bible exposition is that ". . . they shall wander from sea to sea, and from the north even to the east, they shall run to and fro to seek the word of the Lord, and shall not find it."

The culture that ignores the Greek New Testament with its monopolistic solution to man's dilemmas and its cure for his soul sorrow is a culture that produces the man with the hoe. Thus he stands in the bar at the country club - affluent, well dressed, well paid, overfed, oversexed, over entertained and gazes into his drink and wonders why he is so vaguely discontented, while his counterpart stands on the curb in the ghetto, hungry, wretched, rat bitten, undernourished, drug and liquor addicted, sexually exploited, "tongued with censure of the world's blind greed, . . . filled with signs and portents for the soul - . . fraught with menace to the universe."

"Through (these dread shapes) humanity betrayed, Plundered, profaned and disinherited, cries protest to the Judges of the world, a protest that is also prophecy."

Our ship of state has washed up upon the shore the bits and pieces of this flotsam and jetsam of human wreckage because we have ignored the Bible and have therefore failed to appreciate the sweep and scope of its solution to the human problem.

Divine revelation is both cogent and trenchant. It reveals, not all that God knows, for He knows it all, but all that He knows we need to know in order to avoid the frustrations which everyone experiences in his own psyche, which, if not resolved produces the conflicts in society (James 4:1-3). Modern men ". . . turn every one to his own way" (Isa.53:6) and, influenced by environmental forces which he neither fully understands, nor is able to control, he has painted himself into a corner.

Mary Wollstonecraft Shelley, pressured in all philosophical directions by her father, William Godwin, whose theoretical pendulum swung wildly from Sandaman's hyper-calvinism to anarchism and back again, and by her pagan husband, Percy Bysshe Shelley, thought it through and figured it out. The result was *Frankenstein*, a tale of horror, written 160 years ago, about a scientist who created a manlike monster, which, out of control, turned on his inventor and killed him and all of his loved ones. Thus with remarkable prescience this unhappy girl described the plight of the world in the closing quarter of the twentieth century. Frankenstein gave us the industrial revolution, with its sophisticated technology, its urbanization, the affluence of its burgeoning gross national product and the leisure time of its shortened work week, but the monster was armed with smokestacks which belch pollution into the air and sewers that pour chemical poisons into the water. Its voracious maw devours scarce raw materials and its power unit demands more energy than dwindling supplies of fossil fuels can provide. The result? A superfluity of gadgets which we do not need and which only keep us from our Bibles, time on our hands that we have not the sophistication to use profitably, inflation that causes our treasures of earth to erode until all but the idle rich are in poverty, decadent city slums, where rats compete with little children for living space and personality disequilibrium that produces more crime in the streets than the police power of society can control. How could a girl in the early nineteenth century have been so remarkably prophetic? The tragedy is that, while Mary Wollstonecraft Shelley was perceptive enough to predict the zombie more than a century before he began to wreak his vengeance upon society, his victims seem unable to recognize what he is doing to us. Economists understand the monster. We know where he came from, where he is, what he is doing and why he is doing it.

Frankenstein was looking for a higher standard of living. This is legitimate enough. But for all the benefits of the industrial revolution it was not an unmixed blessing. The word benefit, spoken in the presence of an economist, immediately suggests a cost/benefit analysis. We speak of the TANSTAAFL principle which means "There ain't no such thing as a free lunch." Wisdom dictates that Frankenstein's monster can be tolerated only so long as the benefits which he provides exceed his costs. Now it is time for us to ask whether social and personal utility which the monster provides is worth the universal disutility which he imposes upon us.

No one knows at this writing where we are on God's clock. There have been dark days before, but historians know that society has been remarkably resilient. The Italian Renaissance rescued the Middle Ages from its torpor. Embattled farmers at Concord Bridge fired a shot heard round the world to announce that democracy was to be given a chance in an unspoiled environment. The French Revolution checked the excesses of Absolutism in Europe. Though the general moral trend of world society is downward, the plunge has been interrupted again and again by spiritual revivals during which man has returned to the Bible and to Christ. Dwight L.Moody, Billy Sunday and Billy Graham, among others have been used of God to lead the faltering footsteps of sinful man back into the paths of light and social utility.

But the New Testament is clear that for all of the revival fires which burn from time to time, this age is to end in chaos. It is "man's day." He stood before a Roman governor and said, "We will not have this man to reign over us." That was the day that the Light of the World was murdered. On that day the night came when no man can work (John 9:4). The only constructive work done since Calvary, where Jesus Christ finished His work, is that of the Holy Spirit Who has since been engaged in convincing the elect of "sin (because they believe not on Christ), of righteousness (because Jesus went back to the Father and we see Him no more) and of judgment (because at Calvary the prince of this world was judged)" (John 16:7-11).

Not that man has not tried to work. His efforts have been prodigious and now that he thinks his goal is in sight, they are frenetic. He rejected the Son of God, Plato's Philosopher-King, the Light of the World, the Way, the Truth and the Life. He murdered Messiah and sent Him to what was presumed to be a permanent grave. Now that Incarnate Deity has been summarily bowed out of His world and dismissed as unneeded and unwanted, it is up to man to bring in the kingdom and thus demonstrate that he doesn't need the King. But what man has never realized, or if realized has been unwilling to admit, is that "the flesh profiteth nothing" (John 6:63). It is the Holy Spirit Who makes alive. So in economic terms, when we look at this differential equation in a cost/benefit analysis it appears that unregenerate man's little dog and pony show has been all cost and no benefit. God, in His wisdom has allowed it to go on, only because He wanted to "... visit the Gentiles, to take out of them a people for his name." (Acts 15:14).

Adam and Eve rebelled against divine authority in the age of innocence and were driven in tears and sweat from Paradise. The ante-dilluvians rejected God and His laws in the age of conscience and perished in the flood. Then came a period of human government when man became so technological that he began his trip to the moon. He might have made it but for a widespread collapse of communications, as a result of which each man fled in search of someone he could understand. Under law mankind, albeit with fleshly effort, tried to be as moral as God, and ended up murdering God's Son. Now in the age of grace, while the Holy Spirit completes God's program of redemption, man again tries to prove that he is as creative as the Creator, that his moral standards are as high as God's and that he has the wisdom and will to create a viable society upon earth wherein dwelleth righteousness. This too shall fail until finally he will have fouled his nest beyond all repair and Christ will come again to rescue God's experiment upon this planet.

Surely, some may say, we will then learn that God's righteous society is possible only under God's personal supervision. But not even the Second Coming of our Lord and His triumphant reign of millenial peace and progress will persuade those who will still be blinded by the god of this world (II Cor.4:4). One final insane attempt at *coup d'etat* will take place. Read about it in Revelation 20:7-9. Satan and his slaves will never learn, because "the flesh profiteth nothing." There is no remedy but judgment. Our Sovereign God must either judge sin and rebellion or He will Himself be driven from His own universe. The issue is not in doubt. "Greater is He that is in you than he that is in the world" (I John 4:4). The light will always shine in the darkness, but there is no danger that the darkness will overcome the light (John 1:5). Thank God it is the other way around.

What then should the church do? How shall we then live? We have an unfinished commission to preach the gospel to the ends of the earth. The age is darkening but we have no way of knowing how much more time remains before He comes. We are certain that ". . . He that shall come will come and will not tarry" (Heb.10:37), but we do not know when. One thing is certain. We have His message in a Book. Let us study it with scholarly penetration to its very depths. Only thus can Christians escape the sad fate of The Man With the Hoe.

(4) Healing of a Man at Bethesda on the Sabbath And The Action Defended in a Great Discourse
John 5:1-47

John 5:1 - "After this there was a feast of the Jews; and Jesus went up to Jerusalem."

Μετὰ ταῦτα ἦν ἑορτὴ τῶν Ἰουδαίων, καί ἀνέβη Ἰησοῦς εἰς Ἱεροσόλυμα.

Μετὰ (preposition with the accusative of time extent) 50.
ταῦτα (acc.pl.neut.of οὗτος, time extent) 93.
ἦν (3d.per.sing.imp.ind.of εἰμί, customary) 86.
ἑορτὴ (nom.sing.fem.of ἑορτή, subject of ἦν) 1558.
τῶν (gen.pl.masc.of the article in agreement with Ἰουδαίων) 9.
Ἰουδαίων (gen.pl.masc.of Ἰουδαῖος, description) 143.
καὶ (continuative conjunction) 14.
ἀνέβη (3d.per.sing.2d.aor.act.ind.of ἀναβαίνω, constative) 323.
Ἰησοῦς (nom.sing.masc.of Ἰησοῦς, subject of ἀνέβη) 3.
εἰς (preposition with the accusative of extent) 140.
Ἱεροσόλυμα (acc.sing.masc.of Ἱεροσόλυμα, extent) 141.

Translation - "After these things there was a feast of the Jews, and Jesus went up to Jerusalem."

Comment: Dr.A.T.Robertson says, "This feast of John 5:1 was most probably a Passover. . . . If so, we should know that our Lord's public ministry lasted three years and a fraction, and that the great ministry in Galilee lasted some 18 to 20 months. Otherwise, we should know of only two years and a fraction for the former, and 6 to 8 months for the latter; as John gives three Passovers beyond question (John 2:13; 6:4; 12:1), our Lord's ministry began some time before the first of these. If the feast of 5:1 was not a Passover, it is quite impossible to determine what other feast it was." (A.T.Robertson, *A Harmony of the Gospels,* 42). *Cf.*also 267*ff.* Just which feast it was cannot be determined with certainty. It could have been any of the following: Purim, in March; Passover, in April; Pentecost, in May; Tabernacles, in October or Dedication, in December. "It is chiefly between Purim and Passover that opinion is divided, because some feast in May is supposed to be indicated by John 4:35. Against Passover, it is urged that in Chapter 6 another Passover is mentioned; but this is by no means decisive, as John elsewhere passes over equally long intervals of time." (*The Expositors' Greek Testament,* 735).

Fortunately it is not necessary for us to determine without doubt which feast is meant in order to derive spiritual benefit from the passage. Nothing is said as to whether or not the disciples accompanied Jesus on this trip.

Verse 2 - "Now there is at Jerusalem by the sheep market a pool, which is called in the Hebrew tongue Bethesda, having five porches."

ἔστιν δὲ ἐν τοῖς Ἱεροσολύμοις ἐπὶ τῇ προβατικῇ κολυμβήθρα ἡ ἐπιλεγομένη Ἑβραϊστὶ Βηθζαθά, πέντε στοὰς ἔχουσα.

ἔστιν (3d.per.sing.pres.ind.of εἰμί, aoristic) 86.
δὲ (explanatory conjunction) 11.
ἐν (preposition with the locative of place) 80.
τοῖς (loc.pl.masc.of the article in agreement with Ἱεροσόλυμοις) 9.
Ἱεροσολύμοις (loc.pl.masc.of Ἱεροσολύμων, place where) 141.
ἐπὶ (preposition with the locative of place) 47.
τῇ (loc.sing.fem.of the article in agreement with προβατικῇ) 9.

#2091 προβατικῇ (loc.sing.fem.of προβατικός, place where).

sheep market - John 5:2.

Meaning; Cf. πρόβατον (#671). An adjective - pertaining to sheep. The sheep gate - John 5:2.

#2092 κολυμβήθρα (nom.sing.fem.of κολυμβήθρα, subject of ἔστιν).

pool - John 5:2,7; 9:7.

Meaning. Cf. κολυμβάω (#3751). Hence a swimming pool. At Bethesda - John 5:2,7; at Siloam - John 9:7.

ἡ (nom.sing.fem.of the article in agreement with ἐπιλεγομένη) 9.

#2093 ἐπιλεγομένη (pres.pass.part.nom.sing.fem.of ἐπιλέγω, apposition).

call - John 5:2.
choose - Acts 15:40.

Meaning: ἐπί (#47) and λέγω(#66). Hence, to fasten a name to; to name; to call; to give appellation - John 5:2. To choose someone - Acts 15:40.

#2094 Ἑβραϊστὶ (instru.sing., means)

Hebrew - John 5:2; 1;9:13,17,20; 20:16; Rev.9:11; 16:16.

Meaning: The Hebrew language.

#2095 Βηθζαθά (nom.sing.fem.of Βηθζαθά, predicate nominative).

Bethesda - John 5:2.

Meaning: House of Olives. A swimming pool in Jerusalem - John 5:2.

πέντε (numeral) 1119.

#2096 στοὰς (acc.pl.fem.of στοά, direct object of ἔχουσα).

porch - John 5:2; 10:23; Acts 3:11; 5:12.

Meaning: A portico; a covered colonnade where people can stand or walk protected from the rain or snow and from the heat of the sun. Generally - John 5:2; Solomon's Porch - John 10:23; Acts 3:11; 5:12.

ἔχουσα (pres.act.part.nom.sing.fem.of ἔχω, adverbial, circumstantial) 82.

Translation - "Now there is in Jerusalem by the sheep gate, a swimming pool, called in Hebrew Bethesda, having five porticos."

Comment: δὲ is explanatory as John sets the stage for his story. Note the two prepositions ἐν and ἐπί, each with the locative of place where - "*In* Jerusalem *by* the sheep market. . . "* This particular bathing pool was called Bethesda. It was equipped with five porches. The word means a porch with an extended overhead protection from the weather - something perhaps similar to the awning sometimes seen extending from the door to the curb in the better hotels. *Cf.* Neh.3:32; 12:39. *Cf.The Pulpit Commentary*, vol.17, *en loc.* for a discussion of the probable location of this sheep gate.

Verse 3 - "In these lay a great multitude of impotent folk, of blind, halt, withered, waiting for the moving of the water."

ἐν ταύταις κατέκειτο πλῆθος τῶν ἀσθενούντων, τυφλῶν, χωλῶν, ξηρῶν.

ἐν (preposition with the locative of place where) 80.
ταύταις (loc.pl.fem.of οὗτος, place where) 93.
κατέκειτο (3d.per.pl.imp.ind.of κατάκειμαι, duration) 2065.
πλῆθος (nom.sing.masc.of πλῆθος, subject of κατέκειτο) 1792.
τῶν (gen.pl.masc.of the article in agreement with ἀσθενούντων) 9.
ἀσθενούντων (pres.act.part.gen.pl.masc.of ἀσθενέω, adverbial, substantive, partitive) 857.
τυφλῶν (gen.pl.masc.of τυφλός, description) 830.
χωλῶν (gen.pl.masc.of χωλός, description) 908.
ξηρῶν (gen.pl.masc.of ξηρός, description) 972.

Translation - "In these there was lying a large number of the invalids - blind, lame, withered."

Comment: ταύταις has στοὰς of verse 2 as its antecedent . Not all of the invalids were there, but a large number were. Hence τῶν ἀσθενούντων is a partitive genitive, while the genitives which follow are dramatically descriptive. Five colonnades surrounded the pool. Each was crowded with the sick - blind, lame, withered - a heartsickening scene. Though the words are to be taken in their literal physical sense here, they are also used elsewhere to denote spiritual sickness, blindness and lameness, etc. *Cf.#*'s 857,830,908,972. Jesus can help in any case - physical, mental or spiritual.

Verse 4 (not included in the United Bible Societies text) - "For an angel went down at a certain season into the pool, and troubled the water. Whosoever then first after the troubling of the water stepped in was made whole of whatsoever disease he had."

Verse 5 - "And a certain man was there, which had an infirmity thirty and eight years."

ἦν δέ τις ἄνθρωπος ἐκεῖ τριάκοντα (καὶ) ὀκτὼ ἔτη ἔχων ἐν τῇ ἀσθενείᾳ αὐτοῦ.

ἦν (3d.per.sing.imp.ind.of εἰμί, duration) 86.
δέ (explanatory conjunction) 11.
τις (nom.sing.masc.of τις, in agreement with ἄνθρωπος) 486.
ἄνθρωπος (nom.sing.masc.of ἄνθρωπος, subject of ἦν) 341.
ἐκεῖ (adverbial) 204.
τριάκοντα (numeral, accusative of time extent) 1037.
(καὶ) - adjunctive conjunction, joining numerals) 14.
ὀκτὼ (numeral, time extent) 1886.
ἔτη (acc.pl.neut.of ἔτος, time extent) 821.
ἔχων (pres.act.part.nom.sing.masc.of ἔχω, adverbial, circumstantial) 82.
ἐν (preposition with the locative of accompanying circumstance) 80.
τῇ (loc.sing.fem.of the article in agreement with ἀσθενείᾳ) 9.
ἀσθενείᾳ (loc.sing.fem.of ἀσθένεια, accompanying circumstance) 740.
αὐτοῦ (gen.sing.masc.of αὐτός, possession) 16.

Translation - "Now there was a certain man there who had been suffering from his infirmity for thirty-eight years."

Comment: δέ is again explanatory as in verse 2. The adverbial phrase ἔχων ἐν τῇ ἀσθενείᾳ αὐτοῦ with the participle is circumstantial. Note the duration uses of the imperfect . John is beginning to describe the utter helplessness of the man - a point which he pursues further in verses 6 and 7. The man has been in this helpless condition for thirty-eight years. The situation which he describes in verse 7 has served to perpetuate his plight. Our Lord is about to do in a moment what no one had been able to do in a lifetime.

The better manuscripts do not contain the material which the KJV has in verse 4. Metzger says,

Ver.4 is a gloss, whose secondary character is clear from (1) its absence from the earliest and best witnesses (p.66,75 Sinaiticus B C* D Wsupp 33 itd,l,q) the true text of the Latin Vulgate syrc copsa,bomss,ach2 geo Nonnus), (2) the presence of asterisks or obeli to mark the words as spurious in more than twenty Greek witnesses (including S Λ Π 047 1079 2174), (3) the presence of non-Johannine words or expressions (κατὰ καιρόν, ἐμβαίνω (of going into the water), ἐκδέχομαι, κατέρχομαι, κίνησις, ταραχή, and νόσημα - the last three words only here in the New Testament), and (4) the rather wide diversity of variant forms in which the verse was transmitted (see footnotes 6 to 10 on p.338 of the text-volume for variant readings within verse 4). Since the passage is lacking in the earlier and better witnesses, which normally assist in identifying types of text, it is sometimes difficult to make decisions among alternative readings. On the whole, however, the Committee gave preference to the readings that are supported by what was regarded as the preponderant weight of attestation, or that seemed best to account for the origin of the other reading(s).

Bruce M. Metzger, *A Textual Commentary on the Greek New Testament,* 209.

The material in verse 4 sounds like some superstitious legend which may have developed in the area. It seems out of keeping with the miracle working of the Lord. No damage is done to the story by its omission. The man believed that a dip into the pool would heal him and the text makes clear that it was Jesus who performed the miracle.

Verse 6 - "When Jesus saw him lie, and knew that he had been now a long time in that case, he saith unto him, Wilt thou be made whole?"

τοῦτον ἰδὼν ὁ Ἰησοῦς κατακείμενον, καὶ γνοὺς ὅτι πολὺν ἤδη χρόνον ἔχει, λέγει αὐτῷ, Θέλεις ὑγιὴς γενέσθαι;

τοῦτον (acc.sing.masc.of οὗτος, direct object of ἰδών) 93.

ἰδὼν (aor.act.part.nom.sing.masc.of ὁράω, adverbial, temporal) 144.

ὁ (nom.sing.masc.of the article in agreement with Ἰησοῦς) 9.

Ἰησοῦς (nom.sing.masc.of Ἰησοῦς, subject of λέγει) 3.

κατακείμενον (pres.pass.part.acc.sing.masc.of κατάκειμαι, adverbial, circumstantial) 2065.

γνοὺς (2d.aor.act.part.nom.sing.masc.of γινώσκω, adverbial, causal) 131.

ὅτι (conjunction introducing an objective clause in indirect discourse) 211.

πολὺν (acc.sing.neut.of πολύς, in agreement with χρόνον) 228.

ἤδη (adverbial) 291.

χρόνον (acc.sing.masc.of χρόνος, time extent) 168.

ἔχει (3d.per.sing.pres.act.ind.of ἔχω progressive, existing results) 82.

λέγει (3d.per.sing.pres.act.ind.of λέγω, historical) 66.

αὐτῷ (dat.sing.masc.of αὐτός, indirect object of λέγει) 16.

Θέλεις (2d.per.sing.pres.act.ind.of θέλω, direct question) 88.

ὑγιὴς (nom.sing.masc.of ὑγιής, predicate adjective) 979.

γενέσθαι (2d.aor.inf.of γίνομαι, complementary) 113.

Translation - "When Jesus saw this man lying there, and because he already knew that he had already been in this condition for a long time, He said to him, "Do you want to be made healthy?"

Comment: τοῦτον refers to τις ἄνθρωπος of verse 5. Note the two participles - ἰδών and γνούς - the former is temporal and the latter is causal. When Jesus saw the man in question and because He knew about his case, without having been told, He asked the question. γνούς introduces the objective clause in indirect discourse with ὅτι. The verb in the indirect discourse ἔχει carries the same time as in direct. Someone there may have said, "He has a long time . . . " That is, "He has been in this condition a long time." Jesus' question seems almost superfluous, and was designed to elicit the statement of verse 7, which points up the total helplessness of the poor man, whose extremity became God's opportunity.

Verse 7 - "The impotent man answered him, Sir, I have no man, when the water is troubled, to put me into the pool: but while I am coming, another steppeth down before me."

ἀπεκρίθη αὐτῷ ὁ ἀσθενῶν, Κύριε, ἄνθρωπον οὐκ ἔχω ἵνα ὅταν ταραχθῇ τὸ ὕδωρ βάλῃ με εἰς τὴν κολυμβήθραν, ἐν ᾧ δὲ ἔρχομαι ἐγὼ ἄλλος πρὸ ἐμοῦ καταβαίνει.

ἀπεκρίθη (3d.per.sing.aor.ind.of ἀποκρίνομαι, constative) 318.

αὐτῷ (dat.sing.masc.of αὐτός, indirect object of ἀπεκρίθη) 16.

ὁ (nom.sing.masc.of the article in agreement with ἀσθενῶν) 9.

ἀσθενῶν (pres.act.part.nom.sing.masc.of ἀσθενέω, substantival, subject of ἀπεκρίθη) 857.

Κύριε (voc.sing.masc.of κύριος, address) 97.

ἄνθρωπον (acc.sing.masc.of ἄνθρωπος, direct object of ἔχω) 341.

οὐκ (negative conjunction with the indicative) 130.

ἔχω (1st.per.sing.pres.act.ind.of ἔχω, aoristic) 82.

ἵνα (conjunction introducing a purpose clause) 114.

ὅταν (indefinite temporal adverb with the subjunctive introducing a temporal clause) 436.

ταραχθῇ (3d.per.sing.aor.pass.subj.of ταράσσω, indefinite temporal clause) 149.

τὸ (nom.sing.neut.of the article in agreement with ὕδωρ) 9.

ὕδωρ (nom.sing.neut.of ὕδωρ, subject of ταραχθῇ) 301.

βάλῃ (3d.per.sing.aor.act.subj.of βάλλω, purpose) 299.

με (acc.sing.masc.of ἐγώ, direct object of βάλῃ) 123.

εἰς (preposition with the accusative of extent) 140.

τὴν (acc.sing.fem.of the article in agreement with κολυμβήθραν) 9.

κολυμβήθραν (acc.sing.fem.of κολυμβήθρα, extent) 2092.

ἐν (preposition with the locative of time point) 80.

ᾧ (loc.sing.masc.of ὅς, temporal clause) 65.

δὲ (adversative conjunction) 11.

ἔρχομαι (1st.per.sing.pres.act.ind.of ἔρχομαι, aoristic) 146.

ἐγὼ (nom.sing.masc.of ἐγώ, subject of ἔρχομαι) 123.

ἄλλος (nom.sing.masc.of ἄλλος, subject of καταβαίνει) 198.

πρὸ (preposition with the ablative of separation) 442.

ἐμοῦ (abl.sing.masc.of ἐγώ, separation) 123.

καταβαίνει (3d.per.sing.pres.act.ind.of καταβαίνω, customary) 324.

Translation - "The sick man answered Him, 'Sir, I have no one, when the water is agitated, to throw me into the pool. But while I am coming another steps down ahead of me.' "

Comment: ὁ ἀσθενῶν is the participial substantive, the subject of ἀπεκρίθη. Direct discourse without ὅτι. Note ἄνθρωπον οὐκ in emphasis. The indefinite temporal clause with ὅταν is contained within the purpose clause, introduced by ἵνα. The man did not know when the next agitation of the water in the pool would occur. ὅταν with the subjunctive in ταραχθῇ makes this clear. His statement only reveals that the man believed the story that the water was in fact agitated from time to time. There is nothing in the text to indicate that such a phenomenon actually occurred. ἐν ᾧ with the indicative is the temporal clause, which is definite. καταβαίνει is a customary present. It always happened that while the poor man was trying vainly to crawl into the water someone else preceded him. The man's dilemma is well described. In his crippled condition he was never able to be first into the troubled waters. His helplessness is the point to note. He was sick; he knew it and he wanted to be healed, but there was nothing that he could do about it. He had watched many others receive healing - or at least so he thought. His faith in the efficacy of the healing power of the water in the pool was great, albeit it was misplaced faith. But, the redeeming feature in his situation is that his knowledge of his own helplessness was even greater. Any lost sinner in this position is ready for salvation. Some commentators have imagined a mendicant whine in the sick man's tone. Perhaps, but there is nothing in the text to suggest it. He was simply stating the facts in a realistic fashion. There is also nothing in the text to suggest that he looked upon Jesus as one who would be able to heal him, although he may have hoped that Jesus would remain by his side until the next opportunity for healing occurred at which time Jesus would throw him into the water. Little did he realize that his healing was to take place forthwith, without the ritual which he thought to be his only hope for recovery.

Verse 8 - "Jesus saith unto him, Rise, take up thy bed, and walk."

λέγει αὐτῷ ὁ Ἰησοῦς, Ἔγειρε ἆρον τὸν κράβαττόν σου καὶ περιπάτει.

λέγει (3d.per.sing.pres.act.ind.of λέγω, historical) 66.

αὐτῷ (dat.sing.masc.of αὐτός, indirect object of λέγει) 16.

ὁ (nom.sing.masc.of the article in agreement with Ἰησοῦς) 9.

Ἰησοῦς (nom.sing.masc.of Ἰησοῦς, subject of λέγει) 3.

Ἔγειρε (2d.per.sing.pres.act.impv.of ἐγείρω, command) 125.

ἆρον (2d.per.sing.aor.act.impv.of αἴρω, command) 350.

τὸν (acc.sing.masc.of the article in agreement with κράββατόν) 9.
· κράββατόν (acc.sing.masc.of κράββατος, direct object of ἆρον) 2077.
σου (gen.sing.masc.of σύ, possession) 104.
καὶ (adjunctive conjunction, joining verbs) 14.
περιπάτει (2d.per.sing.pres.act.impv.of παριπατέω, command) 384.

Translation - "Jesus said to him, 'Get up, pick up your pallet and walk.' "

Comment: Properly Jesus meant that he should arise, pick up his pallet and walk away. Metaphorically, He meant that he should arise and walk spiritually. *Cf.*#384, 125. We are always to walk in the light as He is in the light (I John 1:7). Now that the Son of God was present, there was no further need to depend upon the mysterious healing waters of Bethesda. In His presence the helpless can be healed as quickly as those who could be first into the pool. Salvation is not for those who by hook or crook are first into the pool, but for those who believe in the word of God's incarnate Son. The effectual call of the Holy Spirit is suggested by this story. *Cf.* John 6:44; I Cor.12:3.

Verse 9 - "And immediately the man was made whole, and took up his bed, and walked: and on the same day was the sabbath."

καὶ εὐθέως ἐγένετο ὑγιὴς ὁ ἄνθρωπος, καὶ ἦρεν τὸν κράβαττον αὐτοῦ καὶ περιεπάτει.Ἦν δὲ σάββατον ἐν ἐκείνῃ τῇ ἡμέρᾳ.

καὶ (inferential conjunction) 14.
εὐθέως (adverbial) 392.
ἐγένετο (3d.per.sing.aor.ind.of γίνομαι, aoristic) 113.
ὑγιὴς (nom.sing.masc.of ὑγιής, pred.adjective) 979.
ὁ (nom.sing.masc.of the article in agreement with ἄνθρωπος) 9.
ἄνθρωπος (nom.sing.masc.of ἄνθρωπος, subject of ἐγένετο) 341.
καὶ (adjunctive conjunction, joining verbs) 14.
ἦρεν (3d.per.sing.aor.act.ind.of αἴρω, aorisitic) 350.
τὸν (acc.sing.masc.of the article in agreement with κράβαττον) 9.
κράββατον (acc.sing.masc.of κράβαττος, direct object of ἦρεν) 2077.
αὐτοῦ (gen.sing.masc.of αὐτός, possession) 16.
καὶ (adjunctive conjunction, joining verbs) 14.
περιεπάτει (3d.per.sing.imp.act.ind.of πατεπατέω, inceptive) 384.
Ἦν (3d.per.sing.imp.ind.of εἰμί, progressive description) 86.
δὲ (explanatory conjunction) 11.
σάββατον (nom.sing.neut.of σάββατον, pred.nominative) 962.
ἐν (preposition with the locative of time point) 80.
ἐκείνῃ (loc.sing.fem.of ἐκεῖνος, in agreement with ἡμέρᾳ) 246.
τῇ (loc.sing.fem.of the article in agreement with ἡμέρᾳ) 9.
ἡμέρᾳ (loc.sing.fem.of ἡμέρα, time point) 135.

Translation - *"Therefore instantly the man was made healthy, and he picked up his pallet and began to walk around. Now that day was the sabbath."*

Comment: καὶ is inferential in the first clause, although only adjunctive later. Note ὑγιὴς in emphasis - the predicate adjective outranking the subject of the verb. Suddenly the man finds himself in perfect health as a result (inferential καὶ) of Jesus' command. What follows is logical. He took up his pallet (*cf.*#2077) and began to move about the area. It was the first time in 38 years that he had walked. δὲ is explanatory, since what follows is necessary if we are to understand the rest of the context. Jesus not only healed a sick man, but He did so on a sabbath day, a fact that precipitated the controversy which follows. The man's obedience is evidence of his great faith in God's Son. To tell an invalid who has not walked in 38 years to get up, pick up his pallet and walk is unusual, but the invalid, by divine grace, arose to the situation.

Verse 10 - *"The Jews therefore said unto him that was cured, It is the Sabbath day; it is not lawful for thee to carry thy bed."*

ἔλεγον οὖν οἱ Ἰουδαῖοι τῷ τεθεραπευμένῳ, Σάββατόν ἐστιν, καὶ οὐκ ἔξεστίν σοι ἆραι τὸν κράβαττόν σου.

ἔλεγον (3d.per.pl.imp.act.ind.of λέγω, inceptive) 66.

οὖν (inferential conjunction) 68.

οἱ (nom.pl.masc.of the article in agreement with Ἰουδαῖοι) 9.

Ἰουδαῖοι (nom.pl.masc.of Ἰουδαῖος, subject of ἔλεγον) 143.

τῷ (dat.sing.masc.of the article in agreement with τεθεραπευμένῳ) 9.

τεθεραπευμένῳ (perf.pass.part.dat.sing.masc.of θεραπεύω, substantival, indirect object of ἔλεγον) 406.

Σάββατόν (nom.sing.neut.of σάβαττον, predicate nominative) 962.

ἐστιν (3d.per.sing.pres.ind.of εἰμί, aoristic) 86.

καὶ (inferential conjunction) 14.

οὐκ (negative conjunction with the indicative) 130.

ἔξεστίν (3d.per.sing.pres.act.ind.of ἔξεστι, aoristic) 966.

σοι (dat.sing.masc.of σύ, personal interest) 104.

ἆραι (aor.act.inf.of αἴρω, complementary) 350.

τὸν (acc.sing.masc.of the article in agreement with κράβαττον) 9.

κράβαττον (acc.sing.masc.of κράβαττος, direct object of ἆραι) 2077.

Translation - *"Therefore the Jews began to protest to the man who was healed, 'It is a Sabbath; therefore it is not lawful for you to carry your pallet.'"*

Comment: οὖν is inferential as also is καὶ. The sight of the healed man walking about the pool area, carrying his bed precipitated the Jews' protest. Note the culminative force of the present passive participle. Having been healed with a complete act of healing, he was therefore healthy. Σάββατόν ἐστιν is in emphasis, John with his Greek syntax indicating the depth of feeling of the self righteous Jews. The infinitive ἆραι completes ἔξεστίν.

For 38 years the Jews were unable to help the man and they cared nothing for him. Now that he is healed, they choose to ignore the notable miracle and quibble over a broken sabbath observance. Society knows how to ignore what it does not understand and to magnify out of all proportion what it considers important. Far better, from the Jews' point of view for the poor cripple to be confined to his couch all of his life than to carry it ten feet on the sabbath. *Cf.* Exod.23:12; Jer.17:21; Neh.13:15. The rabbinical law said, "Whosoever on the Sabbath bringeth anything in, or taketh anything out from a public place to a private one, if he hath done this inadvertently, he shall sacrifice for his sin; but if willfully, he shall be cut off and shall be stoned." Thus we see that the man who carried his pallet willfully was asking for excommunication and death.

Verse 11 - "He answered them, He that made me whole, the same said unto me, Take up thy bed, and walk."

ὁ δὲ ἀπεκρίθη αὐτοῖς, Ὁ ποιήσας με ὑγιῆ ἐκεῖνός μοι εἶπεν, Ἆρον τὸν κράβαττόν σου καὶ περιπάτει.

ὁ (nom.sing.masc.of the article, subject of ἀπεκρίθη) 9.

δὲ (adversative conjunction) 11.

ἀπεκρίθη (3d.per.sing.aor.ind.of ἀποκρίνομαι, constative) 318.

αὐτοῖς (dat.pl.masc.of αὐτός, indirect object of ἀπεκρίθη) 16.

Ὁ (nom.sing.masc.of the article in agreement with ποιήσας) 9.

ποιήσας (aor.act.part.nom.sing.masc.of ποιέω, substantival, nominative absolute) 127.

με (acc.sing.masc.of ἐγώ, direct object of ποιήσας) 123.

ὑγιῆ (nom.sing.masc.of ὑγιής, predicate adjective) 979.

ἐκεῖνος (nom.sing.masc.of ἐκεῖνος, deictic, subject of εἶπεν) 246.

μοι (dat.sing.masc.of ἐγώ, indirect object of εἶπεν) 123.

εἶπεν (3d.per.sing.aor.act.ind.of εἶπον, aoristic) 155.

Ἆρον (2d.per.sing.aor.act.impv.of αἴρω, command) 350.

τὸν (acc.sing.masc.of the article in agreement with κράβαττον) 9.

κράβαττόν (acc.sing.masc.of κράββατος, direct object of ἆρον) 2077.

σου (gen.sing.masc.of σύ, possession) 104.

καὶ (adjunctive conjunction, joining verbs) 14.

περιπάτει (2d.per.sing.pres.act.impv.of περιπατέω, command) 384.

Translation - "But he answered them, 'The One who made me whole - That One said to me, 'Pick up your pallet and walk.' ' "

Comment: δὲ is adversative as the healed man engages the Jews in an argument. There is a great deal of asperity in his response. "You who could do nothing for me in a positive way now try to hedge me about with your religious restrictions. There was One who healed me. That One (deictic ἐκεῖνός) told me to pick up my pallet and walk." This is a sensible view for the man to take. Was not the one who was able to perform such a miracle greater than the petty rule which they sought to impose and enforce? It may be that this appeal to higher authority was made by the man in the hope that Jesus would come to his rescue. Run the references under #962 for other teachings that Jesus Christ is greater than the Sabbath. The question of the Jews in verse 12 is asked as if they did not know.

Verse 12 - "Then asked they him, What man is that which said unto thee, Take up thy bed and walk?"

ἠρώτησαν αὐτόν, Τίς ἐστιν ὁ ἄνθρωπος ὁ εἰπών σοι,Ἀρον καὶ περιπάτει;

ἠρώτησαν (3d.per.pl.aor.act.ind.of ἐρωτάω, constative) 1172.
αὐτόν (acc.sing.masc.of αὐτός, direct object of ἠρώτησαν) 16.
Τίς (nom.sing.masc.of τίς, interrogative pronoun, predicate nominative) 281.
ἐστιν (3d.per.sing.pres.ind.of εἰμί, aoristic) 86.
ὁ (nom.sing.masc.of the article in agreement with ἄνθρωπος) 9.
ἄνθρωπος (nom.sing.masc.of ἄνθρωπος, subject of ἐστιν) 341.
ὁ (nom.sing.masc.of the article in agreement with εἰπών) 9.
εἰπών (aor.act.part.nom.sing.masc.of εἶπον, apposition) 155.
σοι (dat.sing.masc.of σύ, indirect object of εἰπών) 104.
Ἀρον (3d.per.pl.aor.act.impv.of αἴρω, command) 350.
καὶ (adjunctive conjunction, joining verbs) 14.
περιπάτει (2d.per.sing.pres.act.impv.of περιπατέω, command) 384.

Translation - "They asked him, 'Who is the man who said to you, 'Get up and walk?'' "

Comment: Note the direct question in Τίς . . . περιπάτει. Τίς is emphasized. It is the predicate nominative outranking the subject (ὁ ἄνθρωπος) of ἐστιν. "*Who* is the man?" He is further identified with the appositional ὁ εἰπών σοι. . . κ.τ.λ." This is the natural question for the Jews to ask, not because they did not already know the answer, but in order to pursue the matter for their own nefarious designs. Some commentators read contempt into ὁ ἄνθρωπος. If so it comes from the context, not from the text. Perhaps the later behavior of the Jews (verse 16) is a hint. Their question may be construed as their unintentional admission that the Jews had no one in their party capable of performing such a miracle.

Verse 13 - "And he that was healed wist not who it was: for Jesus had conveyed himself away, a multitude being in that place."

ὁ δὲ ἰαθεὶς οὐκ ᾔδει τίς ἐστιν, ὁ γὰρ Ἰησοῦς ἐξένευσεν ὄχλου ὄντος ἐν τῷ τόπῳ.

ὁ (nom.sing.masc.of the article in agreement with ἰαθεὶς) 9.
δὲ (adversative conjunction) 11.
ἰαθεὶς (aor.pass.part.nom.sing.masc.of ἰάομαι, subject of ᾔδει) 721.
οὐκ (negative conjunction with the indicative) 130.
ᾔδει (3d.per.sing.pluperfect ind.of οἶδα, intensive) 144.

τίς (nom.sing.masc.of τίς,subject of ἐστιν) 281.
ἐστιν (3d.per.sing.pres.ind.of εἰμί, aoristic, indirect question) 86.
ὁ (nom.sing.masc.of the article in agreement with Ἰησοῦς) 9.
γάρ (causal conjunction) 105.
Ἰησοῦς (nom.sing.masc.of Ἰησοῦς, subject of ἐξένευσεν) 3.

#2097 ἐξένευσεν (3d.per.sing.aor.act.ind.of ἐκνεύω,culminative).

convey oneself away - John 5:13.

Meaning: To nod or move the head in order to avoid a blow. To "duck" the head. To take oneself away. With reference to Jesus who avoided the crowd that gathered at Bethesda - John 5:13.

ὄχλου (gen.sing.masc.of ὄχλος, genitive absolute) 418.
ὄντος (pres.part.gen.sing.masc.of εἰμί, genitive absolute) 86.
ἐν (preposition with the locative of place) 80.
τῷ (loc.sing.masc.of the article in agreement with τόπῳ) 9.
τόπῳ (loc.sing.masc.of τόπος, place where) 1019.

Translation - "But the man who was healed had never known who he was, because Jesus had left since there was a crowd in the place."

Comment: δέ is adversative. The Jews asked a question but the man did not know the answer. No doubt he would have been glad to answer had he known. Note the intensive pluperfect in ᾔδει. There had been no introductions and he had never known - therefore he did not then know - a present condition as a result of a past completed situation. Nor could he find out who his benefactor was. Why? The causal clause follows in ὁ γάρ . . . ἐξένευσεν Jesus was gone. He had "slipped away" (Williams, *en loc.*). Why did He leave? The genitive absolute clause ὄχλου ὄντος . . . τόπῳ has the causal adverbial participle. Jesus left because there were too many people around. *Cf.*#2097. We might translate, "Jesus ducked out of the crowd." Why did Jesus leave? Perhaps because at this stage in the development of His program to present Himself to Israel He wished to avoid a confrontation with the Jewish Establishment.

Verse 14 - "Afterward Jesus findeth him in the temple, and said unto him, Behold, thou art made whole: sin no more, lest a worse thing come unto thee."

μετὰ ταῦτα εὑρίσκει αὐτὸν ὁ Ἰησοῦς ἐν τῷ ἱερῷ καὶ εἶπεν αὐτῷ, Ἴδε ὑγιὴς γέγονας, μηκέτι ἁμάρτανε, ἵνα μὴ χεῖρόν σοί τι γένηται.

μετά (preposition with the accusative of time extent) 50.
ταῦτα (acc.pl.neut.of οὗτος, time extent) 93.
εὑρίσκει (3d.per.sing.pres.act.ind.of εὑρίσκω, historical) 79.
αὐτὸν (acc.sing.masc.of αὐτός, direct object of εὑρίσκει) 16.

ὁ (nom.sing.masc.of the article in agreement with Ἰησοῦς) 9.

Ἰησοῦς (nom.sing.masc.of Ἰησοῦς, subject of εὑρίσκει and εἶπεν) 3.

ἐν (preposition with the locative of place) 80.

τῷ (loc.sing.neut.of the article in agreement with ἱερῷ) 9.

ἱερῷ (loc.sing.neut.of ἱερόν, place where) 346.

καὶ (adjunctive conjunction, joining verbs) 14.

εἶπεν (3d.per.sing.aor.act.ind.of εἶπον, constative) 155.

αὐτῷ (dat.sing.masc.of αὐτός, indirect object of εἶπεν) 16.

Ἴδε (2d.per.sing.aor.act.impv.of ὁράω, command, exclamation).

ὑγιὴς (nom.sing.masc.of ὑγιής, predicate adjective) 979.

γέγονας (2d.per.sing.perf.ind.of γίνομαι, intensive) 113.

μηκέτι (adverbial) 1368.

ἁμάρτανε (2d.per.sing.pres.act.impv.of ἁμαρτάνω, command) 1260.

ἵνα (final conjunction, introducing a negative purpose clause) 114.

μή (negative conjunction with the subjunctive in a purpose clause) 87.

χεῖρον (nom.sing.neut.of χείρων, predicate adjective) 806.

σοί (dat.sing.masc.of σύ, personal disadvantage) 104.

τι (nom.sing.neut.of τις, subject of γένηται) 486.

γένηται (3d.per.sing.aor.subj.of γίνομαι, negative purpose clause) 113.

Translation - "A little later Jesus found him in the temple and said to him, 'See! You are cured! Do not go on sinning any longer, lest something worse happen to you.' "

Comment: μετὰ ταῦτα does not tell us how long after the man was healed and then challenged by the Jews that Jesus met him in the temple. It was probably not very longs. Note the historical present in εὑρίσκει, which here means, not that Jesus was deliberately seeking for the man, but that He encountered him as if by chance. Note that John used the historical present in εὑρίσκει, but the constative aorist in εἶπεν. The intensive perfect in γέγονας is the usual way of pointing to the present condition as a result of a past completed action. "Having been thoroughly healed a moment ago, you are now in excellent health." μή plus καί plus ἔτι (#1368) is here coupled with the present imperative in ἁμάρτανε and yields "Do not ever again sin in the future." Why not? The negative purpose clause warns about dreadful consequences for the man in the event that he should again transgress God's laws. Jesus implied that the man's invalid condition had been the result of his sin. More sin might bring a worse condition. There are worse results of sin even than 38 years of helplessness.

Note that the man lost Jesus, but that Jesus did not lose the man. So He keeps His eye upon all whom He heals and saves (Mt.10:29). Note also that Jesus did not regard the physical healing as an end in itself, but tied it to the moral and ethical admonition. Antinomians want healing, but they want to go on sinning. "The healing was at least imperfect until the man had learned it spiritual significance" (*The Pulpit Commentary*, en loc.).

John 9:3 makes it clear that not all sickness is directly resultant of sin, though in this case it was, and it often is.

Verse 15 - "The man departed, and told the Jews that it was Jesus, which had made him whole."

ἀπῆλθεν ὁ ἄνθρωπος καὶ ἀνήγγειλεν τοῖς Ἰουδαίοις ὅτι Ἰησοῦς ἐστιν ὁ ποιήσας αὐτὸν ὑγιη.

ἀπῆλθεν (3d.per.sing.aor.act.ind.of ἀπέρχομαι, constative) 239.

ὁ (nom.sing.masc.of the article in agreement with ἄνθρωπος) 9.

ἄνθρωπος (nom.sing.masc.of ἄνθρωπος, subject of ἀπῆλθεν and ἀνήγγειλεν) 341.

καὶ (adjunctive conjunction, joining verbs) 14.

ἀνήγγειλεν (3d.per.sing.aor.act.ind.of ἀναγγέλλω, ingressive) 2012.

τοῖς (dat.pl.masc.of the article in agreement with Ἰουδαίοις) 9.

Ἰουδαίοις (dat.pl.masc.of Ἰουδαῖος, indirect object of ἀνήγγειλεν) 143.

ὅτι (conjunction to introduce an object clause in indirect discourse) 211.

Ἰησοῦς (nom.sing.masc.of Ἰησοῦς, predicate nominative) 3.

ἐστιν (3d.per.sing.pres.ind.of εἰμί, indirect discourse) 86.

ὁ (nom.sing.masc.of the article in agreement with ποιήσας) 9.

ποιήσας (aor.act.part.nom.sing.masc.of ποιέω, substantival, subject of ἐστιν) 127.

αὐτὸν (acc.sing.masc.of αὐτός, direct object of ποιήσας) 16.

ὑγιῆ (acc.sing.masc.of ὑγιής, predicate adjective) 979.

Translation - "The man went away and began to report to the Jews that Jesus was the one who made him whole."

Comment: We have here a good example of the principle that in indirect discourse the tense of the verb is the same as in direct. The direct statement was Ἰησοῦς ἐστιν ὁ ποιήσας με ὑγιῆ. In indirect only the verb follows the direct, while in indirect αὐτὸν is properly the third personal pronoun, rather than με, the first personal pronoun.

The man, thanks to Jesus' encounter with him (vs.14), had now discovered the identity of his benefactor and hastened to identify him. Perhaps he thought that one powerful enough to heal would be prestigious enough to protect him from the wrath of the Jews who were accusing him of Sabbath violation. Jesus had the deeper, truer view of the Sabbath law, which had been held by some of the more scholarly, and therefore less fanatic, teachers, but His views were in diametric opposition to those held by the Jews at that time and place.

That the Jews had Jesus as the target of their intolerance and hatred, and that they were not particularly concerned about the violation of the healed man, is clear from verse 16.

Verse 16 - "And therefore did the Jews persecute Jesus, and sought to slay him, because he had done these things on the sabbath day."

καὶ διὰ τοῦτο ἐδίωκον οἱ Ἰουδαῖοι τὸν Ἰησοῦν, ὅτι ταῦτα ἐποίει ἐν σαββάτῳ.

καὶ (continuative conjunction) 14.

διὰ (preposition with the accusative of cause) 118.

τοῦτο (acc.sing.neut.of οὗτος, cause) 93.

ἐδίωκον (3d.per.pl.imp.act.ind.of διώκω, inceptive) 434.

οἱ (nom.pl.masc.of the article in agreement with Ἰουδαῖοι) 9.

Ἰουδαῖοι (nom.pl.masc.of Ἰουδαῖος, subject of ἐδίωκον) 143.

τὸν (acc.sing.masc.of the article in agreement with Ἰησοῦν) 9.

Ἰησοῦν (acc.sing.masc.of Ἰησοῦς, direct object of ἐδίωκον) 9.

ὅτι (causal conjunction) 211.

ταῦτα (acc.pl.neut.of οὗτος, direct object of ἐποίει) 93.

ἐποίει (3d.per.sing.imp.act.ind.of ποιέω, progressive description) 127.

ἐν (preposition with the locative of time point) 80.

σαββάτῳ (loc.sing.neut.of σάββατον, time point) 962.

Translation - "And because of this the Jews began to hunt down Jesus because He was always doing things like this on the sabbath."

Comment: καὶ is continuative here as we have the causal thought in διὰ τοῦτο. Because of what? The Jews now knew that the man they were looking for was Jesus and that He had not only healed the man with a notable miracle - something that they could not gainsay, nor dared to criticize - but had also directed the man to carry his pallet and depart. In the view of the Jews, this was a violation of the sabbath rule. Obviously Jesus' directive to the man to carry his pallet and the man's compliance was not a violation of the Mosaic rule. This is clear from Mt.5:17. It was a violation of the Jews' interpretation of Moses.

Thus we have an illustration of the difference between naturalism and positivism in jurisprudence. The law of God is moral and hence His *laws* are also rational and moral. This is naturalism. The principles upon which unregenerate man in a democracy operate are neither rational nor moral necessarily; hence the *laws* which men legislate may or may not be reasonable or in keeping with moral principles. Yet, in a society ruled by itself, whether monarchy, oligarchy or democracy a law is a law whether it is moral and sensible or not. Jeremy Bentham, the father of positivistic jurisprudence, laid down the principle that men should ". . . obey punctually but censure freely." Thus the body of law in a democracy may be improved. God's laws are always sensible and moral; hence what Moses received at Sinai and what Jesus came to fulfill are likewise sensible and moral. The fanatic loves to honor *his* law and to seek to enforce it, whether it makes sense or not. This was the position of the Jews. It was *their* law that Jesus had violated, not God's. If God had ruled that a man should not carry his pallet on the Sabbath, Jesus would not have ordered the man to do so.

That Jesus was in a position and therefore fully authorized to ignore the Jewish rule of the sabbath, while fully prepared to fulfill the Divine rule of the sabbath is clear from vss. 17,18.

Note the imperfect tense in ἐδίωκον, which we interpret in its inceptive sense. They *began* to pursue Jesus with hostile intent. *Cf*.#434 for other examples of διώκω in the sense of persecution. Paul, in his days as a self-righteous Pharisee, persecuted Christ and His church - Mt.10:23; 23:34; Acts 9:4,5; 22:4,7,8; 26:11,14,15; I Cor.15:9; Gal.1:13,23; Phil.3:6, and was himself persecuted after he became a Christian - Gal.5:11; 6:12; II Tim.3:12, etc. This is the lot of all Christians. Note that Ishmael tried to kill Isaac - Gal.4:29.

The analogy of Gal.4:25*ff* is apt. Legalism has always persecuted God's grace. The Pharisees were in line with ancient practice. They were sincere - and mistaken! Note the plural in ταῦτα and the progressive imperfect in ἐποίει. Jesus was always doing these things. This is only one instance of repeated offenses against the Pharisaic view of the Sabbath law.

Verse 17 - "But Jesus answered them, My Father worketh hitherto, and I work."

ὁ δὲ Ἰησοῦς ἀπεκρίνατο αὐτοῖς, Ὁ πατήρ μου ἕως ἄρτι ἐργάζεται, κἀγὼ ἐργάζομαι.

ὁ (nom.sing.masc.of the article in agreement with Ἰησοῦς) 9.
δὲ (adversative conjunction) 11.
Ἰησοῦς (nom.sing.masc.of Ἰησοῦς, subject of ἀπεκρίνατο) 3.
ἀπεκρίνατο (3d.per.sing.imp.ind.of ἀποκρίνομαι, progressive duration) 318.
αὐτοῖς (dat.pl.masc.of αὐτός, indirect object of ἀπεκρίνετα) 16.
Ὁ (nom.sing.masc.of the article in agreement with πατήρ) 9.
πατήρ (nom.sing.masc.of πατήρ, subject of ἐργάζεται) 238.
μου (gen.sing.masc.of ἐγώ, relationship) 123.
ἕως (adverbial with ἄρτι) 71.
ἄρτι (an adverb of time description) 320.
ἐργάζεται (3d.per.sing.pres.ind.of ἐργάζομαι, iterative) 691.
κἀγὼ (continuative conjunction, *crasis*) 178.
ἐργάζομαι (1st.per.sing.pres.ind.ofd ἐργάζομαι, iterative) 691.

Translation - "But in reply to them He kept saying, 'My Father has worked from time to time until now and now I am at work."

Comment: #691 lists other usages of ἐργάζομαι, some of which can be used to illuminate this passage. *Cf*.#238 for other passages in which Jesus referred to God as ὁ πατήρ μου, especially those that occurred *before* this occasion and *in Jerusalem, e.g. cf.* John 2:17. The Jews understood that Jesus meant God and not Joseph the carpenter. God the Father has always had a policy of working from time to time (iterative present). He does not continuously perform miracles. It pleases Him for the most part to allow natural law, which is the product of His genius in creation, to run the universe. But He has always reserved the right to intervene in special ways whenever, in His profound wisdom, He chose to do so. Whenever He chooses to intervene it is for good.

Jesus adds that He also has the same policy. When He works (and it is often) it is for good. Furthermore when the occasion arises and He has opportunity to perform a deed for good (Rom.8:28) He will not be hindered by the restrictions that flow from the Pharisaic misinterpretation of the law of the Sabbath. *Cf.#962* for references in which the issue of doing good on the Sabbath comes up.

Two conclusions may be logically inferred from Jesus' statement, and the Jews grasped the significance of each in

Verse 18 - "Therefore the Jews sought the more to kill him, because he not only had broken the Sabbath, but said also that God was His Father, making Himself equal with God."

διὰ τοῦτο οὖν μᾶλλον ἐζήτουν αὐτὸν οἱ Ἰουδαῖοι ἀποκτεῖναι, ὅτι οὐ μόνον ἔλυεν τὸ σάββατον ἀλλὰ καὶ πατέρα ἴδιον ἔλεγεν τὸν θεόν, ἴσον ἑαυτὸν ποιῶν τῷ θεῷ.

διὰ (preposition with the accusative of cause) 118.

τοῦτο (acc.sing.neut.of οὗτος, cause) 93.

οὖν (inferential conjunction) 68.

μᾶλλον (adverbial) 619.

ἐζήτουν (3d.per.pl.imp.act.ind.of ζητέω, inceptive) 207.

αὐτὸν (acc.sing.masc.of αὐτός, direct object of ἀποκτεῖναι) 16.

οἱ (nom.pl.masc.of the article in agreement with Ἰουδαῖοι) 9.

Ἰουδαῖοι (nom.pl.masc.of Ἰουδαῖος, subject of ἐζήτουν) 143.

ἀποκτεῖναι (aor.act.inf.of ἀποκτείνω, complementary) 889.

ὅτι (causal conjunction) 211.

οὐ (negative conjunction with the indicative) 130.

μόνον (adverbial) 339.

ἔλυεν (3d.per.sing.imp.act.ind.of λύω, progressive description) 471.

τὸ (acc.sing.neut.of the article in agreement with σάββατον) 9.

σάββατον (acc.sing.neut.of σάββατον, direct object of ἔλυεν) 962.

ἀλλὰ (adversative conjunction) 342.

καὶ (adjunctive conjunction, joining verbs) 14.

πατέρα (acc.sing.masc.of πατήρ, predicate accusative) 238.

ἴδιον (acc.sing.masc.of ἴδιος, in agreement with πατέρα) 778.

ἔλεγεν (3d.per.sing.imp.act.ind.of λέγω, progressive description) 66.

τὸν (acc.sing.masc.of the article in agreement with θεόν) 9.

θεόν (acc.sing.masc.of θεός, direct object of ἔλεγεν) 124.

ἴσον (acc.sing.masc.of ἴσος, predicate adjective) 1323.

ἑαυτὸν (acc.sing.masc.of ἑαυτός, direct object of ποιῶν) 288.

ποιῶν (pres.act.part.nom.sing.masc.of ποιέω, adverbial, modal) 127.

τῷ (dat.sing.masc.of the article in agreement with θεῷ) 9.

θεῷ (dat.sing.masc.of θεός, reference) 124.

Translation - "Because of what He said therefore the Jews increased their effort to kill Him, because not only was He always breaking the Sabbath, but also He was calling God His own Father, thus making Himself equal to God."

Comment: διὰ τοῦτο refers to Jesus' statement of verse 17. I have translated the first clause loosely. Literally it says, "Because of this, therefore, they began to seek more to kill Him. . . " Note αὐτὸν in emphasis, outranking the infinitive ἀποκτεῖναι of which it is the object. The causal clause with ὅτι gives us two reasons for the increased determination of the Jews to kill Jesus: not only . . . but also (οὐ μόνον. . . ἀλλὰ καὶ) Cf.Rom.1:32. Not only was He always violating their conception of the Sabbath laws, but also He had said something that was equivalent with making Himself equal to God. They were wrong about the first matter. Jesus had never broken God's law of the Sabbath - only their erroneous interpretation of it. But He did indeed make Himself equal with God with His statement of verse 17. He said that God was His Father and that He was going to do now and in the future the same things that the Father had been doing, now and again, in the past. The Jews were quite correct in their analysis of Jesus' thought. Should they have stoned Him? Indeed, yes, if He were not God. But He was and is God incarnate. Judaism is logical but it reasons from the false premise that Jesus Christ was an imposter. If He had not been Deity, He would have been demoniac.

In verses 19-47 we have an unbroken statement from the lips of our Lord which goes to the fullest extreme in asserting His deity and therefore His authority not only for healing the invalid on the Sabbath, but also for ordering him to carry his pallet.

Verse 19 - "Then answered Jesus and said unto them, Verily, verily, I say unto you, The Son can do nothing of himself but what he seeth the Father do: for what things soever he doeth, these also doeth the Son likewise."

Ἀπεκρίνατο οὖν ὁ Ἰησοῦς καὶ ἔλεγεν αὐτοῖς, Ἀμὴν ἀμὴν λέγω ὑμῖν, οὐ δύναται ὁ υἱὸς ποιεῖν ἀφ' ἑαυτοῦ οὐδὲν ἐὰν μή τι βλέπῃ τὸν πατέρα ποιοῦντα, ἃ γὰρ ἂν ἐκεῖνος ποιῇ, ταῦτα καὶ ὁ υἱὸς ὁμοίως ποιεῖ.

ἀπεκρίνατο (3d.per.sing.imp.ind.of ἀποκρίνομαι, inceptive) 318.

οὖν (inferential conjunction) 68.

ὁ (nom.sing.masc.of the article in agreement with Ἰησοῦς) 9.

Ἰησοῦς (nom.sing.masc.of Ἰησοῦς, subject of ἀπεκρίνατο and ἔλεγεν) 3.

καὶ (adjunctive conjunction, joining verbs) 14.

ἔλεγεν (3d.per.sing.imp.act.ind.of λέγω, inceptive) 66.

αὐτοῖς (dat.pl.masc.of αὐτός, indirect object of ἔλεγεν) 16.

Ἀμὴν (explicative) 466.

ἀμὴν (explicative) 466.

λέγω (1st.per.sing.pres.act.ind.of λέγω, aoristic) 66.

ὑμῖν (dat.pl.masc.of σύ, indirect object of λέγω) 104.
οὐ (negative conjunction with the indicative) 130.
δύναται (3d.per.sing.pres.ind.of δύναμαι, customary) 289.
ὁ (nom.sing.masc.of the article in agreement with υἱός) 9.
υἱὸς (nom.sing.masc.of υἱός, subject of δύναται) 5.
ποιεῖν (pres.act.inf.of ποιέω, complementary) 127.
ἀφ' (preposition with the ablative of agency) 70.
ἑαυτοῦ (abl.sing.masc.of ἑαυτός, agency) 288.
οὐδὲν (acc.sing.neut.of οὐδείς, direct object of ποιεῖν) 446.
ἐὰν (conditional particle in a third-class condition) 363.
μή (negative conjunction with the subjunctive) 87.
τι (acc.sing.neut.of τις, direct object of βλέπῃ) 486.
βλέπῃ (3d.per.sing.pres.act.subj.of βλέπω, third-class condition) 499.
τὸν (acc.sing.masc.of the article in agreement with πατέρα) 9.
πατέρα (acc.sing.masc.of πατήρ, direct object of βλέπῃ) 238.
ποιοῦντα (pres.act.part.acc.sing.masc.of ποιέω, adverbial, circumstantial)
127.
ἃ (acc.pl.neut.of ὅς, direct object of ποιῇ) 65.
γὰρ (causal conjunction) 105.
ἂν (conditional particle introducing the subjunctive) 205.
ἐκεῖνος (nom.sing.masc.of ἐκεῖνος, subject of ποιῇ) 246.
ποιῇ (3d.per.sing.pres.act.subj.of ποιέω, third-class condition) 127.
ταῦτα (acc.pl.neut.of οὗτος, direct object of ποιεῖ) 93.
καὶ (adjunctive conjunction, joining substantives) 14.
ὁ (nom.sing.masc.of the article in agreement with υἱός) 9.
υἱὸς (nom.sing.masc.of υἱός, subject of ποιεῖ) 5.
ὁμοίως (adverbial) 1425.
ποιεῖ (3d.per.sing.pres.act.ind.of ποιέω, customary) 127.

*Translation - "Therefore in reply Jesus began to speak to them:'Truly, truly I am
telling you, the Son is not able to do by Himself one thing except that which He
sees the Father doing; because the things which that One may do, those are the
things which also the Son will likewise do."*

Comment: οὖν is inferential. In order to gain His point with the Jews, Jesus must
make a full statement of His unique deity. Only thus can He justify His
overruling of the Sabbath tradition and His strong statement of verse 17. Note
the inceptive imperfects in ἀπεκρίνατο and ἔλεγεν. Jesus' statement is going to
be a long one. The Son has no power to originate action from Himself - ἀφ'
ἑαυτοῦ - an ablative of agency. This statement is qualified by the third-class
condition which follows, introduced by ἐὰν and the subjunctive in βλέπῃ.
Whatever the Son may see the Father doing is that which He also is able to do.
He adds that whatever the Father does is that which He also will do in the same
manner. The third-class conditions which demand the element of some doubt
translate to something like this: "There is a possibility that I may see the Father

doing something. Unless I do see it, I cannot do it of myself."This does not mean that Jesus Christ in incarnation was subordinate to the Father in terms of a diminution of His power. It does mean that both He and the Father are limited, but only by the limitations that derive from the divine nature. They are not limited by any force *outside* themselves. Jesus could not do anything on earth that the Father, for moral reasons, could not do, if He had come to earth. God the Father could not lie, steal, murder or commit adultery. Nor could God the Son.

The claim to deity involved in Jesus' statement is that He was in a position to *see* what the Father did and had the privilege and power to emulate the Father's actions.

In the last sentence we have again ἄν with the subjunctive in ποιῇ. "That which" or "Those things which (ἅ) that One does, if He does them (the subjunctive element of doubt) these things (ταῦτα) also the Son customarily does." Thus the totality of His meaning is that Jesus is equal to the Father in power and authority, but that He has now, in incarnation and therefore temporarily, voluntarily put Himself under the direction of the Father, to do all but only what He sees the Father do. He is also saying, "I healed the man on the Sabbath, only because in my experience, I know that the Father's will is concurrent with my action." In other words there is nothing immoral in healing an invalid on the Sabbath, nor is it immoral for the healed man to obey the command of his Healer and carry his pallet. That was the Jewish addition to God's law - not God's law. The ground of the Son's activity is the Father's will and resultant policy.

δύναται does not mean lack of physical power, but rather it points to the impossibility that the Son should ever originate any action which could be contrary to the will of God. There can never be incompatibility in the Godhead. Meyer phrases it thus: ". . . it is impossible for Him to act with an individual self-assertion independent of the Father, which He could then only do if He were not the Son." (Meyer, *en loc.).*

Verse 20 - "For the Father loveth the Son, and sheweth him all things that him-self doeth: and he will shew him greater works than these, that ye may marvel."

ὁ γὰρ παρὴρ φιλεῖ τὸν υἱὸν καὶ πάντα δείκνυσιν αὐτῷ ἃ αὐτὸς ποιεῖ, καὶ μείζονα τούτων δείξει αὐτῷ ἔργα, ἵνα ὑμεῖς θαυμάζητε.

ὁ (nom.sing.masc.of the article in agreement with πατὴρ) 9.
γὰρ (causal conjunction) 105.
πατὴρ (nom.sing.masc.of πατήρ, subject of φιλεῖ and δείκνυσιν) 238.
φιλεῖ (3d.per.sing.pres.act.ind.of φιλέω, customary) 566.
τὸν (acc.sing.masc.of the article in agreement with υἱὸν) 9.
υἱὸν (acc.sing.masc.of υἱός, direct object of φιλεῖ) 5.
καὶ (adjunctive conjunction, joining verbs) 14.

πάντα (acc.pl.neut.of πᾶς, direct object of δείκνυσιν) 67.
δείκνυσιν (3d.per.sing.pres.act.ind.of δείκνυμι, customary) 359.
αὐτῷ (dat.sing.masc.of αὐτός, indirect object of δείκνυσιν) 16.
ἅ (acc.pl.neut.of ὅς, direct object of ποιεῖ) 65.
αὐτὸς (nom.sing.masc.of αὐτός, subject of ποιεῖ) 16.
ποιεῖ (3d.per.sing.pres.act.ind.of ποιέω, customary) 127.
καὶ (continuative conjunction) 14.
μείζονα (acc.pl.neut.of μείζων, in agreement with ἔργα) 916.
τούτων (abl.pl.neut.of οὗτος, comparison) 93.
δείξει (3d.per.sing.fut.act.ind.of δείκνυμι, prediction) 359.
αὐτῷ (dat.sing.masc.of αὐτός, indirect object of δείξει) 16.
ἔργα (acc.pl.neut.of ἔργον, direct object of δείξει) 460.
ἵνα (consecutive conjunction, introducing a result clause) 114.
ὑμεῖς (nom.pl.masc.of σύ, subject of θαυμάζητε) 104.
θαυμάζητε (2d.per.pl.pres.act.subj.of θαυμάζω, result) 726.

Translation - "For the Father loves the Son and all that which He does He shows to Him, and greater works than these He will show to Him, with the result that you will be astonished."

Comment: The verbs φιλεῖ, δείκνυσιν and ποιεῖ are customary present tenses. δείξει is a predictive future. Customarily (it is always done and is the expected thing) the Father loves the Son and He always shows to the Son that which He does, whatever it may be. There is complete concert of plan and action between the Father and the Son. The Father always keeps the Son informed. This is not all. Greater things will be done in the future, all of which will be shown by the Father to the Son. The divine purpose for future miracles will result in the mystification of the Jews.

That the psychological reaction of the Jews to the future miracles which Jesus was to perform amounted to mystification can be appreciated by running the references under #992.

Note that Jesus began His statement by saying that the Father loved Him. Where there is perfect abiding love there can be no secrets. Jesus had said in verse 19 that He was unable to do anything except that which He saw the Father doing. Were it not for verse 20, we could read into verse 19 the implication that the Son is inferior to the Father because the Father did some things which were *not* revealed to the Son and which the Son thus could not do. But this is all swept away in verse 20. The Son knows and sees everything that the Father does, and therefore He also does it. Why? Because the Father loves the Son.

Jesus then added that the end is not yet. μείζονα . . . ἔργα, *i.e.* than those which the Jews had already seen Jesus do. If they had already marvelled at His works, they were to marvel even more. This power includes resurrection as we shall see in the next few verses.

Note that Jesus did not say, ἵνα ὑμεῖς πιστεύητε. Many of His enemies could not resist marvelling at His works, but they could not believe.

Verse 21 - "For as the Father raiseth up the dead, and quickeneth them; even so the Son quickeneth whom He will."

ὥσπερ γὰρ ὁ πατὴρ ἐγείρει τοὺς νεκροὺς καὶ ζωοποιεῖ, οὕτως καὶ ὁ υἱὸς
οὓς θέλει ζωοποιεῖ.

ὥσπερ (intensive particle introducing a comparative clause) 560.
γὰρ (causal conjunction) 105.
ὁ (nom.sing.masc.of the article in agreement with πατήρ) 9.
πατήρ (nom.sing.masc.of πατήρ, subject of ἐγείρει) 238.
ἐγείρει (3d.per.sing.pres.act.ind.of ἐγείρω, customary) 125.
τοὺς (acc.pl.masc.of the article in agreement with νεκροὺς) 9.
νεκροὺς (acc.pl.masc.of νεκρός, direct object of ἐγείρει) 749.
καὶ (adjunctive conjunction, joining verbs) 14.

#2098 ζωοποιεῖ (3d.per.sing.pres.act.ind.of ζωοποιέω).

give life - II Cor.3:6; Gal.3:21.
make alive - I Cor.15:22.
quicken - John 5:21,21; 6:63; Rom.4:17; 8:11; I Cor.15:36,45; I Pet.3:18.

Meaning: To produce alive; beget or bear living young. Never in this sense in the
N.T., except perhaps Rom.4:17. To give spiritual life; to regenerate as in II
Cor.3:6; Gal.3:21; John 6:63. In passages where the meaning seems to lean more
heavily toward the giving of physical life as in resurrection - Rom.8:11; I
Pet.3:18. The context allows both of the above meanings in I Cor.15:22; John
5:21,21; I Cor.15:45; I Tim.6:13. In I Cor.15:36 it refers to the germination of a
seed in the ground.

οὕτως (demonstrative adverb) 74.
καὶ (adjunctive conjunction, joining clauses) 14.
ὁ (nom.sing.masc.of the article in agreement with υἱός) 9.
υἱὸς (nom.sing.masc.of υἱός, subject of ζωοποιεῖ) 9.
οὓς (acc.pl.masc.of ὅς, direct object of ζωοποιεῖ) 65.
θέλει (3d.per.sing.pres.act.ind.of θέλω, aoristic) 88.
ζωοποιεῖ (3d.per.sing.pres.act.ind.of ζωοποιέω, customary) 2098.

*Translation - "Because precisely as the Father raises up and give life to the dead,
so also the Son gives life to whom He wishes."*

Comment: Here is a case of ὥσπερ and οὕτως used together. "In exactly the
same way (intensive περ) as . . . so also. . . " *Cf.*#560 for other examples. The
intensive form of ὥσπερ again makes the point that there is complete purpose
and action between the Father and the Son. Each raises the dead and gives life.
And they do it in exactly the same way and for the same reasons. *Cf.*#'s 125 and
2098 for comparison of the latter with the former with νεκρός. In ἐγείρει τοὺς
νεκροὺς καὶ ζωοποιεῖ we have an example of repetition for emphasis - - or
perhaps the first clause refers to physical resurrection and the last to spiritual
regeneration. What the Father does, so does also the Son. The clause οὓς θέλει

indicates His sovereignty. He is subject to no control outside Himself. Only His will governs His actions. This is in keeping with the policy of the Father, and it clearly indicates deity in both. οὕς θέλει here recalls καθὼς βούλεται, with reference to the Holy Spirit in I Cor.12:11.

This argument began when the Jews tried to kill Jesus because He healed a man on the Sabbath and then ordered him to pick up his pallet and walk. Did Jesus have the right so to do? How silly to put that question to the One Who has asserted the things of verse 17*ff*! In view of the foregoing the Father's decision of verse 22 is entirely fitting and proper.

Verse 22 - "For the Father judgeth no man, but hath committed all judgment unto the Son."

οὐδὲ γὰρ ὁ πατὴρ κρίνει οὐδένα, ἀλλὰ τὴν κρίσιν πᾶσιν δέδωκεν τῷ υἱῷ.

οὐδὲ (disjunctive particle) 452.
γὰρ (inferential conjunction) 105.
ὁ (nom.sing.masc.of the article in agreement with πατήρ) 9.
πατήρ (nom.sing.masc.of πατήρ, subject of κρίνει and δέδωκεν) 238.
κρίνει (3d.per.sing.pres.act.ind.of κρίνω, customary) 531.
οὐδένα (acc.sing.masc.of οὐδείς, direct object of κρίνει) 446.
ἀλλὰ (alternative conjunction) 342.
τὴν (acc.sing.fem.of the article in agreement with κρίσιν) 9.
κρίσιν (acc.sing.fem.of κρίσις, direct object of δέδωκεν) 478.
πᾶσαν (acc.sing.fem.of πᾶς, in agreement with κρίσιν) 67.
δέδωκεν (3d.per.sing.perf.act.ind.of δίδωμι, consummative) 362.
τῷ (dat.sing.masc.of the article in agreement with υἱῷ) 9.
υἱῷ (dat.sing.masc.of υἱός, indirect object of δέδωκεν) 5.

Translation - "Therefore the Father sits in judgment on no one, but He has entrusted the function of all judgment to the Son."

Comment: οὐδὲ, the disjunctive particle is really not needed here. It might be translated "On the contrary. . ." Contrary to what might normally be thought by the Jews to be the function of God the Father, *viz* that He is the Judge . . . κ.τ.λ. The function of judging has been turned over completely to the Son. That this division of labor in the Godhead is logical in view of the foregoing testimony is clear from inferential γὰρ. Since there is total comprehension and cooperation between Father and Son it is therefore quite in keeping with this harmony of purpose that the Father should have given to Jesus Christ jurisdiction over the universe.

The prime prerequisite for the function of judging is total knowledge of the case. The human judge, presiding over a human court is charged with the responsibility of directing the testimony presented by attorneys who function in an adversary relationship, so that the total truth about the case can be ascertained. Only thus can the judge hand down the proper decision. Of course this ideal result can never be achieved in a human court of law. Witnesses commit perjury, despite all efforts to prevent and threats to punish. Skillful lawyers cloud the issue; half truths prevail. Seldom does the judge and/or jury arrive at the total truth. That the defendant is guilty may be clear to all, but what may not be clear is the motivation that forced the defendant into the action for which he is being held responsible.

It follows that objective judgment can be handed down only when the judge has the entire body of truth that applies to the case before him. Thus only God the Father, God the Son and God the Holy Spirit are qualified to judge the world. Since there is total harmony of opinion within the Godhead, we may be certain that what the Son decides as He sits in judgment upon mankind is consistent with the wishes of the Father and the Holy Spirit.

In addition to the intellectual qualification for the judge, there is also a moral qualification. No one should judge another and sentence him to punishment unless he has paid the supreme sacrifice to redeem him and rescue him from the consequences of his unlawful deeds. Christ alone did this upon the cross and at the empty tomb. *Cf.*Mt.7:1, 2q.v. with comment *en loc.* The transgressor, under a barrage of criticism, admits his guilt, turns to his critic for regeneration and salvation. He who cannot redeem and save should not judge. Thus Christ who alone suffered and who has the power to save, is alone competent to judge.

Error creeps in here. The doctrine of atonement is sometimes represented as a system in which God has condemned the world and then sent Christ, an unwilling victim, to die in order to rescue the world. The truth is that it was Christ who came down from the bench in Heaven's court to die for the defendant. This He did by His own choice. He was not sent to die. He came to die. And thus He alone has the moral right to judge. *Cf.* Rev.5:1-10.

The church is full of bigots who do not understand this fundamental principle. How quick we are to sit in judgment upon the behavior of others and how unlikely we are to recognize that we have no moral right to mount the throne and sit upon the bench and hand down our decisions - decisions that are made when only a small part, if any, of the truth relative to the case is known or can be known. And how little have any of us done to save the poor culprit upon whose defenseless head we pour down our contempt and wrath.

The Jews who went about to kill Jesus because He healed on the Sabbath are told that they are sitting in judgment upon the Judge! The Judge raises up and gives life to whom He will. He does what the Father does. The Father reveals everything to Him. The Father and Son are on a co-eval and co-equal basis. This is a strong statement of the deity of Jesus Christ. *Cf.*John 3:19.

Verse 23 - "That all men should honour the Son, even as they honour the Father. He that honoureth not the Son honoureth not the Father which hath sent him."

ἵνα πάντες τιμῶσι τὸν υἱὸν καθὼς τιμῶσι τὸν πατέρα. ὁ μὴ τιμῶν τὸν υἱὸν οὐ τιμᾷ τὸν πατέρα τὸν πέμφαντα αὐτόν.

ἵνα (conjunction introducing a sub-final clause) 114.

πάντες (nom.pl.masc.of πᾶς, subject of τιμῶσι) 67.

τὸν (acc.sing.masc.of the article in agreement with υἱὸν) 9.

υἱὸν (acc.sing.masc.of υἱός, direct object of τιμῶσι) 5.

καθὼς (comparative adverb) 1348.

τιμῶσι (3d.per.pl.pres.act.ind.of τιμάω, customary) 1142.

τὸν (acc.sing.masc.of the article in agreement with πατέρα) 9.

πατέρα (acc.sing.masc.of πατήρ, direct object of τιμῶσι) 238.

ὁ (nom.sing.masc.of the article in agreement with τιμῶν) 9.

μὴ (negative conjunction with the participle) 87.

τιμῶν (pres.act.part.nom.sing.masc.of τιμάω, substantival, subject of τιμᾷ) 1142.

τὸν (acc.sing.masc.of the article in agreement with υἱὸν) 9.

υἱὸν (acc.sing.masc.of υἱός, direct object of τιμῶν) 5.

οὐ (negative conjunction with the indicative) 130.

τιμᾷ (3d.per.sing.pres.act.ind.of τιμάω, aoristic) 1142.

τὸν (acc.sing.masc.of the article in agreement with πατέρα) 9.

πατέρα (acc.sing.masc.of πατήρ, direct object of τιμᾷ) 238.

τὸν (acc.sing.masc.of the article in agreement with πέμψαντα) 9.

πέμψαντα (aor.act.part.acc.sing.masc.of πέμπω, substantival, apposition) 169.

αὐτόν (acc.sing.masc.of αὐτός, direct object of πέμψαντα) 16.

Translation - ". . . in order (and with the result) that all people will respect the Son just as they respect the Father. He who does not respect the Son does not respect the Father who sent Him."

Comment: The ἵνα clause depends upon all of the foregoing argument beginning with verse 19. There is equality between the Father and Jesus Christ the Son. They coordinate perfectly in purpose, policy and action. The Father loves the Son and entrusts everything to Him, including the all important function of judgment. Why does this relationship exist between the three persons of the Godhead (for the Holy Spirit is also involved in this closest of knit relationships)? Jesus adds in verse 23 that it is for a purpose and since it is a divine purpose, it is also certain to lead to the desired result. Sub-final clauses are examples of a cross between purpose and result. Sometimes it is difficult to distinguish the two. But when the Godhead is involved there is really no distinction between the two, since what God purposes He ordains and brings to historic fruition. It is unthinkable that God should ever purpose anything only to find later that the result failed of achievement. Hence, here in verse 23 we have both purpose and result. All men are going to honor and respect the Judge of all the earth. This is even true in an earthly court, as the lawyers and those whom they represent approach the bench only after permission is granted and address the judge with "Your Honor."

Here we have God's reason for committing all the ministry of judgment to Christ. It is that men may honor Him as they honor the Father. How many? πάντες -for all will be judged (Acts 17:31; *cf.* also John 5:27-29).

ὁ . . . τιμῶν is a participial substantive, the subject of τιμᾷ. Note the use of μὴ and οὐ. The softer negative μὴ is used with ὁ μὴ τιμῶν because there is doubt that all will reject. Perhaps some may honor the Son. Others may not. But there is no doubt (οὐ) that He who honors not the Son, by that attitude dishonors the Father. Men may or may not insult the Son of God, but he who insults Jesus Christ insults God. Of that there is no doubt. τὸν πέμφαντα αὐτόν is a participial clause in apposition with τὸν πατέρα. This language again can be interpreted fairly only to mean that the Father and the Son are on a coordinate basis and therefore equal. Having thus established this point Jesus procedes to show how His ministry as Judge and Life Giver will be conducted.

The student is warned that the exegetical details of this lengthy statement may tend to cause him to lose sight of the fact that the statement is made to the Jews who were trying to kill Jesus because they alleged that He broke the Sabbath. Keep the context in mind and interpret every verse in the light of John 5:10*ff.*

Verse 24 - "Verily, verily I say unto you, He that heareth my word, and believeth on him that sent me, hath everlasting life, and shall not come into condemnation; but is passed from death unto life."

Ἀμὴν ἀμὴν λέγω ὑμῖν ὅτι ὁ τὸν λόγον μου ἀκούων καὶ πιστεύων τῷ πέμφαντί με ἔχει ζωὴν αἰώνιον, καὶ εἰς κρίσιν οὐκ ἔρχεται ἀλλὰ μεταβέβηκεν ἐκ τοῦ θανάτου εἰς τὴν ζωήν.

Ἀμὴν (explicative) 466.

ἀμὴν (explicative) 466.

λέγω (1st.per.sing.pres.act.ind.of λέγω, aoristic) 66.

ὑμῖν (dat.pl.masc.of σύ, indirect object of λέγω) 104.

ὅτι (recitative) 211.

ὁ (nom.sing.masc.of the article in agreement with ἀκούων) 9.

τὸν (acc.sing.masc.of the article in agreement with λόγον) 9.

λόγον (acc.sing.masc.of λόγος, direct object of ἀκούων) 510.

μου (gen.sing.masc.of ἐγώ, possession) 123.

ἀκούων (pres.act.part.nom.sing.masc.of ἀκούω, substantival, subject of ἔχει ἔρχεται and μεταβέβηκεν) 148.

καὶ (adjunctive conjunction, joining substantival participles) 14.

πιστεύων (pres.act.part.nom.sing.masc.of πιστεύω, substantival, subject of ἔχει, ἔρχεται and μεταβέβηκεν) 734.

τῷ (dat.sing.masc.of the article in agreement with πέμφαντί) 9.

πέμφαντί (aor.act.part.dat.sing.masc.of πέμπω, substantival, personal advantage) 169.

με (acc.sing.masc.of ἐγώ, direct object of πέμφαντί) 123.

ἔχει (3d.per.sing.pres.act.ind.of ἔχω, aoristic) 82.

ζωὴν (acc.sing.fem.of ζωή, direct object of ἔχει) 668.

αἰώνιον (acc.sing.fem.of αἰώνιος, in agreement with ζωὴν) 1255.

καὶ (adjunctive conjunction, joining clauses) 14.

εἰς (preposition with the accusative of extent) 140.

κρίσιν (acc.sing.fem.of κρίσις, metaphorical extent) 478.

οὐκ (negative conjunction with the indicative) 130.

ἔρχεται (3d.per.sing.pres.ind.of ἔρχομαι, futuristic) 146.

ἀλλὰ (alternative conjunction) 342.

μεταβέβηκεν (3d.per.sing.perf.act.ind.of μεταβαίνω, consummative) 776.

ἐκ (preposition with the ablative of separation) 19.

τοῦ (abl.sing.masc.of the article in agreement with θανάτου) 9.

θανάτου (abl.sing.masc.of θάνατος, separation) 381.

εἰς (preposition with the accusative of extent) 140.

τὴν (acc.sing.fem.of the article in agreement with ζωήν) 9.

ζωήν (acc.sing.fem.of ζωή, metaphorical extent) 668.

Translation - "Truly, truly I am telling you that the one who is now hearing my message and believing upon the one who has sent me has life eternal, and into judgment he shall not come but he has passed out of (the) death into (the) life."

Comment: We have enclosed the definite article, *the* in parentheses in the last clause to indicate that the article is present in the Greek, whereas it is absent before κρίσιν. Jesus is talking about specific death and life. ὁ τὸν λόγον . . . με is a long subject, joined by three verbs, ἔχει, ἔρχεται and μεταβέβηκεν. Somebody possesses eternal life, is in no danger of judgment but has already passed (consummative perfect) out of the realm of death into the realm of life. Who is this fortunate person? The one who hears the message of the Lord Jesus and believes upon the Father Who sent Him into the world. Since the life is described as eternal (everlasting) both in its qualitative and quantitative aspects and since the verb ἔχει is in the present tense, the sense is that the hearer and believer now possesses a type of life which can never end nor be diminished in its quality. Young preachers, like the writer, forty-eight years ago, who, at that point, have plumbed the depths of Calvinism only far enough to understand the last point, seize upon this verse to *prove* eternal security or "once saved always saved" as we used to call it in western Indiana. Indeed the verse does say something like that, without implying any of the antinomianism which my farmer audiences used to read into it! The statement may comfort Calvinists and distress Arminians, although many of the latter are found not to object to the kind of salvation that changes the life of the hearer and believer from darkness to the marvelous light of the gospel of Christ. On the other hand the Calvinist who insists upon the perseverance of the saints at the expense of the dynamic truths of victorious Christian living is as heretical in his own way as Arminius and his followers are in theirs.

Were it not for verse 25 we might interpret ἔχει of verse 24 to mean that the reason why one hears the message of Christ and believes upon the Father who sent Him is that they *already had* life. Which is to say that the eternal life is the cause, not the result of their hearing and believing. Calvinists might point to Eph.2:1-3; II Cor.4:3,4; John 6:44; I Cor.12:3 and others and ask how one dead in trespasses and sins could hear and believe? It will help to remember that the fact of our salvation is already well known to the God who ordained it and that He who is timeless is not therefore concerned with the chronology of events. It is idle to ask God which comes first and which comes second and third, as though that which came second was the result of that which came first. Were it not for Him no one could have life or hear or believe. We might say that the professional tennis player ". . . who wins the Davis Cup match *has* superior ability" and mean by it that it was his ability that resulted in his victory. So we might say that the hearer and believer demonstrates by those two facts that he *has* eternal life. But verse 25 points to the life with the future tense, which seems to demand that we interpret ἔχει as a futuristic present in verse 24, in which case the better translation would be. . . *will have* eternal life, thus indicating that his possession of life is the result of his hearing and believing.

Because he comes into possession of eternal life he need not fear a future judgment (futuristic present in ἔρχεται). Why? Because *he has passed* (consummative perfect in μεταβέβηκεν) out of the realm of death into the realm of life. Here we have a present condition as a result of the past action. When did he pass from death into life? When he heard the message of Christ and believed upon the Father who sent Him.

On the other side of this exegetical puzzle I now present what I wrote about this verse many years ago. The reader can decide for himself. Then I said, "Whoever this person is he has already passed out of death and into life and at the time of his hearing and believing is already saved. The statement adds comfort to the Calvinists and distress to the Arminians. Is hearing and believing the root and cause of salvation? Is salvation contingent upon hearing and believing? So I preached for many years. But Jesus says that the hearer and believer has already passed out of death and into life and thus he is hearing, believing and having eternal life. The transition out of death and into life produces a divine affinity in the individual which enables him to hear Christ's word and believe on the Father who sent Christ. This is a mystic union. The hearing is more than audible perception. Christ's enemies had that. They heard but they did not *hear*. The hearing did not lead them to believe on the Father, *viz.,* that He had sent Christ. How did Christ do His works? Read the answer in verse 19. How did He perceive what the Father did? Read that answer in verse 20. The Father loved the Son and thus there was complete rapport between them. Thus the Son who saw (in the sense of perceive) all that the Father knew, felt and willed, did the same things. The intimate unity of the Godhead is in view. In verse 24 Jesus says that sinners are also brought into this mystic circle of fellowship. Having passed out of death into life, the sinner now enjoys this rapport with Christ and the Father. Now, as a result, not as a cause, he hears Christ's words, understands them, believes also on the Father who sent Christ and possesses in present possession a kind of life that is characterized qualitatively as communion with the Godhead, and quantitatively as eternal. Negatively described his position is one of being immune to judgment. Nay, he shall judge all things (I Cor.2:15).

Verse 25 - "Verily, verily I say unto you, The hour is coming, and now is, when the dead shall hear the voice of the Son of God: and they that hear shall live."

ἀμὴν ἀμὴν λέγω ὑμῖν ὅτι ἔρχεται ὥρα καὶ νῦν ἐστιν ὅτε οἱ νεκροὶ ἀκούσουσιν τῆς φωνῆς τοῦ υἱοῦ τοῦ θεοῦ καὶ οἱ ἀκούσαντες ζήσουσιν.

ἀμὴν (explicative) 466.

ἀμὴν (explicative) 466.

λέγω (1st.per.sing.pres.act.ind.of λέγω, aoristic) 66.

ὑμῖν (dat.pl.masc.of σύ, indirect object of λέγω) 104.

ὅτι (objective conjunction introducing indirect discourse) 211.

ἔρχεται (3d.per.sing.pres.ind.of ἔρχομαι, futuristic) 146.

καὶ (ascensive conjunction) 14.

νῦν (temporal adverb) 1497.

ἐστιν (3d.per.sing.pres.ind.of εἰμί, aoristic) 86.

ὅτε (adverb introducing a definite contemporaneous temporal clause) 703.

οἱ (nom.pl.masc.of the article in agreement with νεκροὶ) 9.

νεκροὶ (nom.pl.masc.of νεκρός, subject of ἀκούσουσιν) 749.

ἀκούσουσιν (3d.per.pl.fut.act.ind.of ἀκούω, predictive) 148.

τῆς (gen.sing.fem.of the article in agreement with φωνῆς) 9.

φωνῆς (gen.sing.fem.of φωνή, objective genitive) 222.

τοῦ (gen.sing.masc.of the article in agreement with υἱοῦ) 9.

υἱοῦ (gen.sing.masc.of υἱός, possession) 5.

τοῦ (gen.sing.masc.of the article in agreement with θεοῦ) 9.

θεοῦ (gen.sing.masc.of θεός, relationship) 124.

καὶ (continuative conjunction) 14.

οἱ (nom.pl.masc.of the article in agreement with ἀκούσαντες) 9.

ἀκούσαντες (aor.act.part.nom.pl.masc.of ἀκούω, substantival, subject of ζήσουσιν) 148.

ζήσουσιν (3d.per.pl.fut.act.ind.of ζάω, predictive) 340.

Translation - "Truly, truly I am telling you that there is coming an hour - in fact it now is when the dead shall hear the voice of the Son of God and those who have heard shall live."

Comment: Again Jesus emphasizes His statement with ἀμὴν ἀμὴν. Note ὅτι with indirect discourse. Jesus announces the coming of a time (futuristic present in ἔρχεται), but with ascensive καὶ He modifies it to say that He was speaking of that present moment. καὶ νῦν ἐστιν makes it impossible to interpret οἱ νεκροὶ in the sense of physical death. There were no physical resurrections that day. Physical resurrection is prophesied in verse 28. Note the objective genitive in τῆς φωνῆς. We have this construction when the noun in the genitive (φωνῆς in this case) receives the action of the verb ἀκούσουσιν. The grammar here straightens out the order of the hearing and the living. Note that the substantival participle οἱ ἀκούσαντες is aorist and that the verb with which it is joined (ζήτουσιν) if the predictive future. "Those who have heard (in the past) will live (in the future)." This is illustrated by Lazarus who was dead and buried but whose life was restored by the voice of Jesus - "Lazarus, come forth" (John 11:43).

In verse 28 Jesus predicts the resurrection of the physically dead. Note that there He omits the phrase καὶ νῦν ἐστιν. In verse 25 Jesus is speaking about spiritual regeneration. The dead are those alienated from God by sin. *Cf.*#749 for other passages where νεκρός means the spiritually dead. Note that Jesus again asserts His sonship with God. His statement reasserts that of verse 21 and explains verse 24. The voice of the Son of God is enough to give life to the dead. This is not some future experience. It is now - καὶ νῦν ἐστιν. *Cf.*#340 for ζάω in the sense of spiritual life. The participle ἀκούσαντες makes clear that the hearing which originates eternal life and the Christian experience is followed by a continuous presence of eternal life. Those who have eternal life now are those who, in the past, heard. The Christian can say, "I heard (in the past) and now I am living." (Rom.10:17; John 6:63).

Those without faith will scoff at the idea expressed here - that the dead can hear and thus may have life. How can a dead man here? But how could the lame man who had not walked for 38 years do so at Jesus' command? Unbelief says that he could not and therefore that he did not. And the argument ceases. But the spiritually dead are still spiritually dead. All unsaved sinners who attend a gospel service where the Word of God is preached "hear" the voice of the gospel but only the elect *hear* the gospel. A derelict in the Pacific Garden Mission testified, "I heard the gospel and I heard the gospel and I heard the gospel. But one night I *heard* the gospel." What was missing in the man's former visits to the Mission? His hearing was not mixed with faith (Heb.4:2).

In verse 26 we have another statement of the coordinate authority within the Godhead.

Verse 26 - "For as the Father hath life in himself; so hath he given to the Son to have life in himself."

ὥσπερ γὰρ ὁ πατὴρ ἔχει ζωὴν ἐν ἑαυτῷ, οὕτως καὶ τῷ υἱῷ ἔδωκεν ζωὴν ἔχειν ἐν ἑαυτῷ.

ὥσπερ (intensive particle introducing a comparative clause) 560.
γὰρ (causal conjunction) 105.
ὁ (nom.sing.masc.of the article in agreement with πατήρ) 9.
πατὴρ (nom.sing.masc.of πατήρ, subject of ἔχει) 238.
ἔχει (3d.per.sing.pres.act.ind.of ἔχω, aoristic) 82.
ζωὴν (acc.sing.fem.of ζωή, direct object of ἔχει) 668.

ἐν (preposition with the locative of place) 80.
ἑαυτῷ (loc.sing.masc.of ἑαυτός, place where) 288.
οὕτως (demonstrative adverb) 74.
καὶ (adjunctive conjunction joining clauses) 14.
τῷ (dat.sing.masc.of the article in agreement with υἱῷ) 9.
υἱῷ (dat.sing.masc.of υἱός, indirect object of ἔδωκεν) 5.
ἔδωκεν (3d.per.sing.aor.act.ind.of δίδωμι, culminative) 362.
ζωὴν (acc.sing.fem.of ζωή, direct object of ἔχειν) 668.
ἔχειν (pres.act.inf.of ἔχω, epexegetical) 82.
ἐν (preposition with the locative of place) 80.
ἑαυτῷ (loc.sing.masc.of ἑαυτός, place where) 288.

Translation - "Because just as the Father has life by his own authority, so also to the Son He has given to have life by His own authority."

Comment: On whatever basis the Father has life - - on that same basis does Jesus have life, and this by virtue of the Father's gift to the Son. *Cf.*#560 for other examples of ὥσπερ . . . οὕτως καὶ, *e.g.* verse 21. It has pleased the Father to place the Son in a coordinate relationship. This life is not a gift which God received from some source outside Himself. He has it ἐν ἑαυτῷ - *i.e.* "on his own authority." The Son has it on the same basis. That is why the statement of verse 21 is true. The meaning of the verse is made clearer by the last clause of

Verse 27 - "And hath given him authority to execute judgment because he is the son of man."

καὶ ἐξουσίαν ἔδωκεν αὐτῷ κρίσιν ποιεῖν, ὅτι υἱὸς ἀνθρώπου ἐστίν.

καὶ (continuative conjunction) 14.
ἐξουσίαν (acc.sing.fem.of ἐξουσία, direct object of ἔδωκεν) 707.
ἔδωκεν (3d.per.sing.aor.act.ind.of δίδωμι, culminative) 362.
αὐτῷ (dat.sing.masc.of αὐτός, indirect object of ἔδωκεν) 16.
κρίσιν (acc.sing.fem.of κρίσις, direct object of ποιεῖν) 478.
ποιεῖν (pres.act.inf.of ποιέω, epexegetical) 127.
ὅτι (causal conjunction) 211.
υἱὸς (nom.sing.masc.of υἱός, predicate nominative) 5.
ἀνθρώπου (gen.sing.masc.of ἄνθρωπος, relationship) 341.
ἐστίν (3d.per.sing.pres.ind.of εἰμί, aoristic) 86.

Translation - "And He has delegated authority to Him to hand down judicial decisions, because He is the Son of Man."

Comment: καὶ ties the gifts of verse 26 (inherent life) and verse 27 (administration of justice) together. The last clause tells us why the Father gave these gifts to the Son - ὅτι . . . ἐστίν. *Cf.* verse 22. It is Christ's reward for His humiliating incarnation. Mankind will be judged by the God-Man. Man, once cursed by sin and death because of sin, will live because God became a man. All that the Father does for the race He does through the mediation of and in concurrence with the Son of God. Jesus is making these extremely strong and clear-cut statements about His essential deity in order to show that He had authority to heal on the sabbath. Review vss.10-16 for the reason for this discourse. *Cf.#*'s 707 and 478 for cross-reference material on judgment and the authority to execute it.

Verse 28 - "Marvel not at this: for the hour is coming in which all that are in the graves shall hear his voice."

μὴ θαυμάζετε τοῦτο, ὅτι ἔρχεται ὥρα ἐν ᾗ πάντες οἱ ἐν τοῖς μνημείοις ἀκούσουσιν τῆς φωνῆς αὐτοῦ.

μὴ (negative conjunction with the imperative) 87.

θαυμάζετε (2d.per.pl.pres.act.impv.of θαυμάζω, command) 726.

τοῦτο (acc.sing.neut.of οὗτος, cause) 93.

ὅτι (causal conjunction) 211.

ἔρχεται (3d.per.sing.pres.ind.of ἔρχομαι, futuristic) 146.

ὥρα (nom.sing.fem.of ὥρα, subject of ἔρχεται) 735.

ἐν (preposition with the locative of time point) 80.

ᾗ (loc.sing.fem.of ὅς, time point) 65.

πάντες (nom.pl.masc.of πᾶς, in agreement with οἱ ἐν τοῖς μνημείοις) 67.

οἱ (nom.pl.masc.of the article, subject of ἀκούσουσιν) 9.

ἐν (preposition with the locative of place) 80.

τοῖς (loc.pl.neut.of the article in agreement with μνημείοις) 9.

μνημείοις (loc.pl.neut.of μνημεῖον, place where) 763.

ἀκούσουσιν (3d.per.pl.fut.act.ind.of ἀκούω, predictive) 148.

τῆς (gen.sing.fem.of the article in agreement with φωνῆς) 9.

φωνῆς (gen.sing.fem.of φωνή, objective genitive) 222.

αὐτοῦ (gen.sing.masc.of αὐτός, possession) 16.

Translation - "Do not continue to be amazed at this, because there is coming an hour in which all those in the graves shall hear His voice,"

Comment: μὴ with the present imperative indicates that the Jews were already mystified by Jesus' remarks and were pondering their possible meaning. He orders them to stop it. *Cf.#726* for a study of the psychological reaction of Jesus' listeners. τοῦτο, the accusative of cause without εἰς is a little unusual. The ὅτι clause which follows tells us why the Jews should not be wondering at what Jesus had already said, because something even more amazing was going to take place. Why then should they marvel at the foregoing. What is this even more breathtaking event of the future? ἔρχεται . . . αὐτοῦ. Not only those spiritually dead though yet physically alive shall hear the voice of the Son of God (vs.25), but all (and this means literally *all*) physically dead persons, saved and unsaved, shall hear His voice. οἱ νεκροὶ (vs.25) often refer to the unregenerate (#749) but the phrase πάντες οἱ ἐν τοῖς μνημείοις can mean only corpses in the ordinary physical sense. Our Lord here is saying that there is to be a universal summons out of physical death of all persons in whatever age or spiritual condition. Verse 29 declares that they shall all experience a resurrection and judgment, some for life and others for condemnation. Note again as in verse 25 that ἀκούω is followed by the genitive φωνῆς.

Verse 29 - ". . . and shall come forth; they that have done good unto the resurrection of life; and they that have done evil, unto the resurrection of damnation."

καὶ ἐκπορεύσονται, οἱ τὰ ἀγαθὰ ποιήσαντες εἰς ἀνάστασιν ζωῆς, οἱ δὲ τὰ φαῦλα πράξαντες εἰς ἀνάστασιν κρίσεως.

καὶ (adjunctive conjunction, joining verbs) 14.

ἐκπορεύσονται (3d.per.pl.fut.ind.of ἐκπορεύομαι, predictive) 270.

οἱ (nom.pl.masc.of the article in agreement with ποιήσαντες) 9.

τὰ (acc.pl.neut.of the article in agreement with ἀγαθά) 9.

ποιήσαντες (aor.act.part. nom.pl.masc.of ποιέω, subject of ἐκπορεύσονται) 127.

εἰς (preposition with the accusative, purpose) 140.

ἀνάστασιν (acc.sing.fem.of ἀνάστασις, purpose) 1423.

ζωῆς (gen.sing.fem.of ζωή, description) 668.

οἱ (nom.pl.masc.of the article in agreement with πράξαντες) 9.

δὲ (adversative conjunction) 11.

τὰ (acc.pl.neut.of the article in agreement with φαῦλα) 9.

φαῦλα (acc.pl.neut.of φαῦλος, direct object of πράξαντες) 1990.

πράξαντες (aor.act.part.nom.pl.masc.of πράσσω, substantival, subject of ἐκπορεύσονται) 1943.

εἰς (preposition with the accusative, purpose) 140.

ἀνάστασιν (acc.sing.fem.of ἀνάτασις, purpose) 1423.

κρίσεως (gen.sing.fem.of κρίσις, description) 478.

Translation - ". . . and they shall emerge, the ones who had performed good works for a resurrection of life, but the ones who had practised evil deeds for a resurrection of judgment."

Comment: Verse 29 completes the sentence begun in verse 28. All that are in the graves, which at the Second Coming of Christ will include the entire human race except the end-time generation still living, shall hear the voice of the triumphant Son of God as He descends from heaven (I Thess.4:13-18). All will respond. They are divided into two categories, *viz.*, those who did good and those who practised evil. Here the usual word for "do" (#127) is used. But the term for the other category is πράσσω (#1943). Note also that what the last category did was not πονηρά, ordinarily used opposite ἀγαθός but φαῦλα (#1990).

It is noteworthy that in John 3:20; 5:29 and Jas.3:16 φαῦλος is joined with πράσσω or πράγμα and that in Tit.2:8 it is used in opposition to sound speech. Also in Jas.3:16 it is associated with ζῆλος. The Jews were very zealous to the point of strife and contention. They busied themselves, loudly and contentiously with sabbath observance. They criticized the Son of God because He healed a man on the sabbath and transgressed one of *their* rules. They practised little things. They majored on minors. They were unwise stewards. They frittered away their time and energy doing what their culture approbated. They were conformists. They maintained the *status quo*. When a Progressive came along, with His sights on the eternal and rode rough-shod over their little rules they crucified Him. They hated the light because it showed up their littleness in their little battle of the frogs and mice. Study #1990 well with special attention to John 3:20. A great many preachers today are practising little things - zealously carry -ing out the dictates that are handed down from some denominational headquarters corporal, lest the *program* suffer. Each of us will face a resurrection unto discrimination (for this is the real meaning of κρίσις) τὰ ἀγαθά leads to ζωή. τὰ φαῦλα leads to κρίσις. This is the sentence of one who not only broke the sabbath but also made Himself equal to God (John 5:18).

Witnesses to Jesus

Verse 30 - "I can of mine own self do nothing: as I hear, I judge; and my judgment is just; because I seek not mine own will, but the will of the Father which hath sent me."

Οὐ δύναμαι ἐγὼ ποιεῖν ἀπ' ἐμαυτοῦ οὐδέν; καθὼς ἀκούω κρίνω, καὶ ἡ κρίσις ἡ ἐμὴ δικαία ἐστίν, ὅτι οὐ ζητῶ τὸ θέλημα τὸ ἐμὸν ἀλλὰ τὸ θέλημα τοῦ πέμφαντός με.

Οὐ (negative conjunction with the indicative) 130.

δύναμαι (1st.per.sing.pres.ind.of δύναμαι, aoristic) 289.

ἐγὼ (nom.sing.masc.of ἐγώ, subject of δύναμαι) 123.

ποιεῖν (pres.act.inf.of ποιέω, complementary) 127.

ἀπ' (preposition with the ablative of agency) 70.

ἐμαυτοῦ (abl.sing.masc.of ἐμαυτός, agent) 723.

οὐδέν (acc.sing.neut.of οὐδείς, direct object of ποιεῖν) 446.

καθὼς (comparative adverb) 1348.

ἀκούω (1st.per.sing.pres.act.ind.of ἀκούω, aoristic) 148.

κρίνω (1st.per.sing.pres.act.ind.of κρίνω, aoristic) 531.

καὶ (inferential conjunction) 14.

ἡ (nom.sing.fem.of the article in agreement with κρίσις) 9.

κρίσις (nom.sing.fem.of κρίσις, subject of ἐστίν) 478.

ἡ (nom.sing.fem.of the article in agreement with ἐμή) 9.

ἐμὴ (nom.sing.fem.of ἐμός, in agreement with κρίσις) 1267.

δικαία (nom.sing.fem.of δίκαιος, predicate adjective) 85.

ἐστίν (3d.per.sing.pres.ind.of εἰμί, aoristic) 86.

ὅτι (causal conjunction) 211.

οὐ (negative conjunction with the indicative) 130.

ζητῶ (1st.per.sing.pres.act.ind.of ζητέω, aoristic) 207.

τό (acc.sing.neut.of the article in agreement with θέλημα) 9.

θέλημα (acc.sing.neut.of θέλημα, direct object of ζητῶ) 577.

τό (acc.sing.neut.of the article in agreement with ἐμόν) 9.

ἐμόν (acc.sing.neut.of ἐμός, in agreement with θέλημα) 1267.

ἀλλά (alternative conjunction) 342.

τό (acc.sing.neut.of the article in agreement with θέλημα) 9.

θέλημα (acc.sing.neut.of θέλημα, direct object of ζητῶ) 577.

τοῦ (gen.sing.masc.of the article in agreement with πέμφαντός) 9.

πέμφαντός (aor.act.part.gen.sing.masc.of πέμπω, substantival, possession) 169.

με (acc.sing.masc.of ἐγώ, direct object of πέμφαντός) 123.

Translation - "I am not able to do one thing by myself; just as I hear I judge; therefore my judgment is just, because I am not seeking my will but the will of the one who sent me."

Comment: Here Jesus returns to the thought with which He opened the discourse in verse 19. The point of the entire passage is the oneness of the Father and the Son. It is impossible for the Son to do anything without the complete concurrence of the Father. This agreement grows out of the love that flows between Father and Son. The Father agreed with Jesus' decision to heal the man on the sabbath. The Jews professed to love God, but they were about to hold God's Son to a strict account since He had violated one of their insignificant rules. Jesus countered by adding that healing on the sabbath for all of its breathtaking wonder, was insignificant when compared with the greater things which the Godhead had planned for Him (vs.20). These greater things included life giving (vs.21), judgment (vs.22), the gift of salvation by faith (vs.24), regeneration (vs.25), judgment again (vs.26), resurrection of the dead and final judgment (vss.28-29). These things being true, it follows that no man can honor the Father (something which the Jews professed to do) and dishonor the Son (which the Jews were doing). This concurrence between Father and Son depended upon the fact that Jesus was not an empire builder for Himself (vs.30). He was seeking not His own will but the will of the Father Who had sent Him into the world.

Note the emphatic attributive positions in ἡ κρίσις ἡ ἐμὴ and τὸ θέλημα τὸ ἐμόν. Jesus is emphasizing that it is *His* judgment decisions and *His* will.

Verse 31 - "If I bear witness of myself, my witness is not true."

ἐὰν ἐγὼ μαρτυρῶ περὶ ἐμαυτοῦ, ἡ μαρτυρία μου οὐκ ἔστιν ἀληθής.

ἐὰν (conditional particle introducing a third-class condition) 363.

ἐγώ (nom.sing.masc.of ἐγώ, subject of μαρτυρῶ) 123.

μαρτυρῶ (1st.per.sing.pres.act.subj.of μαρτυρέω, third-class condition) 1471.

περὶ (preposition with the genitive of reference) 173.

ἐμαυτοῦ (gen.sing.masc.of ἐμαυτός, reference) 723.

ἡ (nom.sing.fem.of the article in agreement with μαρτυρία) 9.

μαρτυρία (nom.sing.fem.of μαρτυρία, subject of ἔστιν) 1695.

μου (gen.sing.masc.of ἐγώ, possession) 123.

οὐκ (negative conjunction with the indicative) 130.

ἔστιν (3d.per.sing.pres.ind.of εἰμί, aoristic) 86.

ἀληθής (nom.sing.fem.of ἀληθής, predicate adjective) 1415.

Translation - "The fact that I am witnessing about myself does not make my witness true."

Comment: Here I have taken the liberty to give a free translation, since a literal translation makes for awkward English. Literally it reads as the AV has translated it. We have a third-class condition, with ἐὰν and the subjunctive mode in the protasis and the present indicative in the apodosis. Jesus is stating a self-evident proposition that His listeners could well accept. Anyone, be he saint, God or devil could make the statements that Jesus had just made (vss.19-30). To accept them at face value solely on their own authority is naive indeed when we look at it as the empiricist does. Unbelievers, who do not begin their philosophy with the *a priori* assumption that God exists and that He has revealed His truth in the Bible, criticizes the Christian for saying, "I believe the Bible because the Bible says that its testimony is true." This is surely *petitio principii* - "begging the question" - the fallacy of assuming as true the point in litigation and then building a syllogism upon it. Any book can claim infallibility and secure acceptance of all its claims on the same basis. Any man could claim what Jesus claimed. The claim itself does not establish its validity. This is what Jesus is saying here and thus preparing their minds for what follows.

Verse 32 - "There is another that beareth witness of me; and I know that the witness which he witnesseth of me is true."

ἄλλος ἐστὶν ὁ μαρτυρῶν περὶ ἐμοῦ, καὶ οἶδα ὅτι ἀληθής ἐστιν ἡ μαρτυρία ἣν μαρτυρεῖ περὶ ἐμοῦ.

ἄλλος (nom.sing.masc.of ἄλλος, predicate nominative) 198.

ἐστὶν (3d.per.sing.pres.ind.of εἰμί, aoristic) 86.

ὁ (nom.sing.masc.of the article in agreement with μαρτυρῶν) 9.

μαρτυρῶν (pres.act.part.nom.sing.masc.of μαρτυρέω, subject of ἐστὶν) 1471.

περὶ (preposition with the genitive of reference) 173.

ἐμοῦ (gen.sing.masc.of ἐμός, reference) 1267.

καὶ (inferential conjunction) 14.

οἶδα (1st.per.sing.2d.perf. ind.of ὁράω, consummative) 144.
ὅτι (objective conjunction introducing indirect discourse) 211.
ἀληθής (nom.sing.fem.of ἀληθές, predicate adjective) 1415.
ἐστιν (3d.per.sing.pres.ind.of εἰμί, aoristic) 86.
ἡ (nom.sing.fem.of the article in agreement with μαρτυρία) 9.
μαρτυρία (nom.sing.fem.of μαρτυρία, subject of ἐστιν) 1695.
ἥν (acc.sing.fem.of ὅς, direct object of μαρτυρεῖ) 65.
μαρτυρεῖ (3d.per.sing.pres.act.ind.of μαρτυρέω, progressive) 1471.
περὶ (preposition with the genitive of reference) 173.
ἐμοῦ (gen.sing.masc.of ἐμός, reference) 1267.

Translation - "There is another who is preaching about me, therefore I know that the testimony which he is giving about me is true."

Comment: Note that ἄλλος is emphasized, since it is the predicate nominative written ahead of the subject. Jesus is talking now about John the Baptist. John's message, given as the prophesied forerunner of Messiah, has convinced Jesus that John's message is the truth. Note ἀληθής, the predicate adjective in emphasis also. That Jesus means John the Baptist here seems evident from vss.33-35, although Jesus points to even a higher witness in verse 36. Jesus is about to apply the Jewish law that truth must be established in the mouth of two witnesses.

Verse 33 - "Ye sent unto John, and he bare witness unto the truth."

ὑμεῖς ἀπεστάλκατε πρὸς Ἰωάννην, καὶ μεμαρτύρηκεν τῇ ἀληθείᾳ.

ὑμεῖς (nom.pl.masc.of σύ, subject of ἀπεστάλκατε) 104.
ἀπεστάλκατε (2d.per.pl.perf.act.ind.of ἀποστέλλω, consummative) 215.
πρὸς (preposition with the accusative of extent) 197.
Ἰωάννην (acc.sing.masc.of Ἰωάννης, extent) 247.
καὶ (continuative conjunction) 14.
μεμαρτύρηκε (3d.per.sing.perf.act.ind.of μαρτυρέω, consummative) 1471.
τῇ (dat.sing.fem.of the article in agreement with ἀληθείᾳ) 9.
ἀληθείᾳ, reference) 1416.

Translation - "You have sent to John and he has witnessed with reference to the truth."

Comment: John has omitted the direct object of ἀπεστάλκατε. They sent messengers to John, a reference to the material in John 1:19-28. When the messengers arrived John the Baptist gave a clear-cut witness with respect to his own identity (he was *not* the Messiah) and to the identity of Jesus. *Cf.* John 1:19-34. It was on this occasion that John the Baptist referred to the Messiah as the Lamb of God who would take away the sins of the world (John 1:29). John also told the Jews why he was so certain that Jesus was the Messiah. He had seen the

Holy Spirit descend and abide upon Jesus at His baptism. This was the cue, given by God to John, by which he would identify the Messiah as such when he saw him. Thus we have two witnesses thus far - that of Jesus Himself and that of John the Baptist. In addition John's testimony contains his account of the witness of the Father who spoke from heaven when Jesus was baptized, "This is my beloved Son in Whom I am well pleased " (Mt.3:17). The testimonies of Jesus and John the Baptist are parallel. There is no disagreement between them. John had confirmed all that Jesus testified about Himself. But Jesus is not depending upon John's testimony only (vs.36) though He does not repudiate it.

Verse 34 - "But I receive not testimony from man: but these things I say, that ye might be saved."

ἐγὼ δὲ οὐ παρὰ ἀνθρώπου τὴν μαρτυρίαν λαμβάνω, ἀλλὰ ταῦτα λέγω ἵνα ὑμεῖς σωθῆτε.

ἐγὼ (nom.sing.masc.of ἐγώ, subject of λαμβάνω) 123.
δὲ (adversative conjunction) 11.
οὐ (negative conjunction with the indicative) 130.
παρὰ (preposition with the ablative of source, with persons) 154.
ἀνθρώπου (abl.sing.masc.of ἄνθρωπος, source) 341.
τὴν (acc.sing.fem.of the article in agreement with μαρτυρίαν) 9.
μαρτυρίαν (acc.sing.fem.of μαρτυρία, direct object of λαμβάνω) 1695.
λαμβάνω (1st.per.sing.pres.act.ind.of λαμβάνω, customary) 533.
ἀλλὰ (adversative conjunction) 342.
ταῦτα (acc.pl.neut.of οὗτος, direct object of λέγω) 93.
λέγω (1st.per.sing.pres.act.ind.of λέγω, aoristic) 66.
ἵνα (final conjunction introducing a purpose clause) 114.
ὑμεῖς (nom.sing.masc.of σύ, subject of σωθῆτε) 104.
σωθῆτε (2d.per.pl.aor.pass.subj.of σώζω, purpose) 109.

Translation - "But I do not ordinarily accept the testimony from a man, but these things I am saying in order that you might be saved."

Comment: δὲ is adversative, as Jesus hastens to say that under normal circumstances it was not His policy to base His own claims upon the testimony of a mere mortal. John was not the ordinary prophet, but the greatest of the prophets. Even so, Jesus has greater evidence for His claim to deity, even than that which came from John. Jesus did not repudiate John's testimony, but He was not depending upon it to legitimatize His claim to deity. Why then did He mention John? It was, He added, for the purpose of leading them to salvation. Thus the purpose clause ἵνα ὑμεῖς σωθῆτε. Faith comes by hearing the Word of God (Rom.10:17). It was well to establish with the Jews the idea that Jesus' person and works were genuine. According to their law Jesus' claim was established. John had witnessed of Him and He had witnessed about Himself.

It must be admitted that Jesus here seems to support the apologetic approach that saving faith comes to the unsaved on the basis of evidence which is grasped by the unregenerate mind. Here were some Jews who had set about to kill Jesus because He had contributed to the transgression of the law of the sabbath with His command to the man who was healed. Jesus presented His claim to deity, with all of the divine functions which it was His to perform. He then proceeded to *prove* to them, despite the fact that they were unregenerate, that under their law, His claim was valid. This He did by appealing to the testimony of John the Baptist, whom they believed for a short time (vs.35).

We have taken the view that the Christian experience begins with the faith that accepts *a priori* the fact that God exists and that He has spoken to us in His word. Christian evidence is abundantly available and will be apparent to those who take Christ by faith. The evidence comes after we trust Him, not before. Experience confirms truth; it does not create it. The sinner is saved when He accepts Christ's word by faith - not on the basis of the evidence that He spoke the truth. If He is our Lord as we say He is, He need not *prove* to us that He speaks the truth.

Jesus pursues His point in

Verse 35 - "He was a burning and a shining light: and ye were willing for a season to rejoice in his light."

ἐκεῖνος ἦν ὁ λύχνος ὁ καιόμενος καὶ φαίνων, ὑμεῖς δὲ ἠθελήσατε ἀγαλλιαθῆναι πρὸς ὥραν ἐν τῷ φωτὶ αὐτοῦ.

ἐκεῖνος (nom.sing.masc.of ἐκεῖνος, predicate nominative) 246.

ἦν (3d.per.sing.imp.ind.of εἰμί, progressive duration) 86.

ὁ (nom.sing.masc.of the article in agreement with λύχνος) 9.

λύχνος (nom.sing.masc.of λύχνος, subject of ἦν) 454.

ὁ (nom.sing.masc.of the article in agreement with καιόμενος) 9.

καιόμενος (pres.mid.part.nom.sing.masc.of καίω, adjectival, ascriptive) 453.

καὶ (adjunctive conjunction, joining adjectival participles) 14.

φαίνων (pres.act.part.nom.sing.masc.of φαίνω, adjectival, ascriptive) 100.

ὑμεῖς (nom.pl.masc.of σύ, subject of ἠθελήσατε) 104.

ἠθελήσατε (2d.per.pl.aor.act.ind.of θέλω, constative) 88.

ἀγαλλιαθῆναι (aor.pass.inf.of ἀγαλλιάω, complementary) 440.

πρὸς (preposition with the accusative of time extent) 197.

ὥραν (acc.sing.fem.of ὥρα, time extent) 735.

ἐν (preposition with the instrumental of means) 80.

τῷ (instru.sing.neut.of the article in agreement with φωτὶ) 9.

φωτὶ (instru.sing.neut.of φῶς, means) 379.

αὐτοῦ (gen.sing.masc.of αὐτός, possession) 16.

Translation - "The burning and shining lamp was he; and you were willing to rejoice for an hour in his light."

Comment: ἐκεῖνος, the predicate nominative, in emphasis, refers to John the Baptist. He is dramatically described as a torch, an enthused and brilliantly lighted witness. The emphatic attributive positions of the participial adjectives ὁ καιόμενος καὶ φαίνων is to be noted. *Cf.*#453 for other uses of καίω, particularly Lk.24:32. As the hearts of the disciples of Emmaus "burned" with holy emotion, so did that of the Baptist as he preached. It is scant wonder that he shone (#100). And the Jews had gone out to hear him (Mt.3:5,6) as well as to send a delegation to ask questions (John 5:33; 1:19). Jesus is about to point to the fact that the Jews are more severely condemned because they had their chance to be saved. They sent to John - no false prophet, nor a timid trumpet with an uncertain sound - they had listened to one who was aflame with zeal and joy and "shining" in the reflected glory of his soon coming Messiah. Indeed, Jesus adds that they had made a decision to accept John temporarily. Note the aorist in ἠθελήσατε and the middle voice in ἀγαλλιαθῆναι. They heard John and decided to rejoice themselves, *i.e.* to go along with the crowd in the popular acceptance of Israel's hope. But when the Hope appeared, He refused to fit into their preconceived pattern. He healed a man on the sabbath and they were now against Him. They rejoiced πρὸς ὥραν. *Cf.*#197 for other uses of πρός in time expressions. John's light filled them with joy, but the light of Christ offended them. Yet John was shining with Jesus' light. There was something the matter with them - not with Jesus nor with John. They were the hypocrites! John had become for them something of a religious and philosophical toy with which they amused themselves. Meyer points out (*en loc.*) that the Jews rejoiced (ἀγαλλιάω) when they should have repented (μετανοέω).

Verse 36 - "But I have greater witness than that of John: for the works which the Father hath given me to finish, the same works that I do, bear witness of me, that the Father hath sent me."

ἐγὼ δὲ ἔχω τὴν μαρτυρίαν μείζω τοῦ Ἰωάννου, τὰ γὰρ ἔργα ἃ δέδωκέν μοι ὁ πατὴρ ἵνα τελειώσω αὐτά, ανοτὰ τὰ ἃ ποιῶ, μαρτυρεῖ περὶ ἐμοῦ ὅτι ὁ πατήρ με ἀπέσταλκεν.

ἐγὼ (nom.sing.masc.of ἐγώ, subject of ἔχω) 123.

δὲ (adversative conjunction) 11.

ἔχω (1st.per.sing.pres.act.ind.of ἔχω, aoristic) 82.

τὴν (acc.sing.fem.of the article in agreement with μαρτυρίαν) 9.

μαρτυρίαν (acc.sing.fem.of μαρτυρία, direct object of ἔχω) 1695.

μείζω (acc.sing.fem.of μείζων, the comparative of μέγας, in agreement with μαρτυρίαν) 916.

τοῦ (abl.sing.masc.of the article in agreement with Ἰωάννου) 9.

Ἰωάννου (abl.sing.masc.of Ἰωάννης, comparison) 247.

τὰ (nom.pl.neut.of the article in agreement with ἔργα) 9.

γὰρ (causal conjunction) 105.

ἔργα (nom.pl.neut.of ἔργον, subject of μαρτυρεῖ) 460.
ἃ (acc.pl.neut.of ὅς, direct object of δέδωκεν) 65.
δέδωκεν (3d.per.sing.perf.act.ind.of δίδωμι, consummative) 362.
μοι (dat.sing.masc.of ἐγώ, indirect object of δέδωκέν) 123.
ὁ (nom.sing.masc.of the article in agreement with πατήρ) 9.
πατήρ (nom.sing.masc.of πατήρ, subject of δέδωκέν) 238.
ἵνα (sub-final conjunction introducing a purpose/result clause) 114.
τελειώσω (1st.per.sing.aor.act.subj.of τελειόω, sub-final) 1914.
αὐτά (acc.pl.neut.of αὐτός, direct object of τελειώσω) 16.
αὐτὰ (nom.pl.neut.of αὐτός, in agreement with ἔργα) 16.
τὰ (nom.pl.neut.of the article in agreement with ἔργα) 9.
ἔργα (nom.pl.neut.of ἔργον, subject of μαρτυρεῖ) 460.
ἃ (acc.pl.neut.of ὅς, direct object of ποιῶ) 65.
ποιῶ (1st.per.sing.pres.act.ind.of ποιέω, progressive) 127.
μαρτυρεῖ (3d.per.sing.pres.act.ind.of μαρτυρέω, progressive) 1471.
περὶ (preposition with the genitive of reference) 173.
ἐμοῦ (gen.sing.masc.of ἐμός, reference) 1267.
ὅτι (objective conjunction, introducing indirect discourse) 211.
ὁ (nom.sing.masc.of the article in agreement with πατήρ) 9.
πατήρ (nom.sing.masc.of πατήρ, subject of ἀπέσταλκεν) 238.
με (acc.sing.masc.of ἐγω, direct object of ἀπέσταλκεν) 123.
ἀπέσταλκεν (3d.per.sing.perf.act.ind.of ἀποστέλλω, consummative) 215.

Translation - "But I have the greater witness than that of John; therefore the works which the Father has given to me, in order (and with the result) that I carry them out - these works which I am now doing, bear witness of me that the Father has sent me."

Comment: Having gently pointed out to the Jews that they had once apparently accepted John the Baptist's message, though their allegiance to John's message was of short duration (πρὸς ὥραν), Jesus now goes on to say that, while He does not spurn John's testimony - far from it - nevertheless He has greater testimony than that of John. Note μείζω followed by the ablative of comparison. What is this greater testimony? τὰ ἔργα . . . αὐτά. Of these works, He says two things: they were given to Him by the Father, and it is in the divine plan that He should finish them. Christ, the Ω is the Finisher in the Godhead. Study #1914 carefully for a fascinating study of τελειόω in relation to Christ. Notice the consummative perfect tense in δέδωκεν. This delegation of miracle working ministry was given by the Father to the Son as a completed action in the eternal past. But it has resulted in a present matter of fact. Having been given this ministry, Jesus has it now .. These works are always bearing witness about Christ, *viz.* that the Father has sent Him and is still with Him (perfect tense in ἀπέσταλκεν).

Here we have Jesus making an appeal to empiricism, the only language that the Jews, being unregenerate, could understand. Anyone can say that he is the Son of God (vs.31). It should be established by the confirming witness of another (vs.32). Lest they think that the other witness of verse 32 was John the Baptist, He deals with John by saying that when the Jews sent to John and heard his witness, which Jesus approbates, they received him πρὸς ὥραν and then turned away. Should they answer in their thoughts that John also lied and all they did was repudiate the confirming testimony which one liar gave to the word of another, Jesus announces that He is not depending upon John for confirmation, as inspired and truthful as it was, but rather is appealing to the historical record of His works. He declares that they have their source in God the Father and that He is sent by God the Father to finish them. In other words, Israel may expect that from henceforth, all that the God of Israel will do, will be done through Jesus Christ, His Son. What works are they? Of such a supernatural character and so open to public inspection that Jesus submits that they are ample empirical evidence that He is the Son of God and God's Messenger.

Unitarianism, in rejecting the deity of Jesus must face this argument. They do by doubting the historic creditability of the gospel records. They say that if they were convinced that the gospel records were valid, they would have no choice but to accept the Son of God. The acid test of their sincerity therefore would rest upon a return of Christ to earth to perform miracles before their eyes as He did before the eyes of the Jews. Would they then believe? The Jews did not. Hence we see that the highly touted empiricism is not capable of producing certitude. How empirical could Jesus get?! The man had not walked for 38 years!! A man believes or disbelieves in the presence or absence of evidence, whether logical or empirical, because he has the gift of faith in the first instance or lacks it in the second. Witness the stupendous follies believed by some in the total absence of evidence and the obvious truths rejected by the same people though confronted by evidence on every hand. Jesus makes the whole argument rest upon verse 38 - "Ye have not His word abiding in you." Fatal lack. It makes all the difference in the world and in Heaven - - in time and in eternity.

Verse 37 - "And the Father himself, which hath sent me, hath borne witness of me. Ye have neither heard his voice at any time, nor seen his shape."

καὶ ὁ πέμψας με πατὴρ ἐκεῖνος μεμαρτύρηκεν περὶ ἐμοῦ. οὔτε φωνὴν αὐτοῦ πώποτε ἀκηκόατε οὔτε εἶδος αὐτοῦ ἑωράκατε,

καὶ (continuative conjunction) 14.

ὁ (nom.sing.masc.of the article in agreement with πέμψας) 9.

πέμψας (aor.act.part.nom.sing.masc.of πέμπω, substantival, subject of μεμαρτύρηκεν) 169.

με (acc.sing.masc.of ἐγώ, direct object of πέμψας) 123.

πατὴρ (nom.sing.masc.of πατήρ, apposition) 238.

ἐκεῖνος (nom.sing.masc.of ἐκεῖνος, agree with πατήρ) 246.

μεμαρτύρηκεν (3d.per.sing.perf.act.ind.of μαρτυρέω, consummative) 1471.

περὶ (preposition with the genitive of reference) 173.

ἐμοῦ (gen.sing.masc.of ἐμός, reference) 1267.

οὔτε (negative copulative conjunction) 598.
φωνὴν (acc.sing.fem.of φωνή, direct object of ἀκηκόατε) 222.
αὐτοῦ (gen.sing.masc.of αὐτός, possession) 16.
πώποτε (temporal adverb) 1701.
ἀκηκόατε (2d.per.pl.2d.perf.act.ind.of ἀκούω, intensive) 148.
οὔτε (negative copulative conjunction) 598.
εἶδος (acc.sing.neut.of εἶδος, direct object of ἑωράκατε) 1950.
ἑωράκατε (2d.per.pl.perf.act.ind.of ὁράω, intensive) 144.

Translation - "And the One who sent me, the Father himself has testified about me. Neither at any time have you heard His voice nor have you seen His form."

Comment: ὁ πέμψας με is the subject of μεμαρτύρηκεν, while πατὴρ ἐκεῖνος is reflexive. *Cf.#598* for other examples of οὔτε... οὔτε - "neither...nor." The Jews could not testify on empirical grounds about the Father Who sent Jesus. They had not heard His voice nor seen His shape. John 1:18. But Jesus declares that this One Whom the Jews knew so little is the very One Who sent Him into the world and Who also has always witnessed and continues to witness (perfect tense in μεμαρτύρηκεν) περὶ ἐμοῦ. All of the works which Jesus had done before them were evidences that God, of Whom they knew so little, was witnessing through Jesus concerning Himself. The witness of John was great, but the witness of the Father was greater. The Jews rejected John and they were to reject Jesus because they did not have God's Word in them. This is the statement of verse 38. Meyer points out that the perfect tense in μεμαρ. makes it necessary to identify the Father's witness with the scriptures rather than with the miracles of Jesus. "The Father has been telling about me in the Old Testament since the days of old." Had the Jews really believed their scriptures as much as they said they did, they would have accepted both John and Jesus. *Cf.John 5:39.*

Verse 38 - "And ye have not his word abiding in you: for whom he hath sent, him ye believe not."

καὶ τὸν λόγον αὐτοῦ οὐκ ἔχετε ἐν ὑμῖν μένοντα, ὅτι ἀπέστειλεν ἐκεῖνος τούτῳ ὑμεῖς οὐ πιστεύετε.

καὶ (continuative conjunction) 14.
τὸν (acc.sing.masc.of the article in agreement with λόγον) 9.
λόγον (acc.sing.masc.of λόγος, direct object of ἔχετε) 510.
αὐτοῦ (gen.sing.masc.of αὐτός, possession) 16.
οὐκ (negative conjunction with the indicative) 130.
ἔχετε (2d.per.pl.pres.act.ind.of ἔχω, aoristic) 82.
ἐν (preposition with the locative of place where) 80.
ὑμῖν (loc.pl.masc.of σύ, place where) 104.
μένοντα (pres.act.part.acc.sing.masc.of μένω, adjectival, in agreement with λόγον) 864.

ὅτι (causal conjunction) 211.

ὅν (acc.sing.masc.of ὅς, direct object of ἀπέστειλεν) 65.

ἀπέστειλεν (3d.per.sing.aor.act.ind.of ἀποστέλλω, culminative) 215.

ἐκεῖνος (nom.sing.masc.of ἐκεῖνος, subject of ἀπέστειλεν) 246.

τούτῳ (dat.sing.masc.of οὗτος, reference) 93.

ὑμεῖς (nom.pl.masc.of σύ, subject of πιστεύετε) 104.

οὐ (negative conjunction with the indicative) 130.

πιστεύετε (2d.per.pl.pres.act.ind.of πιστεύω, aoristic) 734.

Translation - "And His message you do not have abiding within you, because He whom that one has sent, is the One Whom you do not believe."

Comment: In order to be literal the translation is awkward. The student should understand exactly what Jesus has said. The key to all the trouble which the Jews had is set forth in τὸν λόγον . . . μένοντα. They did not have the message of the Old Testament in their hearts, however much they may have had it in their heads. Verse 39 gives us a hint as to how the Jews regarded the Old Testament scriptures. They had searched the scriptures, but the Word was not mixed with faith (Heb.4:2). Had they received with humility and faith all that the prophets had spoken they would have anticipated the coming of John the Baptist and come to him for help. Furthermore they would have received John's message and accepted Jesus as Messiah when He appeared. Even the Christians were ". . . fools and slow of heart to believe all that the prophets had spoken" (Luke 24:25). Simeon (Luke 2:25-32) is an example of how much light a sincere Bible student can get from the Old Testament scriptures, for he understood clearly that Messiah would come in his lifetime. If Simeon could believe upon Christ, when he saw him only as a tiny baby, why could not the sophisticated Jews, who professed to know so much about the scriptures? The answer is in our verse. Jesus links the lack of the abiding word with their rejection of Him. This is the force of the causal clause introduced by ὅτι.

When the sinner rejects any part of the light of God's revelation, he makes it impossible to accept greater portions of that light. Doubt and unbelief breeds the decision to suppress and cast aside the glimmer of divine light. Thus it breeds greater doubt. *Cf.* Rom.1:18 *ff.* for Paul's analysis of the reason for the apostasy and degradation of the heathen world. The scriptures give us many examples of others who studied the testimony of God in the Old Testament and were anticipating the arrival, both of the Baptist and the Messiah. The main thread of Jesus' argument here is that God's revelation to man is a unit. He gave the Old Testament word, He sent John the Baptist and He sent the Messiah. All are true revelations of God's message to man. When man is receptive to the message he has light. When he is stubborn and doubtful he has nothing but darkness. Only one who had been afflicted with theophobia as long as had the Jews could be blind enough to fail to see the evidence of Jesus' deity in His works and words. Truly prejudice is a crippling disease. None is so blind as the man who refuses to see. Which recalls II Cor.4:3,4.

Verse 39 - "Search the scriptures; for in them ye think ye have eternal life: and they are they which testify of me."

ἐραυνᾶτε τὰς γραφάς, ὅτι ὑμεῖς δοκεῖτε ἐν αὐταῖς ζωὴν αἰώνιον ἔχειν, καὶ ἐκεῖναί εἰσιν αἱ μαρτυροῦσαι περὶ ἐμοῦ.

#2099 ἐραυνᾶτε (2d.per.pl.pres.act.impv.of ἐρευνάω).

search - John 5:39; 7:52; Rom.8:27; I Cor.2:10; I Pet.1:11; Rev.2:23.

Meaning: - ἡ ἔρευνα - a search. To search; do research; look into; examine analytically; investigate. To investigate the teaching of Scripture - John 5:39; 7:52; with reference to God who examines men's hearts - Rom.8:27; Rev.2:23; with reference to the Holy Spirit Who researches everything - I Cor.2:10; of the Old Testament Prophets who sought after the meaning of the things which they testified about - I Pet.1:11.

τὰς (acc.pl.fem.of the article in agreement with γραφάς) 9.
γραφάς (acc.pl.fem.of γραφή, direct object of ἐραυνᾶτε) 1389.
ὅτι (causal conjunction) 211.
δοκεῖτε (2d.per.pl.pres.act.ind.of δοκέω, customary) 287.
ἐν (preposition with the locative of place) 80.
αὐταῖς (loc.pl.fem.of αὐτός, place where) 16.
ζωὴν (acc.sing.fem.of ζωή, direct object of ἔχειν) 668.
αἰώνιον (acc.sing.fem.of αἰώνιος, in agreement with ζωὴν) 1255.
ἔχειν (pres.act.inf.of ἔχω, acc.case, object of δοκεῖτε) 82.
καὶ (emphatic conjunction) 14.
ἐκεῖναί (nom.pl.fem.of ἐκεῖνος, predicate nominative) 246.
εἰσιν (3d.per.pl.pres.ind.of εἰμί, aoristic) 86.
αἱ (nom.pl.fem.of the article in agreement with μαρτυροῦσαι) 9.
μαρτυροῦσαι (pres.act.part.nom.pl.fem.of μαρτυρέω, subject of εἰσιν) 1471.
περὶ (preposition with the genitive of reference) 173.
ἐμοῦ (gen.sing.masc.of ἐμός, reference) 1267.

Translation: "Research the scriptures, because you expect in them to find eternal life; in fact these are the ones which testify about me."

Comment: Here is a challenge. Jesus flings it into the teeth of the Jews to make manifest their intellectual harlotry. The strength of the challenge is in the ὅτι clause of cause. Why go to the Old Testament? "Because you are always thinking (customary present tense in δοκεῖτε) that by means of them you have eternal life." No one professed to believe the Scriptures more than the Jews and in their view, no one understood them as well as they. Yet these Jews were trying to kill Jesus. Yet the scriptures are full of testimony about Him. He stood before them as the living fulfillment of all of the hopes of the nation. Nothing is more revolting than loud protestations of faith in the scriptures accompanied by flagrant violations of their teachings. How could anyone believe the Old

Testament and reject the claims of Jesus Christ? How much of the program of the typical mid-twentieth century church cañ be justified by the scriptures which are read and the creeds which are recited? *Cf.*Lk.24:25-27. Jesus explains how so-called students of the Word can reject Him in

Verse 40 - "And ye will not come to me, that ye might have life."

καὶ οὐ θέλετε ἐλθεῖν πρός με ἵνα ζωὴν ἔχητε.

καὶ (adversative conjunction) 14.

οὐ (negative conjunction with the indicative) 130.

θέλετε (2d.per.pl.pres.act.ind.of θέλω, aoristic) 88.

ἐλθεῖν (aor.inf.of ἔρχομαι, complementary) 146.

πρός (preposition with the accusative of extent) 197.

με (acc.sing.masc.of ἐγώ, extent) 123.

ἵνα (sub-final conjunction introducing a purpose/result clause) 114.

ζωὴν (acc.sing.fem.of ζωή, direct object of ἔχητε) 668.

ἔχητε (2d.per.pl.pres.act.subj.of ἔχω, sub-final) 82.

Translation - "But you are not willing to come to me in order that you might have life."

Comment: Jesus Christ invites the believer into the same close relationship with Him that He enjoyed with the Father. *Cf.*John 1:1; 17:21; I John 1:2. Note πρός τὸν θεόν in John 1:1 and πρὸς τὸν πατέρα in I John 1:2. Compare with πρός με in John 5:40. Jesus is "near to God" (John 1:1); "near to the Father" (I John 1:2). How near? The answer is in John 17:21. Now He invites us to come πρός με - "near to me." What an invitation! To come into a relationship with Christ that is as intimate as that is certainly to have life. But the Jews in Jesus' audience did not want it. The will of man is the final arbiter of his salvation. (John 7:17). The enemies of Jesus knew the scriptures well enough to know who He was and what He could do for them. They did not want His help. *Cf.* Rev.22:17 and note the mistranslation of the KJV. It is not "Whosoever will, let him take the water of life freely" but "Let the willing one take the water of life freely." Back of the fact that the sinner is willing to come is the irresistible conviction of the Holy Spirit who grants repentance (Acts 11:18) and faith (Eph.2:8,9). *Cf.* John 6:44; I Cor.12:3. To be sure, God is willing to save the lost sinner who is willing to allow God to save him. The will of man is involved, for God never saves anyone against his will. But the deeper question asks, "Why do some will to be saved and others do not?"

Verse 41 - "I receive not honor from men."

Δόξαν παρὰ ἀνθρώπων οὐ λαμβάνω.

Δόξαν (acc.sing.fem.of δόξα, direct object of λαμβάνω) 361.

παρὰ (preposition with the ablative of source, with persons) 154.

ἀνϑρώπων (abl.pl.masc.of ἄνϑρωπος, source) 341.
οὐ (negative conjunction with the indicative) 130.
λαμβάνω, (1st.per.sing.pres.act.ind.of λαμβάνω, customary) 533.

Translation - "Honor from men it is not my policy to receive."

Comment: I have interpreted λαμβάνω of verse 41 as a customary present. Our Lord is far too well acquainted with human nature to seek or to expect or accept honor from that source. Glory and honor are given to Him only by those who have been touched by the miraculous finger of divine grace. *Cf.* the list in *The Renaissance New Testament, I, 285,4..* The statement is a further elaboration of the last clause of verse 40. They did not wish to come to Christ that they might be saved. Had they done so they would have honored Him. *Cf.* Lk.14:10; John 5:44a; 7:18a; 8:50,54; 12:43a; I Thess.2:6. We will reserve comment on John 5:44a for the appropriate place. How empty would the δόξα of men be for our Lord! Like "carrying coals to Newcastle." The statement goes on in

Verse 42 - "But I know you, that ye have not the love of God in you."

ἀλλὰ ἔγνωκα ὑμᾶς ὅτι τὴν ἀγάπην τοῦ θεοῦ οὐκ ἔχετε ἐν ἑαυτοῖς.

ἀλλὰ (alternative conjunction) 342.
ἔγνωκα (1st.per.sing.perf.act.ind.of γινώσκω, consummative) 131.
ὑμᾶς (acc.pl.masc.of σύ, direct object of ἔγνωκα) 104.
ὅτι (objective conjunction introducing indirect discourse) 211.
τὴν (acc.sing.fem.of the article in agreement with ἀγάπην) 9.
ἀγάπην (acc.sing.fem.of ἀγάπη, direct object of ἔχετε) 1490.
τοῦ (gen.sing.masc.of the article in agreement with θεοῦ) 9.
θεοῦ (gen.sing.masc.of θεός, possession) 124.
οὐκ (negative conjunction with the indicative) 130.
ἔχετε (2d.per.pl.pres.act.ind.of ἔχω, customary) 82.
ἐν (preposition with the locative of place) 80.
ἑαυτοῖς (loc.pl.masc.of ἑαυτός, place where) 288.

Translation - "On the contrary I have always known you and I know now that you do not have the love of God within you."

Comment: Customarily Jesus had a policy not to expect glory from unregenerate man. ἀλλὰ serves to introduce the alternate situation. Jesus has always known and therefore is now completely aware of the fact (consummative perfect in ἔγνωκα) that (indirect discourse following ὅτι) they customarily and typically had no love for God in their hearts. It is as though Jesus had said, "I have never been honored by men, but this does not surprize and disappoint me, because I have always known your character. You are behaving exactly like men who have no love for God in you." Only God could use the perfective form ἔγνωκα. "I have known you from the beginning and I know you now." Love of God produces faith and the willingness to come to God's Son.

Verse 43 - "I am come in my Father's name, and ye receive me not: if another shall come in his own name, him ye will receive."

ἐγὼ ἐλήλυθα ἐν τῷ ὀνόματι τοῦ πατρός μου καὶ οὐ λαμβάνετέ με; ἐὰν ἄλλος ἔλθῃ ἐν τῷ ὀνόματι τῷ ἰδίῳ, ἐκεῖνον λήμφεσθε.

ἐγὼ (nom.sing.masc.of ἐγώ, subject of ἐλήλυθα) 123.

ἐλήλυθα (1st.per.sing.2d.perf.ind.of ἔρχομαι, consummative) 146.

ἐν (preposition with the dative of accompanying circumstance) 80.

τῷ (dat.sing.neut.of the article in agreement with ὀνόματι) 9.

ὀνόματι (dat.sing.neut.of ὄνομα, accompanying circumstance) 108.

τοῦ (gen.sing.masc.of the article in agreement with πατρός) 9.

πατρός (gen.sing.masc.of πατήρ, possession) 238.

μου (gen.sing.masc.of ἐγώ, relationship) 123.

καὶ (adversative conjunction) 14.

οὐ (negative conjunction with the indicative) 130.

λαμβάνετέ (2d.per.pl.pres.act.ind.of λαμβάνω, progressive) 533.

με (acc.sing.masc.of ἐγώ, direct object of λαμβάνετέ) 123.

ἐὰν (conditional particle introducing a third-class condition) 363.

ἄλλος (nom.sing.masc.of ἄλλος, subject of ἔλθῃ) 198.

ἔλθῃ (3d.per.sing.aor.subj.of ἔρχομαι, third-class condition) 146.

ἐν (preposition with the dative of accompanying circumstance) 80.

τῷ (dat.sing.neut.of the article in agreement with ὀνόματι) 9.

ὀνόματι (dat.sing.neut.of ὄνομα, accompanying circumstance) 108.

τῷ (dat.sing.masc.of the article in agreement with ἰδίῳ) 9.

ἰδίῳ (dat.sing.masc.of ἔδιος, in agreement with ὀνόματι) 778.

ἐκεῖνον (acc.sing.masc.of ἐκεῖνος, direct object of λήμφεσθε, anaphoric) 246.

λήμφεσθε (2d.per.pl.fut.mid.ind.of λαμβάνω, predictive) 533.

Translation - "I am here in my Father's name, but you are not receiving me; if another comes in his own name, that one you will receive."

Comment: Note ἐγώ in emphasis. 2d.perfect in ἐλήλυθα - a present situation as a result of a past completed action - "I have completed the incarnation and here I am." The prepositional phrase ἐν τῷ ὀνόματι seems to be accompanying circumstance. τοῦ πατρός μου - "in the name of my Father" is in contrast to τῷ ἰδίῳ - the latter being in the emphatic attributive position. Jesus is pointing up the enormity of the sinful presumption of one who would dare to come in his own name rather than in the name of the Father. And yet the Jews were not receiving Christ (an established and settled policy on their part) Who came in the name of God His Father, Whom the Jews professed to worship, Who had spoken to Israel in the scriptures and Who had also spoken through the miracles of Jesus before their very eyes.

The third-class condition with ἐὰν and the aorist subjunctive in the protasis and the future indicative in the apodosis, expresses the reasonable doubt that might normally be used for any prediction. "If another shall come in his own name (reasonable doubt) *you will receive him* (no doubt about this)." The man who is so stubborn that he wills not to believe God is sure to be victimized by one who comes to him on lesser authority. The naive credulity of the unregenerate is enough to induce merriment among sophisticated Christians, as we watch those who have rejected Christ consulting their horoscopes, reading palms, tracing patterns on an ouija board or following with fanatical devotion, which includes financial contributions through the mail, some religious fanatic with widespread coverage with radio and television. The California demagogue who led his congregation in Central America to mass suicide is an example of the hellish charisma which Satan grants to those who come in their own name.

College bred infidels find religious fanatics amusing and dismiss them with contempt, yet the radical empiricist, who eschews all statements of faith, procedes to develop his own *weltanschauung* on a mass of assumptions, none of which are subject to verification. They are people of such deep seated prejudices that they are utterly blind to the folly of their philosophy. Fanatics are always like that. At the end of the age Antichrist will come in his own name and the entire world, except those who are members of the body of Christ, will accept him and follow him like sheep into the pit. His coming will be ". . . after the working of Satan with all power and signs and lying wonders, and with all deceivableness of unrighteousness in them that perish, because they received not the love of the truth, that they might be saved" (II Thess.2:9,10). *Cf.* also Rev.13:13-18. A rewarding research project is to study all of the passages in the Revelation where ὄνομα occurs, in the light of John 5:43 (*cf.*#108).

Verse 44 - "How can ye believe, which receive honor one of another, and seek not the honor that cometh from God only?"

πῶς δύνασθε ὑμεῖς πιστεῦσαι, δόξαν παρὰ ἀλλήλων λαμβάνοντες καὶ τὴν δόξαν τὴν παρὰ τοῦ μόνου θεοῦ οὐ ζητεῖτε;

πῶς (interrogative conjunction) 627.

δύνασθε (2d.per.pl.pres.ind.of δύναμαι, direct question) 289.

ὑμεῖς (nom.pl.masc.of σύ, subject of δύνασθε) 104.

πιστεῦσαι (aor.act.inf.of πιστεύω, complementary) 734.

δόξαν (acc.sing.fem.of δόξα, direct object of λαμβάνοντες) 361.

παρὰ (preposition with the ablative of source with persons) 154.

ἀλλήλων (abl.pl.masc.of ἄλληλος, source) 1487.

λαμβάνοντες (pres.act.part.nom.pl.masc.of λαμβάνω, adverbial, conditional) 533.

καὶ (adversative conjunction) 14.

τὴν (acc.sing.fem.of the article in agreement with δόξαν) 9.

δόξαν (acc.sing.fem.of δόξα, direct object of ζητεῖτε) 361.

τὴν (acc.sing.fem.of the article, in agreement with δόξαν) 9.

παρὰ (preposition with the ablative of source, with persons) 154.

τοῦ (abl.sing.masc.of the article in agreement with θεοῦ) 9.

μόνου (abl.sing.masc.of μόνος, in agreement with θεοῦ) 339.
θεοῦ (abl.sing.masc.of θεός, source) 124.
οὐ (negative conjunction with the indicative) 130.
ζητεῖτε (2d.per.pl.pres.act.ind.of ζητέω, aoristic) 207.

Translation - "How are you able to begin the life of faith if you continue to receive praise from one another, while the praise which comes from the only God you are not seeking?

Comment: *Cf.*#627 for other instances of πῶς in rhetorical question where the answer is obvious. Jesus is amazed that the Jews should entertain the notion that approbation from God and man could be sought and enjoyed simultaneously. Note the aorist infinitive in πιστεῦσαι, with its ingressive force. "How can you *begin* to believe? How can you exercise the first step of faith?" Final commitment of one's self to Christ is impossible in a context that demands that we mend our political fences with unsaved men. This statement by Christ presupposes undying antagonism between God and man. God is reconciled to the world through the death of His Son, but the world is rebellious and contemptuous. In the world respect from one's colleagues is the foundation of social, professional and political power. Successful people in this world receive approbation from one another. Nothing must be allowed to interfere with this social interplay. But in such circumstances, Jesus says that such men cannot believe on Christ. Reception of human praise makes impossible the quest for the glory that comes only from God. The same thought is expressed in John 12:42,43; Mt.10:34-38; John 15:18-19; Mt.5:10-12; I Pet.4:12-14.

It has often occurred to me that when a local church becomes socially, financially and politically prestigious, there is danger that the quality of the evangelism suffers. There is little or no social reproach involved in associating with such a church. The offense of the cross of Christ is largely absent. Business men have often found that membership in a given local congregation helped their business. Politicians often boast during their campaigns that they are faithful members of some well known church group. It does not follow from these observations that one's salvation is proved valid because one is disliked by others. Some are disliked because they deserve the contempt of society. Peter pointed out the difference between suffering for the cause of Christ, on the one hand, and suffering as an evil doer on the other (I Pet.4:15,16). A Christian should commend himself as much as possible to society in his sincere effort to win the lost to Christ. We must become all things to all men in order that we might save some (I Cor.9:19-23) so long as there is no basic compromise with the world in regard to the person and work of Christ. The question that separates the Christian world from the world of the unregenerate is this: What think ye of Christ? Whose Son is He? The Jews rejected Jesus and His claim to be the Son of God. In so doing, they made themselves the objects of an accusation that sent them to hell. This accusation came not from Jesus Christ, but from Moses, whom they professed to believe and follow. This is the thought of verse 45.

Verse 45 - "Do not think that I will accuse you to the Father: there is one that accuseth you, even Moses, in whom ye trust."

μὴ δοκεῖτε ὅτι ἐγὼ κατηγορήσω ὑμῶν πρὸς τὸν πατέρα; ἐστιν ὁ κατηγορῶν ὑμῶν Μωϋσῆς, εἰς ὑμεῖς ἠλπίκατε.

μὴ (negative conjunction with the imperative) 87.

δοκεῖτε (2d.per.pl.pres.act.impv.of δοκέω, command) 287.

ὅτι (objective conjunction introducing indirect discourse) 211.

ἐγὼ (nom.sing.masc.of ἐγώ, subject of κατηγορήσω) 123.

κατηγορήσω (1st.per.sing.fut.act.ind.of κατηγορέω, gnomic) 974.

ὑμῶν (gen.pl.masc.of σύ, objective) 104.

πρὸς (preposition with the accusative, after a verb of speaking) 197.

τὸν (acc.sing.masc.of the article in agreement with πατέρα) 9.

πατέρα (acc.sing.masc.of πατήρ, after a verb of speaking) 238.

ἐστιν (3d.per.sing.pres.ind.of εἰμί, aoristic) 86.

ὁ (nom.sing.masc.of the article in agreement with κατηγορῶν) 9.

κατηγορῶν (pres.act.part.nom.sing.masc.of κατηγορέω, substantival, subject of ἐστιν) 974.

ὑμῶν (gen.pl.masc.of σύ, objective) 104.

Μωϋσῆς (nom.sing.masc.of Μωϋσῆς, apposition) 715.

εἰς (preposition with the accusative, cause) 140.

ὃν (acc.sing.masc.of ὅς, cause) 65.

ἠλπίκατε (2d.per.pl.perf.act.ind.of ἐλπίζω, culminative) 991.

Translation - "Stop thinking that I am going to accuse you before the Father; Moses is your prosecutor, in whom you trust."

Comment: μὴ with the present imperative in δοκεῖτε forbids a continuation of what is now going on. The Jews were thinking that Jesus had come to spy upon them and that He would accuse them before God. They had not expressed their fears, but Jesus knew what they were thinking because of His omniscience (John 2:24,25). Jesus said in effect, "I know what you are thinking; you are wrong; do not continue to entertain this thought." Thus He reproved their incipient paranoia. They were already being accused, from a quarter that they little expected - Moses, in whom they had always trusted and in whom their hope for salvation still lay (the perfect tense in ἠλπίκατε). The present participle ὁ κατηγορῶν is substantival, the subject of ἐστιν the present tense verb. These present tenses indicate present tense accusation. They trusted Moses and mistakenly thought therefore that they should reject Jesus, for they thought of Jesus as One Who taught something contrary to Moses. This they thought despite what He said in Mt.5:17. *Cf.* Rom.3:21b; Lk.9:30,31. They did not understand that Moses had pointed forward to Christ, the Messiah and had ordered them to accept Him when He came. It was not that they had too much of Moses, but that they had too little. Faulty in their interpretation of Moses, they were derelict in their duty to him. Hence, Moses was accusing them - not Jesus.

There are contemporary religious leaders, some of whom are probably self-appointed, who have become so zealous in their defense of the Bible that they have not had time to study it. This lack of study of the book that they pretend to revere and in defense of which they exert their quixotic efforts often results in their transgression of its precepts. There is a distinction that must be made between studying *about* the Bible and studying the Bible. A line in *Phinian's Rainbow* says, "I haven't time to read the Constitution; I am too busy defending it." This was true of the Jews in our story and it is also true of some today. The Jews were so sure that Jesus was against Moses and that Moses, when properly interpreted, was against Jesus that they missed Moses' point that Jesus was the fulfillment of the ethics of the law and of the expectations of the prophets. Moses told them to worship Jesus, not try to kill Him. "They were blind to the glory and deaf to the voice of the Father, and so would not come to Him for life." (*The Pulpit Commentary, 17, II, 224).* Bengel interprets Jesus' thought by commenting, "The spirit of Moses is my vindication, the teaching of Moses is typical of mine, the institutions of Moses were symbolic of my coming and work.The predictions of Moses pointed out my coming. The mighty words of Moses will not save you, unless you penetrate to their inner meaning." All of this is underlined in verse 46.

With reference to the point that the Bible, whether in the Old or New Testaments needs defense, we can point to the analogy of the hungry, ferocious, man-eating Bengal tiger, that is nevertheless securely locked in a cage. That tiger needs no defense. He needs liberation. All we need to do is to let him out! So the Bible needs no defense. Indeed we insult it if we substitute its message with our puny defenses. All that the Bible needs is exposition. The expository preacher sees the weight of the argument of the inspired text, when it is fully researched and clearly expounded, fall upon the audience with overwhelming persuasion. This is why Paul told Timothy to "Preach the Word. . . in and out of season. . " and then defined *preach* by saying, ". . . reprove, rebuke, exhort with . . . doctrine" (II Tim.4:2).

Verse 46 - "For had ye believed Moses, you would have believed me: for he wrote of me."

εἰ γὰρ ἐπιστεύετε Μωϋσεῖ, ἐπιστεύετε ἂν ἐμοί, περὶ γὰρ ἐμοῦ ἐκεῖνος ἔγραφεν.

εἰ (conditional particle in a second-class condition) 337.

γὰρ (causal conjunction) 105.

ἐπιστεύετε (2d.per.pl.imperfect act.ind.of πιστεύω, second-class condition, contrary to fact) 734.

Μωϋσεῖ (dat.sing.masc.of Μωϋσῆς, personal advantage) 715.

ἐπιστεύετε (2d.per.pl.imp.act.ind.of πιστεύω, second-class condition, contrary to fact) 734.

ἂν (conditional particle in a second-class condition) 205.

ἐμοί (dat.sing.masc.of ἐμός, personal interest) 1267.

περὶ (preposition with the genitive of reference) 173.
γὰρ (causal conjunction) 105.
ἐμοῦ (gen.sing.masc.of ἐμός, reference) 1267.
ἐκεῖνος (nom.sing.masc.of ἐκεῖνος, subject of ἔγραφεν) 246.
ἔγραφεν (3d.per.sing.aor.act.ind.of γράφω, culminative) 156.

Translation - "Because if you had believed Moses (which you do not) you would have believed upon me (which you do not), because that one has written about me."

Comment: The second-class condition is determined as unfulfilled. The protasis contains εἰ with a secondary tense (imperfect) in the indicative mode (ἐπιστεύετε) and ἂν and the imperfect tense in the apodosis. Since we have the imperfect tense in both ends of the condition (if clause and result clause) the condition deals with the *then* present tense, *i.e.* at the time that Jesus said it. Thus the Jews had never truly believed in Moses and they did not believe in him at the time. Nor did they believe in Jesus. Had they always truly believed in Moses' writings, they would just as truly have accepted Jesus.

Why is this statement by Jesus valid? Because Moses had written about Christ and (culminative aorist in ἔγραφεν) his writings were extant at the time.

The reverse of the same proposition is expressed in the rhetorical question of verse 47, with which Jesus terminated this encounter with the Jews.

Verse 47 - "But if ye believe not his writings, how shall ye believe my words?"

εἰ δὲ τοῖς ἐκείνου γράμμασιν οὐ πιστεύετε, πῶς τοῖς ἐμοῖς ῥήμασιν πιστεύσετε;

εἰ (conditional particle in a first-class condition) 337.
δὲ (adversative conjunction) 11.
τοῖς (dat.pl.neut.of the article in agreement with γράμμασιν) 9.
ἐκείνου (gen.sing.masc.of ἐκεῖνος, possession) 246.

#2100 γράμμασιν (dat.pl.neut.of γράμμα, reference).

bill - Lk.16:6,7.
learning - Acts 26:24.
letter - John 7:15; Acts 28:21; Rom.2:27,29; 7:6; II Cor.3:6; Gal.6:11.
scripture - II Tim.3:15.
writing - John 5:47.
written - II Cor.3:7.

Meaning: That which has been written. A writing. *Cf.#*'s 152, 1389,156, 3843. Memorandum in writing. An evidence of debt - Lk.16:6,7; legal papers of accusation, an indictment sent from one jurisdiction to another - Acts 28:21; of general literary sophistication resulting from much reading - Acts 26:24; John 7:15; with reference to the writings of the Old Testament - Rom.2:27,29; 7:6; I Cor.3:6; II Tim.3:15; John 5:47; the Mosaic law - II Cor.3:7. With reference to the inscription on the cross of Jesus - Lk.23:38. Paul uses the word to refer to the characters of the script which he wrote to the Galatians - Gal.6:11.

οὐ (negative conjunction with the indicative) 130.
πιστεύετε (2d.per.pl.pres.act.ind.of πιστεύω, first-class condition) 734.
πῶς (interrogative conjunction in rhetorical question) 627.
τοῖς (dat.pl.neut.of the article in agreement with ῥήμασιν) 9.
ἐμοῖς (dat.pl.neut.of ἐμός, in agreement with ῥήμασιν) 1267.
ῥήμασιν (dat.pl.neut.of ῥῆμα, personal advantage) 343.
πιστεύσετε (2d.per.pl.fut.act.ind.of πιστεύω, first-class condition) 734.

Translation - "But since you do not believe the writings of that one, how can you believe my words?"

Comment: This is the same proposition in reverse as that put in verse 46. If they had believed Moses they would have believed Christ. If they reject Moses they would be forced to reject Christ. This logic is based on the assumption that Moses and Christ are allies. If this is true the Jews were put in an impossible position. Either they must reject Moses or accept Christ. If they rejected Moses, their own political position with the people would be in jeopardy. Why not yield to public opinion, which at this point was strongly pro-Jesus? This their wicked hearts refused to do, because of the moral commitment involved in following Jesus Christ.

Note that we have a first-class condition (εἰ with the indicative in the protasis and the future indicative in the apodosis). In this construction the statement in the protasis is assumed to be true.

(5) The Disciples Pluck Grain on the Sabbath and the Following Controversy - Mk.2:23-28; Mt.12:1-8; Lk.6:1-5.

Mark 2:23 - "And it came to pass, that he went through the corn fields on the sabbath day; and his disciples began, as they went, to pluck the ears of corn."

Καὶ ἐγένετο αὐτὸν ἐν τοῖς σάββασιν παραπορεύεσθαι διὰ τῶν σπορίμων, καὶ οἱ μαθηταὶ αὐτοῦ ἤρξαντο ὁδὸν ποιεῖν τίλλοντες τοὺς στάχυας.

Καὶ (continuative conjunction) 14.
ἐγένετο (3d.per.sing.aor.ind.of γίνομαι, constative) 113.
αὐτὸν (acc.sing.masc.of αὐτός, general reference) 16.
ἐν (preposition with the locative of time point) 80.
τοῖς (loc.pl.neut.of the article in agreement with σάββασιν) 9.
σάββασιν (loc.pl.neut.of σάββατον, time point) 962.

#2101 διαπορεύεσθαι (pres.inf.of διαπορεύομαι, substantival, subject of ἐγένετο).

go through - Mk.2:23; Lk.6:1; 13:22; Acts 16:4.

pass by - Lk.18:36.
in one's journey - Rom.15:24.

Meaning: A combination of διά (#118) and πορεύομαι (#170). Hence, to pass through. To make a journey into, through and out of a place. Always in the sense of spatial progress in the N.T. Through the fields - Mk.2:23; Lk.6:1; through towns and cities - Lk.13:22; Acts 16:4; Lk.18:36; Rom.15:24.

διά (preposition with the genitive in the sense of physically "through") 118.

τῶν (gen.pl.masc.of the article in agreement with σπορίμων) 9.

σπορίμων (gen.pl.masc.of σπόριμος) 963.

καί (continuative conjunction) 14.

οἱ (nom.pl.masc.of the article in agreement with μαθηταί) 9.

μαθηταί (nom.pl.masc.of μαθητής, subject of ἤρξαντο) 421.

αὐτοῦ (gen.sing.masc.of αὐτός, possession) 16.

ἤρξαντο (3d.per.pl.aor.mid.ind.of ἄρχω, ingressive) 383.

ὁδόν (acc.sing.neut.of ὁδός, direct object of ποιεῖν) 199.

ποιεῖν (pres.act.inf.of ποιεῖν, complementary) 127.

τίλλοντες (pres.act.part.nom.pl.masc.of τίλλω, adverbial, temporal) 964.

τούς (acc.pl.masc.of the article in agreement with στάχυας) 9.

στάχυας (acc.pl.masc.of στάχυς, direct object of τίλλοντες) 965.

Translation - "And He walked through the grain fields on the Sabbath, and His disciples, as they made their way, began to pull off the heads of grain."

Comment: *Cf.*Mt.12:1 and Lk.6:1 for parallel accounts. Mark's grammatical construction is somewhat different. Some have accused Mark of using a "Hebraism" in his καὶ ἐγένετο with the infinitive, but "Moulton finds the inf.with γίνεται in the papyri and rightly sees in the vernacular κοινή the origin of this idiom. There is no essential difference between the inf.with γίνεται and ἐγένετο. *Cf.* Acts 9:32; 16:16; 9:32,37,43; 11:26, etc. Outside of Luke (Gospel and Acts) the inf. with ἐγένετο is confined to Mk.2:23, which Moulton calls 'a primitive assimilation of Lu.6:1.' See Acts 10:25, ἐγένετο τοῦ εἰσελθεῖν. This is Moulton's presentation, which is certainly more just than the mere description of 'Hebraism' for all these constructions." (Burton, *New Testament Moods and Tenses,* 142*ff,* as cited in Robertson, *Grammar,* 1043).

We have taken παραπορεύεσθαι as a verbal noun (perfectly proper for an infinitive), the subject of ἐγένετο. αὐτόν, of course, since it cannot be the subject of an infinitive, is the accusative of general reference. ὁδὸν ποιεῖν is an interesting aside. Matthew and Luke are more direct and omit the explanation that since they were passing through it was quite convenient for them to pluck the grain. Mark says, as it were, "since they were making their way through. . ." Why not? He emphasizes that this is not deliberate pilfering that would take them aside from their path of travel. For further comment *Cf.* Mt.12:1.

Verse 24 - "And the Pharisees said unto him, Behold, why do they on the Sabbath day that which is not lawful?"

καὶ οἱ Φαρισαῖοι ἔλεγον αὐτῷ, Ἴδε τί ποιοῦσιν τοῖς σάββασιν ὃ οὐκ ἔξεστιν;

καὶ (inferential conjunction) 14.
οἱ (nom.pl.masc.of the article in agreement with Φαρισαῖοι) 9.
Φαρισαῖοι (nom.pl.masc.of Φαρισαῖος, subject of ἔλεγον) 276.
ἔλεγον (3d.per.pl.imp.act.ind.of λέγω, inceptive) 66.
αὐτῷ (dat.sing.masc.of αὐτός, indirect object of ἔλεγον) 16.
Ἴδε (2d.per.sing.aor.act.impv.of ὁράω, command) 44.
τί (acc.sing.neut.of τίς, with διά understood, cause) 281.
ποιοῦσιν (3d.per.pl.pres.act.ind.of ποιέω, aoristic) 127.
τοῖς (loc.pl.neut.of the article in agreement with σάββασιν) 9.
σάββασιν (loc.pl.neut.of σάββατον, time point) 962.
ὃ (acc.sing.neut.of ὅς, direct object of ποιοῦσιν) 65.
οὐκ (negative conjunction with the indicative) 130.
ἔξεστιν (3d.per.sing.pres.ind.of ἔξειμι,impersonal verb in a relative clause) 966.

Translation - "Therefore the Pharisees began to demand of Him, 'Look! Why are they doing on the Sabbath day that which is unlawful?' "

Comment: Mark uses the inceptive imperfect ἔλεγον to indicate the frenzied zeal of the Pharisees. Immediately, as a result of what they saw (inferential καὶ) they began to say and continued saying (inceptive ἔλεγον) to Jesus, with their imperious demand (Ἴδε). Why? . . . κ.τ.λ. Matthew and Luke contented themselves with the aorist εἶπαν. Mark, who got most of his information from Peter, who was present, (probably with his mouth full of grain!) has given us the more dramatic picture. Not only were the Pharisees smarting under the sting of His lash as administered in Matthew 11, but also from His analysis of their inconsistencies in John 5. *Cf.* Comment on Mt.12:2. Drowning men grasp at straws in their desperation. Thus the Pharisees engage in nit-picking, like a naughty little girl with a runny nose stalking off in a rage, draging her doll by the foot.

Verse 25 - "And he said unto them, Have ye never read what David did, when he had need and was an hungered, he, and they that were with him?"

καὶ λέγει αὐτοῖς. Οὐδέποτε ἀνέγνωτε τί ἐποίησεν Δαυίδ, ὅτε χρείαν ἔσχεν καὶ ἐπείνασεν αὐτὸς καὶ οἱ μετ' αὐτοῦ;

καὶ (inferential conjunction) 14.
λέγει (3d.per.sing.pres.act.ind.of λέγω, historical) 66.
αὐτοῖς (dat.pl.masc.of αὐτός, indirect object of λέγει) 16.
οὐδέποτε (intensifying negative compound) 689.
ἀνέγνωτε (2d.per.pl.2d.aor.act.ind.of ἀναγινώσκω, direct question) 967.

τί (acc.sing.neut.of τίς, direct object of ἐποίησεν) 281.
Δαυίδ (nom.sing.masc.of Δαυίδ, subject of ἐποίησεν) 6.
ὅτε (temporal conjunction introducing a definite temporal clause) 703.
χρείαν (acc.sing.fem.of χρεία, direct object of ἔσχεν) 317.
ἔσχεν (3d.per.sing.2d.aor.act.ind.of ἔχω, constative) 82.
καὶ (adjunctive conjunction joining verbs) 14.
ἐπείνασεν (3d.per.sing.aor.act.ind.of πεινάω, constative in definite temporal clause) 335.
αὐτὸς (nom.sing.masc.of αὐτός, nominative absolute) 16.
καὶ (adjunctive conjunction, joining substantives) 14.
οἱ (nom.pl.masc.of the article nominative absolute) 9.
μετ' (preposition with the genitive of accompaniment) 50.
αὐτοῦ (gen.sing.masc.of αὐτός, accompaniment) 16.

Translation - "*Therefore He said to them, 'Did you never read what David did, when he had a need and was hungry - he and those with him?'*"

Comment: ὅτε χρείαν ἔσχεν καὶ ἐπείνασεν - Mark points out the necessity under which David and his companions acted. ὅτε with the two indicatives make up a definite temporal clause. Jesus pointed the Pharisees back to a well-known incident in the nation's history. The disciples were also hungry. Eating the shew bread in the temple would normally be considered a worse offense than threshing a bit of grain in the hand. For further comment *cf.*Mt.12:3; Lk.6:3.

Verse 26 - "*How he went into the house of God in the days of Abiathar the high priest, and did eat the shewbread, which is not lawful to eat but for the priests, and gave also to them which were with him?*"

πῶς εἰσῆλθεν εἰς τὸν οἶκον τοῦ θεοῦ ἐπὶ Ἀβιαθὰρ ἀρχιερέως καὶ τοὺς ἄρτους τῆς προθέσεως ἔφαγεν, οὓς οὐκ ἔξεστιν φαγεῖν εἰ μὴ τοὺς ἱερεῖς, καὶ ἔδωκεν καὶ τοῖς σὺν αὐτῷ οὖσιν;

πῶς (interrogative conjunction) 627.
εἰσῆλθεν (3d.per.sing.aor.ind.of εἰσέρχομαι, constative) 234.
εἰς (preposition with the accusative of extent) 140.
τὸν (acc.sing.masc.of the article in agreement with οἶκον) 9.
οἶκον (acc.sing.masc.of οἶκος, extent) 784.
τοῦ (gen.sing.masc.of the article in agreement with θεοῦ) 9.
θεοῦ (gen.sing.masc.of θεός, definition) 124.
ἐπὶ (preposition with the genitive of time description) 47.

#2102 Ἀβιάθαρ (indeclin., genitive of time description).

Abiathar - Mk.2:26.

Meaning: Father of Abimelech, who gave the shew-bread to David and his men (I Sam.21:1ff). Marks says Abiathar was the priest. I Sam.21:2 says that

Ahimelech his son (I Chron.24:6) was priest. The son, Ahimelech, succeeded to the function before Abiathar, his father died. - Mk.2:26.

ἀρχιερέως (gen.sing.masc.of ἀρχιερεύς, apposition) 151.
καὶ (continuative conjunction) 14.
τοὺς (acc.pl.masc.of the article in agreement with ἄρτους) 9.
ἄρτους (acc.pl.masc.of ἄρτος, direct object of ἔφαγεν) 338.
τῆς (gen.sing.fem.of the article in agreement with προθέσεως) 9.
προθέσεως (gen.sing.fem.of πρόθεσις, definition) 968.
ἔφαγεν (3d.per.sing.aor.act.ind.of ἐσθίω, constative) 610.
οὓς (acc.pl.masc.of ὅς, in agreement with ἄρτους, in a relative clause) 65.
οὐκ (negative conjunction with the indicative) 130.
ἔξεστιν (3d.per.sing.pres.ind.of ἔξεστιν, customary) 966.
φαγεῖν (aor.act.inf.of ἐσθίω, epexegetical) 610.
εἰ (conditional particle in a first-class condition) 337.
μὴ (negative conjunction with εἰ in a negative first-class condition) 87.
τοὺς (acc.pl.masc.of the article in agreement with ἱερεῖς) 9.
ἱερεῖς (acc.pl.masc.of ἱερεύς, general reference) 714.
καὶ (continuative conjunction) 14.
ἔδωκεν (3d.per.sing.aor.act.ind.of δίδωμι, constative) 362.
καὶ (ascensive conjunction) 14.
τοῖς (dat.pl.masc.of the article, joined to the participial phrase, indirect object of ἔδωκεν) 9.
σὺν (preposition with the instrumental of association) 1542.
αὐτῷ (instru.sing.masc.of αὐτός, association) 16.
οὖσιν (pres.part.of εἰμί, joined with τοῖς) 86.

Translation - " . . . *how that he went into the house of God, in the time of Abiathar, the priest, and the loaves of the shewbread he ate, which loaves it is unlawful to eat, if the priests (do not); he even gave (bread) to those who were with him.*"

Comment: πῶς here in indirect discourse followed by the indicative. *Cf.*#627 for other examples. ἐπὶ'Αβιάθαρ is an interesting use of ἐπί with the genitive in a temporal phrase. *Cf.*#47 for other examples. Read I Sam.21 for the story. Actually, it was Ahimelech, the son of Abiathar who gave the bread to David. Mark only tells us that it was during the tenure of his father. *Cf.*#968 for other uses of πρόθεσις. οὓς, the relative follows ἄρτους in case and number. Only the priests were permitted under the law to eat the Bread of the Presence. David even (ascensive καὶ) gave this holy bread to those who were with him, whom he had ordered to wait outside the temple. For further comment *cf.* Mt.12:4.

Verse 27 - "And he said unto them, The Sabbath was made for man, and not man for the Sabbath."

καὶ ἔλεγεν αὐτοῖς, Τὸ σάββατον διὰ τὸν ἄνθρωπον ἐγένετο καὶ οὐκ ὁ
ἄνθρωπος διὰ τὸ σάββατον.

καὶ (continuative conjunction) 14.

ἔλεγεν (3d.per.sing.imp.act.ind.of λέγω, inceptive) 66.

αὐτοῖς (dat.pl.masc.of αὐτός, indirect object of ἔλεγεν) 16.

Τὸ (nom.sing.neut.of the article in agreement with σάββατον) 9.

σάββατον (nom.sing.neut.of σάββατον, subject of ἐγένετο) 962.

διὰ (preposition with the accusative of cause) 118.

τὸν (acc.sing.masc.of the article in agreement with ἄνθρωπον) 9.

ἄνθρωπον (acc.sing.masc.of ἄνθρωπος, cause) 341.

ἐγένετο (3d.per.sing.aor.ind.of γίνομαι, culminative) 113.

καὶ (adversative conjunction) 14.

οὐχ (negative conjunction with the indicative) 130.

ὁ (nom.sing.masc.of the article in agreement with ἄνθρωπος) 9.

ἄνθρωπος (nom.sing.masc.of ἄνθρωπος, subject of ἐγένετο understood)
341.

διὰ (preposition with the accusative of cause) 118.

τὸ (acc.sing.neut.of the article in agreement with σάββατον) 9.

σάββατον (acc.sing.neut.of σάββατον, cause) 962.

*Translation - "And He began to say to them, 'The Sabbath was made because of
man and not man because of the Sabbath."*

Comment: διά with the accusative carries the idea of cause and may be rendered
"for the sake of. . " It is because of man's need that the Sabbath was instituted for
his sake. Thus man's need has priority over a rule of sabbath observance, as
David and his men illustrated and as the disciples were illustrating. They were
hungry and needed food. Therefore, since the Sabbath was instituted to help
man, the act of the disciples was not wrong - it only appeared to be wrong to the
Jews who had no real understanding of the purpose of the Sabbath.

Jesus matched the imperfect ἔλεγον (vs.24) with His own imperfect in ἔλεγεν
(vs.27). Here is a case where Jesus put human rights above the Pharisaic
interpretation of the sabbath law. Enacted and established originally because of
the frail nature of man who needed one day in seven for physical recuperation
and relaxation, its purpose is to serve man. It is not the other way around. When
David, who had natural rights which had been given to him by the Creator, and
who was therefore important, was hungry, his need for bread was more
important than the law which forbade him to eat the shew-bread. In this case the
disciples were hungry. They happened to be walking through the grain field. It
happened to be the Sabbath. Should human rights be denied when the disciples
were hungry in order for the Pharisees to be consistent in the application of their
interpretation of the law? The law had said that they might eat the grain. It was
the Pharisaic tradition which regarded the necessary threshing as labor and
hence illegal on the sabbath.

The Pharisees were applying a philosophy of jurisprudence to the law of the sabbath which came to be known in the 18th and 19th centuries as positivism, while Jesus countered with a naturalistic interpretation. Positivism in law was given a full exposition by Jeremy Bentham, who thought of law as having its origin in society. This is consistent with democratic philosophy which assumes that man is rational and good and that, given enough time, he will examine and correct his life style through a thorough democratic process and ultimately bring law into line with morals. In the meantime, however, for the positivist, a law is a law even if it is morally bad, since it is the wish of the people. Positivism believes that *vox populi vox deo* ("the voice of the people is the voice of God") is a true basis for good law.

Naturalism on the other hand believes that all law should be patterned after universal principles and is therefore, if so patterned, consistent with the law of God. For the naturalist in jurisprudence God is the origin of all moral law and man's legislative enactments should conform thereto. The law always means that man should do what is right. Men preceded laws in God's plan. God promulgated laws for the purpose of making man free and happy. When a law subtracts *ultimately* from man's natural rights - from his life, liberty and property as a man, it should be disregarded. It is no law. This is naturalism as Blackstone, the great English jurist expounded it. Andrew Jackson, while a judge on the federal bench in Nashborough, instructed a jury, about to decide a dispute over a line fence, by saying, "Do what is right between these two parties. This is what the law always means." Thus Jackson was true to the Blackstonian philosophy of naturalism.

The Pharisees' philosophy comes down to us in modern times in terms of the Constitutional fanatics who prate about *stare decisis* and property rights and oppose any interpretation that would result in greater freedom for the exercise of human rights. For them the term "property rights" means land, factories, stocks, bonds, money - in short tangible property and cannot be made to include the inalienable rights that Thomas Jefferson mentioned in the Declaration of Independence. Witness the Hammer vs. Dagenhart decision of 1918. The law must not be broken regardless of how many human rights are trampled. Jesus, on the other hand, gave us the "rule of reason" concept. The law is to serve mankind by protecting his natural rights and expediting his pursurance of his divinely destined goal. Jesus demanded mercy and not strict observance of the laws of sacrifice, as the Pharisees were doing. The Pharisees would say that the Bread of the Presence in Ahimelech's court should never have been touched, even if David had starved to death as a result. This is fanaticism. It is the consistency that Ralph Waldo Emerson called "the refuge of the little mind." *Cf.*Mt.12:7 and comment.

If the Pharisees had understood this they would not have condemned as guilty the guiltless disciples. As the true ethical and moral principles of God's spiritual law get smothered by the rules and regulations of man's institutionalism, the institutional leaders become blind leaders of blind people who wander farther and farther from the truth until they all topple into the ditch. But the closer they get to the ditch the more religious and the less Christian they become. The Pharisees cared not one whit for the hunger pangs of the disciples. They thought only of their legal and religious house of cards. In much modern church life, likewise, the means become the end, and clear thinkers are cast out of the synagogue as heterodox and unclean. For further comment *cf.* Mt.12:5-8.

Verse 28 - "Therefore the Son of Man is Lord also of the sabbath."

ὥστε κύριός ἐστιν ὁ υἱὸς τοῦ ἀνθρώπου καὶ τοῦ σαββάτου.

ὥστε (consecutive conjunction introducing a result clause) 752.
κύριός (nom.sing.masc.of κύριος, predicate nominative) 97.
ἐστιν (3d.per.sing.pres.ind.of εἰμί, aoristic) 86.
ὁ (nom.sing.masc.of the article in agreement with υἱός) 9.
υἱὸς (nom.sing.masc.of υἱός, subject of ἐστιν) 5.
τοῦ (gen.sing.masc.of the article in agreement with ἀνθρώπου) 9.
ἀνθρώπου (gen.sing.masc.of ἄνθρωπος, definition) 341.
καὶ (adjunctive conjunction) 14.
τοῦ (gen.sing.neut.of the article in agreement with σαββάτου) 9.
σαββάτου (gen.sing.neut.of σάββατον, definition) 962.

Translation - "The result is that the Son of Man is Lord also of the Sabbath."

Comment: ὥστε introduces result. The foregoing argument carries the thought back to Genesis 2:1-3 and Exodus 20:8-11, which establish the fact that the institution of the sabbath was the direct result of the intention of the Creator, and also that the Creator laid down in the Mosaic law the manner in which it should be observed, together with the reason for its observance. The Sabbath is the creation therefore of Jesus Christ (John 1:3; Col.1:16,17). Obviously therefore the result of this kind of reasoning (ὥστε and the result clause) is that since the Creator made the Sabbath for man and not man for the Sabbath (vs.27) the Creator is the Lord of the Sabbath, in supreme control of the manner in which it is to be observed. Note the emphatic position of κύριος. Jesus doesn't want any doubt about it. He is **LORD** of the Sabbath and what His disciples do on that day is none of the Pharisees' business.

This assertion of His divine authority with which the chapter closes is in line with the high position which He had previously taken for Himself in Matthew 11 and John 5. *Cf.*comment on Mt.12:8.

Luke 6:1 - "And it came to pass on the second sabbath after the first, that he went through the corn fields; and his disciples plucked the ears of corn, and did eat, rubbing them in their hands."

Ἐγένετο δὲ ἐν σαββάτῳ διαπορεύεσθαι αὐτὸν διὰ σπορίμων, καὶ ἔτιλλον οἱ μαθηταὶ αὐτοῦ καὶ ἤσθιον τοὺς στάχυας φώχοντες ταῖς χερσίν.

Ἐγένετο (3d.per.sing.aor.ind.of γίνομαι, constative) 113.

δέ (continuative conjunction) 11.

ἐν (preposition with the locative of time point) 80.

σαββάτῳ (loc.sing.neut.of σάββατον, time point) 962.

διαπορεύεσθαι (pres.inf.of διαπορεύομαι, noun use, subject of ἐγένετο) 2101.

αὐτὸν (acc.sing.masc.of αὐτός, general reference) 16.

διὰ (preposition with the genitive, physically through) 118.

σπορίμων (gen.pl.masc.of σπόριμος, physically through) 963.

καὶ (continuative conjunction) 14.

ἔτιλλον (3d.per.pl.imp.act.ind.of τίλλω, inceptive) 964.

οἱ (nom.pl.masc.of the article in agreement with μαθηταὶ) 9.

μαθηταὶ (nom.pl.masc.of μαθητής, subject of ἔτιλλον) 421.

αὐτοῦ (gen.sing.masc.of αὐτός, possession) 16.

καὶ (adjunctive conjunction, joining verbs) 14.

ἤσθιον (3d.per.pl.imp.act.ind.of ἐσθίω, inceptive) 610.

τοὺς (acc.pl.masc.of the article in agreement with στάχυας) 9.

στάχυας (acc.pl.masc.of στάχυς, direct object of ἤσθιον and ἔτιλλον) 965.

#2103 φώχοντες (pres.act.part.nom.pl.masc.of φώχω, adverbial, instrumental).

rub - Lk.6:1.

Meaning: From an obsolete φώω for φάω. To rub, to rub to pieces. With reference to the threshing of grain in the palm of the hand - Lk.6:1.

ταῖς (instru.pl.fem.of the article in agreement with χερσίν) 9.

χερσίν (instru.pl.fem.of χείρ, means) 308.

Translation - *"One sabbath day He happened to be passing through the grain fields, and His disciples began to pluck and eat the grains after threshing them in their hands."*

Comment: *Cf.* our comment on Mk.2:23. The infinitive is the subject of ἐγένετο. His trip through the field happened on a sabbath day. This is the essence of Luke's greek. It is not important to the story to know which particular Sabbath is meant. The KJV's rendition - ". . . on the second sabbath after the first. . " is based upon a doubtful text.

"In the opinion of a majority of the Committee, although σαββάτῳ δευτεροπρώτῳ is certainly the more difficult reading, it must not for that reason be adopted. The word δευτεροπρῶτος occurs nowhere else, and appears to be a *vox nulla* that arose accidentally through a transcriptional blunder. (Perhaps some copyist introduced πρώτῳ as a correlative of ἐν ἑτέρῳ σαββάτῳ in ver.6, and a second copyist, in view of 4.31, wrote δευτέρῳ, deleting πρώτῳ by using dots over the letters - which was the customary way of cancelling a word. A subsequent transcriber, not noticing the dots, mistakenly combined the two words into one, which he introduced into the text).

Bruce M. Metzger, A Textual Commentary on the Greek New Testament, 139.

Note the inceptive imperfect tenses in ἔτιλλον and ἤσθιον. The disciples "began to pluck and to eat. . . " The adverbial participle ψώχοντες is instrumental, as it describes their action. It was this labor (!) on the sabbath day that the Pharisees objected to. For further comment cf. Mt.12:1-8; Mk.2:23-38.

Verse 2 - "And certain of the Pharisees said unto them, Why do ye that which is not lawful to do on the sabbath days?"

τινὲς δὲ τῶν Φαρισαίων εἶπαν, Τί ποιεῖτε ὃ οὐκ ἔξεστιν τοῖς σάββασιν;

τινὲς (nom.pl.masc.of τις, indefinite pronoun, subject of εἶπαν) 486.
δὲ (adversative conjunction) 11.
τῶν (gen.pl.masc.of the article in agreement with Φαρισαίων) 9.
Φαρισαίων (gen.pl.masc.of Φαρισαῖος, partitive genitive) 276.
εἶπαν (3d.per.pl.aor.act.ind.of εἶπον, ingressive) 155.
Τί (acc.sing.neut.of τίς, interrogative pronoun, cause) 281.
ποιεῖτε (2d.per.pl.pres.act.ind.of ποιέω, direct question) 127.
ὃ (acc.sing.neut.of ὅς, direct object of ποιεῖτε) 65.
οὐκ (negative conjunction with the indicative) 130.
ἔξεστιν (3d.per.sing.pres.ind.of ἔξεστιν, aoristic) 966.
τοῖς (loc.pl.neut.of the article in agreement with σάββασιν) 9.
σάββασιν (loc.pl.neut.of σάββατον, time point) 962.

Translation - "But certain of the Pharisees began to say, 'Why are you doing that which is not lawful during the sabbath week?"

Comment: δὲ is adversative, as the Pharisees decide to start an argument. We have already commented on this story in Mt.12:2 and Mk.2:24. Anent the point of fanatical observance of law and tradition - - "When in 1492, the Jews were expelled from Spain, and were forbidden to enter the city of Fez, lest they should cause a famine, they lived on grass; yet even in this state 'religiously avoided the violation of their sabbath by plucking the grass with their hands.' To avoid this they took the much more laborious method of grovelling on their knees, and cropping it with their teeth!" (*The Pulpit Commentary*, 16, II, 140).

Verse 3 - "And Jesus answering them said, Have ye not read so much as this, what David did, when himself was hungered, and they which were with him;"

καὶ ἀποκριθεὶς πρὸς αὐτοὺς εἶπεν ὁ Ἰησοῦς, Οὐδὲ τοῦτο ἀνέγνωτε ὃ ἐποίησεν Δαυὶδ ὅτε ἐπείνασεν αὐτὸς καὶ οἱ μετ' αὐτοῦ (ὄντες);

καὶ (adversative conjunction) 14.
ἀποκριθεὶς (aor.part.nom.sing.masc.of ἀποκρίνομαι, adverbial, modal) 318.
πρὸς (preposition with the accusative of extent, with persons after a verb of speaking) 197.
αὐτοὺς (acc.pl.masc.of αὐτός, extent) 16.
εἶπεν (3d.per.sing.aor.act.ind.of εἶπον, constative) 155.

ὁ (nom.sing.masc.of the article in agreement with Ἰησοῦς) 9.
Ἰησοῦς (nom.sing.masc.of Ἰησοῦς, subject of εἶπεν) 3.
οὐδὲ (disjunctive particle) 452.
τοῦτο (acc.sing.neut.of οὗτος,direct object of ἀνέγνωτε) 93.
ἀνέγνωτε (2d.per.pl.2d.aor.act.ind.of ἀναγινώσκω, direct question) 967.
ὃ (acc.sing.neut.of ὅς, direct object of ἐποίησεν) 65.
ἐποίησεν (3d.per.sing.aor.act.ind.of ποιέω, constative) 127.
Δαυὶδ (nom.sing.masc.of Δαυίδ, subject of ἐποίησεν) 6.
ὅτε (temporal conjunction introducing a definite temporal clause) 703.
ἐπείνασεν (3d.per.sing.aor.act.ind.of πεινάω, constative) 335.
αὐτὸς (nom.sing.masc.of αὐτός, subject of ἐπείνασεν) 16.
καὶ (adjunctive conjunction, joining substantives) 14.
οἱ (nom.pl.masc.of the article, subject of ἐπείνασεν) 9.
μετ' (preposition with the genitive of accompaniment) 50.
αὐτοῦ (gen.sing.masc.of αὐτός, accompaniment) 16.

Translation - "But Jesus responded to them by saying, 'But did you never read this that David did when he was hungry - he and those with him?' "

Comment: καὶ is adversative as Jesus prepares to counter the criticism of the Pharisees. *Cf.*#452 for other uses of οὐδέ with no other negative. "Did you never even read this?" Like most fanatics the Jews were so busy defending the Word of God that they had never bothered to read it. For other comments *cf.* Mt.12:3 and Mk.2:25.

Verse 4 - "How he went into the house of God, and did take and eat the shewbread, and gave also to them that were with him; which it is not lawful to eat but for the priests alone?"

(ὡς) εἰσῆλθεν εἰς τὸν οἶκον τοῦ θεοῦ καὶ τοὺς ἄρτους τῆς προθέσις λαβὼν ἔφαγεν καὶ ἔδωκεν τοῖς μετ' αὐτοῦ, οὓς ἔξεστιν φαγεῖν εἰ μὴ μόνους τοὺς ἱερεῖς;

(ὡς) - (relative adverb introducing an adverbial clause) 128.
εἰσῆλθεν (3d.per.sing.aor.ind.of εἰσέρχομαι, constative) 234.
εἰς (preposition with the accusative of extent) 140.
τὸν (acc.sing.masc.of the article in agreement with οἶκον) 9.
οἶκον (acc.sing.masc.of οἶκος, extent) 784.
τοῦ (gen.sing.masc.of the article in agreement with θεοῦ) 9.
θεοῦ (gen.sing.masc.of θεός, definition) 124.
καὶ (adjunctive conjunction, joining verbs) 14.
τοὺς (acc.pl.masc.of the article in agreement with ἄρτους) 9.
ἄρτους (acc.pl.masc.of ἄρτος, direct object of ἔφαγεν and ἔδωκεν) 338.
τῆς (gen.sing.fem.of the article in agreement with προθέσεως) 9.
προτέσεως (gen.sing.fem.of πρόθεσις, definition) 968.
λαβὼν (aor.act.part.nom.sing.masc.of λαμβάνω, adverbial, temporal) 533.

ἔφαγεν (3d.per.sing.aor.act.ind.of ἐσθίω, constative) 610.
καὶ (adjunctive conjunction, joining verbs) 14.
ἔδωκεν (3d.per.sing.aor.act.ind.of δίδωμι, constative) 362.
τοῖς (dat.pl.masc.of the article, joined to the prepositional phrase, indirect object of ἔδωκεν) 9.
μετ' (preposition with the genitive of accompaniment) 50.
αὐτοῦ (gen.sing.masc.of αὐτός, accompaniment) 16.
οὓς (acc.pl.neut.of ὅς, in agreement with ἄρτους) 65.
οὐκ (negative conjunction with the indicative) 130.
ἔξεστιν (3d.per.sing.pres.ind.of ἔξεστιν, impersonal verb) 966.
φαγεῖν (aor.act.inf.of ἐσθίω, epexegetical) 610.
εἰ (conditional particle, with μὴ in a first-class condition) 337.
μὴ (negative conjunction with εἰ in a first-class negative condition) 87.
μόνους (acc.pl.masc.of μόνος, in agreement with ἱερεῖς) 339.
τοὺς (acc.pl.masc.of the article in agreement with ἱερεῖς) 9.
ἱερεῖς (acc.pl.masc.of ἱερεύς, general reference) 714.

Translation - "How that he entered into the house of God and when he had seized the loaves of the Presence, he ate and gave to those who were with him, which is not lawful except for the priests alone."

Comment: *Cf.* Mt.12:4; Mk.2:26. Luke adds the temporal adverbial participle λαβὼν.

Verse 5 - "And he said unto them, That the Son of Man is Lord also of the Sabbath."

καὶ ἔλεγεν αὐτοῖς, Κύριός ἐστιν τοῦ σαββάτου ὁ υἱὸς τοῦ ἀνθρώπου.

καὶ (continuative conjunction) 14.
ἔλεγεν (3d.per.sing.imp.act.ind.of λέγω, inceptive) 66.
αὐτοῖς (dat.pl.masc.of αὐτός, indirect object of ἔλεγεν) 16.
Κύριός (nom.sing.masc.of κύριος, predicate nominative) 97.
ἐστιν (3d.per.sing.pres.ind.of εἰμί, aoristic) 86.
τοῦ (gen.sing.neut.of the article in agreement with σαββάτου) 9.
σαββάτου (gen.sing.neut.of σάββατον, definition) 962.
ὁ (nom.sing.masc.of the article in agreement with υἱὸς) 9.
υἱὸς nom.sing.masc.of υἱός, subject of ἐστιν) 5.
τοῦ (gen.sing.masc.of the article in agreement with ἀνθρώπου) 9.
ἀνθρώπου (gen.sing.masc.of ἄνθρωπος, definition) 341.

Translation - "And He began to say to them, 'The Son of Man is Lord of the Sabbath.'"

Comment: Note the imperfect in ἔλεγεν as Jesus emphasized the point. Note also that Κύριός is in emphasis. Further comment in Mt.12:8; Mk.2:28.

Healing of a Man with a Withered Hand on the Sabbath
and the Following Controversy

Mk.3:1-6; Mt.12:9-14; Lk.6:6-11

Mark 3:1 - "And he entered again into the synagogue; and there was a man there
which had a withered hand."

Καὶ εἰσῆλθεν πάλιν εἰς συναγωγήν, καὶ ἦν ἐκεῖ ἄνθρωπος ἐξηραμμένην
ἔχων τὴν χεῖρα.

Καὶ (continuative conjunction) 14.
εἰσῆλθεν (3d.per.sing.aor.ind.of εἰσέρχομαι, constative) 234.
πάλιν (adverbial) 355.
εἰς (preposition with the accusative of extent) 140.
τὴν (acc.sing.fem.of the article in agreement with συναγωγήν) 9.
συναγωγήν (acc.sing.fem.of συναγωγή, extent) 404.
καὶ (continuative conjunction) 14.
ἦν (3d.per.sing.imp.ind.of εἰμί, progressive duration) 86.
ἐκεῖ (adverbial) 204.
ἄνθρωπος (nom.sing.masc.of ἄνθρωπος subject of ἦν) 341.
ἐξηραμμένην (perf.pass.part. acc.sing.fem.of ξηραίνω, adjectival, restrictive)
1033.
ἔχων (pres.act.part.nom.sing.masc.of ἔχω, in agreement with ἄνθρωπος,
adverbial, circumstantical) 82.
τὴν (acc.sing.fem.of the article in agreement with χεῖρα) 9.
χεῖρα (acc.sing.fem.of χείρ, direct object of ἔχων) 308.

Translation - "And He entered again into the synagogue; and there was there a
man having a withered hand."

Comment: The participle ἔχων is joined to ἄνθρωπος as a circumstantial
adverb, while the participle ἐξηραμμένην is a restrictive adjective, joined to
χεῖρα. ἐξηραμμένην is in the perfect tense, indicating a then present condition as
a result of some malady in the past. We do not know how long before the hand
had become affected. Cf.#'s 1033 and 972. Our Lord is abundantly able to heal
any and all things which are atrophied - physically, mentally and spiritually.
Cf.Mt.12:9-14 and Lk.6:6-11 for further comment.

Verse 2 - "And they watched him, whether he would heal him on the sabbath day;
that they might accuse him."

καὶ παρετήρουν αὐτὸν εἰ τοῖς σάββασιν θεραπεύσει αὐτόν, ἵνα κατηγορ -
ήσωσιν αὐτοῦ.

καὶ (continuative conjunction) 14.

#2104 παρετήρουν (3d.per.pl.imp.act.ind.of παρατηρέω, inceptive).

observe - Gal.4:10.
watch - Mk.3:2; Lk.6:7; 14:1; 20:20; Acts 9:24.

Meaning: A combination of παρά (#154) and τηρέω (#1297). Hence to keep by the side of, in order to watch carefully; to give close attention to in view of expected developments. With reference to religious observance - Gal.4:10; of Paul's enemies, who maintained close reconnaissance on Paul - followed by ὅπως and a subjunctive clause of purpose - Acts 9:24; of the Pharisees who were watching Jesus in order to find in His conduct some basis for condemnation, followed by indirect question and ἵνα and the subjective of purpose - Mk.3:2; Lk.6:7 (middle voice); in a periphrastic construction with the middle voice - Lk.14:1; followed by a ἵνα clause of purpose - Lk.20:20.

αὐτὸν (acc.sing.masc.of αὐτός, direct object of παρετήρουν) 16.
εἰ (conditional particle in an indirect question) 337.
τοῖς (loc.pl.neut.of the article in agreement with σάββασιν) 9.
σάββασιν (loc.pl.neut.of σάββατον, time point) 962.
θεραπεύσει (3d.per.sing.fut.act.ind.of θεραπεύω, indirect question) 406.
αὐτόν (acc.sing.masc.of αὐτός, direct object of θεραπεύσει) 16.
ἵνα (final conjunction with a purpose clause) 114.
κατηγορήσωσιν (3d.per.pl.aor.act.subj.of κατηγορέω, purpose) 974.
αὐτοῦ (gen.sing.masc.of αὐτός, objective genitive) 16.

Translation - "And they began to watch him closely (in order to see) if He would heal him on the Sabbath, in order that they might file charges against Him."

Comment: *Cf.* Mt.12:10 and Lk.6:7. The inceptive imperfect in παρετήρουν - "they began and continued to watch him closely" - indicates the zeal, albeit misguided, of these miserable, little people. Those who are sure that they have *all* of the answers to all questions feel called upon, by self appointment, to "ride herd" on their less enlightened fellows. Heresy hunters are very sure that they know what truth is and therefore what heresy is! εἰ and the future indicative is indirect question. The point of Mt.12:7,8, which see *en loc,* and comments, was lost upon them. Positivistic jurisprudence, the legal philosophy of the fanatic, here comes into the picture again and the spirit of the law is ignored if understood at all. The Pharisees were not concerned, either with the hungry disciples in the grain field or the crippled man in the synagogue. They hoped that Jesus would heal him, not for his benefit, but in order that they could procede to destroy Jesus in the courts.

Verse 3 - "And he saith unto the man which had the withered hand, Stand forth."

καὶ λέγει τῷ ἀνθρώπῳ τῷ τὴν ξηρὰν χεῖρα ἔχοντι, Ἔγειρε εἰς τὸ μέσον.

καὶ (inferential conjunction) 14.

λέγει (3d.per.sing.pres.act.ind.of λέγω, historical) 66.

τῷ (dat.sing.masc.of the article in agreement with ἀνθρώπῳ) 9.

ἀνθρώπῳ (dat.sing.masc.of ἄνθρωπος, indirect object of λέγει) 341.

τῷ (dat.sing.masc.of the article in agreement with ἔχοντι) 9.

τὴν (acc.sing.fem.of the article in agreement with χεῖρα) 9.

ξηρὰν (acc.sing.fem.of ξηρός, in agreement with χεῖρα) 972.

χεῖρα (acc.sing.fem.of χείρ, direct object of ἔχοντι) 308.

ἔχοντι (pres.act.part.dat.sing.fem.of ἔχω, in agreement with ἀνθρώπῳ) 82.

Ἔγειρε (2d.per.sing.pres.act.impv.of ἐγείρω, command) 125.

εἰς (preposition with the accusative of extent) 140.

τὸ (acc.sing.neut.of the article in agreement with μέσον) 9.

μέσον (acc.sing.neut.of μέσος, extent) 873.

Translation - *"Therefore He said to the man having the withered hand, 'Step up here into the crowd."*

Comment: Mark wished to emphasize the fact that the man had a withered hand. He did this by modifying ἀνθρώπῳ with the participial phrase τῷ τὴν ξηρὰν χεῖρα ἔχοντι in the emphatic attributive position. The word order in such an idiom is article, noun, article modifier. The modifier here is ξηρὰν χεῖρα ἔχοντι.

Note that Jesus wanted to be certain that everyone in the synagogue saw the miracle and heard the debate which would follow. This is why He commanded the man to leave his place and take a position in the midst of the crowd. The Pharisees had gone too far. Jesus wanted to make an example out of the man with his unfortunate condition and the hardness of the hearts of the Pharisees. *Cf.* Mt.12:13.

Verse 4 - *"And he saith unto them, Is it lawful to do good on the sabbath day, or to do evil? To save life, or to kill? But they held their peace."*

καὶ λέγει αὐτοῖς, Ἔξεστιν τοῖς σάββασιν ἀγαθὸν ποιῆσαι ἢ κακοποιῆσαι, ψυχὴν σῶσαι ἢ ἀποκτεῖναι; οἱ δὲ ἐσιώπων.

καὶ (continuative conjunction) 14.

λέγει (3d.per.sing.pres.act.ind.of λέγω, historical) 66.

αὐτοῖς (dat.pl.masc.of αὐτός, indirect object of λέγει) 16.

Ἔξεστιν (3d.per.sing.pres.ind.of ἔξειμι, customary) 966.

τοῖς (loc.pl.neut.of the article in agreement with σάββασιν) 9.

σάββασιν (loc.pl.neut.of σάββατον, time point) 962.

#2105 ἀγαθοποιῆσαι (aor.act.inf.of ἀγαθοποιέω, compermentary).

do good - Mk.3:4; Lk.6:9,33,33,35; III John 11.
do well - I Pet.2:14,20; 3:6.
for well doing - I Pet.3:17.
with well doing - I Pet.2:15.

Meaning: A combination of ἀγαϑός (#547) and ποιέω (#127). Hence, to do well; to perform deeds of goodness and to behave in an examplary fashion. In contrast to κακοποιέω in Mk.3:4; Lk.6:9; III John 11; I Pet.3:17. To do good to men - Lk.6:33,33,35. As a participial substantive - III John 11; I Pet.2:14; 3:6. *Cf.* also I Pet.3:17; 2:15. As a causal participle - I Pet.2:20.

ἤ (disjunctive particle) 465.

#2106 κακοποιῆσαι (aor.act.inf.of κακοποιέω, complementary).

do evil - Mk.3:4; Lk.6:9; III John 11.
evil doer - I Pet.2:14.
for doing evil - I Pet.3:17.

Meaning: A combination of κακός (#1388) and ποιέω (#127). Hence to do evil. In contrast to #2105 in Mk.3:4; Lk.6:9; III John 11; I Pet.2:14; 3:17.

ψυχήν (acc.sing.fem.of ψυχή, direct object of σῶσαι) 233.
σῶσαι (aor.act.inf.of σώζω, complementary) 109.
ἤ (disjunctive particle) 465.
ἀποκτεῖναι (aor.act.inf.of ἀποκτείνω, complementary) 889.
οἱ (nom.pl.masc.of the article, subject of ἐσιώπων) 9.
δὲ (adversative conjunction) 11.
ἐσιώπων (3d.per.pl.imp.act.ind.of σιωπάω, progressive description) 1337.

Translation - "Then He said to them, 'Is it lawful on the Sabbath to do good or to do evil? to save a life or to kill?' But they remained silent."

Comment: Jesus' question is in reply to their question of Mt.12:10. He counters their question by asking one. His question, had they replied to it, would have forced them to say whether healing is good or bad. And the extension of the thought would then be, whether saving a life is good - or should we kill. For healing is the function to forestall death; if there is no healing ultimately death results. To say that healing is bad is to say that killing is good. Note ἔξεστιν in emphasis. If they were going to emphasize what was legal or illegal, Jesus would do likewise. He presented them with a hard choice. Should one do good or ill? Should one kill or make alive? How could they say that their interpretation of the law forced them to kill (by withholding healing) and otherwise to do evil on the Sabbath? No wonder they found it necessary, in order to accomplish their evil purpose, to maintain a profound silence. Keep in mind that their reason for starting this argument was to force Jesus into a statement and/or act which would provide them with an indictment against Him.

For further comment on the incident review the treatment given the parallel passages in Mt.12:9-14 and Lk.6:6-11.

Verse 5 - "And when he had looked round about on them with anger, being grieved for the hardness of their hearts, he saith unto the man, Stretch forth thine hand. And he stretched it out: and his hand was restored whole as the other."

καὶ περιβλεφάμενος αὐτοὺς μετ' ὀργῆς, συλλυπούμενος ἐπὶ τῇ πωρώσει τῆς καρδίας αὐτῶν, λέγει τῷ ἀνθρώπῳ, Ἔκτεινον τὴν χεῖρα; καὶ ἐξέτεινεν, καὶ ἀπεκατεστάθη ἡ χεὶρ αὐτοῦ.

καὶ (inferential conjunction) 14.

#2107 περιβλεφάμενος (aor.act.part.nom.sing.masc.of περιβλέπω, adverbial, temporal).

> look about on - Mk.3:5.
> look round about - Mk.3:34; 5:32; 9:8.
> look round about on - Mk.10:23.
> look round about upon - Mk.11:11; Lk.6:10.

Meaning: A combination of περί (#173) and βλέπω (#499). Hence, to look around. To sweep the surroundings with one's gaze. To survey the scene. With reference to Jesus in the synagogue before He healed the man with the withered hand - Mk.3:5; Lk.6:10; when His family came to visit - Mk.3:34; in search of the woman who touched His garment - Mk.5:32; in connection with His discourse on riches - Mk.10:23: as He surveyed the temple scene - Mk.11:11. With reference to the disciples on the Transfiguration Mountain - Mk.9:8. Note that six of the seven uses are in Mark's gospel.

αὐτοὺς (acc.pl.masc.of αὐτός, extent after περί in composition) 16.
μετ' (preposition with the genitive in an adverbial sense) 50.
ὀργῆς (gen.sing.fem.of ὀργή, adverbial) 283.

#2108 συνλυπούμενος (pres.mid.part.nom.sing.masc.of συλλυπέω, adverbial, causal).

> grieve - Mk.3:5.

Meaning: A combination of σύν (#1542) and λυπέω (#1113). Hence to be filled with grief. In the middle or passive in Mk.3:5, with reference to our Lord's distress because of the hardness of the hearts of the Pharisees.

ἐπὶ (preposition with the locative, with a verb of emotion) 47.
τῇ (loc.sing.fem.of the article in agreement with πωρώσει) 9.

#2109 πωρώσει (loc.sing.fem.of πώρωσις, with a verb of emotion).

> blindness - Rom.11:25; Eph.4:18.
> hardness - Mk.3:5.

Meaning: Cf.πωρόω (#2282). Hence, properly to cover with a callous. Trop., the deadening and dulling of mental discernment due to prejudice. Twice applied to Israel's rejection of Christ - Mk.3:5; Rom.11:25; once applied to the unregenerate Gentiles - Eph.4:18.

τῆς (gen.sing.fem.of the article in agreement with καρδίας) 9.
καρδίας (gen.sing.fem.of καρδία, definition) 432.
αὐτῶν (gen.pl.masc.of αὐτός, possession) 16.
λέγει (3d.per.sing.pres.act.ind.of λέγω, historical) 66.
τῷ (dat.sing.masc.of the article in agreement with ἀνθρώπῳ) 9.
ἀνθρώπῳ (dat.sing.masc.of ἄνθρωπος, indirect object of λέγει) 341.
Ἔκτεινον (2d.per.sing.aor.act.impv.of ἐκτείνω, command) 710.
τὴν (acc.sing.fem.of the article in agreement with χεῖρα) 9.
χεῖρα (acc.sing.fem.of χείρ, direct object of ἔκτεινον) 308.
καὶ (inferential conjunction) 14.
ἐξέτεινεν (3d.per.sing.aor.act.ind.of ἐκτείνω, constative) 710.
καὶ (continuative conjunction) 14.
ἀπεκατεστάθη (3d.per.sing.aor.pass.ind.of ἀποκαθίστημι, constative) 978.
ἡ (nom.sing.fem.of the article in agreement with χείρ) 9.
χείρ (nom.sing.fem.of χείρ, subject of ἀπεκατεστάθη) 308.
αὐτοῦ (gen.sing.masc.of αὐτός, possession) 16.

Translation - "Therefore when He had looked around at them with anger because He was grieved because of the hardness of their hearts, He said to the man, 'Stretch out your hand.' And he reached out and his hand was restored."

Comment: καὶ is inferential. It was because of the stony·silence of the Pharisees that Jesus looked at them with anger. *Cf.*#47 for ἐπί when joined to a verb of emotion. Other examples are Mt.14:14; 18:26,29; Mk.12:17. We may take τῆς καρδίας either as a genitive of description or an ablative of source. The callous attitude toward the suffering of the crippled man was the result of hearts that had long since rejected the truth and had become totally prejudiced in favor of their own rationalizations. Perverted hearts are the source of callousness and unconcern. Thus we see man's inhumanity to man. A careful study of #432 will show what the καρδία of man will produce. It is not a pretty picture, *e.g.* Lk.1:51. When hearts are regenerated men will not be indifferent to the suffering of others.

The man did with his withered hand what could be done only by faith. He stretched it out in obedience to a command. When God commands, He also enables. The hand was restored. Study #978 carefully for other examples of restoration. Review comment on Mt.12:9-15.

Verse 6 - "And the Pharisees went forth, and straightway took counsel with the Herodians against him, how they might destroy him."

καὶ ἐξελθόντες οἱ Φαρισαῖοι εὐθὺς μετὰ τῶν Ἡρῳδιανῶν συμβούλιον
ἐδίδουν κατ' αὐτοῦ ὅπως αὐτὸν ἀπολέσωσιν.

καὶ (continuative conjunction) 14.
ἐξελθόντες (aor.part.nom.pl.masc.of ἐξέρχομαι, adverbial, temporal) 161.
οἱ (nom.pl.masc.of the article in agreement with Φαρισαῖοι) 9.
Φαρισαῖοι (nom.pl.masc.of Φαρισαῖος, subject of ἐδίδουν) 276.
εὐθὺς (adverbial) 258.
μετὰ (preposition with the genitive of fellowship) 50.
τῶν (gen.pl.masc.of the article in agreement with Ἡρῳδιανῶν) 9.
Ἡρῳδιανῶν (gen.pl.masc.of Ἡρῳδιάνος, fellowship) 1414.
συμβούλιον (acc.sing.neut.of συμβούλιον, direct object of ἐδίδουν) 980.
ἐδίδουν (3d.per.pl.imp.act.ind.of δίδωμι, inceptive) 362.
κατ' (preposition with the genitive of opposition) 98.
αὐτοῦ (gen.sing.masc.of αὐτός, opposition) 16.
ὅπως (final conjunction introducing a purpose clause) 177.
αὐτὸν (acc.sing.masc.of αὐτός, direct object of ἀπολέσωσιν) 16.
ἀπολέσωσιν (3d.per.pl.aor.act.subj.of ἀπόλλυμι, purpose) 208.

*Translation - "And when the Pharisees had gone away immediately they began
to plot against Him with the Herodians in order to destroy Him."*

Comment: We may join εὐθὺς either to the participle ἐξελθόντες or to the main
verb ἐδίδουν. The result is the same. The Pharisees did not wait around to argue
with Jesus about healing the withered hand on the Sabbath. They had seen what
they hoped to see - Jesus had transgressed *their conception* of the law of the
Sabbath, and that was the only version of the law that counted with them.
Unable to reply to Jesus' reasoning that the Creator created the Sabbath for
man's healing and care and therefore that healing was perfectly in order on the
Sabbath, they rushed out to make an alliance with the Herodians. Note the
inceptive imperfect in ἐδίδουν. "They began (and continued) to give advice to the
Herodians. . . " Two political parties, at odds on most issues, found agreement
on one issue - the Truth must be destroyed! κατά with the genitive in the sense of
opposition, a common idiom.

The conference on ways and means to destroy Jesus took some time. Certainly
there was no logical reason to oppose Him. He had won every bout which they
started. He knew their scriptures better than they. Human rights were to be
honored more than Sabbath traditions. If they helped a beast on the Sabbath He
could heal a man. Public opinion at this point was on Jesus' side. The Pharisees
and Herodians were sensitive to this fact. For further comment *cf.* Mt.12:9-14
and the Luke account of the same event which follows in Lk.6:6-11.

*Luke 6:6 - "And it came to pass also on another sabbath, that he entered into the
synagogue and taught: and there was a man whose right hand was withered."*

Ἐγένετο δὲ ἐν ἑτέρῳ σαββάτῳ εἰσελθεῖν αὐτὸν εἰς τὴν συναγωγὴν καὶ
διδάσκειν, καὶ ἦν ἄνθρωπος ἐκεῖ καὶ ἡ χεὶρ αὐτοῦ ἡ δεξιὰ ἦν ξηρά.

'Εγένετο (3d.per.sing.aor.ind.of γίνομαι, constative) 113.
δὲ (explanatory) 11.
ἐν (preposition with the locative of time point) 80.
ἑτέρῳ (loc.sing.neut.of ἕτεροσ, in agreement with σαββάτῳ) 605.
σαββάτῳ (loc.sing.neut.of σάββατον, time point) 962.
εἰσελθεῖν (aor.inf.of εἰσέρχομαι, subject of ἐγένετο) 234.
αὐτὸν (acc.sing.masc.of αὐτός, general reference) 16.
εἰς (preposition with the accusative of extent) 140.
τὴν (acc.sing.fem.of the article in agreement with συναγωγὴν) 9.
συναγωγὴν (acc.sing.fem.of συναγωγή, extent) 404.
καὶ (adjunctive conjunction, joining subject infinitives) 14.
διδάσκειν (pres.act.inf.of διδάσκω, subject of ἐγένετο) 403.
καὶ (continuative conjunction) 14.
ἦν (3d.per.sing.imp.ind.of εἰμί, progressive description) 86.
ἄνθρωπος (nom.sing.masc.of ἄνθρωπος, subject of ἦν) 341.
ἐκεῖ (adverbial) 204.
καὶ (continuative conjunction) 14.
ἡ (nom.sing.fem.of the article in agreement with χεὶρ) 9.
χεὶρ (nom.sing.fem.of χείρ, subject of ἦν) 308.
αὐτοῦ (gen.sing.masc.of αὐτός, possession) 16.
ἡ (nom.sing.fem.of the article in agreement with χεὶρ) 9.
δεξιὰ (nom.sing.fem.of δεξιός, in agreement with χεὶρ) 502.
ἦν (3d.per.sing.imp.ind.of εἰμί, progressive description) 86.
ξηρά (nom.sing.fem.of ξηρός, predicate adjective) 972.

Translation - "Now it happened that on another Sabbath He entered into the synagogue and was teaching, and there was a man there and his right hand was withered."

Comment: δὲ is explanatory. The ἐν clause is temporal. Luke is careful to tell us that the story he is about to tell occurred on a different Sabbath day than did the episode of the grain field of Lk.6:1-5. Luke, the careful historian, who did not write from his own personal observations, but from interviews with the principals in the action, likes to insert into the text little evidences that his history is accurate, even down to the minor details. This policy provides Luke's readers with ample opportunity to check his story against the facts, thus to provide a ground for credibility. Had Luke intended to deceive, he would have taken care *not* to permit these small details from entering in, since any one of them could be the item which proved that his account was inaccurate.

The beginning Greek student may be confused with Luke's idiom here as he uses two infinitives with the verb ἐγένετο. The student should remember that the infinitive is a verbal noun, which in this case is used as a noun, the subject of ἐγένετο. When we look at it like a Greek there is no problem. "Jesus' entrance... and His teaching . . . happened (ἐγένετο) on another Sabbath."

ἦν is imperfect in both usages, indicating that the man had been there for some time and that his hand had been withered also for some time. The verse is used by Luke to establish the setting for what follows. For further comment *cf.* Mt.12:9 and Mk.3:1.

Verse 7 - "And the Scribes and Pharisees watched him, whether he would heal on the sabbath day; that they might find an accusation against him."

παρετηροῦντο δὲ αὐτὸν οἱ γραμματεῖς καὶ οἱ Φαρισαῖοι εἰ ἐν τῷ σαββάτῳ θεραπεύει, ἵνα εὕρωσιν κατηγορεῖν αὐτοῦ.

παρετηροῦντο (3d.per.pl.imp.mid.ind.of παρατηρέω, inceptive) 2104.
δὲ (explanatory conjunction) 11.
αὐτὸν (acc.sing.masc.of αὐτός, direct object of παρετηροῦντο) 16.
οἱ (nom.pl.masc.of the article in agreement with γραμματεῖς) 9.
γραμματεῖς (nom.pl.masc.of γραμματεύς, subject of παρετηροῦντο) 152.
καὶ (adjunctive conjunction joining nouns) 14.
οἱ (nom.pl.masc.of the article in agreement with Φαρισαῖοι) 9.
Φαρισαῖοι (nom.pl.masc.of Φαρισαῖος, subject of παρετηροῦντο) 276.
εἰ (conditional particle in indirect question) 337.
ἐν (preposition with the locative of time point) 80.
τῷ (loc.sing.neut.of the article in agreement with σαββάτῳ) 9.
σαββάτῳ (loc.sing.neut.of σάββατον, time point) 962.
θεραπεύει (3d.per.sing.pres.act.ind.of θεραπεύω, indirect question) 406.
ἵνα (final conjunction introducing a purpose clause) 114.
εὕρωσιν (3d.per.pl.2d.aor.act.subj.of εὑρίσκω, purpose) 79.
κατηγορεῖν (pres.act.inf.of κατηγορεῖν, purpose) 974.
αὐτοῦ (gen.sing.masc.of αὐτός, objective genitive) 16.

Translation - "Now the Scribes and the Pharisees began to watch Him closely, to see whether or not on the Sabbath day He would heal, in order that they might find a reason to indict Him."

Comment: δὲ is either continuative of explanatory. Note the inceptive imperfect in παρετηροῦντο - ". . . they *began* a close scrutiny. . . " a fact that indicates the prejudice in their minds. They had heard of Jesus; possibly they had encountered Him in debate before. The ἵνα clause of purpose reveals their design. They were looking for a chance to take Jesus to court. *Cf.* Mt.12:10 and Mk.3:2.

Verse 8 - "But he knew their thoughts, and said to the man, which had the withered hand, Rise up, and stand forth in the midst. And he arose and stood forth."

αὐτὸς δὲ ᾔδει τοὺς διαλογισμοὺς αὐτῶν, εἶπεν δὲ τῷ ἀνδρὶ τῷ ξηρὰν ἔχοντι τὴν χεῖρα, Ἔγειρε καὶ στῆθι εἰς τὸ μέσον καὶ ἀναστὰς ἔστη.

αὐτὸς (nom.sing.masc.of αὐτός, subject of ᾔδει) 16.

δὲ (adversative conjunction) 11.

ᾔδει (3d.per.sing.pluperfect ind.of οἶδα, intensive) 144.

τοὺς (acc.pl.masc.of the article in agreement with διαλογισμοὺς) 9.

διαλογισμοὺς (acc.pl.masc.of διαλογισμός, direct object of ᾔδει) 1165.

αὐτῶν (gen.pl.masc.of αὐτός, possession) 16.

εἶπεν (3d.per.sing.aor.act.ind.of εἶπον, constative) 155.

δὲ (continuative conjunction) 11.

τῷ (dat.sing.masc.of the article in agreement with ἀνδρὶ) 9.

ἀνδρὶ (dat.sing.masc.of ἀνήρ, indirect object of εἶπεν) 63.

τῷ (dat.sing.masc.of the article in agreement with ἔχοντι) 9.

ξηρὰν (acc.sing.fem.of ξηρός, in agreement with χεῖρα) 972.

ἔχοντι (pres.act.part.dat.sing.masc.of ἔχω, in agreement with ἀνδρὶ) 82.

τὴν (acc.sing.fem.of the article in agreement with χεῖρα) 9.

χεῖρα (acc.sing.fem.of χείρ, direct object of ἔχοντι) 308.

Ἔγειρε (2d.per.sing.pres.act.impv.of ἐγείρω, command) 125.

καὶ (adjunctive conjunction, joining verbs) 14.

στῆθι (2d.per.sing.2d.aor.act.impv.of ἵστημι, command) 180.

εἰς (preposition with the accusative, static use) 140.

τὸ (acc.sing.neut.of the article in agreement with μέσον) 9.

μέσον (acc.sing.neut.of μέσος, static use, like a locative of place) 873.

καὶ (inferential conjunction) 14.

ἀναστὰς (aor.act.part.nom.sing.masc.of ἀνίστημι, adverbial, temporal) 789.

ἔστη (ed.per.sing.2d.aor.act.ind.of ἵστημι, constative) 180.

Translation - "But He had been aware of their schemes, and He said to the man - the one having the withered hand, 'Get up and stand here in the middle.' Therefore when he had arisen he stood.

Comment: δὲ is clearly adversative in the first clause. Jesus' enemies had evil plans, *but* (adversative δὲ) Jesus had always been aware of them and therefore He understood and was master of the situation. This is the force of the pluperfect in ᾔδει. Cf.# 1165 for a study of the word. Note the emphatic attributive position of the adjectival clause τῷ . . . χεῖρα. Luke's use of εἰς with the accusative like ἐν with the locative of a rare example of the static use of εἰς. In Homer, the only case was the accusative and the only preposition with ἐν. As the language evolved other cases, including the locative of place, developed and ἐν while retaining its original form also evolved into εἰς. In the New Testament there are a few cases of εἰς with the accusative serving for ἐν and the locative. Robertson calls this "The Original Static Use" (Robertson, *Grammar,* 591).

Luke gives us information not offered by Matthew or Mark. He adds the evidence of Christ's deity in the keen discernment with which Jesus understood the evil designs of His enemies. The pluperfect in ᾔδει is strongly intensive. He had always known and was not the slightest bit disconcerted by the puny efforts of His enemies to destroy Him.

Verse 9 - "Then said Jesus unto them, I will ask you one thing: Is it lawful on the sabbath days to do good, or to do evil? To save life or destroy it?"

εἶπεν δὲ ὁ Ἰησοῦς πρὸς αὐτούς, Ἐπερωτῶ ὑμᾶς, εἰ ἔξεστιν τῷ σαββάτῳ ἀγαθοποιῆσαι ἢ κακοποιῆσαι, ψυχὴν σῶσαι ἢ ἀπολέσαι;

εἶπεν (3d.per.sing.aor.act.ind.of εἶπον, constative) 155.
δὲ (continuative conjunction) 11.
ὁ (nom.sing.masc.of the article in agreement with Ἰησοῦς) 9.
Ἰησοῦς (nom.sing.masc.of Ἰησοῦς, subject of εἶπεν) 3.
πρὸς (preposition with the accusative, after a verb of speaking) 197.
αὐτούς (acc.pl.masc.of αὐτός, after a verb of speaking) 16.
Ἐπερωτῶ (1st.per.sing.pres.act.ind.of ἐπερωτάω, futuristic) 973.
ὑμᾶς (acc.pl.masc.of σύ, direct object of ἐπερωτῶ) 104.
εἰ (conditional particle in indirect question) 337.
ἔξεστιν (3d.per.sing.pres.ind.of ἔξεστιν, customary) 966.
τῷ (loc.sing.neut.of the article in agreement with σαββάτῳ) 9.
σαββάτῳ (loc.sing.neut.of σάββατον, time point) 962.
ἀγαθοποιῆσαι (aor.act.ind.of ἀγαθοποιέω, complementary) 2105.
ἢ (disjunctive particle) 465.
κακοποιῆσαι (aor.act.inf.of κακοποιέω, complementary) 2106.
ψυχὴν (acc.sing.fem.of ψυχή, direct object of σῶσαι) 233.
ἢ (disjunctive particle) 465.
ἀπολέσαι (aor.act.inf.of ἀπόλλυμι, complementary) 208.

Translation - "Then Jesus said to them, 'I will ask you if it is customary on a Sabbath day to do good or to do evil - to save a life or to destroy?' "

Comment: The spelling of Ἐπερωτῶ is unusual. It is from in B.Tdf. text. Rec.Gr.Sch.Ln.have the future ἐπερωτήσω. No matter. It is a futuristic present. This demand, as reported by Luke followed the analogy of Matthew 12:11-12, about the sheep that fell into the pit and the question whether a man was more or less valuable than a sheep. Read all of the parallel accounts for a full-orbed picture of what happened. For further comments *cf.* Mt.12:9-14; Mk.3:4.

Verse 10 - "And looking round about upon them all, he said unto the man, Stretch forth thy hand. And he did so; and his hand was restored whole as the other."

καὶ περιβλεψάμενος πάντας αὐτοὺς εἶπεν αὐτῷ, Ἔκτεινον τὴν χεῖρά σου. ὁ δὲ ἐποίησεν, καὶ ἀπεκατεστάθη ἡ χεὶρ αὐτοῦ.

καὶ (continuative conjunction) 14.
περιβλεψάμενος (aor.mid.part.nom.sing.masc.of περιβλέπω, adverbial, temporal) 2107.
πάντας (acc.pl.masc.of πάς, in agreement with αὐτοὺς) 67.
αὐτοὺς (acc.pl.masc.of αὐτός, place after περί in composition) 16.
εἶπεν (3d.per.sing.aor.act.ind.of εἶπον, constative) 155.
αὐτῷ (dat.sing.masc.of αὐτός, indirect object of εἶπεν) 16.

Ἔκτεινον (2d.per.sing.aor.act.impv.of ἐκτείνω, command) 710.
τὴν (acc.sing.fem.of the article in agreement with χεῖρά) 9.
χεῖρά (acc.sing.fem.of χείρ, direct object of ἔκτεινον) 308.
σου (gen.sing.mas.of σύ, possession) 104.
ὁ (nom.sing.masc.of the article subject of ἐποίησεν) 9.
δὲ (inferential conjunction) 11.
ἐποίησεν (3d.per.sing.aor.act.ind.of ποιέω, constative) 127.
καὶ (continuative conjunction) 14.
ἀπεκατεστάθη (3d.per.sing.aor.pass.ind.of ἀποκαθίστημι, culminative) 978.
ἡ (nom.sing.fem.of the article in agreement with χείρ) 9.
χείρ (nom.sing.fem.of χείρ, subject of ἀπεκατεστάθη) 308.
αὐτοῦ (gen.sing.masc.of αὐτός, possession) 16.

Translation - *"And after He had looked around at them all, He said to him, 'Stretch out your hand.' And he did so and his hand was restored."*

Comment: *Cf.*Mt.12:13; Mk.3:5. There is nothing difficult in the grammar of the verse. πάντας αὐτοὺς is interesting; it is not "all of them" which would require the partitive genitive αὐτῶν. Rather - "all them" or "them all." Note that Luke put the verb ἀπεκατεσάθη in emphasis ahead of the subject. Here was an outstanding example of divine power at work. Jesus is not reported as having touched the hand. The reaction of the people follows in

Verse 11 - *"And they were filled with madness; and communed one with another what they might do to Jesus."*

αὐτοὶ δὲ ἐπλήσθησαν ἀνοίας, καὶ διελάλουν πρὸς ἀλλήλους τί ἂν ποιήσαιεν τῷ Ἰησοῦ.

αὐτοὶ (nom.pl.masc.of αὐτός, subject of ἐπλήσθησαν) 16.
δὲ (inferential conjunction) 11.
ἐπλήσθησαν (3d.per.pl.aor.pass.ind.of πλήθω, culminative) 1409.

#2110 ἀνοίας (gen.sing.fem.of ἄνοια, partitive genitive).

folly - II Tim.3:9.
madness - Lk.6:11.

Meaning: from ἄνοος. Hence, without understanding. Folly; madness. With reference to the Pharisees, the enemies of Jesus - Lk.6:11; of end-time apostates - II Tim.3:9.

καὶ (inferential conjunction) 14.
διελάλουν (3d.per.pl.imp.act.ind.of διαλαλέω, inceptive) 1848.
πρὸς (preposition with the accusative after a verb of speaking) 197.

ἀλλήλους (acc.pl.masc.of ἄλληλος, after a verb of speaking) 1487.
τί (acc.sing.neut.of τίς, direct object of ποιήσαιεν) 281.
ἄν (particle introducing indirect question) 205.
ποιήσαιεν (3d.per.pl.aor.act.ind.of ποιέω, indirect question) 127.
τῷ (dat.sing.masc.of the article in agreement with Ἰησοῦ) 9.
Ἰησοῦ (dat.sing.masc.of Ἰησοῦς, personal disadvantage) 3.

Translation - "Therefore these men were filled with confusion and they began to confer with one another about what they might do to Jesus."

Comment: δὲ is inferential, since it was Jesus' act of healing that triggered their anger and irrationality. We might translate, less literally, ". . . they became irrational." "Whom the gods destroy they first make mad." One would think (if he did not know the Pharisees) that they would have been filled with admiraion and awe. But they had quite the opposite reaction. Frustration and rage consumed them. Enemies of Christ always have this characteristic. So will it be in the end-time (II Tim.3:9). Note the imperfect in διελάλουν, with its inceptive nature. Hence our translation. τί ἄν ποιήσαιεν - This is an old Aeolic form of the aorist indicative. ἄν introduces the element of doubt as to just what could be done. After all, His power to heal a withered hand with only a word could not be denied and His claim to deity was difficult to gainsay. They knew that they would be compelled to procede with care, since Jesus was popular with the people. For further comment *cf.* Mt.12:14 and Mk.3:6.

PERIOD II. From the Choosing of the Twelve to the Withdrawal into Northern Galilee

A.D. 28-29. *c*.12 months.

(1) Organization of the Kingdom

The Widespread Fame of Jesus - Mk.3:7-12; Mt.12:15-21

Mark 3:7 - "But Jesus withdrew himself with his disciples to the sea; and a great multitude from Galilee followed him, and from Judea."

Καὶ ὁ Ἰησοῦς μετὰ τῶν μαθητῶν αὐτοῦ ἀνεχώρησεν πρὸς τὴν θάλασσαν, καὶ πολὺ πλῆθος ἀπὸ τῆς Γαλιλαίας ἠκολούθησεν, καὶ ἀπὸ τῆς Ἰουδαίας.

Καὶ (continuative conjunction) 14.
ὁ (nom.sing.masc.of the article in agreement with Ἰησοῦς) 9.
Ἰησοῦς (nom.sing.masc.of Ἰησοῦς, subject of ἀνεχώρησεν) 3.
μετὰ (preposition with the genitive of accompaniment) 50.
τῶν (gen.pl.masc.of the article in agreement with μαθητῶν) 9.
μαθητῶν (gen.pl.masc.of μαθητής, accompaniment) 421.
αὐτοῦ (gen.sing.masc.of αὐτός, possession) 16.

ἀνεχώρησεν (3d.per.sing.aor.act.ind.of ἀναχωρέω, ingressive) 200.
πρὸς (preposition with the accusative of extent) 197.
τὴν (acc.sing.fem.of the article in agreement with θάλασσαν) 9.
θάλασσαν (acc.sing.fem.of θάλασσα, extent) 374.
καὶ (continuative conjunction) 14.
πολὺ (nom.sing.neut.of πολύς, in agreement with πλῆθος) 228.
πλῆθος (nom.sing.neut.of πλῆθος, subject of ἠκολούθησεν) 1792.
ἀπὸ (preposition with the ablative of source) 70.
τῆς (abl.sing.fem.of the article in agreement with Γαλιλαίας) 9.
Γαλιλαίας (abl.sing.fem.of Γαλιλαίας, source) 241.
ἠκολούθησεν (3d.per.sing.aor.act.ind.of ἀκολουθέω, ingressive) 394.
καὶ (adjunctive conjunction joining prepositional phrases) 14.
ἀπὸ (preposition with the ablative of source) 70.
τῆς (abl.sing.fem.of the article in agreement with Ἰουδαίας) 9.
Ἰουδαίας (abl.sing.fem.of Ἰουδαίας, source) 134.

Translation - "And Jesus in company with His disciples began to withdraw toward the sea, and a great crowd from Galilee began to follow - also from Judea. . . "

Comment: *Cf.*Mt.4:25; 12:15 καὶ is continuative, although Mark could have used an adversative δὲ, since Jesus' withdrawal can be thought of as a counter-movement to the action of His enemies of Mk.3:6.

He is about to choose from His disciples (μαθητής) twelve apostles (ἀπόστολος). *Cf.*#421 and note that μαθητής, primarily means "learner"; hence a μαθητής could refer to a large number of followers of Jesus who were not included among the twelve. At this time six of the twelve had joined Jesus earlier: Andrew, Simon Peter, Philip and Nathaniel (John 1:40-51); James and John, the sons of Zebedee (Mt.4:21,22) and Matthew (Mt.9:9). The other six were included in the πολὺ πλῆθος which began (ingressive aorist in ἠκολούθησεν) to follow Him. *Cf.* Mt.4:23,24 for an explanation of the great crowds. Some of the people were from Judea and others represented other parts of the country (vs.8). *Cf.*#'s 134 and 141 for evidence that Jesus had also been in Judea attracting attention by His works and words.

Note: We shall avoid the errors of dispensationalism in its extreme form, or be rescued from that pit, in the event that we have already fallen thereinto, if we keep in mind the character of Jesus' ministry at each chronological stage of its development. The contention of some that Jesus said nothing about "church truth" in the sense of His death and blood redemption for individuals who must be born again, until He had made and withdrawn a complete offer of Himself to Israel as Messiah, cannot be sustained when we look at the chronology of events. We offer, therefore, at this point, a recapitulation of the events in their proper chronological sequence, beginning with the immersion of Jesus. These events can be traced by returning in this work to the beginning of the exposition of the Gospel of Mark, which begins following #1693. Notable events that are irreconcilable with the "Kingdom truth first - Church truth later" system of interpretation are: discourse with Nicodemus, discourse with the Samaritan woman (which, at the time of our present story, are history), and the significant fact that the Sermon on the Mount, supposedly the introduction of the kingdom presentation, has not yet been preached! We have pointed out many of the events which have occurred thus far in Jesus' ministry which cannot be reconciled with the Darby school, in our expositions, *en loc.* He has already prophesied His death, burial and resurrection. He has already told a Jewish leader "Ye must be born again" (John 3:3). Everything recorded in Mark from the beginning to Mk.3:6 has already happened. The material in Mt.1:1 - 4:25; 8:2-4, 14-17; 9:1-17; 12:1-14 is already history. So is everything recorded in Lk.1:1-6:11. So is everything recorded through John 5:47. Everything else in the gospel accounts is future at this point. About sixteen months have elapsed (plus the few days He spent in Samaria) since Jesus' baptism. It is now the year A.D.28.

Verse 8 - "And from Jerusalem, and from Idumea, and from beyond Jordan; and they about Tyre and Sidon, a great multitude, when they had heard what great things he did, came unto him."

καὶ ἀπὸ Ἱεροσολύμων καὶ ἀπὸ τῆς Ἰδουμαίας καὶ πέραν τοῦ Ἰορδάνου καὶ περὶ Τύρον καὶ Σιδῶνα, πλῆθος πολύ, ἀκούοντες ὅσα ἐποίει ἦλθον πρὸς αὐτόν,

καὶ (adjunctive conjunction joining prepositional phrases) 14.
ἀπὸ (preposition with the ablative of source) 70.
Ἱεροσολύμων (abl.sing.masc.of Ἱεροσολύμων, source) 141.
καὶ (adjunctive conjunction joining prepositional phrases) 14.
ἀπὸ (preposition with the ablative of source) 70.
τῆς (abl.sing.fem.of the article in agreement with Ἰδουμαίας) 9.

#2111 Ἰδουμαίας (abl.sing.fem.of Ἰδουμαία, source).

Idumaea - Mk.3:8.

Meaning: "The name of the region between southern Palestine and Arabia Petraea, inhabited by Esau or Edom (Gen.36:330) and his posterity." (*Thayer*). Crowds from this region visited Jesus' ministry - Mk.3:8.

καὶ (adjunctive conjunction joining prepositional phrases) 14.
πέραν (improper preposition with the ablative of source) 375.
τοῦ (abl.sing.masc.of the article in agreement with Ἰορδάνου) 9.
Ἰορδάνου (abl.sing.masc.of Ἰορδάνου, source) 272.
καὶ (adjunctive conjunction joining prepositional phrases) 14.
περὶ (preposition with the accusative of extent) 173.
Τύρον (acc.sing.masc.of Τύρος, extent) 939.
καὶ (adjunctive conjunction joining nouns) 14.

Σιδῶνα (acc.sing.masc.of Σιδῶν, extent) 940.

πλῆθος (nom.sing.neut.of πλῆθος, subject of ἦλθον) 1792.

πολύ (nom.sing.neut.of πολύς, in agreement with πλῆθος) 228.

ἀκούοντες (pres.act.part.nom.pl.masc.of ἀκούω, adverbial, temporal and causal) 148.

ὅσα (acc.pl.neut.of ὅς, direct object of ἀκούοντες in a relative clause) 65.

ποιεῖ (3d.per.sing.pres.act.ind.of ποιέω, indirect discourse) 127.

ἦλθον (3d.per.pl.aor.act.ind.of ἔρχομαι, ingressive) 146.

πρός (preposition with the accusative of extent) 197.

αὐτόν (acc.sing.masc.of αὐτός, extent) 16.

Translation - ". . . and from Jerusalem, and from Idumea and from the region beyond the Jordan and around Tyre and Sidon - a great crowd, as soon as they heard what He was doing, began to come to Him."

Comment: These prepositional phrases are joined by καί in the usual way. We may supply ἀπό before πέραν and περί. The region πέραν τοῦ Ἰορδάνου is the territory on the left (east) bank. περί Τύρον καὶ Σιδῶνα can be translated "Tyre and Sidon country." Mark describes it as a great crowd again, this time, please note, with the adjective in the predicate position (vs.8), rather than in the attributive position as in verse 7. ἀκούοντες is adverbial and is both temporal and causal. It was both *when* and *because* they heard what Jesus was doing that they began their trip to His side. The present tense in ἀκούοντες indicates that they started as soon as they heard the news. Note the imperfect in ἐποίει, because the tense in indirect discourse is the same as in direct. The rumor was "Jesus has been doing . . . κ.τ.λ." We may be sure that as they made their way to Jesus' side they spread the rumors along the path. This accounts for the increased size of the crowd as they approached Jesus. Note the relative clause ὅα ἐποιεί, joined to ἀκούοντες. *Cf.* a similar construction in Mt.2:22 where the participle is followed by ὅτι and direct discourse. His fame had spread abroad. Everyone was coming to Him. *Cf.* Mt.4:23-25.

Verse 9 - "And he spoke to his disciples, that a small ship should wait on him because of the multitude, lest they should throng him."

καὶ εἶπεν τοῖς μαθηταῖς αὐτοῦ ἵνα πλοιάριον προσκαρτερῇ αὐτῷ διὰ τὸν ὄχλον ἵνα μὴ θλίβωσιν αὐτόν.

καὶ (inferential conjunction) 14.

εἶπεν (3d.per.sing.aor.act.ind.of εἶπον, constative) 155.

τοῖς (dat.pl.masc.of the article in agreement with μαθηταῖς) 9.

μαθηταῖς (dat.pl.masc.of μαθητής, indirect object of εἶπεν) 421.

αὐτοῦ (gen.sing.masc.of αὐτός, possession) 16.

ἵνα (sub-final conjunction introducing a purpose/result clause) 114.

#2112 πλοιάριον (acc.sing.neut.of πλοιάριον, direct object of προσκαρτερῇ).

boat - John 6:22,24.
little ship - John 21:8.
small ship - Mk.3:9.

Meaning: diminutive of πλοῖον (# 400). Little ship or boat. Always in connection with the ministry of Jesus and His disciples. Mk.4:36 and John 6:22b use πλοῖον instead - John 6:22a; Mk.3:9; John 21:8; 6:24.

#2113 προσκαρτερῇ (3d.per.sing.pres.act.subj.of προσκαρτερέω, purpose).

attend continually upon - Rom.13:6.
continue in - Acts 1:14; 2:46; Col.4:2.
continue instant in - Rom.12:12.
continue steadfastly in - Acts 2:42.
continue with - Acts 8:13.
give one's self continually to - Acts 6:4.
wait on - Mk.3:9.
wait on continually - Acts 10:7.

Meaning: A combination of πρός (#197) and καρτερέω (#5036), from καρτερός ("strong, steadfast") and that from the root of κάρτος for κράτος (#1828) - "strength." Hence, to persevere; to continue faithfully to pursue a given course or policy. To persevere in prayer - Acts 1:14; Col.4:2; Rom.12:12; Acts 6:4; in various acts of worship - Acts 2:42,46; 8:13; with reference to public officials collecting taxes - Rom.13:6; with reference to guarding and attending Cornelius in bodyguard capacity - Acts 10:7; of a small boat anchored near the shore for Jesus' use - Mk.3:9.

αὐτῷ (dat.sing.masc.of αὐτός, personal advantage) 16.
διά (preposition with the accusative, cause) 118.
τόν (acc.sing.masc.of the article in agreement with ὄχλον) 9.
ὄχλον (acc.sing.masc.of ὄχλος, cause) 418.
ἵνα (final conjunction in a negative purpose clause) 114.
μή (negative conjunction with the subjunctive in a negative purpose clause) 87.
θλίβωσιν (3d.per.pl.pres.act.subj.of θλίβω, negative purpose) 667.
αὐτόν (acc.sing.masc.of αὐτός, direct object of θλίβωσιν) 16.

Translation - "Therefore Jesus ordered His disciples to have a small boat waiting for Him because of the crowd, lest they should crush Him."

Comment: καί is inferential, since Jesus' order to His disciples was the result of the quickly gathering crowd of people who in mob-like disregard for His personal safety might push Him into the water. The purpose clause following εἶπεν is a bit unusual for New Testament Greek. He spoke to His disciples with a request that ... κ.τ.λ. The only place in the N.T. where προσκατερέω (#2113) is **applied** to an inanimate object. "Keep the boat moored nearby. I may need to board it in order to escape the crowd." There is no evidence that He entered the boat - only that He ordered it to be held in readiness. αὐτῷ with the dative of personal advantage. Note διὰ with the accusative in a causal construction. *Cf.*#118 for other instances. The danger was that they might throng Him, not maliciously (vss.10,11), but inadvertantly in their desire to benefit from His power and grace.

The world has always imposed its pressures upon Christ and His church. *Cf.*#667.

Verse 10 - "For he had healed many; insomuch that they pressued upon him for to touch him, as many as had plagues."

πολλοὺς γὰρ ἐθεράπευσεν, ὥστε ἐπιπίπτειν αὐτῷ ἵνα αὐτοῦ ἅφωνται ὅσοι εἶχον μάστιγας.

πολλοὺς (acc.pl.masc.of πολύς, direct object of ἐθεράπευσεν) 228.
γὰρ (causal conjunction) 105.
ἐθεράπευσεν (3d.per.sing.aor.act.ind.of θεραπεύω, culminative) 406.
ὥστε (conjunction introducing a result clause) 752.
ἐπιπίπτειν (pres.act.inf.of ἐπιπίπτω, result) 1794.
αὐτῷ (dat.sing.masc.of αὐτός, personal interest) 16.
ἵνα (final conjunction introducing a purpose clause) 114.
αὐτοῦ (gen.sing.masc.of αὐτός, objective genitive) 16.
ἅφωνται (3d.per.pl.aor.mid.subj.of ἅπτω, purpose) 711.
ὅσοι (nom.pl.masc.of ὅσος, subject of εἶχον, in a relative clause) 660.
εἶχον (3d.per.pl.imp.act.ind.of ἔχω, progressive duration) 82.

#2114 μάστιγας (acc.pl.fem.of μάστιξ, direct object of εἶχον).

plauge - Mk.3:10; 5:29,34; Lk.7:21.
scourging - Acts 22:24; Heb.11:36.

Meaning: A whip, scourge - Acts 22:24; Heb.11:36. Metaphorically - a plague of sickness - Mk.3:10; Lk.7:21. Specifically, with reference to the issue of blood - Mk.5:29,34.

Translation - "Because He had healed many, with the result that they were crowding about Him in order that those who had been ill might touch Him."

Comment: γὰρ is causal. It explains the problem of verse 9. Note πολλοὺς in emphasis. ὥστε with the infinitive is "By far the most common way of expressing result. . . " (Mantey, *Manual,* 285). *Cf.*I Cor.13:2; Mk.1:27; 2:12.

Note the dative of personal interest in αὐτῷ, following ἐπί in composition in the infinitive. ". . . it is not always necessary for any preposition to follow the compound verb. Often the preposition with the verb may be followed by the case that is usual with the preposition without much regard to the verb itself. That is to say, the preposition in composition may be tantamount in result to the simple verb followed by that preposition. This is not always true, but it sometimes happens so." (Robertson, *Grammar,* 562. Examples are: Mk.3:10; Gal.5:4; Lk.15:6; 10:42; Acts 14:22; Mt.26:62; 16:18; Acts 28:20, etc.

Cf.#752 for other examples of ὥστε with the infinitive in a result clause. The culminative aorist in ἐθεράπευσεν indicates a present resultant culmination of previous activity. Jesus' record as a healer had become the subject of widespread discussion. His patients, now restored to health, were many. The result was that those not yet healed were pressing upon Him with the hope that they might at least attach themselves to Him (middle voice in ἅφωνται) and thus be healed. The explanation goes on in verse 11. Mt.12:15 adds that He healed them all.

Verse 11 - "And unclean spirits, when they saw him, fell down before him, and cried, saying, Thou art the Son of God."

καὶ τὰ πνεύματα τὰ ἀκάθαρτα, ὅταν αὐτὸν ἐθεώρουν, προσέπιπτον αὐτῷ καὶ ἔκραζον λέγοντες ὅτι Σὺ εἶ ὁ υἱὸς τοῦ θεοῦ.

καὶ (continuative conjunction) 14.

τὰ (nom.pl.neut.of the article in agreement with πνεύματα) 9.

πνεύματα (nom.pl.neut.of πνεῦμα, subject of προσέπιπτον) 83.

τὰ (nom.pl.neut.of the article in agreement with ἀκάθαρτα) 9.

ἀκάθαρτα (nom.pl.neut.of ἀκάθαρτος, in agreement with πνεύματα) 843.

ὅταν (indefinite temporal adverb with the indicative, introducing a temporal clause) 436.

αὐτὸν (acc.sing.masc.of αὐτός, direct object of ἐθεώρουν) 16.

ἐθεώρουν (3d.per.pl.imp.act.ind.of θεωρέω, inceptive) 1667.

προσέπιπτον (3d.per.pl.imp.act.ind.of προσπίπτω, progressive description) 699.

αὐτῷ (loc.sing.masc.of αὐτός, after πρός in composition, with a verb of rest) 16.

καὶ (adjunctive conjunction, joining verbs) 14.

ἔκραζον (3d.per.pl.imp.act.ind.of κράζω, progressive description) 765.

λέγοντα (pres.act.part.nom.pl.neut.of λέγω, adverbial, modal) 66.

ὅτι (recitative conjunction, introducing direct discourse) 211.

Σὺ (nom.sing.masc.of σύ, predicate nominative) 104.

εἶ (2d.per.sing.pres.ind.of εἰμί, aoristic) 86.

ὁ (nom.sing.masc.of the article in agreement with υἱὸς) 9.

υἱὸς (nom.sing.masc.of υἱός, subject of εἶ) 5.

τοῦ (gen.sing.masc.of the article in agreement with θεοῦ) 9.

θεοῦ (gen.sing.masc.of θεός, relationship) 124.

Translation - "And the unclean spirits, as soon as they saw Him fell down before Him and were crying out, saying, 'You are the Son of God.'"

Comment: Note that Mark emphasizes the description of the spirits, with the emphatic attributive position (article, noun, article, adjective). ὅταν with the indicative is somewhat indefinite, due to the use of ὅταν, but it is also definite, as indicated by the indicative mode. The demons did in fact see Jesus, and when they did (*whenever*) - that is, when they first caught a glimpse of Him (inceptive imperfect in ἐθεώρουν), they fell down and began to cry out (inceptive imperfect in ἔκραζον. Satan is a loud-mouthed bore because he is insecure and his subordinate hellions emulate him. One glimpse of the incarnate Son of God and they come bowing and crying out. They admit that which it would have been folly to deny. Jesus was and is indeed the Son of God, as is evident from the fact that He rescued the poor people who were being held captive by the demons. I John 4:4. Note that Σύ, the predicate nominative is emphasized ahead of the subject of εἶ, ὁ υἱὸς τοῦ θεοῦ. The Pharisees and the Herodians might plot to destroy Jesus but the demons recognized and confessed Him.

Verse 12 - "And he straitly charged them that they should not make him known."

καὶ πολλὰ ἐπετίμα αὐτοῖς ἵνα μὴ αὐτὸν φανερὸν ποιήσωσιν.

καὶ (adversative conjunction) 14.
πολλὰ (acc.pl.neut.of πολύς, direct object of ἐπετίμα) 228.
ἐπετίμα (3d.per.sing.imp.act.ind.of ἐπιτιμάω, progressive duration) 757.
αὐτοῖς (dat.pl.masc.of αὐτός, indirect object of ἐπετίμα) 16.
ἵνα (final conjunction introducing a negative purpose clause) 114.
μὴ (negative conjunction with the subjunctive in a prohibition) 87.
αὐτὸν (acc.sing.masc.of αὐτός, direct object of ποιήσωσιν) 16.
φανερὸν (acc.sing.masc.of φανερός, predicate adjective) 981.
ποιήσωσιν (3d.per.pl.aor.act.subj.of ποιέω, prohibition) 127.

Translation - "And He ordered them repeatedly with many words not to make Him known."

Comment: πολλὰ ἐπετίμα αὐτοῖς is an interesting way to say that Jesus insisted to them with many admonitions that they should not tell who He was. The ἵνα clause with μὴ and the subjunctive is the prohibition. For further comment cf. Mt.12:16-21.

(B) The Choosing of the Twelve

Mk.3:13-19; Lk.6:12-16

Mk.3:13 - "And he goeth up into a mountain, and calleth unto him whom he would: and they came unto him."

Καὶ ἀναβαίνει εἰς τὸ ὄρος καὶ προσκαλεῖται οὓς ἤθελεν αὐτός, καὶ ἀπῆλθον πρὸς αὐτόν.

Καὶ (continuative conjunction) 14.
ἀναβαίνει (3d.per.sing.pres.act.ind.of ἀναβαίνω, historical) 323.
εἰς (preposition with the accusative of extent) 140.
τὸ (acc.sing.neut.of the article in agreement with ὄρος) 9.
ὄρος (acc.sing.neut.of ὄρος, extent) 357.
καὶ (adjunctive conjunction, joining verbs) 14.

προσκαλεῖται (3d.per.sing.pres.ind.of προσκαλέομαι,historical) 842.
οὓς (acc.pl.masc.of ὅς, direct object of προσκαλεῖται) 65.
ἤθελεν (3d.per.sing.imp.act.ind.of θέλω, progressive duration) 88.
αὐτός (nom.sing.masc.of αὐτός, subject of ἤθελεν) 16.
καὶ (inferential conjunction) 14.
ἀπῆλθον (3d.per.pl.aor.act.ind.of ἀπέρχομαι, constative) 239.
πρός (preposition with the accusative of extent) 197.
αὐτόν (acc.sing.masc.of αὐτός, extent) 16.

Translation - *"And Jesus went up into the mountain and He called those whom He had always wanted; therefore they came to Him."*

Comment: The ascent into the mountain and the gathering of the disciples is recorded in Mt.5:1, *q.v.* εἰς τὸ ὄρος is a prepositional phrase used adverbially to define ἀναβαίνει. οὓς ἤθελεν indicates His sovereignty. Our Lord was choosing His apostles. All probably thought that they were coming without motivation other than their own. They came of their own free will but they were motivated by His sovereign call. So it is in salvation. καὶ . . . αὐτόν records their response to His call. The parallel passage in Lk.6:12 adds that He had been out upon the mountain side all night in prayer. *Cf.* comment.

The imperfect tense in ἤθελεν with its indication of continuous action in past time speaks of the eternal will of God, the Sovereign. How long had Jesus *always* wanted to call these specific men to be His apostles and not others? They were chosen before the foundation of the world (Eph.1:4). There was a great crowd of people at the foot of the mountain (Mk.3:7). Why did He call the twelve who are named and not twelve others? And why only twelve? Why not twenty or one hundred? (Eph.1:11). It was not because the twelve apostles were better men than others (Rom.9:10-13). Indeed, they were not distinguished for their scholarship or public prominence (I Cor.1:25-29). One, in fact was later declared to be ὁ διάβολός (John 6:70). Jesus had His reasons for choosing Judas (John 17:12).

Verse 14 - "And he ordained twelve, that they should be with him, and that he might send them forth to preach."

καὶ ἐποίησεν δώδεκα, (οὓς καὶ ἀποστόλους ὠνόμασεν,) ἵνα ὦσιν μετ᾽ αὐτοῦ καὶ ἵνα ἀποστέλλῃ αὐτοὺς κηρύσσειν

καὶ (continuative conjunction) 14.
ἐποίησεν (3d.per.sing.aor.act.ind.of ποιέω, constative) 127.
δώδεκα (acc.pl.masc. indeclin., direct object of ἐποίησεν) 820.
οὓς (acc.pl.masc.of ὅς, relative pronoun, direct object of ὠνόμασεν) 65.
καὶ (adjunctive conjunction, joining verbs) 14.
ἀποστόλους (acc.pl.masc.of ἀπόστολος, predicate accusative, in agreement with οὓς) 844.

#2115 ὠνόμασεν (3d.per.sing.aor.act.ind.of ὀνομάζω, constative).

call - Acts 19:13; I Cor.5:11.
name - Mk.3:14; Lk.6:13,14; Rom.15:20; Eph.1:21; 3:15; 5:3; II Tim.2:19.

Meaning: From ὄνομα (#108). To give a name to something or somebody. To designate. To name. To assign a nickname to one already named - Lk.6:14; I Cor.5:11; to assign an official title to one who already has a name - Mk.3:14; Lk.6:13; to pronounce a name in a religious ceremony so as to invoke authority - Acts 19:13; to invoke the name of Christ in a confession of faith - Rom.15:20; II Tim.2:19; Eph.1:21; 3:15; to mention a subject in order to discuss it - I Cor.5:1; Eph.5:3.

ἵνα (sub-final conjunction introducing a purpose/result clause) 114.
ὦσιν (3d.per.pl.pres.subj.of εἰμί, purpose/result) 86.
μετ' (preposition with the genitive of accompaniment) 50.
αὐτοῦ (gen.sing.masc.of αὐτός, accompaniment) 16.
καὶ (adjunctive conjunction, joining infinitives) 14.
ἵνα (sub-final conjunction introducing a purpose/result clause) 114.
ἀποστέλλῃ (3d.per.sing.pres.act.subj.of ἀποστέλλω, purpose/result) 215.
αὐτοὺς (acc.pl.masc.of αὐτός, direct object of ἀποστέλλῃ) 16.
κηρύσσειν (pres.act.inf.of κηρύσσω, complementary) 249.

Translation - "And He appointed twelve whom also He designated apostles, in order (and with the result) that they might accompany Him, and in order (and with the result) that He might send them forth to preach."

Comment: *Cf.*#127 for the basic meaning of ποιέω. The word "ordain" has come to be associated with certain rituals, supposedly of religious significance and deemed utilitarian. No such rituals were practised when our Lord chose the disciple. Note that Jesus did the choosing (John 15:16). He simply picked them out from a larger group and announced that they should henceforth be called "apostles." "Call" here in the sense of *name*, not in the sense of *summon*, which is expressed by καλέω. Jesus had two purposes in His action here and, since it is the sovereign God of the universe Who is acting, purpose is equal to result. Hence we have designated the two clauses as sub-final - both purpose and result. Jesus wanted these twelve men to accompany Him and He wanted to send them out in order to preach His gospel. Only men who have been with Jesus should be sent out to preach. *Cf.* Lk.6:13. Another purpose clause follows in verse 15.

The relative clause οὓς καὶ ἀποστόλους ὠνόμασεν "... may be regarded as an interpolation from Luke (6.13), the Committee was of the opinion that the external evidence is too strong in their favor to warrant their ejection from the text. In order to reflect the balance of probabilities, the words were retained but enclosed with square brackets." (Metzger, *A Textual Commentary on the Greek New Testament*, 80).

Verse 15 - "... and to have power to heal sicknesses, and to cast out devils."

καὶ ἔχειν ἐξουσίαν ἐκβάλλειν τὰ δαιμόνια.

καὶ (adjunctive conjunction joining purpose/result clauses) 14.
ἔχειν (pres.act.inf.of ἔχω, complementary) 82.
ἐξουσίαν (acc.sing.fem.of ἐξουσία, direct object of ἔχειν) 707.
ἐκβάλλειν (pres.act.inf.of ἐκβάλλω, epexegetical) 649.
τὰ (acc.pl.neut.of the article in agreement with δαιμόνια) 9.
δαιμόνια (acc.pl.neut.of δαιμόνιον, direct object of ἐκβάλλειν) 686.

Translation - ". . . and to have power to cast out the demons."

Comment: The verse completes the sentence of verse 14. ἔχειν and κηρύσσειν of verse 14 complete ἀποστέλλῃ, while ἐκβάλλειν explains ἐξουσίαν. The authority of the incarnate Creator over the demon world is now given to His Apostles, and their message was to be authenticated by the exercise of this authority. Thus Christ demonstrated His superiority over the demon world. That they used this power is evident from Luke 10:17 and many other passages.

Verse 16 - "*And Simon he surnamed Peter.*"

(καὶ ἐποίησεν τοὺς δώδεκα,) καὶ ἐπέθηκεν ὄνομα τῷ Σίμωνι Πέτρον,

καὶ (continuative conjunction) 14.
ἐποίησεν (3d.per.sing.aor.act.ind.of ποιέω, constative) 127.
τοὺς (acc.pl.masc.of the article in agreement with δώδεκα) 9.
δώδεκα (acc.pl.masc.indeclin., direct object of ἐποίησεν) 820.
καὶ (continuative conjunction) 14.
ἐπέθηκεν (3d.per.sing.aor.act.ind.of ἐπιτίθημι, constative) 818.
ὄνομα (acc.sing.neut.of ὄνομα, direct object of ἐπέθηκεν) 108.
τῷ (dat.sing.masc.of the article in agreement with Σίμωνα) 9.
Σίμωνι (dat.sing.masc.of Σίμωνα, indirect object of ἐπέθηκεν) 387.
Πέτρον (acc.sing.masc.of Πέτρος, predicate accusative in agreement with ὄνομα) 387.

Translation - "*And He appointed the twelve, and He gave a nickname to Simon - Peter.*"

Comment: Some Mss.omit the clause καὶ . . . δώδεκα, as an unnecessary repetition of verse 14. Note the interesting use of ἐπιτίθημι here. *Cf.*#818. *Cf.* Lk.6:14.

Verse 17 - "*And James the son of Zebedee, and John the brother of James; and he surnamed them Boanerges, which is, The sons of thunder.*"

καὶ Ἰάκωβον τὸν τοῦ Ζεβεδαίου καὶ Ἰωάννην τὸν ἀδελφὸν τοῦ Ἰακώβου, καὶ ἐπέθηκεν αὐτοῖς ὀνόματα Βοανηργές, ὅ ἐστιν Υἱοὶ Βροντῆς;

καί (adjunctive conjunction, joining nouns) 14.
'Ιάκωβον (acc.sing.masc.of 'Ιάκωβον, object of ἐποίησεν) 397.
τὸν (acc.sing.masc.of the article in apposition) 9.
τοῦ (gen.sing.masc.of the article, relationship) 9.
Ζεβεδαίου (gen.sing.masc.of Ζεβεδαίος, relationship) 398.
καί (adjunctive conjunction joining nouns) 14.
'Ιωάννην (acc.sing.masc.of 'Ιωάννης, object of ἐποίησεν) 399.
τὸν (acc.sing.masc.of the article in agreement with ἀδελφὸν) 9.
ἀδελφὸν (acc.sing.masc.of ἀδελφός, apposition) 15.
τοῦ (gen.sing.masc.of the article in agreement with 'Ιακώβου) 9.
'Ιακώβου (gen.sing.masc.of 'Ιάκωβον, relationship) 397.
καί (continuative conjunction) 14.
ἐπέθηκεν (3d.per.sing.aor.act.ind.of ἐπιτίθημι, constative) 818.
αὐτοῖς (dat.pl.masc.of αὐτός, indirect object of ἐπέθηκεν) 16.
ὀνόματα (acc.pl.neut.of ὄνομα, direct object of ἐπέθηκεν) 108.

#2116 Βοανηργές (acc.sing.neut.of Βοανηργές, in apposition).

Meaning: "Sons of Thunder." The name given by Jesus to James and John. The name seems to indicate fiery and destructive zeal, similar to what can be expected in a thunder storm. *Cf.* Lk.9:54.

ὅ (nom.sing.masc.of ὅς, subject of ἐστιν) 65.
ἐστιν (3d.per.sing.pres.ind.of εἰμί, aoristic) 86.
Υἱοὶ (nom.pl.masc.of υἱός, predicate nominative) 5.

#2117 Βροντῆς (gen.sing.fem.of βροντή, definition).

thunder - Mk.3:17; Rev.4:5; 6:1; 8:5; 10:3,4,4; 11:19; 14:2; 16:18; 19:6; John 12:29.

Meaning: Thunder. In the ordinary meterological sense. In connection with the supernatural judgments of the Revelation in all places in that book. In connection with #2116 in Mk.3:17. Properly in John 12:29 as the audience mistakenly interpreted the voice of God.

Translation - ". . and James, the son of Zebedee and John, the brother of James (also He assigned to them names - Boanerges, which means 'Sons of Thunder.'"

Comment: Jesus also included James and John in the chosen group of apostles. Mark repeats the pattern of ἐπέ. . . ὀνόματα in verse 17, which he used in verse 16. *Cf.*Lk.9:54 for comment on the nickname which Jesus gave to the two brothers. That Jesus could read the personality traits of His disciples so well is further evidence of His deity. There are many shortsighted Christians who are remarkably generous with the wrath of God upon others who disagree with them. For nearly two thousand years the Church has been thundering (which is God's prerogative) when she should have been praying (which is her duty).

In 1960 many disciples prayed that the thunder and lightning of political repudiation might fall upon another Christian who happened not to walk in their own denominational camp. Fundamentalists, for all of their commendable zeal for the defense of the historic faith, have too often emulated James and John as they have called down God's wrath on others, whom they thought were astray from the path of theological orthodoxy. A forgotten fundamental of the faith is found in Jesus' statement, "By this shall all men know that ye are my disciples if ye have love one to another" (John 13:35).

The list of apostles becomes complete in vss.18 and 19.

Verse 18 - "And Andrew, and Philip, and Bartholomew, and Matthew, and Thomas, and James the son of Alphaeus, and Thaddaeus, and Simon the Canaanite,"

καὶ Ἀνδρέαν καὶ Φίλιππον καὶ Βαρθολομαῖον καὶ Ματθαῖον καὶ Θωμᾶν καὶ Ἰάκωβον τὸν τοῦ Ἀλφαίου καὶ Θαδδαῖον καὶ Σίμωνα τὸν Καναναῖον,

καὶ (adjunctive conjunction joining nouns) 14.
Ἀνδρέαν (acc.sing.masc.of Ἀνδρέας, direct object of ἐποίησεν) 388.
καὶ (adjunctive conjunction joining nouns) 14.
Φίλιππον (acc.sing.masc.of Φίλιππος, direct object of ἐποίησεν) 845.
καὶ (adjunctive conjunction joining nouns) 14.
Βαρθολομαῖον (acc.sing.masc.of Βαρθολομαῖος, direct object of ἐποίησεν) 846.
καὶ (adjunctive conjunction joining nouns) 14.
Ματθαῖον (acc.sing.masc.of Ματθαῖος, direct object of ἐποίησεν) 788.
καὶ (adjunctive conjunction joining nouns) 14.
Θωμᾶν (acc.sing.masc.of Θωμᾶς, direct object of ἐποίησεν) 847.
καὶ (adjunctive conjunction joining nouns) 14.
Ἰάκωβον (acc.sing.masc.of Ἰάκωβον, direct object of ἐποίησεν) 848.
τὸν (acc.sing.masc.of the article, apposition) 9.
τοῦ (gen.sing.masc.of the article, relationship) 9.
Ἀλφαίου (gen.sing.masc.of Ἀλφαῖος, relationship) 849.
καὶ (adjunctive conjunction joining nouns) 14.
Θαδδαῖον (acc.sing.masc.of Θαδδαῖος, direct object of ἐποίησεν) 850.
καὶ (adjunctive conjunction joining nouns) 14.
Σίμωνα (acc.sing.masc.of Σίμων, direct object of ἐποίησεν) 851.
τὸν (acc.sing.masc.of the article in agreement with Καναναῖον) 9.
Καναναῖον (acc.sing.masc.of Καναναῖος, apposition) 852.

Translation - ". . . and Andrew and Philip and Bartholomew and Matthew and Thomas and James, the son of Alphaeus, and Thaddeus and Simon, the Canaanite. . . "

Comment: Since there are two of the group named James and two named Simon, Mark carefully distinguishes them. James, the son of Zebedee (vs.17) is sometimes called James the Greater; he is the brother of John the Beloved disciple and one of the Sons of Thunder. James (verse 18) is the son of Alphaeus, sometimes called James the Less. Simon Peter (verse 16) is not to be confused with Simon the Canaanite (verse 18). One more was chosen - "... in order that the scripture might be fulfilled" (John 17:12).

Verse 19 - "And Judas Iscariot, which also betrayed him."

καὶ Ἰούδαν Ἰσκαριώθ, ὃς καὶ παρέδωκεν αὐτόν.

καὶ (adjunctive conjunction joining nouns) 14.
Ἰούδαν (acc.sing.masc.of Ἰούδας, direct object of ἐποίησεν) 853.
Ἰσκαριώθ, acc.sing.masc.of Ἰσκαριώτης, in apposition) 854.
ὃς (nom.sing.masc.of ὅς, relative pronoun, subject of παρέδωκεν) 65.
καὶ (emphatic conjunction) 14.
παρέδωκεν (3d.per.sing.aor.act.ind.of παραδίδωμι, constative) 368.
αὐτόν (acc.sing.masc.of αὐτός, direct object of παρέδωκεν) 16.

Translation - "And Judas Iscariot, who in fact betrayed Him."

Comment: It seems proper to translate the second καὶ in an emphatic sense. The student should decide which translation to give in a case like this by trying all the alternatives and picking the one which best fits the context.

It is interesting to note the little bits of information, offered in an incidental manner, about the disciples which the listing gives, in addition to their names. The nicknames of Peter, James and John are given, with an interpretation of the latter, the name of the father of James the Less, in order to distinguish him from James the son of Zebedee, the province of Simon, to distinguish him from Simon Peter and the crime of Judas Iscariat.

We turn now to Luke's account of the same episode in Lk.6:12-16.

Luke 6:12 - "And it came to pass in those days, that he went out into a mountain to pray, and continued all night in prayer to God."

Ἐγένετο δὲ ἐν ταῖς ἡμέραις ταύταις ἐξελθεῖν αὐτὸν εἰς τὸ ὄρος προσεύξασθαι, καὶ ἦν διανυκτερεύων ἐν τῇ προσευχῇ τοῦ θεοῦ.

Ἐγένετο (3d.per.sing.aor.ind.of γίνομαι, constative) 113.
δὲ (explanatory conjunction) 11.
ἐν (preposition with the locative of time point) 80.
ταῖς (loc.pl.fem.of the article in agreement with ἡμέραις) 9.
ἡμέραις (loc.pl.fem.of ἡμέρα, time point) 135.
ταύταις (loc.pl.fem.of οὗτος, in agreement with ἡμέραις) 93.
ἐξελθεῖν (aor.inf.of ἐξέρχομαι, noun use, subject of ἐγένετο) 161.
αὐτὸν (acc.sing.masc.of αὐτός, general reference) 16.
εἰς (preposition with the accusative of extent) 140.
τὸ (acc.sing.neut.of the article in agreement with ὄρος) 9.

ὄρος (acc.sing.neut.of ὄρος, extent) 357.
προσεύξασθαι (aor.inf.of προσεύχομαι, purpose) 544.
καὶ (continuative conjunction) 14.
ἦν (3d.per.sing.imp.ind.of εἰμί, imperfect periphrastic) 86.

#2118 διανυκτερεύων (pres.act.part.nom.sing.masc.of διανυκτερεύω, imperfect periphrastic).

continue all night - Lk.6:12.

Meaning: A combination of διά (#118) and νυκτερεύω - "to pass the night". Opposed to διημερεύω. Hence, to spend the entire night. With reference to Jesus who prayed all night on the mountin. In an imperfect periphrastic- Lk.6:12.

ἐν (preposition with the instrumental of means) 80.
τῇ (instru.sing.fem.of the article in agreement with προσευχῇ) 9.
προσευχῇ (instru.sing.fem.of προσευχή, means) 1238.
τοῦ (gen.sing.masc.of the article in agreement with θεοῦ) 9.
θεοῦ (gen.sing.masc.of θεός, objective genitive) 124.

Translation - "Now during this time He went into the mountain to pray and He continued throughout the night in prayer to God."

Comment: *Cf.*#80 for other examples of ἐν with the locative in a temporal sense. Again we have Luke using the infinitive, with the accusative of general reference as subject of ἐγένετο. Luke is saying that Jesus' exit and journey into the mountain occurred at that time. The purpose infinitive προσεύξασθαι tells us why He went. He went to pray. Note perfective διά in composition with the verb and the point is doubly stressed with the imperfect periphrastic construction in ἦν διανυκτερεύων. Thus, both the preposition and the periphrastic imperfect tell us that Jesus spent the entire night on the mountain. ἐν τῇ προσευχῇ τοῦ θεοῦ - "divine communion" - the sort of fellowship that only God and His Son Jesus would find possible. It is not "prayer to God" but "prayer of God" *i.e.* divine association. This statement is exclusively Lucan. Whom should Jesus call into the inner circle? Boanerges? Impetuous Simon Peter? Thomas the Doubter? Judas the Betrayer? We may be sure that the Holy Trinity thought about it all that night on the mountain.

Verse 13 - "And when it was day, he called unto him his disciples: and of them he chose twelve, whom also he named apostles."

καὶ ὅτε ἐγένετο ἡμέρα, προσεφώνησεν τοὺς μαθητὰς αὐτοῦ, καὶ ἐκλεξάμενος ἀπ᾽ αὐτῶν δώδεκα, οὓς καὶ ἀποστόλους ὠνόμασεν,

καὶ (continuative conjunction) 14.
ὅτε (temporal conjunction introducing a definite temporal clause) 703.
ἐγένετο (3d.per.sing.aor.ind.of γίνομαι, ingressive) 113.

ἡμέρα (nom.sing.fem.of ἡμέρα, subject of ἐγένετο) 135.

προσεφώνησεν (3d.per.sing.aor.act.ind.of προσφωνέω, constative) 925.

τοὺς (acc.pl.masc.of the article in agreement with μαθητὰς) 9.

μαθητὰς (acc.pl.masc.of μαθητής, direct object of προσφώνησεν) 421.

αὐτοῦ (gen.sing.masc.of αὐτός, possession) 16.

καὶ (adjunctive conjunction joining nouns) 14.

#2119 ἐκλεξάμενος (aor.mid.part.nom.sing.masc.of ἐκλέγω, adverbial, temporal).

　　choose - Mk.13:20; Lk.6:13; 10:42; 14:7; John 6:70; 13:18; 15:16,16,19; Acts 1:2,24; 6:5; 13:17; I Cor.1:27,27,28; Eph.1:4; Jas.2:5.
　　make choice - Acts 15:7.
　　beloved - Lk.9:35.
　　chosen - Acts 15:22,25.

Meaning: A combination of ἐκ (#19) and λέγω (#66). Hence to call out; to select; pick; choose. With reference to the election unto spiritual salvation - Mk.13:20; I Cor.1:27,27,28; Eph.1:4; Jas.2:5; with reference to Jesus' selection of the Apostles - Lk.6:13; with ἀπό and the ablative - John 6:70; 13:18; 15:16b,19; Acts 1:2. of the selection of one to replace Judas - Acts 1:24; with ἐκ and the ablative - Acts 6:5. Of God's election of Israel as a chosen people - Acts 13:17; of God's selection of various apostles for specific jobs - Acts 15:7; with reference to the selection of a given policy to which one devotes himself - Lk.10:42; of choosing chief rooms at a public assemblage - Lk.14:7; of God's choice of Christ as the only Saviour - Lk.9:35; of the disciples' choice of Jesus - John 15:16a. Of the choice of Judas Barsabas to accompany Paul - Acts 15:22,25.

ἀπ' (preposition with the ablative, partitive) 70.

αὐτῶν (abl.pl.masc.of αὐτός, partitive) 16.

δώδεκα (acc.sing.masc.of δώδεκα, indeclin., direct object of ἐκλεξάμενος) 820.

οὓς (acc.pl.masc.of ὅς, direct object of ὠνόμασεν) 65.

καὶ (adjunctive conjunction, joining verbs) 14.

ἀποστόλους (acc.pl.masc.of ἀπόστολος, predicate accusative, in agreement with οὓς) 844.

ὠνόμασεν (3d.per.sing.aor.act.ind.of ὀνομάζω, constative) 2115.

Translation - "And as day began to dawn He called to Him His disciples, and He selected from them twelve men, whom He also designated as apostles."

Comment: Note the ingressive aorist in ἐγένετο. "As the day *began* to dawn. . . κ.τ.λ." or "At daybreak." The long night of prayer and fellowship with the Father was over and Jesus was ready to put together His church. He chose the twelve from a greater number and gave to them a new title, to be worn along with that of οἱ μαθηταί. They had been "learners" (#421); not they were "those sent out" (#844).

Cf.#925 for other uses of προσφωνέω. Jesus later reminded the Apostles that He had chosen them; not the other way around (John 15:16).

It is here that we have at least the first date for the founding of the Church of Jesus Christ. Long before Pentecost Christ, the Chief Cornerstone, began building upon the foundation, which consisted of the Apostles and Prophets (Eph.2:20). The building was progressing when He spoke to Peter about it again in Mt.16:18. And it is still going on and will continue to grow until the last member of the body of Christ has been fitted into the perfect building.

In verses 14-16 Luke lists the Apostles.

Verse 14 - "Simon (whom he also named Peter,) and Andrew, his brother, James and John, Philip and Bartholomew,"

Σίμωνα, ὃν καὶ ὠνόμασεν Πέτρον, καὶ Ἀνδρέαν τὸν ἀδελφὸν αὐτοῦ, καὶ Ἰάκωβον καὶ Ἰωάννην καὶ Φίλιππον καὶ Βαρθολομαῖον

Σίμωνα (acc.sing.masc.of Σίμων, direct object of ἐκλεξάμενος) 386.

ὃν (acc.sing.masc.of ὅς, relative pronoun, in agreement with Σίμωνα) 65.

καὶ (adjunctive conjunction joining verbs) 14.

ὠνόμασεν (3d.per.sing.aor.act.ind.of ὀνομάζω, culminative) 2115.

Πέτρον (acc.sing.masc.of Πέτρος, predicate accusative in agreement with Σίμωνα) 387.

καὶ (adjunctive conjunction joining nouns) 14.

Ἀνδρέαν (acc.sing.masc.of Ἀνδρέας, direct object of ἐκλεξάμενος) 388.

τὸν (acc.sing.masc.of the article in agreement with ἀδελφὸν) 9.

ἀδελφὸν (acc.sing.masc.of ἀδελφός, apposition) 15.

αὐτοῦ (gen.sing.masc.of αὐτός, relationship) 16.

καὶ (adjunctive conjunction joining nouns) 14.

Ἰάκωβον (acc.sing.masc.of Ἰάκωβον, direct object of ἐκλεξάμενος) 397.

καὶ (adjunctive conjunction joining nouns) 14.

Ἰωάννην (acc.sing.masc.of Ἰωάννης, direct object of ἐκλεξάμενος) 399.

καὶ (adjunctive conjunction joining nouns) 14.

Φίλιππον (acc.sing.masc.of Φίλιππος, direct object of ἐκλεξάμενος) 845.

καὶ (adjunctive conjunction joining nouns) 14.

Βαρθολομαῖον (acc.sing.masc.of Βαρθολομαῖος, direct object of ἐκλεξάμενος) 846.

Translation - "Simon, whom also He named Peter, and Andrew, his brother, and James and John and Philip and Bartolomew."

Comment: *Cf.* Mk.3:16-19. Note that the evangelists do not list the apostles in the same order, but the identities are the same.

Verse 15 - "Matthew and Thomas, James the son of Alphaeus, and Simon called Zelotes,

καὶ Ματθαῖον καὶ Θωμᾶν καὶ Ἰάκωβον Ἀλφαίου καὶ Σίμωνα τὸν καλούμενον Ζηλωτὴν

καὶ (adjunctive conjunction joining nouns) 14.
Ματθαῖον (acc.sing.masc.of Ματθαῖον, direct object of ἐκλεξάμενος) 788.
καὶ (adjunctive conjunction joining nouns) 14.
Θωμᾶν (acc.sing.masc.of Θωμᾶς, direct object of ἐκλεξάμενος) 847.
καὶ (adjunctive conjunction joining nouns) 14.
Ἰάκωβον (acc.sing.masc.of Ἰάκωβον, direct object of ἐκλεξάμενος) 848.
Ἀλφαίου (gen.sing.masc.of Ἀλφαῖος, relationship) 849.
καὶ (adjunctive conjunction joining nouns) 14.
Σίμωνα (acc.sing.masc.of Σίμων, direct object of ἐκλεξάμενος) 851.
τὸν (acc.sing.masc.of the article in agreement with καλούμενον) 9.
καλούμενον (pres.pass.part.acc.sing.masc.of καλέω, substantival, apposition) 107.

#2120 Ζηλωτὴν (acc.sing.masc.of Ζηλωτής, predicate accusative, in agreement with Σίμωνα).

zealous - Lk.6:15; Acts 1:12; 21:20; 22:3; I Cor.14:12; Gal.1:14; Tit.2:14.
followers - I Pet.3:13.

Meaning: From ζηλόω (#3105). Hence, one burning with zeal; a zealot. As a nickname for one of the Twelve who may have belonged to a political party of the same name - Lk.6:15. Elsewhere as an adjective followed by a genitive of reference: - of the law, Acts 21:20; toward God - Acts 22:3; of spiritual things - I Cor.14:12; of the traditions - Gal.1:14; of good works - Tit.2:14; I Pet.3:13.

Translation - ". . . and Matthew and Thomas and James, the son of Alphaeus and Simon the one who is called a Zealot."

Comment: Here Luke adds more information about Simon whom Mark and Matthew designate as the Canaanite, to distinguish him from Simon Peter. He is also known as a Zealot, perhaps a member of a fanatical political party in Jerusalem.

Verse 16 - ". . . and Judas, the brother of James, and Judas Iscariot, which also was the traitor."

καὶ Ἰούδαν Ἰακώβου καὶ Ἰούδαν Ἰσκαριώθ, ὃς ἐγένετο προδότης.

καὶ (adjunctive conjunction joining nouns) 14.

#2121 Ἰδούδαν (acc.sing.masc.of Ἰούδας, direct object of ἐκλεξάμενος).

Judas - Lk.6:16; Acts 1:13; John 14:22.

Meaning: One of the Apostles, either the son or the brother of Ἰακώβου, who is otherwise unknown in the New Testament.

#2122 Ἰακώβου (gen.sing.masc.of Ἰάκωβον, relationship).

Meaning: Otherwise unknown in the New Testament except as the father (or perhaps brother) of #2121. Not to be confused with #'s397, 848, 1098.

καὶ (adjunctive conjunction joining names) 14.
Ἰούδαν (acc.sing.masc.of Ἰούδας, direct object of ἐκλεξάμενος) 853.
Ἰσκαριώθ (acc.sing.masc.of Ἰσκαριώτης, apposition) 854.
ὅς (nom.sing.masc.of ὅς, relative pronoun, subject of ἐγένετο) 65.
ἐγένετο (3d.per.sing.aor.ind.of γίνομαι, constative) 113.

#2123 προδότης (nom.sing.masc.of προδότης, predicate nominative).

betrayer - Acts 7:52.
traitor - Lk.6:16; II Tim.3:4.

Meaning: from προδίδωμι (#4008). A betrayer; a traitor. With reference to Judas Iscariot - Lk.6:16; of the Jews who murdered Jesus - Acts 7:52; generally of end-time apostates - II Tim.3:4.

Translation - "And Judas, related to James, and Judas Iscariot, who became a traitor."

Comment: This finishes Luke's list of the Apostles. We do not know whether Judas was the brother or the son of the James who is mentioned here. There was some relationship as the genitive indicates. His relative is mentioned, perhaps to be certain to distinguish him from Judas Iscariot, the betrayer. Note that Luke calls Judas Iscariot by the same name that Stephen used in addressing the Jews who crucified Christ and that Paul used in reference to end-time apostates.

(C) - The Sermon on the Mount

Mt.5:1-8:1; Lk.6:17-49

Luke 7:17 - "And he came down with them, and stood on the plain, and the company of his disciples, and a great multitude of people out of all Judea and Jerusalem, and from the sea-coast of Tyre and Sidon, which came to hear him, and to be healed of their diseases;"

Καὶ καταβὰς μετ- αὐτῶν ἔστη ἐπὶ τόπου πεδινοῦ καὶ ὄχλος πολὺς μαθητῶν αὐτοῦ καὶ πλῆθος πολὺ τοῦ λαοῦ ἀπὸ πάσης τῆς Ἰουδαίας καὶ Ἰερουσαλὴμ καὶ τῆς παραλίου Τύρου καὶ Σιδῶνος.

Καὶ (continuative conjunction) 14.
καταβὰς (aor.act.part.nom.sing.masc.of καταβαίνω, adverbial, temporal) 324.
μετ' (preposition with the genitive of accompaniment) 50.
αὐτῶν (gen.pl.masc.of αὐτός, accompaniment) 16.

ἔστη (3d.per.sing.2d.aor.act.ind.of ἵστημι, constative) 180.
ἐπὶ (preposition with the genitive of place description) 47.
τόπου (gen.sing.masc.of τόπος, place description) 1019.

#2124 πεδινοῦ (gen.sing.masc.of πεδινός, in agreement with τόπου).

plain - Lk.6:17.

Meaning: From πεδίον - "a plain." Hence, an adjective - level, flat in a topographical sense. With reference to the place where Jesus stood as He preached the Sermon on the Mount - Lk.6:17.

καὶ (continuative conjunction) 14.
ὄχλος (nom.sing.masc.of ὄχλος, subject of ἦλθον) 418.
πολὺς (nom.sing.masc.of πολύς, in agreement with ὄχλος) 228.
μαθητῶν (gen.pl.masc.of μαθητής, partitive genitive) 421.
αὐτοῦ (gen.sing.masc.of αὐτός, possession) 16.
καὶ (adjunctive conjunction joining nouns) 14.
πλῆθος (nom.sing.neut.of πλῆθος, subject of ἦλθον) 1792.
πολὺ (nom.sing.neut.of πολύς, in agreement with πλῆθος) 228.
τοῦ (gen.sing.masc.of the article in agreement with λαοῦ) 9.
λαοῦ (gen.sing.masc.of λαός, partitive genitive) 110.
ἀπὸ (preposition with the ablative of source) 70.
πάσης (abl.sing.fem.of πᾶς, in agreement with Ἰουδαίας) 67.
τῆς (abl.sing.fem.of the article in agreement with Ἰουδαίας) 9.
Ἰουδαίας (abl.sing.fem.of Ἰουδαίας, source) 134.
καὶ (adjunctive conjunction joining nouns) 14.
Ἰερουσαλὴμ (abl.sing.fem.of Ἰεροσολύμων, source) 141.
καὶ (adjunctive conjunction joining nouns) 14.
τῆς (abl.sing.fem.of the article in agreement with παραλίου) 9.

#2125 παραλίου (abl.sing.fem.of παράλιος, source)

sea coast - Lk.6:17.

Meaning: A combination of παρά (#154) and ἅλιος - "of or pertaining to the sea"; hence, the territory which is beside the sea; sea coast. With reference to the coast-line territory in the Tyre and Sidon region - Lk.6:17

Τύρου (gen.sing.masc.of Τύρος, definition) 939.
καὶ (adjunctive conjunction joining nouns) 14.
Σιδῶνος (gen.sing.masc.of Σιδῶν, definition) 940.

Translation - "*And when He had come down with them, He stood upon a level spot and a great crowd of His disciples, and a large multitude of the people from all Judea and Jerusalem and the Tyre and Sidon coast region, . . .*

Comment: The participle καταβὰς and the aorist indicative verb ἔστη give us the picture. Jesus came down from the mountain with the Twelve disciples, now commissioned as Apostles and He took His stand on a level spot, possibly a little higher than the area where two other groups of people gathered.

Three groups are to be distinguished. (1) The Twelve Apostles who had been with Jesus upon the mountain and who descended μετ' αὐτοῦ - "with Him." (2) another group of disciples of Jesus who came to meet Him and the Twelve Apostles. Note that these are disciples (μαθηταί) but not apostles (ἀπόστολοί). *Cf.*#421 and note that the word means a learner. Jesus had many disciples, twelve of whom became apostles. (3) The third group was made up of those who were neither disciples nor apostles. They are described as a great company of people from the various localities indicated. The Tyre and Sidon country was a long distance up the northern coast-line of the Mediterranean. This great multitude is further described in verse 18. (Note: The Greek text includes the two purpose clauses of verse 17 of KJV in the 18th verse).

Verse 18 - ". . . which came to hear him, and to be healed of their diseases; and they that were vexed with unclean spirits: and they were healed."

οἵ ἦλθον ἀκοῦσαι αὐτοῦ καὶ ἰαθῆναι ἀπὸ τῶν νόσων αὐτῶν; καὶ οἱ ἐνοχλούμενοι ἀπὸ πνευμάτων ἀκαθάρτων ἐθεραπεύοντο.

οἵ (nom.pl.masc.of ὅς, relative pronoun, subject of ἦλθον) 65.
ἦλθον (3d.per.pl.aor.ind.of ἔρχομαι, constative) 146.
ἀκοῦσαι (aor.act.inf.of ἀκούω, purpose) 148.
αὐτοῦ (gen.sing.masc.of αὐτός, objective genitive) 16.
καὶ (adjunctive conjunction joining infinitives) 14.
ἰαθῆναι (aor.pass.inf.of ἰάομαι, purpose) 721.
ἀπὸ (preposition with the ablative of separation) 70.
τῶν (abl.pl.masc.of the article in agreement with νόσων) 9.
νόσων (abl.pl.masc.of νόσος, separation) 407.
αὐτῶν (gen.pl.masc.of αὐτός, possession) 16.
καὶ (continuative conjunction) 14.
οἱ (nom.pl.masc.of the article in agreement with ἐνοχλούμενοι) 9.

#2126 ἐνοχλούμενοι (pres.pass.part.nom.pl.masc.of ἐνοχλέω, substantival, subject of ἐθεραπεύοντο).

vex - Lk.6:18.
trouble - Heb.12:15.

Meaning: A combination of ἐν (#80) and ὀχλέω from ὄχλος (#418). Hence, annoy, vex, trouble. Anyone who loves solitude will understand the annoyance and vexation of the milling throng. Those possessed with evil spirits were "in a crowd of evil spirits." Crowded, pushed around, pressured. With reference to those who were inhabited by evil spirits - Lk.6:18; of one who arises in a Christian assembly to create annoyance - Heb.12:15.

ἀπό (preposition with the ablative of agent) 70.
πνευμάτων (abl.pl.neut.of πνεῦμα, agent) 83.
ἀκαθάρτων (abl.pl.neut.of ἀκάθαρτος, in agreement with πνευμάτων) 843.
ἐθεραπεύοντο (3d.per.pl.imp.pass.ind.of θεραπεύω, progressive description) 406.

Translation - "... *who came to hear Him, and to be healed of their diseases; and those who were being annoyed by unclean spirits were being healed.*"

Comment: Two purpose infinitives complete ἦλθον. They came to hear Jesus speak and to be healed. Another group (οἱ ἐνοχλούμενοι) also came. #2126 is interesting. These poor people were being crowded, pushed and shoved around by the evil spirits. Apply the same thought to the word in Heb.12:15. A missionary testified that when she went with her husband into a desert area in Africa to witness to the natives, she was physically molested by unseen evil spirits. As the crowd pressed about Jesus in order to hear His words, those who needed His healing power were made whole. The level spot at the foot of the mountain where Jesus and the Twelve took their stand made it convenient for the afflicted to approach Him.

Verse 19 - "And the whole multitude sought to touch him: for there went virtue out of him, and he healed them all."

καὶ πᾶς ὁ ὄχλος ἐζήτουν ἅπτεσθαι αὐτοῦ, ὅτι δύναμις παρ᾽ αὐτοῦ ἐξήρχετο καὶ ἰᾶτο πάντας.

καὶ (continuative conjunction) 14.
πᾶς (nom.sing.masc.of πᾶς, in agreement with ὄχλος) 67.
ὁ (nom.sing.masc.of the article in agreement with ὄχλος) 9.
ὄχλος (nom.sing.masc.of ὄχλος, subject of ἐζήτουν) 418.
ἐζήτουν (3d.per.pl.imp.act.ind.of ζητέω, inceptive) 207.
ἅπτεσθαι (pres.mid.inf.of ἅπτω, epexegetical) 711.
αὐτοῦ (gen.sing.masc.of αὐτός, objective) 16.
ὅτι (causal conjunction) 211.
δύναμις (nom.sing.fem.of δύναμις, subject of ἐξήρχετο) 687.
παρ᾽ (preposition with the ablative, with persons) 154.
αὐτοῦ (abl.sing.masc.of αὐτός, source) 16.
ἐξήρχετο (3d.per.sing.imp.ind.of ἐξέρχομαι, inceptive) 161.
καὶ (inferential conjunction) 14.
ἰᾶτο (3d.per.sing.imp.ind.of ἰάομαι, inceptive) 721.
πάντας (acc.pl.masc.of πᾶς, direct object of ἰᾶτο) 67.

Translation - "And the entire crowd begin to try to touch Him, because power began to flow from Him and He healed all."

Comment: The imperfect tenses should be noted. The people *began* (inceptive imperfect) and kept on trying to touch Him. His power to heal began and continued to flow from Him. He continued to heal until He had healed them all. Note the superabundant display of healing power which our Lord manifested. How could one so able to meet man's need be ignored or opposed?

Jesus cared for their physical needs before He spoke to them of spiritual things. The institutional church with its social, economic and political approach to society's needs is not wrong here. The tragedy is that in many cases, once the social, economic, political and psychological needs are met, the spiritual message is forgotten. Jesus did not forget. For the next thirty verses Jesus preaches His gospel. Perhaps one of the reasons why they listened to Him was that He had healed them before He began to preach.

Verse 20 - "And he lifted up his eyes on his disciples, and said, Blessed be ye poor, for yours is the kingdom of God."

Καὶ αὐτὸς ἐπάρας τοὺς ὀφθαλμοὺς αὐτοῦ εἰς τοὺς μαθητὰς αὐτοῦ ἔλεγεν, Μακάριοι οἱ πρωχοί, ὅτι ὑμετέρα ἐστὶν ἡ βασιλεία τοῦ θεοῦ.

Καὶ (continuative conjunction) 14.
αὐτὸς (nom.sing.masc.of αὐτός, subject of ἔλεγεν) 16.
ἐπάρας (aor.act.part.nom.sing.masc.of ἐπαίρω, adverbial, temporal) 1227.
τοὺς (acc.pl.masc.of the article in agreement with ὀφθαλμοὺς) 9.
ὀφθαλμοὺς (acc.pl.masc.of ὀφθαλμός, direct object of ἐπάρας) 501.
αὐτοῦ (gen.sing.masc.of αὐτός, possession) 16.
εἰς (preposition with the accusative of extent) 140.
τοὺς (acc.pl.masc.of the article in agreement with μαθητὰς) 9.
μαθητὰς (acc.pl.masc.of μαθητής, extent) 421.
αὐτοῦ (gen.sing.masc.of αὐτός, possession) 16.
ἔλεγεν (3d.per.sing.imp.act.ind.of λέγω, inceptive) 66.
Μακάριοι (nom.pl.masc.of μακάριος, predicate adjective) 422.
οἱ (nom.pl.masc.of the article in agreement with πτωχοί) 9.
πτωχοί (nom.pl.masc.of πτωχός, subject of εἰσίν, understood) 423.
ὅτι (causal conjunction) 211.

#2127 ὑμετέρα (nom.sing.fem.of ὑμέτερος, in agreement with βασιλεία).

your - John 7:6; 8:17; Acts 27:34; Rom.11:31; I Cor.15:31; II Cor.8:8; Gal.6:13.
yours - Lk.6:20; John 15:20.
that which is your own - Lk.16:12.
on your part - I Cor.16:17.

Meaning: possessive pronoun of the second person plural. Your, yours. With the substantive which expresses what is owned - John 8:17; II Cor.8:8; Gal.6:13; I

Cor.16:17; used as a substantive - Lk.16:12. Alloted to you - Acts 27:34; Rom.11:31; John 7:6; in the predicate - Lk.6:20; proceding from you - John 15:20; used in the attributive position objectively - I Cor.15:31. Of the above, John 7:6 uses the pronoun in the emphatic attributive position; in Lk.6:20, as a predicate adjective; in Lk.16:12 as a substantive, and in all others in the attributive position. In John 15:20 the substantive is missing.

ἐστίν (3d.per.sing.pres.ind.of εἰμί, aoristic) 86.

ἡ (nom.sing.fem.of the article in agreement with βασιλεία) 9.

βασιλεία (nom.sing.fem.of βασιλεία, subject of ἐστίν) 253.

τοῦ (gen.sing.masc.of the article in agreement with θεοῦ) 9.

θεοῦ (gen.sing.masc.of θεός, possession) 124.

Translation - *"And when He had lifted His eyes to His disciples He began to speak: 'Happy are you poor people, because to you belongs the kingdom of God.'"*

Comment: The aorist participle ἐπάρας indicates action prior to that of the inceptive imperfect ἔλεγεν. Jesus stood in the small flat area at the foot of the mountain, with His Apostles by His side, and His other disciples and others crowding about Him. He surveyed the scene before He began to speak (inceptive imperfect in ἔλεγεν). It is probable that the majority of the audience stood on the slopes of the mountain a little below the spot where our Lord stood. *Cf.* comment on Mt.5:1-3, in a part of which I am in error in the statement that "If we are correct that this trip into Galilee is the second such trip, then He may not have called all of the twelve at this point." (*Renaissance New Testament*, I, 329). The Luke account makes it clear that the Sermon on the Mount came after our Lord's commissioning of the twelve Apostles.

The truths of the Word of God reveal themselves only to those who are willing to study long and diligently. The writer was of somewhat more dispensational turn several years ago when he carried this study through the opening chapters of Matthew and discussed Matthew 5-8. I choose now, not to change what I wrote then, but rather to add other comment which will reveal the evolution of my thinking as a result of more study. Some of these statements written years ago are in error, but they shall remain ὅ γέγραφα γέγραφα! I failed then to see what is now clear that the Sermon on the Mount came in the middle of our Lord's second year of ministry. He had said many things both publicly and privately prior to this sermon that were non-dispensational in character. It is a mistake to attempt to interpret Mt.5-7 and Lk.6:20-49 only in a dispensational sense. His audience knew full well that salvation was on an individual basis for those who repented and were born again, not on a basis of national origin. Luke says that He said that "the poor" had the Kingdom of God. Matthew uses the phrase ἡ βασιλεία τῶν οὐρανῶν. Thus the imagined iron-clad distinction between the two phrases is destroyed. *Cf.* comment on #'s 253, 254, *(Renaissance New Testament*, I, 189-193).

Verse 21 - "Blessed are ye that hunger now: for ye shall be filled; Blessed are ye that weep now: for ye shall laugh."

μακάριοι οἱ πεινῶντες νῦν, ὅτι χορτασθήσεσθε; μακάριοι οἱ κλαίοντες νῦν, ὅτι γελάσετε.

μακάριοι (nom.pl.masc.of μακάριος, predicate adjective) 422.

οἱ (nom.pl.masc.of the article in agreement with πεινῶντες) 9.

πεινῶντες (pres.act.part.nom.pl.masc.of πεινάω, substantival, subject of εἰσιν, understood) 335.

νῦν (adverbial) 1497.

ὅτι (causal conjunction) 211.

χορτασθήσεσθε (2d.per.pl.fut.pass.ind.of χορτάζω, predictive) 428.

μακάριοι (nom.pl.masc.of μακάριος, predicate adjective) 422.

οἱ (nom.pl.masc.of the article in agreement with κλαίοντες) 9.

κλαίοντες (pres.act.part.nom.pl.masc.of κλαίω, substantival, subject of εἰσιν, understood) 225.

νῦν (adverbial) 1497.

ὅτι (causal conjunction) 211.

#2128 γελάσετε (2d.per.pl.fut.act.ind.of γελάω, predictive).

laugh - Lk.6:21,25.

Meaning: To laugh. From Homer, down - Lk.6:21,25.

Translation - "Those who hunger now are happy, because they are going to be filled; those who weep now are happy, because they are going to laugh."

Comment: Ellipsis here as in Mt.5:6. The verb is understood. Note how Luke strengthens the present tense condition in πεινῶντες and κλαίοντες with the addition of νῦν, which otherwise is unnecessary, due to the present tense of the participles. But it spotlights the distinction which Jesus wishes us to see between the temporal now and the eternal future. Now, men hunger and weep. In God's **eternal future they shall eat and laugh. He seems to be warning His disciples** who might wish to join Him that the way of the cross is now hazardous and glorious *only* in the long run.
    *Cf.*II Cor.4:17,18.

Verse 22 - "Blessed are ye, when men shall hate you, and when they shall separate you from their company, and shall reproach you, and cast out your name as evil, for the Son of Man's sake."

μακάριοί ἐστε ὅταν μισήσωσιν ὑμᾶς οἱ ἄνθρωποι, καὶ ὅταν ἀφορίσωσιν ὑμᾶς καὶ ὀνειδίσωσιν καὶ ἐκβάλωσιν τὸ ὄνομα ὑμῶν ὡς πονηρὸν ἕνεκα τοῦ υἱοῦ τοῦ ἀνθρώπου.

μακάριοι (nom.pl.masc.of μακάριος, predicate adjective) 422.
ἐστε (2d.per.pl.pres.ind.of εἰμί, aoristic) 86.
ὅταν (temporal conjunction introducing an indefinite temporal clause) 436
μισήσωσιν (3d.per.pl.aor.act.subj.of μισέω, indefinite temporal clause) 542.
ὑμᾶς (acc.pl.masc.of σύ, direct object of μισήσωσιν) 104.
οἱ (nom.pl.masc.of the article in agreement with ἄνθρωποι) 9.
ἄνθρωποι (nom.pl.masc.of ἄνθρωπος, subject of μισήσωσιν, ἀφορίσωσιν,
ὀνειδίσωσιν and ἐκβάλωσιν) 341.
καὶ (adjunctive conjunction joining temporal clauses) 14.
ὅταν (temporal conjunction introducing an indefinite temporal clause) 436.
ἀφορίσωσιν (3d.per.pl.aor.act.subj.of ἀφορίζω, indefinite temporal clause)
1093.
ὑμᾶς (acc.pl.masc.of σύ, direct object of ἀφορίσωσιν) 104.
καὶ (adjunctive conjunction joining verbs) 14.
ἐκβάλωσιν (3d.per.pl.aor.act.subj.of ἐκβάλλω, indefinite temporal clause)
649.
τὸ (acc.sing.neut.of the article in agreement with ὄνομα) 9.
ὄνομα (acc.sing.neut.of ὄνομα, direct object of ἐκβάλωσιν) 108.
ὑμῶν (gen.pl.masc.of σύ, possession) 104.
ὡς (relative adverb in a comparative phrase) 128.
πονηρὸν (acc.sing.neut.of πονηρός, predicate accusative) 438.
ἕνεκα (improper preposition with the genitive of cause) 435.
τοῦ (gen.sing.masc.of the article in agreement with υἱοῦ) 9.
υἱοῦ (gen.sing.masc.of υἱός, cause) 5.
τοῦ (gen.sing.masc.of the article in agreement with ἀνθρώπου) 9.
ἀνθρώπου (gen.sing.masc.of ἄνθρωπος, definition) 341.

*Translation - "Happy are you when men hate you, and when they isolate you and
insult you and cast out your name like an evil thing, because of the Son of Man."*

Comment: ὅταν (#436) is an indefinite temporal conjunction joined with the
subjunctive mode. Jesus is saying that in the future (though He does not name a
definite time, by using ὅτε and the indicative, nor too indefinite by using ὅταν
and the optative) men would hate His disciples (John 15:18-20) and withdraw,
insult and read them out of social circles. "Quarantine" is a good word to
translate ἀφορίσωσιν (#1093). Hatred, discrimination, isolation and social
ostracism are to be the lot of the Christian, not because he deserves such
treatment, but because he has dared to name the name of One whom the world
hates "without a cause" (John 15:25). Unregenerates who arrogate to themselves
a degree of sophistication which they do not possess, love to prate about their
objectivity and look upon Christians as those who act from prejudicial
motives!

Note that in Lk.6:22 the decision to separate is made by the unsaved; in II Cor.6:17 it is made by the Christians. But Paul is speaking of the bonds of local church fellowship, not of social association. This discrimination by the world against the saints is made because of (#435) the Son of Man. Run the references for ἔνεκα and note the various cause and result situations which the word introduces. Who or what has been hated? (#542). Who or what has been alienated from the company of another? (#1093). Who has been reviled? (#437). Character is as easily evaluated for the opposition it arouses as for the praise which it elicits. *Cf.* comment on Mt.5:10,11.

Verse 23 - "Rejoice ye in that day, and leap for joy: for, behold, your reward is great in heaven: for in the like manner did their fathers unto the prophets."

χάρητε ἐν ἐκείνῃ τῇ ἡμέρᾳ καὶ σκιρτήσατε, ἰδοὺ γὰρ ὁ μισθὸς ὑμῶν πολὺς ἐν τῷ οὐρανῷ, κατὰ τὰ αὐτὰ γὰρ ἐποίουν τοῖς προφήταις οἱ πατέρες αὐτῶν.

χάρητε (2d.per.pl.2d.aor.pass.impv.of χαίρω, command) 182.

ἐν (preposition with the locative of time point) 80.

ἐκείνῃ (loc.sing.fem.of ἐκεῖνος, in agreement with ἡμέρᾳ) 246.

τῇ (loc.sing.fem.of the article in agreement with ἡμέρᾳ) 9.

ἡμέρᾳ (loc.sing.fem.of ἡμέρα, time point) 135.

καὶ (adjunctive conjunction joining verbs) 14.

σκιρτήσατε (3d.per.pl.aor.act.impv.of σκιρτάω, command) 1820.

ἰδοὺ (exclamation) 95.

γὰρ (causal conjunction) 105.

ὁ (nom.sing.masc.of the article in agreement with μισθὸς) 9.

μισθὸς (nom.sing.masc.of μισθός, subject of ἐστί, understood) 441.

ὑμῶν (gen.pl.masc.of σύ, possession) 104.

πολὺς (nom.sing.masc.of πολύς, predicate adjective) 228.

ἐν (preposition with the locative of place where) 80.

τῷ (loc.sing.masc.of the article in agreement with οὐρανῷ) 9.

οὐρανῷ (loc.sing.masc.of οὐρανός, place where) 254.

κατὰ (preposition with the accusative, standard rule or measure) 98.

τὰ (acc.pl.neut.of the article in agreement with αὐτὰ) 9.

αὐτὰ (acc.pl.neut.of αὐτός, standard rule or measure) 16.

γὰρ (causal conjunction) 105.

ἐποίουν (3d.per.pl.imp.act.ind.of ποιέω, progressive duration) 127.

τοῖς (dat.pl.masc.of the article in agreement with προφήταις) 9.

προφήταις (dat.pl.masc.of προφήτης, personal disadvantage) 119.

οἱ (nom.pl.masc.of the article in agreement with πατέρες) 9.

πατέρες (nom.pl.masc.of πατήρ, subject of ἐποίουν) 238.

αὐτῶν (gen.pl.masc.of αὐτός, relationship) 16.

Translation - "Rejoice in that day and leap for joy, because, Look! Your reward in the heaven is great, because your ancestors were always doing these things to the prophets."

Comment: Jesus issues two imperatives: "Rejoice" and "Leap for joy." The first is an inner reaction; the second is the physical manifestation of the intensity of the first. "That day" - the time when the Christian is to rejoice is the time of coming persecution. Why rejoice when we are persecuted? "Behold, your reward!" Great reward in heaven as a result and in recompense for persecution on earth. The persecuted Christian is placed in the same category with the prophets who received similar treatment from the ancestors of the persecutors. τὰ αὐτὰ refers to the verbs in vs.22. Note the progressive duration action in the imperfect ἐποίουν. The Jews have always persecuted their men of God. Human behavior has always been the same. Righteous living has never been popular. Saints have never been able to adjust in a world that is filled with prejudice against God. Theophobia is a dreadful malady and all of the unregenerate are afflicted.

Jesus later accused the Scribes and Pharisees of admitting that they were the descendants of those who killed the prophets (Mt.23:29-32) and challenged them to complete the work of their fathers by murdering Him of Whom the prophets spoke.

For further comment *cf.* Mt.5:12.

Verse 24 - "But woe unto you that are rich! for ye have received your consolation."

Πλὴν οὐαὶ ὑμῖν τοῖς πλουσίοις, ὅτι ἀπέχετε τὴν παράκλησιν ὑμῶν.

Πλὴν (adversative conjunction) 944.
οὐαὶ (exclamation) 936.
ὑμῖν (dat.pl.masc.of σύ, personal disadvantage) 104.
τοῖς (dat.pl.masc.of the article in agreement with πλουσίοις) 9.
πλουσίοις (dat.pl.masc.of πλούσιος, apposition) 1306.
ὅτι (causal conjunction) 211.
ἀπέχετε (2d.per.pl.pres.act.ind.of ἀπέχω, progressive) 563.
τὴν (acc.sing.fem.of the article in agreement with παράκλησιν) 9.
παράκλησιν (acc.sing.fem.of παράκλησις, direct object of ἀπέχετε) 1896.
ὑμῶν (gen.pl.masc.of σύ, possession) 104.

Translation - "But woe unto you rich people, because you are now receiving your comfort."

Comment: *Cf.*#944 for the basic meaning - "Furthermore... κ.τ.λ." Verse 24 is the reverse side of the coin as seen in verse 23. The short-run advantage which the rich man has is really his misfortune. He receives all of his comfort in this life and nothing is left for him to anticipate in the future. *Cf.*#1306 for the various ways in which πλούσιος is used in the N.T. *Cf.* also #1896. *Cf.*Lk.16:25.

Verse 25 - *"Woe unto you that are full! for ye shall hunger. Woe unto you that laugh now! for ye shall mourn and weep."*

οὐαί, οἱ ἐμπεπλησμένοι νῦν, ὅτι πεινάσετε; οὐαί, οἱ γελῶντες νῦν, ὅτι πενθήσετε καὶ κλαύσετε.

οὐαί (exclamation) 936.
ὑμῖν (dat.pl.masc.of σύ, personal disadvantage) 104.
οἱ (voc.pl.masc.of the article in agreement with ἐμπεπλησμένοι) 9.
ἐμπεπλησμένοι (perf.pass.part.voc.pl.masc.of ἐμπίπλημι, address) 1833.
νῦν (adverbial) 1497.
ὅτι (causal conjunction) 211.
πεινάσετε (2d.per.pl.fut.act.ind.of πεινάω, predictive) 335.
οὐαί (exclamation) 936.
οἱ (voc.pl.masc.of the article in agreement with γελῶντες) 9.
γελῶντες (pres.act.part.voc.pl.masc.of γελάω, address) 2128.
νῦν (adverbial) 1497.
ὅτι (causal conjunction) 211.
πενθήσετε (2d.per.pl.fut.act.ind.of πενθέω, predictive) 424.
καὶ (adjunctive conjunction joining verbs) 14.
κλαύσετε (2d.per.pl.fut.act.ind.of κλαίω, predictive) 225.

Translation - *"Alas, for you, you who have now become overfed, because you are going to get hungry; alas, you who are laughing now, because you are going to weep and mourn."*

Comment: The perfect passive participle ἐμπεπλησμένοι denotes a filling in the past that results in a present condition of being glutted, gorged and stuffed! It is not a pretty picture. Jesus' remark here recalls Thorstein Veblen's concept of "conspicuous consumption." But the tables will be turned. Those who are surfeited now, to the point where the marginal utility curve becomes zero, or even negative, while others are suffering from malnutrition, will face a time of hunger. Those who are now laughing shall in the future mourn and weep. Jesus again emphasizes the fallacy of short run analysis. Some have wagered their lives on the proposition that this life is the only life. The feasters and the affluent self-appointed comedians are unaware of future judgment. One cannot eat onions in a moral universe and keep it a secret, or as the Apostle Paul put it, "The wages of sin is death" (Rom.6:23). *Cf.*#'s 424, 225 for evidence of future mourning and weeping.

Verse 26 - *"Woe unto you, when all men shall speak well of you! for so did their fathers to the false prophets."*

οὐαὶ ὅταν ὑμᾶς καλῶς εἴπωσιν πάντες οἱ ἄνθρωποι, κατὰ τὰ αὐτὰ γὰρ ἐποίουν τοῖς φευδοπροφήταις οἱ πατέρες αὐτῶν.

οὐαὶ (exclamation) 936.

ὅταν (temporal conjunction in an indefinite temporal clause) 436.

καλῶς (adverbial) 977.

ὑμᾶς (acc.pl.masc.of σύ, direct object of εἴπωσιν) 104.

εἴπωσιν (3d.per.pl.aor.act.subj.of εἶπον, indefinite temporal clause) 155.

πάντες (nom.pl.masc.of πᾶς, in agreement with ἄνθρωποι) 67.

οἱ (nom.pl.masc.of the article in agreement with ἄνθρωποι) 9.

ἄνθρωποι (nom.pl.masc.of ἄνθρωπος, subject of εἴπωσιν) 341.

κατὰ (preposition with the accusative of standard rule or measure) 98.

τὰ (acc.pl.neut.of the article in agreement with αὐτά) 9.

αὐτὰ (acc.pl.neut.of αὐτός, standard rule or measure) 16.

γὰρ (causal conjunction) 105.

ἐποίουν (3d.per.pl.imp.act.ind.of ποιέω, progressive duration) 127.

τοῖς (dat.pl.masc.of the article in agreement with ψευδοπροφήταις) 9.

ψευδοπροφήταις (dative plural masc.of ψευδοπροφήτης, personal advantage) 670.

οἱ (nom.pl.masc.of the article in agreement with πατέρες) 9.

πατέρες (nom.pl.masc.of πατήρ, subject of ἐποίουν) 238.

αὐτῶν (gen.pl.masc.of αὐτός, possession) 16.

Translation - *"Alas, when all men commend you, because in this way the fathers were always speaking of their false prophets!"*

Comment: Note οὐαὶ here without ὑμῖν as we had it in verses 24,25. καλῶς and πάντες are emphasized. κατὰ τὰ αὐτὰ as in verse 23. Also Jesus repeats the imperfect tense in ἐποίουν as in verse 23. The fathers were always speaking well of their false prophets in former days. The universally popular individual is a false prophet. Intellectual prostitution is the only way to be popular in a world inhabited by fools and knaves. Riches, food, laughter and popularity *now* are reasons for coming judgment. This is the messages of verses 24-26. The unregenerate have a misplaced sense of values. Theirs is the short-run analysis. For Jesus, poverty (vs.20), hunger and weeping (vs.21), and unpopularity (vss.22,23) are to be endured now so that the kingdom of God, plenty, laughter and great reward may be ours in the future.

One cannot accept any of this teaching from the lips of our Lord upon an empirical basis. It was Marcus Aurelius who advised young men to spend all of their money while they were young, since they could not be certain that they would survive to old age. The here and now yields present fruit. "Let us eat and drink for tomorrow we die" (I Cor.15:32). So reasoned the "beasts at Ephesus" as they rejected Paul's message of faith in eternal values.

Love For Enemies

Verse 27 - "But I say unto you which hear, Love your enemies, do good to them which hate you."

'Αλλὰ ὑμῖν λέγω τοῖς ἀκούουσιν, ἀγαπᾶτε τοὺς ἐχθροὺς ὑμῶν, καλῶς ποιεῖτε τοῖς μισοῦσιν ὑμᾶς,

'Αλλὰ (adversative conjunction) 342.
ὑμῖν (dat.pl.masc.of σύ, indirect object of λέγω) 104.
λέγω (1st.per.sing.pres.act.ind.of λέγω, aoristic) 66.
τοῖς (dat.pl.masc.of the article in agreement with ἀκούουσιν) 9.
ἀκούουσιν (pres.act.part.dat.pl.masc.of ἀκούω, apposition) 148.
ἀγαπᾶτε (2d.per.pl.pres.act.impv.of ἀγαπάω, command) 540.
τοὺς (acc.pl.masc.of the article in agreement with ἐχθροὺς) 9.
ἐχθροὺς (acc.pl.masc.of ἐχθρός, direct object of ἀγαπᾶτε) 543.
ὑμῶν (gen.pl.masc.of σύ, possession) 104.
καλῶς (adverbial) 977.
ποιεῖτε (2d.per.pl.pres.act.impv.of ποιέω, command) 127.
τοῖς (dat.pl.masc.of the article in agreement with μισοῦσιν) 9.
μισοῦσιν (pres.act.part.dat.pl.masc.of μισέω, personal advantage) 542.
ὑμᾶς (acc.pl.masc.of σύ, direct object of μισοῦσιν) 104.

Translation - "But unto you who hear I say, 'Always love your enemies; always treat those who hate you well.' "

Comment: Luke has omitted a part of the discourse which Matthew supplies in Mt.5:38. Not the Mosaic law of retribution (Mt.5:38) but (adversative ἀλλὰ) love and kindness to those who hate. Note that the imperatives ἀγαπᾶτε and ποιεῖτε are in the present tense. We are to go on loving our enemies and doing good to those who hate us. *Cf.* Mt.5:44.

Verse 28 - "Bless them that curse you, and pray for them which despitefully use you."

εὐλογεῖτε τοὺς καταρωμένους ὑμᾶς, προσεύχεσθε περὶ τῶν ἐπηρεαζόντων ὑμᾶς.

εὐλογεῖτε (2d.per.pl.pres.act.impv.of εὐλογέω, command) 1120.
τοὺς (acc.pl.masc.of the article in agreement with καταρωμένους) 9.
καταρωμένους (pres.act.part.acc.pl.masc.of καταράομαι, direct object of εὐλογεῖτε) 1550.
ὑμᾶς (acc.pl.masc.of σύ, direct object of καταρωμένους) 104.
προσεύχεσθε (2d.per.pl.pres.act.impv.of προσεύχομαι, command) 544.
περὶ (preposition with the genitive of reference) 173.
τῶν (gen.pl.masc.of the article in agreement with ἐπηρεαζόντων) 9.

#2129 ἐπηρεαζόντων (pres.act.part.gen.pl.masc.of ἐπηρεάζω, reference).

accuse falsely - I Pet.3:16.
use despitefully - Lk.6:28.

Meaning: from ἐπήρεια - "spiteful abuse." Hence, to insult, to treat abusively. In a forensic sense, to accuse maliciously and falsely - I Pet.3:16; to upbraid - Lk.6:28.

ὑμᾶς (acc.pl.masc.of σύ, direct object of ἐπηρεαζόντων) 104.

Translation - "Bless those who are cursing you; pray for those who are insulting you."

Comment: *Cf.*#1120 for all uses of εὐλογέω. Also *cf.*#1550. Be always blessing those who are always cursing you. Prayer for those who upbraid the Christian is also enjoined. Luke records elsewhere two literal fulfillments of this admonition - one by our Lord Himself (Lk.23:34) and one by Stephen (Acts 7:60). A world that lived by the Sermon on the Mount in all its parts would be a warless world.

Verse 29 - "And unto him that smiteth thee on the one cheek offer also the other; and him that taketh away thy cloak forbid not to take thy coat also."

τῷ τύπτοντί σε ἐπὶ τὴν σιαγόνα πάρεχε καὶ τὴν ἄλλην, καὶ ἀπὸ τοῦ αἴροντός σου τὸ ἱμάτιον καὶ τὸν χιτῶνα μὴ κωλύσῃς.

τῷ (dat.sing.masc.of the article in agreement with τύπτοντί) 9.
τύπτοντί (pres.act.part.dat.sing.masc.of τύπτω, personal advantage) 1526.
σε (acc.sing.masc.of σύ, direct object of τύπτοντί) 104.
ἐπὶ (preposition with the accusative of extent) 47.
τὴν (acc.sing.fem.of the article in agreement with σιαγόνα) 9.
σιαγόνα (acc.sing.fem.of σιαγών, extent) 529.
πάρεχε (2d.per.sing.pres.act.impv.of παρέχω, command) 1566.
καὶ (adjunctive conjunction, joining substantives) 14.
τὴν (acc.sing.fem.of the article in agreement with ἄλλην) 9.
ἄλλην (acc.sing.fem.of ἄλλος, direct object of πάρεχε) 198.
καὶ (continuative conjunction) 14.
ἀπὸ (preposition with the ablative of separation) 70.
τοῦ (abl.sing.masc.of the article in agreement with αἴροντός) 9.
αἴροντός (pres.act.part.abl.sing.masc.of αἴρω, separation) 350.
σου (gen.sing.masc.of σύ, possession) 104.
τὸ (acc.sing.neut.of the article in agreement with ἱμάτιον) 9.
ἱμάτιον (acc.sing.neut.of ἱμάτιον, direct object of αἴροντός) 534.
καὶ (adjunctive conjunction joining nouns) 14.
τὸν (acc.sing.masc.of the article in agreement with χιτῶνα) 9.
χιτῶνα (acc.sing.masc.of χιτών, direct object of κωλύσῃς) 532.
μὴ (negative conjunction in a prohibition) 87.
κωλύσῃς (2d.per.sing.aor.act.subj.of κωλύω, command) 1296.

Translation - "To the one who is smiting you upon the cheek, turn also the other, and from the one who is taking away your coat do not withhold your shirt either."

Comment: *Cf.* Mt.5:39,40.

Verse 30 - "Give to every man that asketh of theé; and of him that taketh away thy goods ask them not again."

παντὶ αἰτοῦντί σε δίδου, καὶ ἀπὸ τοῦ αἴροντος τὰ σὰ μὴ ἀπαίτει.

παντὶ (dat.sing.masc.of πᾶς, in agreement with αἰτοῦντί) 67.

αἰτοῦντί (pres.act.part.dat.sing.masc.of αἰτέω,substantival, indirect object of δίδου) 537.

σε (acc.sing.masc.of σύ, direct object of αἰτοῦντί) 104.

δίδου (2d.per.sing.pres.act.impv.of δίδωμι, command) 362.

καὶ (continuative conjunction) 14.

ἀπὸ (preposition with the ablative of source) 70.

τοῦ (abl.sing.masc.of the article in agreement with αἴροντος) 9.

αἴροντος (pres.act.part.abl.sing.masc.of αἴρω, substantival, source) 350.

τὰ (acc.pl.neut.of the article direct object of ἀπαίτει) 9.

σὰ (acc.pl.neut.of σός, in agreement with τὰ) 646.

μὴ (negative conjunction, with the imperative) 87.

#2130 ἀπαίτει (2d.per.sing.pres.act.impv.of ἀπαιτέω, command).

ask again - Lk.6:30.
be required - Lk.12:20.

Meaning: A combination of ἀπό (#70) and αἰτέω (#537). Hence, to ask it back; to ask that something be returned. In the Sermon on the Mount - Lk.6:30; to summon the soul in death - Lk.12:20.

Translation - "To all who are asking you be always giving, and from the one who is taking from you, do not ask for the return of your property."

Comment: *Cf.* Mt.5:42. Note that Matthew uses the aorist imperative δός whereas Luke uses the present δίδου. "Give once and for all" in Matthew, and "go on giving" in Luke. Likewise Matthew has the aorist in ἀποστραφῇς, while Luke says ἀπαίτει. In Luke we translate, "Do not continue to ask it back" or "Stop asking it back." Here is an eloquent statement that is in diametric opposition to the worldly spirit of acquisitiveness. "It is more blessed to give than to receive." Christianity gives. The world gets. How opposite the two policies.

Verse 31 - "And as ye would that men should do, to you, do ye also to them likewise."

καὶ καθὼς θέλετε ἵνα ποιῶσιν ὑμῖν οἱ ἄνθρωποι, ποιεῖτε αὐτοῖς ὁμοίως.

καὶ (continuative conjunction) 14.

καθώς (adverbial) 1348.
θέλετε (2d.per.pl.pres.act.ind.of θέλω, progressive) 88.
ἵνα (final conjunction introducing a purpose clause) 114.
ποιῶσιν (3d.per.pl.pres.act.subj.of ποιέω, purpose clause) 127.
ὑμῖν (dat.pl.masc.of σύ, personal advantage) 104.
οἱ (nom.pl.masc.of the article in agreement with ἄνθρωποι) 9.
ἄνθρωποι (nom.pl.masc.of ἄνθρωπος, subject of ποιῶσιν) 341.
ποιεῖτε (2d.per.pl.pres.act.impv.of ποιέω, command) 127.
αὐτοῖς (dat.pl.masc.of αὐτός, personal advantage) 16.
ὁμοίως (adverbial) 1425.

Translation - "*And just as you always wish that men will do for you, in the same way always do for them.*"

Comment: Verse 31 is a summation of verses 27-30. *Cf*.#1348 for other uses of καθώς. - "In the same way. . . κ.τ.λ." καθώς and ὁμοίως go together - "Just as . . in the same way. . . κ.τ.λ.". *Cf*. Mt.7:12 for further comment.

Verse 32 - "*For if ye love them which love you, what thank have ye? For sinners also love those that love them.*"

καὶ εἰ ἀγαπᾶτε τοὺς ἀγαπῶντας ὑμᾶς, ποία ὑμῖν χάρις ἐστίν; καὶ γὰρ οἱ ἁμαρτωλοὶ τοὺς ἀγαπῶντας αὐτοὺς ἀγαπῶσιν.

καὶ (continuative conjunction) 14.
εἰ (conditional conjunction introducing a first-class condition) 337.
ἀγαπᾶτε (2d.per.pl.pres.act.ind.of ἀγαπάω, first-class condition) 540.
τοὺς (acc.pl.masc.of the article in agreement with ἀγαπῶντας) 9.
ἀγαπῶντας (pres.act.part.acc.pl.masc.of ἀγαπάω, substantival, direct object of ἀγαπᾶτε) 540.
ὑμᾶς (acc.pl.masc.of σύ, direct object of ἀγαπῶντας) 104.
ποία (nom.sing.fem.of ποῖος, interrogative pronoun, in agreement with χάρις) 1298.
ὑμῖν (dat.pl.masc.of σύ, personal advantage) 104.
χάρις (nom.sing.fem.of χάρις, subject of ἐστίν) 1700.
ἐστίν (3d.per.sing.pres.ind.of εἰμί, aoristic) 86.
καὶ (ascensive conjunction) 14.
γὰρ (causal conjunction) 105.
οἱ (nom.pl.masc.of the article in agreement with ἁμαρτωλοί) 9.
ἁμαρτωλοὶ (nom.pl.masc.of ἁμαρτωλός, subject of ἀγαπῶσιν) 791.
τοὺς (acc.pl.masc.of the article in agreement with ἀγαπῶντας) 9.
ἀγαπῶντας (pres.act.part.acc.pl.masc.of ἀγαπάω, substantival, direct object of ἀγαπῶσιν) 540.
αὐτοὺς (acc.pl.masc.of αὐτός, direct object of ἀγαπῶντας) 16.
ἀγαπῶσιν (3d.per.pl.pres.act.ind.of ἀγαπάω, customary) 540.

Translation - "Furthermore since you are always loving those who are always loving you, what favorable consideration is due you? Because even sinners are loving those who are loving them."

Comment:Καὶ here serves to further the argument of verse 31. It is a first-class condition, with εἰ and the present indicative in the protasis and the present tense in the apodosis. *Cf.* Mt.5:46 where we have ἐὰν with the subjunctive. These two verses (Mt.5:46 and Lk.6:32) illustrate how μισθός and χάρις are used together. Hence our translation for χάρις - "favorable consideration." Jesus was talking about merit which deserves reward. Also τελῶναι and ἁμαρτωλοί are associated. The Christian ethic is on a higher plane than that of publicans and sinners. Why, therefore, should the child of God expect reward for something that is characteristic of the behavior of unregenerates? It is natural (σαρκικός) for us to love the people who love us. Otherwise sinners could not do it. It requires supernatural motivation, born only of a genuine Christian experience, to love someone who hates you. Verses 33 and 34 express the same philosophy in a slightly different setting.

Verse 33 - "And if ye do good to them which do good to you, what thank have ye? for sinners also do even the same."

καὶ (γὰρ) ἐὰν ἀγαθοποιῆτε τοὺς ἀγαθοποιοῦντας ὑμᾶς, ποία ὑμῖν χάρις ἐστίν; καὶ οἱ ἁμαρτωλοὶ τὸ αὐτὸ ποιοῦσιν.

καὶ (continuative conjunction) 14.

(γὰρ) (emphatic conjunction) 14.

ἐὰν (conditional particle introducing a third-class condition) 363.

ἀγαθοποιῆτε (2d.per.pl.pres.act.subj.of ἀγαθοποιέω, third-class condition) 2105.

τοὺς (acc.pl.masc.of the article in agreement with ἀγαθοποιοῦντας) 9.

ἀγαθοποιοῦντας (pres.act.part.acc.pl.masc.of ἀγαθοποιέω, substantival, direct object of ἀγαθοποιῆτε) 2105.

ὑμᾶς (acc.pl.masc.of σύ, direct object of ἀγαθοποιοῦντας) 104.

ποία (interrogative pronoun, in agreement with χάρις) 1298.

ὑμῖν (dat.pl.masc.of σύ, personal advantage) 104.

χάρις (nom.sing.fem.of χάρις, subject of ἐστίν) 1700.

ἐστίν (3d.per.sing.pres.ind.of εἰμί, customary) 86.

καὶ (adjunctive conjunction, joining verbs) 14.

οἱ (nom.pl.masc.of the article in agreement with ἁμαρτωλοί) 9.

ἁμαρτωλοὶ (nom.pl.masc.of ἁμαρτωλός, subject of ποιοῦσιν) 791.

τὸ (acc.sing.neut.of the article in agreement with αὐτὸ) 9.

αὐτὸ (acc.sing.neut.of αὐτός, direct object of ποιοῦσιν) 16.

ποιοῦσιν (3d.per.pl.pres.act.ind.of ποιέω, customary) 127.

Translation - "Again if, in fact, you are always doing good things for those who always treat you well, what reward is there for you? because the sinners always do the same."

Comment: If γὰρ, enclosed in brackets in the text, is indeed a part of the original, it can be taken as emphatic. Hence, our translation. Note that, unlike the first-class condition of verse 32, Luke here uses a third-class condition, with ἐάν and the subjunctive in the protasis and the present indicative in the result clause. *Cf.*#2105 for other uses of ἀγαθοποιέω.

This passage is devastating to the politician who always has an angle. Sinners, who are by nature self seeking, attend to this carefully. How often we hear it. "Be careful! That man can hurt you." Or, "He is in a position to reward you." Or, "What is in it for me?" True goodness manifests itself when we help other people altruistically. *Cf.* Lk.14:12-14. Luke does not parallel Mt.5:47 but the same idea is expressed.

Verse 34 - "And if ye lend to them of whom ye hope to receive, what thank have ye? for sinners also lend to sinners, to receive as much again."

καὶ ἐὰν δανίσητε παρ' ὧν ἐλπίζετε λαβεῖν, ποία χάρις (ἐστίν) καὶ ἀμαρτωλοὶ ἀμαρτωλοῖς δανείζουσιν ἵνα ἀπολάβωσιν τὰ ἴσα.

καὶ (continuative conjunction) 14.
ἐὰν (conditional particle introducing a third-class condition) 363.
δανίσητε (2d.per.pl.aor.act.subj.of δανείζω, third-class condition) 538.
παρ' (preposition with the ablative of source, with persons) 154.
ὧν (abl.pl.masc.of ὅς, source) 65.
ἐλπίζετε (2d.per.pl.pres.act.ind.of ἐλπίζω, progressive) 991.
λαβεῖν (2d.aor.act.inf.of λαμβάνω, complementary) 533.
ποία (nom.sing.fem.of ποῖος, in agreement with χάρις) 1298.
ὑμῖν (dat.pl.masc.of σύ, personal advantage) 104.
χάρις (nom.sing.fem.of χάρις, subject of ἐστίν) 1700.
(ἐστίν) (3d.per.sing.pres.ind.of εἰμί, customary) 86.
καὶ (ascensive conjunction) 14.
ἀμαρτωλοὶ (nom.pl.masc.of ἀμαρτωλός, subject of δανίζουσιν) 791.
ἀμαρτωλοῖς (dat.pl.masc.of ἀμαρτωλός, personal advantage) 791.
δανίζουσιν (3d.per.pl.pres.act.ind.of δανείζω, customary) 538.
ἵνα (final conjunction introducing a purpose clause) 114.

#2131 ἀπολάβωσιν (3d.per.pl.2d.aor.act.subj.of ἀπολαμβάνω, purpose).

receive - Lk.6:34; 15:27; 16:25; 18:30; 23:41; Rom.1:27; Gal.4:5; Col.3:24; II John 8; III John 8.
take - Mk.7:33.

Meaning: A combination of ἀπό (#70) and λαμβάνω (#533). Hence, to receive back or from; to receive again someone or something which was previously given. With reference to material wealth in return for investment - Lk.6:34; 16:25. With reference to the prodigal's father who received his wayward son back again - Lk.15:27. Of judicial recompense for crime - Lk.23:41; of psychological recompense for sin - Rom.1:27. With reference to the spiritual blessings in return for service - Lk.18:30; Col.3:24; II John 8. With reference to the restoration to sonship of the believer in return for Christ's incarnation - Gal.4:5; of the local church receiving back into membership those missionaries who have been witnessing in other places - III John 8; to take one aside for healing - Mk.7:33.

τὰ (acc.pl.neut.of the article, direct object of ἀπολάβωσιν) 9.
ἴσα (acc.pl.neut.of ἴσος, in agreement with τὰ) 1323.

Translation - "And if you lend (to them) from whom you are hoping to receive, what favorable consideration is due you? Even sinners lend to sinners in order that they may get back an equal amount."

Comment: Jesus adds another illustration in order to make His point. Note that His illustration is couched in a third-class condition. "If you lend . . . " He was not sure that we would, even to one whose credit was considered good. The translation "If you *ever* lend . . . " reflects too much doubt about it, as though we had an optative mode and a fourth-class condition.

Sinners make investments only to a class of borrowers whose credit rating is good - "from whom they expect to recover." This is good business, says Jesus, but it is not an evidence of outstanding Christian service. Hence no reward from heaven should be expected. ποία ὑμῖν χάρις ἐστίν. "What credit should you get for that?" Sinners do as much.

A few years ago administrators of a prominent religious group promoted a scheme whereby Christians were asked to contribute to a fund from which churches might borrow for new church building construction. The rate of interest was advertized at five percent. This was at a time when the national economy was depressed to a point that made a five percent return on an ordinary investment difficult if not impossible. Many sinners in the country would have been glad to have placed money at five percent, but this segment of the money market was monopolized by Christians in the name of our Lord. Meanwhile those who placed their excess liquid capital into the venture were congratulated about what good Christians they were! ποία ὑμῖν χάρις ἐστίν, asks our Lord? Cecil Rhodes believed in "philanthropy plus five percent" but there is no evidence that he tried to involve the Lord in his exploitation.

Verse 35 - "But love ye your enemies, and do good, and lend, hoping for nothing again; and your reward shall be great, and ye shall be the children of the highest; for He is kind unto the unthankful and to the evil."

πλὴν ἀγαπᾶτε τοὺς ἐχθροὺς ὑμῶν καὶ ἀγαθοποιεῖτε καὶ δανείζετε μηδὲν ἀπελπίζοντες, καὶ ἔσται ὁ μισθὸς ὑμῶν πολύς, καὶ ἔσεσθε υἱοὶ ὑψίστου, ὅτι αὐτὸς χρηστός ἐστιν ἐπὶ τοὺς ἀχαρίστους καὶ πονηρούς.

πλὴν (adversative conjunction) 944.
ἀγαπᾶτε (2d.per.pl.pres.act.impv.of ἀγαπάω, command) 540.

τοὺς (acc.pl.masc.of the article in agreement with ἐχθρούς) 9.
ἐχθρούς (acc.pl.masc.of ἐχθρός, direct objct of ἀγαπᾶτε) 543.
ὑμῶν (gen.pl.masc.of σύ, possession) 104.
καὶ (adjunctive conjunction joining verbs) 14.
ἀγαθοποιεῖτε (2d.per.pl.pres.act.impv.of ἀγαθοποιέω, command) 2105.
καὶ (adjunctive conjunction joining verbs) 14.
δανίζετε (2d.per.pl.pres.act.impv.of δανείζω, command) 538.
μηδὲν (acc.sing.neut.of μηδείς, direct object of ἀπελπίζοντες).

#2132 ἀπελπίζοντες (pres.act.part.nom.pl.masc.of ἀπελπίζω, adverbial concessive).

Meaning: A combination of ἀπό (#70) and ἐλπίζω (#991). Hence, to hope for something back again, or in return. With μηδὲν - "nothing aspiring." The idea in Lk.6:35 seems to be that the child of God should lend, even to his enemies, despite the fact that he has no hope that he will be repaid.

καὶ (continuative conjunction) 14.
ἔσται (3d.per.sing.fut.ind.of εἰμί, predictive) 86.
ὁ (nom.sing.masc.of the article in agreement with μισθὸς) 9.
μισθὸς (nom.sing.masc.of μισθός, subject of ἔσται) 441.
ὑμῶν (gen.pl.masc.of σύ, possession) 104.
πολύς (nom.sing.masc.of πολύς, predicate adjective) 228.
καὶ (continuative conjunction) 14.
ἔσεσθε (2d.per.pl.fut.ind.of εἰμί, predictive) 86.
υἱοὶ (nom.pl.masc.of υἱός, predicate nominative) 5.
ὑψίστου (gen.sing.masc.of ὕψιστος, definition) 1353.
ὅτι (causal conjunction) 211.
αὐτὸς (nom.sing.masc.of αὐτός, subject of ἐστιν) 16.
χρηστός (nom.sing.masc.of χρηστός, predicate adjective) 959.
ἐστιν (3d.per.sing.pres.ind.of εἰμί, customary) 86.
ἐπὶ (preposition with the accusative of extent, to express emotion) 47.
τοὺς (acc.pl.masc.of the article in agreement with ἀχαρίστους) 9.

#2133 ἀχαρίστους (acc.pl.masc.of ἀχάριστος, after ἐπὶ).

unthankful - Lk.6:35; II Tim.3:2.

Meaning: α privative plus χαρίζομαι (#2158). *Cf.* also #'s 1700, 1812 and 5295. Ungracious, unpleasant, unthankful.

καὶ (adjunctive conjunction joining adjectives) 14.
πονηρούς (acc.pl.masc.of πονηρός, after ἐπὶ) 438.

Translation - "On the contrary, always love your enemies and always do good and always lend to them despite the fact that you expect to receive nothing in return, and your reward will be great, and you will be sons of the Highest, because He is always kind to the ungracious and evil."

Comment: Verses 32-34 suggest the manner in which sinners interact. They love because they are loved; they do good to others who are good to them; they lend to one another but only because of the certainty of financial gain in return. If Christians behave like this they are neither better nor worse than sinners and should expect no special reward.

The Christian ethic is much sterner. Hence πλὴν may be taken as adversative. We are to love people who hate us, do good generally, and lend specifically, even when the prospect of a favorable return is in doubt. The participle ἀπελπίζοντες is an excellent example of the adverbial participle used concessively. We are to lend *despite the fact that we expect not one thing in return.* This will mean financial loss on earth, but that is only temporal. If we do this we will gain the reward, described here as great, and we shall qualify as Sons of the Highest One in that our behavior has been like unto His. He is available for service to all - even though they be unthankful and evil. Study carefully #959 for this characteristic of God and His children.

The child of God who takes this advice literally is going to be victimized like a naive sheep among sophisticated and rapacious wolves. But this is the clear teaching of our Lord. *Cf.* Mt.5:45 for further comment.

Verse 36 - "Be ye therefore merciful, as your Father also is merciful."

Γίνεσθε οἰκτίρμονες καθὼς (καὶ) ὁ πατὴρ ὑμῶν οἰκτίρμων ἐστίν.

Γίνεσθε (2d.per.pl.pres.impv.of γίνομαι command) 113.

#2134 οἰκτίρμονες (nom.pl.masc.of οἰκτίρμων, predicate adjective).

Meaning: Cf.οἰκτείρω (#3962) and οἰκτιρμός (#4009). "In classic Greek only a poetic term for the more common ἐλεήμων." (*Schmidt, III,* 580). *Cf.* also ἐλεέω (#430). An attribute twice ascribed to the Heavenly Father (Lk.6:36b; Jam.5:11). Jesus enjoined Christians to exercise the same trait (Lk.6:36a).

καθὼς (adverbial) 1348.
ὁ (nom.sing.masc.of the article in agreement with πατὴρ) 9.
πατὴρ (nom.sing.masc.of πατήρ, subject of ἐστίν) 238.
ὑμῶν (gen.pl.masc.of σύ, relationship) 104.
οἰκτίρμων (nom.sing.masc.of οἰκτίρμων, predicate adjective) 2134.
ἐστίν (3d.per.sing.pres.ind.of εἰμί, customary) 86.

Translation - "Be ye always merciful, just as also your Father is always merciful."

Comment: The kind of mercy enjoined here is described in the latter part of verse 35. God is merciful (#959), even to those who are unthankful and evil. This is the perfection described in Mt.5:48.

Judging Others

(Mt.7:1-5)

Verse 37 - "Judge not, and ye shall not be judged: condemn not, and ye shall not be condemned: forgive, and ye shall be forgiven."

Καὶ μὴ κρίνετε, καὶ οὐ μὴ κριθῆτε; καὶ μὴ καταδικάζετε, καὶ οὐ μὴ καταδικασθῆτε. ἀπολύετε, καὶ ἀπολυθήσεσθε;

Καὶ (continuative conjunction) 14.

μὴ (negative conjunction with the imperative) 87.

κρίνετε (2d.per.pl.pres.act.impv.of κρίνω, command) 531.

καὶ (inferential conjunction) 14.

οὐ (negative conjunction, with μὴ and the subjunctive) 130.

μὴ (negative conjunction with οὐ and the subjunctive) 87.

κριθῆτε (2d.per.pl.1st.aor.pass.subjunctive of κρίνω) 531.

καὶ (continuative conjunction) 14.

μὴ (negative conjunction with the imperative) 87.

καταδικάζετε (2d.per.pl.pres.act.impv.of καταδικάζω, command) 971.

καὶ (inferential conjunction) 14.

οὐ (negative conjunction, with μὴ and the subjunctive) 130.

μὴ (negative conjunction, with οὐ, and the subjunctive) 87.

καταδικασθῆτε (2d.per.pl.1st.aor.pass. subjunctive of καταδικάζω) 971.

ἀπολύετε (2d.per.pl.pres.act.impv.of ἀπολύω, command) 92.

καὶ (continuative conjunction) 14.

ἀπολυθήσεσθε (2d.per.pl.fut.pass.ind.of ἀπολύω, predictive) 92.

Translation - "And stop judging, and you will never be judged; also stop condemning, and you will never be condemned. Continue to forgive, and you will always be forgiven."

Comment: Note μὴ here with οὐ and the present imperative in an emphatic prohibition. We are to cease judging and condemning others. The Greek grammar makes it clear that we are now guilty of both of these preemptions of the judgment throne that belongs exclusively to Jesus Christ (John 5:22, comment upon which *Cf.*). The prediction is also emphasized with the double negative - οὐ μὴ. Then Jesus changes the pattern to a positive approach. "Always be forgiving and you will always be forgiven." Judgment and condemnation are the opposites of forgiveness. *Cf.#*'s 971 and 531 for other uses of κρίνω and καταδικάζω. *Cf.#*92. This is the only place where ἀπολύω is used in this sense. *Cf.* comments on Mt.7:1,2. Matthew uses the simple Greek ἵνα μὴ κριθῆτε where the subjunctive is justified by the ἵνα clause of purpose. Luke uses the aorist passive subjunctive, where Matthew would have used the future passive indicative. The Holy Spirit was not dictating to either man, but superintending their choice of words to assure that there would be no contradiction when studied in the light of historical research. This is the verbal inspiration that protects God's message.

Verse 38 - "Give, and it shall be given unto you; good measure, pressed down, and shaken together, and running over, shall men give into your bosom. For with the same measure that ye mete withal it shall be measured to you again."

δίδοτε, καὶ δοθήσεται ὑμῖν, μέτρον καλὸν πεπιεσμένον σεσαλευμένον ὑπερεκχυννόμενον δώσουσιν εἰς τὸν κόλπον ὑμῶν· ᾧ γὰρ μέτρῳ μετρεῖτε ἀντιμετρηθήσεται ὑμῖν.

δίδοτε (2d.per.pl.pres.act.impv.of δίδωμι, command) 362.
καὶ (continuative conjunction) 14.
δοθήσεται (3d.per.sing.fut.pass.ind.of δίδωμι, predictive) 362.
ὑμῖν (dat.pl.masc.of σύ, indirect object of δοθήσεται) 104.
μέτρον (acc.sing.neut.of μέτρος, predicate accusative) 643.
καλὸν (acc.sing.neut.of καλός, in agreement with μέτρον) 296.

#2135 πεπιεσμένον (perf.pass.part.acc.sing.neut.of πιέζω, adverbial, modal).

press down - Lk.6:38.

Meaning: To press together. To compress, thus to pack a greater amount of something into a small space. Only here in Lk.6:38.

σεσαλευμένον (perf.pass.part.acc.sing.neut.of σαλεύω, adverbial, modal) 911.

#2136 ὑπερεκχυννόμενον (perf.mid.part.acc.sing.neut.of ὑπερεκχύνω, adverbial, modal).

run over - Lk.6:38.

Meaning: A combination of ὑπερ (#545), ἐκ (#19) and χύνω, a later form for χέω - "to pour." Hence, to pour (χύνω) out (ἐκ) beyond measure (ὑπερ). To deluge. To innundate. To overwhelm. A very strong word, used here to describe the divine generosity for those who qualify - Lk.6:38.

δώσουσιν (3d.per.pl.fut.act.ind.of δίδωμι, predictive) 362.
εἰς (preposition with the accusative of extent) 140.
τὸν (acc.sing.masc.of the article in agreement with κόλπον) 9.
κόλπον (acc.sing.masc.of κόλπος, extent) 1702.
ὑμῶν (gen.pl.masc.of σύ, possession) 104.
ᾧ (instru.sing.neut.of ὅς, in agreement with μέτρῳ) 65.
γὰρ (causal conjunction) 105.
μέτρῳ (instru.sing.neut.of μέτρον, means) 643.
μετρεῖτε (2d.per.pl.pres.act.ind.of μετρέω, aoristic) 644.

#2137 ἀντιμετρηθήσεται (3d.per.sing.fut.pass.ind.of ἀντιμετρέω, predictive).

measure again - Lk.6:38.

Meaning: A combination of ἀντί (#237) and μετρέω (#644). Hence, to make a reciprocal measurement. To measure back again. To reciprocate.

ὑμῖν (dat.pl.masc.of σύ, indirect object of ἀντιμετρηθήσεται) 104.

Translation - "Keep on giving and it shall continue to be given unto you - ample measure, having been pressed down, shaken together, running over beyond measure - they shall continue to pour into your lap: for by whatever measure you measure, it shall be reciprocally measured unto you."

Comment Note the continuous action in the present and future tenses and the perfect modal participles, indicating present conditions as a result of past completed actions. Having been pressed down and shaken together, the measure is packed. It is no great wonder that it is καλόν! But such a measure, however packed, is no good unless it is poured out. The principle upon which this action operates is then stated in the last clause ᾧ... ὑμῖν. Each Christian selects the size of the measure that governs his giving, and thus automatically he sets the degree to which he will be rewarded. *Cf.* Mt.7:2 for further comment. *Cf.* also Mk.4:24b. This is one of the strongest stewardship texts in scripture. However this principle applies to all of the sacrificial giving which we do, and is not restricted to that which is given to our local church. Jesus taught sharing with all who have need, whether within the scope of the activity of the local church or outside of it.

It is sad that this principle of giving is applied too often only to financial matters! Many are generous with their money and stingy with their time and talents.

Verse 39 - "And he spoke a parable unto them, Can the blind lead the blind: shall they not both fall into the ditch?"

Εἶπεν δὲ καὶ παραβολὴν αὐτοῖς. Μήτι δύναται τυφλὸς τυφλὸν ὁδηγεῖν; οὐχὶ ἀμφότεροι εἰς βόθυνον ἐμπεσοῦνται;

Εἶπεν (3d.per.sing.aor.act.ind.of εἶπον, constative) 155.
δὲ (continuative conjunction) 11.
καὶ (adjunctive conjunction, joining clauses) 14.
παραβολὴν (acc.sing.fem.of παραβολή, direct object of εἶπεν) 1027.
αὐτοῖς (dat.pl.masc.of αὐτός, indirect object of εἶπεν) 16.
μήτι (negative conjunction in direct question expecting a negative reply) 676.
δύναται (3d.per.sing.pres.ind.of δύναμαι, customary) 289.
τυφλὸς (nom.sing.masc.of τυφλός, subject of δύναται) 830.
τυφλὸν (acc.sing.masc.of τυφλός, direct object of ὁδηγεῖν) 830.
ὁδηγεῖν (pres.act.inf.of ὁδηγέω, complementary) 1156.
οὐχὶ (negative conjunction in direct question expecting a positive reply) 130.
ἀμφότεροι (nom.pl.masc.of ἀμφότερος, subject of ἐμπεσοῦνται) 813.
εἰς (preposition with the accusative of extent) 140.
βόθυνον (acc.sing.masc.of βόθυνος, extent) 976.
ἐμπεσοῦνται (3d.per.pl.fut.act.ind.of ἐμπίπτω, direct question) 975.

Translation - *"And He also suggested an analogy to them, 'A blind man is not able to lead a blind man is he? Would not both fall into a pit?'"*

Comment: Here we have δὲ and καὶ together. δὲ is continuative and καὶ is adjunctive, as it joins the material of verse 38 with what follows. Jesus is teaching illustratively as well as by precept. Μήτι introduces a direct question, the anticipated answer to which is negative. It is to be expected that one would relply to the first question by saying, "Of course not." Conversely οὐχὶ introduces a question which must be answered positively. "Would not both the blind leader and the blind man led fall into a pit?" To which rational people would respond, "Of course."

Teachers, no less than guides through the Grand Canyon, should not be blind. In some modern education courses the professor boasts that he is as blind as his students. His message seems to be, "Get your eyes open to the fact that you are blind. Those who think that they can see are blind." There is an element of truth in this empirical approach. To the extent that we recognize that we do not know it *all*, our eyes are open in a way that contributes to our humility and keeps us thinking, researching and debating. The Gnostic who boasts that he is not blind at all is truly as blind as the Existentialist who boasts that he is blind to everything. The only epistemologist who has any sight at all is the one who recognizes some truth and thus recognizes the vast areas in which he is in fact blind. Thus his prayer, "O Lord, give me blindness enough to keep me humble and thinking and give me sight enough to recognize the truth when I see it." He may indeed fall into a pit, but not as often as the "guide" who is blind all of the time and proud of it!

A teacher who stands before a blind student in the classroom needs 20-20 vision, even if this means the use of authority. The teacher or preacher or politician who knows no more than the people he is trying to lead had better find other employment, in the unlikely event that it is available to him.

*Cf.*Mt.15:14b for comment.

Verse 40 - "The disciple is not above his master: but everyone that is perfect shall be as his master."

οὐκ ἔστιν μαθητὴς ὑπὲρ τὸν διδάσκαλον, κατηρτισμένος δὲ πᾶς ἔσται ὡς ὁ διδάσκαλος αὐτοῦ.

οὐκ (negative conjunction with the indicative) 130.
ἔστιν (3d.per.sing.pres.ind.of εἰμί, customary) 86.
μαθητὴς (nom.sing.masc.of μαθητής, subject of ἔστιν) 421.
ὑπὲρ (preposition with the accusative of comparison) 545.
τὸν (acc.sing.masc.of the article in agreement with διδάσκαλον) 9.
διδάσκαλον (acc.sing.masc.of διδάσκαλος, comparison) 742,
κατηρτισμένος (perf.pass.part.nom.sing.masc.of καταρτίζω, substantival, subject of ἔσται) 401.

δε (adversative conjunction) 11.
πᾶς (nom.sing.masc.of πᾶς, in agreement with κατηρτισμένος) 67.
ἔσται (3d.per.sing.fut.ind.of εἰμί, predictive) 86.
ὡς (comparative conjunction) 128.
ὁ (nom.sing.masc.of the article in agreement with διδάσκαλος) 9.
διδάσκαλος (nom.sing.masc.of διδάσκαλος, nominative absolute) 742.
αὐτοῦ (gen.sing.masc.of αὐτός, possession) 16.

Translation - "A pupil is not superior to the teacher, but everyone who is mature will be like his teacher."

Comment: οὐκ ἔστιν has priority of position, outranking the subject μαθητής. Jesus is emphasizing His point that, just as blind guides are not good guides, pupils are not better than teachers. *Cf.#545* for other examples of ὑπέρ with the accusative in comparisons. Verse 40 helps to explain verse 39. If the blind teacher tries to lead the blind pupil, then teacher and pupil are equal - equally blind and hence eqully inept. The learner is never superior in grasp of the subject to the teacher. Hence when the teacher falls into the pit the student falls in with him. A good many college bred middle aged Americans have been in the pit since college days. When the pupil becomes a student he begins to grow. There is a point in his intellectual growth at which he equals his teacher in sophistication. He is not then superior to his teacher - only equal to him; however, he may still procede to a higher level than that achieved by his former teacher, in which case he becomes teacher and his former teacher should seek to learn from him. Jesus does not carry the point this far, except by implication. It is not wise to push κατηρτισμένος to the point of omniscience. If we could in this context, the word would not be fitting for a human analogy. No human teacher, however mature, is that mature. A review of #401 will be rewarding.

Jesus is warning Israel not to listen to their self-appointed teachers - the blind Pharisees. If they listen to Him they will become like Him, as He is the perfect fulfillment of God's plan for Him. So those who follow Him will achieve their own potential development, however high that may be. The unsaved, or even the backslidden Christian, will never eliminate the waste of unused potential assets, until he accepts Jesus as Saviour and then follows Him as far as he is able in His teaching.

There is also a warning to the nation that as long as Israel follows her blind leaders she will become totally blind also and end up in the pit. *Cf.* Rom.11:25. A study of blindness (#830) and its relation to obedience to Christ and His philosophy and ethics will be rewarding. How can blindness be cured? Who is blind? Who can see? What causes blindness? What are the ultimate destinies of blind people?

Verse 41 - "And why beholdest thou the mote that is in thy brother's eye, but perceivest not the beam that is in thine own eye?"

Τί δὲ βλέπεις τὸ κάρφος τὸ ἐν τῷ ὀφθαλμῷ τοῦ ἀδελφοῦ σου, τὴν δὲ δοκὸν
τὴν ἐν τῷ ἰδίῳ ὀφθαλμῷ οὐ κατανοεῖς;

Τί (acc.sing.neut.of τίς, interrogative pronoun) 281.
δὲ (continuative conjunction) 11.
βλέπεις (2d.per.sing.pres.act.ind.of βλέπω, progressive) 499.
τὸ (acc.sing.neut.of the article in agreement with κάρφος) 9.
κάρφος (acc.sing.neut.of κάρφος, direct object of βλέπεις) 645.
τὸ (acc.sing.neut.of the article introducing the prepositional phrase) 9.
ἐν (preposition with the locative of place where) 80.
τῷ (loc.sing.masc.of the article in agreement with ὀφθαλμῷ) 9.
ὀφθαλμῷ (loc.sing.masc.of ὀφθαλμός, place where) 501.
τοῦ (gen.sing.masc.of the article in agreement with ἀδελφοῦ) 9.
ἀδελφοῦ (gen.sing.masc.of ἀδελφός, possession) 15.
σου (gen.sing.masc.of σύ, relationship) 104.
τὴν (acc.sing.fem.of the article in agreement with δοκὸν) 9.
δὲ (adversative conjunction) 11.
δοκὸν (acc.sing.fem.of δοκός, direct object of κατανοεῖς) 647.
τὴν (acc.sing.fem.of the article in agreement with δοκὸν) 9.
ἐν (preposition with the locative of place) 80.
τῷ (loc.sing.masc.of the article in agreement with ὀφθαλμῷ) 9.
ἰδίῳ (loc.sing.masc.of ἴδιος, in agreement with ὀφθαλμῷ) 778.
ὀφθαλμῷ (loc.sing.masc.of ὀφθαλμός, place) 501.
οὐ (negative conjunction with the indicative) 130.
κατανοεῖς (2d.per.sing.pres.act.ind.of κατανοέω, customary) 648.

*Translation - "And why are you always seeing the speck in the eye of your
brother, but the beam in your own eye you do not carefully examine?"*

Comment: *Cf.* Mt.7:3.Note that Luke emphasizes δοκὸν more than Matthew
does. The difference between βλέπω (#499) and κατανοέω (#648) should be
noted. There is no painstaking scrutiny of our own faults but ready and
consistent observation of the faults of otherss. This is true spiritual and
intellectual blindness - the kind that pitches us all headlong into the pit. This
behavior is typical of those who preempt our Lord's position (John 5:22) upon
the judgment throne. There is a great deal of difference between the size and
significance of a "speck" (κάρφος) and a "beam" (δοκός). Thus the self-
appointed critic minimizes his own faults and makes a Hollywood production
out of the faults of others.

Jesus pursues this thought further in

*Verse 42 - "Either how canst thou say to thy brother, Brother, let me pull out the
mote that is in thine eye, when thou thyself beholdest not the beam that is in thine
own eye? Thou hypocrite, cast out first the beam out of thine own eye, and then
shalt thou see clearly to pull out the mote that is in thy brother's eye."*

πῶς δύνασαι λέγειν τῷ ἀδελφῷ σου,'Αδελθέ, ἄφες ἐκβάλω τὸ κάρφος τὸν ἐν τῷ ὀφθαλμῷ σου, αὐτὸς τὴν ἐν τῷ ὀφθαλμῷ σου δοκὸν οὐ βλέπων; ὑποκριτά, ἐκβαλε πρῶτον τὴν δοκὸν ἐκ τοῦ ὀφθαλμοῦ σου, καὶ τότε διαβλέψεις τὸ κάρφος τὸν ἐν τῷ ὀφθαλμῷ τοῦ ἀδελφοῦ σου ἐκβαλεῖν.

πῶς (interrogative conjunction in direct question) 627.

δύνασαι (2d.per.sing.pres.ind.of δύναμαι, aoristic) 289.

λέγειν (pres.act.inf.of λέγω, complementary) 66.

τῷ (dat.sing.masc.of the article in agreement with ἀδελφῷ) 9.

ἀδελφῷ (dat.sing.masc.of ἀδελφός, indirect object of λέγειν) 15.

σου (gen.sing.masc.of σύ, relationship) 104.

'Αδελφέ (voc.sing.masc.of ἀδελφός, address) 15.

ἄφες (2d.per.sing.2d.aor.act.impv.of ἀφίημι, command) 319.

ἐκβάλω (1st.per.sing.2d.aor.act.subj.of ἐκβάλλω, volitive) 649.

τὸ (acc.sing.neut.of the article in agreement with κάρφος) 9.

κάρφος (acc.sing.neut.of κάρφος direct object of ἐκβάλω) 645.

τὸ (acc.sing.neut.of the article in agreement with κάρφος) 9.

ἐν (preposition with the locative of place where) 80.

τῷ (loc.sing.masc.of the article in agreement with ὀφθαλμῷ) 9.

ὀφθαλμῷ (loc.sing.masc.of ὀφθαλμός,place where) 501.

σου (gen.sing.masc.of σύ, possession) 104.

αὐτὸς (nom.sing.masc.of αὐτός, intensive subject of βλέπων) 16.

τὴν (acc.sing.fem.of the article in agreement with δοκὸν) 9.

ἐν (preposition with the locative of place where) 80.

τῷ (loc.sing.masc.of the article in agreement with ὀφθαλῷ) 9.

ὀφθαλμῷ (loc.sing.masc.of ὀφθαλμός, place where) 501.

σου (gen.sing.masc.of σύ, possession) 104.

δοκὸν (acc.sing.fem.of δοκός, direct object of βλέπων) 647.

οὐ (negative conjunction with the participle) 130.

βλέπων (pres.act.part.nom.sing.masc.of βλέπω, adverbial, circumstantial) 499.

ὑποκριτά (voc.sing.masc.of ὑποκριτής, address) 561.

ἐκβαλε (2d.per.sing.2d.aor.act.impv.of ἐκβάλλω, command) 649.

πρῶτον (acc.sing.neut.of πρῶτος, adverbial) 487.

τὴν (acc.sing.fem.of the article in agreement with δοκὸν) 9.

δοκὸν (acc.sing.fem.of δοκός, direct object of ἐκβάλε) 647.

ἐκ (preposition with the ablative of separation) 19.

τοῦ (abl.sing.masc.of the article in agreement with ὀφθαλμοῦ) 9.

ὀφθαλμοῦ (abl.sing.masc.of ὀφθαλμός, separation) 501.

σου (gen.sing.masc.of σύ, possession) 104.

καὶ (continuative conjunction) 14.

τότε (adverb of time) 166.

διαβλέψεις (2d.per.sing.fut.act.ind.of διαβλέπω, predictive) 650.

τὸ (acc.sing.neut.of the article in agreement with κάρφος) 9.

κάρφος (acc.sing.neut.of κάρφος, direct object of ἐκβάλεῖν) 645.
τὸ (acc.sing.neut.of the article in agreement with κάρφος) 9.
ἐν (preposition with the locative of place) 80.
τῷ (loc.sing.masc.of the article in agreement with ὀφθαλμῷ) 9.
ὀφθαλμῷ (loc.sing.masc.of ὀφθαλμός, place) 501.
τοῦ (gen.sing.masc.of the article in agreement with ἀδελφοῦ) 9.
ἀδελφοῦ (gen.sing.masc.of ἀδελφός, possession) 15.
σου (gen.sing.masc.of σύ, relationship) 104.
ἐκβαλεῖν (aor.act.inf.of ἐκβάλλω, complementary) 649.

Translation - *"How can you say to your brother, 'Brother, stand aside. I am going to pluck the speck out of your eye.' Yet you do not see the beam in your own eye! Hypocrite! First pull the beam out of your eye, and then you will see clearly to pull the speck out of your brother's eye."*

Comment: We have an interesting way to use ἄφες (#319) with the volitive subjunctive in ἐκβάλω after ἄφες. "Brugman (*Griech, Grammar, p.500 as cited in Robertson, Grammar, 930)* takes pains to remark that the element of "will" in the volitive subjunctive belongs to the speaker, not to the one addressed. It is purely a matter of the context." The volitive subjunctive instead of the predictive future indicative gives a ring of insolent authority to the demand of the hypocrite. The verse helps to explain verses 39-41.

Few Christians are mature enough in the Christian faith to practise introspection. Most of us are so busy inspecting other people, in our diligent search for their faults, that we forget to turn the critical eye backward upon ourselves. Thus we become exercised about the peccadillos that we see in others and are blissfully unaware of the grave offenses of which we are guilty.

If it be observed that Jesus here suggests that there will be a point in the Christian life when we are justified in assuming the role of judge, let it be further observed that the clear vision required for eye surgery upon our erring brother follows total correction of our own eye trouble. It is doubtful that any Christian ever developed to that point. Even if we were able to rid ourselves of our known faults, we would still be guilty of secret faults, for cleansing of which David prayed (Ps.19:12). The arrogant presumption that we are sufficiently clear sighted to qualify to pick the speck out of our brother's eye, is one of the secret faults which takes on the proportions of a beam. It is therefore doubtful that Jesus intended to say that any child of God would ever develop a spirituality that would equip him to be a judge of others.

The matter of being able to see clearly recalls what Jesus also said in Matthew's account of the same sermon about the single eye *versus* the evil eye (Mt.6:22-23).

A Tree Known by Its Fruit

(Mt.7:17-20; 12:34b-35)

Verse 43 - "For a good tree bringeth not forth corrupt fruit; neither doth a corrupt tree bring forth good fruit."

Οὐ γάρ ἐστιν δένδρον καλὸν ποιοῦν καρπὸν σαπρόν, οὐδὲ πάλιν δένδρον σαπρὸν ποιοῦν καρπὸν καλόν.

οὐ (negative conjunction with the present periphrastic) 130.
γὰρ (causal conjunction) 105.
ἐστιν (3d.per.sing.pres.ind.of εἰμί, present periphrastic) 86.
δένδρον (nom.sing.neut.of δένδρον, subject of ἐστιν) 294.
κὰλὸν (nom.sing.neut.of καλός, in agreement with δένδρου) 296.
ποιοῦν (pres.act.part.nom.sing.neut.of ποιέω, present periphrastic) 127.
καρπὸν (acc.sing.masc.of καρπός, direct object of ποιοῦν) 284.
σαπρόν (acc.sing.masc.of σαπρός, in agreement with καρπὸν) 682.
οὐδὲ (disjunctive particle) 452.
πάλιν (adverbial) 355.
δένδρον (nom.sing.neut.of δένδρον, subject of ποιοῦν) 294.
σαπρὸν (nom.sing.neut.of σαπρός, in agreement with δένδρον) 682.
ποιοῦν (pres.act.part.nom.sing.neut.of ποιέω, present periphrastic) 127.
καρπὸν (acc.sing.masc.of καρπός, direct object of ποιοῦν) 284.
καλόν (acc.sing.masc.of καλός, in agreement with καρπὸν) 296.

Translation - "*Because a good tree is never producing rotten fruit, neither again is a corrupt tree producing good fruit."*

Comment: The verse contains a double present periphrastic with ἐστιν understood in the second half of the sentence. So far, as present knowledge goes, here only do we have οὐδὲ πάλιν. The present periphrastic is used to accentuate the durative idea. Hence we translate, "never" - literally it is ". . . is not . . . bearing fruit at all times." The Greeks said it this way. Pick any moment in all of time and observe. At all times possible the tree is *not* bearing good (bad) fruit. Thus in English we say, "It is *never* bearing good (bad) fruit." The utter impossibility of deriving good fruit from a bad tree (or *vice versa*) is the point.

γὰρ seems to make verse 43 continue the thought of verse 42. The evil fruitage in the lives of the Pharisees indicated that they were corrupt trees, blind leaders, who were making their disciples as evil as themselves. *Cf.* Mt.23:15. For further comment *cf.* Mt.7:17-18.

Verse 44 - "*For every tree is known by his own fruit. For of thorns men do not gather figs, nor of a bramble bush gather they grapes."*

ἕκαστον γὰρ δένδρον ἐκ τοῦ ἰδίου καρποῦ γινώσκεται; οὐ γὰρ ἐξ ἀκανθῶν συλλέγουσιν σῦκα, οὐδὲ ἐκ βάτου σταφυλὴν τρυγῶσιν.

ἕκαστον (nom.sing.neut.of ἕκαστος, in agreement with δένδρον) 1217.
γὰρ (causal conjunction) 105.
δένδρον (nom.sing.neut.of δένδρον, subject of γινώσκεται) 294.

ἐκ (preposition with the ablative, like ἐν with the instrumental) 19.
τοῦ (abl.sing.masc.of the article in agreement with καρποῦ) 9.
ἰδίου (abl.sing.masc.of ἴδιος, in agreement with καρποῦ) 778.
καρποῦ (abl.sing.masc.of καρπός, instrumental) 284.
γινώσκεται (3d.per.sing.pres.pass.ind.of γινώσκω, customary) 131.
οὐ (negative conjunction with the indicative) 130.
γὰρ (causal conjunction) 105.
ἐξ (preposition with the ablative of source) 19.
ἀκανθῶν (abl.pl.neut.of ἄκανθα, source) 678.
συλλέγουσιν (3d.per.pl.pres.act.ind.of συλλέγω, customary) 677.
σῦκα (acc.pl.neut.of σῦκον, direct object of συλλέγουσιν) 681.
οὐδὲ (disjunctive particle) 452.

#2138 βάτου (abl.sing.fem.of βάτος, source)

bramble bush - Lk.6:44.
bush - Mk.12:26; Lk.20:37; Acts 7:30,35.

Meaning: bush, bramble. The plant that burned when God called Moses in Sinai - Mk.12:26; Lk.20:37; Acts 7:30,35. Illustratively - Lk.6:44. *Cf.*ὁ βάτος (#2565).

σταφυλὴν (acc.sing.fem.of σταφυλή, direct object of τρυγῶσιν) 679.

#2139 τρυγῶσιν (3d.per.pl.pres.act.ind.of τρυγάω, customary).

gather - Lk.6:44; Rev.14:18,19.

Meaning: Cf.#677 - συλλέγω. To reap a crop. Gather in. With σταφυλή in Lk.6:44; with ἄμπελος in Rev.14:18,19 in a metaphorical sense.

Translation - "For every tree is known by its own fruit. Because people do not gather figs from thorns, nor do they harvest grapes from a bramble bush."

Comment: Thus verse 44 explains the preceding thought which begins in verse 41.Three ablative phrases, each introduced by ἐκ and indicating source. Every tree is the source of its own fruit and is judged thereby.Thorns trees are not the source of figs; bramble bushes are not the source of grapes. Note the attributive possessive adjective ἰδίου.- "One's own fruit." This is an important point to observe. Evil trees sometimes get transplanted into good organizations. Though an evil man belongs to an organization that is too good for him, he will be judged by *his own fruit*, not that of the group with which he is associated in a superficial social sense. Credit by association is as fallacious as guilt by association. The good deeds of an organization should not be used to whitewash the evil fruit of its individual members. Fig farmers do not approach thorn trees with any degree of expectation, nor do they expect bramble bushes to produce grapes. *Cf.* Mt.7:19; Mk.12:26; Lk.20:37; Acts 7:30,35. Here was a bramble bush that produced no grapes. God burned it as the Baptist said (Mt.7:19), but out of it He spoke to Moses.

Verse 45 - "A good man out of the good treasure of his heart bringeth forth that which is good; and an evil man out of the evil treasure of his heart bringeth forth that which is evil: for of the abundance of the heart his mouth speaketh."

ὁ ἀγαθὸς ἄνθρωπος ἐκ τοῦ ἀγαθοῦ θησαυροῦ τῆς καρδίας προφέρει τὸ ἀγαθόν, καὶ ὁ πονηρὸς ἐκ τοῦ πονηροῦ προφέρει τὸ πονηρόν; ἐκ γὰρ περισσεύματος καρδίας λαλεῖ τὸ στόμα αὐτοῦ.

ὁ (nom.sing.masc.of the article in agreement with ἄνθρωπος) 9.
ἀγαθὸς (nom.sing.masc.of ἀγαθός, in agreement with ἄνθρωπος) 547.
ἄνθρωπος (nom.sing.masc.of ἄνθρωπος, subject of προφέρει) 341.
ἐκ (preposition with the ablative of source) 19.
τοῦ (abl.sing.masc.of the article in agreement with θησαυροῦ) 9.
ἀγαθοῦ (abl.sing.masc.of ἀγαθός, in agreement with θησαυροῦ) 547.
θησαυροῦ (abl.sing.masc.of θησαυρός, source) 189.
τῆς (gen.sing.fem.of the article in agreement with καρδίας) 9.
καρδίας (gen.sing.fem.of καρδία, definition) 432.

#2140 προφέρει (3d.per.sing.pres.act.ind.of προφέρω, customary).

　　bring forth - Lk.6:45,45.

Meaning: A combination of πρό (#442) and φέρω (#683). Hence, to bring forward; bring forth; produce - Lk.6:45,45.

τὸ (acc.sing.neut.of the article in agreement with ἀγαθόν) 9.
ἀγαθόν (acc.sing.neut.of ἀγαθός, direct object of προφέρει) 547.
καὶ (continuative conjunction) 14.
ὁ (nom.sing.masc.of the article in agreement with πονηρὸς) 9.
πονηρὸς (nom.sing.masc.of πονηρός, subject of προφέρει) 438.
ἐκ (preposition with the ablative of source) 19.
τοῦ (abl.sing.neut.of the article in agreement with πονηροῦ) 9.
πονηροῦ (abl.sing.neut.of πονηρός, in agreement with θησαυροῦ, understood) 438.
προφέρει (3d.per.sing.pres.act.ind.of προφέρω, customary) 2140.
τὸ (acc.sing.neut.of the article in agreement with πονηρόν) 9.
πονηρόν (acc.sing.neut.of πονηρός, direct object of προφέρει) 438.
ἐκ (preposition with the ablative of source) 19.
γὰρ (causal conjunction) 105.
περισσεύματος (abl.sing.masc.of περίσσευμα, source) 1003.
καρδίας (gen.sing.fem.of καρδία, definition) 432.
λαλεῖ (3d.per.sing.pres.act.ind.of λαλέω, customary) 815.
τὸ (nom.sing.neut.of the article in agreement with στόμα) 9.
στόμα (nom.sing.neut.of στόμα, subject of λαλεῖ) 344.
αὐτοῦ (gen.sing.masc.of αὐτός, possession) 16.

Translation - "The good man out of the good treasure of the heart brings forward the good thing, and the evil man out of the evil treasure produces the evil. Because out of the emotional overflow his mouth is always speaking."

Comment: *Cf.*Mt.12:34,35. Note the article with καρδίας in the first clause while the last clause has anarthrous καρδίας. Hence in the latter case καρδίας is adjectival. When the heart is abundantly evil the mouth cannot refrain from speaking. The heart is the dictator; the mouth is the servant, always ready at the beck and call of the master. We see this cause and result sequence in Rom.10:9,10. The confession of the mouth is the result of the belief in the heart. But some may object with the question, "Did not the Pharisees open their mouths to confess the Lord? Is this not proof that they had Him in their hearts?" They did indeed confess Him with the mouth, but it was an empty confession as Jesus points out in verse 46. The real question lies in the motive for the confession which the Pharisees gave. The real condition of their hearts is revealed, not in what they say but in what they do.

The Two Foundations

(Mt.7:24-27)

Verse 46 - "And why call ye me, Lord, Lord, and do not the things which I say?"

Τί δέ με καλεῖτε, Κύριε κύριε, καὶ οὐ ποιεῖτε ἃ λέγω;

Τί (acc.sing.neut.of τίς, interrogative pronoun, cause) 281.
δέ (adversative conjunction) 11.
με (acc.sing.masc.of ἐγώ, direct object of καλεῖτε) 123.
καλεῖτε (2d.per.pl.pres.act.ind.of καλέω, progressive) 107.
Κύριε (voc.sing.masc.of κύριος, address) 97.
κύριε (voc.sing.masc.of κύριος, address) 97.
καὶ (adversative conjunction) 14.
οὐ (negative conjunction with the indicative) 130.
ποιεῖτε (2d.per.pl.pres.act.ind.of ποιέω, customary) 127.
ἃ (acc.pl.neut.of ὅς, direct object of ποιεῖτε) 65.
λέγω (1st.per.sing.pres.act.ind.of λέγω, aoristic) 66.

Translation - "But why are you calling me Lord, Lord, but you are not doing the things which I say?"

Comment: δέ is definitely adversative. Evil trees put forth evil fruit, despite what the mouth speaks. If the heart were truly abundant in goodness, actions would suit pious speeches. Here is Jesus' condemnation of dead orthodoxy. How easy it is to parrot, "Lord, Lord." Confessions of faith printed in hymn books and piously intoned on Sunday morning represent the point, although not all ritual is hypocritical. A college graduate dean confided once that though he did not believe a word of the Apostles' Creed he recited it piously along with the rest of the congregation every Sunday morning. Preachers like the phrase "Sound in the faith" in reference to one another, although oftentimes our lives show little inclination that we wish to do as Jesus says.

Jesus clinches the point in the final three verses of the chapter.

Verse 47 - "Whosoever cometh to me, and heareth my sayings, and doeth them, I will show you to whom he is like."

πᾶς ὁ ἐρχόμενος πρός με καὶ ἀκούων μου τῶν λόγων καὶ ποιῶν αὐτούς, ὑποδείξω ὑμῖν τίνι ἐστίν ὅμοιος.

πᾶς (nom.sing.masc.of πᾶς, in agreement with ἐρχόμενος, ἀκούων and ποιῶν) 67.

ὁ (nom.sing.masc.of the article in agreement with ἐρχόμενος, ἀκούων and ποιῶν) 9.

ἐρχόμενος (pres.part.nom.sing.masc.of ἔρχομαι, substantival, nominative absolute) 146.

πρός (preposition with the accusative of extent, metaphorical) 197.

με (acc.sing.masc.of ἐγώ, metaphorical extent) 123.

καὶ (adjunctive conjunction, joining participles) 14.

ἀκούων (pres.act.part.nom.sing.masc.of ἀκούω, substantival, nominative absolute) 148.

μου (gen.sing.masc.of ἐγώ, possession) 123.

τῶν (gen.pl.masc.of the article in agreement with λόγων) 9.

λόγων (gen.pl.masc.of λόγος, description) 510.

καὶ (adjunctive conjunction, joining participles) 14.

ποιῶν (pres.act.part.nom.sing.masc.of ποιέω, substantival, nominative absolute) 127.

αὐτούς (acc.pl.masc.of αὐτός, direct object of ποιῶν) 16.

ὑποδείξω (1st.per.sing.fut.act.ind.of ὑποδείκνυμι, predictive) 282.

ὑμῖν (dat.pl.masc.of σύ, indirect object of ὑποδείξω) 104.

τίνι (dat.sing.masc.of τίς, interrogative pronoun, comparison) 281.

ἐστὶν (3d.per.sing.pres.ind.of εἰμί, aoristic) 86.

ὅμοιος (nom.sing.masc.of ὅμοιος, predicate adjective) 923.

Translation - "Everyone who comes to me and hears my messages and practises them - - - I will show you whom he is like."

Comment: πᾶς is joined to all three of the participles. The man with the house on the rock (vs.48) not only came to Jesus and heard His messages, but he also made them a way of life. Jesus does not finish the sentence, but breaks it off by promising to show us what such a person is like. *Cf.* Mt.7:24 for comment.

Verse 48 - "He is like a man which built an house, and digged deep, and laid the foundation on a rock: and when the flood arose, the stream beat vehemently upon that house, and could not shake it: for it was founded upon a rock."

ὅμοιός ἐστιν ἀνθρώπῳ οἰκοδομοῦντι οἰκίαν ὅς ἔσκαφεν καὶ εβάθυνεν καὶ
ἔθηκεν θεμέλιον ἐπὶ τὴν πέτρον, πλημμύρης δὲ γενομένης προσέρηξεν ὁ
ποταμὸς τῇ οἰκίᾳ ἐκείνῃ, καὶ οὐκ ἴσχυσεν σαλεῦσαι αὐτὴν διὰ τὸ καλῶς
οἰκοδομῆσθαι αὐτήν.

ὅμοιός (nom.sing.masc.of ὅμοιος, predicate adjective) 923.
ἐστιν (3d.per.sing.pres.ind.of εἰμί, aoristic) 86.
ἀνθρώπῳ (dat.sing.masc.of ἄνθρωπος, comparison) 341.
οἰκοδομοῦντι (pres.act.part.dat.sing.masc.of οἰκοδομέω, adjectival,
restrictive, in agreement with ἀνθρώπῳ) 694.
οἰκίαν (acc.sing.fem.of οἰκία, direct object of οἰκοδομοῦντι) 186.
ὅς (relative pronoun, subject of ἔσκαφεν, ἐβάθυνεν and ἔθηκεν) 65.

#2141 ἔσκαφεν (3d.per.sing.aor.act.ind.of σκάπτω, ingressive).

dig - Lk.6:48; 13:8; 16:3.

Meaning: In the New Testament, to excavate in preparation for putting in a
foundation under a building - Lk.6:48; to cultivate around the roots of a tree -
Lk.13:8; to plough or dig for planting a crop - Lk.16:3.

καὶ (adjunctive conjunction joining verbs) 14.

#2142 ἐβάθυνεν (3d.per.sing.imp.act.ind.of βαθύνω, progressive description).

deep - Lk.6:48.

Meaning: to dig deeper; to deepen. To dig a deeper foundation as in Lk.6:48.

καὶ (adjunctive conjunction) 14.
ἔθηκεν (3d.per.sing.aor.act.ind.of τίθημι, culminative) 455.

#2143 θελέλιον (acc.sing.masc.of θεμέλιος, direct object of ἔθηκεν).

foundation - Lk.6:48,49; 14:29; Acts 16:26; Rom.15:20; I Cor.3:10,11,12;
Eph.2:20; I Tim.6:19; II Tim.2:19; Heb.6:1; 11:10; Rev.21:14,19,19.

Meaning: Cf.θεμα - "a thing laid down." Hence, a foundation. Properly in an
architechural sense - Lk.14:29; Acts 16:26; for illustration purposes - Lk.6:48,49;
with reference to the New Jerusalem - Heb.11:10; Rev.21:14,19,19.Christ is the
foundation of the Christian faith - I Cor.3:10,11,12; II Tim.2:19; Rom.15:20;
also used of the Apostles and Prophets - Eph.2:20. With reference to the first step
in the Christian experience - Heb.6:1. Note also I Tim.6:19 in connection with
Lk.6:48.

ἐπὶ (preposition with the accusative of place) 47.
τὴν (acc.sing.fem.of the article in agreement with πέτραν) 9.
πέτραν (acc.sing.fem.of πέτρα, extent after ἐπὶ) 695.

#2144 πλημμύρης (gen.sing.fem.of πλημμύρα, genitive absolute).

flood - Lk.6:48.

Meaning: A flood - Lk.6:48.

δέ (explanatory conjunction) 11.

γενομένης (aor.part.gen.sing.fem.of γίνομαι, genitive absolute, culminat·ve) 113.

#2145 προσέρηξεν (3d.per.sing.aor.act.ind.of προσρήγνυμι, ingressive).

beat vehemently against - Lk.6:48,49.

Meaning: A combination of πρός (#197) and ῥήγνυμι (#654). Hence to press against; put pressure upon. With reference to the river at flood tide beating against a house - Lk.6:48,49.

ὁ (nom.sing.masc.of the article in agreement with ποταμός) 9.

ποταμός (nom.sing.masc.of ποταμός, subject of προσέρηξεν) 274.

τῇ (loc.sing.fem.of the article in agreement with οἰκίᾳ) 9.

οἰκίᾳ (loc.sing.fem.of οἰκία, place with a verb of rest) 186.

ἐκείνῃ (loc.sing.fem.of ἐκεῖνος, in agreement with οἰκίᾳ) 246.

καί (adversative conjunction) 14.

οὐκ (negative conjunction with the indicative) 130.

ἴσχυσεν (3d.per.sing.aor.act.ind.of ἰσχύω, constative) 447.

σαλεῦσαι (aor.act.inf.of σαλεύω, complementary) 911.

αὐτήν (acc.sing.fem.of αὐτός, direct object of σαλεῦσαι) 16.

διά (preposition with the accusative, cause) 118.

τό (acc.sing.neut.of the article, cause) 9.

καλῶς (adverbial) 977.

οἰκοδομῆσθαι (pres.pass.inf.of οἰκοδομέω, accusative of cause, noun use) 694.

αὐτήν (acc.sing.fem.of αὐτός, general reference) 16.

Translation - "He is like a man building a house, who began to excavate and he continued to dig deeper and he laid a foundation upon the rock. Now after the downpour came the river surged against that house, but it was not able to shake it, because it was built solidly."

Comment: The dative of comparison in ἀνθρώπῳ is followed by the adjectival participle in its restrictive use (predicate position). Jesus is restricting the story to a single man who is described as engaged in building a house. The relative clause (ὅς . . . πέτραν) describes him further. He built with an awareness of coming danger. He began to excavate (ingressive aorist), and he continued to dig deeper (progressive description in the imperfect) and finished (culminative aorist in ἔθηκεν) with a foundation laid securely upon a rock. He did not cease to dig deeper until he found bed rock. That is where the foundation must rest. δέ is now explanatory as Jesus adds another element to the story. A heavy rainstorm came and was now past (culminative aorist in the genitive absolute γενομένης). The result is the river out of its banks and beginning to wash against the house (ingressive aorist in προσέρηξεν). καὶ is adversative. But the river, for all of its surging pressure was unable to shake the house. The causal clause with διὰ and the noun infinitive in the accusative case, tell us why the house did not fall, despite the great pressure from the rushing river. It was built solidly. *Cf.* Mt.7:25 for further comment. On foundation building (#2143) *cf.* I Tim.6:17-19.

The social, economic, philosophical and political houses of unregenerate men fall, because their builders are committed to an empirical approach which can never be holistic. Empiricism depends upon the experiences of past and present and must assume that an extrapolation into the future can be made from the experiences of the past. It is statistically probable, within a certain margin of error, that the future will be like the past, although long-range predictions suffer from growing heteroscedasticity. However sincere and thorough the effort of the builder of the system may be to prevent tensions which, under coming pressures, will shake the system to pieces, he cannot succeed because he does not know that his system, in all of its components, is consistent with all of the facts in the universe. For all he knows, his system has built-in contradictions which will become apparent when it is too late.

What we need is an architect like Jesus Christ, Who, being God incarnate and the Creator of the entire universe, with all of its principles of operation, knows the future as He knows the past, since, being eternal, the future and the past are all the same to Him. If we "come to Him and hear His messages and make them the rule of our lives" (vs.47), and if we build into our social, economic and political institutions the ethical principles which He has laid down, we need have no fear of coming storms, since the divine Architect, after Whose blueprint we built knows about the coming storms and was thus able to build safely against them. This is what is meant by the causal clause διὰ τὸ καλῶς οἰκοδομῆσαι αὐτήν- "because it was built solidly." Empiricists, who reject the presuppositional apologetics of the Reformed theologian, may be congratulated for the sincerity of their efforts to build solidly, but they must be criticized for their naive assumption that they know how to draw the blueprint.

The Christian does not know the future any better than the unsaved world, at least not in the short-run and not in terms of minor details. He is no better able than the unsaved to build with safeguards against destruction, once the stresses of life, at present unknown, come. But his wisdom lies in the fact that he recognizes his inability to see the future and therefore plays it safe by following the ethical pattern of the Lord Jesus Christ, Who does in fact know the future as well as the past. If one does not know the road ahead he should allow someone to drive who has been over the road and knows where the danger areas lie.

Verse 49 - "But he that heareth, and doeth not, is like a man that without a foundation built an house upon the earth; against which the stream did beat vehemently, and immediately it fell; and the ruin of that house was great."

ὁ δὲ ἀκούσας καὶ μὴ ποιήσας ὅμοιός ἐστιν ἀνθρώπῳ οἰκοδομήσαντι οἰκίαν
ἐπὶ τὴν γῆν χωρὶς θεμελίου, ᾗ προσέρηξεν ὁ ποταμός, καὶ εὐθὺς συνέπεσεν,
καὶ ἐγένετο τὸ ῥῆγμα τῆς οἰκίας ἐκείνης μέγα.

ὁ (nom.sing.masc.of the article in agreement with ἀκούσας) 9.

δὲ (adversative conjunction) 11.

ἀκούσας (aor.act.part.nom.sing.masc.of ἀκούω, substantival, subject of
ἐστιν) 148.

καὶ (adjunctive conjunction joining participles) 14.

μὴ (negative conjunction with the participle) 87.

ποιήσας (aor.act.part.nom.sing.masc.of ποιέω, substantival, subject of
ἐστιν) 127.

ὅμοιός (nom.sing.masc.of ὅμοιος, predicate adjective) 923.

ἐστιν (3d.per.sing.pres.ind.of εἰμί, aoristic) 86.

ἀνθρώπῳ (dat.sing.masc.of ἄνθρωπος, comparison) 341.

οἰκοδομήσαντι (aor.act.part.dat.sing.masc.of οἰκοδομέω, adjectival,
restrictive, in agreement with ἀνθρώπῳ) 694.

οἰκίαν (acc.sing.fem.of οἰκία, direct object of οἰκοδομήσαντι) 186.

ἐπὶ (preposition with the accusative of place) 47.

τὴν (acc.sing.fem.of the article in agreement with γῆν) 9.

γῆν (acc.sing.fem.of γῆ, extent, place) 157.

χωρὶς (adverbial, with the ablative of separation) 1077.

θεμελίου (abl.sing.masc.of θεμέλιος, separation) 2143.

ᾗ (loc.sing.fem.of ὅς, relative pronoun, place where) 65.

προσέρηξεν (3d.per.sing.aor.act.ind.of προσρήγνυμι, ingressive) 2145.

ὁ (nom.sing.masc.of the article in agreement with ποταμός) 9.

ποταμός (nom.sing.masc.of ποταμός, subject of προσέρηξεν) 274.

καὶ (continuative conjunction) 14.

εὐθὺς (adverbial) 258.

#2146 συνέπεσεν (3d.per.sing.aor.act.ind.of συμπίπτω, culminative).

fall - Lk.6:49.

Meaning: A combination of σύν (#1542) and πίπτω (#187). Hence, literally to
fall (πίπτω) together/in (σύν). Hence, to collapse. To disintegrate centripetally.
This is the logical word for the house of Lk.6:49, since the pressure from the
rising flood waters was exerted from all sides inward.

καὶ (continuative conjunction) 14.

ἐγένετο (3d.per.sing.aor.ind.of γίνομαι, culminative) 113.

τὸ (nom.sing.neut.of the article in agreement with ῥῆγμα) 9.

#2147 ῥῆγμα (nom.sing.neut.of ῥῆγμα, subject of ἐγένετο).

ruin - Lk.6:49.

Meaning: Cf. ῥήγνυμι (#654). That which is fractured, rent asunder, demolished, crushed, split. Of the house of Luke 6:49.

τῇ (gen.sing.fem.of the article in agreement with οἰκίας) 9.

οἰκίας (gen.sing.fem.of οἰκία, description) 186.

ἐκείνης (gen.sing.fem.of ἐκεῖνος, in agreement with οἰκίας) 246.

μέγα (nom.sing.neut.of μέγας, predicate adjective, in agreement with ῥῆγμα) 184.

Translation - "But the one who heard and did not act is like a man who had built a house upon the soil without a foundation, around which the river flooded and immediately it fell in, and the ruin of that house was great."

Comment: δὲ is clearly adversative as Jesus presents the other side of the coin. Everything is different. This man heard Jesus' teachings, but he did not once obey. ὅμοιος is here followed by the dative of comparison in ἀνθρώπῳ as usual. *Cf.#923.* The restrictive adjectival participle οἰκοδομήσαντι is aorist here, unlike the present participle of verse 48, which describes the wise man. This man had built his house, when the storm came. The wise man of verse 48 was still in the process of building when the storm came. Is this not true of the Christian who is rendering obedience to the teachings of Jesus? We never cease to build constructively. Throughout eternity we will be in the process of building our house (Eph.4:13). How unlike the empiricist who has rejected as religious superstition anything that Jesus may have said and has finished his house to his own perfect satisfaction. The builders of the Titanic, which sank on her maiden voyage to America in 1912, announced before she sailed that she was unsinkable! The unsaved tend to ascribe perfection to their productions and announce their perfection with finality, despite coming storms. The house of our passage is without a foundation. Here the student should run the references on #2143 and see what happens when we build without the foundation which is Christ and His teachings. The test came as before but with the opposite result. The house was surrounded by the pounding waters of the rising river. Immediately (εὐθὺς) it collapsed. *Cf.#2146.* Here only in the New Testament though common enough elsewhere in Greek literature. The house fell in like a house of cards. Totally unable to withstand outside pressure, its ruin was great. καὶ . . . μέγα serves only to accentuate the full meaning of συνέπεσεν. For further comment *cf.* Mt.7:26,27.

A vivid picture of the total destruction of the house built by Antichrist and his hellions without a foundation can be seen in Revelation 18. In this passage Jesus diametrically opposes the Pollyannaism of the evolutionary sociologists and their optimistic doctrine of the inevitable perfectability of man and all of his institutions.

(2) The Second Preaching Tour

(A) A Centurion's Servant Healed

(Mt.8:5-13; Lk.7:1-10)

Luke 7:1 - *"Now when he had ended all his sayings in the audience of the people, he entered into Capernaum."*

Ἐπειδὴ ἐπλήρωσεν πάντα τὰ ῥήματα αὐτοῦ εἰς τὰς ἀκοὰς τοῦ λαοῦ, εἰσῆλθεν εἰς Καφαρναούμ.

#2148 Ἐπειδὴ (compound conjunction).

after that - I Cor.1:21.
because - Acts 14:12.
for - Lk.11:6; I Cor.1:22; Phil.2:26.
forasmuch as - Acts 15:24.
seeing - Acts 13:46; I Cor.14:16.
since - I Cor.15:21.
when - Lk.7:1.

Meaning: A combination of ἐπεί (#1281) and δή (#1053). Conjunction. Since now, or when now. In a chronological and causal sense in Lk.7:1. Elsewhere in a causal sense - I Cor.1:21; Acts 14:12; Lk.11:6; I Cor.1:22; Phil.2:26; Acts 13:46; 15:24; I Cor.14:16; 15:21.

ἐπλήρωσεν (3d.per.sing.aor.act.ind.of πληρόω, culminative) 115.
πάντα (acc.pl.neut.of πᾶς, in agreement with ῥήματα) 67.
τὰ (acc.pl.neut.of the article in agreement with ῥήματα) 9.
ῥήματα (acc.pl.neut.of ῥῆμα, direct object of ἐπλήρωσεν) 343.
αὐτοῦ (gen.sing.masc.of αὐτός, possession) 16.
εἰς (preposition with the accusative, static use) 140.
τὰς (acc.pl.fem.of the article in agreement with ἀκοὰς) 9.
ἀκοὰς (acc.pl.fem.of ἀκοή, static use of the accusative) 409.
τοῦ (gen.sing.masc.of the article in agreement with λαοῦ) 9.
λαοῦ (gen.sing.masc.of λαός, definition) 110.
εἰσῆλθεν (3d.per.sing.aor.ind.of εἰσέρχομαι, ingressive) 234.
εἰς (preposition with the accusative of extent) 140.
Καφαρναούμ (acc.sing.of Καφαρναούμ, extent) 370.

Translation - *"Having completed all of His remarks in the hearing of the people, He started toward Capernaum."*

Comment:' Ἐπειδή is used here both in a chronological and causal sense. This is only natural, as cause always precedes result. The culminative aorist in ἐπλήρωσεν reinforces the point. Note the original static use of εἰς with the accusative, like ἐν with the locative. Jesus previously had made Capernaum His headquarters after His rejection at Nazareth (Lk.4:16-31).

Verse 2 - "And a certain centurion's servant, who was dear unto him, was sick, and ready to die."

Ἐκατονάρχου δὲ τινος δοῦλος κακῶς ἔχων ἤμελλεν τελευτᾶν, ὃς ἦν αὐτῷ ἔντιμος.

Ἐκατοντάρχου (gen.sing.masc.of ἑκατοντάρχης, relationship) 717.
δέ (explanatory conjunction) 11.
τινος (gen.sing.masc.of τις, in agreement with ἑκατοντάρχης) 486.
δοῦλος (nom.sing.masc.of δοῦλος, subject of ἤμελλεν) 725.
κακῶς (adverbial) 411.
ἔχων (pres.act.part.nom.sing.masc.of ἔχω, adverbial, circumstantial) 82.
ἤμελλεν (3d.per.sing.imp.act.ind.of μέλλω, inceptive) 206.
τελευτᾶν (pres.act.inf.of τελευτάω, complementary) 231.
ὃς (nom.sing.masc.of ὅς, relative pronoun, subject of ἦν) 65.
ἦν (3d.per.sing.imp.ind.of εἰμί, progressive description) 86.
αὐτῷ (dat.sing.masc.of αὐτός, personal advantage) 16.

#2149 ἔντιμος (nom.sing.masc.of ἔντιμος, predicate adjective).

dear - Lk.7:2.
honourable - Lk.14:8.
precious - I Pet.2:4,6.
reputation - Phil.2:29.

Meaning: Twice (I Pet.2:4,6) applied to Christ. With reference to the prestigious individual who would be seated in the place of honor at a banquet - Lk.14:8. Of the servant of the Centurion - Lk.7:2. Highly valued - precious - Phil.2:29. Held in high esteem. A combination of ἐν (#80) and τιμή (#1619).

Translation - "Now a certain Centurion had a servant whom he held in high regard who was sick and about to die."

Comment: δέ is explanatory, as Luke begins to tell the story. The Roman officer is emphasized here rather than the sick servant. *Cf.*#411 for κακῶς with ἔχω, meaning "illness.' Literally it is "having evil" physical, *i.e.* τελευτᾶν, a present infinitive completes ἤμελλεν. The relative phrase defines δοῦλος. Note the imperfect tense in ἦν. This servant had a long and consistent record of faithful service to his owner, who considered him a valuable asset. The word does not carry the idea of emotional regard although it is not unlikely that the soldier was fond of his servant.

Verse 3 - "And when he heard of Jesus, he sent unto him the elders of the Jews, beseeching him that he would come and heal his servant."

ἀκούσας δὲ περὶ τοῦ Ἰησοῦ ἀπέστειλεν πρὸς αὐτὸν πρεσβυτέρους τῶν Ἰουδαίων, ἐρωτῶν αὐτὸν ὅπως ἐλθὼν διασώσῃ τὸν δοῦλον αὐτοῦ.

ἀκούσας (aor.act.part.nom.sing.masc.of ἀκούω, adverbial, temporal) 148.
δὲ (continuative conjunction) 11.
περὶ (preposition with the genitive of reference) 173.
τοῦ (gen.sing.masc.of the article in agreement with Ἰησοῦ) 9.
Ἰησοῦ (gen.sing.masc.of Ἰησοῦς, reference) 3.
ἀπέστειλεν (3d.per.sing.aor.act.ind.of ἀποστέλλω, constative) 215.
πρὸς (preposition with the accusative of extent) 197.
αὐτὸν (acc.sing.masc.of αὐτός, extent) 16.
πρεσβυτέρους (acc.pl.masc.of πρεσβύτερος, direct object of ἀπέστειλεν) 1141.
τῶν (gen.pl.masc.of the article in agreement with Ἰουδαίων) 9.
Ἰουδαίων (gen.pl.masc.of Ἰουδαῖος, definition) 143.
ἐρωτῶν (pres.act.part.nom.sing.masc.of ἐρωτάω, adverbial, modal) 1172.
αὐτὸν (acc.sing.masc.of αὐτός, direct object of ἐρωτῶν) 16.
ὅπως (final conjunction introducing a purpose clause) 177.
ἐλθὼν (aor.part.nom.sing.masc.of ἔρχομαι, adverbial, temporal) 146.
διασώσῃ (3d.per.sing.aor.act.subj.of διασώζω, purpose) 1138.
τὸν (acc.sing.masc.of the article in agreement with δοῦλον) 9.
δοῦλον (acc.sing.masc.of δοῦλος, direct object of διασώσῃ) 725.
αὐτοῦ (gen.sing.masc.of αὐτός, relationship) 16.

Translation - *"And when he had heard about Jesus he sent to Him elders of the Jews, asking Him that He would come and cure his servant."*

Comment: *Cf.*#148 for other instances of ἀκούω with περί and the genitive of reference. It would have been impossible for the Roman soldier to have not heard about Jesus, the revolutionary Teacher and Healer. Virtually everyone was talking about Jesus. It was a part of the soldier's job to maintain internal security against messiahs of one sort or another who were constantly arising to preach revolt against Rome.

Note that the Centurion had sufficient authority to dispatch Jewish elders to do his bidding. They complied. Perhaps the officer thought that the elders of Israel would have some influence with Jesus. The modal participle ἐρωτῶν is followed by the purpose clause, introduced by the final conjunction ὅπως. #1138 is an example of intensive διά joined to the verb σώζω - "to thoroughly save" or "to cure completely." This request was probably as far as the Roman army officer could go in his unenlightened spiritual condition, but as we shall see he had great respect, if not faith in Jesus' power.

Verse 4 - "And when they came to Jesus, they besought him instantly, saying, That he was worthy for whom he should do this."

οἱ δὲ παραγενόμενοι πρὸς τὸν Ἰησοῦν παρεκάλουν αὐτὸν σπουδαίως, λέγοντες ὅτι Ἄξιός ἐστιν ᾧ παρέξῃ τοῦτο.

οἱ (nom.pl.masc.of the article in agreement with παραγενόμενοι) 9.
δὲ (continuative conjunction) 11.
παραγενόμενοι (2d.aor.part.nom.pl.masc.of παραγίνομαι, substantival, subject of παρεκάλουν) 139.
πρὸς (preposition with the accusative of extent) 197.
τὸν (acc.sing.masc.of the article in agreement with Ἰησοῦν) 9.
Ἰησοῦν (acc.sing.masc.of Ἰησοῦς, extent) 3.
παρεκάλουν (3d.per.pl.imp.act.ind.of παρακαλέω, inceptive) 230.
αὐτὸν (acc.sing.masc.of αὐτός, direct object of παρεκάλουν) 16.

#2150 σπουδαίως (adverbial).

diligently - Tit.3:13.
instantly - Lk.7:4.
the more carefully - Phil.2:28.
very diligently - II Tim.1:17.

Meaning: an adverb - actively, earnestly, zealously, carefully. *Cf.* σπουδή (#1819), σπουδάζω (#4423) and σπουδαῖος (#4340). With reference to Onesiphorous' painstaking search for Paul in Rome - II Tim.1:17. With reference to Titus' conduct to Rome of Zenas and Apollos - Titus 3:13. Of Paul's great care for Epaphroditus' journey to Philippi - Phil.2:28. In a different sense of the elders' urgent pleading with Jesus in behalf of the centurion - Lk.7:4.

λέγοντες (pres.act.part.nom.pl.masc.of λέγω, adverbial, modal) 66.
ὅτι (recitative) 211.
Ἄξιός (nom.sing.masc.of ἄξιος, predicate adjective) 285.
ἐστιν (3d.per.sing.pres.ind.of εἰμί, aoristic) 86.
ᾧ (dat.sing.masc.of ὅς, relative pronoun, personal advantage) 65.
παρέξῃ (3d.per.sing.aor.act.subj.of παρέχω, result) 1566.
τοῦτο (acc.sing.neut.of οὗτος, direct object of παρέξῃ) 93.

Translation - "*And those who came to Jesus began to beg Him earnestly, saying, 'He deserves that you do this for him.'* "

Comment: The elders did not resent the order from the Centurion. On the contrary σπουδαίως makes it clear that they were eager for Jesus to grant the soldier's request. Note the inceptive imperfect in παρεκάλουν. ἄξιος is here used in its pure meaning. *Cf.* note from Liddell and Scott (#285). The Centurion's service to the nation Israel was equal in value to the service of healing for which they now asked. He had done much for them. Could not Jesus now settle the score? They reinforce this argument in verse 5 by a recital of his deeds in behalf of the Jews. The usual arrogance of the orthodox Jewish leader toward the Gentile *dog* is missing here. The Centurion was probably not the typical Roman soldier. He had an interest in his servant and he had built a synagogue for the Jews. *The Pulpit Commentary* suggests that the ethical life of the Jews in Galilee was purer than that in faction-ridden Judea, and that the Roman soldier in Capernaum had seen the true religion shining in the lives of his Jewish neighbors and was thus influenced by it. There is something especially noble about this man.

Verse 5 - "For he loveth our nation and he hath built us a synagogue."

ἀγαπᾷ γὰρ τὸ ἔθνος ἡμῶν καὶ τὴν συναγωγὴν αὐτὸς ᾠκοδόμησεν ὑμῖν.

ἀγαπᾷ (3d.per.sing.pres.act.ind.of ἀγαπάω, aoristic) 540.
γὰρ (causal conjunction) 105.
τὸ (acc.sing.neut.of the article in agreement with ἔθνος) 9.
ἔθνος (acc.sing.neut.of ἔθνος, direct object of ἀγαπᾷ) 376.
ἡμῶν (gen.pl.masc.of ἐγώ, possession) 123.
καὶ (continuative conjunction) 14.
συναγωγὴν (acc.sing.fem.of συναγωγή, direct object of ᾠκοδόμησεν) 404.
αὐτὸς (nom.sing.masc.of αὐτός, subject of ᾠκοδόμησεν) 16.
ᾠκοδόμησεν (3d.per.sing.aor.act.ind.of οἰκοδομέω, culminative) 694.
ἡμῖν (dat.pl.masc.of ἐγώ, personal advantage) 123.

Translation - "Because he loves our nation and he has built the synagogue for us."

Comment: One good turn deserves another. This man is worthy. We owe it to him. He is consistent in his attitude toward us (present tense in ἀπαπᾷ). He has proved his love. Note the emphatic position of τὴν συναγωγὴν, as it outranks the verb. Note also the emphatic αὐτός - "He is the man who built the synagogue for us." The synagogue in Capernaum stood (culminative aorist in ᾠκοδομήσεν) as a beautiful testimony of the Centurion's love for his Jewish friends.

The earnestness with which the elders urge the Centurion's request upon Jesus suggests that they felt inadequate in their own strength to repay him. They realized that he deserved it, but they knew of nothing within their power which would be appropriate. But they also recognized in Jesus a supernatural power which could rise to heights of which they were incapable. By making his own request by faith, the Centurion thus gave occasion for the Jewish elders to give expression to their faith.

Verse 6 - "Then Jesus went with them. And when he was now not far from the house, the centurion sent friends to him, saying unto him, Lord, trouble not thyself: for I am not worthy that thou shouldest enter under my roof."

ὁ δὲ Ἰησοῦς ἐπορεύετο σὺν αὐτοῖς; ἤδη δὲ αὐτοῦ οὐ μακρὰν ἀπέχοντος ἀπὸ τῆς οἰκίας ἔπεμψεν φίλους ὁ ἑκατοντάρχης λέγων αὐτῷ, Κύριε, μὴ σκύλλου, οὐ γὰρ ἱκανός εἰμι ἵνα ὑπὸ τὴν στέγην μου εἰσέλθῃς.

ὁ (nom.sing.masc.of the article in agreement with Ἰησοῦς) 9.
δὲ (inferential conjunction) 11.
Ἰησοῦς (nom.sing.masc.of Ἰησοῦς, subject of ἐπορεύετο) 3.

ἐπορεύετο (3d.per.sing.imp.ind.of πορεύομαι, inceptive) 170.
σὺν (preposition with the instrumental of association) 1542.
αὐτοῖς (instrumental plural masc.of αὐτός, association) 16.
ἤδη (temporal adverb) 291.
δὲ (adversative conjunction) 11.
αὐτοῦ (gen.sing.masc.of αὐτός, genitive absolute) 16.
οὐ (negative conjunction with the indicative) 130.
μακρὰν (an adverb of place) 768.
ἀπέχοντος (pres.act.part.gen.sing.masc.of ἀπέχω, genitive absolute) 563.
ἀπὸ (preposition with the ablative of separation) 70.
τῆς (abl.sing.fem.of the article in agreement with οἰκίας) 9.
οἰκίας (abl.sing.fem.of οἰκία, separation) 186.
ἔπεμψεν (3d.per.sing.aor.act.ind.of πέμπω, constative) 169.
φίλους (acc.pl.masc.of φίλος, direct object of ἔπεμψεν) 932.
ὁ (nom.sing.masc.of the article in agreement with ἑκατοντάρχης) 9.
ἑκατοντάρχης (nom.sing.masc.of ἑκατοντάρχης, subject of ἔπεμψεν) 717.
λέγων (pres.act.part.nom.sing.masc.of λέγω, adverbial, modal) 66.
αὐτῷ (dat.sing.masc.of αὐτός, indirect object of λέγων) 16.
Κύριε (voc.sing.masc.of κύριος, address) 97.
μὴ (negative conjunction with a prohibition) 87.
σκύλλου (2d.per.sing.pres.mid.impv.of σκύλλω, prohibition) 836.
οὐ (negative conjunction with the indicative) 130.
γὰρ (causal conjunction) 105.
ἱκανός (nom.sing.masc.of ἱκανός, predicate adjective) 304.
εἰμι (1st.per.sing.pres.ind.of εἰμί, aoristic) 86.
ἵνα (sub final conjunction introducing a purpose/result clause) 114.
ὑπὸ (preposition with the accusative of extent) 117.
τὴν (acc.sing.fem.of the article in agreement with στέγην) 9.
στέγην (acc.sing.fem.of στέγη, extent) 720.
μου (gen.sing.masc.of ἐγώ, possession) 123.
εἰσέλθῃς (2d.per.sing.aor.subj.of εἰσέρχομαι, purpose/result) 234.

Translation - "Therefore Jesus started with them. But as He approached the house, the centurion dispatched friends, saying to Him, 'Sir, trouble yourself no further, because I am not worthy that you should come under my roof.'"

Comment: δὲ is inferential, as Jesus responded readily to the urgent requests of the elders. He began to go with them (inceptive imperfect in ἐπορεύετο). The next δὲ is adversative. The centurion had other ideas. Note the temporal adverbial clause with ἤδη with its litotes in οὐ μακρὰν. The centurion had another thought about it. His first had been that Jesus could heal his sick servant, and, even though he was a Gentile, perhaps Jesus would come if the centurion sent the Jewish elders to negotiate. This act, in itself reveals humility and the faith which is never present without it. But the centurion now grasps a new concept, as he sees Jesus actually approaching his home. His own sense of unworthiness overwhelms him. Who is he to ask the Son of God to come to his home? What if Jesus should interpret the request of a military official of imperial Rome to visit him as a subpoena? Should a Roman soldier send for the Son of God?

The experience of this soldier is similar to that of Cornelius in Acts 10. Both men, before they were effectually called to repentance and faith by the Holy Spirit, made sincere efforts to live up to the light which they had as unregenerates. And God is always obligated to grant more light to those who use what they have with intellectual honesty. The centurion's philanthropy to the citizens of Capernaum when he built their synagogue is evidence that he was not the average Roman soldier. When he heard the rumors about Jesus he was in a psychological position, at least, to take the matter under advisement and not write it off in a prejudicial manner as another Jewish scheme to influence Rome, of which there was a spate. Hence, when his servant became ill, he knew what to do. And in doing it, he moved a little closer to the humility which he now manifests with his message to Jesus, Who is about to walk into his home.

Jesus of course showed no resentment at the centurion's request. Readily and with good cheer He accompanied the elders of the city. All of this deepened the centurion's humility and augmented his faith. He had no more elders to send, so now he sends his friends (φίλους), whether Jew or Gentile we are not told. Why did not the centurion himself go out to meet Jesus? After all the distance was οὐ μακράν. Verse 7 sheds light on this. Κύριε, though in this context is not "Lord" in the trinitarian sense, is at least a term of highest respect. Note the prohibition with σκύλλου in the present tense. "Do not continue to trouble yourself" or "Stop bothering yourself with it." The word order in the remainder of the centurion's message becomes important. "*Not worthy* am I that under *my* roof you should come." The tone implies the following: "Excuse me, Sir, for my presumption. I am out of line. You should not have to come under my roof."

Verse 7 - "Wherefore neither thought I myself worthy to come unto thee: but say in a word, and my servant shall be healed."

διὸ οὐδὲ ἐμαυτὸν ἠξίωσα πρὸς δὲ ἐλθεῖν; ἀλλὰ εἰπε λόγῳ, καὶ ἰαθήτω ὁ παῖς μου.

διὸ (conjunction introducing a result clause) 1622.

οὐδὲ (disjunctive) 452.

ἐμαυτὸν (acc.sing.masc.of ἐμαυτοῦ, direct object of ἠξίωσα) 723.

#2151 ἠξίωσα (1st.per.sing.aor.act.ind.of ἀξιόω, culminative).

county worthy - II Th.1:11; I Tim.5:17; Heb.3:3.
think worthy - Lk.7:7; Heb.10:29.
desire - Acts 28:22.
think good - Acts 15:38.

Meaning: Cf. #'s 285, 4064. ἀξιόω is the verb form of which #285 is the adjective and #4064 is the adverb. To consider the merits equal and hence worthy. The word always deals in some way with values. Paul prayed that the saints would be *worthy* of the rewards that will be granted at the Revelation - II Thess.1:11. The elders in the church who taught the Word will be worthy of extra financial remuneration - I Tim.5:17. Jesus is counted worthy of more glory than Moses - Heb.3:3. The centurion thought himself unworthy to approach Jesus - Lk.7:7. Sinners who reject the blood of Christ are worthy of sorer punishment than Jews under the law - Heb.10:29. In Acts 15:38 it is used of Paul's decision, after careful consideration, not to take Mark. The Jews in Rome desired to hear Paul's philosophy - Acts 28:22.

πρὸς (preposition with the accusative of extent) 197.
σὲ (acc.sing.masc.of σύ, extent) 104.
ἐλθεῖν (aor.inf.of ἔρχομαι, complementary) 146.
ἀλλὰ (alternative conjunction) 342.
εἰπὲ (2d.per.sing.aor.act.impv.of εἶπον, entreaty) 155.
λόγῳ (instru.sing.masc.of λόγος, means) 510.
καὶ (adjunctive conjunction joining verbs) 14.
ἰαθήτω (3d.per.sing.aor.pass.impv.of ἰάομαι, peremptory command) 721.
ὁ (nom.sing.masc.of the article in agreement with παῖς) 9.
παῖς (nom.sing.masc.of παῖς, subject of ἰαθήτω) 217.
μου (gen.sing.masc.of ἐγώ, relationship) 123.

Translation - "Therefore neither did I consider myself worthy to you **to come,** *but speak by a single word and my little boy will be healed."*

Comment: διὸ depends for its meaning on the last clause of verse 6. There he had said that he was not worthy to act as host. Since that is true, it follows that he was also unworthy to call upon Jesus. Hence he sent his Jewish friends, whom he supposed Jesus, the Jewish Messiah would find more acceptable. But now he adds that even that was unnecessary. Jesus needs only to speak a word of command and the healing will be accomplished by remote control. Note the growth in this man's humility and hence the growth in his faith. For the two - humility and growth in faith go together. And humility grows by a growing appreciation of Jesus' person and His worth, and hence, by comparison, our own worthlessness.

First, he is confronted with a problem which he cannot solve. His little servant is critically ill and the centurion is helpless. He hears that Jesus is coming. He believes in Jesus' healing power but he feels unworthy to ask for His services. So he appeals to the Jewish leaders for help, thus admitting that he believes that their influence with Jesus is greater than his own. This is strange philosophy for a Roman army officer in Galilee!

The Jewish elders comply with his request and succeed in persuading Jesus to come, whereupon the centurion thinks more deeply into the problem and sees (a) that Jesus does not need personally to come, only to speak and heal with a word, and (b) that he, being unworthy that Jesus should enter his home, is even unworthy to approach Jesus. So he sends his Jewish friends to ask Jesus only to speak and heal by a word (instrumental of means in λόγῳ). *Cf.*#2151 for other uses of ἀξιόω. εἰπὲ λόγῳ - "speak only once (aorist tense) by a single word (no article with λόγῳ)" Here the centurion confesses his faith in Jesus' great authority. Now, speaking of authority, a Roman army officer is talking about something that he knows about. Jesus has the same authority over illness (even at a distance) that the centurion has over his men in the Roman army (vs.8).

On the unusual ἰαθήτω, Metzger says, "The more peremptory tone of the imperative ἰαθήτω was softened by scribal assimilation to the Matthean ἰαθήσεται (Mt.8:8)." (*A Textual Commentary on the Greek New Testament*, 142). It was natural for the centurion to use an imperative here since he was thinking about giving orders and having them obeyed, not because the order came from him but because it came from Jesus!

Verse 8 - "For I also am a man set under authority, having under me soldiers, and I say unto one, Go, and he goeth; and to another, Come, and he cometh; and to my servant, Do this, and he doeth it."

καὶ γὰρ ἐγὼ ἄνθρωπος εἰμι ὑπὸ ἐξουσίαν τασσόμενος , ἔχων ὑπ' ἐμαυτὸν στρατιώτας, καὶ λέγω τούτῳ, Πορεύθητι καὶ πορεύεται, καὶ ἄλλῳ, Ἔρχου, καὶ ἔρχεται, καὶ τῷ δούλῳ μου, Ποίησον τοῦτο, καὶ ποιεῖ.

καὶ (adjunctive conjunction, joining pronouns) 14.

γὰρ (causal conjunction) 105.

ἐγὼ (nom.sing.masc.of ἐγώ, subject of εἰμί) 123.

ἄνθρωπος (nom.sing.masc.of ἄνθρωπος, predicate nominative) 341.

εἰμι (1st.per.sing.pres.ind.of εἰμί, aoristic) 86.

ὑπὸ (preposition with the accusative, metaphorical "under") 117.

ἐξουσίαν (acc.sing.fem.of ἐξουσία, metaphorical "under" with ἐπί) 707.

τασσόμενος (pres.pass.part.nom.sing.masc. adjectival, restrictive, in agreement with ἄνθρωπος) 722.

ἔχων (pres.act.part.nom.sing.masc.of ἔχω, adjectival, restrictive, in agreement with ἄνθρωπος) 82.

ὑπ' (preposition with the accusative, metaphorical "under") 117.

ἐμαυτὸν (acc.sing.masc.of ἐμαυτοῦ, reflexive pronoun) 723.

στρατιώτας (acc.pl.masc.of στρατιώτης, direct object of ἔχων) 724.

καὶ (inferential conjunction) 14.

λέγω (1st.per.sing.pres.act.ind.of λέγω, customary) 66.

τούτῳ (dat.sing.masc.of οὗτος, indirect object of λέγω) 93.

πορεύθητι (2d.per.sing.aor.impv.of πορεύομαι, command) 170.

καὶ (inferential conjunction) 14.

πορεύεται (3d.per.sing.pres.mid.ind.of πορεύομαι, customary) 170.

καὶ (continuative conjunction) 14.

ἄλλῳ (dat.sing.masc.of ἄλλος, indirect object of λέγω) 198.
Ἔρχου (2d.per.sing.pres.impv.of ἔρχομαι, command) 146.
καὶ (inferential conjunction) 14.
ἔρχεται (3d.per.sing.pres.ind.of ἔρχομαι, customary) 146.
καὶ (continuative conjunction) 14.
τῷ (dat.sing.masc.of the article in agreement with δούλῳ) 9.
δούλῳ (dat.sing.masc.of δοῦλος, indirect object of λέγω) 725.
μου (gen.sing.masc.of ἐγώ, relationship) 123.
ποίησον (2d.per.sing.aor.act.impv.of ποιέω, command) 127.
τοῦτο (acc.sing.neut.of οὗτος, direct object of ποίησον) 93.
καὶ (inferential conjunction) 14.
ποιεῖ (3d.per.sing.pres.act.ind.of ποιέω, customary) 127.

Translation - "Because I also am a man to whom is delegated authority who has under my command soldiers. Therefore I say to this one, 'Go' and he goes; and to another I say, 'Come'. And he comes. And to my servant I say, 'Do this.' And he does it."

Comment: Note the interesting ways in which καὶ fits into this context, either as adjunctive, inferential or continuative. Jesus is not the only One to Whom authority has been given. The centurion also (adjunctive καὶ) has some authority. The adjectival participles τασσόμενος and ἔχων describe him in a restrictive way. He is the only one to whom authority is delegated and the only one with soldiers in his command who are subject to his commands. The centurion understands the chain of command. Our Lord is at the top, able even to command sickness to disappear. The centurion recognizes Caesar as his superior, for Caesar appointed him. But Jesus is superior to Caesar - else why did not the centurion appeal to Caesar for the healing needed? Under Caesar's appointment, however, even the centurion has authority over the soldiers who serve under him. He needs but to speak and they go or come or do whatever he orders. Since this is proper, should not Jesus employ the superior authority which He has by virtue of His superior position and accomplish the healing the easy way - by speaking a word of command? This would obviate the necessity for Jesus' visit. How much authority does Jesus have? (Mt.28:18). The choppy sentence gives us a picture of the discipline the centurion had over his command. "Go! Come! Do this!" No back talk! His word was law within the sphere of his authority. Much more, then, the word of Jesus. Jesus also had an army at His command. *Cf.* Lk.2:13; Mt.26:53.

Augustine well said that when the centurion said, "I am not worthy" he made it possible for Jesus to come, not only within his walls, but within his heart.

Verse 9 - "When Jesus heard these things, he marvelled at him, and turned him about, and said unto the people that followed him, I say unto you, I have not found so great faith, no, not in Israel."

ἀκούσας δὲ ταῦτα ὁ Ἰησοῦς ἐθαύμασεν αὐτόν, καὶ στραφεὶς τῷ ἀκολουθοῦντι αὐτῷ ὄχλῳ εἶπεν, Λέγω ὑμῖν, οὐδὲ ἐν τῷ Ἰσραὴλ τοσαύτην πίστιν εἶρον.

ἀκούσας (aor.act.part.nom.sing.masc.of ἀκούω, adverbial, temporal) 148.

δὲ (explantory conjunction) 11.

ταῦτα (acc.pl.neut.of οὗτος, direct object of ἀκούσας) 93.

ὁ (nom.sing.masc.of the article in agreement with Ἰησοῦς) 9.

Ἰησοῦς (nom.sing.masc.of Ἰησοῦς, subject of ἐθαύμασεν and εἶπεν) 3.

ἐθαύμασεν (3d.per.sing.aor.act.ind.of θαυμάζω, ingressive) 726.

αὐτόν (acc.sing.masc.of αὐτός, after an intransitive verb) 16.

καὶ (adjunctive conjunction joining verbs) 14.

στραφεὶς (2d.aor.pass.part.nom.sing.masc.of στρέφω, adverbial, temporal)
530.

τῷ (dat.sing.masc.of the article in agreement with ὄχλῳ) 9.

ἀκολουθοῦντι (pres.act.part.dat.sing.masc.of ἀκολουθέω, adjectival,
ascriptive, in agreement with ὄχλῳ) 394.

αὐτῷ (dat.sing.masc.of αὐτός, personal interest) 16.

ὄχλῳ (dat.sing.masc.of ὄχλος, indirect object of εἶπεν) 418.

εἶπεν (3d.per.sing.aor.act.ind.of εἶπον, constative) 155.

Λέγω (1st.per.sing.pres.act.ind.of λέγω, aoristic) 66.

ὑμῖν (dat.pl.masc.of σύ, indirect object of λέγω) 104.

οὐδὲ (disjunctive) 452.

ἐν (preposition with the locative of sphere) 80.

τῷ (loc.sing.masc.of the article in agreement with Ἰσραήλ) 9.

Ἰσραήλ (loc.sing.masc.of Ἰσραήλ, sphere) 165.

τοσαύτην (acc.sing.fem.of τοσοῦτος, in agreement with πίστιν) 727.

πίστιν (acc.sing.fem.of πίστις, direct object of εὖρον) 728.

εὖρον (1st.per.sing.2d.aor.act.ind.of εὑρίσκω, culminative) 79.

*Translation - "Now when Jesus heard these things He began to marvel at him,
and when He had turned around He said to the crowd following Him, 'I tell you,
not even in Israel have I found such faith.' "*

Comment: The accusative αὐτόν following ἐθαύμασεν need not disturb us. Just
as it is true that not all transitive verbs have the accusative, it is also true that
there is a list of verbs that are not always transitive, but sometimes have the
accusative. (Robertson, *Grammar,* 472.) Θαυμάζω has the accusative in Lu.7:9;
Acts 7:31 and Jude 16. (*Ibid,*474). Jesus admired the centurion's faith, yet it was
Jesus Himself Who inspired and elicited it. Note the ascriptive adjectival
participle in the attributive position, modifying ὄχλῳ. *Cf.*Mt.8:10,11 for further
comment.

*Verse 10 - "And they that were sent, returning to the house, found the servant
whole that had been sick."*

καὶ ὑποστρέψαντες εἰς τὸν οἶκον οἱ πεμφθέντες εὖρον τὸν δοῦλον
ὑγιαίνοντα.

καὶ (continuative conjunction) 14.

ὑποστρέψαντες (aor.act.part.nom.pl.masc.of ὑποστρέφω, adverbial, temporal) 1838.

εἰς (preposition with the accusative of extent) 140.

τὸν (acc.sing.masc.of the article in agreement with οἶκον) 9.

οἶκον (acc.sing.masc.of οἶκος, extent) 784.

οἱ (nom.pl.masc.of the article in agreement with πεμφθέντες) 9.

πεμφθέντες (aor.pass.part.nom.pl.masc.of πέμπω, substantival, subject of εἷρον) 169.

εὗρον (3d.per.pl.aor.act.ind.of εὑρίσκω, constative) 79.

τὸν (acc.sing.masc.of the article in agreement with δοῦλον) 9.

δοῦλον (acc.sing.masc.of δοῦλος, direct object of εὗρον) 725.

ὑγιαίνοντα (pres.part.acc.sing.masc.of ὑγιαίνω, adverbial, circumstantial) 2088.

Translation - *"And when they had returned to the house, those who had been sent found the servant in good health."*

Comment: We do not know which delegation - possibly both - the elders and the centurion's friends. It is not likely that anyone involved would have failed to return in order to see the outcome of it all. The servant, formerly near death, was now in the best of health, as noted in the present participle ὑγιαίνοντα - "continuing in a state of good health." *Cf*.#2088 for Paul's use of the word with reference to sound doctrine, - something that is more important even than a sound body. *Cf*. Mt.8:12 which adds the information that the servant recovered at the same time that Jesus ordered that it should be so.

The next section (Lk.7:11-17) records an incident not found in the other Synoptic gospels nor in John.

(B) A Widow's Son Raised From the Dead

(Lk.7:11-17)

Lk.7:11 - *"And it came to pass the day after, that he went into a city called Nain; and many of his disciples went with him and much people."*

Καὶ ἐγένετο ἐν τῷ ἑξῆς ἐπορεύθη εἰς πόλιν καλουμένην Ναΐν, καὶ συνεπορεύοντο αὐτῷ οἱ μαθηταὶ αὐτοῦ καὶ ὄχλος πολύς.

Καὶ (continuative conjunction) 14.

ἐγένετο (3d.per.sing.aor.ind.of γίνομαι, constative) 113.

ἐν (preposition with the locative of time point) 80.

τῷ (loc.sing.masc.of the article, time point) 9.

#2152 ἑξῆς (adverb of succession).

next - Acts 27:18; Lk.9:37.

the morrow - Acts 25:17.
the day after - Lk.7:11.
the day following - Acts 21:1.

Meaning: An adverb. The next in succession; the immediately following item. Used in the New Testament to denote the next day, but never with ἡμέρᾳ except in Lk.9:37. With τῇ in Acts 27:18; 25:17; 21:1, as it ought in order to conform with ἡμέρᾳ (understood) in gender. With τῷ in Lk.7;11, although we have τῇ here also in the margin. *Cf.* Metzger's comment *infra.*

ἐπορεύθη (3d.per.sing.aor.mid.ind.of πορεύομαι, ingressive) 170
εἰς (preposition with the accusative of extent) 140.
πόλιν (acc.sing.fem.of πόλις, extent) 243.
καλουμένην (pres.pass.part.acc.sing.fem.of καλέω, adjectival, restrictive, in agreement with Ναΐν) 107.

#2153 Ναΐν (acc.sing.fem.of Ναΐν, extent).

Nain - Lk.7:11.

Meaning: A city about 25 miles southwest of Capernaum. 10 miles west of the Jordan River.South of the southern end of the Sea of Galilee - Lk.7:11.

καὶ (continuative conjunction) 14.

#2154 συνεπορεύοντο (3d.per.pl.imp.ind.of συμπορεύομαι).

go with - Lk.7:11; 14:25; 24:15.
resort - Mk.10:1.

Meaning: A combination of σύν (1542) and πορεύομαι (#170). Hence, to go along with; to accompany. With reference to the people following Jesus in His journeys - Lk.7:11; 14:25; Mk.10:1. Of Jesus who went with the Emmaus travellers in Lk.24:15.

αὐτῷ (instru.sing.masc.of αὐτός, association) 16.
οἱ (nom.pl.masc.of the article in agreement with μαθηταὶ) 9.
μαθηταὶ (nom.pl.masc.of μαθητής, subject of συνεπορεύοντο) 421.
αὐτοῦ (gen.sing.masc.of αὐτός, possession) 16.
καὶ (adjunctive conjunction joining nouns) 14.
ὄχλος (nom.sing.masc.of ὄχλος, subject of συνεπορεύοντο) 418.
πολύς (nom.sing.masc.of πολύς, in agreement with ὄχλος) 228.

Translation - "*Not long after He happened to begin His journey unto a city called Nain, and His disciples and a large crowd went along with Him.*"

Comment: Some textual authorities have ἐν τῇ ἑξῆς, though the United Bible Socieities committee prefers ἐν τῷ ἑξῆς. Metzger says, "With ἐν τῇ ἑξῆς the reader is to supply ἡμέρᾳ ("on the next day"); with ἐν τῷ ἑξῆς one supplies χρόνῳ (" soon afterward"). Elsewhere, however, when Luke writes τῇ ἑξῆς the does not prefix ἐν (Lk.9:37; Ac.21:1; 25:17; 27:18); on the other hand, when χρόνῳ is to be understood, Luke uses ἐν τῳς καθεξῆς (Lk.8:1). On the whole, it is more probable that the less definite expression of time would be altered to the more definite than vice versa. Likewise the external evidence supporting τῷ ἑξῆς is slightly better than that supporting τῇ ἑξῆς." (Metzger, *A Textual Commentary on the Greek New Testament*, 142).

From Capernaum to Nain is probably 25 miles. (*Cf.*Edersheim, *Life and Times of Jesus*, I, 552*ff*). Capernaum is on the north end of the Sea of Galilee, while Nain lies perhaps 10 miles southwest of the southern end of the Sea. The road into Nain goes through Endor. Nain is near Little Hermon.   Sepulchral caves line the path on both sides, into one of which, no doubt, the young man was about to be placed.

Verse 12 - "Now when he came nigh to the gate of the city, behold, there was a dead man carried out, the only son of his mother, and she was a widow: and much people of the city was with her."

ὡς δὲ ἤγγισεν τῇ πύλῃ τῆς πόλεως, καὶ ἰδοὺ ἐξεκομίζετο τεθνηκὼς μονογενὴς υἱὸς τῇ μητρὶ αὐτοῦ, καὶ αὐτὴ ἦν χήρα, καὶ ὄχλος τῆς τῆς πόλεως ἱκανὸς ἦν σὺν αὐτῇ.

ὡς (temporal conjunction, introducing a definite temporal clause) 128.

δὲ (continuative conjunction) 11.

ἤγγισεν (3d.per.sing.aor.act.ind.of ἐγγίζω, ingressive) 252.

τῇ (loc.sing.fem.of the article in agreement with πύλη) 9.

πύλη (loc.sing.fem.of πύλη, place where) 662.

τῆς (gen.sing.fem.of the article in agreement with πόλεως) 9.

πόλεως (gen.sing.fem.of πόλις, definition) 243.

καὶ (continuative conjunction) 14.

ἰδοὺ (exclamation) 95.

#2155 ἐξεκομίζετο (3d.per.sing.imp.pass.ind.of ἐκκομίζω, progressive description).

carry out - Lk.7:12.

Meaning: A combination of ἐκ (#19) and κομίζω (#1541). Hence, to carry out. With reference to the funeral procession at Nain - Lk.7:12.

τεθνηκὼς (perf.part.nom.sing.masc.of θνήσκω, adjectival, ascriptive, in agreement with υἱός) 232.

μονογενὴς (nom.sing.masc.of μονογενής, in agreement with υἱός) 1699.

υἱὸς (nom.sing.masc.of υἱός, subject of ἐξεκομίζετο) 5.

τῇ (dat.sing.fem.of the article in agreement with ματρὶ) 9.

μᾱτρὶ (dat.sing.fem.of μήτηρ, personal relation) 76.
αὐτοῦ (gen.sing.masc.of αὐτός, relationship) 16.
καὶ (emphatic conjunction) 14.
αὐτὴ (nom.sing.fem.of αὐτός, subject of ἦν) 16.
ἦν (3d.per.sing.imp.ind.of εἰμί, progressive duration) 86.
χήρα (nom.sing.fem.of χήρα, predicate nominative) 1910.
καὶ (continuative conjunction) 14.
ὄχλος (nom.sing.masc.of ὄχλος, subject of ἦν) 418.
τῆς (abl.sing.fem.of the article in agreement with πόλεως) 9.
πόλεως (abl.sing.fem.of πόλις, source) 243.
ἱκανὸς (nom.sing.masc.of ἱκανός, in agreement with ὄχλος) 304.
ἦν (3d.per.sing.imp.ind.of εἰμί, progressive description) 86.
σὺν (preposition with the instrumental of association) 1542.
αὐτῇ (instru.sing.fem.of αὐτός, association) 16.

Translation - "And as He approached the gate of the city, look! There was being carried out a dead man - the only son of His mother. In fact she was a widow; and a great crowd from the city was with her."

Comment: The καὶ here before ἰδοὺ seems unnecessary. As Jesus approached the gate of the city, on His way in, He met the funeral procession on the other side, on its way out. The son is described both by the perfect passive participle and by the adjective μονογενής. He was her only son and he was dead. Emphatic καὶ introduces addition information that she was in fact a widow. Finally Luke adds that a large number of citizens of Nain, possibly everyone in town (ἱκανός) was in company with her. It is a dramatic situation. Jesus, the Source of all life (John 1:4; 11:25; Acts 3:15) walks into a situation that has bred nothing but despair. A poverty stricken widow is about to bury her only son, the sole source of her support.

Verse 13 - "And when the Lord saw her, he had compassion on her, and said unto her, Weep not."

καὶ ἰδὼν αὐτὴν ὁ κύριος ἐσπλαγχνίσθη ἐπ᾽ αὐτῇ καὶ εἶπεν αὐτῇ, Μὴ κλαῖε.

καὶ (continuative conjunction) 14.
ἰδὼν (aor.act.part.of ὁράω, adverbial, temporal) 144.
αὐτὴν (acc.sing.fem.of αὐτός, direct object of ἰδὼν) 16.
ὁ (nom.sing.masc.of the article in agreement with κύριος) 9.
κύριος (nom.sing.masc.of κύριος, subject of ἐσπλαγχνίσθη and εἶπεν) 97.
ἐσπλαγχνίσθη (3d.per.sing.aor.pass.ind.of σπλαγχνίζομαι, ingressive) 835.
ἐπ᾽ (preposition with the locative with a verb of emotion) 47.
αὐτῇ (loc.sing.fem.of αὐτός, with a verb of emotion) 16.
καὶ (adjunctive conjunction joining verbs) 14.
εἶπεν (3d.per.sing.aor.act.ind.of εἶπον, constative) 155.
αὐτῇ (dat.sing.fem.of αὐτός, indirect object of εἶπεν) 16.

Μή (negative conjunction with the imperative in a prohibition) 87.
κλαῖε (2d.per.sing.pres.act.impv.of κλαίω, prohibition) 225.

Translation - "And when He saw her the Lord was moved with pity for her and said to her, 'Stop weeping.' "

Comment: Note the ingressive aorist in ἐσπλαγχνίσθη, as in the translation. "Jesus was seized with pity." We have a similar construction in John 11:35 - "Jesus burst into tears." The careless translator who neglects to fit the tense with its various possible uses into the context misses these points and thus cheapens the production. The constative aorist is colorless; the culminative aorist does not fit the context. The ingressive aorist, with its emphasis upon the onset of the action is the best.

Jesus saw the situation (ἰδών), analyzed it and immediately reacted with sorrow for the poor mother, as we would expect the Son of Man to do. Cf.#835 for various ways the verb fits into a sentence. Here it is followed by ἐπί and the locative. Cf.#47 for other examples.

Note also that the prohibition is in the present tense, not the aorist. Thus "Do not weep" or "Weep not" is incorrect. The present tense demands the translation "Do not go on weeping" or "Do not continue to weep" or "Stop weeping." If Luke had written it aorist it would have implied that the widowed mother, on the way to the cemetery with her only son, was not weeping! Of course she was weeping and it would seem cruel for Jesus to command her to cease, had He not been able to raise her son from the dead. He, who only a short time before had dried the tears of worry for a Roman soldier, now dries the tears of grief for a Jewish peasant widow. Bengel says, "The consolation before the deed shows the power of certainly working the future deed." (Meyer, Gospel of Mark and Luke, 346). Indeed, how presumptuous for a mere mortal, with no power to raise the dead, to tell a weeping mother not to cry! The woman may have resented Jesus' curt order to stop weeping. Her resentment quickly faded and turned to joy when He proved that He alone had the power to turn a tragic moment into one of rapturous joy.

Verse 14 - "And he came and touched the bier: and they that bare him stood still. And he said, Young man, I say unto thee, Arise."

καὶ προσελθὼν ἥψατο τῆς σοροῦ, οἱ δὲ βαστάζοντες ἔστησαν, καὶ εἶπεν Νεανίσκε, σοὶ λέγω, ἐγέρθητι.

καὶ (continuative conjunction) 14.
προσελθών (aor.part.nom.sing.masc.of προσέρχομαι, adverbial, temporal) 336.
ἥψατο (3d.per.sing.aor.mid.ind.of ἅπτω, constative) 711.
τῆς (gen.sing.fem.of the article in agreement with σοροῦ) 9.

#2156 σοροῦ (gen.sing.fem.of σορός, objective genitive).

bier - Lk.7:14.

Meaning: Thayer, "An urn or receptacle for keeping the bones of the dead (Hom. *Il.*,23,91). A coffin (Gen.50:26). . . . The funeral couch or bier on which the Jews carried their dead forth to burial." Edersheim says it was a wicker basket. *Cf.* Edersheim, *Life and Times of Jesus The Messiah*, I, 555*ff* for an excellent description of this entire scene. Lk.7:14.

οἱ (nom.pl.masc.of the article in agreement with βαστάζοντες) 9.

δὲ (inferential conjunction) 11.

βαστάζοντες (pres.act.part.nom.pl.masc.of βαστάζω, substantival, subject of ἔστησαν) 306.

ἔστησαν (3d.per.pl.aor.act.ind.of ἵστημι, constative) 180.

καὶ (continuative conjunction) 14.

εἶπεν (3d.per.sing.aor.act.ind.of εἶπον, constative) 155.

Νεανίσκε (voc.sing.masc.of νεανίσκος, address) 1300.

σοὶ (dat.sing.masc.of σύ, indirect object of λέγω) 104.

λέγω (1st.per.sing.pres.act.ind.of λέγω, aoristic) 66.

ἐγέρθητι (2d.per.sing.aor.pass.impv.of ἐγείρω, command) 125.

Translation - "And when He had come forward He touched the coffin; therefore the pallbearers stood still and He said, 'Young man, I am commanding you to stand up.'"

Comment: Jesus of course, walked toward the bier before He touched it. This is obvious, but we point it out for the benefit of the Greek beginner, in order to show that the action of the aorist participle προσελθών, since it is aorist, is antecedent to (comes before) the action of the main verb, which is ἥψατο. Jesus' action caused the pallbearers to stop. Hence δὲ is inferential. Something about the bearing of this stranger fascinated them. Jesus ignored them and spoke directly to the corpse.

We do not know the precise age of the dead man, but study #1300 for others in this category. He was between 22 and 28 years old. Note the emphatic position of σοὶ, as it outranks the verb λέγω. Literally "be raised up," or as we have taken the liberty to say, "Stand up." "Wake up" (Goodspeed) is wrong, since it implies that the young man was not dead - only asleep, perhaps in a deep coma. One cannot read resurrection into ἐγέρθητι either; hence "Stand up" *could* also imply that he was not dead, were it not for verse 12, coupled with the actions of the people of Nain, who were about to bury him. Williams' translation "Arise" is better. I translated it "Stand up" since one cannot imagine that the young man remained prone when he became alive!! #125 is used most often in the New Testament in connection with resurrection from the dead, but this is due to the context, not to the meaning of the word itself.

Three such resurrections are recorded though Jesus may have performed others. Jairus' daughter (Mt.9:18-26); the young man of Nain (Lk.7:11-17) and Lazarus (John 11:1-46). Note that only Matthew and John record the story of Jairus' daughter; Luke only tells us the Nain story and John alone relates the Lazarus account. Mark records none of these.

It is worth noting that these three recorded instances illustrate three stages of physical decomposition. Jairus' daughter had only just died. There was no onset of rigor mortis. The young man in our story had been dead long enough for funeral arrangements to have been made and partially carried out. Lazarus had been dead for four days and decomposition had indeed set in! Infidels may doubt that the girl was dead - only asleep or perhaps in a deep coma, and that Jesus recognized the fact and used His power only to resuscitate. There can be little doubt that the young man of Nain and Lazarus were dead, or at least everyone thought they were! There was olfactory evidence available to prove the point (John 11:39). To our Lord, the condition of the dead body makes no difference.

The author remembers the suggestion of a professor in a Greek class that physical resurrection of the body would be impossible in the case of a Christian sailor, long since buried at sea and subsequently subject to the decomposing impact of the gastric juices of a whale which swallowed him! He reinforced his point by adding that the whale also died and his body, utterly decomposed by the sea water, then sank to the bottom of the ocean floor as sediment or was circulated throughout the waters of the seven seas by ocean currents!! How then, the professor demanded, could God raise *that* body from the dead?

A student in the class then offered another case which he considerd even more disastrous for one like me, who believes in the resurrection of the body. He said that he was born and reared in Gary, Indiana and that a man, walking across a catwalk above a huge bucket of white-hot molten steel, lost his footing and fell into it. The body immediately was lost in the solution. He added that the steel company gave the steel Christian burial since it contained in solution the poor man's body.

Both the professor and the young man from Gary demanded of me how God could raise from the dead the bodies of the sailor and/or the steel worker; to which I replied, "I don't know." But I reminded them that we are not dealing with some human chemist, but with the incarnate Son of God who created human bodies in the beginning and would thus not find it difficult to create again in such extreme cases, as they described.

As a matter of fact the decomposition of all dead bodies is complete after burial, if enough time is allowed. Arguments such as these miss the point. The point is that resurrection from the dead is a miracle and that only the God of Creation and Preservation can perform miracles. To the pre-suppositional apologist, who accepts *a priori* the fact of God and revelation, there is no problem. It altogether depends upon the point at which one begins to build his system.

Verse 15 - "And he that was dead sat up, and began to speak. And he delivered him to his mother."

καὶ ἀνεκάθισεν ὁ νεκρὸς καὶ ἤρξατο λαλεῖν, καὶ ἔδωκεν αὐτὸν τῇ μητρὶ αὐτοῦ.

καὶ (inferential conjunction) 14.

#2157 ἀνεκάθισεν (3d.per.sing.aor.act.ind.of ἀνακαθίζω, constative).

sit up - Lk.7:15; Acts 9:40.

Meaning: A combination of ἀνά (#1059) and καθίζω (#420). Hence, to sit up. To raise oneself up. To sit erect. With reference to the son of the widow of Nain - Lk.7:15. Of the girl whom Peter raised from death - Acts 9:40.

ὁ (nom.sing.masc.of the article in agreement with νεκρὸς) 9.
νεκρὸς (nom.sing.masc.of νεκρός, subject of ἀνεκάθισεν and ἤρξατο) 749.
καὶ (adjunctive conjunction joining verbs) 14.
ἤρξατο (3d.per.sing.aor.mid.ind.of ἄρχω, ingressive) 383.
λαλεῖν (complementary infinitive) 815.
καὶ (continuative conjunction) 14.
ἔδωκεν (3d.per.sing.aor.act.ind.of δίδωμι, constative) 362.
αὐτὸν (acc.sing.masc.of αὐτός, direct object of ἔδωκεν) 16.
τῇ (dat.sing.fem.of the article in agreement with μητρὶ) 9.
μητρὶ (dat.sing.fem.of μήτηρ, indirect object of ἔδωκεν) 76.
αὐτοῦ (gen.sing.masc.of αὐτός, relationship) 16.

Translation - "Therefore he sat up and began to speak, and He gave him to his mother."

Comment: We may imagine the action in ἔδωκεν. Jesus perhaps took the young man by the hand, as he sat up and assisting him to stand up, He led him into the arms of the astounded and joyous mother. When the dead are raised by the power of God, they are certain to speak. It would be impossible to remain silent about such an experience. The daughter of Jairus (Lk.8:55) probably asked for something to eat - an evidence that the little girl was in good health. One often wonders when we note the sealed lips of the saints, when it comes to witnessing for Christ, if they have ever truly been raised from the dead.

There was no doubt about the young man as we see the reaction of the people to the miracle in

Verse 16 - "And there came a fear on all: and they glorified God, saying, That a great prophet is risen up among us; and, That God hath visited his people."

ἔλαβεν δὲ φόβος πάντας, καὶ ἐδόξαζον τὸν θεὸν λέγοντες ὅτι Προφήτης μέγας ἠγέρθη ἐν ἡμῖν, καὶ ὅτι Ἐπεσκέψατο ὁ θεὸς τὸν λαὸν αὐτοῦ.

ἔλαβεν (3d.per.sing.aor.act.ind.of λαμβάνω, ingressive) 533.
δὲ (inferential conjunction) 11.

φόβος (nom.sing.masc.of φόβος, subject of ἔλαβεν) 1131.
πάντας (acc.pl.masc.of πᾶς, direct object of ἔλαβεν) 67.
καὶ (continuative conjunction) 14.
ἐδόξαζον (3d.per.pl.imp.act.ind.of δοξάζω, inceptive) 461.
τὸν (acc.sing.masc.of the article in agreement with θεὸν) 9.
θεὸν (acc.sing.masc.of θεός, direct object of ἐδόξαζον) 124.
λέγοντες (pres.act.part.nom.pl.masc.of λέγω, adverbial, modal) 66.
ὅτι (recitative, introducing direct discourse) 211.
Προφήτης (nom.sing.masc.of προφήτης, subject of ἠγέρθη) 119.
μέγας (nom.sing.masc.of μέγας, in agreement with προφήτης) 184.
ἐν (preposition with the locative of place with plural nouns and/or pronouns) 80.
ἡμῖν (loc.pl.masc.of ἐγώ, place where) 123.
καὶ (adjunctive conjunction, joining clauses in direct discourse) 14.
ὅτι (recitative, introducing direct discourse) 211.
Ἐπεσκέψατο (3d.per.sing.aor.mid.ind.of ἐπισκέπτομαι, ingressive) 1549.
ὁ (nom.sing.masc.of the article in agreement with θεὸς) 9.
θεὸς (nom.sing.masc.of θεός, subject of ἐπεσκέψατο) 124.
τὸν (acc.sing.masc.of the article in agreement with λαὸν) 9.
λαὸν (acc.sing.masc.of λαός, direct object of ἐπεσκέψατο) 110.
αὐτοῦ (gen.sing.masc.of αὐτός, relationship) 16.

Translation - *"Therefore fear began to seize all and therefore they began to glorify God, saying, 'A great prophet has been raised up among us,' and 'God has begun to look upon His people.'"*

Comment: φόβος here in the sense, not of terror, but of great awe in the presence of the supernatural. *Cf*.#1131. Fear began (ingressive aorist in ἔλαβεν) to seize them all. The student should try to imagine how he would have felt if he had been there. They began (inceptive imperfect in ἐδόξαζον) to give glory to God. The inceptive idea suggests a sudden burst of expressions of praise to God which continued for some time. Luke uses direct discourse to suggest what the people were saying. Note ἐν with the locative plural of the first personal pronoun ἡμῖν, which means, not within any one person, but "in the midst of all of them" and compare with Lk.17:21 where we have in this much misunderstood passage ἐντὸς ὑμῶν ἐστιν - which means "in your midst", *i.e.* as a group, not "within each of you." This is clear from the plural forms of the pronouns.

"God has begun to look in upon His people." This is the cry of those who had perhaps begun to believe that God had forgotten them. *Cf*.#1549 for other uses of this interesting word. It denotes a visit of inspection with a view to offering help. Moses visited his brethren in Egypt. Note especially Heb.2:6.

Verse 17 - *"And this rumour of him went forth throughout all Judea, and throughout all the region round about."*

καὶ ἐξῆλθεν ὁ λόγος οὗτος ἐν ὅλῃ τῇ Ἰουδαίᾳ περὶ αὐτοῦ καὶ πάσῃ τῇ περιχώρῳ.

καὶ (continuative conjunction) 14.
ἐξῆλθεν (3d.per.sing.aor.ind.of ἐξέρχομαι, ingressive) 161.
ὁ (nom.sing.masc.of the article in agreement with λόγος) 9.
λόγος (nom.sing.masc.of λόγος, subject of ἐξῆλθεν) 510.
οὗτος (nom.sing.masc.of οὗτος, in agreement with λόγος) 93.
ἐν (preposition with the locative of place where) 80.
ὅλῃ (loc.sing.fem.of ὅλος, in agreement with Ἰουδαίᾳ) 112.
τῇ (loc.sing.fem.of the article in agreement with Ἰουδαίᾳ) 9.
Ἰουδαίᾳ (loc.sing.fem.of Ἰουδαῖος, place where) 134.
περὶ (preposition with the genitive of reference) 173.
αὐτοῦ (gen.sing.masc.of αὐτός, reference) 16.
καὶ (adjunctive conjunction joining phrases) 14.
πάσῃ (loc.sing.fem.of πᾶς, in agreement with περιχώρῳ) 67.
τῇ (loc.sing.fem.of the article in agreement with περιχώρῳ) 9.
περιχώρῳ (loc.sing.fem.of περίχωρος, place where) 271.

Translation - *"And this rumour spread throughout the entire provice of Judea about Him, and throughout all the surrounding territory."*

Comment: What was said by the citizens of Nain about Jesus, as reported in verse 16, became a topic of conversation in all Judea and surrounding territory. A great Prophet had arisen. God was beginning to pay some attention to His covenant people. The province of Judea would include Jerusalem and environs. Hence we know that the Jewish Establishment heard about this notable miracle in the little Galilean village up north and were apprehensive about what impact this Nazarene carpenter's ministry would have upon their own hold upon society. The common people had nothing to lose and everything to gain by endorsing Jesus. He healed their sick, fed their hungry and preached His gospel to them. And He did not challenge their position in society since they had no position which could be exploited. *Contra* the Establishment.

(C). The Baptist's Inquiry and Jesus' Response

(Mt.11:2-19; Lk.7:18-35)

Luke 7:18 - "And the disciples of John shewed him of all these things."

Καὶ ἀπήγγειλαν Ἰωάννῃ οἱ μαθηταὶ αὐτοῦ περὶ πάντων τούτων. καὶ προσκαλεσάμενος δύο τινὰς τῶν μαθητῶν αὐτοῦ ὁ Ἰωάννης

(Note: The KJV includes only the first clause of verse 18. The Greek text includes in verse 18 the first participial clause, which follows in verse 19 of the KJV. We have followed the Greek arrangement while dividing the English text in keeping with the KJV.)

Καὶ (explanatory conjunction) 11.

ἀπήγγειλαν (3d.per.pl.aor.act.ind.of ἀπαγγέλλω, constative) 176.

Ἰωάννῃ (dat.sing.masc.of Ἰωάννης, indirect object of ἀπήγγειλαν) 247.

οἱ (nom.pl.masc.of the article in agreement with μαθηταὶ) 9.

μαθηταὶ (nom.pl.masc.of μαθητής, subject of ἀπήγγειλαν) 421.

αὐτοῦ (gen.sing.masc.of αὐτός, relationship) 16.

περὶ (preposition with the genitive of reference) 173.

πάντων (gen.pl.neut.of πᾶς, in agreement with τούτων) 67.

τούτων (gen.pl.neut.of οὗτος, reference) 93.

καὶ (inferential conjunction) 14.

προσκαλεσάμενος (aor.mid.part.nom.sing.masc.of προσκαλέω, adverbial, temporal) 842.

δύο (indeclinable numeral, object of προσκαλεσάμενος) 385.

τινὰς (acc.pl.masc.of τίς, direct object of προσκαλεσάμενος) 486.

μαθητῶν (gen.pl.masc.of μαυητής, partitive genitive) 421.

αὐτοῦ (gen.sing.masc.of αὐτός, relationship) 16.

ὁ (nom.sing.masc.of the article in agreement with Ἰωάννης) 9.

Ἰωάννης (nom.sing.masc.of Ἰωάννης, subject of ἔπεμψεν) 247.

Translation - "Now the disciples of John told him about all of these things and when he had called two of them . . . "

Comment:The verb ἀπήγγειλαν is emphasized. As the rumors spread throughout the country from Nain the disciples of John the Baptist found their leader, now imprisoned and soon to be beheaded, and reported it all to him. These were men who had been immersed by John and who had followed him about and listened to his message. From them John heard the account of Jesus' miracle at Nain and perhaps of our Lord's healing ministry in Capernaum.

John came with a clear understanding of his mission. He was not the Messiah, although some of his disciples may have thought he was. He had expressly denied that he was either the Messiah or Elijah or the promised Prophet of Deut.18:15 (John 1:19-28). He added to this denial of his own role as Messiah, the testimony that Jesus was the Lamb of God who would take away the sin of the world.This testimony came "the next day" (John 1:29) after John had baptized Jesus and was based upon what John saw when Jesus came out of the water the day before (Mt.3:16,17). John had gone on to predict his own decline in authority (John 3:22-30), and to add that the Body of Christ would increase until at the end of the age the elect would all have been called to salvation.

A little later John was imprisoned, but his disciples were allowed to remain free and to visit him in the prison. Now after hearing of Jesus' exploits he seeks reassurance of something that he ought already to know for certain - that Jesus was the Messiah of Israel.

Verse 19 - "And John calling unto him two of his disciples sent them to Jesus, saying, Art thou he that should come? Or look we for another?"

ἔπεμφεν πρὸς τὸν κύριον λέγων, Σὺ εἶ ὁ ἐρχόμενος ἢ ἄλλον προσδοκῶμεν;

ἔπεμφεν (3d.per.sing. aor.act.ind.of πέμπω, constative) 169.

πρὸς (preposition with the accusative of extent) 197.

τὸν (acc.sing.masc.of the article in agreement with κύριον) 9.

κύριον (acc.sing.masc.of κύριος, extent) 97.

λέγων (pres.act.part.nom.sing.masc.of λέγω, adverbial, modal) 66.

Σὺ (nom.sing.masc.of σύ, predicate nominative) 104.

εἶ (2d.per.sing.pres.ind.of εἰμί, aoristic) 86.

ὁ (nom.sing.masc.of the article in agreement with ἐρχόμενος) 9.

ἐρχόμενος (pres.part.nom.sing.masc.of ἔρχομαι, substantival, subject of εἶ) 146.

ἢ (disjunctive) 465.

ἕτερον (acc.sing.masc.of ἕτερος, direct object of προσδοκῶμεν) 605.

προσδοκῶμεν (1st.per.pl.pres.act.ind.of προσδοκάω,progressive) 906.

Translation - "*. . . he sent to the Lord saying, 'You are the One Who is to come are you not, or should we continue to look for another?'*"

Comment: As soon as John the Baptist received the news about Jesus from some of his disciples he called two others. This is clear from δύο τινὰς - "a certain two", *i.e.* two, specifically selected from the ranks of John's followers who could be trusted on an important mission. *Cf.*#486 for examples of τίς untranslated in the AV. The participle λέγων introduces the direct question which expects an affirmative reply. Note that the predicate nominative Σὺ is emphasized ahead of the copulative verb εἶ. "You, Sir, you are the coming One are you not?" ἐρχόμενος is the participial substantive, the subject of the verb.

In view of the fact that John the Baptist already had the evidence that Jesus was the real Messiah (John 1:29-34), the question arises as to why he should have sought for further assurance? For the answer, *cf.* the parallel passage in Mt.11:2-19. Before we condemn the Baptist too much for his lack of faith and need for reassurance, let us remember that he had been in prison for a long time (Mt.4:12). If Jesus is truly the Messiah, then John's role as a prisoner makes sense (John 3:30). Review John 3:25-36.

But John was charged with a commission to preach until Messiah came upon the scene. As if to strengthen his faith, Jesus points to His miracles just as the Father had pointed John to the abiding Holy Spirit at Jesus' immersion. Many of the early church expositors thought that John did not ask this question for his own sake, but rather to strengthen the faith of his disciples. This seems to me to

be a farfetched view. There can be no doubt that John *should have known better* than to ask the question, but faith may falter, especially if one is incarcerated and perhaps tortured in a prison. John's faith needed a tonic.

Verse 20 - "When the men were come unto him, they said, John Baptist hath sent us unto thee saying, Art thou he that should come? Or look we for another?"

παραγενόμενοι δὲ πρὸς αὐτὸν οἱ ἄνδρες εἶπαν, Ἰωάννης ὁ βαπτιστὴς ἀπέστειλεν ὑμᾶς πρὸς σὲ λέγων, Σὺ εἶ ὁ ἐρχόμενος ἢ ἄλλον προσδοκῶμεν;

παραγενόμενοι (aor.part.nom.pl.masc.of παραγίνομαι, adverbial, temporal) 139.
δὲ (inferential conjunction) 11.
πρὸς (preposition with the accusative of extent) 197.
αὐτὸν (acc.sing.masc.of αὐτός, extent) 14.
οἱ (nom.pl.masc.of the article in agreement with ἄνδρες) 9.
ἄνδρες (nom.pl.masc.of ἀνήρ, subject of εἶπαν) 63.
εἶπαν (3d.per.pl.aor.act.ind.of εἶπον, constative) 155.
Ἰωάννης (nom.sing.masc.of Ἰωάννης, subject of ἀπέστειλεν) 247.
ὁ (nom.sing.masc.of the article in agreement with βαπτιστὴς) 9.
βαπτιστὴς (nom.sing.masc.of βαπτιστής, apposition) 248.
ἀπέστειλεν (3d.per.sing.aor.act.ind.of ἀποστέλλω, culminative) 215.
ἡμᾶς (acc.pl.masc.of ἐγώ, direct object of ἀπέστειλεν) 123.
πρὸς (preposition with the accusative of extent) 197.
Σὺ (nom.sing.masc.of σύ, predicate nominative) 104.
λέγων (pres.act.part.nom.sing.masc.of λέγω, adverbial, modal) 66.
Σὺ (nom.sing.masc.of σύ, subject of εἶ) 104.
εἶ (2d.per.sing.pres.ind.of εἰμί, aoristic) 86.
ὁ (nom.sing.masc.of the article in agreement with ἐρχόμενος) 9.
ἐρχόμενος (pres.act.part.nom.sing.masc.of ἔρχομαι, substantival, subject of εἶ) 146.
ἢ (disjunctive) 465.
ἄλλον (acc.sing.masc.of ἄλλος, direct object of προσδοκῶμεν) 198.
προσδοκῶμεν (1st.per.pl.pres.act.ind.of προσδοκάω, futuristic) 906.

Translation - "Therefore the men approached Him and said, 'John the Baptist has sent us to you with this question: 'Are you the One who is to come, or should we expect another?' "

Comment: δὲ is inferential. It was because of John's mission of verse 19 that the men of verse 20 made the trip. παραγίνομαι is a favorite with Luke. *Cf.*#139 - "to happen alongside." One gathers that John's disciples were a bit timid as they approached Jesus and hastened to say that it was John the Baptist, not they, who was responsible for the visit. Again, as in verse 19, Σὺ, the predicate nominative, is emphasized ahead of the subject and verb. The disciples of John carried out the mission and asked the question exactly as they got it from John.

Luke adds verse 21 as necessry information to explain verses 22 and 23.

Verse 21 - "And in that same hour he cured many of their infirmities and plagues, and of evil spirits; and unto many that were blind he gave sight."

ἐν ἐκείνῃ τῇ ὥρᾳ ἐθεράπευσεν πολλοὺς ἀπὸ νόσων καὶ μαστίγων καὶ
πνευμάτων πονηρῶν, καὶ τυφλοῖς πολλοῖς ἐχαρίσατο βλέπειν.

ἐν (preposition with the locative of time point) 80.
ἐκείνῃ (loc.sing.fem.of ἐκεῖνος, in agreement with ὥρᾳ) 246.
τῇ (loc.sing.fem.of the article in agreement with ὥρᾳ) 9.
ὥρᾳ (loc.sing.fem.of ὥρα, time point) 735.
ἐθεράπευσεν (3d.per.sing.aor.act.ind.of θεραπεύω, constative) 406.
πολλοὺς (acc.pl.masc.of πολύς, direct object of ἐθεράπευσεν) 228.
ἀπὸ (preposition with the ablative of separation) 70.
νόσων (abl.pl.masc.of νόσος, separation) 407.
καὶ (adjunctive conjunction joining nouns) 14.
μαστίγων (abl.pl.fem.of μάστιξ, separation) 2114.
καὶ (adjunctive conjunction joining nouns) 14.
πνευμάτων (abl.pl.neut.of πνεῦμα, separation) 83.
πονηρῶν (abl.pl.neut.of πονηρός, in agreement with πνευμάτων) 438.
καὶ (continuative conjunction) 14.
τυφλοῖς (dat.pl.masc.of τυφλός, indirect object of ἐχαρίσατο) 830.
πολλοῖς (dat.pl.masc.of πολύς, in agreement with τυφλοῖς) 228.

#2158 ἐχαρίσατο (3d.per.sing.aor.ind.of χαρίζομαι, constative).

deliver - Acts 25:11,16.
forgive - Lk.7:43; II Cor.2:7,10,10,10; 12:13; Eph.4:32,32; Col.2:13; 3:13.
forgive frankly - Lk.7:42.
give - Lk.7:21; Acts 27:24; Gal.3:18; Phil.1:29; 2:9; Phm.22.
give freely - Rom.8:32.
grant - Acts 3:14.
things that are freely given - I Cor.2:12.

Meaning: Related to χάρις (#1700); χάρισμα (#3790) and χαριτόω (#1812).
Hence, to do a favor; to render some service of an agreeable nature. To act for
someone so as to please. Used in a variety of contexts. (1) To deliver a prisoner
into the hands of the authorities, thus to please the authorities - Acts 25:11,16. (2)
To deliver to the mob Barabbas, thus to set him free. This favored the mob, since
it was their wish - Acts 3:14. (3) To grant to Paul the favor of saving from
shipwreck all those on board - Acts 27:24. (4) To grant to Philemon the
happiness of another visit from Paul - Philemon 22. (5) To forgive a debt of
money, *i.e.* to forego collection - Lk.7:42,43. (6) To favor the blind with the
ability to see - Lk.7:21. (7) God favored Abraham with the promise of
inheritance - Gal.3:18. (8) God gave to Christ the highest name - Phil.2:9. (9) To
some saints are given the honor of martyrdom - Phil.1:29. (10) With reference to
one's forgiveness for another - II Cor.2:7,10,10,10; 12:13; Eph.4:32a; Col.3:13.
(11) With reference to God's forgiveness of our sins - Eph.4:32b; Col.2:13. (12).
Of God's grace to us generally - Rom.8:32; I Cor.2:12.

βλέπειν (pres.act.inf.of βλέπω, epexegetical) 499.

Translation - "During that hour He healed many of their infirmities and plagues and evil spirits, and to many blind people He granted ability to see."

Comment: ἐν ... ὥρᾳ is a temporal phrase, denoting the same time for the arrival of John's messengers as for the healing described. "At the same time. . . " Goodspeed well translates "Just then ... " Note that θεραπεύω (#406) in classical Greek meant to do general service. Jesus busied Himself doing for the people whatever needed to be done. Infirmities, weaknesses, general debilitation, general sicknesses, plagues that lashed the people with pain and misery. *Cf.#2114.* The insane, beset by evil spirits who deranged their thinking - all received His healing touch as the fascinated disciples of John looked on. The blind were there in great numbers. Jesus favored them with the restored ability to see. *Cf.#2158,* with βλέπειν. *Cf.* #70 for a few other instances of ἀπό in the same sense, always with the ablative.

The list of services which Jesus rendered for the people is expanded in

Verse 22 - "Then Jesus answering said unto them, Go your way, and tell John what things ye have seen and heard; how that the blind see, the lame walk, the lepers are cleansed, the deaf hear, the dead are raised, tothe poor the gospel is preached."

καὶ ἀποκριθεὶς εἶπεν αὐτοῖς, Πορευθέντες ἀπαγγείλατε Ἰωάννῃ ἃ εἴδετε καὶ ἠκούσατε. τυφλοὶ ἀναβλέπουσιν, χωλοὶ περιπατοῦσιν, λεπροὶ καθαρίζονται καὶ κωφοὶ ἀκούουσιν, νεκροὶ ἐγείρονται, πτωχοὶ εὐαγγελίζονται.

καὶ (inferential conjunction) 14.
ἀποκριθεὶς (aor.part.nom.sing.masc.of ἀποκρίνομαι, adverbial, modal) 318.
εἶπεν (3d.per.sing.aor.act.ind.of εἶπον, constative) 155.
αὐτοῖς (dat.pl.masc.of αὐτός, indirect object of εἶπεν) 16.
Πορευθέντες (aor.part.nom.pl.masc.of πορεύομαι, adverbial, temporal) 170.
ἀπαγγείλατε (2d.per.pl.aor.act.impv.of ἀπαγγέλλω, command) 176.
Ἰωάννῃ (dat.sing.masc.of Ἰωάννης, indirect object of ἀπαγγείλατε) 247.
ἃ (acc.pl.neut.of ὅς, relative pronoun, direct object of εἴδετε and ἠκούσατε) 65.
εἴδετε (2d.per.pl.2d.aor.act.ind.of ὁράω, culminative) 144.
ἠκούσατε (2d.per.pl.aor.act.ind.of ἀκούω, culminative) 148.
τυφλοὶ (nom.pl.masc.of τυφλός, subject of ἀναβλέπουσιν) 830.
ἀναβλέπουσιν (3d.per.pl.pres.act.ind.of ἀναβλέπω, progressive) 907.
χωλοὶ (nom.pl.masc.of χωλός, subject of περιπατοῦσιν) 908.
περιπατοῦσιν (3d.per.pl.pres.act.ind.of περιπατέω, progressive) 384.
λεπροὶ (nom.pl.masc.of λεπρός, subject of καθαρίζονται) 708.
καθαρίζονται (3d.per.pl.pres.pass.ind.of καθαρίζω, progressive) 709.

καὶ (continuative conjunction) 14.

κωφοὶ (nom.pl.masc.of κωφός, subject of ἀκούουσιν) 833.

ἀκούουσιν (3d.per.pl.pres.act.ind.of ἀκούω, progressive) 148.

νεκροὶ (nom.pl.masc.of νεκρός, subject of ἐγείρονται) 749.

ἐγείρονται (3d.per.pl.pres.pass.ind.of ἐγείρω, progressive) 125.

πτωχοὶ (nom.pl.masc.of πτωχός, subject of εὐαγγελίζονται) 423.

εὐαγγελίζονται (3d.per.pl.pres.pass.ind.of εὐαγγελίζω, progressive) 909.

Translation - "Therefore He said in reply, 'Go and tell John what you have seen and heard: blind people see; lame people are walking around; lepers are cleansed and deaf people hear, the dead are raised to life; poor people are evangelized."

Comment: Jesus will make a similar appeal to the disciples at the last supper (John 14:11). This is the empirical test. Explain Jesus and His miracles on any other basis, if you can. The disciples of John are told to go back and report that blind, lame, leprous, deaf, dead and poor people are all being helped in a way that was never available to them before, and has not been since. Has Israel or, in fact, any part of the human race seen the like before?

John had heard from his disciples before of these same miracles. Now Jesus recounts them as fulfillment of Isa.29:18 and Isa.35:1-10. The Baptist was not mistaken. Jesus was indeed the Messiah. He, upon Whom the Holy Spirit descended at the immersion (John 1:32-34) now authenticates Himself by miracles which John recognized as fulfillment of the kingdom prophecies. What was still obscure to them, however, was the concept that Messiah must first die to redeem the world before exercizing Messianic functions of world government. This is the meaning of the Beatitudes of

Verse 23 - "And blessed is he, whosoever shall not be offended in me."

καὶ μακάριος ἐστιν ὅς ἐὰν μὴ σκανδαλισθῇ ἐν ἐμοί.

καὶ (continuative conjunction) 14.

μακάριος (nom.sing.masc.of μακάριος, predicate adjective) 422.

ἐστιν (3d.per.sing.pres.ind.of εἰμί, aoristic) 86.

ὅς (nom.sing.masc.of ὅς, relative pronoun, subject of σκανδαλισθῇ) 65.

ἐὰν (conditional particle in a third-class condition) 363.

μὴ (negative conjunction with the subjunctive) 87.

σκανδαλισθῇ (3d.per.sing.aor.pass.subj.of σκανδαλίζω, third-class condition) 503.

ἐν (preposition with the instrumental of cause) 80.

ἐμοί (instrumental sing.masc.of ἐμός, cause) 1267.

Translation - "And happy is the man if he is not embarrassed because of me."

Comment: Jesus, by His miracles, was attracting great public attention. He was certain to incur the enmity of the political powers and pressure groups. This unpopularity which Jesus was to suffer would be certain to transfer to His followers. Only those who had the faith to see the ultimate end of the Kingdom plan would be indeed μακάριος. Jesus is saying to John, "I am truly the Coming One. And ultimately the kingdoms of this world will be mine. But before that day there is a cross, a tomb, a resurrection and the Church Age, while kingdom matters are held in abeyance. My followers will be persecuted. You, John, will lose your head. But, no matter. Take the long look. Believe in me and you will be blessed." *Cf.*# 503 for other verses which deal with the offence of the cross. Note that even the twelve disciples of Jesus did not escape this offense though they were with Him three years (Mt.26:31,33,33), despite our Lord's best efforts to prevent it (John 16:1).

The visit of John's disciples prompted our Lord to discuss the role of John the Baptist in the Kingdom plan, a discussion of which role was favourably received by the common people and the publicans, but rejected by the Pharisees and the lawyers.

Jesus' Testimony to John the Baptist

(Lk.7:24-29; Mt.11:7-15)

Verse 24 - "And when the messengers of John were departed he began to speak unto the people concerning John. What went ye out into the wilderness for to see? A reed shaken with the wind?"

'Απελθόντων δὲ τῶν ἀγγέλων Ἰωάννου ἤρξατο λέγειν πρὸς τοὺς ὄχλους περὶ Ἰωάννου, Τί ἐξήλθατε εἰς τὴν ἔρημον θεάσασθαι; κάλαμον ὑπὸ ἀνέμου σαλευόμενον;

'Απελθόντων (aor.part.gen.pl.masc. of ἀπέρχομαι, genitive absolute) 239.
δὲ (continuative conjunction) 11.
τῶν (gen.pl.masc.of the article in agreement with ἀγγέλων) 9.
ἀγγέλων (gen.pl.masc.of ἄγγελος, genitive absolute) 96.
Ἰωάννου (gen.sing.masc.of Ἰωάννης, relationship) 247.
ἤρξατο (3d.per.sing.aor.mid.ind.of ἄρχω, ingressive) 383.
λέγειν (pres.act.inf.of λέγω, complementary) 66.
πρὸς (preposition with the accusative of extent) 197.
τοὺς (acc.pl.masc.of the article in agreement with ὄχλους) 9.
ὄχλους (acc.pl.masc.of ὄχλος, extent, after a verb of speaking) 418.
περὶ (preposition with the genitive of reference) 173.
Ἰωάννου (gen.sing.masc.of Ἰωάννης, reference) 247.
Τί (acc.sing.neut.of τίς, interrogative pronoun in direct question, direct object of ἐξήλθατε) 281.
ἐξήλθατε (2d.per.pl.aor.ind.of ἐξέρχομαι, constative) 161.
εἰς (preposition with the accusative of extent) 140.
τὴν (acc.sing.fem.of the article in agreement with ἔρημον) 9.

ἔρημον (acc.sing.fem.of ἔρημος, extent) 250.
θεάσασθαι (1st.aor.inf.of θεάομαι, purpose) 556.
κάλαμον (acc.sing.masc.of κάλαμος, direct object of θεάσασθαι) 910.
ὑπό (preposition with the abiative of agent) 117.
ἀνέμου (abl.sing.masc.of ἄνεμος, agent) 698.
σαλευόμενον (pres.pass.part.acc.sing.masc.of σαλεύω, adjectival, restrictive) 911.

Translation - *"And after the messengers of John had gone away He began to speak to the crowds about John; 'What did you go out into the desert to see? A reed being shaken by wind?' "*

Comment: The forerunner might be shaken by fear and doubt, as John, being only human, then was. He had been imprisoned because of his message of righteousness and he began to doubt that Jesus was the Messiah, despite the evidence which he had at his immersion (Mt.3:16,17). But the Messiah before Whose face John went out to minister will never be shaken (Acts 2:25). Note the genitive absolute in the aorist tense. After John's messengers left to return to John with their account of Jesus' miracles, Jesus began to discuss the ministry of the Baptist with the crowds gathered about Him. He demands to know what the people expected to find in John. There was many weeds in the desert swaying back and forth by desert winds. The figure of verse 24 is in contrast to that of verse 25. They found neither the weeds nor a man dressed in fine clothing. They found the greatest prophet of all time, because he had a unique mission, given to none other. His ministry would serve to introduce Messiah to the nation Israel. John had been wavering - swept by winds of doubt (*cf*.#698), but Jesus had solidified the Baptist's resolution. He was soon to lose his head.

Verse 25 - "But what went ye out for to see? A man clothed in soft raiment: Behold, they which are gorgeously apparelled, and live delicately, are in king's courts."

ἀλλὰ τί ἐξήλθατε ἰδεῖν; ἄνθρωπον ἐν μαλακοῖς ἱματίοις ἠμφιεσμένον; ἰδοὺ οἱ ἐν ἱματισμῷ ἐνδόξῳ καὶ τρυφῇ ὑπάρχοντες ἐν τοῖς βασιλείοις εἰσίν.

ἀλλὰ (adversative conjunction) 342.
τί (acc.sing.neut.of τίς, interrogative pronoun, direct object of ἰδεῖν) 281.
ἐξήλθατε (2d.per.pl.aor.ind.of ἐξέρχομαι, constative) 161.
ἰδεῖν (aor.inf.of ὁράω, purpose) 144.
ἄνθρωπον (acc.sing.masc.of ἄνθρωπος, direct object of ἰδεῖν) 341.
ἐν (preposition with the locative of place where) 80.
μαλακοῖς (loc.pl.neut.of μαλακός, in agreement with ἱματίοις) 912.
ἱματίοις (loc.pl.neut.of ἱμάτιον, place where) 534.
ἠμφιεσμένον (perf.pass.part.acc.sing.masc.of ἀμφιέννυμι, in agreement with ἄνθρωπον) 635.

ἰδού (exclamation) 95.
οἱ (nom.pl.masc.of the article in agreement with ὑπάρχοντες) 9.
ἐν (preposition with the locative of place) 80.

#2159 ἱματισμῷ (loc.sing.masc.of ἱματισμός, place).

apparel - Acts 20:33.
array - I Tim.2:9.
raiment - Lk.9:29.
vesture - John 19:24.
apparelled - Lk.7:25.

Meaning: Clothing; apparel. *Cf.*#534 and ἱματίζω (#2223). Seems synonymous with the neuter ἱμάτιον (#534), which is used more often in the New Testament. With reference to the clothing of Jesus - Lk.9:29; John 19:24. Generally in Acts 20:33. Must be modified when expensive fabrics are in view as in I Tim.2:9, with πολυτελεῖ and Lk.7:25 with ἐνδόξῳ.

#2160 ἐνδόξῳ (loc.sing.masc.of ἔνδοξος, in agreement with ἱματισμῷ).

glorious - Lk.13:17; Eph.5:27.
honourable - I Cor.4:10.
gorgeously - Lk.7:25.

Meaning: A combination of ἐν (#80) and δόξα (1361). Hence, endued with glory. Glorious. Used as a substantive, with reference to the miracles of Jesus - "glorious things" - Lk.13:17. An adjective in the predicate position with reference to the raptured church - Eph.5:27. As a predicate adjective of the high prestige of the Corinthian church as opposed to Paul's unpopularity - I Cor.4:10. As an adjective in the predicate position to denote the expensive apparel of the Scribes - Lk.7:25.

καὶ (adjunctive conjunction joining a phrase with an adverb) 14.

#2161 τρυφῇ (instru.sing.fem.of τρυφή)

to riot - II Pet.2:13.
delicately - Lk.7:25.

Meaning: From θρύπτω - "to break down; to enervate." In middle and passive voices to debilitate oneself. To destroy one's health. Hence the noun τρυφή means softness, delicacy, luxurious living. Of the luxury of the apostates in II Pet.2:13 and that of the Scribes in Lk.7:25. With ἐν in Lk.7:25, like an adverb - "living in softness."

ὑπάρχοντες (pres.act.part.nom.pl.masc.of ὑπάρχω, substantival, subject of εἰσίν) 1303.
ἐν (preposition with the locative of place where) 80.
τοῖς (loc.pl.masc.of the article in agreement with βασιλείοις) 9.

#2162 βασιλείοις (loc.pl.masc.of βασίλειος, place where).

royal - I Pet.2:9.
king's court - Lk.7:25.

Meaning: Related to βασιλεία (#253), βασιλεύω (#236); βασιλεύς (#31); βασιλικός (#2017) and βασίλισσα (#1014). Pertaining to royalty. Kingly; splendid.As an adjective in the attributive position with ἱεράτευμα - "a royal priesthood" of the priesthood of the believer in I Pet.2:9; as a substantive in Lk.7;25 - "king's court."

εἰσίν (3d.per.pl.pres.ind.of εἰμί, customary) 86.

Translation - "But what did you go out to see? A man clothed in soft garments? Look! Those who are dressed in gloriously luxurious apparel live in royal palaces."

.Comment: The syntax of the passage is difficult but the meaning is none-the-less plain. Jesus is presenting the people with alternatives. Did they expect to find in John the Baptist an insignificant weed, helplessly influenced by the winds of a social and political environment over which he had no control? Or, perhaps, they expected to find one of their own Scribes or other prestigious religious leaders. These Jesus described as those who dressed lavishly and lived in voluptuous ease in Herod's court If they looked for the latter, they would not find them in the desert but in the court of Herod the King, perhaps present when Herod granted the head of John the Baptist to Salome.

Jesus is preparing to praise John, despite the Baptist's temporary lapse of faith (vs.19). But He must make a contrast between the rugged Forerunner and the current crop of Scribes whose luxurious living made them defenders of the status quo - not preachers of revolt, like John. One cannot imagine the Scribes laying the axe to the root of Herod's tree - not while it supported them in such luxury as Jesus has described.

They were not looking for a useless weed when they went out into the desert to hear John preach. If so, they would never have gone. Nor were they looking for the Scribes. If so, they knew where to find them - in Herod's court. Apparently they thought that John was important and apparently they thought he had a message for them which the Scribes could not provide. They went out to find a prophet. And Jesus now tells them that they found in John much more than a Prophet.

Verse 26 - "But what went ye out for to see? A prophet? Yea, I say unto you, and much more than a prophet."

ἀλλὰ τί ἐξήλθατε ἰδεῖν; προφήτην; ναί, λέγω ὑμῖν, καὶ περισσότερον προφήτου.

ἀλλά (adversative conjunction) 342.
τί (acc.sing.neut.of τίς, interrogative pronoun, direct object of ἰδεῖν) 281.
ἐξήλθατε (2d.per.pl.aor.ind.of ἐξέρχομαι, constative) 161.
ἰδεῖν (aor.inf.of ὁράω, purpose) 144.
προφήτην (acc.sing.masc.of προφήτης, direct object of ἰδεῖν) 119.
ναί (affirmative particle) 524.
λέγω (1st.per.sing.pres.act.ind.of λέγω, aoristic) 66.
ὑμῖν (dat.pl.masc.of σύ, indirect object of λέγω) 104.
καὶ (emphatic conjunction) 14.
περισσότερον (acc.sing.neut. comp.of περισσός) 525.
προφήτου (abl.sing.masc.of προφήτης, comparison) 119.

Translation - "But what did you go out to see? A prophet? Indeed! I am telling you in fact, more than a prophet!"

Comment: Again the adversative ἀλλά. Not a reed shaken by the wind, nor a Scribe of Herod's luxurious court, but a prophet. Not just any prophet, but a special prophet. In fact (emphatic καὶ) the greatest of the prophets as we learn in verse 28.

Scribes were interpreters of the law and the prophets, not the sources of either. Prophets enjoyed greater distinction, having been sent by God to rescue the nation in times of national peril. What is greater than a prophet? The Messiah Himself? Perhaps some of John's disciples thought as much. But as Jesus goes on to say that between the prophets and Messiah stood one, lower in prestige than Messiah, but the greatest of all the prophets - the forerunner of Messiah. John the Baptist is the fulfillment of the prophecy of Malachi 3:1. *Cf.* also Exodus 23:20.

Verse 27 - "This is he of whom it is written, Behold I send my messenger before thy face, which shall prepare thy way before thee."

οὗτός ἐστιν περὶ οὗ γέγραπται, Ἰδοὺ ἀποστέλλω τὸν ἄγγελόν μου πρὸ προσώπου σου, ὃς κατασκευάσει τὴν ὁδόν σου ἔμπροσθέν σου.

οὗτός (nom.sing.masc.of οὗτος, subject of ἐστιν) 93.
ἐστιν (3d.per.sing.pres.ind.of εἰμί, aoristic) 86.
περὶ (preposition with the genitive of reference) 173.
οὗ (gen.sing.masc.of ὅς, reference) 65.
γέγραπται (3d.per.sing.perf.pass.ind.of γράφω, consummative) 156.
ἰδοὺ (exclamation) 95.
ἀποστέλλω (1st.per.sing.pres.act.ind.of ἀποστέλλω, futuristic) 215.
τὸν (acc.sing.masc.of the article in agreement with ἄγγελον) 9.
ἄγγελόν (acc.sing.masc.of ἄγγελος, direct object of ἀποστέλλω) 96.
μου (gen.sing.masc.of ἐγώ, possession) 123.
πρὸ (preposition with the ablative of separation) 442.
προσώπου (abl.sing.neut.of πρόσωπον, separation) 588.
σου (gen.sing.masc.of σύ, possession) 104.

ὅς (nom.sing.masc.of ὅς, subject of κατασκευάσει) 65.
κατασκευάσει (3d.per.sing.fut.act.ind.of κατασκευάζω, predictive) 914.
τὴν (acc.sing.fem.of the article in agreement with ὁδόν) 9.
σου (gen.sing.masc.of σύ, possession) 104.
ἔμπροσθέν (improper preposition with the ablative) 459.
σου (abl.sing.masc.of σύ, separation) 104.

Translation - *"This man is the one about whom it has been written, 'Behold I send my messenger before my face, who shall prepare your way before you.'"*

Comment: οὗτός is emphatic and deictic. It points back to προφήτην of verse 26. It refers to John the Baptist. Note the consummative perfect in γέγραπται - " having been written, it stands written" - a present condition as a result of a past completed action. *Cf.*#442 for πρό in this expression. *Cf.* Lk.1:17, where the prophecy cited here (Mal.3:1) is cited by Zacharias, before John's birth. Jesus, speaking through Malachi had phrased it differently. "Behold I *will send* my messenger and he shall prepare *the* way before *me*." Now, this same Jesus says, "Behold *I am sending* my messenger *before thy face* who shall prepare *thy* way before *thee*." It was too early in Jesus' ministry for Him to announce openly, "I am He." But there is a strong hint here. For indeed the Messiah stood before the people saying that the prophet in the prison, whose baptism many in the audience had received, was the forerunner - the fulfillment of Mal.3:1.Then Jesus had said, "I *will send* my messenger." Now He says, "*I am sending* my messenger." Then He had said, "*the* way before *me*." Now He puts the words into the Father's mouth and says "*thy* way before *thee*.". Jesus thus claims Sonship and Messiahship but He does it by inference rather than by direct statement.

Verse 28 - *"For I say unto you, Among those that are born of women there is not a greater prophet than John the Baptist: but he that is least in the kingdom of the God is greater than he."*

λέγω ὑμῖν, μείζων ἐν γεννητοῖς γυναικῶν Ἰωάννου οὐδείς ἐστιν, ὁ δὲ μικρότερος ἐν τῇ βασιλείᾳ τοῦ θεοῦ μείζων αὐτοῦ ἐστιν.

λέγω (1st.per.sing.pres.act.ind.of λέγω, aoristic) 66.
ὑμῖν (dat.pl.masc.of σύ, indirect object of λέγω) 104.
μείζων (nom.sing.masc.of μείζων, in agreement with οὐδείς, pred.adjective) 916.
ἐν (preposition with the locative with plural nouns/pronouns) 80.
γεννητοῖς (loc.pl.masc.of γεννητός, periphrasis for *men*) 915.
γυναικῶν (abl.pl.fem.of γυνή, source) 103.
Ἰωάννου (abl.sing.masc.of Ἰωάννης, comparison) 247.
οὐδείς (nom.sing.masc.of οὐδείς, subject of ἐστιν) 446.
ἐστιν (3d.per.sing.pres.ind.of εἰμί, aoristic) 86.
ὁ (nom.sing.masc .of the article in agreement with μικρότερος) 9.

δέ (adversative conjunction) 11.

μικρότερος (nom.sing.masc.comp.of μικρός, subject of ἐστιν) 917.

ἐν (preposition with the locative of sphere) 80.

τῇ (loc.sing.fem.of the article in agreement with βασιλείᾳ) 9.

βασιλείᾳ (loc.sing.fem.of βασιλεία, sphere) 253.

τοῦ (gen.sing.masc.of the article in agreement with θεοῦ) 9.

θεοῦ (gen.sing.masc.of θεός, definition) 124.

μείζων (nom.sing.masc.of μείζων, predicate adjective) 916.

αὐτοῦ (abl.sing.masc.of αὐτός, comparison) 16.

ἐστιν (3d.per.sing.pres.ind.of εἰμί, aoristic) 86.

Translation - "I am telling you that there is not one man born of woman who is greater than John, but the man of little importance in the kingdom of God is greater than he."

Comment: Note the ablatives of comparison in Ἰωάννου and αὐτοῦ. John is the greatest of the prophets, but one of scant significance in the Kingdom of God outranks the greatest prophet. John, indeed, is said to be the greatest man in the human family. This is the sense of ἐν γεννητοῖς γυναικῶν.

John was a prophet and the greatest of them all, but he was preaching the gospel of the kingdom of heaven, a kingdom which will indeed come, but not now. The Messiah will ultimately fulfill John's predictions, but in the meantime another kingdom message must be preached. The Kingdom of God will include all sinners, Jew and Gentile, who trust in Messiah's shed blood and resurrection. John had known nothing of this when he first came preaching. *Cf.* comments on Mt.3:13-17 and John 1:29-34. Jesus is saying that the sinner who sees his need of salvation from sin, trusts Him and His sacrifice and becomes a member of the Kingdom of God, though he be among the less significant in the Kingdom of God, shall be greater than John. Those who see no distinction at all in any way, between the Kingdom of the Heavens and the Kingdom of God, and thus miss the fact that Messiah's earthly kingdom for Israel is held in abeyance, while the church is called, should have trouble with Jesus' statement here. If the weakest saint in the Kingdom is greater than the greatest prophet in the Kingdom, and if it is the same kingdom, in what sense is he greater? What Jesus meant was that *at that time* - at the time when He was making the statement, John, the mighty prophet was forced to withdraw, because his kingdom was dispensationally out of place, in God's plan of the ages.

John himself understood this clearly after he immersed Jesus and received the confirmation from heaven that (a) Jesus was indeed the Messiah, and, (b) that Jesus, although the Messiah of Israel in God's good time, had come to earth to die upon a cross and call out from among the Gentiles a people for His name (Acts 15:14).

As we struggle with this passage it is well to recognize that Jesus was speaking to a divided audience. Some of the people had received John's baptism (vs.29); other rejected it (vs.30). Jesus' task was to congratulate and endorse the action of the disciples of John and at the same time tell them that they must look to Messiah in a new sense. He must also condemn the Pharisees and lawyers. The first group is introduced in

Verse 29 - "And all the people that heard him, and the publicans, justified God, being baptized with the baptism of John."

(Καὶ πᾶς ὁ λαὸς ἀκούσας καὶ οἱ τελῶναι ἐδικαίωσαν τὸν θεόν, βαπτισθέντες τὸ βάπτισμα Ἰωάννου.

Καὶ (inferential conjunction) 14.
πᾶς (nom.sing.masc.of πᾶς, in agreement with λαὸς) 67.
ὁ (nom.sing.masc.of the article in agreement with λαὸς) 9.
λαὸς (nom.sing.masc.of λαός, subject of ἐδικαίωσαν) 110.
ἀκούσας (aor.act.part.nom.sing.masc.of ἀκούω, adverbial, causal) 148.
καὶ (adjunctive conjunction joining nouns) 14.
οἱ (nom.pl.masc.of the article in agreement with τελῶναι) 9.
τελῶναι (nom.pl.masc.of τελώνης, subject of ἐδικαίωσαν) 550.
ἐδικαίωσαν (3d.per.pl.aor.act.ind.of δικαιόω, ingressive) 933.
τὸν (acc.sing.masc.of the article in agreement with θεόν) 9.
θεόν (acc.sing.masc.of θεός, direct object of ἐδικαίωσαν) 124.
βαπτισθέντες (aor.pass.part.nom.pl.masc.of βαπτίζω, adverbial, circumstantial) 273.
τὸ (acc.sing.neut.of the article in agreement with βάπτισμα) 9.
βάπτισμα (acc.sing.neut.of βάπτισμα, general reference) 278.
Ἰωάννου (gen.sing.masc.of Ἰωάννης, definition) 247.

Translation - "And when all the people and the publicans had heard, they began to agree that God was just, because they were immersed by the immersion of John."

Comment: πᾶς need not mean the quantitative all, but all of the people who were standing there and who had been immersed with John's baptism. The publicans also heard Jesus' remark and rejoiced. The Pharisees and lawyers reacted differently as we see in verse 30.

It was natural that those who had been baptized by John should have some doubts since John was now in prison. But Jesus' appraisal of the Baptist restored their faith in the validity of his ministry. Note the accusative in τὸ βάπτισμα without a transitive verb.

Verse 30 - "But the Pharisees and lawyers rejected the counsel of God against themselves, being not baptized of him."

οἱ δὲ Φαρισαῖοι καὶ οἱ νομικοὶ τὴν βουλὴν τοῦ θεοῦ ἠθέτησαν εἰς ἑαυτούς, μὴ βαπτισθέντες ὑπ' αὐτοῦ.

οἱ (nom.pl.masc.of the article in agreement with Φαρισαῖοι) 9.

170   *The Renaissance New Testament*   Lk.7:30

δέ (adversative conjunction) 11.

Φαρισαῖοι (nom.pl.masc.of Φαρισαῖος, subject of ἠθέτησαν) 276.

καὶ (adjunctive conjunction joining nouns) 14.

οἱ (nom.pl.masc.of the article in agreement with νομικοὶ) 9.

νομικοὶ (nom.pl.masc.of νομικός, subject of ἠθέτησαν) 1427.

τὴν (acc.sing.fem.of the article in agreement with βουλὴν) 9.

#2163 βουλὴν (acc.sing.fem.of βουλή, direct object of ἠθέτησαν).

counsel - Lk.7:30; 23:51; Acts 2:23; 4:28; 5:38; 20:27; 27:42; I Cor.4:5; Eph.1:11; Heb.6:17.
will - Acts 13:36.
advise - Acts 27:12.

Meaning: Related to βούλημα (#3750), βουλευτής (#2873), βουλεύομαι (#90) and βούλομαι (#953). A studied conclusion. A philosophy or policy, or both, arrived at by someone and held as truth. With reference to the counsel of God, *i.e.* His wise plan of operation in relation to the universe and man - Lk.7:30; Acts 2:23; 4:28; 5:38; 20:27; Eph.1:11; Heb.6:17; Acts 13:36. With reference to the counsel of men - San Hedrin against God - Lk.23:51; of the soldiers to kill the prisoners - Acts 27:42; of the philosophies and motivations of men - I Cor.4:5. Of those on board ship with regard to plans for sailing - Acts 27:12.

τοῦ (gen.sing.masc.of the article in agreement with θεοῦ) 9.

θεοῦ (gen.sing.masc.of θεός, definition) 124.

#2164 ἠθέτησαν (3d.per.pl.aor.act.ind.of ἀθετέω, constative).

bring to nothing - I Cor.1:19.
cast off - I Tim.5:12.
despise - Lk.10:16,16,16,16; I Thess.4:8,8; Heb.10:28; Jude 8.
disannul - Gal.3:15.
frustrate - Gal.2:21.
reject - Mk.6:26; 7:9; Lk.7:30; John 12:48.

Meaning: To reject as false and unworthy of consideration a philosophy or doctrine. To spurn. To cast aside. To repudiate. In the New Testament most often of men rejecting the counsel of God as in I Tim.5:12; Lk.10:16,16,16,16; I Thess.4:8,8; Heb.10:28 (Moses' law); Jude 8; Gal.2:21; Mk.7:9; Lk.7:30; John 12:48 where it is used in connection with the reverse idea - ὁ ἀθετῶν ἐμὲ καὶ μὴ λαμβάνων τὰ ῥήματά μου . . . Also of God showing up as falacious the wisdom of unregenerate man - I Cor.1:19. In an analogy - no man rejects another man's contract - Gal.3:15. With reference to Herod honoring the promise to Salome for John the Baptist's head - Mk.6:26.

εἰς (preposition with the accusative, hostility) 140.

ἑαυτούς (acc.pl.masc.of ἑαυτός, hostility) 288.

μὴ (negative conjunction with the participle) 87.

βαπτισθέντες (aor.pass.part.nom.pl.masc.of βαπτίζω, adverbial, causal)
273.
ὑπ' (preposition with the ablative of agent) 117.
αὐτοῦ (abl.sing.masc.of αὐτός, agent) 16.

Translation - *"But the Pharisees and the lawyers repudiated the counsel of God against themselves because they had not been immersed by him."*

Comment: δὲ here is definitely adversative. The common people and the publicans believed Jesus' explanation of John the Baptist and his place in the divine plan of the ages, *but* (adversative δὲ) the Pharisees and lawyers rejected it. τὴν βουλὴν τοῦ θεοῦ - *Cf.*#2163 for other interesting uses of the word. It is a tonic to faith to see what God has counselled, how immutable His counsel is, and what happens to those who by rejecting it, place themselves outside God's *weltanschauung* and thus condemn themselves to everlasting frustration. εἰς ἑαυτοὺς - This is clearly opposition - "against themselves." John the Baptist was certainly opposed to the *status quo* society of the Pharisees (Mt.3:7-12). *Cf.*#140 for other uses of εἰς in the sense of hostility or opposition. But we might also translate, "They rejected the counsel of God as it related to them" *i.e.* insofar as they were concerned. Luke tells us how they expressed this rejection. It was by the fact that at the time of our story they had already refused John's baptism. This is the force of the aorist causal participle βαπτισθέντες. αὐτοῦ refers directly to John the Baptist and, of course indirectly to God by whose authority John came preaching (Lk.10:16,16).

Verses 31-35 are directed against the Pharisees and lawyers. Thus we have Jesus' use of the occasion which brought from the prison John's question: (1) John the Baptist is the Mal.3:1 prophet despite his evident lapse of faith; (2) He is the greatest of the prophets; in fact the greatest man who ever lived, with the exception of our Lord Himself; (3) But a new era has dawned while the heavenly kingdom on earth for Israel nationally is in abeyance. This new era, The Kingdom of God, is one in which the least saint shall be greater than the greatest Kingdom Prophet; (4) Therefore those people who stood there with John's baptism needed to take an additional step of faith in the crucified and risen Messiah. Repentance was not enough. They needed the positive faith in blood redemption, but (5) the lawyers and Pharisees had a totally indefensible position for they had accepted neither John nor Jesus. (The student should reread the comment on Mt.11:2-19).

In the remaining verses of this episode Luke points out the devastating analysis of Jesus by which He showed up the pitiable inconsistency of the Pharisees and lawyers, as well as all others who accepted neither John the Baptist nor the Messiah Whom he came to announce.

Verse 31 - *"And the Lord said, Whereunto then shall I liken the men of this generation? And to what are they like?"*

Τίνι οὖν ὁμοιώσω τοὺς ἀνθρώπους τῆς γενεᾶς ταύτης, καὶ τίνι εἰσὶν ὅμοιοι;

Τίνι (dat.sing.neut.interrogative of τίς, comparison) 281.
οὖν (inferential conjunction) 68.
ὁμοιώσω (1st.per.sing.fut.act.ind.of ὁμοιόω, deliberative) 575.
τοὺς (acc.pl.masc.of the article in agreement with ἀνθρώπους) 9.
ἀνθρώπους (acc.pl.masc.of ἄνθρωπος, direct object of ὁμοιώσω) 341.
τῆς (gen.sing.fem.of the article in agreement with γενεᾶς) 9.
γενεᾶς (gen.sing.fem.of γενεά, definition) 922.
ταύτης (gen.sing.fem.of οὗτος, in agreement with γενεᾶς) 93.
καὶ (emphatic conjunction) 14.
τίνι (dat.sing.neut.of the interrogative τίς, comparison) 281.
εἰσὶν (3d.per.pl.pres.ind.of εἰμί, aoristic) 86.
ὅμοιοι (nom.pl.masc.of ὅμοιος, predicate adjective) 923.

Translation - "Unto what therefore shall I compare the men of this generation? Indeed, what are they like?"

Comment: The KJV has "And the Lord said . . . κ.τ.λ." The better manuscripts do not support this reading. Note the two datives of comparison with the verb and the predicate adjective. Note the comment on Mt.11:60 on γενεά. *Cf.*#922. No good reason occurs to me at this point why Jesus should have repeated the question except for emphasis. Hence I have taken καὶ as emphatic. Jesus is not asking for information. This is the deliberative use of the future tense. It is a psychological device designed to set the stage for the devastating analogy in

Verse 32 - "They are like unto children sitting in the marketplace, and calling one to another, and saying, We have piped unto you, and ye have not danced; we have mourned to you, and ye have not wept."

ὅμοιοί εἰσιν παιδίοις τοῖς ἐν ἀγορᾷ καθημένοις καὶ προσφωνοῦσιν ἀλλήλοις, ἃ λέγει,
    Ηὐλήσαμεν ὑμῖν καὶ οὐκ ὠρχήσασθε,
    ἐθρηνήσαμεν καὶ οὐκ ἐκλαύσατε.

ὅμοιοι (nom.pl.masc.of ὅμοιος, predicate adjective) 923.
εἰσιν (3d.per.pl.pres.ind.of εἰμί, progressive) 86.
παιδίοις (dat.pl.neut.of παιδίον, comparison) 174.
τοῖς (dat.pl.neut.of the article in agreement with παιδίοις) 9.
ἐν (preposition with the locative of place where) 80.
ἀγορᾷ (loc.sing.fem.of ἀγορά, place where) 924.
καθημένοις (pres.mid.part.dat.pl.neut.of κάθημαι, adjectival, restrictive, in agreement with παιδίοις) 377.
καὶ (continuative conjunction) 14.
προσφωνοῦσιν (3d.per.pl.pres.act.ind.of προσφωνέω, customary) 925.
ἀλλήλοις (dat.pl.masc.of ἀλλήλων, indirect object of προσφωνοῦσιν) 1487.

ἁ (nom.pl.neut.of ὅς, subject of λέγει) 65.

λέγει (3d.per.sing.pres.act.ind.of λέγω, customary) 66.

Ηὐλήσαμεν (1st.per.pl.aor.act.ind.of αὐλέω, culminative) 926.

ὑμῖν (dat.pl.masc.of σύ, personal advantage) 104.

καὶ (adversative conjunction) 14.

οὐκ (negative conjunction with the indicative) 130.

ὠρχήσασθε (2d.per.pl.aor.mid.ind.of ὀρχέω, ingressive) 927.

ἐθρηνήσαμεν (1st.per.pl.aor.act.ind.of θρηνέω, culminative) 928.

καὶ (adversative conjunction) 14.

οὐκ (negative conjunction with the indicative) 130.

ἐκλαύσατε (2d.per.pl.aor.act.ind.of κλαίω, ingressive) 225.

Translation - "They are like the children who seat themselves in the marketplace and call out to the others, who say, 'We have played the flute for you, but you did not begin to dance; we have lamented but you did not begin to weep."

Comment: Note the adjectival participle καθημένοις used in a restrictive sense. Jesus is speaking only of children who seat themselves (middle voice) in the marketplace. Note that instead of using another adjectival participle, Luke uses a coordinate clause, introduced by continuative καὶ as Jesus describes the scene. Note the singular number in λέγει with the neuter plural ἁ, - a good classical Greek idiom, which we have come to expect from the pen of Luke. Note also the culminative aorists in Ηὐλήσαμεν and ἐθρηνήσαμεν and the ingressive aorists in ὠρχήσασθε and ἐκλαύσατε. The flute playing, in which the children imitated the musicians at a wedding had been done and was an accomplished fact. But the dance did not begin. The weeping, in which the children sought to emulate the mourners at a funeral was also over (culminative aorist), but the weeping had not begun (ingressive aorist). Whatever the children did, whether for joy or for sorrow, their fellows did not respond appropriately. They refused to be pleased. The children are complaining that it would seem that everything they did was wrong.

The application of the analogy is found in verses 33 and 34, with Jesus' comment on their behavior in verse 35.

Verse 33 - "For John the Baptist came neither eating bread nor drinking wine; and ye say, He hath a devil."

ἐλήλυθεν γὰρ Ἰωάννης ὁ βαπτιστὴς μὴ ἐσθίων ἄρτον μήτε πίνων οἶνον, καὶ λέγετε, Δαιμόνιον ἔχει.

ἐλήλυθεν (3d.per.sing.2d.per.ind.of ἔρχομαι, consummative) 146.

γὰρ (causal conjunction) 105.

Ἰωάννης (nom.sing.masc.of Ἰωάννης, subject of ἐλήλυθεν) 247.

ὁ (nom.sing.masc.of the article in agreement with βαπτιστὴς) 9.

βαπτιστὴς (nom.sing.masc.of βαπτιστής, apposition) 248.

μὴ (negative conjunction with the participle) 87.

ἐσθίων (pres.act.part.nom.sing.masc.of ἐσθίω, adverbial, modal) 610.
ἄρτον (acc.sing.masc.of ἄρτος, direct object of ἐσθίων) 338.
μήτε (disjunctive) 518.
πίνων (pres.act.part.nom.sing.masc.of πίνω, adverbial, modal) 611.
οἶνον (acc.sing.masc.of οἶνος, direct object of πίνων) 808.
καὶ (inferential conjunction) 14.
λέγετε (2d.per.pl.pres.act.ind.of λέγω, customary) 66.
Δαιμόνιον (acc.sing.neut.of δαιμόνιον, direct object of ἔχει) 686.
ἔχει (3d.per.sing.pres.act.ind.of ἔχω, aoristic) 82.

Translation - *"Because John the Baptist has come neither eating bread nor drinking wine; therefore you keep saying, 'He has a demon.' "*

Comment: γὰρ is causal, as Jesus explains His point in the analogy of verse 32. Note that Luke matches the culminative aorists of verse 32 with the consummative perfect in ἐλήλυθεν of verse 33. The coming of John the Baptist was an accomplished fact. John the Baptist was still on the scene, with a ministry that displeased the Pharisees and lawyers, because he was a Nazarite. He came neither eating bread nor drinking wine. The two participles ἐσθίων and πίνων are modal. They describe how John came and the character of his ministry. John's abstemious way of life was not acceptable to the Establishment. The reaction was that John was deranged. Note the direct discourse in which Δαιμόνιον is emphasized ahead of the verb ἔχει. If John wanted to reform the nation why did he not commend himself to his audience with a little more conformity to the currently lax morals? On the contrary John mourned, but they did not lament.

The reason the Pharisees and lawyers rejected John the Baptist and his message was not the fact that he was a Nazarite. The real reason was the ethical character of his message, with its emphasis upon repentance, confession of sin and the social implications of his ethics which challenged the hold which the Establishment had upon society. It is always the moral commitment of the gospel which turns the sinner away, not the particular way of life of the preacher who brings the message. If, in fact, the Pharisees and lawyers were offended by the Baptist's asceticism, they would have been happy to accept Jesus and His message, since He came both eating and drinking. Yet they rejected Him also for the same reason that they rejected John the Baptist.

Verse 34 - *"The son of man is come eating and drinking; and ye say, Behold a gluttonous man, and a winebibber, a friend of publicans and sinners!"*

ἐλήλυθεν ὁ υἱὸς τοῦ ἀνθρώπου ἐσθίων καὶ πίνων, καὶ λέγετε, Ἰδοὺ ἄνθρωπος φάγος καὶ οἰνοπότης, φίλος τελωνῶν καὶ ἁμαρτωλῶν.

ἐλήλυθεν (3d.per.sing.2d.perf.mid.ind.of ἔρχομαι, consummative) 146.
ὁ (nom.sing.masc.of the article in agreement with υἱὸς) 9.

υἱὸς (nom.sing.masc.of υἱός, subject of ἐλήλυθεν) 5.
τοῦ (gen.sing.masc.of the article in agreement with ἀνθρώπου) 9.
ἀνθρώπου (gen.sing.masc.of ἄνθρωπος, definition) 341.
ἐσθίων (pres.act.part.nom.sing.masc.of ἐσθίω, adverbial, modal) 610.
καὶ (adjunctive conjunction joining participles) 14.
πίνων (pres.act.part.nom.sing.masc.of πίνω, adverbial, modal) 611.
καὶ (inferential conjunction) 14.
λέγετε (2d.per.pl.pres.act.ind.of λέγω, customary) 66.
Ἰδοὺ (exclamation) 95.
ἄνθρωπος (nom.sing.masc.of ἄνθρωπος, nominative absolute) 341.
φάγος (nom.sing.masc.of φάγος, in agreement with ἄνθρωπος) 930.
καὶ (adjunctive conjunction joining nouns) 14.
οἰνοπότης (nom.sing.masc.of οἰνοπότης, nominative absolute) 931.
φίλος (nom.sing.masc.of φίλος, nominative absolute) 932.
τελωνῶν (gen.pl.masc.of τελώνης, definition) 550.
καὶ (adjunctive conjunction joining nouns) 14.
ἁμαρτωλῶν (gen.pl.masc.of ἁμαρτωλός, definition) 791.

Translation - "The Son of Man is here eating and drinking; therefore you are saying, 'Look at the man! A glutton and a drunkard! A friend of publicans and sinners!'"

Comment: This is the other side of the analogy. Jesus was no Nazarite, though He did not condemn John for being one. He ate and drank and fraternized socially with those He was trying to help. The Pharisees and lawyers criticized Him for doing what they criticized John the Baptist for not doing. Jesus is saying, "You cannot have it both ways." The real opposition in Israel's leadership, both to John the Baptist and to Jesus, was that both were preaching the same ethical message and putting the divine finger upon the sins of men. The Establishment wanted a religion that did not ask meddlesome questions about sin. Their privileged position from which they exploited society was threatened by all of this talk about the "straight paths" which Messiah would travel. They wanted political power with no ethical commitments.

Jesus sums it up in

Verse 35 - "But wisdom is justified of all her children."

καὶ ἐδικαιώθη ἡ σοφία ἀπὸ πάντων τῶν τέκνων αὐτῆς.

καὶ (emphatic conjunction) 14.
ἐδικαιώθη (3d.per.sing.aor.pass.ind.of δικαιόω, constative) 933.
ἡ (nom.sing.fem.of the article in agreement with σοφία) 9.
σοφία (nom.sing.fem.of σοφία, subject of ἐδικαιώθη) 934.
ἀπὸ (preposition with the ablative of means) 70.
πάντων (abl.pl.neut.of πᾶς, in agreement with τέκνων) 67.
τῶν (abl.pl.neut.of the article in agreement with τέκνων) 9.
τέκνων (abl.pl.neut.of τέκνον, means) 229.

αὐτῆς (gen.sing.fem.of αὐτός, metaphorical relationship) 16.

Translation - "Indeed! Wisdom is vindicated by all of her children."

Comment: This is a choice observation. Wisdom gives birth (#229) to her children, who, truly born out of wisdom justify and vindicate her. They think logically, speak coherently and consistently and behave wisely. By the same token those not born of wisdom think, speak and act like fools and knaves. And that is how the men of that generation were behaving. After exposing their inconsistencies Jesus closes the incident with this quiet observation. Note the empirical nature of His observation. The practical test of one's philosophy is one's behavior. Note how Matthew reports this (Mt.11:19).

In the chronological sequence of events parts D and E follow, after which we take up the Luke story.

(D) Woes Upon the Cities of Opportunity

(Mt.11:20-24)

(E) Christ's Prayer and Claim for Himself

(Mt.11:25-30)

(F) The Anointing of Jesus' Feet in the House of Simon and the Parable of the Two Debtors

(Lk.7:36-50)

Luke 7:36 - "And one of the Pharisees desired him that he would eat with him. And he went into the Pharisee's house, and sat down to meat."

Ἠρώτα δέ τις αὐτὸν τῶν Φαρισαίων ἵνα φάγῃ μετ' αὐτοῦ, καὶ εἰσελθὼν εἰς τὸν οἶκον τοῦ Φαρισαίου κατεκλίθη.

Ἠρώτα (3d.per.sing.imp.act.ind.of ἐρωτάω, inceptive) 1172.

δέ (continuative conjunction) 11.

τις (nom.sing.masc.of τις, indefinite pronoun, subject of ἠρώτα) 486.

αὐτὸν (acc.sing.masc.of αὐτός, direct object of ἠρώτα) 16.

τῶν (gen.pl.masc.of the article in agreement with Φαρισαίων) 9.

Φαρισαίων (gen.pl.masc.of Φαρισαῖος, partitive genitive) 276.

ἵνα (final conjunction introducing a purpose clause) 114.

φάγῃ (3d.per.sing.2d.aor.act.subj.of Φάγω, purpose) 610.

μετ' (preposition with the genitive of accompaniment) 50.

αὐτοῦ (gen.sing.masc.of αὐτός, accompaniment) 16.

καὶ (inferential conjunction) 14.

εἰσελθὼν (aor.mid.part.nom.sing.masc.of εἰσέρχομαι, adverbial, temporal) 234.

εἰς (preposition with the accusative of extent) 140.

τὸν (acc.sing.masc.of the article in agreement with οἶκον) 9.
οἶκον (acc.sing.masc.of οἶκος, extent) 784.
τοῦ (gen.sing.masc.of the article in agreement with Φαρισαίου) 9.
Φαρισαίου (gen.sing.masc.of φαρισαῖος, possession) 276.

#2165 κατεκλίθη (3d.per.sing.aor.pass.ind.of κατακλίνω, constative).

sat down - Lk.7:36; 14:8.
make sit down - Lk.9:14,15.
sit at meat - Lk.24:30.

Meaning: A combination of κατά (#98) and κλίνω (#746). Hence, to sit down; to recline. To recline on a couch to eat a meal - Lk.7;36; 24:30. To sit down on the ground on a mountain side - Lk.9:14,15. To sit down to a wedding feast - Lk.14:8.

Translation - *"And a certain member of the Pharisee party invited Him to eat with him. Therefore, when he had walked into the house, He was seated at the table."*

Comment: ἠρώτα is an inceptive imperfect, denoting the repeated invitation which the Pharisee pressed upon Jesus. δὲ might be considered as adversative in the light of Jesus' remarks of vss.31-35, since it would seem unlikely that a Pharisee would invite Jesus to dinner after our Lord's devastating analysis. However, we have taken it as continuative. The Pharisee offered his hospitality, although it is clear from what follows that he did not recognize any great need for the salvation which only Jesus could provide. Having entered the house (aorist participle in εἰσελθών) Jesus was ushered to the couch by the side of the table.

In order fully to appreciate the significance of the events in the house of Simon, the Pharisee, the student should review with care the material in Mt.11:20-30, which fits chronologically between His analogy about the children in the marketplace and his visit to the house of Simon. In this passage, Jesus turned away from national Israel with His excoriation of the cities where His mighty works had been performed, prayed a prayer to the Father which is strongly Calvinistic, and then offered salvation on a personal, individual basis to those who recognized the burden of the heavy load. This description of Mt.11:28 describes the poor woman who came to anoint His feet - not her proud host.

Verse 37 - *"And, behold a woman in the city, which was a sinner, when she knew that Jesus sat at meat in the Pharisee's house, brought an alabaster box of ointment."*

καὶ ἰδοὺ γυνὴ ἥτις ἦν ἐν τῇ πόλει ἁμαρτωλός, καὶ ἐπιγνοῦσα ὅτι κατάκειται ἐν τῇ οἰκίᾳ τοῦ Φαρισαίου, κομίσασα ἀλάβαστρον μύρου.

καὶ (continuative conjunction) 14.
ἰδού (exclamation) 95.

γυνή (nom.sing.fem.of γυνή, subject of ἤρξατο, ἐξέμασσεν, κατεφίλει and ἤλειφεν) 103.

ἥτις (nom.sing.fem.of the relative ὅστις, subject of ἦν) 163.

ἦν (3d.per.sing.imp.ind.of εἰμί, progressive description) 86.

ἐν (preposition with the locative of place) 80.

τῇ (loc.sing.fem.of the article in agreement with πόλει) 9.

πόλει (loc.sing.fem.of πόλις, place where) 243.

ἁμαρτωλός, (nom.sing.masc.of ἁμαρτωλός, predicate nominative) 791.

καί (continuative conjunction, *see comment infra*) 14.

ἐπιγνοῦσα (aor.act.part.nom.sing.fem.of ἐπιγινώσκω, adverbial, temporal) 675.

ὅτι (conjunction introducing a declarative clause, indirect assertion) 211.

κατάκειται (3d.per.sing.pres.ind.of κατάκειμαι, indirect assertion) 2065.

ἐν (preposition with the locative of place) 80.

τῇ (loc.sing.fem.of the article in agreement with οἰκίᾳ) 9.

οἰκίᾳ (loc.sing.fem.of οἰκία, place where) 186.

τοῦ (gen.sing.masc.of the article in agreement with Φαρισαίου) 9.

Φαρισαίου (gen.sing.masc.of φαρισαῖος, possession) 276.

κομίσασα (aor.act.part.nom.sing.fem.of κομίζω, adverbial, temporal) 1541.

ἀλάβαστρον (acc.sing.neut.of ἀλάβαστρον, direct object of κομίσασα) 1561.

μύρου (gen.sing.neut.of μύρος, description) 1562.

Translation - "And Look! A woman who in the city was a sinner, when she heard that He was dining in the house of the Pharisee, brought an alabaster vase of myrhh . . . "

Comment: We must look in verse 38 for the main verbs which are joined to the subject γυνή. They are indicated above. Joined with them are four adverbial participles and a complementary infinitive. We also have ἦν in the relative clause and κατάκειται in the declarative clause. The imperfect ἦν indicates that the woman had lived in the city for some time and that her reputation was not good, although ἁμαρτωλός, does not necessarily mean that she was a prostitute, or a woman of loose morals, since the Pharisees used the term to apply to everyone outside their own party. However verse 39 strongly implies that she was a woman of the street. Also verse 47 seems to bear it out. ἐπιγνοῦσα (#675) is stronger than γινώσκω (#131), as perfective knowledge is always greater than durative. The woman made certain that the rumor was true. Otherwise she would not have dared to crash the dinner party. Note that the indirect discourse carries the present tense as it had in direct discourse. "He is dining with the Pharisee." This fact having been established, she went to fetch (κομίσασα) the vase of ointment. We encounter two more adverbial participles in verse 38 (στᾶσα and κλαίουσα), the former an aorist and the latter a present tense, before we reach the main verb with its complementary infinitive (ἤρξατο βρέχειν). The entire sentence says, "The woman . . . having made certain that Jesus was having dinner in the house. . . having brought the vase. . . having stood behind him. . .

weeping. . . began to wash . . . κ.τ.λ."

The Expositors' Bible describes the eastern custom on such occasions. The door to the guest chamber was left open and the uninvited, even comparative strangers, might come and go at will, or they might sit by the wall and watch and listen to the procedings. Thus it is not strange that the woman was free to come near the table as she did.

καὶ before ἐπιγνοῦσα seems unnecessary to the structure of the sentence, since it follows the relative clause and is followed by the participle. If we omit it, the sentence does not bleed. Verse 38 continues to describe the woman's actions.

Verse 38 - ". . . and stood at his feet behind him weeping, and began to wash his feet with tears, and did wipe them with the haris of her head, and kissed his feet, and anointed them with the ointment."

καὶ στᾶσα ὀπίσω παρὰ τοὺς πόδας αὐτοῦ κλαίουσα, τοῖς δάκρυσιν ἤρξατο βρέχειν τοὺς πόδας αὐτοῦ καὶ ταῖς θριξὶν τῆς κεφαλῆς αὐτῆς ἐξέμασσεν, καὶ κατεφίλει τοὺς πόδας αὐτοῦ καὶ ἤλειφεν τῷ μύρῳ.

καὶ (adjunctive conjunction joining participles) 14.
στᾶσα (2d.aor.act.part.nom.sing.fem.of ἵστημι, adverbial, temporal) 180.
ὀπίος (an adverb of place) 302.
παρά (preposition with the accusative of place - "alongside") 154.
τοὺς (acc.pl.masc.of the article in agreement with πόδας) 9.
πόδας (acc.pl.masc.of πούς, physically "alongside") 353.
αὐτοῦ (gen.sing.masc.of αὐτός, possession) 16.
κλαίουσα (pres.act.part.nom.sing.fem.of κλαίω, adverbial, modal) 225.
τοῖς (instrumental pl.neut.of the article in agreement with δάκρυσιν) 9.

#2166 δάκρυσιν (instru.pl.neut.of δάκρυ, means).

tear - Lk.7:38,44; Acts 20:19,31; II Cor.2:4; II Tim.1:4; Heb.5:7; 12:17; Rev.7:17; 21:4.

Meaning: From Homer down. Regular in the New Testament. A tear. With reference to the tears of the woman in the Pharisee's house - Lk.7:38,44. Of Paul's tears - the evidence of his earnestness in the gospel - Acts 20:19,31; II Cor.2:4. Of the tears of Timothy - II Tim.1:4. Of Jesus' tears as He became perfected through the things which He suffered - Heb.5:7; of all tears of the saints to be wiped away in Heaven - Rev.7:17; 21:4. Of Esau's tears - Heb.12:17.

ἤρξατο (3d.per.sing.aor.ind.of ἄρχω, ingressive) 383.
βρέχειν (pres.act.inf.of βρέχω, complementary) 548.
τοὺς (acc.pl.masc.of the article in agreement with πόδας) 9.
πόδας (acc.pl.masc.of πούς, direct object of βρέχειν) 353.
αὐτοῦ (gen.sing.masc.of αὐτός, possession) 16.

καὶ (continuative conjunction) 14.
ταῖς (instru.pl.fem.of the article in agreement with θριξὶν) 9.
θριξὶν (instru.pl.fem.of θρίξ, means) 261.
τῆς (gen.sing.fem.of the article in agreement with καφαλῆς) 9.
κεφαλῆς (gen.sing.fem.of κεφαλή, definition) 521.
αὐτῆς (gen.sing.fem.of αὐτός, possession) 16.

#2167 ἐξέμασσεν (3d.per.sing.imp.act.ind.of ἐκμάσσω, inceptive).

wipe - Lk.7:38,44; John 11:2; 12:3; 13:5.

Meaning: To wipe off or away. With an accusative of direct object and an instrumental of means. Always in the New Testament except John 13:5 of wiping Jesus' feet with the hair. In John 13:5 of wiping the disciples' feet with a towel.

καὶ (continuative conjunction) 14.
κατεφίλει (3d.per.sing.imp.act.ind.of καταφιλέω, ingressive) 1591.
τοὺς (acc.pl.masc.of the article in agreement with πόδας) 9.
πόδας (acc.pl.masc.of πούς, direct object of κατεφίλει) 353.
αὐτοῦ (gen.sing.masc.of αὐτός, possession) 16.
καὶ (continuative conjunction) 14.
ἤλειφεν (3d.per.sing.imp.act.ind.of ἀλείφω, ingressive) 589.
τῷ (instru.sing.masc.of the article in agreement with μύρῳ) 9.
μύρῳ (instru.sing.masc.of μύρος, means) 1562.

Translation - "And when she had taken a position behind Him, by the side of His feet, as she sobbed, she began with her tears to wash His feet, and she began to wipe them with her hair, and she began to kiss His feet and she began to anoint them with myrhh."

Comment: The literal English translation is rough, but it faithfully translates the Greek. One can picture the scene if we remember how the guests reclined on one side, on a couch that was set at some angle from the table upon which the food was served and from which it was eaten. The woman took up her place behind Jesus' back and parallel to His feet. Thus He was not in a position to see her as she ministered unto Him. This was doubtless her wish. This was modesty for a woman of her reputation. Jesus was not forced to look at her. The present tense participle κλαίουσα indicates that she was weeping throughout the performance. With her tears she began to flood His feet (#548). The poor woman burst out sobbing and her tears fell as rain. With her hair she began to wipe His feet. This is the force of the inceptive imperfect tense used throughout the sentence. She also began to kiss His feet and to anoint them with the ointment in her vase. Thus the long sentence, beginning with καὶ ἰδοὺ in verse 37 comes to a close in verse 38. It is packed with drama, when we pay regard to all of the diction, grammar and syntax. Try to imagine the scene! For a moment, with our eyes fixed upon the woman, we forget Simon the Pharisee, who is the host and the other guests at the party. We almost forget our Lord as the action focuses upon the woman. She may have been physically attractive - voluptuously so. What repentance. Her body wracked with sobs, tears flowing and falling down, hair in disarray as she continues to use it to wipe His feet, lips covering the scarred, trail-worn feet of her Lord, repeated applications of the precious, fragrant ointment. Behold, how she loved Him! No sex appeal here - the resurrection power of our Sovereign Lord had burned out her lust and transformed it into love.

As we turn from the touching scene to the host, we see a self-righteous bigot with a mind and heart corrupted by prejudice and self interest. He could see nothing glorious about it. For the Christian who appreciates the spiritual blessing of verse 38 to the full, it is a rude shock to be forced into grim reality as we are forced to consider the caustic unbelief of the host in

Verse 39 - "Now when the Pharisee which had bidden him saw it, he spake within himself, saying, This man, if he were a prophet, would have known who and what manner of woman this is that toucheth him: for she is a sinner."

ἰδὼν δὲ ὁ Φαρισαῖος ὁ καλέσας αὐτὸν εἶπεν ἐν ἑαυτῷ λέγων, Οὗτος εἰ ἦν προφήτης, ἐγίνωσκεν ἂν τίς καὶ ποταπὴ ἡ γυνὴ ἥτις ἅπτεται αὐτοῦ, ὅτι ἁμαρτωλός ἐστιν.

ἰδὼν (aor.part.nom.sing.masc.of ὁράω, adverbial, temporal) 144.
δὲ (adversative conjunction) 11.
ὁ (nom.sing.masc.of the article in agreement with Φαρισαῖος) 9.
Φαρισαῖος (nom.sing.masc.of Φαρισαῖος, subject of εἶπεν) 276.
ὁ (nom.sing.masc.of the article in agreement with καλέσας) 9.
καλέσας (aor.act.part.nom.sing.masc.of καλέω, substantival, apposition) 107.
αὐτὸν (acc.sing.masc.direct object of καλέσας) 16.
εἶπεν (3d.per.sing.aor.act.ind.of εἶπον, constative) 155.
ἐν (preposition with the locative, with ἑαυτῷ) 80.
ἑαυτῷ (loc.sing.masc.of ἑαυτός, metaphorical place) 288.
λέγων (pres.act.part.nom.sing.masc.of λέγω, adverbial, recitative) 66.
Οὗτος (nom.sing.masc.of οὗτος, subject of ἦν) 93.
εἰ (conditional particle in a second-class condition) 337.
ἦν (3d.per.sing.imp.ind.of εἰμί, second-class condition, contrary to fact) 86.
προφήτης (nom.sing.masc.of προφήτης, predicate nominative) 119.
ἐγίνωσκεν (3d.per.sing.imp.act.ind.of γινώσκω, second-class, contrary to fact, condition) 131.
ἂν (conditional particle in a second-class condition) 205.
τίς (nom.sing.fem.of the interrogative pronoun in an indirect question) 281.
καὶ (adjunctive conjunction, joining interrogative pronouns) 14.
ποταπὴ (nom.sing.fem.of ποταπός, interrogative pronoun in indirect question) 759.
ἡ (nom.sing.fem.of the article in agreement with γυνὴ) 9.
γυνὴ (nom.sing.fem.of γυνή, subject of ἐστίν understood) 103.

ἥτις (nom.sing.fem.of ὅστις, relative pronoun, subject of ἅπτεται) 163.
ἅπτεται (3d.per.sing.pres.mid.ind.of ἅπτω, progressive) 711.
αὐτοῦ (gen.sing.masc.of αὐτός, objective genitive) 16.
ὅτι (causal conjunction) 211.
ἁμαρτωλός (nom.sing.fem.of ἁμαρτωλός, predicate nominative) 791.
ἐστιν (3d.per.sing.pres.ind.of εἰμί, aoristic) 86.

Translation - "But when the Pharisee who had invited Him saw it he said to himself, 'This man, if he were a prophet, would know who and of what sort the woman who keeps fondling him is, because she is a sinner.' "

Comment: δὲ is most definitely adversative as the Pharisee is certain to oppose what was going on. The woman's thoughts about Jesus were certainly opposite to those of His host. The substantival participle ὁ καλέσας is in apposition to ὁ Φαρισαῖος. The main verb is εἶπεν. Cf.#80 for other examples of ἐν with ἑαυτός. You find the same data under #288 where the list of ἑαυτός after ἐν is given. Note the contemptuous use of emphatic Οὗτος, in a second-class, contrary to fact, condition. "*This man* if he *were* a prophet would know... κ.τ.λ." - but He is not a prophet and He does not know. The second-class condition always uses one of the secondary tenses (in this case the imperfect) with εἰ in the protasis and ἄν usually is found in the apodosis. The premise (if clause) is assumed to be contrary to fact. "The condition states a thing as if it were untrue or unreal, although in actual fact it may be true." (Mantey, *Manual*, 289). Jesus actually was and is a Prophet, but the Pharisee believed that He was not. Since he was wrong in his premise, he was also wrong in his conclusion. Jesus *did know* who the woman was and of what sort she was. The host only thought He did not. "If He were (I do not believe that He is) a prophet, He would have known (which I do not believe He does) what kind of woman she is." Jesus is a Prophet and He did know, but these words were in the mouth of Simon the Pharisee who believed otherwise. "In this somewhat difficult condition only past tenses of the indicative occur. The premise is assumed to be contrary to fact. The thing in itself may be true, but it is treated as untrue. Here again the condition has only to do with the *statement*, not with the actual fact. The Pharisee here assumes that Jesus is not a prophet because He allowed the sinful woman to wash His feet. Jesus is therefore bound to be ignorant of her true character. The form of the condition reveals the state of mind of the Pharisee, not the truth about Jesus' nature and powers. As a matter of fact it is the Pharisee who is ignorant. . . Surely the indicative is the mode for positive and negative statements, for directness of statement and clarity of expression. But one must emphasize the words "statement" and "expression." The indicative does not go behind the face value of the record. Most untruths are told in the indicative mode. The statement of unreality here from the standpoint of the speaker or writer is as clear cut and positive as that of reality in the first class condition. The term "unreal" as applied to this use of the indicative properly belongs only to the standpoint of the user. To him the case is impossible and he makes a positive statement to that effect in the indicative. By the indicative mode the condition is determined. Whether it is fulfilled or unfulfilled is a more difficult matter. This idea has to be conveyed by suggestion. It is not a question of positive or negative, but of definite assumption of unreality. The "unreality" does not come from the indicative. That in its origin is a matter wholly of the context." (A.T.Robertson, *A Grammar of the Greek New Testament in the Light of Historical Research*, 1934 ed., 1012,1013).

The Pharisee's thought was erroneous because he believed that Jesus should avoid all contact with "sinners" and he also thought that the woman's motives were impure. His first error arose from his own view that he was so good that he also ought to avoid sinners. His second error arose from his habit of judging others. Pharisees were like that. Assuming virtual perfection for themselves, they arrogated to themselves the right to judge others. As a man thinketh in his heart, so is he. That a woman of her stripe could be touched supernaturally by faith in the Son of God and thus be rendered capable of pure worship was beyond Simon's twisted powers of comprehension. Why the display? Why should she love Him more than I do? Jesus answers the questions with the parable of the two debtors in verses 40-47.

Verse 40 - "And Jesus answering said unto him, Simon, I have somewhat to say unto thee. And he saith, Master, say on."

καὶ ἀποκριθεὶς ὁ Ἰησοῦς εἶπεν πρὸς αὐτόν, Σίμων, ἔχω σοί τι εἰπεῖν. ὁ δὲ Διδάσκαλε, εἰπέ, φησίν.

καὶ (inferential conjunction) 14.
ἀποκριθεὶς (aor.part.nom.sing.masc.of ἀποκρίνομαι, adverbial, modal) 318.
ὁ (nom.sing.masc.of the article in agreement with Ἰησοῦς) 9.
Ἰησοῦς (nom.sing.masc.of Ἰησοῦς, subject of εἶπεν) 3.
εἶπεν (3d.per.sing.aor.act.ind.of εἶπον, constative) 155.
πρὸς (preposition with the accusative after a verb of speaking) 197.
αὐτόν (acc.sing.masc.of αὐτός, after a verb of speaking) 16.

#2168 Σίμων (voc.sing.masc.of Σίμων, address).

Simon - Lk.7:40,43,44.

Meaning: Thought to be the same as Σίμων ὁ λεπρός (#1560). We think not. At any rate, I have given him a separate number. The Pharisee in whose house the woman anointed Jesus' feet - Lk.7:40,43,44.

ἔχω (1st.per.sing.pres.act.ind.of ἔχω, aoristic) 82.
σοί (dat.sing.masc.of σύ, indirect object of εἰπεῖν) 104.
τι (acc.sing.neut.of τις, direct object of ἔχω) 486.
εἰπεῖν (aor.act.inf.of εἶπον, complementary) 155.
ὁ (nom.sing.masc.of the article, subject of φησίν) 9.
δὲ (continuative conjunction) 11.
Διδάσκαλε (voc.sing.masc.of διδάσκαλος, address) 742.
εἰπέ (2d.per.sing.aor.act.impv.of εἶπον, command) 155.
φησίν (3d.per.sing.pres.ind.of φημί, aoristic) 354.

Translation - "*Therefore in reply Jesus said to him, 'Simon, I have something to say to you.' And he said, 'Teacher, say it.'* "

Comment:καὶ is inferential. It was because Jesus knew what Simon was thinking that He said to him what is recorded. Note that Simon the Pharisee did not speak his thoughts aloud (vs.39). But this did not prevent our Lord from knowing all that he was thinking. Jesus' statement to His host sounds aggressive. Our Lord was probably irked by the stinking bigotry and ignorance of this Pharisee who had no good reason for having invited Jesus home to dinner in the first place. Simon's reply is with eclat and aplomb. He is the host in perfect possession of his feelings. Why should he be troubled with any question from this Nazarene carpenter? At this point he thinks that he is in a strong position fully able to bandy words with this ill-taught peasant who claims to be a prophet.

Verse 41 - "*There was a certain creditor which had two debtors: the one owed five hundred pence, and the other fifty.*"

δύο χρεοφειλέται ἦσαν δανειστῇ τινι. ὁ εἷς ὤφειλεν δηνάρια πεντακόσια, ὁ δὲ ἕτερος πεντήκοντα.

δύο (numeral) 385.

#2169 χρεοφειλέται (nom.pl.masc.of χρεοφειλέτης, subject of ἦσαν).

　debtor - Lk.7:41; 16:5.

Meaning: A combination of χρεός - "debt" and ὀφειλέτης (#581). Hence, a debtor. One owing money to a creditor. In Jesus' parables - Lk.7:41; 16:5.

ἦσαν (3d.per.pl.imp.ind.of εἰμί, progressive duration) 86.

#2170 δανιστῇ (dat.sing.masc.of δανειστής, personal advantage).

　creditor - Lk.7:41.

Meaning: Related to δάνειον (#1275), δανείζω (#538). A creditor. One who loans money to a debtor - Lk.7:41.

τινι (dat.sing.masc.of τις, in agreement with δανειστῇ) 486.
ὁ (nom.sing.masc.of the article in agreement with εἷς) 9.
εἷς (nom.sing.masc.of εἷς, subject of ὤφειλεν) 469.
ὤφειλεν (3d.per.sing.imp.act.ind.of ὀφείλω, progressive duration) 1277.
δηνάρια (acc.pl.neut.of δηνάριον, direct object of ὤφειλεν) 1278.

#2171 πεντακόσια (acc.pl.neut.of πεντακόσιοι, in agreement with δηνάρια).

　five hundred - Lk.7:41; I Cor.15:6.

Meaning: Five hundred. Joined with δηνάρια in Lk.7:41; with ἀδελφοῖς in I Cor.15:6.

ὁ (nom.sing.masc.of the article in agreement with ἕτερος) 9.

δέ (continuative conjunction) 11.

ἕτερος (nom.sing.masc.of ἕτερος, subject of ὤφειλεν, understood) 605.

#2172 πεντήκοντα (acc.pl.neut.of πεντήκοντα, direct object of ὤφειλεν).

fifty - Lk.7:41; 9:14; 16:6; John 8:57; 21:11; Acts 13:20; Mk.6:40.

Meaning: Related to #'s 4382, 1125, 1119, 1927, 2171, 2956. Fifty. Joined to δηνάρια in Lk.7:41; βάτους in Lk.16:6; ἔτη in John 8:57. With reference to the number of fish - John 21:11; with τετρακοσίοις καὶ πεντήκοντα ἔτεσιν in Acts 13:20. *Cf.* also Lk.9:14.

Translation - *"Two debtors were under obligation to a certain creditor. The one owed $83.34 and the other $8.34."*

Comment: A literal translation is "Two debtors were for the personal advantage of a certain creditor." There is no other verb to go with ἦσαν. The dative of personal advantage in δανειστῇ supplies the key. The meaning is clear. Two men owed money to the same man - the first ten times more than the second. *Cf.*#1278 and the amounts owed respectively are as translated. The exact size of the debts cannot be computed due to the devaluation of the denarius under Roman rule. It is not important however that we know with precision how much they owed. The point is that one was ten times as deep in debt as the other.

Verse 42 - *"And when they had nothing to pay, he frankly forgave them both. Tell me therefore, which of them will love him most?"*

μὴ ἐχόντων αὐτῶν ἀποδοῦναι ἀμφοτέροις ἐχαρίσατο. τίς οὖν αὐτῶν πλεῖον ἀγαπήσει αὐτόν;

μή (negative conjunction with the participle) 87.

ἐχόντων (pres.act.part.gen.pl.masc.of ἔχω, genitive absolute) 82.

αὐτῶν (gen.pl.masc.of αὐτός, genitive absolute) 16.

ἀποδοῦναι (2d.aor.act.inf.of ἀποδίδωμι, epexegetical) 495.

ἀμφοτέροις (dat.pl.masc.of ἀμφότερος, personal advantage) 813.

ἐχαρίσατο (3d.per.sing.aor.ind.of χαρίζομαι, constative) 2158.

τίς (nom.sing.masc.of τίς, interrogative pronoun, subject of ἀγαπήσει) 281.

οὖν (inferential conjunction) 68.

αὐτῶν (gen.pl.masc.of αὐτός, partitive genitive) 16.

πλεῖον (acc.sing.neut.of πλείων, adverbial) 474.

ἀγαπήσει (3d.per.sing.fut.act.ind.of ἀγαπάω, deliberative) 540.

αὐτόν (acc.sing.masc.of αὐτός, direct object of ἀγαπήσει) 16.

Translation - *"Because they had nothing to pay, he cancelled the debt for both. Which of them, therefore, will love him more?"*

Comment: The genitive absolute in the present tense is causal. It was *because* they had nothing to pay that the creditor cancelled the debts. *Cf.*#2158 for the variety of ways in which this verb is used - always "to favor" in some way, in each case dependent upon the context. In this context it means to grant favor by cancelling a debt.τίς . . . αὐτῶν, a partitive genitive. "Which one of them . . . ?" *i.e.* of the two debtors.

It was a simple problem and Simon, although thoroughly confused at the moment was not totally benighted. He is about to give the correct answer iñ

Verse 43 - "Simon answered and said, I suppose that he, to whom he forgave most. And he said unto him, Thou hast rightly judged."

ἀποκριθεὶς Σίμων εἶπεν, Ὑπολαμβάνω ὅτι ᾧ τὸ πλεῖον ἐχαρίσατο. ὁ δὲ εἶπεν αὐτῷ, Ὀρθῶς ἔκρινας.

ἀποκριθεὶς (aor.part.nom.sing.masc.of ἀποκρίνομαι, adverbial, modal) 318.
Σίμων (nom.sing.masc.of Σίμων, subject of εἶπεν) 2168.
εἶπεν (3d.per.sing.aor.act.ind.of εἶπον, constative) 155.

#2173 Ὑπολαμβάνω (1st.per.sing.pres.act.ind.of ὑπολαμβάνω, aoristic).

answer - Lk.10:30.
receive - Acts 1:9; III John 8.
suppose - Lk.7:43; Acts 2:15.

Meaning: A combination of ὑπό (#117) and λαμβάνω (#533). Hence, "to take up" or "to take under." Physically, to lift up from the earth and to receive under a cloud so as to disappear from earthly sight - Acts 1:9. To "take up" an argument; therefore to reply; to interrupt, *i.e.* "to take up the point in conversation" - Lk.10:30. Intellectually, to take under advisement; therefore to suppose or assume - Lk.7:43; Acts 2:15. To take a visitor into a home - III John 8.

ὅτι (conjunction introducing an object clause) 211.
ᾧ (dat.sing.masc.of ὅς, personal advantage) 65.
τὸ (acc.sing.neut.of the article in agreement with πλεῖον) 9.
πλεῖον (acc.sing.neut.of πλείων, direct object of ἐχαρίσατο) 474.
ἐχαρίσατο (3d.per.sing.aor.ind.of χαρίζομαι, culminative) 2158.
ὁ (nom.sing.masc.of the article in agreement with εἶπεν) 9.
δὲ (inferential conjunction) 11.
εἶπεν (3d.per.sing.aor.act.ind.of εἶπον, constative) 155.
αὐτῷ (dat.sing.masc.of αὐτός, indirect object of εἶπεν) 16.

#2174 ὀρθῶς (adverbial).

plain - Mk.7:35.
right - Lk.10:28.
rightly - Lk.7:43; 20:21.

Meaning: Related to #'s 4426, 3314, 4824. Correct; right; in line with what is considered truthful and sound. In Mk.7:35, as it relates to correct enunciation;

as it relates to logic - Lk.7:43; as it relates to correct theological and philosophical thought - Lk.10:28; 20:21.

ἔκρινας (2d.per.sing.aor.act.ind.of κρίνω, culminative) 531.

Translation - "Simon replied by saying, 'I assume that it is he for whom he forgave more.' Therefore He said to him,'You have reached a right conclusion.'"

Comment: Jesus may have smiled a bit as He congratulated Simon on his orthodox thinking! Simon may have expected a trap. Hence his cautious use of ὑπολαμβάνω, as if he were thinking, "What is he driving at?" So, "On the face of it, and for the sake of the argument, I assume . . . κ.τ.λ." Jesus agrees and pursues His point in

Verse 44 - "And he turned to the woman, and said unto Simon, Seest thou this woman? I entered thine house, thou gavest me no water for my feet: but she hath washed my feet with tears, and wiped them with the hairs of her head."

καὶ στραφεὶς πρὸς τὴν γυναῖκα τῷ Σίμωνι ἔφη, Βλέπεις ταύτην τὴν γυναῖκα; εἰσῆλθόν σου εἰς τὴν οἰκίαν, ὕδωρ μοι ἐπὶ πόδας οὐκ ἔδωκας; αὕτη δὲ τοῖς δάκρυσιν ἔβρεξέν μου τοὺς πόδας καὶ ταῖς θριξὶν αὐτῆς ἐξέμαξεν.

καὶ (continuative conjunction) 14.
στραφεὶς (2d.aor.act.part.nom.sing.masc.of στρέφω, adverbial, temporal) 530.
πρὸς (preposition with the accusative of extent) 197.
τὴν (acc.sing.fem.of the article in agreement with γυναῖκα) 9.
γυναῖκα (acc.sing.fem.of γυνή, extent) 103.
τῷ (dat.sing.masc.of the article in agreement with Σίμωνι) 9.
Σίμωνι (dat.sing.masc.of Σίμων, indirect object of ἔφη) 2168.
ἔφη (3d.per.sing.2d.aor.act.ind.of φημί, constative) 354.
Βλέπεις (2d.per.sing.pres.act.impv.of βλέπω, direct question) 499.
ταύτην (acc.sing.fem.of οὗτος, in agreement with γυναῖκα) 93.
τὴν (acc.sing.fem.of the article in agreement with γυναῖκα) 9.
γυναῖκα (acc.sing.fem.of γυνή, direct object of βλέπεις) 103.
εἰσῆλθόν (1st.per.sing.aor.ind.of εἰσέρχομαι, culminative) 234.
σου (gen.sing.masc.of σύ, possession) 104.
εἰς (preposition with the accusative of extent) 140.
τὴν (acc.sing.fem.of the article in agreement with οἰκίαν) 9.
οἰκίαν (acc.sing.fem.of οἰκία, extent) 186.
ὕδωρ (acc.sing.neut.of ὕδωρ, direct object of ἔδωκας) 301.
μοι (dat.sing.masc.of ἐγώ, indirect object of ἔδωκας) 123.
ἐπὶ (preposition with the accusative of extent) 47.
πόδας (acc.pl.masc.of πούς, extent) 353.
οὐκ (negative conjunction with the indicative) 130.
ἔδωκας (2d.per.sing.aor.act.ind.of δίδωμι, culminative) 362.
αὕτη (nom.sing.fem.of οὗτος, subject of ἔβρεξέν and ἐξέμαξεν) 93.

δέ (adversative conjunction) 11.

τοῖς (instru.pl.neut.of the article in agreement with δάκρυσιν) 9.

δάκρυσιν (instru.pl.neut.of δάκρυ, means) 2166.

ἔβρεξέν (3d.per.sing.aor.act.ind.of βρέχω, culminative) 548.

μου (gen.sing.masc.of ἐγώ, possession) 123.

τοὺς (acc.pl.masc.of the article in agreement with πόδας) 9.

πόδας (acc.pl.masc.of πούς, direct object of ἔβρεξέν) 353.

καὶ (adjunctive conjunction joining verbs) 14.

ταῖς (instru.pl.fem.of the article in agreement with θριξὶν) 9.

θριξὶν (instru.pl.fem.of θρίξ, means) 261.

αὐτῆς (gen.sing.fem.of αὐτός, possession) 16.

ἐξέμαξεν (3d.per.sing.aor.act.ind.of ἐκμάσσω, culminative) 2167.

Translation - "And when He had turned to the woman, He said to Simon, 'Do you see this woman? I came into your house; you gave me no water for my feet, but she has washed my feet with tears and she has wiped them with her hair.'"

Comment: στραφεὶς πρὸς τὴν γυναῖκα contrasts beautifully with ὀπίσω παρὰ τοὺς πόδας αὐτοῦ of verse 38. Because she was self-conscious, due to her character, she had taken her place behind Him. Now He turns "near to the woman." This gesture, motivated by pure divine love and not by sinful attraction to her sensual charms, was as natural for Jesus as it was necessary. Her sins had attacked her and brought her to degradation. God, in holy wrath had attacked her and brought her, lowly and weeping, to approach her Saviour from behind; the self-righteous Pharisee had also attacked her in his thoughts. It was time that somebody came to her defense. Who else but Jesus, the only One Who could help her? He, whose divine love had granted her repentance and faith, now turns "near" to her (the basic meaning of πρός #197). Jesus' gesture must have thrilled her heart. What if Jesus had never turned to her, after her acts of worship? Not even a human gentleman would spurn a woman who did what she did! Much less the Son of God. Suppose that Jesus had not come to her defense? What would the poor woman have done? And what would she have thought? The hurt, as of a knife, plunged deep into her spirit, might have driven her back into the streets.

There is another thought here. Jesus seems to be taunting Simon. The Pharisee would have thought the slightest touch contaminating. If he was shocked because Jesus accepted her ministrations without protest, how much more to see Jesus turn His body and come nearer to her? For Jesus to have shrunk from her touch would have been approval for Simon's wicked pride, and a negation of the whole concept of Divine forgiveness. When God forgives a sinner, the basis for pure, close, human association is established. The Christian with racist prejudices, who says that the black Christian is a member of the body of Christ, but should not associate closely with white Christians in the same church building, should take heed.

Having proved to Simon whose side He is on, Jesus attacks him. "Do you see this woman?" if we take βλέπεις as indicative, or "Look at this woman" if we take it as imperative. (The forms are the same). Simon had been looking at her with eyes less pure than those of Jesus. Now Jesus spells out Simon's boorish lack of hospitality. "I came into your house." σου is emphatic. "Water for my feet you did not give." The Westcott & Hort text has μοι ἐπί, but the better reading is μου ἐπὶ τοὺς πόδας. This is better grammar and translates "water for (or upon) my feet, κ.τ.λ." The thought is clear in any case. Jesus' wrath is evident from the emphatic positions of the words in the text. The road had been dusty and hot and Jesus' sandals provided scant protection. Simon should have washed Jesus' feet. He did not.But the poor woman, whom Simon regarded as a "sinner" did. She supplied the customary service which the host neglected. Why? Because she loved Him. Why? Because He had forgiven her many sins. This is the point of the passage. But her foot bath was not the usual basin of water and a towel. "*She with tears flooded my feet* and *with her hair she wiped them.*" The italcized words are emphasized in the Greek. *The Expositors' Greek Testament* points to the "sharply marked antithesis (which) runs through the description" in verses 44-46. ὕδωρ as contrasted with δάκρυσιν; φίλημα with καταφιλοῦσα; ἐλαίῳ (common oil) with μύρῳ (precious ointment); κεφαλὴν with πόδας. "There is a kind of poetic rhythm in the words, as is apt to be the case when men speak under deep emotion."

There are two reasons why Simon's response to Jesus was inferior to that of the woman: (1) His faith was not as strong. He was still stumbling over the "if" in verse 39. Apparently the woman had no doubt that Jesus was the Son of God and the Messiah. (2) Simon was not aware of his sin debt and hence felt no gratitude for the cancellation of the obligation. In his view his need for forgiveness was not as great as hers (vs.47).

Jesus continues in His analysis of the quality of the hospitality of his host as contrasted with the behavior of the woman in

Verse 45 - "*Thou gavest me no kiss: but this woman since the time I came in hath not ceased to kiss my feet.*"

φίλημά μοι οὐκ ἔδωκας, αὕτη δὲ ἀφ᾽ ἧς εἰσῆλθον οὐ διέλιπεν καταφιλοῦσά μου τοὺς πόδας.

#2175 φίλημά (acc.sing.neut.of φίλημα, direct object of ἔδωκας).

kiss - Lk.7:45; 22:48; Rom.16:16; I Cor.16:20; II Cor.13:12; I Thess.5:26; I Pet.5:14.

Meaning: Related to other words beginning with φίλ, e.g. #'s 4023, 5198, 5324, 4880, 4892, 3756, 3675, 4785, 2573, 4836, 2542, 4841, 566, 5141. A kiss. The result (μα) of friendship. In Simon's house - Lk.7:45; in the Garden of Betrayal - Lk.22:48; with reference to the kiss of greeting used in the early church - with ἁγίῳ - in Rom.16:16; I Cor.16:20; II Cor.13:12; I Thess.5:26. With ἀγάπης in I Pet.5:14.

μοι (dat.sing.masc.of ἐγώ, indirect object of ἔδωκας) 123.

οὐκ (negative conjunction with the indicative) 130.

ἔδωκας (2d.per.sing.2d.aor.act.ind.of δίδωμι, constative) 362.
αὕτη (nom.sing.fem.of οὗτος, subject of διέλιπεν) 93.
δὲ (adversative conjunction) 11.
ἀπ' (preposition with the ablative of time separation) 70.
ἧς (abl.sing.fem.of ὅς, time separation) 65.
εἰσῆλθον (1st.per.sing.aor.ind.of εἰσέρχομαι, constative) 234.
οὐ (negative conjunction with the indicative) 130.

#2176 διέλιπεν (3d.per.sing.aor.act.ind.of διαλείπω, constative).

cease - Lk.7:45.

Meaning: A combination of διά (#118) and λείπω (#2636). Hence to cease completely (intensive διά). To stop whatever is going on. With the present participle καταφιλοῦσα - "she did not stop kissing" - continued kissing - Lk.7:45.

καταφιλοῦσα (pres.act.part.nom.sing.fem.of καταφιλέω, adverbial, modal) 1591.
μου (gen.sing.masc.of ἐγώ, possession) 123.
τοὺς (acc.pl.masc.of the article in agreement with πόδας) 9.
πόδας (acc.pl.masc.of πούς, direct object of καταφιλοῦσα) 353.

Translation - "A kiss to me you did not give, but she, from the moment I came in, has not ceased repeatedly to kiss my feet."

Comment: The contrast between φίλημά (#2175) and καταφιλοῦσα (#1591) is important. Run the references to see that the former is likely to be more perfunctory - even deceitful (Lk.22:48), whereas the latter is tender and meaningful (Lk.15:20; Acts 20:37). Yet Matthew (Mt.26:49) uses καταφιλέω for Judas' kiss! It is a safe conjecture that had Simon the Pharisee kissed Jesus, it would have been cold and formal. δὲ is strongly adversative as Jesus contrasts Simon's behavior with that of the woman. Note ἀπ' ἧς - the preposition with the relative in a time expression. *Cf.*#70 for other time expressions with ἀπό. οὐ διέλιπεν - "did not cease once", hence "continually without cessation." The durative time force of the present participle reinforces οὐ with the punctiliar action in the aorist διέλιπεν. Both expressions are non-punctiliar, hence strongly durative. Had Simon kissed Jesus, it would have been upon the cheek. The woman did not so presume but covered His feet with tears, kisses and ointment and with her crowing glory - her hair.
    Jesus continues His odious comparison in

Verse 46 - "My head with oil thou didst not anoint: but this woman hath anointed my feet with ointment."

ἐλαίῳ τὴν κεφαλήν μου οὐκ ἤλειψας, αὕτη δὲ μύρῳ ἤλειφεν τοὺς πόδας μου.

ἐλαίῳ (instru.sing.neut.of ἔλαιον, means) 1530.
τὴν (acc.sing.fem.of the article in agreement with κεφαλήν) 9.
κεφαλήν (acc.sing.fem.of κεφαλή, direct object of ἤλειφας) 521.
μου (gen.sing.masc.of ἐγώ, possession) 123.
οὐκ (negative conjunction with the indicative) 130.
ἤλειφας (2d.per.sing.aor.act.ind.of ἀλείφω, constative) 589.
αὕτη (nom.sing.fem.of οὗτος, subject of ἤλειφεν) 93.
δὲ (adversative conjunction) 11.
μύρῳ (instru.sing.neut.of μύρον, means) 1562.
ἤλειφεν (3d.per.sing.aor.act.ind.of ἀλείφω, culminative) 589.
τοὺς (acc.pl.masc.of the article in agreement with πόδας) 9.
πόδας (acc.pl.masc.of πούς, direct object of ἤλειφεν) 353.
μου (gen.sing.masc.of ἐγώ, possession) 123.

Translation - *"With olive oil my head you did not once anoint, but this woman with ointment has anointed my feet.*

Comment: The literal translation which is designed to show the emphases, should not be used in public worship, except as the reader uses voice stress to bring out emphasis. Of course in exposition the fact that the text emphasizes certain words above others should be pointed out. Contrast ἔλαιον (#1530) with μύρον (#1562). The cheapest versus the most costly. Also contrast κεφαλή with πούς. The woman apparently felt that the anointing of Jesus' head would have been misinterpreted. Hence she expended her costly contribution upon His feet.
    The point of the episode is brought out in

Verse 47 - *"Wherefore I say unto thee, Her sins, which are many, are forgiven; for she loved much: but to whom little is forgiven, the same loveth little."*

οὗ χάριν, λέγω σοι, ἀφέωνται αἱ ἁμαρτίαι αὐτῆς αἱ πολλαί, ὅτι ἠγάπησεν πολύ. ᾧ δὲ ὀλίγον ἀφίεται, ὀλίγον ἀγαπᾷ.

οὗ (gen.sing.masc.of ὅς, relative pronoun with χάριν, definition) 65.

#2177 χάριν (improper preposition of cause).

    because of - Gal.3:19; Jude 16.
    for . . . cause - Eph.3:1,14; Tit.1:5.
    wherefore - I John 3:12; Lk.7:47.
    for the sake of - Tit.1:11.
    reproachfully - (λοιδορίας χάριν) - I Tim.5:14.

Meaning: Always in the New Testament with the genitive. With τίνος - I John 3:12; with ὠφελείας - Jude 16. Because of, on account of. Because of transgressions - Gal.3:19; τούτου χάριν - "for this cause" - Eph.3:1,14; Tit.1:5,11; with οὗ in Lk.7:47.

λέγω (1st.per.sing.pres.act.ind.of λέγω, aoristic) 66.

σοι (dat.sing.masc.of σύ, indirect object of λέγω) 104.

ἀφέωνται (3d.per.pl.perf.pass.ind.of ἀφίημι, consummative) 319.

αἱ (nom.pl.fem.of the article in agreement with ἁμαρτίαι) 9.

ἁμαρτίαι (nom.pl.fem.of ἁμαρτία, subject of ἀφέωνται) 111.

αὐτῆς (gen.sing.fem.of αὐτός, possession) 16.

αἱ (nom.pl.fem.of the article in agreement with πολλαί) 9.

πολλαί (nom.pl.fem.of πολύς, in agreement with ἁμαρτίαι) 228.

ὅτι (epexegetic use in prolepsis) 211.

ἠγάπησεν (3d.per.sing.aor.act.ind.of ἀγαπάω, constative) 540.

πολύ (adverbial) 228.

ᾧ (dat.sing.masc.of ὅς, personal advantage) 65.

δὲ (adversative conjunction) 11.

ὀλίγον (acc.sing.neut.of ὀλίγος, direct object of ἀφίεται) 669.

ἀφίεται (3d.per.sing.pres.pass.ind.of ἀφίημι, aoristic) 319.

ὀλίγον (acc.sing.neut.of ὀλίγος, adverbial) 669.

ἀγαπᾷ (3d.per.sing.pres.act.ind.of ἀγαπάω, aoristic) 540.

Translation - "Therefore I am telling you her sins, though they are many have been forgiven, which explains why she has loved so much; but for the one for whom little is forgiven - that one loves little."

Comment: οὗ χάριν is an infrequent idiom in which the relative in the genitive is joined to the improper preposition. The relative has no antecedent with which it agrees in case. Obviously it refers to the material in verses 44-46. If it were ἧς we could join it to the woman of verse 46 and translate "Because of her. . . " It is "Because of the contrast between your (Simon's) treatment of me and that of the woman." What Simon saw when Jesus said, "Look at this woman" (vs.44) - her tears, her kisses, her tender ministrations upon her Saviour and Lord - this is the basis for what Jesus says in verse 47. The principle here laid down is that the woman had real repentance and faith in the Son of God, as is manifested by her behavior. She was not forgiven because she came to the dinner party and behaved as she did. She was forgiven because she was granted repentance and faith and her good works, there demonstrated, were the fruit, not the root of her salvation. Salvation is never contingent upon works, however sincerely they are expended. But works are contingent upon faith. Her works demonstrated her faith. What Jesus is saying is that her great faith is demonstrated by her love. This is the reason why we cannot take the ὅτι clause as causal, but a prolepsis, and thus epexegetical. It explains the woman's love, which in turn explains her behavior.

The reason Simon did not enthuse over Jesus was that he did not realize the depth of his sin and therefore he could not appreciate the magnitude of his forgiveness. His love for Jesus was only in proportion to his repentance and faith, which in turn was in proportion to the extent of his forgiveness, which in turn was in proportion to his realization of his own depravity. Simon was not impressed by the gravity of his own sinful condition. The woman was devastated by hers. Hence, when forgiveness came, her depth of sinful despair was replaced by depths of love for her Saviour. When and if forgiveness should come to Simon his reaction to his great good fortune would be demonstrated by something more than the perfunctory invitation to a dinner party. He had not thus far been sufficiently impressed with his debt to Jesus to administer the usual social amenities which were customary for a host. The Arminians who take the ὅτι clause as causal, are justified in their conclusion that the woman's love for Jesus, with its resultant ministry of love was the reason for her forgiveness. It does not help to point out that ἀφέωνται is a consummative perfect. This only says that her forgiveness was an accomplished fact *before* she came into the room. The Calvinist cannot prove his point from this passage. But he dare not take ὅτι in a causal sense without forcing this statement into conflict with other passages such as Eph.2:8,9; Tit.3:5 and many others.

On the other hand the Antinomian will twist this passage by arguing that in order to love Christ much we must sin much. Therefore let us plumb the depths of depravity! To which Godet has replied, "We need add nothing to what each of us already has, for the sum of the whole matter is - to the noblest and purest of us, what is wanting in order to love much, is not sin, but the knowledge of it." (*The Pulpit Commentary*, en loc., Lk.7:47).

Jesus then announced to the woman what He had already told Simon, the Pharisee in

Verse 48 - "And he said unto her, Thy sins are forgiven."

εἶπεν δὲ αὐτῇ, Ἀφέωνταί σου αἱ ἁμαρτίαι.

εἶπεν (3d.per.sing.aor.act.ind.of εἶπον, constative) 155.
δὲ (continuative conjunction) 11.
αὐτῇ (dat.sing.fem.of αὐτός, indirect object of εἶπεν) 16.
ἀφέωνταί (3d.per.pl.perf.pass.ind.of ἀφίημι, consummative) 319.
σου (gen.sing.fem.of σύ, possession) 104.
αἱ (nom.pl.fem.of the article in agreement with ἁμαρτίαι) 9.
ἁμαρτίαι (nom.pl.fem.of ἁμαρτία, subject of ἀφέωνται) 111.

Translation - "And He said to her, 'Your sins have been forgiven.' "

Comment: Jesus has finished His long statement to Simon (vss.44-47) and turns back to the woman. Note that the perfect passive consummative ἀφέωνται is emphasized ahead of the subject and the possessive pronoun. The important point her is not sins, however great, nor that they are hers, but that *they have been and therefore now are forgiven*. In fact, under the blood and by Divine grace atoned. God has also forgotten about them! The perfect tense speaks of a present condition as a result of a past completed action. By forgiving her sins and saving her (vs.50) Jesus takes His place as Incarnate God. Thus only can He justify His action. If Jesus had not been God, the woman in this piece would have been demonstrated to be a frustrated, distraught and oversexed sensualist. His deity is the factor in the pattern that lends dignity and reason to her action. And since His is God, Who, by divine power could purify her motives, He has authority on earth to forgive her sins. His announcement to the woman triggered comment from the other guests, who, until this point, have not figured in the story.

Verse 49 - "And they that sat at meat with him began to say within themselves, Who is this man that forgiveth sins also?"

καὶ ἤρξαντο οἱ συνανακείμενοι λέγειν ἐν ἑαυτοῖς, Τίς οὗτός ἐστιν ὅς καὶ ἁμαρτίας ἀφίησιν;

καὶ (inferential conjunction) 14.

ἤρξαντο (3d.per.pl.aor.mid.ind.of ἄρχω, ingressive) 383.

οἱ (nom.pl.masc.of the article in agreement with συνανακείμενοι) 9.

συνανακείμενοι (pres.part.nom.pl.masc.of συνανάκειμαι, substantival, subject of ἤρξαντο) 792.

λέγειν (pres.act.inf.of λέγω, complementary) 66.

ἐν (preposition with the locative, with plural nouns and pronouns) 80.

ἑαυτοῖς (loc.pl.masc.of ἑαυτός, metaphorical place) 288.

Τίς (nom.sing.masc.of τίς, interrogative pronoun in direct question) 281.

οὗτος (nom.sing.masc.of οὗτος, subject of ἐστιν) 93.

ἐστιν (3d.per.sing.pres.ind.of εἰμί, aoristic) 86.

ὅς (nom.sing.masc.of ὅς, relative pronoun, subject of ἀφίησιν) 65.

καὶ (ascensive conjunction) 14.

ἁμαρτίας (acc.pl.fem.of ἁμαρτία, direct object of ἀφίησιν) 111.

ἀφίησιν (3d.per.sing.pres.act.ind.of ἀφίημι, customary) 319.

Translation - "And those who were dining with Him began to say to themselves, 'Who is this man who even forgives sins?' "

Comment: Jesus' remark to the woman (vs.48) caused this stir among the other guests. They did not say aloud what they were thinking. *Cf.*#288 for other examples of ἐν ἑαυτοῖς. Note that Τίς in the direct question is emphasized. "*Who* is He? The relative clause explains their amazement. ". . . who *even* (ascensive καὶ) is forgiving sins?"

Jesus had been performing many miracles (Lk.7:17,22), not the least of which was the miracle the guests had just witnessed - that of touching a sinful life with the redemptive grace of God. But they could not read the woman's heart, as Jesus did, and hence could have misunderstood or perhaps underestimated her motives. Authority to forgive sin can be found only in the One with power to cleanse a sinful life.

If Jesus replied to their thoughts, it is not recorded. Rather He speaks again to the woman in

Verse 50 - "And he said to the woman, Thy faith hath saved thee; go in peace."

εἶπεν δὲ πρὸς τὴν γυναῖκα, Ἡ πίστις σου σέσωκέν σε. πορεύου εἰς εἰρήνην.

εἶπεν (3d.per.sing.aor.act.ind.of εἶπον, constative) 155.
δὲ (continuative conjunction) 11.
πρὸς (preposition with the accusative, after a verb of speaking) 197.
τὴν (acc.sing.fem.of the article in agreement with γυναῖκα) 9.
γυναῖκα (acc.sing.fem.of γυνή, after a verb of speaking) 103.
ἡ (nom.sing.fem.of the article in agreement with πίστις) 9.
πίστις (nom.sing.fem.of πίστις, subject of σέσωκέν) 728.
σου (gen.sing.fem.of σύ, possession) 104.
σέσωκέν (3d.per.sing.perf.act.ind.of σώζω, consummative) 109.
σε (acc.sing.fem.of σύ, direct object of σέσωκέν) 104.
πορεύου (2d.per.sing.pres.act.impv.of πορεύομαι, command) 170.
εἰς (preposition with the accusative, static use) 140.
εἰρήνην (acc.sing.fem.of εἰρήνη, like an instrumental, static, original use of εἰς) 865. ·

Translation - "And He said to the woman, "Your faith has saved you. Go in peace.'"

Comment: Jesus, of course, knew what the other guests were thinking, and He could have entered into controversy with them, but He ignored them in order to devote His attention to the new Christian at His feet. Note the perfect tense in σέσωκέν, which matches the consummative perfect in ἀφέωνται of verse 48. Her sins had been forgiven and salvation was hers, as a result of a past completed action. Note also that it was her faith that saved her - not her beautiful good works that the story tells us about. Faith had saved her. She is now saved. When, in relation to the events at the dinner party did she exercise faith? She would not have taken steps in the first place to ascertain that Jesus was Simon's guest had she not believed upon Him and loved Him. Note again ἐπιγνοῦσα ὅτι κατάκειται (vs.37). Also she had brought the ointment with her (κομίσασα #1541). This action was not on the spur of the moment. Since faith saved her, all subsequent acts of service and worship represent its fruit, not its root. Which bears out comments on verse 47. Note εἰς in the adverbial sense. *Cf.*#140 for other examples.

(G) Christ's Companions on His Second Tour of Galilee

(Luke 8:1-3)

Luke 8:1 - "And it came to pass afterward, that he went throughout every city and village, preaching and shewing the glad tidings of the kingdom of God: and the twelve were with him."

Καὶ ἐγένετο ἐν τῷ καθεξῆς καὶ αὐτὸς διώδευεν κατὰ πόλιν καὶ κώμην κηρύσσων καὶ εὐαγγελιζόμενος τὴν βασιλείαν τοῦ θεοῦ, καὶ οἱ δώδεκα σὺν αὐτῷ,

Καὶ (continuative conjunction) 14.
ἐγένετο (3d.per.sing.aor.ind.of γίνομαι, constative) 113.
ἐν (preposition with the locative of time point) 80.
τῷ (loc.sing.masc.of the article in agreement with χρόνῳ, understood) 9.
καθεξῆς (adverb of time) 1711.
καὶ (adjunctive conjunction) 14.
αὐτὸς (nom.sing.masc.of αὐτός, subject of διώδευεν) 16.

#2178 διώδευεν (3d.per.sing.imp.act.ind.of διοδεύω, inceptive).

go throughout - Lk.8:1.
pass through - Acts 17:1.

Meaning: A combination of διά (#118) and ὁδεύω - "to travel." Hence, to travel through or throughout. Followed by geographic place names both in Lk.8:1 and Acts 17:1.

κατὰ (preposition with the accusative, horizontal extension) 98.
πόλιν (acc.sing.fem.of πόλις, extension) 243.
καὶ (adjunctive conjunction joining nouns) 14.
κώμην (acc.sing.fem.of κώμη, extension) 834.
κηρύσσων (pres.act.part.nom.sing.masc.of κηρύσσω, adverbial, modal) 249.
καὶ (adjunctive conjunction joining participles) 14.
εὐαγγελιζόμενος (pres.mid.part.nom.sing.masc.of εὐαγγελίζω, adverbial, modal) 909.
τὴν (acc.sing.fem.of the article in agreement with βασιλείαν) 9.
βασιλείαν (acc.sing.fem.of βασιλεία, direct object of εὐαγγελιζόμενος) 253.
τοῦ (gen.sing.masc.of the article in agreement with θεοῦ) 9.
θεοῦ (gen.sing.masc.of θεός, description) 124.
καὶ (adjunctive conjunction joining substantives) 14.
οἱ (nom.pl.masc.of the article in agreement with δώδεκα) 9.
δώδεκα (nom.pl.masc.indeclin.of δώδεκα, subject of ἦσαν, understood) 820.
σὺν (preposition with the instrumental of accompaniment) 1542.
αὐτῷ (instru.sing.masc.of αὐτός, accompaniment) 16.

Translation - "And it happened a short time after that both He and the twelve with Him began to visit every city and village, preaching and telling the good news of the kingdom of God."

Comment: The adverb καθεξῆς means "according to order" of whatever sort - chronological, geographical, logical, etc., etc. In this context we supply χρόνῳ after ἐν to get the translation *supra.* The verb διώδευεν indicates that they went from city to city and from village to village. It was a thorough coverage of the territory. Note the inceptive imperfect in the verb - "He began the journey..." The modal participles tell us what He and the disciples did on this preaching tour. They preached and spread the good news of the Kingdom of God. Jesus was really preaching Himself for He is the embodiment of the Kingdom of God.

This is after His turn from Israel as a nation to the offer of the Kingdom on an individual basis (Mt.11:20-30). He was engaged in soul winning as we should practise it today. Luke adds, almost as an afterthought, that the twelve disciples were with Him. Some women also accompanied Him as we learn in verses 2 and 3.

Verse 2 - "And certain women, which had been healed of evil spirits and infirmities, Mary called Magdalene, out of whom went seven devils. . . "

καὶ γυναῖκες τινες αἱ ἦσαν τεθεραπευμέναι ἀπὸ πνευμάτων πονηρῶν καὶ ἀσθενειῶν, Μαρία ἡ καλουμένη Μαγδαληνή, ἀφ' ἧς δαιμόνια ἑπτὰ ἐξεληλύθει,

καὶ (continuative conjunction) 14.

γυναῖκες (nom.pl.fem.of γυνή, subject of verb understood) 103.

τινες (nom.pl.fem.of τις, in agreement with γυναῖκες) 486.

αἱ (nom.pl.fem.of ὅς, relative pronoun, subject of ἦσαν) 65.

ἦσαν (3d.per.pl.imp.ind.of εἰμί, pluperfect periphrastic) 86.

τεθεραπευμέναι (perf.pass.part.nom.pl.fem.of θεραπεύω, pluperfect periphrastic) 406.

ἀπὸ (preposition with the ablative of separation) 70.

πνευμάτων (abl.pl.neut.of πνεῦμα, separation) 83.

πονηρῶν (abl.pl.neut.of πονηρός, in agreement with πνευμάτων) 438.

καὶ (adjunctive conjunction, joining nouns) 14.

ἀσθενειῶν (ablative plural fem.of ἀσθένεια, separation) 740.

Μαρία (nom.sing.fem.of Μαρία, apposition with γυναῖκες) 1668.

ἡ (nom.sing.fem.of the article in agreement with καλουμένη) 9.

καλουμένη (pres.pass.part.nom.sing.fem.of καλέω, substantival, in apposition with Μαρία) 107.

Μαγδαληνή (nom.sing.fem.of Μαγδαληνή, appellation) 1669.

ἀφ' (preposition with the ablative of separation) 70.

ἧς (abl.sing.fem.of ὅς, separation) 65.

δαιμόνια (nom.pl.neut.of δαιμόνιον, subject of ἐξεληλύθει) 686.

ἑπτὰ (numeral) 1024.

ἐξεληλύθει (3d.per.sing.pluperfect act.ind.of ἐξέρχομαι, consummative) 161.

Translation - "And certain women who had been healed of evil spirits and general ill health - Mary, known as Magdalene, from whom seven demons had gone out."

Comment: The pluperfect periphrastic ἦσαν τεθεραπευμέναι and the pluperfect ἐξεληλύθει both indicate past healing with permanent results of good health. Luke the physician may be expected to diagnose their previous illnesses. He gives special attention to Mary Magdalene who had been an especially difficult case.

Verse 3 - "And Joanna the wife of Chuza, Herod's steward, and Susanna, and many others, which ministered unto him of their substance."

καὶ Ἰωάννα γυνὴ Χουζᾶ ἐπιτρόπου Ἡρῴδου καὶ Σουσάννα καὶ ἔτεραι
πολλαί, αἵτινες διηκόνουν αὐτοῖς ἐκ τῶν ὑπαρχόντων αὐταῖς.

καὶ (adjunctive conjunction joining nouns) 14.

#2179 Ἰωάννα (nom.sing.fem.of Ἰωάννα, in apposition with γυναῖκες).

Joanna - Lk.8:3; 24:10.

Meaning: The wife of Chuza, Herod's steward. One of the women with Jesus on
His second Galilean tour (Lk.8:3) and one of the group at the empty tomb
(Lk.24:10).

γυνή (nom.sing.fem.of γυνή, in apposition with Ἰωάννα) 103.

#2180 Χουζᾶ (gen.sing.masc.of Χουζᾶς, relationship).

Chuza - Lk.8:3.

Meaning: Steward of Herod Antipas and husband of Joanna (#2179).

ἐπιτρόπου (gen.sing.masc.of ἐπίτροπος, in apposition with Χουζᾶ) 1321.
Ἡρῴδου (gen.sing.masc.of Ἡρῴδης, relationship) 136A.
καὶ (adjunctive conjunction joining nouns) 14.

#2181 Σουσάννα (nom.sing.fem.of Σουσάννα, in apposition with γυναῖκες).

Susanna - Lk.8:3.

Meaning: One of the women who accompanied Jesus on His second Galilean
tour. The name means "Lily." Lk.8:3.

καὶ (adjunctive conjunction joining a noun with a pronoun) 14.
ἔτεραι (nom.pl.fem.of ἔτερος, in agreement with γυναῖκες) 605.
πολλαί (nom.pl.fem.of πολύς, in agreement with ἔτεραι) 228.
αἵτινες (nom.pl.fem.of ὅστις, subject of διηκόνουν) 163.
διηκόνουν (3d.per.pl.imp.act.ind.of διακονέω, progressive duration) 367.
αὐτοῖς (dat.pl.masc.of αὐτός, personal advantage) 16.
ἐκ (preposition with the ablative of source) 19.
τῶν (abl.pl.neut.of the article in agreement with ὑπαρχόντων) 9.
ὑπαρχόντων (pres.act.part.abl.pl.neut.of ὑπάρχω, substantival, source)
1303.
αὐταῖς (dat.pl.fem.of αὐτός, possession) 16.

Translation - ". . . and Joanna, the wife of Chuza, steward of Herod Antipas, and
Susanna, and many other women, who were constantly taking care of them from
their own possessions."

Comment: The imperfect διηκόνουν indicates the constant care which the
women provided for Jesus and the disciples.

(3) A Day of Teaching and a Blasphemous Accusation
of League with Beelzebub

(Mark 3:20-30; Matthew 12:22-37)

Mark 3:20 - *"And the multitude cometh together again, so that they could not so much as eat bread."*

Καὶ ἔρχεται εἰς οἶκον, καὶ συνέρχεται πάλιν ὄχλος, ὥστε μὴ δύνασθαι αὐτοὺς μηδὲ ἄρτον φαγεῖν.

(Note:The first clause - "And they went into an house," is included in Mk.3:19 in the KJV. The better Greek manuscripts include the clause in verse 20).

Καὶ (continuative conjunction) 14.

ἔρχεται (3d.per.sing.pres.ind.of ἔρχομαι, historical) 146.

εἰς (preposition with the accusative of extent) 140.

οἶκον (acc.sing.masc.of οἶκος, extent) 784.

καὶ (continuative conjunction) 14.

συνέρχεται (3d.per.sing.pres.ind.of συνέρχομαι, historical) 78.

πάλιν (adverbial) 355.

ὁ (nom.sing.masc.of the article in agreement with ὄχλος) 9.

ὄχλος (nom.sing.masc.of ὄχλος, subject of συνέρχεται) 418.

ὥστε (consecutive conjunction introducing a result clause) 752.

μὴ (negative conjunction with the infinitive) 87.

δύνασθαι (pres.inf.of δύναμαι, result) 289.

αὐτοὺς (acc.pl.masc.of αὐτός, general reference) 16.

μηδὲ (negative paratactic disjunctive) 612.

ἄρτον (acc.sing.masc.of ἄρτος, direct object of φαγεῖν) 338.

φαγεῖν (aor.act.inf.of ἐσθίω, complementary) 610.

Translation - *"And He came into a house; and again the crowd assembled, with the result that they were not able even to eat bread."*

Comment: The first clause is found in the KJV in verse 19. The story is more coherent if we consider it a part of what follows in verse 20. The selection of the twelve apostles is the thought of verse 19. Now the account moves on. Note the historical present tenses, which is typical of Mark's writings. Once again the people gathered about the house and invaded the premises in such number that they were not even able to eat their meals. The result clause with ὥστε and the infinitive is the most common way to express result. *Cf.*#752 for other examples. Note the μὴ . . . μηδὲ sequence. His friends, who were travelling with Him (Lk.8:1-3) became worried about Jesus, as we see in

Verse 21 - *"And when his friends heard of it, they went out to lay hold on him: for they said, He is beside Himself."*

καὶ ἀκούσαντες οἱ παρ' αὐτοῦ ἐξῆλθον κρατῆσαι αὐτόν, ἔλεγον γὰρ ὅτι ἐξέστη.

καὶ (continuative conjunction) 14.
ἀκούσαντες (aor.act.part.nom.pl.masc.of ἀκούω, adverbial, temporal) 148.
οἱ (nom.pl.masc.of the article, subject of ἐξῆλθον) 9.
παρ' (preposition with the ablative, with persons) 154.
αὐτοῦ (abl.sing.masc.of αὐτός, with παρά) 16.
ἐξῆλθον (3d.per.pl.aor.ind.of ἐξέρχομαι, constative) 161.
κρατῆσαι (aor.act.inf.of κρατέω, purpose) 828.
αὐτόν (acc.sing.masc.of αὐτός, direct object of κρατῆσαι) 16.
ἔλεγον (3d.per.pl.imp.act.ind.of λέγω, inceptive) 66.
γὰρ (causal conjunction) 105.
ὅτι (objective conjunction introducing indirect discourse) 211.
ἐξέστη (3d.per.sing.2d.aor.act.ind.of ἐξίστημι, culminative) 992.

Translation - "And when those who were with Him heard about it, they went out to take Him into their custody, because they began to say that He had become deranged."

Comment: The crowd was getting out of hand. His friends heard about it and went out to protect Jesus. *Cf.*#828. They wished to provide Him with protective custody. The phrase οἱ παρ' αὐτοῦ - "Those who were with Him" refers to the group named in Lk.8:1-3. Their concern for Jesus' safety is explained by the causal clause introduced by γὰρ. We take it that those who began to say (inceptive imperfect in ἔλεγον) that Jesus was out of His mind were the people in the crowd, not His disciples and the women with them. The rumor began and persisted, and there was danger that the mob would arrest Jesus and turn Him over to the authorities, or there might have been danger of mob violence. At least Jesus' friends thought so. The Scribes move in for the attack in

Verse 22 - "And the scribes which came down from Jerusalem said, He hath Beelzebub, and by the prince of the devils casteth he out devils."

καὶ οἱ γραμματεῖς οἱ ἀπὸ Ἱεροσολύμων καταβάντες ἔλεγον ὅτι Βεελζεβοὺλ ἔχει, καὶ ὅτι ἐν τῷ ἄρχοντι τῶν δαιμονίων ἐκβάλλει τὰ δαιμόνια.

καὶ (continuative conjunction) 14.
οἱ (nom.pl.masc.of the article in agreement with γραμματεῖς) 9.
γραμματεῖς (nom.pl.masc.of γραμματεύς, subject of ἔλεγον) 152.
οἱ (nom.pl.masc.of the article in agreement with καταβάντες) 9.
ἀπὸ (preposition with the ablative of separation) 70.
Ἱεροσολύμων (abl.sing.masc.of Ἱεροσολύμων, separation) 141.
καταβάντες (2d.aor.act.part.nom.pl.masc.of καταβαίνω, apposition with γραμματεῖς) 324.
ἔλεγον (3d.per.pl.imp.act.ind.of λέγω, inceptive) 66.
ὅτι (objective conjunction introducing indirect discourse) 211.

Βεελζεβοὺλ (acc.sing.masc.of Βεελζεβούλ, direct object of ἔχει) 883.
ἔχει (3d.per.sing.pres.act.ind.of ἔχω, progressive) 82.
καὶ (adjunctive conjunction joining objective clauses) 14.
ὅτι (conjunction introducing an object clause in indirect discourse) 211.
ἐν (preposition with the instrumental of agent) 80.
τῷ (instru.sing.masc.of the article in agreement with ἄρχοντι) 9.
ἄρχοντι (instru.sing.masc.of ἄρχων, agent) 816.
τῶν (gen.pl.neut.of the article in agreement with δαιμονίων) 9.
δαιμονίων (gen.pl.neut.of δαιμόνιον, relationship) 686.
ἐκβάλλει (3d.per.sing.pres.act.ind.of ἐκβάλλω, customary) 649.
τὰ (acc.pl.neut.of the article in agreement with δαιμόνια) 9.
δαιμόνια (acc.pl.neut.of δαιμόνιον, direct object of ἐκβάλλει) 686.

Translation - *"And the scribes who had come down from Jerusalem began to spread the rumor that He had Beelzeboul, and that through the agency of the prince of the demons He was casting out the demons."*

Comment: The scribes are described as those who had recently come down from Jerusalem (*down* because it is down the mountain). Matthew says that it was the Pharisees who also started the rumor, here ascribed by Mark to the Scribes. No doubt both groups did so. The inceptive imperfect in ἔλεγον indicates that they started the rumor which probably spread rapidly throughout the crowd. They were saying that Jesus had Beelzeboul, or more properly that Beelzeboul had Him. Another rumor had it that Jesus was using the chief demon as His agent by whom He cast out other demons. *Cf.* comment on Mt.12:24.

Verse 23 - *"And he called them unto him, and said unto them in parables, How can Satan cast out Satan?"*

καὶ προσκαλεσάμενος αὐτοὺς ἐν παραβολαῖς ἔλεγεν αὐτοῖς, Πῶς δύναται Σατανᾶς Σατανᾶν ἐκβάλλειν;

καὶ (inferential conjunction) 14.
προσκαλεσάμενος (aor.mid.part.nom.sing.masc.of προσκαλέω, adverbial, temporal) 842.
αὐτοὺς (acc.pl.masc.of αὐτός, direct object of προσκαλεσάμενος) 16.
ἐν (preposition with the instrumental of means) 80.
παραβολαῖς (instru.pl.fem.of παραβολή, means) 1027.
ἔλεγεν (3d.per.sing.imp.act.ind.of λέγω, inceptive) 66.
αὐτοῖς (dat.pl.masc.of αὐτός, indirect object of ἔλεγεν) 16.
Πῶς (interrogative conjunction, introducing direct question) 627.
δύναται (3d.per.sing.pres.ind.of δύναμαι, direct question) 289.
Σατανᾶς (nom.sing.masc.of Σατανᾶς, subject of δύναται) 365.
Σατανᾶν (acc.sing.masc.of Σατανᾶς, direct object of ἐκβάλλειν) 365.
ἐκβάλλειν (pres.act.inf.of ἐκβάλλω, complementary) 649.

Translation - "Therefore when He had called them to Him He began to speak to them in parables: 'How can Satan cast out Satan?' "

Comment:καὶ is inferential. Jesus heard the rumors that were circulating about and summoned the people to His side in order to counteract the argument of the Scribes and Pharisees. Jesus' authority is evident in the fact that He was able to command the people to come near so that He could speak to them. The blasphemy was unspeakble. *Cf.*#883 to see that Βεελζεβούλ was the "god of filth" and "god of flies." A lesser person than Jesus would have gone about among the people asking them to listen to his rebuttal. Jesus calls them to His side. Why did they obey the summons? In view of the charge that Jesus was in league with Beelzeboul they should have avoided Him. Yet they could not - dared not resist His summons. He stood majestically in their midst and said, "Come to me." They came. Note the inceptive imperfect in ἔλεγεν. "He began to speak to them." He made the same point in a different way with His question in

Verse 24 - "And if a kingdom be divided against itself, that kingdom cannot stand."

καὶ ἐὰν βασιλεία ἐφ' ἑαυτὴν μερισθῇ, οὐ δύναται σταθῆναι ἡ βασιλεία ἐκείνη.

καὶ (emphatic conjunction) 14.
ἐὰν (conditional particle introducing a third-class condition) 363.
βασιλεία (nom.sing.fem.of βασιλεία, subject of μερισθῇ) 253.
ἐφ' (preposition with the accusation to express hostility) 47.
ἑαυτὴν (acc.sing.fem.of ἑαυτός, hostility) 288.
μερισθῇ (3d.per.sing.aor.pass.subj.of μερίζω, third-class condition) 993.
οὐ (negative conjunction with the indicative) 130.
δύναται (3d.per.sing.pres.act.ind.of δύναμαι, customary) 289.
σταθῆναι (aor.pass.inf.of ἴστημι, complementary) 180.
ἡ (nom.sing.fem.of the article in agreement with βασιλεία) 9.
βασιλεία (nom.sing.fem.of βασιλεία, subject of δύναται) 253.
ἐκείνη (nom.sing.fem.of ἐκεῖνος, in agreement with βασιλεία) 246.

Translation - "In fact, if a kingdom is divided against itself, that kingdom is not able to stand."

Comment: We have a third-class condition with ἐὰν and the subjunctive μερισθῇ in the protasis and the present indicative in the apodosis. It is a hypothetical case. Jesus is not speaking of any specific kingdom thus disunited. The conclusion states with finality that such a kingdom is not viable. ἐπί with the accusative often expresses hostility or opposition. *Cf.*#47 for other examples.

This passage of scripture was used by Abraham Lincoln in his famous Cooper's Union speech in New York during his presidential campaign in 1860.

Verse 25 - *"And if a house be divided against itself, that house cannot stand."*

καὶ ἐὰν οἰκία ἐφ' ἑαυτὴν μερισθῇ, οὐ δύνήσεται ἡ οἰκία ἐκείνη σταθῆναι.

καὶ (continuative conjunction) 14.
ἐὰν (conditional particle introducing a third-class condition) 363.
οἰκία (nom.sing.fem.of οἰκία, subject of μερισθῇ) 186.
ἐφ' (preposition with the accusative, expressing hostility) 47.
ἑαυτὴν (acc.sing.fem.of ἑαυτός, hostility) 288.
μερισθῇ (3d.per.sing.aor.pass.subj.of μερίζω, third-class condition) 993.
οὐ (negative conjunction with the indicative) 130.
δύνήσεται (3d.per.sing.fut.ind.of δύναμαι, predictive) 289.
ἡ (nom.sing.fem.of the article in agreement with οἰκία) 9.
οἰκία (nom.sing.fem.of οἰκία, subject of δύνήσεται) 186.
ἐκείνη (nom.sing.fem.of ἐκεῖνος, in agreement with οἰκία) 246.
σταθῆναι (aor.act.inf.of ἵστημι, complementary) 180.

Translation - *"And if a house is divided against itself, that house shall not be able to stand."*

Comment: Here Jesus changed the grammatical pattern. We still have the third-class condition, but with the future indicative in the apodosis rather than the indicative as in verse 24. The thought is essentially the same. The divided house cannot stand at the moment (verse 24) nor can it stand at any future time (verse 25). Divisions bring discord and ultimate destruction, whether in political kingdoms, social structures, households or philosophical systems.

The Scribes had started this argument with their talk about Satan and his alleged occupation of Jesus. Jesus replied in kind (verse 24) Then He established His principle that enduring systems are not internally discordant (vss.24,25). Now He returns to the application of all of this to Satan himself, in

Verse 26 - *"And if Satan rise up against himself, and be divided, he cannot stand, but hath an end."*

καὶ εἰ ὁ Σατανᾶς ἀνέστη ἐφ' ἑαυτὸν καὶ ἐμερίσθη, οὐ δύναται στῆναι, ἀλλὰ τέλος ἔχει.

καὶ (inferential conjunction) 14.
εἰ (conditional particle in a first-class condition) 337.
ὁ (nom.sing.masc.of the article in agreement with Σατανᾶς) 9.
Σατανᾶς (nom.sing.masc.of Σατανᾶς, subject of ἀνέστη and ἐμερίσθη) 993.
ἀνέστη (3d.per.sing.aor.act.ind.of ἀνίστημι, constative) 789.
ἐφ' (preposition with the accusative, expressing hostility) 47.
ἑαυτὸν (acc.sing.masc.of ἑαυτός, hostility) 288.
καὶ (adjunctive conjunction joining verbs) 14.
ἐμερίσθη (3d.per.sing.aor.pass.ind.of μερίζω, constative) 993.

οὐ (negative conjunction with the indicative) 130.

δύναται (3d.per.sing.pres.ind.of δύναμαι, customary) 289.

στῆναι (aor.act.inf.of ἵστημι, complementary) 180.

ἀλλά (alternative conjunction) 342.

τέλος (acc.sing.neut.of τέλος, direct object of ἔχει) 881.

ἔχει (3d.per.sing.pres.act.ind.of ἔχω, customary) 82.

Translation - *"Therefore since Satan has risen up against himself and has been divided, he is not able to stand, but has an end."*

Comment:Here Jesus changed the form of the conditional sentence more basicly than the change between verse 24 and verse 25. In those verses both sentences were third-class conditions. The only change was from the present tense in the apodosis of the first to the future tense in the apodosis of the second. Here the condition changes from a third-class to a first-class condition. εἰ with the indicative in both protasis and apodosis. That it is not a second-class contrary to fact condition is clear from the fact that the present tense is used in the apodosis. Second-class conditions use only secondary tenses. In the third-class conditions Jesus was saying, "If a kingdom (house) should be divided . . . κ.τ.λ. - I am not saying that it is. . . " But in verse 26, with His use of εἰ and the indicative, both in "if clause" and conclusion, Jesus is reasoning like the Scribes. For the sake of the argument Jesus assumes the Scribes' attitude. They had said that Satan's kingdom was divided. Jesus was casting out demons, but He was doing it through the agency of the prince of the demon world. Beelzeboul was casting out his own demons! Jesus is not saying that He really believes that that is true, but He is assuming as true what they said they really believed to be true. "Satan is rising up against himself and is being divided." Thus in the conclusion, Jesus drove them to logical confusion. Satan shall not be able to stand, but is heading for collapse. If he is stupid enough to fight against himself, his kingdom is destined to fall. All of this goes to prove how faulty the reasoning of the Scribes really was. The truth was that Satan was not fighting Satan. The Son of God was in full battle array against the kingdom of darkness. Let us remember what had just occurred (Mt.12:22). Jesus had healed a demoniac so completely that the blind and dumb both spake and saw and the people were frightened out of their wits. This was not Satan against Satan, as the Scribes were saying. This was the Son of God against Satan and the evidence is that He was greater than Satan, else He could not have healed the demoniac.

It is this principle that Jesus now lays down in

Verse 27 - *"No man can enter into a strong man's house and spoil his goods, except he will first bind the strong man; and then he will spoil his house."*

ἀλλ' οὐ δύναται οὐδεὶς εἰς τὴν οἰκίαν τοῦ ἰσχυροῦ εἰσελθὼν τὰ σκεύη αὐτοῦ διαρπάσαι ἐὰν μὴ πρῶτον τὸν ἰσχυρὸν δήσῃ, καὶ τότε τὴν οἰκίαν αὐτοῦ διαρπάσει.

ἀλλ' (alternative conjunction) 342.

οὐ (negative conjunction with the indicative) 130.
δύναται (3d.per.sing.pres.ind.of δύναμαι, aoristic) 289.
οὐδεὶς (nom.sing.masc.of οὐδείς, subject of δύναται) 446.
εἰς (preposition with the accusative of extent) 140.
τὴν (acc.sing.fem.of the article in agreement with οἰκίαν) 9.
οἰκίαν (acc.sing.fem.of οἰκία, extent) 186.
τοῦ (gen.sing.masc.of the article in agreement with ἰσχυροῦ) 9.
ἰσχυροῦ (gen.sing.masc.of ἰσχυρός, possession) 303.
εἰσελθὼν (aor.part.nom.sing.masc.of εἰσέρχομαι, adverbial, temporal) 234.
τὰ (acc.pl.neut.of the article in agreement with σκεύη) 9.
σκεύη (acc.pl.neut.of σκεῦος, direct object of διαρπάσαι) 997.
αὐτοῦ (gen.sing.masc.of αὐτός, possession) 16.
διαρπάσαι (aor.act.inf.of διαρπάζω, complementary) 999.
ἐὰν (conditional particle in a third-class condition) 363.
μὴ (negative conjunction with the subjunctive) 87.
πρῶτον (acc.sing.neut.of πρῶτος, adverb of time) 487.
τὸν (acc.sing.masc.of the article in agreement with ἰσχυρὸν) 9.
ἰσχυρὸν (acc.sing.masc.of ἰσχυρός, direct object of δήσῃ) 303.
δήσῃ (3d.per.sing.aor.act.subj.of δέω, third-class condition, constative) 998.
καὶ (continuative conjunction) 14.
τότε (temporal conjunction) 166.
τὴν (acc.sing.fem.of the article in agreement with οἰκίαν) 9.
οἰκίαν (acc.sing.fem.of οἰκία, direct object of διαρπάσει) 186.
αὐτοῦ (gen.sing.masc.of αὐτός, possession) 16.
διαρπάσει (3d.per.sing.fut.act.ind.of διαρπάζω, predictive) 999.

Translation - *"On the contrary no man is able to enter into the house of the strong man and plunder his household goods if he does not first tie up the strong man; only then will he ransack his house."*

Comment: One can enter the strong man's house without violence, but once his intent is to rob, the strong man resists and must first of all be bound before the pillage can take place. In this context σκεύη (#997) means general household property - personal possessions. The third-class condition indicates that first the strong man must be bound.

Jesus had just robbed Satan of his property (Mt.12:22). Thus, according to Jesus' parable He must already have entered the strong man's (Satan's) house (the world), and He must already have bound the strong man. Is Satan bound, and, if so, when was he bound? Cf.#998 for passages where δέω applies to Satan. When the Scribes said that Jesus was in league with Satan, they were talking about the Sovereign God Incarnate in human flesh, who, having entered the strong man's house, in incarnation, had just given evidence (Mt.12:22) that He had tied up the strong man. How heinous, then, their crime of ascribing unto Jesus an unclean spirit. (I John 4:4).

The unfolding of these events made it particularly apropos for Jesus to speak next about the unpardonable sin in verses 28 and 29.

Verse 28 - "Verily I say unto you, All sins shall be forgiven unto the sons of men, and blasphemies wherewith soever they shall blaspheme,"

'Αμὴν λέγω ὑμῖν ὅτι πάντα ἀφεθήσεται τοῖς υἱοῖς τῶν ἀνθρώπων, τὰ ἁμαρτήματα καὶ αἱ βλασφημίαι ὅσα ἐὰν βλασφημήσωσιν.

'Αμὴν (explicative) 466.
λέγω (1st.per.sing.pres.act.ind.of λέγω, aoristic) 66.
ὑμῖν (dat.pl.masc.of σύ, indirect object of λέγω) 104.
ὅτι (conjunction introducing an object clause in indirect discourse) 211.
πάντα (nom.pl.neut.of πᾶς, in agreement with ἁμαρτήματα) 67.
ἀφεθήσεται (3d.per.sing.fut.pass.ind.of ἀφίημι, predictive) 319.
τοῖς (dat.pl.masc.of the article in agreement with υἱοῖς) 9.
υἱοῖς (dat.pl.masc.of υἱός, personal advantage) 5.
τῶν (gen.pl.masc.of the article in agreement with ἀνθρώπων) 9.
ἀνθρώπων (gen.pl.masc.of ἄνθρωπος, definition) 341.
τὰ (nom.pl.neut.of the article in agreement with ἁμαρτήματα) 9.

#2182 ἁμαρτήματα (nom.pl.neut.of ἁμάρτημα, subject of ἀφεθήσεται).

sin - Mk.3:28; Rom.3:25; I Cor.6:18.
damnation - Mk.3:29.

Meaning: Cf.#'s 111, 1260, 791.Apparently ἁμάρτημα is more nefarious - a more deliberate sin while ἁμαρτία is used of any shortcoming. Translated "damnation" in Mk.3:29.

καὶ (adjunctive conjunction joining nouns) 14.
αἱ (nom.pl.fem.of the article in agreement with βλασφημίαι) 9.
βλασφημίαι (nom.pl.fem.of βλασφημία, subject of ἀφεθήσεται) 1001.
ὅσα (nom.pl.fem.of ὅσος, in agreement with βλασφημίαι) 660.
ἐὰν (conditional particle in a third-class condition) 363.
βλασφημήσωσιν (3d.per.pl.aor.act.subj.of βλασφημέω, third-class condition) 781.

Translation - "Truly I am telling you that all shall be forgiven for the sons of men, whatever sins (they may commit) and blasphemies which they may utter."

Comment: Jesus has established His analogy and made His point (verse 27). Now He gets specific in verses 28-30. ὅτι introduces indirect discourse. Note that πάντα is in emphasis. Everything shall be forgiven for the sons of men. This is a sweeping general statement of available salvation for the human race. This forgiveness includes τὰ ἁμαρτήματα καὶ αἱ βλασφημίαι - nefarious and deliberate sins (#2182) and evil speakings (#1001). But there is one exception to this which He tells us about in

Verse 29 - "But he that shall blaspheme against the Holy Ghost hath never forgiveness, but is in danger of eternal damnation."

ὅς δ' ἂν βλασφημήσῃ εἰς τὸ πνεῦμα τὸ ἅγιον οὐκ ἔχει ἄφεσιν εἰς τὸν αἰῶνα, ἀλλὰ ἔνοχός ἐστιν αἰωνίου ἁμαρτήματος —

ὅς (nom.sing.masc.of ὅς, subject of βλασφημήσῃ) 65.

δ' (adversative conjunction) 11.

ἂν (conditional particle in a relative clause, more probable condition) 205.

βλασφημήσῃ (3d.per.sing.aor.act.ind.of βλασφημέω, more probable condition) 781.

εἰς (preposition with the accusative, hostility) 140.

τὸ (acc.sing.neut.of the article in agreement with πνεῦμα) 9.

πνεῦμα (acc.sing.neut.of πνεῦμα, hostility) 83.

τὸ (acc.sing.neut.of the article in agreement with ἅγιὸν)9.

ἅγιον (acc.sing.neut.of ἅγιος, in agreement with πνεῦμα) 84.

οὐκ (negative conjunction with the indicative) 130.

ἔχει (3d.per.sing.pres.act.ind.of ἔχω, aoristic) 82.

ἄφεσιν (acc.sing.fem.of ἄφεσις, direct object of ἔχει) 1576.

εἰς (preposition with the accusative of time extent) 140.

τὸν (acc.sing.masc.of the article in agreement with αἰῶνα) 9.

αἰῶνα (acc.sing.masc.of αἰών, time extent) 1002.

ἀλλὰ (alternative conjunction) 342.

ἔνοχός (nom.sing.masc.of ἔνοχος, predicate adjective) 477.

ἐστιν (3d.per.sing.pres.ind.of εἰμί, aoristic) 86.

αἰωνίου (gen.sing.masc.of αἰώνιος, in agreement with ἁμαρτήματος) 1255.

ἁμαρτήματος (gen.sing.masc.of ἁμάρτημα, definition) 2182.

Translation - "But whoever shall blaspheme against the Holy Spirit has no forgiveness ever - rather he is liable for a sin that persists forever."

Comment: The relative clause with ὅς has ἂν and the subjunctive in βλασφημήσῃ. The protasis is a more probable future condition. Jesus is saying that the sin which the Scribes had just committed, when they said that what was actually done by the Holy Spirit had been done by Beelzeboul, would be committed again by someone. The Scribes had blasphemed against (εἰς with the accusative) the Holy Spirit. Since the function of the Holy Spirit is to call the sinner to repentance and faith (John 16:7-11; I Cor.12:3; John 6:44), rejection of His call is blasphemy against Him. Thus the sin for which there is no forgiveness is the sin for which there is no atonement, *viz.*, the sin of rejecting the Holy Spirit's invitation to partake of the nature of Christ.

Note that we also have εἰς with the accusative of time extent. There will be no forgiveness "into the ages" which agrees with the adjective αἰωνίου which defines ἁμαρτήματος. The sin described is one which cannot be obliterated; hence there is no forgiveness of it. Note that βλασφημήσῃ εἰς τὸ πνεῦμα τὸ ἅγιον of Mk.3:29 is parallel to ὅς δ' ἂν εἴπῃ κατὰ τοῦ πνεύματος τοῦ ἁγίου of Mt.12:32. Reread Mt.12:32 for comment on the passage.

Verse 30 - "Because they said, He hath an unclean spirit."

ὅτι ἔλεγον, Πνεῦμα ἀκάθαρτον ἔχει.

ὅτι (causal conjunction) 211.
ἔλεγον (3d.per.pl.imp.act.ind.of λέγω, progressive duration) 66.
Πνεῦμα (acc.sing.neut.of πνεῦμα, direct object of ἔχει) 83.
ἀκάθαρτον (acc.sing.neut.of ἀκάθαρτος, in agreement with Πνεῦμα) 843.
ἔχει (3d.per.sing.pres.act.ind.of ἔχω, aoristic) 82.

Translation - "Because they were saying, 'He has an unclean spirit.' "

Comment: Here Mark tells us why Jesus' words of verses 28 and 29 were spoken. The entire passage from verse 22 contributes to the thought. In order to point out their illogicality (verse 22) Jesus spoke the material of verses 23-27, after which He issued the warning of verses 28 and 29. Cf. Mt.12:32 for comment on the unpardonable sin.

The Scribes and Pharisees Demand a Sign

(Mt.12:38-45)

The True Kindred of Christ

(Mk.3:31-35; Mt.12:46-50; Lk.8:19-21)

Mark 3:31 - "There came then his brethren and his mother, and, standing without, sent unto him, calling him."

Καὶ ἔρχεται ἡ μήτηρ αὐτοῦ καὶ οἱ ἀδελφοὶ αὐτοῦ καὶ ἔξω στήκοντες ἀπέστειλαν πρὸς αὐτὸν καλοῦντες αὐτόν.

Καὶ (continuative conjunction) 14.
ἔρχεται (3d.per.sing.pres.ind.of ἔρχομαι, historical) 146.
ἡ (nom.sing.fem.of the article in agreement with μήτηρ) 9.
μήτηρ (nom.sing.fem.of μήτηρ, subject of ἔρχεται) 76.
αὐτοῦ (gen.sing.masc.of αὐτός, relationship) 16.
καὶ (adjunctive conjunction joining nouns) 14.
οἱ (nom.pl.masc.of the article in agreement with ἀδελφοὶ) 9.
ἀδελφοὶ (nom.pl.masc.of ἀδελφός, subject of ἔρχεται) 15.
αὐτοῦ (gen.sing.masc.of αὐτός, relationship) 16.
καὶ (continuative conjunction) 14.
ἔξω (adverbial) 449.
στήκοντες (perf.act.part.nom.pl.masc.of ἵστημι, adverbial, temporal) 180.
απέστειλαν (3d.per.pl.aor.act.ind.of ἀποστέλλω, constative) 215.
πρὸς (preposition with the accusative of extent) 197.
αὐτὸν (acc.sing.masc.of αὐτός, extent) 16.

καλοῦντες (pres.act.part.nom.pl.masc.of καλέω, adverbial, modal) 107.
αὐτόν (acc.sing.masc.of αὐτός, direct object of καλοῦντες) 16.

Translation - "And His mother and His brothers came, and when they had taken their place outside they sent to Him calling Him."

Comment: Note the double subject. His mother and His brothers came, seeking a chance to speak to Jesus. They grew tired of waiting outside the house and sent in a messenger to Him. *Cf.* the parallel accounts in Mt.12:46,47 and Luke 8:19-21.

Verse 32 - "And the multitude sat about him, and they said unto him, Behold, thy mother and thy brethren without seek for thee."

καὶ ἐκάθητο περὶ αὐτὸν ὄχλος, καὶ λέγουσιν αὐτῷ, Ἰδοὺ ἡ μήτηρ σου καὶ οἱ ἀδελφοί σου ἔξω ζητοῦσίν σε.

καὶ (continuative conjunction) 14.
ἐκάθητο (3d.per.sing.imp.mid.ind.of κάθημαι, progressive duration) 377.
περὶ (preposition with the accusative of extent, place) 173.
αὐτὸν (acc.sing.masc.of αὐτός, extent) 16.
ὄχλος (nom.sing.masc.of ὄχλος, subject of ἐκάθητο and λέγουσιν) 418.
καὶ (adjunctive conjunction joining verbs) 14.
λέγουσιν (3d.per.pl.pres.act.ind.of λέγω, historical) 66.
αὐτῷ (dat.sing.masc.of αὐτός, indirect object of λέγουσιν) 16.
Ἰδοὺ (exclamation) 95.
ἡ (nom.sing.fem.of the article in agreement with μήτηρ) 9.
μήτηρ (nom.sing.fem.of μήτηρ, subject of ζητοῦσιν) 76.
σου (gen.sing.masc.of σύ, relationship) 104.
καὶ (adjunctive conjunction joining nouns) 14.
οἱ (nom.pl.masc.of the article in agreement with ἀδελφοί) 9.
ἀδελφοί (nom.pl.masc.of ἀδελφός, subject of ζητοῦσιν) 15.
σου (gen.sing.masc.of σύ, relationship) 104.
ἔξω (adverbial) 449.
ζητοῦσίν (3d.per.pl.pres.act.ind.of ζητέω, progressive) 207.
σε (acc.sing.masc.of σύ, direct object of ζητοῦσίν) 104.

Translation - "And a crowd was seated around Him, and they said to Him, 'Look, your mother and your brothers are outside seeking you."

Comment: The messengers from Jesus' family got as close to Him as possible and asked someone to convey the message. They could not get close enough to deliver the message themselves because of περὶ αὐτὸν ὄχλος. *Cf.*#173 for other examples of περί with the accusative in this spatial sense.

Verse 33 - "And he answered them saying, 'Who is my mother or my brethren?'"

καὶ ἀποκριθεὶς αὐτοῖς λέγει, Τίς ἐστιν ἡ μήτηρ μου καὶ οἱ ἀδελφοί (μου);

καὶ (continuative conjunction) 14.

ἀποκριθεὶς (aor.part.nom.sing.masc.of ἀποκρίνομαι, adverbial, modal) 318.

αὐτοῖς (dat.pl.masc.of αὐτός, indirect object of λέγει) 16.

λέγει (3d.per.sing.pres.act.ind.of λέγω, historical) 66.

Τίς (nom.sing.masc.of τίς, interrogative pronoun, in direct question, predicate nominative) 281.

ἡ (nom.sing.fem.of the article in agreement with μήτηρ) 9.

μήτηρ (nom.sing.fem.of μήτηρ, subject of ἐστιν) 76.

μου (gen.sing.masc.of ἐγώ, relationship) 123.

καὶ (adjunctive conjunction joining nouns) 14.

οἱ (nom.pl.masc.of the article in agreement with ἀδελφοί) 9.

ἀδελφοί (nom.pl.masc.of ἀδελφός, subject of ἐστιν) 15.

(μου) (gen.sing.masc.of ἐγώ, relationship) 123.

Translation - "*And He replied by saying to them, 'Who is my mother and my brothers?'* "

Comment: Direct question, as Jesus sets the stage for verses 34 and 35. *Cf.*Mt.12:48 for comment.

Verse 34 - "*And he looked about on them which sat about him, and said, Behold my mother and my brethren.*"

καὶ περιβλεφάμενος τοὺς περὶ αὐτὸν κύκλῳ καθημένους λέγει,Ἴδε ἡ μήτηρ μου καὶ οἱ ἀδελφοί μου.

καὶ (continuative conjunction) 14.

περιβλεφάμενος (aor.part.nom.sing.masc.of περιβλέπομαι, adverbial, temporal) 2107.

τοὺς (acc.pl.masc.of the article in agreement with καθημένους) 9.

περὶ (preposition with the accusative of extent, place) 173.

αὐτὸν (acc.sing.masc.of αὐτός, extent) 16.

#2183 κύκλῳ (instru.sing.masc.of κύκλος, manner).

round about - Mk.3:34; 6:6,36; Lk.9:12; Rom.15:19; Rev.4:6; 5:11; 7:11.

Meaning: κύκλος means a ring or circle. In the N.T. κύκλῳ, the instrumental is found in all places. Hence "by means of" or "in a circle." Round about. Always in spatial relation to a fixed point in the center.

καθημένους (pres.part.acc.pl.masc.of κάθημαι, direct object of περιβλεφάμενος) 377.

λέγει (3d.per.sing.pres.act.ind.of λέγω, historical) 66.

Ἴδε (2d.per.sing.aor.act.impv.of ὁράω, command) 144.

ἡ (nom.sing.fem.of the article in agreement with μήτηρ) 9.

μήτηρ (nom.sing.fem.of μήτηρ, nominative absolute) 76.

μου (gen.sing.masc.of ἐγώ, relationship) 123.

καὶ (adjunctive conjunction joining nouns) 14.
οἱ (nom.pl.masc.of the article in agreement with ἀδελφοί) 9.
ἀδελφοί (nom.pl.masc.of ἀδελφός, nominative absolute) 15.
μου (gen.sing.masc.of ἐγώ, relationship) 123.

Translation - *"And when He had swept the circle of those seated around Him with His gaze, He said, 'See my mother and my brothers.' "*

Comment: The "round about" idea is here three times: first, in the participle περιβλεψάμενος; second, in περὶ αὐτὸν and third, in κύκλῳ. Jesus gazed about Him. They were seated all around Him - on the furniture and on the floor. "You who are here listening to my preaching, taking advantage of my miracles and finding in me a new way of life - you are closer to me by spiritual ties than anyone could be because of physical blood ties." Of course, Mary and her children (Jesus' half-brothers and half-sisters) could also participate in personal faith in the Son of God, in which case He meant more to them as Saviour and Lord than as brother and son. This scene accentuates again His change in emphasis from national to individual salvation. His earthly ties, even those of His immediate family, must make way for the spiritual ties which are made by faith in His Person and work and obedience to His commands. This is His point in

Verse 35 - *"For whosoever shall do the will of God, the same is my brother, and my sister, and mother."*

ὅς (γὰρ) ἂν ποιήσῃ τὸ θέλημα τοῦ θεοῦ, οὗτος ἀδελφός μου καὶ ἀδελφὴ καὶ μήτηρ ἐστίν.

ὅς (nom.sing.masc.of ὅς, subject of ποιήσῃ, in a relative clause, the subject of ἐστίν) 65.
γὰρ (inferential conjunction) 105.
ἂν (conditional particle in a more probable condition relative clause) 205.
ποιήσῃ (3d.per.sing.aor.act.subj.of ποιέω, more probable condition) 127.
τὸ (acc.sing.neut.of the article in agreement with θέλημα) 9.
θέλημα (acc.sing.neut.of θέλημα, direct object of ποιήσῃ) 577.
τοῦ (gen.sing.masc.of the article in agreement with θεοῦ) 9.
θεοῦ (gen.sing.masc.of θεός, definition) 124.
οὗτος (nom.sing.masc.of οὗτος, subject of ἐστιν, deictic) 93.
ἀδελφός (nom.sing.masc.of ἀδελφός, predicate nominative) 15.
μου (gen.sing.masc.of ἐγώ, relationship) 123.
καὶ (adjunctive conjunction, joining nouns) 14.
ἀδελφή (nom.sing.fem.of ἀδελφή, predicate nominative) 1025.
καὶ (adjunctive conjunction joining nouns) 14.
μήτηρ (nom.sing.fem.of μήτηρ, predicate nominative) 76.
ἐστίν (3d.per.sing.pres.ind.of εἰμί, aoristic) 86.

Translation - *"Therefore whoever shall do the will of God - that one is my brother and sister and mother."*

Comment: The relative clause with ὅς . . . ἂν ποιήσῃ presents a more probable condition. Jesus is suggesting that some will indeed do the will of the Father and thus qualify as His brother, sister or mother. ὅς is followed by the deictic οὗτος,the subject of ἐστιν. Note that ἀδελφός μου καὶ ἀδελφή καὶ μήτηρ are emphasized ahead of the verb. *Cf.*Mt.7:24,25. For further comment *cf.* Mt.12:50.

We turn now to Luke's brief account of this episode in

Luke 8:19 - "Then came to him his mother and his brethren, and could not come at him for the press."

Παρεγένετο δὲ πρὸς αὐτὸν ἡ μήτηρ καὶ οἱ ἀδελφοὶ αὐτοῦ, καὶ οὐκ ἠδύναντο συντυχεῖν αὐτῷ διὰ τὸν ὄχλον.

παρεγένετο (3d.per.sing.aor.ind.of παραγίνομαι, constative) 139.
δὲ (continuative conjunction) 11.
πρὸς (preposition with the accusative of extent) 197.
αὐτὸν (acc.sing.masc.of αὐτός, extent) 16.
ἡ (nom.sing.fem.of the article in agreement with μήτηρ) 9.
μήτηρ (nom.sing.fem.of μήτηρ, subject of παρεγένετο) 76.
καὶ (adjunctive conjunction, joining nouns) 14.
οἱ (nom.pl.masc.of the article in agreement with ἀδελφοὶ) 9.
ἀδελφοὶ (nom.pl.masc.of ἀδελφός, subject of παρεγένετο) 15.
αὐτοῦ (gen.sing.masc.of αὐτός, relationship) 16.
καὶ (adversative conjunction) 14.
οὐκ (negative conjunction with the indicative) 130.
ἠδύναντο (3d.per.pl.imp.act.ind.of δύναμαι, progressive description) 289.

#2184 συντυχεῖν (2d.aor.act.inf.of συντυγχάνω, complementary).

come at - Lk.8:19.

Meaning: A combination of σύν (#1542) and τυγκάνω (#2699). Hence, to come to the mark. To come to some point in space. Only in the New Testament of Jesus' mother and brothers who were trying to reach Jesus in a crowded house - Lk.8:19. Followed by the instrumental of association.

αὐτῷ (instrumental sing.masc.of αὐτός, association) 16.
διὰ (preposition with the accusative, cause) 118.
τὸν (acc.sing.masc.of the article in agreement with ὄχλον) 9.
ὄχλον (acc.sing.masc.of ὄχλος, cause) 418.

Translation - "And His mother and His brothers came to Him, but they were not able to reach Him because of the crowd."

Comment: Mary, the mother of Jesus and His brothers (the word can also mean His relatives) approached the house. #2184 is an interesting word, used only here in the New Testament. They were unable to "come at Him." τυγκάνω - "to hit the mark" is the opposite of ἁμαρτάνω (#1260), "to miss the mark." "To hit with the mark" is the resultant meaning of συντυχεῖν. The objective of Mary and her children was to reach Jesus, perhaps with a view of persuading Him to leave the crowd and come with them. Matthew says they were "seeking to speak to Him" (Mt.12:47). Mark says they were calling Him (Mk.3:31). Now Luke points up their frustrated efforts to make their way through the crowd to reach His side. διὰ τὸν ὄχλον is causal. Cf.#118 for other instances.

Verse 20 - "And it was told him by certain which said, Thy mother and thy brethren stand without, desiring to see thee."

ἀπηγγέλη δὲ αὐτῷ, Ἡ μήτηρ σου καὶ οἱ ἀδελφοί σου ἑστήκασιν ἔξω ἰδεῖν θέλοντές σε.

ἀπηγγέλη (3d.per.sing.2d.aor.pass.ind.of ἀπαγγέλλω, constative) 176.
δὲ (continuative conjunction) 11.
αὐτῷ (dat.sing.masc.of αὐτός, indirect object of ἀπηγγέλη) 16.
Ἡ (nom.sing.fem.of the article in agreement with μήτηρ) 9.
μήτηρ (nom.sing.fem.of μήτηρ, subject of ἑστήκασιν) 76.
σου (gen.sing.masc.of σύ, relationship) 104.
καὶ (adjunctive conjunction joining nouns) 14.
οἱ (nom.pl.masc.of the article in agreement with ἀδελφοί) 9.
ἀδελφοί (nom.pl.masc.of ἀδελφός, subject of ἑστήκασιν) 15.
σου (gen.sing.masc.of σύ, relationship) 104.
ἑστήκασιν (3d.per.pl.perf.act.ind.of ἵστημι, consummative) 180.
ἔξω (adverbial) 449.
ἰδεῖν (aor.act.inf.of ὁράω, complementary) 144.
θέλοντες (pres.act.part.nom.pl.masc.of θέλω, adverbial, circumstantial) 88.
σε (acc.sing.masc.of σύ, direct object of ἰδεῖν) 104.

Translation - "And the message was given to Him, 'Your mother and your brothers have been standing outside, wishing to see you.' "

Comment: Note the direct discourse without ὅτι. Someone relayed the message to Jesus - in fact more than one did as the plural λέγουσιν (Mk.3:32) reveals. The message implies that Jesus was expected to take more interest in His immediate family than in anyone else. This idea militates against the universality of Jesus' ministry and in favor of a local, tribal, provincial or nationalistic type of ministry. The idea needed to be opposed and Jesus procedes in verse 21 to oppose it. The Scribes' unpardonable sin (Mt.12:31*ff*) and Jesus' castigation of Israel as a nation is coupled with His universal offer of salvation (Mt.11:28-30). Reread the entire argument from Mt.11:7-30, to see this shift in emphasis from a nationalistic Messianic offer to Israel, to a personal offer. Jesus now replies as Matthew and Mark have recorded elsewhere (Mt.12:49,50; Mk.3:34,35) in

Verse 21 - "And he answered and said unto them, My mother and my brethren are these which hear the word of God, and do it."

ὁ δὲ ἀποκριθεὶς εἶπεν πρὸς αὐτούς, Μήτηρ μου καὶ ἀδελφοί μου οὗτοί εἰσιν οἱ τὸν λόγον τοῦ θεοῦ ἀκούοντες καὶ ποιοῦντες.

ὁ (nom.sing.masc.of the article subject of εἶπεν) 9.

δὲ (adversative conjunction) 11.

ἀποκριθεὶς (aorist participle, nom.sing.masc.of ἀποκρίνομαι, adverbial, modal) 318.

εἶπεν (3d.per.sing.aor.act.ind.of εἶπον, constative) 155.

πρὸς (preposition with the accusative, after a verb of speaking) 197.

αὐτούς (acc.pl.masc.of αὐτός, extent, after a verb of speaking) 16.

Μήτηρ (nom.sing.fem.of μήτηρ, predicate nominative) 76.

μου (gen.sing.masc.of ἐγώ, relationship) 123.

καὶ (adjunctive conjunction joining nouns) 14.

ἀδελφοί (nom.pl.masc.of ἀδελφός, predicate nominative) 15.

μου (gen.sing.masc.of ἐγώ, relationship) 123.

οὗτοι (nom.pl.masc.of οὗτος, subject of εἰσιν) 93.

εἰσιν (3d.per.pl.pres.ind.of εἰμί, aoristic) 86.

οἱ (nom.pl.masc.of the article in agreement with ἀκούοντες and ποιοῦντες) 9.

τὸν (acc.sing.masc.of the article in agreement with λόγον) 9.

λόγον (acc.sing.masc.of λόγος, direct object of ἀκούοντες and ποιοῦντες) 510.

τοῦ (gen.sing.masc.of the article in agreement with θεοῦ) 9.

θεοῦ (gen.sing.masc.of θεός, definition) 124.

ἀκούοντες (pres.act.part.nom.pl.masc.of ἀκούω, substantival, in apposition with οὗτοι) 148.

καὶ (adjunctive conjunction joining participles) 14.

ποιοῦντες (pres.act.part.nom.pl.masc.of ποιέω, substantival, in apposition with οὗτοι) 127.

Translation - *"But in reply He said to them, 'These who are hearing and putting into practice the message of God are my mother and my brothers.'"*

Comment: δὲ is adversative, for Jesus is about to define μήτηρ and ἀδελφοί in a different way. The passage is very emphatic. The predicate nominatives μήτηρ μου καὶ ἀδελφοί μου are emphasized ahead of the subject, the participles in apposition and the verb. It is possible to take μητήρ μου καὶ ἀδελφοί μου in an absolute sense, in which case the translation might be, "My mother and my brothers?" Then, with a sweep of His hand (Mt.12:49) and a sweeping glance (Mk.3:34), He may have added, "These are (οὗτοι εἰσιν... κ.τ.λ.) my mother and brothers."

Thus every Christian who has heard the message of God and sought to live by its precepts is in a familial relationship with Jesus Christ which is closer than physical blood ties.

(Mk.4:1-34; Mt.13:1-53; Lk.8:4-18).

Mark 4:1 - "And he began again to teach by the sea side: and there was gathered unto him a great multitude, so that he entered into a ship, and sat in the ship; and the whole multitude was by the sea on the land."

Καὶ πάλιν ἤρξατο διδάσκειν παρὰ τὴν θάλασσαν, καὶ συνάγεται πρὸς αὐτὸν ὄχλος πλεῖστος, ὥστε αὐτὸν εἰς πλοῖον ἐμβάντα καθῆσθαι ἐν τῇ θαλάσσῃ, καὶ πᾶς ὁ ὄχλος πρὸς τὴν θάλασσαν ἐπὶ τῆς γῆς ἦσαν.

Καὶ (continuative conjunction) 14.

πάλιν (adverbial) 355.

ἤρξατο (3d.per.sing.aor.mid.ind.of ἄρχω, inceptive) 383.

διδάσκειν (pres.act.inf.of διδάσκω, complementary) 403.

παρὰ (preposition with the accusative of extent, alongside) 154.

τὴν (acc.sing.fem.of the article in agreement with θάλασσαν) 9.

θάλασσαν (acc.sing.fem.of θάλασσα, extent) 374.

καὶ (continuative conjunction) 14.

συνάγεται (3d.per.sing.pres.pass.ind.of συνάγω, historical) 150.

πρὸς (preposition with the accusative of extent) 197.

αὐτὸν (acc.sing.masc.of αὐτός, extent) 16.

ὄχλος (nom.sing.masc.of ὄχλος, subject of συνάγεται) 418.

πλεῖστος (nom.sing.masc.of πλεῖστος, in agreement with ὄχλος) 935.

ὥστε (consecutive conjunction introducing a result clause) 752.

αὐτὸν (acc.sing.masc.of αὐτός, general reference) 16.

εἰς (preposition with the accusative of extent) 140.

πλοῖον (acc.sing.neut.of πλοῖον, extent) 400.

ἐμβάντα (2d.aor.act.part.acc.sing.masc.of ἐμβαίνω, adverbial, temporal) 750.

καθῆσθαι (pres.mid.inf.of κάθημαι, result) 377.

ἐν (preposition with the locative of place where) 80.

τῇ (loc.sing.fem.of the article in agreement with θαλάσσῃ) 9.

θαλάσσῃ (loc.sing.fem.of θάλασσα, place where) 374.

καὶ (continuative conjunction) 14.

πᾶς (nom.sing.masc.of πᾶς, in agreement with ὄχλος) 67.

ὁ (nom.sing.masc.of the article in agreement with ὄχλος) 9.

ὄχλος (nom.sing.masc.of ὄχλος, subject of ἦσαν) 418.

πρὸς (preposition with the accusative of extent) 197.

τὴν (acc.sing.fem.of the article in agreement with θάλασσαν) 9.

θάλασσαν (acc.sing.fem.of θάλασσα, extent) 374.

ἐπὶ (preposition with the genitive of physical place) 47.

τῆς (gen.sing.fem.of the article in agreement with γῆς) 9.

γῆς (gen.sing.fem.of γῆ, physical place) 157.

ἦσαν (3d.per.pl.imp.ind.of εἰμί, progressive description) 86.

Translation - "And again He began to teach by the sea, and a great multitude crowded toward Him, with the result that He stepped into a boat in the water and sat down. And all the people were on the land near the seashore.

Comment: καὶ πάλιν - "and again" because He had been teaching them in the house (Mk.3:31-35). Jesus left the house and walked down to the seashore. Of course the crowd followed Him and assembled (middle voice in συνάγεται) in a semicircle about Jesus. It was a large crowd (πλεῖστος). The number was so great that it created a space problem, as those who brought up the rear pushed those ahead of them forward, so as to gain a better position to see Jesus and hear His words. They had created a similar problem in the house a short time before. In fact they now forced Jesus into the boat. Note the result clause with ὥστε and the infinitive. Jesus stepped into the boat and seated Himself. Mt.13:1,2 gives a clear account which, together with Mark, gives us a clear picture. Jesus stepped into the boat on the sea (εἰς πλοῖον ἐν τῇ θαλάσσῃ) while the peole were "near the sea on the land" (πρὸς τὴν θάλασσαν ἐπὶ τῆς γῆς). For further comment *Cf.* Mt.13:1,2.

Verse 2 - "And he taught them many things by parables, and said unto them in his doctrine,"

καὶ ἐδίδασκεν αὐτοὺς ἐν παραβολαῖς πολλά, καὶ ἔλεγεν αὐτοῖς ἐν τῇ διδαχῇ αὐτοῦ,

καὶ (continuative conjunction) 14.
ἐδίδασκεν (3d.per.sing.imp.act.ind.of διδάσκω, inceptive) 403.
αὐτοὺς (acc.pl.masc.of αὐτός, direct object of ἐδίδασκεν) 16.
ἐν (preposition with the instrumental of means) 80.
παραβολαῖς (instrumental pl.fem.of παραβολή, means) 1027.
πολλά (acc.pl.neut.of πολύς, direct object of ἐδίδασκεν) 228.
καὶ (continuative conjunction) 14.
ἔλεγεν (3d.per.sing.imp.act.ind.of λέγω, progressive duration) 66.
αὐτοῖς (dat.pl.masc.of αὐτός, indirect object of ἔλεγεν) 16.
ἐν (preposition with the locative of sphere) 80.
τῇ (loc.sing.fem.of the article in agreement with διδαχῇ) 9.
διδαχῇ (loc.sing.fem.of διδαχή, sphere) 706.
αὐτοῦ (gen.sing.masc.of αὐτός, possession) 16.

Translation - "And He began to teach them many things by parables, and He continued to speak to them about His teaching."

Comment: We have taken the first imperfect as inceptive, with emphasis upon the beginning of the action and the second imperfect as durative. He *began* to teach them and He *continued to speak* to them. Jesus began His discourse with the parabolic method, but later spoke to them in explanation of the parables. His teaching approach was parabolic, but when they asked for clarification He used a didactic method. The explantion of the parables is what is meant by ἔλεγεν. *Cf.* Luke's statement which is much simpler (Lk.8:7) and Matthew's (Mt.13:3). A parable "is the truth presented by a similitude. It differs from the proverb inasmuch as it is necessarily figurative. The proverb may be figurative, but it need not of necessity be figurative. The parable is often an expanded proverb, and the proverb is a condensed parable. There is but one Hebrew word for the two English words "parable" and "proverb," which may account for their being frequently interchanged. The proverb (Latin) is a common sentiment generally accepted. The parable (Greek) is something put by the side of something else. Theologically, it is something in the world of nature which finds its counterpart in the world of spirit. The parable attracts attention and so becomes valuable as a test of character. It reveals the seekers after truth, those who love the light. It withdraws the light from those who love darkness." (*The Pulpit Commentary*, en. loc.).

Here Jesus is teaching ἡ βασιλεία τοῦ θεοῦ truth essentially, and ἡ βασιλεία τῶν οὐρανῶν truth only as it relates to it. The emphasis is no more Kingdom but Church truth. Chronologically we are beyond Mt.11:28-30. *Cf.* comment on Mt.13:1-3.

Verse 3 - "Hearken. Behold, there went out a sower to sow."

Ἀκούετε. ἰδοὺ ἐξῆλθεν ὁ σπείρων σπεῖραι.

Ἀκούετε (2d.per.pl.pres.act.impv.of ἀκούω, command) 148.
ἰδοὺ (exclamation) 95.
ἐξῆλθεν (3d.per.sing.aor.ind.of ἐξέρχομαι, ingressive) 161.
ὁ (nom.sing.masc.of the article in agreement with σπείρων) 9.
σπείρων (pres.act.part.nom.sing.masc.of σπείρω, substantival, subject of ἐξῆλθεν) 616.
σπεῖραι (1st.aor.act.inf.of σπείρω, purpose) 616.

Translation - "Pay attention! Behold there went out the sower to sow."

Comment:Ἀκούετε - "Hear ye," or as the Navy says, "Now hear this!" It is an attention getter. We have this also in ἰδοὺ which serves the same purpose. The participial substantive as subject of the verb is followed by the infinitive of purpose of the same word. Sowers must *go out* in order to sow. ἐξῆλθεν is emphasized. *Cf.* Mt.13:3 for comment. Jesus' exposition of the parable of the sower is expounded in Mt.13:18-23, *q.v.* We shall comment more at length on Mk.4:14-20.

Verse 4 - "And it came to pass, as he sowed, some fell by the way side, and the fowls of the air came and devoured it up."

καὶ ἐγένετο ἐν τῷ σπείρειν ὁ μὲν ἔπεσεν παρὰ τὴν ὁδόν, καὶ ἦλθεν τὰ πετεινὰ καὶ κατέφαγεν αὐτό.

καὶ (continuative conjunction) 14.
ἐγένετο (3d.per.sing.aor.ind.of γίνομαι, constative) 113.
ἐν (preposition with the locative of time point) 80.
τῷ (loc.sing.neut.of the article, time point) 9.

σπείρειν (pres.act.inf.of σπείρω, noun use, time point) 616.
ὅ (nom.sing.neut.of ὅς, subject of ἔπεσεν) 65.
μὲν (particle of affirmation) 300.
ἔπεσεν (3d.per.sing.2d.aor.act.ind.of πίπτω, constative) 187.
παρὰ (preposition with the accusative of extent) 154.
τὴν (acc.sing.fem.of the article in agreement with ὁδόν) 9.
ὁδόν (acc.sing.fem.of ὁδός, extent) 199.
καὶ (continuative conjunction) 14.
ἦλθεν (3d.per.sing.aor.ind.of ἔρχομαι, constative) 146.
τὰ (nom.pl.neut.of the article in agreement with πετεινά) 9.
πετεινὰ (nom.pl.neut.of πετεινόν, subject of ἦλθεν and κατέφαγεν) 615.
καὶ (adjunctive conjunction joining verbs) 14.
κατέφαγεν (3d.per.sing.aor.act.ind.of κατεσθίω, constative) 1028.
αὐτό (acc.sing.neut.of αὐτός, direct object of κατέφαγεν) 16.

Translation - *"And as he sowed some seed fell by the side of the road and the birds came and ate it."*

Comment: ἐν τῷ σπείρειν is an articular infinitive in the locative case denoting time point, after ἐν. This construction with ἐν denotes time simultaneous with that of the main verb - in this case ἔπεσεν.

The seed in this part of the parable did not germinate because the birds ate it. All the other seed in the parable did in fact germinate, though only the last portion with profit. This is the heart of the interpretation of the parable.

Some interesting preaching material on "devouring" can be unearthed with a study of #1028, an interesting word with a variety of uses. It is sometimes an unfriendly word.

Verse 5 - *"And some fell on stony ground, where it had not much earth; and immediately it sprang up, because it had no depth of earth."*

καὶ ἄλλο ἔπεσεν ἐπὶ τὸ πετρῶδες ὅπου οὐκ εἶχεν γῆν πολλήν, καὶ εὐθὺς ἐξανέτειλεν διὰ τὸ μὴ ἔχειν βάθος γῆς.

καὶ (continuative conjunction) 14.
ἄλλο (nom.sing.neut.of ἄλλος, subject of ἔπεσεν) 198.
ἔπεσεν (3d.per.sing.aor.act.ind.of πίπτω, constative) 187.
ἐπὶ (preposition with the accusative of extent) 47.
τὸ (acc.sing.neut.of the article in agreement with πετρῶδες) 9.
πετρῶδες (acc.sing.neut.of πατρώδης, extent, place) 1029.
ὅπου (relative adverb of place) 592.
οὐκ (negative conjunction with the indicative) 592.
εἶχεν (3d.per.sing.imp.act.ind.of ἔχω, progressive description) 82.
γῆν (acc.sing.fem.of γῆ, direct object of εἶχεν) 157.
πολλήν (acc.sing.fem.of πολύς, in agreement with γῆν) 228.
καὶ (continuative conjunction) 14.

εὐθὺς (adverbial) 258.
ἐξανέτειλεν (3d.per.sing.aor.act.ind.of ἐξανατέλλω, ingressive) 1030.
διὰ (preposition with the accusative of cause) 118.
τὸ (acc.sing.neut.of the article, cause) 9.
μὴ (negative conjunction with the infinitive) 87.
ἔχειν (pres.act.inf.of ἔχω, articular infinitive, cause) 82.
βάθος (acc.sing.neut.of βάθος, general reference) 1031.
γῆς (gen.sing.fem.of γῆ, definition) 157.

Translation - "And some other seed fell upon the stony ground, where there was not much soil, and immediately it began to grow because it had no deep seed bed."

Comment: ἄλλο is joined in case,number and gender agreement with ὅ in verse 4. "Some fell . . . and other fell . . κ.τ.λ." πετρῶδες - "looks like rock" *Cf.*#1029. The stony soil οὐκ εἶχεν τὴν πολλήν - "had not much earth." Immediately it germinated and sprang up. There was no depth of soil and a root system which makes for permanence and fruit bearing could not develop. All of the strength therefore in the seed contributed to an immediate and temporary flowering of the plant. Note διὰ and the articular infinitive in the accusative case, denoting cause. The lack of soil depth was the reason for the immediate and temporary growth of the seed. The botany of it is explained further in

Verse 6 - "But when the sun was up, it was scorched; and because it had no root, it withered away."

καὶ ὅτε ἀνέτειλεν ὁ ἥλιος ἐκαυματίσθη, καὶ διὰ τὸ μὴ ἔχειν ῥίζαν ἐξηράνθη.

καὶ (inferential conjunction) 14.
ὅτε (temporal conjunction, introducing a definite temporal clause) 703.
ἀνέτειλεν (3d.per.sing.1st.aor.act.ind.of ἀνατέλλω, constative) 382.
ὁ (nom.sing.masc.of ἥλιος, subject of ἀνέτειλεν) 546.
ἐκαυματίσθη (3d.per.sing.aor.pass.ind.of καυματίζω, constative) 1032.
καὶ (continuative conjunction) 14.
διὰ (preposition with the accusative of cause) 118.
τὸ (acc.sing.neut.of the article, cause) 9.
μὴ (negative conjunction with the infinitive) 87.
ἔχειν (pres.act.inf.of ἔχω, accusative of cause) 82.
ῥίζαν (acc.sing.fem.of ῥίζα, direct object of ἔχειν) 293.
ἐξηράνθη (3d.per.sing.1st.aor.pass.ind.of ξηραίνω, constative) 1033.

Translation - "Therefore when the sun arose it was scorched and because it had no root system it was withered."

Comment: ὅτε with the indicative provides a definite temporal clause. *Cf.*#382 and note that ἀνατέλλω also refers to Christ's appearance (Heb.7:14) as the Sun of Righteousness. At His return sinners will be scorched - καυματίζω (#1032) because they have not the Root of David (#293). διά introduces another articular infinitive in the accusative case, denoting cause. Luxuriant growth atop the ground, but no root in depth means scorching and withering when the heat is on! *Cf.*Col.2:7.

Verse 7 - *"And some fell among thorns, and the thorns grew up, and choked it, and it yielded no fruit."*

καὶ ἄλλο ἔπεσεν εἰς τὰς ἀκάνθας, καὶ ἀνέβησαν αἱ ἄκανθαι καὶ συνέπνιξαν αὐτό, καὶ καρπὸν οὐκ ἔδωκεν.

καὶ (continuative conjunction) 14.
ἄλλο (nom.sing.neut.of ἄλλος, subject of ἔπεσεν) 198.
ἔπεσεν (3d.per.sing.aor.act.ind.of πίπτω, constative) 187.
εἰς (preposition with the accusative of extent) 140.
τὰς (acc.pl.fem.of the article in agreement with ἀκάνθας) 9.
ἀκάνθας (acc.pl.fem.of ἄκανθα, extent) 678.
καὶ (continuative conjunction) 14.
ἀνέβησαν (3d.per.pl.aor.act.ind.of ἀναβαίνω, constative) 323.
αἱ (nom.pl.fem.of the article in agreement with ἄκανθαι) 9.
ἄκανθαι (nom.pl.fem.of ἄκανθα, subject of ἀνέβησαν and συνέπνιξαν) 678.
καὶ (continuative conjunction) 14.
συνέπνιξαν (3d.per.pl.aor.act.ind.of συμπνίγω, constative) 1051.
καὶ (continuative conjunction) 14.
καρπὸν (acc.sing.masc.of καρπός, direct object of ἔδωκεν) 284.
οὐκ (negative conjunction with the indicative) 130.
ἔδωκεν (3d.per.sing.aor.act.ind.of δίδωμι, culminative) 362.

Translation - *"And other seed fell among the thorns and the thorns grew up and they choked it and it yielded no fruit."*

Comment: Note the simple Greek style of Mark as he uses καί again and again to connect the narrative with short, choppy paratactic clauses. This is the style of a young person who is more excited about telling a story than he is in putting it down in a sophisticated manner. The thorns sprang up and choked the plant with the sad result that it yielded no fruit. In this case, as in the case immediately preceding it the seed germinated, but though the soil in this case was deep and rich, it also grew thorns which choked the good plant and rendered it fruitless. Parallel passages in Mt.13:7 and Lk.8:7, *q.v.*

Verse 8 - *"And other fell on good ground, and did yield fruit that sprang up and increased; and brought forth, some thirty, and some sixty, and some an hundred."*

καὶ ἄλλα ἔπεσεν εἰς τὴν γῆν τὴν καλήν, καὶ ἐδίδου καρπὸν ἀναβαίνοντα καὶ αὐξανόμενα, καὶ ἔφερεν ἓν τριάκοντα καὶ ἓν ἑξήκοντα καὶ ἓν ἑκατόν.

καὶ (adversative conjunction) 14.

ἄλλα (nom.pl.neut.of ἄλλος, subject of ἔπεσεν) 198.

ἔπεσεν (3d.per.sing. aor.act.ind.of πίπτω, constative) 187.

εἰς (preposition with the accusative of extent) 140.

τὴν (acc.sing.fem.of the article in agreement with γῆν) 9.

γῆν (acc.sing.fem.of γῆ, extent) 157.

τὴν (acc.sing.fem.of the article in agreement with καλήν) 9.

καλήν (acc.sing.fem.of καλός, in agreement with γῆν) 296.

καὶ (continuative conjunction) 14.

ἐδίδου (3d.per.sing.imp.act.ind.of δίδωμι, inceptive) 362.

καρπὸν (acc.sing.masc.of καρπός, direct object of ἐδίδου) 284.

ἀναβαίνοντα (pres.act.part.nom.pl.neut.of ἀναβαίνω, adverbial, modal) 323.

καὶ (adjunctive conjunction, joining participles) 14.

αὐξανόμενα (pres.pass.part.nom.pl.neut.of αὐξάνω, adverbial, modal) 628.

ἔφερεν (3d.per.sing.imp.act.ind.of φέρω, inceptive) 683.

ἐν (nom.sing.neut.of ἐς, subject of ἔφερεν, understood) 469.

τριάκοντα (acc.sing.neut.of τριάκοντα, numeral) 1037.

καὶ (adjunctive conjunction joining phrases) 14.

ἐν (nom.sing.neut.of εἷς, subject of ἔφερεν) 469.

ἑξήκοντα (acc.sing.neut.of ἑξήκοντα, numeral) 1036.

καὶ (adjunctive conjunction joining phrases) 14.

ἐν (nom.sing.neut.of εἷς, subject of ἔφερεν understood) 469.

ἑκατόν (acc.sing.neut.of ἑκατόν, numeral) 1035.

Translation - "But other seed fell into the good soil, and began to bear fruit as it grew and was multiplied; and it bore thirty-to-one, and sixty-to-one and one hundred-to-one."

Comment: Note that in verses 5 and 7, Mark uses ἄλλο, the nominative neuter singular, while in verse 8 he uses ἄλλα, the nominative neuter plural. The seed on stony ground and among the thorns are treated as a single category. That seed germinated quickly, sprang up and died quickly for lack of root, or it was choked by thorns. But the seed on the good soil is treated in multi-category fashion. It was all fruitful, but some yielded in a ratio of thirty to one, others sixty to one and even some one hundred to one. *Cf.* comment on Mt.13:1-8; 18-23 and Luke 8:5-15. Note that it was lack of a root system, due to lack of soil depth that caused the quick germination but subsequent lack of production in the seed on the stony soil. One of the reasons perhaps why some Christians produce only thirty fold while other produce more is the difference in intellectual depth through genetic endowment. High intelligence is necessary to the victorious life viewed in its fullest sense. This is not to say, however that the highly endowed Christians are *per se* better Christians than those less highly endowed. Other factors must also be present. But certainly it can be said that intelligence imposes some ceiling on Christian efficiency even when all other positive factors for victorious Christian are present. Our Lord, the faithful Judge of all the earth (John 5:22) asks only that each of us live for Him up to the limit of our highest potential.

Note the geometric progression of fruit production implied in αὐξανόμενα. Cf.#628. Note also the inceptive imperfect in ἐδίδου. "It began a process of continuous fruit bearing." (John 15:2). It takes faith of a high order to believe that Christians of this category are always fruitful, even in moments when they personally are defeated. Yet Jesus said it. A backslidden soul winner may be said to be bearing fruit indirectly, through the lives of others whom he led to Christ before he backslid.

Note the change in the text from the W-H ἐν to ἓν. . . . . Doctor Bruce Metzger comments: "The reading that predominates in the manuscripts is εν, whether accented ἐν or ἓν. In favor of the latter is the probability that underlying the variants was the Aramaic sign of multiplication ("times" or "fold"), . . . , which also is the numeral "one." (Metzger, *A Textual Commentary on the Greek New Testament*, 83).

Verse 9 - "And he said unto them, He that hath ears to hear, let him hear."

καὶ ἔλεγεν,ʺΟς ἔχει ὦτα ἀκούειν ἀκουέτω.

καὶ (continuative conjunction) 14.
ἔλεγεν (3d.per.sing.imp.act.ind.of λέγω, progressive duration) 66.
ʺΟς (nom.sing.masc.of ὅς, subject of ἔχει) 65.
ἔχει (3d.per.sing.pres.act.ind.of ἔχω, progressive) 82.
ὦτα (acc.pl.neut.of οὖς, direct object of ἔχει) 887.
ἀκούειν (pres.act.inf.of ἀκούω, purpose) 148.
ἀκουέτω, 3d.per.sing.pres.act.impv.of ἀκούω, command) 148.

Translation - "And He continued to admonish them, 'Whoever has ears to hear, let him be hearing.' "

Comment: Note that ὅς, the relative pronoun here, has no antecedent. The statement is metaphorical. Everyone has ears, but some lack the ability to grasp the real meaning of life or of God's revelation to man. This is indeed unfortunate. Jesus said something similar to this in His prayer of Mt.11:25,26. Jesus invites those who can do so to probe the depths of His parable to find His true meaning. Note in #887 that οὖς is used metaphorically more often than properly. It will be profitable to study the context to determine all of the situations in which οὖς is used metaphorically. What parts of divine truth, all of which can be *heard* (audibly) are hard to *hear* (spiritually)?

The Purpose of the Parables

(Mt.13:10-17; Lk.8:9-10)

Verse 10 -"And when he was alone, they that were about him with the twelve asked of him the parable."

Καὶ ὅτε ἐγένετο κατὰ μόνας, ἠρώτων αὐτὸν οἱ περὶ αὐτὸν σὺν τοῖς δώδεκα τὰς παραβολάς.

Καὶ (continuative conjunction) 14.
ὅτε (temporal conjunction introducing a definite temporal clause) 703.
ἐγένετο (3d.per.sing.aor.ind.of γίνομαι, constative) 113.
κατὰ (preposition with the accusative, general reference, adverbial) 98.
μόνας (acc.pl.fem.of μόνος, adverbial) 339.
ἠρώτων (3d.per.pl.imp.act.ind.of ἐρωτάω, inceptive) 1172.
αὐτὸν (acc.sing.masc.of αὐτός, direct object of ἠρώτων) 16.
οἱ (nom.pl.masc.of the article introducing the prepositional phrase, subject of ἠρώτων) 9.
περὶ (preposition with the accusative of place description) 173.
αὐτὸν (acc.sing.masc.of αὐτός, place description) 16.,
σὺν (preposition with the instrumental of association) 1542.
τοῖς (instru.pl.masc.of the article, association) 9.
δώδεκα (numeral) 820.
τὰς (acc.pl.fem.of the article in agreement with παραβολάς) 9.
παραβολάς (acc.pl.fem.of παραβολή, object of ἠλώτων) 1027.

Translation - "And when they were alone, those who surrounded Him, along with the twelve, began to ask Him about the parables."

Comment: Note κατὰ here with the accusative used adverbially. This is sometimes called general reference. Jesus escaped the crowd and was alone except for a small group which included the twelve disciples. The vast multitude that almost pushed Him into the Sea of Galilee was gone temporarily. Note the inceptive imperfect in ἠρώτων - "they began to ask Him. . . κ.τ.λ." Those non-twelve disciples along with the Apostles, all of whom had remained by Jesus' side, after the multitude had dispersed, were eager to hear Jesus' further exposition of His teaching. Note the parallel passages in Mt.13:10 and Luke 8:9.

Verse 11 - "And he said unto them, Unto you it is given to know the mystery of the kingdom of God: but unto them that are without, all these things are done in pr~ables."

καὶ ἔλεγεν αὐτοῖς, Ὑμῖν τὸ μυστήριον δέδοται τῆς βασιλείας τοῦ θεοῦ, ἐκείνοις δὲ τοῖς ἔξω ἐν παραβολαῖς τὰ πάντα γίνεται,

καὶ (inferential conjunction) 14.
ἔλεγεν (3d.per.sing.imp.act.ind.of λέγω, inceptive) 66.
αὐτοῖς (dat.pl.masc.of αὐτός, indirect object of ἔλεγεν) 16.

Ὑμῖν (dat.pl.masc.of σύ, indirect object of δέδοται) 104.

τό (acc.sing.neut.of the article in agreement with μυστήριον) 9.

μυστήριον (acc.sing.neut.of μυστήριον, direct object of δέδοται) 1038.

δέδοται (3d.per.sing.perf.pass.ind.of δίδωμι, consummative) 362.

τῆς (gen.sing.fem.of the article in agreement with βασιλείας) 9.

βασιλείας (gen.sing.fem.of βασιλεία, definition) 253.

τοῦ (gen.sing.masc.of the article in agreement with θεοῦ) 9.

θεοῦ (gen.sing.masc.of θεός, definition) 124.

ἐκείνοις (dat.pl.masc.of ἐκεῖνος, personal advantage) 246.

δὲ (adversative conjunction) 11.

τοῖς (dat.pl.masc.of the article in agreement with ἐκείνοις) 9.

ἔξω (adverbial) 449.

ἐν (preposition with the instrumental of means) 80.

παραβολαῖς (instru.pl.fem.of παραβολή, means) 1027.

τά (nom.pl.neut.of the article in agreement with πάντα) 9.

πάντα (nom.pl.neut.of πᾶς, subject of γίνεται) 67.

γίνεται (3d.per.sing.pres.ind.of γίνομαι, aoristic) 113.

Translation - "And He began to explain to them, 'Unto you the mystery of the Kingdom of God has already been given; but to those who are outside these things are given in parables.' "

Comment: Jesus began (inceptive imperfect in ἔλεγεν) to explain to the smaller inside group. Note Ὑμῖν in emphasis, to distinguish them from ἐκείνοις δὲ τοῖς ἔξω - "those on the outside." The perfect tense in δέδοται is consummative. The gift has already been given and therefore it is now ours. The gift is their understanding of what to other less fortunate people is a mystery - a mystery about the Kingdom of God. Luke follows Mark with τῆς βασιλείας τοῦ θεοῦ while Matthew uses τῆς βασιλείας τῶν οὐρανῶν. (Lk.8:10; Mt.13:11). This stubborn fact of the inspired text makes it difficult for those dispensationalists who imagine that there is *always* a difference between the two terms.

The last half of the verse is adversative. Note postpositive δὲ. To the outsiders (*i.e.* those who are not among the elect) the kingdom of God is truly a mystery and as such is presented in a mysterious fashion, *i.e.* in parables. *Cf.*#449 for the places where ἔξω is used to denote the non-elect and unsaved - "The outsiders" - *cf.* especially Lk.13:25. The understanding of the mystery of the Kingdom of God is the possession of the saints - no thanks to them, since to them it was the gift of God's grace. To us it has been given and thus we now possess it. A parable presents truth but only for those who have been given the ability to discern its deeper meaning. Those without understand the story but fail to grasp the concept which the Author intends to convey. They hear, but not with spiritual perception. The reason God has chosen to conduct it this way is given in verse 21. The passage is intensely Calvinistic and hence difficult for babes in Christ, while, of course, it is taboo for sinners.

Verse 12 - "That seeing they may see, and not perceive; and hearing they may hear, and not understand; lest at any time they should be converted, and their sins should be forgiven them."

ἴνα βλέποντες βλέπωσιν καὶ μὴ ἴδωσιν, καὶ ἀκούοντες ἀκούωσιν καὶ μὴ συνιῶσιν, μήποτε ἐπιστρέφωσιν καὶ ἀφεθῇ αὐτοῖς.

ἴνα (final conjunction introducing a purpose clause) 114.

βλέποντες (pres.act.part.nom.pl.masc.of βλέπω, adverbial, concessive) 499.

βλέπωσιν (3d.per.pl.pres.act.subj.of βλέπω, purpose) 499.

καὶ (adversative conjunction) 14.

μὴ (negative conjunction with the subjunctive) 87.

ἴδωσιν (3d.per.pl.aor.act.subj.of ὁράω, purpose) 144.

καὶ (adjunctive conjunction joining clauses) 14.

ἀκούοντες (pres.act.part.nom.pl.masc.of ἀκούω, adverbial, concessive) 148.

ἀκούωσιν (3d.per.pl.pres.act.subj.of ἀκούω, purpose) 148.

καὶ (adversative conjunction) 14.

μὴ (negative conjunction with the subjunctive) 87.

συνιῶσιν (3d.per.pl.pres.act.subj.of συνίημι, purpose) 1039.

μήποτε (prohibitory conjunctive particle introducing a negative final clause) 351.

ἐπιστρέφωσιν (3d.per.pl.1st.aor.act.subj.of ἐπιστρέφω, purpose) 866.

καὶ (adjunctive conjunction joining clauses) 14.

ἀφεθῇ (3d.per.sing.1st.aor.pass.subj.of ἀφίημι, purpose) 319.

αὐτοῖς (dat.pl.masc.of αὐτός, personal advantage) 16.

Translation - ". . . in order that although seeing, they may see, but not perceive, and although hearing, they may hear but not understand, lest they turn around and it be forgiven for them."

Comment: The ἴνα purpose clause runs throughout the verse, which quotes Isa.6:9-10. *Cf.*John 12:40; Acts 28:26,27.

Jesus had spoken to the outsiders, who now were not with Him, but He used the parabolic approach in order that although they see (concessive participle in βλέποντες), they saw only in the βλέπω sense, but did not perceive in a deeper, more intellectual and spiritual sense. This deeper insight is gained by ὁράω (#144). This verse points up beautifully the difference between βλέπω (#499) and ὁράω (#144), and also the difference between ἀκούω (#148) and συνίημι (#1039). The gospel of Jesus Christ is superficially intelligible to the unsaved. They "see" and "hear" but they do not "perceive" and "identify with" it. To do so is to accept Christ and this gift of salvation is for the elect only. This deliberate parabolic approach in the teaching methods of Jesus is to achieve the purpose intended as expressed in "μήποτε . . . κ.τ.λ." - "Lest they turn around in repentance and their previous sin of rejection of Christ be forgiven for them." *Cf.* Mt.13:14,15.

Israel's heart had been hardened when they rejected the messages of the prophets. The treatment they are receiving now is in just retribution for their hardness of heart. God is under no obligation to take measures to enlighten minds and hearts that do not wish the light. *Cf.*comment on Mt.13:14,15.

The Parable of the Sower Explained

(Mt.13:18-23; Lk.8:11-15)

Verse 13 - "And he said unto them, Know ye not this parable? And how then will ye know all parables?"

Καὶ λέγει αὐτοῖς, Οὐκ οἴδατε τὴν παραβολὴν ταύτην, καὶ πῶς πάσας τὰς παραβολὰς γνώσεσθε;

Καὶ (continuative conjunction) 14.
λέγει (3d.per.sing.pres.act.ind.of λέγω, historical) 66.
αὐτοῖς (dat.pl.masc.of αὐτός, indirect object of λέγει) 16.
Οὐκ (negative conjunction with the indicative in rhetorical question) 130.
οἴδατε (2d.per.pl.aor.act.impv.of ὁράω, rhetorical question) 144.
τὴν (acc.sing.fem.of the article in agreement with παραβολὴν) 9.
παραβολὴν (acc.sing.fem.of παραβολή, direct object of οἴδατε) 1027.
ταύτην (acc.sing.fem.of οὗτος, in agreement with παραβολὴν) 93.
καὶ (emphatic conjunction) 14.
πῶς (interrogative conjunction in direct question) 627.
τὰς (acc.pl.fem.of the article in agreement with παραβολὰς) 9.
παραβολὰς (acc.pl.fem.of παραβολή, direct object of γνώσεσθε) 1027.
γνώσεσθε (2d.per.pl.fut.mid.ind.of γινώσκω, deliberative) 131.

Translation - "And He said to them, 'You know this parable do you not? Otherwise how will you understand all the other parables?"

Comment: A rhetorical question which expects an affirmative reply is followed by a question of credulity, with the deliberative future. In the light of what He had just said about the mysteries of the Kingdom of God being understood by the in-group and hidden only from the out-group, Jesus seems astonished that the disciples did not grasp the true and hidden import of His words. *Cf.* Mk.4:11. His second question implies that if they did not understand the parable of the sower it was doubtful that they would understand any of those which were to follow. Then He condescends to help them with the first one, in the hope that perhaps they would learn the technique and be able to understand them all.

Verse 14 - "The sower soweth the word."

ὁ σπείρων τὸν λόγον σπείρει.

ὁ (nom.sing.masc.of the article in agreement with σπείρων) 9.
σπείρων (pres.act.part.nom.sing.masc.of σπείρω, subject of σπείρει) 616.
τὸν (acc.sing.masc.of the article in agreement with λόγον) 9.
λόγον (acc.sing.masc.of λόγος, direct object of σπείρει) 510.
σπείρει (3d.per.sing.pres.act.ind.of σπείρω, customary) 616.

Translation - "The sower sows the word."

Comment: Note that τὸν λόγον is emphasized ahead of the verb. Jesus did not spell out for the disciples all of the details. Since it is given to them as God's elect, to know the mysteries, they should be able to interpret some of this story for themselves. The seed is not literal seed, but the Word of God. *Cf.#*510 for other places where λόγος is so used. Thus the sower is not necessarily a farmer, but any witness of the Word of God. Witnessing for Christ is sowing the seed of the Word of God broadcast, without discrimination as to where it should be sowed. The preacher is not given the authority of selecting the seed bed. He must not think of this. He sows the seed everywhere and leaves the harvest up to God. It would be a mistake to avoid the stony places by the way side or those places infested with thorns. How can the preacher tell what is good ground in every case? Too much time would be wasted in trying to select the proper seed bed. Our commission (Mt.28:18-20; Acts 1:7,8) is to preach the Word - sow the seed - scatter it far and wide. We are sowers *not* the Lord of the harvest. Keep in mind that even the unproductive seed, which fell upon shallow or thorny soil, germinated. There was resurrection of life from the tiny seed, albeit destined to become unproductive due to hot sun, thin soil and thorns. Does the parable teach that germination of seed means salvation? "He that hath ears to hear, let him hear."

Verse 15 - "And these are they by the way side, where the word is sown; but when they have heard, Satan cometh immediately, and taketh away the word that was sown in their hearts."

οὗτοι δέ εἰσιν οἱ παρὰ τὴν ὁδὸν ὅπου σπείρεται ὁ λόγος, καὶ ὅταν ἀκούσωσιν εὐθὺς ἔρχεται ὁ Σατανᾶς καὶ αἴρει τὸν λόγον τὸν ἐσπαρμένον εἰς αὐτούς.

οὗτοι (nom.pl.masc.of οὗτος, subject of εἰσιν) 93.
δέ (explanatory conjunction) 11.
εἰσιν (3d.per.pl.pres.ind.of εἰμί, aoristic) 86.
οἱ (nom.pl.masc.of the article, predicate nominative) 9.
παρὰ (preposition with the accusative of extent) 154.
τὴν (acc.sing.fem.of the article in agreement with ὁδὸν) 9.
ὁδὸν (acc.sing.fem.of ὁδός, extent, place) 199.
ὅπου (relative adverb of place) 592.
σπείρεται (3d.per.sing.pres.pass.ind.of σπείρω, aoristic) 616.
ὁ (nom.sing.masc.of the article in agreement with λόγος) 9.
λόγος (nom.sing.masc.of λόγος, subject of σπείρεται) 510.
καὶ (adversative conjunction) 14.
ὅταν (indefinite temporal adverb with the subjunctive) 436.
ἀκούσωσιν (3d.per.pl.aor.act.subj.of ἀκούω, in an indefinite temporal clause) 148.
εὐθὺς (adverbial) 258.
ἔρχεται (3d.per.sing.pres.ind.of ἔρχομαι, aoristic) 146.
ὁ (nom.sing.masc.of the article in agreement with Σατανᾶς) 9.
Σατανᾶς (nom.sing.masc.of Σατανᾶς, subject of ἔρχεται and αἴρει) 365.

καὶ (adjunctive conjunction joining verbs) 14.

αἴρει (3d.per.sing.pres.act.ind.of αἴρω, aoristic) 350.

τὸν (acc.sing.masc.of the article in agreement with λόγον) 9.

λόγον (acc.sing.masc.of λόγος, direct object of αἴρει) 510.

τὸν (acc.sing.masc.of the article in agreement with ἐσπαρμένον) 9.

ἐσπαρμένον (perf.pass.part.acc.sing.masc.of σπείρω, adjectival, restrictive) 616.

εἰς (preposition with the accusative of extent) 140.

αὐτούς (acc.pl.masc.of αὐτός, extent) 16.

Translation - "Now these are they by the side of the road, where the word is sown, but when they hear immediately Satan comes and catches up the seed which was sown among them."

Comment: δὲ is explanatory, as Jesus continues to explain the parable. The sower has positive ideas in verse 14, but Satan awaits to oppose. παρὰ τὴν ὁδόν, a prepositional phrase in the accusative case, is joined to οἱ, the predicate nominative in agreement with οὗτοι. "These are they. . . " "Who?" The ones by the road. What road? ὅπου . . . ὁ λόγος - Where the seed was sown. Now that they are properly identified, what about them? ὅταν introduces the indefinite temporal clause with the subjunctive. "When they hear. . . " Jesus is not speaking of a specific sermon on a specific occasion. But *when* and if they hear, Satan comes and catches up the seed which was sown in their hearts. Satan is in a hurry to do this as εὐθὺς indicates. Matthew 13:19 calls Satan "the evil one" - ὁ πονηρός and Luke calls him ὁ διάβολος (Lk.8:12). All three are correct since Satan, the Devil is also the Evil One. Satan is on the alert to combat the preaching of the gospel (II Cor.4:3,4) and comes as soon as the Word of God is preached to take it away. He must be fast because the seed is the supernatural Word of God and is sure to germinate quickly unless it is taken away. *Cf.* Mt.13:19 and Lk.8:12 for further comment. Note that the seed was sown εἰς αὐτούς (Mk.4:15), ἐν τῇ καρδίᾳ αὐτοῦ (Mt.13:19 but was taken ἀπὸ τῆς καρδίας αὐτῶν (Lk.8:12). Lest Matthew's phrase "in his heart" be misinterpreted as salvation, Luke adds ἵνα μὴ πιστεύσαντες σωθῶσιν - "lest having believed, they might be saved."

Verse 16 - "And these are they likewise which are sown on stony ground; who, when they have heard the word, immediately receive it with gladness."

καὶ οὗτοί εἰσιν οἱ ἐπὶ τὰ πετρώδη σπειρόμενοι, οἳ ὅταν ἀκούσωσιν τὸν λόγον εὐθὺς μετὰ χαρᾶς λαμβάνουσιν αὐτόν,

καὶ (continuative conjunction) 14.

οὗτοί (nom.pl.masc.of οὗτος, subject of εἰσιν) 93.

οἱ (nom.pl.masc.of the article, in agreement with σπειρόμενον) 9.

ἐπὶ (preposition with the accusative of extent, place) 47.

τὰ (acc.pl.neut.of the article in agreement with πετρώδη) 9.

πετρώδη (acc.pl.neut.of πετρώδης, extent) 1029.

σπειρόμενον (pres.pass.part.nom.pl.masc.of σπείρω, pred.nominative) 616.

οἱ (relative pronoun, nom.pl.masc.of ὅς, subject of ἀκούσωσιν and λαμβάνουσιν) 65.

ὅταν (indefinite temporal adverb with the subjunctive) 436.

ἀκούσωσιν (3d.per.pl.aor.act.subj.of ἀκούω , indefinite temporal clause) 148.

τὸν (acc.sing.masc.of the article in agreement with λόγον) 9.

λόγον (acc.sing.masc.of λόγος, direct object of ἀκούσωσιν) 510.

εὐθὺς (adverbial) 258.

μετὰ (preposition with the genitive, adverbial) 50.

χαρᾶς (gen.sing.fem.of χαρά, adverbial) 183.

λαμβάνουσιν (3d.per.pl.pres.act.ind.of λαμβάνω, aoristic) 533.

αὐτόν (acc.sing.masc.of αὐτός, direct object of λαμβάνουσιν) 16.

Translation - "And these are the seeds sown upon the rocky soil, which, when they hear the word immediately with joy receive it."

Comment: οἱ ἐπὶ τὰ πετρώδη σπειρόμενοι is the participial phrase used as the predicate nominative to agree with οὗτοι. The copula is εἰσιν. "These are the ones sown .. κ.τ.λ." They are further defined by the relative clause with ὅταν and the subjunctive, indicating an indefinite time. They do hear the word but Jesus does not tell us definitely when. But when they hear it, immediately they receive it. Note, however, that it is λαμβάνουσιν rather than συνίωσιν .. of .. verse 12. There is little intellectual depth in this case and hence there is no deep perceptive acceptance, which συνίημι implies. But there is germination and life as a result. Many shallow Christians will not live consistently with their faith nor stoutly defend it because they have not enough depth to understand it. Christian theology, for the intellectual, who is deeply committed to it, joins issue with the philosophy of the God of this world. The shallow Christian is not even aware that there is a war going on. Others do know (verse17) and see no reason for it and are thus offended by the controversy and withdraw from the fight.

Verse 17 - ". . . and have not root in themselves, and so endure but for a time; afterward, when affliction or persecution ariseth for the word's sake, immediately they are offended."

καὶ οὐκ ἔχουσιν ῥίζαν ἐν ἑαυτοῖς ἀλλὰ πρόσκαιροί εἰσιν, εἶτα γενομένης θλίψεως ἢ διωγμοῦ διὰ τὸν λόγον εὐθὺς σκανδαλίζονται.

καὶ (adversative conjunction) 14.

οὐκ (adversative conjunction) 130.

ἔχουσιν (3d.per.pl.pres.act.ind.of ἔχω, aoristic) 82.

ῥίζαν (acc.sing.fem.of ῥίζα, direct object of ἔχουσιν) 293.

ἐν (preposition with the locative, with plural nouns and pronouns) 80.

ἑαυτοῖς (loc.pl.masc.of ἑαυτός, place where) 288.

ἀλλὰ (alternative conjunction) 342.

πρόσκαιροί (nom.pl.masc.of πρόσκαιρος, predicate adjective) 1045.
εἰσιν (3d.per.pl.pres.ind.of εἰμί, progressive) 86.

#2185 εἶτα (an adverb of time).

after that - Mk.4:28; 8:25; John 13:5.
afterward - Mk.4:17.
furthermore - Heb.12:9.
then - Mk.4:28; Lk.8:12; John 19:27; 20:27; I Cor.15:5,7,24; I Tim.2:13; 3:10;
Jam.1:15.

Meaning: An adverb of time. Then, after that, next, etc., etc. *Cf.*ἔπειτα (#2566).
In a sequence, showing chronological arrangement as in Mk.4:28,28 which has
εἶτεν before πρῶτον. In the sequence εἶτα. . . ἔπειτα - I Cor.15:5; in reverse order
as ἔπειτα . . εἶτα in I Cor.15:7. With πρῶτον, both in logical and chronological
order - I Tim.3:10. Following πρόσκαιρος in Mk.4:17. Joined by a verb of action
or command, in which cases εἶτα moves the action of the story as in John 13:5 -
"He girded Himself. . . εἶτα he poured water. . κ.τ.λ." In this sense also in
Mk.8:25; Lk.8:12; John 19:27; 20:27; I Tim.2:13; Jam.1:15. Showing the logical
order of the resurrection - I Cor.15:24. Once in a sense foreign to all other New
Testament usage - as a pivot word in an argument as in Heb.12:9, following the
statement of verse 8 - "Furthermore. . . κ.τ.λ."

γενομένης (aor.part.gen.sing.fem.of γίνομαι, genitive absolute) 113.
θλίφεως (gen.sing.fem.of θλῖφσις, genitive absolute) 1046.
ἤ (disjunctive) 465.
διωγμοῦ (gen.sing.masc.of διωγμός, genitive absolute) 1047.
διά (preposition with the accusative of cause) 118.
τὸν (acc.sing.masc.of the article in agreement with λόγον) 9.
λόγον (acc.sing.masc.of λόγος, cause) 510.
εὐθὺς (adverbial) 258.
σκανδαλίζονται (3d.per.pl.pres.pass.ind.of σκανδαλίζω, ingressive) 503.

Translation - ". . . *but they have no root in themselves, but they are there only a
short time after which, when social pressure and persecution begin because of
the word, they quickly begin to take offense."*

Comment: The shallow earth did not provide plant food for the development of
a viable root system. All of the strength of the plant was devoted to germination
and sudden growth upward. No root in themselves. *Cf.* Col.2:7. Run the
references under #293 on roots for valuable sermon material. Christ is the ῥίζα
(Rom.15:12; Rev.5:5). Roots provide stability and nourishment. No plant can
live long without them. These people, though genuinely born again were only
temporary insofar as an effective Christian witness is concerned. Note
πρόσκαιρος in II Cor.4:18 - temporal. εἶτα *i.e.*following a temporary flowering -
- γενομένης . . . τὸν λόγον - a genitive absolute with the aorist tense - - after
pressure and persecution developed, immediately they were offended. They had
received the Word εὐθὺς with joy. Now they are just as quick to be offended.

These people are quick reactors. They yield readily to environmental circumstances. Surround them with gospel seed and immediately they receive it joyously. Surround them with pressure and persecution and immediately they are offended. Why? No root system. Shallow people. The world is full of them. Run the references on #1046 to see how deep rooted Christians react to pressure. *Cf.*also #1047 and note the difference between ϑλίφσις and διωγμός. *Cf.* also #434 for the word διώκω. Pressure (ϑλίφσις) and persecution always accompany true Christianity. It is how we react to them that determines whether we shall be victorious Christians. Note I Thess. 1:6, where the saints received the seed of the word with ϑλίφσις and χαρᾷ. Pressure from the unsaved world and joy from the Holy Spirit. How tragic that pressure should bring offence! The Christian who gets bitter when pressure hits him had better look to his root system.

Verse 18 - "And these are they which are sown among thorns; such as hear the word,. . . "

καὶ ἄλλοι εἰσὶν οἱ εἰς τὰς ἀκάνϑας σπειρόμενοι, cὗτοί εἰσιν οἱ τὸν λόγον ἀκούσαντες, . . .

καὶ (continuative conjunction) 14.
ἄλλοι (nom.pl.masc.of ἄλλος, subject of εἰσὶν) 198.
εἰσὶν (3d.per.pl.pres.ind.of εἰμί, aoristic) 86.
οἱ (nom.pl.masc.of the article in agreement with σπειρόμενοι) 9.
εἰς (preposition with the accusative of extent) 140.
τὰς (acc.pl.fem.of the article in agreement with ἀκάνϑας) 9.
ἀκάνϑας (acc.pl.fem.of ἄκανϑα, extent) 678.
σπειρόμενοι (pres.pass.part.nom.pl.masc.of σπείρω, predicate nominative) 616.
οὗτοί (nom.pl.masc.of οὗτος, subject of εἰσιν) 93.
εἰσιν (3d.per.pl.pres.ind.of εἰμί, aoristic) 86.
οἱ (nom.pl.masc.of the article in agreement with ἀκούσαντες) 9.
τὸν (acc.sing.masc.of the article in agreement with λόγον) 9.
λόγον (acc.sing.masc.of λόγος, direct object of ἀκούσαντες) 510.
ἀκούσαντες (aor.act.part.nom.pl.masc. of ἀκούω, predicate nominative) 148.

Translation - "And there are others which are sown among thorns; these are they who heard the word . . . "

Comment: Our Lord moves on to the third category of seed. ἄλλοι to distinguish from οὗτοι in verse 16. The predicate nominative in agreement with ἄλλοι is οἱ . . . σπειρόμενοι. Note the locative use of εἰς with the accusative. *Cf.*#140. The οὗτοί refers to ἄλλοι and is identified by another predicate nominative οἱ τὸν λόγον ἀκούσαντες. The sentence is finished in verse 19. Note in Mt.27:29 that ἄκανϑα were still fighting the living Word of God as He died on the cross, just as they fight the new Christian who happens to germinate and grow among them.

Verse 19 - "And the cares of this world, and the deceitfulness of riches, and the lusts of other things entering in, choke the word, and it becometh unfruitful."

καὶ αἱ μέριμναι τοῦ αἰῶνος καὶ ἡ ἀπάτη τοῦ πλούτου καὶ αἱ περὶ τὰ λοιπὰ ἐπιθυμίαι εἰσπορευόμεναι συμπνίγουσιν τὸν λόγον, καὶ ἄκαρπος γίνεται.

καὶ (adversative conjunction) 14.

αἱ (nom.pl.fem.of the article in agreement with μέριμναι) 9.

μέριμναι (nom.pl.fem.of μέριμνα, subject of συμπνίγουσιν) 1048.

τοῦ (gen.sing.masc.of the article in agreement with αἰῶνος) 9.

αἰῶνος (gen.sing.masc.of αἰών, definition) 1002.

καὶ (adjunctive conjunction joining nouns) 14.

ἡ (nom.sing.fem.of the article in agreement with ἀπάτη) 9.

ἀπάτη (nom.sing.fem.of ἀπάτη, subject of συμπνίγουσιν) 1049.

τοῦ (gen.sing.masc.of the article in agreement with πλούτου) 9.

πλούτου (gen.sing.masc.of πλοῦτος, definition) 1050.

καὶ (adjunctive conjunction, joining nouns) 14.

αἱ (nom.pl.fem.of the article in agreement with ἐπιθυμίαι) 9.

περὶ (preposition with the accusative of reference) 173.

τὰ (acc.pl.neut.of the article in agreement with λοιπὰ) 9.

λοιπὰ (acc.pl.neut.of λοιπός, reference) 1402.

#2186 ἐπιθυμίαι (nom.pl.fem.of ἐπιθυμία, subject of συμπνίγουσιν).

desire - Lk.22:15; Phil.1:23; I Thess.2:17.

concupiscence - Rom.7:8; I Thess.4:5; Col.3:5.

lust - Rev.18:14; Mk.4:19; Rom.7:7; Jam.1:14,15; II Pet.1:4; Gal.5:24; I Tim.6:9; II Tim.2:22; 4:3; I Pet.1:14; 4:2; II Pet.2:10; Rom.1:24; I John 2:17; Rom.6:12; 13:14; Eph.4:22; I John 2:16,16; II Pet.2:18; Gal.5:16; I Pet.2:11; Tit.2:12; Rom.13:14; John 8:44; Tit.3:3; II Tim.3:6; I Pet.4:3; Jude 16,18; II Pet.3:3; Eph.2:3.

Meaning: Related to ἐπιθυμέω (#500), which is made up of ἐπί (#47) and θυμός (#2034), which is made up of θύω (#1398). θύω means "to breathe violently," "to be in a heat" as with an urge to kill - θύω plus μα (result suffix) hence the result of passion, which is θυμός. When one keeps θυμός concentrated upon (ἐπί) a desire it becomes intense. Hence, ἐπιθυμία means intense desire. There is nothing in the word itself, from a etymological point of view, to denote evil desire. The evil in ἐπιθυμία is not in the word but in the adjuncts of the context. It is associated in the New Testament most often with evil - hence the English word "lust" has been most often used.

Intense desires of a godly sort are found in Lk.22:15, of our Lord's desire to eat the Passover with His disciples, and in Phil.1:23, of Paul's desire to die and go to heaven. Also in a good sense in I Thess.2:17. In all other passages the context makes clear that ἐπιθυμία is a fierce and compelling drive to commit sin.

εἰσπορευόμεναι (pres.part.nom.pl.fem.of εἰσπορεύομαι, adverbial, temporal) 1161.
συμπνίγουσιν (3d.per.pl.pres.act.ind.of συμπνίγω, aoristic) 1051.
τὸν (acc.sing.masc.of the article in agreement with λόγον) 9.
λόγον (acc.sing.masc.of λόγος, direct object of συμπνίγουσιν) 510.
καὶ (continuative conjunction) 14.
ἄκαρπος (nom.sing.masc.of ἄκαρπος, predicate adjective) 1052.
γίνεται (3d.per.sing.pres.ind.of γίνομαι, aoristic) 113.

Translation - "... *and the conflicting pressures of the age and the deceitfulness of wealth and the intense desires for the other things, having entered in, choke the word and it becomes unfruitful.*"

Comment: Here is a formula for the defeated Christian life. Three subjects of the same verb show that αἱ μέριμναι, ἡ ἀπάτη and αἱ ἐπιθυμίαι join together to choke the seed and render it unfruitful. Frustrations, deceitfulness of riches and evil desires combine to bring defeat to the Christian. Study carefully each word in the verse by number. "The cares of the age. . . " Society is becoming increasingly complex and life in modern society is more difficult, even for non-Christians. The word μέριμνα (#1048) means the result of being pulled in opposite directions. Hence we have translated "conflicting pressures." "Dilemmas" will serve as well. "Cares" of the KJV is too general - not specific enough. "Frustrations" tends to carry the idea. Note #1002 for other passages where αἰών is used to denote the present church age. A check of all of these passages will reveal characteristics of the age which impose pressures upon the saints. There is much valuable preaching material here. Jesus warned us against them (Lk.21:34); Peter tells us what to do with them (I Pet.5:7). *Cf.*#1049 for programs of deceit. How many ways does Satan have to deceive us? Riches (πλούτου) is one of them. Here it has reference to material wealth as also in Mt.13:22; Lk.8:14 (the parallel accounts) and II Cor.8:2; I Tim.6:17; Jam.5:2; Rev.18:17. They are uncertain (I Tim.6:17); they are subject to corruption (Jam.5:2) and they come to nothing (Rev.18:17). But there are heavenly riches. *Cf.*#1050 for a list of God's riches for the saints. I Tim.6:17 sets the two types of riches against each other. Material wealth will deceive the Christian if we let it, but it need not do so. Many deeply dedicated Christians are affluent, because they do not trust in riches, but in the living God. When we worship material wealth, we have been victimized by "the deceitfulness of riches." We can rise above the dilemmas of the age; we can escape the deceit of riches. What about the intense desire for the other things? *Cf.*#2186 - "Intense desire, passion, lust, overwhelming drive, compulsion, concentrated craving. This is what the word means. It is not evil except when it is directed toward evil. In this passage, it is evil desire. The point here is the intensity of it. Modern psychology has taught us that ἐπιθυμία is irresistible - that men must yield to it, because they have no choice. Hence there is no moral responsibility for acts committed under its spell.

The M'Naughton doctrine (that if a criminal knows the difference between right and wrong at the time of the crime, he may not plead innocence on grounds of insanity) has been overthrown in a United States Circuit Court of Appeals. Psychologists convinced the judges that mere knowledge of right and wrong in itself is not enough. Insane people know, but they cannot escape the compulsion to act. The ἐπιθυμία is too strong for them. The Christian should not allow θυμός to concentrate (ἐπί) upon the thing desired. "Whatsoever things are pure. . . . think on these things" (Phil.4:8). Desire earnestly the best gifts (I Cor.12:31). The stronger the drive in ἐπιθυμία, the more enslaved the Christian among the thorns. Note that the thorns cannot choke the Word until they enter in. Christians should not allow them to enter. But since they spring up simultaneously with germination, it is a problem that confronts the infant Christian, who cannot be expected, in his days of spiritual infancy, to discern the danger. This is why pastors should devote extra time to the babes in Christ. The verse states clearly the problem which the new Christian faces. To analyze it properly is to know how to combat it. A formula for the defeated Christian life suggests a counte-formula for the victorious Christian life.

For further comment *Cf.* Mt.13:22 and Lk.8:14.

Verse 20 - "And there are they which are sown on good ground; such as hear the word, and receive it, and bring forth fruit, some thirtyfold, some sixty and some an hundred."

καὶ ἐκεῖνοί εἰσιν οἱ ἐπὶ τὴν γῆν τὴν καλὴν σπαρέντες, οἵτινες ἀκούουσιν τὸν λόγον καὶ παραδέχονται καὶ καρποφοροῦσιν ἐν τριάκοντα καὶ ἐν ἑξήκοντα καὶ ἐν ἑκατόν.

καὶ (continuative conjunction) 14.

ἐκεῖνοί (nom.pl.masc.of ἐκεῖνος, subject of εἰσιν) 246.

εἰσιν (3d.per.pl.pres.ind.of εἰμί, aoristic) 86.

οἱ (nom.pl.masc.of the article in agreement with σπαρέντες) 9.

ἐπὶ (preposition with the accusative of extent) 47.

τὴν (acc.sing.fem.of the article in agreement with γῆν) 9.

γῆν (acc.sing.fem.of γῆ, extent) 157.

τὴν (acc.sing.fem.of the article in agreement with καλὴν) 9.

καλὴν (acc.sing.fem.of καλός, in agreement with γῆν) 296.

σπαρέντες (2d.aor.pass.part.nom.pl.masc.of σπείρω, predicate nominative) 616.

οἵτινες (nom.pl.masc.of ὅστις, subject of ἀκούουσιν, παραδέχονται and καρποφοροῦσιν) 163.

ἀκούουσιν (3d.per.pl.pres.act.ind.of ἀκούω, aoristic) 148.

τὸν (acc.sing.masc.of the article in agreement with λόγον) 9.

λόγον (acc.sing.masc.of λόγος, direct object of ἀκούουσιν) 510.

καὶ (adjunctive conjunction joining verbs) 14.

#2187 παραδέχονται (3d.per.pl.pres.ind.of παραδέχομαι, aoristic).

receive - Mk.4:20; Acts 15:4; 16:21; 22:18; I Tim.5:19; Heb.12:6.

Meaning: A combination of παρά (#154) and δέχομαι (#867). Hence to receive along side. To receive, accept, claim as one's own. With reference to intellectual and spiritual acceptance of the truth of the gospel of Christ - Mk.4:20; Acts 16:21; 22:18; of believing a rumor against an elder - I Tim.5:19; with reference to God's acceptance of believers as His children - Heb.12:6. To receive visitors - Acts 15:4.

καὶ (adjunctive conjunction joining verbs) 14.
καρποφοροῦσιν (3d.per.pl.pres.act.ind.of καρποφορέω,progressive) 1054.
ἓν (nom.sing.neut.of εἷς, nominative absolute) 469.
τριάκοντα (numeral) 1037.
καὶ (adjunctive conjunction joining substantives) 14.
ἓν (nom.sing.neut.of εἷς, nominative absolute) 469.
ἑξήκοντα (numeral) 1036.
καὶ (adjunctive conjunction joining substantives) 14.
ἓν (nom.sing.neut.of εἷς, nominative absolute) 469.
ἑκατόν (numeral) 1035.

Translation - "*And these are they who were sown upon the good soil, who hear the word and receive (it) and continue to bear fruit - one thirty fold and one sixty and one an hundred.*"

Comment: Note the emphatic attributive position of τὴν καλήν. *Cf.*#2187. παραδέχομαι means to receive favourably. They heard, they accepted and they bore fruit in varying amounts. Why the varying amounts? Were there no thorns for the saints? In the parable, the distinction is in the place of sowing, not the sower, nor the seed. Wayside, stony ground, thorny ground, good ground. We are not told whether the thorny ground was deep, although it was deep enough to support thorns. It is dangerous to push a parable too far. *Cf.* Lk.8:15.

A Light Under a Bushel

(Lk.8:16-18)

Verse 21 - "*And he said unto them, Is a candle brought to be put under a bushel, or under a bed? And not to be set on a candlestick?*"

Καὶ ἔλεγεν αὐτοῖς, Μήτι ἔρχεται ὁ λύχνος ἵνα ὑπὸ τὸν μόδιον τεθῇ ἢ ὑπὸ τὴν κλίνην; οὐχ ἵνα ἐπὶ τὴν λυχνίαν τεθῇ;

Καὶ (continuative conjunction) 14.
ἔλεγεν (3d.per.sing.imp.act.ind.of λέγω, inceptive) 66.
αὐτοῖς (dat.pl.masc.of αὐτός, indirect object of ἔλεγεν) 16.
Μήτι (negative conjunction in direct question which expects a negative reply) 676.
ἔρχεται (3d.per.sing.pres.pass.ind.of ἔρχομαι, customary) 146.
ὁ (nom.sing.masc.of the article in agreement with λύχνος) 9.
λύχνος (nom.sing.masc.of λύχνος, subject of ἔρχεται) 454.
ἵνα (final conjunction introducing a purpose clause) 114.

ὑπό (preposition with the accusative, extent) 117.
τὸν (acc.sing.masc.of the article in agreement with μόδιον) 9.
μόδιον (acc.sing.masc.of μόδιος, extent) 456.
τεθῇ (3d.per.sing.1st.aor.pass.subj.of τίθημι, purpose) 455.
ἤ (disjunctive) 465.
ὑπό (preposition with the accusative of extent) 117.
τὴν (acc.sing.fem.of the article in agreement with κλίνην) 9.
κλίνην (acc.sing.fem.of κλίνη, extent) 779.
οὐχ (negative conjunction with the indicative implied) 130.
ἵνα (final conjunction introducing a purpose clause) 114.
ἐπί (preposition with the accusative of extent) 47.
τὴν (acc.sing.fem.of the article in agreement with λυχνίαν) 9.
λυχνίαν (acc.sing.fem.of λυχνία, extent) 457.
τεθῇ (3d.per.sing.1st.aor.pass.subj.of τίθημι) 455.

Translation - *"And He began to ask them, 'The candle is not brought in order that it may be placed under the bushel or under the bed, is it? Is it not that it may be placed upon the candlestick?' "*

Comment: Jesus resumed His address, this time with a rhetorical question, the answer to which is properly in the negative. The second question with οὐχ expects an affirmative reply. Candles shed no light under a bushel or under a bed, but they are useful if placed upon a candlestick. The candle is designed to give light and therefore should not be hidden. The thought is reinforced in

Verse 22 - *"For there is nothing hid, which shall not be manifested; neither was anything kept secret, but that it should come abroad."*

οὐ γὰρ ἐστιν κρυπτὸν ἐὰν μὴ ἵνα φανερωθῇ, οὐδὲ ἐγένετο ἀπόκρυφον ἀλλ' ἵνα ἔλθῃ εἰς φανερόν.

οὐ (negative conjunction with the indicative) 130.
γάρ (causal conjunction) 105.
ἐστιν (3d.per.sing.pres.ind.of εἰμί, aoristic) 86.
κρυπτὸν (nom.sing.neut.of κρυπτός, predicate nominative) 565.
ἐὰν (conditional particle in a third-class condition) 363.
μὴ (negative conjunction with the subjunctive, in a third-class condition) 87.
ἵνα (final conjunction in a purpose clause) 114.
φανερωθῇ (3d.per.sing.aor.pass.subj.of φανερόω, purpose) 1960.
οὐδὲ (disjunctive particle) 452.
ἐγένετο (3d.per.sing.aor.ind.of γίνομαι, constative) 113.

#2188 ἀπόκρυφον (nom.sing.neut.of ἀπόκρυφος, predicate adjective).

hid - Lk.8:17; Co.2:3.
be kept secret - Mk.4:22.

Meaning: A combination of ἀπό (#70) and κρύπτω (#451). Hence, an adjective - hidden, kept secret, concealed. In the parallel passages - Mk.4:22; Lk.8:17. In Col.2:3, the treasures of wisdom and knowledge are hidden in Christ.

ἀλλ' (alternative conjunction) 342.
ἵνα (final conjunction introducing a purpose clause) 114.
ἔλθῃ (3d.per.sing.aor.pass.subj.of ἔρχομαι, purpose) 146.
εἰς (preposition with the accusative of extent) 140.
φανερόν (acc.sing.neut.of φανερός, extent) 981.

Translation - "Because nothing is hidden except for the purpose of future manifestation, nor was anything kept secret except that it may be brought to light."

Comment: Candles are for the production of light. Light is for shining. Hence, candles should be placed on candlesticks, not under bushels or beds. All light is going to shine somewhere. There is not one thing now hidden, but that in God's eternal purpose is destined for revelation. The second sentence says essentially the same thing and is repeated only for emphasis. ἀπόκρυφον (#2188) is a stronger word than κρυπτόν (#565). It means "hidden away from" not simply "hidden." The phrase ἵνα ἔλθῃ εἰς φανερόν indicates a definite purpose on God's part. Hidden things are going to be brought to light. When we note in Col.2:3 that these hidden things include all of the treasures of wisdom and knowledge which are now hidden in Christ, it is indeed a wonderful promise. All of these things shall be included in the curriculum in God's eternal university. Not one treasure will be forever hidden.

Verse 23 - "If any man have ears to hear, let him hear."

εἴ τις ἔχει ὦτα ἀκούειν ἀκουέτω.

εἴ (conditional particle in a first-class condition) 337.
τις (nom.sing.masc.of τις, subject of ἔχει) 486.
ἔχει (3d.per.sing.pres.act.ind.of ἔχω, first-class condition) 82.
ὦτα (acc.pl.neut.of οὖς, direct object of ἔχει) 887.
ἀκούειν (pres.act.inf.of ἀκούω, epexegetical) 148.
ἀκουέτω (3d.per.sing.pres.act.impv.of ἀκούω, command) 148.

Translation - "If anyone has ears to hear, let him hear."

Comment: This statement which occurs frequently (Mt.11:15; 13:9,43; Mk.4:9,23; 7:16; Lk.8:8; 14:35; Rev.2:7,11,17,29; 3:6,13,22; 13:9) along with other related statements (#887), seems always to be a divine invitation for man to probe as deeply into what has been said as possible. In Mk.4:23 it follows the statement that no wisdom and knowledge will be permanently hidden from everyone. The depths of God's wisdom can be plumbed by those willing to have the ears that are able to hear. It is indeed a challenge. The next verses are to the point.

Verse 24 - "And he said unto them, Take heed what ye hear: with what measure ye mete, it shall be measured to you: and unto you that hear shall more be given."

Καὶ ἔλεγεν αὐτοῖς, Βλέπετε τί ἀκούετε. ἐν ᾧ μέτρῳ μετρεῖτε μετρηθήσεται ὑμῖν καὶ προστεθήσεται ὑμῖν.

Καὶ (continuative conjunction) 14.
ἔλεγεν (3d.per.sing.imp.act.ind.of λέγω, progressive duration) 66.
αὐτοῖς (dat.pl.masc.of αὐτός, indirect object of ἔλεγεν) 16.
Βλέπετε (2d.per.pl.pres.act.impv.of βλέπω, command) 499.
τί (acc.sing.neut.of τίς, direct object of ἀκούετε) 281.
ἀκούετε (2d.per.pl.pres.act.ind.of ἀκούω, progressive) 148.
ἐν (preposition with the instrumental of means) 80.
ᾧ (instru.sing.neut.of ὅς, relative pronoun) 65.
μέτρῳ (instru.sing.neut.of μέτρον, means) 643.
μετρεῖτε (2d.per.pl.pres.act.ind.of μετρέω, aoristic) 644.
μετρηθήσεται (3d.per.sing.fut.pass.ind.of μετρέω, predictive) 644.
ὑμῖν (dat.pl.masc.of σύ, personal interest) 104.
καὶ (adjunctive conjunction joining verbs) 14.
προστεθήσεται (3d.per.sing.fut.pass.ind.of προστίθημι, predictive) 621.
ὑμῖν (dat.pl.masc.of σύ, personal interest) 104.

Translation - "And He continued to speak to them, 'Be careful what you listen to: with what measure you use to measure it shall be measured for you and and it shall be even more for you."

Comment: Mark says, "Be careful *what* you hear." Luke says, "Be careful therefore *how* you hear." If everything among the hidden treasures of wisdom and knowledge in Christ (Col.2:3) is to be revealed to those with ears to hear (Mk.4:23), how much the Christian grows in grace will depend upon what he hears (Mk.4:23) and how he hears it (Lk.8:18). Both ideas - *what* and *how* are important to the thought. Many Christians attend worship services where the *what* is settled satisfactorily, but the *how* is lacking. A recent comment: "Pastor's Bible preaching would help this church, if they would listen to him." When one gives attention to a parable, the benefit we derive from it will depend upon *how* we hear. The Christian who fills his ears with the drivel from Madison Avenue should take heed. The rest of the verse lays down the principle that the measure of faith and grace which we bring to the Lord and His Word, determines the measure of what we receive. Further, that if we get some of our Lord's meaning, more will be added, since the supernatural Word of God is so vital that a little divine light stimulates reflection until an exponential growth can be expected. Jesus reinforces this idea in

Verse 25 - "For he that hath, to him shall be given: and he that hath not, from him shall be taken even that which he hath."

ὅς γὰρ ἔχει, δοθήσεται αὐτῷ, καὶ ὅς οὐκ ἔχει, καὶ ὅ ἔχει ἀρθήσεται ἀπ'
αὐτοῦ,

ὅς (nom.sing.masc.of ὅς, relative pronoun, subject of ἔχει) 65.
γὰρ (causal conjunction) 105.
ἔχει (3d.per.sing.pres.act.ind.of ἔχω, aoristic) 82.
δοθήσεται (3d.per.sing.fut.pass.ind.of δίδωμι, predictive) 362.
αὐτῷ (dat.sing.masc.of αὐτός, indirect object of δοθήσεται) 16.
καὶ (adversative conjunction) 14.
ὅς (nom.sing.masc.of the relative pronoun ὅς, subject of ἔχει) 65.
οὐκ (negative conjunction with the indicative) 130.
ἔχει (3d.per.sing.pres.act.ind.of ἔχω, aoristic) 82.
καὶ (ascensive conjunction) 14.
ὅ (nom.sing.neut.of ὅς, subject of ἀρθήσεται) 65.
ἔχει (3d.pers.sing.pres.act.ind.of ἔχω, aoristic) 82.
ἀρθήσεται (3d.per.sing.fut.pass.ind.of αἴρω, predictive) 350.
ἀπ' (preposition with the ablative of separation) 70.
αὐτοῦ (abl.sing.masc.of αὐτός, separation) 16.

*Translation - "Because to him who has shall be given, but from him who does not
have shall be taken even that which he has."*

Comment: Our translation says essentially what the Greek says, but we have
smoothed out the English. Literally, with full attention given to the relative
pronouns, it reads, "Because whoever has, to him shall be given, but whoever
does not have, even that which he has shall be taken from him."

This verse must be interpreted in the light of the entire context beginning at
verse 1. Jesus taught the multitudes by parables and the disciples asked Him why
He used the parabolic method (Mt.13:12) and what the parable of the sower
meant (Mk.4:10). These questions elicited from our Lord His reply in
Mk.4:11,12. Then, after explaining the parable of the sower (Mk.4:14-20) He
adds that light is for shining, not for being hidden (Mk.4:21), and that all the
light shall be manifested somewhere, sometime, to someone, but that it all
depends upon *what* we hear and *how* we listen. He holds out the promise that if
we listen with some spiritual discernment, we shall have some light and be able
even to receive more light (verse 24).

But verse 24 also contains the veiled threat that if we listen from sinful motives
and receive only darkness and confusion from the very parable that would have
given us light and faith, had we listened from purer motives, we shall then go on
to greater darkness and confusion. Verse 25 adds that the one who has some of
God's light is going to get more, but that the one who has only intellectual light to
understand the outer symbols of the parable is going to lose even that light.

These things being true, there is no place for the Christian to stop growing
until there is not one thing yet kept secret. Christian growth and illumination
goes on until we reach the fulfillment of Paul's prayer in Eph.3:14-19. *Cf.*
comment on Mt.25:29 and Luke 19:26, as well as the parallel passages in
Mt.13:12 and Lk.8:18.

After this penetrating study into the importance of listening humbly to Jesus' teachings, so that having ears to hear, we shall hear *what* He has to say and *all* He has to say to us, Jesus goes on to another parable in verse 26.

The Parable of the Growing Seed

Verse 26 - "And he said, So is the kingdom of God, as if a man should cast seed into the ground."

Καὶ ἔλεγεν, Οὗτως ἐστὶν ἡ βασιλεία τοῦ θεοῦ ὡς ἄνθρωπος βάλῃ τὸν σπόρον ἐπὶ τῆς γῆς.

Καὶ (continuative conjunction) 14.
ἔλεγεν (3d.per.sing.imp.act.ind.of λέγω, progressive duration) 66.
Οὗτως (demonstrative adverb) 74.
ἐστὶν (3d.per.sing.pres.ind.of εἰμί, aoristic) 86.
ἡ (nom.sing.fem.of the article in agreement with βασιλεία) 9.
βασιλεία (nom.sing.fem.of βασιλεία, subject of ἐστὶν) 253.
τοῦ (gen.sing.masc.of the article in agreement with θεοῦ) 9.
θεοῦ (gen.sing.masc.of θεός, definition) 124.
ὡς (relative adverb introducing a comparative clause) 128.
ἄνθρωπος (nom.sing.masc.of ἄνθρωπος, subject of βάλῃ) 341.
βάλῃ (3d.per.sing.aor.act.subj.of βάλλω, in a contingent comparative clause) 299.
τὸν (acc.sing.masc.of the article in agreement with σπόρον) 9.

#2189 σπόρον (acc.sing.masc.of σπόρος, direct object of βάλῃ).

seed sown - Mk.4:26,27.
seed - Lk.8:5,11; II Cor.9:10.

Meaning: Seed for sowing as distinct from σπέρμα (#1056), which means spermatozoa. Properly in parables - Mk.4:26,27; Lk.8:5,11. Spiritually, with reference to the seed of the gospel - II Cor.9:10. But note in #1056 that σπέρμα is also used for botanical seed.

ἐπὶ (preposition with the genitive of place description) 47.
τῆς (gen.sing.fem.of the article in agreement with γῆς) 9.
γῆς (gen.sing.fem.of γῆ, place description) 157.

Translation - "And He continued to speak: 'Thus is the kingdom of God - as if a man were to scatter the seed upon the ground.' "

Comment: Mark loves the imperfect ἔλεγεν. It is his way of saying that Jesus continued His remarks. Note under #74 how οὗτως is used as a demonstrative adverb which serves as a tie between antitype and type. Note that Jesus here is speaking of the Kingdom of God in its broadest aspect, not of the more nationalistic Jewish Kingdom of the Heavens. ὡς should read "as if" since the verbβάλῃ is in the subjunctive, which carries the idea of contingency. ἐπὶ with the genitive means "upon" rather than "into." *Cf.*#47.

Mark is the only writer who records this parable. The intervening material in the Harmony of the Gospels is the parable of the tares in Mt.13:24-30, comment upon which the student should read before going further. Also *cf.*Mt.13:36-43, where Jesus expounds the parable. The audience which heard the parable before us (Mk.4:26-29) had just heard the parable of the tares in Mt.13:24-30 and its exposition (Mt.13:36-43). They were asked to picture a field (the world) in which the sower (Christ) sowed good seed (Christians), but in which another sower (Satan) sowed darnel (the sons of Satan). In this field appeared both wheat and tares which at first are so similar in appearance that they cannot be distinguished. But when harvest time comes the tares are revealed in their true worthless and evil character. Then comes the misguided request that the tares (whose root system is intertwined with the wheat) should be uprooted, and the owner's veto on the ground that to so do will also uproot the wheat. The alternative advice is to wait until the harvest (the consummation of the age) when the reapers (angels) will be sent to gather first the tares for burning after which the wheat will be harvested and stored safely in the barn (heaven). Thus the co-existence with the church of false teachers is set forth. This is a condition that has existed since the beginning of the church age. Moral reforms (rooting out the tares) is forbidden to the church. The fact that both wheat and tares eventually will be ripe for harvest is set forth. The fact that the separation of the two must wait until the end of the age and must be carried out by angels, not preachers and other moral reformers is clearly taught.

Into this picture Jesus introduces Mk.4:26-29. When the gospel seed is sown, it begins a process of fruition which is not known to the sower. He leaves the field, retires to his house to sleep and awakes again to work, but all of the time, whether he sleeps or wakes the seed is growing. Finally the fruit is borne and the harvest is gathered. The parable seems to teach patience. God's will in the world will be done. It is inevitable. God's *weltanschauung* will be carried out in complete conformity to His eternal purpose (Eph.1:11).

If more Christians understood this parable, there would be less disregard for and positive disobedience to the parable of the tares.

Verse 27 - "And should sleep and rise night and day, and the seed should spring and grow up, he knoweth not how."

καὶ καθεύδῃ καὶ ἐγείρηται νύκτα καί ἡμέραν, καὶ ὁ σπόρος βλαστᾷ καὶ μηκύνηται ὡς οὐκ οἶδεν αὐτός.

καὶ (continuative conjunction) 14.

καθεύδῃ (3d.per.sing.pres.act.subj.of καθεύδω, contingency in a comparative clause) 755.

καὶ (adjunctive conjunction joining verbs) 14.

ἐγείρηται (3d.per.sing.pres.subj.of ἐγείρω, contingency in a comparative clause) 125.

νύκτα (acc.sing.fem.of νύξ, time extent) 209.
καὶ (adjunctive conjunction joining nouns) 14.
ἡμέραν (acc.sing.fem.of ἡμέρα, time extent) 135.
καὶ (continuative conjunction) 14.
ὁ (nom.sing.masc.of the article in agreement with σπόρος) 9.
σπόρος (nom.sing.masc.of σπόρος, subject of βλαστᾷ and μηκύνηται) 2189.
βλαστᾷ (3d.per.sing.pres.act.subj.of βλαστάνω, contingency in a comparative clause) 1060.
καὶ (adjunctive conjunction joining verbs) 14.

#2190 μηκύνηται (3d.per.sing.pres.mid.subj.of μηκύνω, contingency in a comparative clause).

grow up - Mk.4:27.

Meaning: To make long; lengthen. Cause to grow. Parabolically of seed - Mk.4:27.

ὡς (relative adverb in indirect question) 128.
οὐκ (negative conjunction with the indicative) 130.
οἶδεν (3d.per.sing.aor.ind.of ὁράω, constative) 144.
αὐτός (nom.sing.masc.of αὐτός, subject of οἶδεν) 16.

Translation - "... *and were to sleep and get up, night and day, and the seed were to germinate and grow up, he knows not how.*"

Comment: The verse is the continuation of the sentence which began in verse 26. ὡς of verse 26 is still calling for the subjunctive mode, since we have a series of comparative clauses in each of which the element of contingency is present. Jesus is describing a hypothetical case. "Suppose a man should . . .plant. . . sleep and rise. . . and it should sprout and grow. . . κ.τ.λ." The ὡς of verse 27 introduces the indirect question. It means "in a way" that he does not understand. The farmer was not a botanist who understood the science of plant life, but he did know how to sow wheat and he had sense enough to wait for the harvest.

The point is that the only task the man has is seed sowing. After that he goes about his daily routine, rising by day and lying down to sleep by night, while the seed is germinating and growing, despite the man's ignorance of botany. Seed, once sown, must be allowed to have the time required for harvest. Arrest the botanical process through impatience by rooting up tares and/or investigating the good seed to ascertain whether or not it has germinated, and we stop the harvest. When good seed is sown the earth does the rest without the sower's further concern.

Verse 28 - "For the earth bringeth forth fruit of herself; first the blade, then the ear, after that the full corn in the ear."

αὐτομάτη ἡ γῆ καρποφορεῖ, πρῶτον χόρτον, εἶτεν στάχυν, εἶτεν πλήρη σῖτον ἐν τῷ στάχυϊ.

#2191 αὐτομάτη (adverbial).

of one's own accord - Acts 12:10.
of one's self - Mk.4:28.

Meaning: A combination of αὐτός (#16) and μέμαα (from μάω) - "to desire eagerly." Hence to be motivated by oneself, without outside stimulation. Automatic. With reference to the earth producing fruit without cultivation - Mk.4:28. With reference to prison doors opening automatically - Acts 12:10. It declines like an adjective, following its adjunct in number, gender and case, but is used like an adverb. In Mk.4:28 it is nominative, singular, feminine in agreement with ἡ γῆ, which follows.

ἡ (nom.sing.fem.of the article in agreement with γῆ) 9.
γῆ (nom.sing.fem.of γῆ, subject of καρποφορεῖ) 157.
καρποφορεῖ (3d.per.sing.pres.act.ind.of καρποφορέω, customary) 1054.
πρῶτον (adverbial) 487.
χόρτον (acc.sing.masc.of χόρτος, direct object of καρποφορεῖ) 632.
εἶτεν (rare form of εἶτα, temporal adverb) 2185.
στάχυν (acc.sing.masc.of στάχυς, direct object of καρποφορεῖ) 965.
εἶτεν (rare form of εἶτα, temporal adverb) 2185.
πλήρη (acc.sing.masc.of πλήρης, in agreement with σῖτον) 1124.
σῖτον (acc.sing.masc.of σῖτος, direct object of καρποφορεῖ) 311.
ἐν (preposition with the locative of place where) 80.
τῷ (loc.sing.masc.of the article in agreement with στάχυϊ) 9.
στάχυϊ (loc.sing.masc.of στάχυς) 965.

Translation - "Automatically the earth bears fruit - first a blade, then an ear, then full corn in the ear."

Comment: The reason for the sower's lack of concern of vss.26,27 is here given. Once the seed is committed to the soil (the sower's obligation) the process is automatic, due to the built in qualities of seed and soil. This the Lord of Harvests provided in creation. He understands the biochemistry, and perhaps some scientists do also, at least in part, but it is not necessary for the sower to understand it in order to grow luxuriant harvests. The most ignorant farmer can realize rich harvests if only he will do what is required of him. He must sow the seed. This does not require a graduate degree in agronomy. God does not need experts, though He does not repudiate expertise, if it is humble. All God needs is a faithful sower who can be patient and wait.

Note πρῶτον. . . εἶτεν . . . εἶτεν here in chronological sequence. *Cf.*#487 and 2185 for other examples. The order will not be reversed. God's order is blade, ear and full grain. Some pastors expect at least ears if not full grain from the people after the first night of the revival. Babes in Christ must be given time to grow, though it need not take as long as most of them do. *Cf.*#632 and note that χόρτος is included in the works "to be burned" in I Cor.3:12. Remember from the parable of the tares that in early development the blade resembles the wheat. The children of the Wicked One who also grow in the field (the world) have a development also, but their fruit is not true full grain - at least, not for the glory of God.

It is well for the Christian social reformer to remember that the judgment of the tares is as inevitable as is the harvesting of the wheat. The angels in judgment at the Second Coming of our Lord will perform both functions, at the direction of the King, unto Whom all judgment has been committed (John 5:22). Christians who, like just Lot, are vexed with the wickedness of the unsaved in this age, should keep in mind that it is not ours to judge (Mt.7:1-3). We need not fear that Satan's program will achieve his wicked final goal. It assuredly will not. (I John 4:4).

Verse 29 - *"But when the fruit is brought forth, immediately he putteth in the sickle, because the harvest is come."*

ὅταν δὲ παραδοῖ ὁ καρπός, εὐθὺς ἀποστέλλει τὸ δρέπανον, ὅτι παρέστηκεν ὁ θερισμός.

ὅταν (temporal conjunction introducing an indefinite temporal clause) 436.
δὲ (continuative conjunction) 11.
παραδοῖ (3d.per.sing.2d.aor.subj.of παραδίδωμι, indefinite temporal clause) 368.
ὁ (nom.sing.masc.of the article in agreement with καρπός) 9.
καρπός (nom.sing.masc.of καρπός, subject of παραδοῖ) 284.
εὐθὺς (adverbial) 258.
ἀποστέλλει (3d.per.sing.pres.act.ind.of ἀποστέλλω, futuristic) 215.
τὸ (acc.sing.neut.of the article in agreement with δρέπανον) 9.

#2192 δρέπανον (acc.sing.neut.of δρέπανον, direct object of ἀποστέλλει).

sickle - Mk.4:29; Rev.14:14,15,16,17,18,18,19.

Meaning: From δρέπω - "to pluck." Hence, a plucking tool; pruning hook; sickle; reaping instrument. Parabolically in Mk.4:29. Used by the angels in judgment, in a metaphorical sense, in the passages in Revelation.

ὅτι (causal conjunction) 211.
παρέστηκεν (3d.per.sing.perf.act.ind.of παρίστημι, consummative) 1596.
ὁ (nom.sing.masc.of the article in agreement with θερισμός) 9.
θερισμός (nom.sing.masc.of θερισμός, subject of παρέστηκεν) 839.

Translation - *"And when the fruit will allow it, he goes in with the sickle, because the harvest has come."*

Comment: ὅταν with the subjunctive in παραδοῖ is an indefinite temporal clause. Jesus is not setting a definite time for harvest, but pointing to it as a future fulfillment of the sowing and growing process. *Cf.*#368 for the basic idea in παραδίδωμι. To give alongside; to surrender; to give up. The idea of giving permission pervades this passage. "When the fruit is ready to be harvested." Until that time the reaper is forbidden to harvest the crop. Verse 28 has described the cycle that must be completed in terms of blade, ear and full development. Only in the third stage is the harvest ready. When it is - then comes harvest. Only then does the sower put in his sickle.

The parable can be applied to the parable of the tares as well as to this one. When the wheat is fully developed, and only then, will the Christians be finished with this life. *Cf.* Rev.3:2. Some of the saints at Sardis remained (had escaped a previous martyrdom) because their God-assigned works on earth were not yet finished. The same is true of the tares. The Amorites were spared judgment for 400 years because they had not developed their wickedness to the "full corn in the ear " stage. *Cf.* Gen.15:16. Also II Thess.2:7,8.

G.H.Lang says of the parable of spontaneous growth, "This exhibits (a) that the affairs of the kingdom of God go on though man perceiveth it not. This is because the Son of Man and His Enemy uninterruptedly continue their activites, even as the forces of nature go on automatically: "the earth beareth fruit spontaneously" automatically (αὐτοματᾳ). (b) Growth is a process and takes time: blade, ear, and full grain. (c) Harvest is determined by ripeness, not by calendar clock: "when the fruit permits straightway he sends forth the sickle, because the harvest has come." ("permits" points to a definite season and action; παραδοῖ - aorist subjunctive).

"Thus God's judgments are at proper seasons, which, though in His foreknowledge known and controlled by Him, are not determined by the calendar as are human assizes, but by the moral consideration of ripeness of character and ways." (G.H.Lang, *The Parabolic Teaching of Scripture*, Wm.B.Eerdmans Pub.Co., 1956, p.82).

"The iniquity of the Amorites is not yet full" (Gen.15:16), and therefore full judgment on them was delayed for 400 years. This gave opportunity for repentance in humble hearts (II Pet.3:9).

The connection between the parable of the growing seed and the great commission with its work of world evangelism is seen in Paul's comments to the Corinthians (I Cor.1:11-17; 3:5-8).

The Parable of the Mustard Seed

(Mt.13:31-32; Lk.13:18-19)

Verse 30 - "And he said, Whereunto shall we liken the kingdom of God? or with what comparison shall we compare it?"

Καὶ ἔλεγεν, Πῶς ὁμοιώσωμεν τὴν βασιλείαν τοῦ θεοῦ, ἢ ἐν τίνι αὐτὴν παραβολῇ θῶμεν;

Καὶ (continuative conjunction) 14.
ἔλεγεν (3d.per.sing.imp.act.ind.of λέγω, progressive duration) 66.
Πῶς (interrogative conjunction with the deliberative subjunctive) 627.
ὁμοιώσωμεν (1st.per.pl.aor.act.subj.of ὁμοιόω, deliberative) 575.
τὴν (acc.sing.fem.of the article in agreement with βασιλείαν) 9.
βασιλείαν (acc.sing.fem.of βασιλεία, direct object of ὁμοιώσωμεν) 253.
τοῦ (gen.sing.masc.of the article in agreement with θεοῦ) 9.
θεοῦ (gen.sing.masc.of θεός, definition) 124.
ἤ (disjunctive) 465.
ἐν (preposition with the instrumental of means) 80.
τίνι (instru.sing.fem.of τίς, in agreement with παραβολῇ) 281.
αὐτὴν (acc.sing.fem.of αὐτός, direct object of θῶμεν) 16.
παραβολῇ (instru.sing.fem.of παραβολή, means) 1027.
θῶμεν (1st.per.pl.2d.aor.act.subj.of τίθημι, deliberative) 455.

Translation - "And He continued to speak: 'Unto what shall we compare the Kingdom of God, or by what parable shall we discuss it?' "

Comment:καὶ ἔλεγεν in Mark can be thought of as "He continued to say," or "He continued by saying." πῶς introduces the deliberative subjunctive. *Cf.*#627 for other examples. Jesus is struggling to find an analogy that will serve to make clear His teaching about the Kingdom of God. They had had the parable of the sower, the parable of the tares and the wheat and now the parable of spontaneous growth. How shall He continue in His effort to make them understand the divine *weltanschauung.* That God exercises a sovereign rule over the course of history on this planet is obvious. But how will He carry it out? What is the divine scenario? How long will it take to run its course? We know that it will end happily and for the total glory of God, but where are we on God's clock and what does the future hold? In the meantime, what should be the role of the Christian? These are important questions for the saints.

In the last half of the verse Jesus repeats His question as He muses, as though in soliloquy. "By what parable shall we set it forth?" - an interesting use of τίθημι. Verses 31 and 32 provide us with the parable of the mustard seed.

Verse 31 - "It is like a grain of mustard seed, which, when it is sown in the earth, is less than all the seeds that be in the earth."

ὡς κόκκῳ σινάπεως, ὃς ὅταν σπαρῇ ἐπὶ τῆς γῆς, μικρότερον ὂν πάντως τῶν σπερμάτων τῶν ἐπὶ τῆς γῆς,

ὡς (relative adverb introducing a comparative clause, with the indicative 128.
κόκκῳ (dat.sing.masc.of κόκκος, comparison) 1067.
σινάπεως (gen.sing.neut.of σίναπι, definition) 1068.
ὃς (relative pronoun, nom.sing.masc.of ὅς, subject of σπαρῇ) 65.

ὅταν (temporal conjunction introducing an indefinite temporal clause) 436.
σπαρῇ (3d.per.sing.2d.aor.pass.subj.of σπείρω, indefinite temporal clause) 616.
ἐπὶ (preposition with the genitive of place description) 47.
τῆς (gen.sing.fem.of the article in agreement with γῆς) 9.
γῆς (gen.sing.fem.of γῆ, place description) 157.
μικρότερον (nom.sing.neut.comparative of μικρός, in agreement with σινάπεως) 917.
ὄν (pres.part.nom.sing.neut.of εἰμί, adverbial, concessive) 86.
πάντων (abl.pl.neut.of πᾶς, in agreement with σπερμάτων) 67.
τῶν (abl.pl.neut.of the article in agreement with σπερμάτων) 9.
σπερμάτων (abl.pl.neut.of σπέρμα, comparison) 1056.
τῶν (abl.pl.neut.of the article in agreement with σπερμάτων) 9.
ἐπὶ (preposition with the genitive of place description) 47.
τῆς (gen.sing.fem.of the article in agreement with γῆς) 9.
γῆς (gen.sing.fem.of γῆ, place description) 157.

Translation - "... *like a mustard seed, which when sown upon the soil, although smaller than all the seeds upon the earth,* ... "

Comment: Mark has his syntax problems in this verse but his meaning is very clear, which is all that the Holy Spirit expected from him. We know what he means to say. He goes on breathlessly from the question of verse 30. How? He omits the verb, but after a pause, (indicated by our dash in the translation) presents the analogy - ὡς κόκκῳ σινάπεως - "... like a mustard seed." This mustard seed is then discussed in the relative clauses ὅταν σπαρῇ ἐπὶ τῆς γῆς (verse 31) and ὅταν σπαρῇ (verse 32). The sentence ends only with verse 32. Note that the two temporal clauses are indefinite, as indicated by the subjunctive mode in σπαρῇ. Jesus is not saying that the mustard seed will be planted, but if and when it is planted, it will behave as described in verse 32. And, furthermore, this behavior bears a similarity, in a parabolic manner, to the Kingdom of God.

Mark emphasizes the relative insignificance of the mustard seed, in comparison with all other seeds by the concession participle ὄν and the ablative of comparison. "Despite the fact that (although) it is the smaller of all the seeds on earth... κ.τ.λ."

So what has He said? Jesus is going to build spiritual truth about the Kingdom of God around a tiny mustard seed. What are its characteristics? At the time that it is sown it is the tiniest seed on earth. What happens then?

Verse 32 - "*But when it is sown, it groweth up, and becometh greater than all herbs and shooteth out great branches, so that the fowls of the air may lodge under the shadow of it.*"

καὶ ὅταν σπαρῇ, ἀναβαίνει καὶ γίνεται μεῖζον πάντων τῶν λαχάνων καὶ ποιεῖ κλάδους μεγάλους, ὥστε δύνασθαι ὑπὸ τὴν σκιάν αὐτοῦ τὰ πετεινωὰ τοῦ οὐρανοῦ κατασκηνοῦν.

καί (adversative conjunction) 14.

ὅταν (temporal conjunction introducing an indefinite temporal clause) 436.

σπαρῇ (3d.per.sing.2d.aor.pass.subj.of σπείρω, indefinite temporal clause) 616.

ἀναβαίνει (3d.per.sing.pres.act.ind.of ἀναβαίνω, customary) 323.

καί (adjunctive conjunction joining verbs) 14.

γίνεται (3d.per.sing.pres.ind.of γίνομαι, customary) 113.

μεῖζον (acc.sing.neut.of μεῖζων, predicate adjective) 916.

πάντων (abl.pl.neut.of πᾶς, in agreement with λαχάνων) 67.

τῶν (abl.pl.neut.of the article in agreement with λαχάνων) 9.

λαχάνων (abl.pl.neut.of λάχανον, comparison) 1069.

καί (adjunctive conjunction joining verbs) 14.

ποιεῖ (3d.per.sing.pres.act.ind.of ποιέω, customary) 127.

κλάδους (acc.pl.masc.of κλάδος, direct object of ποιεῖ) 1071.

μεγάλους (acc.pl.masc.of μέγας, in agreement with κλάδους) 184.

ὥστε (consecutive conjunction introducing a result clause) 752.

δύνασθαι (pres.inf.of δύναμαι, result clause) 289.

ὑπό (preposition with the accusative of extent) 117.

τήν (acc.sing.fem.of the article in agreement with σκιάν) 9.

σκιάν (acc.sing.fem.of σκιά, extent) 380.

αὐτοῦ (gen.sing.neut.of αὐτοῦ, possession) 16.

τά (nom.pl.neut.of the article in agreement with πετεινά) 9.

πετεινά (nom.pl.neut.of πετεινόν, subject of κατασκηνοῦν) 615.

τοῦ (gen.sing.masc.of the article in agreement with οὐρανοῦ) 9.

οὐρανοῦ (gen.sing.masc.of οὐρανός, definition) 254.

κατασκηνοῦν (pres.act.inf.of κατασκηνόω, complementary) 1070.

Translation - ". . . nevertheless when it is sown it grows up and becomes greater than all of the plants and puts out large branches, with the result that the birds of the heaven are able to bed down under its shadow."

Comment: Mark brings this long sentence to a close. Another indefinite temporal clause with ὅταν σπαρῇ. Before it we have adversative καί. "Although (concessive ὄν) it is small . . . nevertheless (adversative καί) when it is sown, the results follow. Now the verbs become indicative in mode and customarily present in tense. The nature of the seed is such that once planted, it germinates, grows and becomes greater than all plants and produces large branches, which have the result described in the ὥστε consecutive clause. Note result expressed here, as most commonly in the New Testament with ὥστε and the infinitive. Here too we have a complementary infinitive κατασκηνοῦν completing a result infinitive δύνασθαι. With reference to this result clause Burton says, "Tendency or conceived result which it is implied is an actual result. In this case the result is thought of as that which the action of the principal verb is adapted or sufficient to produce, and it is the context or the nature of the case only which shows that this result is actually produced." (*Moods and Tenses,* 148).

The three principal verbs are ἀναβαίνει, γίνεται and ποιεῖ. Certainly their action is sufficient to produce the result, *viz.* that the birds found rest under the shadow of the great branches. *Cf.*#1069 to see that the word means a cultivated plant.

The Kingdom of God began with an insignificant beginning. Philosophical systems developed by man seemed far more sophisticated than the gospel of the cross. Yet the tiny mustard seed grows to exceed in greatness the cultivated systems of mens' minds. The least of all seeds (vs.31) produces the greatest of all trees (vs.32). One of its branches is Israel (Rom.11:16,17,18,19,21). *Cf.*#1071. There is much good preaching here. The shade of the tree is gracious for all birds, saved and unsaved, including those who bed down like David did in Christ - (Acts 2:26). Many unsaved fowls of the air lodge permanently under the shadows instead of trusting in the substance. *Cf.*#380 and note particularly Col.2:17; Heb.8:5; 10:1. Those who confuse ἡ βασιλεία τοῦ θεοῦ with ἡ ἐκκλεσία (the kingdom of God with the Church) have misinterpreted this parable to mean that the Church, beginning small, will become the institution which ultimately will dominate the entire world for good. It teaches only that when the Kingdom of God becomes great, it becomes abnormal, because the mustard plant normally was not the largest tree. It grew normally to a height of ten feet. This plant is described as a monstrosity. The more it grew the greater became the number of branches. Church history abounds with evidence that church organization without God's guidance or His blessing has produced split after split until there are many "branches" of the church, each condemning all of the others. The Moravians understand this danger and pray, "From the unhappy desire of becoming great, Good Lord, deliver us." The Plymouth Brethren started small and were used of God. They grew and organized and became a monstrosity. So with many other groups. In fact, most organized Christianity has fallen into this trap.

Who are the birds? Jesus has already told us in the parable of the sower (Mt.13:19; Mk.4:15; Lk.8:12). The Evil One, Satan, the Devil and his hellish representatives. So every speckled bird of false philosophy finds rest and comfort under the countless branches of this grotesque tree. We all know of nominal Christians, who have repudiated the trinitarian theology of the New Testament, who go to church every Sunday and piously intone, "I believe in God the Father Almighty. . . and in Jesus Christ His only begotten Son. . . born of a virgin. . . crucified. . . He arose, etc., etc." This is bird talk. Like magpies arguing in a deal tree or owls hooting in a barn. For further comment *cf.* Mt.13:31,32; Lk.13:18,19.

Verse 33 - "And with many such parables spoke he the word unto them, as they were able to hear it."

Καὶ τοιαύταις παραβολαῖς πολλαῖς ἐλάλει αὐτοῖς τὸν λόγον, καθὼς ἠδύναντο ἀκούειν.

Καὶ (continuative conjunction) 14.

τοιαύταις (instru.pl.fem.of τοιοῦτος, in agreement with παραβολαῖς) 785.
παραβολαῖς (instru.pl.fem.of παραβολή, means) 1027.
πολλαῖς (instru.pl.fem.of πολύς, in agreement with παραβολαῖς) 228.
ἐλάλει (3d.per.sing.imp.act.ind.of λαλέω, progressive duration) 815.
αὐτοῖς (dat.pl.masc.of αὐτός, indirect object of ἐλάλει) 16.
τὸν (acc.sing.masc.of the article in agreement with λόγον) 9.
λόγον (acc.sing.masc.of λόγος, direct object of ἐλάλει) 510.
καθὼς (adverbial) 1348.
ἠδύναντο (3d.per.pl.imp.ind.,Attic for ἐδύναντο, progressive description) 289.
ἀκούειν (pres.act.inf.of ἀκούω, epexegetical) 148.

Translation - *"And with many such parables He continued to speak to them as they were able to hear."*

Comment: Whether Mark is referring to some parables which neither he, nor Matthew nor Luke record is not told us. It is doubtful that the writers recorded all of Jesus' parabolic teaching (John 21:25). Note that He taught only at their perception pace - καθὼς ἠδύναντο ἀκούειν - "as they were able to hear." The imperfect in ἠδύναντο indicates that they enjoyed a growing capacity to understand His message. Jesus was not preaching over their heads in order to achieve the purpose of Mk.4:11,12. The difference is that since verse 10, Jesus' audience has consisted only of the Twelve and a small group of sympathetic followers. These had followed Him with the proper attitude. Only through the virtue of intellectual humility can knowledge be increased (II Pet.1:5; Mt.5:3,5,6,8; 11:25-27; 18:3). Only those disciples of Jesus who qualify in terms of the passages cited shall be given His truths more abundantly. Hence we see Jesus' patient pedagogy. But because His audience often included those who had already turned against Him, He always used the parabolic method and then clarified the material for His true disciples when they were alone. This is the sense of

Verse 34 - *"But without a parable spake He not unto them: and when they were alone, He expounded all things to His disciples."*

χωρὶς δὲ παραβολῆς οὐκ ἐλάλει αὐτοῖς, κατ᾽ ἰδίαν δὲ τοῖς ἰδίοις μαθηταῖς ἐπέλυεν πάντα.

χωρὶς (improper preposition with the ablative of separation) 1077.
δὲ (adversative conjunction) 11.
παραβολῆς (abl.sing.fem.of παραβολή, separation) 1027.
οὐκ (negative conjunction with the indicative) 130.
ἐλάλει (3d.per.sing.imp.act.ind.of λαλέω, progressive duration) 815.
αὐτοῖς (dat.pl.masc.of αὐτός, indirect object of ἐλάλει) 16.
κατ᾽ (preposition with the accusative, adverbial) 98.
ἰδίαν (acc.sing.fem.of ἴδιος, adverbial) 778.
δὲ (adversative conjunction) 11.

τοῖς (dat.pl.masc.of the article in agreement with μαθηταῖς) 9.
ἰδίοις (dat.pl.masc.of ἴδιος, in agreement with μαθηταῖς) 778.
μαθηταῖς (dat.pl.masc.of μαθητής, indirect object of ἐπέλυεν) 421.

#2193 ἐπέλυεν (3d.per.sing.imp.act.ind.of ἐπιλύω, progressive duration).

determine - Acts 19:39.
expound - Mk.4:34.

Meaning: A combination of ἐπί (#47) and λύω (#471). Hence, to unloose; untie; to set free whatever is bound. In the New Testament in an intellectual way - Jesus explained His parables to His disciples- Mk.4:34. With reference to the remarks of the Ephesian official to the mob - Acts 19:39.

πάντα (acc.pl.neut.of πᾶς, direct object of ἐπέλυεν) 67.

Translation - "But without the use of a parable He was not speaking to them; however when He was alone with His own disciples He began to explain everything."

Comment: *Cf.* comment at the end of verse 33. κατ' ἰδίαν is an idiom used elsewhere to denote time when a small group is alone. *Cf.* Mt.14:13,23; 17:1,19; 20:17; 24:3, etc.*Cf.*#98. Those closed sessions with Jesus must have been unspeakably uplifting for the Disciples. The marvel is that they should have been so slow to grasp His meaning. Yet we should probably had been as slow. This was before the time when the Holy Spirit was given to them in the special way as indicated by John 20:22; Acts 1:8; 2:1-4. This special instruction which He gave to His disciples was in preparation for their function as the co-builders with Him of His church. I Cor.3:9.

We turn now to the parallel account as recorded by Luke.

Luke 8:4 - "And when much people were gathered together, and were come to him out of every city, he spoke by a parable."

Συνιόντος δὲ ὄχλου πολλοῦ καὶ τῶν κατὰ πόλιν ἐπιπορευομένων πρὸς αὐτὸν εἶπεν διὰ παραβολῆς,

#2194 Συνιόντος (pres.part.gen.sing.masc.of συνείμι, genitive absolute, simultaneous time).
be with - Lk.9:18; Acts 22:11.
be gathered together - Lk.8:4.

Meaning: A combination of σύν (#1542) and εἰμί (#86). Hence to be present; to accompany. It speaks of the fact that people are associated together in a physical and spatial sense - Lk.8:4, of the people who gathered about Jesus. With reference to the disciples and Jesus - Lk.9:18. With reference to Paul and his companions on the Damascus road - Acts 22:11.

δὲ (continuative conjunction) 11.

ὄχλου (gen.sing.masc.of ὄχλος, genitive absolute) 418.

πολλοῦ (gen.sing.masc.of πολύς, in agreement with ὄχλου) 228.

καὶ (adjunctive conjunction joining participles) 14.

τῶν (gen.pl.masc.of the article in agreement with ἐπιπορευομένων) 9.

κατὰ (preposition with the accusative, distribution) 98.

πόλιν (acc.sing.fem.of πόλις, distribution) 243.

#2195 ἐπιπορευομένων (pres.part.gen.pl.masc.of ἐπιπορεύομαι, genitive absolute, simultaneous time).

come to - Lk.8:4.

Meaning: A combination of ἐπί (#47) and πορεύομαι (#170); Hence, to come upon; come to. With reference to the crowds coming to Jesus for teaching - Lk.8:4.

πρὸς (preposition with the accusative of extent) 197.

αὐτὸν (acc.sing.masc.of αὐτός, extent) 16.

εἶπεν (3d.per.sing.aor.act.ind.of εἶπον, ingressive) 155.

διὰ (preposition with the genitive of means) 118.

παραβολῆς (gen.sing.fem.of παραβολή, means) 1027.

Translation - "*And as a great crowd was assembled and as others were coming to Him from various cities He began to speak parabolically.*"

Comment: The two genitive absolute participles are in the present tense, indicating simultaneity with the action of the main verb εἶπεν. It is an ingressive aorist - "He began to speak in a parable." Part of the crowd was present (συνιόντος) and the rest of the people were approaching (ἐπιπορευομένων). κατὰ πόλιν is an idiom indicating each one came to Jesus from his own city. Montgomery translates, "As a great crowd was gathering and men of town after town kep resorting to Him, He spoke a parable to them." Goodspeed has, "When a great throng was gathering and people were coming to him from one town after another, he said in his figurative way." This is parallel to Mt.13:2 and Mk.4:12, for comment upon which *cf.* Note that Luke uses διὰ with the genitive rather than ἐν with the instrumental as did Matthew and Mark.

Verse 5 - "*A sower went out to sow his seed: and as he sowed some fell by the way side; and it was trodden down, and the fowls of the air devoured it.*"

Ἐξῆλθεν ὁ σπείρων τοῦ σπεῖραι τὸν σπόρον αὐτοῦ, καὶ ἐν τῷ σπείρειν αὐτὸν ὃ μὲν ἔπεσεν παρὰ τὴν ὁδόν, καὶ κατεπατήθη καὶ τὰ πετεινὰ τοῦ οὐρανοῦ κατέφαγεν αὐτό.

Ἐξῆλθεν (3d.per.sing.aor.ind.of ἐξέρχομαι, constative) 161.

ὁ (nom.sing.masc.of the article in agreement with σπείρων) 9.

σπείρων (pres.act.part.nom.sing.masc.of σπείρω, substantival, subject of
ἐξῆλθεν) 616.
τοῦ (gen.sing.masc.of the article in agreement with σπεῖραι, purpose) 9.
σπεῖραι (1st.aor.act.inf.of σπείρω, purpose) 616.
τὸν (acc.sing.masc.of the article in agreement with σπόρον) 9.
σπόρον (acc.sing.masc.of σπόρος, direct object of σπεῖραι) 2189.
αὐτοῦ (gen.sing.masc.of αὐτός, possession) 16.
καὶ (continuative conjunction) 14.
ἐν (preposition with the locative of time point) 80.
τῷ (loc.sing.masc.of the article in agreement with σπείρειν) 9.
σπείρειν (pres.act.inf.of σπείρω, loc.sing.masc., time point) 616.
αὐτὸν (acc.sing.masc.of αὐτός, general reference) 16.
ὃ (nom.sing.neut.of ὅς, relative pronoun, subject of ἔπεσεν) 65.
μὲν (particle of affirmation) 300.
ἔπεσεν (3d.per.sing.2d.aor.act.ind.of πίπτω, constative) 187.
παρὰ (preposition with the accusative of extent) 154.
τὴν (acc.sing.fem.of the article in agreement with ὁδόν) 9.
ὁδόν (acc.sing.fem.of ὁδός, extent) 199.
καὶ (adversative conjunction) 14.
κατεπατήθη (3d.per.sing.aor.pass.ind.of καταπατέω, constative) 450.
καὶ (continuative conjunction) 14.
τὰ (nom.pl.neut.of the article in agreement with πετεινά) 9.
πετεινὰ (nom.pl.neut.of πετεινόν, subject of κατέφαγεν) 615.
τοῦ (gen.sing.masc.of the article in agreement with οὐρανοῦ) 9.
οὐρανοῦ (gen.sing.masc.of οὐρανός, definition) 254.
κατέφαγεν (3d.per.sing.aor.act.ind.of κατεσθίω, constative) 1028.
αὐτό (acc.sing.neut.of αὐτός, direct object of κατέφαγεν) 16.

Translation - *"The sower went out to sow his seed, but as he was sowing some in
fact fell by the way side, and it was trodden down and the birds of the heaven ate
it up."*

Comment: For interpretation of the parable *cf.* Mt.13:4,5, 18-23 and Mk.4:3-5;
13-20. Luke's sophisticated Greek, as always, is interesting. Note the participial
substantive ὁ σπείρων as subject of the verb. τοῦ σπεῖραι is an articular infinitive
in the genitive case indicating purpose. "The normal use of τοῦ with the inf. was
undoubtedly final as it was developed by Thucydides, and in the N.T. that is still
its chief use," (Moulton, *Prol.,216*, as cited in Robertston, *Grammar*, 1067).
But many of the examples are not final or consecutive. It is only in Luke (Gospel
24, Acts 24) and Paul (13) that τοῦ with the inf.(without prepositons) is
common" (*Ibid.*, 217, as cited in Robertson, *Ibid.*) They have five-sixths of the
examples. And Luke has himself two-thirds of the total in the N.T. Matthew has
seven. John avoids it." (Robertson, *Ibid.*, 1067).
    The locative of time point is seen in another articular infinitive with ἐν τῷ
σπείρειν αὐτόν. - "During the time that (while) he was sowing. . . κ.τ.λ." *Cf.*#80
for other examples of ἐν with the locative articular infinitive to show time point.

The neuter relative pronoun ὅ is the subject of the last part of the verse and governs the gender and number of αὐτό at the end, of which ὅ is the antecedent. The holy seed of the Word of God which fell by the way side was trampled by the swine who passed by (*cf.* Mt.7:6 for his use of κατεπατέω). See also in this connection Heb.10:29. Some good preaching here on the subject of unholy feet. We already know who τὰ πετεινὰ τοῦ οὐρανοῦ are. The emissaries of the Wicked One are good at devouring. *Cf.* Lk.8:5 (devouring the seed of the Word of God before it has the opportunity to germinate) with Mt.23:14; Mk.12:40; Lk.20:47. The avaricious son of Satan who devours the seed of the gospel soon translates his hatred for God and His word into hatred for God's people in the economic, social and political world. The unsaved are gluttonous predators.

Verse 6 - "And some fell upon a rock; and as soon as it was sprung up, it withered away, because it lacked moisture."

καὶ ἕτερον κατέπεσεν ἐπὶ τὴν πέτραν, καὶ φυὲν ἐξηράνθη διὰ τὸ μὴ ἔχειν ἰκμάδα.

καὶ (continuative conjunction) 14.
ἕτερον (nom.sing.neut.of ἕτερος, subject of κατέπεσεν) 605.

#2196 κατέπεσεν (3d.per.sing.aor.act.ind.of καταπίπτω, constative).

fall - Lk.8:6; Acts 26:14.
fall down - Acts 28:6.

Meaning: A combination of κατά (#98) and πίπτω (#187). Hence, to fall down. Physically in all New Testament references. With reference to the seed sown - Lk.8:6. Of Paul, falling down before Christ at his conversion - Acts 26:14 and of Paul on Malta - Acts 28:6.

ἐπὶ (preposition with the accusative of extent) 47.
τὴν (acc.sing.fem.of the article in agreement with πέτραν) 9.
πέτραν (acc.sing.fem.of πέτρα, extent) 695.
καὶ (adversative conjunction) 14.

#2197 φυὲν (2d.aor.pass.part.nom.sing.neut.of φύω, adverbial, temporal).

spring up - Lk.8:6,8; Heb.12:15.

Meaning: To beget; produce; bring forth. In the passive voice, to be born; to spring up; to grow. Without an object, to spring up - Of seed sown - Lk.8:6,8. With reference to hostility arising between people - Heb.12:15.

ἐξηράνθη (3d.per.sing.1st.aor.pass.ind.of ξηραίνω, ingressive) 1033.
διὰ (preposition with the accusative of cause) 118.
τὸ (acc.sing.neut.of the article, cause in an articular infinitive) 9.
μὴ (negative conjunction with the infinitive) 87.

ἔχειν (pres.act.inf.of ἔχω, cause) 82.

#2198 ἰκμάδα (acc.sing.fem.of ἰκμάς, direct object of ἔχειν).

moisture - Lk.8:6.

Meaning: Moisture. With reference to the soil in the parable of the sower - Lk.8:6.

Translation - "And other seed fell down upon the rock, but once sprouted it was withered because it had no moisture.

Comment: ἕτερον is joined to ὅ of verse 5. "Some fell by the way side. . . other fell. . κ.τ.λ." Note our comment on πέτρα (#695) which is particularly pertinent here. There was no moisture. Luke introduces φύω here, which usage he shares with the writer of Hebrews. διά with the articular infinitive in the accusative case, denoting cause. A review of #1033 on "withering" will provide some interesting preaching material- *Cf.* John 15:6. Here we have seed (the Word of God) having germinated (φυὲν new birth?) and then withered due to a lack of root structure which was in turn due to lack of moisture. Jesus says that the branch was ἐν ἐμοί (in Him). Is there a connection here? See also James 1:11 and I Pet.1:24 where the context makes it pretty clear that the unsaved are in view. The Matthew and Mark parallel accounts discuss the parable itself more fully. *Cf.* Mt.13:4,5,18-23; Mk.4:3-5, 13-20).

Verse 7 - "And some fell among thorns; and the thorns sprang up with it, and choked it."

καὶ ἕτερον ἔπεσεν ἐν μέσῳ τῶν ἀκανθῶν, καὶ συμφυεῖσαι αἱ ἄκανθαι ἀπέπνιξαν αὐτό.

καὶ (continuative conjunction) 14.

ἕτερον (nom.sing.neut.of ἕτερος, subject of ἔπεσεν) 605.

ἔπεσεν (3d.per.sing.aor.act.ind.of πίπτω, constative) 187.

ἐν (preposition with the locative of place where) 80.

μέσῳ (loc.sing.masc.of μέσος, place where) 873.

τῶν (gen.pl.fem.of the article in agreement with ἀκανθῶν) 9.

ἀκανθῶν (gen.pl.fem.of ἄκανθα, definition) 678.

καὶ (adjunctive conjunction joining verbs) 14.

συμφυεῖσαι (2d.aor.pass.part.nom.pl.fem.of συμφύω, adverbial, temporal).

spring up with - Lk.8:7.

Meaning: A combination of σύν (#1542) and φύω (#2197). Hence, to spring up with. Of the good seed and the thorns - Lk.8:7.

αἱ (nom.pl.fem.of the article in agreement with ἄκανθαι) 9.

ἄκανθαι (nom.pl.fem.of ἄκανθα, subject of ἀπέπνιξαν) 1034.

ἀπέπνιξαν (3d.per.pl.aor.act.ind.of ἀποπνίγω, ingressive) 1034.
αὐτό (acc.sing.neut.of αὐτός, direct object of ἀπέπνιξαν) 16.

Translation - *"And other seed fell in the midst of the thorns and when they had grown up together, the thorns began to choke it."*

Comment: The grammar here is perfectly regular. The thorns grew together with the good seed and the choking action began. ἀπέπνιξαν can also be taken as constative or culminative. The thorns won the battle for survival and the good seed was fruitless. Further comment in Matthew and Mark, *q.v.*

Verse 8 - *"And other fell on good ground, and sprang up, and bare fruit an hundredfold. And when he had said these things, he cried, He that hath ears to hear, let him hear."*

καὶ ἕτερον ἔπεσεν εἰς τὴν γῆν τὴν ἀγαθήν, καὶ φυὲν ἐποίησεν καρπὸν ἑκατονταπλασίονα. ταῦτα λέγων ἐφώνει, Ὁ ἔχων ὦτα ἀκούειν ἀκουέτω.

καὶ (continuative conjunction) 14.
ἕτερον (nom.sing.neut.of ἕτερος, subject of ἔπεσεν and ἐποίησεν) 605.
ἔπεσεν (3d.per.sing.aor.act.ind.of πίπτω, constative) 187.
εἰς (preposition with the accusative of extent) 140.
τὴν (acc.sing.fem.of the article in agreement with γῆν) 9.
γῆν (acc.sing.fem.of γῆ, extent) 157.
τὴν (acc.sing.fem.of the article in agreement with γῆν) 9.
ἀγαθήν (acc.sing.fem.of ἀγαθός, in agreement with γῆν) 547.
καὶ (continuative conjunction) 14.
φυὲν (2d.aor.pass.part.nom.sing.neut.of φύω, adverbial, temporal) 2197.
ἐποίησεν (3d.per.sing.aor.act.ind.of ποιέω, constative) 127.
καρπὸν (acc.sing.masc.of καρπός, direct object of ἐποίησεν) 284.

#2200 ἑκατονταπλασίονα (acc.pl.neut.of ἑκατονταπλασίων, adverbial).

hundred fold - Mk.10:30; Lk.8:8.

Meaning: Multiplied by one hundred. Of the reward of the faithful Christian - Mk.10:30. With reference to the fruitage of the seed in the good ground - Lk.8:8.

ταῦτα (acc.pl.neut.of οὗτος, direct object of λέγων) 93.
λέγων (pres.act.part.nom.sing.masc.of λέγω, adverbial, temporal) 66.
ἐφώνει (3d.per.sing.imp.act.ind.of φωνέω, inceptive) 1338.
Ὁ (nom.sing.masc.of the article in agreement with ἔχων) 9.
ἔχων (pres.act.part.nom.sing.masc.of ἔχω, substantival, subject of ἀκουέτω) 82.
ὦτα (acc.pl.neut.of οὖς, direct object of ἔχων) 887.
ἀκούειν (pres.act.inf.of ἀκούω, epexegetical) 148.
ἀκουέτω (3d.per.sing.pres.act.impv.of ἀκούω, command) 148.

Translation - *"And other seed fell into the good soil, and when it had germinated produced fruit one hundred fold. As He said these things, He began to cry out, 'He that has ears to hear, let him hear.' "*

Comment: Note the emphatic attributive position in τὴν γῆν τὴν ἀγαθήν. Luke says that Jesus put the stress of His voice behind His challenge'O ἔχων . . . ἀκουέτω. Cf.#1338 for φωνέω. Notice also the inceptive imperfect in ἐφώνει. This material has been discussed in Mt.13:1-9 and Mk.4:1-9.

Verse 9 - *"And his disciples asked him, saying, What might this parable be?"*

Ἐπηρώτων δὲ αὐτὸν οἱ μαθηταὶ αὐτοῦ τίς αὕτη εἴη ἡ παραβολή.

ἐπηρώτων (3d.per.pl.imp.act.ind.of ἐπερωτάω, inceptive) 973.
δὲ (continuative conjunction) 11.
αὐτὸν (acc.sing.masc.of αὐτός, direct object of ἐπωρώτων) 16.
οἱ (nom.pl.masc.of the article in agreement with μαθηταί) 9.
μαθηταὶ (nom.pl.masc.of μαθητής, subject of ἐπηρώτων) 421.
αὐτοῦ (gen.sing.masc.of αὐτός, relationship) 16.
τίς (nom.sing.masc.of the interrogative pronoun in indirect question) 281.
αὕτη (nom.sing.fem.of οὗτος, in agreement with παραβολή) 93.
εἴη (3d.per.sing.pres.optative of εἰμί) 86.
ἡ (nom.sing.fem.of the article in agreement with παραβολή) 9.
παραβολή (nom.sing.fem.of παραβολή, subject of εἴη) 1027.

Translation - *"And His disciples began to ask Him what this parable might mean?"*

Comment: He had just challenged them to think deeply and seek to understand the parable of the sower. Their ability to understand would depend upon their spiritual capacity to do so. It all depended upon *how* they heard *what* they heard. The disciples were willing to admit that they needed His help. Hence they began (inceptive imperfect in ἐπηρώτων) to ask Him to explain the parable. They were in great doubt. Hence Luke's use of the optative in εἴη, the mode of greatest contingency. *Cf.* Mt.13:10 and Mk.4:10 for further comment.

Verse 10 - *"And he said, Unto you it is given to know the mysteries of the kingdom of God: but to others in parables; that seeing they might not see, and hearing they might not understand."*

ὁ δὲ εἶπεν,Ὑμῖν δέδοται γνῶναι τὰ μυστήρια τῆς βασιλείας τοῦ θεοῦ, τοῖς δὲ λοιποῖς ἐν παραβολαῖς, ἵνα βλέποντες μὴ βλέπωσιν καὶ ἀκούοντες μὴ συνιῶσιν.

ὁ (nom.sing.masc.of the article, subject of εἶπεν) 9.
δὲ (continuative conjunction) 11.
εἶπεν (3d.per.sing.aor.act.ind.of εἶπον, constative) 155.

Ὑμῖν (dat.pl.masc.of σύ, indirect object of δέδοται) 104.

δέδοται (3d.per.sing.perf.pass.ind.of δίδωμι, consummative) 362.

γνῶναι (2d.aor.act.inf.of γινώσκω, epexegetical) 131.

τὰ (acc.pl.neut.of the article in agreement with μυστήρια) 9.

μυστήρια (acc.pl.neut.of μυστήριον, direct object of γνῶναι) 1038.

τῆς (gen.sing.fem.of the article in agreement with βασιλείας) 9.

βασιλείας (gen.sing.fem.of βασιλεία, definition) 253.

τοῦ (gen.sing.masc.of the article in agreement with θεοῦ) 9.

θεοῦ (gen.sing.masc.of θεός, definition) 124.

τοῖς (dat.pl.masc.of the article in agreement with λοιποῖς) 9.

δὲ (adversative conjunction) 11.

λοιποῖς (dat.pl.masc.of λοιπός, personal interest) 1402.

ἐν (preposition with the instrumental of means) 80.

παραβολαῖς (instru.pl.fem.of παραβολή, means) 1027.

ἵνα (conjunction introducing a sub-final clause) 114.

βλέποντες (pres.act.part.nom.pl.masc.of βλέπω, adverbial, concessive) 499.

μὴ (negative conjunction with the subjunctive in a sub-final clause) 87.

βλέπωσιν (3d.per.pl.pres.act.subj.of βλέπω, purpose/result) 499.

καὶ (adjunctive conjunction joining clauses) 14.

ἀκούοντες (pres.act.part.nom.pl.masc.of ἀκούω, adverbial, concessive) 148.

μὴ (negative conjunction with the subjunctive in a sub-final clause) 87.

συνίωσιν (3d.per.pl.pres.act.subj.of συνίημι, purpose/result) 1039.

Translation - "And He said, 'To you it has been given to know the mysteries of the kingdom of God, but for the others by parables, in order (and with the result) that, although they see they do not perceive and, although they hear, they do not understand."

Comment: This is essentially the same statement as reported in Mt.13:11-13 and Mk.4:11,12, *q.v.* Matthew uses ὅτι with the indicative (Mt.13:13) while Mark and Luke use ἵνα and the subjunctive with μὴ (Mk.4:12; Lk.8:10). The theology of this passage has been discussed in the parallel passages.

The Parable of the Sower Explained

(Mt.13:18-23; Mk.4:13-20)

Verse 11 - "Now the parable is this: The seed is the Word of God."

Ἔστιν δὲ αὕτη ἡ παραβολή, Ὁ σπόρος ἐστὶν ὁ λόγος τοῦ θεοῦ.

Ἔστιν (3d.per.sing.pres.ind.of εἰμί, aoristic) 86.

δὲ (explantory conjunction) 11.

αὕτη (nom.sing.fem.of οὗτος, predicate nominative) 93.

ἡ (nom.sing.fem.of the article in agreement with παραβολή) 9.

παραβολή (nom.sing.fem.of παραβολή, subject of ἐστὶν) 1027.

Ὁ (nom.sing.masc.of the article in agreement with σπόρος) 9.

σπόρος (nom.sing.masc.of σπόρος, subject of ἐστὶν) 2189.
ἐστὶν (3d.per.sing.pres.ind.of εἰμί, aoristic) 86.
ὁ (nom.sing.masc.of the article in agreement with λόγος) 9.
λόγος (nom.sing.masc.of λόγος, predicate nominative) 510.
τοῦ (gen.sing.masc.of the article in agreement with θεοῦ) 9.
θεοῦ (gen.sing.masc.of θεός, definition) 124.

Translation - "*Now the parable is this: The seed is the Word of God.*"

Comment: God's purpose with reference to His enemies is served by parables (vs.10), but Jesus is willing to expound it to His disciples, to whom is given the privilege of understanding the mysteries of the kingdom of God. The principles involved in the parable have been expounded elsewhere (Mt.13:18-23; Mk.4:13-20).

Verse 12 - "*Those by the way side are they that hear; then cometh the devil, and taketh away the word out of their hearts, lest they should believe and be saved.*"

οἱ δὲ παρὰ τὴν ὁδόν εἰσιν οἱ ἀκούσαντες, εἶτα ἔρχεται ὁ διάβολος καὶ αἴρει τὸν λόγον ἀπὸ τῆς καρδίας αὐτῶν, ἵνα μὴ πιστεύσαντες σωθῶσιν.

οἱ (nom.pl.masc.of the article, subject of εἰσιν) 9.
δὲ (continuative conjunction) 11.
παρὰ (preposition with the accusative of place) 154.
τὴν (acc.sing.fem.of the article in agreement with ὁδόν) 9.
ὁδόν (acc.sing.fem.of ὁδός, place where) 199.
εἰσιν (3d.per.pl.pres.ind.of εἰμί, aoristic) 86.
οἱ (nom.pl.masc.of the article in agreement with ἀκούσαντες) 9.
ἀκούσαντες (aor.act.part.nom.pl.masc.of ἀκούω, predicate nominative) 148.
εἶτα (temporal adverb) 2185.
ἔρχεται (3d.per.sing.pres.ind.of ἔρχομαι, customary) 146.
ὁ (nom.sing.masc.of the article in agreement with διάβολος) 9.
διάβολος (nom.sing.masc.of διάβολος, subject of ἔρχεται) 331.
καὶ (adjunctive conjunction joining verbs) 14.
αἴρει (3d.per.sing.pres.act.ind.of αἴρω, customary) 350.
τὸν (acc.sing.masc.of the article in agreement with λόγον) 9.
λόγον (acc.sing.masc.of λόγος, direct object of αἴρει) 510.
ἀπὸ (preposition with the ablative of separation) 70.
τῆς (gen.sing.fem.of the article in agreement with καρδίας) 9.
καρδίας (gen.sing.fem.of καρδία, separation) 432.
αὐτῶν (gen.pl.masc.of αὐτός, possession) 16.
ἵνα (conjunction introducing a sub-final clause) 114.
μὴ (negative conjunction with the subjunctive in a sub-final clause) 87.
πιστεύσαντες (aor.act.part.nom.pl.masc.of ἀκούω, adverbial, temporal) 734.
σωθῶσιν (3d.per.pl.1st.aor.pass.subj.of σώζω, purpose/result) 109.

Translation - "*And those by the wayside are the ones who heard, after which the devil comes and takes the word away from their heart, lest, after they have heard, they be saved."*

Comment: The prepositional phrase, introduced by οἱ is the subject of the verb, while the participial substantive οἱ ἀκούσαντες is the predicate nominative. εἶτα, the temporal adverb moves the story. *Cf.#2185* - "Then. . . ," *i.e.* after those by the wayside heard the word - enter the devil. He comes and takes the word away from their hearts. (II Cor.4:4). Satan is successful only because the Sovereign God permits this to happen. The ἵνα clause with the subjunctive is sub-final, *i.e.* it is both purpose and result. When God purposes the result is always forthcoming (Eph.1:11). If Satan did not remove the seed of the Word of God from their hearts, having heard,they would then believe and be saved (Rom.10:17). Luke's statement is a little fuller than that of Mark 4:15 or Matthew 13:19, *q.v.*

Verse 13 - "They on the rock are they, which, when they hear, receive the word with joy; and these have no root, which for a while believe, and in time of temptation fall away."

οἱ δὲ ἐπὶ τῆς πέτρας οἳ ὅταν ἀκούσωσιν μετὰ χαρᾶς δέχονται τὸν λόγον, καὶ οὗτοι ῥίζαν οὐκ ἔχουσιν, οἳ πρὸς καιρὸν πιστεύουσιν καὶ ἐν καιρῷ πειρασμοῦ ἀφίστανται.

οἱ (nom.pl.masc.of the article, subject of εἰσιν, understood) 9.

δὲ (continuative conjunction) 11.

ἐπὶ (preposition with the genitive of place description) 47.

τῆς (gen.sing.fem.of the article in agreement with πέτρας) 9.

πέτρας (gen.sing.fem.of πέτρα, place description) 695.

οἳ (nom.pl.masc.of ὅς, relative pronoun, subject of δέχονται) 65.

ὅταν (indefinite temporal adverb with the subjunctive) 436.

ἀκούσωσιν (3d.per.pl.pres.act.subj.of ἀκούω, indefinite temporal clause) 148.

μετὰ (preposition with the genitive, adverbial) 50.

χαρᾶς (gen.sing.fem.of χαρά, adverbial) 183.

δέχονται (3d.per.pl.pres.ind.of δέχομαι, customary) 867.

τὸν (acc.sing.masc.of the article in agreement with λόγον) 9.

λόγον (acc.sing.masc.of λόγος, direct object of δέχονται) 510.

καὶ (continuative conjunction) 14.

οὗτοι (nom.pl.masc.of οὗτος, subject of ἔχουσιν) 93.

ῥίζαν (acc.sing.fem.of ῥίζα, direct object of ἔχουσιν) 293.

οὐκ (negative conjunction with the indicative) 130.

ἔχουσιν (3d.per.pl.pres.act.ind.of ἔχω, progressive) 82.

οἳ (nom.pl.masc.of ὅς, relative pronoun, subject of πιστεύουσιν and ἀφίστανται.) 65.

πρὸς (preposition with the accusative of time extent) 197.

καιρὸν (acc.sing.masc.of καιρός, time extent) 767.

πιστεύουσιν (3d.per.pl.pres.act.ind.of πιστεύω, progressive) 734.

καὶ (adversative conjunction) 14.

ἐν (preposition with the locative of time point) 80.

καιρῷ (loc.sing.masc.of καιρός, time point) 767.

πειρασμοῦ (gen.sing.masc.of πειρασμός, definition) 583.
ἀφίστανται (3d.per.pl.pres.mid.ind.of ἀφίστημι, customary) 1912.

Translation - "And those upon the rock are they who, when they hear, with joy, receive the Word, but these have no root, who for a time believe, but in a time of testing they withdraw."

Comment: The verb must be supplied in the first clause. "Those upon the rock are those who . . . κ.τ.λ." We have an indefinite temporal clause within the first relative clause. It is when they hear the word that they receive it with joy. καὶ is then adversative. Unfortunately, these have no root and demonstrate the fact by what we find in the second relative clause. They believe for a time but in the time of trial they forsake the cause. Note πρὸς καιρὸν and ἐν καιρῷ, an accusative of time extent and a locative of time point. *Cf.*#867 to find, if possible, in what sense they received the Word. Was it intellectually only or with God given faith? It is to some degree emotional - "with joy." Unfortunately Luke adds that they have no root. *Cf.* Col.2:7. For a time they believe. What causes the apostasy? Temptation is the test. When that comes they take themselves away. Note that Matthew and Mark define πειρασμός more clearly as "pressure and persecution because of the Word." (Mt.13:20,21; Mk.4:16,17). It is the offense of the cross of Christ. For further comment *cf.* the parallel accounts.

Verse 14 - "And that which fell among thorns are they which when they have heard, go forth, and are choked with cares and riches and pleasures of this life, and bring no fruit to perfection."

τὸ δὲ εἰς τὰς ἀκάνθας πεσόν, οὗτοί εἰσιν οἱ ἀκούσαντες, καὶ ὑπὸ μεριμνῶν καὶ πλούτου καὶ ἡδονῶν τοῦ βίου πορευόμενοι συμπνίγονται καὶ οὐ τελεσφοροῦσιν.

τὸ (nom.sing.neut.of the article in agreement with πεσόν) 9.
δὲ (continuative conjunction) 11.
εἰς (preposition with the accusative of extent) 140.
τὰς (acc.pl.fem.of the article in agreement with ἀκάνθας) 9.
ἀκάνθας (acc.pl.fem.of ἄκανθα, extent) 678.
πεσόν (2d.aor.act.part.nom.sing.neut.of πίπτω, nominative absolute) 187.
οὗτοι (nom.pl.masc.of οὗτος, deictic, subject of εἰσιν) 93.
εἰσιν (3d.per.pl.pres.ind.of εἰμί, aoristic) 86.
οἱ (nom.pl.masc.of the article in agreement with ἀκούσαντες) 9.
ἀκούσαντες (aor.act.part.nom.pl.masc.of ἀκούω, predicate nominative) 148.
καὶ (adversative conjunction) 14.
ὑπὸ (preposition with the ablative of cause) 117.
μεριμνῶν (abl.pl.fem.of μέριμνα, cause) 1048.
καὶ (adjunctive conjunction joining nouns) 14.
πλούτου (abl.sing.masc.of πλοῦτος, cause) 1050.
καὶ (adjunctive conjunction joining nouns) 14.

#2201 ἡδονῶν (abl.pl.fem.of ἡδονή, cause).

lust - Jam.4:1,3.
pleasure - Lk.8:14; Tit.3:3; II Pet.2:13.

Meaning: Pleasure. Desire for fleshly gratification. The source of conflict between Christians - Jam.4:1; the cause of misguided prayer - Jam.4:3. A characteristic of the unregenerate life: with reference to the former lives of saints - Tit.3:3. Of the present lives of apostates - II Pet.2:13. With reference to the desires that normally grow out of social contact with an unregenerate world in this age - Lk.8:14. Care should be exercised not to restrict the meaning to carnality. Desire for status and its trappings are included - anything that gives pleasure - be in physical or psychological.

τοῦ (gen.sing.masc.of the article in agreement with βίου) 9.

#2202 βίου (gen.sing.masc.of βίος, definition).

good - I John 3:17.
life - Lk.8:14; I Tim.2:2; I John 2:16; II Tim.2:4.
living - Mk.12:44; Lk.8:43; 15:12,30; 21:4.

Meaning: Life, as we think of it upon this earth. Never in the New Testament for eternal life. With reference to the financial and physical necessities for life in a competitive society - I John 3:17; II Tim.2:4; Mk.12:44; Lk.15:12,30; 21:4. This idea fits also into the context in Lk.8:14 and I John 2:16. In I Tim.2:2, Paul wishes for a peaceable "life," *i.e.* an ordered society where social and economic pressures are minimized.

πορευόμενοι (pres.part.nom.pl.masc.of πορεύομαι, adverbial, temporal) 170.
συμπνίγονται (3d.per.pl.pres.pass.ind.of συμπνίζω, customary) 1051.
καὶ (adjunctive conjunction joining verbs) 14.
οὐ (negative conjunction with the indicative) 130.

#2203 τελεσφοροῦσιν (3d.per.pl.pres.act.ind.of τελεσφορέω, customary).

bring fruit to perfection - Lk.8:14.

Meaning: A combination of τέλος (#881) and φέρω (#683). Hence, to bear fruit; to carry out the fruition process. In classical Greek used both botanically and with reference to child bearing. In the New Testament only of the seed among the thorns - Lk.8:14.

Translation - "And with reference to that which fell among the thorns - these are those who heard, but because of frustrations and riches and pleasures of this life, as they went forth they were choked out and did not fulfill their spiritual destiny."

Comment: Luke introduces this group with the participial phrase τὸ δὲ εἰς τὰς ἀκάνϑας πεσόν - "That which fell among thorns." This is a nominative absolute. Luke then goes on with οὗτοι - masculine gender and plural number; not quite a match with τό . . . πεσόν. But we know Luke's meaning. The ones represented in the parable by the seed which fell among the thorns are interpreted as those who heard the word, but for various reasons failed to become victorious Christians. Thus the first καί is adversative. Note ὑπό with the ablatives of cause. Frustrations, love of riches and the pleasures of this life - all of these militate against spiritual development. *Cf.* the longer discussion of this in Mt.13:22 and Mk.4:18,19.

Verse 15 - "But that on the good ground are they, which in an honest and good heart, having heard the word, keep it, and bring forth fruit with patience."

τό δέ ἐν τῇ καλῇ γῇ, οὗτοί εἰσιν οἵτινες ἐν καρδίᾳ καλῇ καί ἀγαθῇ ἀκούσαντες τόν λόγον κατέχουσιν καί καρποφοροῦσιν ἐν ὑπομονῇ.

τό (nom.sing.neut.of the article, nominative absolute) 9.

δέ (adversative conjunction) 11.

ἐν (preposition with the locative of place where) 80.

τῇ (loc.sing.fem.of the article in agreement with γῇ) 9.

καλῇ (loc.sing.fem.of καλός, in agreement with γῇ) 296.

γῇ (loc.sing.fem.of γῆ, place where) 157.

οὗτοι (nom.pl.masc.of οὗτος, subject of εἰσιν) 93.

εἰσιν (3d.per.pl.pres.ind.of εἰμί, aoristic) 86.

οἵτινες (nom.pl.masc.of ὅστις, subject of κατέχουσιν and καρπορφοροῦσιν) 163.

ἐν (preposition with the instrumental of means) 80.

καρδίᾳ (instru.sing.fem.of καρδία, means) 432.

καλῇ (instru.sing.fem.of καλός, in agreement with καρδίᾳ) 296.

καί (adjunctive conjunction joining adjectives) 14.

ἀγαθῇ (instru.sing.fem.of ἀγαθός, in agreement with καρδίᾳ) 547.

ἀκούσαντες (aor.act.part.nom.pl.masc.of ἀκούω, adverbial, temporal) 148.

τόν (acc.sing.masc.of the article in agreement with λόγον) 9.

λόγον (acc.sing.masc.of λόγος, direct object of ἀκούσαντες) 510.

κατέχουσιν (3d.per.pl.pres.act.ind.of κατέχω, progressive) 2071.

καί (adjunctive conjunction joining verbs) 14.

καρποφοροῦσιν (3d.per.pl.pres.act.ind.of καρποφορέω, progressive) 1054.

ἐν (preposition with the instrumental of accompanying circumstance) 80.

#2204 ὑπομονῇ (instru.sing.fem.of ὑπομονή, accompanying circumstance).

enduring - II Cor.1:6.
patience - Lk.8:15; 21:19; Rom.5:3,4; 8:25; 15:4,5; II Cor.6:4; 12:12; Col.1:11; I Thess.1:3; II Thess.1:4; I Tim.6:11; II Tim.3:10; Tit.2:2; Heb.10:36; 12:1; Jam.1:3,4; 5:11; II Pet.1:6,6; Rev.1:9; 2:2,3,19; 3:10; 13:10; 14:12.

patient continuance - Rom.2:7.
patient waiting - II Thess.3:5.

Meaning: A combination of ὐπό (#117) and μένω (#864). Hence, to remain under. The ability to remain under a burden rather than to escape it, is patience. Often in a context of the suffering of the saints. Rev.3:10 - "the word of my patience" in an interesting use. *Cf.*comment *en loc.*. Willingness to remain under - hence, to be patient is necessarily connected with hope that things will improve. Hence, "patience of hope" as in I Thess.1:3. Many passages speak of the patience of the saints in the midst of persecution.

Translation - "But with reference to that on the good ground: these are they who with a noble and good heart, having heard the word, are keeping it steadfast and bearing fruit with patience."

Comment: Luke again begins with a neuter prepositional phrase, this time with no verb at all and then follows with οὖτοι εἰσιν οἵτινες - "these are they who. . . κ.τ.λ." Their hearts are noble and good. These adjectives may mean a number of complimentary things. καλός (#296) can mean "beautiful" but when applied to καρδία, the aesthetic is not in view. ἀγαθός (#547) means "good" but this is too general when applied to the heart. Luke is not referring to efficiency, though regularity of the blood pump is essential to prolonged fruit bearing. The point is that these people had the proper attitude, and recalls Jesus warning that we should take care as to *what* and *how* we hear (Mk.4:24; Lk.8:18).

κατέχουσιν (#2071) - "hold the word fast." These were pressured also as were those among the thorns (vs.14) but they were not choked and rendered unfruitful, because of their patience. Note καρποφορέω in Rom.7:4,5; Col.1:6,10. *Cf.* also Gal.5:22,23. This brings us to the end of the parables by the seaside. Note again parallel passages in Mt.13 and Mk.4.

A Light under a Vessel

(Mk.4:21-25)

Verse 16 - "No man, when he hath lighted a candle, covereth it with a vessel or putteth it under a bed; but setteth it on a candlestick, that they which enter in may see the light."

Οὐδεὶς δὲ λύχνον ἅψας καλύπτει αὐτὸν σκεύει ἢ ὑποκάτω κλίνης τίθησιν, ἀλλ' ἐπὶ λυχνίας τίθησιν ἵνα οἱ εἰσπορευόμενοι βλέπωσιν τὸ φῶς.

Οὐδεὶς (nom.sing.masc.of οὐδείς, subject of καλύπτει and τίθησιν) 446.
δὲ (continuative conjunction) 11.
λύχνον (acc.sing.masc.of λύχνος, direct object of ἅψας) 454.
ἅψας (aor.act.part.nom.sing.masc.of ἅπτω, adverbial, temporal) 711.
καλύπτει (3d.per.sing.pres.act.ind.of καλύπτω, customary) 753.

αὐτὸν (acc.sing.masc.of αὐτός, direct object of καλύπτει) 16.

σκεύει (instru.sing.neut.of σκεῦος, means) 997.

ἤ (disjunctive) 465.

ὑποκάτω (improper preposition with the ablative of place separation) 1429.

κλίνης (abl.sing.fem.of κλίνη, place description) 779.

τίθησιν (3d.per.sing.pres.act.ind.of τίθημι, customary) 455.

ἀλλ᾽ (alternative conjunction) 342.

ἐπὶ (preposition with the genitive of place description) 47.

λυχνίας (gen.sing.fem.of λυχνία, place description) 457.

τίθησιν (3d.per.sing.pres.act.ind.of τίθημι, customary) 455.

ἵνα (final conjunction introducing a purpose clause with the subjunctive) 114.

οἱ (nom.pl.masc.of the article in agreement with εἰσπορευόμενοι) 9.

εἰσπορευόμενοι (pres.part.nom.sing.masc.of εἰσπορεύομαι, substantival, subject of βλέπωσιν) 1161.

βλέπωσιν (3d.per.pl.pres.act.subj.of βλέπω, purpose clause) 499.

τό (acc.sing.neut.of the article in agreement with φῶς) 9.

φῶς (acc.sing.neut.of φῶς, direct object of βλέπωσιν) 379.

Translation - "And no man, when he has lighted a candle, covers it with a vessel or places it under a bed, but he places it upon a candlestick, in order that those who come in may see the light."

Comment: Οὐδεὶς is emphatic here. "No one . . . " indulges in such foolishness. Candles are for giving light, not for concealment. ἅψας is an interesting use of ἅπτω (#711). To touch a candle with a match is to light it. The purpose clause with ἵνα of course has the subjunctive in βλέπωσιν. *Cf.* comment on Mk.4:21 and Mt.5:15. Verses 17 and 18 reinforce the point in verse 16.

Verse 17 - "For nothing is secret, that shall not be made manifest; neither anything hid, that shall not be known and come abroad."

οὐ γὰρ ἐστιν κρυπτὸν ὃ οὐ φανερὸν γενήσεται, οὐδὲ ἀπόκρυφον ὃ οὐ μὴ γνωσθῇ καὶ εἰς φανερὸν ἔλθῃ.

οὐ (negative conjunction with the indicative) 130.

γὰρ (causal conjunction) 105.

ἐστιν (3d.per.sing.pres.ind.of εἰμί, aoristic) 86.

κρυπτὸν (nom.sing.neut.of κρυπτός, predicate adjective) 565.

ὃ (nom.sing.neut.of ὅς, relative pronoun, subject of γενήσεται) 65.

οὐ (negative conjunction with the indicative) 130.

φανερὸν (nom.sing.neut.of φανερός, predicate adjective) 981.

γενήσεται (3d.per.sing.fut.ind.of γίνομαι, predictive) 113.

οὐδὲ (disjunctive particle) 452.

ἀπόκρυφον (nom.sing.neut.of ἀπόκρυφος, predicate adjective) 2188.

ὃ (nom.sing.neut.of ὅς, relative pronoun, subject of γνωσθῇ and ἔλθῃ) 65.

μὴ (negative conjunction with the subjunctive) 87.

γνωσθῇ (3d.per.sing.aor.pass.subj.of γινώσκω, emphatic negation) 131.

καὶ (adjunctive conjunction joining verbs) 14.

εἰς (preposition with the accusative of general reference, adverbial) 140.

φανερὸν (acc.sing.neut.of φανερός, predicate adverb) 981.

ἔλθῃ (3d.per.sing.aor.subj.of ἔρχομαι, emphatic negation) 146.

Translation - "Because there is nothing now secret which shall not become well known, nor hidden which shall not be known and come to light."

Comment: Note the subjunctive in γνωσθῇ with μή in emphatic negation, and again in ἔλθῃ.

The statement is similar to its parallel in Mk.4:22. *Cf.* also Mt.10:26. Though this passage has been expounded elsewhere in this work, let us say it again in different words. It comes at the end of a time when Jesus had been preaching in parables. He had had a mixed audience. Part of the time His listeners consisted of (1) His disciples, not only the twelve, but other who loved Him, or were at least friendly and were humbly eager to be helped; (2) a large neutral audience, neither deeply committed to Him nor bitterly antagonistic against Him. Some of these would believe on Him; others would not. But they were curious enough to listen; (3) a third group were His enemies - some openly opposed; others covertly plotting against Him.

At other times Jesus withdrew from the larger, mixed audience and conversed only with His disciples and closest friends. When His audience consisted of numbers 2 and 3 *supra*, or either 2 or 3, He spoke in parables. When only group 1 was present He expounded His parables openly to them and urged them to deeper insights into His teaching.

All of this was designed to separate the elect from the non-elect. Those who misunderstood His meaning to their own destruction had already rejected God's light and were now only being further blinded by their own prejudice. The neutrals, with humble attitudes, could pick up a little light and thus be assured of more light. Read again Mt.13:11-17; Mk.4:21-25; Lk.8:16-18. Through all of these passages runs His challenge, "He that hath ears to hear, let him hear." "To him that hath shall more be given." "It will be measured unto you in accordance with your own measure."

Now He says, "Nothing shall be forever hidden from everyone. Everything shall be brought to light for someone." Just as men do not hide candles under beds or dishpans, so God does not intend His light to be hidden. He will put it upon the candelstick where it belongs, so that it will give *all of its light* to those who grow spiritually to the point *where they are able to receive it.*

There is nothing in the context to indicate that hidden sins will become common knowledge, though they may be so known. It is possible to push these negatives οὐ . . . οὐδὲ to extremes. The context means that nothing of God's truth shall forever remain hidden. Whether it is hidden from any one Christian depends upon *how* he hears and *what* he hears. Some will have greater visual and oral acuity than others. A humble use of what acuity we have carries the promise that we shall become more acute in our grasp of God's thoughts.

The section closes with Luke's record of Christ's warning in

Verse 18 - "Take heed therefore how ye hear; for whosoever hath, to him shall be

given; and whosoever hath not, from him shall be taken even that which he
seemeth to have."

βλέπετε οὖν πῶς ἀκούετε, ὃς ἂν γὰρ ἔχῃ, δοθήσεται αὐτῷ, καὶ ὃς ἂν μὴ ἔχῃ,
καὶ ὃ δοκεῖ ἔχειν ἀρθήσεται ἀπ' αὐτοῦ.

βλέπετε (2d.per.pl.pres.act.impv.of βλέπω, command) 499.

οὖν (inferential conjunction) 68.

πῶς (adverbial) 627.

ἀκούετε (2d.per.pl.pres.act.ind.of ἀκούω, progressive) 148.

ὃς (nom.sing.masc.of ὅς, relative pronoun, subject of ἔχῃ) 65.

ἂν (particle in a relative clause, more probable condition) 205.

γὰρ (causal conjunction) 105.

ἔχῃ (3d.per.sing.pres.act.subj.of ἔχω, more probable condition) 82.

δοθήσεται (3d.per.sing.fut.pass.ind.of δίδωμι, predictive) 362.

αὐτῷ (dat.sing.masc.of αὐτός, indirect object of δοθήσεται) 16.

καὶ (adversative conjunction) 14.

ὃς (nom.sing.masc.of ὅς, relative pronoun, subject of ἔχῃ) 65.

ἂν (particle in a relative clause, more probable condition) 205.

μὴ (negative conjunction with the subjunctive) 87.

ἔχῃ (3d.per.sing.pres.act.subj.of ἔχω, more probable condition) 82.

καὶ (ascensive conjunction) 14.

ὃ (acc.sing.neut.of ὅς, direct object of ἀρθήσεται) 65.

δοκεῖ (3d.per.sing.pres.act.ind.of δοκέω, progressive) 287.

ἔχειν (pres.act.inf.of ἔχω, epexegetical) 82.

ἀρθήσεται (3d.per.sing.fut.pass.ind.of αἴρω, predictive) 350.

ἀπ' (preposition with the ablative of separation) 70.

αὐτοῦ (abl.sing.masc.of αὐτός, separation) 16.

Translation - "Be careful therefore how you hear, because to whomever has it
shall be given, but from whomever has not shall be taken even that which he
seems to have."

Comment: In view of the eternal consequences of our reaction to Jesus'
preaching, and the social spin-off of this reaction, in social, political, economic
and psychological areas, our Lord's warning takes on tremendous significance.
We have pointed out before that Mark warns us about what we hear (Mk.4:24),
while Luke warns us about how we hear. The relative clause with ὃς ἂν . . . ἔχῃ
provides a more probable condition. Jesus is saying that some will probably
profit from His teachings, whoever they may be and to those who do so profit,
more light will be given, but (adversative καὶ) He is also saying that others will
get nothing from His teaching and He adds the warning that from these
unfortunate people, whoever they may be, will be taken that which they
mistakenly think that they have.

The first relative clause opens up a wide vista of mental improvement
stretching across time into eternity and encompassing every field of human
knowledge. This is the reward for those who listen with sufficient grace and

humility to our Lord and thus grasp a little of His meaning. The promise is that we shall have more light as time rolls onward into eternity. Blessed hope! How this should increase our faith and thus increase the efficiency of our prayer life. The virtue of intellectual humility, which is the product of faith, is prerequisite to an addition of knowledge (II Pet.1:5). Only those who have faith can become humble and only humble people can learn anything. Not all who have faith probe the depths of its committment, thus to acquire the virtue of intellectual humility. The reason seems to be that some quit thinking as soon as they are assured of salvation. To them Christ is only a "fire escape." But to study the Scriptures and reflect upon the depths of God's wisdom, love and grace in providing salvation is to equip oneself for advance learning in the eternal treasures of wisdom and knowledge which are hid in Jesus Christ (Col.2:3). In view of these things the term *Christian Education* is tautology. There really isn't any other kind.

The other side of the coin is indeed sad. Some in Jesus' audience thought they understood a great deal, whereas in fact that understood nothing. They only seemed to know. They were Scribes, Pharisees, Lawyers - respectable people all who thought that they possessed above average morals and intelligence. But it was all fantasy. They only *seemed* to have a foundation for a future superstructure. They were not tuned in on Jesus' wavelength. They were marching to the cadence of Satan's drum and following it with rhythmic fidelity (Eph.2:1-3; II Cor.4:4; I John 5:19). All of their highly touted wisdom and ingenuity will come to nothing. There is no truth in hell and no remedy for such - only judgment.

(4) A Day of Miracles

Jesus Stills the Tempest

(Mk.4:35-41; Mt.8:18,23-27; Lk.8:22-25)

Mark 4:35 - *"And the same day, when the even was come, he saith unto them, Let us pass over unto the other side."*

Καὶ λέγει αὐτοῖς ἐν ἐκείνῃ τῇ ἡμέρᾳ ὀψίας γενομένης, Διέλθωμεν εἰς τὸ πέραν.

Καὶ (continuative conjunction) 14.
λέγει (3d.per.sing.pres.act.ind.of λέγω, histo:ical) 66.
αὐτοῖς (dat.pl.masc.of αὐτός, indirect object of λέγει) 16.
ἐν (preposition with the locative of time point) 80.
ἐκείνῃ (loc.sing.fem.of ἐκεῖνος, in agreement with ἡμέρᾳ) 246.
τῇ (loc.sing.fem.of the article in agreement with ἡμέρᾳ) 9.
ἡμέρᾳ (loc.sing.fem.of ἡμέρα, time point) 135.
ὀψίας (gen.sing.fem.of ὄψιος, genitive absolute) 739.
γενομένης (2d.aor.part.gen.sing.fem.of γίνομαι, genitive absolute) 113.

Διέλθωμεν (1st.per.pl.aor.act.subj.of διέρχομαι, hortatory) 1017.
εἰς (preposition with the accusative of extent) 140.
τὸ (acc.sing.neut.of the article in agreement with πέραν) 9.
πέραν (acc.sing.neut.of πέραν, extent) 375.

Translation - *"And on that day as night fell He said to them, 'Let us go over to the other side.'"*

Comment: The day of teaching by parables was drawing to a close. The antecedent of αὐτοῖς is τοῖς ἰδίοις μαθηταῖς of Mk.4:34 - clearly the twelve disciples. *Cf.*#80 for other examples of ἐν ἐκείνῃ τῇ ἡμέρᾳ, denoting time point. The genitive absolute tells us that evening had come and the night was at hand. Note the hortatory subjunctive in Διέλθωμεν with the accusative of extent with εἰς. "Let us go over to the other side."

The disciples had heard some hard teaching that day - enough to test their faith in the authority of the Teacher. They needed a miracle. They were about to see one!

Verse 36 - *"And when they had sent away the multitude, they took him even as he was in the ship. And there were also with him other little ships."*

καὶ ἀφέντες τὸν ὄχλον παραλαμβάνουσιν αὐτὸν ὡς ἦν ἐν τῷ πλοίῳ, καὶ ἄλλα πλοῖα ἦν μετ' αὐτοῦ.

καὶ (inferential conjunction) 14.
ἀφέντες (aor.act.part.nom.pl.masc.of ἀφίημι, adverbial, temporal) 319.
τὸν (acc.sing.masc.of the article in agreement with ὄχλον) 9.
ὄχλον (acc.sing.masc.of ὄχλος, direct object of ἀφέντες) 418.
παραλαμβάνουσιν (3d.per.pl.pres.act.ind.of παραλαμβάνω, historical) 102.
αὐτὸν (acc.sing.masc.of αὐτός, direct object of παραλαμβάνουσιν) 16.
ὡς (relative adverb) 128.
ἦν (3d.per.sing.imp.ind.of εἰμί, progressive description) 86.
ἐν (preposition with the locative of place where) 80.
τῷ (loc.sing.neut.of the article in agreement with πλοίῳ) 9.
πλοίῳ (loc.sing.neut.of πλοῖον, place where) 400.
καὶ (continuative conjunction) 14.
ἄλλα (nom.pl.neut.of ἄλλος, in agreement with πλοῖα) 198.
πλοῖα (nom.pl.neut.of πλοῖον, subject of ἦν) 400.
μετ' (preposition with the genitive of accompaniment) 50.
αὐτοῦ (gen.sing.masc.of αὐτός, accompaniment) 16.

Translation - *"And having left the crowd they took Him in the boat in which He had been sitting. And other boats were with Him."*

Comment: *Cf.* Mt.13:36. Recall that Jesus was in the boat, just off shore and the people were thronging about the shore line as He spoke to them. Now the disciples, in response to Jesus' suggestion of verse 35, leave the people standing on the shore and put out to sea. Mark adds the unnecessary information that it was the same boat in which Jesus had been sitting as He taught the people. Peter, who probably was the source of Mark's information, being a fisherman was interested in the number of boats at the dock and thus we have the added information that the others embarked in other boats as Jesus left the shore and headed eastward into the gathering darkness.

Note Mark's correct grammar as he uses the singular ἦν with the neuter plural subject πλοῖα. There is no hint in any of the parallel accounts to tell us how far the other boats accompanied Jesus. Matthew 8:24 says τὸ πλοῖον καλύπτεσθαι ὑπὸ τῶν κυμάτων, without mentioning the peril, if any, to any other craft.

Verse 37 - "And there arose a great storm of wind, and the waves beat into the ship, so that it was now full."

καὶ γίνεται λαῖλαψ μεγάλη ἀνέμου, καὶ τὰ κύματα ἐπέβαλλεν εἰς τὸ πλοῖον, ὥστε ἤδη γεμίζεσθαι τὸ πλοῖον.

καὶ (continuative conjunction) 14.
γίνεται (3d.per.sing.pres.ind.of γίνομαι, historical) 113.

#2205 λαῖλαψ (nom.sing.fem.of λαῖλαψ, subject of γίνεται).

    storm - Mk.4:37; Lk.8:23.
    tempest - II Pet.2:17.

Meaning: Thayer says, "According to Schmidt, λαῖλαψ is never a single gust, nor a steadily blowing wind, however violent; but a storm breaking forth from black thunderclouds in furious gusts, with floods of rain, and throwing everything topsy-turvy; acc. to Aristotle (*de mund. 4 p.395, 7)* it is a whirlwind revolving from below upwards." This sound like a good description of a tornado. Twice properly in Mk.4:37; Lk.8:23. Once metaphorically of philosophical, theological and ethical chaos - II Pet.2:17.

μεγάλη (nom.sing.fem.of μέγας, in agreement with λαῖλαψ) 184.
ἀνέμου (gen.sing.masc.of ἄνεμος, description) 698.
καὶ (continuative conjunction) 14.
τὰ (nom.pl.neut.of the article in agreement with κύματα) 9.
κύματα (nom.pl.neut.of κῦμα, subject of ἐπέβαλλεν) 754.
ἐπέβαλλεν (3d.per.sing.imp.act.ind.of ἐπιβάλλω, inceptive) 800.
εἰς (preposition with the accusative of extent) 140.
τὸ (acc.sing.neut.of the article in agreement with πλοῖον) 9.
πλοῖον (acc.sing.neut.of πλοῖον, extent) 400.
ὥστε (consecutive conjunction introducing a result clause) 752.
ἤδη (adverbial) 291.
γεμίζεσθαι (pres.pass.inf.of γεμίζω, result) 1972.
τὸ (acc.sing.neut.of the article in agreement with πλοῖον) 9.
πλοῖον (acc.sing.neut.of πλοῖον, general reference with the infinitive in a result clause) 400.

Translation - *"And a great tornado developed, and the waves began to crash into the boat, with the result that immediately the boat was filled."*

Comment: Two main verbs γίνεται and ἐπέβαλλεν describe the coming of the storm and the action of the waves upon the boat, with the result in the ὥστε clause. The Prince of the Power of the Air (Eph.2:1) made a pitiably futile effort to drown the Sovereign of the Universe in the bottom of the Sea of Galilee. Had he been successful the Lamb of God would never have gone to a cross to redeem the elect. But ". . . the Lamb slain from the foundation of the world" (Rev.13:8) rose to the occasion as He will again, to discomfit the evil forces which sought to destroy Him. *Cf.*#754. End time apostates will attack our Lord also as "raging waves of the sea" as they did on this occasion (Jude 13). Job 1,2 seem to teach that Satan as the "prince of the power of the air" has temporary control over the elements. Striking deceptively, as he always does, Satan waited until Jesus was asleep before he loosed the tornado on the little boat and its occupants.

Verse 38 - *"And he was in the hinder part of the ship, asleep on a pillow: and they awake him, and say unto him, Master, carest thou not that we perish?"*

καὶ αὐτὸς ἦν ἐν τῇ πρύμνῃ ἐπὶ τὸ προσκεφάλαιον καθεύδων. καὶ ἐγείρουσιν αὐτὸν καὶ λέγουσιν αὐτῷ, Διδάσκαλε, οὐ μέλει σοι ὅτι ἀπολλύμεθα;

καὶ (continuative conjunction) 14.

αὐτὸς (nom.sing.masc.of αὐτός, subject of ἦν) 16.

ἦν (3d.per.sing.imp.ind.of εἰμί, imperfect periphrastic) 86.

ἐν (preposition with the locative of place where) 80.

τῇ (loc.sing.fem.of the article in agreement with πρύμνῃ) 9.

#2206 πρύμνῃ (loc.sing.fem.of πρύμνα, place where).

hinder part - Acts 27:41.
hinder part of the ship - Mk.4:38.
stern - Acts 27:29.

Meaning: The feminine form of πρυμνός - "last" or "hind part." Recessive accent in the noun. The stern of a boat or ship - Mk.4:38; Acts 27:29,41.

ἐπὶ (preposition with the accusative of place where) 47.

τὸ (acc.sing.neut.of the article in agreement with προσκεφάλαιον) 9.

#2207 προσκεφάλαιον (acc.sing.neut.of προσκεφάλαιον, extent).

pillow - Mk.4:38.

Meaning: A combination of πρός (#197) and κεφαλή (#521). Near the head; hence, a pillow - Mk.4:38.

κατεύδων (pres.act.part.nom.sing.masc.of καθεύδω, imperfect periphrastic) 755.

καί (continuative conjunction) 14.

ἐγείρουσιν (3d.per.pl.pres.act.ind.of ἐγείρω, historical) 125.

αὐτόν (acc.sing.masc.of αὐτός, direct object of ἐγείρουσιν) 16.

καί (continuative conjunction) 14.

λέγουσιν (3d.per.pl.pres.act.ind.of λέγω, historical) 66.

αὐτῷ (dat.sing.masc.of αὐτός, indirect object of λέγουσιν) 16.

Διδάσκαλε (voc.sing.masc.of διδάσκαλος, address) 742.

οὐ (negative conjunction with the indicative in rhetroical question) 130.

μέλει (3d.per.sing.pres.act.ind.of μέλω, aoristic) 1417.

σοι (dat.sing.masc.of σύ, personal interest) 104.

ὅτι (causal conjunction) 211.

ἀπολλύμεθα (1st.per.pl.pres.pass.ind.of ἀπόλλυμι, rhetorical question) 208.

Translation - *"And He was sleeping in the stern upon a pillow, and they awakened Him and said to Him, 'Teacher, you care, do you not, that we are going down?' "*

Comment: The imperfect periphrastic in ἦν . . . καθεύδων, with its continuous action is interesting. Satan in his fury lashes up the storm. Winds howl about the boat. The sea heaves and waves roll in and crash in until the decks are awash. Disciples, some of whom are fishermen who have been in storms before, are now distraught. They run about, wild eyed and crying out with fear. And through it all Jesus remains asleep on a pillow in the stern. His sleep indicates His very real humanity. He had had a hard day and He was tired and hungry. He had preached to the people all day long. A fellow has to get his rest!

One moment the human Jesus sleeps peacefully in a storm that bids fair to take His life. The next the Divine Son of God rises calmly and with stern authority rebukes the winds and the waves. There is no more dramatic evidence of the hypostatic union of deity and humanity in the incarnate Son of God. For another *cf.* John 11:35-44 where the human Jesus burst into tears because His friend Lazarus was dead and then, snorting with rage, raised him from the dead and restored him to his sisters and friends.

The disciples awakened Jesus with a mild rebuke in

Verse 39 - *"And he arose, and rebuked the wind, and said unto the sea, Peace, be still. And the wind ceased, and there was a great calm."*

καί διεγερθεὶς ἐπετίμησεν τῷ ἀνέμῳ καί εἶπεν τῇ θαλάσσῃ, Σιώπα, πεφίμωσο. καί ἐκόπασεν ὁ ἄνεμος, καί ἐγένετο γαλήνη μεγάλη.

καί (continuative conjunction) 14.

#2208 διεγερθεὶς (aor.mid.part.nom.sing.masc.of διεγείρω, adverbial, temporal).

     awake - Lk.8:24.
     stir up - II Pet.1:13; 3:1.
     arise - Mk.4:39; John 6:18; Lk.8:24.

Meaning: A combination of διά (#118) and ἐγείρω (#125). Hence, to raise up thoroughly. διά adds the intensive element. To awaken; to arouse completely. The disciples awakened Jesus during the storm - Mk.4:39; Lk.8:24,24. The wind lashed the sea into huge waves - John 6:18. In a psychological sense, Peter wished to arouse the sleeping saints - II Pet.1:13; 3:1.

ἐπετίμησεν (3d.per.sing.aor.act.ind.of ἐπιτιμάω, constative) 757.

τῷ (dat.sing.masc.of the article in agreement with ἀνέμῳ) 9.

ἀνέμῳ (dat.sing.masc.of ἄνεμος, indirect object of ἐπετίμησεν) 698.

καὶ (adjunctive conjunction joining verbs) 14.

εἶπεν (3d.per.sing.aor.act.ind.of εἶπον, constative) 155.

τῇ (dat.sing.fem.of the article in agreement with θαλάσσῃ) 9.

θαλάσσῃ (dat.sing.fem.of θάλασσα, indirect object of εἶπεν) 374.

Σιώπα (2d.per.sing.pres.impv.of σιωπάω, command) 1337.

πεφίμωσο (2d.per.sing.perf.pass.impv.of φιμόω, command) 1410.

καὶ (inferential conjunction) 14.

ἐκόπασεν (3d.per.sing.aor.act.ind.of κοπάζω, constative) 1135.

ὁ (nom.sing.masc.of the article in agreement with ἄνεμος) 9.

ἄνεμος (nom.sing.masc.of ἄνεμος, subject of ἐκκόπασεν) 698.

καὶ (inferential conjunction) 14.

ἐγένετο (3d.per.sing.aor.ind.of γίνομαι, constative) 113.

γαλήνη (nom.sing.fem.of γαλήνη, subject of ἐγένετο) 758.

μεγάλη (nom.sing.fem.of μέγας, in agreement with γαλήνη) 184.

Translation - "And when He had been awakened He rebuked the wind and said to the sea, 'Be silent. Since you have been muzzled continue to be still.' Therefore the wind ceased and there was a great calm."

Comment: Having been aroused from His nap, Jesus took command. When He came into His own world (John 1:11), although His own people did not receive Him, the world which He had created, which operates on the scientific principles which He in creation ordained, obeyed His every command. Thus the meteorological elements accepted His rebuke and there was a great calm. *Cf.*#757. He said to the sea, "Be always silent" - a present tense imperative. This was enough. His will calmed the sea, but He adds, "Having been muzzled, continue to be still." This is a literal translation of the perfect passive imperative. The perfect tense speaks of a completed action in the past which result in a present continuous condition. This does not mean that the Sea of Galilee has never again been agitated, but it remained placid for the duration of our story. Jesus gave the sea a cease and desist order. There was not a gradual lessening of the intensity of the storm. Suddenly the tornado subsided and the sea became calm. We note this same thoroughness in Jesus' healing ministry. His patients did not get better. Suddenly they were made whole. No natural scientific process was at work here. The elements immediately obeyed Him. What a mighty demonstration! One moment, in human weakness, asleep on a pillow; the next moment the Sovereign Lord of fierce elements of wind and water.

Verse 40 - *"And he said unto them, Why are ye so fearful? How is it that ye have no faith?"*

καὶ εἶπεν αὐτοῖς, Τί δειλοί ἐστε; οὔπω ἔχετε πίστιν;

καὶ (continuative conjunction) 14.
εἶπεν (3d.per.sing.aor.act.ind.of εἶπον, constative) 155.
αὐτοῖς (dat.pl.masc.of αὐτός, indirect object of εἶπεν) 16.
Τί (acc.sing.neut.of τίς, interrogative pronoun in direct question, cause) 281.
ἐστε (2d.per.pl.pres.ind.of εἰμί, aoristic) 86.
οὔπω (adverbial) 1198.
ἔχετε (2d.per.pl.pres.act.ind.of ἔχω, aoristic) 82.
πίστιν (acc.sing.fem.of πίστις, direct object of ἔχετε) 728.

Translation - *"And He said to them, 'Why are you afraid? Do you not yet have faith?' "*

Comment: Τί here without διά (διὰ τί - "on account of what?" "Why?"). οὔπω is emphasized. "Not yet?!" There was evidence that though they had ears to hear, they had not heard - at least not yet enough but that a storm, even with Jesus Christ aboard, was fearful to them. What a testimony of human unwillingness and inability to receive the things of the Spirit of God.

It has been a source of some amazement to us to see Christians exhibit fear in the midst of a severe electrical storm. Surely a child of God should have grasped the significance of the fact that Jesus Christ is sovereign over His universe, and that we are members of His body, with a foreordained destiny to fulfill. It follows that accidents cannot happen to the child of God who is totally yielded to His will. This seems to be the clear teaching of Romans 8:28.

The terror caused by the tornado now changes to reverential fear as the disciples talk it over in

Verse 41 - *"And they feared exceedingly, and said one to another, What manner of man is this, that even the wind and the sea obey him?"*

καὶ ἐφοβήθησαν φόβον μέγαν, καὶ ἔλεγον πρὸς ἀλλήλους, Τίς ἄρα οὗτός ἐστιν ὅτι καὶ ὁ ἄνεμος καὶ ἡ θάλασσα ὑπακούει αὐτῷ;

καὶ (inferential conjunction) 14.
ἐφοβήθησαν (3d.per.pl.aor.mid.ind.of φοβέομαι, ingressive) 101.
φόβον (acc.sing.masc.of φόβος, cognate accusative) 1131.
μέγαν (acc.sing.masc.of μέγας, in agreement with φόβον) 184.
καὶ (continuative conjunction) 14.
ἔλεγον (3d.per.pl.imp.act.ind.of λέγω, inceptive) 66.
πρὸς (preposition with the accusative after a verb of speaking) 197.
ἀλλήλους (acc.pl.masc.of ἀλλήλων, extent, after a verb of speaking) 1487.
Τίς (nom.sing.masc.of τίς, interrogative pronoun) 281.
ἄρα (illative particle in direct question with a causal clause) 995.

οὗτός (nom.sing.masc.of οὗτος, subject of ἐστιν) 93.
ἐστιν (3d.per.sing.pres.ind.of εἰμί, aoristic) 86.
ὅτι (conjunction introducing an epexegetical clause) 211.
καὶ (ascensive conjunction) 14.
ὁ (nom.sing.masc.of the article in agreement with ἄνεμος) 9.
ἄνεμος (nom.sing.masc.of ἄνεμος, subject of ὑποακούει) 698.
καὶ (adjunctive conjunction joining nouns) 14.
ἡ (nom.sing.fem.of the article in agreement with θάλασσα) 9.
θάλασσα (nom.sing.fem.of θάλασσα, subject of ὑποακούει) 374.
ὑποακούει (3d.per.sing.pres.act.ind.of ὑπακούω, customary) 760.
αὐτῷ (dat.sing.masc.of αὐτός, personal advantage) 16.

Translation - "*Therefore they were seized with great fear and they began to say to one another, 'What kind of man is this that even the wind and the sea obey Him?'*"
Comment: Note the cognate accusative of inner content in ἐφοβήθησαν φόβον. *Cf.*Mt.2:10 (ἐχάρησαν χαρὰν) for another example. This juxtaposition of paronymous is perfectly good Greek. There are many examples in the Greek New Testament. The disciples reacted with great astonishment and reverential fear to this notable miracle. The inceptive nature of ἔλεγον - "they began to speak and continued speaking" - indicates the consternation and amazement among the disciples. #995 for other examples of τίς ἄρα. καὶ is ascensive. The disciples had seen sickness, blindness, leprosy, insanity and other diseases yield to Jesus' command but *even* (ascensive καὶ) the wind and the sea were subject to His command. The elements bowed to His word and will. His "Peace and remain quiet" was enough. It should be enough to quiet all of the storms in the Christian's life. Note that ὑποακούει is singular. Jesus' word commands separate obedience from wind and sea. The wind obeys! Even the sea obeys Him! The wicked are like the troubled sea, but the Christian, who has heard His "Peace" are like the sea over which the great calm has spread. All of this because He is the Son of God.

We turn now to Luke's account of the same event in

Luke 8:22 - "*Now it came to pass on a certain day, that he went into a ship with his disciples: and he said unto them, Let us go over unto the other side of the lake. And they launched forth.*"

Ἐγένετο δὲ ἐν μιᾷ τῶν ἡμερῶν καὶ αὐτὸς ἐνέβη εἰς πλοῖον καὶ οἱ μαθηταὶ αὐτοῦ, καὶ εἶπεν πρὸς αὐτούς, Διέλθωμεν εἰς τὸ πέραν τῆς λίμνης, καὶ ἀνήχθησαν.

Ἐγένετο (3d.per.sing.aor.ind.of γίνομαι, constative) 113.
δὲ (explanatory conjunction) 11.
ἐν (preposition with the locative of time point) 80.
μιᾷ (loc.sing.fem.of εἷς, time point) 469.
τῶν (gen.pl.fem.of the article in agreement with ἡμερῶν) 9.
ἡμερῶν (gen.pl.fem.of ἡμέρα, partitive genitive) 135.

καί (continuative conjunction) 14.
αὐτός (nom.sing.masc.of αὐτός, subject of ἐνέβη and εἶπεν) 16.
εἰς (preposition with the accusative of extent) 140.
πλοῖον (acc.sing.neut.of πλοῖον, extent) 400.
καί (adjunctive conjunction joining nouns) 14.
οἱ (nom.pl.masc.of the article in agreement with μαθηταί) 9.
μαθηταί (nom.pl.masc.of μαθητής, subject of ἐνέβη) 421.
αὐτοῦ (gen.sing.masc.of αὐτός, possession) 16.
καί (adjunctive conjunction joining verbs) 14.
εἶπεν (3d.per.sing.aor.act.ind.of εἶπον, constative) 155.
πρός (preposition with the accusative after a verb of speaking) 197.
αὐτούς (acc.pl.masc.of αὐτός, after a verb of speaking) 16.
Διέλθωμεν (1st.per.pl.aor.subj.of διέρχομαι, hortatory) 1017.
εἰς (preposition with the accusative of extent) 140.
τό (acc.sing.neut.of the article in agreement with πέραν) 9.
πέραν (acc.sing.neut.of πέραν, extent) 375.
τῆς (gen.sing.fem.of the article in agreement with λίμνης) 9.
λίμνης (gen.sing.fem.of λίμνη, definition) 2041.
καί (continuative conjunction) 14.
ἀνήχθησαν (3d.per.pl.1st.aor.pass.ind.of ἀνάγω, constative) 329.

Translation - *"And now it happened one day that He and His disciples entered a boat and He said to them, 'Let us go to the other side of the lake.' And they got under way."*

Comment: Literally ἐν μιᾷ ἡμερῶν translates to "on one of the days." The verb ἐνέβη is singular and is thus attached to αὐτός. There is no verb in the plural to go with the plural οἱ μαθηταί αὐτοῦ. The direct discourse with the hortatory subjunctive διέλθωμεν is regular enough. The passive verb ἀνήχθησαν is literally translated "They were led up" or (in the middle voice) "They led themselves up." *Cf.*#329 for comment on the prepositional prefix ἀνά. The meaning simply is that they set sail. Perhaps Luke means that the wind filled their sails and they were driven by full sails "up." It always appears to one standing on the shore, that a ship, putting out to sea, is going up. Mark 4:35 is the parallel passage, *q.v.*

Verse 23 - *"But as they sailed he fell asleep: and there came down a storm of wind on the lake; and they were filled with water, and were in jeopardy."*

πλεόντων δὲ αὐτῶν ἀφύπνωσεν, καὶ κατέβη λαῖλαψ ἀνέμου εἰς τὴν λίμνην, καὶ συνεπληροῦντο καὶ ἐκινδύνευον.

#2209 πλεόντων (pres.act.part.gen.pl.masc.of πλέω, genitive absolute).

sail - Lk.8:23; Acts 21:3; 27:6,24.
sail by - Acts 27:2.
in ships - Rev.18:17.

Meaning: To sail; to travel by ship or boat. With reference to Jesus' trip across Galilee - Lk.8:23. Paul's voyage in the Mediterranean - Acts 21:3; 27:2,6,24. Generally in Rev.18:17.

δέ (continuative conjunction) 11.
αὐτῶν (gen.pl.masc.of αὐτός, genitive absolute) 16.

#2210 ἀφύπνωσεν (3d.per.sing.1st.aor.act.ind.of ἀφυπνόω).

fall asleep - Lk.8:23.

Meaning: A combination of ἀπό (#70) and ὑπνόω - "to sleep." *Cf.* ὕπνος (#126). To fall to sleep. The old Greeks used καθυπνόω for this.

καί (continuative conjunction) 14.
κατέβη (3d.per.sing.aor.act.ind.of καταβαίνω, constative) 324.
λαῖφας (nom.sing.fem.of λαῖφας, subject of κατέβη) 2205.
ἀνέμου (gen.sing.masc.of ἄνεμος, definition) 698.
εἰς (preposition with the accusative of extent) 140.
τὴν (acc.sing.fem.of the article in agreement with λίμνην) 9.
λίμνην (acc.sing.fem.of λίμνη, extent) 2041.
καί (continuative conjunction) 14.

#2211 συνεπληροῦντο (3d.per.pl.imp.pass.ind.of συμπληρόω, inceptive).

fill - Lk.8:23.
be fully come - Acts 2:1.
come - Lk.9:51.

Meaning: A combination of σύν (#1542) and πληρόω (#115). Hence, to fill or fulfill, entirely or completely. With reference to a boat filled with water - Lk.8:23; with reference to a time that had arrived - of the transfiguration of Jesus Christ - Lk.9:51; of the day of Pentecost - Acts 2:1.

καί (continuative conjunction) 14.

#2212 ἐκινδύνευον (3d.per.pl.imp.act.ind.of κινδυνεύω, inceptive).

be in danger - Acts 19:27,40.
be in jeopardy - Lk.8:23.
stand in jeopardy - I Cor.15:30.

Meaning: To be in danger; to be placed in jeopardy. With reference to the economic threat to the silversmith industry in Ephesus due to Paul's preaching against idols - Acts 19:27. Of the danger that the officials in Ephesus would be held responsible for the riot - Acts 19:40. Of the boat in jeopardy because of the storm - Lk.8:23. Paul's security, he felt, was shaken if the fact of the resurrection should be in doubt - I Cor.15:30.

Translation - "And as they were sailing, He fell asleep. And there descended upon the lake a tornado and they began to be swamped and were in danger."

Comment: πλεόντων δὲ αὐτῶν is a genitive absolute in the present tense indicating action simultaneous to that of the main verb. As they were sailing out upon the lake Jesus fell asleep. The action is ingressive, with emphasis upon its inception; hence, the translation. Mark 4:38 tells us that He was in the stern of the ship where the helmsman often rested, and that His head rested upon a pillow. The storm swept down upon the lake and two results followed, indicated by the inceptive actions of the two imperfect tense verbs συνεπληροῦντο and ἐκινδύνευον. They began rapidly to be swamped with water as the waves came crashing in and they began to be in danger. The verse introduces four new words, #'s 2209, 2210, 2211 and 2212. Luke's vocabulary was different from that of Matthew and Mark. Matthew says that the ship was covered by the waves (Mk.8:24). The greater the jeopardy the greater the miracle that rescued them.

Verse 24 - "And they came to him, and awoke him saying, Master, master, we perish. Then he arose, and rebuked the wind and the raging of the water: and they ceased, and there was a calm."

προσελθόντες δὲ διήγειραν αὐτὸν λέγοντες, Ἐπιστάτα ἐπιστάτα, ἀπολλύμεθα. ὁ δὲ διεγερθεὶς ἐπετίμησεν τῷ ἀνέμῳ καὶ τῷ κλύδωνι τοῦ ὕδατος, καὶ ἐπαύσαντο, καὶ ἐγένετο γαλήνη.

προσελθόντες (aor.part.nom.pl.masc.of προσέρχομαι, adverbial, temporal) 336.

δὲ (inferential conjunction) 11.

διήγειραν (3d.per.pl.aor.act.ind.of διεγείρω, constative) 2208.

αὐτὸν (acc.sing.masc.of αὐτός, direct object of διήγειραν) 16.

λέγοντες (pres.act.part.nom.pl.masc.of λέγω, recitative) 66.

Ἐπιστάτα (voc.sing.masc.of ἐπιστάτης, address) 2047.

ἐπιστάτα (voc.sing.masc.of ἐπιστάτης, address) 2047.

ἀπολλύμεθα (1st.per.pl.pres.ind.of ἀπόλλυμι, aoristic) 208.

ὁ (nom.sing.masc.of the article subject of ἐπετίμησεν) 9.

δὲ (inferential conjunction) 11.

διεγερθεὶς (aor.pass.part.nom.sing.masc.of διεγείρω, adverbial, temporal) 2208.

ἐπετίμησεν (3d.per.sing.aor.act.ind.of ἐπιτιμάω, constative) 757.

τῷ (dat.sing.masc.of the article in agreement with ἀνέμῳ) 9.

ἀνέμῳ (dat.sing.masc.of ἄνεμος, personal disadvantage) 698.

καὶ (adjunctive conjunction joining nouns) 14.

τῷ (dat.sing.masc.of the article in agreement with κλύδωνι) 9.

#2213 κλύδωνι (dat.sing.masc.of κλύδων, personal disadvantage).

raging - Lk.8:24.
wave - Jam.1:6.

Meaning: A wave. Cf.κλυδωνίζομαι (#4495). A surging wave, as distinct from κῦμα (#754), which suggests uninterrupted succession, while κλύδων means a billow, surge. Properly in Lk.8:24; in simile in James 1:6.

τοῦ (gen.sing.neut.of the article in agreement with ὕδατος) 9.
ὕδατος (gen.sing.neut.of ὕδωρ, definition) 301.
καὶ (inferential conjunction) 14.
ἐπαύσαντο (3d.per.pl.aor.mid.ind.of παύω, constative) 2044.
καὶ (continuative conjunction) 14.
ἐγένετο (3d.per.sing.aor.ind.of γίνομαι, constative) 113.
γαλήνη (nom.sing.fem.of γαλήνη, subject of ἐγένετο) 758.

Translation - *"And they went to Him and woke Him up, saying, 'Master, Master, we are perishing!' Therefore He stood up and rebuked the wind and the violent action of the water and they ceased and calm was restored."*

Comment: There is something interesting in the action of the disciples, which indicates that they recognized in Jesus something more than human, even though they were not totally convinced that He was the Messiah. Why would fishermen in the midst of a storm, of which they had seen and survived many, consult a carpenter for advice? Yet when they knew that their own efforts to forestall disaster were futile, they rushed to the side of Jesus to awaken Him and ask for His help. *Cf.*#2047 - "Overseer." He was truly that - more than they knew. All day long He had been διδάσκαλος - "teacher." They had seen Him as a great physician. Now they were to see Him in action as Overseer, Supreme Supervisor, for He was about to supervise and direct wind and wave. *Cf.*#2213 for the difference between κλύδωνι and κῦμα (#754). These were raging waves, leaping high, seemingly out of control, dashing their waves of water into the reeling ship. I stood upon the bridge of the Aroso Star, a little ten thousand ton banana boat, and saw her bury the forward third of her length beneath the towering waves of the north Atlantic as they came rushing to meet her. The waves in our story were covering the ship (Mt.8:24) and filling its hold with water. Jesus spoke only two words - one to the wind and the other to the sea. Luke simply says ἐπαύσαντο - "they ceased." As a result the sea became as glass with scarcely a ripple upon its placid surface.

Verse 25 - *"And he said unto them, Where is your faith? And they being afraid, wondered, saying one to another, What manner of man is this! for he commandeth even the winds and water, and they obey him."*

εἶπεν δὲ αὐτοῖς, Ποῦ ἡ πίστις ὑμῶν; φοβηθέντες δὲ ἐθαύμασεν, λέγοντες πρὸς ἀλλήλους, Τίς ἄρα οὗτός ἐστιν ὅτι καὶ τοῖς ἀνέμοις ἐπιτάσσει καὶ τῷ ὕδατι, καὶ ὑπακούουσιν αὐτῷ;

εἶπεν (3d.per.sing.aor.act.ind.of εἶπον, constative) 155.
δὲ (continuative conjunction) 11.
αὐτοῖς (dat.pl.masc.of αὐτός, indirect object of εἶπεν) 16.
Ποῦ (interrogative adverb of place) 142.
ἡ (nom.sing.fem.of the article in agreement with πίστις) 9.
πίστις (nom.sing.fem.of πίστις, subject of ἐστίν, understood) 728.

ὑμῶν (gen.pl.masc.of σύ, possession) 104.

φοβηθέντες (1st.aor.mid.part.nom.pl.masc.of φοβέομαι, adverbial, circumstantial) 101.

δὲ (inferential conjunction) 11.

ἐθαύμασαν (3d.per.pl.aor.act.ind.of θαυμάζω, ingressive) 726.

λέγοντες (pres.act.part.nom.pl.masc.of λέγω, adverbial, temporal) 66.

πρὸς (preposition with the accusative after a verb of speaking) 197.

ἀλλήλους (acc.pl.masc.of ἀλλήλων, after a verb of speaking) 1487.

Τίς (interrogative pronoun, nom.sing.masc.of τίς, in direct question) 281.

ἄρα (illative particle introducing a causal clause) 995.

οὗτός (nom.sing.masc.of οὗτος, subject of ἐστιν) 93.

ἐστιν (3d.per.sing.pres.ind.of εἰμί, aoristic) 86.

ὅτι (causal conjunction) 211.

καὶ (ascensive conjunction) 14.

τοῖς (dat.pl.masc.of the article in agreement with ἀνέμοις) 9.

ἀνέμοις (dat.pl.masc.of ἄνεμος, personal disadvantage) 698.

ἐπιτάσσει (3d.per.sing.pres.act.ind.of ἐπιτάσσω, customary) 2061.

καὶ (adjunctive conjunction joining nouns) 14.

τῷ (dat.sing.neut.of the article in agreement with ὕδατι) 9.

ὕδατι (dat.sing.neut.of ὕδωρ, personal disadvantage) 301.

καὶ (inferential conjunction) 14.

ὑπακούουσιν (3d.per.pl.pres.act.ind.of ὑπακούω, customary) 760.

αὐτῷ (dat.sing.masc.of αὐτός, personal advantage) 16.

Translation - "*And He said to them, 'Where is your faith?' And filled with awe they began to be amazed as they said to one another, 'What sort of man is this because He even commands the winds and the water, and they always obey Him?'*"

Comment: The storm is over. Calm prevails, but not in the hearts of the disciples. Jesus redirects His rebuke from the obedient elements to the disobedient disciples. Where? *Cf.*#142 for the list of references where ποῦ is used in rhetorical question as here. "Where is your faith?" as if Jesus did not know. It is a strong way of saying, "You have no faith." The disciples were upset. All day long they had listened to His parables and had tried hard to understand. Then came the storm and their anxiety for their personal safety. Now it is the reverential fear of Jesus which turns to amazement. Then the whispered conferences among themselves. Τίς ἄρα οὗτός ἐστιν ὅτι καὶ . . . κ.τ.λ." *Cf.*#995 for other examples of τίς ἄρα as here. καὶ is ascensive. "He dares to command the winds and the water and, what is more, they obey Him!" Review the entire account from Mt.8:18-27 and Mark 4:35-41.

A Gergesene Demoniac Healed

(Mk.5:1-20; Mt.8:28-34; Lk.8:26-39)

Mark 5:1 - "*And they came over unto the other side of the sea, into the country of the Gadarenes.*"

Καὶ ἦλθον εἰς τὸ πέραν τῆς θαλάσσης εἰς τὴν χώραν τῶν Γερασηνῶν.

Καὶ (continuative conjunction) 14.
ἦλθον (3d.per.pl.aor.ind.of ἔρχομαι, constative) 146.
εἰς (preposition with the accusative of extent) 140.
τὸ (acc.sing.neut.of the article in agreement with πέραν) 9.
πέραν (acc.sing.neut.of πέραν, extent) 375.
τῆς (gen.sing.fem.of the article in agreement with θαλάσσης) 9.
θαλάσσης (gen.sing.fem.of θάλασσα, definition) 374.
εἰς (preposition with the accusative of extent) 140.
τὴν (acc.sing.fem.of the article in agreement with χώραν) 9.
χώραν (acc.sing.fem.of χώρα, extent) 201.
τῶν (gen.pl.masc.of the article in agreement with Γερασηνῶν) 9.

#2214 Γερασηνῶν (gen.pl.masc.of Γερασηνός, definition).

Gadarenes - Mk.5:1; Lk.8:26,37.

Meaning: Same as Γαδαρήνης (#761).

Translation - "And they arrived at the other side of the sea in Gadarene country."

Comment: No further incidents characterized the remainder of their passage to the east side of the lake. We may be certain that the disciples could not cease speaking of the storm and Jesus' control over it.

Jesus had no more than set foot on the opposite shore that He precipitated a crisis among the citizens ! My wonderful Lord!!!

Verse 2 - "And when he was come out of the ship, immediately there met him out of the tombs a man with an unclean spirit."

καὶ ἐξελθόντος αὐτοῦ ἐκ τοῦ πλοίου (εὐθὺς) ὑπήντησεν αὐτῷ ἐκ τῶν μνημείων ἄνθρωπος ἐν πνεύματι ἀκαθάρτῳ,

καὶ (continuative conjunction) 14.
ἐξελθόντος (aor.act.part.gen.sing.masc.of ἐξέρχομαι, genitive absolute) 161.
αὐτοῦ (gen.sing.masc.of αὐτός, genitive absolute) 16.
ἐκ (preposition with the ablative of separation) 19.
τοῦ (abl.sing.neut.of the article in agreement with πλοίου) 9.
πλοίου (abl.sing.neut.of πλοῖον, separation) 400.
(εὐθὺς) - (adverbial) 258.
ὑπήντησεν (3d.per.sing.aor.act.ind.of ὑπαντάω, constative) 762.
αὐτῷ (dat.sing.masc.of αὐτός, personal interest) 16.
ἐκ (preposition with the ablative of separation) 19.
τῶν (abl.pl.neut.of the article in agreement with μνημείων) 9.
μνημείων (abl.pl.neut.of μνημεῖον, separation) 763.
ἄνθρωπος. (nom.sing.masc.of ἄνθρωπος, subject of ὑπήντησεν) 341.
ἐν (preposition with the locative of accompanying circumstance) 80.

πνεύματι (loc.sing.neut.of πνεῦμα, accompanying circumstance) 83.
ἀκαθάρτῳ (loc.sing.neut.of ἀκάθαρτος, in agreement with πνεύματι) 843.

Translation - "And as soon as He left the ship immediately there met him a man with a foul spirit who came out of the cemetery."

Comment: The genitive absolute is aorist, thus indicating that the insane man waited to approach Jesus until after He had left the ship. The ship touched shore; Jesus disembarked. Then came the man. The meeting took place immediately - εὐθύς. The phrase ἐν πνεύματι ἀκαθάρτῳ is an interesting and unusual use of ἐν. Robertson (*Grammar*, 589) citing Mk.1:23, calls it accompanying circumstance. Blass (*Grammar of New Testament Greek*, 131) points to Mk.3:30 where we have Πνεῦμα ἀκάθαρτον ἔχει.

In ancient Greek ἐν served for many ideas and was followed originally by the accusative case, before the oblique cases (locative, instrumental, dative) developed.

An interesting sermon idea can be found in a study of μνημεῖον (#763). Run the references and get the story of Jesus' record with tombs. A suggested title - "Jesus, the Grave Robber." Every time Jesus came near a cemetery dynamic things happened.

Verse 3 - "Who had his dwelling among the tombs; and no man could bind him, no, not with chains."

ὃς τὴν κατοίκησιν εἶχεν ἐν τοῖς μνήμασιν, καὶ οὐδὲ ἁλύσει οὐκέτι οὐδεὶς ἐδύνατο αὐτὸν δῆσαι,

ὃς (nom.sing.masc.of ὅς, relative pronoun, subject of εἶχεν) 65.
τήν (acc.sing.fem.of the article in agreement with κατοίκησιν) 9.

#2215 κατοίκησιν (acc.sing.fem.of κατοίκησις, direct object of εἶχεν).

dwelling - Mk.5:3.

Meaning: Cf.κατοικέω (#242). Dwelling place. Not necessarily a house. With reference to the insane man among the tombs - Mk.5:3.

εἶχεν (3d.per.sing.imp.act.ind.of ἔχω, progressive duration) 82.
ἐν (preposition with the locative of place where) 80.
τοῖς (loc.pl.neut.of the article in agreement with μνήμασιν) 9.
μνήμασιν (loc.pl.neut.of μνῆμα, place where) 2876.

NOTE: *When this passage was analyzed in the longhand manuscript the word μνῆμα was inadvertently confused with μνημεῖον and assigned to #763. When the error was discovered it was too late to correct it since by doing so the numbering system would have been confused. The first occurrence of μνῆμα is in Mk.15:46 and the number is #2876. Cf. our discussion en loc of the difference between μνῆμα and μνημεῖον.*

καὶ (ascensive conjunction) 14.
οὐδὲ (disjunctive particle) 452.

#2216 ἁλύσει (instru.sing.fem.of ἅλυσις, means).

bonds - Eph.6:20.
chain - Acts 28:20; II Tim.1:6; Rev.20:1; Mk.5:3,4,4; Lk.8:29; Acts 12:6,7; 21:33.

Meaning: α privative plus λύω (#471). Hence the opposite of that which releases - a chain, bond or manacle with which prisoners are bound. With reference to the demoniac at Gadara - Mk.5:3,4,4; Lk.8:29 where it is used with πέδη. Elsewhere of the chains that bound Paul - Eph.6:20; Acts 28:20; II Tim.1:16, or Peter - Acts 12:6,7; 21:33. Once of the chain used to bind Satan - Rev.20:1. *Cf.*#2217.

οὐκέτι (adverb of denial) 1289.
οὐδεὶς (nom.sing.masc.of οὐδείς, subject of ἐδύνατο) 446.
ἐδύνατο (3d.per.sing.imp.act.ind.of δύναμαι, progressive description) 289.
αὐτὸν (acc.sing.masc.of αὐτός, direct object of δῆσαι) 16.
δῆσαι (aor.act.inf.of δέω, complementary) 998.

Translation - "Who had been living among the tombs, but not even with a chain had anyone been able to keep him bound."

Comment: Mark is so excited about this insane man's strength and the consequent inability of any man any longer to bind him that he piles up the negatives until the verse makes smooth translation difficult. οὐδὲ. . . οὐκέτι οὐδεὶς - "but no. . . not yet, but not one." Montgomery makes it simple with "Not even with a chain could any man bind him" which leaves out the thought that once the man had been successfully bound.

The tragic life of this poor demented man was indeed pitiable. His only asset was savage brute strength, employed with demonic fury against all who came against him. He was a total manic. Everyone was afraid of him - that is, everyone but Jesus.

The word μνῆμα (#2876) probably is distinguished from μνημεῖον (#763) as a tomb for the rich as distinct from a grave in the potter's field. Mark goes on to expand the point in

Verse 4 - "Because that he had been often bound with fetters and chains, and the chains had been plucked asunder by him, and the fetters broken in pieces: neither could any man tame him."

διὰ τὸ αὐτὸν πολλάκις πέδαις καὶ ἁλύσεσιν δεδέσθαι καὶ διεσπάσθαι ὑπ' αὐτοῦ τὰ ἁλύσεις καὶ τὰς πέδας συντετρῖφθαι, καὶ οὐδεὶς ἴσχυεν αὐτὸν δαμάσαι.

διὰ (preposition with the accusative, cause) 118.
τὸ (acc.sing.neut.of the article, joined to the infinitives δεδέσθαι, διεσπάσθαι

and συντετρῖφθαι) 9.
αὐτὸν (acc.sing.masc.of αὐτός, general reference) 16.
πολλάκις (adverbial) 1230.

#2217 πέδαις (instru.pl.fem.of πέδη, means).

fetter - Mk.5:4,4; Lk.8:29.

Meaning: From πέζα - "the foot" or "instep." Therefore a shackle for the feet. A fetter. Distinct from ἅλυσις (#2216), which means "chains" and could be used anywhere. When used together, it means that the prisoner was bound hand and foot.

καὶ (adjunctive conjunction, joining nouns) 14.
ἁλύσει (instru.pl.fem.of ἅλυσις, means) 2216.
δεδέσθαι (perf.pass.inf.of δέω, articular, accusative of cause) 998.
καὶ (adjunctive conjunction joining infinitives) 14.

#2218 διεσπάσθαι (perf.pass.inf.of διασπάω, articular, accusative of cause).

pluck asunder - Mk.5:4.
pull in pieces - Acts 23:10.

Meaning: A combination of διά (#118) and σπάω (#2802). Hence, to separate thoroughly; to tear in pieces. With reference to the chains of the demoniac - Mk.5:4. With reference to Paul who was in jeopardy by the mob - Acts 23:10.

ὑπ' (preposition with the ablative of agent) 117.
αὐτοῦ (abl.sing.masc.of αὐτός, agent) 16.
τὰς (acc.pl.fem.of the article in agreement with ἁλύσεις) 9.
ἁλύσεις (acc.pl.fem.of ἅλυσις, general reference) 2216.
καὶ (adjunctive conjunction joining infinitive clauses) 14.
τὰς (acc.pl.fem.of the article in agreement with πέδας) 9.
πέδας (acc.pl.fem.of πέδη, general reference) 2217.
συντετρῖφθαι (perf.pass.inf.of συντρίβω, articular, accusative of cause) 985.
καὶ (inferential conjunction) 14.
οὐδεὶς (nom.sing.masc.of οὐδείς, subject of ἴσχυεν) 446.
ἴσχυεν (3d.per.sing.imp.act.ind.of ἰσχύω, progressive description) 447.
αὐτὸν (acc.sing.masc.of αὐτός, direct object of δαμάσαι) 16.

#2219 δαμάσαι (aor.act.inf.of δαμάζω, complementary).

tame - Mk.5:4; Jam.3:7,7,8.

Meaning: To tame. With reference to an insane man - Mk.5:4; wild life - Jam.3:7,7. Metaphorically to control an unruly tongue - Jam.3:8.

Translation - ". . . because often he had been bound with shackles and chains and the chains had been pulled apart and the shackles had been broken and therefore no man had been able to subdue him."

Comment: διὰ here introduces three articular infinitives of cause. They are served by a single article, τὸ, in the accusative case. This causal construction supports the statement of the last clause of verse 3, that no one was able to bind the man permanently. He had in fact been bound (τὸ . . . δεδέσθαι), but the chains had been pulled apart (διεσπάσθαι) and the fetters about his feet had been shattered (συντετρίφθαι). These three perfect passive infinitives are all joined to the same article. Mark, having supported his statement of verse 3 with the evidence, now reiterates his statement in the last clause of verse 4 that "no man was able to bind him." Truly the poor man was sick and dangerous. The pitiable condition is further described in

Verse 5 - "And always, night and day, he was in the mountains, and in the tombs, crying, and cutting himself with stones."

καὶ διὰ παντὸς νυκτὸς καὶ ἡμέρας ἐν τοῖς μνήμασιν καὶ ἐν τοῖς ὄρεσιν ἦν κράζων καὶ κατακόπτων ἑαυτὸν λίθοις.

καὶ (continuative conjunction) 14.

διὰ (preposition with the genitive of time description) 118.

παντὸς (gen.sing.fem.of πᾶς, in agreement with νυκτὸς and ἡμέρας) 67.

νυκτὸς (gen.sing.fem.of νύξ, time description) 209.

καὶ (adjunctive conjunction joining nouns) 14.

ἡμέρας (gen.sing.fem.of ἡμέρα, time description) 135.

ἐν (preposition with the locative of place where) 80.

τοῖς (loc.pl.neut.of the article in agreement with μνήμασιν) 9.

μνήμασιν (loc.pl.neut.of μνῆμα, place where) 2876.

καὶ (adjunctive conjunction joining prepositional phrases) 14.

ἐν (preposition with the locative of place where) 80.

τοῖς (loc.pl.neut.of the article in agreement with ὄρεσιν) 9.

ὄρεσιν (loc.pl.neut.of ὄρος, place where) 357.

ἦν (3d.per.sing.imp.ind.of εἰμί, imperfect periphrastic) 86.

κράζων (pres.act.part.nom.sing.masc.of κράζω, imperfect periphrastic) 765.

καὶ (adjunctive conjunction joining participles) 14.

#2220 κατακόπτων (pres.act.part.nom.sing.masc.of κατακόπτω, imperfect periphrastic).

cut - Mk.5:5.

Meaning: A combination of κατά (#98) and κόπτω (#929). Hence, to cut up; to cut into pieces. To lacerate - with reference to the demoniac in Gadara - Mk.5:5.

ἑαυτὸν (acc.sing.masc.of ἑαυτός, direct object of κατακόπτων) 288.

λίθοις (instru.pl.masc.of λίθος, means) 290.

Translation - ". . . and all of the time, every night and day, among the tombs and in the mountains, he continued to cry out and to cut himself with stones."

Comment:διὰ with the genitives of time description indicates nighttime and daytime as distinct from summertime or wintertime, while παντὸς adds that Mark is speaking of *every* night and day. διὰ says that every period of time, whether it be by night or by day, was *completely* occupied with the man's activity. Thus the essence of διὰ παντὸς νυκτὸς καὶ ἡμέρας is *always* or *all of the time*. This is further strengthened by the durative character of the two imperfect periphrastics. He was always crying out and always cutting himself with stones. Either in the mountains or among the tombs the poor man shrieked out his insane frustration and lacerated his body with sharp stones. The picture is verses 3-5 is bleak indeed. What a pitiable case, but Jesus is equal to it just as He was equal to the storm at sea.

Verse 6 - *"But when he saw Jesus afar off, he ran and worshipped him."*

καὶ ἰδὼν τὸν Ἰησοῦν ἀπὸ μακρόθεν ἔδραμεν καὶ προσεκύνησεν αὐτῷ.

καὶ (adversative conjunction) 14.
ἰδὼν (aor.part.nom.sing.masc.of ὁράω, adverbial, temporal) 144.
τὸν (acc.sing.masc.of the article in agreement with Ἰησοῦν) 9.
Ἰησοῦν (acc.sing.masc.of Ἰησοῦς, direct object of ἰδὼν) 3.
ἀπὸ (preposition with the adverb to show space separation) 70.
μακρόθεν (adverbial) 1600.
ἔδραμεν (3d.per.sing.2d.aor.act.ind.of τρέχω, ingressive) 1655.
καὶ (adjunctive conjunction joining verbs) 14.
προσεκύνησεν (3d.per.sing.aor.act.ind.of προσκυνέω, ingressive) 147.
αὐτῷ (dat.sing.masc.of αὐτός, personal advantage) 16.

Translation - *"But having seen Jesus from afar he ran and began to worship Him."*

Comment: This is more than the Pharisees did, and they were supposed to be sane!

Verse 7 - *"And cried with a loud voice and said, What have I to do with thee, Jesus, thou Son of the most high God? I adjure thee by God, that thou torment me not."*

καὶ κράξας φωνῇ μεγάλῃ λέγει. Τί ἐμοὶ καὶ σοί, Ἰησοῦ υἱὲ τοῦ θεοῦ τοῦ ὑψίστου; ὁρκίζω σε τὸν θεόν, μὴ με βασανίσῃς.

καὶ (adjunctive conjunction) 14.
κράξας (aor.act.part.nom.sing.masc.of κράζω, adverbial, temporal) 765.
φωνῇ (instru.sing.fem.of φωνή, means) 222.
μεγάλῃ (instru.sing.fem.of μέγας, in agreement with φωνῇ) 184.
λέγει (3d.per.sing.pres.act.ind.of λέγω, historical) 66.
Τί (nom.sing.neut.of τίς, interrogative pronoun in direct question) 281.
ἐμοὶ (dat.sing.masc.of ἐμός, personal interest) 1267.
καὶ (adjunctive conjunction joining pronouns) 14.

σοί (dat.sing.masc.of σύ, personal interest) 104.
'Ιησοῦ (voc.sing.masc.of 'Ιησοῦς, address) 3.
υἱὲ (voc.sing.masc.of υἱός, apposition) 5.
τοῦ (gen.sing.masc.of the article in agreement with θεοῦ) 9.
θεοῦ (gen.sing.masc.of θεός, relationship) 124.
τοῦ (gen.sing.masc.of the article in agreement with ὑψίστου) 9.
ὑψίστου (gen.sing.masc.of ὕψιστος, apposition) 1353.

#2221 ὀρκίζω (1st.per.sing.pres.act.ind.of ὀρκίζω, aoristic).

adjure - Mk.5:7; Acts 19:13.

Meaning: Cf. ἐνορκίζω (#4673) in I Thess.5:27. Related to ὅρκος (#515). Hence, to force one to take an oath. To adjure, solemnly implore, charge, call upon. With reference to the demoniac speaking to Jesus - Mk.5:7. Of the exorcists in Acts 19:13.

σε (acc.sing.masc.of σύ, direct object of ὀρκίζω) 104.
τὸν (acc.sing.masc.of the article in agreement with θεόν) 9.
θεόν (acc.sing.masc.of θεός, general reference) 124.
μὴ (negative conjunction with the subjunctive in a prohibition) 87.
με (acc.sing.masc.of ἐγώ, direct object of βασανίσῃς) 123.
βασανίσῃς (2d.per.sing.1st.aor.act.subj.of βασανίζω, prohibition) 719.

Translation - "And when he had finished shrieking at the top of his voice he said, 'What have you and I in common, Jesus, Son of the Most High God? I call upon you in God's name not to torment me.' "

Comment: It is grammatically not possible to take κράξας as modal, as Goodspeed does. The participle is aorist and denotes action prior to that in λέγει. This forbids the interpretation that the man screamed at Jesus at the top of his lungs. His shrieking ceased and he became calm as he spoke to Jesus.

It is hard to imagine the poor man prostrate before our Lord raving like a maniac. His speech to Jesus was probably delivered in a subdued voice. The demon's cry was inarticulate. What the man said to Jesus made good sense. The man realized that in his demon possessed condition he really had nothing in common with our Lord, Whom he correctly designated as the Son of the Most High God. The Son of God and a demon possessed man find little common ground. Cf.#1353 for other places where the adjective applies to Jesus. The demons know more theology than some religious leaders. τὸν θεόν after σε is an example of a double accusative. τὸν θεόν is an accusative of general reference. σε is the object of ὀρκίζω. "I charge you and call God to witness. . . κ.τ.λ." The prohibition is couched in the aorist subjunctive, βασανίσῃς which is ingressive - "... do not begin to torment me." Apparently the demon thought that Jesus was going to send him immediately to hell. This is supported by γὰρ in

Verse 8 - "For he said unto him, Come out of the man, thou unclean spirit."

ἔλεγεν γὰρ αὐτῷ, Ἔξελθε τὸ πνεῦμα τὸ ἀκάθαρτον ἐκ τοῦ ἀνθρώπου.

ἔλεγεν (3d.per.sing.imp.act.ind.of λέγω, progressive duration) 66.
γὰρ (causal conjunction) 105.
αὐτῷ (dat.sing.masc.of αὐτός, indirect object of ἔλεγεν) 16.
Ἔξελθε (2d.per.sing.aor.act.impv.of ἐξέρχομαι, command) 161.
τὸ (voc.sing.neut.of the article in agreement with πνεῦμα) 9.
πνεῦμα (voc.sing.neut.of πνεῦμα, address) 83.
τὸ (voc.sing.neut.of the article in agreement with ἀκάθαρτον) 9.
ἀκάθαρτον (voc.sing.neut.of ἀκάθαρτος, in agreement with πνεῦμα) 843.
ἐκ (preposition with the ablative of separation) 19.
τοῦ (abl.sing.masc.of the article in agreement with ἀνθρώπου) 9.
ἀνθρώπου (abl.sing.masc.of ἄνθρωπος, separation) 341.

Translation - "*Because He was saying to him, 'Come, you unclean spirit, out of the man.'*"

Comment: This is why the demon was begging Jesus not to assign him to torment. Already Jesus was ordering (continuous action in ἔλεγεν) him out of the man. Whither? Is there any other place but hell? Not to the demon's knowledge. Note that, in addressing him, Jesus used the emphatic attributive position - τὸ πνεῦμα τὸ ἀκάθαρτον. Running through the entire story is evidence of our Lord's superiority over the demon, just as He had shown His superiority over the storm and waves, a short time before.

Verse 9 - "*And he asked him, What is thy name? And he answered, saying, My name is Legion: for we are many.*"

καὶ ἐπηρώτα αὐτόν, Τί ὄνομά σοι; καὶ λέγει αὐτῷ, Λεγιὼν ὄνομά μοι, ὅτι πολλοί ἐσμεν.

καὶ (continuative conjunction) 14.
ἐπηρώτα (3d.per.sing.imp.act.ind.of ἐπερωτάω, iterative) 973.
αὐτόν (acc.sing.masc.of αὐτός, direct object of ἐπηρώτα) 16.
Τί (nom.sing.neut.of τίς, predicate nominative) 281.
ὄνομά (nom.sing.neut.of ὄνομα, subject of ἐστιν understood) 108.
σοι (dat.sing.neut.of σύ, possession) 104.
καὶ (continuative conjunction) 14.
λέγει (3d.per.sing.pres.act.ind.of λέγω, historical) 66.
αὐτῷ (dat.sing.masc.of αὐτός, indirect object of λέγει) 16.
Λεγιὼν (nom.sing.masc.of λεγιών, predicate nominative) 1597.
ὄνομά (nom.sing.neut.of ὄνομα, subject of ἐστιν understood) 108.
μοι (dat.sing.neut.of ἐγώ, possession) 123.
ὅτι (causal conjunction) 211.
πολλοί (nom.pl.neut.of πολύς, predicate adjective) 228.
ἐσμεν (1st.per.pl.pres.ind.of εἰμί, aoristic) 86.

Translation - "*And He asked him repeatedly, 'What is your name?' And he said to Him, 'Legion is my name, because there are many of us.' "*

Comment: The imperfect in ἐπηρώτα is iterative. Jesus insisted that the demon identify himself. He also insisted that the demons leave their victim despite their frantic entreaties. Perhaps as long as the demons controlled the body of the man they would not permit him to reply to Jesus, in which case we have the struggle for power between Jesus and the demons as in Mk.3:11 and Mt.12:22. Once the demons were cast out, the man could speak. He had lived wìth the demons so long that he identified with them. πολλοί ἐσμεν - "I am more than one. I am controlled by many." Once cast out, the demons were at the complete mercy of the Son of God, as we see in verses 10-14.

Verse 10 - "*And he besought him much that he would not send them away out of the country.*"

καὶ παρεκάλει αὐτὸν πολλὰ ἵνα μὴ αὐτοὺς ἀποστείλῃ ἔξω τῆς χώρας.

καὶ (continuative conjunction) 14.
παρεκάλει (3d.per.sing.imp.act.ind.of παρακαλέω, inceptive) 230.
αὐτὸν (acc.sing.masc.of αὐτός, direct object of παρεκάλει) 16.
πολλὰ (adverbial) 228.
ἵνα (final conjunction introducing a purpose clause) 114.
μὴ (negative conjunction with the subjunctive in a negative purpose clause) 87.
αὐτοὺς (acc.pl.masc.of αὐτός, direct object of ἀποστείλῃ) 16.
ἀποστείλῃ (3d.per.sing.1st.aor.act.subj.of ἀποστέλλω, purpose) 215.
ἔξω (improper preposition with the ablative of separation) 449.
τῆς (abl.sing.fem.of the article in agreement with χώρας) 9.
χώρας (abl.sing.fem.of χώρα, separation) 201.

Translation - "*And he began to beg him earnestly that He not send them out of the country.*"

Comment: We have for the first time in this story a clear grammatical distinction between the man and the demons - perhaps because this is the earliest moment when the demons are outside his body. In verses 2-9 the man and the demons seem inextricably bound together. See it is verse 2. It seems in verse 6 that the man ran. The man in verse 7 begged for no torment because (γὰρ in verse 8) Jesus was ordering the demons to leave. But in verse 9 - ὅτι πολλοί ἐσμεν - again he identifies with them. Now in verse 10, it seems clear who is who. The man begs Jesus with great earnestness that He (Jesus) not send them (the demons) out of the country. One wonders why? It would seem that he would be glad to see them leave. Grotius suggests that Decapolis was full of Hellenizing apostate Jews and hence a favorite haunt for demons. (*The Expositors' Greek Testament, en loc.*).

Verse 11 - "Now there was there nigh unto the mountains a great herd of swine feeding."

Ἦν δὲ ἐκεῖ πρὸς τῷ ὄρει ἀγέλη χοίρων μεγάλη βοσκομένη.

Ἦν (3d.per.sing.imp.ind.of εἰμί, imperfect periphrastic) 86.
δὲ (explanatory conjunction) 11.
ἐκεῖ (adverb of place) 204.
πρὸς (preposition with the locative of place) 197.
τῷ (loc.sing.neut.of the article in agreement with ὄρει) 9.
ὄρει (loc.sing.neut.of ὄρος, place where) 357.
ἀγέλη (nom.sing.fem.of ἀγέλη, subject of ἦν) 769.
χοίρων (gen.pl.masc.of χοῖρος, definition) 653.
μεγάλη (nom.sing.fem.of μέγας, in agreement with ἀγέλη) 184.
βοσκομένη (pres.pass.part.nom.sing.fem.of βόσκω, imperfect periphrastic) 770.

Translation - "Now there near the mountain a large herd of swine had been feeding."

Comment: δὲ is explanatory as Mark introduces a new element into the story. The imperfect periphrastic (ἦν ... βοσκομένη) is durative in character. The spot there on the hillside, not far from the mountain had been devoted by the natives to swine feeding.

The man had interceded in behalf of the demons that they might be allowed to remain in the area. Now they intercede for themselves in

Verse 12 - "And all the devils besought him saying, Send us into the swine, that we may enter into them."

καὶ παρεκάλεσαν αὐτὸν λέγοντες, Πέμφον ὑμᾶς εἰς τοὺς χοίρους, ἵνα εἰς αὐτοὺς εἰσέλθωμεν.

καὶ (continuative conjunction) 14.
παρεκάλεσαν (3d.per.pl.aor.act.ind.of παρακαλέω, ingressive) 230.
αὐτὸν (acc.sing.masc.of αὐτός, direct object of παρεκάλεσαν) 16.
λέγοντες (pres.act.part.nom.pl.masc.of λέγω, recitative) 66.
Πέμφον (2d.per.sing.aor.act.impv.of πέμπω, entreaty) 169.
ἡμᾶς (acc.pl.neut.of ἐγώ, direct object of πέμφον) 123.
εἰς (preposition with the accusative of extent) 140.
τοὺς (acc.pl.masc.of the article in agreement with χοίρους) 9.
χοίρους (acc.pl.masc.of χοῖρος, extent) 653.
ἵνα (sub-final conjunction introducing a purpose/result clause) 114.
εἰς (preposition with the accusative of extent) 140.
αὐτοὺς (acc.pl.masc.of αὐτός, extent) 16.
εἰσέλθωμεν (1st.per.pl.aor.subj.of εἰσέρχομαι, sub-final purpose/result) 234.

Translation - "*And they began to beg Him, 'Send us into the swine in order that we may enter into them.'* "

Comment: The subject of παρεκάλεσαν is the group of demons themselves. Thus we have the plural form of the verb. This is the first time that the demons have spoken to Jesus since they were cast out of their victim. They were now without a home. They could have been sent to hell where they belong, but the man, their former victim, did not want that. He wanted them to remain in Decapolis for some reason not disclosed in the text. They needed somewhere to go. Hence their request. And what a request! Any port in a storm!!

Verse 13 - "*And forthwith Jesus gave them leave. And the unclean spirits went out,and entered into the swine: and the herd ran violently down a steep place into the sea, (they were about two thousand;) and were choked in the sea.*"

καὶ ἐπέτρεψεν αὐτοῖς, καὶ ἐξελθόντα τὰ πνεύματα τὰ ἀκάθαρτα εἰσῆλθον εἰς τοὺς χοίρους, καὶ ὥρμησεν ἡ ἀγέλη κατὰ τοῦ κρημνοῦ εἰς τὴν θάλασσαν, ὡς δισχίλιοι, καὶ ἐπνίγοντο ἐν τῇ θαλάσσῃ.

καὶ (continuative conjunction) 14.
ἐπέτρεψεν (3d.per.sing.aor.act.ind.of ἐπιτρέπω, constative) 747.
αὐτοῖς (dat.pl.neut.of αὐτός, personal advantage) 16.
καὶ (continuative conjunction) 14.
ἐξελθόντα (2d.aor.act.part.nom.pl.neut.of ἐξέρχομαι, adverbial, temporal) 161.
τὰ (nom.pl.neut.of the article in agreement with πνεύματα) 9.
πνεύματα (nom.pl.neut.of πνεῦμα, subject of εἰσῆλθον) 83.
τὰ (nom.pl.neut.of the article in agreement with ἀκάθαρτα) 9.
ἀκάθαρτα (nom.pl.neut.of ἀκάθαρτος, in agreement with πνεύματα) 843.
εἰσῆλθον (3d.per.pl.aor.ind.of εἰσέρχομαι, constative) 234.
εἰς (preposition with the accusative of extent) 140.
τοὺς (acc.pl.masc.of the article in agreement with χοίρους) 9.
χοίρους (acc.pl.masc.of χοῖρος, extent) 653.
καὶ (continuative conjunction) 14.
ὥρμησεν (3d.per.sing.aor.act.ind.of ὁρμάω, ingressive) 772.
ἡ (nom.sing.fem.of the article in agreement with ἀγέλη) 9.
ἀγέλη (nom.sing.fem.of ἀγέλη, subject of ὥρμησεν) 769.
κατὰ (preposition with the genitive of place description, "down upon" - perpendicular) 98.
τοῦ (gen.sing.masc.of the article in agreement with κρημνοῦ) 9
κρημνοῦ (gen.sing.masc.of κρημνός, place description) 773.
εἰς (preposition with the accusative of extent) 140.
τὴν (acc.sing.fem.of the article in agreement with θάλασσαν) 9.
θάλασσαν (acc.sing.fem.of θάλασσα, extent) 374.
ὡς (relative adverb introducing a comparative clause) 128.

#2222 δισχίλιοι (numeral).

two thousand - Mk.5:13.

Meaning: Two thousand. The estimated number of swine killed at Gadara - Mk.5:13.

καὶ (continuative conjunction) 14.
ἐπνίγοντο (3d.per.pl.imp.pass.ind.of πνίγω, progressive description) 1279.
ἐν (preposition with the locative of place where) 80.
τῇ (loc.sing.fem.of the article in agreement with θαλάσσῃ) 9.
θαλάσσῃ (loc.sing.fem.of θάλασσα, place where) 374.

Translation - *"And He gave them permission, and when they had left the man the unclean spirits entered into the swine, and the stampeded herd rushed pell-mell down the precipice into the sea (about two thousand in number) and they were drowned in the sea."*

Comment: Jesus gave His permission, thus demonstrating His total authority over the demons, a fact which they recognized. They asked His permission, awaited His assent and obeyed forthwith. The hogs, suddenly seized with the insanity of demon possession, rushed precipitantly down the precipice into the sea where they were drowned. Mark adds the detail that there were about two thousand of them. Any farm boy who has tried to drive a hog anywhere, to say nothing of driving one over a cliff, will sense the demonic character of the story. The student should read our comment on ὁρμάω (#772). Demon possessed men and demon possessed pigs have done all of the rushing in the New Testament. One could well ask the child of God, "What's the rush?" "The fruit of the Spirit is . . . gentleness. . . " (Gal.5:22,23).

The poor demoniac is healed. The demons are gone. The hogs are dead. And the hog farmers are bereft of their property. As a result the Gerasenes are amazed and eager to be rid of this divine trouble maker.

Verse 14 - *"And they that fed the swine fled, and told it in the city, and in the country. And they went out to see what it was that was done."*

καὶ οἱ βόσκοντες αὐτοὺς ἔφυγον καὶ ἀπήγγειλαν εἰς τὴν πόλιν καὶ εἰς τοὺς ἀγροὺς, καὶ ἦλθον ἰδεῖν τί ἐστιν τὸ γεγονός.

καὶ (inferential conjunction) 14.
οἱ (nom.pl.masc.of the article in agreement with βόσκοντες) 9.
βόσκοντες (pres.act.part.nom.pl.masc.of βόσκω, subject of ἔφυγον and ἀπήγγειλαν) 770.
αὐτοὺς (acc.pl.masc.of αὐτός, direct object of βόσκοντες) 16.
ἔφυγον (3d.per.pl.1st.aor.act.ind.of φεύγω, constative) 202.
καὶ (adjunctive conjunction joining verbs) 14.
ἀπήγγειλαν (3d.per.pl.1st.aor.act.ind.of ἀπαγγέλλω, constative) 176.
εἰς (preposition with the accusative, static use) 140.
τὴν (acc.sing.fem.of the article in agreement with πόλιν) 9.

πόλιν (acc.sing.fem.of πόλις, static use of the accusative with εἰς, place where) 243.
καὶ (adjunctive conjunction joining prepositional phrases) 14.
τοὺς (acc.pl.masc.of the article in agreement with ἀγρούς) 9.
ἀγρούς (acc.pl.masc.of ἀγρός, static use place where) 626.
καὶ (continuative conjunction) 14.
ἦλθον (3d.per.pl.aor.ind.of ἔρχομαι, constative) 146.
ἰδεῖν (aor.act.inf.of ὁράω, purpose) 144.
τί (nom.sing.neut.of τίς, subject of ἐστιν) 281.
ἐστιν (3d.per.sing.pres.ind.of εἰμί, indirect discourse) 86.
τὸ (nom.sing.neut.of the article in agreement with γεγονός) 9.
γεγονός (2d.perf.part.nom.sing.neut.of γίνομαι, predicate nominative) 113.

Translation - "And the swineherds fled and reported in the city and in the surrounding territories, and they came to see what had happened."

Comment: Those who had been feeding the swine probably felt the need to clear themselves of blame for the loss of the swine. Certainly they could not be held responsibile for having lost control of the animals. The people came from the city and from the surrounding countryside to assess the damage. No doubt the owners were concerned about so great a loss. Jews were forbidden to eat pork but there was nothing to forbid them selling it to the Romans and the Hellenized apostate Jews who lived in Decapolis. The first thing they saw was the evidence of Jesus' healing power in

Verse 15 - "And they came to Jesus, and see him that was possessed with the devil, and had the legion, sitting, and clothed, and in his right mind: and they were afraid."

καὶ ἔρχονται πρὸς τὸν Ἰησοῦν, καὶ θεωροῦσιν τὸν δαιμονιζόμενον καθήμενον ἱματισμένον καὶ σωφρονοῦντα, τὸν ἐσχηκότα τὸν λεγιῶνα, καὶ ἐφοβήθησαν.

καὶ (continuative conjunction) 14.
ἔρχονται (3d.per.pl.pres.ind.of ἔρχομαι, historical) 146.
πρὸς (preposition with the accusative of extent) 197.
τὸν (acc.sing.masc.of the article in agreement with Ἰησοῦν) 9.
Ἰησοῦν (acc.sing.masc.of Ἰησοῦς, extent) 3.
καὶ (continuative conjunction) 14.
θεωροῦσιν (3d.per.pl.pres.act.ind.of θεωρέω, historical) 1667.
τὸν (acc.sing.masc.of the article in agreement with δαιμονιζόμενον) 9.
δαιμονιζόμενον (pres.pass.part.acc.sing.masc.of δαιμονίζομαι, substantival, direct object of θεωροῦσιν) 415.
καθήμενον (pres.mid.part.acc.sing.masc.of κάθημαι, adverbial, circumstantial) 377.

#2223 ἱματισμένον (pres.pass.part.acc.sing.masc.of ἱματίζω, adverbial, circumstantial).

clothe - Mk.5:15; Lk.8:35.

Meaning: Cf.ἱμάτιον (#534) and *ἱματισμός* (#2159). To clothe; to put on wearing apparel - Mk.5:15; Lk.8:35.

καὶ (adjunctive conjunction, joining participles) 14.

#2224 σωφρονοῦντα (pres.part.acc.sing.masc.of σωφρονέω, adverbial, circumstantial).

be in one's right mind - Mk.5:15; Lk.8:35.
be sober - II Cor.5:13; I Pet.4:7.
be sober minded - Tit.2:6.
soberly - Rom.12:3.

Meaning: Sane. With respect to one restored to sanity after demon possession - Mk.5:15; Lk.8:35. Opposed to ἐξεστῆναι in II Cor.5:13. To put a modest estimate upon one's self - Rom.12:3. To put a curb on passions - Tit.2:6. To be sober - I Pet.4:7.

τὸν (acc.sing.masc.of the article in agreement with ἐσχηκότα) 9.
ἐσχηκότα (perf.part.acc.sing.masc.of ἔχω, substantival, in apposition with δαιμονιζόμενον) 82.
τὸν (acc.sing.masc.of the article in agreement with λεγιῶνα) 9.
λεγιῶνα (acc.sing.masc.of λεγιών, direct object of ἐσχηκότα) 1597.
καὶ (inferential conjunction) 14.
ἐφοβήθησαν (3d.per.pl.aor.pass.ind.of φοβέομαι, ingressive) 101.

Translation - "And they came to Jesus and they saw the demoniac seated, clothed and sane - the one who had had the legion. Therefore they began to be afraid."

Comment: Mark uses the historical present - ἔρχονται. . . καὶ θεωροῦσιν. - "They come and see." The one formerly demon possessed is sitting, clothed and in full possession of his mental faculties. Note these three adverbial circumstantial participles. ἐσχηκότα is substantival, in apposition with δαιμονιζόμενον. The student should go back and read Mark's dramatic description of the man in verses 3-5 and note the contrast with verse 15. This is the transformation that Jesus makes. In view of the man's previous belligerence and now his quiet humility it is scant wonder that the people began to be afraid. Is it harder to tame a tornado or a crazy man? For our Lord it is all a simple matter, for He is Sovereign.

That Legion was now healed was cause for amazement and rejoicing. That two thousand pigs were dead was another matter.

Verse 16 - "And they that saw it told them how it befell to him that was possessed with the devil, and also concerning the swine."

καὶ διηγήσαντο αὐτοῖς οἱ ἰδόντες πῶς ἐγένετο τῷ δαιμονιζομένῳ καὶ περὶ τῶν χοίρων.

καὶ (continuative conjunction) 14.

#2225 διηγήσαντο (3d.per.pl.1st.aor.ind.of διηγέομαι, constative).

declare - Acts 8:33; 9:27; 12:17.
show - Lk.8:39.
tell - Mk.5:16; 9:9; Lk.9:10; Heb.11:32.

Meaning: A combination of διά (#118) and ἡγέομαι (#162). Hence, to lead or carry a narrative through to the end. To relate fully. To give a thorough account of. Followed by an accusative - Acts 8:33; with πῶς - Acts 9:27; 12:17; with πῶς and περί - Mk.5:16. With ὅσα - Lk.8:39; 9:10. With ἅ - Mk.9:9; with περί - Heb.11:32.

αὐτοῖς (dat.pl.masc.of αὐτός, indirect object of διηγήσαντο) 16.
οἱ (nom.pl.masc.of the article in agreement with ἰδόντες) 9.
ἰδόντες (aor.act.part.nom.pl.masc.of ὁράω, subject of διηγήσαντο) 144.
πῶς (adverbial) 627.
ἐγένετο (3d.per.sing.aor.ind.of γίνομαι, constative) 113.
τῷ (dat.sing.masc.of the article in agreement with δαιμονιζομένῳ) 9.
δαιμονιζομένῳ (pres.mid.part.dat.sing.masc.of δαιμονίζομαι, personal advantage) 415.
καὶ (adjunctive conjunction, joining an adverbial and a prepositional phrase) 14.

περὶ (preposition with the genitive of reference) 173.
τῶν (gen.pl.masc.of the article in agreement with χοίρων) 9.
χοίρων (gen.pl.masc.of χοῖρος, reference) 653.

Translation - "And those who saw it related fully to them what happened to the demoniac and about the swine."

Comment: The identity of οἱ ἰδόντες seems clearly to be οἱ βόσκοντες of verse 14. There may have been other spectators present who were not mentioned before in the text, other than the disciples. They gave a full account. *Cf.*#2225 for this interesting verb. The narrators left nothing out, we may be sure. The antecedent of αὐτοῖς is the unexpressed subject of ἦλθον in verse 14. The people from the cities and fields round about came to see what happened.

The insane wild man (or men, for Matthew says that there were two of them - Mt.8:28) is healed, clothed and sitting at Jesus' feet in his right mind. But two thousand head of hogs are lost! What a rest for the sense of values of the citizenry! They failed it miserably.

Verse 17 - "And they began to pray him to depart out of their coasts."

καὶ ἤρξαντο παρακαλεῖν αὐτὸν ἀπελθεῖν ἀπὸ τῶν ὁρίων αὐτῶν.

καὶ (inferential conjunction) 14.
ἤρξαντο (3d.per.pl.aor.ind.of ἄρχω, ingressive) 383.
παρακαλεῖν (pres.act.inf.of παρακαλέω, epexegetical) 230.
αὐτὸν (acc.sing.masc.of αὐτός, direct object of παρακαλεῖν) 16.
ἀπελθεῖν (aor.inf.of ἀπέρχομαι, epexegetical) 239.
ἀπὸ (preposition with the ablative of separation) 70.
τῶν (abl.pl.neut.of the article in agreement with ὁρίων) 9.
ὁρίων (abl.pl.neut.of ὅριος, separation) 218.
αὐτῶν (gen.pl.masc.of αὐτός, possession) 16.

Translation - "Therefore they began to beg Him to go away from their territory."

Comment: When the infinitive is joined to a noun we say that it is in apposition; when it is joined to a verb it is either complementary or epexegetical. The complementary and epexegetical ideas are closely related. Each explains the verb. We may take παρακαλεῖν as complementary. It completes ἤρξαντο, as ἀπελθεῖν explains παρακαλεῖν. The Gerasenes wanted Jesus to leave them alone. This request went to the man who had turned a raving manic into a quiet rational member of society. This is typical Chamber of Commerce. "We have an insanity problem in our community, we admit. We cannot cope with it despite the fetters and handcuffs which we have designed for their feet and hands. In fact, for the sake of public safety, we have turned a part of our territory over to them, because it isn't safe for sane people to go near them. They have taken over that section of the tombs and mountains. You have healed them and now they are rehabilitated and useful citizens. But the pigs! There were two thousand of them. And now they are dead. It is a great loss of property. The story will spread. It will hurt the image of Decapolis. Our Industrial Relations Commission is working hard to induce the swine industry to move in here with large investments. It will boost our economy and wipe out unemployment, although it may add to our air pollution problem. But we will have better schools and playgrounds as a result of the increased wealth. But not if you run all of our pigs into the sea! Sir, we are sorry but if we must choose between our pigs and our insane men, give us the pigs. Will you please leave town?"

It is small wonder that the man whom Jesus healed, now in his right mind, reacted as he did in

Verse 18 - "And when he was come into the ship he that had been possessed with the devil prayed him that he might be with him."

καὶ ἐμβαίνοντος αὐτοῦ εἰς τὸ πλοῖον παρεκάλει αὐτὸν ὁ δαιμονισθεὶς ἵνα μετ᾽ αὐτοῦ ᾖ.

καὶ (inferential conjunction) 14.
ἐμβαίνοντος (pres.act.part.gen.sing.masc.of ἐμβαίνω, genitive absolute) 750.

αὐτοῦ (gen.sing.masc.of αὐτός, genitive absolute) 16.
εἰς (preposition with the accusative of extent) 140.
τό (acc.sing.neut.of the article in agreement with πλοῖον) 9.
πλοῖον (acc.sing.neut.of πλοῖον, extent) 400.
παρεκάλει (3d.per.sing.imp.act.ind.of παρακαλέω, inceptive) 230.
αὐτόν (acc.sing.masc.of αὐτός, direct object of παρεκάλει) 16.
ὁ (nom.sing.masc.of the article in agreement with δαιμονισθείς) 9.
δαιμονισθείς (aor.pass.part.nom.sing.masc.of δαιμονίζομαι, substantival,
subject of παρεκάλει) 415.
ἵνα (final conjunction introducing a purpose clause) 114.
μετ' (preposition with the genitive of accompaniment) 50.
αὐτοῦ (gen.sing.masc.of αὐτός, accompaniment) 16.
ᾖ (3d.per.sing.pres.subj.of εἰμί, purpose) 86.

Translation - "Therefore as He went on board the ship the man who had been demon possessed began to beg Him that he might go with Him."

Comment: The genitive absolute construction has the present tense participle indicating simultaneous action with that of the main verb παρεκάλει. Jesus was stepping into the ship when the man who had been demon possessed (aorist participle in ὁ δαιμονισθείς) began to beg Him (inceptive imperfect in παρεκάλει). For what? The purpose clause with ἵνα and the subjunctive in ᾖ, tells us what he wanted. He wanted to go with Jesus. "... that he might always be with Him." Jesus was leaving in acquiescence to the request of the Gerasenes. He and His disciples made their way back to the shore where the boat had been secured. His new friend was following, no longer under the control of the demons, but sober minded, gentle, clothed, no longer crying out nor masochistic, but shocked and humiliated that the citizens of Decapolis thought more of their hogs than of him. One thing he wished above all else - that he might leave the place forever and spend the rest of his life in the presence of Jesus, Who had rescued him from the scenes of his former torment. Hence his persistent entreaty. Every step of the way to the boat he hoped against hope that his request might be granted; and yet he was reluctant to ask. At the last moment, as Jesus stepped into the boat, he realized that he must ask now or never. Thus he began to beg Jesus - "Let me be with you always."

It might be worthwhile to research the question as to how those who were healed, saved or otherwise supernaturally helped by Jesus immediately reacted. How many of them wanted to follow Jesus? .e.g. Lk.18:43. How many examples are there?

The man in our story had his request denied as we see in

Verse 19 - "Howbeit Jesus suffered him not, but saith unto him, Go home to thy friends, and tell them how great things the Lord hath done for thee, and hath had compassion on thee."

καὶ οὐκ ἀφῆκεν αὐτόν, ἀλλὰ λέγει αὐτῷ,Ὕπαγε εἰς τὸν οἰκόν σου πρὸς τοὺς
σούς, καὶ ἀπάγγειλον αὐτοῖς ὅσα ὁ κύριός σοι πεποίηκεν καὶ ἠλέησέν σε.

καὶ (adversative conjunction) 14.
οὐκ (negative conjunction with the indicative) 130.
ἀφῆκεν (3d.per.sing.aor.act.ind.of ἀφίημι, constative) 319.
αὐτόν (acc.sing.masc.of αὐτός, direct object of ἀφῆκεν) 16.
ἀλλὰ (alternative conjunction) 342.
λέγει (3d.per.sing.pres.act.ind.of λέγω, historical) 66.
αὐτῷ (dat.sing.masc.of αὐτός, indirect object of λέγει) 16.
Ὕπαγε (2d.per.sing.pres.act.impv.of ὑπάγω, command) 364.
εἰς (preposition with the accusative of extent) 140.
τὸν (acc.sing.masc.of the article in agreement with οἰκόν) 9.
οἰκόν (acc.sing.masc.of οἶκος, extent) 784.
σου (gen.sing.masc.of σύ, possession) 104.
πρὸς (preposition with the accusative of extent) 197.
τοὺς (acc.pl.masc.of the article in agreement with σούς) 9.
σούς (acc.pl.masc.of σός, extent) 646.
καὶ (continuative conjunction) 14.
ἀπάγγειλαν (2d.per.sing.1st.aor.act.impv.of ἀπαγγέλλω, command) 176.
αὐτοῖς (dat.pl.masc.of αὐτός, indirect object of ἀπάγγειλον) 16.
ὅσα (acc.pl.neut.of ὅσος, direct object of ἀπάγγειλον) 660.
ὁ (nom.sing.masc.of the article in agreement with κύριός) 9.
κύριός (nom.sing.masc.of κύριος, subject of πεποίηκεν and ἠλέησεν) 97.
σοι (dat.sing.masc.of σύ, personal advantage) 104.
πεποίηκεν (3d.per.sing.perf.act.ind.of ποιέω, consummative) 127.
καὶ (continuative conjunction) 14.
ἠλέησέν (3d.per.sing.aor.act.ind.of ἐλεέω, culminative) 430.
σε (acc.sing.masc.of σύ, direct object of ἠλέησέν) 104.

*Translation - "But He did not permit him, but said to him, 'Go back to your
home to your own people, and tell them what the Lord has done for you and has
had mercy on you."*

Comment: καὶ here is adversative as Jesus refused to grant the man's request.
Cf.#319 for a review of the meaning. Jesus did not stand aside and thus permit
the man to go with Him, but offered an alternative policy, as indicated by ἀλλὰ.
He gave the man a commission, which is clearly prophetic of Mt.28:18-20. "Go
home to your friends." That is a good place for any young Christian to start his
witness. The citizens of Decapolis no doubt represented the power structure of
the city establishment. They were not his friends. They cared less for him than
they did for the pigs. They had already indicated how they evaluated the work
which Jesus did for the man. We are not to cast pearls before swine nor give that
which is holy to dogs (Mt.7:6). The man should not waste his time in Decapolis.
But he had a home in which he once lived before the demons possessed him.
There his own people - perhaps a wife and children, parents and friends, who
would receive him with joy and listen to his testimony.

"Tell them" - for their personal advantage - αὐτοῖς. Note the consummative perfect in πεποίηκεν. Mark then promptly adds καὶ ἠλέησέν σε. He could have written smoother Greek had he inserted πῶς before ἠλέησέν. The man was to go home and give his testimony where it would count the most. Men would say, "Is not this the man from the tombs, who was insane?" The notorious sinner who has been saved, can do his most effective witnessing among those who know all about his past life. The man was faithful to his commission as we see in

Verse 20 - "And he departed, and began to publish in Decapolis how great things Jesus had done for him: and all men did marvel."

καὶ ἀπῆλθεν καὶ ἤρξατο κηρύσσειν ἐν τῇ Δεκαπόλει ὅσα ἐποίησεν αὐτῷ ὁ Ἰησοῦς, καὶ πάντες ἐθαύμαζον.

καὶ (inferential conjunction) 14.
ἀπῆλθεν (3d.per.sing.aor.ind.of ἀπέρχομαι, constative) 239.
καὶ (adjunctive conjunction joining verbs) 14.
ἤρξατο (3d.per.sing.aor.act.ind.of ἄρχω, ingressive) 383.
κηρύσσειν (pres.act.inf.of κηρύσσω, complementary) 249.
ἐν (preposition with the locative of place where) 80.
τῇ (loc.sing.fem.of the article in agreement with Δεκαπόλει) 9.
Δεκαπόλει (loc.sing.fem.of Δεκαπόλεως, place where) 419.
ὅσα (acc.pl.neut.of ὅσος, direct object of κηρύσσειν) 660.
ἐποίησεν (3d.per.sing.aor.act.ind.of ποιέω, culminative) 127.
αὐτῷ (dat.sing.masc.of αὐτός, personal advantage) 16.
ὁ (nom.sing.masc.of the article in agreement with Ἰησοῦς) 9.
Ἰησοῦς (nom.sing.masc.of Ἰησοῦς, subject of ἐποίησεν) 3.
καὶ (continuative conjunction) 14.
πάντες (nom.pl.masc.of πᾶς, subject of ἐθαύμαζον) 67.
ἐθαύμαζον (3d.per.pl.imp.act.ind.of θαυμάζω, inceptive) 726.

Translation - "Therefore he went away and began to proclaim in Decapolis those things which Jesus did for him, and everyone was seized with amazement."

Comment: The man wasted no time. He wanted to go with Jesus, but no sooner than he had his orders from our Lord, he was gone. Mark does not use εὐθύς, one of his favorite expressions, but we may be sure that he wasted no time. ἤρξατο κηρύσσειν - "he began to preach", not only in his own home to his family and friends, as Jesus had modestly suggested, but ἐν Δεκαπόλει. In all of the ten cities. He had only one message - "See what Jesus did for me."Everyone was seized (inceptive imperfect) with wonder. We now proceed to Luke's account of the story in Lk.8:26-39. *Cf.* comment on Matthew's version in Mt.8:28-34.

Lk.8:26 - "And they arrived at the country of the Gadarenes, which is over against Galilee."

Καὶ κατέπλευσαν εἰς τὴν χώραν τῶν Γεργεσηνῶν ἥτις ἐστὶν ἀντιπέρα τῆς Γαλιλαίας.

Καὶ (continuative conjunction) 14.

#2226 κατέπλευσαν (3d.per.pl.aor.act.ind.of καταπλέω, culminative).

arrive - Lk.8:26.

Meaning: A combination of κατά (#98) and πλέω (#2209). Hence, to sail down from the sea to the land. Followed in Lk.8:26 by εἰς τὴν χώραν...κ.τ.λ. "Down from" because of the optical illusion from the shore that an incoming ship is coming *down* to the shore.

εἰς (preposition with the accusative of extent) 140.
τὴν (acc.sing.fem.of the article in agreement with χώραν) 9.
χώραν (acc.sing.fem.of χώρα, extent) 201.
τῶν (gen.pl.masc.of the article in agreement with Γεργεσηνῶν) 9.
Γεργεσηνῶν (gen.pl.masc.of Γερασηνῶν, definition) 2214.
ἥτις (relative pronoun, nom.sing.fem.of ὅστις, subject of ἐστὶν) 163.
ἐστὶν (3d.per.sing.pres.ind.of εἰμί, aoristic) 86.

#2227 ἀντιπέρα (improper preposition with the genitive/ablative).

over against - Lk.8:26.

Meaning: A combination of ἀντί (#237) and πέραν (#375). Hence, an improper preposition used adverbially. On the opposite side; on the other shore, or over against. Followed by the genitive in Lk.8:26.

(NOTE: "The case is open to dispute, since ἀντί comes with the genitive and πέραν with the ablative. 'Over against' would be genitive, 'on the other side of' would be ablative. Either will make sense in Lk.8:26. Probably genitive is the case here." (Robertson, *Grammar*, 639).

τῆς (gen.sing.fem.of the article in agreement with Γαλιλαίας) 9.
Γαλιλαίας (gen.sing.fem.of Γαλιλαίας, place description) 241.

Translation - "And they sailed down to the coast of the Gerasenes, which is opposite Galilee."

Comment: The storm at sea has stopped in obedience to our Lord's command and the story moves on. "They sailed *down* to the coast." The optical illusion, from the point of view of the shore line, makes it look like that. They landed on the southern coast of the Sea of Galilee near Gadara.

Verse 27 - "And when he went forth to land, there met him out of the city a certain man, which had devils long time, and wore no clothes, neither abode in any house, but in the tombs."

ἐξελθόντι δὲ αὐτῷ ἐπὶ τὴν γῆν ὑπήντησεν ἀνήρ τις ἐκ τῆς πόλεως ἔχων δαιμόνια, καὶ χρόνῳ ἱκανῷ οὐκ ἐνεδύσατο ἱμάτιον, καὶ ἐν οἰκίᾳ οὐκ ἔμενεν ἀλλ' ἐν τοῖς μνήμασιν.

ἐξελθόντι (2d.aor.part.instru.sing.masc.of ἐξέρχομαι, adverbial, temporal) 161.

δέ (continuative conjunction) 11.

αὐτῷ (dat.sing.masc.of αὐτός, personal interest) 16.

ἐπί (preposition with the accusative of extent) 47.

τήν (acc.sing.fem.of the article in agreement with γῆν) 9.

γῆν (acc.sing.fem.of γῆ, extent) 157.

ὑπήντησεν (3d.per.sing.aor.act.ind.of ὑπαντάω, constative) 762.

ἀνήρ (nom.sing.masc.of ἀνήρ, subject of ὑπήντησεν) 63.

τις (indefinite pronoun, nom.sing.masc.of τις, in agreement with ἀνήρ) 486.

ἐκ (preposition with the ablative of separation) 19.

τῆς (abl.sing.fem.of the article in agreement with πόλεως) 9.

πόλεως (abl.sing.fem.of πόλις, separation) 243.

ἔχων (pres.act.part.nom.sing.masc.of ἔχω, adverbial, circumstantial) 82.

δαιμόνια (acc.pl.neut.of δαιμόνιον, direct object of ἔχων) 686.

καί (explanatory conjunction) 14.

χρόνῳ (instru.sing.masc.of χρόνος, time) 168.

ἱκανῷ (instru.sing.masc.of ἱκανός, in agreement with χρόνῳ) 304.

οὐκ (negative conjunction with the indicative) 130.

ἐνεδύσατο (3d.per.sing.1st.aor.mid.ind.of ἐνδύω) 613.

ἱμάτιον (acc.sing.neut.of ἱμάτιον, direct object of ἐνεδύσατο) 534.

καί (adjunctive conjunction joining verbs) 14.

ἐν (preposition with the locative of place where) 80.

οἰκίᾳ (loc.sing.fem.of οἰκία, place where) 186.

ἔμενεν (3d.per.sing.imp.act.ind.of μένω, progressive duration) 864.

ἀλλ' (alternative conjunction) 342.

ἐν (preposition with the locative of place where) 80.

τοῖς (loc.pl.neut.of the article in agreement with μνήμασιν) 9.

μνήμασιν (loc.pl.neut.of μνῆμα, place where) 2876.

Translation - "And when He stepped out upon the shore a certain demon possessed man from the city met him. Now for a long time he had not worn clothing nor lived in a house, but among the tombs."

Comment: ἐξελθόντι δέ αὐτῷ is not a dative absolute contruction. There is no such thing. Absolute constructions are found in the nominative, genitive and accusative cases - not in the dative. If αὐτῷ were a part of an absolute construction there would be nothing to join to ὑπήντησεν. But αὐτῷ is joined to ὑπήντησεν, which takes a dative and ἐλθόντι is therefore an adverbial participle, temporal in character and instrumental in case to describe the time when the meeting occurred. Accusative of extent in ἐπί τήν γῆν. Note the ablative of separation in ἐκ τῆς πόλεως. There is a fine distinction between the locative of time point and the instrumental of time description, which we have in χρόνῳ ἱκανῷ. *Cf.* comment on Mt.8:28 and Mk.5:2.

Verse 28 - *"When he saw Jesus, he cried out and fell down before him, and with a loud voice said, What have I to do with thee, Jesus, thou Son of God most high? I beseech thee, torment me not."*

ἰδὼν δὲ τὸν Ἰησοῦν ἀνακράξας προσέπεσεν αὐτῷ καὶ φωνῇ μεγάλῃ εἶπεν, Τί ἐμοὶ καὶ σοί, Ἰησοῦ υἱὲ τοῦ θεοῦ τοῦ ὑψίστου; δέομαί σου, μή με βασανίσῃς.

ἰδὼν (aor.part.nom.sing.masc.of ὁράω, adverbial, temporal) 144.
δὲ (continuative conjunction) 11.
τὸν (acc.sing.masc.of the article in agreement with Ἰησοῦν) 9.
Ἰησοῦν (acc.sing.masc.of Ἰησοῦς, direct object of ἰδὼν) 3.
ἀνακράξας (aor.act.part.nom.sing.masc.of ἀνακράζω, adverbial, temporal) 2057.
προσέπεσεν (3d.per.sing.aor.act.ind.of προσπίπτω, constative) 699.
αὐτῷ (loc.sing.masc.of αὐτός, place where with verbs of rest, after πρός in composition) 16.
καὶ (continuative conjunction) 14.
φωνῇ (instru.sing.fem.of φωνή, means) 222.
μεγάλῃ (instru.sing.fem.of μέγας, in agreement with φωνῇ) 184.
εἶπεν (3d.per.sing.aor.act.ind.of εἶπον, constative) 155.
Τί (interrogative pronoun, nom.sing.neut.of τίς, nom.absolute) 281.
ἐμοὶ (dat.sing.masc.of ἐμός, personal interest) 1267.
καὶ (adjunctive conjunction joining pronouns) 14.
σοί (dat.sing.masc.of σύ, personal interest) 104.
Ἰησοῦ (voc.sing.masc.of Ἰησοῦς, address) 3.
υἱὲ (voc.sing.masc.of υἱός, apposition) 5.
τοῦ (gen.sing.masc.of the article in agreement with θεοῦ) 9.
θεοῦ (gen.sing.masc.of θεός, relationship) 124.
τοῦ (gen.sing.masc.of the article in agreement with ὑψίστου) 9.
ὑψίστου (gen.sing.masc.of ὕψιστος, apposition) 1353.
δέομαί (1st.per.sing.pres.act.ind.of δέομαι, aoristic) 841.
σου (abl.sing.masc.of σύ, with a verb of asking) 104.
μή (negative conjunction with the subjunctive in a prohibition) 87.
με (acc.sing.masc.of ἐγώ, direct object of βασανίσῃς) 123.
βασανίσῃς (2d.per.sing.aor.act.subj.of βασανίζω, prohibition) 719.

Translation - "And when he saw Jesus he cried out and fell down before Him and with a loud voice he said, 'What do you and I have in common, Jesus, Son of the Most High God? I beg you, do not torture me.'"

Comment: δὲ here can be taken either as continuative or adversative. The man had been living among the tombs, but (adversative δὲ) he now came forward to meet Jesus. Verse 28 goes back over the ground covered by Matthew and Mark and adds detail. The logical order is (1) he saw Jesus; (2) he went to meet Him; (3) he cried out with a loud voice; (4) he fell at Jesus' feet; (5) he made his request. Note the locative in αὐτῷ after πρός in composition in a verb of resting. σοῦ is ablative, after a verb of asking and hearing. (Robertson, *Grammar*, 519).

Verse 29 - *"For he had commanded the unclean spirit to come out of the man. For oftentimes it had caught him: and he was kept bound with chains and fetters; and he brake the bands, and was driven of the devil into the wilderness."*

παρήγγειλεν γὰρ τῷ πνεύματι τῷ ἀκαθάρτῳ ἐξελθεῖν ἀπὸ τοῦ ἀνθρώπου· πολλοῖς γὰρ χρόνους συνηρπάκει αὐτόν, καὶ ἐδεσμεύετο ἀλύσεσιν καὶ πέδαις φυλασσόμενος, καὶ διαρρήσσων τὰ δεσμὰ ἠλαύνετο ὑπὸ τοῦ δαιμονίου εἰς τὰ ἐρήμους.

παρήγγειλεν (3d.per.sing.imp.act.ind.of παραγγέλλω, progressive duration) 855.

γὰρ (causal conjunction) 105.

τῷ (dat.sing.neut.of the article in agreement with πνεύματι) 9.

πνεύματι (dat.sing.neut.of πνεῦμα, indirect object of παρήγγειλεν) 83.

τῷ (dat.sing.neut.of the article in agreement with ἀκαθάρτῳ) 9.

ἀκαθάρτῳ (dat.sing.neut.of ἀκάθαρτος, in agreement with πνεύματι) 843.

ἐξελθεῖν (aor.inf.of ἐξέρχομαι, complementary) 161.

ἀπὸ (preposition with the ablative of separation) 70.

τοῦ (abl.sing.masc.of the article in agreement with ἀνθρώπου) 9.

ἀνθρώπου (abl.sing.masc.of ἄνθρωπος, separation) 341.

πολλοῖς (instru.pl.masc.of πολύς, in agreement with χρόνοις) 228.

γὰρ (causal conjunction) 105.

χρόνοις (instru.pl.masc.of χρόνος, time description) 168.

#2228 συνηρπάκει (3d.per.sing.pluperf.act.ind.of συναρπάζω, intensive).

catch - Lk.8:29; Acts 6:12; 19:29; 27:15.

Meaning: A combination of σύν (#1542) and ἁρπάζω (#920). Hence, to seize upon; to seize and carry away by force. The resultant idea is clear from the context. With reference to Stephen - Acts 6:12; of Gaius and Aristarchus - Acts 19:29; of a ship caught up in a storm - Acts 27:15. Of demons seizing an insane man - Lk.8:29.

αὐτόν (acc.sing.masc.of αὐτός, direct object of συνηρπάκει) 16.

καὶ (continuative conjunction) 14.

ἐδεσμεύετο (3d.per.sing.imp.pass.ind.of δεσμεύω, progressive description) 1431.

ἀλύσεσιν (instru.pl.fem.of ἅλυσις, means) 2216.

καὶ (adjunctive conjunction joining nouns) 14.

πέδαις (inst.pl.fem.of πέδη, means) 2217.

φυλασσόμενος (pres.pass.part.nom.sing.masc.of φυλάσσω, adverbial, circumstantial) 1301.

καὶ (continuative conjunction) 14.

διαρήσσων (pres.act.part.nom.sing.masc.of διαρρήγνυμι, adverbial, temporal) 1605.

τὰ (acc.pl.neut.of the article in agreement with δεσμὰ) 9.

#2229 δεσμὰ (acc.pl.neut.of δεσμός, direct object of διαρήσσων).

band - Lk.8:29; Acts 16:26.
bond - Lk.13:16; Acts 20:23; 23:29; 26:29,31; Phil.1:7,13,14,16; Col.4:18; II Tim.2:9; Philemon 10,13; Heb.11:36.
chain - Jude 6.
string - Mk.7:35.

*Meaning: Cf.*δέω (#998). Therefore, that which binds. Associated in Lk.8:29 with ἅλυσις and πέδη. Of whatever impediment, anatomical or psychological, which tied the tongue of the dumb man in Mk.7:35; with the genitive of description - ἀπὸ τοῦ δεσμοῦ τούτου, where τούτου refers in the context to a spinal injury. With reference to the chains that bind the wicked angels - Jude 6. Elsewhere of prison manacles and fetters. In Philemon 13 with the genitive of description, in a metaphorical sense - τοῦ εὐαγγελίου.

#2230 ἠλαύνετο (3d.per.sing.imp.pass.ind.of ἐλαύνω, progressive description).

carry - II Pet.2:17.
drive - Lk.8:29; Jam.3:4.
row - Mk.6:48; John 6:19.

Meaning: To drive or propel. With reference to winds driving clouds, in a metaphorical sense - II Pet.2:17; ships - Jam.3:4; of men propelling a ship with oars and sails - Mk.6:48; John 6:19. Of a demon dominating an insane man - Lk.8:29.

ἀπὸ (preposition with the ablative of agent) 70.
τοῦ (abl.sing.neut.of the article in agreement witf δαιμονίου) 9.
δαιμονίου (abl.sing.neut.of δαιμόνιον, agent) 686.
εἰς (preposition with the accusative of extent) 140.
τὰ (acc.pl.fem.of the article in agreement with ἐρήμους) 9.
ἐρήμους (acc.pl.fem.of ἔρημος, extent) 250.

Translation - "Because He had been ordering the unclean spirit to come out of the man; for on many occasions it had caught him and he had been kept bound with chains and fetters, and when he ripped the bonds apart he was driven by the demon into the desert."

Comment: The man's plea "Don't begin to torture me" at the close of verse 28 is explained by the first clause of verse 29. This is the force of causal γὰρ. Jesus had been ordering the demon to leave the man. ἀπὸ τοῦ ἀνθρώπου is a simple ablative of separation. Jesus' command to rid the poor wretch of his tormentor is based upon the treatment he had received in the past, which is now described. πολλοῖς . . . χρόνοις does not mean "for a long time" - a concept which would be expressed by the accusative of time extent. This is an instrumental description. Hence our translation - "On many occasions" - in the past, as expressed by the pluperfect in συνηρπάκει. On these occasions when the evil spirit possessed the man, body, mind and soul, it was necessary for his friends to tie him up. He then, although kept (φυλασσόμενος) by virtue of having been bound (imperfect tense in ἐδεσμεύετο) with chains and fetters, was strong enough in the manic stages of his affliction to break τὰ δεσμὰ (a general term, including both ἅλυσις and πέδη) after which he was driven by his demon into the desert. The ablative of agent in ἀπὸ τοῦ δαιμονίου, though agency is generally expressed with ὑπό and the ablative. Indeed the Westcott/Hort text has ὑπό in the margin.

Note that the victim was always being acted upon. Jesus had to order the demon to leave the man since he had no power to rid himself of it. The demon caught him. Men kept him by binding him with manacles. His only action by his own strength was in breaking the bonds that held him, after which the demon took command again and drove him into the desert. Mark 5:4,5 and Luke 8:29, taken together, give a pitiable picture indeed of this poor man. For further comment *Cf.* the parallel passages in Matthew and Mark.

Verse 30 - "And Jesus asked him, saying, What is thy name? And he said, Legion: because many devils were entered into him."

ἐπηρώτησεν δὲ αὐτὸν ὁ Ἰησοῦς, Τί σοι ὄνομά ἐστιν; ὁ δὲ εἶπεν, Λεγιών, ὅτι εἰσῆλθεν δαιμόνια πολλὰ εἰς αὐτόν.

ἐπηρώτησεν (3d.per.sing.aor.act.ind.of ἐπερωτάω, ingressive) 973.
δὲ (continuative conjunction) 11.
αὐτὸν (acc.sing.masc.of αὐτός, direct object of ἐπηρώτησεν) 16.
ὁ (nom.sing.masc.of the article in agreement with Ἰησοῦς) 9.
Ἰησοῦς (nom.sing.masc.of Ἰησοῦς, subject of ἐπηρώτησεν) 9.
Τί (interrogative pronoun, nom.sing.neut. of τίς, in direct question, subject of ἐστιν) 281.
σοι (dat.sing.masc.of σύ, possession) 104.
ὄνομά (nom.sing.neut.of ὄνομα, predicate nominative) 108.
ἐστιν (3d.per.sing.pres.ind.of εἰμί, aoristic) 86.
ὁ (nom.sing.masc.of the article, subject of εἶπεν) 9.
δὲ (continuative conjunction) 11.
εἶπεν (3d.per.sing.aor.act.ind.of εἶπον, constative) 155.
Λεγιών (nom.sing.masc.of Λεγιών, appellation) 1597.
ὅτι (causal conjunction) 211.
εἰσῆλθεν (3d.per.sing.aor.ind.of εἰσέρχομαι, culminative) 161.
δαιμόνια (nom.pl.neut.of δαιμόνιον, subject of εἰσῆλθεν) 686.
πολλὰ (nom.pl.neut.of πολύς, in agreement with δαιμόνια) 228.
εἰς (preposition with the accusative of extent) 140.
αὐτόν (acc.sing.masc.of αὐτός, extent) 16.

Translation - "And Jesus began to ask him, 'What is your name?' And he said, 'Legion,' because many demons had entered into him."

Comment: *Cf.*Mark 5:9 for comment.

Verse 31 - "And they besought him that he would not command them to go into the deep."

καὶ παρεκάλουν αὐτὸν ἵνα μὴ ἐπιτάξῃ αὐτοῖς εἰς τὴν ἄβυσσον ἀπελθεῖν.

καὶ (continuative conjunction) 14.
παρεκάλουν (3d.per.pl.imp.act.ind.of παρακαλέω, inceptive) 230.
αὐτὸν (acc.sing.masc.of αὐτός, direct object of παρεκάλουν) 16.
ἵνα (final conjunction introducing a purpose clause) 114.
μὴ (negative conjunction with the subjunctive) 87.
ἐπιτάξῃ (3d.per.sing.aor.act.subj.of ἐπιτάσσω, purpose) 2061.
αὐτοῖς (dat.pl.masc.of αὐτός, personal disadvantage, after ἐπί in composition) 16.
εἰς (preposition with the accusative of extent) 140.
τὴν (acc.sing.fem.of the article in agreement with ἄβυσσον) 9.

#2231 ἄβυσσον (acc.sing.fem.of ἄβυσσος, extent)

bottomless pit - Rev.9:11; 11:7; 17:8; 20:1,3.
deep - Lk.8:31; Rom.10:7.
bottomless - Rev.9:1,2.

Meaning: A place of unsounded depth. The abode of the dead - Rev.10:7; in all other places in the New Testament of the abode of demons - Rev.9:1,2,11; 11:7; 17:8; 20:1,3; Lk.8:31.

ἀπελθεῖν (aor.inf.of ἀπέρχομαι, complementary) 239.

Translation - "And they began to beg Him that He not order them to go away into the abyss."

Comment: The demons were frantic. Note the dative in αὐτοῖς after ἐπί in composition. It denotes personal disadvantage. *Cf.*#47 for other examples. Matthew adds πρὸ καιροῦ (Mt.8:29) - "before the time." The demons were only asking that their inevitable judgment not be visited upon them in advance. The implication seems clear that they recognized in Jesus their Sovereign, who would eventually judge them. They called Him υἱὲ τοῦ θεοῦ ὑψίστου (Mk.5:7). The god of this world (II Cor.4:4) who is also the dictator of the demons as well as commander over the unregenerate has not chosen to hide the fact of inevitable judgment from the demons. He does, however, blind the minds of the unsaved to this obvious fact, even though it is plainly revealed in scripture. There is no reason why the demons should not know in advance that their ultimate destiny is in hell.

Verse 32 - "And there was there an herd of many swine feeding on the mountain: and they besought him that he would suffer them to enter into them. And he suffered them."

Ἦν δὲ ἐκεῖ ἀγέλη χοίρων ἱκανῶν βοσκομένη ἐν τῷ ὄρει, καὶ παρεκάλεσαν αὐτὸν ἵνα ἐπιτρέψῃ αὐτοῖς εἰς ἐκείνους εἰσελθεῖν, καὶ ἐπέτρεψεν αὐτοῖς.

Ἦν (3d.per.sing.imp.ind.of εἰμί imperfect periphrastic) 86.
δὲ (explanatory conjunction) 11.
ἐκεῖ (adverb of place) 204.
ἀγέλη (nom.sing.fem.of ἀγέλη, subject of ἦν) 769.
χοίρων (gen.pl.masc.of χοῖρος, definition) 653.
ἱκανῶν (gen.pl.masc.of ἱκανός, in agreement with χοίρων) 304.
βοσκομένη (pres.pass.part.nom.sing.fem.of βόσκω, imperfect periphrastic) 770.
ἐν (preposition with the locative of place) 80.
τῷ (loc.sing.neut.of the article in agreement with ὄρει) 9.
ὄρει (loc.sing.neut.of ὄρος, place where) 357.
καὶ (continuative conjunction) 14.
παρεκάλεσαν (3d.per.pl.1st.aor.act.ind.of παρακαλέω, ingressive) 230.
αὐτὸν (acc.sing.masc.of αὐτός, direct object of παρεκάλεσαν) 16.
ἵνα (final conjunction introducing a purpose clause) 114.
ἐπιτρέφῃ (3d.per.sing.aor.act.subj.of ἐπιτρέπω, purpose) 747.
αὐτοῖς (dat.pl.masc.of αὐτός, personal advantage) 16.
εἰς (preposition with the accusative of extent) 140.
ἐκείνους (acc.pl.masc.of ἐκεῖνος, extent) 246.
εἰσελθεῖν (aor.inf.of εἰσέρχομαι, complementary) 234.
καὶ (continuative conjunction) 14.
ἐπέτρεφεν (3d.per.sing.aor.act.ind.of ἐπιτρέπω, constative) 747.
αὐτοῖς (dat.pl.masc.of αὐτός, personal advantage) 16.

Translation - *"Now there was a herd of many swine feeding on the mountain; and they began to beg Him that He would permit them to enter into them. And He gave them permission."*

Comment: The participle in the imperfect periphrastic βοσκομένη can be either middle or passive voice. The sense is the same. They were either feeding themselves or being fed. Note that the demons were more concerned about escaping the abyss (verse 31) than they were about their request to enter the swine. The antecedents must be kept straight. "They asked Him (Jesus) that He would permit them (the demons) to enter them (the swine). And He permitted them (the demons)." The rule is that a pronoun agrees with its antecedent in gender and number, but not necessarily in case, since it derives its case from its use in its own clause.

Verse 33 - *"Then went the devils out of the man, and entered into the swine: and the herd ran violently down a steep place into the lake, and were choked."*

ἐξελθόντα δὲ τὰ δαιμόνια ἀπὸ τοῦ ἀνθρώπου εἰσῆλθον εἰς τοὺς χοίρους, καὶ ὥρμησεν ἡ ἀγέλη κατὰ τοῦ κρημνοῦ εἰς τὴν λίμνην καὶ ἀπεπνίγη.

ἐξελθόντα (aor.part.nom.pl.neut.of ἐξέρχομαι, constative) 161.
δὲ (continuative conjunction) 11.
τὰ (nom.pl.neut.of the article in agreement with δαιμόνια) 9.
δαιμόνια (nom.pl.nuet.of δαιμόνιον, subject of εἰσῆλθον) 686.

ἀπό (preposition with the ablative of separation) 70.
τοῦ (abl.sing.masc.of the article in agreement with ἀνθρώπου) 9.
ἀνθρώπου (abl.sing.masc.of ἄνθρωπος, separation) 341.
εἰσῆλθον (3d.per.pl.aor.ind.of εἰσέρχομαι, constative) 234.
εἰς (preposition with the accusative of extent) 140.
τοὺς (acc.pl.masc.of the article in agreement with χοίρους) 9.
χοίρους (acc.pl.masc.of χοῖρος, extent) 653.
καὶ (continuative conjunction) 14.
ὥρμησεν (3d.per.sing.aor.act.ind.of ὁρμάω, constative) 772.
ἡ (nom.sing.fem.of the article in agreement with ἀγέλη) 9.
κατά (preposition with the genitive of description - "down upon" - perpendicular) 98.
τοῦ (gen.sing.masc.of the article in agreement with κρημνοῦ) 9.
κρημνοῦ (gen.sing.masc.of κρημνός, genitive of description) 773.
εἰς (preposition with the accusative of extent) 140.
τὴν (acc.sing.fem.of the article in agreement with λίμνην) 9.
λίμνην (acc.sing.fem.of λίμνη, extent) 2041.
καὶ (continuative conjunction) 14.
ἀπεπνίγη (3d.per.sing.2d.aor.pass.ind.of ἀποπνίγω, constative) 1034.

Translation - "And when the demons had gone out of the man they entered into the swine, and the herd rushed down the slope into the lake, and was drowned."

Comment: These prepositional phrases are interesting grammar. The student should remember that the case is determined by function, not by case endings or prepositional adjuncts, though the endings here are all regular - "out of the man" - "into the swine" - down the slope" - "into the lake." Cf.Mk.5:13; Mt.8:32.

Verse 34 - "When they that fed them saw what was done, they fled, and went and told it in the city and in the country."

ἰδόντες δὲ οἱ βόσκοντες τὸ γεγονὸς ἔφυγον καὶ ἀπήγγειλαν εἰς τὴν πόλιν καὶ εἰς τοὺς ἀγρούς.

ἰδόντες (aor.act.part.nom.pl.masc.of ὁράω, adverbial, temporal) 144.
δὲ (continuative conjunction) 11.
οἱ (nom.pl.masc.of the article in agreement with βόσκοντες) 9.
βόσκοντες (pres.act.part.nom.pl.masc.of βόσκω, substantival, subject of ἔφυγον and ἀπήγγειλαν) 770.
τὸ (acc.sing.neut.of the article in agreement with γεγονὸς) 9.
γεγονὸς (2d.perf.part.acc.sing.neut.of γίνομαι, consummative, substantival, direct object of ἰδόντες) 113.
ἔφυγον (3d.per.pl.2d.aor.act.ind.of φεύγω, constative) 202.
καὶ (adjunctive conjunction joining verbs) 14.
ἀπήγγειλαν (3d.per.pl.aor.act.ind.of ἀπαγγέλλω, ingressive) 176.
εἰς (preposition with the accusative, static use, like a locative) 140.
τὴν (acc.sing.fem.of the article in agreement with πόλιν) 9.

πόλιν (acc.sing.fem.of πόλις, static use, like a locative) 243.
καὶ (adjunctive conjunction joining prepositional phrases) 14.
τοὺς (acc.pl.masc.of the article in agreement with ἀγρούς) 9.
ἀγρούς (acc.pl.masc.of ἀγρός, static use, like a locative) 626.

Translation - *"And when they saw what happened the herdsmen fled and
reported it in the city and in the surrounding countryside."*

Comment: The two εἰς phrases at the end of the verse are examples of the
original static use of εἰς in the same way that later Greek used ἐν with the
locative. For further comment *Cf.*Mk.5:14 and Mt.8:33.

Verse 35 - *"Then they went out to see what was done; and came to Jesus, and
found the man, out of whom the devils were departed, sitting at the feet of Jesus,
clothed, and in his right mind: and they were afraid."*

ἐξῆλθον δὲ ἰδεῖν τό γεγονὸς καὶ ἦλθον πρὸς τὸν Ἰησοῦν, καὶ εὗρον
καθήμενον τὸν ἄνθρωπον ἀφ' οὗ τὰ δαιμόνια ἐξῆλθεν ἱματισμένον καὶ
σωφρονοῦντα παρὰ τοὺς πόδας τοῦ Ἰησοῦ, καὶ ἐφοβήθησαν.

ἐξῆλθον (3d.per.pl.aor.ind.of ἐξέρχομαι, constative) 161.
δὲ (continuative conjunction) 11.
ἰδεῖν (aor.act.inf.of ὁράω, purpose) 144.
τό (acc.sing.neut.of the article in agreement with γεγονὸς) 9.
γεγονὸς (2d.perf.part.acc.sing.neut.of γίνομαι, consummative, substantival,
direct object of ἰδεῖν) 113.
καὶ (continuative conjunction) 14.
ἦλθον (3d.per.pl.aor.ind.of ἔρχομαι, constative) 146.
πρὸς (preposition with the accusative of extent) 197.
τὸν (acc.sing.masc.of the article in agreement with Ἰησοῦν) 9.
Ἰησοῦν (acc.sing.masc.of Ἰησοῦς, extent) 3.
εὗρον (3d.per.pl.2d.aor.act.ind.of εὑρίσκω, constative) 79.
καθήμενον (pres.part.acc.sing.masc.of κάθημαι, adverbial, circumstantial)
377.
τὸν (acc.sing.masc.of the article in agreement with ἄνθρωπον) 9.
ἄνθρωπον (acc.sing.masc.of ἄνθρωπος, direct object of εὗρον) 341.
ἀφ' (preposition with the ablative of separation) 70.
οὗ (abl.sing.masc.of ὅς, separation) 65.
τὰ (nom.pl.neut.of the article in agreement with δαιμόνια) 9.
δαιμόνια (nom.pl.neut.of δαιμόνιον, subject of ἐξῆλθεν) 686.
ἐξῆλθεν (3d.per.sing.aor.act.ind.of ἐξέρχομαι, culminative) 161.
ἱματισμένον (perf.pass.part.acc.sing.masc.of ἱματίζω, adverbial, circumstantial) 2223.
καὶ (adjunctive conjunction joining participles) 14.
σωφρονοῦντα (pres.part.acc.sing.masc.of σωφρονέω, adverbial, circumstantial) 2224.
παρὰ (preposition with the accusative, "alongside of" with verbs of rest) 154.
τοὺς (acc.pl.masc.of the article in agreement with πόδας) 9.

πόδας (acc.pl.masc.of πούς, with a verb of rest) 353.
τοῦ (gen.sing.masc.of the article in agreement with Ἰησοῦ) 9.
Ἰησοῦ (gen.sing.masc.of Ἰησοῦς, possession) 3.
καὶ (continuative conjunction) 14.
ἐφοβήθησαν (3d.per.pl.aor.pass.ind.of φοβέομαι, ingressive) 101.

Translation - "And they went out to see what had happened and they came to Jesus and found sitting at the feet of Jesus the man out of whom the demons had come, clothed and in his right mind. And they were seized with fear."

Comment: Note that the circumstantial participle καθήμενον is out of position for emphasis. What they least expected to find is what they found. The man, previously insanely belligerent, now sits at Jesus' feet. He is also fully clothed and totally rational. It is no great wonder that they were seized with fear (ingressive aorist in ἐφοβήθησαν). *Cf.*Mk.5:14,15 for further comment.

Verse 36 - "They also which saw it told them by what means he that was possessed of the devils was healed."

ἀπήγγειλαν δὲ αὐτοῖς οἱ ἰδόντες πῶς ἐσώθη ὁ δαιμονισθείς.

ἀπήγγειλαν (3d.per.pl.aor.act.ind.of ἀπαγγέλλω, ingressive) 176.
δὲ (continuative conjunction) 11.
αὐτοῖς (dat.pl.masc.of αὐτός, indirect object of ἀπήγγειλαν) 16.
οἱ (nom.pl.masc.of the article in agreement with ἰδόντες) 9.
ἰδόντες (aor.act.part.nom.pl.masc.of ὁράω, substantival, subject of ἀπήγγειλαν) 144.
πῶς (adverb in indirect discourse, followed by the indicative) 627.
ἐσώθη (3d.per.sing.aor.pass.ind.of σώζω, indirect discourse) 109.
ὁ (nom.sing.masc.of the article in agreement with δαιμονισθείς) 9.
δαιμονισθείς (aor. pass.part.nom.sing.masc.of δαιμονίζομαι, substantival, subject of ἐσώθη) 415.

Translation - "And those who had seen it told them how the demon possessed man was saved."

Comment: Mark adds καὶ περὶ τῶν χοίρων, upon which passage see comment - Mk.5:16.

Verse 37 - "Then the whole multitude of the country of the Gadarenes round about besought him to depart from them, for they were taken with great fear: and he went up into the ship and returned back again."

καὶ ἠρώτησεν αὐτὸν ἅπαν τὸ πλῆθος τῆς περιχώρου τῶν Γερεσηνῶν ἀπελθεῖν ἀπ' αὐτῶν, ὅτι φόβῳ μεγάλῳ συνείχοντο, αὐτὸς δὲ ἐμβὰς εἰς πλοῖον ὑπέστρεφεν.

καὶ (continuative conjunction) 14.

ἠρώτησεν (3d.per.sing.aor.act.ind.of ἐρωτάω, ingressive) 1172.

αὐτόν (acc.sing.masc.of αὐτός, direct object of ἠρώτησεν) 16.

ἅπαν (nom.sing.neut.of ἅπας, in agreement with πλῆθος) 639.

τό (nom.sing.neut.of the article in agreement with πλῆθος) 9.

πλῆθος (nom.sing.neut.of πλῆθος, subject of ἠρώτησεν) 1792.

τῆς (gen.sing.fem.of the article in agreement with περιχώρου) 9.

περιχώρου (gen.sing.fem.of περίχωρος, description) 271.

τῶν (gen.pl.masc.of the article in agreement with Γεργεσηνῶν) 9.

Γεργεσηνῶν (gen.pl.masc.of Γερασηνός, definition) 2214.

ἀπελθεῖν (aor.act.inf.of ἀπέρχομαι, complementary) 239.

ἀπ' (preposition with the ablative of separation) 70.

αὐτῶν (abl.pl.masc.of αὐτός, separation) 16.

ὅτι (causal conjunction) 211.

φόβῳ (instru.sing.masc.of φόβος, means) 1131.

μεγάλῳ (instru.sing.masc.of μέγας, in agreement with φόβῳ) 184.

συνείχοντο (3d.per.pl.imp.pass.ind.of συνέχω, inceptive) 414.

αὐτός (nom.sing.masc.of αὐτός, subject of ὑπέστρεφεν) 16.

δὲ (continuative conjunction) 11.

ἐμβὰς (2d.aor.act.part.nom.sing.masc.of ἐμβαίνω, adverbial, temporal) 750.

εἰς (preposition with the accusative of extent) 140.

πλοῖον (acc.sing.neut.of πλοῖον, extent) 400.

ὑπέστρεφεν (3d.per.sing.aor.act.ind.of ὑποστρέφω, constative) 1838.

Translation - "*And the entire populace of the Gadarene country round about began to beg Him to depart from them, because they had been seized with great consternation. And He stepped into a boat and returned.*"

Comment: φόβῳ μεγάλῃ συνείχοντο. Here is an example of means expressed by the instrumental case without a preposition joined to the substantive φόβῳ. In such a case the verb is always in the middle or passive voice. Luke makes a more complete statement of this part of the story than do either Matthew or Mark (*Cf.* Mt.8:34; Mk.5:17). Luke stresses the unanimity of opinion in the community that Jesus should leave. We have discussed why elsewhere. ἅπαν... Γερασηνῶν is a strong statement. He also refers again to their fear (Lk.8:35; Mk.5:15) as a reason for their desire to be rid of Jesus. *Cf.*#1131 for other instances of φόβος as fear caused by the supernatural power of God.

Jesus left Gadara, so far as is known, never to return again. "Within forty years this district was the scene of one of the terrible calamities of the great Roman war. The sack of Gadara, and the desolation and ruin which was the hapless lot of this once wealthy but evil-living district, is one of the melancholy chapters of the hopeless Jewish revolt. (*Cf.* Josephus, '*Bell. Jud.*' III, 7,1; IV, 7,4). A modern traveller, Dr. Thomson, remarks, singularly enough, that the old district of Gadara at the present day is infested with wild, fierce hogs: 'Everywhere,' he writes, 'the land is ploughed up by wild hogs in search of roots on which they live.' " (*The Land and the Book,* II, Chap.25).

Verse 38 - "Now the man out of whom the devils were departed besought him that he might be with him; but Jesus sent him away, saying, . . . "

ἐδεῖτο δὲ αὐτοῦ ὁ ἀνὴρ ἀφ' οὗ ἐξεληλύθει τὰ δαιμόνια εἶναι σὺν αὐτῷ, ἀπέλυσεν δὲ αὐτὸν λέγων,

ἐδεῖτο (3d.per.sing.imp.act.ind.of δέομαι, inceptive) 841.
δὲ (explanatory conjunction) 11.
αὐτοῦ (gen.sing.masc.of αὐτός) 16
ὁ (nom.sing.masc.of the article in agreement with ἀνήρ) 9.
ἀνὴρ (nom.sing.masc.of ἀνήρ, subject of ἐδεῖτο) 63.
ἀφ' (preposition with the ablative of separation) 70.
οὗ (abl.sing.masc.of ὅς, separation) 65.
ἐξεληλύθει (3d.per.sing.pluperf.act.ind.of ἐξέρχομαι, consummative) 161.
τὰ (nom.pl.neut.of the article in agreement with δαιμόνια) 9.
δαιμόνια (nom.pl.neut.of δαιμόνιον, subject of ἐξεληλύθει) 686.
εἶναι (pres.inf.of εἰμί, purpose) 86.
σὺν (preposition with the instrumental of association) 1542.
αὐτοῦ (abl.sing.masc.of αὐτός, source, with a verb of asking) 16.
ἀπέλυσεν (3d.per.sing.aor.act.ind.of ἀπολύω, constative) 92.
δὲ (adversative conjunction) 11.
αὐτὸν (acc.sing.masc.of αὐτός, direct object of ἀπέλυσεν) 16.
λέγων (pres.act.part.nom.sing.masc.of λέγω, adverbial, modal) 66.

Translation - "Now the man out of whom the demons had come began to beg Him that he might come with Him. But He sent him away, saying . . . "

Comment: Note the imperfect tense in ἐδεῖτο, indicating the intense desire of the man to accompany Jesus. Mark conveys the same idea with παρεκάλει. Another interesting variation between Mark and Luke is Mark's ἵνα clause of purpose with the subjunctive as opposed to Luke's infinitive of purpose with εἶναι completing ἐδεῖτο. Both are good Greek and each conveys the idea. For further comment *Cf.* Mk.5:18.

Verse 39 - "Return to thine own house and show how great things God hath done unto thee. And he went his way, and published throughout the whole city how great things Jesus had done unto him."

Ὑπόστρεφε εἰς τὸν οἶκόν σου, καὶ διηγοῦ ὅσα σοι ἐποίησεν ὁ θεός. καὶ ἀπῆλθεν καθ' ὅλην τὴν πόλιν κηρύσσων ὅσα ἐποίησεν αὐτῷ ὁ Ἰησοῦς.

Ὑπόστρεφε (2d.per.sing.pres.act.impv.of ὑποστρέφω, command) 1838.
εἰς (preposition with the accusative of extent) 140.
τὸν (acc.sing.masc.of the article in agreement with οἶκόν) 9.
οἶκόν (acc.sing.masc.of οἶκος, extent) 784.
σου (gen.sing.masc.of σύ, possession) 104.
καὶ (continuative conjunction) 14.

διηγοῦ (2d.per.sing.pres.act.impv.of διηγέομαι, command) 2225.

ὅσα (acc.pl.neut.of ὅς, relative pronoun, introducing a demonstrative clause) 65.

σοι (dat.sing.masc.of σύ, personal advantage) 104.

ἐποίησεν (3d.per.sing.aor.act.ind.of ποιέω, culminative) 127.

ὁ (nom.sing.masc.of the article in agreement with θεός) 9.

θεός (nom.sing.masc.of θεός, subject of ἐποίησεν) 124.

καὶ (inferential conjunction) 14.

ἀπῆλθεν (3d.per.sing.aor.ind.of ἀπέρχομαι, constative) 239.

καθ' (preposition with the accusative, standard rule of measure) 98.

ὅλην (acc.sing.fem.of ὅλος, in agreement with πόλιν) 112.

τὴν (acc.sing.fem.of the article in agreement with πόλιν) 9.

πόλιν (acc.sing.fem.of πόλις, standard rule of measure) 243.

κηρύσσων (pres.act.part.nom.sing.masc.of κηρύσσω, adverbial, complementary) 249.

ὅσα (acc.pl.neut.of ὅς, direct object of κηρύσσων) 65.

ἐποίησεν (3d.per.sing.aor.act.ind.of ποιέω, culminative) 127.

αὐτῷ (dat.sing.masc.of αὐτός, personal advantage) 16.

ὁ (nom.sing.masc.of the article in agreement with Ἰησοῦς) 9.

Ἰησοῦς (nom.sing.masc.of Ἰησοῦς, subject of ἐποίησεν) 3.

Translation - "Go back to your house and give a complete account of those things which God has done for you. Therefore he went throughout the entire city telling the things which Jesus had done for him."

Comment: *Cf.*#2225 for the exact meaning. ὅσα in each case is used like a demonstrative pronoun. Ordinarily the demonstratives (οὗτος, ἐκεῖνος) would be used, or the article in its demonstrative sense. Occasionally the relative is used as here, though usually with μέν and δέ which are absent here. καθ' with the accusative indicates the standard rule of measure. Wherever the boundaries of the city extended, the man went preaching. The participle κηρύσσων complements the verb ἀπῆλθεν. Note that Jesus told him to report on what *God* had done for him, but Luke reports that he went telling what *Jesus* had done for him. Thus the man, now thoroughly sane, and forever free from hellish influences identifies Jesus with God. In fact even Legion had called Jesus υἱὲ τοῦ θεοῦ ὑψίστου - "son of God most high." The demons, destined for hell know more theology than some preachers.

Luke says καθ' ὅλην τὴν πόλιν. Mark says ἐν τῇ Δεκαπόλει. Luke thus thinks of the ten cities as a single metropolitan area. Mark also speaks of it in the singular.

It had been quite a day. Jesus had taught the parables of the kingdom (Mk.4:1-34). "On the same day at even" (Mk.4:35) He made the trip across the Lake to Decapolis and quieted the storm enroute (Mk.4:35-41). Upon arrival He healed the demoniac by driving out Legion (Mk.5:1-20). Now He returns to the Galilee (west) side of the Lake, where He meets Jairus (Mk.5:21-43). Is all of this on the same day? It was evening when He started to Decapolis. How long did it take to cross? To enact the Legion episode? To return? Mark gives us no further chronological hint. Nor does Luke.

In any case, wherever Jesus went supernatural teachings and events took place!

The Raising of the Daughter of Jairus and the Healing
of the Woman with an Issue of Blood

(Mk.5:21-43; Mt.9:18-26; Lk.8:40-56)

Mark 5:21 - "And when Jesus was passed over again by ship unto the other side, much people gathered unto him: and he was nigh unto the sea."

Καὶ διαπεράσαντος τοῦ Ἰησοῦ πάλιν εἰς τὸ πέραν συνήχθη ὄχλος πολὺς ἐπ' αὐτόν, καὶ ἦν παρὰ τὴν θάλασσαν.

Καὶ (continuative conjunction) 14.

διαπεράσαντος (aor.act.part.gen.sing.masc.of διαπεράω, genitive absolute) 777.

τοῦ (gen.sing.masc.of the article in agreement with Ἰησοῦ) 9.

Ἰησοῦ (gen.sing.masc.of Ἰησοῦς, genitive absolute) 3.

πάλιν (adverbial) 355.

εἰς (preposition with the accusative of extent) 140.

τὸ (acc.sing.neut.of the article, extent) 9.

πέραν (adverbial) 1016.

συνήχθη (3d.per.sing.1st.aor.pass.ind.of συνάγω, constative) 150.

ὄχλος (nom.sing.masc.of ὄχλος, subject of συνήχθη) 418.

πολὺς (nom.sing.masc.of πολύς, in agreement with ὄχλος) 228.

ἐπ' (preposition with the accusative of extent) 47.

αὐτόν (acc.sing.masc.of αὐτός, extent) 16.

καὶ (ascensive conjunction) 14.

ἦν (3d.per.sing.imp.ind.of εἰμί, progressive description) 86.

παρὰ (preposition with the accusative "alongside" - place description) 154.

τὴν (acc.sing.fem.of the article in agreement with θάλασσαν) 9.

θάλασσαν (acc.sing.fem.of θάλασσα, place description) 374.

Translation - "And when Jesus had passed over again to the other side, a great crowd gathered about Him, even when He was at the water's edge."

Comment: "The parallel in Luke (ἐν δὲ τῷ ὑποστρέφειν τὸν Ἰησοῦν ἀπεδέξατο αὐτὸν ὁ ὄχλος, Lk.8:40) presupposes the Markan reading πάλιν εἰς τὸ πέραν. The reading of Sinaiticus D 565 700 *al*, which places πάλιν next to συνήχθη ὄχλος πολύς ("again a great crowd gathered"), looks back to 4.1. Both the omission of πάλιν by Θ *al* and the omission of εἰς τὸ πέραν by p 45vid *al* seem to be the result of palaeographical confusion." (Metzger, *A Textual Commentary on the Greek New Testament*, 85).

We have taken the καὶ in the last clause as ascensive. The crowd was so eager to see and hear Jesus that they crowded about Him *even* as He stepped out of the boat and stood at the water's edge. This followed, in point of time, His passage back to Galilee, as is clear from the aorist tense in διαπεράσαντος. The crowd was so great that He was unable to make His way from the shoreline. The Galilee revival was in full swing as a result of His healing and other miracles. Many of the people were "fair weather friends" of Jesus who would forsake Him when His theology became too severe for them (John 6:60-66). For further comment *Cf.* Lk.8:40.

Verse 22 - "And, behold, there cometh one of the rulers of the synagogue, Jairus, by name; and when he saw him, he fell at his feet."

καὶ ἔρχεται εἰς τῶν ἀρχισυναγώγων, ὀνόματι Ἰάϊρος, καὶ ἰδὼν αὐτὸν πίπτει πρὸς τοὺς πόδας αὐτοῦ

καὶ (continuative conjunction) 14.

ἔρχεται (3d.per.sing.pres.ind.of ἔρχομαι, historical) 146.

εἰς (nom.sing.masc.of εἷς, subject of ἔρχεται) 469.

τῶν (gen.pl.masc.of the article in agreement with ἀρχισυναγώγων) 9.

#2232 ἀρχισυναγώγων (gen.pl.masc.of ἀρχισυνάγωγος, partitive genitive).

chief ruler of the synagogue - Mk.5:22,35,36,38; Lk.8:49; 13:14; Acts 13:15; 18:8,17.

Meaning: A combination of ἀρχή (#1285) and συναγωγή (#404). The chief administrative official of the local synagogue. With reference to Jairus, whose daughter Jesus raised from the dead - Mk.5:22,35,36,38; Lk.8:49. The synagogue rulers in Antioch of Pisidia - Acts 13:15; Crispus - Acts 18:8; Sosthenes - Acts 18:17. Plural in Acts 13:15, thus indicating that more than one could share the honor in the same synagogue. *Cf.* Lk.13:14.

ὀνόματι (dat.sing.neut.of ὄνομα, possession) 108.

#2233 Ἰάϊρος (nom.sing.masc.of Ἰάϊρος, appellation).

Jairus - Mk.5:22; Lk.8:49.

Meaning: The word means "whom Jehovah enlightens." The ruler of the synagogue in Capernaum, whose daughter Jesus raised from the dead - Mk.5:22; Lk.8:49.

καὶ (continuative conjunction) 14.

ἰδὼν (aor.act.part.nom.sing.masc.of ὁράω, adverbial, temporal) 144.

αὐτὸν (acc.sing.masc.of αὐτός, direct object of ἰδὼν) 16.

πίπτει (3d.per.sing.pres.act.ind.of πίπτω, historical) 187.

πρὸς (preposition with the accusative of extent, "near to") 197.

τοὺς (acc.pl.masc.of the article in agreement with πόδας) 9.

πόδας (acc.pl.masc.of πούς, near to, extent) 353.

αὐτοῦ (gen.sing.masc.of αὐτός, possession) 16.

Translation - "And one of the rulers of the synagogue named Jairus approached and when he saw Him he fell at His feet . . . "

Comment: Mark uses the historical present in ἔρχεται and πίπτει. Jairus came down to the beach with the rest of the great crowd. When he saw Jesus he fell at His feet. The prostrate form of this Jewish religious leader tends to indicate that at this point Jesus was highly respected in Capernaum. *Cf.* Lk.8:41 for further comment.

Verse 23 - "And besought him greatly, saying, My little daughter lieth at the point of death: I pray thee, come and lay thy hands on her, that she may be healed; and she shall live."

καὶ παρακαλεῖ αὐτὸν πολλὰ λέγων ὅτι Τὸ θυγάτριόν μου ἐσχάτως ἔχει, ἵνα ἐλθὼν ἐπιθῇς τὰς χεῖρας αὐτῇ ἵνα σωθῇ καὶ ζήσῃ.

καὶ (continuative conjunction) 14.
παρακαλεῖ (3d.per.sing.pres.act.ind.of παρακαλέω, historical) 230.
αὐτὸν (acc.sing.masc.of αὐτός, direct object of παρακαλεῖ) 16.
πολλὰ (acc.pl.neut.of πολύς, adverbial) 228.
λέγων (pres.act.part.nom.sing.masc.of λέγω, adverbial, modal) 66.
ὅτι (recitative) 211.
Τὸ (nom.sing.neut.of the article in agreement with θυγάτριόν) 9.

#2234 θυγάτριόν (nom.sing.neut.of θυγάτριον, subject of ἔχει).

little daughter - Mk.5:23.
young daughter - Mk.7:25.

Meaning: The diminutive of θυγάτηρ (#817). Little daughter. Jairus' daughter - Mk.5:23; the child of the Syrophenician woman - Mk.7:25.

μου (gen.sing.masc.of ἐγώ, relationship) 123.

#2235 ἐσχάτως (adverb, used here in the idiom ἐσχάτως ἔχει).

lie at the point of death - Mk.5:23.

Meaning: The adverb related to ἔσχατος (#496). Here only in the New Testament. In the context the idiom ἐσχάτως ἔχει means "she is at the point of death." Literally, "she has it in the final stages."

ἔχει (3d.per.sing.pres.act.ind.of ἔχω, progressive description) 82.
ἵνα (final conjunction introducing a purpose clause) 114.
ἐλθὼν (aor.part.nom.sing.masc.of ἔρχομαι, adverbial, temporal) 146.
ἐπιθῇς (2d.per.sing.2d.aor.act.subj.of ἐπιτίθημι, purpose) 818.
τὰς (acc.pl.fem.of the article in agreement with χεῖρας) 9.

χεῖρας (acc.pl.fem.of χείρ, direct object of ἐπιθῆς) 308.
αὐτῇ (loc.sing.fem.of αὐτός, place where) 16.
ἵνα (sub-final conjunction introducing a purpose/result clause) 114.
σωθῇ (3d.per.sing.1st.aor.pass.subj.of σώζω, purpose/result) 109.
καὶ (continuative conjunction) 14.
ζήσῃ (3d.per.sing.1st.aor.act.subj.of ζάω, purpose/result) 340.

Translation - "And he pleaded with Him earnestly, saying, 'My little daughter has a terminal illness - that you come and lay your hands upon her in order that she may be saved and live."

Comment: The garbled Greek indicates the almost incoherent utterances of a distraught father. αὐτὸν πολλὰ is an interesting double accusative, the objects of παρακαλεῖ - one personal and the other impersonal. ἐσχάτως ἔχει. Jairus tries to use an adverb as the object of ἔχει. He omits the main verb to introduce his two ἵνα clauses of purpose and result. But his meaning is very clear. He apparently had great faith in Jesus' power to heal, although he lacked the degree of faith of the Roman Centurion who suggested that Jesus needed only to speak and it would be done (Mt.8:5-10). But at least Jairus recognized Jesus' deity and His power to save and heal. Robertson calls the asyndeton ἵνα ἐλθὼν ἐπιθῆς an elliptical imperative and cites in addition to Mk.5:23, Mt.20:32; I Cor.7:29; II Cor.8:7; Eph.4:29; 5:33. We have another asyndeton without ἵνα is Mk.10:36 where we have Τί θέλετε (με) ποιήσω ὑμῖν. (Robertson, *Grammar*, 994).

The κοινή ". . . has some idiomatic constructions with the adverb that are difficult from the English point of view. Thus τοὺς κακῶς ἔχοντας (Mt.14:35), and with the instrumental case in Mk.1:34. *Cf.*Lk.7:2. In English we prefer the predicate adjective with have (He has it bad), whereas the Greek likes the adverb with ἔχω. So ἐσχάτως ἔχει (Mk.5:23) and in John 4:52 κομφότερον ἔσχεν the comparative adverb. One must be willing for the Greek to have his standpoint." (Robertson, *Ibid.*, 546).

However fractured Mark's record of Jairus' Greek may be, the synagogue official was granted Jesus' full cooperation as we see in

Verse 24 - "And Jesus went with him; and much people followed him, and thronged him."

καὶ ἀπῆλθεν μετ᾽ αὐτοῦ. Καὶ ἠκολούθει αὐτῷ ὄχλος πολύς, καὶ συνέθλιβον αὐτόν.

καὶ (continuative conjunction) 14.
ἀπῆλθεν (3d.per.sing.aor.ind.of ἀπέρχομαι, ingressive) 239.
μετ᾽ (preposition with the genitive of accompaniment) 50.
αὐτοῦ (gen.sing.masc.of αὐτός, accompaniment) 16.
Καὶ (continuative conjunction) 14.
ἠκολούθει (3d.per.sing.imp.act.ind.of ἀκολουθέω, inceptive) 394.
αὐτῷ (dat.sing.masc.of αὐτός, personal interest) 16.
ὄχλος (nom.sing.masc.of ὄχλος, subject of ἠκολούθει and συνέθλιβον) 418.

πολύς (nom.sing.masc.of πολύς, in agreement with ὄχλος) 228.
καὶ (continuative conjunction) 14.

#2236 συνέθλιβον (3d.per.pl.imp.act.ind.of συνθλίβω, inceptive).

throng - Mk.5:24,31.

Meaning: A combination of σύν (#1542) and θλίβω (#667). Hence, to press together; to press upon something or someone from all sides. With reference to a thronging multitude of people - Mk.5:24,31.

αὐτόν (acc.sing.masc.of αὐτός, direct object of συνέθλιβον) 16.

Translation - "And He went away with him; and a large crowd began to follow Him and they were crowding around Him."

Comment: Jesus at this time was popular in Capernaum. It was His temporary home. The news about the storm had spread, as had the episode in Gadara. Now Jairus makes his dramatic and humble plea. As Jesus and Jairus hurry away to the bedside of the dying child, the crowd begins to follow in order that they can witness another miracle. It becomes difficult for Jesus to make His way through the throng.

Enroute to Jairus' home another incident occurs, which we will deal with here and return to the Jairus story in verses 35-43.

Verse 25 - "And a certain woman, which had an issue of blood twelve years, . . . "

καὶ γυνὴ οὖσα ἐν ῥύσει αἵματος δώδεκα ἔτη

καὶ (continuative conjunction) 14.
γυνὴ (nom.sing.fem.of γυνή, subject of ἥψατο) 103.
οὖσα (pres.part.nom.sing.fem.of εἰμί, adjectival, restrictive) 86.
ἐν (preposition with the instru.of means) 80.

#2237 ῥύσει (instru.sing.fem.of ῥύσις, means).

issue - Mk.5:25; Lk.8:43,44.

Meaning: From an unused pres. ῥύω, from which several of the tenses of ῥέω are borrowed. A flowering: an issue of blood. Followed by the genitive of description - Mk.5:25; Lk.8:43,44.

αἵματος (gen.sing.neut.of αἵμα, description) 1203.
δώδεκα (numeral, indeclin.with ἔτη) 820.
ἔτη (acc.pl.neut.of ἔτος, time extent) 821.

Translation - "And a woman who had had an issue of blood for twelve years, . . . "

Comment: The story turns our attention away from Jairus and Jesus, as they hurried to the bedside of the little girl, to a poor sick woman who intrudes into the scenario. It is a long involved sentence which is complete only at the end of verse 27 where we find ἥψατο as the main verb, of which γυνή is the subject. In between we have a series of participles, the first of which is οὖσα, an ascriptive adjectival participle in the predicate position. It agrees with γυνή, which it modifies and ascribes to her a fact: - this woman had been menstruating for twelve years. *Cf.*Mk.5:2 for a similar use of ἐν. Robertson calls it accompanying circumstance. The accusative case in δώδεκα ἔτη tells us that throughout the entire extent of the twelve year period the woman continued to be afflicted (present tense in οὖσα). Verse 26 continues to paint the sad picture of the woman's hopeless condition.

Verse 26 - "And had suffered many things of many physicians, and had spent all that she had, and was nothing bettered, but rather grew worse,"

καὶ πολλὰ παθοῦσα ὑπὸ πολλῶν ἰατρῶν καὶ δαπανήσασα τὰ παρ' αὐτῆς πάντα καὶ μηδὲν ὠφεληθεῖσα ἀλλὰ μᾶλλον εἰς τὸ χεῖρον ἐλθοῦσα,

καὶ (adjunctive conjunction joining participles) 14.
πολλὰ (acc.pl.neut.of πολύς, direct object of παθοῦσα) 228.
παθοῦσα (2d.aor.part.nom.sing.fem.of πάσχω, adjectival, ascriptive) 1208.
ὑπὸ (preposition with the ablative of agent) 117.
πολλῶν (abl.pl.masc.of πολύς, in agreement with ἰατρῶν) 228.
ἰατρῶν (abl.pl.masc.of ἰατρός, agent) 793.
καὶ (adjunctive conjunction joining participles) 14.

#2238 δαπανήσασα (1st.aor.act.part.nom.sing.fem.of δαπανάω).

be at charges - Acts 21:24.
consume - Jam.4:3.
spend - Mk.5:26; Lk.15:14; II Cor.12:15.

Meaning: To spend; expend; incur obligation. With reference to the assumption of certain obligations in connection with religious vows - Acts 21:24. To spend assets for something to be desired, in an evil sense - Jam.4:3. To spend money for medical help - Mk.5:26. For subsistence and pleasure in an evil sense - Lk.15:14. Paul spent his own money for food and lodging, rather than be burdensome to the Corinthians - II Cor.12:15.

τὰ (acc.pl.neut.of the article in agreement with πάντα) 9.
παρ' (preposition with the ablative of source) 154.
αὐτῆς (abl.sing.fem.of αὐτός, source) 16.
πάντα (acc.pl.neut.of πᾶς, direct object of δαπανήσασα) 67.
καὶ (adversative conjunction) 14.
ὠφεληθεῖσα (1st.aor.pass.part.nom.sing.fem.of ὠφελέω, adjectival, ascriptive) 1144.
ἀλλὰ (alternative conjunction) 342.

μᾶλλον (adverbial) 619.
εἰς (preposition with the accusative of measure) 140.
τό (acc.sing.neut.of the article in agreement with χεῖρον) 9.
χεῖρον (acc.sing.neut.of χείρων, accusative of measure) 806.
ἐλθοῦσα (2d.aor.part.nom.sing.fem.of ἔρχομαι, adjectival, ascriptive) 146.

Translation - "... and had suffered much at the hands of many doctors and had
spent all that she possessed, but was never cured but grew worse..."

Comment: These participles, like οὖσα in verse 25 are all ascriptive adjectival
participles, in agreement with γυνή and used more fully to ascribe to the woman
characteristics by which she was known. Thus in addition to οὖσα, we have
παθοῦσα, δαπανήσασα, ὠφεληθεῖσα and ἐλθοῦσα. Being for twelve years ill
(verse 25) she had suffered, spent, but profited nothing but instead had come to a
worse condition. Verse 27 presents two more participles - ἀκούσασα and
ἐλθοῦσα, but they are not ascriptive adjectives. They are adverbial temporals.
They shed light on the main verb ἥψατο and hence are adverbial. Note that
πολλά is emphasized ahead of its participle παθοῦσα. Lightfoot (p.614ff) has
pointed out the variety of experiments tried by Jewish doctors upon women who
were menstruating. τὰ παρ' αὐτῆς πάντα is interesting. παρ' αὐτῆς, an ablative
of source, is used like an adjective in the attributive position, between the article
τά and the substantive to which it is joined, πάντα. "Everything which she had
by her" *i.e.* all of her assets which she could expend for more doctor bills and
medicine. Results? Not one evidence of recovery; on the contrary (ἀλλὰ
μᾶλλον) she had come εἰς τὸ χεῖρον. The article makes χεῖρον emphatic. The
poor woman had reached her extremity. The woman is in a pitiable condition.
Her health is gone; her money is gone; there are no more physicians to consult
and no more remedies to try. But there is still faith in the Eternal Son of God and
this is enough. The woman's extremity became God's opportunity. Only in our
most devastated situations do we really trust in God and turn to Him for help.
This is what the woman did as we see in

Verse 27 - "When she had heard of Jesus, came in the press behind, and touched
his garment."

ἀκούσασα περὶ τοῦ Ἰησοῦ, ἐλθοῦσα ἐν τῷ ὄχλῳ ὄπισθεν ἥψατο τοῦ ἱματίου
αὐτοῦ, ..."

ἀκούσασα (aor.act.part.nom.sing.fem.of ἀκούω, adverbial, temporal) 148.
περὶ (preposition with the genitive of reference) 173.
τοῦ (gen.sing.masc.of the article in agreement with Ἰησοῦ) 9.
Ἰησοῦ (gen.sing.masc.of Ἰησοῦς, reference) 3.
ἐλθοῦσα (aor.part.nom.sing.fem.of ἔρχομαι, adverbial, temporal) 146.
ἐν (preposition with the locative of place where) 80.
τῷ (loc.sing.masc.of the article in agreement with ὄχλῳ) 9.
ὄχλῳ (loc.sing.masc.of ὄχλος, place where) 418.

ὅπισθεν (adverbial) 822.

ἥψατο (3d.per.sing.aor.mid.ind.of ἅπτω, constative) 711.

τοῦ (gen.sing.neut.of the article in agreement with ἱματίου) 9.

ἱματίου (gen.sing.neut.of ἱμάτιον, description) 534.

αὐτοῦ (gen.sing.masc.of αὐτός, possession) 16.

Translation - "... *when she heard about Jesus came in the crowd behind him and touched His garment."*

Comment: As we stated in comment on verse 26 ἀκούσασα is a temporal participle, used adverbially to throw light, not upon γυνή, as did the attributive participles in verses 25 and 26, but upon the main verb ἥψατο. ἐλθοῦσα is also temporal. The woman heard about Jesus and His power to heal those who could find no healing elsewhere and were in despair. Then she came to Him. The text does not tell us where the woman came from. She may not have been a local resident as she would have known about Jesus before had she lived in Capernaum. The article τοῦ with Ἰησοῦ makes it definite, as though she asked, "Who is this Jesus?" and got a reply, "Haven't you heard?" followed by a full recital of His deeds. Her decision to lose herself in the crowd and then approach Jesus from behind is explained in

Verse 28 - "For she said, If I may touch but his clothes, I shall be whole."

ἔλεγεν γὰρ ὅτι Ἐὰν ἅψωμαι κἂν τῶν ἱματίων αὐτοῦ σωθήσομαι.

ἔλεγεν (3d.per.sing.imp.act.ind.of λέγω, progressive duration) 66.

γὰρ (causal conjunction) 105.

ὅτι (recitative) 211.

Ἐὰν (conditional particle in a third-class condition) 363.

ἅψωμαι (1st.per.sing.aor.mid.subj.of ἅπτω, third-class condition) 711.

κἂν (ascensive conditional particle in a third-class condition) 1370.

τῶν (gen.pl.neut.of the article in agreement with ἱματίων) 9.

ἱματίων (gen.pl.neut.of ἱμάτιον, description) 534.

αὐτοῦ (gen.sing.masc.of αὐτός, possession) 16.

σωθήσομαι (1st.per.sing.fut.pass.ind.of σώζω, third-class condition, predictive) 109.

Translation - "Because she kept repeating, 'If I even touch His clothing I will be recovered."

Comment: Ἐὰν ... σωθήσομαι is a more probable future conditional clause. κἂν is a combination of ἂν, which we expect to find in a third-class condition and καί in its ascensive sense. There was a great deal of doubt in the woman's mind about her ability to fulfill the condition. There was no doubt in her mind that the result would be forthcoming. "If I touch (and I do not think that I can) even (ascensive καὶ in κἂν) His garments, I shall get well" (no doubt in her mind about that). The result (σωθήσομαι) is certain but contingent upon the fulfillment of the protasis.

Here is where the uncertainty lies. This is a typical third-class condition with κἄν added to heighten both the uncertainty of the fulfillment of the protasis and also to heighten the statement of the woman's faith. She had some doubt that she would ever get close enough to Jesus, as she fought her way through the crowd, to even touch His clothing. But her faith was so great that she thought that *if only* she could touch His garments the miracle would take place. Thus her doubt had to do only with her ability. There was no doubt about Jesus' ability to heal. The woman's faith in the outcome is not in question. She only doubts her ability to fulfill the condition. She could have been more doubtful than she was. Mark could have reported the incident in a fourth-class less vivid future clause with εἰ with the optative in the protasis and the optative with ἄν in the apodosis.

Some commentators have pointed to an element of heathen mysticism in the woman, because she thought that the garment of the great Healer might have some magical qualities. Perhaps so, but, mystic or not, she had enough faith to secure the result. Matthew (Mt.9:20) and Luke (Lk.8:44) say τοῦ κρασπέδου τοῦ ἱματίου αὐτοῦ - "the hem of His garment" where the blue band at the bottom indicated His special mission.

The story makes clear that saving faith neither precludes nor even suggests that human decision and action is not essential to the salvation equation. The woman indeed had sufficient faith to gain her total recovery. But had she never put her faith to work at the almost impossible task of struggling though that dense crowd of people until she commanded a position directly behind Jesus, she would never have been healed. A predestinarian concept of salvation that concludes that since God will save whom He will we are to do nothing but wait to see what God has willed is sadly anti-biblical. To be sure, God has willed the salvation of the elect, but He has also willed that in the process the elect must hear, believe, commit themselves, confess and accept. The subjective elements in the atonement are prerequisite to those elements that are objective.

Verse 29 - "And straightway the fountain of her blood was dried up; and she felt in her body that she was healed of that plague.

καὶ εὐθὺς ἐξηράνθη ἡ πηγὴ τοῦ αἵματος αὐτῆς, καὶ ἔγνω τῷ σώματι ὅτι ἴαται ἀπὸ τῆς μάστιγος.

καὶ (continuative conjunction) 14.
εὐθὺς (adverbial) 258.
ἐξηράνθη (3d.per.sing.1st.aor.pass.ind.of ξηραίνω, constative) 1033.
ἡ (nom.sing.fem.of the article in agreement with πηγή) 9.
πηγὴ (nom.sing.fem.of πηγή, subject of ἐξηράνθη) 2001.
τοῦ (gen.sing.neut.of the article in agreement with αἵματος) 9.
αἵματος (gen.sing.neut.of αἷμα, description) 1203.
αὐτῆς (gen.sing.fem.of αὐτός, possession) 16.
καὶ (continuative conjunction) 14.
ἔγνω (3d.per.sing.2d.aor.act.ind.of γινώσκω, constative) 131.
τῷ (loc.sing.neut.of the article in agreement with σώματι) 9.

σώματι (loc.sing.neut.of σῶμα, sphere) 507.
ὅτι (conjunction introducing an object clause) 211.
ἴαται (3d.per.sing.perf.pass.ind.of ἰάομαι, consummative) 721.
ἀπό (preposition with the ablative of separation) 70.
τῆς (abl.sing.fem.of the article in agreement with μάστιγος) 9.
μάστιγος (abl.sing.fem.of μάστιξ, separation) 2114.

Translation - "And immediately the flow of her blood ceased and she knew that her body had been healed of the plague."

Comment: Faith was instantly rewarded. Mark's favorite εὐθὺς is here to tell the story. We have τῷ σώματι without a preposition to help us decide between the dative ("with reference/for the advantage of her body"),instrumental ("by means of her body") or locative, which could translate "in her body" or "in the bodily sphere." Any of these ideas can be made to fit the context, without destroying the point. We have elected to think of it in terms of the locative of sphere. She knew, so far as her body was concerned, that she had been healed. Our Lord, the Giver of the healing power, also knew ἐν ἑαυτῷ that something wonderful had happened to the woman (vs.30).

The perfect tense in ἴαται is a good example of the consummative perfect. The healing took place when she touched Him, and when she felt the surge of health, something that she had not felt for twelve years, the healing was an accomplished fact - a present condition as the result of a past completed action.

Verse 30 - "And Jesus immediately knowing in himself that virtue had gone out of him, turned him about in the press, and said, Who touched my clothes?"

καὶ εὐθὺς ὁ Ἰησοῦς ἐπιγνοὺς ἐν ἑαυτῷ τὴν ἐξ αὐτοῦ δύναμιν ἐξελθοῦσαν ἐπιστραφεὶς ἐν τῷ ὄχλῳ ἔλεγεν, Τίς μου ἥψατο τῶν ἱματίων;

καὶ (continuative conjunction) 14.
εὐθὺς (adverbial) 258.
ὁ (nom.sing.masc.of the article in agreement with Ἰησοῦς) 9.
Ἰησοῦς (nom.sing.masc.of Ἰησοῦς, subject of ἔλεγεν) 3.
ἐπιγνοὺς (2d.aor.act.part.nom.sing.masc.of ἐπιγινώσκω, adverbial, temporal) 675.
ἐν (preposition with the instrumental of manner) 80.
ἑαυτῷ (instrumental sing.masc.of ἑαυτός, manner) 288.
τὴν (acc.sing.fem.of the article in agreement with δύναμιν) 9.
ἐξ (preposition with the ablative of separation) 19.
αὐτοῦ (abl.sing.masc.of αὐτός, separation) 16.
δύναμιν (acc.sing.fem.of δύναμις, direct object of ἐπιγνοὺς) 687.
ἐξελθοῦσαν (aor.part.acc.sing.fem.of ἐξέρχομαι, adjectival, restrictive) 161.
ἐπιστραφεὶς (aor.act.part.nom.sing.masc.of ἐπιστρέφω, adverbial, temporal) 866.
ἐν (preposition with the locative of place where) 80.
τῷ (loc.sing.masc.of the article in agreement with ὄχλῳ) 9.

ὄχλῳ (loc.sing.masc.of ὄχλος, place where) 418.
ἔλεγεν (3d.per.sing.imp.act.ind.of λέγω, progressive duration) 66.
Τίς (nom.sing.masc.of τίς, in direct question) 281.
μου (gen.sing.masc.of ἐγώ, possession) 123.
ἥψατο (3d.per.sing.aor.mid.ind.of ἅπτω, constative) 711.
τῶν (gen.pl.neut.of the article in agreement with ἱματίων) 9.
ἱματίων (gen.pl.neut.of ἱμάτιον, description) 534.

Translation - "And immediately when Jesus had sensed within Himself the fact that the power had flowed out from Him, He turned around in the crowd and began to ask, 'Who touched my clothing?' "

Comment: The participles ἐπιγνοὺς and ἐπιστραφεὶς are adverbially temporal, thus indicating the order of events. Jesus knew with perfect perception (the basic meaning of ἐπιγνοὺς) about the departing power (τὴν ἐξ αὐτοῦ δύναμιν ἐξελθοῦσαν), and then He turned around in the crowd (ἐπιστραφεὶς), and then He spoke. Note carefully how ἐξελθοῦσαν is adjectival in a restrictive sense, modifying δύναμιν. It was the specific power that had flown from Him (ἐξ αὐτοῦ, an ablative of separation) that Jesus was aware of at that point. He still had plenty of other power left. Jesus knew about "the having gone out from Him power." This perfect perception caused Him to turn around in the thronging multitude of people and begin to ask His searching question, as if He didn't already know.

When a needy sinner has a vital personal encounter with his Sovereign Saviour, both the sinner and the Saviour know about it. The woman knew that Jesus' power had healed her. Jesus knew ἐν ἑαυτῷ that the power had gone out from Him. The passage strongly upholds the personal relationship involved in salvation between Christ and the repentant and humble believer. "His Spirit bears witness with our spirit . . . " (Rom.8:16).

The disciples thought Jesus' question stupid, as is clear in

Verse 31 - "And his disciples said unto him, Thou seest the multitude thronging thee, and sayest thou, Who touched me?"

καὶ ἔλεγον αὐτῷ οἱ μαθηταὶ αὐτοῦ, Βλέπεις τὸν ὄχλον συνθλίβοντά σε, καὶ λέγεις, Τίς μου ἥψατο;

καὶ (inferential conjunction) 14.
ἔλεγον (3d.per.pl.imp.act.ind.of λέγω, progressive duration) 66.
αὐτῷ (dat.sing.masc.of αὐτός, indirect object of ἔλεγον) 16.
οἱ (nom.pl.masc.of the article in agreement with μαθηταὶ) 9.
μαθηταὶ (nom.pl.masc.of μαθητής, subject of ἔλεγον) 421.
αὐτοῦ (gen.sing.masc.of αὐτός, relationship) 16.
Βλέπεις (2d.per.sing.pres.act.ind.of βλέπω, aoristic) 499.
τὸν (acc.sing.masc.of the article in agreement with ὄχλον) 9.
ὄχλον (acc.sing.masc.of ὄχλος, direct object of Βλέπεις) 418.

συνθλίβοντά (pres.act.part.acc.sing.masc.of συνθλίβω, adjectival, ascriptive) 2236.

σε (acc.sing.masc.of σύ, direct object of συνθλίβοντά) 104.

καί (emphatic conjunction) 14.

λέγεις (2d.per.sing.pres.act.ind.of λέγω, aoristic) 66.

Τίς (nom.sing.masc.of τίς, subject of ἥψατο) 281.

μου (gen.sing.masc.of ἐγώ, description) 123.

ἥψατο (3d.per.sing.aor.mid.ind.of ἅπτω, constative, direct question) 711.

Translation - "Therefore His disciples were saying to Him, 'You see the crowd thronging you, yet you say, 'Who touched me?!'"

Comment: This bit of sarcasm from the disciples is natural enough. They may have been expending themselves as body guards to keep the people at least far enough away so that Jesus could walk. Everyone was trying to get close enough to Jesus to touch Him. Until we understand Jesus' meaning His question, "Who touched my clothing?" does appear stupid. And so His disciples interpreted it. They were all touching Jesus, but only the woman really *touched* Him. It is the difference between the touch of faith, born out of desperation, and the touch of idle curiosity born only out of the desire to see the unusual. Most of the people were there for the same reason that they would have gone to a fire. Jesus was unusual. He was doing things not ordinarily done in Capernaum - or anywhere else.

Attendance in the Sunday School class at the First Baptist Church of Washington, D.C. is always larger on the Sunday when *The Washington Post* announces that the President of the United States will be there.

The people in Capernaum may have conceded Jesus' greatness. They may have admired Him temporarily, but they were not accepting Him as Messiah and the Incarnate Son of God. The sick woman, insofar as she understood these things, did accept Jesus Christ. The reason is simple. She knew that she needed Him. The other people needed Him also, but they did not realize it as she did. Her experience included everything in verse 26. Her extremity was Christ's opportunity.

Any Easter Sunday morning in any church, one can see the people thronging Jesus. They are present, perhaps not because they know that they need Jesus and what He can do for them, but because sociology says that in Western cultures people go to church on Easter. The people who go to church every Sunday are more likely to be the people who recognize their need for Jesus, although in certain institutional churches, which enjoy political, economic and social prestige there may be scant recognition by sinners for the unique salvation available only through the death and resurrection of the Son of God.

Luke 8:45 says that Peter was the spokesman for the disciples as he was so often. *Cf.* the Luke parallel account for further comment in verse 32.

Verse 32 - "And he looked round about to see her that had done this thing."

καί περιεβλέπετο ἰδεῖν τὴν τοῦτο ποιήσασαν.

καὶ (continuative conjunction) 14.
περιεβλέπετο (3d.per.sing.imp.mid.ind.of περιβλέπω, inceptive) 2107.
ἰδεῖν (aor.act.inf.of ὁράω, purpose) 144.
τὴν (acc.sing.fem.of the article in agreement with ποιήσασαν) 9.
τοῦτο (acc.sing.neut.of οὗτος, direct object of ποιήσασαν) 93.
ποιήσασαν (aor.act.part.acc.sing.fem.of ποιέω, substantival, direct object of ἰδεῖν) 127.

Translation - "And He began to turn around in order to see the woman who had done this."

Comment: *Cf.*#2107, a favorite with Mark, who uses it six of the seven times it occurs. Since it is middle voice the idea is that Jesus acted upon Himself. In order to know who she was (ἰδεῖν) He wished to see (βλέπω) all about Him (περί). Thus He turned His body around. Or at least He started to do so, as the inceptive imperfect in περιεβλέπετο indicates. Mark adds the complementary infinitive of purpose. He, Who knew all things and had no need that any man tell Him about other people (John 2:24,25), already knew perfectly well who the woman was and the reason for her act of desperate faith. But had He singled her out, without her coming forward voluntarily, He would have embarrassed her and robbed her of the joy of the spiritual exercise of open confession of her faith in Him and her testimony of the glorious result. This confession of faith she made humbly, gladly and with utmost gratitude. None can say that Jesus wrung her testimony from unwilling lips.

Jesus' omniscience which enabled Him to know all about others is seen also in His innocent request of the Samaritan woman at the well that she go and call her husband, when He knew that she was a prostitute (John 4:16).

Jesus apparently had not completed His "about-face" (the inceptive imperfect translates "He *began* to turn around") when the woman hastened to identify herself in

Verse 33 - "But the woman fearing and trembling, knowing what was done in her, came and fell down before him, and told him all the truth."

ἡ δὲ γυνὴ φοβηθεῖσα καὶ τρέμουσα, εἰδυῖα ὃ γέγονεν αὐτῇ, ἦλθεν καὶ προσέπεσεν αὐτῷ καὶ εἶπεν αὐτῷ πᾶσαν τὴν ἀλήθειαν.

ἡ (nom.sing.fem.of the article in agreement with γυνή) 9.
δὲ (adversative conjunction) 11.
γυνὴ (nom.sing.fem.of γυνή, subject of ἦλθεν, προσέπεσεν and εἶπεν) 103.
φοβηθεῖσα (1st.aor.part.nom.sing.fem.of φοβέομαι, adverbial, circumstantial) 101.
καὶ (adjunctive conjunction joining participles) 14.

#2239 τρέμουσα (pres.act.part.nom.sing.fem.of τρέμω, adverbial, circumstantial).

be afraid - II Pet.2:10.

tremble - Mk.5:33; Lk.8:47.

Meaning: To tremble; to be afraid. *Cf.*φοβέομαι (#101). φοβέομαι seems to be the psychological state, while τρέμω is the physical reaction to the fear. Hence φοβηθεῖσα καὶ τρέμουσα, as Mark puts them together in Mk.5:33 is logical. Also in the parallel passage in Lk.8:47. With οὐ in II Pet.2:10. In the margin, of Paul at his conversion in Acts 9:6, though not in Westcott and Hort.

εἰδυῖα (perf.part.nom.sing.fem.of ὁράω, adverbial, circumstantial) 144.

ὅ (nom.sing.neut.of ὅς, subject of γέγονεν, relative pronoun) 65.

γέγονεν (3d.per.sing.perf.ind.of γίνομαι, consummative) 113.

αὐτῇ (dat.sing.fem.of αὐτός, personal advantage) 16.

ἦλθεν (3d.per.sing.aor.ind.of ἔρχομαι, constative) 146.

προσέπεσεν (3d.per.sing.aor.act.ind.of προσπίπτω, constative) 699.

αὐτῷ (loc.sing.masc.of αὐτός, after πρός in composition with a verb of rest) 16.

καὶ (adjunctive conjunction joining verbs) 14.

εἶπεν (3d.per.sing.aor.act.ind.of εἶπον, constative) 155.

αὐτῷ (dat.sing.masc.of αὐτός, indirect object of εἶπεν) 16.

πᾶσαν (acc.sing.fem.of πᾶς, in agreement with ἀλήθειαν) 67.

ἀλήθειαν (acc.sing.fem.of ἀλήθεια, direct object of εἶπεν) 1416.

Translation - "But the woman, seized with fear and trembling, knowing what had happened to her, came and fell down before Him and told Him the whole truth."

Comment: There are three circumstantial participles, each in a different tense. φοβηθεῖσα is an ingressive aorist. τρέμουσα is in the present tense. It describes the physical agitation of the woman as a result of the fact that she had been *seized with fear* (ingressive aorist in φοβ.). εἰδυῖα is a perfect participle, which is consummative. As a result of the woman's perception she knew what had happened to her - present knowledge as a result of having experienced healing in the immediate past. γέγονεν is also perfect tense. That which had happened to her resulted in her present happiness and obligation to tell Jesus all. Notice that her testimony was given as she trembled (present continuous action in τρέμουσα). It was not easy for her to speak publicly. She had been humiliated for twelve years by her physical condition. Despite her fear she gave her testimony because she knew what had happened. Christians who know what their experience with Christ has been, the depths of the pit of degradation from which they have been rescued and the glory of the heavenly position to which they have been called, will not hesitate to speak for Christ publicly, though they might tremble as they speak. The whole story came out - εἶπεν αὐτῷ πᾶσαν τὴν ἀλήθειαν. As she poured out her story Jesus saw in it the evidence of her faith as we see in

Verse 34 - "And he said unto her, Daughter, thy faith hath made thee whole; go in peace, and be whole of thy plague."

ὁ δὲ εἶπεν αὐτῇ, Θυγάτηρ, ἡ πίστις σου σέσωκέν σε. ὕπαγε εἰς εἰρήνην, καὶ ἴσθι ὑγιὴς ἀπὸ τῆς μάστιγός σου.

ὁ (nom.sing.masc.of the article, subject of εἶπεν) 9.
δὲ (continuative conjunction) 11.
εἶπεν (3d.per.sing.aor.act.ind.of εἶπον, constative) 155.
αὐτῇ (dat.sing.fem.of αὐτός, indirect object of εἶπεν) 16.
Θυγάτηρ (voc.sing.fem.of θυγάτηρ, address) 817.
ἡ (nom.sing.fem.of the article in agreement with πίστις) 9.
πίστις (nom.sing.fem.of πίστις, subject of σέσωκέν) 728.
σου (gen.sing.fem.of σύ, possession) 104.
σέσωκέν (3d.per.sing.perf.act.ind.of σώζω, consummative) 109.
σε (acc.sing.fem.of σύ, direct object of σέσωκέν) 104.
ὕπαγε (2d.per.sing.pres.act.impv.of ὑπάγω, command) 364.
εἰς (preposition with the accusative of general reference, adverbial) 140.
εἰρήνην (acc.sing.fem.of εἰρήνη, general reference, adverbial) 865.
καὶ (adjunctive conjunction joining verbs) 14.
ἴσθι (2d.per.sing.pres.impv.of εἰμί, command) 86.
ὑγιὴς (nom.sing.fem.of ὑγιής, predicate adjective) 979.
ἀπὸ (preposition with the ablative of separation) 70.
τῆς (abl.sing.fem.of the article in agreement with μάστιγός) 9.
μάστιγός (abl.sing.fem.of μάστιξ, separation) 2114.
σου (gen.sing.fem.of σύ, possession) 104.

Translation - "And He said to her, 'Daughter, your faith has saved you. Go in peace and always be free from your disease.' "

Comment: Jesus expresses two thoughts here. To say that σέσωκέν refers to physical salvation from the disease is to charge Jesus with needless repetition. The woman's faith which she translated into action saved her soul. Now she is told to go her way with the peace of God in her mind and heart. Incidentally, she also has healing for her physical needs. Note the perfect tense in σέσωκέν σε. The past completed action (her faith that *if* she could make her way through the dense crowd and touch His clothing she would be healed) resulted in her present condition. She is saved from sin. Note #140 for εἰς with the adverbial accusative of general reference.

The story of the woman's healing has been an interlude in the other story of Jairus' concern over his daughter. Jesus was enroute to Jairus' house to heal his daughter when the woman came to touch His garment. Now we resume the other story in

Verse 35 - "While he yet spake, there came from the ruler of the synagogue's house certain which said, Thy daughter is dead: why troublest thou the Master any further?"

Ἔτι αὐτοῦ λαλοῦντος ἔρχονται ἀπὸ τοῦ ἀρχισυναγώγου λέγοντες ὅτι Ἡ θυγάτηρ σου ἀπέθανεν. τί ἔτι σκύλλεις τὸν διδάσκαλον;

Ἔτι (adverbial) 448.

αὐτοῦ (gen.sing.masc.of αὐτός, genitive absolute) 16.

λαλοῦντος (pres.act.part.gen.sing.masc.of λαλέω, genitive absolute) 815.

ἔρχονται (3d.per.pl.pres.ind.of ἔρχομαι, historical) 146.

ἀπό (preposition with the ablative of separation) 70.

τοῦ (abl.sing.masc.of the article in agreement with ἀρχισυναγώγου) 9.

ἀρχισυναγώγου (abl.sing.masc.of ἀρχισυνάγωγος, separation) 2232.

λέγοντες (pres.act.part.nom.pl.masc.of λέγω, adverbial, temporal) 66.

ὅτι (recitative) 211.

Ἡ (nom.sing.fem.of the article in agreement with θυγάτηρ) 9.

θυγάτηρ (nom.sing.fem.of θυγάτηρ, subject of ἀπέθανεν) 817.

σου (gen.sing.masc.of σύ, relationship) 104.

ἀπέθανεν (3d.per.sing.2d.aor.act.ind.of ἀποθνήσκω, culminative) 774.

τί (interrogative pronoun, acc.sing.neut.of τίς, cause) 281.

ἔτι (adverbial) 448.

σκύλλεις (2d.per.sing.pres.act.ind.of σκύλλω, static) 836.

τὸν (acc.sing.masc.of the article in agreement with διδάσκαλον) 9.

διδάσκαλον (acc.sing.masc.of διδάσκαλος, direct object of σκύλλεις) 742.

Translation - "As He was speaking they came from the (house) of the ruler of the synagogue saying, 'Your daughter is dead. Why do you continue to trouble the teacher?'"

Comment: Mark does not need ἔτι before the genitive absolute, as the participle λαλοῦντος is in the present tense giving the notion of simultaneity with the main verb ἔρχονται. As Jesus spoke the words of verse 34, someone (Lk.8:49 has τις) came from Jairus' home with bad news. τοῦ ἀρχισυναγώγου cannot be all of the prepositional phrase introduced by ἀπό. If so, the Greek says that those who brought the death message came from the ruler. But they did not. They came *to* the ruler, not *from* him and told him of his daughter's death and suggested that there was no further need to bother Jesus about it. We assume that the little girl was at home at the time of her death. If so, the word οἴκου should be inserted. Luke write the passage τις παρὰ τοῦ ἀρχισυναγώγου which translates "someone came to the ruler's side." Mark's use of ἀπό ("from") demands οἴκου.

The message is abrupt and devastating to the distraught father, who probably resented the intrusion of the sick woman as he and Jesus hurried to his home. But Jesus is still in command.

Note the culminative aorist in ἀπέθανεν and the static present in σκύλλεις. The question implies that Jairus will continue to bother Jesus indefinitely. Mantey discusses the Static Present by saying, "The present tense may be used to represent a condition which is assumed as perpetually existing, or to be ever taken for granted as a fact. . . The idea of progress in a verb of action finds its natural counterpart in an idea of perpetual state in a verb of being. This use is practically the present of duration applied to a verb of being." (Mantey, *Manual Grammar*, 186).

Verse 36 - "As soon as Jesus heard the word that was spoken, he saith unto the ruler of the synagogue, Be not afraid, only believe."

ὁ δὲ'Ιησοῦς παρακούσας τὸν λόγον λαλούμενον λέγει τῷ ἀρχισυναγώγου, Μὴ φοβοῦ, μόνον πίστευε.

ὁ (nom.sing.masc.of the article in agreement with 'Ιησοῦς) 9.

δὲ (adversative conjunction) 11.

'Ιησοῦς (nom.sing.masc.of 'Ιησοῦς, subject of λέγει) 3.

παρακούσας (aor.act.part.nom.sing.masc.of παρακούω, adverbial, causal) 1264.

τὸν (acc.sing.masc.of the article in agreement with λόγον) 9.

λόγον (acc.sing.masc.of λόγος, direct object of παρακούσας) 510.

λαλούμενον (pres.pass.part.acc.sing.masc.of λαλέω, adjectival, restrictive) 815.

λέγει (3d.per.sing.pres.act.ind.of λέγω, historical) 66.

τῷ (dat.sing.masc. of the article in agreement with ἀρχισυναγώγῳ) 9.

ἀρχισυναγώγῳ (dat.sing.masc.of ἀρχισυνάγωγος, indirect object of λέγει) 2232.

Μὴ (negative conjunction with the imperative in a prohibition) 87.

φοβοῦ (2d.per.sing.pres.impv.of φοβέομαι, prohibition) 101.

μόνον (acc.sing.neut.of μόνος, adverbial) 339.

πίστευε (2d.per.sing.pres.act.impv.of πιστεύω, command) 734.

Translation - "But Jesus ignored the message spoken and said to the ruler of the synagogue, 'Try not to be afraid. Only continue to believe.' "

Comment: This time δὲ is adversative. What Jesus was about to say to the father was quite opposite to what he had just heard. *Cf.*#1264 for a close look at παρακούω. In Mt.18:17,17 it means to hear carelessly, with a view to reject what is heard - "to let it go in one ear and out the other." We have the same meaning hear. Jesus overheard what the messengers said, but He was not worried. He knew what He was going to do.

Note the adjectival participle, used in a restrictive sense, to modify τὸν λόγον. Jesus was also ignoring (παρακούω) the chatter of the people surrounding Him, but He had a special reason for paying no attention to the sad news about the little girl's death.

Μὴ φοβοῦ - "Try not to be afraid." We have translated thus because μὴ is a weaker negative conjunction than οὐκ (#130). Μὴ is generally used with the imperative where the speaker is not sure that the one commanded will be able (or willing) to obey. Jesus is being very gentle with Jairus, the distraught father. To say, "Fear not," using οὐκ with the aorist imperative, would be unkind and unrealistic. One does not imperiously order a father who has just been told that his daughter is dead, not to fear at all. Μὴ is not an order, but a gentle negative suggestion. φοβοῦ is present tense - hence, "Try not to go on fearing." Then Jesus gave him the antidote to fear - "Continue to be believing." The father had already believed on Jesus, to some extent, at least. Else he would not have come to Him in the first place. He could believe that Jesus could heal his desperately sick child. Could he go on believing that Jesus could even raise her from the dead? Jesus gave him this tonic for faith now. Jairus, while not opposed to the episode of the sick woman, understandably was impatient with the interruption. Could not the woman wait? She was ill, but not critically so, whereas haste was needed if Jesus was to reach her bedside before his daughter died. Yet Jesus had seemed to be in no real hurry. It mattered not to our Lord whether He reached Jairus' house before or after the child's death. The result was going to be the same in either case. Thus Jesus knew, but Jairus did not. So Jesus took the time to heal the woman and even to secure her public confession, so necessary for her future spiritual development.

The delay served Jesus' purpose in another way. It assured the death of the girl and thus presented Jesus with the opportunity for a greater miracle, and thus, a stronger basis for Jairus' faith. We hear no more directly of Jairus, but it is a safe guess that he followed Jesus as a devoted disciple until he (Jairus) died. He would have had less human reason to trust Jesus had our Lord's service in his home been only that of healing a sick child.

On another occasion, when Jesus' healing ministry was in demand, He deliberately stayed away until the patient died and then He went to raise him from the dead - *Cf.*John 11:1-15 with special attention to verse 15. Jesus was about to perform His second resurrection from death in the gospel record. On the first occasion (Lk.7:11-18) there was a large crowd present.This was unavoidable, as He interrupted a funeral procession. So as not to cast genuine pearls before genuine swine, Jesus decides now to restrict this audience to those who were motivated, not by vulgar curiosity, but by genuine Christian faith.

Verse 37 - "And he suffered no man to follow him, save Peter, and James, and John, the brother of James."

καὶ οὐκ ἀφῆκεν οὐδένα μετ' αὐτοῦ συνακολουθῆσαι εἰ μὴ τὸν Πέτρον καὶ Ἰάκωβον καὶ Ἰωάννην τὸν ἀδελφὸν Ἰακώβου.

καὶ (adversative conjunction) 14.

οὐκ (summary negative particle with the indicative) 130.

ἀφῆκεν (3d.per.sing.1st.aor.act.ind.of ἀφίημι, constative) 319.

οὐδένα (acc.sing.masc.of οὐδείς, direct object of ἀφῆκεν) 446.

μετ' (preposition with the genitive of accompaniment) 50.

αὐτοῦ (gen.sing.masc.of αὐτός, accompaniment) 16.

#2240 συνακολουθῆσαι (aor.act.inf.of συνακολουθέω, epexegetical).

follow - Mk.5:37; 14:51; Lk.23:49.

Meaning: A combination of σύν (#1542) and ἀκολουθέω (#394). Hence to follow with; to follow along; to accompany. To accompany but at a short distance behind. (If the preposition in composition were παρά, accompaniment "by the side of" would be the meaning). With reference to Peter, James and John with Jesus and Jairus - Mk.5:37. Of His friends who had followed Jesus to Calvary -

Lk.23:49. With reference to Mark who followed Jesus to Gethsemane - Mk.14:51.

εἰ (conditional conjunction with the negative particle μή) 337.
μή (qualified negative particle, with εἰ) 87.
τὸν (acc.sing.masc.of the article in agreement with Πέτρον) 9.
Πέτρον (acc.sing.masc.of Πέτρος, direct object of ἀφῆκεν understood) 387.
καὶ (adjunctive conjunction, joining nouns) 14.
Ἰάκωβον (acc.sing.masc.of Ἰάκωβον, direct object of ἀφῆκεν understood) 397.
καὶ (adjunctive conjunction) 14.
Ἰωάννην (acc.sing.masc.of Ἰωάννης, object of ἀφῆκεν understood) 399.
τὸν (acc.sing.masc.of the article in agreement with ἀδελφὸν) 9.
ἀδελφὸν (acc.sing.masc.of ἀδελφός, apposition) 15.
Ἰακώβου (gen.sing.masc.of Ἰάκωβον, relationship) 397.

Translation - "But He did not permit anyone to go along with Him except Peter and James and John, the brother of James."

Comment: Jesus was emphatic about this as οὐκ the summary negative particle indicates. Note also that we have οὐκ in composition in οὐδένα - "but not one." Had Jesus not forbid the multitude which up to that point had followed Him, the people would only have added to the confusion that Jesus found at Jairus' home when He arrived.

Verse 38 - "And he cometh to the house of the ruler of the synagogue, and seeth the tumult, and them that wept and wailed greatly."

καὶ ἔρχονται εἰς τὸν οἶκον τοῦ ἀρχισυναγώγου, καὶ θεωρεῖ θόρυβον καὶ κλαίοντας καὶ ἀλαλάζοντας πολλά,

καὶ (continuative conjunction) 14.
ἔρχονται (3d.per.pl.pres.ind.of ἔρχομαι, historical) 146.
εἰς (preposition with the accusative of extent) 140.
τὸν (acc.sing.masc.of the article in agreement with οἶκον) 9.
οἶκον (acc.sing.masc.of οἶκος, extent) 784.
τοῦ (gen.sing.masc.of the article in agreement with ἀρχισυναγώγου) 9.
ἀρχισυναγώγου (gen.sing.masc.of ἀρχισυνάγωγος, possession) 2232.
καὶ (continuative conjunction) 14.
θεωρεῖ (3d.per.sing.pres.act.ind.of θεωρέω, historical) 1667.
θόρυβον (acc.sing.masc.of θόρυβος, direct object of θεωρεῖ) 1559.
καὶ (adjunctive conjunction joining substantives) 14.
κλαίοντας (pres.act.part.acc.pl.fem.of κλαίω, substantival, direct object of θεωρεῖ) 225.
καὶ (adjunctive conjunction joining participles) 14.

#2241 ἀλαλάζοντας (pres.act.part.acc.pl.fem.of ἀλαλάζω, direct object of θεωρεῖ).

tinkle - I Cor.13:1.
wail - Mk.5:38.

Meaning: Prop. to repeat frequently the cry ἀλαλά as soldiers used to do when entering battle. Univ., to utter a joyful shout - Ps.46:2; 65:2 and in profane writings. To wail and lament like hired mourners at a funeral - Mk.5:38. With reference to the reverberations coming from a cymbal as it vibrates after being struck - I Cor.13:1. *Cf.*ὀλολύζω and the Latin *ululare..*

πολλά (acc.pl.neut.of πολύς, adverbial) 228.

Translation - "And they entered the house of the ruler of the synagogue and He witnessed the uproar with women weeping and much ululation."

Comment: "They came . . . " - plural in ἔρχονται - *viz.,* Jesus, Jairus, Peter, James and John. Mark then narrows the account to Jesus - "He saw . . . " θεωρεῖ. #1559 is an interesting study in mob behavior. Jesus saw one here. Capernaum had its professional funeral weepers as most little towns do. κλαίοντας and ἀλαλάζοντας are substantival participles. It was a disgusting picture. Scarcely nothing is as revolting as insincere grief at a funeral. *Cf.*#2241. Jesus put an end to the nonesense forthwith, as we see in

Verse 39 - " And when he was come in, he saith unto them, Why make ye this ado, and weep? the damsel is not dead, but sleepeth."

καὶ εἰσελθὼν λέγει αὐτοῖς Τί θορυβεῖσθε καὶ κλαίετε; τὸ παιδίον οὐκ ἀπέθανεν ἀλλὰ καθεύδει.

καὶ (continuative conjunction) 14.
εἰσελθὼν (aor.part.nom.sing.masc.of εἰσέρχομαι, adverbial, temporal) 234.
λέγει (3d.per.sing.pres.act.ind.of λέγω,historical) 66.
αὐτοῖς (dat.pl.masc.of αὐτός, indirect object of λέγει) 16.
Τί (acc.sing.neut.of τίς, cause, in direct question) 281.
θορυβεῖσθε (2d.per.pl.pres.pass.ind.of θορυβέω, progressive) 825.
καὶ (adjunctive conjunction joining verbs) 14.
κλαίετε (2d.per.pl.pres.act.ind.of κλαίω, progressive) 225.
τὸ (nom.sing.neut.of the article in agreement with παιδίον) 9.
παιδίον (nom.sing.neut.of παιδίον, subject of ἀπέθανεν and καθεύδει) 174.
οὐκ (summary negative conjunction with the indicative) 130.
ἀπέθανεν (3d.per.sing.2d.aor.act.ind.ofd ἀποθνήσκω, culminative) 774.
ἀλλὰ (alternative conjunction) 342.
καθεύδει (3d.per.sing.pres.act.ind.of καθεύδω, progressive) 755.

Translation - "And He walked in and said to them, 'Why are you upset and weeping? The child is not dead. She is asleep.' "

Comment: Verse 38 says ἔρχονται εἰς τὸν οἶκον. Now verse 39 adds εἰσελθὼν - "He entered in and said to them. . . κ.τ.λ." Jesus, Jairus, Peter, James and John entered the house, but Jesus was alone when He entered the room where the dead child and mourners were. θορυβεῖσθε can be either middle or passive. If passive - "Why are you thrown into tumult?" If middle - "Why do you make such noise?" In any case - "Why the noise?" οὐκ is the summary negative. Jesus was sure of it. But He was using ἀπέθανεν and καθεύδει in His own way. ἀλλὰ is also more strongly adversative than δέ. For further comment *Cf.* Mt.9:23-26 and Lk.8:40-56.

Verse 40 - "And they laughed him to scorn. But when he had put them all out, he taketh the father and the mother of the damsel, and them that were with him, and entereth in where the damsel was lying."

καὶ κατεγέλων αὐτοῦ. αὐτὸς δὲ ἐκβαλὼν πάντας παραλαμβάνει τὸν πατέρα τοῦ παιδίου καὶ τὴν μητέρα καὶ τοὺς μετ᾽ αὐτοῦ, καὶ εἰσπορεύεται ὅπου ἦν τὸ παιδίον,

καὶ (continuative conjunction) 14.

κατεγέλων (3d.per.pl.imp.act.ind.of καταγελάω, inceptive) 827.

αὐτοῦ (gen.sing.masc.of αὐτός, description) 16.

αὐτὸς (nom.sing.masc.of αὐτός, subject of παραλαμβάνει and εἰσπορεύεται) 16.

δὲ (adversative conjunction) 11.

ἐκβαλὼν (2d.aor.act.part.nom.sing.masc.of ἐκβάλλω, adverbial, temporal) 649.

πάντας (acc.pl.masc.of πᾶς, direct object of ἐκβαλὼν) 67.

παραλαμβάνει (3d.per.sing.pres.act.ind.of παραλαμβάνω, historical) 102.

τὸν (acc.sing.masc.of the article in agreement with πατέρα) 9.

πατέρα (acc.sing.masc.of πατήρ, direct object of παραλαμβάνει) 238.

τοῦ (gen.sing.neut.of the article in agreement with παιδίου) 9.

παιδίου (gen.sing.neut.of παιδίον,relationship) 174.

καὶ (adjunctive conjunction joining nouns) 14.

τὴν (acc.sing.fem.of the article in agreement with μητέρα) 9.

μητέρα (acc.sing.fem.of μήτηρ, direct object of παραλαμβάνει) 76.

καὶ (adjunctive conjunction joining substantives) 14.

τοὺς (acc.pl.masc.of the article direct object of παραλαμβάνει) 9.

μετ᾽ (preposition with the genitive of accompaniment) 50.

αὐτοῦ (gen.sing.masc.ofd αὐτός, accompaniment) 16.

καὶ (continuative conjunction) 14.

εἰσπορεύεται (3d.per.sing.pres.ind.of εἰσπορεύομαι, historical) 1161.

ὅπου (relative adverb of place introducing a local clause) 592.

ἦν (3d.per.sing.imp.ind.of εἰμί, progressive duration) 86.

τὸ (nom.sing.neut.of the article in agreement with παιδίον) 9.

παιδίον (nom.sing.neut.of παιδίον, subject of ἦν) 174.

Translation - "And they began to laugh at Him in derision. But He put everyone out and conducted the father of the child and the mother and those with him, and He went into where the child was."

Comment: The reaction of the mourners to Jesus' good news is typical of little people. It is no wonder that Jesus put them out, and that without ceremony! He selected the little group - Jairus, his wife, Peter, James and John and they approached the silent form of the little girl.

Verse 41 - "And he took the damsel by the hand, and said unto her, Talitha cumi, *which is, being interpreted, Damsel, I say unto thee, arise."*

καὶ κρατήσας τῆς χειρὸς τοῦ παιδίου λέγει αὐτῇ, Ταλιθα κουμ, ὅ ἐστιν μεθερμηνευόμενον Τὸ κοράσιον, σοὶ λέγω, ἔγειρε.

καὶ (continuative conjunction) 14.
κρατήσας (aor.act.part.nom.sing.masc.of κρατέω, adverbial, temporal) 828.
τῆς (gen.sing.fem.of the article in agreement with χειρὸς) 9.
χειρὸς (gen.sing.fem.of χείρ, description) 308.
τοῦ (gen.sing.neut.of the article in agreement with παιδίου) 9.
παιδίου (gen.sing.neut.of παιδίον, possession) 174.
λέγει (3d.per.sing.pres.act.ind.of λέγω, aoristic) 66.
αὐτῇ (dat.sing.fem.of αὐτός, indirect object of λέγει) 16.

#2242 Ταλιθα.

Talitha - Mk.5:41.

Meaning: A Chaldean word for maiden, damsel - Mk.5:41.

#2243 κουμ.

Cumi - Mk.5:41.

Meaning: Arise - Mk.5:41.

ὅ (nom.sing.neut.of ὅς, subject of ἐστιν) 65.
ἐστιν (3d.per.sing.pres.ind.of εἰμί, aoristic) 86.
μεθερμηνευόμενον (pres.pass.part.nom.sing.neut.of μεθερμηνεύω, adverbial, circumstantial) 122.
Τὸ (voc.sing.neut.of the article joined to κοράσιον) 9.
κοράσιον (voc.sing.neut.of κοράσιον, address) 826.
σοὶ (dat.sing.fem.of σύ, indirect object of λέγω) 104.
λέγω (1st.per.sing.pres.act.ind.of λέγω, aoristic) 66.
ἔγειρε (2d.per.sing.pres.act.impv.of ἐγείρω, command) 125.

Translation - "And when He had grasped the head of the child, He said to her, Talitha cumi, *which, when translated, means, 'Little girl, to you I say, Arise.'"*

Comment: *Cf.*#828. The word carries a great deal of authority. Our Lord was in complete control of the situation as always. ὅ ἐστιν μεθερμηνευόμενον. . . ἐγείρω is a relative clause which more fully explains the substantive Ταλιθα κουμ. To infinite authority a miracle of this nature is no more difficult than any other. Jesus was under no more stress here than at other times. To say that Deity finds some things more difficult than others is to suggest that Deity finds anything difficult - a concept which is out of harmony with the concept of sovereignty. The only things that a sovereign God cannot do are those things which, if done, would be inconsistent with His own perfect nature. He is limited only by His eternal character, not by anything outside Himself.

In the twenty four hours immediately antecedent to this episode, Jesus had taught supernaturally, stopped a tornado, cast demons out of an insane man, ruined a good herd of pigs, healed a woman whom the doctors could not cure in twelve years, and raised a twelve year old girl from the dead. Trench points to the fact that Elisha cleared the room before he raised the son of the Shunammite (II Kings 4:33). On three occasions Jesus singled out Peter, James and John to witness scenes not permitted to the other disciples. This is the first. The other two are the Transfiguration and the agony in Gethsemane.

Verse 42 - "And straightway the damsel arose and walked; for she was of the age of twelve years. And they were astonished with a great astonishment."

καὶ εὐθὺς ἀνέστη τὸ κοράσιον καὶ περιεπάτει, ἦν γὰρ ἐτῶν δώδεκα. καὶ ἐξέστησαν εὐθὺς ἐκστάσει μεγάλῃ.

καὶ (inferential conjunction) 14.

εὐθὺς (adverbial) 258.

ἀνέστη (3d.per.sing.2d.aor.act.ind.of ἀνίστημι, constative) 789.

τὸ (nom.sing.neut.of the article in agreement with κοράσιον) 9.

κοράσιον (nom.sing.neut.of κοράσιον, subject of ἀνέστη and περιεπάτει) 826.

καὶ (adjunctive conjunction joining verbs) 14.

περιεπάτει (3d.per.sing.imp.act.ind.of περιπατέω, inceptive) 384.

ἦν (3d.per.sing.imp.ind.of εἰμί, progressive description) 86.

γὰρ (causal conjunction) 105.

ἐτῶν (gen.pl.neut.of ἔτος, time description) 821.

δώδεκα (numeral) 820.

καὶ (inferential conjunction) 14.

ἐξέστησαν (3d.per.pl.aor.act.ind.of ἐξίστημι, ingressive) 992.

εὐθὺς (adverbial) 258.

ἐκστάσει (instru.sing.fem.of ἔκστασις, means) 2083.

μεγάλῃ (instru.sing.fem.of μέγας, in agreement with ἐκστάσει) 184.

Translation - "Therefore forthwith the little girl stood up and began to walk around (she was twelve years old). Therefore immediately they were seized with overwhelming ecstasy."

Comment: The inceptive imperfect περιεπάτει gives us the picture. Mark felt it necessary to tell us her age, lest his readers interpret τὸ κοράσιον as being a child too young to walk. There was nothing miraculous about her walking about the room, now that she was alive. Had she opened her eyes, smiled weakly and perhaps waved her hand, she would have proved that she was alive, but not with the dramatic demonstration that she gave. She proved conclusively that Jesus had not only given her life but robust health as well. So also with Lazarus as he sat joyously at the supper table in his home in Bethany as the enemies of Jesus watched him narrowly. Had he been afflicted with the hypochondria which seems characteristic of many backslidden Christians, he would not have been much of a testimony of Jesus' power to raise from the dead. One would be inclined to observe that if *that* was the result of resurrection, Jesus might better have left him in the grave. So here the little girl arises from her bed and begins to explore the premises - perhaps to look for her doll or raid the refrigerator!

The reaction of her parents and the disciples was natural. *Cf.*#'s 992 and 2083, for the exact meaning of these words.Titillation beyond compare! Jesus occasionally frightened people almost out of their minds. A good sermon outline might use these occasions listed under #992. Skeptics have often argued that Jesus raised no one from the dead. He only resuscitated sick people who appeared dead to superficial observation. Jairus' daughter had been dead the shortest time of the three whom Jesus raised. She had just died. The son of the widow of Nain had been dead long enough for funeral procedures to be followed. Lazarus had been dead long enough for decomposition to set in. But the greatest miracle of all is our Lord's own resurrection from the dead. If that did not happen, neither did any of the other three - nor is there resurrection for anyone.

Verse 43 - "And he charged them straitly that no man should know it; and commanded that something should be given her to eat."

καὶ διεστείλατο αὐτοῖς πολλὰ ἵνα μηδεὶς γνοῖ τοῦτο, καὶ εἶπεν δοθῆναι αὐτῇ φαγεῖν.

καὶ (continuative conjunction) 14.

#2244 διεστείλατο (3d.per.sing.1st.aor.mid.ind.of διαστέλλομαι).

charge - Mk.5:43; 7:36,36; 8:15; 9:9.
give commandment - Acts 15:24.
be commanded - Heb.12:20.

Meaning: A combination of διά (#118) and στέλλω (#4342). To draw asunder, divide, distinguish, dispose, order. In a thorough way (the force of διά). In the middle, to open one's mind; to set forth distinctly; hence, to admonish, order, charge. With reference to Jesus' order to those who witnessed the resurrection of Jairus' daughter - Mk.5:43. In connection with the deaf man - Mk.7:36,36. To the disciples about the leaven of the Pharisees - Mk.8:15. To the three disciples after the transfiguration - Mk.9:9. In Peter's sermon at the Jerusalem Council in regard to religious observance - Acts 15:24. With reference to God's injunction to Israel at Sinai - Heb.12:20. In each case, the order is a summary command which brooks no disobedience. With the dative in all cases except in Heb.12:20 where the form is participial.

αὐτοῖς (dat.pl.masc.of αὐτός, indirect object of διεστείλατο) 16.

πολλά (acc.pl.neut.of πολύς, adverbial) 228.

ἵνα (final conjunction introducing a purpose clause) 114.

μηδεὶς (nom.sing.masc.of μηδείς, subject of γνοῖ) 713.

γνοῖ (3d.per.sing.2d.aor.act.subj.of γινώσκω, purpose) 131.

τοῦτο (acc.sing.neut.of οὗτος, direct object of γνοῖ) 93.

εἶπεν (continuative conjunction) 155.

δοθῆναι (1st.aor.pass.inf.of δίδωμι, epexegetical) 362.

αὐτῇ (dat.sing.fem.of αὐτός, indirect object of δοθῆναι) 16.

φαγεῖν (aor.act.inf.of ἐσθίω, complementary) 610.

Translation - "*And He gave them emphatic orders that no one should know about this, and He suggested that she be given something to eat.*"

Comment: διεστείλατο (#2244) means to command thoroughly or insistently. The intensity of the command (intensive διά) lies in the quality of the voice in which it was given, with perhaps an assist from the expression on Jesus' face. The tense is aorist, and hence forbids the notion that He repeated the order. The adverbial πολλά adds to the intensity. Montgomery translates, "He . . . repeatedly cautioned them, κ.τ.λ." Weymouth says, "He gave strict injunctions (note the plural) κ.τ.λ." Goodspeed has ". . . he strictly forbade them. . . κ.τ.λ."

διεστείλατο is completed, not with a complementary infinitive but with ἵνα and the subjunctive of purpose in γνοῖ - "in order that no one should know this." Note the demonstrative pronoun τοῦτο. In δοθῆναι we have a substantival use of the infinitive in the accusative case as the object of εἶπεν.

One of the surest signs of good health is a good appetite. The little girl was so healthy that she was hungry. Jesus, of course, knew this. Her parents were so esctatic over her resurrection that they failed to notice. Hence our Lord's quiet suggestion, "Feed her. She is hungry."

Jesus forbade them to report the incident for the same reason that He did not allow the mob to witness it in the first place. He had already taught against casting pearls before swine. The gainsayers would not have believed it even if they had been told. Note the same charge in Mk.7:36; 9:9. For further comment *Cf.* Luke 8:40-56 we which we now turn.

Luke 8:40 - "And it came to pass, that, when Jesus was returned, the people gladly received him: for they were all waiting for him."

Ἐν δὲ τῷ ὑποστρέφειν τὸν Ἰησοῦν ἀπεδέξατο αὐτὸν ὁ ὄχλος, ἦσαν γὰρ πάντες προσδοκῶντες αὐτόν.

Ἐν (preposition introducing the articular infinitive, loc.of time) 80.

δὲ (continuative conjunction) 11.

τῷ (loc.sing.neut.of the article, loc.of time point) 9.

ὑποστρέφειν (pres.act.inf.of ὑποστρέφω, loc.of time) 1838.

τὸν (acc.sing.masc.of the article in agreement with Ἰησοῦν) 9.

Ἰησοῦν (acc.sing.masc.of Ἰησοῦς, general reference) 3.

#2245 ἀπεδέξατο (3d.per.sing.aor.ind.of ἀποδέχομαι, constative).

accept - Acts 24:3.
gladly receive - Lk.8:40; Acts 2:41; 21:17.
receive - Acts 18:27; 28:30; Lk.9:11.

Meaning: A combination of ἀπό (#70) and δέχομαι (#867). Hence, to receive from, i.e. to receive someone or something, coming from another place. To receive a visitor or a favor offered by someone. Tertullus said the Jewish nation was happy to receive the political favors of Felix - Acts 24:3; the Jews in Jerusalem received the Word of God by faith on Pentecost - Acts 2:41; the brethren received Apollos and gave him hospitality in response to letters from the brethren - Acts 18:27; the Jerusalem chucrh received the brethren who came in Acts 21:17; Paul in his home in Rome received visitors who came to him in Acts 28:30; the citizens of Capernaum received Jesus upon His return from Gadara - Lk.8:40. Jesus received the multitude at Bethsaida - Lk.9:11.

αὐτόν (acc.sing.masc.of αὐτός, direct object of ἀπεδέξατο) 16.
ὁ (nom.sing.masc.of the article in agreement with ὄχλος) 9.
ὄχλος (nom.sing.masc.of ὄχλος, subject of ἀπεδέξατο) 418.
ἦσαν (3d.per.pl.imp.ind.of εἰμί, imperfect periphrastic) 86.
γὰρ (causal conjunction) 105.
πάντες (nom.pl.masc.of πᾶς, subject of ἦσαν) 67.
προσδοκῶντες (pres.act.part.nom.pl.masc.of προσδοκάω, imperfect periphrastic) 906.
αὐτόν (acc.sing.masc.of αὐτός, direct object of προσδοκῶντες) 16.

Translation - "And when Jesus returned the people received Him because they had been expecting Him."

Comment: ἐν introduces the articular infinitive in the locative case indicating time point. This is a verbal use of the infinitive, not a substantival use. Keep in mind that infinitives are verbal nouns. Hence both verb and noun ideas are always present, but one idea in each case dominates the other. Here ὑποστρέφειν is more verb than noun. It is also a noun however, and has τῷ, the article in the locative case. Mantey says, "The infinitive may be used as the equivalent of a temporal clause" (Mantey, *Manual*, 215), while Robertson adds ".. temporal relations are only vaguely expressed by the infinitive." (Robertson, *Grammar*, 1091). Mantey continues, "It does not have within itself any significance of time, but may derive a temporal meaning from the context and its use with a preposition or particle." (Mantey, *Ibid.*). Here ὑποστρέφειν with ἐν and the locative of time in τῷ make clear that the construction is used like a temporal clause. ἐν τῷ also denotes contemporaneous time. *Cf.*#80 for other examples., *e.g.* Mt.27:12; Lk.1:21; 2:27,43; 3:21; 5:12; 8:40; Mt.13:4; Acts 9:3 κ.τ.λ. The people in Capernaum were expecting their hero back. Currently He was very popular in their city. *Cf.*#2245 for the exact meaning of ἀποδέχομαι. ἦσαν γὰρ πάντες προσδοκῶντες is an imperfect periphrastic, which is durative in nature.

They had been waiting there for Him for a long time. *Cf.*#906 - προσδοκάω - "to think or suppose one close by" - hence, expecting. Put Mark 5:21 together with Lk.8:40 and the picture demands that προσδοκῶντες be rendered "they were expecting Him" which is exactly what it means. Expecting Him momentarily to return from Gadard, they hastened to the sea side as soon as He docked. For further comment *Cf.* Mk.5:21.

Verse 41 - "And, behold, there came a man named Jairus, and he was a ruler of the synagogue: and he fell down at Jesus' feet, and besought him that he would come into his house."

καὶ ἰδοὺ ἦλθεν ἀνὴρ ᾧ ὄνομα Ἰάϊρος, καὶ οὗτος ἄρχων τῆς συναγωγῆς ὑπῆρχεν, καὶ πεσὼν παρὰ τοὺς πόδας τοῦ Ἰησοῦ παρεκάλει αὐτὸν εἰσελθεῖν εἰς τὸν οἶκον αὐτοῦ,

καὶ (continuative conjunction) 14.

ἰδοὺ (exclamation) 95.

ἦλθεν (3d.per.sing.aor.act.ind.of ἔρχομαι, constative) 146.

ἀνὴρ (nom.sing.masc.of ἀνήρ, subject of ἦλθεν) 63.

ᾧ (dat.sing.masc.of ὅς, possession) 65.

ὄνομα (nom.sing.neut.of ὄνομα, subject of the verb understood) 108.

Ἰάϊρος (nom.sing.masc.of Ἰάϊρος, appellation) 2233.

καὶ (continuative conjunction) 14.

οὗτος (nom.sing.masc.of οὗτος, demonstrative pronoun, subject of ὑπῆρχεν) 93.

ἄρχων (nom.sing.masc.of ἄρχων, predicate nominative) 816.

τῆς (gen.sing.fem.of the article in agreement with συναγωγῆς) 9.

συναγωγῆς (gen.sing.fem.of συναγωγή, definition) 404.

ὑπῆρχεν (3d.per.sing.imp.act.ind.of ὑπάρχω, progressive duration) 1303.

καὶ (continuative conjunction) 14.

πεσὼν (aor.act.part.nom.sing.masc.of πίπτω, adverbial, temporal) 187.

παρὰ (preposition with the accusative of extent) 154.

τοὺς (acc.pl.masc.of the article in agreement with πόδας) 9.

πόδας (acc.pl.masc.of πούς, extent) 353.

τοῦ (gen.sing.masc.of the article in agreement with Ἰησοῦ) 9.

Ἰησοῦ (gen.sing.masc.of Ἰησοῦς, possession) 3.

παρεκάλει (3d.per.sing.imp.act.ind.of παρακαλέω, inceptive) 230.

αὐτὸν (acc.sing.masc.of αὐτός, direct object of παρεκάλει) 16.

εἰσελθεῖν (aor.inf.of εἰσέρχομαι, epexegetical) 234.

εἰς (preposition with the accusative of extent) 140.

τὸν (acc.sing.masc.of the article in agreement with οἶκον) 9.

οἶκον (acc.sing.masc.of οἶκος, extent) 784.

αὐτοῦ (gen.sing.masc.of αὐτός, possession) 16.

Translation - "And behold a man named Jairus who was ruler of the synagogue came and fell down at the feet of Jesus and began to beg Him to come to his house."

Comment: ᾧ ὄνομα Ἰάϊρος is a relative clause in the dative case, indicating possession. Note the demonstrative pronoun οὗτος in the emphatic position. Luke introduces Jairus simply as a man who came to Jesus. Then he points to him emphatically (οὗτος) as a man of some distinction - he was a ruler of the local synagogue, and therefore an authority on religious questions among the Jews. He had been in that position for some time as the imperfect tense in ὑπῆρχεν reveals. Another imperfect in παρεκάλει is inceptive. Jairus began to plead and continued to do so. Before he began to beg Jesus to come to his home he fell down at His feet. One of the leaders in Capernaum society is in great distress and down on his face before the Son of God.

Verse 42 - "For he had one only daughter, about twelve years of age, and she lay a dying. But as he went the people thronged him."

ὅτι θυγάτηρ μονογενὴς ἦν αὐτῷ ὡς ἐτῶν δώδεκα καὶ αὐτὴ ἀπέθνῃσκεν. Ἐν δὲ τῷ ὑπάγειν αὐτὸν οἱ ὄχλοι συνέπνιγον αὐτόν.

ὅτι (causal conjunction) 211.
θυγάτηρ (nom.sing.fem.of θυγάτηρ, subject of ἦν) 817.
μονογενὴς (nom.sing.fem.of μονογενής, in agreement with θυγάτηρ) 1699.
ἦν (3d.per.sing.imp.ind.of εἰμί, progressive duration) 86.
αὐτῷ (dat.sing.masc.of αὐτός, possession) 16.
ὡς (comparative particle) 128.
ἐτῶν (gen.pl.neut.of ἔτος, description) 821.
δώδεκα (numeral) 820.
καὶ (continuative conjunction) 14.
αὐτὴ (nom.sing.fem.of αὐτός, subject of ἀπέθνῃσκεν) 16.
ἀπέθνῃσκεν (3d.per.sing.imp.act.ind.of ἀποθνῄσκω, progressive description) 774.
Ἐν (preposition introducing the articular infinitive in the locative case) 80.
δὲ (adversative conjunction) 11.
τῷ (loc.sing.neut.of the article, time point) 9.
ὑπάγειν (pres.act.inf.of ὑπάγω, time point) 364.
αὐτὸν (acc.sing.masc.of αὐτός, general reference) 16.
οἱ (nom.pl.masc.of the article in agreement with ὄχλοι) 9.
ὄχλοι (nom.pl.masc.of ὄχλος, subject of συνέπνιγον) 418.
συνέπνιγον (3d.per.pl.imp.act.ind.of συμπνίγω, inceptive) 1051.
αὐτόν (acc.sing.masc.of αὐτός, direct object of συνέπνιγον) 16.

Translation - "Because he had an only daughter about twelve years old, and she was dying. But as He was going the people crowded about Him."

Comment: Note Luke's use of the dative of possession in αυτῷ. He could have written it εἶχεν θυγάτηρ μονογενήν. We have another articular infinitive with ἐν and the locative of time as in verse 40. It is also of interest to note Luke's use of συμπνίγω (#1051) rather than συνθλίβω (#2236), Mark's word. For further comment *Cf.* Mk.5:23,24. In *re* Luke's use of συμπνίγω, this mob who followed

Jesus was similar to the thorns which choke the Word. In that case (Mt.13:22) their presence made the Word of God unfruitful. In this case so would the people have done. This is why Jesus excluded these "thorns" when He arrived at Jairus' house.

Verse 43 - "And a woman having an issue of blood twelve years, which had spent all her living upon physicians, neither could be healed of any."

καὶ γυνὴ οὖσα ἐν ῥύσει αἵματος ἀπὸ ἐτῶν δώδεκα, ἥτις οὐκ ἴσχυσεν ἀπ' οὐδενὸς θεραπευτῆναι,

(Note: Another reading encloses in brackets after ἥτις (ἰατροῖς προσαναλώσασα ὅλον τὸν βίον). Metzger explains, "The clause ἰατροῖς προσαναλώσασα ὅλον τὸν βίον looks like a digest of Mk.5:26. The question is whether anyone except Luke himself would rewrite Mark in this way - with skillful condensation and the substitution of προσαναλώσασα (a hapax legomenon in the New Testament for δαπανήσασα). On the other hand, the early and diversified evidence for the shorter text (*p 75 B (D) (itd syrs pal mss copsa arm geo)* is well-nigh compelling. As a resolution of these conflicting considerations a majority of the Committee decided to retain the words in the text but to enclose them within square brackets, indicating doubt whether they have a right to stand there." (Metzger, *A Textual Commentary on the Greek New Testament*, 145).

καὶ (continuative conjunction) 14.
γυνὴ (nom.sing.fem.of γυνή, subject of ἥψατο) 103.
οὖσα (pres.act.part.nom.sing.fem.of εἰμί, adjectival, ascriptive) 86.
ἐν (preposition with the instrumental of means) 80.
ῥύσει (instru.sing.fem.of ῥύσις, means) 2237.
αἵματος (gen.sing.neut.of αἷμα, description) 1203.
ἀπὸ (preposition with the ablative of time separation) 70.
ἐτῶν (abl.pl.neut.of ἔτος, time separation) 821.
δώδεκα (numeral) 820.
ἥτις (nom.sing.fem.of ὅστις, subject of ἴσχυσεν) 163.
οὐκ (negative conjunction with the indicative) 130.
ἴσχυσεν (3d.per.sing.aor.act.ind.of ἰσχύω, constative) 447.
ἀπ' (preposition with the ablative of agent) 70.
οὐδενὸς (abl.sing.masc.of οὐδείς, agent) 446.
θεραπευθῆναι (1st.aor.pass.inf.of θεραπεύω, epexegetical) 406.

Translation - "And a woman who had been menstruating for twelve years, who was unable to be healed by anyone . . . "

Comment: Mark 5:26 gives the most vivid account of the woman's pitiable condition.

Verse 44 - "Came behind him, and touched the border of his garment: and immediately her issue of blood stanched."

προσελθοῦσα ὄπισθεν ἥψατο τοῦ κρασπέδου τοῦ ἱματίου αὐτοῦ, καὶ παραχρῆμα ἔστη ἡ ῥύσις τοῦ αἵματος αὐτῆς.

προσελθοῦσα (aor.part.nom.sing.fem.of προσέρχομαι, adverbial, temporal) 336.

ὄπισθεν (adverbial) 822.

ἥψατο (3d.per.sing.aor.mid.ind.of ἅπτω, constative) 711.

τοῦ (gen.sing.neut.of the article in agreement with κρασπέδου) 9.

κρασπέδου (gen.sing.neut.of κράσπεδον, description) 823.

τοῦ (gen.sing.neut.of the article in agreement with ἱματίου) 9.

ἱματίου (gen.sing.neut.of ἱμάτιον, description) 534.

αὐτοῦ (gen.sing.masc.of αὐτός, possession) 16.

καὶ (continuative conjunction) 14.

παραχρῆμα (adverbial) 1369.

ἔστη (3d.per.sing.2d.aor.act.ind.of ἵστημι, constative) 180.

ἡ (nom.sing.fem.of the article in agreement with ῥύσις) 9.

ῥύσις (nom.sing.fem.of ῥύσις, subject of ἔστη) 2237.

τοῦ (gen.sing.neut.of the article in agreement with αἵματος) 9.

αἵματος (gen.sing.neut.of αἷμα, description) 1203.

αὐτῆς (gen.sing.fem.of αὐτός, possession) 16.

Translation - " . . . approached him from behind and touched the hem of His garment, and immediately her hemorrhage ceased.

Comment: The participle οὖσα is an adjective, ascriptive in character and joined to γυνή of verse 43, but the participle προσελθοῦσα is a temporal adverb, joined to ἥψατο. We have an interesting use of ἵστημι (#180) here. The flow of blood stood still. Her faith in the touch, not the touch itself, healed the woman.

Verse 45 - "And Jesus said, Who touched me? When all denied, Peter and they that were with him said, Master, the multitude throng thee and press thee, and sayest thou, Who touched me?"

καὶ εἶπεν ὁ Ἰησοῦς, Τίς ὁ ἁψάμενός μου; ἀρνουμένων δὲ πάντων εἶπεν ὁ Πέτρος, Ἐπιστάτα, οἱ ὄχλοι συνέχουσίν σε καὶ ἀποθλίβουσιν,

καὶ (continuative conjunction) 14.

εἶπεν (3d.per.sing.aor.act.ind.of εἶπον, constative) 155.

ὁ (nom.sing.masc.of the article in agreement with Ἰησοῦς) 9.

Ἰησοῦς (nom.sing.masc.of Ἰησοῦς, subject of εἶπεν) 3.

Τίς (nom.sing.masc.of the interrogative pronoun τίς, predicate nominative) 281.

ὁ (nom.sing.masc.of the article in agreement with ἁψάμενός) 9.

ἁψάμενός, pres.mid.part.nom.sing.masc.of ἅπτω, subject of ἐστιν understood) 711.

μου (gen.sing.masc.of ἐγώ, description) 123.

ἀρνουμένων (pres.part.gen.pl.masc.of ἀρνέομαι, genitive absòlute) 895.

δέ (adversative conjunction) 11.

πάντων (gen.pl.masc.of πᾶς, genitive absolute) 67.

εἶπεν (3d.per.sing.aor.act.ind.of εἶπον, constative) 155.

ὁ (nom.sing.masc.of the article in agreement with Πέτρος) 9.

Πέτρος (nom.sing.masc.of Πέτρος, subject of εἶπεν) 387.

Ἐπιστάτα (voc.sing.masc.of Ἐπιστάτης, address) 2047.

οἱ (nom.pl.masc.of the article in agreement with ὄχλοι) 9.

ὄχλοι (nom.pl.masc.of ὄχλος, subject of συνέχουσίν and ἀποθλίβουσιν) 418.

συνέχουσίν (3d.per.pl.pres.act.ind.of συνέχω, aoristic) 414.

σε (acc.sing.masc.of σύ, direct object of συνέχουσίν) 104.

καὶ (adjunctive conjunction joining verbs) 14.

#2246 ἀποθλίβουσιν (3d.per.pl.pres.act.ind.of ἀποθλίβω, aorist).

press - Lk.8:45.

Meaning: A combination of ἀπό (#70) and θλίβω (#667). To press from all sides; squeeze; press hard. *Cf.* LXX, Numbers 22:25 - the ass squeezed Balaam's foot against the wall. Of the pressure of the Capernaum mob upon Jesus - Lk.8:45.

Translation - "And Jesus said, 'Who touched me?' (Literally, The one who is touching me is who?) But as everyone denied it Peter said, 'Master the crowds are thronging and pressing upon you from all sides.' "

Comment: The subject in Jesus' question is the participial substantive ὁ ἀφάμενός, the subject of ἔστιν understood, while the predicate nominative is the interrogative pronoun Τίς. Luke omitted the copula.

　　Everyone denied it. This shows how the people felt about Jesus. Half afraid of Him, and with great respect, yet they did not wish to displease Him in any way, because they did not really trust Him as the poor woman did. As they were registering their denials ("Who, me?" "Not me.") Peter replied with some sarcasm. Mark 5:31 says that the disciples replied to Him. Peter said, "They have you surrounded and are pressing in upon you from all sides." In view of this fact Peter thought that Jesus' question was stupid. *Cf.*#'s 414 and 2246 for the full meaning of these words. *Cf.* Mark 5:31 for a fuller comment.

Verse 46 - "And Jesus said, Somebody hath touched me: for I perceive that virtue is gone out of me."

　　ὁ δὲ Ἰησοῦς εἶπεν, Ἥφατό μού τις, ἐγὼ γὰρ ἔγνων δύναμιν ἐξεληλυθυῖαν ἀπ' ἐμοῦ.

ὁ (nom.sing.masc.of the article in agreement with Ἰησοῦς) 9.

δέ (adversative conjunction) 11.

Ἰησοῦς (nom.sing.masc.of Ἰησοῦς, subject of εἶπεν) 3.

εἶπεν (3d.per.sing.aor.act.ind.of εἶπον, constative) 155.

Ἡφατό (3d.per.sing.aor.mid.ind.of ἅπτω, culminative) 711.

μού (gen.sing.masc.of ἐγώ, description) 123.

τις (nom.sing.masc.of the indefinite pronoun τις, subject of ἡφατό) 486.

ἐγώ (nom.sing.masc.of ἐγώ, subject of ἔγνων) 123.

γάρ (causal conjunction) 105.

ἔγνων (1st.per.sing.2d.aor.act.ind.of γινώσκω, aoristic) 131.

δύναμιν (acc.sing.fem.of δύναμις, direct object of ἔγνων) 687.

ἐξεληλυθυῖαν (perf.part.acc.sing.fem.of ἐξέρχομαι, adjectival, ascriptive) 161.

ἀπ' (preposition with the ablative of separation) 70.

ἐμοῦ (abl.sing.masc.of ἐμός, separation) 1267.

Translation - "But Jesus said, 'Someone has touched me, because I am aware that power has gone from me.' "

Comment:Ἡφατο is in the emphatic position. The aorist ἔγνων together with the perfect tense in the participle ἐξεληλυθυῖαν gives us a continuous action situation in past time. "I knew (past time) and therefore I now know (culminative) that power has been passing from me and therefore (at the present moment) that power is gone." Mark handles this material earlier in the story. *Cf.* Mk.5:30.

Jesus statement to Peter, overheard by the woman, who is now healed forces her into the open with her confession as we see in

Verse 47 - "And when the woman saw that she was not hid, she came trembling and falling down before him, she declared unto him before all the people for what cause she had touched him, and how she was healed immediately."

ἰδοῦσα δὲ ἡ γυνὴ ὅτι οὐκ ἔλαθεν τρέμουσα ἦλθεν καὶ προσπεσοῦσα αὐτῷ δι' ἣν αἰτίαν ἥψατο αὐτοῦ ἀπήγγειλεν ἐνώπιον παντὸς τοῦ λαοῦ καὶ ὡς ἰάθη παραχρῆμα.

ἰδοῦσα (aor.part.nom.sing.fem.of ὁράω, adverbial, temporal) 144.

δὲ (inferential conjunction) 11.

ἡ (nom.sing.fem.of the article in agreement with γυνή) 9.

γυνὴ (nom.sing.fem.of γυνή, subject of ἦλθεν and ἀπήγγειλεν) 103.

ὅτι (conjunction introducing an objective clause in indirect discourse) 211.

οὐκ (negative conjunction with the indicative) 130.

#2247 ἔλαθεν (3d.per.sing.2d.aor.ind.of λανθάνω, culminative).

be hid - Mk.7:24; Lk.8:47.
be hidden - Acts 26:26.
be ignorant of - II Pet.3:5,8.
unawares - Heb.13:2.

Meaning: To be hidden; to be unknown to someone. Jesus found it impossible to be incognito in Tyre and Sidon - Mk.7:24. The woman could not conceal the fact from Jesus that she had been healed - Lk.8:47. The story of first century Christianity development was not hidden from Agrippa - Acts 26:26. End time apostates are willingly ignorant of certain things - II Pet.3:5,8.* Abraham entertained angels without knowing them - Heb.13:2.

*A charge to Christians.

τρέμουσα (pres.act.part.nom.sing.fem.of τρέμω, adverbial, modal) 2239.

ἦλθεν (3d.per.sing.aor.act.ind.of ἔρχομαι, constative) 146.

καὶ (adjunctive conjunction joining verbs) 14.

προσπεσοῦσα (aor.act.part.nom.sing.fem.of προσπίπτω, adverbial, temporal) 699.

αὐτῷ (loc.sing.masc.of αὐτός, after πρός with a verb of rest) 16.

δι' (preposition with the accusative, cause) 118.

ἣν (acc.sing.fem.of the relative pronoun ὅς, in agreement with αἰτίαν) 65.

αἰτίαν (acc.sing.fem.of αἰτία, cause) 1283.

ἥψατο (3d.per.sing.aor.mid.ind.of ἅπτω, constative) 711.

αὐτοῦ (gen.sing.masc.of αὐτός, description) 16.

ἀπήγγειλεν (3d.per.sing.1st.aor.act.ind.of ἀπαγγέλλω, constative) 176.

ἐνώπιον (improper preposition with the genitive, adverbial) 1798.

παντὸς (gen.sing.masc.of πᾶς, in agreement with λαοῦ) 67.

τοῦ (gen.sing.masc.of the article in agreement with λαοῦ) 9.

λαοῦ (gen.sing.masc.of λαός, place where after ἐνώπιον) 110.

καὶ (adjunctive conjunction joining a prepositional phrase with a comparative clause) 14.

ὡς (conjunction introducing a comparative clause) 128.

ἰάθη (3d.per.sing.aor.pass.ind.of ἰάομαι, culminative) 721.

παραχρῆμα (adverbial) 1369.

Translation - *"Therefore the woman, when she realized that she was not hidden came trembling and fell down before Him and declared before all the people the reason why she touched Him and how she was healed immediately."*

Comment: This is Luke's Greek at its best. Note the use of the participles. The woman no doubt had been ashamed to speak of her illness during the dreadful twelve years when she had spent all of her money and gone to every doctor. Now that she is healed the shame is gone and she is filled with delight and love for her Lord, to whom she gives all the credit. *Cf.* Mk.5:33 for further comment.

Verse 48 - *"And he said unto her, Daughter, be of good comfort: thy faith hath made thee whole; go in peace."*

ὁ δὲ εἶπεν αὐτῇ, Θυγάτηρ, ἡ πίστις σου σέσωκέν σε. πορεύου εἰς εἰρήνην.

ὁ (nom.sing.masc.of the article, subject of εἶπεν) 9.

δὲ (continuative conjunction) 11.

εἶπεν (3d.per.sing.aor.act.ind.of εἶπον, constative) 155.

αὐτῇ (dat.sing.fem.of αὐτός, indirect object of εἶπεν) 16.

Θυγάτηρ (voc.sing.fem.of θυγάτηρ, address) 817.

ἡ (nom.sing.fem.of the article in agreement with πίστις) 9.
πίστις (nom.sing.fem.of πίστις, subject of σέσωκέν) 728.
σου (gen.sing.fem.of σύ, possession) 104.
σέσωκέν (3d.per.sing.perf.act.ind.of σώζω, consummative) 109.
σε (acc.sing.fem.of σύ, direct object of σέσωκέν) 104.
πορεύου (2d.per.sing.pres.act.impv.of πορεύομαι, command) 170.
εἰς (preposition with the accusative, original static use) 140.
εἰρήνην (acc.sing.fem.of εἰρήνη, static use, adverbial) 865.

Translation - "And He said to her, 'Daughter, your faith has saved you. Go in peace.'"

Comment: σέσωκέν σε - A consummative perfect tense indicating a present durative condition as a result of a past completed action. Her faith was exercised when she believed in Him enough to struggle through the crowd and make the desperate effort to touch His garment. Then she was healed and her soul was saved. Both healings, physical and spiritual were permanent. *Cf.* Mark 5:33,34 for further comment.

We now turn our attention again to Jairus and his problem in

Verse 49 - "While he yet spake, there cometh one from the ruler of the synagogue's house saying to him, Thy daughter is dead; trouble not the Master.'"

Ἔτι αὐτοῦ λαλοῦντος ἔρχεταί τις παρὰ τοῦ ἀρχισυναγώγου λέγων ὅτι Τέθνηκεν ἡ θυγάτηρ σου, μηκέτι σκύλλε τὸν διδάσκαλον.

Ἔτι (adverbial) 448.
αὐτοῦ (gen.sing.masc.of αὐτός, genitive absolute) 16.
λαλοῦντος (pres.act.part.gen.sing.masc.of λαλέω, genitive absolute) 815.
ἔρχεται (3d.per.sing.pres.ind.of ἔρχομαι, historical) 146.
τις (nom.sing.masc.of the indefinite pronoun τις, subject of ἔρχεται) 486.
παρὰ (preposition with the ablative of source) 154.
τοῦ (gen.sing.masc.of the article in agreement with ἀρχισυναγώγου) 9.
ἀρχισυναγώγου (gen.sing.masc.of ἀρχισυνάγωγος, possession) 2232.
λέγων (pres.act.part.nom.sing.masc.of λέγω, adverbial, temporal) 66.
ὅτι (conjunction introducing an objective clause in indirect discourse) 211.
Τέθνηκεν (3d.per.sing.perf.act.ind.of θνήσκω, consummative) 232.
ἡ (nom.sing.fem.of the article in agreement with θυγάτηρ) 9.
θυγάτηρ (nom.sing.fem.of θυγάτηρ, subject of τέθνηκεν) 817.
σου (gen.sing.masc.of σύ, relationship) 104.
μηκέτι (adverb of time) 1368.
σκύλλε (2d.per.sing.pres.act.impv.of σκύλλω, command) 836.
τὸν (acc.sing.masc.of the article in agreement with διδάσκαλον) 9.
διδάσκαλον (acc.sing.masc.of διδάσκαλος, direct object of σκύλλε) 742.

Translation - "As He was speaking someone came from (the house) of the ruler of the synagogue saying, 'Your daughter is dead. Do not trouble the Teacher any longer.'"

Comment: Mark says that more than one came to Jairus. Luke does not deny it; he singles out one. Mark uses ἀπό with the ablative. Luke has παρὰ with the ablative and the genitive of possession. "From the house of the ruler of the synagogue" is the apparent meaning. Mark has the aorist ἀπέθανεν; Luke the perfect τέθνηκεν. Mark has the rhetorical question; Luke the imperative. These do not constitute any essential differences in communication of thought. For comment *cf.* Mk.5:35.

We could hardly expect these men to believe that Jesus could raise the dead, though they might have believed with Jairus that He could heal the sick. For them, death was final. But when Jesus is present, death is never final! (I Cor.15:26). This is why, though Jesus heard them (vs.50), He ignored them (Mk.5:36).

Verse 50 - "But when Jesus heard it, he answered him, saying, Fear not: believe only, and she shall be made whole."

ὁ δὲ Ἰησοῦς ἀκούσας ἀπεκρίθη αὐτῷ, Μὴ φοβοῦ, μόνον πίστευσον, καὶ σωθήσεται.

ὁ (nom.sing.masc.of the article in agreement with Ἰησοῦς) 9.

δὲ (adversative conjunction) 11.

Ἰησοῦς (nom.sing.masc.of Ἰησοῦς, subject of ἀπεκρίθη) 3.

ἀκούσας (aor.act.part.nom.sing.masc.of ἀκούω, adverbial, temporal) 148.

αὐτῷ (dat.sing.masc.of αὐτός, indirect object of ἀπεκρίθη) 16.

Μὴ (qualified negative conjunction with the imperative) 87.

φοβοῦ (2d.per.sing.pres.impv.of φοβέομαι, command) 101.

μόνον (acc.sing.neut.of μόνος, adverbial) 339.

πίστευσον (2d.per.sing.aor.act.impv.of πιστεύω, command) 734.

καὶ (continuative conjunction) 14.

σωθήσεται (3d.per.sing.fut.pass.ind.of σώζω, predictive) 109.

Translation - "But when Jesus heard it He answered him, 'Try not to be afraid. Only believe one more time and she will be saved."

Comment: Jesus heard the remark of the one who came to tell Jairus that his daughter was dead, but He did not respond to it. Instead He spoke to Jairus. Μὴ φοβοῦ is the imperative of entreaty. μή is a qualified negative, used with the imperative, where there is some doubt that the order will be obeyed. Jesus knew that it was too much to expect that Jairus would not be devastated by the news. Hence our translation. That Jairus had lost faith seems clear from Jesus' use of the aorist in μόνον πίστευσον - "Believe one more time." It is Jesus' plea for Jairus to exercise extreme faith. He strengthens it with the prediction of the future passive σωθήσεται - "she shall be saved."

Cf. Mark 5:36 for a fuller discussion.

Verse 51 - "And when he came into the house, he suffered no man to go in, save Peter, and James, and John, and the father and the mother of the maiden."

ἐλθὼν δὲ εἰς τὴν οἰκίαν οὐκ ἀφῆκεν εἰσελθεῖν τινα σὺν αὐτῷ εἰ μὴ Πέτρον καὶ Ἰωάννην καὶ Ἰάκωβον καὶ τὸν πατέρα τῆς παιδὸς καὶ τὴν μητέρα.

ἐλθὼν (aor.act.part.nom.sing.masc.of ἔρχομαι, adverbial, temporal) 146.
δὲ (continuative conjunction) 11.
εἰς (preposition with the accusative of extent) 140.
τὴν (acc.sing.fem.of the article in agreement with οἰκίαν) 9.
οἰκίαν (acc.sing.fem.of οἰκία, extent) 186.
οὐκ (summary negative conjunction with the indicative) 130.
ἀφῆκεν (3d.per.sing.aor.act.ind.of ἀφίημι, constative) 319.
εἰσελθεῖν (aor.inf.of εἰσέρχομαι, epexegetical) 234.
τινα (acc.sing.masc.of τις, direct object of ἀφῆκεν) 486.
σὺν (preposition with the instrumental of accompaniment) 1542.
αὐτῷ (instru.sing.masc.of αὐτός, accompaniment) 16.
εἰ (conditional particle) 337.
μὴ (qualified negative conjunction with εἰ) 87.
Πέτρον (acc.sing.masc.of Πέτρος, direct object of ἀφῆκεν) 387.
καὶ (adjunctive conjunction joining nouns) 14.
Ἰωάννην (acc.sing.masc.of Ἰωάννης, direct object of ἀφῆκεν) 399.
καὶ (adjunctive conjunction joining nouns) 14.
Ἰάκωβον (acc.sing.masc.of Ἰάκωβον, direct object of ἀφῆκεν) 397.
καὶ (adjunctive conjunction joining nouns) 14.
τὸν (acc.sing.masc.of the article in agreement with πατέρα) 9.
πατέρα (acc.sing.masc.of πατήρ, direct object of ἀφῆκεν) 238.
τῆς (gen.sing.fem.of the article in agreement with παιδὸς) 9.
παιδὸς (gen.sing.fem.of παῖς, relationship) 217.
καὶ (adjunctive conjunction joining nouns) 14.
τὴν (acc.sing.fem.of the article in agreement with μητέρα) 9.
μητέρα (acc.sing.fem.of μήτηρ, direct object of ἀφῆκεν) 76.

Translation - "And when He came into the house He did not allow to enter in with Him anyone except Peter, and John, and James and the father of the little girl and her mother."

Comment: There seems to be a slight discrepancy in the accounts of Mark and Luke as to when Jesus banned the curious followers. Mark says that He forbade them to follow with Him (Mk.5:37) and then that the five, Jesus, Jairus, Peter, James and John "came into the house" (Mk.5:38), put the minstrels out and joined by the girl's mother, entered the room where the child lay (Mk.5:40). Luke says that the ban on the followers came after they entered the house (Lk.8:51), unless we translate εἰς τὴν οἰκίαν with "unto the house" which is better expressed by πρὸς τὴν οἰκίαν. It is a small point and really makes no difference in the main lines of the story. It is interesting also to note Mark's μετ᾽ αὐτοῦ against Luke's σὺν αὐτῷ. On the point as to why Jesus banned the audience, cf. Mk.5:36.

Verse 52 - "And all wept, and bewailed her: but he said, Weep not; she is not dead, but sleepeth."

ἔκλαιον δὲ πάντες καὶ ἐκόπτοντο αὐτήν. ὁ δὲ εἶπεν, Μὴ κλαίετε, οὐ γὰρ ἀπέθανεν ἀλλὰ καθεύδει.

ἔκλαιον (3d.per.pl.imp.act.ind.of κλαίω, progressive duration) 225.
δὲ (continuative conjunction) 11.
πάντες (nom.pl.masc.of πᾶς, subject of ἔκλαιον and ἐκόπτοντο) 67.
καὶ (adjunctive conjunction joining verbs) 14.
ἐκόπτοντο (3d.per.pl.imp.mid.ind.of κόπτω, progressive duration) 929.
αὐτήν (acc.sing.fem.of αὐτός, general reference, cause) 16.
ὁ (nom.sing.masc.of the article subject of εἶπεν) 9.
δὲ (adversative conjunction) 11.
εἶπεν (3d.per.sing.aor.act.ind.of εἶπον, constative) 155.
Μὴ (qualified negative conjunction with the imperative) 87.
κλαίετε (2d.per.pl.pres.act.impv.of κλαίω, command) 225.
οὐ (summary negative conjunction with the indicative) 130.
γὰρ (causal conjunction) 105.
ἀπέθανεν (3d.per.sing.aor.act.ind.of ἀποθνήσκω, culminative) 774.
ἀλλὰ (alternative conjunction) 342.
καθεύδει (3d.per.sing.pres.act.ind.of καθεύδω, aoristic) 755.

Translation - "And everyone was weeping and beating himself because of her. But He said, 'Try to stop crying, because she is not dead, but she is sleeping.'"

Comment: The first δὲ is continuative. The minstrels had no reason to think that Jesus could help at this point. However, after He spoke, the thought becomes strongly adversative. The second δὲ is therefore adversative. Jesus strongly disagreed with their behavior. Anyone who mourns when Jesus is present is misguided. Note the imperfect continuous action in both ἔκλαιον and ἐκόπτοντο. They "continued to wail and to beat themselves." Why? αὐτήν in the accusative indicates cause. Cf.#929 for the exact meaning. It is a pagan practice still observed as a mark of social distinction in some communities, as any funeral director can testify. Since neither verb is transitive αὐτὴν cannot be the direct object.

Note the qualified negative Μὴ with the imperative. Jesus knew that they would not obey His order. On the contrary they laughed at Him (vs.53). But Jesus got dogmatic with it as He added His statement with the summary οὐκ and the dogmatic indicative. "She is not dead, but she is sleeping."

It requires a look at all three parallel accounts to get the complete picture. Cf. Mt.9:23; Mk.5:38 and our passage under discussion.

Verse 53 - "And they laughed him to scorn, knowing that she was dead."

καὶ κατεγέλων αὐτοῦ, εἰδότες ὅτι ἀπέθανεν.

καὶ (adversative conjunction) 14.

κατεγέλων (3d.per.pl.imp.act.ind.of καταγελάω, inceptive) 827.
αὐτοῦ (gen.sing.masc.of αὐτός, hostility, after κατά in composition) 16.
εἰδότες (aor.part.nom.pl.masc.of ὁράω, adverbial, causal) 144.
ὅτι (conjunction introducing an object clause, in indirect discourse) 211.
ἀπέθανεν (3d.per.sing.aor.act.ind.of ἀποθνήσκω, culminative) 774.

Translation - "But they began to laugh at Him, because they knew that she was dead."

Comment: The inceptive imperfect in κατεγέλων indicates the reaction of the mourners and the insincerity of their motives. One minute they were wailing and beating their breasts; the next minute they were laughing in derision at the Son of God. His statement that she was not dead had precipitated their laughter - "They *began* (inceptive) to laugh at Him. Why? The participle εἰδότες is adverbial and causal. Because they knew something. What? The object clause with ὅτι - "that she had died and was therefore dead" (culminative aorist).

Shakespeare quotes the phrase "laugh to scorn" in Macbeth, *Act 5, Sc.5* - "... our castles strength will laugh a siege to scorn." But the hired mourners in Jairus' house had no more respect for Jesus' power to conquer death, than Macbeth had for the forests of "Great Birnam wood" to overthrow "high Dunsinane hill" (Macbeth, *Act IV, Sc.I).* Yet neither the scorn of the mourners, nor Macbeth's misplaced faith in his castle, could frustrate the superior power present. Dunsinane fell and Macbeth died. Jairus' daughter lived.

Verse 54 - "And he put them all out, and took her by the hand, and called, saying, Maid, arise."

αὐτὸς δὲ κρατήσας τῆς χειρὸς αὐτῆς ἐφώνησεν λέγων, Ἡ παῖς ἔγειρε.

αὐτὸς (nom.sing.masc.of αὐτός, 3d.personal pronoun, subject of ἐφώνησεν) 16.
δὲ (adversative conjunction) 11.
κρατήσας (aor.act.part.nom.sing.masc.of κρατέω, adverbial, temporal) 828.
τῆς (gen.sing.fem.of the article in agreement with χειρὸς) 9.
χειρὸς (gen.sing.fem.of χείρ, description) 308.
αὐτῆς (gen.sing.fem.of αὐτός, possession) 16.
ἐφώνησεν (3d.per.sing.aor.act.ind.of φωνέω, constative) 1338.
λέγων (pres.act.part.nom.sing.masc.of λέγω, adverbial, modal) 66.
ἡ (voc.sing.fem.of the article in agreement with παῖς) 9.
παῖς (voc.sing.fem.of παῖς, address) 217.
ἔγειρε (2d.per.sing.pres.act.impv.of ἐγείρω, command) 125.

Translation - "But when He had taken her hand, He called, saying, 'Maid, arise.'
"

Comment: Jesus called Lazarus out of the tomb in the same way. *Cf.* John 12:17, #1338. See also #828 for the authority involved in κρατέω. αὐτὸς - twice here; the first time as subject of the verb and then in the genitive of possession. ἡ παῖς ἔγειρε - Jesus made it definite. *Cf.* Mt.9:25; Mk.5:41 for further comment.

Verse 55 - "And her spirit came again, and she arose straightway: and he commanded to give her meat."

καὶ ἐπέστρεφεν τὸ πνεῦμα αὐτῆς, καὶ ἀνέστη παραχρῆμα, καὶ διέταξεν αὐτῇ δοθῆναι φαγεῖν.

καὶ (inferential conjunction) 14.

ἐπέστρεφεν (3d.per.sing.aor.act.ind.of ἐπιστρέφω, constative) 866.

τὸ (nom.sing.neut.of the article in agreement with πνεῦμα) 9.

πνεῦμα (nom.sing.neut.of πνεῦμα, subject of ἐπέστρεφεν) 83.

αὐτῆς (gen.sing.fem.of αὐτός, possession) 16.

καὶ (continuative conjunction) 14.

ἀνέστη (3d.per.sing.2d.aor.act.ind.of ἀνίστημι, constative) 789.

παραχρῆμα (adverbial) 1369.

καὶ (continuative conjunction) 14.

διέταξεν (3d.per.sing.1st.aor.act.ind.of διατάσσω, constative) 904.

αὐτῇ (dat.sing.fem.of αὐτός, indirect object of δοθῆναι) 16.

δοθῆναι (1st.aor.pass.inf.of δίδωμι, epexegetical) 362.

φαγεῖν (aor.act.inf.of ἐσθίω, epexegetical) 610.

Translation - "Therefore her spirit returned, and she stood up immediately, and He ordered that something be given to her to eat."

Comment: There is real action in this dramatic scene. Three coordinate clauses stand paratactically. Her spirit returned. She stood up forthwith. He ordered them to feed her. *Cf.*#866 - "to turn back." This verb proves that the girl was lifeless when Jesus walked in. It was for Luke, the physician, to give us the diagnosis. Matthew says, "She was raised up" (Mt.9:25. Mark 5:42 says, "she stood up and walked around." Both of these permit the theory that she had only fainted and that Jesus only revived her. But Luke tells us that her human spirit came back, which means that the spirit had already left. She was dead. Luke adds then, in agreement with the other reporters that she stood up immediately (#1369). *Cf.*#904 for the exact meaning. Jesus gave specific orders for her feeding. Does this mean that He prescribed the menu? διά plus τάσσω means to arrange thoroughly even in the small details. The mother was too overjoyed to do her duty momentarily. Any girl whom Jesus raises from the dead is in good health and every healthy girl of twelve years is hungry. The two infinitives are epexegetical. δοθῆναι explains διέταξεν and φαγεῖν explains δοθῆναι.

Verse 56 - "And her parents were astonished: but he charged them that they should tell no man what was done."

καὶ ἐξέστησαν οἱ γονεῖς αὐτῆς, ὁ δὲ παρήγγειλεν αὐτοῖς μηδενὶ εἰπεῖν τὸ γεγονός.

καὶ (inferential conjunction) 14.

ἐξέστησαν (3d.per.pl.aor.act.ind.of ἐξίστημι, constative) 992.

οἱ (nom.pl.masc.of the article in agreement with γονεῖς) 9.

γονεῖς (nom.pl.masc.of γονεύς, subject of ἐξέστησαν) 878.

αὐτῆς (gen.sing.fem.of αὐτός, possession) 16.

ὁ (nom.sing.masc.of the article subject of παρήγγειλεν) 9.

δὲ (adversative conjunction) 11.

παρήγγειλεν (3d.per.sing.aor.act.ind.of παραγγέλλω, ingressive) 855.

αὐτοῖς (dat.pl.masc.of αὐτός, indirect object of παρήγγειλεν) 16.

μηδενὶ (dat.sing.masc.of μηδείς, indirect object of εἰπεῖν) 713.

εἰπεῖν (aor.inf.of εἶπον, complementary) 155.

τό (acc.sing.neut.of the article in agreement with γεγονός) 9.

γεγονός (2d.perf.part.acc.sing.neut.of γίνομαι, substantival, direct object of εἰπεῖν) 113.

Translation - "*Therefore her parents were beside themselves. But He began to order them to tell no one about that which had been done.*"

Comment: *Cf.*#992 for the exact meaning. "They were standing outside themselves." We might say, "Frightened out of their wits." It was a natural reaction. Contrast the father's mood in Lk.8:40,41 and Mk.5:22,23. Our Lord can transform our deepest depths of despair into heights of ecstatic joy! #855 denotes authority as διέταξεν did in verse 55 and ἔγειρε in verse 54. The substantival participle τό γεγονός is the direct object of the infinitive εἰπεῖν. Jesus' popularity in Capernaum at this point was at its height. The mob was about to get out of hand. Why add fuel to the flames? Jesus, Who knows the heart of every man (John 2:24,25) was well aware that the superficial enthusiasm of the people, based upon His ability to raise from the dead a little girl, would turn to the hatred that demanded His blood later. Who needs the acclaim of people like that? Hence He told Jairus and his wife not to mention the event.

(Note: The student should now turn to Mt.9:27-34 for the account of the healing of the two blind men and a dumb demoniac.)

The Third Preaching Tour

The Second Rejection at Nazareth

(Mk.6:1-6; Mt.13:54-58)

Mark 6:1 - "*And he went out from thence, and came into his own country; and his disciples follow him.*"

Καὶ ἐξῆλθεν ἐκεῖθεν, καὶ ἔρχεται εἰς τὴν πατρίδα αὐτοῦ, καὶ ἀκολουθοῦσιν αὐτῷ οἱ μαθηταὶ αὐτοῦ.

Καὶ (continuative conjunction) 14.

ἐξῆλθεν (3d.per.sing.aor.act.ind.of ἐξέρχομαι, constative) 161.

ἐκεῖθεν (adverbial) 396.

καὶ (adjunctive conjunction joining verbs) 14.

ἔρχεται (3d.per.sing.pres.ind.of ἔρχομαι,historical) 146.
εἰς (preposition with the accusative of extent) 140.
τὴν (acc.sing.fem.of the article in agreement with πατρίδα) 9.
πατρίδα (acc.sing.fem.of πατρίς, extent) 1096.
αὐτοῦ (gen.sing.masc.of αὐτός, possession) 16.
καὶ (continuative conjunction) 14.
ἀκολουθοῦσιν (3d.per.pl.pres.act.ind.of ἀκολουθέω, historical) 394.
αὐτῷ (dat.sing.masc.of αὐτός, personal interest) 16.
οἱ (nom.pl.masc.of the article in agreement with μαθηταί) 9.
μαθηταὶ (nom.pl.masc.of μαθητής, subject of ἀκολουθοῦσιν) 421.
αὐτοῦ (gen.sing.masc.of αὐτός, relationship) 16.

Translation - "And He left there and came into His home town, and His disciples followed Him."

Comment: After using the aorist ἐξῆλθεν, Mark continues with the historical present. εἰς τὴν πατρίδα αὐτοῦ - "into His fatherland." His home town, Nazareth, where Joseph and Mary lived and where Jesus spent His childhood, although Capernaum was now, temporarily at least, His headquarters.

Matthew records two healing incidents in Capernaum, following the resurrection of Jairus' daughter in Mt.9:27-34. This He did before leaving Capernaum to return to Nazareth. It will be recalled that this is Jesus' second trip to Nazareth since He left there at the age of thirty to be baptized by John. Read the account of His first rejection in Lk.4:16-30. Then He had read Isa.61:1-2a in the synagogue and had said things which enraged the Nazarenes who tried to kill Him by throwing Him off a cliff. "No prophet is accepted in His own country" (Lk.4:24) He had said on that occasion. Things had not changed in Nazareth since Jesus was there before, as we shall see. His ministry began in the same place and on a similar occasion as on His previous visit, as we see in

Verse 2 - "And when the sabbath day was come, he began to teach in the synagogue: and many hearing him were astonished, saying, From whence hath this man these things? And what wisdom is this which is given unto him, that even such mighty works are wrought by his hands?"

καὶ γενομένου σαββάτου ἤρξατο διδάσκειν ἐν τῇ συναγωγῇ, καὶ πολλοὶ ἀκούοντες ἐξεπλήσσοντο λέγοντες, Πόθεν τούτῳ ταῦτα, καὶ τίς ἡ σοπφία ἡ δοθεῖσα τούτῳ ἵνα καὶ δυνάμεις τοιαῦται διὰ τῶν χειρῶν αὐτοῦ γίνωνται;

καὶ (continuative conjunction) 14.
γενομένου (aor.part.gen.sing.neut.of γίνομαι, genitive absolute) 113.
σαββάτου (gen.sing.neut.of σάββατον, genitive absolute) 962.
ἤρξατο (3d.per.sing.aor.mid.ind.of ἄρχω, ingressive) 383.
διδάσκειν (pres.act.inf.of διδάσκω, complementary) 403.
ἐν (preposition with the locative of place) 80.
τῇ (loc.sing.fem.of the article in agreement with συναγωγῇ) 9.
συναγωγῇ (loc.sing.fem.of συναγωγή, place where) 404.

καὶ (continuative conjunction) 14.

πολλοὶ (nom.pl.masc.of πολύς, subject of ἐξεπλήσσοντο) 228.

ἀκούοντες (pres.act.part.nom.pl.masc.of ἀκούω, adverbial, temporal) 148.

ἐξεπλήσσοντο (3d.per.pl.imp.pass.ind.of ἐκπλήσσομαι, inceptive) 705.

λέγοντες (pres.act.part.nom.pl.masc.of λέγω, adverbial, circumstantial) 66.

Πόθεν (interrogative conjunction) 1061.

τούτῳ (dat.sing.masc.of οὗτος, personal advantage) 93.

ταῦτα (nom.pl.neut.of οὗτος, subject of verb understood) 93.

καὶ (adjunctive conjunction joining clauses) 14.

τίς (interrogative pronoun, nom.sing.neut.of τίς, predicate nominative, in agreement with σοφία) 281.

ἡ (nom.sing.fem.of the article in agreement with σοφία) 9.

σοφία (nom.sing.fem.of σοφία, subject of verb understood) 934.

ἡ (nom.sing.fem.of the article in agreement with δοθεῖσα) 9.

δοθεῖσα (2d.aor.pass.part.nom.sing.fem.of δίδωμι, adjectiveal, ascriptive in the emphatic attributive position) 362.

τούτῳ (dat.sing.masc.of οὗτος, indirect object of δοθεῖσα) 93.

καὶ (adjunctive conjunction joining nouns) 14.

αἱ (nom.pl.fem.of the article in agreement with δυνάμεις) 9.

δυνάμεις (nom.pl.fem.of δύναμις, subject of verb understood) 687.

τοιαῦτα (nom.pl.fem.of τοιοῦτος, in agreement with δυνάμεις) 785.

διὰ (preposition with the ablative of agent) 118.

τῶν (abl.pl.fem.of the article in agreement with χειρῶν) 9.

χειρῶν (abl.pl.fem.of χείρ, agent) 308.

αὐτοῦ (gen.sing.masc.of αὐτός, possession) 16.

γινόμεναι (pres.part.nom.pl.fem.of γίνομαι, adjectival, ascriptive, in agreement with δυνάμεις) 113.

Translation - "And on the sabbath day He began to teach in the synagogue. And many when they heard were seized with amazement, saying, 'Where did these things which this man is doing come from? And what is the wisdom which has been given to this man. And what about such miracles which are being performed by His hands?"

Comment: Jesus did not wait long to begin His ministry in His old home town. γενομένου σαββάτου - *i.e.* the first sabbath day after He arrived in town. He began to teach in the synagogue. This had been His old custom during His days as a carpenter (Lk.4:16). He had resumed it briefly on His first return. Now He is back at His old place. There was a large audience - οἱ πολλοὶ ἀκούοντες. They were unusually impressed with Jesus' teaching as the inceptive imperfect tense of ἐξεπλήσσοντο indicates. They were seized with amazement. The synagogue buzzed with half whispered comment. One gets a picture of the audience, as, amazed almost beyond control, they visited with one another about it. One said, Πόθεν τούτῳ ταῦτα - "Where did this man get all of this?" Another said, "What wisdom has been given to this man!" There may be a touch of sarcasm here. One does not use a demonstrative pronoun when speaking in a friendly way about an old acquaintance. This is what is known as the contemptuous use of the demonstrative. The emphatic attributive position given to δοθεῖσα, the ascriptive participle, is a reflection of their contempt and scorn. "This wisdom had to be given to him, because we know him. He has not been to Rabbinical school. He is only an uneducated carpenter.

Some one else was saying, "What miracles at His hands are being manifested." Many may have remembered Jesus' ministry at His last visit, when He had said that Isa.61:1,2a was even then being fulfilled by Him, but that He would fulfill only that part of it having to do with God's mercy, while the judgment phase must await His second coming. He had said other things then which reflected unfavorably upon upon the local gentry. In fact, they had become so enraged that they had tried to push Him off a cliff. Study carefully the comments on Lk.4:16-30. Grudgingly they were being forced to admit that their old friend and neighbor was the best preacher they had ever heard, and there was no doubt about His miracles. But the wickedness and blight of their benighted, prejudiced hearts turned their grudging admission of His greatness into envy and resentment. What horrid fruitage of unbelief!

Verse 3 - "Is not this the carpenter, the son of Mary, the brother of James, and Joses and of Juda, and Simon? And are not his sisters here with us? And they were offended at him."

οὐκ οὗτός ἐστιν ὁ τέκτων, ὁ υἱὸς τῆς Μαρίας καὶ ἀδελφὸς Ἰακώβου καὶ Ἰωσῆτος καὶ Ἰούδα καὶ Σίμωνος; καὶ οὐκ εἰσὶν αἱ ἀδελφαὶ αὐτοῦ ὧδε πρὸς ἡμᾶς; καὶ ἐσκανδαλίζοντο ἐν αὐτῷ.

οὐχ (summary negative conjunction in rhetorical question) 130.
οὗτός (nom.sing.masc.of οὗτος, subject of ἐστιν, contemptuous use) 93.
ἐστιν (3d.per.sing.pres.ind.of εἰμί, aoristic) 86.
ὁ (nom.sing.masc.of the article in agreement with τέκτων) 9.
τέκτων (nom.sing.masc.of τέκτων, predicate nominative) 1097.
ὁ (nom.sing.masc.of the article in agreement with υἱὸς) 9.
υἱὸς (nom.sing.masc.of υἱός, apposition) 5.
τῆς (gen.sing.fem.of the article in agreement with Μαρίας) 9.
Μαρίας (gen.sing.fem.of Μαρίας, relationship) 64.
καὶ (adjunctive conjunction joining nouns) 14.
ἀδελφὸς (nom.sing.masc.of ἀδελφός, apposition) 15.
Ἰακώβου (gen.sing.masc.of Ἰάκωβος, relationship) 1098.
καὶ (adjunctive conjunction joining nouns) 14.
Ἰωσῆτος (gen.sing.masc.of Ἰωσήφ, relationship) 1099.
καὶ (adjunctive conjunction joining nouns) 14.
Ἰούδα (gen.sing.masc.of Ἰούδας, relationship) 1101.
καὶ (adjunctive conjunction joining nouns) 14.
Σίμωνος (gen.sing.masc.of Σίμων, relationship) 1100.
καὶ (emphatic conjunction) 14.
οὐκ (summary negative conjunction in rhetorical question) 130.
εἰσὶν (3d.per.pl.pres.ind.of εἰμί, aoristic) 86.

αἱ (nom.pl.fem.of the article in agreement with ἀδελφαὶ) 9.
ἀδελφαὶ (nom.pl.fem.of ἀδελφή, subject of εἰσίν) 1025.
αὐτοῦ (gen.sing.masc.of αὐτός, relationship) 16.
ὧδε (adverbial, place) 766.
πρὸς (preposition with the accusative of extent - "near to" - with persons) 197.
ἡμᾶς (acc.pl.masc.of ἐγώ, extent) 123.
καὶ (continuative conjunction) 14.
ἐσκανδαλίζοντο (3d.per.pl.imp.pass.ind.of σκανδαλίζω, inceptive) 503.
ἐν (preposition with the instrumental of cause) 80.
αὐτῷ (instru.sing.masc.of αὐτός, cause) 16.

Translation - "Is not this fellow the carpenter - the son of Mary and brother of James and Joses and Juda and Simon? In fact are not His sisters here, well known to us? And they began to be offended because of Him."

Comment: The passage reeks with small town prejudice. οὐχ in interrogation is rhetorical question expecting an affirmative in reply. It is a strong negation in effect therefore. The use of οὗτός in contempt indicates that Jesus was a nobody to the Nazarenes. "Was he not . . . ?" Of course, everybody in town knew Jesus, not as Incarnate Son of God, but as the local carpenter, illegitimate child of Mary and brother to the other boys and girls who were born *after* Joseph and Mary got married. His half-brothers and sisters show up only infrequently in the Scriptures and never in a good light (Mt.13:55,56, the parallel passage; Mk.3:31-35; Mt.12:46-50; Lk.8:19-21). Note the inceptive imperfect in ἐσκανδαλίζοντο. "They began to be offended because of Him" or "They were seized with offense" or "They took offense. . . " All of these translations point to the emphasis *at the beginning* of the action of the verb. Like the little babies, intellectually, morally and spiritually that they were, they were easily hurt and they wanted to cry. Jesus was too big for them - a spiritual and intellectual Gulliver tied down by the Lilliputians. Why could He not be ordinary, average and mediocre like others in Nazareth? For further comment *cf.* Mt.13:54-58.

Verse 4 - "But Jesus said unto them, A prophet is not without honour, but in his own country, and among his own kin, and in his own house."

καὶ ἔλεγεν αὐτὸς ὁ Ἰησοῦς ὅτι Οὐκ ἔστιν προφήτης ἄτιμος εἰ μὴ ἐν τῇ πατρίδι αὐτοῦ καὶ ἐν τοῖς συγγενεῦσιν αὐτοῦ καὶ ἐν τῇ οἰκίᾳ αὐτοῦ.

καὶ (adversative conjunction) 14.
ἔλεγεν (3d.per.sing.imp.act.ind.of λέγω, inceptive) 66.
αὐτοῖς (dat.pl.masc.of αὐτός, indirect object of ἔλεγεν) 16.
ὁ (nom.sing.masc.of the article in agreement with Ἰησοῦς) 9.
Ἰησοῦς (nom.sing.masc.of Ἰησοῦς, subject of ἔλεγεν) 3.
ὅτι (recitative) 211.
Οὐκ (summary negative conjunction with the indicative) 130.
ἔστιν (3d.per.sing.pres.ind.of εἰμί, static) 86.
προφήτης (nom.sing.masc.of προφήτης, subject of ἔστιν) 119.

ἄτιμος (nom.sing.masc.of ἄτιμος, predicate adjective) 1102.
εἰ (conditional particle with μή) 337.
μή (qualified negative conjunction with εἰ in a conditional clause) 87.
ἐν (preposition with the locative of place where) 80.
τῇ (loc.sing.fem.of the article in agreement with πατρίδι) 9.
πατρίδι (loc.sing.fem.of πατρίς, place where) 1096.
αὐτοῦ (gen.sing.masc.of αὐτός, possession) 16.
καὶ (adjunctive conjunction joining prepositional phrases) 14.
ἐν (preposition with the locative with plural nouns) 80.
τοῖς (loc.pl.masc.of the article in agreement with συγγενεῦσιν) 9.
συγγενεῦσιν (loc.pl.masc.of συγγενής, "among") 1815.
αὐτοῦ (gen.sing.masc.of αὐτός, relationship) 16.
καὶ (adjunctive conjunction joining prepositional phrases) 14.
ἐν (preposition with the locative of place where) 80.
τῇ (loc.sing.fem.of the article in agreement with οἰκίᾳ) 9.
οἰκίᾳ (loc.sing.fem.of οἰκία, place where) 186.
αὐτοῦ (gen.sing.masc.of αὐτός, possession) 16.

Translation - "But Jesus began to say to them, 'A prophet is not without honor except in his home town and among his relatives and in his own house' "

Comment: ὅτι here introduces direct discourse. Prophets are certain to be respected (summary negative in οὐκ with the indicative) so long as they stay clear of their most familiar haunts. One's home town, his relatives and those of his immediate family - - these should hear the prophet and heed his message but they will not honor him for it. The passage does not say that the prophet should stay out of his home town, though it is often used to support this idea. If so, Jesus never would have gone back to Nazareth, once He left it. It does say that prophets who expect accolades from those who know them best have missed the point. But a true prophet is not concerned with accolades anyway. What he is concerned with, if he is a true prophet, is the reaction which he gets from his audience. If they are listening with a receptive spirit he procedes. If not he terminates his ministry, lest he "cast pearls before swine" and "give that which is holy to the dogs" (Mt.7:6). Jesus was the truest of prophets. Hence His reaction in

Verse 5 - "And he could there do no mighty work, save that he laid his hands upon a few sick folk and healed them."

καὶ οὐκ ἐδύνατο ἐκεῖ ποιῆσαι οὐδεμίαν δύναμιν, εἰ μὴ ὀλίγοις ἀρρώστοις ἐπιθεὶς τὰς χεῖρας ἐθεράπευσεν.

καὶ (inferential conjunction) 14.
οὐκ (summary negative conjunction with the indicative) 130.
ἐδύνατο (3d.per.sing.imp.ind.of δύναμαι, progressive description) 289.
ἐκεῖ (adverb of place) 204.
ποιῆσαι (aor.act.inf.of ποιέω, complementary) 127.

οὐδεμίαν (acc.sing.fem.of οὐδείς, in agreement with δύναμιν) 446.

δύναμιν (acc.sing.fem.of δύναμις, direct object of ποιῆσαι) 687.

εἰ (conditional particle with μή in a conditional clause) 337.

μή (qualified negative conjunction in a conditional clause) 87.

ὀλίγοις (loc.pl.masc.of ὀλίγος, in agreement with ἀρρώστοις) 669.

ἀρρώστοις (loc.pl.masc.of ἄρρωστος, place where) 1117.

ἐπιθεὶς (2d.aor.act.part.nom.sing.masc.of ἐπιτίθημι, adverbial, modal) 818.

τὰς (acc.pl.fem.of the article in agreement with χεῖρας) 9.

χεῖρας (acc.pl.fem.of χείρ, direct object of ἐπιθεὶς) 308.

ἐθεράπευσεν (3d.per.sing.aor.act.ind.of θεραπεύω, constative) 406.

Translation - "Therefore He was unable to perform a single miracle there, except that by placing His hands upon a few sick people He healed them."

Comment: οὐδεμίαν is a strong negative. "He was not able to do *but not one* miracle. . κ.τ.λ.*" However Mark qualifies this strong negation with the εἰ μή clause. The passage does not tell us why Jesus could not perform the ministry which He performed in Capernaum. We may be certain on other scriptural grounds that His was not a physical inability. Their unbelief made Him morally unable to do as He would like to have done. There were some there who believed upon Him. For these He exercised His healing powers. Just as the throngs in Capernaum had touched Him, although only one sick woman really *touched* Him, so here in Nazareth, the healing that was available for all was offered only to those with open minds. These people were the Master's minority in Nazareth. Everything is possible for the one who believes. Few in Nazareth could qualify as we see in

Verse 6a - "And he marvelled because of their unbelief . . . "

καὶ ἐθαύμαζεν διὰ τὴν ἀπιστίαν αὐτῶν.

καὶ (continuative conjunction) 14.

ἐθαύμαζεν (3d.per.sing.imp.act.ind.of θαυμάζω, inceptive) 726.

διὰ (preposition with the accusative of cause) 118.

τὴν (acc.sing.fem.of the article in agreement with ἀπιστίαν) 9.

ἀπιστίαν (acc.sing.fem.of ἀπιστία, cause) 1103.

αὐτῶν (gen.pl.masc.of αὐτός, possession) 16.

Translation - "And He was seized with amazement because of their unbelief."

Comment: The probability is that the Nazarenes had disliked Jesus for years. Though not yet openly revealed as Messiah and Son of God while He remained in Joseph's home, He must have manifested qualities of goodness and greatness that would be certain to antagonize such little people. Once baptized by John, anointed by the Holy Spirit and publicized throughout Galilee as a miracle worker and teacher, He could not and did not expect to be admired by His former fellow citizens of Nazareth. Yet the text says that their lack of faith was the cause of His surprize. He never returned to Nazareth.

The Third Tour in Galilee

(Mk.6:6b; Mt.9:35)

Mk.6:6b - *"And he went round about the villages teaching."*

Καὶ περιῆγεν τὰς κώμας κύκλῳ διδάσκων.

Καὶ (continuative conjunction) 14.
περιῆγεν (3d.per.sing.imp.act.ind.of περιάγω, progressive duration) 402.
τὰς (acc.pl.fem.of the article in agreement with κώμας) 9.
κώμας (acc.pl.fem.of κώμη, place after περί in composition) 834.
κύκλῳ (instru.sing.masc.of κύκλος, manner) 2183.
διδάσκων (pres.act.part.nom.sing.masc.of διδάσκω, adverbial, temporal) 403.

Translation - *"And He went around among the villages teaching."*

Comment: So as not to waste the time, Jesus took a swing around the circle (*cf.*#2183) and taught the people. He had shaken the dust of Nazareth from His feet. What they refused to hear, Jesus offered to others. Mt.9: 35, the parallel account, upon which see comment, reports that He was much more respectfully received on this tour than in Nazareth.

The Mission of the Twelve

(Mk.6:7-13; Mt.9:36-11:1; Lk.9:1-6)

Mk.6:7 - *"And he called unto him the twelve, and began to send them forth by two and two; and gave them power over unclean spirits."*

καὶ προσκαλεῖται τοὺς δώδεκα, καὶ ἤρξατο αὐτοὺς ἀποστέλλειν δύο δύο, καὶ ἐδίδου αὐτοῖς ἐξουσίαν τῶν πνευμάτων τῶν ἀκαθάρτων.

καὶ (continuative conjunction) 14.
προσκαλεῖται (3d.per.sing.pres.mid.ind.of προσκαλέω, historical) 842.
τοὺς (acc.pl.masc.of the article in agreement with δώδεκα) 9.
δώδεκα (acc.pl.masc.of δώδεκα, direct object of προσκαλεῖται) 820.
καὶ (adjunctive conjunction joining verbs) 14.
ἤρξατο (3d.per.sing.aor.mid.ind.of ἄρχω, ingressive) 383.
αὐτοὺς (acc.pl.masc.of αὐτός, direct object of ἀποστέλλειν) 16.
ἀποστέλλειν (pres.act.inf.of ἀποστέλλω, complementary) 215.
δύο (distributive numeral in the idiom δύο δύο) 385.
δύο 385.
καὶ (adjunctive conjunction joining verbs) 14.
ἐδίδου (3d.per.sing.imp.act.ind.of δίδωμι, inceptive) 362.
αὐτοῖς (dat.pl.masc.of αὐτός, indirect object of ἐδίδου) 16.
ἐξουσίαν (acc.sing.fem.of ἐξουσία, direct object of ἐδίδου) 707.
τῶν (gen.pl.neut.of the article in agreement with πνευμάτων) 9.

πνευμάτων (gen.pl.neut.of πνεῦμα, description) 83.

τῶν (gen.pl.neut.of the article in agreement with ἀκαθάρτων) 9.

ἀκαθάρτων (gen.pl.neut.of ἀκάθαρτος, in agreement with πνευμάτων) 843.

Translation - "And He called the twelve to Him and began to send them out, two by two and He began to give to them authority over the obscene spirits."

Comment: προσκαλεῖτα is middle voice. Jesus summoned the Twelve to Himself. Note the ingressive character of ἤρξατο αὐτοὺς ἀποστέλλειν. Also the inceptive imperfect in ἐδίδου, which results in the same idea. This was the *beginning* of Jesus' policy in His establishment of the missionary enterprise. "He *began* to send them forth," and "He *began* to give to them authority over foul spirits." Note that the uncleanness of the spirits is emphasized by the emphatic attributive position of ἀκαθάρτων. What Jesus began at the beginning of the church age, He has been doing since. (Mt.28:18-20; Acts 1:8). He is still sending His witnesses out to witness and He still gives us all of His power which is abundantly able to combat successfully the obscene spirits. δύο δύο is an idiom which uses the numerals in a distributive manner. "By twos" or "two together" or "two by two."

Until this time the disciples had spent their time with Jesus. The introductory phase of their training, at least, is now complete and it is time for them to strike out upon their own. There is comfort in numbers, as Jesus sends them out in pairs. In view of their timidity it is not likely that they would have braved the gainsaying world alone. The new phase is an "on the job training" program, for they returned from their sorties to report to Jesus and gain new inspiration from time to time. Jesus also equipped them with partial power - at least enough to enable them to prove that they were disciples of Him Who is Sovereign over the demon world and everything else. Plenary power in their hands at this point would have been dangerous. They had not the spiritual perception as yet to know how to use it. They also were given power to cure diseases. The secret of fruit bearing for Christ is to go out and begin. Note the "fruit, more fruit, much fruit" sequence in John 15:2,8.

*Cf.*Mt.10:1 for further comment, particularly as it relates to dispensational truth.

Verse 8 - "And commanded them that they should take nothing for their journey, save a staff only; no scrip, no bread, no money in their purse."

καὶ παρήγγειλεν αὐτοῖς ἵνα μηδὲν ἄρωσιν εἰς ὁδὸν εἰ μὴ ῥάβδον μόνον, μὴ ἄρτον, μὴ πήραν, μὴ εἰς τήν ζώνην χαλκόν.

καὶ (continuative conjunction) 14.

παρήγγειλεν (3d.per.sing.aor.act.ind.of παραγγέλλω, constative) 855.

αὐτοῖς (dat.pl.masc.of αὐτός, indirect object of παρήγγειλεν) 16.

ἵνα (final conjunction introducing a purpose clause) 114.

μηδὲν (acc.sing.neut.of μηδείς, direct object of ἄρωσιν) 713.

αἴρωσιν (United Bible Societies text has ἄρωσιν) - (3d.per.pl.pres.act.subj.of αἴρω, purpose) 350.

εἰς (preposition with the accusative of extent) 140.

ὁδὸν (acc.sing.fem.of ὁδός, extent) 199.

εἰ (conditional particle with μὴ in a conditional clause) 337.

μὴ (qualified negative with εἰ in a conditional clause) 87.

ῥάβδον (acc.sing.fem.of ῥάβδος, direct object of αἴρωσιν) 863.

μόνον (acc.sing.neut.of μόνος, adverbial) 339.

μὴ (qualified negative conjunction with αἴρωσιν) 87.

ἄρτον (acc.sing.masc.of ἄρτος, direct object of αἴρωσιν) 338.

μὴ (qualified negative with αἴρωσιν) 87.

πήραν (acc.sing.fem.of πήρα, direct object of αἴρωσιν) 862.

μὴ (qualified negative with αἴρωσιν) 87.

εἰς (preposition with the accusative, original static use, like a locative) 140.

τὴν (acc.sing.fem.of the article in agreement with ζώνην) 9.

ζώνην (acc.sing.fem.of ζώνη, original static use of εἰς with the accustive like a locative) 263.

χαλκόν (acc.sing.masc.of χαλκός, direct object of αἴρωσιν) 861.

Translation - "And He ordered them to carry nothing on their trip except a staff only, - no bread, no wallet, no brass coins in their girdles."

Comment: *Cf.*#855. παραγγέλλω carries a great deal of authority. εἰς ὁδὸν means "for purposes of the journey." See other examples where the purpose idea is introduced by εἰς and the accusative (#140). εἰ μὴ ῥάβδον μόνον - "If you take no staff, then take nothing." The staff was to be their sole equipment, for the Lord's work is to be done ". . . not by might, nor by power, but by my spirit, saith the Lord of Hosts" (Zech.4:6). They were to take no food. Since πήραν (#862) means "wallet" not "scrip" we have two means of carrying money mentioned, for it was the custom to carry metal money, such as brass, in the girdle which they wore inside the tunic, like a money belt. *Cf.*#263. No wallet with its obvious evidence of money, nor any hidden money in your girdle. Matthew adds that gold and silver were also forbidden. *Cf.* Mt.10:9; Lk.9:3 for further comment. It will be noted that Mt.10:10 forbids a ῥάβδον also in the event that they had none and would otherwise have gone out to purchase one for the trip. If they already had one Mark says that they might take it with them. Luke 9:3 agrees with Matthew's ban on ῥάβδον. The point is "Do not make special preparations for the journey. Travel lightly. Live off the land." Note in Mt.10:7 that they were commanded to preach the kingdom message as John the Baptist had first preached it, before he baptized Jesus. Preachers in the church age are to go equipped (Luke 22:35,36).

Verse 9 - "But be shod with sandals; and not put on two coats."

ἀλλὰ ὑποδεδεμένους σανδάλια καὶ μὴ ἐνδύσασθαι δύο χιτῶνας.

ἀλλὰ (alternative conjunction) 342.

#2248 ὑποδεδεμένους (perf.pass.part.acc.pl.masc.of ὑποδέω, adverbial, circumstantial).

be shod with - Mk.6:9.
bind on - Acts 12:8.
have shod - Eph.6:15.

Meaning: A combination of ὑπό (#117) and δέω (#998). Hence, to bind beneath. To put on shoes; to bind on footwear that rests primarily *under* not *around* the foot, as sandles. *Cf.*#305 and see discussion on this verse. Of the footware of the disciples - Mk.6:9; Acts 12:8. Metaphorically in Eph.6:15.

#2249 σανδάλια (acc.pl.neut.of σανδάλιον, direct object of αἴρωσιν).

Meaning: A sandal; a sole of wood or hide, covering the bottom of the foot and bound on with leather thongs. Footware for the disciples - Mk.6:9; Acts 12:8. *Cf.*#305.

καὶ (adjunctive conjunction joining an infinitive and a noun) 14.
μὴ (qualified negative conjunction with the imperative infinitive) 87.
ἐνδύσασθαι (1st.aor.pass.inf.of ἐνδύω, imperative infinitive) 613.
δύο (numeral) 385.
χιτῶνας (acc.pl.masc.of χιτών, general reference) 532.

Translation - "... *but sandal-shod and not clothed with two coats.*"

Comment: The verse completes the sentence which began in verse 8. Note the use of the purpose clause (ἵνα ἄρωσιν) in verse 8 followed by the infinitive in verse 9. Robertson thinks that Mark is guilty of anacoluthon here (Robertson, *Grammar*, 437-438). Mantey suggests (*Manual*, 216) that we have here what is "commonly called "the imperative infinitive." It is the only independent use of the Greek infinitive, and is not of very frequent occurrence." Burton (*New Testament Moods and Tenses*, 146) says, "It is of ancient origin, being especially frequent in Homer." "The construction suggests a close kinship between the infinitive and imperative" (Mantey, *Ibid.*) and Robertson adds that "... the probability is that imperative forms like δεῖξαι ... are infinitive in origin" (Robertson, *Ibid.*, 943).

It is interesting to note that Peter still had his sandals the night the angel let him out of jail (Acts 12:8).

Verse 10 - "*And he said unto them, In what places soever ye enter into an house, there abide till ye depart from that place.*"

καὶ ἔλεγεν αὐτοῖς, Ὅπου ἐὰν εἰσέλθητε εἰς οἰκίαν, ἐκεῖ μένετε ἕως ἂν ἐξέλθητε ἐκεῖθεν.

καὶ (continuative conjunction) 14.
ἔλεγεν (3d.per.sing.imp.act.ind.of λέγω, progressive duration) 66.
αὐτοῖς (dat.pl.masc.of αὐτός, indirect object of ἔλεγεν) 16.
Ὅπου (relative adverb of place in an indefinite local clause) 592.
ἐὰν (conjunction with the subjunctive in an indefinite local clause) 363.
εἰσέλθητε (2d.per.pl.2d.aor.subj.of εἰσέρχομαι, indefinite local clause) 234.

εἰς (preposition with the accusative of extent) 140.
οἰκίαν (acc.sing.fem.of οἰκία, extent) 186.
ἐκεῖ (an adverb of place) 204.
μένετε (2d.per.pl.pres.act.impv.of μένω, command) 864.
ἕως (adverb of time extent) 71.
ἄν (conditional particle in an indefinite temporal clause) 205.
ἐξέλθητε (2d.per.pl.2d.aor.subj.of ἐξέρχομαι, indefinite temporal clause) 161.
ἐκεῖθεν (adverbial) 396.

Translation - "Jesus went on to say to them, 'Wherever you enter a house, remain there until such time as you leave it.' "

Comment: The literal translation as given above of course is obvious. Everyone who enters into a house stays until he leaves! But Jesus meant that the disciples were to consider the house their temporary home while they ministered in that locality. They would come and go as the demands of their ministry dictated, until the day when they left the community. The verse has two indefinite clauses, the first local and the second temporal. Jesus did not stipulate where they were to go or how long they were to stay. *Cf.*Mt.10:11 and Lk.9:4 for further comment.

Verse 11 - "And whosoever shall not receive you, nor hear you, when ye depart thence, shake off the dust under your feet for a testimony against them. Verily I say unto you, It shall be more tolerable for Sodom and Gomorrha in the day of judgment, than for that city."

καὶ ὃς ἂν τόπος μὴ δέξηται ὑμᾶς μηδὲ ἀκούσωσιν ὑμῶν, ἐκπορευόμενοι ἐκεῖθεν ἐκτινάξατε τὸν χοῦν τὸν ὑποκάτω τῶν ποδῶν ὑμῶν εἰς μαρτύριον αὐτοῖς.

καὶ (continuative conjunction) 14.
ὃς (nom.sing.masc.of the relative ὅς, in agreement with τόπος) 65.
ἂν (particle with the subjunctive in an indefinite local clause) 205.
τόπος (nom.sing.masc.of τόπος, subject of δέξηται) 1019.
μὴ (qualified negative conjunction with the subjunctive in an indefinite local clause) 87.
δέξηται (3d.per.sing.aor.subj.of δέχομαι, indefinite clause local) 867.
ὑμᾶς (acc.pl.masc.of σύ, direct object of δέξηται) 104.
μηδὲ (disjunctive particle) 612.
ἀκούσωσιν (3d.per.pl.aor.act.subj.of ἀκούω, indefinite local clause) 148.
ὑμῶν (gen.pl.masc.of σύ, description) 104.
ἐκπορευόμενοι (pres.mid.part.nom.pl.masc.of ἐκπορεύομαι, adverbial, temporal) 270.
ἐκεῖθεν (adverbial) 396.
ἐκτινάξατε (2d.per.pl.aor.act.impv.of ἐκτινάσσω, command) 868.
τὸν (acc.sing.masc.of the article in agreement with χοῦν) 9.

#2250 χοῦν (acc.sing.masc.of χόος, direct object of ἐκτινάξατε).

dust - Mk.6:11; Rev.18:19.

Meaning: from χέω - "to pour." Earth dug or poued out. Hence, dust - Mk.6:11; Rev.18:19.

τὸν (acc.sing.masc.of the article in agreement with χοῦν) 9.
ὑποκάτω (improper preposition with the ablative of place separation) 1429.
τῶν (abl.pl.masc.of the article in agreement with ποδῶν) 9.
ποδῶν (abl.pl.masc.of πούς, separation) 353.
ὑμῶν (gen.pl.masc.of σύ, possession) 104.
εἰς (preposition with the accusative, purpose) 140.
μαρτύριον (acc.sing.neut.of μαρτύριον purpose) 716.
αὐτοῖς (dat.pl.masc.of αὐτός, personal disadvantage) 16.

Translation - "And whatever place does not receive you nor listen to you, when you leave there shake off the dust under your feet for a witness against them."

Comment: Note εἰς with the accusative for purpose. *Cf*.#140 for other examples. ὅς as joined to a noun (τόπος in this case) is a little unusual. "Whatever place . . . κ.τ.λ." It is indefinite as ἄν and the subjunctive in δέξηται and ἀκούσωσιν indicate. The burden of moral responsibility for reaction to the message of the gospel of the kingdom rests upon the host who takes the preacher in and listens to his message. The idea that the genitive after ἀκούω means a superficial hearing, without necessarily involving understanding of what was said, does not always hold in the New Testament, but it is interesting to note that we have it here. Had Mark written ὑμᾶς after ἀκούσωσιν it could have meant that what was *heard* also penetrated into the deeper consciousness, which might imply salvation, in which case the act of shaking off the dust would be inappropriate. Apparently the host referred to in this passage, heard only in the superficial sense. The act of shaking off the dust symbolizes the fact that the preacher would never again return to the place. Note well that this is the kingdom message, not the gospel of the crucified and risen Saviour. The gospel preacher in the church age, with a different message, will return again and again.

Verse 12 - "And they went out and preached that men should repent."

Καὶ ἐξελθόντες ἐκήρυξαν ἵνα μετανοῶσιν,

Καὶ (continuative conjunction) 14.
ἐξελθόντες (aor.part.nom.pl.masc.of ἐξέρχομαι, adverbial, temporal) 161.
ἐκήρυξαν (3d.per.pl.aor.act.ind.of κηρύσσω, ingressive) 249.
ἵνα (final conjunction introducing a purpose clause) 114.
μετανοῶσιν (3d.per.pl.pres.act.subj.of μετανοέω, purpose) 251.

Translation - "And they went out and began to preach in order that men might repent."

Comment: *Cf*.again Mt.10:5,7. These disciples were forbidden to go to the Gentiles or the Samaritans, who were half Jewish and half Gentile. Their

Gentiles or the Samaritans, who were Jewish/Gentile hybrids. Their commission was only πρὸς τὰ πρόβατα τὰ ἀπολωλότα οἴκου Ἰσραήλ (Mt.10:6) - "to the lost sheep of the house of Israel." They preached exactly what John the Baptist first preached - "The Kingdom of the Heavens is at hand." Their message assumed that Israel as a nation as represented both by its leadership and the common people would receive Jesus as Messiah, the Anointed, and that, as a result, He would sit upon David's throne to rule the world. They knew little at this time, if anything clearly, of Christ's death, resurrection and ascension. The Age of the Holy Spirit when God would call out from among the Gentiles a people for His name (Acts 15:14) was a part of the divine plan which was at that time unrevealed to them.

Verse 13 - "And they cast out many devils, and anointed with oil many that were sick, and healed them."

καὶ δαιμόνια πολλὰ ἐξέβαλλον, καὶ ἤλειφον ἐλαίῳ πολλοὺς ἀρρώστους καὶ ἐθεράπευον.

καὶ (continuative conjunction) 14.
δαιμόνια (acc.pl.neut.of δαιμόνιον, direct object of ἐξέβαλλον) 686.
πολλὰ (acc.pl.neut.of πολύς, in agreement with δαιμόνια) 228.
ἐξέβαλλον (3d.per.pl.imp.act.ind.of ἐκβάλλω, inceptive) 649.
καὶ (adjunctive conjunction joining verbs) 14.
ἤλειφον (3d.per.pl.imp.act.ind.of ἀλείφω, inceptive) 589.
ἐλαίῳ (instru.sing.neut.of ἔλαιον, means) 1530.
πολλοὺς (acc.pl.masc.of πολύς, in agreement with ἀρρώστους) 228.
ἀρρώστους (acc.pl.masc.of ἄρρωστος, direct object of ἤλειφον and ἐθεράπευον) 1117.
καὶ (adjunctive conjunction joining verbs) 14.
ἐθεράπευον (3d.per.pl.imp.act.ind.of θεραπεύω, inceptive) 406.

Translation - "And they began a ministry of casting out many demons, and anointing with oil many sick people and healing them."

Comment: The inceptive imperfect tenses indicate that the disciples were very busy. They were using the power which Jesus gave them to dominate the demon world and to heal the sick. These miraculous signs were designed to authenticate the validity of the Apostles' message. This is why Jesus gave them the power to perform miracles. Israel had no logical reason to reject Jesus and His claims to Messiahship. Neither He nor His apostles ever did anything except good for the people. At the foot of the cross official Jewry stood absolutely without excuse. The contention of Catholicism that the use of oil by the disciples was an instance of final unction is erroneous. The people whom the disciples anointed with oil recovered. *Cf.* James. 5:14.

At this point, before the student goes on to study the parallel account in Luke 9:1-6, the long Matthew story of the mission of the disciples should be studied. *Cf.* Mt.9:36-11:1.

Luke 9:1 - "Then he called his twelve disciples together, and gave them power and authority over all devils, and to cure diseases."

Συγκαλεσάμενος δὲ τοὺς δώδεκα ἔδωκεν αὐτοῖς δύναμιν καὶ ἐξουσίαν ἐπὶ πάντα τὰ δαιμόνια καὶ νόσους θεραπεύειν,

#2251 Συγκαλεσάμενος (aor.mid.part.nom.sing.masc.of συγκαλέω, adverbial, temporal).

call together - Mk.15:16; Lk.9:1; 15:6,9; 23:13; Acts 5:21; 10:24; 28:17.

Meaning: A combination of σύν (#1542) and καλέω (#107). Hence, to call together. To assemble a group of persons by a voice summons. With reference to a military assembly - Mk.15:16; with reference to Jesus' call to His apostles - Lk.9:1. Parabolically in Lk.15:6,9. Of Pilate's summons to the political leaders in Israel - Lk.23:13. See also Acts 5:21. Cornelius' summons - Acts 10:24; Paul's call to the chief Jews - Acts 28:17.

δὲ (continuative conjunction) 11.
τοὺς (acc.pl.masc.of the article in agreement with δώδεκα) 9.
δώδεκα (numeral, here used to modify μαθητής understood) 820.
ἔδωκεν (3d.per.sing.1st.aor.act.ind.of δίδωμι, ingressive) 362.
αὐτοῖς (dat.pl.masc.of αὐτός indirect object of ἔδωκεν) 16.
δύναμιν (acc.sing.fem.of δύναμις, direct object of ἔδωκεν) 687.
καὶ (adjunctive conjunction joining nouns) 14.
ἐξουσίαν (acc.sing.fem.of ἐξουσία, direct object of ἔδωκεν) 707.
ἐπὶ (preposition with the accusative, general reference) 47.
πάντα (acc.pl.neut.of πᾶς, in agreement with δαιμόνια) 67.
τὰ (acc.pl.neut.of the article in agreement with δαιμόνια) 9.
δαιμόνια (acc.pl.neut.of δαιμόνιον, general reference) 686.
καὶ (adjunctive conjunction joining a prepositional phrase with an infinitive) 14.
νόσους (acc.pl.masc.of νόσος, direct object of θεραπεύειν) 407.
θεραπεύειν (pres.act.inf.of θεραπεύω, complementary) 406.

Translation - "And when He had called the twelve together He began to give to them power and authority over all the demons and to heal diseases."

Comment: Συγκαλεσάμενος is adverbially temporal. Mt.10:1 and Mk.6:7 (the parallel passages) use προσκαλέω instead of συνκαλέω. Jesus called the twelve together (συνκαλέω) to Himself (προσκαλέω). It was a tightly knit group that gathered about Jesus. Each had been given a special call. Each had made sacrifices to follow Jesus. One was destined to betray Him; another to deny Him; the others to forsake Him and flee precipitately into the night rather than face the Romans who came to arrest Him. But all of that was future. Now they look upon Him only as their long awaited Messiah. They have seen Him perform miracles; even raise the dead. They have heard Him teach and preach as no other man. Now He gives that power to them at least in part. They will demonstrate God's superior authority over the demon world, which is destined eventually for hell. They will heal the sick and they will announce, as the Baptist did, that the earthly Messianic Kingdom of Messiah upon earth is the next event on God's schedule of events. This message must be preached because Israel must have a fully authenticated and freely proferred invitation to accept her Messiah. Otherwise she would be justified in rejecting Him. Reject and crucify Him she will, but her revolt will procede without a shred of evidence to justify the murder of the Son of God incarnate. For further comment *cf.* Mk.6:7; Mt.10:1.

Verse 2 - "And he sent them to preach the kingdom of God, and to heal the sick."

καὶ ἀπέστειλεν αὐτοὺς κηρύσσειν τὴν βασιλείαν τοῦ θεοῦ καὶ ἰᾶσθαι (τοὺς ἀσθενεῖς),

καὶ (adjunctive conjunction joining verbs) 14.
ἀπέστειλεν (3d.per.sing.aor.act.ind.of ἀποστέλλω, ingressive) 215.
αὐτοὺς (acc.pl.masc.of αὐτός, direct object of ἀπέστειλεν) 16.
κηρύσσειν (pres.act.inf.of κηρύσσω, purpose) 249.
τὴν (acc.sing.fem.of the article in agreement with βασιλείαν) 9.
βασιλείαν (acc.sing.fem.of βασιλεία, direct object of κηρύσσειν) 253.
τοῦ (gen.sing.masc.of the article in agreement with θεοῦ) 9.
θεοῦ (gen.sing.masc.of θεός, description) 124.
καὶ (adjunctive conjunction joining infinitives) 14.
ἰᾶσθαι (pres.inf.of ἰάομαι, purpose) 721.
τοὺς (acc.pl.masc.of the article in agreement with ἀσθενεῖς) 9.
ἀσθενεῖς (acc.pl.masc.of ἀσθενής, direct object of ἰᾶσθαι) 1551.

Translation - "And He began to send them away to preach the kingdom of God and to heal the sick."

Comment: Two complementary infinitives of purpose complete the main verb ἀπέστειλεν. They were to do two things: preach and heal. Matthew (10:7,8) expands the commission. What was their message? And to whom did they preach it? Matthew is clear on both points. The audience? The lost sheep of the house of Israel. No more. Not even the Samaritans who had some Jewish blood in their veins and were quasi-Jewish in their culture. This is clear from Mt.10:6-8. The message? "Repent for the kingdom of the heavens is at hand" (Mt.10:6-8). They did indeed also preach what Luke reports *viz.,* τὴν βασιλείαν τοῦ θεοῦ - "the kingdom of God," for the whole is the sum of all its parts. Whoever therefore preaches that Messiah shall reign on David's throne over Israel as a nation forever, is preaching the Kingdom of God for he is preaching that God will dominate all things in heaven and on the earth and under the earth. The Kingdom of God simply means the divine rule. Wherever, whenever and in whatever manner God's will is being done, the Kingdom of God is in force.

We cannot, as some have tried to do, restrict the phrase ἡ βασιλεία τοῦ θεοῦ to the church message and ἡ βασιλεία τῶν οὐρανῶν to Israel's kingdom message. ἡ βασιλεία τῶν οὐρανῶν is indeed Israel's earthly kingdom message but ἡ βασιλεία τοῦ θεοῦ includes both - indeed all messages about God's sovereign rule over men, demons and angels, in all ages and in all spheres. The disciples indeed preached both kingdom messages. At first they preached ἡ βασιλεία τῶν οὐρανῶν is at hand. Messiah is here. Rome shall be subject to Him and to Israel. After the full and free offer to Israel and her rejection, they continued to preach the gospel of the grace of God for all men on the ground of Christ's shed blood. Hence Luke is not in contradiction. They did preach one of the messages of the Kingdom of God immediately, *viz.,* the Kingdom of the Heavens. Later they preached another part of the Kingdom of God message, *viz.,* that God would call out from among the Gentiles a people for His name (Acts 15:14). *Cf.* comment on βασιλεία, #253.

Verse 3 - "And he said unto them, Take nothing for your journey, neither staves, nor scrip, neither bread, neither money; neither have two coats apiece."

καὶ εἶπεν πρὸς αὐτούς, Μηδὲν αἴρετε εἰς τὴν ὁδόν, μήτε ῥάβδον μήτε πήραν μήτε ἄρτον μήτε ἀργύριον, μήτε (ἀνὰ) δύο χιτῶνας ἔχειν.

καὶ (continuative conjunction) 14.
εἶπεν (3d.per.sing.aor.act.ind.of εἶπον, constative) 155.
πρὸς (preposition with the accusative, after a verb of speaking) 197.
αὐτούς (acc.pl.masc.of αὐτός, extent after a verb of speaking) 16.
Μηδὲν (acc.sing.neut.of μηδείς, direct object of αἴρετε) 713.
αἴρετε (2d.per.pl.pres.act.impv.of αἴρω, command) 350.
εἰς (preposition with the accusative, purpose) 140.
τὴν (acc.sing.fem.of the article in agreement with ὁδόν) 9.
ὁδόν (acc.sing.fem.of ὁδός, purpose) 199.
μήτε (negative disjunctive) 518.
ῥάβδον (acc.sing.masc.of ῥάβδος, direct object of αἴρετε) 863.
μήτε (negative disjunctive) 518.
πήραν (acc.sing.fem.of πήρα, direct object of αἴρετε) 862.
μήτε (negative disjunctive) 518.
ἄρτον (acc.sing.masc.of ἄρτος, direct object of αἴρετε) 338.
μήτε (negative disjunctive) 518.
ἀργύριον (acc.sing.neut.of ἀργύριον, direct object of αἴρετε) 1535.
μήτε (negative disjunctive) 518.
ἀνὰ (preposition with the accusative, distributive) 1059.
δύο (numeral) 385.
χιτῶνας (acc.pl.masc.of χιτών, direct object of ἔχειν) 532.
ἔχειν (pres.act.inf.of ἔχω, imperative infinitive) 82.

Translation - "And He said to them, 'Take nothing for your journey, neither a staff, nor a wallet, nor food, nor silver nor have two coats each."

Comment: For comment *cf.* Mk.6:8; Mt.10:9,10. *The Pulpit Commentary* quotes Farrar, "The general spirit of the instructions merely is, 'Go forth in the simplest, humblest manner, with no hindrances to your movements, and in perfect faith." History seems to show that this has always been the method of the most successful mission programs.

"The reading with ἀνά appears to be an elucidation of the meaning implicit in the context (i.e. not simply that the Twelve but that no individual should have two coats); but was this an addition made originally by Luke or by later copyists? Or did Alexandrian scribes, taking for granted that readers would correctly understand the passage, delete ἀνά in accord with the parallels (Mt.10:10; Mk.6:9)? To reflect these alternative possibilities, the Committee decided to include the word in the text but to enclose it within square brackets. (Among the versions only itd syrh and goth express the force of ἀνά; but whether the others simply omit to render the word or whether they rest upon a Greek text that lacked it, it is difficult to say. Syrs reads, "and not even two coats.") (Metxger, *A Textual Commentary on the Greek New Testament*, 147).

Verse 4 - "And whatsoever house ye enter into, there abide, and thence, depart."

καὶ εἰς ἣν ἂν οἰκίαν εἰσέλθητε, ἐκεῖ μένετε καὶ ἐκεῖθεν ἐξέρχεσθε.

καὶ (continuative conjunction) 14.
εἰς (preposition with the accusative of extent) 140.
ἣν (acc.sing.fem.of ὅς, in agreement with οἰκίαν) 65.
ἂν (conditional particle, contingency with the subjunctive) 205.
οἰκίαν (acc.sing.fem.of οἰκία, extent) 186.
εἰσέλθητε (2d.per.pl.aor.subj.of εἰσέρχομαι, indefinite local clause) 234.
ἐκεῖ (adverb of place) 204.
μένετε (2d.per.pl.pres.act.impv.of μένω, command) 864.
καὶ (adjunctive conjunction joining verbs) 14.
ἐκεῖθεν (adverbial) 396.
ἐξέρχεσθε (2d.per.pl.pres.impv.of ἐξέρχομαι, command) 161.

Translation - "And into whatever house you enter, remain there and leave from there."

Comment: One host, hostess and home for each community. Pick a house when you get to town. Move in and stay until you are ready to leave that community. Your hosts may not believe your message nor accept your Messiah. The time to register this fact is not while you are a guest in their home, but when you leave. Care should be exercised in the selection of the house. When the disciples came to a new community they were to enquire as to who in the city was worthy (Mt.10:11) before they moved in. Once moved in, that house was to be headquarters for the duration. *Cf.* Acts 16:40. The ceremony of condemnation, described in verse 5, is against any and/or all disbelievers in the community, not simply those in the house where the apostles stayed. For further comment *cf.* Mk.6:10,11; Mt.10:11-13.

Verse 5 - "And whosoever will not receive you, when ye go out of that city, shake off the very dust from your feet for a testimony against them."

καὶ ὅσοι ἂν μὴ δέχωνται ὑμᾶς, ἐξερχόμενοι ἀπὸ τῆς πόλεως ἐκείνης τὸν κονιορτὸν ἀπὸ τῶν ποδῶν ὑμῶν ἀποτινάσσετε εἰς μαρτύριον ἐπ' αὐτούς.

καί (continuative conjunction) 14.

ὅσοι (nom.pl.masc.of ὅσος, subject of δέχωνται) 660.

ἄν (conditional particle in a conditional clause) 205.

μή (qualified negative conjunction in a conditional clause) 87.

δέχωνται (3d.per.pl.pres.subj.of δέχομαι, conditional clause) 867.

ὑμᾶς (acc.pl.masc.of σύ, direct object of δέχωνται) 104.

ἐξερχόμενοι (pres.mid.part.nom.pl.masc.of ἐξέρχομαι, adverbial, temporal) 161.

ἀπό (preposition with the ablative of separation) 70.

τῆς (abl.sing.fem.of the article in agreement with πόλεως) 9.

πόλεως (abl.sing.fem.of πόλις, separation) 243.

ἐκείνης (abl.sing.fem.of ἐκεῖνος, in agreement with πόλεως) 246.

τόν (acc.sing.masc.of the article in agreement with κονιορτόν) 9.

κονιορτόν (acc.sing.masc.of κονιορτός, direct object of ἀποτινάσσετε) 869.

ἀπό (preposition with the ablative of separation) 70.

τῶν (abl.pl.masc.of the article in agreement with ποδῶν) 9.

ποδῶν (abl.pl.masc.of πούς, separation) 353.

ὑμῶν (gen.pl.masc.of σύ, possession) 104.

#2252 ἀποτινάσσετε (2d.per.pl.pres.act.impv.of ἀποτινάσσω, command).

shake off - Lk.9:5; Acts 28:5.

Meaning: A combination of ἀπό (#70) and τινάσσω - "to shake." Hence, to shake off or away from. With reference to our Lord's instructions to the apostles - Lk.9:5. With reference to Paul's experience with the serpent - Acts 28:5.

εἰς (preposition with the accusative, purpose) 140.

μαρτύριον (acc.sing.neut.of μαρτύριον, purpose) 716.

ἐπ' (preposition with the accusative, hostility) 47.

αὐτούς (acc.pl.masc.of αὐτός, hostility) 16.

Translation - "And whoever does not receive you, when you leave that city, shake off the dust from your feet for a witness against them."

Comment: The relative pronoun ὅσοι is used here like a demonstrative. "The relative was originally identical with the demonstrative. . . In Homer ὅς is used alternately as demonstrative and relative. . . This usage continues into the κοινή and is found in the New Testament," (Mantey, *Manual*, 125). We have an example of it here. *Cf.* also Mk.6:11; Mt.10;14. Note the demonstrative ἐκείνης in the predicate position. This is strong. Jesus wants the city that rejects the kingdom message singled out. Matthew adds that Sodom and Gomorrah will fare better in the judgment than the city that turns a deaf ear to the message of the apostles.

Verse 6 - "And they departed, and went through the towns, preaching the gospel, and healing everywhere."

ἐξερχόμενοι δὲ διήρχοντο κατὰ τὰς κώμας εὐαγγελιζόμενοι καὶ θεραπεύοντες πανταχοῦ.

ἐξερχόμενοι (pres.part.nom.pl.masc.of ἐξέρχομαι, adverbial, temporal) 161.
δὲ (continuative conjunction) 11.
διήρχοντο (3d.per.pl.imp.act.ind.of διέρχομαι, inceptive) 1017.
κατὰ (preposition with the accusative, distributive) 98.
τὰς (acc.pl.fem.of the article in agreement with κώμας) 9.
κώμας (acc.pl.fem.of κώμη, distributive, extent) 834.
εὐαγγελιζόμενοι (pres.part.nom.pl.masc.of εὐαγγελίζομαι, adverbial, modal) 909.
καὶ (adjunctive conjunction joining participles) 14.
θεραπεύοντες (pres.act.part.nom.pl.masc.of θεραπεύω, adverbial, modal) 406.
πανταχοῦ (adverbial) 2062.

Translation - *"And when they had gone out they began a trip through the villages, preaching the good news and healing everywhere."*

Comment: διήρχοντο, the inceptive imperfect indicates the beginning and consistent pursuit of a preaching mission by the apostles which went from village to village. κατὰ with the accusative in a distributive sense - "from village to village." This was blanket coverage. Everywhere they proclaimed the good news and healed the people. The message to the lost sheep of the house of Israel was that the disciples had seen the Messiah and had been sent by Him and were preaching in His name. The admonition was to repent, since the nation was soon to be delivered from political, moral and spiritual bondage.

It is idle to speculate about what might have been but was not. Had Israel obeyed the message of the gospel of the kingdom, Christ would not have died and man's sin debt would not have been paid. But Israel rejected her Messiah (John 1:11), although she will accept Him when He comes again.

Death of John the Baptist

(Mk.6:14-29; Mt.14:1-12; Lk.9:7-9)

Mark 6:14 - *"And king Herod heard of him; (for his name was spread abroad:) and he said, That John the Baptist was risen from the dead, and therefore mighty works do shew forth themselves in him,"*

Καὶ ἤκουσεν ὁ βασιλεὺς Ἡρῴδης, φανερὸν γὰρ ἐγένετο τὸ ὄνομα αὐτοῦ, καὶ ἔλεγεν ὅτι Ἰωάννης ὁ βαπτίζων ἐγήγερται ἐκ νεκρῶν, καὶ διὰ τοῦτο ἐνεργοῦσιν αἱ δυνάμεις ἐν αὐτῷ.

Καὶ (continuative conjunction) 14.
ἤκουσεν (3d.per.sing.aor.act.ind.of ἀκούω, ingressive) 148.

ὁ (nom.sing.masc.of the article in agreement with βασιλεὺς) 9.
βασιλεὺς (nom.sing.masc.of βασιλεύς, subject of ἤκουσεν) 31.
Ἡρῴδης (nom.sing.masc.of Ἡρῴδης, apposition) 136a.
φανερὸν (nom.sing.neut.of φανερός, predicate adjective) 981.
γὰρ (causal conjunction) 105.
ἐγένετο (3d.per.sing.aor.ind.of γίνομαι, ingressive) 113.
τὸ (nom.sing.neut.of the article in agreement with ὄνομα) 9.
ὄνομα (nom.sing.neut.of ὄνομα, subject of ἐγένετο) 108.
αὐτοῦ (gen.sing.masc.of αὐτός, possession) 16.
καὶ (inferential conjunction) 14.
ἔλεγον (3d.per.pl.imp.act.ind.of λέγω, progressive duration) 66.
ὅτι (conjunction introducing an object clause in indirect discourse) 211.
Ἰωάννης (nom.sing.masc.of Ἰωάννης, subject of ἐγήγερται) 247.
ὁ (nom.sing.masc.of the article in agreement with βαπτίζων) 9.
βαπτίζων (pres.act.part.nom.sing.masc.substantival, apposition) 273.
ἐγήγερται (3d.per.sing.perf.pass.ind.of ἐγείρω, consummative) 125.
ἐκ (preposition with the ablative of separation) 19.
νεκρῶν (abl.pl.masc.of νεκρός, separation) 749.
καὶ (continuative conjunction) 14.
διὰ (preposition with the accusative, cause) 118.
τοῦτο (acc.sing.neut.of οὗτος, cause) 93.
ἐνεργοῦσιν (3d.per.pl.pres.ind.of ἐνεργέω, progressive) 1105.
αἱ (nom.pl.fem.of the article in agreement with δυνάμεις) 9.
δυνάμεις (nom.pl.fem.of δύναμις, subject of ἐνεργοῦσιν) 687.
ἐν (preposition with the instrumental of means) 80.
αὐτῷ (instru.sing.masc.of αὐτός, means) 16.

Translation - "And King Herod began to hear about it, for His name was beginning to be well known, and they were saying that John the Baptist had been raised from the dead, and therefore the miracles were working by him."

Comment: Wherever the disciples went, preaching the same message that John had preached and accompanying the preaching with miracles of healing, they announced Jesus as the Messiah. In view of the widespread geographical character of their ministry (Lk.9:6) the name of Jesus had become widely publicized. Herod heard about it. It was natural for him to associate this miracle working with John the Baptist. It was the same message, but something had been added - he was now performing miracles! John's resurrection was a logical explanation to a superstitious mind, fed by a guilty conscience. *Cf.* Mt.14:1,2; Lk.9:7 for further comment.

Verse 15 - "Others said, That it is Elias. And others said, That it is a prophet, or as one of the prophets."

ἄλλοι δὲ ἔλεγον ὅτι Ἠλίας ἐστίν, ἄλλοι δὲ ἔλεγον ὅτι προφήτης ὡς εἷς τῶν προφητῶν.

ἄλλοι (nom.pl.masc.of ἄλλος, subject of ἔλεγον) 198.
δὲ (adversative conjunction) 11.
ἔλεγον (3d.per.pl.imp.act.ind.of λέγω, progressive duration) 66.
ὅτι (conjunction introducing an object clause in indirect discourse) 211.
Ἡλίας (nom.sing.masc.of Ἡλίας, predicate nominative) 921.
ἐστίν (3d.per.sing.pres.ind.of εἰμί, aoristic, indirect discourse) 86.
ἄλλοι (nom.pl.masc.of ἄλλος, subject of ἔλεγον) 198.
δὲ (adversative conjunction) 11.
ἔλεγον (3d.per.pl.imp.act.ind.of λέγω, progressive duration) 66.
ὅτι (conjunction introducing an object clause in indirect discourse) 211.
προφήτης (nom.sing.masc.of προφήτης, predicate nominative) 119.
ὡς (comparative adverb) 128.
εἷς (nom.sing.masc.of εἷς, predicate nominative) 469.
τῶν (gen.pl.masc.of the article in agreement with προφητῶν) 9.
προφητῶν (gen.pl.masc.of προφήτης, partitive genitive) 119.

Translation - "*But others were saying that he was Elijah; but others were saying that he was a prophet like one of the (ancient) prophets.*"

Comment: The general public, not sharing Herod's guilt complex, had various opinions. *Cf.* Mt.16:13-16. The work of the disciples and Jesus could not be that of John the Baptist. He was dead and only Herod believed that he might have been resurrected. But it could be Elijah. They had asked John if he was Elijah and got a denial (John 1:21). John was not Elijah, nor the Prophet promised in Mal.4:5,6 or in Deut.18:15. But perhaps John's successor was Eliajh or a prophet like one of the ancient prophets of Israel. Thus all public opinion with regard to Jesus was plausible. Herod's crazed brain and guilty conscience were playing tricks on him.

"The plural ἔλεγον, read by B W ita,b,d,ff2 and supported by the intention of Dgr (ἐλέγοσαν), seems to be the original reading. Copyists altered it to ἔλεγεν in agreement with ἤκουσεν, not observing that after the words καὶ ἤκουσεν ὁ βασιλεὺς Ἡρῴδης the sentence is suspended, in order to introduce parenthetically three specimens of the opinions held about Jesus (καὶ ἔλεγον . . . ἄλλοι δὲ ἔλεγον. . . ἄλλοι δὲ ἔλεγον), and is taken up again at ver.16, ἀκούσας δὲ ὁ Ἡρῴδης. . . " (Metzger, *Textual Commentary*, 89).

Verse 16 - "*But when Herod heard thereof he said, It is John, whom I beheaded: he is risen from the dead.*"

ἀκούσας δὲ ὁ Ἡρῴδης ἔλεγεν, Ὃν ἐγὼ ἀπεκεφάλισα Ἰωάννην, οὗτος ἠγέρθη.

ἀκούσας (aor.act.part.nom.sing.masc.of ἀκούω, adverbial, temporal) 148.
δὲ (adversative conjunction) 11.
ὁ (nom.sing.masc.of the article in agreement with Ἡρῴδης, subject of ἔλεγεν) 136a.
ἔλεγεν (3d.per.sing.imp.act.ind.of λέγω, progressive duration) 66.
ὃν (acc.sing.masc.of ὅς, direct object of ἀπεκεφάλισα, indirect attraction) 65.

ἐγώ (nom.sing.masc.of ἐγώ, subject of ἀπεκεφάλισα) 123.
ἀπεκεφάλισα (1st.per.sing.aor.act.ind.of ἀποκεφαλίζω, constative) 1114.
Ἰωάννην (acc.sing.masc.of Ἰωάννης, apposition) 247.
οὗτος (nom.sing.masc.of οὗτος, subject of ἠγέρθη) 93.
ἠγέρθη (3d.per.sing.aor.pass.ind.of ἐγείρω, culminative) 125.

Translation - *"But when Herod heard it he began to say, 'The one whom I beheaded, John - he has been raised from the dead.' "*

Comment: Herod heard the rumors going around the court as to who this mighty prophet was. He disagreed with them all. Note the emphatic position of the relative clause ὅν ἐγώ ἀπεκεφάλισα. This gruesome fact was uppermost in Herod's tormented mind. This man John had been raised from the dead. We have an example of indirect attraction of the antecedent, Ἰωάννην, being attracted in case to the relative pronoun ὅν, which is accusative by virtue of its use in its clause as object of ἀπεκεφάλισα. Mark devotes verses 17-29 to the story in explanation of Herod's problem. What follows is a description of what happened previous to the time of the story contained in vss.14-16.

Verse 17 - *"For Herod himself had sent forth and laid hold upon John and bound him in prison for Herodias' sake, his brother Philip's wife: for he had married her."*

Αὐτὸς γὰρ ὁ Ἡρῴδης ἀποστείλας ἐκράτησεν τὸν Ἰωάννην καὶ ἔδησεν αὐτὸν ἐν φυλακῇ διὰ Ἡρῳδιάδα τὴν γυναῖκα Φιλίππου τοῦ ἀδελφοῦ αὐτοῦ, ὅτι αὐτὴν ἐγάμησεν.

Αὐτὸς (nom.sing.masc.of αὐτός, intensive personal pronoun, in agreement with Ἡρῴδης) 16.
γὰρ (causal conjunction) 105.
ὁ (nom.sing.masc.of the article in agreement with Ἡρῴδης) 9.
Ἡρῴδης (nom.sing.masc.of Ἡρῴδης, subject of ἐκράτησεν, ἔδησεν and ἐγάμησεν) 136a.
ἀποστείλας (1st.aor.act.part.nom.sing.masc.of ἀποστέλλω, adverbial, temporal) 215.
ἐκράτησεν (3d.per.sing.aor.act.ind.of κρατέω, constative) 828.
τὸν (acc.sing.masc.of the article in agreement with Ἰωάννην) 9.
Ἰωάννην (acc.sing.masc.of Ἰωάννης, direct object of ἐκράτησεν) 247.
καὶ (adjunctive conjunction joining verbs) 14.
ἔδησεν (3d.per.sing.aor.act.ind.of δέω, constative) 998.
αὐτὸν (acc.sing.masc.of αὐτός, direct object of ἔδησεν) 16.
ἐν (preposition with the locative of place) 80.
φυλακῇ (loc.sing.fem.of φυλακή, place where) 494.
διὰ (preposition with the accusative, cause) 118.
Ἡρῳδιάδα (acc.sing.fem.of Ἡρῳδιάς, cause) 1107.
τὴν (acc.sing.fem.of the article in agreement with γυναῖκα) 9.
γυναῖκα (acc.sing.fem.of γυνή, apposition) 103.

Φιλίππου (gen.sing.masc.of Φίλιππος, relationship) 1108.
τοῦ (gen.sing.masc.of the article in agreement with ἀδελφοῦ) 9.
ἀδελφοῦ (gen.sing.masc.of ἀδελφός, apposition) 15.
αὐτοῦ (gen.sing.masc.of αὐτός, relationship) 16.
ὅτι (causal conjunction) 211.
αὐτήν (acc.sing.fem.of αὐτός, direct object of ἐγάμησεν) 16.
ἐγάμησεν (3d.per.sing.aor.act.ind.of γαμέω, culminative) 512.

Translation - *"For Herod himself sent and arrested John and tied him up in prison on account of Herodias, the wife of Philip, his brother, because he had married her."*

Comment: The first αὐτος is an intensive use of the third personal pronoun, calling special attention to Herod. Herod himself was personally responsible for John's arrest and imprisonment. διά with the accusative tells us why. It was because Herod had married Herodias, his sister-in-law, the wife of his brother, Philip. This, in itself, would not have brought about John's arrest had the Baptist remained silent about it. But he did not. John warned Herod repeatedly, as we see in

Verse 18 - *"For John had said unto Herod, It is not lawful for thee to have thy brother's wife."*

ἔλεγεν γὰρ ὁ Ἰωάννης τῷ Ἡρῴδῃ ὅτι Οὐκ ἔξεστίν σοι ἔχειν τὴν γυναῖκα τοῦ ἀδελφοῦ σου.

ἔλεγεν (3d.per.sing.imp.act.ind.of λέγω, progressive duration) 66.
γάρ (causal conjunction) 105.
ὁ (nom.sing.masc.of the article in agreement with Ἰωάννης) 9.
Ἰωάννης (nom.sing.masc.of Ἰωάννης, subject of ἔλεγεν) 247.
τῷ (dat.sing.masc.of the article in agreement with Ἡρῴδῃ) 9.
Ἡρῴδῃ (dat.sing.masc.of Ἡρῴδης, indirect object of ἔλεγεν) 135a.
ὅτι (recitative) 211.
Οὐκ (summary negative with the indicative) 130.
ἔξεστίν (impersonal verb, predicate adjective) 966.
σοι (dat.sing.masc.of σύ, reference) 104.
ἔχειν (pres.act.inf.of ἔχω, complementary) 82.
τήν (acc.sing.fem.of the article in agreement with γυναῖκα) 9.
γυναῖκα (acc.sing.fem.of γυνή, direct object of ἔχειν) 103.
τοῦ (gen.sing.masc.of the article in agreement with ἀδελφοῦ) 9.
ἀδελφοῦ (gen.sing.masc.of ἀδελφός, relationship) 15.
σου (gen.sing.masc.of σύ, relationship) 104.

Translation - *"For John kept saying to Herod, 'It is not lawful for you to have your brother's wife.'"*

Comment: The continuous action in the imperfect in ἔλεγεν speaks of John the Baptist's repeated warning to the king that his relation with Herodias was adulterous. That John found it necessary to repeat the warning proves that Herod was just as consistent in his rejection of the divine warning.

John the Baptist belonged to no school of ethical relativism. He believed that some things were wrong, regardless of circumstances and he did not hesitate to say so. The fact that the sinner in this case was the king made no difference to John. The excess of democracy which expresses itself in modern educational theory would favor giving Herod and Herodias three hours of academic credit for indulging in new experience. The forthright message of John elicited hatred from Herodias, as we see in

Verse 19 - " Therefore Herodias had a quarrel against him, and would have killed him, but she could not."

ἡ δὲ Ἡρῳδιὰς ἐνεῖχεν αὐτῷ καὶ ἤθελεν αὐτὸν ἀποκτεῖναι, καὶ οὐκ ἠδύνατο.

ἡ (nom.sing.fem.of the article in agreement with Ἡρῳδιὰς) 9.
Ἡρῳδιὰς (nom.sing.fem.of Ἡρῳδιὰς, subject of ἐνεῖχεν) 1107.

#2253 ἐνεῖχεν (3d.per.sing.imp.act.ind.of ἐνέχω, progressive description).

    have a quarrel against - Mk.6:19.
    urge - Lk.11:53.
    be entangled with - Gal.5:1.

Meaning: A combination of ἐν (#80) and ἔχω (#82). Hence, to have or to hold in or within. To become involved with. In modern usage we say, "You and I are going to have it" meaning "We are going to get involved in a quarrel or fight." Herodias quarreled with John - Mk.6:19; the Pharisees engaged in controversy with Jesus - Lk.11:53; Christians who enjoy liberty in Christ should not get involved with the legalisms of Moses - Gal.5:1.

    αὐτῷ (dat.sing.masc.of αὐτός, personal interest) 16.
    καὶ (adjunctive conjunction joining verbs) 14.
    ἤθελεν (3d.per.sing.imp.act.ind.of θέλω, progressive duration) 88.
    αὐτὸν (acc.sing.masc.of αὐτός, direct object of ἀποκτεῖναι) 16.
    ἀποκτεῖναι (1st.aor.act.inf.of ἀποκτείνω, epexegetical) 889.
    καὶ (adversative conjunction) 14.
    οὐκ (summary negative conjunction with the indicative) 130.
    ἠδύνατο (3d.per.sing.imp.ind.of δύναμαι, progressive description) 289.

Translation - "But Herodias was always quarreling with him and she always wanted to kill him, but she could not."

Comment: Mark continues to use the imperfect tense in all of the verbs. Herodias hated John and quarreled with him on every occasion, while she continued to indulge the urge to kill him, but was never able to bring it off for the reasons given in verse 20. Note the Attic form of the imperfect of δύναμαι, rather than the κοινή form ἐδύνατο.

The epexegetical infinitive ἀποκτεῖναι explains the verb ἤθελεν. This running fight between John on God's side and Herodias on the other, put Herod in the middle. He wanted also to kill John, but Herod still had a bit of decency about him, as we shall see in

Verse 20 - "For Herod feared John knowing that he was a just man and an holy, and observed him; and when he heard him, he did many things, and heard him gladly.

ὁ γάρ Ἡρώδης ἐφοβεῖτο τὸν Ἰωάννην, εἰδὼς αὐτὸν ἄνδρα δίκαιον καὶ ἅγιον, καὶ συνετήρει αὐτόν, καὶ ἀκούσας αὐτοῦ πολλὰ ἐποίει, καὶ ἡδέως αὐτοῦ ἤκουεν.

ὁ (nom.sing.masc.of the article in agreement with Ἡρώδης) 9.

γάρ (causal conjunction) 105.

Ἡρώδης (nom.sing.masc.of Ἡρώδης, subject of all of the verbs in the sentence) 136a.

ἐφοβεῖτο (3d.per.sing.imp.mid.ind.of φοβέομαι, inceptive) 101.

τὸν (acc.sing.masc.of the article in agreement with Ἰωάννην) 9.

Ἰωάννην (acc.sing.masc.of Ἰωάννης, direct object of ἐφοβεῖτο) 247.

εἰδὼς (pres.part.nom.sing.masc.of ὁράω, adverbial, causal) 144.

αὐτὸν (acc.sing.masc.of αὐτός, direct object of εἰδὼς) 16.

ἄνδρα (acc.sing.masc.of ἀνήρ, general reference) 63.

δίκαιον (acc.sing.masc.of δίκαιος, in agreement with ἄνδρα) 85.

καὶ (adjunctive conjunction joining adjectives) 14.

ἅγιον (acc.sing.masc.of ἅγιος, in agreement with ἄνδρα) 84.

καὶ (adjunctive conjunction joining verbs) 14.

συνετήρει (3d.per.sing.imp.act.ind.of συντηρέω, progressive duration) 814.

αὐτόν (acc.sing.masc.of αὐτός, direct object of συνετήρει) 16.

καὶ (adjunctive conjunction joining verbs) 14.

ἀκούσας (aor.act.part.nom.sing.masc.of ἀκούω, adverbial, temporal) 148.

αὐτοῦ (gen.sing.masc.of αὐτός, description) 16.

πολλὰ (acc.pl.neut.of πολύς, direct object of ἠπόρει) 228.

#2254 ἠπόρει (3d.per.sing.imp.act.ind.of ἀπορέω, inceptive).

doubt - John 13:22; Acts 25:20.
be perplexed - II Cor.4:8; Lk.24:4.
stand in doubt - Gal.4:20.
do - Mk.6:20.

Meaning: α privative plus πόρος - "a transit, ford, way, revenue, resource." Hence, to be without a way to procede. To be in doubt; to be in a dilemma. To be in a state of not knowing what to do. Joined by the accusative in Mk.6:20 - Herod was in doubt about many things after he heard John the Baptist preach. Followed by περὶ τίνος λέγει - the disciples had doubts about whom Jesus spoke - John 13:22. Followed by περὶ τούτων - Acts 25:20; II Cor.4:8. By ἐν ὑμῖν - "I am in doubt because of you" - Gal.4:20. Followed by περὶ τούτου - the women at the tomb - Lk.24:4.

καὶ (adjunctive conjunction joining verbs) 14.

#2255 ἡδέως (adverbial).

gladly - Mk.6:20; 12:37; II Cor.11:19.

Meaning: gladly. With ἤκουεν αὐτοῦ in Mk.6:20; 12:37. With ἀνέχεσθε in 11 Cor.11:19.

αὐτοῦ (gen.sing.masc.of αὐτός, after ἤκουεν) 16.
ἤκουεν (3d.per.sing.imp.act.ind.of ἀκούω, inceptive) 148.

Translation - "*Because Herod was beginning to have respect for John because he knew that he was a holy and righteous man and he kept in touch with him, and after he heard him he was in great doubt and he began to hear him gladly.*"

Comment: The verse outlines the history of Herod's attitude toward John. It manifests ambivalence. First of all Herod respected John because he knew him to be a holy and righteous man. There was nothing in John's personal record to subtract from the power of his message. Herod kept himself informed about John, in reference to his whereabouts and ministry, which may also mean that the king was protecting the prophet from the wrath of Herodias. This seems to be the meaning of συνετήρει αὐτόν. *Cf.*#814. Wherever John went and whatever he preached, Herod took measures to find out all about it. Then Herod heard John preach and we already know what John told the king. *Cf.* verse 18. John's message impacted upon Herod in opposing ways. Thus the king was in a dilemma. Here is a man, torn by a guilty conscience, yet desiring to hear God's message and grudgingly admitting to himself at least that John was telling the truth. Thus he *began* (inceptive imperfect tense in ἤκουεν) to listen gladly. But Herod had family connections and social and political pressures which spelled his doom.

(Note: This portion of *The Renaissance New Testament* was originally prepared before the textual research of the United Bible Societies Committee was available. The text followed was that of Westcott/Hort, which reads ἠπόρει, the imperfect active indicative of ἀπορέω. This being the first appearance of the word in our study, we gave it the approriate number (#2254) and proceded. The Aland Committee of the United Bible Societies have opted for ἐποίει in the text and have indicated an average degree of certitude in the matter. In our view Metzger's explanation of the thinking of the committee is not convincing. He says, "On the one hand, the reading ἐποίει, which has been thought to reflect a Semitic original, is supported by a broad spectrum of Greek and versional witnesses. On the other hand, the reading ἠπόρει, though sometimes suspected of having arisen by scribal assimilation to the Lukan statement concerning Herod's being "much perplexed" (διηπόρει, Lk.9:7) on another occasion, was preferred by a majority of the Committee on the grounds of (a) strong external support (Sinaiticus B L (W) Θ copsa, bo); (b) the usage, in this case of πολλά as an adverb, in keeping with Markan style; and (c) the intrinsic superiority of meaning in contrast to the banality of the clause when ἐποίει is read." (Metzger, *Textual Commentary*, 89).

It appears to me that when we read πολλὰ ἐποίει - "he began to do many things" we are left wondering what things Herod began to do, whereas when we read πολλὰ ἠπόρει - "he began to be confused" it is what we would normally expect from a man who was caught between the obvious facts of his illicit behavior and the conviction that John was a holy and righteous man who was telling God's truth when he said that Herod was an adulterer. The ἐποίει reading is indeed banal as the majority of the Aland Committee has suggested. No great damage is being done to the overall point of the story whether we are to read ἐποίει or ἠπόρει, but the latter, it seems to me, fits into the context much, much better. Herod's regret that he had given a sacred oath to grant Salome's bloody request, albeit given when he was drunk, reinforces the dilemma between the horns of which he hesitated - a psychological state clearly indicated by ἠπόρει, but not by ἐποίει.

Verse 21 - "And when a convenient day was come, that Herod on his birthday made a supper to his lords, high captains, and chief estates of Galilee,"

Καὶ γενομένης ἡμέρας εὐκαίρου ὅτε Ἡρῴδης τοῖς γενεσίοις αὐτοῦ δεῖπνον ἐποίησεν τοῖς μεγιστᾶσιν αὐτοῦ καὶ τοῖς χιλιάρχοις καὶ τοῖς πρώτοις τῆς Γαλιλαίας,

Καὶ (continuative conjunction) 14.
γενομένης (aor.part.gen.sing.fem.of γίνομαι, genitive absolute) 113.
ἡμέρας (gen.sing.fem.of ἡμέρα, genitive absolute) 135.

#2256 εὐκαίρου (gen.sing.fem.of εὔκαιρος, in agreement with ἡμέρας).

convenient - Mk.6:21.
in time of need - Heb.4:16.

Meaning: A combination of εὐ (#1536) and καιρός (#767). Hence, a good time; a good opportunity. A convenient time. As an adjective in the attributive position - Heb.4:16; in the predicate position - Mk.6:21.

ὅτε (temporal conjunction, introducing a definite temporal clause) 703.
Ἡρῴδης (nom.sing.masc.of Ἡρῴδης, subject of ἐποίησεν) 136a.
τοῖς (loc.pl.masc.of the article in agreement with γενεσίοις) 9.
γενεσίοις (loc.pl.masc.of γενέσια, time point) 1109.
αὐτοῦ (gen.sing.masc.of αὐτός, possession) 16.
δεῖπνον (acc.sing.neut.of δεῖπνον, direct object of ἐποίησεν) 1440.
ἐποίησεν (3d.per.sing.aor.act.ind.of ποιέω, constative) 127.
τοῖς (dat.pl.masc.of the article in agreement with μεγιστᾶσιν) 9.

#2257 μεγιστᾶσιν (dat.pl.masc.of μεγιστάν, personal advantage).

great men - Rev.6:15; 18:23.

lords - Mk.6:21.

Meaning: Cf.μέγεθος (#4465) and *μέγιστος* (#5227). The grandees, magnates, noble, chief men. The associates and courtiers of a king. *μεγιστᾶνες τῆς γῆς* in Rev.6:15; 18:23. Attached to Herod's court - Mk.6:21.

αὐτοῦ (gen.sing.masc.of αὐτός, possession) 16.
καὶ (adjunctive conjunction joining nouns) 14.
τοῖς (dat.pl.masc.of the article in agreement with χιλιάρχοις) 9.

#2258 χιλιάρχοις (dat.pl.masc.of χιλίαρχος, personal advantage).

captain - John 18:12; Rev.19:18.
chief captain - Mk.6:21; Acts 21:31,32,33,37; 22:24,26,27,28,29; 23:10,15,17, 18,19,22; 24:7,22; 25:23; Rev.6:15.
Meaning: A combination of χίλιοι (#5278) and ἄρχω (#383). Hence, a chiliarch; a commander of a thousand soldiers. Commander of a Roman cohort (a military tribune). The context makes clear whether in a Jewish, Galilean or Roman army. Generally in Rev.6:15; 19:18.

καὶ (adjunctive conjunction joining nouns) 14.
τοῖς (dat.pl.masc.of the article in agreement with πρώτοις) 9.
πρώτοις (dat.pl.masc.of πρῶτος, personal advantage) 487.
τῆς (gen.sing.fem.of the article in agreement with Γαλιλαίας) 9.
Γαλιλαίας (gen.sing.fem.of Γαλιλαίας, definition) 241.

Translation - "And on a convenient ·day, when, during Herod's birthday celebrations, he gave a dinner party for his lords and the chief captains and the Galilean establishment . . . "

Comment: The grammar is a bit difficult here. Normally we would think of γενομένης ἡμέρας εὐκαίρου as a genitive absolute in the aorist tense, indicating time antecedent to that of the main verb. But Mark follows it with a definite temporal clause with ὅτε and indicative ἐποίησεν. The convenient day which came occurred during the period when Herod was celebrating his birthday feasts (note the plural in τοῖς γενεσίοις). The main verb is ἤρεσεν in verse 22, a grammatical fact which we are likely to overlook due to the unusual syntax. We can translate, "When, a convenient day having come, Herod during his birthday feasts, gave a dinner party . . . κ.τ.λ." The sense is clear in any case. On one of the days of his birthday celebration it was convenient for Herod to give the dinner party. The Establishment of course was present - Politicians, Joint Chiefs of Staff and the civilian Establishment generally. All of the "influential" people in Galilee were on hand. εὐκαίρου may refer more to Herodias' evil designs than to Herod's plans. The evil woman sought opportunity to catch Herod in an unguarded moment when she could move him from his resolute determination to protect John the Baptist from her murderous hatred.

Verse 22 - "And when the daughter of the said Herodias came in, and danced, and pleased Herod and them that sat with him, the king said unto the damsel,

Ask of me whatsoever thou wilt, and I will give it thee."

καὶ εἰσελθούσης τῆς θαγατρὸς αὐτοῦ Ἡρἰδιάδος καὶ ὀρχησαμένης ἤρεσεν
τῷ Ἡρῴδῃ καὶ τοῖς συνανακειμένους ὁ δὲ βασιλεὺς εἶπεν τῷ κορασίῳ Αἴτησόν
με ὃ ἐὰν θέλῃς καὶ δώσω σοι.

καὶ (continuative conjunction) 14.
εἰσελθούσης (aor.part.gen.sing.fem.of εἰσέρχομαι, genitive absolute) 234.
τῆς (gen.sing.fem.of the article in agreement with θυγατρὸς) 9.
θυγατρὸς (gen.sing.fem.of θυγάτηρ, genitive absolute) 817.
αὐτοῦ (gen.sing.masc.of αὐτός, intensive pronoun) 16.
Ἡρῳδιάδος (gen.sing.fem.of Ἡρῳδιάς, relationship) 1107.
καὶ (adjunctive conjunction joining participles) 14.
ὀρχησαμένης (aor.mid.part.gen.sing.fem.of ὀρχέω, genitive absolute) 927.
ἤρεσεν (3d.per.sing.aor.act.ind.of ἀρέσκω, constative) 1110.
τῷ (dat.sing.masc.of the article in agreement with Ἡρῴδῃ) 9.
Ἡρῴδῃ (dat.sing.masc.of Ἡρῴδης, personal advantage) 136a.
καὶ (adjunctive conjunction joining substantives) 14.
τοῖς (dat.pl.masc.of the article in agreement with συνανακειμένους) 9.
συνανακειμένους (pres.part.dat.pl.masc.of συνανάκειμαι, substantival,
personal advantage) 792.
ὁ (nom.sing.masc.of the article in agreement with βασιλεὺς) 9.
δὲ (continuative conjunction) 11.
βασιλεὺς (nom.sing.masc.of βασιλεύς, subject of εἶπεν) 31.
εἶπεν (3d.per.sing.aor.act.ind.of εἶπον, constative) 155.
τῷ (dat.sing.neut.of the article in agreement with κορασίῳ) 9.
κορασίῳ (dat.sing.neut.of κοράσιον, indirect object of εἶπεν) 826.
Αἴτησόν (2d.per.sing.aor.act.impv.of αἰτέω, command) 537.
με (acc.sing.masc.of ἐγώ, direct object of αἴτησόν) 123.
ὃ (acc.sing.neut.of ὅς, direct object of θέλῃς) 65.
ἐὰν (conditional particle with the subjunctive) 363.
θέλῃς (2d.per.sing.pres.act.subj.of θέλω, conditional clause) 88.
καὶ (continuative conjunction) 14.
δώσω (1st.per.sing.fut.act.ind.of δίδωμι, predictive) 362.
σοι (dat.sing.fem.of σύ, indirect object of δώσω) 104.

*Translation - " . . . the daughter of the esteemed Herodias came in, danced and
pleased Herod and those reclining at the table with him. And the king said to the
girl, 'Ask me whatever you wish, and I will give it to you.' "*

Comment: Mark continues to use the genitive absolute construction by putting
τῆς θυγατρὸς in the genitive. Yet it is not absolute, for, if so, there is no subject
for the main clause, except as it is implicit in ἤρεσεν.

Another reading has θυγ ατρὸς αὐτῆς τῆς Ἡρῳδιάδος, which at least has the
pronoun in the correct gender to agree with Ἡρῳδιάδος. None of the readings
are grammatically sound. "It is very difficult to decide which reading is the least
unsatisfactory. According to the reading with αὐτοῦ the girl is herself named

Herodias and is described as Herod's daughter. But in ver.24 she is Herodias's daughter, who, according to other sources, was named Salome, a grand-niece of Herod. The reading with αὐτῆς τῆς must mean something like "the daughter of Herodias herself," unless αὐτῆς be taken as the redundant pronoun anticipating a noun (an Aramaism). The reading with τῆς, read by *f1* and (presumably) Greek witnesses lying behind several early versions, is the easiest and seems to have arisen from an accidental omission of αὐτῆς.

"A majority of the Committee decided, somewhat reluctantly, that the reading with αὐτοῦ, despite the historical and contextual difficulties, must be adopted on the strength of its external attestation." (Metzger, *Textual Commentary*, 89,90).

As is always the case when there is doubt about the precise reading of the text the main thrust of the story is not threatened regardless of which reading we take. It is possible to assume that Mark's αὐτοῦ, should have been the feminine αὐτῆς, in which case it would agree with Ἡρῳδιάδος (genitive singular) and would thus be intensive. Thus we have translated.

The girl, having entered and danced, pleased the king and his guests with her performance, so much that he gave her the promise recorded in vss.22,23. Whether Herodias was party to the scheme is not told. If not, she was quick to take advantage of the king's rash offer. *Cf.* Mt.14:8; Mk.6:24. There is no necessary contradiction. How long before the girl made her request to Herod, she had received instructions from her mother is not clear. Matthew's account, taken alone, sounds as if Herodias instructed the girl before she entered and danced. Mark says that having entered, danced and pleased the king, the girl then got the suggestion from Herodias and made it to Herod. It was Herodias' idea - not Salome's.

Verse 23 - "And he sware unto her, Whatsoever thou shalt ask of me, I will give it thee, unto the half of my kingdom."

καὶ ὤμοσεν αὐτῇ (πολλά), Ὅ τι ἐάν με αἰτήσῃς δώσω ἕως ἡμίσους τῆς βασιλείας μου.

καὶ (continuative conjunction) 14.
ὤμοσεν (3d.per.sing.aor.act.ind.of ὄμνυμι, constative) 516.
αὐτῇ (dat.sing.fem.of αὐτός, indirect object of ὤμοσεν) 16.
(πολλά) (acc.pl.neut.of πολύς, adverbial) 228.
Ὅ (acc.sing.neut.of ὅς, direct object of αἰτήσῃς) 65.
τι (acc.sing.neut.of τις, indefinite pronoun) 486.
ἐάν (conditional particle with the subjunctive) 363.
με (acc.sing.masc.of ἐγώ, direct object of αἰτήσῃς) 123.
αἰτήσῃς (2d.per.sing.aor.act.subj.of αἰτέω, conditional clause) 537.
δώσω (1st.per.sing.fut.act.ind.of δίδωμι, predictive) 363.
σοι (dat.sing.fem.of σύ, indirect object of δώσω) 104.
ἕως (preposition with the genitive of description of extent) 71.

#2259 ἡμίσους (gen.sing.neut.of ἥμισυς, extent description).

half - Mk.6:23; Lk.19:8; Rev.11:9,11; 12:14.

Meaning: Half. With reference to Herod's kingdom - Mk.6:23; with reference to Zaccheus' wealth - Lk.19:8. Of time extent - days - Rev.11:9,11; years - Rev.12:14. It takes the gender and number of the annexed substantive.

τῆς (gen.sing.fem.of the article in agreement with βασιλείας) 9.
βασιλείας (gen.sing.fem.of βασιλεία, description) 253.
μου (gen.sing.masc.of ἐγώ, possession) 123.

Translation - "And he swore unto her again and again, 'Whatever you may ask me, I will give it unto half my kingdom."

Comment: "It is likely that ὅ was inserted by copyists who, coming upon the letters οτι, took them as ὅτι (rather than ὅ τι) and thus felt need of a relative pronoun to introduce the subsequent clause." (Metzger, *Textual Commentary*, 90). The subjunctive in αἰτήσῃς introduces contingency. Herod is not sure what the girl will ask him but promises to give it whatever it may be. His only qualification is that it will be no more than half his kingdom. He was drunk; he was sexually aroused; he was surrounded by his influential friends. He was also being maneuvered by his wife.

Verse 24 - "And she went forth, and said unto her mother, What shall I ask? And she said, The head of John the Baptist."

καὶ ἐξελθοῦσα εἶπεν τῇ μητρὶ αὐτῆς, Τί αἰτήσωμαι; ἡ δὲ εἶπεν, Τὴν κεφαλὴν Ἰωάννου τοῦ βαπτίζοντος.

καὶ (continuative conjunction) 14.
ἐξελθοῦσα (aor.part.nom.sing.fem.of ἐξέρχομαι, adverbial, temporal) 161.
εἶπεν (3d.per.sing.aor.act.ind.of εἶπον, constative) 155.
τῇ (dat.sing.fem.of the article in agreement with μητρὶ) 9.
μητρὶ (dat.sing.fem.of μήτηρ, indirect object of εἶπεν) 76.
αὐτῆς (gen.sing.fem.of αὐτός, relationship) 16.
Τί (acc.sing.neut.of τίς, interrogative pronoun, direct object of αἰτήσωμαι) 281.
αἰτήσωμαι (1st.per.sing. 1st.aor.mid.subj.of αἰτέω, deliberative) 537.
ἡ (nom.sing.fem.of the article subject of εἶπεν) 9.
δὲ (continuative conjunction) 11.
εἶπεν (3d.per.sing.aor.act.ind.of εἶπον, constative) 155.
Τὴν (acc.sing.fem.of the article in agreement with κεφαλὴν) 9.
κεφαλὴν (acc.sing.fem.of κεφαλή, direct object of the verb understood) 521.
Ἰωάννου (gen.sing.masc.of Ἰωάννης, possession) 247.
τοῦ (gen.sing.masc.of the article in agreement with βαπτίζοντος) 9.
βαπτίζοντος (pres.act.part.gen.sing.masc.of βαπτίζω, substantival, apposition) 273.

Translation - "And she left the room and said to her mother, 'What shall I ask?'

And she said, 'The head of John the Baptist.' "

Comment: ἐξελθοῦσα indicates that Herodias was not immediately present during the dance. No doubt she was not far away, although the girl had to leave the room where she had danced in order to consult her mother. Note the middle voice in αἰτήσωμαι - "what shall I ask for myself?" The girl's request would indicate that though she may have known something of her mother's wicked plan, she did not know the end result. Herodias replied immediately.

Verse 25 - "And she came in straightway with haste unto the king, and asked, saying, I will that thou give me by and by in a charger the head of John the Baptist."

καὶ εἰσελθοῦσα εὐθὺς μετὰ σπουδῆς πρὸς·τὸν βασιλέα ᾐτήσατο λέγουσα, Θέλω ἵνα ἐξαυτῆς δῶς μοι ἐπὶ πίνακι τὴν κεφαλὴν Ἰωάννου τοῦ βαπτιστοῦ.

καὶ (continuative conjunction) 14.
εἰσελθοῦσα (aor.part.nom.sing.fem.of εἰσέρχομαι, adverbial, temporal) 234.
εὐθὺς (adverbial) 258.
μετὰ (preposition with the genitive, adverbial) 50.
σπουδῆς (gen.sing.fem.of σπουδή, adverbial) 1819.
πρὸς (preposition with the accusative of extent) 197.
τὸν (acc.sing.masc.of the article in agreement with βασιλέα) 9.
βασιλέα (acc.sing.masc.of βασιλεύς, extent) 31.
ᾐτήσατο (3d.per.sing.aor.mid.ind.of αἰτέω, constative) 537.
λέγουσα (pres.act.part.nom.sing.fem.of λέγω, adverbial, modal) 66.
Θέλω (1st.per.sing.pres.act.ind.of θέλω, aoristic) 88.
ἵνα (final conjunction with the subjunctive in a purpose clause) 114.

#2260 ἐξαυτῆς (adverbial).

by and by - Mk.6:25.
immediately - Acts 10:33; 11:11; 21:32.
presently - Phil.2:23.

Meaning: Instantly, forthwith; on the instant; immediately.

δῶς (2d.per.sing.2d.aor.act.subj.of δίδωμι, purpose) 362.
μοι (dat.sing.masc.of ἐγώ, indirect object of δῶς) 123.
ἐπὶ (preposition with the locative of place) 47.
πίνακι (loc.sing.masc.of πίναξ, place) 1112.
τὴν (acc.sing.fem.of the article in agreement with κεφαλὴν) 9.
κεφαλὴν (acc.sing.fem.of κεφαλή, direct object of δῶς) 521.
Ἰωάννου (gen.sing.masc.of Ἰωάννης, possession) 247.
τοῦ (gen.sing.masc.of the article in agreement with βαπτιστοῦ) 9.
βαπτιστοῦ (gen.sing.masc.of βαπτιστής, apposition) 248.

Translation - "And she came running in immediately to the king and asked, saying,'I want you immediately to give to me on a platter the head of John the Baptist.' "

Comment: Salome obeyed her mother promptly. εὐθὺς μετὰ σπουδῆς indicates this. *Cf*.#1819. She hastened, perhaps running back into Herod's presence, motivated by Herodias' wicked and murderous suggestion. Θέλω is here followed by a purpose clause with ἵνα and the subjunctive in δῷς. Her demand indicates some impatience. "I want it *now*." - ἐξαυτῆς *Cf*.#2260. The serving platter (#1112) was made out of a pine board.

Verse 26 - "And the king was exceeding sorry; yet for his oath's sake, and for their sakes which sat with him, he would not reject her."

καὶ περίλυπος γενόμενος ὁ βασιλεὺς διὰ τοὺς ὅρκους καὶ τοὺς ἀνακειμένους οὐκ ἠθέλησεν ἀθετῆσαι αὐτήν.

καὶ (continuative conjunction) 14.

περίλυπος (nom.sing.masc.of περίλυπος, predicate adjective) 1586.

γενόμενος (2d.aor.part.nom.sing.masc.of γίνομαι, adverbial, concessive) 113.

ὁ (nom.sing.masc.of the article in agreement with βασιλεὺς) 9.

βασιλεὺς (nom.sing.masc.of βασιλεύς, subject of ἠθέλησεν) 31.

διὰ (preposition with the accusative of cause) 118.

τοὺς (acc.pl.masc.of the article in agreement with ὅρκους) 9.

ὅρκους (acc.pl.masc.of ὅρκος, cause) 515.

καὶ (adjunctive conjunction joining a noun with a participle) 14.

τοὺς (acc.pl.masc.of the article in agreement with ἀνακειμένους) 9.

ἀνακειμένους (pres.mid.part.acc.pl.masc.of ἀνάκειμαι, substantival, cause) 790.

οὐκ (summary negative conjunction with the indicative) 130.

ἠθέλησεν (3d.per.sing.aor.act.ind.of θέλω, constative) 88.

ἀθετῆσαι (aor.act.inf.of ἀθετέω, epexegetical) 2164.

αὐτήν (acc.sing.fem.of αὐτός, direct object of ἀθετῆσαι) 16.

Translation - "And although overcome with sorrow, because of the oaths and his guests sitting there, the king was not willing to retract his promise to her."

Comment: καὶ is continuative, but only because it is followed by the concessive participle γενόμενος. *Cf*.#1586 for an understanding of the depths of sorrow felt by Herod. Review verse 20 for Herod's secret admiration for John. Note the dilemma of this unfortunate tyrant. Impelled by his deeply felt conviction that John was God's man, to set him free, Herod was nevertheless bound by a series of drunken oaths (note the plural in ὅρκους) and by his craven desire to please his influential guests who reclined with him at the festive board. Hence Herod was unwilling to renege on his promise to Salome. Vss.27 and 28 finish the gruesome story.

Verse 27 - "And immediately the king sent an executioner, and commanded his head to be brought: and he went and beheaded him in the prison."

καὶ εὐθὺς ἀποστείλας ὁ βασιλεὺς σπεκουλάτορα ἐπέταξεν ἐνέγκαι τὴν κεφαλὴν αὐτοῦ, καὶ ἀπελθὼν ἀπεκεφάλισεν αὐτὸν ἐν τῇ φυλακῇ.

καὶ (continuative conjunction) 14.

εὐθὺς (adverbial) 258.

ἀποστείλας (aor.act.part.nom.sing.masc.of ἀποστέλλω, adverbial, temporal) 215.

ὁ (nom.sing.masc.of the article in agreement with βασιλεὺς) 9.

βασιλεὺς (nom.sing.masc.of βασιλεύς, subject of ἐπέταξεν) 31.

#2261 σπεκουλάτορα (acc.sing.masc.of σπεκουλάτωρ, direct object of ἀποστείλας).

Meaning: Latin, *speculator.* Prop. *scout.* In the Roman Imperial Army, one of the *principales,* a member of the headquarters staff of a legionary commander or a provincial governor. His duties included that of an executioner. *Cf.* δορυφόρος - "a spear bearer."

ἐπέταξεν (3d.per.sing.aor.act.ind.of επιτάσσω, constative) 2061.

ἐνέγκαι (aor.act.inf.of φέρω, epexegetical) 683.

τὴν (acc.sing.fem.of the article in agreement with κεφαλὴν) 9.

κεφαλὴν (acc.sing.fem.of κεφαλή, direct object of ἐνέγκαι) 521.

αὐτοῦ (gen.sing.masc.of αὐτός, possession) 16.

καὶ (continuative conjunction) 14.

ἀπελθὼν (aor.part.nom.sing.masc.of απέρχομαι, adverbial, temporal) 239.

ἀπεκεφάλισεν (3d.per.sing.aor.act.ind.of ἀποκεφαλίζω, constative) 1114.

αὐτὸν (acc.sing.masc.of αὐτός, direct object of ἀπεκεφάλισεν) 16.

ἐν (preposition with the locative of place) 80.

τῇ (loc.sing.fem.of the article in agreement with φυλακῇ) 9.

φυλακῇ (loc.sing.fem.of φυλακή, place where) 494.

Translation - "*And immediately the king sent away and ordered an executioner to bring his head, and he went away and beheaded him in the prison.*"

Comment: It is not clear whether the executioner was present at the banquet or not. If not the messenger who carried Herod's order to him is not mentioned. If so, Herod sent him (the object of ἀποστείλας) and ordered him (the object of ἐπέταξεν) to bring back John's head. The murder took place in the prison. The executioner went away (ἀπελθὼν), beheaded John (απεκεφάλισεν) and brought his head back (ἤνεγκεν, verse 28) and gave it to Salome (ἔδωκεν, verse 28).

Verse 28 - "*And brought his head in a charger, and gave it to the damsel: and the damsel gave it to her mother.*"

καὶ ἤνεγκεν τὴν κεφαλὴν αὐτοῦ ἐπὶ πίνακι καὶ ἔδωκεν αὐτὴν τῷ κορασίῳ, καὶ τὸ κοράσιον ἔδωκεν αὐτὴν τῇ μητρὶ αὐτῆς.

καὶ (continuative conjunction) 14.
ἤνεγκεν (3d.per.sing.aor.act.ind.of φέρω, constative) 683.
τὴν (acc.sing.fem.of the article in agreement with κεφαλὴν) 9.
κεφαλὴν (acc.sing.fem.of κεφαλή, direct object of ἤνεγκεν) 521.
αὐτοῦ (gen.sing.masc.of αὐτός, possession) 16.
ἐπὶ (preposition with the locative of place where) 47.
πίνακι (loc.sing.masc.of πίναξ, place where) 1112.
καὶ (adjunctive conjunction joining verbs) 14.
ἔδωκεν (3d.per.sing.aor.act.ind.of δίδωμι, constative) 362.
αὐτὴν (acc.sing.fem.of αὐτός, direct object of ἔδωκεν) 16.
τῷ (dat.sing.neut.of the article in agreement with κορασίῳ) 9.
κορασίῳ (dat.sing.neut.of κοράσιον, indirect object of ἔδωκεν) 826.
καὶ (continuative conjunction) 14.
τὸ (nom.sing.neut.of the article in agreement with κοράσιον) 9.
κοράσιον (nom.sing.neut.of κοράσιον, subject of ἔδωκεν) 826.
ἔδωκεν (3d.per.sing.aor.act.ind.of δίδωμι, constative) 362.
αὐτὴν (acc.sing.fem.of αὐτός, direct object of ἔδωκεν) 16.
τῇ (dat.sing.fem.of the article in agreement with μητρὶ) 9.
μητρὶ (dat.sing.fem.of μήτηρ, indirect object of ἔδωκεν) 76.
αὐτῆς (gen.sing.fem.of αὐτός, relationship) 16.

Translation - ". . . and he carried his head upon a pine board and he gave it to the girl and the girl gave it to her mother."

Comment: Verse 28 is a continuation of the sentence which began in verse 27. The pine board was the serving platter of the day, no doubt similar to those in use on the table at the king's dinner party. Mark gives us no account of Salome's reaction to this dramatic incident. He only says that she received it from the executioner and in turn gave it to her mother. Since αὐτὴν, following ἔδωκεν is feminine, while πίνακι is masculine, the antecedent of αὐτὴν must be κεφαλὴν, not πίνακι. Thus we glean the information that Salome gave the head, not the platter to her mother. Does this mean that she took the head from the platter and carried it, dripping with blood (!), to her mother and that her mother finally, no doubt with great satisfaction got her hands on the Baptist's head? Is this the source of the threat one sometimes hears, "I will have his head"? *Cf.*Mt.14:1-12.

Verse 29 - "And when his disciples heard of it, they came and took up his corpse, and laid it in a tomb."

καὶ ἀκούσαντες οἱ μαθηταὶ αὐτοῦ ἦλθον καὶ ἦραν τὸ πτῶμα αὐτοῦ καὶ ἔθηκαν αὐτὸ ἐν μνημείῳ.

καὶ (continuative conjunction) 14.
ἀκούσαντες (aor.act.part.nom.pl.masc.of ἀκούω, adverbial, temporal) 148.
οἱ (nom.pl.masc.of the article in agreement with μαθηταὶ) 9.
μαθηταὶ (nom.pl.masc.of μαθητής, subject of ἦλθον, ἦραν and ἔθηκαν) 421.

αὐτοῦ (gen.sing.masc.of αὐτός, relationship) 16.

ἦλθον (3d.per.pl.aor.ind.of ἔρχομαι, constative) 146.

καὶ (adjunctive conjunction joining verbs) 14.

ἦραν (3d.per.pl.1st.aor.act.ind.of αἴρω, constative) 350.

τὸ (acc.sing.neut.of the article in agreement with πτῶμα) 9.

πτῶμα (acc.sing.neut.of πτῶμα, direct object of ἦραν) 1115.

αὐτοῦ (gen.sing.masc.of αὐτός, possession) 16.

καὶ (adjunctive conjunction joining verbs) 14.

ἔθηκαν (3d.per.pl.aor.act.ind.of τίθημι, constative) 455.

αὐτὸ (acc.sing.neut.of αὐτός, direct object of ἔθηκαν) 16.

ἐν (preposition with the locative of place where) 80.

μνημείῳ (loc.sing.neut.of μνημεῖον, place where) 763.

Translation - "And when they heard about it his disciples came and picked up his dead body and laid it in a tomb."

Comment: It is interesting to reflect whether or not, as John's disciples went about the sad task of claiming and burying the body of their teacher, they remembered and perhaps discussed his statement "He must increase, but I must decrease" (John 3:30). If so, they realized how completely fulfilled John's prophecy, at least his part of it, was being fulfilled. This is the last time we hear of John the Baptist except for our Lord's evaluation of him and references to his ministry by the apostles in later statements.

John's function was to introduce Messiah to Israel as her King. This he had done. His work was finished. It was not in God's plan that Jesus should be enthroned over Israel in a political and earthly sense at His first coming. That will take place when He comes again. Then, at Christ's second coming the following prophecies will be as literally fulfilled as were those immediately adjoined to them: Isa.9:6 (3d.clause); Isa.61:2 (second phrase);Lk.1:32 (last half), 33. Students who refuse to recognize a gap between clauses and phrases in the passage listed *supra* take refuge in an allegorical interpretation of the portions which refer to Christ's second coming. To which we reply: if the right to declare a part of a sentence allegorical while accepting the other part as literal be granted, why cannot I declare the entire sentence allegorical. If ". . . the Lord God shall give unto Him the throne of His father David, and He shall reign over the house of Israel forever, and of His kingdom there shall be no end" (Lk.1:32b,33) is allegorical why not say that "Behold thou shalt conceive in thy womb and bear a Son and thou shalt call His name Jesus; He shall be great, and He shall be called the Son of the Highest. . . " is also allegorical, in which case Mary never had a baby, and Mary Baker Eddy may be right that Mary conceived the idea of God, *i.e.* that she had a pure thought!

John the Baptist was dispensationally ahead of his time. Israel not only beheaded the forerunner but she also crucified her King.

We turn now to Luke's brief comment about the death of John the Baptist in

Luke 9:7 - "Now Herod the tetrarch heard of all that was done by him: and he was perplexed because that it was said of some, that John was risen from the dead."

Ἤκουσεν δὲ Ἡρῴδης ὁ τετραάρχης τὰ γινόμενα πάντα, καὶ διηπόρει διὰ τὸ λέγεσθαι ὑπὸ τινων ὅτι Ἰωάννης ἠγέρθη ἐκ νεκρῶν.

Ἤκουσεν (3d.per.sing.aor.act.ind.of ἀκούω, constative) 14.
δὲ (explanatory conjunction) 11.
Ἡρῴδης (nom.sing.masc.of Ἡρῴδης, subject of ἤκουσεν and διηπόρει) 136a.
ὁ (nom.sing.masc.of the article in agreement with τετραάρχης) 9.
τετραάρχης (nom.sing.masc.of τετραάρχης, apposition) 1104.
τὰ (acc.pl.neut.of the article in agreement with γινόμενα) 9.
γινόμενα (pres.part.acc.pl.neut.of γίνομαι, substantival, direct object of ἤκουσεν) 113.
πάντα (acc.pl.neut.of πᾶς, in agreement with γινόμενα) 67.
καὶ (adjunctive conjunction) 14.

#2262 διηπόρει (3d.per.sing.imp.act.ind.of διαπορέω, inceptive).

be in doubt - Acts 2:12.
be perplexed - Lk.9:7.
doubt - Acts 5:24; 10:17.

Meaning: A combination of διά (#118) and ἀπορέω (#2254). Hence, to be thoroughly (διά) confused (ἀπορέω); at a complete loss to explain. In a dilemma. *Cf.*#2254 and add διά in its intensive sense. To be greatly perplexed. With reference to the reaction of those who saw the miracle at Pentecost - Acts 2:12. With reference to Herod's reaction to the fame of Jesus - Lk.9:7. Of the High Priest when told of the escape of the Apostles - Acts 5:24. Of Peter, perplexed about the vision of the sheet - Acts 10:17. Used only by Luke in the New Testament. Not found in profane Greek.

διὰ (preposition with the accusative of cause) 118.
τὸ (acc.sing.neut.of the article, cause) 9.
λέγεσθαι (pres.pass.inf.of λέγω, in the accusative case, cause, substantival) 66.
ὑπὸ (preposition with the ablative of agent) 117.
τινῶν (abl.pl.masc.of τις, agent) 486.
ὅτι (conjunction introducing an object clause in indirect discourse) 211.
Ἰωάννης (nom.sing.masc.of Ἰωάννης, subject of ἠγέρθη) 247.
ἠγέρθη (3d.per.sing.aor.pass.ind.of ἐγείρω, culminative) 125.
ἐκ (preposition with the ablative of separation) 19.
νεκρῶν (abl.pl.masc.of νεκρός, separation) 749.

Translation - "*Now Herod the Tetrarch heard about all the things which were happening and He began to be thoroughly confused, because it was being said by some that John had been raised from the dead.*"

Comment: This is Herod Antipas, the Tetrarch. Originally a Tetrarch ruled one-fourth of the empire. Later the term applied to a ruler of any portion. *Cf.*#1104. Note the substantival participle, modified by πάντα, the direct object of ἤκουσεν. The time of γινόμενα (present tense) is simultaneous with that of ἤκουσεν. Herod was keeping abreast of the situation as Jesus went about the country. There was always some new story to tell about our Lord's latest miracle or statement and Herod insisted upon keeping informed. He was also becoming perplexed as the inceptive imperfect in διηπόρει indicates. Why? Luke uses the articular infinitive in the accusative case after διὰ to tell us. It is a causal construction. The student will have no difficulty with this infinitive construction if he remembers that an infinitive is a verbal noun. In this case its noun use predominates. "Because (διὰ) of the fact that some people were saying (τὸ λέγεσθαι ὑπ' τινων) that... κ.τ.λ." More literally, "Because it was being said by some people . . . . κ.τ.λ." ὅτι introduces indirect discourse. Read the parallel accounts in Mt.14:1-12 and Mk.6:14-29 for the full story of John's death, which is capsulated here by Luke.

The king's confusion arose from conflicting reports about the identity of Jesus, as we see in

Verse 8 - "And of some that Elias had appeared; and of others, that one of the old prophets was risen again."

ὑπὸ τινων δὲ ὅτι 'Ηλίας ἐφάνη, ἄλλων δὲ ὅτι προφήτης τις τῶν ἀρχαίων ἀνέστη.

ὑπὸ (preposition with the ablative of agent) 117.
τινων (abl.pl.masc.of τις, agent) 486.
δὲ (adversative conjunction) 11.
ὅτι (conjunction introducing an object clause in indirect discourse) 211.
'Ηλίας (nom.sing.masc.of 'Ηλίας, subject of ἐφάνη) 921.
ἐφάνη (3d.per.sing.2d.aor.pass.ind.of φαίνω, culminative) 100.
ἄλλων (abl.pl.masc.of ἄλλος, agent) 198.
δὲ (adversative conjunction) 11.
ὅτι (conjunction introducing an object clause in indirect discourse) 211.
προφήτης (nom.sing.masc.of προφήτης, subject of ἀνέστη) 119.
τις (nom.sing.masc.of τις, in agreement with προφήτης) 486.
τῶν (gen.pl.masc.of the article in agreement with ἀρχαίων) 9.
ἀρχαίων (gen.pl.masc.of ἀρχαῖος, partitive genitive) 475.
ἀνέστη (3d.per.sing.2d.aor.act.ind.of ἀνίστημι, culminative) 789.

Translation - ". . . but by some that Elijah had appeared, but by others that a prophet from the past had arisen."

Comment: δὲ is adversative in both usages as various opinions are advanced to explain Jesus and His miraculous work. "It was said by some κ.τ.λ. (vs.7), but by some κ.τ.λ. (vs.8), but by others κ.τ.λ. (vs.8). The rumor that the miracle worker was Elijah stems from their understanding of Mal.4:5,6. They had also thought that John the Baptist was Elijah when he first appeared (John 1:21). Public opinion was not in agreement, which caused Herod's perplexity (vs.7). Was it John the Baptist, alive again and back to haunt Herod, or Elijah or . . . "but others, a prophet, one of the old ones, has risen." Clearly Jesus' miracles and His teachings were of a quality and quantity that forced Israel to explain them as another divine visitation. Meyer says of Herod's perplexity - διηπόρει (vs.7), "This was the uncertainty of an evil conscience." (Heinrich August Wilhelm Meyer, *Critical and Exegetical Hand-Book to the Gospels of Mark and Luke*, 365). *Cf.*#789 for other interesting uses of ἀνίστημι.

Verse 9 - "And Herod said, John have I beheaded: but who is this, of whom I hear such things? And he desired to see him."

εἶπεν δὲ Ἡρῴδης, Ἰωάννην ἐγὼ ἀπεκεφάλισα, τίς δέ ἐστιν οὗτος περὶ οὗ ἀκούω τοιαῦτα; καὶ ἐζήτει ἰδεῖν αὐτόν.

εἶπεν (3d.per.sing.aor.act.ind.of εἶπον, constative) 155.
δὲ (adversative conjunction) 11
Ἡρῴδης (nom.sing.masc.of Ἡρῴδης, subject of εἶπεν) 136a.
Ἰωάννην (acc.sing.masc.of Ἰωάννης, direct object of ἀπεκεφάλισα) 247.
ἐγὼ (nom.sing.masc.of ἐγώ, subject of ἀπεκεφάλισα) 123.
ἀπεκεφάλισα (1st.per.sing.aor.act.ind.of ἀποκεφαλίζω, culminative) 1114.
τίς (interrogative pronoun, nom.sing.masc.of τίς, predicate nominative) 281.
δέ (adversative conjunction) 11.
ἐστιν (3d.per.sing.pres.ind.of εἰμί, aoristic) 86.
οὗτος (nom.sing.masc.of οὗτος, subject of ἐστιν) 93.
περὶ (preposition with the genitive of reference) 173.
οὗ (gen.sing.masc.of ὅς, reference) 65.
ἀκούω (1st.per.sing.pres.act.ind.of ἀκούω, progressive) 148.
τοιαῦτα (acc.pl.neut.of τοιοῦτος, direct object of ἀκούω) 785.
καὶ (continuative conjunction) 14.
ἐζήτει (3d.per.sing.imp.act.ind.of ζητέω, inceptive) 207.
ἰδεῖν (aor.inf.of ὁράω, epexegetical) 144.
αὐτόν (acc.sing.masc.of αὐτός, direct object of ἰδεῖν) 16.

Translation - "But Herod said, 'John I have beheaded, but who is this fellow about whom I keep hearing such things?' And he began to try to see him."

Comment: Opinions as to the identity of Jesus were being circulated about the court. Some said one thing; some another. Herod entered the discussion with a positive statement. Note in Herod's statement that Ἰωάννην is in the emphatic position, which proves that Herod had the Baptist on his conscience. No one had suggested that the miracle worker might be John. Why should Herod have mentioned him? He rules him out as a possibility, with the statement that John is dead, the victim of the king's own order. Note ἐγὼ also in emphasis, since it is not needed, being implicit in the verb. "*John, I* beheaded." Meyer says, "The twofold ἐγώ has the emphasis of the terrified heart." (Meyer, *Ibid.*, 366). The second δέ is definitely adversative. "John is dead, but who κ.τ.λ.?" Note also the contemptuous use of οὗτος. The present continuous action of ἀκούω indicates that stories were pouring into Herod's palace. It was fear and remorse mixed with curiosity. Herod had to know the truth. This, he could discover only by seeing the miracle worker. Hence, καὶ ... αὐτόν. The imperfect tense in ἐζήτει is inceptive and is explained by the epexegetical infinitive ἰδεῖν. Herod began his efforts, which were to continue, to see the man whose ministry had stirred up all of the controversy. How hard did Herod really try to see Jesus? Did Jesus deliberately avoid seeing him? They never met until the evening before our Lord's crucifixion.

We now enter the 6th phase of Period II, which extends for about twelve months from A.D. 28-29. It records the crisis at Capernaum and begins with the return of the Twelve. Review Mt.14:13. *Cf.* also Lk.9:10 and Mk.6:30-32 which follows:

Mark 6:30 - "And the apostles gathered themselves together unto Jesus, and told him all things, both what they had done, and what they had taught."

Καὶ συνάγονται οἱ ἀπόστολοι πρὸς τὸν Ἰησοῦν, καὶ ἀπήγγειλαν αὐτῷ πάντα ὅσα ἐποίησαν καὶ ὅσα ἐδίδαξαν.

Καὶ (continuative conjunction) 14.
συνάγονται (3d.per.pl.pres.mid.ind.of συνάγω, historical) 150.
οἱ (nom.pl.masc.of the article in agreement with ἀπόστολοι) 9.
ἀπόστολοι (nom.pl.masc.of ἀπόστολος, subject of συνάγονται) 844.
πρὸς (preposition with the accusative of extent) 197.
τὸν (acc.sing.masc.of the article in agreement with Ἰησοῦν) 9.
Ἰησοῦν (acc.sing.masc.of Ἰησοῦς, extent) 3.
καὶ (adjunctive conjunction joining verbs) 14.
ἀπήγγειλαν (3d.per.pl.imp.act.ind.of ἀπαγγέλλω, inceptive) 176.
αὐτῷ (dat.sing.masc.of αὐτός, indirect object of ἀπήγγειλαν) 16.
πάντα (acc.pl.neut.of πᾶς, direct object of ἀπήγγειλαν) 67.
ὅσα (acc.pl.neut.of the relative pronoun ὅσος, direct object of ἐποίησαν) 660.
ἐποίησαν (3d.per.pl.aor.act.ind.of ποιέω, culminative) 127.
καὶ (adjunctive conjunction joining relative clauses) 14.
ὅσα (acc.pl.neut.of ὅσος, relative pronoun, direct object of ἐδίδαξαν) 660.
ἐδίδαξαν (3d.per.pl.aor.act.ind.of διδάσκω, culminative) 403.

Translation - "And the Apostles returned to Jesus and began to tell Him all they had done and what they had taught."

Comment: This is the first time since Mk.3:14 and Lk.6:13 that the word ἀπόστολος occurs. In the two parallel passages listed above, which records Jesus' commission to the Twelve disciples to preach, the distinction is made between the words disciple (μαθητής, #421) and apostle (ἀπόστολος, #844). The former means "a learner" and the latter "one who is sent away" on a special mission. The inceptive imperfect in ἀπήγγειλαν indicates that the Apostles could scarcely wait until they got back to Jesus to begin their recital of their experiences and, once begun, could scarcely cease. This was their first tour of duty and the first ministry of the Church (Eph.2:19-22), for when Jesus sent out the disciples and called them Apostles we have the first association of ". . . the foundation of the apostles and prophets. . . " with "Jesus Christ himself (as) the Chief corner stone. . . " into whom "the building fitly framed together (will grow) unto an holy temple in the Lord" (Eph.2:20,21).

There is nothing parallel in Matthew. *Cf.* Lk.9:10 for his account of the "homecoming." Not only was Jesus able to perform many wonderful works, but also He was able to impart this miracle working power as He chose to those whom He selected and dispatched. No wonder Herod was perplexed.

The tender loving care of the Shepherd and Bishop of our souls (I Pet.2:25) is demonstrated for some tired preachers who needed a vacation in

Verse 31 - "And he said unto them, Come ye yourselves apart into a desert place, and rest a while: for there were many coming and going, and they had no leisure so much as to eat."

καὶ λέγει αὐτοῖς Δεῦτε ὑμεῖς αὐτοὶ κατ' ἰδίαν εἰς ἔρημον τόπον καὶ ἀναπαύσασθε ὀλίγον, ἦσαν γὰρ οἱ ἐρχόμενοι καὶ οἱ ὑπάγοντες πολλοί, καὶ οὐδὲ φαγεῖν εὐκαίρουν.

καὶ (continuative conjunction) 14.

λέγει (3d.per.sing.pres.act.ind.of λέγω, historical) 66.

αὐτοῖς (dat.pl.masc.of αὐτός, indirect object of λέγει) 16.

Δεῦτε (2d.per.pl.pres.act.impv.of δεῦτε, command) 391.

ὑμεῖς (voc.pl.masc.of σύ, address) 104.

αὐτοὶ (voc.pl.masc.of αὐτός, intensive pronoun) 16.

κατ' (preposition with the accusative, adverbial) 98.

ἰδίαν (acc.sing.fem.of ἴδιος, adverbial) 778.

εἰς (preposition with the accusative of extent) 140.

ἔρημον (acc.sing.masc.of ἔρημος, in agreement with τόπον) 250.

τόπον (acc.sing.masc.of τόπος, extent) 1019.

καὶ (adjunctive conjunction joining verbs) 14.

ἀναπαύσασθε (2d.per.pl.aor.mid.impv.of ἀναπαύω, command) 955.

ὀλίγον (acc.sing.neut.of ὀλίγος, adverbial) 669.

ἦσαν (3d.per.pl.imp.ind.of εἰμί, progressive duration) 86.

γὰρ (causal conjunction) 105.

οἱ (nom.pl.masc.of the article in agreement with ἐρχόμενοι) 9.

ἐρχόμενοι (pres.act.part.nom.pl.masc.of ἔρχομαι, substantival, subject of ἦσαν) 146.

καὶ (adjunctive conjunction joining participial substantives) 14.

οἱ (nom.pl.masc.of the article in agreement with ὑπάγοντες) 9.

ὑπάγοντες (pres.act.part.nom.pl.masc.of ὑπάγω, substantival, subject of ἦσαν) 364.

πολλοί (nom.pl.masc.of πολύς, predicate adjective) 228.

καὶ (inferential conjunction) 14.

οὐδὲ (disjunctive particle) 452.

φαγεῖν (2d.aor.act.inf.of ἐσθίω, epexegetical) 610.

#2263 εὐκαίρουν (3d.per.pl.imp.act.ind.of εὐκαιρέω, progressive description).

have convenient time - I Cor.16:12.
have leisure - Mk.6:31.
spend one's time - Acts 17:21.

Meaning: A combination of εὖ (#1536) and καιρός (#767). To have a good opportunity; to have a convenient time. With reference to Apollos' trip to Corinth - I Cor.16:12; with reference to the Athenian philosophers who take advantage of every good opporunity to debate - Acts 17:21. Of Jesus and His Apostles who had no opportunity to eat - Mk.6:31.

Translation - "And He said to them, 'Come away by yourselves unto a secluded spot and rest a little while.' Because those coming and going were so many and they did not even have a chance to eat."

Comment: The loving care of the Great, Good and Chief Shepherd (Heb.13:19; John 10:9; I Pet.5:4) for His sheep is clearly manifested here. Jesus wants us to rest (#955) and eat (#610). A study of these verbs will provide much good preaching material on resting and eating, both in physical and spiritual realms, for the child of God. In their excitement over their recent exploits in His name the Apostles seem to have forgotten their need for food and relaxation. But our Lord, the Sovereign of Eternity, who planned it all from before the beginning, is not frenetic. Since it is His program, not ours, He is responsible for its success and we can relax occasionally. Many were coming and going. Jesus said, "Come ye, *yourselves.* . . " Note the intensive use of αὐτοί. κατ᾽ ἰδίαν - an idiom which means "by yourselves." *Cf.*#98 for the complete list. The last sentence in the verse is illative, introduced by post-positive γὰρ which is causal. Why did Jesus order a temporary withdrawal? Those coming and going were so numerous (πολλοί) that Jesus and His Apostles were never able to find an opportunity to eat. (imperfect tense in εὐκαίρουν). So they took a short vacation as we see in

Verse 32 - "And they departed into a desert place by ship privately."

καὶ ἀπῆλθον ἐν τῷ πλοίῳ εἰς ἔρημον τόπον κατ᾽ ἰδίαν.

καὶ (continuative conjunction) 14.
ἀπῆλθον (3d.per.pl.aor.act.ind.of ἀπέρχομαι, constative) 239.
ἐν (preposition with the locative of place) 80.
τῷ (loc.sing.neut.of the article in agreement with πλοίῳ) 9.
πλοίῳ (loc.sing.neut.of πλοῖον, place where) 400.
εἰς (preposition with the accusative of extent) 140.
ἔρημον (acc.sing.masc.of ἔρημος, in agreement with τόπον) 250.
τόπον (acc.sing.masc.of τόπος, extent) 1019.
κατ᾽ (preposition with the accusative, adverbial) 98.
ἰδίαν (acc.sing.neut.of ἴδιος, adverbial) 778.

Translation - "And they went away in the boat to a secluded spot by themselves."

Comment: The prepositional phrase ἐν τῷ πλοίῳ is an example of how the grammar permits the exegete to take either of two possible interpretations, without lessening the "Word" of God. It can be taken as a locative phrase, and translated "in the ship" or as an instrumental phrase and translated "by means of the ship." Both ideas amount to the same thing. They did not go by car, bus, plane or submarine; they went *by* ship and it is obvious that when they went *by* the ship they also went *in* the ship. They went by/in the ship to a desert?! The word ἔρημον (#250) means a deserted place, not a dry place. Most dry places are also deserted, since men need water, but a place can be isolated and deserted without being dry. So there is nothing wrong about saying that a group of men took a ship and went to a desert. *Cf.* comment on the parallel passage, Mt.14:13, which follows the account of the death of John the Baptist.

Jesus' departure in the ship with His disciples to escape the crowd temporarily was only partially successful. They followed Him on foot from out the cities (Mt.14:13). Luke in the parallel passage, says,

Luke 9:10 - "And the apostles when they were returned told him all that they had done. And he took them, and went aside privately into a desert place belonging to the city called Bethsaida."

Καὶ ὑποστρέψαντες οἱ ἀπόστολοι διηγήσαντο αὐτῷ ὅσα ἐποίησαν. καὶ παραλαβὼν αὐτοὺς ὑπεχώρησεν κατ' ἰδίαν εἰς πόλιν καλουμένην Βηθσαϊδά.

Καὶ (continuative conjunction) 14.

ὑποστρέψαντες (aor.act.part.nom.pl.masc.of ὑποστρέφω, adverbial, temporal) 1838.

οἱ (nom.pl.masc.of the article in agreement with ἀπόστολοι) 9.

ἀπόστολοι (nom.pl.masc.of ἀπόστολος, subject of διηγήσαντο) 844.

διηγήσαντο (3d.per.pl.aor.act.ind.of διηγέομαι, ingressive) 2225.

αὐτῷ (dat.sing.masc.of αὐτός, indirect object of διηγήσαντο) 16.

ὅσα (acc.pl.neut.of ὅσος, direct object of ἐποίησαν) 660.

ἐποίησαν (3d.per.pl.aor.act.ind.of ποιέω, culminative) 127.

καὶ (continuative conjunction) 14.

παραλαβὼν (aor.act.part.nom.sing.masc.of παραλαμβάνω adverbial, temporal) 102.

ὑπεχώρησεν (3d.per.sing.aor.act.ind.of ὑποχωρέω, constative) 2074.

κατ' (preposition with the accusative, adverbial) 98.

ἰδίαν (acc.sing.neut.of ἴδιος, adverbial) 778.

εἰς (preposition with the accusative of extent) 140.

πόλιν (acc.sing.fem.of πόλις, extent) 243.

καλουμένην (pres.pass.part.acc.sing.fem.of καλέω, adjectival, restrictive) 107.

Βηθσαϊδά (nom.sing.fem.of Βηθσαϊδά, appellation) 938.

Translation - "And when they returned the Apostles gave Him a full account of what they had accomplished. And He took them with Him and withdrew privately unto a city called Bethsaida."

Comment: The Apostles returned and entered breathlessly (Mk.6:30) and exhaustively (*cf.*#2225) into their account of the things which they had accomplished - ὅσα ἐποίησαν. There is in παραλαβὼν (#102) the idea of protective custody. John the Baptist had just been beheaded by Herod's order. The Twelve were in the spotlight. Jesus chose to avoid further publicity and possible controversy. Mk.6:31 show His concern that they should rest and be fed. Luke here adds Jesus determination to protect them. Note #2074 in the sense of a withdrawal. κατ' ἰδίαν helps out the idea. Our Lord did not sneak away furtively in craven fear. He quietly withdrew to Bethsaida. We shall see soon that the crowds did not permit Jesus and the Apostles to remain alone very long.

The Feeding of the Five Thousand

(Mt.14:13-21; Lk.9:11-17; John 6:1-13; Mk.6:33-44)

Mk.6:33 - "And the people saw them departing, and many knew him, and ran afoot thither out of all the cities, and outwent them, and came together unto him."

καὶ εἶδον αὐτοὺς ὑπάγοντας καὶ ἐπέγνωσαν πολλοί   καὶ πεζῇ ἀπὸ πασῶν τῶν πόλεων συνέδραμον ἐκεῖ καὶ προῆλθον αὐτούς.

καὶ (continuative conjunction) 14.

εἶδον (3d.per.pl.aor.ind.of ὁράω, constative) 144.

αὐτοὺς (acc.pl.masc.of αὐτός, direct object of εἶδον) 16.

ὑπάγοντας (pres.act.part.acc.pl.masc.of ὑπάγω, adverbial, circumstantial) 364.

καὶ (continuative conjunction) 14.

ἐπέγνωσαν (3d.per.pl.aor.act.ind.of ἐπιγινώσκω, constative) 675.

πολλοί (nom.pl.masc.of πολύς, subject of ἐπέγνωσαν) 228.

καὶ (adjunctive conjunction joining verbs) 14.

πεζῇ (dat.sing.fem.of πεζός, adverbial) 1116.

ἀπὸ (preposition with the ablative of separation) 70.

πασῶν (abl.pl.fem.of πᾶς, in agreement with πόλεων) 67.

τῶν (abl.pl.fem.of the article in agreement with πόλεων) 9.

πόλεων (abl.pl.fem.of πόλις, separation) 243.

#2264 συνέδραμον (3d.per.pl.2d.aor.act.ind.of συντρέχω, ingressive).

run - Mk.6:33; Acts 3:11; I Pet.4:4.

Meaning: A combination of σύν (#1542) and τρέχω (#1655). Hence, to run together in a physical sense. A multitude of people hastily congregates - Mk.6:33; Acts 3:11. In a metaphorical sense of persons engaging in the same activities, as we say, "They run around together," or "With whom are you going?" as in I Pet.4:4.

ἐκεῖ (adverb of place) 204.

καὶ (adjunctive conjunction joining verbs) 14.

προῆλθον (3d.per.pl.aor.act.ind.of προέρχομαι, constative) 1587.
αὐτούς (acc.pl.masc.of αὐτός, direct object of προῆλθον) 16.

Translation - "And many people saw them going away and they understood and they began to hasten on foot from all the cities and got there before them."

Comment: Note that Mark puts the substantive πολλοί, at the end of the clause, emphasizing all of the action ahead of the actors. The people saw Jesus and the twelve Apostles going away and they knew where they were going. Note the intensive ἐπέγνωσαν instead of the milder γινώσκω (#'s 675, 131). The people went by land (πεζῇ) in contrast to Jesus and the Apostles who went ἐν τῷ πλοίῳ, *i.e.* they ran around the lake. They came from all of the towns in the neighborhood. We cannot push πασῶν to mean all of the towns in Palestine! ἐκεῖ refers to their destination. The people could run around the lake in less time than it took Jesus and the Apostles to sail across by boat. They were waiting for Him when the boat was beached at Bethsaida.

The eager desire of the people to be with Jesus, hear His teaching and perhaps receive His healing is touching, as we see in

Verse 34 - "And Jesus, when he came out, saw much people, and was moved with compassion toward them because they were as sheep not having a shepherd; and he began to teach them many things."

καὶ ἐξελθὼν εἶδεν πολὺν ὄχλον, καὶ ἐσπλαγχνίσθη ἐπ᾽ αὐτοὺς ὅτι ἦσαν ὡς πρόβατα μὴ ἔχοντα ποιμένα, καὶ ἤρξατο διδάσκειν αὐτοὺς πολλά.

καὶ (continuative conjunction) 14.
ἐξελθὼν (aor.act.part.nom.sing.masc.of ἐξέρχομαι, adverbial, temporal) 161.
εἶδεν (3d.per.sing.aor.act.ind.of ὁράω, constative) 144.
πολὺν (acc.sing.masc.of πολύς, in agreement with ὄχλον) 228.
ὄχλον (acc.sing.masc.of ὄχλος, direct object of εἶδεν) 418.
καὶ (inferential conjunction) 14.
ἐσπλαγχνίσθη (3d.per.sing.aor.act.ind.of σπλαγχνίζομαι, ingressive) 835.
ἐπ᾽ (preposition with the accusative, to express emotion) 47.
αὐτοὺς (acc.pl.masc.of αὐτός, emotion) 16.
ὅτι (causal conjunction) 211.
ἦσαν (3d.per.pl.imp.ind.of εἰμί, imperfect periphrastic) 86.
ὡς (particle introducing a comparative phrase) 128.
πρόβατα (nom.pl.neut.of πρόβατον, predicate nominative) 671.
μὴ (qualified negative conjunction with the participle) 87.
ἔχοντα (pres.act.part.nom.pl.neut.of ἔχω, imperfect periphrastic) 82.
ποιμένα (acc.sing.masc.of ποιμήν, direct object of ἔχοντα) 838.
καὶ (continuative conjunction) 14.
ἤρξατο (3d.per.sing.aor.mid.ind:of ἄρχω, ingressive) 383.
διδάσκειν (pres.act.inf.of διδάσκω, epexegetical) 403.
αὐτοὺς (acc.pl.masc.of αὐτός, direct object of διδάσκειν) 16.

πολλά (acc.pl.neut.of πολύς, direct object of διδάσκειν) 228.

Translation - "And when He got out of the boat He saw a great crowd; therefore He was seized with compassion for them because they had always been like sheep without a shepherd. And He began to teach them many things."

Comment: Since Mark has said that the people arrived before Jesus and the Apostles did, it is not clear why Jesus should not have seen them waiting at the shore line before His boat landed. Perhaps some detail in the terrain, not included in Mark's account, explains it. In any case the Greek says that Jesus emerged from the ship before He saw the people. It is a minor point. Jesus was "seized with compassion" - thus we interpret the ingressive action of the aorist ἐσπλαγχνίσθη. *Cf.* John 11:35 - "Jesus burst into tears." *Cf.*#835 for other uses of the word. Beaten down and exploited by Roman tyrants and their own exploitative religious leaders, the common people, sick in sin and sick of sin, finally found One Whom they thought they could trust and Who would deliver them. Hot and exhausted from their hasty trip around the lake from Capernaum and across the ford of the Jordan they crowded about the boat. Their eager zeal to see Jesus was moving. Because of them Jesus was moved with pity. *Cf.*#47 for other examples of ἐπί with the accusative to express emotion. Mark tells us why. The ὅτι clause is causal. The imperfect periphrastic is decidedly durative in character. Their sad condition was continually that which could be compared to sheep who had no shepherd. No one in the Roman government, not even Israel's so-called spiritual leaders really cared for the downtrodden masses of the people. Jesus' pity for the masses overcame His desire to rest and eat. So He began to teach them many things. Mt.14:14 adds that He also healed them. Lk.9:11 adds that He spoke to them about the Kingdom of God. No one tells us what the Apostles did. Perhaps they rested and ate, since that is what they came over there to do.

Jesus reaction to the people and His ministry in their behalf recalls the prophecy of Gabriel to His mother before He was born. He was destined to ". . . exhalt them of low degree and fill the hungry with good things" (Lk.1:52,53). Thus Jesus is the social and economic revolutionary. He was also said to be preparing a philosophical and political revolution (Lk.1:51,52).

Verse 35 - "And when the day was now far spent, his disciples came unto him, and said, This is a desert place, and now the time is far passed."

Καὶ ἤδη ὥρας πολλῆς γενομένης προσελθόντες (αὐτῷ) οἱ μαθηταὶ αὐτοῦ ἔλεγον ὅτι Ἐρημός ἐστιν ὁ τόπος, καὶ ἤδη ὥρα πολλή.

Καὶ (continuative conjunction) 14.
ἤδη (adverbial) 291.
ὥρας (gen.sing.fem.of ὥρα, genitive absolute) 735.
πολλῆς (gen.sing.fem.of πολύς, in agreement with ὥρας) 228.
γενομένης (aor.part.gen.sing.fem.of γίνομαι, genitive absolute) 113.

προσελθόντες (aor.part.nom.pl.masc.of προσέρχομαι, adverbial, temporal) 336.

(αὐτῷ) (loc.sing.masc.of αὐτός, after πρός in composition, with a verb of rest) 16.

οἱ (nom.pl.masc.of the article in agreement with μαθηταί) 9.
μαθηταί (nom.pl.masc.of μαθητής, subject of ἔλεγον) 421.
αὐτοῦ (gen.sing.masc.of αὐτός, relationship) 16.
ἔλεγον (3d.per.pl.imp.act.ind.of λέγω, inceptive) 66.
ὅτι (recitative) 211.
Ἔρημός (nom.sing.masc.of ἔρημος, predicate adjective) 250.
ἐστιν (3d.per.sing.pres.ind.of εἰμί, aoristic) 86.
ὁ (nom.sing.masc.of the article in agreement with τόπος) 9.
τόπος (nom.sing.masc.of τόπος, subject of ἐστιν) 1019.
καὶ (continuative conjunction) 14.
ἤδη (adverbial) 291.
ὥρα (nom.sing.fem.of ὥρα, subject of the verb understood) 735.
πολλή (nom.sing.fem.of πολύς, predicate adjective) 228.

Translation - "And now that it was late in the afternoon His disciples came to Him and began to say, 'The place is deserted and the hour is late.' "

Comment: ἤδη . . . γενομένης is the genitive absolute in the aorist tense, indicating antecedent time to that of ἔλεγον. An advanced hour in the day had come. It was late - perhaps five or six o'clock in the evening. The disciples began to insist (inceptive imperfect with durative action in ἔλεγον) that the place was deserted and that night was approaching, as if Jesus did not already know. They were full of advice, as we see in verse 36.

Note that the disciples came to Jesus (προσελθόντες) to tell Him the time and to offer their suggestion, which proves that when they landed they did indeed withdraw to rest and eat, even though Jesus remained behind to teach and heal the people. It was only after some time, as dusk approached, that they returned from rest to find Jesus still teaching. The disciples were saying in effect, "We came here at your suggestion to rest and to eat, but we cannot feed this crowd."

Verse 36 - "Send them away, that they may go into the country round about and into the villages, and buy themselves bread; for they have nothing to eat."

ἀπόλυσον αὐτούς, ἵνα ἀπελθόντες εἰς τοὺς κύκλῳ ἀγροὺς καὶ κώμας ἀγοράσωσιν ἑαυτοῖς τί φάγωσιν.

ἀπόλυσον (2d.per.sing.aor.act.impv.of ἀπολύω, entreaty) 92.
αὐτούς (acc.pl.masc.of αὐτός, direct object of ἀπόλυσον) 16.
ἵνα (final conjunction introducing a purpose clause) 114.
ἀπελθόντες (aor.part.nom.pl.masc.of ἀπέρχομαι, adverbial, temporal) 239.
εἰς (preposition with the accusative of extent) 140.
τοὺς (acc.pl.masc.of the article in agreement with ἀγρούς) 9.
κύκλῳ (loc.sing.neut.of κύκλος, adverbial, place where) 2183.

ἀγροὺς (acc.pl.masc.of ἀγρός, extent) 626.
καὶ (adjunctive conjunction joining nouns) 14.
κώμας (acc.pl.fem.of κώμη, extent) 834.
ἀγοράσωσιν (3d.per.pl.aor.act.subj.of ἀγοράζω, purpose) 1085.
ἑαυτοῖς (dat.pl.masc.of ἑαυτός, personal advantage) 288.
τί (acc.sing.neut.of τις, direct object of ἀγοράσωσιν) 486.
φάγωσιν (3d.per.pl.aor.act.subj.of ἐσθίω, purpose) 610.

Translation - "*Dismiss them in order that they may go around into the fields and villages and buy for themselves something to eat.*"

Comment: The imperative in ἀπόλυσον sounds officious. The Apostles, rested and fed, refreshed by a few hours of solitude while Jesus ministered to the pitiable mob for whom He felt so much compassion, are full of advice. The place had no facilities for feeding the people. The hour was late. The people needed to be released from the dynamic personality of Jesus so that they might provide for their evening meal. "Into the fields and villages in a circle - hence, roundabout." *Cf.*#2183 for other uses of κύκλῳ in this adverbial sense. Mark could have reintroduced ἵνα before φάγωσιν but he did not. *Cf.* Mt.14:15 and Lk.9:12 for the parallel passages. Read also John 6:5 which records that Jesus asked Philip the test question. There is no contradiction. The Apostles could have begun the conversation with the suggestion to send the people away, after which Jesus put the question to Philip. J.F.& B. say that the precise order cannot be determined, and dismiss it as being of slight importance. Meyer, as usual, accuses the record of contradiction. I say that had the Holy Spirit deemed the exact order of events important enough to require precision He would have superintended the writing of all the writers in such a way as to make it clear to us. Since He did not the order of events is not important. To quibble over it is to miss the real point in the story.

Verse 37 - "*He answered and said unto them, Give ye them to eat. And they say unto him, Shall we go and buy two hundred pennyworth of bread, and give them to eat.*"

ὁ δὲ ἀποκριθεὶς εἶπεν αὐτοῖς, Δότε αὐτοῖς ἡμεῖς φαγεῖν. καὶ λέγουσιν αὐτῷ, Ἀπελθόντες ἀγοράσωμεν δηναρίων διακοσίων ἄρτους καὶ δώσωμεν αὐτοῖς φαγεῖν;

ὁ (nom.sing.masc.of the article, subject of εἶπεν) 9.
δὲ (adversative conjunction) 11.
ἀποκριθεὶς (aor.part.nom.sing.masc.of ἀποκρίνομαι, adverbial, modal) 318.
εἶπεν (3d.per.sing.aor.act.ind.of εἶπον, constative) 155.
αὐτοῖς (dat.pl.masc.of αὐτός, indirect object of εἶπεν) 16.
Δότε (2d.per.pl.aor.act.impv.of δίδωμι, command) 362.
αὐτοῖς (dat.pl.masc.of αὐτός, indirect object of Δότε) 16.
ὑμεῖς (voc.pl.masc.of σύ, address) 104.
φαγεῖν (aor.act.inf.of ἐσθίω, purpose) 610.
καὶ (adversative conjunction) 14.

λέγουσιν (3d.per.pl.pres.act.ind.of λέγω,historical) 66.
αὐτῷ (dat.sing.masc.of αὐτός, indirect object of λέγουσιν) 16.
Ἀπελθόντες (aor.part.nom.pl.masc.of ἀπέρχομαι, adverbial, temporal) 239.
ἀγοράσωμεν (1st.per.pl.aor.act.subj.of ἀγοράζω, deliberative) 1085.
δηναρίων (gen.pl.neut.of δηνάριον, description) 1278.

#2265 διακοσίων (gen.pl.masc.of διακόσιοι, numeral).

two hundred - Mk.6:37; John 6:7; 21:8; Acts 23:23,23; 27:37; Rev.11:3; 12:6.

Meaning: Two hundred pennies - Mk.6:37; John 6:7; two hundred cubits - John 21:8; two hundred soldiers - Acts 23:23; two hundred, seventy-six people - Acts 27:37; one thousand two hundred and sixty days - Rev.11:3; 12:6.

ἄρτους (acc.pl.masc.of ἄρτος, direct object of ἀγοράσωμεν) 338.
καὶ (adjunctive conjunction joining verbs) 14.
δώσωμεν (1st.per.pl.aor.act.subj.of δίδωμι, deliberative) 362.
αὐτοῖς (dat.pl.masc.of αὐτός, indirect object of δώσωμεν) 16.
φαγεῖν (aor.act.inf.of ἐσθίω, complementary) 610.

Translation - "But in reply He said to them, 'You give them something to eat.' But they said to Him, 'Do you expect us to go away and buy $33.34 worth of bread and give it to them to eat?' "

Comment:δὲ and the first καὶ are adversative, as Jesus and the Apostles argue about it. The original suggestion of the Apostles was that the people should be allowed to go and buy food for themselves. But Jesus had other ideas. His suggestion seemed preposterous to the Apostles. Note the incredulity in their rebuttal question. Note emphatic ὑμεῖς in Jesus' order, as though Jesus meant, "If you are so concerned about their welfare, why do you not feed them yourselves?" And thus Jesus got an immediate sarcastic response from His friends. Of course they expected "No" as a reply to their incredulous question, as their use of the subjunctives ἀγοράσωμεν and δώσωμεν indicates.

Human nature is never quite so repulsive as when an exaggerated sarcastic question is put rhetorically. *Cf.*#1278. τὸ δηνάριον was worth about 16 2/3 cents, though it was debased after Nero's time. Whether this represents all the money the disciples had or not is not clear. Divided among 5000 men (leaving out of account the women and children) that would provide six tenths of a cent per man! The Apostles had had some experience with Jesus as a miracle worker, but they were totally unprepared for what happened. They were looking at the problem naturalistically. Perhaps we should not blame them. *Cf.* Mt.14:16. Matthew reports that Jesus prefaced Δότε αὐτοῖς ὑμεῖς φαγεῖν with οὐ χρείαν ἔχουσιν ἀπελθεῖν, which makes Mark's δὲ more strongly adversative.

Verse 38 - "He saith unto them, How many loaves have ye? Go and see. And when they knew, they say, Five, and two fishes."

ὁ δὲ λέγει αὐτοῖς, Πόσους ἄρτους ἔχετε; ὑπάγετε ἴδετε. καὶ γνόντες λέγουσιν, Πέντε, καὶ δύο ἰχθύας.

ὁ (nom.sing.masc.of the article, subject of λέγει) 9.
δὲ (continuative conjunction) 11.
λέγει (3d.per.sing.pres.act.ind.of λέγω historical) 66.
αὐτοῖς (dat.pl.masc.of αὐτός, indirect object of λέγει) 16.
Πόσους (acc.pl.masc.of πόσος, in agreement with ἄρτους) 603.
ἄρτους (acc.pl.masc.of ἄρτος, direct object of ἔχετε) 338.
ἔχετε (2d.per.pl.pres.act.ind.of ἔχω, aoristic) 82.
ὑπάγετε (2d.per.pl.pres.act.impv.of ὑπάγω, command) 364.
ἴδετε (2d.per.pl.aor.act.impv.of ὁράω, command) 144.
καὶ (continutative conjunction) 14.
γνόντες (aor.act.part.nom.pl.masc.of γινώσκω, adverbial, temporal) 131.
λέγουσιν (3d.per.pl.pres.act.ind.of λέγω, historical) 66.
Πέντε (numeral, acc.case, object of ἔχομεν, understood) 1119.
καὶ (adjunctive conjunction joining nouns) 14.
δύο (numeral, joined with ἰχθύας) 385.
ἰχθύας (acc.pl.masc.of ἰχθύς, direct object of ἔχομεν, understood) 657.

Translation - "And He said to them, 'How many loaves do you have? Go and see.' And when they had counted they said, 'Five and two fish.' "

Comment: Our Lord is willing to perform a miracle for the people if necessary. They must know that their own resources are inadequate, but they must be willing to give all that they have. Hence the question, "How many? Go and see." The disciples went away and took an inventory and came back with the information. "Five loaves and two fish." John 6:9 adds the information that Andrew reported that the five barley loaves and two fish were the property of a little boy. John also tells us that this interchange between Jesus and the Apostles was our Lord's method of testing them. Their skepticism matches that of Moses who also asked a sarcastic rhetorical question (Numbers 11:22).

Verse 39 - "And he commanded them to make all sit down by companies upon the green grass."

καὶ ἐπέταξεν αὐτοῖς ἀνακλῖναι πάντας συμπόσια συμπόσια ἐπὶ τῷ χλωρῷ χόρτῳ.

καὶ (continuative conjunction) 14.
ἐπέταξεν (3d.per.sing.aor.act.ind.of ἐπιτάσσω, constative) 2061.
αὐτοῖς (dat.pl.masc.of αὐτός, personal interest) 16.
ἀνακλῖναι (aor.act.inf.of ἀνακλίνω, epexegetical) 731.
πάντας (acc.pl.masc.of πᾶς, direct object of ἀνακλῖναι) 67.

#2266 συμπόσια (acc.pl.neut.of συμπόσιον, distributive).

company - Mk.6:39.

Meaning: A combination of σύν (#1542) and πίνω (#611). Hence, a party staged for the purpose of drinking together. A drinking party. A convivial assembly for purposes of entertainment. Synonymous with the Latin *convivium*. By metonymy, the party itself; the guests. In the plural, groups or rows of guests. Hence, companies or groups in Mk.6:39. Normally, in Greek, we would say κατὰ συμπόσια - "according to companies" or "by companies." Thayer thinks that Mark's συμπόσια συμπόσια is a Hebraism. Robertson disagrees - "The repetition is not a mere Hebraism, since the papyri show examples of it. See Eccl.2:16 κ.τ.λ. (Robertson, *Grammar*, 460).

συμπόσια (acc.pl.neut.of συμπόσιον, distributive) 2266.
ἐπὶ (preposition with the locative of place) 47.
τῷ (loc.sing.masc.of the article in agreement with χόρτῳ) 9.

#2267 χλωρῷ (loc.sing.masc.of χλωρός, in agreement with χόρτῳ).

green - Mk.6:39; Rev.8:7.
green thing - Rev.9:4.
pale - Rev.6:8.

Meaning: Green. As an adjective with χόρτος in Mk.6:39; Rev.8:7. Of vegetation generally - Rev.9:4. The sickly green that we associate with death - Rev.6:8. From χλοερός - the first green shoots of corn or other newly planted vegetation.

χόρτῳ (loc.sing.masc.of χόρτος, place where) 632.

Translation - "And He ordered them to seat everyone in groups upon the green grass."

Comment: The Westcott/Hort text has ἀνακλιθῆναι, the aorist passive infinitive, with ἀνακλῖναι, the aorist active infinitive in the margin. If we read the passive form, there is no way to explain the accusative case in πάντας. But the United Bible Societies text has the better ἀνακλῖναι reading. Thus αὐτοῖς refers, not to the people but to the disciples who were directed to seat πάντας. *Cf.*συμπόσια συμπόσια with πρασιαὶ πρασιαὶ in verse 40. Be seating the people in rows or blocks they facilitated the problem of serving the food. There was a very great multitude present - 5000 men plus women and children. To utilize His man power most efficiently (Jesus had 12 men on His serving team) it was necessary to seat the people in this fashion. Had Jesus asked the people to form a long line, only one person could have been served at a time. Under this arrangement twelve people could be served at the same time. Jesus, as usual gets an A for His time/motion efficiency. Under His system all of the disciples were working at the same time without the chaos of a crowd of perhaps 10,000 people milling about and pushing forward in order to get fed.

Verse 40 - "And they sat them down in ranks, by hundreds and by fifties."

καὶ ἀνέπεσαν πρασιαὶ πρασιαὶ κατὰ ἑκατὸν καὶ κατὰ πεντήκοντα.

καὶ (inferential conjunction) 14.
ἀνέπεσαν (3d.per.pl.aor.act.ind.of ἀναπίπτω, constative) 1184.

#2268 πρασιαὶ (nom.pl.fem.of πρασιά)

ranks - Mk.6:40,40.

Meaning: Some have imagined that πρασιαὶ πρασιαὶ here permits a variety of colors (perhaps on the assumption that the people wore bright colors) but regularity of seating arrangement is all that can be read since the word denotes a garden of herbs, probably leeks from πράσον. The translation "They sat down in flower beds" while forceful and interesting cannot be justified. They sat down in regular rectangular and square groups of fifty and/or one hundred - five rows of ten persons each to form a rectangle and ten rows of ten persons each to form a square. This facilitated serving by creating aisles between groups in which the disciples walked as they passed the bread and fish down each aisle.

πρασιαὶ (nom.pl.fem.of πρασιά) 2268.
κατὰ (preposition with the accusative, distributive) 98.
ἑκατον (acc.sing.neut.of ἑκατον, distributive) 1035.
καὶ (adjunctive conjunction joining prepositional phrases) 14.
κατὰ (preposition with the accusative, distributive) 98.
πεντήκοντα (acc.sing.neut.of πεντήκοντα, distributive) 2172.

Translation - "Therefore they reclined in orderly groups of hundreds and fifties."

Comment: *Cf.*#1184 for the exact meaning of ἀναπίπτω. If a table had been present equipped with reclining couches as in their homes, the people would have assumed the reclining position. On the grass they probably assumed a position as near to the reclining position (perhaps on one elbow) as was possible. The orderly geometric arrangement with the disciples passing through the aisles and passing the food to the people must have been an inspiring sight. In the middle of the array stood the Creator, not only of bread and fish, but of the entire universe, Who, unwilling to turn stones into bread for His own benefit, now creates enough bread and fish to feed ten thousand hungry people.

Verse 41 - "And when he had taken the five loaves and the two fishes, he looked up to heaven, and blessed, and brake the loaves, and gave them to his disciples to set before them; and the two fishes divided he among them all."

καὶ λαβὼν τοὺς πέντε ἄρτους καὶ τοὺς δύο ἰχθύας ἀναβλέψας εἰς τὸν οὐρανὸν εὐλόγησεν καὶ κατέκλασεν τοὺς ἄρτους καὶ ἐδίδου τοῖς μαθηταῖς (αὐτοῦ) ἵνα παρατιθῶσιν αὐτοῖς, καὶ τοὺς δύο ἰχθύας ἐμέρισεν πᾶσιν.

καὶ (continuative conjunction) 14.
λαβὼν (aor.act.part.nom.sing.masc.of λαμβάνω, adverbial, temporal) 533.
τοὺς (acc.pl.masc.of the article in agreement with ἄρτους) 9.
πέντε (numeral) 1119.
ἄρτους (acc.pl.masc.of ἄρτος, direct object of λαβὼν) 338.

καὶ (adjunctive conjunction joining nouns) 14.
τοὺς (acc.pl.masc.of the article in agreement with ἰχθύας) 9.
δύο (numeral) 385.
ἰχθύας (acc.pl.masc.of ἰχθύς, direct object of λαβὼν) 657.
ἀναβλέψας (aor.act.part.nom.sing.masc.of ἀναβλέπω, adverbial, temporal) 907.
εἰς (preposition with the accusative of extent) 140.
τὸν (acc.sing.masc.of the article in agreement with οὐρανὸν) 9.
οὐρανὸν (acc.sing.masc.of οὐρανός, extent) 254.
εὐλόγησεν (3d.per.sing.aor.act.ind.of εὐλογέω, constative) 1120.
καὶ (adjunctive conjunction joining verbs) 14.

#2269 κατέκλασεν (3d.per.sing.aor.act.ind.of κατακλάω, ingressive).

break - Mk.6:41; Lk.9:16.

Meaning: A combination of κατά (#98) and κλάω (#1121). Hence, to break into pieces. With a view to division and distribution as in Mk.6:41; Lk.9:16.
τοὺς (acc.pl.masc.of the article in agreement with ἄρτους) 9.
ἄρτους (acc.pl.masc.of ἄρτος, direct object of κατέκλασεν) 338.
καὶ (adjunctive conjunction joining verbs) 14.
ἐδίδου (3d.per.sing.imp.act.ind.of δίδωμι, inceptive) 362.
τοῖς (dat.pl.masc.of the article in agreement with μαθηταῖς) 9.
μαθηταῖς (dat.pl.masc.of μαθητής, indirect object of ἐδίδου) 421.
(αὐτοῦ) - (gen.sing.masc.of αὐτός, relationship) 16.
ἵνα (final conjunction introducing a purpose clause) 114.
παρατιθῶσιν (3d.per.pl.aor.act.subj.of παρατίθημι, purpose) 1055.
αὐτοῖς (dat.pl.masc.of αὐτός, indirect object of παρατιθῶσιν) 16.
καὶ (adjunctive conjunction joining verbs) 14.
τοὺς (acc.pl.masc.of the article in agreement with ἰχθύας) 9.
δύο (numeral) 385.
ἰχθύας (acc.pl.masc.of ἰχθύς, direct object of ἐμέρισεν) 657.
ἐμέρισεν (3d.per.sing.aor.act.ind.of μερίζω, ingressive) 993.
πᾶσιν (dat.pl.masc.of πᾶς, personal advantage) 67.

Translation - *"And when He had taken the five loaves and the two fish, He looked up into the heaven and blessed and began to break the loaves and He began to give to His disciples, in order that they might serve to them, and the two fish He began to divide among all."*

Comment: The participles are temporal, antecedent to the two main verbs εὐλόγησεν and κατέκλασεν. εὐλόγησεν is constative, but κατέκλασεν is ingressive, since Jesus spent the next two hours breaking the loaves and giving them to the disciples to serve to the people. Thus the imperfect ἐδίδου is also inceptive, putting the emphasis upon the beginning of the action. Of course inceptive action implies also continuous action as Jesus "began to give and *kept on giving* to His disciples. The disciples took the bread, set it before the group to which each had been assigned and came back to Jesus again and again for more! Just as the pot of oil continued to pour until all vessels were filled (II Kings 4:5-7) so the bread and fish continued to pass from Jesus' creative fingers into the hands of the disciples and into the mouths and stomachs of the people until all were filled!

There is only one explanation. It was a case of direct and special creation on the spot. Science of course knows nothing of such a thing, but science has nothing whatever to say on the subject of a miracle. The Christian has no difficulty believing the story because he has already accepted by faith (*a priori*) the proposition that Jesus of Nazareth is God incarnate. Those who reject miracles, of course, do so only because they have already rejected the deity of Jesus Christ. καὶ . . . πᾶσιν seems almost to be an afterthought. The plural in πᾶσιν shows that everyone present got fish as well as bread.

It is interesting to speculate about how much time was required for 12 men to serve perhaps 10,000 people. If half were seated in groups of 50 and half in groups of 100, then there were 50 large groups and 100 small groups. I am assuming that the women and children equalled the men in number. Twelve men serving 150 groups would average twelve and one-half groups each. Each man served 833 people (if 10,000 were served!). It must have taken two hours, during all of which time Jesus kept on giving out bread and fish!

The attempts of unbelievers to explain the miracle on natural grounds are pitiable. It takes far more faith to believe a scientific explanation of a miracle than to believe the miracle in the first place . *Cf.*#993 for references to God's division among the saints, not only of physical but also of spiritual blessings. Review parallel accounts in Mt.14:19; Lk.9:16 and John 6:11.

Verse 42 - "And they did all eat and were filled."

καὶ ἔφαγον πάντες καὶ ἐχορτάσθησαν.

καὶ (continuative conjunction) 14.
ἔφαγον (3d.per.pl.aor.act.ind.of ἐσθίω, constative) 610.
πάντες (nom.pl.masc.of πᾶς, subject of ἔφαγον and ἐχορτάσθησαν) 67.
καὶ (adjunctive conjunction joining verbs) 14.
ἐχορτάσθησαν (3d.per.pl.aor.pass.ind.of χορτάζω, culminative) 428.

Translation - "And all ate and everyone had enough."

Comment: χορτάζω (#428) does not mean that they ate to excess, but it does indicate that each guest had all that he wanted. No one left the place hungry.

Verse 43 - "And they took up twelve baskets full of fragments, and of the fishes."

καὶ ἦραν κλάσματα δώδεκα κοφίνων πληρώματα καὶ ἀπὸ τῶν ἰχθύων.

καὶ (continuative conjunction) 14.
ἦραν (3d.per.pl.1st.aor.act.ind.of αἴρω, constative) 350.
κλάσματα (acc.pl.neut.of κλάσμα, direct object of ἦραν) 1122.

δώδεκα (numeral) 820.

κοφίνων (gen.pl.masc.of κόφινος, description) 1123.

πληρώματα (acc.pl.neut.of πλήρωμα, extent) 805.

καὶ (adjunctive conjunction joining a noun and a prepositional phrase) 14.

ἀπὸ (preposition with the ablative of source) 70.

τῶν (abl.pl.masc.of the article in agreement with ἰχθύων) 9.

ἰχθύων (abl.pl.masc.of ἰχθύς, source) 657.

Translation - "And they picked up twelve baskets full of fragments and of the fish."

Comment: κοφίνων, a genitive of description, tells us how many fragments. I have called the accusative in πληρώματα, extent, since it does not seem logical to connect it to κλάσματα. The fragments were not "full." The baskets were "full" but πληρώματα does not agree in case with κοφίνων. The fragments which they picked up are described as being in quantity such that twelve baskets were filled to the extent which is described as "full." The bits of fish which the people had dropped or cast aside also helped to fill the baskets. There is no question that an act of special creation had occurred. The little lad's lunch certainly did not require a 12 basket capacity to carry. A multitude eats until completely satisfied. The remainder is more than we started with. Eph.3:20.

The unbelieving Sunday School teacher told her class that Jesus broke not the literal bread of barley but the spiritual bread of the Word of God - that Jesus preached and the people were filled spiritually. Whereupon an irrepressible Junior boy raised his hand and asked, "What was it they took up in baskets?" *Cf.*Mk.8:19,20. When Jesus fed the 4000 on a later occasion they used not κόφινος but σπυρίδων (#1186). On the occasion under discussion the pilgrims were on their way to the Passover (John 6:3) and carried the special κόφινος for the trip. Later (Mk.8:19,20) a different type of basket was used. If the stories were fabricated would the evangelists have been so careful to make the distinction?

Verse 44 - "And they that did eat of the loaves were about five thousand men."

καὶ ἦσαν οἱ φαγόντες (τοὺς ἄρτους) πεντακισχίλιοι ἄνδρες.

καὶ (continuative conjunction) 14.

ἦσαν (3d.per.pl.imp.ind.of εἰμί, progressive description) 86.

οἱ (nom.pl.masc.of the article in agreement with φαγόντες) 9.

φαγόντες (aor.act.part.nom.pl.masc.of ἐσθίω, substantival, subject of ἦσαν) 610.

(τοὺς) (acc.pl.masc.of the article in agreement with ἄρτους) 9.

(ἄρτους) (acc.pl.masc.ofd ἄρτος, direct object of φαγόντες) 338.

πεντακισχίλιοι (nom.pl.masc.of πεντακισχίλιος, in agreement with ἄνδρες) 1125.

ἄνδρες (nom.pl.masc.of ἀνήρ, predicate nominative) 63.

Translation - "And the men who ate the loaves numbered five thousand."

Comment: Mt.14:21 adds χωρὶς γυναικῶν καὶ παιδίων - "beside women and children." How many? We do not know. John 6:10 agrees in the number of men who sat down to eat.

We now examine Luke's account in Lk.9:11-17. Review Mt.14:15-21.

Luke 9:11 - "And the people when they knew it followed him: and he received them, and spoke unto them of the kingdom of God, and healed them that had need of healing."

οἱ δὲ ὄχλοι γνόντες ἠκολούθησαν αὐτῷ, καὶ ἀποδεξάμενος αὐτοὺς ἐλάλει αὐτοῖς περὶ τῆς βασιλείας τοῦ θεοῦ, καὶ τοὺς χρείαν ἔχοντας θεραπείας ἰᾶτο.

οἱ (nom.pl.masc.of the article in agreement with ὄχλοι) 9.

δὲ (adversative conjunction) 11.

ὄχλοι (nom.pl.masc.of ὄχλος, subject of ἠκολούθησαν) 418.

γνόντες (2d.aor.act.part.nom.pl.masc.of γινώσκω, adverbial, temporal, causal) 131.

ἠκολούθησαν (3d.per.pl.aor.act.ind.of ἀκολουθέω, ingressive) 394.

αὐτῷ (dat.sing.masc.of αὐτός, personal interest) 16.

καὶ (inferential conjunction) 14.

ἀποδεξάμενος (aor.part.nom.sing.masc.of ἀποδέχομαι, adverbial, temporal) 2245.

αὐτοὺς (acc.pl.masc.of αὐτός, direct object of ἀποδεξάμενος) 16.

ἐλάλει (3d.per.sing.imp.act.ind.of λαλέω, inceptive) 815.

αὐτοῖς (dat.pl.masc.of αὐτός, indirect object of ἐλάλει) 16.

περὶ (preposition with the genitive of reference) 173.

τῆς (gen.sing.fem.of the article in agreement with βασιλείας) 9.

βασιλείας (gen.sing.fem.of βασιλεία, reference) 253.

τοῦ (gen.sing.masc.of the article in agreement with θεοῦ) 9.

θεοῦ (gen.sing.masc.of θεός, possession) 124.

καὶ (adjunctive conjunction joining verbs) 14.

τοὺς (acc.pl.masc.of the article in agreement with ἔχοντας) 9.

χρείαν (acc.sing.fem.of χρεία, direct object of ἔχοντας) 317.

ἔχοντας (pres.act.part.acc.pl.masc.of ἔχω, direct object of ἰᾶτο) 82.

#2270 θεραπείας (gen.sing.fem.of θεραπεία, description).

healing - Lk.9:11; Rev.22:2.
household - Lk.12:42.

Meaning: Cf.θεραπεύω (#406). In Lk.9:11 and Rev.22:2 in the accommodated sense of healing. In Lk.12:42 in the classical sense of service. Luke also uses θεραπεύω once in the classical sense in Acts 17:25.

ἰᾶτο (3d.per.sing.imp.ind.of ἰάομαι, progressive duration) 721.

Translation - "But when the multitudes learned of it they began to follow Him; so He received them and began to speak to them about the Kingdom of God, and those who had need of healing He cured."

Comment: δὲ is adversative. Jesus wanted to take the Apostles away for a little rest and relaxation (Mk.6:31) but the people insisted upon seeing Jesus. γνόντες, the adverbial participle is therefore both temporal and causal, in relation to ἠκολούθησαν. *When* and *because* the people found out where Jesus went, they began (ingressive aorist) to follow Him. Jesus pitied them (Mk.6:34) and received them hospitably. *Cf.*#2245 for other examples of ἀποδέχομαι. The idea of genuine hospitality seems always to be present. ἐλάλει and ἰᾶτο are imperfect tenses, the former inceptive and the latter progressive duration. Jesus began immediately to speak to them about the Kingdom of God and as He noted their physical infirmities He carried on His usual healing ministry. This ministry continued until evening (Lk.9:12; Mk.6:35). *Cf.*#317 for other examples of χρεία, followed by a genitive of description - in this case, "need of healing." Jesus was adequate to their needs, intellectually, spiritually, physically and, as we shall see, gastronomically.

Verse 12 - "And when the day began to wear away, then came the twelve, and said unto him, Send the multitude away, that they may go into the towns and country round about, and lodge, and get victuals; for we are here in a desert place."

Ἡ δὲ ἡμέρα ἤρξατο κλίνειν προσελθόντες δὲ οἱ δώδεκα εἶπαν αὐτῷ, Ἀπόλυσον τὸν ὄχλον ἵνα πορευθέντες εἰς τὰς κύκλῳ κώμας καὶ ἀγροὺς καταλύσωσιν καὶ εὕρωσιν ἐπισιτισμόν, ὅτι ὧδε ἐν ἐρήμῳ τόπῳ ἐσμέν.

Ἡ (nom.sing.fem.of the article in agreement with ἡμέρα) 9.

δὲ (adversative conjunction) 11.

ἡμέρα (nom.sing.fem.of ἡμέρα, subject of ἤρξατο) 135.

ἤρξατο (3d.per.sing.aor.mid.ind.of ἄρχω, ingressive) 383.

κλίνειν (pres.act.inf.of κλίνω, complementary) 746.

προσελθόντες (aor.part.nom.pl.masc.of προσέρχομαι, adverbial, temporal) 336.

δὲ (inferential conjunction) 11.

οἱ (nom.pl.masc.of the article in agreement with δώδεκα) 9.

δώδεκα (numeral, used here as subject of εἶπαν) 820.

εἶπαν (3d.per.sing.aor.act.ind.of εἶπον, constative) 155.

αὐτῷ (dat.sing.masc.of αὐτός, indirect object of εἶπαν) 16.

Ἀπόλυσον (2d.per.sing.aor.act.impv.of ἀπολύω, entreaty) 92.

τὸν (acc.sing.masc.of the article in agreement with ὄχλον) 9.

ὄχλον (acc.sing.masc.of ὄχλος, direct object of ἀπόλυσον) 418.

ἵνα (final conjunction introducing a purpose clause) 114.

πορευθέντες (aor.part.nom.pl.masc.of πορεύομαι, adverbial, temporal) 170.

εἰς (preposition with the accusative of extent) 140.

τὰς (acc.pl.fem.of the article in agreement with κώμας) 9.

κύκλῳ (loc.sing.masc.of κύκλος, adverbial, place where) 2183.

κώμας (acc.pl.fem.of κώμη, extent) 834.

καὶ (adjunctive conjunction joining nouns) 14.

ἀγροὺς (acc.pl.masc.of ἀγρός, extent) 626.

καταλύσωσιν (3d.per.pl.aor.act.subj.of καταλύω, purpose) 463.

καὶ (adjunctive conjunction joining verbs) 14.

εὕρωσιν (3d.per.pl.aor.act.subj.of εὑρίσκω, purpose) 79.

#2271 ἐπισιτισμόν (acc.sing.masc.of ἐπισιτισμός, direct object of εὕρωσιν).

victuals - Lk.9:12.

*Meaning: Cf.*ἐπισιτίζομαι - "to provide for one's self. To forage for food."
Hence, food. Lk.9:12.

ὅτι (causal conjunction) 211.

ὧδε (adverb of place) 766.

ἐν (preposition with the locative of place) 80.

ἐρήμῳ (loc.sing.masc.of ἔρημος, in agreement with τόπῳ) 250.

τόπῳ (loc.sing.masc.of τόπος, place where) 1019.

ἐσμέν (1st.per.pl.pres.ind.of εἰμί, aoristic) 86.

*Translation - "But the daylight began to fade; so the twelve came and said to
Him, 'Send the crowd away, in order that when they have gone into the
surrounding villages and fields they may bed down and find food, because we are
here in a deserted spot.' "*

Comment: The people were crowding about Jesus as He continued to teach and
heal. But (adversative δὲ) it was getting late in the afternoon. Soon it would be
dark. The pressures of their physical position and needs interfered with the
provision of blessings which Jesus was continuing to give. *Cf.*#746 for the other
uses of κλίνω. Only in Lk.24:29 in the sense in which we find it here. "The day
began to fade" and hence it was beginning to get dark.

The twelve Apostles had spent the day in isolation, resting and eating, in
accordance with Jesus' suggestion (Mk.6:31). Now they approached Jesus with
what they thought was a practical suggestion. Physical needs, for them, held
priority over spiritual. The Apostles knew that the people would not disperse as
long as Jesus taught and healed them. Only on His command would they go
away. The people were closer to an appreciation of spiritual matters at this point
than the disciples. Apparently no one in the audience had thought of food or the
need for lodging. But the Twelve did. There were villages and farms round
about. *Cf.* Lk.19:7 for καταλύω in the same sense - "to bed down." Luke uses a
rare Greek word for forage. The disciples defended their crass suggestion by
pointing out the obvious - ὅτι . . . ἐσμέν, as though they were half ashamed of
their suggestion.

*Verse 13 - "But he said unto them, Give ye them to eat. And they said, We have
no more but five loaves and two fishes; except we should go and buy meat for all
this people."*

εἶπεν δὲ πρὸς αὐτοῖς, Δότε αὐτοῖς ὑμεῖς φαγεῖν. οἱ δὲ εἶπαν, Οὐκ εἰσὶν ἡμῖν πλεῖον ἢ ἄρτοι πέντε καὶ ἰχθύες δύο, εἰ μήτι πορευθέντες ἡμεῖς ἀγοράσωμεν εἰς πάντα τὸν λαὸν τοῦτον βρώματα.

εἶπεν (3d.per.sing.aor.act.ind.of εἶπον, constative) 155.

δὲ (adversative conjunction) 11.

πρὸς (preposition with the accusative after a verb of speaking) 197.

αὐτούς (acc.pl.masc.of αὐτός, extent after a verb of speaking) 16.

Δότε (2d.per.pl.aor.act.impv.of δίδωμι, command) 362.

αὐτοῖς (dat.pl.masc.of αὐτός, indirect object of δότε) 16.

φαγεῖν (aor.act.inf.of ἐσθίω, complementary) 610.

ὑμεῖς (nom.pl.masc.of σύ, emphatic) 104.

οἱ (nom.pl.masc.of the article subject of εἶπαν) 9.

δὲ (adversative conjunction) 11.

εἶπαν (3d.per.pl.aor.act.ind.of εἶπον, constative) 155.

Οὐκ (summary negative conjunction with the indicative) 130.

εἰσὶν (3d.per.pl.pres.ind.of εἰμί, aoristic) 86.

ἡμῖν (dat.pl.masc.of ἐγώ, personal advantage) 123.

πλεῖον (acc.sing.neut.of πλείων, adverbial) 474.

ἢ (disjunctive) 465.

ἄρτοι (nom.pl.masc.of ἄρτος, subject of εἰσὶν) 338.

πέντε (numeral) 1119.

καὶ (adjunctive conjunction joining nouns) 14.

ἰχθύες (nom.pl.masc.of ἰχθύς, subject of εἰσὶν) 657.

δύο (numeral) 385.

εἰ (conditional particle) 337.

μήτι (negative conjunction in a conditional clause) 676.

πορευθέντες (pres.mid.part.nom.pl.masc.of πορεύομαι, adverbial, temporal) 170.

ἡμεῖς (nom.pl.masc.of ἐγώ, subject of ἀγοράσωμεν) 123.

ἀγοράσωμεν (1st.per.pl.aor.act.subj.of ἀγοράζω, conditional clause) 1085.

εἰς (preposition with the accusative, purpose) 140.

πάντα (acc.sing.masc.of πᾶς, in agreement with λαόν) 67.

τὸν (acc.sing.masc.of the article in agreement with λαόν) 9.

λαόν (acc.sing.masc.of λαός, purpose) 110.

τοῦτον (acc.sing.masc.of οὗτος, in agreement with λαόν) 93.

βρώματα (acc.pl.neut.of βρῶμα, direct object of ἀγοράσωμεν) 1118.

Translation - "But He said to them, 'Give them something to eat yourselves.' But they said, 'There are here available to us not more than five loaves and two fish, unless we go and buy food for all these people.' "

Comment: δὲ is adversative in both instances, as Jesus and the Apostles argue about what is to be done. Note the emphatic use of ὑμεῖς. It is emphatic because otherwise it is unnecessary since it is implicit in the verb Δότε. "The pronominal subject of a finite verb is ordinarily not expressed, the person and number of the subject being indicated by the verbal ending. When the personal pronoun is used, it is for emphasis." (Mantey, *Manual*, 123). The Apostles had said, "Give the people a chance to find food and shelter." Jesus said, "Feed them yourselves." They countered with an inventory report - five loaves and two fish. οὐκ εἰσὶν is emphatic. πλεῖον ἤ - "more than." *Cf.*#465 for other examples of ἤ with πλεῖον. εἰ μήτι - literally, "if we do not κ.τ.λ." Unless they went out and bought food, they were compelled, they thought, to divide five small loaves and two fish among ten thousand people. They moved from an emphatic indicative "we have only five loaves and two fish" to a sarcastic doubting subjunctive - "unless we go out and buy food for all of these people." This was a preposterous idea since the next verse says that there were 5000 men. εἰς with the accusative in a purpose construction. Mark joins Luke in expressing the disciples' skepticism with the subjunctive ἀγοράσωμεν. Matthew 14:21 reminds us that in addition to the 5000 men there were women and children present.

Verse 14 - "For they were about five thousand men. And he said to his disciples, Make them sit down by fifties in a company."

ἦσαν γὰρ ὡσεὶ ἄνδρες πεντακισχίλιοι. εἶπεν δὲ πρὸς τοὺς μαθητὰς αὐτοῦ, Κατακλίνατε αὐτοὺς κλισίας (ὡσεὶ) ἀνὰ πεντήκοντα.

ἦσαν (3d.per.pl.imp.ind.of εἰμί, progressive duration) 86.

γὰρ (causal conjunction) 105.

ὡσεὶ (comparative adverb) 325.

ἄνδρες (nom.pl.masc.of ἀνήρ, subject of ἦσαν) 63.

πεντακισχίλιοι (nom.pl.masc.of πεντακισχίλιος, in agreement with ἄνδρες) 1125.

εἶπεν (3d.per.sing.aor.act.ind.of εἶπον, constative) 155.

δὲ (adversative conjunction) 11.

πρὸς (preposition with the accusative of extent after a verb of speaking) 197.

τοὺς (acc.pl.masc.of the article in agreement with μαθητὰς) 9.

αὐτοῦ (gen.sing.masc.of αὐτός, relationship) 16.

Κατακλίνατε (2d.per.pl.pres.act.impv.of κατακλίνω, command) 2165.

αὐτοὺς (acc.pl.masc.of αὐτός, direct object of κατακλίνατε) 16.

#2272 κλισίας (gen.sing.fem.of κλισία, adverbial).

company - Lk.9:14.

Meaning: *Cf.* κλίνω (#746). Prop. a place to recline; a place to lie down. Hence a couch or a hut in which to spend the night. A tent or a reclining chair. Also used of a company of people reclining as in Lk.9:14. Josephus (*Antiq.12,2,12*) also uses κλισία in this sense.

(ὡσεὶ) - (comparative adverb) 325.

ἀνὰ (preposition with accusative, distributive) 1059.

πεντήκοντα (numeral) 2172.

Translation - ". . . for there were about five thousand men present. But He said to

His disciples, 'Seat them in groups of about fifty each.' "

Comment: Luke offers an illative clause, ἦσαν . . . πεντακισχίλιοι, with postpositive γὰρ to explain why the disciples were so skeptical in verse 13. Five thousand men is too large a crowd to feed when you have assets of only five loaves and two fish. Nevertheless (adversative δὲ) Jesus persisted. The order was to seat the people on the ground. *Cf.*#2272 - ὡσεὶ ἀνὰ - "as if up to fifty in a group." There was no further argument from the disciples. They obeyed in

Verse 15 - "And they did so, and made them all sit down."

καὶ ἐποίησαν οὕτως καὶ κατέκλιναν ἅπαντας.

καὶ (inferential conjunction) 14.
ἐποίησαν (3d.per.pl.aor.act.ind.of ποιέω, constative) 127.
οὕτως (demonstrative adverb) 74.
καὶ (adjunctive conjunction joining verbs) 14.
κατέκλιναν (3d.per.pl.imp.act.ind.of κατακλίνω, inceptive) 2165.
ἅπαντας (acc.pl.masc.of ἅπας, direct object of κατέκλιναν) 639.

Translation - "Therefore they did as He said and began to tell everyone to sit down."

Comment: The disciples began to comply with Jesus' order, although it seemed illogical both to them and to the people. Why should a crowd of more than five thousand hungry people be seated on the grass in regularly organized groups to facilitate serving food which consisted only of five loaves and two fish? Prior planning and execution of the plan takes place rationally only for the One who is able to control the future. To those mortals who cannot see the future, planning sometimes does not make sense. The Christian can see examples of this in his daily life. In order to use us in some way, plain indeed to Him, but as yet unrevealed to us, our Lord must put us into a given position. He does not often allow us to see the future, any more than He chose to tell the people in advance that He was going to feed them. Hence making us do this or that or go here or there makes sense to Him who sees the end result, but not to us who grope in the dark (Rom.8:28; Eph.1:11). The Christian position involves a teleological cosmology. Often we resist being forced "to sit down on the ground in groups of fifty" as much as the people did at Bethsaida. The disciples may have had some difficulty with the people who saw no point in the procedure. They did not know that they were going to get a free meal. Jesus plans "free meals" for all of His children. Note ἅπαντας, the intensive form of πᾶς (#67, 639). Everybody there, barring no one - man, woman and child, sat down and ate. Mt.14:21 assures us that the women and children were also present.

Verse 16 - "Then he took the five loaves and the two fish, and looking up to heaven, he blessed them, and brake, and gave to the disciples to set before the multitude."

λαβὼν δὲ τοὺς πέντε ἄρτους καὶ τοὺς δύο ἰχθύας ἀναβλέψας εἰς τὸν
οὐρανὸν εὐλόγησεν αὐτοὺς καὶ κατέκλασεν καὶ ἐδίδου τοῖς μαθηταῖς
παραθεῖναι τῷ ὄχλῳ.

λαβὼν (aor.act.part.nom.sing.masc.of λαμβάνω, adverbial, temporal) 533.

δὲ (continuative conjunction) 11.

τοὺς (acc.pl.masc.of the article in agreement with ἄρτους) 9.

πέντε (numeral) 1119.

ἄρτους (acc.pl.masc.of ἄρτος, direct object of λαβὼν) 338.

καὶ (adjunctive conjunction joining nouns) 14.

τοὺς (acc.pl.masc.of the article in agreement with ἰχθύας) 9.

δύο (numeral) 385.

ἰχθύας (acc.pl.masc.of ἰχθύς, direct object of λαβὼν) 657.

ἀναβλέψας (aor.act.part.nom.sing.masc.of ἀναβλέπω, adverbial, temporal)
907.

εἰς (preposition with the accusative of extent) 140.

τὸν (acc.sing.masc.of the article in agreement with οὐρανὸν) 9.

οὐρανὸν (acc.sing.masc.of οὐρανός, extent) 254.

εὐλόγησεν (3d.per.sing.aor.act.ind.of εὐλογέω, constative) 1120.

αὐτοὺς (acc.pl.masc.of αὐτός, direct object of εὐλόγησεν, κατέκλασεν and
ἐδίδου) 16.

καὶ (adjunctive conjunction joining verbs) 14.

κατέκλασεν (3d.per.sing.aor.act.ind.of κατακλάω, ingressive) 2269.

καὶ (adjunctive conjunction joining verbs) 14.

ἐδίδου (3d.per.sing.imp.act.ind.of δίδωμι, inceptive) 362.

τοῖς (dat.pl.masc.of the article in agreement with μαθηταῖς) 9.

μαθηταῖς (dat.pl.masc.of μαθητής, indirect object of ἐδίδου) 421.

παραθεῖναι (aor.act.inf.of παρατίθημι, purpose) 1055.

τῷ (loc.sing.masc.of the article in agreement with ὄχλῳ) 9.

ὄχλῳ (loc.sing.masc.of ὄχλος, place where) 418.

*Translation - "And He took the five loaves and the two fish, looked up to heaven
and blessed them and began to break and give to the disciples to serve to the
crowd."*

Comment: The participles establish the sequence of events. Jesus took the food,
looked up to heaven and blessed it. Then He *began* (ingressive aorist and
inceptive imperfect) to break the food into pieces and to give it to the disciples
that they might serve it to the people. The aorist infinitive παραθεῖναι is purpose.
How long did it take? *Cf.* comments on Mk.6:41. Whether we read the ingressive
aorist ἔδωκεν in Mt.14:19 or the inceptive imperfect ἐδίδου as in Mk.6:41 and
Lk.9:16, both constructions put the emphasis upon the beginning of the action.
Hence there is no contradiction. Plenary inspiration does not mean that the
Holy Spirit robs the writer of his individuality, so long as what he writes is clear
to later exegetes who know what they are doing.

The decision as to whether an aorist tense in ingressive, constative, culminative, gnomic, epistolary or dramatic, and whether an imperfect tense is progressive, customary, iterative, tendential, voluntative or inceptive depends upon the context, not upon the form itself. The blessing which Jesus gave to the food was a simple act of grace, with no particular emphasis upon either the beginning or the end. Hence εὐλόγησεν is constative. But it took perhaps two hours for Jesus to break into pieces and give them to the disciples. Hence the emphasis is upon the beginning of the action (ingressive in κατέκλασεν and inceptive in ἐδίδου). That these actions were also completed is clear from the other elements in the story. Any action that begins and continues for some time (inceptive and progressive imperfect) ultimately ceases. If the text said that Jesus fired a gun and used the imperfect tense, we would be involved in grammatical difficulty.

Further evidence that divine plenary verbal inspiration does not mean dictation, as though the writers were robots, is found in the grammatical variety between Matthew, Mark and Luke in the use of παρατίθημι. Mark uses a purpose clause with ἵνα and the subjunctive (Mk.6:41). Luke uses the complementary aorist infinitive to complete ἐδίδου (Lk.9:16). Matthew asks us to supply ἔδωκεν and follows with the dative of indirect object (Mt.14:19). All are good Greek and the message conveyed is exactly the same in each case. John leaves the disciples out of it (John 6:1), while not denying that they served as waiters.

For the spiritual implications of this event *Cf.* our comments on John 6:22-71. We close Luke's account of the episode with

Verse 17 - "And they did eat, and were filled: and there was taken up of fragments that remained to them twelve baskets."

καὶ ἔφαγον καὶ ἐχορτάσθησαν πάντες, καὶ ἤρθη τὸ περισσεῦσαν αὐτοῖς κλασμάτων κόφινοι δώδεκα.

καὶ (continuative conjunction) 14.

ἔφαγον (3d.per.pl.aor.act.ind.of ἐσθίω, constative) 610.

καὶ (adjunctive conjunction joining verbs) 14.

ἐχορτάσθησαν (3d.per.pl.aor.pass.ind.of χορτάζω, culminative) 428.

πάντες (nom.pl.masc.of πᾶς, subject of ἔφαγον and ἐχορτάσθησαν) 67.

καὶ (continuative conjunction) 14.

ἤρθη (3d.per.sing.aor.pass.ind.of αἴρω, culminative) 350.

τὸ (nom.sing.neut.of the article in agreement with περισσεῦσαν) 9.

περισσεῦσαν (aor.act.part.nom.sing.neut.of περισσεύω, substantival, subject of ἤρθη) 473.

αὐτοῖς (dat.pl.masc.of αὐτός, personal advantage) 16.

κλασμάτων (gen.pl.neut.of κλάσμα, partitive genitive) 1122.

κόφινοι (nom.pl.masc.of κόφινος, predicate nominative) 1123.

δώδεκα (numeral) 820.

Translation - "And they ate and everyone was filled and there was picked up of the fragments that remained to them twelve baskets full."

Comment: All were filled. No one went away hungry. One wonders what they did with the excess production. Perhaps it was taken home by some and given to other hungry people, since Jesus insisted that it not be wasted (John 6:12). We turn now to John's parallel account of the story in John 6:1-13.

John 6:1 - "After these things Jesus went over the sea of Galilee, which is the sea of Tiberias."

Μετὰ ταῦτα ἀπῆλθεν ὁ Ἰησοῦς πέραν τῆς θαλάσσης τῆς Γαλιλαίας τῆς Τιβεριάδος.

Μετὰ (preposition with the accusative in a time expression) 50.

ταῦτα (acc.pl.neut.of οὗτος, time extent) 93.

ἀπῆλθεν (3d.per.sing.aor.ind.of ἀπέρχομαι, constative) 239.

ὁ (nom.sing.masc.of the article in agreement with Ἰησοῦς) 9.

Ἰησοῦς (nom.sing.masc.of Ἰησοῦς, subject of ἀπῆλθεν) 3.

πέραν (improper preposition with the ablative of separation, adverbial) 375.

τῆς (abl.sing.fem.of the article in agreement with θαλάσσης) 9.

θαλάσσης (abl.sing.fem.of θάλασσα, separation) 374.

τῆς (gen.sing.fem.of the article in agreement with Γαλιλαίας) 9.

Γαλιλαίας (gen.sing.fem.of Γαλιλαίας, designation) 241.

τῆς (gen.sing.fem.of the article in agreement with Τιβεριάδος) 9.

Τιβεριάδος, (gen.sing.fem.of Τιβέριας, apposition) 1929.

Translation - "After these things Jesus went away across the Sea of Galilee, otherwise known as the Sea of Tiberias."

Comment: Μετὰ ταῦτα does not necessarily mean that Jesus' departure to the other side of the Sea of Galilee followed immediately upon the close of His remarks as recorded in John 5. When He finished His discussion with His detractors (John 5:17-47) we have no record from John as to what He did. The departure in the boat was from Capernaum in Galilee to Bethsaida, before which the Sermon on the Mount (Mt.5:1 - 7:29) and many other events occurred.

John's purpose is to show the essential deity of the incarnate Son of God in the historic Jesus of Nazareth. This John does by putting together a series of vignettes which serves his purpose. The chronological order, in places, fits into that of the Synoptic gospels, as John offers little hints, here and there, such as John 3:24. Μετὰ ταῦτα often serves as a mark of John's continuation of the story and should not be held to strict chronological account in all instances.

John, writing to a Greek audience in Ephesus in the tenth decade of the first century, found it necessary to identify the Sea of Galilee as the Sea of Tiberias, something which he would not have found necessary had his audience been composed of native Palestinians. It is not likely that many, if any, of John's audience in A.D.90 had been to Palestine and therefore they knew little of its geography and toponomy. *Cf.*#375 for other uses of πέραν with the ablative. It is an improper preposition because it is never found in composition with a verb. Used like an adverb, in this case, it defines ἀπῆλθεν to tell us where Jesus went.

Verse 2 - "And a great multitude followed him, because they saw his miracles which he did on them that were diseased."

ἠκολούθει δὲ αὐτῷ ὄχλος πολύς, ὅτι ἐθεώρουν τὰ σημεῖα ἃ ἐποίει ἐπὶ τῶν ἀσθενούντων.

ἠκολούθει (3d.per.sing.imp.act.ind.of ἀκολουθέω, inceptive) 394.
δὲ (continuative conjunction) 11.
αὐτῷ (dat.sing.masc.of αὐτός, personal interest) 16.
ὄχλος (nom.sing.masc.of ὄχλος, subject of ἠκολούθει and ἐθεώρουν) 418.
πολύς (nom.sing.masc.of πολύς, in agreement with ὄχλος) 228.
ὅτι (causal conjunction) 211.
ἐθεώρουν (3d.per.pl.imp.act.ind.of θεωρέω, progressive duration) 1667.
τὰ (acc.pl.neut.of the article in agreement with σημεῖα) 9.
σημεῖα (acc.pl.neut.of σημεῖον, direct object of ἐθεώρουν) 1005.
ἃ (acc.pl.neut.of ὅς, direct object of ἐποίει) 65.
ἐποίει (3d.per.sing.imp.act.ind.of ποιέω, progressive duration) 127.
ἐπὶ (preposition with the genitive, basis) 47.
τῶν (gen.pl.masc.of the article in agreement with ἀσθενούντων) 9.
ἀσθενούντων (pres.act.part.gen.pl.masc.of ἀσθενέω, basis) 857.

Translation - "And a great crowd began to follow Him because they had been watching the signs which He had been performing for those who were sick."

Comment: We know from the synoptic accounts that Jesus' withdrawal was for purposes of rest and relaxation (Mk.6:31) as well as to avoid further controversy which might arise from the undue publicity which arose over the murder of John the Baptist (Mt.14:13). Hence, for us who have the advantage of reading the other gospel accounts, δὲ is adversative. But for John's audience who may or may not have seen the synoptics, there was no reason to interpret δὲ as adversative. Hence we have called it continuative.

The imperfect tenses are eloquent. The people *began* to follow Jesus because they *had been watching* His miracles which He *had been performing* for the sick. Every verb in the verse is linear in action while the first is inceptive. The crowds had seen enough to excite their curiosity and genuine interest. They had been treated to repeated evidence (imperfect progressive duration in ἐθεώρουν) as they watched His miracles which He had continued to perform (imperfect tense in ἐποίει), for those who were chronically ill (present participle in ἀσθενούντων).

John could have written ἐποίει τοῖς ἀσθενούντοις - the dative of personal advantage, but he chose ἐπὶ with the genitive of basis. Robertson calls it "a natural metaphor" and cites Lk.4:25; Gal.3:16 and Mt.18:16 as other examples. (Roberston, *Grammar*, 604).

Verse 3 - "And Jesus went up into a mountain, and there he sat with his disciples."

ἀνῆλθεν δὲ εἰς τὸ ὄρος Ἰησοῦς, καὶ ἐκεῖ ἐκάθητο μετὰ τῶν μαθητῶν αὐτοῦ.

#2273 ἀνῆλθεν (3d.per.sing.aor.ind.of ἀνέρχομαι, constative).

go up - John 6:3; Gal.1:17,18.

Meaning: A combination of ἀνά (#1059) and ἔρχομαι (#146). Hence, to go up. Topographically in John 6:3, where it is followed by εἰς τὸ ὄρος. Perhaps topographically also in Gal.1:17,18, but certainly also "up" in terms of authority and prestige, since Jerusalem was considered the seat of Jewish authority to Saul of Tarsus.

δὲ (adversative conjunction) 11.
εἰς (preposition with the accusative of extent) 140.
τὸ (acc.sing.neut.of the article in agreement with ὄρος) 9.
ὄρος (acc.sing.neut.of ὄρος, extent) 357.
Ἰησοῦς (nom.sing.masc.of Ἰησοῦς, subject of ἀνῆλθεν and ἐκάθητο) 3.
καὶ (adjunctive conjunction joining verbs) 14.
ἐκεῖ (adverb of place) 204.
ἐκάθητο (3d.per.sing.imp.act.ind.of κάθημαι, progressive duration) 377.
μετὰ (preposition with the genitive of accompaniment) 50.
τῶν (gen.pl.masc.of the article in agreement with μαθητῶν) 9.
μαθητῶν (gen.pl.masc.of μαθητής, accompaniment) 421.
αὐτοῦ (gen.sing.masc.of αὐτός, relationship) 16.

Translation - "But Jesus went up into the mountain and there He was sitting with His disciples."

Comment: The order of events is as follows: John the Baptist was murdered and his disciples buried him (Mt.14:1-12; Mk.6:14-29; Lk.9:7-9); the Apostles returned from their first preaching mission and reported with enthusiasm the results to Jesus (Mk.6:30). John's disciples also reported John's death to Jesus (Mt.14:12); Jesus and the Twelve got into a ship and sailed to Bethsaida, on the northeast side of the Sea of Galilee (Lk.9:10); they arrived and proceded up the mountain to a secluded spot where they sat down (John 6:3; Mt.14:13; Mk.6:32). Meanwhile the people discerned Jesus' destination and followed by land around the northwest corner of the Galilee and across the Jordan River and approached Jesus on the mountainside (Mt.14:13; Mk.6:33; Lk.9:11). Jesus saw them and had compassion on them (Mt.14:14; Mk.6:34), preached to them and healed the sick (Lk.9:11), while the Apostles, in obedience to His suggestion rested.

Verse 4 - "And the passover, a feast of the Jews, was nigh."

ἦν δὲ ἐγγὺς τὸ πάσχα, ἡ ἑορτὴ τῶν Ἰουδαίων.

ἦν (3d.per.sing.imp.ind.of εἰμί, progressive description) 86.
δὲ (explanatory conjunction) 11.
ἐγγὺς (nom.sing.neut.of ἐγγύς, predicate adjective) 1512.
τὸ (nom.sing.neut.of the article in agreement with πάσχα) 9.
πάσχα (nom.sing.neut.of πάσχα, subject of ἦν) 1553.

ἡ (nom.sing.fem.of the article in agreement with ἑορτῇ) 9.
ἑορτὴ (nom.sing.fem.of ἑορτή, apposition) 1558.
τῶν (gen.pl.masc.of the article in agreement with Ἰουδαίων) 9.
Ἰουδαίων (gen.pl.masc.of Ἰουδαῖος, description) 143.

Translation - "Now the Passover, the feast of the Jews was at hand."

Comment: Since John is writing to a Greek audience who knows little of Jewish culture and traditions we can take δὲ as explanatory. Otherwise they would have had no idea of the significance of this annual festival which required that every Jew make his annual pilgrimage to Jerusalem. This explains why the crowd was so great. They were not all local people from the immediate vicinity, but pilgrims, enroute to Jerusalem, eighty miles to the southwest.

Verse 5 - "When Jesus then lifted up His eyes and saw a great company come unto Him, he saith unto Philip, Whence shall we buy bread, that these may eat?"

ἐπάρας οὖν τοὺς ὀφθαλμοὺς ὁ Ἰησοῦς καὶ θεασάμενος ὅτι πολὺς ὄχλος ἔρχεται πρὸς αὐτὸν λέγει πρὸς Φίλιππον, Πόθεν ἀγοράσωμεν ἄρτους ἵνα φάγωσιν οὗτοι;

ἐπάρας (aor.act.part.nom.sing.masc.of ἐπαίρω, adverbial, temporal) 1227.
οὖν (inferential conjunction) 68.
τοὺς (acc.pl.masc.of the article in agreement with ὀφθαλμοὺς) 9.
ὀφθαλμοὺς (acc.pl.masc.of ὀφθαλμός, direct object of ἐπάρας) 501.
ὁ (nom.sing.masc.of the article in agreement with Ἰησοῦς) 9.
Ἰησοῦς (nom.sing.masc.of Ἰησοῦς, subject of λέγει) 3.
καὶ (adjunctive conjunction joining participles) 14.
θεασάμενος (aor.act.part.nom.sing.masc.of θεάομαι, adverbial, temporal) 556.
ὅτι (conjunction introducing an object clause in indirect discourse) 211.
πολὺς (nom.sing.masc.of πολύς, in agreement with ὄχλος) 228.
ὄχλος (nom.sing.masc.of ὄχλος, subject of ἔρχεται) 418.
ἔρχεται (3d.per.sing.pres.ind.of ἔρχομαι, aoristic) 146.
πρὸς (preposition with the accusative of extent) 197.
αὐτὸν (acc.sing.masc.of αὐτός, extent) 16.
λέγει (3d.per.sing.pres.act.ind.of λέγω, historical) 66.
πρὸς (preposition with the accusative of extent, after a verb of speaking) 197.
Φίλιππον (acc.sing.masc.of Φίλιππος, extent, after a verb of speaking) 845.
Πόθεν (interrogative conjunction in direct question) 1061.
ἀγοράσωμεν (1st.per.pl.aor.act.subj.of ἀγοράζω, deliberative) 1085.
ἄρτους (acc.pl.masc.of ἄρτος, direct object of ἀγοράσωμεν) 338.
ἵνα (sub-final conjunction introducing a sub-final clause) 114.
φάγωσιν (3d.per.pl.aor.act.subj.of ἐσθίω, purpose/result) 610.
οὗτοι (nom.pl.masc.of οὗτος, subject of φάγωσιν) 93.

Translation - "Therefore Jesus looked up and saw that a great crowd was coming toward Him, and He said to Philip, 'Where can we buy food so that these people can eat?'"

Comment: οὖν is inferential. Jesus and the disciples had crossed the Lake to escape the crowds temporarily so they could get some rest, but the people made the great sacrifice of walking the long distance around the lake in order to hear more of Jesus' teachings. They were so pitiable that when Jesus looked up and saw them coming He had compassion upon them. He knew how He was going to feed them, but He wanted to test Philip's faith. Hence the question. Πόθεν ἀγοράσωμεν is a deliberative subjunctive, as though Jesus had some doubt about the answer. He did not assume that Philip had the answer. It was a rhetorical device to point up to Philip the gravity of the situation. For other examples of the subjunctive mode in deliberation *cf.* Rom.10:14; I Cor.11:22; Lk.3:10; Mk.12:14. The ἵνα clause is sub-final - both purpose and result. If indeed they could go out and buy enough food, they would accomplish their purpose and the result would be that the people would eat.

John does not mention the flood of compassion in which Jesus was engulfed when He saw the people as the synoptic writers do (Mt.14:14; Mk.6:34).

Verse 6 - "And this he said to prove him: for he himself knew what he would do."

τοῦτο δὲ ἔλεγεν πειράζων αὐτόν, αὐτὸς γὰρ ᾔδει τί ἔμελλεν ποιεῖν.

τοῦτο (acc.sing.neut.of οὗτος, direct object of ἔλεγεν) 93.
δὲ (adversative conjunction) 11.
ἔλεγεν (3d.per.sing.imp.act.ind.of λέγω, tendential) 66.
πειράζων (pres.act.part.nom.sing.masc.of πειράζω, adverbial, telic) 330.
αὐτὸν (acc.sing.masc.of αὐτός, direct object of πειράζων) 16.
αὐτὸς (nom.sing.masc.of αὐτός, subject of ᾔδει, emphatic) 16.
γὰρ (causal conjunction) 105.
ᾔδει (3d.per.sing.pluperfect active indicative of ὁράω, consummative) 144.
τί (acc.sing.neut.of τίς, direct object of ᾔδει) 281.
ἔμελλεν (3d.per.sing.imp.act.ind.of μέλλω, progressive description) 206.
ποιεῖν (pres.act.inf.of ποιέω, complementary) 127.

Translation - "But this He was saying in order to test him, because He himself had always known what He was about to do."

Comment: δὲ is adversative as John explains. He had already indicated in the deliberative subjunctive of verse 5 that Jesus was not asking for information. Now John strengthens the point with δὲ, as if to hasten to correct any wrong impression that his readers might have. "But He was saying this, contrary to what you might think, not for information, but in order to test Philip." The participle is telic - it indicates the purpose which Jesus had in mind. Note the emphatic use of the personal pronoun αὐτός. The subject is implicit in ᾔδει, but John adds it for emphasis. Jesus *Himself* had always known (pluperfect in ᾔδει) what He was going to do. *Cf.*#330 for comment on God in the role of a tempter. No conflict here with James 1:13,14. An object lesson was in store for the disciples as well as for the people.

Verse 7 - "Phillip answered him, Two hundred pennyworth of bread is not sufficient for them, that everyone of them may take a little.

ἀπεκρίθη αὐτῷ ὁ Φίλιππος, Διακοσίων δηναρίων ἄρτοι οὐκ ἀρκοῦσιν αὐτοῖς ἵνα ἕκαστος βραχύ τι λάβῃ.

ἀπεκρίθη (3d.per.sing.aor.ind.of ἀποκρίνομαι, constative) 318.
αὐτῷ (dat.sing.masc.of αὐτός, indirect object of ἀπεκρίθη) 16.
ὁ (nom.sing.masc.of the article in agreement with Φίλιππος) 9.
Φίλιππος (nom.sing.masc.of Φίλιππος, subject of ἀπεκρίθη) 845.
Διακοσίων (gen.pl.masc.of διακόσιοι, description) 2265.
δηναρίων (gen.pl.neut.of δηνάριον, partitive) 1278.
ἄρτοι (nom.pl.masc.of ἄρτος, subject of ἀρκοῦσιν) 338.
οὐκ (summary negative conjunction with the indicative) 130.
ἀρκοῦσιν (3d.per.pl.pres.act.ind.of ἀρκέω, aoristic) 1534.
αὐτοῖς (dat.pl.masc.of αὐτός, personal advantage) 16.
ἵνα (final conjunction introducing a purpose clause) 114.
ἕκαστος (nom.sing.masc.of ἕκαστος, subject of λάβῃ) 1217.

#2274 βραχύ (acc.sing.neut.of βραχύς, direct object of λάβῃ).

a little - John 6:7; Acts 27:28; Heb.2:7,9; Lk.22:58; Acts 5:34.
few words - Heb.13:22.

Meaning: short,small. With reference to amount - John 6:7; Heb.13:22; with reference to distance - Acts 5:34; 27:28; with reference to time - Lk.22:58; with reference to degree - Heb.2:7,9.

λάβῃ (3d.per.sing.aor.act.subj.of λαμβάνω, purpose) 533.

Translation - "Philip replied to Him, 'Thirty-three dollars and thirty-four cents worth of bread is not enough for them, if each one took but a little.' "

Comment: Goodspeed translates it "Forty dollars." *Cf.*#1278. The δηνάριον replaced the *drachma* which was in use before the time of Diocletian. The Neronian denarius, reintroduced by Diocletian, being reckoned equal to the drachma and was 1/6000 of the talent. (*Moulton and Milligan*, 145). Thayer says it was rapidly debased from Nero on and was worth about 16 2/3 cents at the end of the century, which makes the amount cited by Philip as $33.34. Mrs. Montgomery's translation is closer than Goodspeed's. She says, "$35.00 worth of bread." In any case Philip was pointing up the hopelessness of the situation.

Verse 8 - "One of his disciples, Andrew, Simon Peter's brother, saith unto him . . .

λέγει αὐτῷ εἷς ἐκ τῶν μαθητῶν αὐτοῦ, Ἀνδρέας ὁ ἀδελφὸς Σίμωνος Πέτρου,

λέγει (3d.per.sing.pres.act.ind.of λέγω, historical) 66.
αὐτῷ (dat.sing.masc.of αὐτός, indirect object of λέγει) 16.
εἷς (nom.sing.masc.of εἷς, subject of λέγει) 469.

ἐκ (preposition with the genitive, partitive) 19.
τῶν (gen.pl.masc.of the article in agreement with μαθητῶν) 9.
μαθητῶν (gen.pl.masc.of μαθητής, partitive genitive) 421.
αὐτοῦ (gen.sing.masc.of αὐτός, relationship) 16.
'Ανδρέας (nom.sing.masc.of 'Ανδρέας, apposition) 388.
ὁ (nom.sing.masc.of the article in agreement with ἀδελφός) 9.
ἀδελφός (nom.sing.masc.of ἀδελφός, apposition) 15.
Σίμωνος (gen.sing.masc.of Σίμων, relationship) 386.
Πέτρου (gen.sing.masc.of Πέτρος, apposition) 387.

*Translation - "One of His disciples, Andrew, Simon Peter's brother, said to Him
. . ."*

Comment: Again John, writing to a Greek audience in Ephesus, remembers that his readers know nothing about Palestine and the people in it, so he is careful to identify each character. He had mentioned the two brothers before (John 1:40,42).

Verse 9 - "There is a lad here, which hath five barley loaves and two small fishes; but what are they among so many?"

Ἔστιν παιδάριον ὧδε ὃς ἔχει πέντε ἄρτους κριθίνους καὶ δύο ὀψάρια, ἀλλὰ ταῦτα τί ἐστιν εἰς τοσούτους;

Ἔστιν (3d.per.sing.pres.ind.of εἰμί, aoristic) 86.

#2275 παιδάριον (nom.sing.neut.of παιδάριον, subject of ἔστιν).

lad - John 6:9.

Meaning: Diminutive of παῖς (#217). Hence, a little boy; a lad. Used only by John. *Cf.*γυναικάριον in II Tim.3:6.

ὧδε (adverb of place) 766.
ὃς (nom.sing.masc.of ὅς, subject of ἔχει) 65.
ἔχει (3d.per.sing.pres.act.ind.of ἔχω, aoristic) 82.
πέντε (numeral) 1119.
ἄρτους (acc.pl.masc.of ἄρτος, direct object of ἔχει) 338.

#2276 κριθίνους (acc.pl.masc.of κρίθινος, in agreement with ἄρτους).

barley - John 6:9,13.

*Meaning: Cf.*κριθή (#5352) in Rev.6:6. Hence, here as an adjective - made of barley.

καὶ (adjunctive conjunction joining nouns) 14.
δύο (numeral) 385.

#2277 ὀψάρια (acc.pl.neut.of ὀψάριον, direct object of ἔχει).

fish - John 6:11; 21:9,10,13.
small fish - John 6:9.

Meaning: diminutive for ὄφον, which means "cooked food." Not necessarily fish, though context reveals that it means this in the New Testament. Any little delicacy which has been prepared to eat with something else - like bread. With reference to the little lad's lunch - John 6:9,11. With reference to the food in preparation by Jesus on the seashore - John 21:9,10,13.

ἀλλὰ (adversative conjunction) 342.

ταῦτα (nom.pl.neut.of οὗτος, predicate nominative) 93.

τί (nom.sing.neut.of τίς, interrogative pronoun, subject of ἔστιν) 281.

ἔστιν (3d.per.sing.pres.ind.of εἰμί, aoristic) 86.

εἰς (preposition with the accusative, original static use, like ἐν with the locative) 140.

τοσούτους (acc.pl.masc.of τοσοῦτος, original static use) 727.

Translation - "There is a little boy here who has five barley loaves and two little fish, but what are these among so many?!"

Comment: "A little child" - #2275. Used here only in the N.T. ὅς is a definite relative pronoun, with a direct attraction in case (nominative) to its antecedent (παιδάριον). The little boy had two small morsels of some sort of prepared food to eat with his bread - probably fish. ἀλλὰ is a strong adversative as is indicated by the rhetorical question which follows. To support Andrew's skepticism we have the contemptuous use of ταῦτα, here in emphasis.

John had learned his Greek grammar well during his stay in Ephesus. Note his singular ἔστιν with the neuter plural subject and predicate nominative. This is good Greek. The writer of the ἀποκάλυψις did not understand this rule. Note also the original static use of εἰς with the accusative like ἐν with the locative. Cf.#727 for other examples of τοσοῦτος with reference to numbers. Philip's skepticism was apparent in verse 7. Andrew adds his in verses 8 and 9. - "If we bought $33 worth it would not be enough." Both were being empirical about it. Five loaves and two fish were not enough. They hadn't time or money to buy more. The task of feeding the multitude was impossible. Neither of them understood that the Creator of the universe was present.

Verse 10 - "And Jesus said, Make the men sit down. Now there was much grass in the place. So the men sat down, in number about five thousand."

εἶπεν ὁ Ἰησοῦς, Ποιήσατε τοὺς ἀνθρώπους ἀναπεσεῖν. ἦν δὲ χόρτος πολὺς ἐν τῷ τόπῳ. ἀνέπεσεν οὖν οἱ ἄνδρες τὸν ἀριθμὸν ὡς πεντακισχίλιοι.

εἶπεν (3d.per.sing.aor.act.ind.of εἶπον, constative) 155.

ὁ (nom.sing.masc.of the article in agreement with Ἰησοῦς) 9.

Ἰησοῦς (nom.sing.masc.of Ἰησοῦς, subject of εἶπεν) 3.

Ποιήσατε (2d.per.pl.aor.act.impv.of ποιέω, command) 127.

τοὺς (acc.pl.masc.of the article in agreement with ἀνθρώπους) 9.

ἀνθρώπους (acc.pl.masc.of ἄνθρωπος, direct object of ποιήσατε) 341.
ἀναπεσεῖν (aor.act.inf.of ἀναπίπτω, complementary) 1184.
ἦν (3d.per.sing.imp.ind.of εἰμί,progressive description) 86.
δὲ (explanatory conjunction) 11.
χόρτος (nom.sing.masc.of χόρτος, subject of ἦν) 632.
πολὺς (nom.sing.masc.of πολύς, in agreement with χόρτος) 228.
ἐν (preposition with the locative of place where) 80.
τῷ (loc.sing.masc.of the article in agreement with τόπῳ) 9.
τόπῳ (loc.sing.masc.of τόπος, place where) 1019.
ἀνέπεσαν (3d.per.pl.aor.act.ind.of ἀναπίπτω, ingressive) 1184.
οὖν (continuative conjunction) 68.
οἱ (nom.pl.masc.of the article in agreement with ἄνδρες) 9.
ἄνδρες (nom.pl.masc.of ἀνήρ, subject of ἀνέπεσαν) 63.
τὸν (acc.sing.masc.of the article in agreement with ἀριθμὸν) 9.

#2278 ἀριθμὸν (acc.sing.masc.of ἀριθμός, accusative of measure).

number - Lk.22:3; John 6:10; Acts 4:4; 5:36; 6:7; 11:21; 16:5; Rom.9:27; Rev.5:11; 7:4; 9:16,16; 13:17,18,18,18; 15:2; 20:8.

Meaning: Number. Followed by ὡς and a number - John 6:10; Acts 4:4; 5:36; followed by a genitive of description - Lk.22:3; Acts 6:7; Rom.9:27; Rev.5:11; 9:16,16; 13:17,18a; 15:2; followed by a participle in the nominative case - Acts 11:21; in the genitive case - Rev.7:4. Absolutely in Acts 16:5; followed by a predicate nominative - Rev.13:18b. As a subject in Rev.13:18c. Followed by ὡς and a comparative clause - Rom.9:27; Rev.20:8.

ὡς (comparative adverb) 128.
πεντακισχίλιοι (nom.pl.masc.of πεντακισχίλιος, in agreement with ἄνδρες) 1125.

Translation - "*Jesus said, 'Make the men sit down.' Now there was much grass in the place. Then the men sat down the number of whom was about five thousand.*"

Comment: Matthew calls the spot ἔρημον τόπον, but John describes it as displaying a luxuriant growth of grass. ἔρημος does not mean a desert in the sense of a place devoid of moisture, but a place of solitude. *Cf.*#1184 - "to sit down but in a position commonly assumed, *i.e.* leaning upon one arm as át a table." Note ἀριθμὸν - in the accusative. The basic accusative idea of limitation - in this case limited in number to about 5000. *Cf.*#2278 for other instances of ἀριθμός followed by ὡς and a definite number. ἄνδρες means males only, not human beings in the generic sense, a meaning which ἄνθρωπος includes. Jesus told the disciples to seat everyone including the women and children. John tells us that the men in the crowd numbered about 5000. How many women and children? This data is not revealed. John's careful distinction between ἄνθρωπος and ἄνδρες is exact, precise and interesting. Meyer is astray when he says that only the men sat down. *Cf.*Mk.6:39.

Verse 11 - "And Jesus took the loaves; and when he had given thanks, he distributed to the disciples, and the disciples to them that were set down; and likewise of the fishes as much as they would."

ἔλαβεν οὖν τοὺς ἄρτους ὁ Ἰησοῦς καὶ εὐχαριστήσας διέδωκεν τοῖς ἀνακειμένοις, ὁμοίως καὶ ἐκ τῶν ὀφαρίων ὅσον ἤθελον.

ἔλαβεν (3d.per.sing.aor.act.ind.of λαμβάνω, constative) 533.
οὖν (continuative conjunction) 68.
τοὺς (acc.pl.masc.of the article in agreement with ἄρτους) 9.
ἄρτους (acc.pl.masc.of ἄρτος, direct object of ἔλαβεν) 338.
ὁ (nom.sing.masc.of the article in agreement with Ἰησοῦς) 9.
Ἰησοῦς (nom.sing.masc.of Ἰησοῦς, subject of ἔλαβεν and διέδωκεν) 3.
καὶ (adjunctive conjunction joining verbs) 14.
εὐχαριστήσας (aor.act.part.nom.sing.masc.of εὐχαριστέω, adverbial, temporal) 1185.

#2279 διέδωκεν (3d.per.sing.aor.act.ind.of διαδίδωμι, ingressive).

distribute - Lk.18:22; John 6:11.
divide - Lk.11:22.
make distribution - Acts 4:35

Meaning: A combination of δια (#118) and δίδωμι (#362). Hence to make a complete gift. To give totally, thoroughly and through (or among) all the recipients. Hence, to distribute; to divide. Jesus distributed the food to the people - John 6:11; the rich ruler was ordered to distribute his wealth to the poor - Lk.18:22. A thief divides the stolen property - Lk.11:22. With reference to economic distribution in the early church - Acts 4:35.

τοῖς (dat.pl.masc.of the article in agreement with ἀνακειμένοις) 9.
ἀνακειμένοις (pres.mid.part.dat.pl.masc.of ἀνάκειμαι, substantival, indirect object of διέδωκεν) 790.
ὁμοίως (adverbial) 1425.
καὶ (adjunctive conjunction joining nouns) 14.
ἐκ (preposition with the ablative of source) 19.
τῶν (abl.pl.neut.of the article in agreement with ὀφαρίων) 9.
ὀφαρίων (abl.pl.neut.of ὀφάριον, source) 2277.
ὅσον (acc.sing.neut.of ὅσος, direct object of διέδωκεν) 660.
ἤθελον (3d.per.pl.imp.act.ind.of θέλω, progressive duration) 88.

Translation - "Then Jesus took the loaves and when He had given thanks He began to divide them among those who were seated; similarly also of the fish (He gave) as much as they wanted."

Comment: Jesus took the loaves and gave thanks and *began to divide* (ingressive aorist in διέδωκεν) them among the people. Mt.14:19 says that Jesus did this by first giving the food to the disciples who, in turn, gave it to the people. There is no contradiction. John uses διέδωκεν (#2279). Matthew uses ἔδωκεν (#362). Jesus made the distribution; the disciples made the delivery. καὶ often follows ὁμοίως (cf.#1425) in which case it is adjunctive and is translated "also." Note the ablative of source in ἐκ τῶν ὀφαρίων. That Jesus was able to give to 10,000 people all of the fish they wanted to eat, out of an original store of only two fish is, of course, impossible. Jesus kept on feeding the people until they wanted no more. John handles this with ὅσον ἤθελον, while Matthew and Mark tell us that all ate and were filled - ἔφαγον πάντες καὶ ἐχορτάσθησαν (Mt.14:20; Mk.6:42). When one is "filled" he doesn't want anymore. No one went away hungry. Cf. also Luke 9:17.

Meyer refuses to follow other German higher critics as they explain away the miracle. Cf. his comments on Mt.14:20,21 and Lk.9:17. We have commented in the exposition of the parallel accounts on the intellectual poverty of the attempts to accept this story without also accepting the fact that the Creator created, by a special act, enough bread and fish to feed all of the people. Why cannot infidels be honest enough to say boldly and clearly that they do not believe the clear record of the text?

Verse 12 - "When they were filled, he said unto his disciples, Gather up the fragments that remain, that nothing be lost."

ὡς δὲ ἐνεπλήσθησαν λέγει τοῖς μαθηταῖς αὐτοῦ, Συναγάγετε τὰ περισσεύσαντα κλάσματα, ἵνα μή τι ἀπόληται.

ὡς (temporal conjunction, introducing a definite temporal clause) 128.

δὲ (continuative conjunction) 11.

ἐνεπλήσθησαν (3d.per.pl.aor.pass.ind.of ἐμπίπλημι, culminative) 1833.

λέγει (3d.per.sing.pres.act.ind.of λέγω, historical) 66.

τοῖς (dat.pl.masc.of the article in agreement with μαθηταῖς) 9.

μαθηταῖς (dat.pl.masc.of μαθητής, indirect object of λέγει) 421.

αὐτοῦ (gen.sing.masc.of αὐτός, relationship) 16.

Συναγάγετε (2d.per.p.pres.act.impv.of συνάγω, command) 150.

τὰ (acc.pl.neut.of the article in agreement with κλάσματα) 9.

περισσεύσαντα (aor.act.part.acc.pl.neut.of περισσεύω, adjectival, ascriptive, in agreement with κλάσματα) 473.

κλάσματα (acc.pl.neut.of κλάσμα, direct object of Συναγάγετε) 1122.

ἵνα (final conjunction introducing a purpose clause) 114.

μή (qualified negative conjunction with the subjunctive in a purpose clause) 87.

τι (indefinite pronoun, nom.sing.neut.of τις, subject of ἀπόληται) 486.

ἀπόληται (3d.per.sing.2d.aor.mid.subj.of ἀπόλλυμι, purpose) 208.

Translation - "And when they were filled He said to His disciples, 'Gather together the excess fragments in order that nothing be lost.' "

Comment: ὡς here introduces a definite temporal clause with the indicative mode in ἐνεπλήσθησαν, John's verb to match ἐχορτάσθησαν of Matthew,

Mark and Luke. (Mt.14:20; Mk.6:42; Lk.9:17). The people could not eat another bite. *Cf.*#1833. When Jesus feeds people they are filled physically and spiritually - Rom.15:24; Acts 14:17; Lk.1:53. *Cf.*#473 for a list of spiritual blessings that abound beyond our needs. Our Lord provides abundantly whether it be food or spiritual blessings. ἵνα introduces the purpose clause with the subjunctive. Jesus never loses what is His, either by right of creation or by right of redemption (John 17:12).

Verse 13 - "Therefore they gathered them together, and filled twelve baskets with the fragments of the five barley loaves, which remained over and above unto them that had eaten.

συνήγαγον οὖν, καὶ ἐγέμισαν δώδεκα κοφίνους κλασμάτων ἐκ τῶν πέντε ἄρτων τῶν κριθίνων ἃ ἐπερίσσευσαν τοῖς βεβρωκόσιν.

συνήγαγον (3d.per.pl.2d.aor.act.ind.of συνάγω, constative) 150.
οὖν (inferential conjunction) 68.
καὶ (adjunctive conjunction joining verbs) 14.
ἐγέμισαν (3d.per.pl.aor.act.ind.of γεμίζω, culminative) 1972.
δώδεκα (numeral) 820.
κοφίνους (acc.pl.masc.of κόφινος, direct object of ἐγέμισαν) 1123.
κλασμάτων (gen.pl.neut.of κλάσμα, description) 1122.
ἐκ (preposition with the ablative of source) 19.
τῶν (abl.pl.masc.of the article in agreement with ἄρτων) 9.
πέντε (numeral) 1119.
ἄρτων (abl.pl.masc.of ἄρτος, source) 338.
τῶν (abl.pl.masc.of the article in agreement with κριθίνων) 9.
κριθίνων (abl.pl.masc.of κρίθινος, in agreement with ἄρτων) 2276.
ἃ (nom.pl.neut.of ὅς, subject of ἐπερίσσευσαν) 65.
ἐπερίσσευσαν (3d.per.pl.aor.act.ind.of περισσεύω, constative) 473.
τοῖς (dat.pl.masc.of the article in agreement with βεβρωκόσιν) 9.

#2280 βεβρωκόσιν (perf.act.part.dat.pl.masc.of βιβρώσκω, personal advantage).

eat - John 6:13.

Meaning: To eat. Often in the LXX. Only here in the N.T.

Translation - "Therefore they began to gather, and they filled twelve baskets with the fragments of the five loaves of barley which were left after the people had eaten."

Comment: κόφινος (#1123) is not the type of basket they used in a later feeding miracle when Jesus fed 4000 (Mk.8:19,20) but a wicket basket carried only when the Jews were enroute to the Passover feast. *Cf.* notes on Mk.6:43. ἃ, the definite relative pronoun has a direct attraction in case to its antecedent κοφίνους.

This completes all versions of the feeding of the 5000, the only miracle reported by all four gospel writers. Review Mt.14:13-21; Mk.6:33-44; Lk.9:11-17 and John 6:1-13.

In Mt.14:22,23 (*q.v.*), John 6:14,15 and Mk.6:45,46 the disciples and the multitudes are sent away and Jesus retires for prayer. We shall take up Mark's account first.

Mark 6:45 - "And straightway he constrained his disciples to get into the ship, and to go to the other side before unto Bethsaida, while he sent away the people."

Καὶ εὐθὺς ἠνάγκασεν τοὺς μαθητὰς αὐτοῦ ἐμβῆναι εἰς τὸ πλοῖον καὶ προάγειν εἰς τὸ πέραν πρὸς Βηθσαϊδάν, ἕως αὐτὸς ἀπολύει τὸν ὄχλον.

Καὶ (continuative conjunction) 14.

εὐθὺς (adverbial) 258.

ἠνάγκασεν (3d.per.sing.aor.act.ind.of ἀναγκάζω, constative) 1126.

τοὺς (acc.pl.masc.of the article in agreement with μαθητὰς) 9.

μαθητὰς (acc.pl.masc.of μαθητής, direct object of ἠνάγκασεν) 421.

αὐτοῦ (gen.sing.masc.of αὐτός, relationship) 16.

ἐμβῆναι (aor.act.inf.of ἐμβαίνω, complementary) 750.

εἰς (preposition with the accusative of extent) 140.

τὸ (acc.sing.neut.of the article in agreement with πλοῖον) 9.

πλοῖον (acc.sing.neut.of πλοῖον, extent) 400.

καὶ (adjunctive conjunction joining infinitives) 14.

προάγειν (pres.act.inf.of προάγω, complementary) 179.

εἰς (preposition with the accusative of extent) 140.

τὸ (acc.sing.neut.of the article in agreement with πέραν) 9.

πέραν (adverbial) 375.

πρὸς (preposition with the accusative of extent) 197.

Βηθσαϊδάν (acc.sing.fem.of Βηθσαϊδα, extent) 938.

ἕως (conjunction introducing a definite temporal clause with the indicative) 71.

αὐτὸς (nom.sing.masc.of αὐτός, emphatic, subject of ἀπολύει) 16.

ἀπολύει (3d.per.sing.pres.act.ind.of ἀπολύω, historical) 92.

τὸν (acc.sing.masc.of the article in agreement with ὄχλον) 9.

ὄχλον (acc.sing.masc.of ὄχλος, direct object of ἀπολύει) 418.

Translation - "And immediately thereafter He persuaded His disciples to get into the boat and to go ahead unto the other side to Bethsaida, while He himself sent the crowd away."

Comment: καὶ εὐθὺς - Mark's distinct approach. Jesus lost no time. As soon as the fragments of food had been gathered, Jesus, very much in need of rest and relaxation which He had sought for Himself and His disciples when they came to the spot much earlier in the day, at last was free to be alone with His Father. He had suggested this short vacation when the Twelve came back from their first preaching mission (Mk.6:30-31). But before Jesus could retire to pray He had to get rid of the Disciples and the vast multitude who were still aghast at the great miracle. ἠνάγκασεν (#1126). The word implies a little more persuasion than an ordinary order. The disciples did not want to leave Him. The order is followed by two complementary infinitives. They were to get into the boat and to go ahead to the other side to Bethsaida. Meanwhile, as they were rowing across the Sea of Galilee He was going to dismiss the crowd. Note ἕως here in introduction of the definite temporal clause with the indicative in ἀπολύει. Note Mark's use of the adverb πέραν here following τό the article of the accusative of extent, following εἰς. There was less constraint in Jesus' order to the crowd (ἀπολύει) than in His order to the disciples. The people were taught; those who were sick were healed; all had been fed. But their view of Jesus was not that of the disciples. Jesus sent them away. They left without an argument, and Jesus was at last alone. The Bethsaida to which the disciples proceeded was on the west coast. Lk.9:10 says that the feeding of the multitude was at a place called Bethsaida, which was on the northeast side of Tiberias.

Verse 46 - "And when he had sent them away, he departed into a mountain to pray."

καὶ ἀποταξάμενος αὐτοῖς ἀπῆλθεν εἰς τὸ ὄρος προσεύξασθαι.

καὶ (continuative conjunction) 14.

#2281 ἀποταξάμενος (aor.mid.part.nom.sing.masc.of ἀποτάσσομαι, adverbial).

   bid farewell - Lk.9:61; Acts 18:21.
   forsake - Lk.14:33.
   send away - Mk.6:46.
   take leave of - Acts 18:18; II Cor.2:13.

Meaning: A combination of ἀπό (#70) and τάσσω (#722). Hence, to set apart; to separate; to take leave of; to say goodbye to; to forsake. Jesus dismissed the people and sent them away - Mk.6:46. With reference to leaving others and saying goodbye - Acts 18:18,21; II Cor.2:13. Of one saying goodbye to his family to follow Christ - Lk.9:61. With reference to the decision to renounce the world - Lk.14:33.

   αὐτοῖς (dat.pl.masc.of αὐτός, indirect object of ἀποταξάμενος) 16.
   ἀπῆλθεν (3d.per.sing.aor.act.ind.of ἀπέρχομαι, constative) 239.
   εἰς (preposition with the accusative of extent) 140.
   τό (acc.sing.neut.of the article in agreement with ὄρος) 9.
   ὄρος (acc.sing.neut.of ὄρος, extent) 357.
   προσεύξασθαι (aor.mid.inf.of προσεύχομαι, purpose) 544.

Translation - "And having said goodbye to them, He went away unto the mountain to pray."

Comment: Rather than use a purpose clause with ἵνα and the subjunctive, John uses the infinitive. Jesus went up upon the mountain to pray. *Cf.*#544 for a study of the prayer life of Jesus. Review the parallels in Mt. 14:22,23 and the two verses in John 6 which follow:

John 6:14 - "Then those men when they had seen the miracle that Jesus did said, This is of a truth that prophet that should come into the world."

Οἱ οὖν ἄνθρωποι ἰδόντες ὃ ἐποίησεν σημεῖον ἔλεγον ὅτι Οὗτός ἐστιν ἀληθῶς ὁ προφήτης ὁ ἐρχόμενος εἰς τὸν κόσμον.

Οἱ (nom.pl.masc.of the article in agreement with ἄνθρωποι) 9.

οὖν (inferential conjunction) 68.

ἄνθρωποι (nom.pl.masc.of ἄνθρωπος, subject of ἔλεγον) 341.

ἰδόντες (aor.act.part.nom.pl.masc.of ὁράω, adverbial, temporal, causal) 144.

ὃ (acc.pl.neut.of ὅς, attracted to σημεῖα) 65.

ἐποίησεν (3d.per.sing.aor.act.ind.of ποιέω, culminative) 127.

σημεῖα (acc.pl.neut.of σημεῖον, direct object of ἰδόντες) 1005.

ἔλεγον (3d.per.pl.imp.act.ind.of λέγω, inceptive) 66.

ὅτι (recitative) 211.

Οὗτός (nom.sing.masc.of οὗτος, deictic, subject of ἐστιν) 93.

ἀληθῶς (adverbial) 1136.

ὁ (nom.sing.masc.of the article in agreement with προφήτης) 9.

προφήτης (nom.sing.masc.of προφήτης, predicate nominative) 119.

ὁ (nom.sing.masc.of the article in agreement with ἐρχόμενος) 9.

ἐρχόμενος (pres.part.nom.sing.masc.of ἔρχομαι, substantival, apposition) 146.

εἰς (preposition with the accusative of extent) 140.

τὸν (acc.sing.masc.of the article in agreement with κόσμον) 9.

κόσμον (acc.sing.masc.of κόσμος, extent) 360.

Translation - "Therefore when (and because) the people saw the miracles which He performed they began to say, 'This man is really the Prophet who is to come into the world.' "

Comment: The miracles which Jesus performed, climaxed by the feeding of the multitude, convinced the people that He was their promised Messiah. They had in mind Deut.18:15. Enroute to Jerusalem to celebrate the Passover Feast (John 6:4), their minds were occupied with the religious question, closely allied to their nationalistic hopes, as to when the promised Deliverer would appear. Now they believe that they have found Him. This is the force of the inferential conjunction οὖν, which is supported by what had occurred as reported in John 6:1-13. The participle ἰδόντες is adverbial and can be taken both as temporal and causal. *After* (temporal) they saw Jesus' miracles and *because* (causal) they saw them, they reached the conclusion to which they began (inceptive imperfect in ἔλεγον) to give expression. ὅτι here is recitative, introducing direct discourse. Note the emphatic position of deictic οὗτός, the subject of ἐστιν while ὁ προφήτης is the predicate nominative. The substantival participle ὁ ἐρχόμενος is in apposition.

The rumor spread like wildfire among the men, women and children who comprized the company. We may be sure that when they arrived in Jerusalem they were still talking about Him. Their enthusiastic reporting served to heighten the tension which had already begun to develop between Jesus and the Jewish Establishment. The crowd's reaction to Jesus and His miracles explains

Verse 15 - "When Jesus therefore perceived that they would come and take him by force to make him a king, he departed again into a mountain himself alone."

Ἰησοῦς οὖν γνοὺς ὅτι μέλλουσιν ἔρχεσθαι καὶ ἁρπάζειν αὐτὸν ἵνα ποιήσωσιν βασιλέα ἀνεχώρησεν πάλιν εἰς τὸ ὄρος αὐτὸς μόνος.

Ἰησοῦς (nom.sing.masc.of Ἰησοῦς, subject of ἀνεχώρησεν) 3.
οὖν (inferential conjunction) 68.
γνοὺς (aor.act.part.nom.sing.masc.of γινώσκω, adverbial, causal) 131.
ὅτι (conjunction introducing an object clause in indirect discourse) 211.
μέλλουσιν (3d.per.pl.pres.act.ind.of μέλλω, progressive) 206.
ἔρχεσθαι (pres.inf.of ἔρχομαι, complementary) 146.
καὶ (adjunctive conjunction joining infinitives) 14.
ἁρπάζειν (pres.act.inf.of ἁρπάζω, complementary) 920.
αὐτὸν (acc.sing.masc.of αὐτος, direct object of ἁρπάζειν) 16.
ἵνα (final conjunction introducing a purpose clause with the subjunctive) 114.
ποιήσωσιν (3d.per.pl.aor.act.subj.of ποιέω, purpose) 127.
βασιλέα (acc.sing.masc.of βασιλεύς, predicate accusative) 31.
ἀνεχώρησεν (3d.per.sing.aor.act.ind.of ἀναχωρέω, constative) 200.
πάλιν (adverbial) 355.
εἰς (preposition with the accusative of extent) 140.
τὸ (acc.sing.neut.of the article in agreement with ὄρος) 9.
ὄρος (acc.sing.neut.of ὄρος, extent) 357.
αὐτὸς (nom.sing.masc.of αὐτός, emphatic) 16.
μόνος (nom.sing.masc.of μόνος, predicate adjective) 339.

Translation - "Jesus therefore, when He realized that they were about to come and seize Him in order to make Him a king, withdrew again into the mountain where He could be alone."

Comment: Οὖν is inferential. Jesus' decision to escape into the mountain was contingent upon His appraisal of the situation described in verse 14. ὅτι is the objective conjunction introducing indirect discourse, which, of course, carries the same tenses as it had in direct discourse. The people were saying, "They are about to come and seize Him to make Him a king." It was not some plan for future development. The people were about to come and seize Him and crown Him king immediately. Hence the need for a speedy retreat up the mountain. ἵνα and the subjunctive tells us their purpose.

Jesus had retreated before when He and His disciples had sought rest and solitude, only to find themselves unable to elude the eager people (Mt.14:13; Mk.6:33; Lk.9:11; John 6:2). Now that they are taught, healed and fed, the people insist upon forcing upon Him the Messiahship which, of course, He is entitled to enjoy. They suspected it and based their view on His miracles. He knew it, but what He also knew, which was unknown to them, was that the plan of salvation called Him first to Calvary and an empty tomb before (after 2000 years of church history) He could return to earth and take His place upon David's throne as their King (II Sam.7:12-17: Heb.1:5: Lk.1:30-33). The people were 2000 years ahead of God's schedule. This they could not have known. He, the Author of the plan, knew its every detail and hence ἀνεχώρησεν πάλιν εἰς τὸ ὄρος αὐτὸς μόνος. John alone, of the four gospel writers, gives us this detail about the Messianic intent of the people. Dispensationalism, so cruelly tortured by some Bible students and rejected out of hand by unbelievers, is nevertheless taught in scripture and only when rightly understood permits us to "rightly divide the Word." Mt.14:23 and Mk.6:46 tell us that Jesus sought the mountain solitude to pray.

We shall learn in John 6 that the current popularity which Jesus enjoyed was superficial. It was probably based upon the benefits which His healing and feeding miracles could provide. Any politician who promises to put the people on the "gravy train," who performs the economic miracle of something for nothing and who can support his campaign with a few sleight-of-hand tricks will have a following among the gullible people who ask to be deceived. The people who had just had a free meal at Jesus' creative hand were unwilling to face the moral commitments of the gospel which He preached. When He spelled it out in John 6, they decided that the cost of discipleship was too great and "... many of his disciples went back, and walked no more with him" (John 6:66). Only the Twelve Apostles, who had a deeper insight into the purpose of God and the Person and work of Jesus chose to remain at His side. Their decision was based upon the fact that there was nowhere else to turn, since Christ alone "ha(d) the words of eternal life" (John 6:67,68).

The next episode in the Crisis at Capernaum finds Jesus walking upon the water to rescue His hapless disciples from a storm. The student should review Mt.14:24-33, read in advance John 6:16-21 and now examine Mark's account in Mk.6:47-52.

Walking on the Water

(Mt.14:22-33; John 6:15-21; Mk.6:47-52)

Mark 6:47 - "And when even was come, the ship was in the midst of the sea, and he alone on the land."

καὶ ὀψίας γενομένης ἦν τὸ πλοῖον ἐν μέσῳ τῆς θαλάσσης, καὶ αὐτὸς μόνος ἐπὶ τῆς γῆς.

καὶ (continuative conjunction) 14.
ὀψίας (gen.sing.fem.of ὄψιος, genitive absolute) 739.
γενομένης (aor.part.gen.sing.fem.of γίνομαι, genitive absolute) 113.
ἦν (3d.per.sing.imp.ind.of εἰμί, progressive description) 86.
τὸ (nom.sing.neut.of the article in agreement with πλοῖον) 9.

πλοῖον (nom.sing.neut.of πλοῖον, subject of ἦν) 400.
ἐν (preposition with the locative of place where) 80.
μέσῳ (loc.sing.masc.of μέσος, place where) 873.
τῆς (gen.sing.fem.of the article in agreement with θαλάσσης) 9.
θαλάσσης (gen.sing.fem.of θάλασσα, description) 374.
καὶ (continuative conjunction) 14.
αὐτὸς (nom.sing.masc.of αὐτός, emphatic, subject of ἦν understood) 16.
μόνος (nom.sing.masc.of μόνος, predicate adjective) 339.
ἐπὶ (preposition with the genitive of place description) 47.
τῆς (gen.sing.fem.of the article in agreement with γῆς) 9.
γῆς (gen.sing.fem.of γῆ, place description) 157.

Translation - *"And when evening came the boat was in the middle of the sea and He Himself was alone upon the land."*

Comment: Note the genitive absolute ὀψίας γενομένης. When evening came it found the disciples in the boat half way across the Sea of Tiberias enroute to Bethsaida. Jesus had remained behind on the land. It had been quite a day. Jesus had gone up the hill to pray and now had returned to the shore, from which point He could see that the disciples were in trouble. They were going to need Him soon, not for food for their empty stomachs but for protection from the storm at sea that threatened to engulf them.

Verse 48 - *"And he saw them toiling in rowing: for the wind was contrary unto them: and about the fourth watch of the night he cometh unto them, walking upon the sea, and would have passed by them."*

καὶ ἰδὼν αὐτοὺς βασανιζομένους ἐν τῳ ἐλαύνειν, ἦν γὰρ ὁ ἄνεμος ἐναντίος αὐτοῖς, περὶ τετάρτην φυλακὴν τῆς νυκτὸς ἔρχεται πρὸς αὐτοὺς περιπατῶν ἐπὶ τῆς θαλάσσης. καὶ ἔθελεν παρελθεῖν αὐτούς.

καὶ (continuative conjunction) 14.
ἰδὼν (aor.act.part.nom.sing.masc.of ὁράω, adverbial, temporal) 144.
αὐτοὺς (acc.pl.masc.of αὐτός, direct object of ἰδὼν) 16.
βασανιζομένους (pres.pass.part.acc.pl.masc.of βασανίζω, adverbial, circumstantial) 719.
ἐν (preposition with the locative of time point in a temporal clause, with the infinitive) 80.
τῳ (loc.sing.neut.of the article, time point) 9.
ἐλαύνειν (pres.act.inf.of ἐλαύνω, time point, in a temporal clause) 2230.
ἦν (3d.per.sing.imp.ind.of εἰμί, progressive description) 86.
γὰρ (causal conjunction) 105.
ὁ (nom.sing.masc.of the article in agreement with ἄνεμος) 9.
ἄνεμος (nom.sing.masc.of ἄνεμος, subject of ἦν) 698.
ἐναντίος (nom.sing.masc.of ἐναντίος, predicate adjective) 1128.
αὐτοῖς (dat.pl.masc.of αὐτός, personal disadvantage) 16.
περὶ (preposition with the accusative in a time expression) 173.

τετάρτην (acc.sing.fem.of τέταρτος, in agreement with φυλακὴν) 1129.

φυλακὴν (acc.sing.fem.of φυλακή, time expression) 494.

τῆς (gen.sing.fem.of the article in agreement with νυκτὸς) 9.

νυκτὸς (gen.sing.fem.of νύξ, description) 209.

ἔρχεται (3d.per.sing.pres.ind.of ἔρχομαι, historical) 146.

πρὸς (preposition with the accusative of extent) 197.

αὐτοὺς (acc.pl.masc.of αὐτός, extent) 16.

περιπατῶν (pres.act.part.nom.sing.masc.of περιπατέω, adverbial, modal) 384.

ἐπὶ (preposition with the genitive of place description) 47.

τῆς (gen.sing.fem.of the article in agreement with θαλάσσης) 9.

θαλάσσης (gen.sing.fem.of θάλασσα, place description) 374.

καὶ (adversative conjunction) 14.

ἤθελεν (3d.per.sing.imp.act.ind.of θέλω, inceptive) 88.

παρελθεῖν (aor.inf. of παρέρχομαι, complementary) 467.

αὐτούς (acc.pl.masc.of αὐτός, direct object of παρελθεῖν) 16.

Translation - "And when He saw them straining at the oars, because the wind was blowing against them, about the fourth watch of the night He came toward them, walking about on the sea, and was thinking of passing them by."

Comment: The verse is full of interesting grammar. ἰδὼν is the temporal participle in the aorist tense. It was *after* Jesus saw them that He went out to help. The participle βασανιζομένους is also an adverb used here in a circumstantial way. Under what circumstance did Jesus see them? As they were being severely tested (the basic meaning of βασανίζω #719) as they tried to propel (the basic meaning of ἐλαύνω #2230) the boat. Hence, in this context "rowing." Hence our translation, "straining at the oars." The temporal clause consists of ἐν τῷ and the infinitive and means "while" or "during the time that." Then comes causal γὰρ as Mark tells us why the disciples were having such a hard time rowing. The wind was against them. *Cf.*II Pet.2:8 where Lot was buffeted by the opposing mores of a wicked city. Christians must always "toil at the oars" because we live in a social and philosophical environment that is unfriendly (Eph.6:12). The social, economic, philosophical and political winds are against us. *Cf.*#698 for the winds of doctrine (Eph.4:4; Jude 12) which always oppose Christian theology and ethics. *Cf.*#1128 where ἐναντίος is used of spiritual opposition to Christians, *e.g.* Acts 28:17; 26:9; I Thess.2:15; Tit.2:8.

With the appropriate and much needed warning that symbolism in exegesis is always wrong *unless what we see in symbol is exegetically clear elsewhere in scripture*, we may point out that this story is rich indeed in symbolism. Having been fed miraculously by Jesus upon the Bread from heaven (John 6:35) and ordered by Him to put out upon the troubled sea of man's sinful society (Mt.28:18-20; Acts 1:8; Mt.10:16; John 15:18; Mt.5:10-12; I Pet.4:12-16), we toil at the task of obeying Him. Our task is onerous because the winds of heretical dogma oppose us constantly. But Jesus, Who meanwhile is praying for us upon the exalted heights, is not unaware of our plight (Heb.9:24). Our Great

Shepherd, the Shepherd and Bishop of our souls (Heb.13:20; I Pet.2:25), intercedes at God's right hand, far above the storms and contrary winds of earth's troubled sea (Eph.1:20-23; Phil.2:9-11; Col.3:1; I John 2:1,2). He knows about our struggles, prays for us and eventually will come to us (Heb.9:28; 10:37), contemptuously treading beneath His feet the waves that frighten us. Christians are in the gospel boat, obeying Him, toiling at the oars, resisting contrary winds. He will come! *Cf.* comments on Mt.24:33. *Cf.*#173 for other examples of περί in a time sense.τῆς νυκτός is description of φυλακήν. The fourth watch of the night would be sometime after 2:00 A.M.

Jesus approached the boat with quiet and deliberate dignity. It was almost a saunter. He was "walking around on the sea." Now here, now there. Moving from one wave to another, like a gardener inspecting the flowers in his garden. He who had just indulged in direct creation of food was having no trouble overriding the law of gravity, since it was His law.

παρελθεῖν can be translated either as "coming near or along side" or as "coming by or coming parallel to" the boat. Jesus was already near enough to the boat that the disciples could see Him, although they thought that He was a ghost! If we take the verb to mean "bypass" we have an insight into a characteristic of Jesus, purely human and perfectly legitimate that is not often seen. He may have been teasing the disciples. Of course He did not intend to allow them to drown, but He may have thought that it would be fun to make them think that He was going on without them, thus to leave them to the tender mercies of the storm. He had already given them one demonstration of His authority over a tornade at sea (Mk.4:35-41). He who commands the winds and the waves that they obey Him was not concerned about this storm at sea, which had the disciples in jeopardy.

The violence of the wind can be gauged by the fact that from the onset of evening (ὀψίας γενομένης in verse 47) until the 4th watch (eight hours later) they had got only halfway across. John 6:19 says that they had rowed about 25 or 30 furlongs - a little more than halfway across. The lake at that point is about seven miles wide. Three and one half miles in eight hours. Slow progress. Much windy opposition. Threatening waves. Dispirited disciples. But a warchful Sovereign Lord, who may have been having a little fun at their expense, but was certain not to let them drown.

Verse 49 - "But when they saw him walking upon the sea, they supposed it had been a spirit, and cried out."

οἱ δὲ ἰδόντες αὐτὸν ἐπὶ τῆς θαλάσσης περιπατοῦντα ἔδοξαν ὅτι φάντασμά ἐστιν, καὶ ἀνέκραξαν.

οἱ (nom.pl.masc.of the article subject of ἔδοξαν and ἀνέκραξαν) 9.
δὲ (adversative conjunction) 11.
ἰδόντες (aor.act.part.nom.pl.masc.of ὁράω, adverbial, temporal) 144.
αὐτὸν (acc.sing.masc.of αὐτός, direct object of ἰδόντες) 16.
ἐπὶ (preposition with the genitive of place description) 47.
τῆς (gen.sing.fem.of the article in agreement with θαλάσσης) 9.

θαλάσσης (gen.sing.fem.of θάλασσα, place description) 374.

περιπατοῦντα (pres.act.part.acc.sing.masc.of περιπατέω, adverbial, circumstantial) 384.

ἔδοξαν (3d.per.pl.aor.act.ind.of δοκέω, constative) 287.

ὅτι (objective conjunction introducing an object clause in indirect discourse) 211.

φάντασμά (nom.sing.neut.of φάντασμα, predicate nominative) 1130.

ἐστιν (3d.per.sing.pres.ind.of εἰμί, indirect discourse) 86.

καὶ (adjunctive conjunction joining verbs) 14.

ἀνέκραξαν (3d.per.pl.aor.act.ind.of ἀνακράζω, ingressive) 2057.

Translation - "But when they saw Him walking around upon the sea they thought that it was a ghost and they began to cry out."

Comment: δὲ is adversative. The reaction of the disciples was not one of comfort. One would think that, pressed almost beyond endurance by the continued toil at the oars against the buffeting winds, the disciples would be delighted to see Jesus coming to their rescue. But He was walking around on the water! It should have been no problem for them since they had already seen so many of His miracles that they should have been surprized at nothing He did. But walking on the water?! Thus their reaction was in terms of something that their faith could handle. It was easier to believe in ghosts than to believe that Jesus could walk on the water, so they allowed their minds to follow the line of least resistance. They saw Him where? On the sea. Doing what? Walking around. Note that the verb is not πατέω - "to walk" but περιπατέω - "to walk around." And note that it is continuous present tense action. He was continuing to walk around. Strolling casually here and there, although His general line of progress was πρὸς αὐτοὺς - "toward them." A direct line of march in the direction of the struggling disciples in the boat would be expressed by πατέω (#2415), not περιπατέω (#384). Thus our Lord strolls about, demonstrating His contempt for the storm by calmly treading its waves beneath His sovereign feet. Symbolically the lesson it that as we struggle against the world's opposition with its buffeting winds of doctrine, He calmly walks with us in the midst of our distress. (I John 4:4; John 1:5; Mt.28:20). Should we think it strange and imagine Him to be a ghost and shriek in fear? The reaction of the disciples was more natural than ours should be under the same circumstances. For them His death, burial, resurrection and ascension and Pentecost and the gift of the New Testament revelation was yet future. For us these events are history. *Zeitgeist* , "the spirit of the times" would dictate that we should not judge the disciples too harshly. On the basis of what they thought they saw, they screamed! Who wouldn't?

Verse 50 - "For they all saw him, and were troubled. And immediately he talked with them, and saith unto them, Be of good cheer. It is I; be not afraid."

πάντες γὰρ αὐτὸν εἶδον καὶ ἐταράχθησαν, ὁ δὲ εὐθὺς ἐλάλησεν μετ' αὐτῶν, καὶ λέγει αὐτοῖς, Θαρσεῖτε, ἐγώ εἰμι, μὴ φοβεῖσθε.

πάντες (nom.pl.masc.of πᾶς, subject of εἶδον and ἐταράχθησαν) 67.
γάρ (causal conjunction) 105.
αὐτόν (acc.sing.masc.of αὐτός, direct object of εἶδον) 16.
εἶδον (3d.per.pl.aor.act.ind.of ὁράω, constative) 144.
καί (adjunctive conjunction joining verbs) 14.
ἐταράχθησαν (3d.per.pl.aor.pass.ind.of ταράσσω, ingressive) 149.
ὁ (nom.sing.masc.of the article, subject of ἐλάλησαν and λέγει) 9.
δέ (inferential conjunction) 11.
εὐθύς (adverbial) 258.
ἐλάλησεν (3d.per.sing.aor.act.ind.of λαλέω, ingressive) 815.
μετ' (preposition with the genitive of fellowship) 50.
αὐτῶν (gen.pl.masc.of αὐτός, fellowship) 15.
καί (adjunctive conjunction joining verbs) 14.
λέγει (3d.per.sing.pres.act.ind.of λέγω, historical) 66.
αὐτοῖς (dat.pl.masc.of αὐτός, indirect object of λέγει) 16.
Θαρσεῖτε (2d.per.pl.pres.act.impv.of θαρσέω, entreaty) 780.
ἐγώ (nom.sing.masc.of ἐγώ, subject of εἰμί) 123.
εἰμι (1st.per.sing.pres.ind.of εἰμί, aoristic) 86.
μή (qualified negative conjunction in a prohibition with the imperative) 87.
φοβεῖσθε (2d.per.pl.pres.mid.impv.of φοβέομαι, entreaty) 101.

Translation - *"Because they all saw Him and they were seized with consternation. So immediately He began to speak with them, and He said to them, 'Cheer up. I, I Am! Put away your fear.' "*

Comment: Mark explains why they cried out, as γάρ is causal. They all saw Jesus and they were upset, confused and seized with consternation (ingressive aorist). Jesus birth had caused Herod and all Jerusalem consternation. *Cf.* Mt.2:3. Now He is confusing His own disciples. Peter later warned the saints not to be confused (I Pet.3:14) because of the "hard   rowing" on the sea of sin and unbelief. It is easy for the Christian, surrounded as he is by the hellish winds and waves of unbelief, to be confused. *Cf.* Acts 15:24; Gal.1:7; 5:10, all of which use ταράσσω. Perfect love casts out fear and perfect knowledge banishes confusion. The disciples were not yet perfected. δέ is inferential. Jesus saw the need to comfort His friends, therefore He began immediately to speak to them.

Cf.#'s 66, 815. There may or may not be any fine distinction between these words in any given context. λαλέω seems in our passage to refer to the comforting solace of our Lord's cheerful and gentle voice. He comforted the disciples by the sound of His voice and He also comforted them by what He said (λέγει). Paul uses λαλέω and λέγω interchangeably in Rom.3:19 and I Cor.9:8. Or does he? There does seem to be a clear distinction in Heb.5:11, where the writer carefully uses λέγω in speaking of his difficulty in communicating with his audience. In any case, if λαλέω means sounds but not necessarily intelligible sound, while λέγω means intelligible speech, the distinction in Mk.6:50 is clear-cut. While they were shrieking in fear and confusion, He εὐθύς ἐλάλησεν - "He began to speak with them" (ingressive aorist). μετ' αὐτῶν speaks of fellowship, while λέγει αὐτοῖς is the dative of indirect object. They may or may not have understood what Jesus said when He first began to speak with them (λαλέω). The wind was howling about them and the waves were roaring, but when He said clearly Θαρσεῖτε, ἐγώ εἰμι. Μὴ φοβεῖσθε - that they understood. *Cf.*#780 for Jesus admonition for the saints to "Cheer Up!" In Mt.9:2, we have the *Cheerio!* of sins forgiven; in Mt.14:27; Mk.6:50, the *Cheerio!* of companionship in the storm, and in John 16:33 we have the *Cheerio!* of victory over the world.

Ἐγώ εἰμι is the name of Him who spoke to Moses at the bush on fire (Ex.3:14). See it again in John 4:26; 8:12; 10:7; 11:25; 14:6; 18:5,6. It was the Great I AM who tread the waves that night. Who could fear in His presence ? Hence His entreaty - "Do not go on fearing." Where Jesus is there can be no continued fear. (Ps.27:1).

Verse 51 - *"And he went up unto them into the ship; and the wind ceased; and they were sore amazed in themselves beyond measure, and wondered."*

καὶ ἀνέβη πρὸς αὐτοὺς εἰς τὸ πλοῖον, καὶ ἐκόπασεν ὁ ἄνεμος. καὶ λίαν (ἐκ περισσοῦ) ἐν ἑαυτοῖς ἐξίσταντο,

καὶ (continuative conjunction) 14.
ἀνέβη (3d.per.sing.aor.act.ind.of ἀναβαίνω, constative) 323.
πρὸς (preposition with the accusative of extent) 197.
αὐτοὺς (acc.pl.masc.of αὐτός, extent) 16.
εἰς (preposition with the accusative of extent) 140.
τὸ (acc.sing.neut.of the article in agreement with πλοῖον) 9.
πλοῖον (acc.sing.neut.of πλοῖον, extent) 400.
καὶ (continuative conjunction) 14.
ἐκόπασεν (3d.per.sing.aor.act.ind.of κοπάζω, constative) 1135.
ὁ (nom.sing.masc.of the article in agreement with ἄνεμος) 9.
ἄνεμος (nom.sing.masc.of ἄνεμος, subject of ἐκόπασεν) 698.
καὶ (inferential conjunction) 14.
λίαν (adverbial) 214.
(ἐκ) - (preposition with the ablative of comparison) 19.
(περισσοῦ) - (abl.sing.masc.of περισσός, comparison) 525.
ἐν (preposition with the locative, with plural pronouns) 80.
ἑαυτοῖς (loc.pl.masc.of ἑαυτός) 288.
ἐξίσταντο (3d.per.pl.imp.mid.ind.of ἐξίστημι, progressive description) 992.

Translation - *"And He climbed up with them into the boat, and the wind ceased; therefore they were frightened out of their wits."*

Comment: Mark's greek is hard to translate smoothly into English. The parenthetical ἐκ περισσοῦ means that their fright was of an intensity that defied measurement. The prepositonal phrase ἐν ἑαυτοῖς means that all of the disciples were smitten. The verb (#992) means "out of their wits" or "beside themselves."

Jesus had to do His own climbing as He entered the ship. The disciples were so smitten that no one gave Him a hand. The wind had had experience with Jesus before (Mk.4:39) and had learned its lesson well. There was no more wind that night. λίαν, the adverb is emphasized to give strength to ἐξίσταντο. *Cf.*#992 for the meaning of ἐξίστημι. The disciples were beside themselves - almost mentally deranged, so great was their astonishment. Again we point out that by this time they should have expected unusual behavior out of Jesus. Why, then, their astonishment? Mark explains in

Verse 52 - "For they considered not the miracle of the loaves; for their heart was hardened."

οὐ γὰρ συνῆκαν ἐπὶ τοῖς ἄρτοις, ἀλλ᾽ ἦν αὐτῶν ἡ καρδία πεπωρωμένη.

οὐ (summary negative conjunction with the indicative) 130.
γὰρ (causal conjunction) 105.
συνῆκαν (3d.per.pl.aor.act.ind.of συνίημι, culminative) 1039.
ἐπὶ (preposition with the locative, occasion) 47.
τοῖς (loc.pl.masc.of the article in agreement with ἄρτοις) 9.
ἄρτοις (loc.pl.masc.of ἄρτος, occasion) 338.
ἀλλ᾽ (alternative conjunction) 342.
ἦν (3d.per.sing.imp.ind.of εἰμί, pluperfect periphrastic) 86.
αὐτῶν (gen.pl.masc.of αὐτός, possession) 16.
ἡ (nom.sing.fem.of the article in agreement with καρδία) 9.
καρδία (nom.sing.fem.of καρδία, subject of πεπωρωμένη) 432.

#2282 πεπωρωμένη (perf.pass.part.nom.sing.fem.of πωρόω, pluperfect periphrastic).

blind - Rom.11:7; II Cor.3:14.
harden - Mk.6:52; 8:17; John 12:40.

Meaning: Cf.#2109. From πῶρος - "hard skin." Hence, prop. to cover with a hard skin. To harden. Metaphorically in the N.T. To be made obdurate. To stiffen one's resistance against persuasion. To resist acceptance of a person or a theory. With reference to Israel and her refusal to accept Jesus as Messiah in all N.T. references.

Translation - "Because they did not come to a logical conclusion about the loaves, but their heart had been made obdurate."

Comment: This is Mark's explanation as to why the disciples reacted as they did to Jesus' miraculous performance of walking on the water. They had not thought through about the miracle of the feeding of the multitude which had occurred only a few hours before. Cf.#1039 for the precise meaning. The disciples had not put it all together. They had not arrived at a logical conclusion about Jesus. If He could feed the multitude with five loaves and two fish, there was no reason to doubt that He could do whatever comes within the powers of the Creator of the universe, which certainly would include the small matter of defying the law of gravity long enough to walk upon the water. When we think in a structured fashion, we are said in modern parlance to be "getting it all together." Had the Twelve done that they would not have been frightened, but rather, might have shaken their heads in amusement and said, "What next?!"

On the contrary (ἀλλὰ) "their heart had been made hard" (#2282). The construction ἦν . . . πεπωρωμένη is a pluperfect periphrastic, consisting of the imperfect of the verb εἰμί and the perfect participle. It denotes a decidedly durative present condition as a result of a past action. At this point in the spiritual development of the disciples they chose to ignore the implications of the ministry of Jesus and thus, with it put out of their minds, they backslid to a purely natural outlook.

Mark omits the episode of Mt.14:28-31 about Peter trying to walk on the water to Jesus, his failure and Jesus' rescue. John 6:21 says that the disciples wanted to take Jesus into the boat, doubtless in reaction to Jesus' pretended attempt to pass them up (Mk.6:48). In order that we understand all of the elements of the story, in an attempt to understand how the disciples felt and why, all of the elements of the three gospel accounts (Luke does not mention it) must be put together. We turn now to John's account, written thirty years later, in John 6:16-21.

John 6:16 - "And when even was now come, his disciples went down unto the sea."

Ὡς δὲ ὀψία ἐγένετο κατέβησαν οἱ μαθηταὶ αὐτοῦ ἐπὶ τὴν θάλασσαν,

Ὡς (conjunction introducing a definite temporal clause with the indicative) 128.

δὲ (continuative conjunction) 11.

ὀψία (nom.sing.fem.of ὀψία, subj.of ἐγένετο) 739.

ἐγένετο (3d.per.sing.aor.ind.of γίνομαι, culminative) 113.

κατέβησαν (3d.per.pl.aor.act.ind.of καταβαίνω, constative) 324.

οἱ (nom.pl.masc.of the article in agreement with μαθηταὶ) 9.

μαθηταὶ (nom.pl.masc.of μαθητής, subject of κατέβησαν) 421.

αὐτοῦ (gen.sing.masc.of αὐτός, relationship) 16.

ἐπὶ (preposition with the accusative of extent) 47.

τὴν (acc.sing.fem.of the article in agreement with θάλασσαν) 9.

θάλασσαν (acc.sing.fem.of θαλάσση, extent) 374.

Translation - "And when evening came His disciples went down unto the sea."

Comment: Verse 15 tells of the crowd's desire to make Jesus a king. Vss.16 and 17 relate, not to Jesus' reaction to the popular movement, but to the departure of the disciples. They were going under orders from Jesus (Mt.14:22; Mk.6:45).

Note again as in John 6:12 the definite temporal clause introduced by ὡς and the indicative mode. Now the time is evening and upon Jesus' insistence, the Twelve go down the mountainside (κατέβησαν, # 324) to the sea. ἐπὶ with the accusative of extent - "to the sea" is followed in verse 17 by another compound verb of motion which is followed by εἰς and another accusative of extent. They went "unto" the sea (ἐπὶ) and "into" the boat

Verse 17 - "And entered into a ship, and went over the sea toward Capernaum, and it was now dark, and Jesus was not come to them."

καὶ ἐμβάντες εἰς πλοῖον ἤρχοντο πέραν τῆς θαλάσσης εἰς Καφαρναούμ. καὶ σκοτία ἤδη ἐγεγόνει καὶ οὔπω ἐληλύθει πρὸς αὐτοὺ ὁ Ἰησοῦς,

καὶ (continuative conjunction) 14.
ἐμβάντες (aor.act.part.nom.pl.masc.of ἐμβαίνω, adverbial, temporal) 750.
εἰς (preposition with the accusative of extent) 140.
πλοῖον (acc.sing.neut.of πλοῖον, extent) 400.
ἤρχοντο (3d.per.pl.imp.ind.of ἔρχομαι, inceptive) 146.
πέραν (adverbial) 375.
τῆς (gen.sing.fem.of the article in agreement with θαλάσσης) 9.
θαλάσσης (gen.sing.fem.of θάλασσα, definition) 374.
εἰς (preposition with the accusative of extent) 140.
Καφαρναούμ (acc.sing.of καφαρναούμ, extent) 370.
καὶ (continuative conjunction) 14.
σκοτία (nom.sing.fem.of σκοτία, subject of ἐγεγόνει) 378.
ἤδη (adverbial) 291.
ἐγεγόνει (3d.per.sing.pluperfect ind.of γίνομαι, consummative) 113.
καὶ (adversative conjunction) 14.
οὔπω (adverbial) 1198.
ἐληλύθει (3d.per.sing.pluperfect ind.of ἔρχομαι, consummative) 146.
πρὸς (preposition with the accusative of extent) 197.
αὐτοὺς (acc.pl.masc.of αὐτός, extent) 16.
ὁ (nom.sing.masc.of the article in agreement with Ἰησοῦς) 9.
Ἰησοῦς (nom.sing.masc.of Ἰησοῦς, subject of ἐληλύθει) 3.

Translation - "And they boarded a ship and started across the sea toward Capernaum; and darkness had already fallen, but Jesus had not yet come to them."

Comment: Following the aorist temporal participle ἐμβάντες, we have the inceptive imperfect ἤρχοντο. With the emphasis at the beginning of the action, and looking toward πέραν we can translate, "They began to come across the sea in the direction of Capernaum."
Darkness had fallen as the pluperfect ἐγεγόνει indicates and Jesus had not yet joined them as the other pluperfect ἐληλύθει indicates. Mt.14:23 says that He was on the mountain in prayer.

Verse 18 - "And the sea arose by reason of a great wind that blew."

ἥ τε θάλασσα ἀνέμου μεγάλου πνέοντος διεγείρετο.

ἥ (nom.sing.fem.of the article in agreement with θάλασσα) 9.
τε (continuative particle) 1408.
θάλασσα (nom.sing.fem.of θάλασσα, subject of διεγείρετο) 374.
ἀνέμου (gen.sing.masc.of ἄνεμος, genitive absolute) 698.

μεγάλου (gen.sing.masc.of μέγας, in agreement with ἀνέμου) 184.

πνέοντος (pres.act.part.gen.sing.masc.of πνέω, genitive absolute, adverbial, causal) 697.

διεγείρετο (3d.per.sing.imp.pass.ind.of διεγείρω, inceptive) 2208.

Translation - "And the sea, due to a strong wind blowing, began to get rough."

Comment: τε here instead of καὶ or δὲ and used alone. *Cf.*#1408 for other examples. The genitive absolute in the present tense indicates the cause for the agitation of the sea. The main verb is imperfect with emphasis upon the beginning of the action. Hence - "the sea began to be tossed" literally, since the verb is in the passive voice. A study of #2208 reveals that spiritual and intellectual as well as physical agitation can result from the winds of false doctrine that blow - *Cf.*II Pet.1:13; 3:1. *Cf.* Mt.14:24 and Mk.6:48 for parallel descriptions of the scene.

Verse 19 - "So when they had rowed about five and twenty or thirty furlongs, they see Jesus walking on the sea, and drawing nigh unto the ship: and they were afraid."

ἐληλακότες οὖν ὡς σταδίους εἴκοσι πέντε ἢ τριάκοντα θεωροῦσιν τὸν Ἰησοῦν περιπατοῦντα ἐπὶ τῆς θαλάσσης καὶ ἐγγὺς τοῦ πλοίου γινόμενον, καὶ ἐφοβήθησαν.

ἐληλακότες (perf.act.part.nom.pl.masc.of ἐλαύνω, adverbial, temporal) 2230.

οὖν (continuative conjunction) 68.

ὡς (comparative conjunction introducing a comparative clause) 128.

σταδίους (acc.pl.masc.of στάδιος, extent) 1127.

#2283 εἴκοσι (numeral with πέντε).

twenty - Lk.14:31; John 6:19; Acts 1:15; 27:28; I Cor.10:8; Rev.4:4,4,10; 5:8; 11:16; 19:4.

Meaning: twenty. Used in combination of a larger number in all cases except Acts 27:28 where it is used alone.

πέντε (numeral, with εἴκοσι) 1119.

ἢ (disjunctive particle) 465.

τριάκοντα (numeral) 1037.

θεωροῦσιν (3d.per.pl.pres.act.ind.of θεωρέω, historical) 1667.

τὸν (acc.sing.masc.of the article in agreement with Ἰησοῦν) 9.

Ἰησοῦν (acc.sing.masc.of Ἰησοῦς, direct object of θεωροῦσιν) 9.

περιπατοῦντα (pres.act.part.acc.sing.masc.of περιπατέω, adverbial, circumstantial) 384.

ἐπὶ (preposition with the genitive of place description) 47.

τῆς (gen.sing.fem.of the article in agreement with θαλάσσης, place description) 374.

θαλάσσης (gen.sing.fem.of θάλασσα, description) 374.

καὶ (adjunctive conjunction joining participles) 14.

ἐγγὺς (adverbial) 1512.

τοῦ (gen.sing.neut.of the article in agreement with πλοίου) 9.

πλοίου (gen.sing.neut.of πλοῖον, description) 400.

γινόμενον (pres.part.acc.sing.masc.of γίνομαι, adverbial, circumstantial) 113.

καὶ (inferential conjunction) 14.

ἐφοβήθησαν (3d.per.pl.aor.pass.ind.of φοβέομαι, ingressive) 101.

Translation - "And when they had rowed about three and one-half miles they saw Jesus walking around upon the sea and approaching the boat; therefore they were seized with terror."

Comment: The perfect participle ἐληλακότες indicates the position of the ship. ὁ στάδιος is equal to 606 feet and 9 inches by English measurement. Thus they were about 3 1/2 miles from Bethsaida. This squares with Mark 6:47 which says that they were ἐν μέσῳ τῆς θαλάσσης - "in the midst of the sea" or about half way across, since the sea is about seven miles wide at this point. They saw Jesus, but under a strange circumstance. He was walking around upon the sea, although His general direction brought Him closer and closer to the boat. He was not in any hurry. The continuous action of both circumstantial participles indicates that our Lord was calmly strolling about among the waves. As the breakers rolled high, so did He and as they completed the cycle He momentarily disappeared from their sight, only to rise again upon the next wave. A straightforward advance toward the boat would indicate that He was anxious to arrive before He sank. Not our Lord. The result of this most unusual phenomenon was that the disciples were seized with terror. Mk.6:52 tells us why the disciples reacted as they did. Their hearts had been hardened because they refused to think holistically about the miracle of the feeding of the five thousand.

Our experiences provide us with an opportunity to ask why and then think about it. This is the function of a rational man who is humbly and sincerely looking for more truth. It is the basis of the inductive method employed by science. But the disciples let the incident pass without giving it much thought. How one could ignore a miracle like the bread and fish feast for the multitude is difficult to understand. But the disciples did so and they paid for their intellectual sloth.

Verse 20 - "But he saith unto them, It is I; be not afraid."

ὁ δὲ λέγει αὐτοῖς, Ἐγώ εἰμι, μὴ φοβεῖσθε.

ὁ (nom.sing.masc.of the article subject of λέγει) 9.

δὲ (adversative conjunction) 11.

λέγει (3d.per.sing.pres.act.ind.of λέγω, historical) 66.

αὐτοῖς (dat.pl.masc.of αὐτός, indirect object of λέγει) 16.

Ἐγώ (nom.sing.masc.of ἐγώ, subject of εἰμί) 123.

εἰμι (1st.per.sing.pres.ind.of εἰμί, aoristic) 86.

μή (qualified negative conjunction with the imperative) 87.

φοβεῖσθε (2d.per.pl.pres.impv.of φοβέομαι, entreaty) 101.

Translation - "But He said to them, 'I Am. Put away your fears.' "

Comment:δὲ is adversative. What Jesus said to them was designed to allay the disciples' fear, expressed in ἐφοβήθησαν in verse 19. The Great I Am speaks again. *Cf.*Mk.6:50; John 4:26; Ex.3:14; John 18:5,6 and others. The present imperative translates to "Do not continue to fear", "Stop fearing," or "Put away your fears." It was at this point (Mt.14:28) that Peter tried to walk to Jesus on the water. Mark and John omit the incident.

Verse 21 - "Then they willingly received him into the ship: and immediately the ship was at the land whither they went."

ἤθελον οὖν λαβεῖν αὐτὸν εἰς τὸ πλοῖον, καὶ εὐθέως ἐγένετο τὸ πλοῖον ἐπὶ τῆς γῆς εἰς ἣν ὑπῆγον.

ἤθελον (3d.per.pl.imp.act.ind.of θέλω, inceptive) 88.

οὖν (inferential conjunction) 68.

λαβεῖν (aor.act.inf.of λαμβάνω, complementary) 533.

αὐτὸν (acc.sing.masc.of αὐτός, direct object of λαβεῖν) 16.

εἰς (preposition with the accusative of extent) 140.

τὸ (acc.sing.neut.of the article in agreement with πλοῖον) 9.

πλοῖον (acc.sing.neut.of πλοῖον, extent) 400.

καὶ (continuative conjunction) 14.

εὐθέως (adverbial) 392.

ἐγένετο (3d.per.sing.aor.ind.of γίνομαι, culminative) 113.

τὸ (nom.sing.neut.of the article in agreement with πλοῖον) 9.

πλοῖον (nom.sing.neut.of πλοῖον, subject of ἐγένετο) 400.

ἐπὶ (preposition with the genitive of place description) 47.

τῆς (gen.sing.fem.of the article in agreement with γῆς) 9.

γῆς (gen.sing.fem.of γῆ, place description) 157.

εἰς (preposition with the accusative of extent) 140.

ἣν (acc.sing.fem.of ὅς, extent) 65.

ὑπῆγον (3d.per.pl.imp.act.ind.of ὑπάγω, progressive duration) 364.

Translation - "Therefore they began to want to take Him into the boat, and immediately the boat arrived at the shore unto which they were going."

Comment: οὖν is clearly inferential. When they knew who He was (Εγώ εἰμι) they changed their minds and *became* willing (inceptive imperfect in ἤθελον) to take Jesus into the boat. Before they thought that He was a ghost and to have Him in the boat was the last thing they wanted. The boat was suddenly at the shore, at the spot they had been trying almost all night to reach. Note that the relative has no attraction in case to its antecedent γῆς, but gets its case from εἰς the preposition which precedes it. The durative action of the imperfect ὑπῆγον indicates the extent of their efforts at the oars (Mk.6:48). Note that the text does not say that Jesus entered the ship. The disciples began to want Him to come in, but the next thing we learn is that the ship is at the shore forthwith (ἐνθέως). They covered the last three and one-half miles instantly, a fact which made it unnecessary for Jesus to come on board. Mt.14:32 and Mk.5:51 however agree that Jesus actually went on board. John does not deny it, but only refers to the change of attitude of the disciples on board.

The narrative now takes us to Gennesaret and Jesus' reception there. Review Mt.14:34-36. We turn now to Mark's account of it in Mk.6:53-56.

Mark 6:53 - "And when they had passed over, they came into the land of Gennesaret, and drew to the shore."

Καὶ διαπεράσαντες ἐπὶ τὴν γῆν ἦλθον εἰς Γεννησαρὲτ καὶ προσωρμίσθησαν.

Καὶ (continuative conjunction) 14.

διαπεράσαντες (aor.act.part.nom.pl.masc.of διαπεράω, adverbial, temporal) 777.

ἐπὶ (preposition with the accusative of extent) 47.

τὴν (acc.sing.fem.of the article in agreement with γῆν) 9.

γῆν (acc.sing.fem.of γῆ, extent) 157.

ἦλθον (3d.per.pl.aor.ind.of ἔρχομαι, constative) 146.

εἰς (preposition with the accusative of extent) 140.

Γεννησαρὲτ (acc.sing.fem.of Γεννησαρέτ, extent) 1137.

καὶ (adjunctive conjunction joining verbs) 14.

#2284 προσωρμίσθησαν (3d.per.pl.aor.pass.ind.of προσορμίζω, culminative).

draw to the shore - Mk.6:53.

Meaning: A combination of πρός (#197) and ὁρμίζω, from ὅρμος - "a cord or chain." ὅρμος came to denote the inner circle of ships anchored in a circle inside a harbor; hence, an anchorage. Hence προσορμίζω means to bring a ship to anchor inside a harbor to be secured in a chain of ships. Used only in Mk.6:53.

Translation - "And when they had passed over to the land, they came to Gennesaret and dropped anchor in the harbor."

Comment: Mark gives us a more detailed account of the progress of the disciples and Jesus in the boat than does Matthew (Mt.14:34). Matthew simply says that they passed over the sea and came to shore at Gennesaret. Mark says they passed over ἐπὶ τὴν γῆν and came (ἦλθον) εἰς Γεννησαρέτ where they were anchored. The exact spot where the boat docked is not stated by any of the writers. John 6:21 says that the ship was at the shore toward which they were proceding, as a result of the miracle of transport when Jesus and Peter came on board. Were they trying to reach Gennesaret before the storm arose? It is a minor point not made clear by the writers. In any case, all agree that the ship ultimately came to rest in the harbor at Gennesaret. Moffatt translates, "On crossing over they came to land at Gennesaret and moored to the shore." Montgomery says, "When they had crossed over they landed at Gennesaret and moored to the shore." Goodspeed is better with "They crossed over to the other side and came to Gennesaret and moored the boat." The action of the clause διαπερασάντες ἐπὶ τὴν γῆν is antecedent to the action of the clause ἦλθον εἰς Γεννησαρὲτ.

As the boat tied up the curious onlookers gazed at Jesus and the disciples. What happened next is told by Mark in vss.54-56.

Verse 54 - "And when they were come out of the ship, straightway they knew him."

καὶ ἐξελθόντων αὐτῶν ἐκ τοῦ πλοίου εὐθὺς ἐπιγνόντες αὐτὸν

καὶ (continuative conjunction) 14.
ἐξελθόντων (aor.part.gen.pl.masc.of ἐξέρχομαι, genitive absolute) 161.
αὐτῶν (gen.pl.masc.of αὐτός, genitive absolute) 16.
ἐκ (preposition with the ablative of separation) 19.
τοῦ (abl.sing.neut.of the article in agreement with πλοίου) 9.
πλοίου (abl.sing.neut.of πλοῖον, separation) 400.
εὐθὺς (adverbial) 258.
ἐπιγνόντες (aor.act.part.nom.pl.masc.of ἐπιγινώσκω,adverbial, causal) 675.
αὐτὸν (acc.sing.masc.of αὐτός, direct object of ἐπιγνόντες) 16.

Translation - "And when they had left the boat, immediately the people recognized Him,"

Comment: The verse is the beginning of a long sentence which runs through the end of verse 55. The subject is understood to be the people of Gennesaret. The main verbs are περιέδραμον and ἤρξαντο. Verse 54 consists of a genitive absolute with αὐτῶν meaning Jesus and the Twelve. When they had disembarked from the boat the people in the town recognized Jesus. ἐπιγνόντες, another temporal participle which is also causal is antecedent to the main verbs of verse 55. It was when and because the natives recognized Jesus that they ran to get those who needed healing. The order of events then is (1) Jesus and the Twelve disembark; (2) the people at dockside in Gennesaret recognize Jesus; (3) they run to spread the word that Jesus is in town; (4) the sick people are carried to Him for healing. Note that ἐπιγινώσκω (#675) is perfective knowledge. They were sure that it was Jesus. No doubt about Him! Anyone who ever really sees Him will know for certain Who He is!

Verse 55 - "And ran through that whole region round about, and began to carry in beds those that were sick, where they heard he was."

περιέδραμον ὅλην τὴν χώραν ἐκείνην καὶ ἤρξαντο ἐπὶ τοῖς κραβάττοις τοὺς κακῶς ἔχοντας περιφέρειν ὅπου ἤκουον ὅτι ἐστίν.

#2285 περιέδραμον (3d.per.pl.aor.act.ind.of περιτρέχω, ingressive).

run through - Mk.6:55.

Meaning: A combination of περί (#173) and τρέχω (#1655). Hence, to run around; to run hither and yon, here and there. With reference to the frantic excitement created among the people in Gennesaret when Jesus arrived - Mk.6:55. Followed by the accusative of extent.

ὅλην (acc.sing.fem.of ὅλος, in agreement with χώραν) 112.
τὴν (acc.sing.fem.of the article in agreement with χώραν) 9.
χώραν (acc.sing.fem.of χώρα, extent after περί) 201.
ἐκείνην (acc.sing.fem.of ἐκεῖνος, in agreement with χώραν) 246.
καὶ (adjunctive conjunction joining verbs) 14.
ἤρξαντο (3d.per.pl.1st.aor.mid.ind.of ἄρχω, ingressive) 383.
ἐπὶ (preposition with the locative of place where) 47.
τοῖς (loc.pl.masc.of the article in agreement with κραβάττοις) 9.
κραβάττοις (loc.pl.masc.of κράββατος, place where) 2077.
τοὺς (acc.pl.masc.of the article in agreement with ἔχοντας) 9.
κακῶς (adverbial) 411.
ἔχοντας (pres.act.part.acc.pl.masc.of ἔχω, substantival, direct object of περιφέρειν) 82.

#2286 περιφέρειν (pres.act.inf.of περιφέρω, complementary).

bear about - II Cor.4:10.
carry about - Mk.6:55; Eph.4:14.

Meaning: A combination of περί (#173) and φέρω (#683). To carry around. To transport from one place to another. With reference to the sick being carried by others who were seeking Jesus for healing - Mk.6:55; in a metaphorical sense, of being influenced intellectually by various opposing theories - Eph.4:14. With reference to Paul carrying in his body the scars inflicted upon him by his persecutors - II Cor.4:10.

ὅπου (relative adverb in an indefinite local clause with the indicative) 592.
ἤκουον (3d.per.pl.imp.act.ind.of ἀκούω, in an indefinite local clause) 148.
ὅτι (objective conjunction in indirect discourse) 211.
ἔστιν (3d.per.sing.pres.ind.of εἰμί, indirect discourse) 86.

Translation - ". . . and they began to run around throughout that entire countryside and they began to carry with them upon their pallets those who were sick wherever they had heard that He was."

Comment: The reason for the frenetic activity of the citizens was that they had recognized Jesus as soon as He left the boat. His reputation as a healer had gone before Him. The natives *began* (inceptive imperfect in περιέδραμον) to run hither and thither and they *began* (ingressive aorist in ἤρξαντο) to carry with them those who needed healing. Their search for the sick extended to the entire region. Their method of transport was ἐπὶ τοῖς κραβάττοις - "upon their pallets." That was the only way to get the sick to Jesus. The local clause with ὅπου is indefinite, even though the indicative mode is used in ἤκουον because the action described took place before Mark wrote about it. "The indicative is used in *indefinite* (Mantey's emphasis) local clauses when the action took place prior to the writing, but the subjunctive occurs when the action is expected to take place in the future. . . " (Mantey, *Manual*, 278). The people took the sick with them upon their pallets until they found Jesus. They depended upon local gossip to tell them where Jesus might be found. That this involved a great deal of trouble and some expense is proof that the people had great faith that *if* they could get the sick to Jesus, He certainly could and would heal them. We are reminded of the men who let the invalid down through a hole in the roof (Mk.2:1-5). *Cf.*#2077 for the difference between κράββτος and κλινή (#779). περιφέρειν indicates an uncertainty as to where they should go with the sick. It depended upon the latest report as to where Jesus could be found. ὅτι introduces indirect discourse, with the tense of ἐστίν the same as in direct. The people were saying, "Jesus is here" or "Jesus is there." It must have been a frustrating experience for the healthy people who were trying to help. Mass confusion for a noble purpose. The result was that wherever Jesus went He found the sick awaiting His arrival, as we learn in

Verse 56 - "And whithersoever he entered, into villages or cities, or country, they laid the sick in the streets, and besought him that they might touch if it were but the border of his garment: and as many as touched him were made whole."

καὶ ὅπου ἂν εἰσεπορεύετο εἰς κώμας ἢ εἰς πόλεις ἢ εἰς ἀγροὺς ἐν ταῖς ἀγοραῖς ἐτίθεσαν τοὺς ἀσθενοῦντας, καὶ παρεκάλουν αὐτὸν ἵνα κἂν τοῦ κρασπέδου τοῦ ἱματίου αὐτοῦ ἅψωνται, καὶ ὅσοι ἂν ἥψαντο αὐτοῦ ἐσῴζοντο.

καὶ (inferential conjunction) 14.

ὅπου (relative adverb in an indefinite local clause with the indicative) 592.

ἂν (conditional particle in an indefinite local clause) 205.

εἰσεπορεύετο (3d.per.sing.imp.ind.of εἰσπορεύομαι, inceptive) 1161.

εἰς (preposition with the accusative of extent) 140.

κώμας (acc.pl.fem.of κώμη, extent) 834.

ἢ (disjunctive conjunction) 465.

εἰς (preposition with the accusative of extent) 140.

πόλεις (acc.pl.masc.of πόλις, extent) 243.

ἢ (disjunctive conjunction) 465.

εἰς (preposition with the accusative of extent) 140.

ἀγροὺς (acc.pl.masc.of ἀγρός, extent) 626.

ἐν (preposition with the locative of place where) 80.

ταῖς (loc.pl.fem.of the article in agreement with ἀγοραῖς) 9.

ἀγοραῖς (loc.pl.fem.of ἀγορά, place where) 924.

ἐτίθεσαν (3d.per.pl.imp.act.ind.of τίθημι, progressive duration) 455.

τοὺς (acc.pl.masc.of the article in agreement with ἀσθενοῦντας) 9.

ἀσθενοῦντας (pres.act.part.acc.pl.masc.of ἀσθενέω, substantival, direct object of ἐτίθεσαν) 857.

καὶ (adjunctive conjunction joining verbs) 14.

παρεκάλουν (3d.per.pl.imp.act.ind.of παρακαλέω progressive duration) 230.

αὐτὸν (acc.sing.masc.of αὐτός, direct object of παρεκάλουν) 16.

ἵνα (final conjunction introducing a purpose clause) 114.

κἂν (conditional particle with the subjunctive) 1370.

τοῦ (gen.sing.neut.of the article in agreement with κρασπέδου) 9.

κρασπέδου (gen.sing.neut.of κράσπεδον, definition) 823.

τοῦ (gen.sing.neut.of the article in agreement with ἱματίου) 9.

ἱματίου (gen.sing.neut.of ἱμάτιον, definition) 534.

αὐτοῦ (gen.sing.masc.of αὐτός, possession) 16.

ἅφωνται (3d.per.pl.aor.act.subj.of ἅπτω, third-class condition) 711.

καὶ (continuative conjunction) 14.

ὅσοι (nom.pl.masc.of the relative pronoun ὅσος, subject of ἥφαντο and ἐσώζοντο) 660.

ἂν (conditional particle in an indefinite relative clause) 205.

ἥφαντο (3d.per.pl.aor.mid.ind.of ἅπτω, indefinite relative clause) 711.

αὐτοῦ (gen.sing.masc.of αὐτός, description) 16.

ἐσώζοντο (3d.per.pl.imp.pass.ind.of σώζω, progressive description) 109.

Translation - "*Therefore wherever He entered into villages or into cities or into rural areas, they were laying the sick in the market places, and they were begging Him for permission to touch the hem of His garment. And whoever touched Him was saved.*"

Comment: Mark uses ἂν twice to introduce speculation as to where Jesus went and who was fortunate enough to get close enough to touch Him. Wherever He went and whoever was there and touched Him, was healed. The imperfect tenses are always significant. Remember that if there is no special point to be made about the action in past time, the aorist tense is used. Even when the aorist is used the time element comes, not from the aorist stem, which reveals nothing, but from the augment. It follows therefore that when past time action is expressed either by the imperfect or the perfect, the exegete should look for something special. In other words the imperfect or perfect tenses are used only when there is a special reason for doing so. Jesus was going everywhere in the region, as is indicated by the imperfect tense in εἰσεπορεύετο. In and out of villages, cities and fields, constantly on the move, our Lord made His way and wherever He went He found the sick there waiting for His help. The strong continued to place the sick before Him (imperfect tense in ἐτίθεσαν). Also they continued to ask Him (imperfect tense in παρεκάλουν) for permission to touch the hem of His garment. Some did touch and were healed.

For the full effect of this graphic picture verses 54,55 and 56 should be read in a single breath! The disciples and Jesus leave the boat and step out upon the shore; some people recognize Jesus immediately; the rumor spreads; runners begin to scurry in all directions to bring the sick; confusion abounds as rumors fly about as to where Jesus is and where He is going next; strong men carry sick people on their pallets. Wherever Jesus goes, whether in the small villages, the larger cities or into the fields the scene is the same. The marketplace is full. Voices clamor for attention. Eager hands reach out. Some touch Him, are healed and rejoice.

Others fail to reach Him in the crush of people and are carried away in disappointment. Review again the parallel account in Mt.14:35-36. αὐτοῦ in the last clause refers not to the hem of His garment but to Jesus Himself. Meyer remarks, "They were saved, no matter where they touched him."

We turn now to the discourse of Jesus on the Bread of Life in John 6:22-71 where He made the eternal spiritual application to temporal and physical facts.

Jesus the Bread of Life

John 6:22 - "The day following, when the people which stood on the other side of the sea saw that there was none other boat there, save that one whereinto his disciples were entered, and that Jesus went not with his disciples into the boat, but that his disciples were gone away alone, . . . "

Τῇ ἐπαύριον ὁ ὄχλος ὁ ἑστηκὼς πέραν τῆς θαλάσσης εἶδον ὅτι πλοιάριον ἄλλο οὐκ ἦν ἐκεῖ εἰ μὴ ἕν, καὶ ὅτι οὐ συνεισῆλθεν τοῖς μαθηταῖς αὐτοῦ ὁ Ἰησοῦς εἰς τὸ πλοῖον ἀλλὰ μόνοι οἱ μαθηταὶ αὐτοῦ ἀπῆλθον,

Τῇ (loc.sing.fem.of the article, time point) 9.
ἐπαύριον (adverbial) 1680.
ὁ (nom.sing.masc.of the article in agreement with ὄχλος) 9.
ὄχλος (nom.sing.masc.of ὄχλος, subject of εἶδον) 418.
ὁ (nom.sing.masc.of the article in agreement with ἑστηκὼς) 9.
ἑστηκὼς (perf.act.part.nom.sing.masc.of ἵστημι, adjectival, restrictive) 180.
πέραν (adverbial) 375.
τῆς (gen.sing.fem.of the article in agreement with θαλάσσης) 9.
θαλάσσης (gen.sing.fem.of θάλασσα, description) 374.
εἶδον (3d.per.sing.aor.ind.of ὁράω, constative) 144.
ὅτι (conjunction introducing an object clause) 211.
πλοιάριον (nom.sing.neut.of πλοιάριον, subject of ἦν) 2112.
ἄλλο (nom.sing.neut.of ἄλλος in agreement with πλοιάριον) 198.
οὐκ (summary negative conjunction with the indicative) 130.
ἦν (3d.per.sing.imp.ind.of εἰμί, progressive description) 86.
ἐκεῖ (adverbial) 204.
εἰ (conditional particle with μή) 337.
μὴ (qualified negative conjunction in a conditional clause) 87.
ἕν (nom.sing.neut.of εἷς, subject of ἦν) 469.
καὶ (adjunctive conjunction joining object clauses) 14.
ὅτι (conjunction introducing an object clause) 211.
οὐ (summary negative conjunction with the indicative) 130.

#2287 συνεισῆλθεν (3d.per.sing.aor.ind.of συνεισέρχομαι, constative).

go into with - John 6:22.
go in with - John 18:15.

Meaning: A combination of σύν (#1542), εἰς (#140) and ἔρχομαι (#146). Hence, to go in with. Followed by εἰς τὸ πλοῖον in John 6:22; by εἰς τὴν αὐλὴν τοῦ ἀρχιερέως in John 18:15.

τοῖς (instrumental pl.masc.of the article in agreement with μαθηταῖς) 9.

μαθηταῖς (instrumental pl.masc.of μαθητής, association) 421.

αὐτοῦ (gen.sing.masc.of αὐτός, relationship) 16.

ὁ (nom.sing.masc.of the article in agreement with Ἰησοῦς) 9.

Ἰησοῦς (nom.sing.masc.of Ἰησοῦς, subject of συνεισῆλθεν) 3.

εἰς (preposition with the accusative of extent) 140.

τὸ (acc.sing.neut.of the article in agreement with πλοῖον) 9.

πλοῖον (acc.sing.neut.of πλοῖον, extent) 400.

ἀλλὰ (alternative conjunction) 342.

μόνοι (nom.pl.masc.of μόνος, in agreement with μαθηταὶ, predicate adjective) 339.

οἱ (nom.pl.masc.of the article in agreement with μαθηταὶ) 9.

μαθηταὶ (nom.pl.masc.of μαθητής, subject of ἀπῆλθον) 421.

ἀπῆλθον (3d.per.pl.aor.ind.of ἀπέρχομαι, constative) 239.

Translation - "The next day the crowd standing on the other side of the sea saw that there was no other boat there except one, and that Jesus had not got into the ship with His disciples, but that the disciples only had gone away . . . "

Comment: ὁ ὄχλος ὁ ἑστηκὼς πέραν τῆς θαλάσσης - note the emphatic attributive position of the perfect participle ἑστηκὼς - "the crowd *viz* the one that *had stood* (perfect tense) on the other side of the sea. . . " On the other side from the standpoint of Gennesaret where Jesus and the disciples now were. The time is the next morning after the storm. During the night while the disciples were toiling in the waves and Jesus was praying upon the mountain, the people in Bethsaida had probably had a good night's sleep. But the next morning they came back to the shore and they were still there, looking for Jesus, Who is now, with His disciples at Gennesaret carrying on another fantastic healing ministry (Mk.6:56). The people in Bethsaida saw two things introduced by the two object clauses, each introduced by ὅτι. First, that there was only one little boat there, the disciples having embarked in the larger ship on the previous evening, and Second, that Jesus had not gone into the boat with His disciples. This second fact must have been known from their knowledge of what had taken place the evening before. The disciples had taken the only ship big enough to accommodate those who wished to go. All they had was the little boat, but we learn in verse 23 that there were other ships not far away. Note John's distinction between τὸ πλοῖον which the disciples took and τὸ πλοιάριον, the smaller boat which was still there. They deduced that the disciples were across the sea, but they had no way of knowing where Jesus was since the events of the night before were unknown to them. They wished to follow and seek Jesus but could not because only one small boat was available, clearly insufficient in size to carry across Tiberias all who wished to go. The problem was solved in

Verse 23 - "Howbeit there came other boats from Tiberias night unto the place

where they did eat bread, after that the Lord had given thanks."

ἄλλα ἦλθεν πλοῖα ἐκ Τιβεριάδος ἐγγὺς τοῦ τόπου ὅπου ἔφαγον τὸν ἄρτον (εὐχαριστήσαντος τοῦ κυρίου).

ἄλλα (nom.pl.neut.of ἄλλος, in agreement with πλοῖα) 198.

ἦλθεν (3d.per.sing.aor.ind.of ἔρχομαι, culminative) 146.

πλοῖα (nom.pl.neut.of πλοῖον, subject of ἦλθεν) 400.

ἐκ (preposition with the ablative of source) 19.

Τιβεριάδος (ablative sing.masc.of Τιβέριας, source) 1929.

ἐγγὺς (adverb of place) 1512.

τοῦ (gen.sing.masc.of the article in agreement with τόπου) 9.

τόπου (gen.sing.masc.of τόπος, place description) 1019.

ὅπου (relative adverb of place introducing a definite local clause) 592.

ἔφαγον (3d.per.pl.aor.act.ind.of ἐσθίω, constative) 610.

τὸν (acc.sing.masc.of the article in agreement with ἄρτον) 9.

ἄρτον (acc.sing.masc.of ἄρτος, direct object of ἔφαγον) 338.

εὐχαριστήσαντος (aor.act.part.gen.sing.masc.of εὐχαριστέω, genitive absolute) 1185.

τοῦ (gen.sing.masc.of the article in agreement with κυρίου) 9.

κυρίου (gen.sing.masc.of κύριος, genitive absolute) 97.

Translation - "However ships came off Tiberias, near the place where they ate the bread after the Lord had given thanks."

Comment: It is not necessary to believe that the entire crowd of 5000 had returned to the shore or had remained throughout the night, but a large crowd nevertheless stood helplessly on the shore wishing to go in search of Jesus. But there was only one little boat available (πλοιάριον). However other boats were landing nearby, as the morning traffic on the Lake began to move. Note John's proper Greek grammar as he joins a singular verb with a neuter plural subject (ἄλλος ἦλθεν πλοῖα). John who had spent thirty years in Ephesus before writing the Gospel had refined his Greek. Note the definite local clause in ὅπου and the indicative in ἔφαγον. The genitive absolute at the end is tacked on almost as an afterthought. John wishes his audience to remember that the miraculous multiplication of loaves and fish was the work of Jesus Who had taken proper steps to thank God for it. Verse 23 is a parenthesis between vss. 22 and 24 in a complicated bit of Greek rhetoric, very unlike John, who is trying to explain precisely what the problem was. The people never would have found Jesus and the remainder of John 6 might never have been spoken except for the fact that the people took advantage of the greater availability of ships as normal shipping business began.

Verse 24 - "When the people therefore saw that Jesus was not there, neither his disciples, they also took shipping and came to Capernaum, seeking for Jesus."

ὅτε οὖν εἶδεν ὁ ὄχλος ὅτι Ἰησοῦς οὐκ ἔστιν οὐδὲ οἱ μαθηταὶ αὐτοῦ, ἐνέβησαν αὐτοὶ εἰς τὰ πλοιάρια καὶ ἦλθον εἰς Καφαρναοὺμ ζητοῦντες τὸν Ἰησοῦν. Ἰησοῦν.

ὅτε (temporal conjunction introducing a definite temporal clause) 703.

οὖν (inferential conjunction) 68.

εἶδεν (3d.per.sing.aor.act.ind.of ὁράω, constative) 144.

ὁ (nom.sing.masc.of the article in agreement with ὄχλος) 9.

ὄχλος (nom.sing.masc.of ὄχλος, subject of εἶδεν and ἐνέβησαν) 418.

ὅτι (conjunction introducing an object clause in indirect discourse) 211.

Ἰησοῦς (nom.sing.masc.of Ἰησοῦς, subject of ἔστιν) 3.

οὐκ (summary negative conjunction with the indicative) 130.

ἔστιν (3d.per.sing.pres.ind.of εἰμί, aoristic) 86.

ἐκεῖ (adverb of place) 204.

οὐδὲ (disjunctive particle) 452.

οἱ (nom.pl.masc.of the article in agreement with μαθηταὶ) 9.

μαθηταὶ (nom.pl.masc.of μαθητής, subject of εἰσίν, understood) 421.

αὐτοῦ (gen.sing.masc.of αὐτός, relationship) 16.

ἐνέβησαν (3d.per.pl.aor.act.ind.of ἐμβαίνω, ingressive) 750.

αὐτοὶ (nom.pl.masc.of αὐτός, emphatic, subject of ἐνέβησαν and ἦλθον) 16.

εἰς (preposition with the accusative of extent) 140.

τὰ (acc.pl.neut.of the article in agreement with πλοιάρια) 9.

πλοιάρια (acc.pl.neut.of πλοιάριον, extent) 2112.

καὶ (adjunctive conjunction joining verbs) 14.

ἦλθον (3d.per.pl.aor.ind.of ἔρχομαι, constative) 146.

εἰς (preposition with the accusative of extent) 140.

Καφαρναούμ (acc.sing.fem.of Καφαρναούμ, extent) 370.

ζητοῦντες (pres.act.part.nom.pl.masc.of ζητέω, adverbial, telic) 207.

τὸν (acc.sing.masc.of the article in agreement with Ἰησοῦν) 9.

Ἰησοῦν (acc.sing.masc.of Ἰησοῦς, direct object of ζητοῦντες) 3.

Translation - "*When therefore the crowd realized that Jesus was not there, nor were His disciples, they themselves went on board the little boats and they came to Capernaum in search of Jesus.*"

Comment: John is still struggling with the complicated sentence, after having introduced the parenthetical clauses of verse 23. He reviews in part what he said in verse 22. They realized that Jesus was not there; nor were His disciples. One thing was changed. At first there was only one little boat (vs.22); now there are many, the morning lake traffic having arrived from off the lake. Note that the word is verse 23 is πλοῖα (a large ship) while in verse 24 they embarked in πλοιάρια (little boats). Apparently both types arrived and the people, not permitted to take the larger ships, availed themselves of several smaller boats. This indicates that the sea was calm, after the cold front which caused the storm of the night before. Otherwise small craft would have been unsafe in choppy seas. The flotilla of small boats, crowded with people, crossed over and came to Capernaum, where they disembarked and went about, here and there (present tense in the participle) in search of Jesus. Their search did not go unrewarded as we see in

Verse 25 - "*And when they had found him on the other side of the sea, they said*

unto him, Rabbi, when comest thou hither?"

καὶ εὑρόντες αὐτὸν πέραν τῆς θαλάσσης εἶπον αὐτῷ, Ῥαββί, πότε ὧδε γέγονας;

καὶ (continuative conjunction) 14.

εὑρόντες (2d.aor.act.part.nom.pl.masc.of εὑρίσκω, adverbial, temporal) 79.

αὐτὸν (acc.sing.masc.of αὐτός, direct object of εὑρόντες) 16.

πέραν (adverbial) 375.

τῆς (gen.sing.fem.of the article in agreement with θαλάσσης) 9.

θαλάσσης (gen.sing.fem.of θάλασσα, description) 374.

εἶπον (3d.per.sing.aor.act.ind.of εἶπον, constative) 155.

αὐτῷ (dat.sing.masc.of αὐτός, indirect object of εἶπον) 16.

Ῥαββί (voc.sing.masc.of Ῥαββί, address) 1443.

πότε (direct interrogative adverb) 1233.

ὧδε (an adverb of place) 766.

γέγονας (2d.per.sing.perf.impv.of γίνομαι, consummative) 113.

Translation - "And when they found Him on the other side of the sea they said to Him, 'Rabbi, since when have you been here?"

Comment: They found Him across the sea, after which they asked Him the question. In view of their deductions of vss.22-24 they should not have expected to find Him in Gennesaret. The disciples had taken the ship the night before and they knew that Jesus had not gone with them. The next morning they found the ship gone but the little boat still moored at Bethsaid. They knew nothing about Jesus' walk upon the water. Thus they could only deduce that Jesus had walked around the north end of the lake during the night, since they knew that He did not take the little boat. Their search had led them across the lake, although logic dictated that it was a fruitless search. But they found Him and asked what Jesus probably regarded as an impertinent question, since He did not choose to answer it. If He had told them they would not have believed it. πότε ὧδε γέγονας - the perfect tense translates "at what time in the past did you arrive here as a result of which you are now present?"- a present situation as a result of a past completed action. It comes down in loose translation to "When did you come?" "How long have you been here?" Implicit in the question is another - "How did you get over here?" Wicked and ignorant presumption, since it implies that Jesus was bound to time and space as were they. And yet they were asking this of One Who had created enough bread and fish to feed 10,000 people! They should have been ready to believe that He could do anything in anyway He wished. They were still evaluating Jesus as if He were only a man. Apparently they had had the same heart hardening experience as did the disciples (Mk.6:52).

Jesus replied, not by answering their question, but with a penetrating and devastating analysis of their motives for coming and then introduced them to some of the greatest depths of theological truth in the entire body of Christian revelation. Verses 26-71 give us the sum and substance of Christian theology in its greatest depths and broadest sweep and scope. All restraints are off. Jesus unloaded the whole truth upon them. After this speech there is no turning back. The Incarnate Deity is out in the open with His entire program of redemption. Bengel says of the people's question to Jesus, *"quaestro de tempore includit quaestionem de modo"* - "The question of *when* included the question of *how*."

Verse 26 - "Jesus answered them and said, Verily, verily I say unto you, Ye seek me not because ye saw the miracles but because ye did eat the loaves and were filled."

ἀπεκρίθη αὐτοῖς ὁ Ἰησοῦς καὶ εἶπεν, Ἀμὴν ἀμὴν λέγω ὑμῖν, ζητεῖτέ με οὐχ ὅτι εἴδετε σημεῖα ἀλλ' ὅτι ἐφάγετε ἐκ τῶν ἄρτων καὶ ἐχορτάσθητε.

ἀπεκρίθη (3d.per.sing.aor.ind.of ἀποκρίνομαι, constative) 318.
αὐτοῖς (dat.pl.masc.of αὐτός, indirect object of ἀπεκρίθη) 16.
ὁ (nom.sing.masc.of the article in agreement with Ἰησοῦς) 9.
Ἰησοῦς (nom.sing.masc.of Ἰησοῦς, subject of ἀπεκρίθη and εἶπεν) 3.
καὶ (adjunctive conjunction joining verbs) 14.
εἶπεν (3d.per.sing.aor.act.ind.of εἶπον, constative) 155.
Ἀμὴν (explicative) 466.
ἀμὴν (explicative) 466.
λέγω (1st.per.sing.pres.act.ind.of λέγω, aoristic) 66.
ὑμῖν (dat.pl.masc.of σύ, indirect object of λέγω) 104.
ζητεῖτε (2d.per.pl.pres.act.ind.of ζητέω, aoristic) 207.
με (acc.sing.masc.of ἐγώ, direct object of ζητεῖτε) 123.
οὐχ (summary negative conjunction with the indicative) 130.
ὅτι (causal conjunction introducing a causal clause) 211.
εἴδετε (2d.per.pl.aor.act.ind.of ὁράω, constative) 144.
σημεῖα (acc.pl.neut.of σημεῖον, direct object of εἴδετε) 1005.
ἀλλ' (alternative conjunction) 342.
ὅτι (causal conjunction introducing a causal clause) 211.
ἐφάγετε (2d.per.pl.aor.act.ind.of ἐσθίω, constative) 610.
ἐκ (preposition with the ablative of source) 19.
τῶν (abl.pl.masc.of the article in agreement with ἄρτων) 9.
ἄρτων (abl.pl.masc.of ἄρτος, source) 338.
καὶ (adjunctive conjunction joining verbs) 14.
ἐχορτάσθητε (2d.per.pl.aor.pass.ind.of χορτάζω, culminative) 428.

Translation - "In reply Jesus said to them, 'Truly, truly I am telling you, you are looking for me not because you saw miracles, but because you ate of the loaves and you were filled.' "

Comment: Jesus' reply to their presumptuous question has an element of asperity. They were impertinent in asking it. Jesus is keenly perceptive in diagnosis, eloquently articulate in formulation and brutally frank. Montgomery translates Ἀμὴν ἀμὴν - "in solemn truth." "You are looking for me . . . οὐχ ὅτι . . . ἀλλ' ὅτι . . " Not for the reason that you want me to think but for the real reason. "Not because . . . but because . . κ.τ.λ." They had seen His signs but they had also gorged upon the bread and fish which he multiplied in creation.

The diagnosis sets the stage for the sermon which He gave them, without answering the question that arose from their vulgar curiosity as to how He got across the lake. Their concern was for the material welfare of their stomachs and also for their desire to see him perform "stunts." They probably asked one another after their meal the evening before, "How do you suppose he did that?"

Should they not have reasoned that the man who could do such miracles was the Son of God incarnate, the Messiah of Israel, and should they not therefore have been concerned, not with their stomachs, but with their need for spiritual awakening and nourishment?

The primacy of the spiritual over the physical is the opening theme of His discourse.

Nicodemus (John 3:2) reasoned correctly from Jesus' signs to a valid conclusion about Jesus' personality and status. The people in Capernaum did not make the leap in logic. Jesus' opening remarks and the argument which followed occupies us throughout the remainder of the chapter.

Verse 27 - "Labour not for the meat which perisheth, but for the meat which endureth unto everlasting life, which the Son of Man shall give ynto you; for him hath God the Father sealed."

ἐργάζεσθε μὴ τὴν βρῶσιν τὴν ἀπολλυμένην ἀλλὰ τὴν βρῶσιν τὴν μένουσαν εἰς ζωὴν αἰώνιον, ἣν ὁ υἱὸς τοῦ ἀνθρώπου ὑμῖν δώσει, τοῦτον γὰρ ὁ πατὴρ ἐσφράγισεν ὁ θεός.

ἐργάζεσθε (2d.per.pl.pres.impv.of ἐργάζομαι, command) 691.

μὴ (qualified negative conjunction in a prohibition, with the imperative) 87.

τὴν (acc.sing.fem.of the article in agreement with βρῶσιν) 9.

βρῶσιν (acc.sing.fem.of βρῶμα, direct object of ἐργάζεσθε) 1118.

τὴν (acc.sing.fem.of the article in agreement with ἀπολλυμένην) 9.

ἀπολλυμένην (pres.mid.part.acc.sing.fem.of ἀπόλλυμι, adjectival, restrictive) 208.

ἀλλὰ (alternative conjunction) 342.

τὴν (acc.sing.fem.of the article in agreement with βρῶσιν) 9.

βρῶσιν (acc.sing.fem.of βρῶμα, direct object of ἐργάζεσθε) 1118.

τὴν (acc.sing.fem.of the article in agreement with μένουσαν) 9.

μένουσαν (pres.act.part.acc.sing.fem.of μένω, adjectival, restrictive) 864.

εἰς (preposition with the accusative, purpose) 140.

ζωὴν (acc.sing.fem.of ζωή, purpose) 668.

αἰώνιον (acc.sing.fem.of αἰώνιος, in agreement with ζωὴν) 1255.

ἣν (relative pronoun, direct object of δώσει) 65.

ὁ (nom.sing.masc.of the article in agreement with υἱὸς) 9.

υἱὸς (nom.sing.masc.of υἱός, subject of δώσει) 5.

τοῦ (gen.sing.masc.of the article in agreement with ἀνθρώπου) 9.

ἀνθρώπου (gen.sing.masc.of ἄνθρωπος, definition) 341.

ὑμῖν (dat.pl.masc.of σύ, indirect object of δώσει) 104.

δώσει (3d.per.sing.fut.act.ind.of δίδωμι, predictive) 362.

τοῦτον (acc.sing.masc.of οὗτος, direct object of ἐσφράγισεν) 93.

γὰρ (causal conjunction) 105.

ὁ (nom.sing.masc.of the article in agreement with πατήρ) 9.

πατήρ (nom.sing.masc.of πατήρ, subject of ἐσφράγισεν) 238.

ἐσφράγισεν (3d.per.sing.aor.act.ind.of σφραγίζω, culminative) 1686.

ὁ (nom.sing.masc.of the article in agreement with θεός) 9.

θεός (nom.sing.masc.of θεός, apposition) 124.

Translation - "Do not work for the meat that is perishable, but for the meat that remains unto eternal life, which the Son of Man will give to you, because upon this one God the Father has placed His seal of approval."

Comment: The tense of ἐργάζεσθε is present indicating continuous action - "Go on working, but not for the meat. . . but for . . κ.τ.λ." Jesus did not condemn them for their zeal but He did say that it was misdirected. We must not strive for perishable goals, but for eternal goals. The people had been spending their time and maintaining their interest only in goals which, when and if achieved, could satisfy only temporarily. This was Jesus' observation about the water from Jacob's well which the woman sought so diligently (John 4:13,14). The "meat" in each case is defined emphatically by participial adjectives in the emphatic attributive positions - article, substantive, article, adjectival participle. It is the meat "the perishing kind" as opposed to the meat "the enduring kind." The heavenly food is for purpose of eternal life (εἰς ζωὴν αἰώνιος). The adjective αἰώνιος refers as much to the quality of life as to its extended duration.

Spiritual food abides eternally. Physical food is biodegradable. The spiritual food is further defined by the relative clause which follows. It is what we can expect as the gift of the Son of Man, Who will surely give it to those who ask. What Jesus is willing to give is something far more lasting than what Jesus had given to them the afternoon before. Its nourishment, while immediately effective, was now gone. During the night, though gorged in the evening by the delicious meal which Jesus served to them, they had digested the food and now they were hungry again, just as the Samaritan woman knew that although she drank with refreshment from the well at the moment she would soon thirst again. Yet another meal of the perishable type was all that they wanted. And they had rowed across the lake in order to get it. A long row across the lake to Capernaum measures their desire for that which was only temporarily satisfying. Jesus told them that they should be concerned with the spiritual food which continues to endure εἰς ζωὴν αἰώνιος.

If they were doubting His authority and power to fulfill this promise, they should know that it was He (deictic τοῦτον) upon Whom God the Father had placed His seal, with its authorization to come to the world for this specific purpose. *Cf.*#1686 for the meaning of σφραγίζω. Note ἀλλὰ, the strong adversative which distinguishes between perishing food and enduring food. The Father's official seal upon Jesus is the ground for His statement that He alone is the source of the enduring meat. Jesus will give them spiritual food because (causal γὰρ) the Father had authorized Him to do so. When? At His immersion (Mt.3:11-15) upon earth, but before the foundation of the world in eternity past.

There was to be a final authorization as God placed the supreme stamp of His approval upon Jesus when He raised Him from the dead (Eph.1:19-23; Phil.2:9-11).

God the Father has sealed Christ (John 6:27) as His duly authorized representative, with eternal power of attorney. Whatever Jesus Christ does on earth is ratified in heaven. When the sinner receives Jesus' testimony God the Father also seals the believing sinner (Eph.4:30). The certification expressed in σφραγίζω is thus threefold: The Father seals the Son; the believer agrees; the Father seals the believer .

Thus Jesus presented to the people an analysis of their philosophy and behavior, a rebuke, a positive suggestion and a challenge. They were there, having gone to all the trouble of the trip across the lake and the search, only to receive a meal of temporary value. This is a poor allocation of their scarce time and energy resources and it reveals that their sense of values was all wrong. "Why do you spend your money for that which is not bread?" (Isa.55:2).

Modern society has its axiology all wrong. Modern man should rather seek eternal bread. The challenge is that they must believe that Jesus Christ is the sole source of this bread. Him alone has God the Father certified with His seal. If the people could digest all of this strong teaching they would forget their stomachs and ask Jesus how to be saved.

Since Jesus is the sole source of the eternal bread and since we must accept Him in His unique character in order to eat this eternal bread, are there any specific instructions that will help us to believe upon Him? This question was in the minds of the people as they respond with the question of

Verse 28 - "Then said they unto him, What shall we do, that we might work the works of God?"

εἶπον οὖν πρὸς αὐτόν, Τί ποιῶμεν ἵνα ἐργαζώμεθα τὰ ἔργα τοῦ θεοῦ;

εἶπον (3rd.per.pl.aor.act.ind.of εἶπον, constative) 155.

οὖν (inferential conjunction) 68.

πρὸς (preposition with the accusative of extent, after a verb of speaking) 197.

αὐτόν (acc.sing.masc.of αὐτός, extent) 16.

Τί (acc.sing.neut.of the interrogative pronoun τίς, direct object of ποιῶμεν) 281.

ποιῶμεν (1st.per.pl.pres.act.subj.of ποιέω, deliberative) 127.

ἵνα (final conjunction introducing a purpose clause) 114.

ἐργαζώμεθα (1st.per.pl.pres.act.subj.of ἐργάζομαι, purpose) 691.

τὰ (acc.pl.neut.of the article in agreement with ἔργα) 9.

ἔργα (acc.pl.neut.of ἔργον, direct object of ἐργαζώμεθα) 460.

τοῦ (gen.sing.masc.of the article in agreement with θεοῦ) 9.

θεοῦ (gen.sing.masc.of θεός, description) 124.

Translation - "Therefore they said to Him, 'What shall we do to carry out the activities of God?'"

Comment: οὖν is inferential. Their question was motivated by Jesus' remark that they should work for eternal results. Therefore they responded with a direct question. "What shall we do (deliberative subjunctive) in order that (purpose clause) . . . κ.τ.λ." *Cf.*#691 for a list of the activities of God. Satan also works - Jam.2:9; Mt.7;23. Evidence of God's seal upon Jesus, thus identifying God's work with Jesus' work is found in John 5:17,17. *Cf.* also John 9:4,4. The works of God, by Jesus, and by Jesus through the believers who are sealed (Eph.4:30) as Jesus was (John 6:27) make much material for preaching.

The question from the people indicates their willingness at least to hear Jesus out. They did not immediately press Him for His answer to their first question - "How did you get here and when?", though they could not have missed noticing that He ignored it. They seemed willing to accept His rebuke about their misplaced values and seemed willing to work for the everlasting rather than the temporal reward. How shall we go about it? What shall we do? What works shall we perform? *Cf.* Acts 16:31.

Their question indicates that they expected to merit God's blessing by doing something good, but Jesus was soon to dispossess them of this falacious notion. Apparently they missed ἥν ὁ υἱὸς τοῦ ἀνθρώπου ὑμῖν δώσει of verse 27. Just as perishable bread had been given to them by the bounty of the Son of God, so also will the eternal bread be given - not earned. Note the parallel between temporal and eternal bread in John 6 and temporal and eternal water in John 4:13,14. Jesus gives water (John 4:10). He also gives bread (John 6:27).

Verse 29 - "Jesus answered and said unto them, This is the work of God, that ye believe on Him whom He hath sent."

ἀπεκρίθη ὁ Ἰησοῦς καὶ εἶπεν αὐτοῖς, Τοῦτό ἐστιν τὸ ἔργον τοῦ θεοῦ, ἵνα πιστεύητε εἰς ὃν ἀπέστειλεν ἐκεῖνος.

ἀπεκρίθη (3d.per.sing.aor.ind.of ἀποκρίνομαι, constative) 318.
ὁ (nom.sing.masc.of the article in agreement with Ἰησοῦς) 9.
Ἰησοῦς (nom.sing.masc.of Ἰησοῦς, subject of ἀπεκρίθη and εἶπεν) 3.
καὶ (adjunctive conjunction joining verbs) 14.
εἶπεν (3d.per.sing.aor.act.ind.of εἶπον, constative) 155.
αὐτοῖς (dat.pl.masc.of αὐτός, indirect object of εἶπεν) 16.
Τοῦτό (nom.sing.neut.of οὗτος, predicate nominative) 93.
ἐστιν (3d.per.sing.pres.ind.of εἰμί, aoristic) 86.
τὸ (nom.sing.neut.of the article in agreement with ἔργον) 9.
ἔργον (nom.sing.neut.of ἔργον, subject of ἐστιν) 460.
τοῦ (gen.sing.masc.of the article in agreement with θεοῦ) 9.
θεοῦ (gen.sing.masc.of θεός, designation) 124.
ἵνα (final conjunction introducing a purpose clause) 114.
πιστεύητε (2d.per.pl.pres.act.subj.of πιστεύω, purpose) 734.
εἰς (preposition with the accusative of cause) 140.
ὃν (acc.sing.masc.of ὅς, cause) 65.
ἀπέστειλεν (3d.per.sing.aor.act.ind.of ἀποστέλλω, culminative) 215.
ἐκεῖνος (nom.sing.masc.of ἐκεῖνος, subject of ἀπέστειλεν) 246.

Translation - "In reply Jesus said to them, 'This is the work of God - that you believe upon the One whom that one himself has sent.'"

Comment: Note that Jesus emphasized the predicate nomintive Τοῦτο ahead of the subject τὸ ἔργον. Note also that the remote demonstrative ἐκεῖνος is employed. This is emphatic since the pronominal subject of ἀπέστειλεν is implict in the personal endings. - "The work of God is *this!* That you believe on the One Whom *that one* has sent." This activity of God originates in Him Who is a higher source than physical hunger for food. Animals seek food when they are hungry. Divine activity is at a higher level. *Cf.*#140 for other examples of εἰς adjoined to πιστεύω.

Jesus is making clear to the people that He is on earth by divine commission. This repeats the thought of τοῦτον . . . ὁ θεός in verse 27. Jesus is saying that it would be better for the people to believe upon Him as Incarnate God than to receive from His miraculous hands another free meal. He asserts His divine origin and commission emphatically and asks openly for their trust in and acceptance of Him. If they did they would have the food that endures unto life eternal. They were willing to be convinced but asked for evidence. "Why should we believe on you and accept you for what and whom you claim to be?" It is a challenge for Jesus to perform another startling miracle. They are saying in effect, "You may as well be practical about it, if you want us to accept you. How about some breakfast like the supper we had last night?"

Verse 30 - "They said therefore unto him, What sign shewest thou then, that we may see and believe thee? What does thou work?"

εἶπον οὖν αὐτῷ, Τί οὖν ποιεῖς σὺ σημεῖον, ἵνα ἴδωμεν καὶ πιστεύσωμέν σοι; τί ἐργάζῃ;

εἶπον (3d.per.pl.aor.act.ind.of εἶπον, constative) 155.
οὖν (inferential conjunction) 68.
αὐτῷ (dat.sing.masc.of αὐτός, indiret object of εἶπον) 16.
Τί (acc.sing.neut.of τίς, interrogative pronoun, joined with σημεῖον) 281.
οὖν (inferential conjunction) 68.
ποιεῖς (2d.per.sing.pres.act.ind.of ποιέω, futuristic) 127.
σὺ (nom.sing.masc.of σύ, subject of ποιεῖς, emphatic) 104.
σημεῖον (acc.sing.neut.of σημεῖον, direct object of ποιεῖς) 1005.
ἵνα (final conjunction introducing a sub-final clause) 114.
ἴδωμεν (1st.per.pl.aor.act.subj.of ὁράω, purpose/result) 144.
καὶ (adjunctive conjunction joining verbs) 14.
πιστεύσωμέν (1st.per.pl.aor.act.subj.of πιστεύω, purpose/result) 734.
σοι (dat.sing.masc.of σύ, dative of reference) 104.
τί (acc.sing.neut.of τίς, direct object of ἐργάζῃ) 281.
ἐργάζῃ (2d.per.sing.pres.mid.ind.of ἐργάζομαι, futuristic) 691.

Translation - "Therefore they said to Him, 'What sign then are you going to perform, in order (and with the result) that we may believe you? What are you going to show us?'"

Comment: οὖν is inferential here in both usages. The question of the people was triggered by His challenge to them to believe upon Him. Note that σύ is emphatic - "What sign do *you* do?" What was Jesus doing at the moment that justified their faith in Him? They were implying this - "If you want us to believe upon you, give us a good reason. Motivate us. Why, otherwise, should we?" The ἵνα clause which follows is sub-final, *i.e.* it is both purpose and result. Perform a miracle in order that (purpose) and with the result that (result) we may see it and as a result believe upon you. The impertinence of the question is apparent when we recall that these people had seen the miraculous multiplication of bread and fish and had participated in the feast less than 24 hours before. Their contentious attitude is clear also from the repetition of their demand. τί ἐργάζη?

Christian faith in Jesus Christ is faith in the absence of evidence. The unregenerate who must be convinced with logic and empirical investigation before he is willing to commit his soul to Christ has a faith that stands only in the wisdom of men and not in the power of God (I Cor.2:1-5). Apologetics belongs in the message of the evangelist whose audience is made up of the unsaved to whom he is witnessing the good news of the gospel. But Christian Evidences are for the ears of the believers only. They appeal to the mind which has now been regenerated and thus they are a part of the Christian's growth in grace and knowledge (II Pet.3:18). But the evangelist is the apologist who offers no evidence that what he says is true. He only tells his audience that they must start where he did and where every sinner must - they must begin by accepting *a priori* the idea that God exists and that He has spoken to the world in propositional revelation, which is the Word of God. He then challenges - he even *dares* his listeners to believe it. Christ is not looking for convinced people. He is looking for humble sinners who are distressed about their lost condition and who, like little children, are willing to accept on faith what neither human reason nor empirical evidence can provide for them.

When a sinner, under the conviction of the Holy Spirit (John 16:7-11), decides to argue with Christ about it, he is certain to think of much which at the moment appears to him to be valid reason why he should reject the Saviour. Satan will fill his mind with confusion and his mouth with loud arguments (II Cor.4:3,4). Note the zeal with which the people pursue the debate with Jesus, as they make what to them was a valid appeal to their own national history, in

Verse 3₁   ına in the desert, as it is written, He gave them
bread fıuı.   to

οἱ πα   γον ἐν τῇ ἐρήμῳ, καθώς ἐστιν γεγραμμένον,
Ἄρτον ἐκ τоυ оυρανου εοωκεν αυτοῖς φαγεῖν.

οἱ (nom.pl.masc.of the article in agreement with πατέρες) 9.
πατέρες (nom.pl.masc.of πάτηρ, subject of ἔφαγον) 238.
ἡμῶν (gen.pl.masc.of ἐγώ, relationship) 123.
τό (acc.sing.neut.of the article in agreement with μάννα) 9.

#2288 μάννα (acc.sing.neut.of μάννα, direct object of ἔφαγον).

manna - John 6:31,49; Heb.9:4; Rev.2:17.

Meaning: Thayer says, ". . . according to the accounts of travellers a very sweet dew-like juice, which in Arabia and other oriental countries exudes from the leaves (acc.to others only from the twigs and branches) of certain trees and shrubs, particularly in the summer of rainy years. It hardens into little white pellucid grains, and is collected before sunrise by the inhabitants of those countries and used as an article of food, very sweet like honey. the Israelites in their journey through the wilderness met with a gread quantity of food of this kind." The food of Israel in the wilderness - John 6:31, 49, some of which was preserved as a memorial in the heavenly ark of the covenant - Heb.9:4; in a metaphorical sense, perhaps, of the food of overcomers in heaven - Rev.2:17.

ἔφαγον (3d.per.pl.aor.act.ind.of ἐσθίω, constative) 610.
ἐν (preposition with the locative of place where) 80.
τῇ (loc.sing.fem.of the article in agreement with ἐρημῳ) 9.
ἐρήμῳ (loc.sing.fem.of ἔρημος, place where) 250.
καθώς (adverb to introduce a comparative clause) 1348.
ἐστιν (3d.per.sing.pres.ind.of εἰμί, perfect periphrastic) 86.
γεγραμμένον (perf.pass.part.acc.sing.masc.of γράφω, perfect periphrastic) 156.
Ἄρτον (acc.sing.masc.of ἄρτος, direct object of ἔδωκεν) 338.
ἐκ (preposition with the ablative of source) 19.
τοῦ (abl.sing.masc.of the article in agreement with οὐρανοῦ) 9.
οὐρανοῦ (abl.sing.masc.of οὐρανός, source) 254.
ἔδωκεν (3d.per.sing.aor.act.ind.of δίδωμι, constative) 362.
αὐτοῖς (dat.pl.masc.of αὐτός, indirect object of ἔδωκεν) 16.
φαγεῖν (aor.act.inf.of ἐσθίω, purpose) 610.

Translation - "Our forefathers ate the manna in the desert, just as it stands written, 'Bread out of heaven He gave to them to eat.' "

Comment: τὸ μάννα is emphasized ahead of the verb. The Jews were gloating over a glorious event in their national history, as if to say to Jesus, "We are a chosen people, descended from those who ate manna in the desert. This manna was God's gift to them. We have the Scriptures to prove it. You are going to have to be pretty good to beat that!" The perfect passive periphrastic construction ἐστιν γεγραμμένον, is decidedly durative - a present condition as a result of a completed past action - "it has been written in the past and therefore now stands written." For a Jew to say this is to appeal to Biblical authority and rightly so. *Cf.*Ex.16:15; Num.11:7-9; Neg.9:15; Ps.78:24; 105:40.

Few are as bigoted as a superficial thinker with a Bible under his arm and a proof-text in his mouth! ἐκ τοῦ οὐρανοῦ - the source of the manna was heavenly. The argument is this: Moses gave us manna in the wilderness. Yesterday you did the same thing. We are willing to admit that you are a great leader who has arisen in Israel - a modern Moses. We are willing to give you an honored place on a par with him. Thus they damned our Lord with faint praise, as did a prominent city church when it adorned its building with a sculpturesque likeness of Jesus standing beside other great leaders of religion. The world today is full of philosophers who are willing to grant to Jesus His place in the galaxy of great teachers, but who deny Him His claim to unique and essential deity.

The people in our story were making the same mistake that Nicodemus and the Samaritan woman made in John 3 and 4. In this case also, as in theirs, Jesus was thinking metaphorically of spiritual bread from heaven, just as He was speaking of spiritual birth to Nicodemus and of spiritual drink to the woman at the well, while Nicodemus, the woman and the hungry mob in our story were thinking only upon the natural level. In each case Jesus made His prospect see the difference between the natural and the spiritual levels. Nicodemus forgot about obstetrics and was born from above. The Samaritan woman forgot about the water in the well and found a drink of the water of everlasting life. Some of those hungry people in John six began to see the value of the everlasting bread from heaven as opposed to the earthly bread of which we eat only to hunger again. Jesus' task was to make them see the difference between food that filled their stomachs temporarily, whether it be manna or bread and fish, and the spiritual food that nourishes the soul. This He sets out to do in

Verse 32 - "Then Jesus said unto them, Verily, verily I say unto you. Moses gave you not that bread from heaven; but my Father giveth you the true bread from heaven."

εἶπεν οὖν αὐτοῖς ὁ Ἰησοῦς, Ἀμὴν ἀμὴν λέγω ὑμῖν, οὐ Μωϋσῆς δέδωκεν ὑμῖν τὸν ἄρτον ἐκ τοῦ οὐρανοῦ, ἀλλ' ὁ πατήρ μου δίδωσιν ὑμῖν τὸν ἄρτον ἐκ τοῦ οὐρανοῦ τὸν ἀληθινόν.

εἶπεν (3d.per.sing.aor.act.ind.of εἶπον, constative) 155.

οὖν (inferential conjunction) 68.

αὐτοῖς (dat.pl.masc.of αὐτός, indirect object of εἶπεν) 16.

ὁ (nom.sing.masc.of the article in agreement with Ἰησοῦς) 9.

Ἰησοῦς (nom.sing.masc.of Ἰησοῦς, subject of εἶπεν) 3.

Ἀμὴν (explicative) 466.

ἀμὴν (explicative) 466.

λέγω (1st.per.sing.pres.act.ind.of λέγω, aoristic) 66.

ὑμῖν (dat.pl.masc.of σύ, indirect object of λέγω) 104.

οὐ (summary negative conjunction with the indicative) 130.

Μωϋσῆς (nom.sing.masc.of Μωϋσῆς, subject of ἔδωκεν) 715.

ἔδωκεν (3d.per.sing.aor.act.ind.of δίδωμι, constative) 362.

ὑμῖν (dat.pl.masc.of σύ, indirect object of ἔδωκεν) 104.

τὸν (acc.sing.masc.of the article in agreement with ἄρτον) 9.

ἄρτον (acc.sing.masc.of ἄρτος, direct object of ἔδωκεν) 338.

ἐκ (preposition with the ablative of source) 19.

τοῦ (abl.sing.masc.of the article in agreement with οὐρανοῦ) 9.

οὐρανοῦ (abl.sing.masc.of οὐρανός, source) 254.

ἀλλ᾽ (alternative conjunction) 342.

ὁ (nom.sing.masc.of the article in agreement with πατήρ) 9.

πατήρ (nom.sing.masc.of πατήρ, subject of δίδωσιν) 238.

μου (gen.sing.masc.of ἐγώ, relationship) 123.

δίδωσιν (3d.per.sing.pres.act.ind.of δίδωμι, futuristic) 362.

ὑμῖν (dat.pl.masc.of σύ, indirect object of δίδωσιν) 104.

τὸν (acc.sing.masc.of the article in agreement with ἄρτον) 9.

ἄρτον (acc.sing.masc.of ἄρτος, direct object of δίδωσιν) 338.

ἐκ (preposition with the ablative of source) 19.

τοῦ (abl.sing.masc.of the article in agreement with οὐρανοῦ) 9.

οὐρανοῦ (abl.sing.masc.of οὐρανός, source) 254.

τὸν (acc.sing.masc.of the article in agreement with ἀληθινόν) 9.

ἀληθινόν (acc.sing.masc.of ἀληθινός, in agreement with ἄρτον) 1696.

Translation - *"Therefore Jesus said to them, 'Truly, truly I am telling you that Moses gave you* **not** *the bread out of heaven, but my Father will give you the bread out of heaven which is the* **real** *bread.' "*

Comment: The negative οὐ belongs, not with Μωϋσῆς, but with τὸν ἄρτον ἐκ τοῦ οὐρανοῦ. Under Moses' administration they did indeed eat of the manna in the wilderness, but it was not the bread from heaven. Had it been they would not have needed to gather and eat every day. The manna in the wilderness is contrasted with the bread from heaven, which is here described in the emphatic attributive position as τοῦ οὐρανοῦ τὸν ἀληθινόν. *Cf.*#1696 for the meaning of the adjective. Not "true" as opposed to "false" but as opposed to "counterfeit."

οὖν is inferential. In this spirited exchange each comment calls for rebuttal. They had just alluded to the manna in the wilderness as bread *out of heaven*. - ἄρτον ἐκ τοῦ οὐρανοῦ (vs.31). Jesus disputes this by saying that what Moses provided was *not* heavenly bread, despite the fact that it was produced supernaturally, any more than what He had given to them the evening before. It also was supernaturally produced. But the point is not the manner in which the food was produced but the quality of that which was produced. Moses' manna and Jesus' bread and fish were both good food, clean, nutritious and delicious to be sure, but only temporarily satisfying. In contrast the true bread from heaven which the Father will give to those who ask for it, satisfies eternally. The people must come to understand that the quality of the food is the issue, whether produced supernaturally or otherwise. The miraculous manner in which the children of Israel were given their daily manna did not endow the manna with perpetual nourishment. Otherwise they would not have needed to gather it daily, just as the people in our story would not have needed to follow Jesus around the lake for another meal.

This then was their error. Jesus must set them straight. While not denying that Moses had fed their forefathers, He denigrates the quality as contrasted with the true bread from heaven which the Father will give. They were talking about two different kinds of bread, just as Jesus and Nicodemus were talking about two different kinds of birth in John 3 and He and the Samaritan woman two different kinds of water in John 4. In John 5 the lame man did not understand at first that Jesus could give him a different kind of healing than he felt that he needed.

It is now time for Jesus to define this real heavenly bread which He does in

Verse 33 - "For the bread of God is he which cometh down from heaven, and giveth life unto the world."

ὁ γὰρ ἄρτος τοῦ θεοῦ ἐστιν ὁ καταβαίνων ἐκ τοῦ οὐρανοῦ καὶ ζωὴν διδοὺς τῷ κόσμῳ.

ὁ (nom.sing.masc.of the article in agreement with ἄρτος) 9.

γὰρ (causal conjunction) 105.

ἄρτος (nom.sing.masc.of ἄρτος, subject of ἐστιν) 338.

τοῦ (abl.sing.masc.of the article in agreement with θεοῦ) 9.

θεοῦ (abl.sing.masc.of θεός, source) 124.

ἐστιν (3d.per.sing.pres.ind.of εἰμί, aoristic) 86.

ὁ (nom.sing.masc.of the article in agreement with καταβαίνων) 9.

καταβαίνων (pres.act.part.nom.sing.masc.of καταβαίνω, substantival, predicate nominative) 324.

ἐκ (preposition with the ablative of source) 19.

τοῦ (abl.sing.masc.of the article in agreement with οὐρανοῦ) 9.

οὐρανοῦ (abl.sing.masc.of οὐρανός, source) 254.

καὶ (adjunctive conjunction joining participles) 14.

ζωὴν (acc.sing.fem.of ζωή, direct object of διδοὺς) 668.

διδοὺς (pres.act.part.nom.sing.masc.of δίδωμι, substantival, predicate nominative) 362.

τῷ (dat.sing.masc.of the article in agreement with κόσμῳ) 9.

κόσμῳ (dat.sing.masc.of κόσμος, indirect object of διδοὺς) 360.

Translation - "Because the Bread that comes from God is the One coming down out of heaven and giving life to the world."

Comment: γὰρ is causal as Jesus supports His objection of verse 32. The bread that Moses gave was not the bread from heaven *because* (causal γὰρ) the heavenly bread is about to be identified in altogether different terms. The bread that has its source in God (ablative of source) must come down from heaven, and when He does He will give life to the world, not temporary relief from physical hunger. Jesus has not yet identified Himself as ὁ ἄρτος τοῦ θεοῦ. This comes in verse 35. There is a connection between the true spiritual bread and everlasting life. Simply to eat physical bread, albeit miraculously produced, is not to escape physical death (vs.48). The Jews in the wilderness who ate the manna are all dead and the people who ate the bread and fish that Jesus provided were hungry again and destined some time to die physically.

Verse 34 - "Then said they unto him, Lord, evermore give us this bread."

Εἶπον οὖν πρὸς αὐτόν, Κύριε, πάντοτε δὸς ὑμῖν τὸν ἄρτον τοῦτον.

Εἶπον (3d.per.sing.aor.act.ind.of εἶπον, constative) 155.
οὖν (continuative conjunction) 68.
πρὸς (preposition with the accustive of extent after a verb of speaking) 197.
αὐτόν (acc.sing.masc.of αὐτός, extent after a verb of speaking) 16.
Κύριε (voc.sing.masc.of κύριος, address) 97.
πάντοτε (adverbial) 1567.
δὸς (2d.per.sing.aor.act.impv.of δίδωμι, entreaty) 362.
ὑμῖν (dat.pl.masc.of ἐγώ, indirect object of δὸς) 123.
τὸν (acc.sing.masc.of the article in agreement with ἄρτον) 9.
ἄρτον (acc.sing.masc.of ἄρτος, direct object of δὸς) 338.
τοῦτον (acc.sing.masc.of οὗτος, in agreement with ἄρτον, deictic) 93.

Translation - "Then they said to Him, 'Sir, always give to us this bread.' "

Comment: Note πρὸς with the accusative of extent after εἶπον, a verb of speaking, instead of the dative of indirect object. *Cf.* John 4:48; 6:28 for John's use of the same construction. It is good Greek, used by all of the gospel writers. Since πρός (#197) means "near to" it speaks of intimacy, and when used after a verb of speaking (λέγω, λαλέω, εἶπον) it may indicate a high degree of rapport between the speaker and the one addressed. In this case the people were genuinely interested in their request, even if for the wrong reasons. Κύριε - a term of high respect, without the overtones of Christian worship, and hence translated "Sir." Their request echos that of the Samaritan worman who wanted a satisfying drink (John 4:15). This request does not indicate their desire for spiritual salvation, since they do not yet believe upon Him (vs.41).

Cf. John 3:13. When Jesus was dealing with Nicodemus He impressed him with His own heavenly origin, just as now He points out that He is the One Who has come down from heaven (ὁ καταβαίνων ἐκ τοῦ οὐρανοῦ, verse 33). No commitment to Jesus Christ results in salvation except that which recognizes that Jesus is Incarnate God. Thus Jesus so presented Himself to Nicodemus (John 3:13), to the woman at the well (John 4:26) and to the Jews after He had healed the lame man (John 5:17-18). It is fitting therefore that He should tell the hungry crowd before Him in our story that the only source of the eternal bread from heaven is the One who has come down from heaven - ὁ καταβαίνων τοῦ οὐρανοῦ (John 6:33,35).

That the people were still thinking of physical food seems evident from their use of πάντοτε, the adverb which implies that they wanted a miracuous meal of loaves and fishes every day from that time on. God had provided food every day for thirty eight years in the wilderness; why should not Jesus give them bread and fish every day? Jesus cannot allow this fallacy to persist. He is talking about a kind of salvation that far transcends what they were thinking about with this shallow request. They wanted the benefits of the welfare state without the moral commitments which should be involved. Verses 35-40 make it clear that those who finally come to understand what is meant by "the bread of life" (vs.35) are the special objects of electing grace, irresistible call and eternal preservation. It is scant wonder that what Jesus had to say in the next six verses triggered the opposition of the Jewish establishment and ultimately resulted in Jesus losing most of His crowd.

Verse 35 - "And Jesus said unto them, I am the bread of life: he that cometh to me shall never hunger; and he that believeth on me shall never thirst."

εἶπεν αὐτοῖς ὁ Ἰησοῦς, Ἐγώ εἰμι ὁ ἄρτος τῆς ζωῆς, ὁ ἐρχόμενος πρός με οὐ μὴ πεινάσῃ, καὶ ὁ πιστεύων εἰς ἐμὲ οὐ μὴ διψήσει πώποτε.

εἶπεν (3d.per.sing.aor.act.ind.of εἶπον, constative) 155.
αὐτοῖς (dat.pl.masc.of αὐτός, indirect object of εἶπεν) 16.
ὁ (nom.sing.masc.of the article in agreement with Ἰησοῦς) 9.
Ἰησοῦς (nom.sing.masc.of Ἰησοῦς, subject of εἶπεν) 3.
Ἐγώ (nom.sing.masc.of ἐγώ, subject of εἰμι) 123.
εἰμι (1st.per.sing.pres.ind.of εἰμί, aoristic) 86.
ὁ (nom.sing.masc.of the article in agreement with ἄρτος) 9.
ἄρτος (nom.sing.masc.of ἄρτος, predicate nominative) 338.
τῆς (gen.sing.fem.of the article in agreement with ζωῆς) 9.
ζωῆς (gen.sing.fem.of ζωή, description) 668.
ὁ (nom.sing.masc.of the article in agreement with ἐρχόμενος) 9.
ἐρχόμενος (pres.part.nom.sing.masc.of ἔρχομαι, substantival, subject of πεινάσῃ) 146.
πρός (preposition with the accusative of extent) 197.
ἐμὲ (acc.sing.masc.of ἐμός, extent) 1267.
οὐ (negative conjunction with μή and the subjunctive) 130.
μή (negative conjunction with οὐ and the subjunctive) 87.
πεινάσῃ (3d.per.sing.aor.act.subj.of πεινάω, emphatic negation) 335.
καὶ (continuative conjunction) 14.
ὁ (nom.sing.masc.of the article in agreement with πιστεύων) 9.
πιστεύων (pres.act.part.nom.sing.masc.of πιστεύω, substantival, subject of διψήσει) 734.
εἰς (preposition with the accusative of cause) 140.
ἐμὲ (acc.sing.masc.of ἐμός, cause) 1267.
οὐ (negative conjunction with μή and the future indicative) 130.
μή (negative conjunction with οὐ and the future indicative) 87.
διψήσει (3d.per.sing.fut.act.ind.of διψάω, futuristic subjunctive) 427.
πώποτε (adverbial) 1701.

Translation - "Jesus said to them, 'I AM - The Bread of Life. The one who comes to me shall never never hunger and the one who believes upon me shall never ever thirst."

Comment: Though John follows εἶπον with πρός and the accusative in verse 34, he uses the usual dative (αὐτοῖς) in verse 35. Ἐγώ is emphatic since the first personal pronoun is implicit in the verb endings of εἰμι. But there is a special reason why Jesus said it like this. Ἐγώ εἰμι is the Greek translation of the tetragrammaton in Exodus 3:14 which stands in Hebrew for the name of God. Translated "I AM THAT I AM" in the King James Version, the Hebrew is translated by the LXX as Ἐγώ εἰμι ὁ ὤν - "I AM, THE CONTINUING ONE." Exodus 3:15 continues as Jehovah says to Moses, "Thus shall you say to the sons of Israel, 'The Lord, the God of your fathers, God of Abraham, God of Isaac and God of Jacob, has sent me to you. This is my *eternal name and a memorial of generations to generations.'* " In the expression Ἐγώ εἰμι ὁ ὤν - the participle ὤν is in apposition. It is the present participle of the verb εἰμί and means "One who survives (always is, continues, has no end, etc.)" Thus He is eternal. This indicates that He is sovereign. He is unaffected by contrary forces that otherwise would impinge upon Him and alter His character and ultimately destroy Him. Man survives in the natural world because he either adjusts to his environment or overcomes it. God will always survive because He is greater than His environment, as the Creator is always *a fortiori* greater than that which He has created. So we need not worry about whether or not God is viable. Indeed He is the only one in the universe who is viable by means of His own resources. If man is destroyed it will be his environment, whether physical, social, economic or psychological, that will destroy him. God is in no such danger. Thus to say Ἐγώ εἰμι ὁ ὤν - is to assert eternal sovereignty. Jesus used this formula for His name which He had told Moses at the bush was to be His memorial for succeeding generations, whenever He wished to assert His deity and authority. Thus in John 4:26 He introduced Himself to the woman at the well. It is scant wonder that she believed upon Him, and forgetting her water pot, which a few moments before had been her most important treasure, rushed back into town to announce that she had found the Messiah. Now in John 6:35 Jesus uses His name again to convince His audience that His "bread of life" is superior to Moses' manna. *Cf.* it again in John 6:48,51; 8:12 ("the light of the world"); 8:58 (where He said that He antedated Abraham); John 11:25 ("I am the resurrection and the life"); John 14:6 ("I am the way, the truth and the life"); John 18:5,6 (when He identified Himself to the arresting officers, with a force that sent them sprawling) and John 6:20 (spoken as He walked upon the water and comforted His panic stricken disciples). It is significant that we find this formula for the name of our Lord only in John's gospel, where we would expect to find it since John is particularly concerned with demonstrating the essential deity of the incarnate Son of God. Matthew's King of the Jews, Mark's servant and Luke's Son of Man is also Ἐγώ εἰμι indeed, but it is for John to bring the eternal memorial from the burning bush at Sinai and remind his readers that we are dealing with the Eternal God of Abraham, Isaac and Jacob, Who is essentially sovereign and therefore eternally viable.

As the student examines the passages in which Ἐγώ εἰμι occurs, he will note that it is always in connection with some context in which Jesus' deity is the important issue. The water of life, the master of the tornado, the bread of life, the light of the world, He Who was before Abraham, the resurrection and the life, the way, the truth and the life and Jesus of Nazareth Whom they came to arrest and were allowed to do so only because of His cooperation.

It is particularly fitting that Jesus should use His eternal name in John 6:35 because at this point He is about to make one of the strongest Calvinistic statements in the New Testament, as a result of which many who heard Him found His theology unacceptable and the next time we see them they are adding their voices to the mob before Pilate in demanding His death.

The idiom οὐ μὴ πεινάσῃ - the double negative with the subjunctive is common enough as an example of the subjunctive of emphatic negation. But it is followed in the next clause by οὐ μὴ διφήσει - the double negative with the future indicative, which seems also to be emphatically negative. Robertson (*Grammar, 928-930*) has a long discussion of the problem in his section on the Futuristic Subjunctive. Burton (*Moods and Tenses, 78*) says, "The Aorist Subjunctive is used with οὐ μή in the sense of an emphatic Future Indicative" and cites Heb.13:5; Mt.5:18; Mk.13:30; Lk.9:27 representative of frequent examples. Robertson adds, "The ancient Greek sometimes employed the present subjunctive in this sense, but the N.T. does not use it. But the LXX has it, as in Jer.1:19. So in Is.11:9 we find οὐ μὴ κακοποιήσουσιν οὐδὲ μὴ δύνωνται. The future ind. with οὐ μή is rare in the N.T., but οὐ μή with the aorist sub. appears in the W. H. text 100 times. It cannot be said that the origin of this οὐ μή construction has been solved. Goodwin states the problem well. The two negatives ought to neutralize each other, being *simplex* but they do not (*cf.μή οὐ*). The examples are partly futuristic and partly prohibitory. Ellipsis is not satisfactory nor complete separation (Gildersleeve) of the two negatives. Perhaps οὐ expresses the emphatic denial and μή the prohibition which come to be blended into the one construction. At any rate it is proper to cite the examples of emphatic denial as instances of the futuristic subjunctive. Thus οὐ μή σε ἀνῶ, οὐδ᾽ οὐ μή σε ἐγκαταλίπω (Heb.13:5); οὐ μὴ ἀπολέσῃ (Mk.9:41); οὐκέτι οὐ μὴ πίω (Mk.14:25). Cf. Lu.6:37, etc. See οὐ μή in both principal and subordinate clauses in Mk.13:2."

That we have strong negative emphasis in the last two clauses of John 6:35, the first with the subjunctive and the second with the future indicative, is clear. *Cf.#*'s 335 and 427 for examples of spiritual hunger and thirst in other passages. Especially note Lk.1:53; Mt.5:6; Lk.6:21; Rev.21:6; 22:17.

Once they have asked for bread, even though they are still thinking of bread in the physical sense, though perhaps of some special quality because miraculously produced, Jesus introduces them to the very heart of Christian theology - the Incarnate God, Jesus Christ. "What think ye of Christ? Whose son is He?" Sinners must come into intimate relationship with Him - ὁ ἐρχόμενος πρὸς ἐμέ. Having come they must believe because of Him - here εἰς with πιστεύω in a causal sense. To believe *upon* Him, is to believe *because of* Him. *Cf.#140* for other examples. That they were not coming to Him and believing upon (because of) Him in the saving sense, is clear in

Verse 36 - "*But I said unto you, That ye also have seen me, and believe not.*"

ἀλλ᾽ εἶπον ὑμῖν ὅτι καὶ ἐωράκατέ (με) καὶ οὐ πιστεύετε.

ἀλλ᾽ (adversative conjunction) 342.
εἶπον (1st.per.sing.aor.act.ind.of εἶπον, constative) 155.
ὑμῖν (dat.pl.masc.of σύ, indirect object of εἶπον) 104.
ὅτι (objective conjunction introducing indirect discourse) 211.
καὶ (concessive conjunction) 14.

ἐωράκατέ (2d.per.pl.perf.ind.of ὀράω, consummative) 144.
(με) acc.sing.masc.of ἐγώ, direct object of ἐωράκατέ) 123.
καὶ (adversative conjunction) 14.
οὐ (summary negative conjunction with the indicative) 130.
πιστεύετε (2d.per.pl.pres.act.ind.of πιστεύω, aoristic) 734.

Translation - "But I told you that although you have understood me yet you do not believe."

Comment: The first καὶ is concessive; the second adversative. Despite the fact that on the day before they had witnessed His miracle of the loaves and fish and had been fed, yet they did not believe upon Him. Note that the verb is ἐρώκατέ (to perceive, understand), not βλέπω (to see physically), though of course they also saw Jesus in the optical sense. He is saying that the people had some insight into who He was and what His purpose in coming was. Despite this gleam of light they did not believe. They had the same experience that the disciples had who, after witnessing the miracle of the loaves and fish were frightened by His appearance during the storm at sea (Mk.6:52). This observation is preliminary to what follows to the effect that neither experience nor reason can induce repentance, faith and our personal acceptance of Christ. The people were forced to admit that Jesus was supernatural. They had seen the evidence. Their minds were forced to a conclusion that He was the Son of God, the Messiah of Israel. They had all of the Christian Evidences. But they were not believers - not yet and Jesus will soon tell them why.

He is now engaged in showing the contrast between those who see His miracles and come to Him in personal commitment and faith, and eat and drink with eternal satisfaction, and others who see His miracles and fail to come and believe, except for the temporal satisfaction of physical bread.Some were true spiritual believers - the eleven disciples, for example. But there were others who had seen as much. Yet they were not believers. Hence the strong adversative ἀλλά to begin verse 36. Two groups, both present, had seen His miracles. One group (vs.35) believed and were saved. The other group (vs.36) did not believe and were still lost. Jesus, having analyzed the situation, now explains it in

Verse 37 - "All that the Father giveth me shall come to me; and him that cometh to me I will in no wise cast out."

Πᾶν ὃ δίδωσίν μοι ὁ πατὴρ πρὸς ἐμὲ ἥξει, καὶ τὸν ἐρχόμενον πρὸς ἐμὲ οὐ μὴ ἐκβάλω ἔφω,

Πᾶν (nom.sing.neut. of πᾶς, subject of ἥξει) 67.
ὃ (acc.sing.neut.of the relative ὅς, direct object of δίδωσιν) 65.
δίδωσιν (3d.per.sing.pres.act.ind.of δίδωμι, aoristic) 362.
μοι (dat.sing.masc.of ἐγώ, indirect object of δίδωσίν) 123.
ὁ (nom.sing.masc.of the article in agreement with πατήρ) 9.
πατὴρ (nom.sing.masc.of πατήρ, subject of δίδωσίν) 238.
πρὸς (preposition with the accusative of extent) 197.
ἐμὲ (acc.sing.masc.of ἐμός, extent) 1267.

ἐμὲ (acc.sing.masc.of ἐμός, extent) 1267.

ἥξει (3d.per.sing.fut.act.ind.of ἥκω, predictive) 730.

καὶ (continuative conjunction) 14.

τὸν (acc.sing.masc.of the article in agreement with ἐρχόμενον) 9.

ἐρχόμενον (pres.part.acc.sing.masc.of ἔρχομαι, substantival, direct object of ἐκβάλω) 146.

πρὸς (preposition with the accusative of extent) 197.

ἐμὲ (acc.sing.masc.of ἐμός, extent) 1267.

οὐ (negative conjunction with μή and the subjunctive) 130.

μὴ (negative conjunction with οὐ and the subjunctive) 87.

ἐκβάλω (1st.per.sing.aor.act.subj.of ἐκβάλλω, emphatic negation) 649.

ἔξω (adverbial) 449.

Translation - "Everyone whom the Father gives to me shall come to me, and the one coming to me I will never cast out."

Comment: Πᾶν is the subject of ἥξει, but it is qualifed by the relative pronoun phrase ὃ δίδωσίν μοι ὁ πατήρ. Not everyone will come to Christ, but everyone *whom the Father gives to Christ* shall come to Him. Note that the preposition is πρός (#197), not εἰς (#140). πρός means "near to" with an intimacy not indicated by εἰς which means "toward" or "in the direction of." The gift of the Father of the elect is a gift which speaks of this intimacy. The Father gives them πρὸς ἐμὲ - "into an intimate relationship" and when they come to Christ, as a result of their having been given to Him, they come πρὸς Χριστόν. Thus they enjoy the same intimacy of relationship with Christ that He enjoys with the Father (John 1:1; I John 1:1; John 17:21). *Cf.* In John 17:2,6,9,11 and 24 Jesus spoke to the Father about those whom the Father had given to Him. They are His people for whose salvation He came into the world (Mt.1:21). To be sure, when Joseph the carpenter was told to name Mary's son Jesus because he would save "his people" from their sins, he thought of "his people" as the Jews in a national sense, not of the broader redemptive program which would also include the Gentiles, but although Joseph did not see all that can be seen in the statement when it is viewed in the light of scripture later to be inspired, Mt.1:21 comports with John 6:37 and the passages in John 17 listed supra.

Those so given to Christ in the eternal covenant of election are certain to be brought to Christ by the conviction of the Holy Spirit (John 16:7-11) without Whose help they cannot call Jesus Lord (I Cor.12:3). And when they come (not *if* they come) they come with the assurance that Christ will never never reject them. Note the emphatic negation in οὐ μή and the subjunctive in ἐκβάλω. Of course He will not cast them out because they are His - the Father's gift to Him and He has died for them and redeemed them with His own precious blood. *Cf.*#'s 649 and 449 for ἐκβάλω and ἔξω in passages where sinners and demons, indeed Satan himself, will be cast out. Here in bold statement is the doctrine of unconditional election as later taught by Paul and the other apostles.

The difference between coming to Christ (εἰς Χριστόν) for a free meal and coming πρὸς Χριστόν for salvation lies in the fact that the coming πρὸς Χριστόν is contingent upon the Father's will to give the sinner to Christ. Those so chosen and given to Christ come in the spiritual sense and their acceptance is certain, not because they came but because the Father gave them to Christ. This is the heart of the gospel. Jesus will explore this thought and all that relates to it in the remainder of this discourse.

The "Back to Jesus" movement of the 1920's, which implied that Paul taught something foreign and in addition to Jesus' teachings overlooks John 6. *Cf.* Wilkinson, *Paul and the Revolt Against Him,* Philadelphia: Griffith and Rowland Press, 1914.

Lest there arise the notion that the Father and His Incarnate Son Jesus are working at cross purposes Jesus speaks to the point in

Verse 38 - "For I came down from heaven, not to do mine own will, but the will of him that sent me."

ὅτι καταβέβηκα ἀπὸ τοῦ οὐρανοῦ οὐχ ἵνα ποιῶ τὸ θέλημα τὸ ἐμὸν ἀλλὰ τὸ θέλημα τοῦ πέμφαντός με.

ὅτι (causal conjunction) 211.

καταβέβηκα (1st.per.sing.perf.act.ind.of καταβαίνω, consummative) 324.

ἀπὸ (preposition with the ablative of separation) 70.

τοῦ (abl.sing.masc.of the article in agreement with οὐρανοῦ) 9.

οὐρανοῦ (abl.sing.masc.of οὐρανός, separation) 254.

οὐχ (summary negative conjunction with a purpose clause) 130.

ἵνα (final conjunction introducing a purpose clause) 114.

ποιῶ (1st.per.sing.pres.act.subj.of ποιέω, purpose) 127.

τὸ (acc.sing.neut.of the article in agreement with θέλημα) 9.

θέλημα (acc.sing.neut.of θέλημα, direct object of ποιῶ) 577.

τὸ (acc.sing.neut.of the article in agreement with ἐμὸν) 9.

ἐμὸν (acc.sing.neut.of ἐμός, in agreement with θέλημα) 1267.

ἀλλὰ (alternative conjunction) 342.

τὸ (acc.sing.neut.of the article in agreement with θέλημα) 9.

θέλημα (acc.sing.neut.of θέλημα, direct object of ποιῶ) 577.

τοῦ (gen.sing.masc.of the article in agreement with πέμφαντος) 9.

πέμφαντος (aor.act.part.gen.sing.masc.of πέμπω, substantival, possession) 169.

με (acc.sing.masc.of ἐγώ, direct object of πέμφαντός) 123.

Translation - "Because here I am, having come down from heaven, not in order to do my own will but the will of the One Who sent me."

Comment: The consummative perfect in καταβέβηκα justifies my translation. The perfect tense speaks of a present state or condition as a result of a past completed action. Jesus points back to His incarnation and to its present result. Having come down from heaven, He was there speaking to the people. Why did He come? And why not? Not for the purpose (the ἵνα clause of purpose) of doing what He wanted, necessarily, but (the alternative conjunction ἀλλὰ) to do the will of the Father Who had sent Him. We do not yet know what the will of the Father is. That is revealed in verse 39, but whatever it may be, we know that Jesus will concern Himself with doing the will of the Father rather than His own will, in the event that the two wills are in conflict. Note that Jesus does not say that His will is ever contrary to that of His Father. What He does say is that He will always do that which comports with the Father's will. (John 8:29; Mt.3:17).

Verse 38 is a causal clause introduced by ὅτι and it serves to give the reason for Jesus' last statement of verse 37 to the effect that the one who comes to Christ will never be cast out. The question might arise as to what would happen in the event that the will of the Father and that of His Son were not in harmony, in which case, pursuant to the Father's will, the sinner who had been given to the Son by the Father would come to the Son for salvation, only to find that the Son did not want to accept him in which case he would be rejected. This can never happen. Why will Jesus never reject the one who comes to Him for salvation? Because Jesus' purpose on earth is to carry out the will of the Father, not His own. The agreement between Father and Son came in the eternal counsels of the Godhead in eternity past. The elect were then "chosen in (Christ) before the foundation of the world . . . " (Eph.1:4) and it was then that the plan of redemption called for Christ's mission into the world. But for the fact that the emphasis is upon what Jesus will *not* do, as opposed to what He *will* do, the sentence would read more smoothly like this: ἵνα ποιῶ οὐχ τὸ θέλημα . . . κ.τ.λ." Οὐχ is emphasized by its priority of position. To carry out the idea of contrast ἀλλὰ the alternative conjunction is used rather than the weaker adversative δέ. Also note that Jesus' will is described in the emphatic attributive position τὸ θέλημα τὸ ἐμὸν, thus pointing out the contrast that might conceivably exist between the two wills.

The ablative phrase ἀπὸ τοῦ οὐρανοῦ emphasizes His heavenly origin as does τοῦ πέμψαντός με, which points up the fact that Jesus was here on earth as a result of a definite divine mission. "My Father Who is in heaven has sent me, His Son, on a specific mission out of heaven and down to earth. Now that I am here I am to do His will, not my own." He does not say that His will is in contrast to that of the Father. He is explaining that only those whom the Father has given to Him, in accord with the Father's purpose, will come to Him. Jesus will accept those who thus come, because those who come are precisely those who were involved in the covenant of redemption agreed upon between Father and Son before the world was. Jesus is issuing a disclaimer. It was not His decision as to who should come. He only receives those who come. It does not include those who came without faith (verse 36) and whose purpose was to get a free meal, or perhaps to satisfy a vulgar curiosity in the man who did unusual things. Some come and believe and are accepted and saved. Others come but in unbelief. What is the difference? The will of the Father is the difference and Jesus is not authorized to act independently of and in contrariety to it. Jesus here takes what appears from a human point of view to be a subordinate position to the Father. He further explains His divine orders in verses 39 and 40.

Verse 39 - "And this is the Father's will which hath sent me, that of all which he hath given me I should lose nothing, but should raise it up again at the last day."

τοῦτο δέ ἐστιν τὸ θέλημα τοῦ πέμφαντός με, ἵνα πᾶν ὃ δέδωκέν μοι μὴ
ἀπολέσω ἐξ αὐτοῦ ἀλλὰ ἀναστήσω αὐτὸ (ἐν) τῇ ἐσχάτῃ ἡμέρᾳ.

τοῦτο (nom.sing.neut.of οὗτος, predicate nominative) 93.

δέ (continuative conjunction) 11.

ἐστιν (3d.per.sing.pres.ind.of εἰμί, aoristic) 86.

τὸ (nom.sing.neut.of the article in agreement with θέλημα) 9.

θέλημα (nom.sing.neut.of θέλημα, subject of ἐστιν) 577.

τοῦ (gen.sing.masc.of the article in agreement with πέμφαντος) 9.

πέμφαντος (aor.act.part.gen.sing.masc.of πέμπω, possession) 169.

με (acc.sing.masc.of ἐγώ, direct object of πέμφαντος) 123.

ἵνα (sub-final conjunction introducing a purpose/result clause) 114.

πᾶν (acc.sing.neut.of πᾶς, direct object of ἀπολέσω) 67.

ὃ (acc.sing.neut.of ὅς, relative pronoun, attracted to πᾶν) 65.

δέδωκέν (3d.per.sing.perf.act.ind.of δίδωμι, consummative) 362.

μοι (dat.sing.masc.of ἐγώ, indirect object of δέδωκέν) 123.

μὴ (negative conjunction with the subjunctive in a negative sub-final clause)
87.

ἀπολέσω (1st.per.sing.aor.act.subj.of ἀπόλλυμι, sub-final clause) 208.

ἐξ (preposition with the partitive genitive) 19.

αὐτοῦ (gen.sing.neut.of αὐτός, partitive genitive) 16.

ἀλλὰ (alternative conjunction) 342.

ἀναστήσω (1st.per.sing.fut.act.ind.of ἀνίστημι, predictive) 789.

αὐτὸ (acc.sing.neut.of αὐτός, direct object of ἀναστήσω) 16.

(ἐν) (preposition with the locative of time point) 80.

τῇ (loc.sing.fem.of the article in agreement with ἡμέρᾳ) 9.

ἐσχάτῃ (loc.sing.fem.of ἔσχατος, in agreement with ἡμέρᾳ) 496.

ἡμέρᾳ (loc.sing.fem.of ἡμέρα, time point) 135.

*Translation - "And this is the will of the One Who sent me - that I should not lose
all of that (that I should lose none of that) which He has given to me; on the
contrary I will raise it up at the last day."*

Comment: In recent years Madison Avenue, which flunked Freshman English,
has been bombarding our ears with the same mistake which the Greek makes
when we translate it literally into English. How often we have heard the radio
and television advertizers says, "All aspirins are not alike" when they obviously
mean that "Not all aspirins are alike" or at least we hope that is what they mean
since what they say is that every Bayer aspirin which they offer for sale is
different from every other Bayer, despite the fact that they all come from the
same box! John did not mean to have Jesus say that it was the Father's will that
Jesus might lose some of those whom He had given to Him, so long as He did not
lose all of them. It is not the Father's will that Jesus should lose *any* of those who
have been given to Him. He must save all of them. Note that the relative pronoun
ὃ is singular and that the antecedent of αὐτὸ, also singular number and neuter

gender, is δ. Note also that in the partitive genitive phrase ἐξ αὐτοῦ, αὐτοῦ is also singular number and neuter gender. Thus that which the Father has given to Jesus Christ is considered as a unit and the Father wills that Jesus should not lose it. πᾶν modifies δ and thus Jesus means the *entire* unit must be saved. That is why He predicted that He would raise *it* (αὐτό) up at the last day. Note the deictic use of τοῦτο as John places the predicate nominative ahead of the subject of the verb. "The will of the One Who sent me is *this*." The ἵνα clause is both purpose and result, since that which the sovereign God purposes is certain to result. God wanted it that way (purpose) and that is how it is going to be (result). Here again Jesus refers to those whom God has given to Him and adds that the Father's will is that He should lose none of it. Since the gift is looked upon in the text as a package, the result is that every individual component of the package is safe from destruction and destined to be resurrected on the last day. This is the Father's will and Jesus is sworn to perform it without regard to how His own will might possibly differ (verse 38), although, as we have stated before, He does not say that His will is any different from that of His Father. Jesus reported to His Father that He had lost none of those whom the Father gave to Him, although He had lost one whom He had chosen, in order that the scripture might be fulfilled (John 17:12).

If the Father has given to Christ the quantitative whole of the human race, then, in the light of these passages, we must conclude that Universalism is the correct soteriology. There can be no final eternal punishment for any of Adam's fallen race under the assumption that the election of God is universal. How many of Adam's descendants did the Father give to Christ? Only the Godhead knows. That is why the great commission orders the church to preach the good news universally. The Calvinist is presumptuous indeed if he refuses to preach the gospel to some on the ground that they are not a part of the gift package which the Father gave to Jesus Christ. How indeed should he know? Therefore we broadcast the seed of the Word of God on a worldwide and universal basis, depending upon the Lord of the harvest to give the harvest in terms of the parable of the sower (Mt.13:1-9; 18-23).

The famous Calvinistic TULIP with its theological terminology is not found in the Greek text of the New Testament, but Calvinists believe that the principles are clearly taught. Unconditional election (the second point in the acrostic) is inferred in verse 37. At least the election is there, although we must look to other passages for the point that its is not conditioned upon human merit, *e.g.* Eph.2:1-3. Perseverance (preservation) of the saints is clearly taught in verse 39. Limited atonement (particular redemption) is implied in verse 39 and irresistible grace is suggested in verse 37. Total depravity, with its teaching that the elect can do nothing to save themselves until God first moves, is clearly taught in verse 44.

It is well to remember that no scripture stands upon the basis of its own interpretation (II Pet.1:20) and thus that the total message of the Word of God is the result of a proper interrelationship of all scriptures as we rightly divide the Word of truth. No sound theology can be built upon isolated proof texts. To put it another way no single passage teaches anything until all other passages have been allowed to shed upon it whatever extra light they may have that is germane to the point.

The corollary of this proposition is that, just as no single proof text can support a theology, no theology can survive despite the plain statement of a single passage to the contrary. Of course all exegesis must be based upon sound grammatical, lexicographical and syntactical principles with due regard to the principle of *zeitgeist*.

Our Lord points forward to the resurrection of the saints ἐν τῇ ἐσχάτῃ ἡμέρᾳ - "at the last day." This day is not specifically defined in this passage, but other scriptures shed light upon the time of the resurrection in relation to other end-time events.

Cf.# 208 for other uses of ἀπόλλυμι in the sense of spiritual destruction. For ἡμέρα as the last day in an eschatological sense *cf.#* 135.

To those who are lost, what Jesus has to say is foolishness (I Cor.1:18). Their eyes are blinded (II Cor.4:3). To them the gospel is a means of death (II Cor.2:15). On the contrary they will believe Satan's lie (II Thess.2:10). Jesus had already spoken of the judgment day (Mt.7:22; 10:15; 11:22,24; 12:36). In strict accounting the resurrection day for the saints whom God has given to Christ is not ἡ ἐσχάτη ἡμέρα. Jesus means the last day of the Church Age, after which 1000 years of Kingdom rule will pass before God's eternal day begins. Jesus is not teaching the details of eschatological events. He is saying that the Father's will, to which He is voluntarily subordinate, is that some should come to Him and that those who do so come, He will never cast out. Furthermore that these who come shall never be lost to Him. Verse 39 is the negative statement of which verse 37 is the positive. In between is verse 38 which says that all of this is contingent upon the will of the Father, not that of the Son, although He never says that His own will is contrary to that of the Father. Thus God's gift to Christ of the elect means that (a) they will come to Christ in a sense in which others will not come; (b) when they come they shall never be cast out; (c) on the contrary He shall lose none of them, except Judas; (d) He will raise them up in the resurrection at the last day. (I Thess.4:13-18; I Cor.15:51-58; Phil.3:20,21; Mt.24:29-31; Rev.11:15-19). The so-called doctrine of eternal security for the elects stands upon these assurances. How shall the elect be distinguished from others? We are told in

Verse 40 - "And this is the will of him that sent me, that every one which seeth the Son and believeth on him may have everlasting life: and I will raise him up at the last day."

τοῦτο γάρ ἐστιν τὸ θέλημα τοῦ πατρός μου, ἵνα πᾶς ὁ θεωρῶν τὸν υἱὸν καὶ πιστεύων εἰς αὐτὸν ἔχῃ ζωὴν αἰώνιον, καὶ ἀναστήσω αὐτὸν ἐγὼ (ἐν) τῇ ἐσχάτῃ ἡμέρᾳ.

τοῦτο (nom.sing.neut.of οὗτος, predicate nominative, deictic) 93.
γάρ (causal conjunction) 105.
ἐστιν (3d.per.sing.pres.ind.of εἰμί, aoristic) 86.
τὸ (nom.sing.neut.of the article in agreement with θέλημα) 9.
θέλημα (nom.sing.neut.of θέλημα, subject of ἐστιν) 577.

τοῦ (gen.sing.masc.of the article in agreement with πατρός) 9.

πατρός (gen.sing.masc.of πατήρ, possession) 238.

μου (gen.sing.masc.of ἐγώ, relationship) 123.

ἵνα (sub-final conjunction introducing a purpose/result clause) 114.

πᾶς (nom.sing.masc.of πᾶς, in agreement with θεωρῶν and πιστεύων) 67.

ὁ (nom.sing.masc.of the article in agreement with θεωρῶν) 9.

θεωρῶν (pres.act.part.nom.sing.masc.of θεωρέω, substantival, subject of ἔχῃ) 1667.

τὸν (acc.sing.masc.of the article in agreement with υἱόν) 9.

υἱὸν (acc.sing.masc.of υἱός, direct object of θεωρῶν) 5.

καὶ (adjunctive conjunction joining participles) 14.

πιστεύων (pres.act.part.nom.sing.masc.of πιστεύω, substantival, subject of ἔχῃ) 734.

εἰς (preposition with the accusative of cause) 140.

αὐτὸν (acc.sing.masc.of αὐτός, cause) 16.

ἔχῃ (3d.per.sing.pres.act.subj.of ἔχω, purpose/result) 82.

ζωὴν (acc.sing.fem.of ζωή, direct object of ἔχῃ) 668.

αἰώνιον (acc.sing.fem.of αἰώνιος, in agreement with ζωὴν) 1255.

καὶ (continuative conjunction) 14.

ἀναστήσω (1st.per.sing.fut.act.ind.of ἀνίστημι, predictive) 789.

αὐτὸν (acc.sing.masc.of αὐτός, direct object of ἀναστήσω) 16.

ἐγὼ (nom.sing.masc.of ἐγώ, subject of ἀναστήσω, emphatic) 123.

(ἐν) (preposition with the locative of time point) 80.

τῇ (loc.sing.fem.of the article in agreement with ἡμέρᾳ) 9.

ἐσχάτῃ (loc.sing.fem.of ἔσχατος, in agreement with ἡμέρᾳ) 496.

ἡμέρᾳ (loc.sing.fem.of ἡμέρα, time point) 135.

Translation - "Because the will of my Father is this, that everyone who sees the Son and believes because of Him will have life eternal, and I will raise Him up at the last day."

Comment: γὰρ is causal and serves to tie verse 40 to verse 39. Why should Jesus be so careful to lose none of those whom the Father has given to Him? Because it is also the Father's will that these fortunate elect shall become identified as such by seeing Jesus and believing upon Him. Verse 36 had made it clear that not everyone who see also believes. John's grammar is better here than in verse 39. πᾶς ὁ θεωρῶν τὸν υἱὸν - "everyone (singular in πᾶς) who sees the Son and (adjunctive καὶ) believes because of Him." πᾶς is also joined to the participle πιστεύων. Believing εἰς αὐτόν is a more intimate relationship than believing about Him. We noted in verse 37 that following ὁ ἐρχόμενος, πρός with the accusative is a more intimate relationship than εἰς with the accusative, because the latter can mean only a physical approach whereas the former means a personal psychological trust. But here, in verse 40 εἰς with the accusative follows πιστεύων, not ἐρχόμενος. The accusative of extent cannot follow a verb of believing (trusting). It makes no sense to say, "believing toward Him," but "believing because of Him" makes very good sense indeed. εἰς with the accusative of cause is the common idiom for personal trust in and commitment to Jesus Christ, *e.g.* John 3:16.

When the sovereign God purposes we may think of the clause that expresses it as sub-final, *i.e.* both telic and consecutive, purpose and result, since that which He purposes never fails in result. Here the ἵνα clause is sub-final. His purpose is that His elect, His gift to His Son, Jesus Christ, will see the Son and believe upon Him because of the motivating and enabling power of the Holy Spirit. Otherwise they could not call Jesus Lord (II Cor.12:3). When they see and believe they will have eternal life. Thus the result is gained. The conclusion is the same as in verse 39 except that (a) in verse 40 the masculine αὐτὸν has as its antecedents the two participles, ὁ θεωρῶν and πιστεύων, whereas in verse 39 He used the neuter αὐτὸ with its antecedent the relative ὅ, and (b) in verse 40, Jesus emphasizes that it is He who will raise the dead at the last day, with the inclusion of emphatic ἐγώ, whereas in verse 39, the personal pronoun is implicit only in the verb ending of ἀναστήσω. The division of labor in the Godhead is thus set forth. The Father gives the elect to the Son. When they see Him they are so attracted to Him that because of Him they believe upon Him. He gives them the eternal bread (verse 27); He preserves them (verse 39) and He raises them from the dead in the resurrection on the last day (verse 40). *Cf.* I Thess.4:13-18. Meyer points to the change in tenses. ἔχῃ is present tense and ἀναστήσω is future. Everlasting life at the moment in time when they see the Son and believe upon Him and make their commitment. Resurrection from death in the future - but as certain as though presently possessed. *Cf.* Rom.8:29,30.

This statement completes Jesus' opening salvo. During all of this time they had spoken to Him only four times: "How did you get here?" (verse 25); "What shall we do?" (verse 28); "Prove yourself to us" (verses 30,31) and "Give us the bread," (verse 34). Their concepts rise no higher than that this miracle worker, whoever he is, can feed us for nothing and therefore we should join ourselves to him for purely economic reasons. But Jesus' keen distinctions have offended them as we see in their next response in

Verse 41 - "The Jews then murmered at him, because he said, 'I am the bread which came down from heaven."

Ἐγόγγυζον οὖν οἱ Ἰουδαῖοι περὶ αὐτοῦ ὅτι εἶπεν Ἐγώ εἰμι ὁ ἄρτος ὁ καταβὰς ἐκ τοῦ οὐρανοῦ,

Ἐγόγγυζον (3d.per.pl.imp.act.ind.of γογγύζω, inceptive) 1322.

οὖν (inferential conjunction) 68.

οἱ (nom.pl.masc.of the article in agreement with Ἰουδαῖοι) 9.

Ἰουδαῖοι (nom.pl.masc.of Ἰουδαῖος, subject of ἐγόγγυζον) 143.

περὶ (preposition with the genitive of reference) 173.

αὐτοῦ (gen.sing.masc.of αὐτός, reference) 16.

ὅτι (causal conjunction) 211.

εἶπεν (3d.per.sing.aor.act.ind.of εἶπον, constative) 155.

Ἐγώ (nom.sing.masc.of ἐγώ, subject of εἰμι) 123.

εἰμι (1st.per.sing.pres.ind.of εἰμί, aoristic) 86.

ὁ (nom.sing.masc.of the article in agreement with ἄρτος) 9.
ἄρτος (nom.sing.masc.of ἄρτος, predicate nominative) 338.
ὁ (nom.sing.masc.of the article in agreement with καταβὰς) 9.
καταβὰς (aor.act.part.nom.sing.masc.of καταβαίνω, apposition) 324.
ἐκ (preposition with the ablative of source) 19.
τοῦ (abl.sing.masc.of the article in agreement with οὐρανοῦ) 9.
οὐρανοῦ (abl.sing.masc.of οὐρανός, source) 254.

Translation - "Therefore the Jews began to complain about Him because He said, 'I am the bread which came down out of heaven.' "

Comment: οὖν is inferential. Jesus' bold statements about His heavenly origin, His relationship to God and the plan of salvation irritated the Jews and they began (inceptive imperfect in ἐγόγγυζον) to complain about Him (genitive of reference). The ὅτι clause is causal. It was because He had said that He was the bread that came down from heaven. Such a positive declaration of His heavenly origin would be certain to elicit dissatisfaction only in those not elected to salvation. They did not really see Jesus and believe upon Him in the sense of verse 40. Saving faith is not irrational, but it is superrational. It provides certitude but it transcends human reason. Therefore human reason, not mixed with faith militates against saving faith. Saints must become as little children (Mt.18:3) if they are to receive God's revelation message (Mt.11:25-27) and inherit the earth (Mt.5:5). The Jews were resorting only to human reason. It will always support unbelief and never fails to promote pride and skepticism, the antithesis of saving faith.

The heart of the gospel is the incarnation of the historic Jesus of Nazareth. Christianity begins here. There is no vicarious atonement without a virgin born God-Man, the Man Christ Jesus. This gospel never fails to separate the elect from the non-elect. To the former the gospel smells like life; to the latter it smells like death (II Cor.2:15).

So long as the preacher avoids any mention of the trinitarian theology with its incarnate Jesus he can keep His crowds. Even Jesus lost His audience that day beside the Sea of Galilee. Because the Jews rejected the virgin birth they rejected Jesus' claim to a heavenly origin. This is the thought of

Verse 42 - "And they said, Is not this Jesus, the son of Joseph whose father and mother we know? How is it then that he saith, I came down from heaven?"

καὶ ἔλεγον, Οὐχ οὗτός ἐστιν Ἰησοῦς ὁ υἱὸς Ἰωσήφ, οὗ ἡμεῖς οἴδαμεν τὸν πατέρα καὶ τὴν μητέρα; πῶς νῦν λέγει ὅτι Ἐκ τοῦ οὐρανοῦ καταβέβηκα;

καὶ (continuative conjunction) 14.
ἔλεγον (3d.per.pl.imp.act.ind.of λέγω, inceptive) 66.
Οὐχ (summary negative conjunction with the indicative in rhetorical question) 130.
ἐστιν (3d.per.sing.pres.ind.of εἰμί, aoristic) 86.
Ἰησοῦς (nom.sing.masc.of Ἰησοῦς, predicate nominative) 3.

ὁ (nom.sing.masc.of the article in agreement with υἰὸς) 9.

υἰὸς (nom.sing.masc.of υἰός, apposition) 5.

'Ιωσήφ (gen.sing.masc.of 'Ιωσήφ, relationship) 62.

οὗ (gen.sing.masc.of ὅς, relationship) 65.

ἡμεῖς (nom.pl.masc.of ἐγώ, subject of οἴδαμεν) 123.

οἴδαμεν (1st.per.pl.2d.perf.ind.of ὁράω, consummative) 144.

τὸν (acc.sing.masc.of the article in agreement with πατέρα) 9.

πατέρα (acc.sing.masc.of πατήρ, direct object of οἴδαμεν) 238.

καὶ (adjunctive conjunction joining nouns) 14.

τὴν (acc.sing.fem.of the article in agreement with μητέρα) 9.

μητέρα (acc.sing.fem.of μήτηρ, direct object of οἴδαμεν) 76.

πῶς (interrogative conjunction) 627.

νῦν (temporal adverb) 1497.

λέγει (3d.per.sing.pres.act.ind.of λέγω, aoristic) 66.

ὅτι (recitative introducing direct discourse) 211.

'Εκ (preposition with the ablative of source) 19.

τοῦ (abl.sing.masc.of the article in agreement with οὐρανοῦ) 9.

οὐρανοῦ (abl.sing.masc.of οὐρανός, source) 254.

καταβέβηκα (1st.per.sing.perf.act.ind.of καταβαίνω, consummative) 324.

Translation - "And they began to say, 'Is not this man Jesus, the son of Joseph, the father and the mother of whom we have known? Why now is He saying, Out of the heaven I have come down?'"

Comment: The whining complaints (#1322) accelerated as the tongues began to wag. The people were trying to reconcile what Jesus said with what they thought they knew about Him. This is another illustration of the way in which fallible human reason intercepts saving faith. Their question is rhetorical. They are not asking for information. They think they have all of the facts. Their question challenges any to deny their logic. They are driving home a point. Note the contemptuous use of οὗτος - "Is not this fellow Jesus, the son of Joseph . . . κ.τ.λ." To which question the obvious answer seemed to be, "Of course it is." Their wickedness is evident in their mention of Joseph the carpenter as His father. They had all heard the scandal at Nazareth. Perhaps a knowing wink and a lecherous leer accompanied this snide remark. They emphasized what they knew with ἡμεῖς - unnecessary except for emphasis since it is implicit in the verb endings in οἴδαμεν. They were emphasizing what they thought they knew and judging Jesus upon that basis. This is the way all unbelievers make up their minds about Jesus - they judge Him on the basis of what they know. Believers judge themselves on the basis of the Son of God. Note the perfect tense in οἴδαμεν - "We have known His father and mother for years and are well acquainted with them now." Jesus had heard this reaction to His teaching before in Nazareth (Mt.14:54-58). Both cases indicate unbelief. πῶς often introduces rhetorical question. Cf.#627 for the complete list.

Their confusion about His birth could have been cleared up by Jesus. For them Messiah was to come in clouds of great glory, not as the illegitimate son of a Nazarene carpenter. Jesus had grown up among them in quiet solitude and had gained the reputation of a good little boy, a well-behaved teen-ager and a fine young man (Lk.2:40,52). We can thus understand their mental confusion. If they were right about His origins their conclusion that He was mistaken when He said that He had come down from heaven was sound. In a sentimental sense all little babies "come down from heaven" but hardly in a genetic sense and it was in this genetic sense that they understood Jesus to be speaking.

We may wonder why Jesus who certainly understood the ground of their confusion did not explain to them. He tells us why He did not in verses 43-44.

Verse 43 - "Jesus therefore answered and said unto them, Murmer not among yourselves."

ἀπεκρίθη Ἰησοῦς καὶ εἶπεν αὐτοῖς, Μὴ γογγύζετε μετ' ἀλλήλων.

ἀπεκρίθη (3d.per.sing. aor.ind.of ἀποκρίνομαι, constative) 318.
Ἰησοῦς (nom.sing.masc.of Ἰησοῦς, subject of ἀπεκρίθη and εἶπεν) 3.
καὶ (adjunctive conjunction joining verbs) 14.
εἶπεν (3d.per.sing.aor.act.ind.of εἶπον, constative) 155.
αὐτοῖς (dat.pl.masc.of αὐτός, indirect object of εἶπεν) 16.
Μὴ (qualified negative with the imperative) 87.
γογγύζετε (2d.per.pl.pres.act.impv.of γογγύζω, prohibition) 1322.
μετ' (preposition with the genitive, adverbial) 50.
ἀλλήλων (gen.pl.masc.of ἀλλήλων, adverbial) 1487.

Translation - "In reply Jesus said to them, 'Stop complaining among yourselves.'
"

Comment: The prohibition in the present tense means "Do not continue to complain" - therefore "Stop complaining among youselves (to one another)." γογγύζω (#1322) is a splendid example of onomatopoeia, the use of words whose sound suggests the meaning. The pronunciation provides an audible hint of the meaning. Transliterated into English it sounds like this: *gongedzo* (long e and long o) with the accent upon the long e. In classical Greek it was used of the cooing of doves. Pronounce and compare with the whine of a spoiled child. Accented properly with appropriate sing-song inflection and it suggests the paranoid little girl dragging her doll through the mud by the foot and mournfully proclaiming "You won't let me do *anything!*" Reread verse 42 with this in mind. Jesus said, "Stop your whining!"

Why did Jesus not explain? To have removed the intellectual basis for their doubts by explaining to them His virgin birth would have been casting genuine pearls before genuine swine. They would not have believed Him if He had told them. They had not believed in Him thus far, despite the evidence of the multiplication of the bread and fish and they would only have rejected His story of the incarnation.

Men do not repent and believe the gospel because of their intellectual understanding of its message. A sinner does not reason his way to salvation by the inductive method. Many unbelievers understand the theology of Christianity quite well. They simply cannot believe it. This truth has deep implications for the proper approach to personal evangelism. No one was ever brought to Christ because he lost an argument with a Christian. This point Jesus makes very clear in

Verse 44 - *"No man can come to me except the Father, which hath sent me draw him; and I will raise him up at the last day."*

οὐδεὶς δύναται ἐλθεῖν πρός με ἐὰν μὴ ὁ πατὴρ ὁ πέμψας με ἑλκύσῃ αὐτόν, κἀγὼ ἀναστήσω αὐτὸν ἐν τῇ ἐσχάτῃ ἡμέρᾳ.

οὐδεὶς (nom.sing.masc.of οὐδείς, subject of δύναται) 446.

δύναται (3d.per.sing.pres.ind.of δύναμαι, aoristic) 289.

ἐλθεῖν (aor.inf.of ἔρχομαι, complementary) 146.

πρός (preposition with the accusative of extent) 197.

με (acc.sing.masc.of ἐγώ, extent) 123.

ἐὰν (particle introducing a third-class condition) 363.

μὴ (qualified negative conjunction with the subjunctive in a third-class condition) 87.

ὁ (nom.sing.masc.of the article in agreement with πατήρ) 9.

πατήρ (nom.sing.masc.of πατήρ, subject of ἑλκύσῃ) 238.

ὁ (nom.sing.masc.of the article in agreement with πέμψας) 9.

πέμψας (aor.act.part.nom.sing.masc.of πέμπω, apposition) 169.

με (acc.sing.masc.of ἐγώ, direct object of πέμψας) 123.

#2289 ἑλκύσῃ (3d.per.sing.aor.act.subj.of ἑλκύω, third-class condition).

draw - John 6:44; 12:32; 18:10; 21:6,11; Acts 16:19.

Meaning: To draw; to pull a person or thing toward one. To attract, either physically or psychologically. Peter unsheathed a sword - John 18:10; the disciples dragged a net into a boat - John 21:6, and to the shore - John 21:11. With reference to conveying a prisoner against his will - Acts 16:19. With reference to spiritual attraction, involving the will, intellect and emotion, to Christ - When God the Father exercises the force - John 6:44; when Christ pulls - John 12:32. In certain contexts the force may be applied in the face of personal resistance as in Acts 16:19, or impersonal friction - John 18:10; 21:6,11. It does not necessarily involve coercion, though it does involve persuasion and motivation - John 6:44; 12:32.

αὐτόν (acc.sing.masc.of αὐτός, direct object of ἑλκύσῃ) 16.

κἀγὼ (continuative conjunction) 178.

ἀναστήσω (1st.per.sing.fut.act.ind.of ἀνίστημι, predictive) 789

αὐτὸν (acc.sing.masc.of αὐτός, direct object of ἀναστήσω) 16.

ἐν (preposition with the locative of time point) 80.

τῇ (loc.sing.fem.of the article in agreement with ἡμέρᾳ) 9.

ἐσχάτῃ (loc.sing.fem.of ἔσχατος, in agreement with ἡμέρᾳ) 496.

ἡμέρᾳ (loc.sing.fem.of ἡμέρα, time point) 135.

Translation - "No one is able to come to me if the Father who sent me does not draw him, and I will raise him up at the last day."

Comment: The translation is literal. This is an inverted third-class condition. The apodosis (result clause) comes before the protasis (if clause). So we could translate "If the Father who sent me does not draw him, no man is able to come to me" or "Except the Father . . . draw him no man is able . . . κ.τ.λ." Note that Jesus uses πρός and the accusative after the infinitive ἐλθεῖν, an example of πρός rather than εἰς after a verb of coming, when the issue is salvation. Again Jesus points to the fact that His Father had sent Him into the world, in order that the Father might have Someone to Whom He might draw His elect whom He has given to His Son. Since the elect is the Father's gift to His Son and since the Father has drawn the elect to His Son, the Son, whose will always coincides with that of His Father will accept the sinner and preserve him unto the last day at which time physical resurrection will rescue his body from the grave.

The distinction between πρός and εἰς after ἔρχομαι or one of its forms is important. πρός speaks of the more intimate rapport which the true believer enters into with Christ. Anyone who walked up to Jesus in the physical sense could be said to have come to Him. This idea is expressed by ἔρχομαι, followed by εἰς and the accusative of extent. The most blatant unbeliever can do this though he has not the slightest spiritual or intellectual interest in Jesus. Witness the Roman soldiers and many others, including most of Jesus' audience on this occasion who had come to Him but only for another free meal. But to come πρὸς Ἰησοῦν is a different, more glorious matter. *Cf.*#146 for all the cases in which ἔρχομαι is followed by πρός.

The main thrust of the verse is that if the Father does not first of all draw the sinner, he cannot come to Christ and enjoy the πρός "saving" relationship. The condition is third-class with ἐάν and the subjunctive indicating some element of doubt as to whether or not the Father will draw the sinner. Jesus does not doubt that the Father will draw some to Him, but He is not stating specifically the identity of the elect ones. The result in the apodosis is contingent upon the fulfillment of the protasis. If the Father draws . . . men can come. Otherwise not. Jesus is making no statement as to whether or not the Father will draw anyone. This depends solely upon the Father's will and His purpose will be carried out without regard to Jesus or anyone else. Jesus is only saying that the coming of the sinner to Him will not take place unless the Father first of all draws him. ἑλκύσῃ (#2289) does not imply coercion in the two places where it is applied to the elect. Swords, fish nets and political prisoners (John 18:10; 21:6,11; Acts 16:19) may resist, but the *element* of resistance is not implicit in the word itself. One who is convinced (impelled, motivated, courted, influenced, attracted, lured) is also "drawn" as the intellect and the emotions influence the will to act in accord with the wishes of the one who draws. No sinner ever came to Christ against His will, and no sinner ever wished to come to Christ whose will was not first of all acted upon by the Father's drawing power. That is why Jesus told them in verse 43 to stop whining. Their feeble attempts to solve their dilemma with human logic had nothing whatever to do with it. If the Father draw them they will come to Christ whether they understand Him or not. (Whoever qualified as an accomplished theologian on the day that he came to Christ for salvation?!). If they understood all of the correct theology with reference to Christ they would not come to Him without the Father's drawing power first exerted. Why then should Jesus waste time, His and theirs, by applying intellectual persuasion? This is why He ignored the question of verse 25 and why He did not enlighten them about how the Nazarene carpenter, Mary's son, could nevertheless be the Incarnate Son of God. Christians who try to win souls by intellectualizing the theology of salvation and Christology may win intellectual converts. But those, thus converted, do not necessarily come πρὸς τὸν Χριστόν. He explains further in

Verse 45 - "It is written in the prophets, And they shall be all taught of God. Every man therefore that hath heard, and hath learned of the Father, cometh unto me."

ἐστιν γεγραμμένον ἐν τοῖς προφήταις, Καὶ ἔσονται πάντες διδακτοὶ θεοῦ. πᾶς ὁ ἀκούσας παρὰ τοῦ πατρὸς καὶ μαθὼν ἔρχεται πρὸς ἐμέ.

ἔστιν (3d.per.sing.pres.ind.of εἰμί, perfect periphrastic) 86.

γεγραμμένον (perfect passive participle, nom.sing.neut.of γράφω, perfect periphrastic) 156.

ἐν (preposition with the locative of place where) 80.

τοῖς (loc.pl.masc.of the article in agreement with προφήταις) 9.

προφήταις (loc.pl.masc.of προφήτης, place where) 119.

Καὶ (explanatory conjunction) 14.

ἔσονται (3d.per.pl.fut.ind.of εἰμί, predictive) 86.

πάντες (nom.pl.masc.of πᾶς, subject of ἔσονται) 67.

#2290 διδακτοὶ (nom.pl.masc.of διδακτός, predicate adjective).

taught - John 6:45.
which teacheth - I Cor.2:13,13.

Meaning: - taught, instructed. With θεοῦ in John 6:45. Followed by ἀνθρωπίνης σοφίας λόγοις in I Cor.2:13a, and by πνεύματος in I Cor.2:13b.

θεοῦ (abl.sing.masc.of θεός, source) 124.

πᾶς (nom.sing.masc.of πᾶς, in agreement with ἀκούσας and μαθὼν) 67.

ὁ (nom.sing.masc.of the article in agreement with ἀκούσας) 9.

ἀκούσας (aor.act.part.nom.sing.masc.of ἀκούω, subject of ἔρχεται) 148.

παρὰ (preposition with the ablative, with persons, "from the side of") 154.

τοῦ (abl.sing.masc.of the article in agreement with πατρὸς) 9.

πατρὸς (abl.sing.masc.of πατήρ, "from the side of") 238.

μαθὼν (2d.aor.act.part.nom.sing.masc.of μανθάνω, subject of ἔρχεται) 794.

ἔρχεται (3d.per.sing.pres.ind.of ἔρχομαι, customary) 146.

πρὸς (preposition with the accusative of extent) 197.

ἐμέ (acc.sing.masc.of ἐμός, extent) 1267.

Translation - "It is written in the prophets, 'Now all men shall be divine students.'
Everyone who heard from the Father and became a learner comes to me."

Comment: The quotation is from Isa.54:13 where the LXX has καὶ πάντας
τοὺς υἱούς σου διδακτοὺς ϑεοῦ. *Cf.* I Thess.4:9 where we have αὐτοὶ γὰρ ὑμεῖς
ϑεοδίδακτοί ἐστε. The perfect periphrastic ἐστιν γεγραμμένον denotes a
current linear state of being. "Having in past time been written it now stands
written." We must say "in the prophets" (*i.e.* in the prophetic scrolls), the locative
of place where, rather than "by the prophets", the instrumental of agent, since
the prophets wrote centuries before Jesus spoke these words.

We cannot push πάντες to mean the quanatative whole of the human race
since that would include those who died in infancy, but it does include all the race
who survived to the age of discretion, even though millions, because of
geographical isolation, died without ever having had the privilege of hearing the
Bible read and discussed. διδακτοὶ ϑεοῦ need not depend wholly upon the
teaching ministry of a gospel missionary. God has other ways to teach men.
διδακτοὶ is a predicate adjective and is followed by the genitive of description in
ϑεοῦ *without the article.* Hence the translation, "divine students." When the
genitive follows a substantive without the intervening article it is definitive. God
has appealed to all men in that He created man with the power of reason - "the
light that lightens every man that comes into the world" (John 1:9). This gift of
the power of deduction was not given to the beasts. Given to man it is, in itself
evidence that God wants to communicate with him. Also *Cf.* Psalm 19:1,2. In
these senses all men who have attained the age of intellectual discretion and
moral responsibility shall become students of God.

But there is a difference between being in the number of the διδακτοὶ ϑεοῦ and
those described by Jesus as πᾶς ὁ ἀκούσας παρὰ τοῦ πατρὸς καὶ μαϑὼν - "all
those who heard with understanding at the side of the Father and became
learners." All matriculate in the divine school and all attend the lectures. They
learn something. Paul describes the extent of their learning in Romans 1:19-20
and goes on in verse 21 to describe their reaction to what they learned. Thus it is
clear that not all who are "divine students" come πρὸς Χριστόν, because only
some hear and submit to discipleship.

A special kind of hearing is seen in ὁ ἀκούσας παρὰ τοῦ πατρός. Παρά (#154)
has a basic meaning of "alongside" or "the the side of." The Latin *pari passu* -
"step by step with," "with equal step" or "at an equal rate or pace" expresses it.
To hear παρὰ τοῦ πατρός is to learn all that God means to convey as He conveys
it. This is the kind of rapport, mentally and spiritually, that results when God,
who sent Jesus to earth, draws men to His Son (vs. 44). A good conversationalist
carries his listeners with him; a good listener stays with (alongside) the speaker.
This is apparent in a university classroom. The A students hear in the best sense
while the B,C and D students are less alert. The F students may as well not be
there.

Though we cannot push to extremes this principle, it seems that in many
contexts the distinction between the accusative and the genitive following ἀκούω
is to be noted. The accusative with its basic idea of extension indicates that what

was heard extended (penetrated) into the consciousness, while the genitive of description need only mean that the sound was heard, although the essence of what was said did not register. Thus we explain what has been called a contradiction between Acts 9:7 on the one hand and Acts 22:9; 26:14 on the other. In Acts 9:7 the genitive case follows ἀκούοντες, whereas in the two later passages, the accusative follows ἤκουσαν in Acts 22:9 and ἤκουσα in Acts 26:14. Paul's companions heard the sound (Acts 9:7) but they did not understand what was said (Acts 22:9) although Paul did understand (Acts 26:14). When we apply this grammatical principle it is interesting to note that in John 5:24 the accusative of extent (penetration) is joined with ἀκούων to indicate genuine understanding and hence salvation.

Some seed never germinates. The same seed, falling in more receptive soil, grows immediately. And yet the difference between those who hear and those who do not hear παρὰ τοῦ πατρός is not in the listener. God draws some and they hear παρὰ τοῦ πατρός. Others He does not draw and though the voice of the teacher is physically audible and the testimony of nature is intellectually clear, the listener does not *hear*. Dr. Walter Taylor, the famous director of the Pacific Garden Mission in the 1930's said to the author with reference to the men who attended the services, "They hear the gospel and hear the gospel and hear the gospel, and then one night they **HEAR THE GOSPEL.**" It was on that last night that they were subjected to the Holy Spirit's effectual call. This is what the Calvinists call irresistible grace.

Those who hear the gospel παρὰ τοῦ πατρός also become learners (μαθών). That is, they have taken their proper position as "learners" (disciples). This is a humble position. Those who take this position have given up the quest for certitude in the realms of reason and/or experience. Neither deductive reason nor inductive science can give us more certitude than is available in statistical probability. Those who understand this have undergone a humiliating experience. They become like the little child of Mt.18:3 and the babe of Mt.11:25. Intellectual humility and spiritual humility go hand in hand. Only the intellectually humble are meek and they alone will inherit the earth (Mt.5:3). This is the one that Jesus was talking about when He said ἔρχεται πρὸς ἐμέ. To be that close to Jesus is to be as close to Him as He was to God (John 1:1) and the Father (I John 1:1). *Cf.* John 17:21. The student should check #197 to see if πρός is ever used of the relationship of the unsaved to God and Christ. In this discourse it seems that Jesus uses πρός to denote a more intimate and hence saving relationship with Him than is expressed by εἰς which could denote only physical proximity. It is the difference between the multitudes who touched Jesus and the sick woman who *touched* Him (Lk.8:45). If ἀκούσας παρὰ τοῦ πατρός denotes a rapport with the Father of such close intimacy it might be concluded that those who have been so blessed have been close enough to God to see Him. This Jesus denies in verse 46.

The *Expositors' Bible* says that verse 45 may not teach "irresistible grace" though it does support Augustine against Pelagius. This writer believes that the verse strongly supports "irresistible grace." If so the Calvinistic TULIP is complete in this discourse by our Lord. Total depravity (John 6:44); Unconditional Election (John 6:37); Irresistible grace (John 6:45); Limited Atonement or Particular Redemption (John 6:39); and Preservation (Perseverance) of the Saints (John 6:35,37,39,40,44,47,50,54,57). The student should remember that no verse teaches what you think it does if it is plainly contradicted by another verses, taken in context and with due regard to grammar, diction, syntax and *zeitgeist*. The Holy Spirit has not written a self-contradictory book. The contradictions are in the mind of the beholder, not in that which is beheld.

Verse 46 - "Not that any man hath seen the Father, save he which is of God, he hath seen the Father."

οὐχ ὅτι τὸν πατέρα ἐώρακέν τις εἰ μὴ ὁ ὢν παρὰ τοῦ θεοῦ, οὗτος ἑώρακεν τὸν πατέρα.

οὐχ (summary negative conjunction with the indicative understood) 130.
ὅτι (objective conjunction introducing an object clause) 211.
τὸν (acc.sing.masc.of the article in agreement with πατέρα) 9.
πατέρα (acc.sing.masc.of πατήρ, direct object of ἐώρακέν) 238.
τις (nom.sing.masc.of τις, the indefinite pronoun, subject of ἑρώκέν) 486.
εἰ (conditional particle with μὴ with the indicative) 337.
μὴ (qualified negative conjunction with εἰ, and the indicative) 87.
ὁ (nom.sing.masc.of the article in agreement with ὢν) 9.
ὢν (pres.part.nom.sing.masc.of εἰμί, substantival, subject of ἑρώκεν) 86.
παρὰ (preposition with the genitive, with persons, "by the side of") 154.
τοῦ (gen.sing.masc.of the article in agreement with θεοῦ) 9.
θεοῦ (gen.sing.masc.of θεός, "by the side of") 124.
οὗτος (nom.sing.masc.of οὗτος, subject of ἑώρακεν) 93.
ἑώρακεν (3d.per.sing.perf.act.ind.of ὁράω, consummative) 144.
τὸν (acc.sing.masc.of the article in agreement with πατέρα) 9.
πατέρα (acc.sing.masc.of πατήρ, direct object of ἑώρακεν) 238.

Translation - "Not that anyone has understood the Father, except the One Who is always by the side of God. That One understands the Father."

Comment: τις, the subject of ἑώρακέν yields the prior position of emphasis to τὸν πατέρα. Jesus is emphasizing that the Father is inaccessible to all except (εἰ μὴ) the One who is always by God's side. ἑώρακεν here (#144) refers to intellectual, not physical sight. It might be supposed that mortals who have been in the divine school as God's students and who have heard παρὰ τοῦ πατρός, have learned all that there is to know about Him. This is what Jesus denies. To hear the voice of God in effectual call and thus to become His disciple assures salvation, but it is not a graduate diploma in all that can be known about God. Only Christ knows that much about it, and that is because He has always been παρὰ τοῦ θεοῦ - "by the side of God." This expresses as intimate a relationship as does πρὸς τὸν θεόν in John 1:1 and πρὸς τὸν πατέρα of I John 1:1. That παρά refers to spiritual and intellectual fellowship rather than physical proximity is clear since Jesus, when He said this, was on earth while God was in heaven. We are indulging in undue anthropomorphic ideas when we speak of physical relationships with God the Father. Jesus here asserts that He is παρὰ τοῦ θεοῦ - "by the side of God." The last clause emphasizes the deictic οὗτος. "That one (referred to in the previous clause) has seen the Father." Without this statement some might conclude from verse 45 that it is possible to sit under God's instruction, hear with complete rapport and become a learner, without the intermediate agency of Christ. He claims monopoly on the experience of understanding all that the Father understands. No one else has been or is παρὰ τοῦ θεοῦ. No one else has seen Him. If we are to be saved our faith must begin with acceptance of the essential deity of the historic Jesus. He cannot be bypassed. The revelation of God to sinners is Christocentric.

Verse 47 - "Verily, verily I say unto you, He that believeth on me hath everlasting life."

ἀμὴν ἀμὴν λέγω ὑμῖν, ὁ πιστεύων ἔχει ζωὴν αἰώνιον.

ἀμὴν (explicative) 466.
ἀμὴν (explicative) 466.
λέγω (1st.per.sing.pres.act.ind.of λέγω, aoristic) 66.
ὑμῖν (dat.pl.masc.of σύ, indirect object of λέγω) 104.
ὁ (nom.sing.masc.of the article in agreement with πιστεύων) 9.
πιστεύων (pres.act.part.nom.sing.masc.of πιστεύω, substantival, subject of ἔχει) 734.
ἔχει (3d.per.sing.pres.act.ind.of ἔχω, aoristic) 82.
ζωὴν (acc.sing.fem.of ζωή, direct object of ἔχει) 668.
αἰώνιον (acc.sing.fem.of αἰώνιος, in agreement with ζωὴν) 1255.

Translation - "Truly, truly I am telling you that the believer has life everlasting."

Comment: Possession of eternal life is contingent upon faith. Some manuscripts add εἰς ἐμὲ after πιστεύων. The context demands this in any case. Metzger explains, "The addition of εἰς ἐμέ as the object of the verb "believe" was both natural and inevitable; the surprising thing is that relatively many copyists resisted the temptation. If the words had been present in the original text, no good reason can be suggested to account for their omission. The reading of the Old Syriac has been assimilated to 14.1." (Metzger, *A Textual Commentary on the Greek New Testament*, 213,214).

The author remembers how, as a young preacher in western Indiana, enthusiastically, if not fanatically commited to the doctrine of "eternal security" he employed this verse to prove his point. The method is first to stress the present tense of ἔχει. "The believer has whatever he has right now!" Now, what has he? Life. What kind of life? Eternal. How long is eternity and what kind of life is eternal life? If one possesses at the present moment a kind of life described as eternal, then he must live forever. It seemed at the time to be a conclusive argument. It still does, although there is much more to eternal life than the idea of existence somewhere forever. The unsaved have that. The quality of that life that is eternally viable is assured because in being saved the believer is brought πρὸς αὐτόν - "into intimate relationship with Him" as He prayed in John 17:21. If this is not recognized and appropriated by faith the "eternal security" becomes antinomianism and we say that we ought to continue in sin that grace may abound - a concept that Paul thought horrible (Rom.6:1-4). Verse 47 is linked to everything that Jesus said about Himself in previous as well as in following verses.

Verse 48 - "I am that bread of life."

ἐγώ εἰμι ὁ ἄρτος τῆς ζωῆς.

ἐγώ (nom.sing.masc.of ἐγώ, subject of εἰμι) 123.
εἰμι (1st.per.sing.pres.ind.of εἰμί, aoristic) 86.
ὁ (nom.sing.masc.of the article in agreement with ἄρτος) 9.
ἄρτος (nom.sing.masc.of ἄρτος, predicate nominative) 338.
τῆς (gen.sing.masc.of the article in agreement with ζωῆς) 9.
ζωῆς (gen.sing.masc.of ζωή, description) 668.

Translation - "I am the bread of life."

Comment: Here we have Jesus introducing Himself again with the name which He gave to Moses at the bush (Ex.3:12-14). Note its use also in John 4:26; 6:20,35,48,51; 8:12,58; 11:25; 14:6; 18:5,6. He is Jehovah (Joshua, Jesus, Jehovah is the Saviour). This statement following immediately upon verse 47 makes εἰς ἐμέ after πιστεύων (supplied by A C₂ D K Δ Π Ψ and others) unnecessary. This is a repetition of a part of verse 35. The Jews had implied in verse 31 that Jesus' performance in feeding them was no greater than Moses' in the wilderness. Judged on that basis alone, they were saying that Jesus could rise no higher in their esteem than did Moses. Jesus proceded in verses 49-50 to refute this argument. Moses, to be sure, was used of God to feed a nation miraculously for 38 years. But the quality of the produce was not equal to that which Jesus, in the spiritual realm, could give to those who would believe.

What happened to their forefathers who ate Moses' manna for 38 years? This is the subject of

Verse 49 - "Your fathers did eat manna in the wilderness and are dead."

οἱ πατέρες ὑμῶν ἔφαγον ἐν τῇ ἐρήμῳ τὸ μάννα καὶ ἀπέθανον.

οἱ (nom.pl.masc.of the article in agreement with πατέρες) 9.
πατέρες (nom.pl.masc.of πατήρ, subject of ἔφαγον and ἀπέθανον) 238.
ἡμῶν (gen.pl.masc.of σύ, relationship) 104.
ἔφαγον (3d.per.pl.aor.act.ind.of ἐσθίω, constative) 610.
ἐν (preposition with the locative of place where) 80.
τῇ (loc.sing.fem.of the article in agreement with ἐρήμῳ) 9.
ἐρήμῳ (loc.sing.fem.of ἐρημός, place where) 250.

τό (acc.sing.neut.of the article in agreement with μάννα) 9.
μάννα (acc.sing.neut.of μάννα, direct object of ἔφαγον) 2288.
καί (adversative conjunction) 14.
ἀπέθανον (3d.per.pl.2d.aor.ind.of ἀποθνήσκω, culminative) 774.

Translation - "Your forefathers ate the manna in the wilderness, but they are dead."

Comment: This is a reference to their history to which they alluded in verse 31. They had appealed to the experience of the past - οἱ πατέρες ἡμῶν. Jesus counters with οἱ πατέρες ὑμῶν - "Your forefathers? What about them?" καί is adversative and the aorist in ἀπέθανον is culminative. "But they are now dead," despite the fact that they ate Moses' manna, of which you seem to be so proud. Moses was a miracle worker, but he could not forestall death except temporarily. The manna, supernaturally produced was not of a supernatural quality. They gathered and ate it daily or they starved. Jesus' bread and fish, served so lavishly the day before, was also miraculously produced, although not of any greater nutrient quality than Moses' manna. They ate but hungered again just as their forefathers in the desert did.

The point is not in the comparison between the two miracles. The point is in the metaphorical use to which Jesus is about to put the entire incident. This He does in

Verse 50 - "This is the bread which cometh down from heaven that a man may eat thereof, and not die."

οὗτός ἐστιν ὁ ἄρτος ὁ ἐκ τοῦ οὐρανοῦ καταβαίνων ἵνα τις ἐξ αὐτοῦ φάγη καὶ μὴ ἀποθάνη.

οὗτός (nom.sing.masc.of οὗτος, deictic, subject of ἐστιν) 93.
ἐστιν (3d.per.sing.pres.ind.of εἰμί, aoristic) 86.
ὁ (nom.sing.masc.of the article in agreement with ἄρτος) 9.
ἄρτος (nom.sing.masc.of ἄρτος, predicate nominative) 338.
ὁ (nom.sing.masc.of the article in agreement with καταβαίνων) 9.
ἐκ (preposition with the ablative of source) 19.
τοῦ (abl.sing.masc.of the article in agreement with οὐρανοῦ) 9.
οὐρανοῦ (abl.sing.masc.of οὐρανός, source) 254.
καταβαίνων (pres.act.part.nom.sing.masc.of καταβαίνω, apposition) 324.
ἵνα (sub-final conjunction introducing a purpose/result clause) 114.
τις (nom.sing.masc.of τις, subject of φάγη and ἀποθάνη) 486.
ἐξ (preposition with the ablative of source) 19.
αὐτοῦ (abl.sing.masc.of αὐτός, source) 16.
φάγη (3d.per.sing.aor.act.subj.of ἐσθίω, purpose/result) 610.
καί (adjunctive conjunction joining sub-final clauses) 14.
μή (qualified negative conjunction with the subjunctive in a sub-final clause) 87.
ἀποθάνη (3d.per.sing.aor.act.subj.of ἀποθνήσκω, purpose/result) 774.

Translation - "This is the bread that has come down out of heaven in order that anyone can eat of it and not die."

Comment: οὗτός is emphatic. Jesus is speaking about Himself as He made clear in verses 35-38, 48 and as He will repeat in verse 51. He is the Bread of Life and He reasserts His heavenly origin and the reason for it. It is that men may eat the Bread from Heaven and, unlike their forefathers in the wilderness, who also had eaten what they thought was heavenly bread, never die. Thus Jesus is doing what He did in John 3 with Nicodemus, in John 4 with the Samaritan woman, and in John 5 with the lame man. He is using earthly things to teach heavenly things. Spiritual birth from above, spiritual water that satisfies forever, permanent healing and now heavenly bread which gives everlasting life. This is better than eating heavenly manna every day for 38 years.

Jesus had repeatedly identified Himself with ὁ ἄρτος (vss.33,35,48,50). The Jews so understood Him (verse 41). Now He introduces a new thought into the discussion. Men may, indeed they *must* eat Him if they wish to escape eternal death. Their forefathers ate the manna (vss.31,49). Now Jesus suggests that they must *eat* the true bread from heaven. He reiterates the point and makes it even stronger in

Verse 51 - "I am the living bread which came down from heaven; if any man eat of this bread he shall live forever: and the bread that I will give him is my flesh, which I will give for the life of the world."

ἐγώ εἰμι ὁ ἄρτος ὁ ζῶν ὁ ἐκ τοῦ οὐρανοῦ καταβάς. ἐάν τις φάγῃ ἐκ τούτου τοῦ ἄρτου ζήσει εἰς τὸν αἰῶνα, καὶ ὁ ἄρτος δὲ ὃν ἐγὼ δώσω ἡ σάρξ μού ἐστιν ὑπὲρ τῆς τοῦ κόσμου ζωῆς.

ἐγώ (nom.sing.masc.of ἐγώ, subject of εἰμι) 123.

εἰμι (1st.per.sing.pres.ind.of εἰμί, aoristic) 86.

ὁ (nom.sing.masc.of the article in agreement with ἄρτος) 9.

ἄρτος (nom.sing.masc.of ἄρτος, predicate nominative) 338.

ὁ (nom.sing.masc.of the article in agreement with ζῶν) 9.

ζῶν (pres.act.part.nom.sing.masc.of ζάω, adjectival, restrictive) 340.

ὁ (nom.sing.masc.of the article in agreement with καταβάς) 9.

ἐκ (preposition with the ablative of source) 19.

τοῦ (abl.sing.masc.of the article in agreement with καταβάς) 9.

καταβάς (aor.act.part.nom.sing.masc.of καταβαίνω, substantival, apposition with ἄρτος) 324.

ἐάν (conditional particle in a third-class condition) 363.

τις (indefinite pronoun, nom.sing.masc.of τις, subject of φάγῃ and ζήσει) 486.

φάγῃ (3d.per.sing.aor.act.subj.of ἐσθίω, third-class condition) 610.

ἐκ (preposition with the ablative of source) 19.

τούτου (abl.sing.masc.of οὗτος, in agreement with ἄρτου) 93.

τοῦ (abl.sing.masc.of the article in agreement with ἄρτου) 9.

ἄρτου (abl.sing.masc.of ἄρτος, source) 338.

ζήσει (3d.per.sing.fut.act.ind.of ζάω, predictive) 340.

εἰς (preposition with the accusative, time extent) 140.

τὸν (acc.sing.masc.of the article in agreement with αἰῶνα) 9.

αἰῶνα (acc.sing.masc.of αἰών, time extent) 1002.

καὶ (continuative conjunction) 14.

ὁ (nom.sing.masc.of the article in agreement with ἄρτος) 9.

ἄρτος (nom.sing.masc.of ἄρτος, subject of ἐστιν) 338.

δὲ (intensive conjunction) 11.

ὃν (acc.sing.masc.of ὅς, direct object of δώσω) 65.

ἐγὼ (nom.sing.masc.of ἐγώ, subject of δώσω) 123.

δώσω (1st.per.sing.fut.act.ind.of δίδωμι, predictive) 362.

ἡ (nom.sing.fem.of the article in agreement with σάρξ) 9.

σάρξ (nom.sing.fem.of σάρξ, predicate nominative) 1202.

μού (gen.sing.masc.of ἐγώ, possession) 123.

ἐστιν (3d.per.sing.pres.ind.of εἰμί, aoristic) 86.

ὑπὲρ (preposition with the ablative, "for the sake of.") 545.

τῆς (abl.sing.fem.of the article in agreement with ζωῆς) 9.

τοῦ (gen.sing.masc.of the article in agreement with κόσμου) 9.

κόσμου (gen.sing.masc.of κόσμος, definition) 360.

ζωῆς (abl.sing.fem.of ζωή, "for the sake of.") 668.

Translation - "I AM - the Bread, the Living Bread, Who has come down out of heaven. If anyone will eat of this bread, he will live into the ages, and the bread which I will give for the life of the world is, in fact, my flesh."

Comment: Again Jesus identifies Himself as Jehovah of the Burning Bush. *Cf.* comment on John 4:26. Two participles follow ἄρτος, the first is a restrictive adjective. There is only one living bread of which we can eat and not die. The second identifies the Living Bread as the One Who has only recently come down out of heaven. Thus Jesus deals with His audience as He did with Nicodemus (John 3:13) by stating that He is on an incarnate visit from the heavenly realms. This thought had been a large part of the confrontation with the Jews on this occasion (*cf.* vss.33,38,41,42,50,51,58). It presents the heart of the matter. If Jesus is in fact the Son of God, come down from heaven in incarnation, then what He has to say about eternal life and how to get it is valid. If not the Jews were justified in turning away from Him. Note the sequence in the two participles after ὁ ἄρτος. He is ὁ ἄρτος ὁ ζῶν ὁ . . . . καταβὰς - "the Bread, the Living Bread, the out of heaven having descended Bread."

He now introduces a third-class condition. If anyone eats of this bread (the if clause) he will live forever (the result clause). As in all third-class conditions there is no positive assertion that anyone will eat. There is dogma in the statement of the result if anyone eats. Eat what? ἐκ τούτου τοῦ ἄρτου. Again He is emphatic with τούτου. The result is that those fortunate enough to eat of this bread will live into the ages - εἰς τὸν αἰῶνα - the New Testament expression for eternity. *Cf.*#1002. *Cf.*#'s 340 and 668 for the complete list of verses where spiritual life is in view.

Jesus has one more assertion in this remarkable statement. He must identify this Heavenly Bread which bestows eternal life more closely. Again He is intensive - this time with δὲ in one of its rare intensive uses. "And indeed (in fact, as a matter of fact, really) the bread which I will give is my flesh." For what? - ὑπὲρ τῆς τοῦ κόσμου ζωῆς. Cf.#545,III, 3 for other uses of ὑπέρ in the sense of "instead of" "in behalf of" or "for the sake of." ὑπέρ is "the most usual preposition for the notion of substitution" (Robertson, *Short Grammar*, 262). Now Jesus has added to His statement of the theology of incarnation, the theology of substitutionary sacrifice. His flesh is the Bread of which He has been speaking. Freely given it will be broken upon the cross. And because of this some will live forever.

His previous statement that He had come down out of heaven had triggered their resentment (vss.41,42). Now this further statement about giving His flesh for the life of the world upsets them again, as we see in

Verse 52 - "The Jews therefore strove among themselves, saying, How can this man give us his flesh to eat?"

Ἐμάχοντο οὖν πρὸς ἀλλήλους οἱ Ἰουδαῖοι λέγοντες, Πῶς δύναται οὗτος ἡμῖν δοῦναι τὴν σάρκα (αὐτοῦ) φαγεῖν;

#2291 Ἐμάχοντο (3d.per.pl.imp.ind.of μάχομαι, inceptive).

fight - Jam.4:2.
strive - John 6:52; Acts 7:26; II Tim.2:24.

Meaning: Cf.μάχαιρα (#896), μάχη (#4327) and διαμάχομαι (#3595). To fight; to engage in physical combat. Properly, as in Acts 7:26. To engage in heated argument - John 6:52; II Tim.2:24; with πολεμέω in Jam.4:2.

οὖν (inferential conjunction) 68.
πρὸς (preposition with the accusative of extent) 197.
ἀλλήλους (acc.pl.masc.of ἀλλήλων, extent, after a verb of speaking) 1487.
οἱ (nom.pl.masc.of the article in agreement with Ἰουδαῖοι) 9.
Ἰουδαῖοι (nom.pl.masc.of Ἰουδαῖος, subject of ἐμάχοντο) 143.
λέγοντες (pres.act.part.nom.pl.masc.of λέγω, recitative) 66.
Πῶς (interrogative conjunction) 627.
δύναται (3d.per.sing.pres.ind.of δύναμαι, aoristic) 289.
οὗτος (nom.sing.masc.of οὗτος, subject of δύναται, contemptuous use) 93.
ἡμῖν (dat.pl.masc.of ἐγώ, indirect object of δοῦναι) 123.
δοῦναι (aor.act.inf.of δίδωμι, complementary) 362.
τὴν (acc.sing.fem.of the article in agreement with σάρκα) 9.
σάρκα (acc.sing.fem.of σάρξ, direct object of δοῦναι) 1202.
αὐτοῦ (gen.sing.masc.of αὐτός, possession) 16.
φαγεῖν (aor.act.inf.of ἐσθίω, telic) 610.

Translation - "Therefore the Jews started an argument among themselves saying, 'How is this fellow able to give us His flesh to eat?' "

Comment: οὖν is inferential. Small wonder! For Jesus to speak of His flesh being bread to eat, thus to give life eternal, is as mysterious as a "birth from above" for an old man (John 3:3,7) or water which permanently quenches thirst (John 4:14). Just as Nicodemus and the Samaritan woman were confused so also were the Jews on this occasion. Nicodemus reacted with sarcasm (John 3:4), the woman with evasion (John 4:17) and the Jews, under great tension, with belligerence. They started a fight among themselves (inceptive imperfect in ἐμάχοντο). The word can mean fisticuffs (#2291) but it is not likely that it came to that in this case. At least the argument was heated, which may suggest that some were willing to hear Jesus out, while others were already prepared to reject Him totally (John 6:60-71). Πῶς here introduces rhetorical question, indicating the emotional tension of the audience. They were so surprized, even shocked at what was said, that they did not know what to believe. *Cf.*#627, I, C for other examples.

It is a natural reaction for one trained to think objectively to take words without equivocation and then, if when interpreted for their face value, they do not make sense to look for metaphorical meanings. Few are totally devoid of intellectual humility. At least some of the people there, who were also in the dark, were yet willing to wait for Jesus' own explanation of phraseology which was at that moment, admittedly obscure.

We note the contemptuous use of οὗτος, with its sarcasm, as it is unnecessarily emphasized. "How is *this fellow* able to give . . . κ.τ.λ.?" Then instead of a ἵνα clause of purpose with the subjunctive, John completes with a complementary telic infinitive. The infinitive to express purpose is common in the New Testament. *Cf.* Mt.2:2; 5:17; Lk.1:77; with τοῦ in Acts 9:15; with εἰς in I Thess.3:5; πρός - Mt.6:1; ὥστε - Lk.4:29; ὡς - Lk.9:52, *etc.*

Jesus made no further effort to explain His mysterious language. He only reiterated with a significant addition to His thought in verse 56. He knew who would believe and who would not (vs.64) and He repeated in verse 65 the Calvinistic thought of verse 44, as an explanation of the reason why there was no further point in making the truth of the gospel rational to sub-rational unregenerate man. He only reasserted, as He did to Nicodemus that birth (John 3), water (John 4), healing (John 5) and meat and bread (John 6) are of heavenly, not earthly origin.

Our Sovereign Lord, Who had always known the end from the beginning, therefore knew that after His passion, resurrection and reentry into glory, the Holy Spirit would fill the church and inspire the writing of the New Testament in which the full explanation of Jesus' words about His flesh and blood being meat and drink to the believer would be given. With Paul's writings before us, believers need no further explanation, for the Holy Spirit has brought everything to our remembrance and understanding. When the perfect revelation came that which was partial was done away (I Cor.13:10).

Verse 53 - "Then Jesus said unto them, Verily, verily, I say unto you, Except ye eat the flesh of the Son of Man and drink his blood, ye have no life in you."

εἶπεν οὖν αὐτοῖς ὁ'Ιησοῦς,'Αμὴν ἀμὴν λέγω ὑμῖν, ἐὰν μὴ φάγητε τὴν σάρκα τοῦ υἱοῦ τοῦ ἀνθρώπου καὶ πίητε αὐτοῦ τὸ αἷμα, οὐκ ἔχετε ζωὴν ἐν ἑαυτοῖς.

εἶπεν (3d.per.sing.aor.act.ind.of εἶπον, constative) 155.

οὖν (inferential conjunction) 68.

αὐτοῖς (dat.pl.masc.of αὐτός, indirect object of εἶπεν) 16.

ὁ (nom.sing.masc.of the article in agreement with 'Ιησοῦς) 9.

'Ιησοῦς (nom.sing.masc.of 'Ιησοῦς, subject of εἶπεν) 3.

'Αμὴν (explicative) 466.

ἀμὴν (explicative) 466.

λέγω (1st.per.sing.pres.act.ind.of λέγω, aoristic) 66.

ὑμῖν (dat.pl.masc.of σύ, indirect object of λέγω) 104.

ἐὰν (conditional particle in a third-class condition) 363.

μὴ (qualified negative conjunction in a third-class condition) 87.

φάγητε (2d.per.pl.aor.act.subj.of ἐσθίω, third-class condition) 610.

τὴν (acc.sing.fem.of the article in agreement with σάρκα) 9.

σάρκα (acc.sing.fem.of σάρξ, direct object of φάγητε) 1202.

τοῦ (gen.sing.masc.of the article in agreement with υἱοῦ) 9.

υἱοῦ (gen.sing.masc.of υἱός, possession) 5.

τοῦ (gen.sing.masc.of the article in agreement with ἀνθρώπου) 9.

ἀνθρώπου (gen.sing.masc.of ἄνθρωπος, definition) 341.

καὶ (adjunctive conjunction joining verbs) 14.

πίητε (2d.per.pl.aor.act.subj.of πίνω, third-class condition) 611.

αὐτοῦ (gen.sing.masc.of αὐτός, possession) 16.

τὸ (acc.sing.neut.of the article in agreement with αἷμα) 9.

αἷμα (acc.sing.neut.of αἷμα, direct object of πίητε) 1203.

οὐκ (summary negative conjunction with the indicative) 130.

ἔχετε (2d.per.pl.pres.act.ind.of ἔχω, aoristic) 82.

ζωὴν (acc.sing.fem.of ζωή, direct object of ἔχετε) 668.

ἐν (preposition with the locative with plural pronouns) 80.

ἑαυτοῖς (loc.pl.masc.of ἑαυτός, place where) 288.

Translation - "Jesus therefore said to them, 'Truly, truly I am telling you, if you do not eat the flesh of the Son of Man and drink His blood, you do not have life which is self-generated."

Comment: Again, as in all third-class conditions, Jesus makes no positive statement as to whether anyone would eat His flesh and drink His blood, but He is positive that *if* no one does, then no one has the potential to generate eternal life from his own inner resources. Lost man can never be his own saviour. Dead man can never raise himself from the dead. This is why Jesus, "The Son of Man" had to become incarnate, thus to become "The Son of Man" - ὁ υἱὸς τοῦ ἀνθρώπου. Jesus returns here to this designation which He had used only once before in this discourse (vs.27). He will use it again in verse 62. It is His official title when the context is dealing specifically with the incarnation.

Note the emphasis of αὐτοῦ, which outranks τὸ αἷμα in the second clause of the protasis.

What then does the unbeliever who does not eat and drink have in Him? Not life - only a living death like the Jews who, though they ate Moses' manna, nevertheless died, all of them physically and, unfortunately, some of them also in a spiritual sense. Goodspeed translates ζωὴν ἐν ἑαυτοῖς as "self-existent life." Life in man, in order to be truly viable must be the eternal life, the gift of Christ to man, made possible by His death, burial and resurrection, the Holy Spirit's effectual call, man's acceptance and Christ's acquiescence.

Verse 53 is the negative way of stating what Jesus repeats in a positive way in

Verse 54 - "Whoso eateth my flesh and drinketh my blood hath eternal life; and I will raise him up at the last day."

ὁ τρώγων μου τὴν σάρκα καὶ πίνων μου τὸ αἷμα ἔχει ζωὴν αἰώνιον, κἀγὼ ἀναστήσω αὐτὸν τῇ ἐσχάτῃ ἡμέρᾳ.

ὁ (nom.sing.masc.of the article in agreement with τρώγων) 9.

τρώγων (pres.act.part.nom.sing.masc.of τρώγω, substantival, subject of ἔχει) 1516.

μου (gen.sing.masc.of ἐγώ, possession) 123.

τὴν (acc.sing.fem.of the article in agreement with σάρκα) 9.

σάρκα (acc.sing.fem.of σάρξ, direct object of τρώγων) 1202.

καὶ (adjunctive conjunction joining participles) 14.

πίνων (pres.act.part.nom.sing.masc.of πίνω, substantival, subject ἔχει) 611.

μου (gen.sing.masc.of ἐγώ, possession) 123.

τὸ (acc.sing.neut.of the article in agreement with αἷμα) 9.

αἷμα (acc.sing.neut.of αἷμα, direct object of πίνων) 1203.

ἔχει (3d.per.sing.pres.act.ind.of ἔχω, aoristic) 82.

ζωὴν (acc.sing.fem.of ζωή, direct object of ἔχει) 668.

αἰώνιον (acc.sing.fem.of αἰώνιος, in agreement with ζωὴν) 1255.

κἀγὼ (continuative conjunction) 178.

ἀναστήσω (1st.per.sing.fut.act.ind.of ἀνίστημι, predictive) 789.

αὐτὸν (acc.sing.masc.of αὐτός, direct object of ἀναστήσω) 16.

τῇ (loc.sing.fem.of the article in agreement with ἡμέρᾳ) 9.

ἐσχάτῃ (loc.sing.fem.of ἔσχατος, in agreement with ἡμέρᾳ) 496.

ἡμέρᾳ (loc.sing.fem.of ἡμέρα, time point) 135.

Translation - "The one who eats my flesh and drinks my blood has life everlasting, and I will raise him up at the last day."

Comment: Why Jesus should employ τρώγω here and in vss. 56,57 and 68, after having used ἐσθίω previously in this discourse is not clear. *Cf.*#1516 for the original meaning of τρώγω, though by New Testament times ἐσθίω and τρώγω had become synonymous. In Patristic Greek (A.D. 4th/5th century) a song of Diogenes ". . . who, when he saw a certain man eating (ἔσθοντα) remarked - ἡ νύξ τὴν ἡμέραν τρώγει - ("the night is eating up the day" - *our translation*). There seems no good reason for assuming the survival of any difference in meaning between the two verbs that supplied a present stem ofr φαγεῖν, but see

Haussleiter in *Archiv. für lat. Lexicographie* ix. (1896), p.300*ff.* In MGr πρώ(γ)ω is the usual word for "eat." (Moulton and Milligan, *The Vocabulary of the Greek Testament*, 644).

Having said in verse 53 that there is no life except as we eat and drink of the body of Christ, He now says that life is certain for those who do so appropriate Christ unto themselves, even though physical death intervenes, because He promises κἀγὼ . . . ἡμέρᾳ. Those to whom spiritual discernment was granted saw the significance of the analogy. Just as they had appropriated the loaves and fishes the previous day for their own temporary advantage, so now they can appropriate the person of Christ for an eternal advantage. He who eats bread and fish at the creative hands of Jesus lives temporarily. He who eats what the bread typifies (ἐγὼ εἰμι ὁ ἄρος τῆς ζωῆς) lives eternally. But the bread must be broken and the blood must be shed. He had prophesied His sacrificial death before (John 2:19; 3:14-18). Once again He points forward to the cross.

Jesus' refusal to spell out the analogy in theological terms for the benefit of His audience recalls His reason for speaking in parables, as He gave it to the disciples in Mt.13:10-17, upon which *cf.* comment.

Having identified Himself as ὁ ἄρτος He now procedes to identify His flesh with meat and His blood with drink in

Verse 55 - "For my flesh is meat indeed, and my blood is drink indeed."

ἡ γὰρ σάρξ μου ἀληθής ἐστιν βρῶσις, καὶ τὸ αἷμά μου ἀληθής ἐστιν πόσις.

ἡ (nom.sing.fem.of the article in agreement with σάρξ) 9.

γὰρ (causal conjunction) 105.

σάρξ (nom.sing.fem.of σάρξ, subject of ἐστιν) 1202.

μου (gen.sing.masc.of ἐγώ, possession) 123.

ἀληθής (nom.sing.fem.of ἀληθής, in agreement with βρῶσις) 1415.

ἐστιν (3d.per.sing.pres.ind.of εἰμί, aoristic) 86.

βρῶσις (nom.sing.fem.of βρῶσις, predicate nominative) 594.

καὶ (continuative conjunction) 14.

τὸ (nom.sing.neut.of the article in agreement with αἷμά) 9.

αἷμά (nom.sing.neut.of αἷμα, subject of ἐστιν) 1203.

μου (gen.sing.masc.of ἐγώ, possession) 123.

ἀληθής (nom.sing.fem.of ἀληθής, in agreement with πόσις) 1415.

ἐστιν (3d.per.sing.pres.ind.of εἰμί, aoristic) 86.

#2292 πόσις (nom.sing.fem.of πόσις, predicate nominative).

drink - John 6:55; Rom.14:17; Col.2:16.

Meaning: Cf.#611 πίνω. The act of drinking or that which is drunk. Drink. Applied to the blood of Christ in John 6:55. The act of drinking in a proper sense in Rom.14:17; Col.2:16.

Translation - "Because my flesh is real food and my blood is real drink."

Comment: γὰρ is causal as verse 55 gives us the reason for the statement of verse 54, *Cf.*#594 - the result of eating - hence, food. Note that Paul says in Rom.14:17 that οὐ γάρ ἐστιν ἡ βασιλεία τοῦ θεοῦ βρῶσις καὶ πόσις. He is referring to food and drink in the metaphorical, not in the proper sense. Metaphorically the basis for the kingdom of God is βρῶσις καὶ πόσις because in the metaphor you mean ἡ βρῶσις καὶ ἡ πόσις as referring to ἡ σάρξ καὶ τὸ αἷμα τοῦ Χριστοῦ. In Col.2:16 Paul admonishes that we allow no man to judge our meat and drink. Indeed the believer, who has chosen the true meat and drink is beyond all human ability to condemn. The child of God, in Christ, lives beyond the jurisdiction of the unsaved world, although we are admonished to put ourselves under the political jurisdiction of the state (Rom.13:1-7).

Up to this point in the discourse Jesus has said nothing about the personal intimacy which exists between Him and the believer. It has been represented simply as a matter of accepting Him in the unique character of His person, His miraculous incarnation and the efficacy of His sacrificial death. What sort of personal relationship shall those enjoy who "eat His flesh and drink His blood?" Jesus answers this in

Verse 56 - "He that eateth my flesh and drinketh my blood dwelleth in me, and I in him."

ὁ τρώγων μου τὴν σάρκα καὶ πίνων μου τὸ αἷμα ἐν ἐμοὶ μένει κἀγὼ ἐν αὐτῷ.

ὁ (nom.sing.masc.of the article in agreement with τρώγων) 9.

τρώγων (pres.act.part.nom.sing.masc.of τρώγω, substantival, subject of μένει) 1516.

μου (gen.sing.masc.of ἐγώ, possession) 123.

τὴν (acc.sing.fem.of the article in agreement with σάρκα) 9.

σάρκα (acc.sing.fem.of σάρξ, direct object of τρώγων) 1202.

καὶ (adjunctive conjunction joining participles) 14.

πίνων (pres.act.part.nom.sing.masc.of πίνω, substantival, subject of μένει) 611.

μου (gen.sing.masc.of ἐγώ, possession) 123.

τὸ (acc.sing.neut.of the article in agreement with αἷμα) 9.

αἷμα (acc.sing.neut.of αἷμα, direct object of πίνων) 1203.

ἐν (preposition with the instrumental of means to denote the mystic union of the believer with Christ) 80.

ἐμοὶ (instrumental sing.masc.of ἐμός, means) 1267.

μένει (3d.per.sing.pres.act.ind.of μένω, progressive) 864.

κἀγὼ (adjunctive conjunction joining phrases, crasis) 14.

ἐν (preposition with the dative of personal advantage) 80.

αὐτῷ (dat.sing.masc.of αὐτός, personal advantage) 16.

Translation - "The one who eats my flesh and drinks my blood abides in me forever and I in him."

Comment: The prepositional phrases ἐν ἐμοὶ and ἐν αὐτῷ can, from the purely grammatical point of view, be locative, instrumental or dative, since the oblique cases all use the same ending. We can eliminate the concept of physical place where. To live physically *in Christ* does not make sense. The dative, which indicates personal interest or personal advantage/disadvantage, is a possible interpretation. He who eats and drinks abides for Christ's advantage and certainly the arrangement is for his own personal advantage. But the analogy in Jesus' teaching has reference to what happened the day before when they ate the loaves and fishes. Just as they lived physically for a few hours "by means of" (instrumental) the food, so the believer lives eternally (present tense in μένει) by means of Christ. It is His eternal essence which sustains the believer forever. The last phrase κἀγὼ ἐν αὐτῷ eliminates the locative and instrumental ideas, but clearly indicates the dative. The believer lives "by means of" Christ, and Christ abides in the believer "for the believer's advantage." *Cf.*Mι.10:32a,b; 17:12 for a similar construction. Our interpretation finds an explanation (instrumental in ἐν ἐμοί and dative in ἐν αὐτῷ) without resorting to the mystical explanation of Deissmann who says, "There cannot be any doubt that 'Christ in me' means the exalted Christ living in Paul. . . and Paul is in Christ. Christ, the exalted Christ, is Spirit. Therefore He can live in Paul and Paul in Him." (Mantey, *A Manual Grammar of the Greek New Testament*, 106). I object to this view on the grounds that the exalted Christ is also a body and hence Christ in the believer in a locative sense is nonesense. But that the passage can mean the mystic relationship between Christ and the believer of which He speaks in John 17:21 is clear. There is a long list of such passages in the New Testament. *Cf.*#80 in the Appendix. The instrumental concept is underscored in verse 57 which closes with the words κἀκεῖνος ζήσει δι' ἐμέ - "that one shall live because of me."

Verse 57 - "As the living Father hath sent me and I live by the Father, so he that eateth me, even he shall live by me."

καθὼς ἀπέστειλέν με ὁ ζῶν πατὴρ κἀγὼ ζῶ διὰ τὸν πατέρα, καὶ ὁ τρώγων με κἀκεῖνος ζήσει δι' ἐμέ.

καθὼς (adverb introducing a comparative clause) 1348.

ἀπέστειλεν (3d.per.sing.aor.act.ind.of ἀποστέλλω, culminative) 215.

με (acc.sing.masc.of ἐγώ, direct object of ἀπέστειλέν) 123.

ὁ (nom.sing.masc.of the article in agreement with πατήρ) 9.

ζῶν (pres.act.part.nom.sing.masc.of ζάω, adjectival, ascriptive, in agreement with πατήρ) 340.

πατὴρ (nom.sing.masc.of πατήρ, subject of ἀπέστειλέν) 238.

κἀγὼ (adjunctive conjunction joining clauses) 14.

ζῶ (1st.per.sing.pres.act.ind.of ζάω, aoristic) 340.

διὰ (preposition with the accusative, cause) 118.

τὸν (acc.sing.masc.of the article in agreement with πατέρα) 9.

πατέρα (acc.sing.masc.of πατήρ, cause) 238.

καὶ (emphatic conjunction) 14.

ὁ (nom.sing.masc.of the article in agreement with τρώγων) 9.

τρώγων (pres.act.part.nom.sing.masc.of τρώγω, substantival, subject of

με (acc.sing.masc.of ἐγώ, direct object of τρώγων) 123.
κἀκεῖνος (nom.sing.masc.of κἀκεῖνος, subject of ζήσει) 1164.
ζήσει (3d.per.sing.fut.act.ind.of ζάω, predictive) 340.
δι' (preposition with the accusative of cause) 118.
ἐμέ (acc.sing.masc.of ἐμός, cause) 1267.

Translation - *"Just as the living Father sent me and I am living because of the Father, (so) also the one who eats me - that one will always live because of me."*

Comment: Only the incredibly naive or one who feigns naivete will interpret ὁ τρώγων με κἀκεῖνος ζήσει δι' ἐμέ literally. The language is metaphorical. Obviously the believer does not *eat* Jesus' flesh nor *drink* His blood. His flesh, forever glorified, is at the right hand of God (Heb.1:3; Ps.110:1; Col.3:1), and His blood is sprinkled on the heavenly mercy seat witnessing that our sin debt is forever paid. The analogy relates to assimilation. Just as we ingest meat and drink and our bodies digest them, with the result that physical life and health are sustained, so our union with Christ provides His life. We identify totally with what we eat and drink and the Christian identifies totally with our ascended Lord (John 17:21).

Note καθώς . . . κἀγώ . . . καὶ in the "just as . . . and just as I . . . even so" sequence. The Father sent the Son and thus the Son lives because of the Father. In this same way the believer who believes upon and is identified with the Son will live because of the Son. διά with the genitive indicates means or agency; with the ablative it indicates source; with the accusative as in this passage it indicates cause. In verse 57 there is little difference between cause and means. "I live because of (by means of) the Father and he who eats me, that one lives because of (by means of) me." The καθώς . . . καὶ sequence says that the same relationship which exists between Jesus and the Father, as it pertains to life, also exists between the believer and Jesus. This is real homogeneity and it is supported by Jesus' prayer in John 17:21 to which we have alluded. To live by means of, or through the instrumentality of someone is to live because of that someone. If the someone did not exist and provide the means to the end, the end could not be accomplished. Thus Jesus is saying that the fortunes of the believer are tied to the hypostatic union of the Godhead - Father, Son and Holy Spirit. *Cf.* John 5:26 to support John 6:57.

The language indicates the subordination of Jesus to His Father. The sender takes precedence over the one sent. This is a part of the price which Jesus paid in incarnation (Phil. 2:5-8). That the incarnate Son of God is sovereign, coequal, coeval and coeternal with His Father is clearly taught in other scriptures. That for purposes of redemption He voluntarily divested Himself of the utilities of these characteristics is also clearly taught. This is a mystery as Paul admitted (I Tim.3:16).

Jesus closed His discourse by reiterating the thought of verse 49 in

Verse 58 - *"This is that bread which came down from heaven: not as your fathers did eat manna, and are dead: he that eateth of this bread shall live forever."*

οὖτός ἐστιν ὁ ἄρτος ὁ ἐκ τοῦ οὐρανοῦ καταβάς, οὐ καθὼς ἔφαγον οἱ πατέρες καὶ ἀπέθανον. ὁ τρώγων τοῦτον τὸν ἄρτον ζήσει εἰς τὸν αἰῶνα.

οὖτός (nom.sing.masc.of οὖτος, predicate nominative) 93.

ἐστιν (3d.per.sing.pres.ind.of εἰμί, aoristic) 86.

ὁ (nom.sing.masc.of the article in agreement with ἄρτος) 9.

ἄρτος (nom.sing.masc.of ἄρτος, subject of ἐστιν) 338.

ὁ (nom.sing.masc.of the article in agreement with καταβάς) 9.

ἐκ (preposition with the ablative of source) 19.

τοῦ (abl.sing.masc.of the article in agreement with οὐρανοῦ) 9.

οὐρανοῦ (abl.sing.masc.of οὐρανός, source) 254.

καταβάς (aor.act.part.nom.sing.masc.of καταβαίνω, adjectival, restrictive) 324.

οὐ (summary negative conjunction with the indicative in a comparative clause) 130.

καθὼς (comparative adverb introducing a comparative clause) 1348.

ἔφαγον (3d.per.pl.aor.act.ind.of ἐσθίω, constative) 610.

οἱ (nom.pl.masc.of the article in agreement with πατέρες) 9.

πατέρες (nom.pl.masc.of πατήρ, subject of ἔφαγον and ἀπέθανον) 238.

καὶ (adversative conjunction) 14.

ἀπέθανον (3d.per.pl.aor.act.ind.of ἀποθνήσκω, culminative) 774.

ὁ (nom.sing.masc.of the article in agreement with τρώγων) 9.

τρώγων (pres.act.part.nom.sing.masc.of τρώγω, substantival, subject of ζήσει) 1516.

τοῦτον (acc.sing.masc.of οὖτος, in agreement with ἄρτον) 93.

τὸν (acc.sing.masc.of the article in agreement with ἄρτον) 9.

ἄρτον (acc.sing.masc.of ἄρτος, direct object of ἔφαγον) 338.

ζήσει (3d.per.sing.fut.act.ind.of ζάω, predictive) 340.

εἰς (preposition with the accusative of time extent) 140.

τὸν (acc.sing.masc.of the article in agreement with αἰῶνα) 9.

αἰῶνα (acc.sing.masc.of αἰών, time extent) 1002.

Translation - "This is the bread which has come down out of heaven. It is not like what the fathers ate, but are now dead. The one who eats this bread will live into the ages."

Comment: Note that οὖτός, the predicate nominative (anarthrous) is emphasized, as it outranks ὁ ἄρτος in position. The subject is defined with the restrictive adjectival participle ὁ ἐκ τοῦ οὐρανοῦ καταβάς. Jesus is the only bread that had its source in heaven. Thus it is distinct and superior to the bread with which He is about to contrast it. What their forefathers ate in the wilderness for 38 years was miraculously provided, but (adversative καὶ), despite the miracle of its provision it was not miraculously qualitative. They ate it but they died and at the time that Jesus spoke this were then dead (culminative aorist). Jesus is talking about *bread* which gives life into the ages to those who eat it. There is positive and negative definition of the true bread. It was heavenly in origin and therefore in quality (positive definition), but it was unlike the manna in the wilderness since (negative definition) those who eat it, unlike Israel in the wilderness will not die. Moses' provision for the nation was miraculously produced and it enjoyed a great place in Israel's history. They loved to talk about it (vs.31). Yet those who ate it are dead. After all it was only physical food, designed to sustain a nation, day by day, throughout a 38 year trip through a desert to the promised land. Contrary to that ὁ τρώγων . . . εἰς τὸν αἰῶνα. There is nothing new in this verse. It is a reiteration of what had been said before. Thus Jesus laid before a hostile audience the essence of Christian theology in its Christological and soteriological aspects, with a touch of eschatology thrown in.

As Jesus taught Nicodemus to distinguish between the physical and the spiritual as they relate to birth (John 3), the Samaritan woman as they relate to drink (John 4), and the cripple as they relate to healing (John 5), so now He teaches the multitude that physical food, though good and necessary to sustain life temporarily cannot be compared with the spiritual food from heaven which is best because it gives life permanently.

In the closing verses of the chapter we shall see that Jesus lost His audience, though, of course, that did not surprize Him.

Verse 59 - "These things said he in the synagogue, as he taught in Capernaum.

Ταῦτα εἶπεν ἐν συναγωγῇ διδάσκων ἐν Καφαρναούμ.

Ταῦτα (acc.pl.neut.of οὗτος, direct object of εἶπεν) 93.
εἶπεν (3d.per.sing.aor.act.ind.of εἶπον, constative) 155.
ἐν (preposition with the locative of place where) 80.
συναγωγῇ (loc.sing.fem.of συναγωγή, place where) 404.
διδάσκων (pres.act.part.nom.sing.masc.of διδάσκω, adverbial, temporal) 403.
ἐν (preposition with the locative of place where) 80.
Καφαρναούμ (loc.sing.fem.of Καφαρναούμ, place where) 370.

Translation - "These things He said in a synagogue while teaching in Capernaum."

Comment: Ταῦτα in deictic emphasis refers to everything Jesus said beginning in verse 26. He certainly had said some emphatic things which penetrate to the roots of the Reformed theology. e.g.vss.37,39,44. These truths bring the sword of division into human society. What smells like life to some smells like death to others (II Cor.2:14-17). To most in Jesus' audience that day His gospel, which defies rational analysis when lost sinners bring to the task only human mental equipment, it smelled like death as we see in

Verse 60 - "Many therefore of his disciples, when they had heard this, said, This is a hard saying; who can hear it?"

Πολλοὶ οὖν ἀκούσαντες ἐκ τῶν μαθητῶν αὐτοῦ εἶπαν, Σκληρός ἐστιν ὁ λόγος οὗτος. τίς δύναται αὐτοῦ ἀκούειν;

Πολλοὶ (nom.pl.masc.of πολύς, subject of εἶπαν) 228.
οὖν (inferential conjunction) 68.
ἀκούσαντες (aor.act.part.nom.pl.masc.of ἀκούω, adverbial, causal) 148.
ἐκ (preposition with the partitive genitive) 19.
τῶν (gen.pl.masc.of the article in agreement with μαθητῶν) 9.
μαθητῶν (gen.pl.masc.of μαθητής, partitive genitive) 421.
αὐτοῦ (gen.sing.masc.of αὐτός, relationship) 16.
εἶπαν (3d.per.pl.aor.act.ind.of εἶπον, ingressive) 155.
Σκληρός (nom.sing.masc.of σκληρός, predicate adjective) 1537.
ἐστιν (3d.per.sing.pres.ind.of εἰμί, aoristic) 86.
ὁ (nom.sing.masc.of the article in agreement with λόγος) 9.
λόγος (nom.sing.masc.of λόγος, subject of ἐστιν) 510.
οὗτος (nom.sing.masc.of οὗτος, in agreement with λόγος) 93.
τίς (nom.sing.masc.of τίς, subject of δύναται) 281.
δύναται (3d.per.sing.pres.ind.of δύναμαι, direct question) 289.
αὐτοῦ (gen.sing.masc.of αὐτός, description) 16.
ἀκούειν (pres.act.inf.of ἀκούω, epexegetical) 148.

Translation - "Many of His disciples therefore because they had heard, began to say, 'This concept is harsh. Who can listen to it?'"

Comment: οὖν is definitely inferential. It is possible to take ἀκούσαντες as a substantival participle, modified by Πολλοὶ and the subject of εἶπαν. We have taken it as a causal adverbial. The large number who heard Jesus spoke (εἶπαν), to be sure. The large number (Πολλοὶ) spoke (εἶπαν) *because* and *when* (ἀκούσαντες) they heard what Jesus said. Both ideas are true and either can legitimately be derived from the Greek. *Cf.*#421 for the list of passages where μαθητής means (a) the twelve, (b) the eleven, without Judas, or (c) a larger group of "learners." Verse 66 makes it clear that μαθητῶν of verse 60 means the larger, more general group of listeners. Verse 66 could not be speaking of the eleven faithful disciples, or, indeed, of Judas Iscariot.

We have taken εἶπαν as an ingressive aorist. "They *began* to say ... κ.τ.λ." We may be sure that they said it more than once. The non-elect say the same thing all the time and advance it as their reason for rejecting Christ. Σκληρός is in the emphatic position. *Cf.*#1537 for other uses of this interesting adjective. Note αὐτοῦ, the genitive, joined to ἀκούειν. Broadus says, "With verbs the genitive means this and no other, while the accusative with verbs means this and no more." (as cited in Robertson, *Short Grammar*, 230). The skeptics were singling out Jesus and His teaching as impossible to understand and therefore intolerable to listen to. When one talks over the head of an intellectual lightweight boredom for the listener is the result. They could understand much of what Jesus said - not this. ἀκούειν means "to listen," as ἀκούσαντες makes clear. They heard in the auditory sense but they were not a part of πᾶς ὁ ἀκούσας παρὰ τοῦ πατρός of verse 45. Review comment on verse 45. The preaching of the cross (vs.56) has always been foolishness to them that perish. *Cf.* John 12:34; I Cor.1:18,23; Gal.5:11. Note even Peter's reaction in Mt.16:21,22. The rapport necessary if we are to understand the gospel of Christ is the gift of the sovereign Holy Spirit (John 3:8; I Cor.12:3; John 16:7-11; Mt.11:25-27). Jesus returns to this thesis in the verses that follow.

Euripides distinguishes σκληρ' ἀληθῆ - "hard, distasteful, uncompromising truths" from μαλθακά φευδή - "flattering lies." Apparently the Jews were particularly worried about what He said in verse 58, judging from His challenge in verse 62, although none of His discourse found acquiescence in their hearts.

Verse 61 - "When Jesus knew in himself that his disciples murmered at it, he said unto them, Doth this offend you?"

εἰδὼς δὲ ὁ Ἰησοῦς ἐν ἑαυτῷ ὅτι γογγύζουσιν περὶ τούτου οἱ μαθηταὶ αὐτοῦ εἶπεν αὐτοῖς, Τοῦτο ὑμᾶς σκανδαλίζει;

εἰδὼς (aor.part.nom.sing.masc.of ὁράω, adverbial, causal) 144.
δὲ (continuative conjunction) 11.
ὁ (nom.sing.masc.of the article in agreement with Ἰησοῦς) 9.
Ἰησοῦς (nom.sing.masc.of Ἰησοῦς, subject of εἶπεν) 3.
ἐν (preposition with the locative of place where) 80.
ἑαυτῷ (loc.sing.masc.of ἑαυτός, place where) 288.
ὅτι (conjunction introducing an object clause in indirect discourse) 211.
γογγύζουσιν (3d.per.pl.pres.act.ind.of γογγύζω, progressive) 1322.
περὶ (preposition with the genitive of reference) 173.
τούτου (gen.sing.neut.of οὗτος, reference) 93.
οἱ (nom.pl.masc.of the article in agreement with μαθηταὶ) 9.
μαθηταὶ (nom.pl.masc.of μαθητής, subject of γογγύζουσιν) 421.
αὐτοῦ (gen.sing.masc.of αὐτός, relationship) 16.
εἶπεν (3d.per.sing.aor.act.ind.of εἶπον, constative) 155.
αὐτοῖς (dat.pl.masc.of αὐτός, indirect object of εἶπεν) 16.
Τοῦτο (nom.sing.neut.of οὗτος, subject of σκανδαλίζει) 93.
ὑμᾶς (acc.pl.masc.of σύ, direct object of σκανδαλίζει) 104.
σκανδαλίζει (3d.per.sing.pres.act.ind.of σκανδαλίζω, progressive) 503.

Translation - "And because Jesus was aware that His disciples were complaining about this, He said to them, 'This? Does this annoy you?' "

Comment: Apparently the murmering was gong on behind Jesus' back. They were afraid to criticize Him to His face! But such cryptic tactics are ineffective when Jesus is involved. "Because He was aware. . . " (causal adverb in εἰδὼς). ἐν ἑαυτῷ is probably locative, but it could be instrumental - "by means of His own divine perceptive resources" (*cf.*John 2:24). Jesus does not need to be told what others are thinking or saying. He knows! ὅτι after a verb of perceiving introduces an object clause and indirect discourse, where the tense of the verb is the same as in direct discourse.

Jesus knew that the Twelve as well as the others were perplexed. That is why He gave them a further promise in verse 62. Of course, Judas did not see the fulfillment of the promise of verse 62, while only Peter, James and John witnessed the transfiguration, although Judas may have heard their account of it. This is a part of the reason why Jesus mentions the apostasy of Judas in vss.64,70,71.

Jesus' question seems rhetorical, although John does not use the summary negative conjunction. "This? Dos this annoy even you?" To strengthen their faith He makes them a promise in

Verse 62 - "What and if ye shall see the Son of Man ascend up where he was before?"

ἐὰν οὖν θεωρῆτε τὸν υἱὸν τοῦ ἀνθρώπου ἀναβαίνοντα ὅπου ἦν τὸ πρότερον;

ἐὰν (conditional particle in an elliptical condition, aposiopesis).363.

οὖν (inferential conjunction) 68.

θεωρῆτε (2d.per.pl.pres.subj.of θεωρέω, elliptical condition) 1667.

τὸν (acc.sing.masc.of the article in agreement with υἱὸν) 9.

υἱὸν (acc.sing.masc.of υἱός, direct object of θεωρῆτε) 5.

τοῦ (gen.sing.masc.of the article in agreement with ἀνθρώπου) 9.

ἀνθρώπου (gen.sing.masc.of ἄνθρωπος, description) 341.

ἀναβαίνοντα (pres.act.part.acc.sing.masc.of ἀναβαίνω, adverbial, circumstantial) 323.

ὅπου (adverb introducing a definite local clause) 592.

ἦν (3d.per.sing.imp.ind.of εἰμί, progressive duration) 86.

τὸ (acc.sing.neut.of the article in agreement with πρότερον) 9.

#2293 πρότερον (acc.sing.neut.of πρότερος, adverbial accusative, temporal).

by night - John 7:50.
former - Eph.4:22.
at the first - Gal.4:13.
before - John 6:62; 9:8; II Cor.1:15; I Tim.1:13.
first - Heb.4:6; 7:27.
former - Heb.10:32; I Pet.1:14.

Meaning: Cf.#487. An adjective. Former, previous, prior. In the attributive position - Eph.4:22; Heb.10:32. With the neuter article - τὸ πρότερον, like an adverb of time - Gal.4:13; John 6:62; Heb.10:32; 9:8; I Tim.1:13. Without the article, an accusative of general reference, used like an adverb - II Cor.1:15; Heb.7:27; John 7:50; Heb.4:6; I Pet.1:14.

Translation - "What then if you shall see the Son of Man ascending to (the place) where He was before?"

Comment: We have the protasis of a third-class condition but without the apodosis. This the grammarians call an elliptical conditional clause. It is a case of aposiopesis in which the thought is suddenly left incomplete. Had He finished it, He probably would have said, "Would you still be offended?" The subjunctive *in ϑεωρῆτε* in the protasis introduces some doubt. Jesus is not promising to ascend to heaven; He is only presenting a hypothetical question. "Let us suppose that you . . . κ.τ.λ." What then? Would that help you to overcome your skepticism and confusion? The imperfect in *ἦν* is progressive duration indicating continuous eternal existence in the past. *Cf.* John 1:1,3.

τὸ πρότερον - an accusative of general reference used adverbially to indicate a time point. Jesus used this same argument on Nicodemus (John 3:13), Nathaniel (John 1:49,51) and on Mary (John 20:17). Peter alluded to it in Acts 2:34. *Cf.* also John 13:3.

We have seen before in this discourse that Jesus refused to present in clearer terms the rationale of His person and work on the grounds that saving faith does nor arise from a clear intellectual understanding, except in the cases of those whom the Father has given to Him (vs.37) and whom He draws to Christ (vs.44). Others are mystified by His metaphorical language, but He does not clarify their confusion, because He knows that they would not come to Him if they did understand it. But for Jesus to know who will not come, is also to know who will. And with this latter elect group He provides a tender Shepherd's care. Speaking to the twelve (Judas present) He promises two visual aids which will support their faltering faith. Peter, James and John will see Him transfigured (Mt.17: Lk.9) and all, except Judas who shall by that time have fulfilled his own destiny, will see His ascension (Acts 1:10,11). It is as if Jesus is saying to His disciples, "Wait and see. Reserve your judgment until all of the evidence is in⌣."

The doubters were reacting as the flesh always reacts. They are warned in verse 63 that there is nothing profitable in the flesh. Only the Holy Spirit gives life.

Verse 63 - "It is the spirit that quickeneth; the flesh profiteth nothing. The words that I speak unto you, they are spirit and they are life."

τὸ πνεῦμά ἐστιν τὸ ζωοποιοῦν, ἡ σάρξ οὐκ ὠφελεῖ οὐδέν, τὰ ῥήματα ἃ ἐγὼ λελάληκα ὑμῖν πνεῦμά ἐστιν καὶ ζωή ἐστιν.

τὸ (nom.sing.neut.of the article in agreement with πνεῦμα) 9.

πνεῦμά (nom.sing.neut.of πνεῦμα, subject of ἐστιν) 83.

ἐστιν (3d.per.sing.pres.ind.of εἰμί, aoristic) 86.

τὸ (nom.sing.neut.of the article in agreement with ζωοποιοῦν) 9.

ζωοποιοῦν (pres.act.part.nom.sing.neut.of ζωοποιέω, substantival, predicate nominative) 2098.

ἡ (nom.sing.fem.of the article in agreement with σάρξ) 9.

σάρξ (nom.sing.fem.of σάρξ, subject of ὠφελεῖ) 1202.

οὐκ (summary negative conjunction with the indicative) 130.

ὠφελεῖ (3d.per.sing.pres.act.ind.of ὠφελέω, customary)

οὐδέν (acc.sing.neut.of οὐδείς, direct object of ὠφελεῖ) 446.

τὰ (nom.pl.neut.of the article in agreement with ῥήματα) 9.

ῥήματα (nom.pl.neut.of ῥῆμα, subject of ἐστιν) 343.

ἃ (nom.pl.neut.of the relative pronoun ὅς, case attraction to the antecedent) 65.

ἐγὼ (nom.sing.masc.of ἐγώ, subject of λελάληκα) 123.

λελάληκα (1st.per.sing.perf.act.ind.of λαλέω, consummative) 815.

ὑμῖν (dat.pl.masc.of σύ, indirect object of λελάληκα) 104.
πνεῦμά (nom.sing.neut.of πνεῦμα, predicate nominative) 83.
ἐστιν (3d.per.sing.pres.ind.of εἰμί, aoristic) 86.
καὶ (continuative conjunction joining coordinate clauses) 14.
ζωή (nom.sing.fem.of ζωή, predicate nominative) 668.
ἐστιν (3d.per.sing.pres.ind.of εἰμί, aoristic) 86.

Translation - "The Spirit is the Lifegiver; the flesh does not produce a single gain. The words which I have spoken to you are spirit and are life."

Comment: A profitable exercise in research which will provide many good preaching and teaching leads is the study of #2098. How and where else is the word used, both in spiritual and physical senses? Paul says the same thing in II Cor.3:6. He also agrees that the flesh is without profit in Gal.3:21. Jesus has implied that His death is the only hope for salvation for sinners (vs.53). He now hints at His bodily resurrection as a function of the Holy Spirit (Rom.8:11; I Pet.3:18). He also promises that believers shall live in resurrected flesh (I Cor.15:22,45). *Cf.* also John 5:21,21; I Tim.6:13. *Cf.*#1144 for a study on "profit making." This is good preaching material. οὐκ ὠφελεῖ οὐδέν - a very strong negative. The flesh does not produce a profit. That says it, but Jesus adds οὐδέν, in which δέ is ascensive - "not even one thing." τὰ ῥήματα, the subject is defined by the relative pronominal clause ἃ . . . ὑμῖν. Note the consummative perfect tense in λελάληκα - "which I have spoken and which are therefore now in the record."

If the distinction between λέγω (#66) and λαλέω (#815) is real we can see it here. Jesus had been speaking to them and they had heard Him audibly (λαλέω) though with only imperfect understanding (λέγω).

John's Greek here follows the Classical usage of a singular verb ἐστιν with a neuter plural subject τὰ ῥήματα. Christ's words are spirit and also life, which practically amounts to the same thing since τὸ πνεῦμά ἐστιν ζωοποιοῦν. The doubts, the sarcastic questions, the argumentative spirit, the heated debates and snide rebuttals of His audience (vss.26,28,30,31,41,42,52,60) are all manifestations of σάρξ. That is why Jesus did not encourage debate. Debate would only mean more flesh and Jesus said that ἡ σάρξ οὐκ ὠφελεῖ οὐδέν. Since His words are πνεῦμα, it is a fleshly, profitless practice to resist them. *Cf.*#668 for ζωή, both in the sense of spiritual life and of the resurrection of the body of the believer.

Jesus had made much of His cooperation with God the Father, *e.g.* vs.38. Here He also brings the Holy Spirit into the salvation equation. It was through the Eternal Spirit that He offered Himself without spot to God (Heb.9:14).

Christ's words - both Spirit and Life - are of no avail to the unbeliever. This is the thought of

Verse 64 - "But there are some of you that believe not. For Jesus knew from the beginning who they were that believed not, and who should betray him."

ἀλλ' εἰσὶν ἐξ ὑμῶν τινες οἳ οὐ πιστεύουσιν. ᾔδει γὰρ ἐξ ἀρχῆς ὁ Ἰησοῦς τίνες εἰσὶν οἱ μὴ πιστεύοντες καὶ τίς ἐστιν ὁ παραδώσων αὐτόν.

ἀλλ' (adversative conjunction) 342.

εἰσὶν (3d.per.pl.pres.ind.of εἰμί, aoristic) 86.

ἐξ (preposition with the partitive genitive) 19.

ὑμῶν (gen.pl.masc.of σύ, partitive) 104.

τινες (nom.pl.masc.of τις, indefinite pronoun, subject of εἰσὶν) 486.

οἳ (nom.pl.masc.of ὅς, subject of πιστεύουσιν) 65.

οὐ (summary negative conjunction with the indicative) 130.

πιστεύουσιν (3d.per.pl.pres.act.ind.ofd πιστεύω, aoristic) 734.

ᾔδει (3d.per.sing.pluperfect act. ind.of ὁράω, consummative) 144.

γὰρ (causal conjunction) 105.

ἐξ (preposition with the ablative in a time separation phrase) 19.

ἀρχῆς (abl.sing.fem.of ἀρχή, time separation) 1285.

ὁ (nom.sing.masc.of the article in agreement with Ἰησοῦς) 9.

Ἰησοῦς (nom.sing.masc.of Ἰησοῦς, subject of ᾔδει) 3.

τίνες (nom.pl.masc.of τίς, the interrogative pronoun, predicate nominative) 281.

εἰσὶν (3d.per.pl.pres.ind.of εἰμί, aoristic) 86.

οἱ (nom.pl.masc.of the article in agreement with πιστεύοντες) 9.

μὴ (negative conjunction with the participle) 87.

πιστεύοντες (pres.act.part.nom.pl.masc.of πιστεύω, subject of εἰσὶν) 734.

καὶ (ascensive conjunction) 14.

τίς (nom.sing.masc.of τίς, the interrogative pronoun, predicate nominative) 281.

ἐστιν (3d.per.sing.pres.ind.of εἰμί, aoristic) 86.

ὁ (nom.sing.masc.of the article in agreement with παραδώσων) 9.

παραδώσων (fut.act.part.nom.sing.masc.of παραδίδωμι, substantival, subject of ἐστιν) 368.

αὐτόν (acc.sing.masc.of αὐτός, direct object of παραδώσων) 16.

Translation - " 'But there are certain ones of you who do not believe.' Because Jesus had known from the beginning who the unbelievers are, even who is the one who would betray Him."

Comment: ἀλλ' is a strong adversative. Despite the fact that Jesus' words are spirit and life, yet, He adds there are certain ἐξ ὑμῶν - "of your number" - defined by the relative clause with the personal pronoun, the subject of πιστεύουσιν. It can be viewed as an object clause and indirect discourse with ὅτι omitted. That is why the verbs are in the present tense, since in indirect discourse the tenses are the same as in direct. Direct discourse was "The unbelievers are these and the the betrayer is this man." γὰρ is causal as John explains to his readers how Jesus could declare that some of them would not believe. It was because our Lord had always known (pluperfect tense in ᾔδει) who would believe and who would not. He even knew (ascensive καὶ) that Judas would betray Him. ἐξ ἀρχῆς - from the beginning of eternity (!), from the beginning of His ministry and from the beginning of this episode. *Cf.*#1285. The eternal ἀρχή includes all subsequent ἀρχαί.

That our Lord had always known the roster of the personnel of His bride is consistent with John 6:37 and John 5:17, 19-20. To know the sheep is also to know those who are not the sheep. To know them all is to know all about the betrayer. He had voiced His skepticism about some of them in verse 26. Why were some of the people there unbelievers? Verse 44 provides the answer. Jesus had foretold His death and resurrection. He could have told them also that one of the Twelve would betray Him. There is no way to explain it except to say that Jesus of Nazareth is God incarnate and that He is sovereign.

Note John's good Greek. οὐ with οἷ, the relative, but μή with the articular participle οἱ πιστεύοντες.

Jesus repeats the thought of verse 44 in

Verse 65 - "And he said, Therefore said I unto you that no man can come unto me, except it were given unto him of my Father."

καὶ ἔλεγεν, Διὰ τοῦτο εἴρηκα ὑμῖν ὅτι οὐδεὶς δύναται ἐλθεῖν πρός με ἐὰν μὴ ᾖ δεδομένον αὐτῷ ἐκ τοῦ πατρός.

καὶ (continuative conjunction) 14.

ἔλεγεν (3d.per.sing.imp.act.ind.of λέγω, inceptive) 66.

Διὰ (preposition with the accusative of cause) 118.

τοῦτο (acc.sing.neut.of οὗτος, cause) 93.

εἴρηκα (1st.per.sing.perf.act.ind.of ῥέω, Attic form) 116.

ὑμῖν (dat.pl.masc.of σύ, indirect object of εἴρηκα) 104.

ὅτι (conjunction introducing an object clause in indirect discourse) 211.

οὐδεὶς (nom.sing.masc.of οὐδείς, subject of δύναται) 446.

δύναται (3d.per.sing.pres.ind.of δύναμαι, aoristic) 289.

ἐλθεῖν (aor.inf.of ἔρχομαι, complementary) 146.

πρός (preposition with the accusative of extent) 197.

με (acc.sing.masc.of ἐγώ, extent) 123.

ἐὰν (particle introducing a third-class condition) 363.

μὴ (qualified negative conjunction with the subjunctive) 87.

ᾖ (3d.per.sing.pres.subj.of εἰμί, third-class condition) 86.

δεδομένον (perf.pass.part.acc.sing.neut.of δίδωμι, adverbial, temporal) 362.

αὐτῷ (dat.sing.masc.of αὐτός, indirect object of δεδομένον) 16.

ἐκ (preposition with the ablative of source) 19.

τοῦ (abl.sing.masc.of the article in agreement with πατρός) 9.

πατρός (abl.sing.masc.of πατήρ, source) 238.

Translation - "And He began to say, 'This is why I have said to you that no one can come to me if the desire has not been given to him from the Father.' "

Comment: The previous statement to this effect was in verse 44. The third-class condition has the apodosis before the protasis. If the desire to come to Christ is not present, having been given (consummative perfect in δεδομένον) to the man from the Father, no man can come. The will to come to Christ, manifest in the elect at the time of his repentance and faith, is the result of a past action, indicated by the perfect passive participle δεδομένον. The participle is consummative, *i.e.* ". . . it is not an existing state, but a consummated process which is presented" (Mantey, *Manual*, 202), to which I would add that the "consummated process" is the result of a previous act, as Burton says (Burton, *New Testament Moods and Tenses*, 38), ". . . the writer had in mind both the past act and the present result" - a statement which Mantey quotes with approval (Mantey, *Ibid*, 203). The cause and result sequence is this: the Father gives the desire to come to Christ to the elect, hence such desire exists, hence he comes to Christ, hence he is saved. His coming is contingent upon δεδομένον αὐτῷ ἐκ τοῦ πατρός. This is strong support for the Reformed theology, but that is precisely what Jesus said. We shall not help the cause of God by explaining it away.

The alternative to this view is that the sinner, in and of himself, and with the use of his own resources, decides to come to Christ. This is a rational decision, arrived at by weighing the alternative course. The sinner decides that it is better to come to Christ and be rescued than to reject Him and be lost. That he has the good sense to do this is the view of the Thomist since Aquinas taught that man's intellect escaped the depravity, visited upon his will and emotions by the fall. It is also the view of the Pelagians who were certain that man could decide by himself to come to Christ. If this view is correct a logical question to be asked is this: Is that part of man which motivates him to make the right choice and come to Christ, good or bad? There could be only one reply to that. It is good. Then what becomes of the doctrine of total depravity? When Reformed theologians say that man is totally depraved, they do not mean that at any given time in his life he is so bad that he cannot get worse. The depravity of which we speak is *extensive* not intensive. That is, it extends to every component of his personality, *viz.,* his will, his emotional nature and his intellect. The Judaizers whom Paul opposed, Pelagius whom Augustine opposed, St.Thomas Aquinas whom the Reformed theologians opposed, Erasmus whom Luther opposed, Arminius whom Calvin opposed and current thinkers who reject Calvinism must say that they do not believe in total depravity, only in a depravity that has ruined two-thirds of man's personality. This is not to say that such thinkers are unsaved or that they are not, in many cases, wonderfully charming and brilliant people. It is only to say that from the Calvinist's point of view, they have not thought it through to a logical conclusion.

Calvinists cannot with any logic support democracy as a viable system of government, since it assumes that man is a rational creature and that his judgment can be trusted. It happens to be the best system that is available to us *now*, since Plato's Philosopher-King at the right hand of God is currently unavailable. It was Winston Churchill who said that democracy is the worst possible form of human government devised by the mind of man except one - its alternative. I want democracy now, since to the left is anarchy and to the right are oligarchy, close at hand, and monarchy at the extreme, all of which are worse, but it does not follow that the Reformed theologian looks to democracy as the ultimate solution to man's soul sorrow.

A caveat is needed when we think of the phrase "come to Christ." The Greek text has ἐλθεῖν πρός με - "to come to me." Note that the preposition is πρός (#197), which is used elsewhere (John 1:1,3; I John 1:2) to denote a relationship which is particularly intimate. *Cf. The Renaissance New Testament*, 4, 4. πρός with the accusative of extent is used for spatial extension, but it is also used of spiritual, intellectual and moral extension, such as exists in the intimacy which exists between God the Father and His Son. It is possible to come "near to" Christ in a physical sense, but to be spiritually remote from Him. It is possible to come "near to" an altar at the front of a church auditorium and to approach a minister who stands there ready to grasp one's hand, and yet not come "near to" Christ in the sense that Christ is πρὸς τὸν θεόν (John 1:1) and πρὸς τὸν πατέρα (I John 1:2).

I remember a gospel invitation which I once extended at the close of a sermon in a little country school house not far from Stillwater, Oklahoma. A little man responded. He came whimpering down the center aisle, fell upon his knees and began to beat his forehead rapidly and with more force than was good for it upon a rude two-by-four altar. I have always been interested in research into the nature of unusual phenomena. Since I had never seen such behavior before my insatiable curiosity impelled me to get down on my knees beside the little man and ask, "What are you doing?" He replied, "I'm gettin' it." Naturally I wanted to know what he was getting and asked him to tell me. I added the observation that if he did not stop beating his head on that two-by-four he was going to get a headache, because I doubted that that was what he had in mind. He responded that he had to "get it this way." With an open Bible as I knelt beside him, I asked him if he was willing to surrender his life completely to Christ. This was precisely what he did not wish to do. Thus he struggled on seeking an emotional outlet for pent-up frustration. I was unable to persuade him to trust Christ for salvation in simple child-like faith and was compelled to leave him there beating his forehead upon a piece of wood. His thinking and behavior is typical of the religious activity of certain groups who give such priority to emotion that they virtually ignore the intellect and, most important of all, the will. I do not believe that the poor man in Oklahoma had been given the gift from the Father of the desire to "come to Christ." He was trying in a fleshly way to generate an experience. Those who are called by the Holy Spirit need not "pray through." If God had not been willing to save them, He would not have called them in the first place.

This analysis guards against a superficial interpretation of the last half of John 6:37. Ignoring the first half of the verse it is easy to say, ". . . him that cometh to me I will in no wise cast out" and then, on the basis of that plain statement walk down an aisle and "come to Christ." Unless the decision and act are induced by the Holy Spirit the sinner is not "coming to Christ." He is only coming "to the altar" or "down the aisle" or "to the enquiry room." A tight television camera shot of the hundreds who were "coming forward" in a recent meeting revealed one penitent with a camera who was taking pictures of the other sinners who, like him, were trying to "get it." I could only remember the night that I came down an aisle to accept Christ. I had no camera. The Holy Spirit had taken a picture of me which I did not like at all, and I had come, by divine grace, to realize that the only One who could change that was Jesus Christ.

The evangelist should exercise more care with the preparation and delivery of his sermon than with the effectiveness of his invitation. There is great danger that, in his commendable desire to see the unsaved respond, he will, albeit unconsciously, turn his invitation into an exercise in mob psychology. If what he preaches is the true gospel of Christ, consistent with the κήρυγμα (#1013) of the Apostles the Holy Spirit will apply his message to the audience. To some it will smell like life and they will be saved, with or without a trip down the aisle. To the others it will smell like death and they will not be saved regardless of what they do or do not. *Cf.* our comments on II Cor.2:14-17 and note that Paul asks "Who is sufficient for these things?" after which he observes that his preaching, unlike others does not corrupt the Word of God, but is sincere and has its source in God. If preachers would cease and desist from worrying about what the audience thinks of their sermons and worry rather about what the Holy Spirit thinks of them, the evangelistic efforts of the church would be far more effective. If the local churches were as effective in witnessing for Christ and winning souls as the first century churches, the office of "professional evangelist" could safely be terminated.

Verse 66 - "From that time many of his disciples went back, and walked no more with him."

Ἐκ τούτου (οὖν) πολλοὶ ἐκ τῶν μαθητῶν αὐτοῦ ἀπῆλθον εἰς τὰ ὀπίσω καὶ οὐκέτι μετ' αὐτοῦ περιεπάτουν.

Ἐκ (preposition with the ablative of cause) 19.

τούτου (abl.sing.neut.of οὗτος, cause) 93.

πολλοὶ (nom.pl.masc.of πολύς, subject of ἀπῆλθον and περιεπάτουν) 228.

ἐκ (preposition with the partitive genitive) 19.

τῶν (gen.pl.masc.of the article in agreement with μαθητῶν) 9.

μαθητῶν (gen.pl.masc.of μαθητής, partitive genitive) 421.

αὐτοῦ (gen.sing.masc.of αὐτός, relationship) 16.

ἀπῆλθον (3d.per.pl.aor.ind.of ἀπέρχομαι, ingressive) 239.

εἰς (preposition with the accusative of extent) 140.

τὰ (acc.pl.neut.of the article, joined with the adverb of place, ὀπίσω, to show extent) 9.

ὀπίσω (adverb of place) 302.

καὶ (adjunctive conjunction joining verbs) 14.

οὐκέτι (adverb of denial) 1289.

μετ' (preposition with the genitive of accompaniment) 50.

αὐτοῦ (gen.sing.masc.of αὐτός, accompaniment) 16.

περιεπάτουν (3d.per.pl.imp.act.ind.of περιπατέω, progressive duration) 384.

Translation - "Because of this many of His disciples began to leave and walked about with Him no more."

Comment: The King James Version assumes that the translator should supply χρόνου after τούτον and thus read "From that time . . . " in a chronological sense. This translation is open to question. In all other places where ἐκ is employed with the ablative to indicate a point in time it is joined to a substantive to make the point clear, (*Cf.*#19,III) except Mt.26:42,44, where it is followed by δευτέρου (vs.42) and τρίτου (vs.44). These are adjectives with the substantive omitted. But Mt.26:42,44 are clear from the context. Jesus prayed the second time and the third time. But in John 6:66 it is not clear what, if anything, should follow τούτου. ἐκ is also joined with substantives in the ablative to indicate cause (*Cf.*#19,VI). So there is precedent for either idea. "From this" *viz.* from what Jesus said many withdrew. Hence we can agree with Goodspeed who reads it "In consequence of this . . .κ.τ.λ." or Montgomery's "Therefore. . . κ.τ.λ." Moffatt follows the KJV with "After that . . . κ.τ.λ." If τούτου is causal and not temporal it is deictic and points backward to Jesus' entire discourse, not to verse 65 only, since what He said in verse 65 He had said before. Certainly both the temporal and causal ideas are true. It is the context that supplies the former and the grammar that supplies the latter. Those who forsook Jesus did so at this time and they did so because of the strictures of Jesus' teaching. In John 19:12 we have ἐκ τούτου and the same problem. *The Expositors' Greek Testament*, (I, 760) agrees with me - "ἐκ τούτου, "on this"; neither exclusively "from this time" ἔκτοτε (Euthymius), "from this moment onwards" (Lücke), nor exclusively "on this account," but a combination of both. *Cf.*John xix.12. Here the time is in the foreground, as is shown by the οὐκ ἔτι following."

ἐκ . . . αὐτοῦ, partitive, indicating that μαθητῶν here includes the larger group since the Twelve, even Judas, did not forsake Him. The ἀπῆλθον εἰς τὰ ὀπίσω sounds like the action of a deserter in a battle. Literally it reads "They began to depart unto the things in the rear," *i.e.* they forsook the line of battle. They terminated their practice of following Jesus wherever He went, despite the fact that they thus were forced to forego a free meal on occasion. ἀπῆλθον may be taken as ingressive - "they *began* to depart, and περιεπάτουν is progressive duration - "no longer did they continue to walk around with Him."

Sinners in whatever age do not receive sound doctrine. The blindness with which the "god of this world" has afflicted them (II Cor.4:4) and the innate prejudice of the NIH syndrome ("Not Invented Here") forbid it. All of God's revelations are new since man is incapable of thinking like that and it is the characteristic of the depraved human mind to say that anything which is new to him cannot be true since he did not think of it first! This is why the Russians insist that all of the new inventions were produced by them. So the plain terms of the Gospel of Christ do not fit the philosophy of the natural man (I Cor.1:18; 2:14). That is why the gospel of Christ smells like death to all except those who are called by the Holy Spirit. To us it smells like life - no thanks to us, since, but for the grace of God we too would resist divine truth.

Some wanted Jesus because He could feed them without expended effort on their part. Others wanted Him because He seemed for a time to fulfill their selfish political ambitions. Everyone wants Him for a "fire escape." Few wanted to be told that only if the Father enabled them could they fellowship with Him. This offended their sinful pride. There is no greater rebuff to an unsaved man than that. Jesus lost His crowd. One wonders why some preachers today speak to such large audiences! In most cases the great crowds that assemble every Sunday to hear a preacher are composed of regenerates. The preacher who preaches what Jesus preached in John 6 is not likely to have many listeners among the unsaved. Our Lord invited His closest associates to leave in

Verse 67 - "Then said Jesus unto the twelve, Will ye also go away?"

εἶπεν οὖν ὁ Ἰησοῦς τοῖς δώδεκα, Μὴ καὶ ὑμεῖς θέλετε ὑπάγειν;

εἶπεν (3d.per.sing.aor.act.ind.of εἶπον, constative) 155.

οὖν (continuative conjunction) 68.

ὁ (nom.sing.masc.of the article in agreement with Ἰησοῦς) 9.

Ἰησοῦς (nom.sing.masc.of Ἰησοῦς, subject of εἶπεν) 3.

τοῖς (dat.pl.masc.of the article in agreement with δώδεκα) 9.

δώδεκα (dat.pl.masc., indeclin., of δώδεκα, indirect object of εἶπεν) 820.

Μὴ (qualified negative conjunction with the indicative in direct question) 87.

καὶ (adjunctive conjunction) 14.

ὑμεῖς (nom.pl.masc.of σύ, subject of θέλετε) 104.

θέλετε (2d.per.pl.pres.act.ind.of θέλω, in rhetorical question) 88.

ὑπάγειν (pres.act.inf.of ὑπάγω, complementary) 364.

Translation - "Jesus then said to the Twelve, 'You do not also wish to go away do you?' "

Comment: οὖν is continuative. Most of the people were leaving - saddened, disgusted, confused and angry. Their departure motivated Jesus' appeal to the Twelve. Μὴ with the indicative poses a rhetorical question which expects a negative reply. The humanity of our Lord comes through in this wistful question filled with unfulfilled longing or desire. As the Son of God Jesus was sure of Himself. He knew ἐξ ἀρχῆς (vs.64) who would believe and who would not. Nothing surprizes the omniscient God. He had chosen twelve with perfect foreknowledge that Judas was a slanderer (vss.70,71). Why then the question? Because as the Son of Man He needed the assurance that Peter gave in his reply in the next verse. No preacher is happy when the audience walks out on him. Would they all forsake Him?

Verse 68 - "Then Simon Peter answered him, Lord, to whom shall we go? Thou hast the words of eternal life."

ἀπεκρίθη αὐτῷ Σίμων Πέτρος, Κύριε, πρὸς τίνα ἀπελευσόμεθα; ῥήματα ζωῆς αἰωνίου ἔχεις.

ἀπεκρίθη (3d.per.sing.aor.ind.of ἀποκρίνομαι, constative) 318.

αὐτῷ (dat.sing.masc.of αὐτός, indirect object of ἀπεκρίθη) 16.

Σίμων (nom.sing.masc.of Σίμων, subject of ἀπεκρίθη) 386.

Πέτρος (nom.sing.masc.of Πέτρος, appellation) 387.

Κύριε (voc.sing.masc.of κύριος, address) 97.

πρὸς (preposition with the accusative of extent) 197.

τίνα (acc.sing.masc.of τίς, interrogative pronoun, extent) 281.
ἀπελευσόμεθα (1st.per.pl.fut.mid.ind.of ἀπέρχομαι, deliberative) 239.
ῥήματα (acc.pl.neut.of ῥῆμα, direct object of ἔχεις) 343.
ζωῆς (gen.sing.fem.of ζωή, description) 668.
αἰωνίου (gen.sing.fem.of αἰώνιος, in agreement with ζωῆς) 1255.
ἔχεις (2d.per.sing.pres.act.ind.of ἔχω, aoristic) 82.

Translation - *"Simon Peter replied to Him, 'Lord, to whom shall we go? You have the words of eternal life.' "*

Comment: Jesus had asked a rhetorical question. Simon Peter's reply is also in a sense rhetorical since he employed the deliberative future. "To whom shall we go, if we walk out?" Which is another way for Peter to say that there is no one else to whom the disciples could go and hear what they had just heard. Then comes Peter's positive statement, which continues throughout verse 69. Peter did not expect Jesus to answer his question. When one has heard all that Jesus said in this great discourse he has heard it all. Where else could he go and to whom could he possibly listen who could improve upon the message of the gospel which he had just heard? Rhetorical question is a most dogmatic way to make a positive assertion. "Who else?" - perhaps with raised eyebrows and a shrug of the shoulders, as though Jesus had asked a stupid question.

The first time that Peter heard an exposition of the Reformed theology he accepted it, although he did not understand all of its implications and acted and talked against it several times after that. After Pentecost, of course, Peter redeemed himself for all of his theological missteps before that. We do not praise Peter for his statement on this occasion. The ability and desire to receive Christ had been given to him from the Father (vs.65). He had been previously drawn by the Holy Spirit (vs.44). So, when Jesus spoke what is in verse 63, Peter accepted it at face value and made it the rule of his action. *Cf.* Mt.16:16, which came a little later. To have God's gift of faith so that one can say, "You are the Messiah, the Son of the Living God" (Mt.16:16) is evidence that one has repudiated all dependence upon the flesh, in which there is no profit, and accepted with childlike faith the revelation of the Father which is in heaven (John 6:63; Mt.16:17; 11:25-27). Peter had felt the surge of eternal life in its divine and heavenly quality, flow from Jesus' words into his own consciousness. The rest of his confession is in

Verse 69 - *"And we believe and are sure that thou art that Christ, the Son of the living God."*

καὶ ἡμεῖς πεπιστεύκαμεν καὶ ἐγνώκαμεν ὅτι σὺ εἶ ὁ ἅγιος τοῦ θεοῦ.

καὶ (emphatic conjunction) 14.
ἡμεῖς (nom.pl.masc.of ἐγώ, subject of πεπιστεύκαμεν and ἐγνώκαμεν) 123.
πεπιστεύκαμεν (1st.per.pl.perf.act.ind.of πιστεύω, consummative) 734.
καὶ (adjunctive conjunction joining verbs) 14.

ἐγνώκαμεν (1st.per.pl.perf.act.ind.of γινώσκω, consummative) 131.
ὅτι (conjunction introducing an object clause) 211.
σὺ (nom.sing.masc.of σύ, subject of εἶ) 104.
εἶ (2d.per.sing.pres.ind.of εἰμί, aoristic) 86.
ὁ (nom.sing.masc.of the article in agreement with ἅγιος) 9.
ἅγιος (nom.sing.masc.of ἅγιος, predicate nominative) 84.
τοῦ (abl.sing.masc.of the article in agreement with θεοῦ) 9.
θεοῦ (abl.sing.masc.of θεός, source) 124.

Translation - "In fact we have come to the conclusion and now we know that you are the Holy One from God."

Comment: The first καὶ can be taken as emphatic, as Peter supports in verse 69 his strong statement of verse 68. The perfect tenses must not be overlooked. They speak of a past revelation of the truth on the basis of which the disciples were now in possesion of a positive faith. "We have believed and therefore we now believe. We have come to know and now we are positive that . . . κ.τ.λ." Goodspeed says, "We are satisfied . . . κ.τ.λ." Peter, speaking for the disciples pointed backward to some previous occasion(s) when they had received insights from Jesus' teachings and works and found it possible to believe. The will and capacity to believe had been given to them from the Father (vs.65).

The problem that the unregenerate face when they find it impossible to accept the miracles and the teachings of Jesus is that they find it impossible to accept the fact that He is "the Holy One from God." Once the incarnation of the Son of God is accepted, there is no further difficulty with His miracles or His teachings, even those in His discourse in John 6. I have never seen one who rejected the virgin birth of Jesus Christ and the other clear New Testament statements about His essential deity, who did not also find it necessary to explain away the supernatural elements in His words and deeds. Peter's statement of faith was about the Person of Jesus, not about His teachings or works. "You are the Holy One from God" or, as he said it a little later "You are the Messiah, the Son of the Living God" (Mt.16:16). The real question is not, "What did Jesus do or teach." It is "Who is this man Jesus of Nazareth?"

If we take ὁ ἅγιος τοῦ θεοῦ as an ablative, we get "You are the Holy One *from* God." If we construe it as a genitive we read, "You are the One endowed with God's holiness." Both ideas are true.

The variant reading has been adopted by the Aland Committee with an A degree of certitude. Metzger explains, "The reading adopted for the text, decisively supported by *p75,* Sinaiticus, B C* D L W Ψ *al,* was expanded in various ways by copyists, perhaps in inmitation of expressions in 1.49; 11.27 and Mt.16.16. (Metzger, *A Textual Commentary on the Greek New Testament,* 215).

What Peter said applies only to the eleven disciples, though he could not have known at that time that it did not also apply to Judas. Jesus does not identify the traitor (though John tells us in verse 71), but he does correct Peter by saying that of the twelve, He had chosen one who was a slanderer.

It is idle to speculate in regard to the chronological order of πιστεύω and γινώσκω and the results that flow from each. *Cf.* John 1:40-41; 8:32; 17:8; Phil.3:10; I John 4:16.

Verse 70 - "Jesus answered them, Have not I chosen you twelve, and one of you is a devil?"

ἀπεκρίθη αὐτοῖς ὁ Ἰησοῦς, Οὐκ ἐγὼ ὑμᾶς τοὺς δώδεκα ἐξελεξάμην, καὶ ἐξ ὑμῶν εἰς διάβολοσ ἐστιν;

ἀπεκρίθη (3d.per.sing.aor.ind.of ἀποκρίνομαι, constative) 318.

αὐτοῖς (dat.pl.masc.of αὐτός, indirect object of ἀπεκρίθη) 16.

ὁ (nom.sing.masc.of the article in agreement with Ἰησοῦς) 9.

Ἰησοῦς (nom.sing.masc.of Ἰησοῦς, subject of ἀπεκρίθη) 3.

Οὐκ (summary negative conjunctio in rhetorical question) 130.

ἐγὼ (nom.sing.masc.of ἐγώ, subject of ἐξελεξάμην) 123.

ὑμᾶς (acc.pl.masc.of σύ, direct object of ἐξελεξάμην) 104.

τοὺς (acc.pl.masc.of the article in agreement with δώδεκα) 9.

δώδεκα (acc.pl.masc.of δώδεκα, apposition) 820.

ἐξελεξάμην (1st.per.sing.aor.mid.ind.of ἐκλέγω, culminative) 2119.

καὶ (concessive conjunction) 14.

ἐξ (preposition with the partitive genitive) 19.

ὑμῶν (gen.pl.masc.of σύ, partitive) 104.

εἰς (nom.sing.masc.of εἷς, subject of ἐστιν) 469.

διάβολός (nom.sing.masc.of διάβολος, predicate nominative) 331.

ἐστιν (3d.per.sing.pres.ind.of εἰμί, aoristic) 86.

Translation - "Jesus replied to them, 'Did not I myself select you, the Twelve, even though one of you is a slanderer?' "

Comment: The direct question with οὐκ expects an affirmative response. Note ἐγώ is emphasis - "I made the selection myself." καὶ is concessive - "even though (despite the fact that) one . . . κ.τ.λ." *Cf.*#331 for the exact meaning of διάβολος. *Cf.*#2119 for a study on election. *Cf.* John 17:12 which tells us why Jesus, with perfect knowledge of past, present and future (with Whom time is not a factor) nevertheless chose Judas. This is an inscrutable doctrine, but none-the-less the plain teaching of Jesus. Do not ask why until you see Him!

Thus Jesus modifies Peter's statement in verse 69, where ἡμεῖς included Judas. Note again that Jesus does not identify ὁ διάβολος in the group, though of course He knew who he was. John tells us, his readers, whom Jesus meant.

On the question of Judas and his "election" *cf.* Meyer (*John*, 225,226) in an interesting but unsuccessful attempt to "get off the hook" though he does not challenge the statement in the record. With reference to the entire discourse (John 6:26-71) Meyers says that Jesus was "sowing for the future in the bosom of the present."

Verse 71 - "He spake of Judas Iscariot, the son of Simon; for he it was that should betray him, being one of the twelve."

ἔλεγεν δὲ τὸν Ἰούδαν Σίμωνος Ἰσκαριώτου. οὗτος γὰρ ἔμελλεν παραδιδόναι αὐτόν, εἷς (ὢν) ἐκ τῶν δώδεκα.

ἔλεγεν (3d.per.sing.imp.act.ind.of λέγω, progressive description) 66.

δὲ (explanatory conjunction) 11.

τὸν (acc.sing.masc.of the article in agreement with Ἰούδαν) 9.

Ἰούδαν (acc.sing.masc.of Ἰούδας, general reference) 853.

#2294 Σίμωνος (gen.sing.masc.of Σιμών, relationship).

Simon - John 6:71; 13:2, 26.

Meaning: The father of Judas and a citizen of Carioth.

Ἰσκαριώτου (abl.sing.masc.of Ἰσκαριώτης, source) 854.

οὗτος (nom.sing.masc.of οὗτος, subject of ἔμελλεν) 93.

γὰρ (causal conjunction) 105.

ἔμελλεν (3d.per.sing.imp.act.ind.of μέλλω, progressive) 206.

παραδιδόναι (pres.act.inf.of παραδίδωμι, complementary) 368.

αὐτόν (acc.sing.masc.of αὐτός, direct object of παραδιδόναι) 16.

εἷς (nom.sing.masc.of εἷς, apposition) 469.

τῶν (genitive pl.masc.of the article in agreement with δώδεκα) 9.

δώδεκα (indeclin., gen.pl.masc.of δώδεκα, partitive) 820.

Translation - "Now he was speaking of Judas, the son of Simon the Iscariot Because though he was one of the twelve he it was who was going to betray Him."

Comment: δὲ is explanatory. Note ἔλεγεν with the accusative τὸν . . . Ἰσκαρ., of general reference instead of περὶ and the genitive of reference. We have a similar usage in Mark 14:71 - "He was speaking about Judas." Causal γὰρ follows as John explains to his Ephesian audience who Judas was and what his connection with Jesus was. Note the contemptuous use of οὗτος. "He it was although one of the Twelve (concessive adverbial participle in ὢν) κ.τ.λ. . . ἔμελλεν παραδιδόναι αὐτόν - "on the verge of (drifting toward the moment when) betraying Him." The concessive participle ὢν omitted from the Westcott & Hort text is included in brackets in the text of the United Bible Societies Committee.

This concludes the long discourse on the Bread of Life and the crisis it precipitated in the synagogue in Capernaum. We now turn to a discourse on the traditions of men. It is significant that a spiritual interpretation of the λάλαι Ἰησοῦς should be followed by a critical interpretation of man's traditions. Review Mt.15:1-20 and we shall now examine the parallel account in Mk.7:1-23.

Mark 7:1 - "Then came together unto him the Pharisees and certain of the scribes, which came from Jerusalem."

Καὶ συνάγονται πρὸς αὐτὸν οἱ Φαρισαῖοι καί τινες τῶν γραμματέων ἐλθόντες ἀπὸ Ἰεροσολύμων.

Καὶ (continuative conjunction) 14.
συνάγονται (3d.per.pl.pres.mid.ind.of συνάγω, historical) 150.
πρὸς (preposition with the accusative of extent) 197.
αὐτὸν (acc.sing.masc.of αὐτός, extent) 16.
οἱ (nom.pl.masc.of the article in agreement with Φαρισαῖοι) 9.
Φαρισαῖοι (nom.pl.masc.of Φαρισαῖος, subject of συνάγονται) 276.
καὶ (adjunctive conjunction joining substantives) 14.
τινες (nom.pl.masc.of τις, subject of συνάγονται) 486.
τῶν (gen.pl.masc.of the article in agreement with γραμματέων) 9.
γραμματέων (gen.pl.masc.of γραμματεύς, partitive) 152.
ἐλθόντες (aor.participle, nom.pl.masc.of ἔρχομαι, adjectival, restrictive) 146.
ἀπὸ (preposition with the ablative of separation) 70.
Ἱεροσολύμων (abl.sing.indeclin.of Ἱεροσολύμων, separation) 141.

Translation - *"And there came together to Him the Pharisees and some of the Scribes who had come from Jerusalem."*

Comment: πρὸς αὐτὸν cannot be pushed here to mean an intimacy of spiritual relationship as in John 1:1 and John 6:37. Mark merely used πρὸς to denote a proximity in a spatial sense. The participle ἐλθόντες is adjectival and restrictive. Not all of the Scribes came to Him - only some of them and these are confined to those who had come from Jerusalem. Does ἐλθόντες apply to the Pharisees as well as to the Scribes? The grammar permits it but the syntax is not very helpful. Did the Pharisees who had encountered Jesus before send for the Scribes to assist them in the legal and philosophical bouts with Jesus? At any rate the Jewish brain trust from Establishmentarian Jerusalem was on hand. They were looking for a fight and soon found occasion to attack Jesus.

Verse 2 - *"And when they saw some of his disciples eat bread with defiled, that is to say, with unwashen hands, they found fault."*

καὶ ἰδόντες τινὰς τῶν μαθητῶν αὐτοῦ ὅτι κοιναῖς χερσίν, τοῦτ' ἔστιν ἀνίπτοις ἐσθίουσιν τοὺς ἄρτους.

καὶ (continuative conjunction) 14.
ἰδόντες (aor.act.part.nom.pl.masc.of ὁράω, adverbial, temporal) 144.
τινὰς (acc.pl.masc.of τις, direct object of ἰδόντες) 486.
τῶν (gen.pl.masc.of the article in agreement with μαθητῶν) 9.
μαθητῶν (gen.pl.masc.of μαθητής, partitive genitive) 421.
αὐτοῦ (gen.sing.masc.of αὐτός, relationship) 16.
ὅτι (conjunction introducing an object clause) 211.

#2295 κοιναῖς (instru.pl.fem.of κοινός, in agreement with χερσίν).

common - Acts 2:44; 4:32; 10:14,28; 11:8; Tit.1:4; Jude 3.
defiled - Mk.7:2; Rev.21:27.
unwashen - Mk.7:5.
unclean - Rom.14:14,14,14.
unholy thing - Heb.10:29.

Meaning: Common. Belonging to the generality of things. With reference to wealth not monopolistically held but shared by all - Acts 2:44; 4:32. Profane, as opposed to that which is ceremonially and ritually set apart (with ἀκάθαρτον) in Acts 10:14,28; 11:8. With reference to faith, Titus 1:4, and salvation, Jude 3, the possession alike of all true believers. Physically and therefore ceremonially unclean hands - Mk.7:2,5. With reference to that which is low, base, taboo or sinful as opposed to that which is aristocratic and acceptable - Rom.14:14,14,14. Ordinary, lacking in unique dignity and worth - Heb.10:29; Rev.21:21.

χερσίν (instrumental pl.fem.of χείρ, means) 308.
τοῦτ' (nom.sing.neut.of οὗτος, subject of ἐστιν) 93.
ἐστιν (3d.per.sing.pres.ind.of εἰμί, aoristic, apposition) 86.
ἀνίπτοις (instru.pl.neut.of ἄνιπτος, in agreement with χερσίν) 1170.
ἐσθίουσιν (3d.per.pl.pres.act.ind.of ἐσθίω, progressive, indirect discourse) 610.
τοὺς (acc.pl.masc.of the article in agreement with ἄρτους) 9.
ἄρτους (acc.pl.masc.of ἄρτος, direct object of ἐσθίουσιν) 338.

Translation - "And when they noticed that some of His disciples were eating the loaves with ceremonially, (that is to say) unwashed hands. . . "

Comment: The sentence beginning in verse 2, is interrupted with Mark's long parenthesis in verses 3 and 4 and never finished, as he begins a new sentence in verse 5. ἰδόντες, the aorist participle is temporally relative to the verbs of verse 5. ὅτι introduces the object clause in indirect discourse which explains the present tense in ἐσθίουσιν, since the tense in indirect discourse follows the tense in direct. κοιναῖς χερσίν is out of place for emphasis. "For shame," said the critics, as they held up their hands in holy horror! Mark explains to any non-Jewish readers what κοιναῖς χερσίν means to a Jew. Since the hands of the disciples were unwashed they were ceremonially unclean. Mark procedes in verses 3 and 4 to give a long parenthetical explanation of the religious attitudes and practices of the Jews.

Verse 3 - "For the Pharisees, and all the Jews, except they wash their hands oft, eat not, holding the tradition of the elders."

-οἱ γὰρ Φαρισαῖοι καὶ πάντες οἱ Ἰουδαῖοι ἐὰν μὴ νίφωνται τὰς χεῖρας οὐκ ἐσθίουσιν, κρατοῦντες τὴν παράδοσιν τῶν πρεσβυτέρων.

οἱ (nom.pl.masc.of the article in agreement with Φαρισαῖοι) 9.
γὰρ (causal conjunction) 105.
Φαρισαῖοι (nom.pl.masc.of Φαρισαῖος, subject of ἐσθίουσιν) 276.
καὶ (adjunctive conjunction joining nouns) 14.
πάντες (nom.pl.masc.of πᾶς, in agreement with Ἰουδαῖοι) 67.
οἱ (nom.pl.masc.of the article in agreement with Ἰουδαῖοι) 9.
Ἰουδαῖοι (nom.pl.masc.of Ἰουδαῖος, subject of ἐσθίουσιν) 143.
ἐὰν (conditional particle in a third-class condition) 363.
μὴ (qualified negative conjunction with the subjunctive in a third-class condition) 87.

#2296 πυγμῇ (adverbial).

oft - Mk.7:3.

Meaning: fist. *Cf.*Edersheim, *Life and Times of Jesus the Messiah*, II, 11 - "In the 'first affusion' which was all that was originally required when the hands were Levitically 'defiled', the water had to run down to the wrist. If the water remained short of the wrist the hands were not clean.

Accordingly, the words of St. Mark can only mean that the Pharisees eat not 'except they wash their hands to the wrist.' "

νίφωνται (3d.per.pl.pres.mid.subj.of νίπτω, third-class condition) 590.
τὰς (acc.pl.fem.of the article in agreement with χεῖρας) 9.
χεῖρας (acc.pl.fem.of χείρ, direct object of νίφωνται) 308.
οὐκ (summary negative conjunction with the indicative) 130.
ἐσθίουσιν (3d.per.pl.pres.act.ind.of ἐσθίω, third-class condition) 610.
κρατοῦντες (pres.act.part.nom.pl.masc.of κρατέω, adverbial, telic) 828.
τὴν (acc.sing.fem.of the article in agreement with παράδοσιν) 9.
παράδοσιν (acc.sing.fem.of παράδοσις, direct object of κρατοῦντες) 1140.
τῶν (gen.pl.masc.of the article in agreement with πρεσβυτέρων) 9.
πρεσβυτέρων (gen.pl.masc.of πρεσβύτερος, definition) 1141.

Translation - "Because the Pharisees and all the Jews, if they do not wash their hands down to the wrist (in a specific way) never eat, in order to maintain the tradition of the elders."

Comment: γὰρ is causal, as Mark explains why the Pharisees were so offended by the alleged violation of the code by the disciples. Not only the Pharisees, but all of the Jews were influenced by the tradition. ἐὰν μὴ introduces the third-class condition. Hands must be washed before eating. If there is no washing, there can be no eating. πυγμῇ (#2296) - here only in the New Testament. The word literally means "fist" and since it is adverbial it can be translates "with the fist" - *i.e.* by rubbing each hand with the other fist, to assure thorough cleaning, like a surgeon "scrubbing" before an operation. Read the Edersheim comment noted above. In order that the water used, originally clean and hence Levitically pure, but rendered unclean by its contact with the dirt on the hands, not run down on the fingers and thumbs, thus to contaminate them again, the Pharisees held their hands up with fingers pointing up. Thus, in the process of washing, they applied pure water to the tips of the fingers and thumbs which, when contaminated ran down to the wrist. Thus the hands were cleansed of all dirt, including the dirt in the unclean water! Hence we translate, "down to the wrist." It follows that they were careful not to touch the food which they ate with any part of the arm above the wrist or with any other part of the body.

The reader will gasp at the ridiculous lengths to which the religious bigots of Jesus' day went to protect their vested interest in the maintenance of the traditions of the elders. We need only look about us to see modern parallels in organized *churchianity*, as self-appointed "priests" display intemperate zeal to maintain, not the demands of the Word of God, but their own rationalized interpretations of them. We leave this exercise to the research, imagination and incisive analysis of the reader. A college president in Ohio objected when a Christian who smokes a pipe was asked to pray in a public worship service. It was later revealed that the one asked to pray also chewed chewing gum. Thus the tradition of the elders is guarded by the Pharisees.

Cf.#828 for the basic meaning of κρατέω and the way it is used in the New Testament. Note especially Col.2:19; II Thess.2:15; Heb.4:14; Mk.9:10; Heb.6:18; Rev.2:13,25. There is nothing wrong with steadfast observance of a truth if it is God's truth. The Pharisees were guilty of subverting what they should have guarded by guarding what they should have abandoned.

Mark continues his parenthetical explanation in

Verse 4 - "And when they come from the market, except they wash, they eat not. And many other things there be, which they have received to hold, as the washing of cups, and pots, brasen vessels, and of tables."

καὶ ἀπ' ἀγορᾶς ἐὰν μὴ βαπτίσωνται οὐκ ἐσθίουσιν, καὶ ἄλλα πολλά ἐστιν ἃ παρέλαβον κρατεῖν, βαπτισμοὺς ποτηρίων καὶ ξεστῶν καὶ χαλκίων (καὶ κλινῶν) —"

καὶ (continuative conjunction) 14.
ἀπ' (preposition with the ablative of source) 70.
ἀγορᾶς (abl.sing.fem.of ἀγορά, source) 924.
ἐὰν (conditional particle in a third-class condition) 363.
μὴ (qualified negative conjunction with the subjunctive in a third-class condition) 87.

#2297 ῥαντίσωνται (3d.per.pl.1st.aor.mid.subj.of ῥαντίζω, third-class condition).

sprinkle - Heb.9:13,19,21; 10:22.
wash - Mk.7:4.

(Note: The United Bible Societies Committee have opted for βαπτίσωνται rather than ῥαντίσωνται, of the Westcott/Hort text, which was being followed when this verse was analyzed. In order, therefore not to disrupt the numerical order of the words we present ῥαντίσωνται here, with its appropriate number and present Metzger's explanation for their decision.

"Although it can be argued that the less familiar word (ῥαντίσωνται), was replaced by the more familiar one (βαπτίσωνται), it is far more likely that Alexandrian copyists, either wishing to keep βαπτίζειν for the Christian rite, or, more probably, taking ἀπ' ἀγορᾶς as involving a partitive construction, introduced ῥαντίσωνται as more appropriate to express the meaning, "except they sprinkle (what is) from the market place, they do not eat (it)." (Metzger, *A Textual Commentary on the Greek New Testament*, 93).

Meaning: to sprinkle; from ῥαίνω. To cleanse by sprinkling. Objects purchased in the market place - Mk.7:4, in which water was used. With reference to the sprinkling of blood and ashes upon people and article in the temple - Heb.9:13,19,21. Metaphorically in Heb.10:22.

οὐκ (summary negative conjunction with the indicative) 130.
ἐσθίουσιν (3d.per.pl.pres.act.ind.of ἐσθίω, aoristic) 610.
καὶ (continuative conjunction) 14.
ἄλλα (nom.pl.neut.of ἄλλος, subject of ἐστιν) 198.
πολλά (nom.pl.neut.of πολύς, in agreement with ἄλλα) 228.
ἐστιν (3d.per.sing.pres.ind.of εἰμί, aoristic) 86.
ἃ (acc.pl.neut.of ὅς, relative pronoun, object of παρέλαβον) 65.
παρέλαβον (3d.per.pl.aor.act.ind.of παραλαμβάνω, constative) 102.
κρατεῖν (pres.act.inf.of κρατέω, telic) 828.

#2298 βαπτισμοὺς (acc.pl.masc.of βαπτισμός, apposition, in agreement with ἃ).

baptism - Heb.6:2; Col.2:12.
washing - Mk.7:4; Heb.9:10.

Meaning: Cf. βαπτίζω (#273), βάπτισμα (#278), βαπτιστής (#248) and βάπτω (#2584). The act of dipping or submerging. In reference to washing ποτήριον, ξέστης and χαλκίον, all of which are properly immersed in water when washed, in Mk.7:4. In reference to the ceremonial washing of Mk.7:4 in Heb.6:2; 9:10. With reference to the symbolism of Christian baptism - Col.2:12.

ποτηρίων (gen.pl.neut.of ποτήριον, description) 902.
καὶ (adjunctive conjunction joining nouns) 14.

#2299 ξεστῶν (gen.pl.masc.of ξέστης, description).

pot - Mk.7:4.

Meaning: A corruption of the Latin *sextarius*, a vessel for measuring liquid - pint capactiy. The Vulgate uses *urceus* to translate it.

καὶ (adjunctive conjunction joining nouns) 14.

#2300 χαλκίων (gen.pl.neut.of χαλκίον, description).

brazen vessel - Mk.7:4.

Meaning: from χαλκός. *Cf.*χαλκολίβανον (#5326), χαλκός (#861), χαλκεύς (#4871), χάλκεος (#5378) and χαλκηδών (# 5430). A copper or brazen vessel.

Translation - "And they will not eat anything from the market if they do not first wash it, and many other (customs) there are which they have received in order to observe - washing of cups and pots and brass vessels and pallets."

(Note:There is some manuscript authority for adding καὶ κλινῶν at the end of the sentence. "It is difficult to decide whether the words καὶ κλινῶν were added by copyists who were influenced by the legislation of Lv.15, or whether the words were omitted (a) accidentally because of homoeoteleuton or (b) deliberately because the idea of washing or sprinkling beds seemed to be quite incongruous. In view of the balance of probabilities, as well as the strong witnesses that support each reading, a majority of the Committee preferred to retain the words, but to enclose them within square brackets."

(Metzger, *A Textual Commentary on the Greek New Testament*, 93,94).

With reference to the incongruity involved in washing beds by immersion in water, a study of κλινή (#779) indicates that the word probably means a pallet, not a bed in the modern sense, in which case there is nothing incongruous about using βαπτισμός (#2298) and κλινή together. Any wash woman knows that sheets, blankets, quilts and pillow cases are washed by immersion in water. The argument of the pedobaptists that Greek words in βαπ do not always mean immersion because of Mk.7:4 is therefore idle.

Another variant reading has attempted to clear up the passage by adding ἀγορᾶς ὅταν ἔλθωσιν or ὅταν δὲ εἰσέλθωσιν. If this is the original reading (though the better manuscript evidence is against it) the passage says that the Jews washed themselves when they came from the market, rather than those articles which they had purchased. Having arrived from a trip to the town square (#924), where they were forced to mingle too closely with sinners, they never ate until first they had a bath - a shower bath if we accept ῥαντίσωνται as the proper text, though the margin has βαπτίσωνται, in which case they submerged themselves in the pool. In any case, whether ῥαν or βαπ, they cleansed themselves thoroughly before eating, and Mark's point is made that they were fanatics about ceremonial cleansing. Cleanliness indeed is a virtue but they were not bathing for reasons of health but to maintain the validity of religious tradition.

Metzger comments, "The abruptness of καὶ ἀπ' ἀγορᾶς ἐὰν μὴ βαπτίσωνται οὐκ ἐσθίουσιν was relieved by the addition of several witnesses (D W *al*) of ὅταν ἔλθωσιν ("*when they come* from the market place, they do not eat unless they wash themselves"), (*Ibid.,* 93).

Here we have a good example of the way in which the Holy Spirit inspired the Word of God. The text which in His sovereign wisdom He has allowed to come down to us is totally adequate to transmit the total message which He wants us to have. The point in the passage is not whether the Pharisees washed themselves or the articles which they purchased in the market, but that they washed something or someone, not for purposes of hygienics but in order to keep alive a religious tradition. They were fanatics. This is the fate of all who refuse the intellectual light which comes only from a commitment to ὁ λόγος - the incarnate Son of God.

Mark now adjoins more proof of their religious fanaticism. ἄλλα πολλά ἐστιν - ". . many other things there are. . . " Note the singular verb with the neuter plural subject - good Greek grammar. He says that the Pharisees had accepted these rules from their fathers in order that (telic infinitive in κρατεῖν) they might observe them. Then, in apposition, Mark lists objects which the Pharisees thought in great need of cleansing - cups, pots and pans, brass vessels and bed clothing, all of which are small enough to be immersed in water when they are washed.

Verses 3 and 4 do not occur in some manuscripts and may not be a part of the original inspired autograph of Mark, though the material presented is essentially correct. With or without the interpolation, if indeed it is that, the point is clear that the Pharisees regarded as highly important many fanatical ideas which Jesus did not endorse. Their beliefs and actions illustrate Jesus' point in John 5:39a, 44 and Paul's statement in Rom.10:1-4.

Verse 4 ends the parenthesis and we return to the main story in

Verse 5 - "Then the Pharisees and Scribes asked him, Why walk not thy disciples according to the tradition of the elders, but eat bread with unwashen hands?"

καὶ ἐπερωτῶσιν αὐτὸν οἱ Φαρισαῖοι καὶ οἱ γραμματεῖς, Διὰ τί οὐ περιπατοῦσιν οἱ μαθηταί σου κατὰ τὴν παράδοσιν τῶν πρεσβυτέρων, ἀλλὰ κοιναῖς χερσὶν ἐσθίουσιν τὸν ἄρτον;

καὶ (inferential conjunction) 14.
ἐπερωτῶσιν (3d.per.pl.pres.act.ind.of ἐπερωτάω, historical) 973.
αὐτὸν (acc.sing.masc.of αὐτός, direct object of ἐπερωτῶσιν) 16.
οἱ (nom.pl.masc.of the article in agreement with Φαρισαῖοι) 9.
Φαρισαῖοι (nom.pl.masc.of Φαρισαῖος, subject of ἐπερωτῶσιν) 276.
καὶ (adjunctive conjunction joining nouns) 14.
οἱ (nom.pl.masc.of the article in agreement with γραμματεῖς) 9.
γραμματεῖς (nom.pl.masc.of γραμματεύς, subject of ἐπερωτῶσιν) 152.
Διὰ (preposition with the accusative, cause) 118.
τί (acc.sing.neut.of τίς, interrogative pronoun, cause) 281.
οὐ (summary negative conjunction with the indicative in direct question) 130.
περιπατοῦσιν (3d.per.pl.pres.act.ind.of περιπατέω, aoristic) 384.
οἱ (nom.pl.masc.of the article in agreement with μαθηταί) 9.
μαθηταί (nom.pl.masc.of μαθητής, subject of περιπατοῦσιν) 421.
σου (gen.sing.masc.of σύ, relationship) 104.
κατὰ (preposition with the accusative, standard rule of measure) 98.
τὴν (acc.sing.fem.of the article in agreement with παράδοσιν) 9.
παράδοσιν (acc.sing.fem.of παράδοσις, standard rule of measure) 1140.
τῶν (gen.pl.masc.of the article in agreement with πρεσβυτέρων) 9.
πρεσβυτέρων (gen.pl.masc.of πρεσβύτερος, definition) 1141.
ἀλλὰ (negative alternative conjunction) 342.
κοιναῖς (instru.pl.fem.of κοινός, in agreement with χερσὶν) 2295.
χερσὶν (instru.pl.fem.of χείρ, means) 308.
ἐσθίουσιν (3d.per.pl.pres.act.ind.of ἐσθίω, customary) 610.
τὸν (acc.sing.masc.of the article in agreement with ἄρτον) 9.
ἄρτον (acc.sing.masc.of ἄρτος, direct object of ἐσθίουσιν) 338.

Translation - "Therefore the Pharisees and the Scribes asked Him, 'Why do not your disciples conduct themselves in keeping with the traditions of the elders, but rather with dirty hands eat their bread?'"

Comment: The verse joins verse 2 since verses 3 and 4 are parenthetical. καὶ is inferential, influenced by the aorist temporal participle ἰδόντες of verse 2. What they saw in verse 2 triggered their question of verse 5. Having seen the disciples eat their food without going through all of the ceremonial nonsense which the

Pharisees and Scribes thought important, they started an argument. *Cf.*#118 for other examples of διὰ τί in the sense of "Why?" or "On account of (because of) what?" *Cf.*#384 for περιπατέω in the same sense. "Why does not the religious behavior of your disciples conform to ... κ.τ.λ.?" κατά with the accusative often in this sense. *Cf.*#98. Note the strong adversative ἀλλά. Again, as in verse 2, κοιναῖς χερσὶν is emphasized. The outraged sense of decency, propriety and orthodoxy which these bigots felt in verse 2 they express in verse 5. Thus the power structure in the institutional church rides herd on the morals of everyone. Jesus' rebuttal is devastating in

Verse 6 - "He answered and said unto them, Well hath Esaias prophesied of you hypocrites, as it is written, This people honoreth me with their lips, but their heart is far from me."

ὁ δὲ εἶπεν αὐτοῖς, Καλῶς ἐπροφήτευσεν Ἡσαΐας περὶ ὑμῶν τῶν ὑποκριτῶν, ὡς γέγραπται ὅτι Οὗτος ὁ λαὸς τοῖς χείλεσίν με τιμᾷ, ἡ δὲ καρδία αὐτῶν πόρρω ἀπέχει ἀπ' ἐμοῦ.

ὁ (nom.sing.masc.of the article, subject of εἶπεν) 9.
δὲ (adversative conjunction) 11.
εἶπεν (3d.per.sing.aor.act.ind.of εἶπον, constative) 155.
αὐτοῖς (dat.pl.masc.of αὐτός, indirect object of εἶπεν) 16.
Καλῶς (adverbial) 977.
ἐπροφήτευσεν (3d.per.sing.aor.act.ind.of προφητεύω, culminative) 685.
Ἡσαΐας (nom.sing.masc.of Ἡσαΐα, subject of ἐπροφήτευσεν) 255.
περὶ (preposition with the genitive of reference) 173.
ὑμῶν (gen.pl.masc.of σύ, reference) 104.
τῶν (gen.pl.masc.of the article in agreement with ὑποκριτῶν) 9.
ὑποκριτῶν (gen.pl.masc.of ὑποκριτής, apposition) 561.
ὡς (relative adverb introducing a comparative clause) 128.
γέγραπται (3d.per.sing.perf.pass.ind.of γράφω, consummative) 156.
ὅτι (recitative) 211.
Οὗτος (nom.sing.masc.of οὗτος, in agreement with λαὸς, contemptuous use) 93.
ὁ (nom.sing.masc.of the article in agreement with λαὸς) 9.
λαὸς (nom.sing.masc.of λαός, subject of τιμᾷ) 110.
τοῖς (instru.pl.masc.of the article in agreement with χείλεσίν) 9.
χείλεσίν (instru.pl.masc.of χεῖλος, means) 1146.
με (acc.sing.masc.of ἐγώ, direct object of τιμᾷ) 123.
τιμᾷ (3d.per.sing.pres.act.ind.of τιμάω, customary) 1142.
ἡ (nom.sing.fem.of the article in agreement with καρδία) 9.
δὲ (adversative conjunction) 11.
καρδία (nom.sing.fem.of καρδία, subject of ἀπέχει) 432.
αὐτῶν (gen.pl.masc.of αὐτός, possession) 16.
πόρρω (adverbial) 1147.
ἀπέχει (3d.per.sing.pres.act.ind.of ἀπέχω, aoristic) 563.
ἀπ' (preposition with the ablative of separation) 70.

ἐμοῦ (abl.sing.masc.of ἐμός, separation) 1267.

Translation - *"But He said to them, 'Well has Isaiah prophesied about you hypocrites, as it is written, This people honor me with the lips, but their heart is far removed from me."*

Comment: δὲ is adversative as Jesus ignores their question and rushes to the attack. Note that He emphasizes Καλῶς. The direct discourse, introduced by ὅτι continues through verse 7. Note the contemptuous use of οὗτος. *Cf.*#1146 for lips in insincere worship or for genuine praise as in Heb.13:15; I Pet.3:10. Note also Heb.11:12 for an interesting metaphor. δὲ in the quotation is adversative again. Despite what the lips say, the heart stands afar off. *Cf.*#1147 for a study of πόρρω. ἀπ' ἐμοῦ in a spiritual sense as in Mt.15:8 and Mk.4:25. Jesus spells it out in detail in vss.7-13. Thus did Jesus begin His castigation of the sinners who elicited from Him His blazing righteous anger. So gentle with the fallen who were humble and contrite, whose sins were chiefly of the flesh, He was a tiger on the attack against those who were duplicit. His incisive analysis of the motivation of the Pharisees who contrived spurious holiness in order to escape the obligations of true holiness proves that though man looks only on the outward appearance, God looks upon the heart.

The Greek idiom that uses an adverb with ἔχω or some composite verb that contains it, "is difficult from the English point of view." *Cf.* Mt.14:35; Mk.1:34; Lk.7:2. "In English we prefer the predicate adjective with have (He has it bad), whereas the Greek likes the adverb with ἔχω." *Cf.* Mk.5:23 and John 4:52, where we have the comparative adverb. "One must be willing for the Greek to have his standpoint." *Cf.* also Acts 7:1; 15:36. (Robertson, *Grammar*, 546).

Verse 7 - *"Howbeit in vain do they worship me, teaching for doctrines the commandments of men."*

μάτην δὲ σέβονταί με, διδάσκοντες διδασκαλίας ἐντάλματα ἀνθρώπων.

μάτην (adverbial) 1148.
δὲ (adversative conjunction) 11.
σέβονταί (3d.per.pl.pres.mid.ind.of σέβομαι, customary) 1149.
με (acc.sing.masc.of ἐγώ, direct object of σέβονταί) 123.
διδάσκοντες (pres.act.part.nom.pl.masc.of διδάσκω, adverbial, causal) 403.
διδασκαλίας (acc.pl.fem.of διδασκαλία, direct object of διδάσκοντες) 1150.
ἐντάλματα (acc.pl.neut.of ἔνταλμα, direct object of διδάσκοντες) 1151.
ἀνθρώπων (gen.pl.masc.of ἄνθρωπος, description) 341.

Translation - *"But they offer me only empty worship, because they are teaching doctrines which are only human commandments."*

Comment: δὲ is adversative. Despite the sonorous folderol of their litany, designed to impress the naive sinner in the congregation, at least until the offering plates are passed, the performance is in vain. Jesus pointed to insincere words in verse 6 and empty worship and false theology in verse 7. The perfidy of these hypocrites augments. They were elevating human commands, based only on human wisdom, to the dignity of dogma to be handed down. ἐντάλματα ἀνθρώπων - the genitive without the article is descriptive - "human commands." No one is as dogmatic and didactic as the teacher who is pushing some human system upon the mind of the student. Perhaps such teachers are overreacting to their own feeling of insecurity and inferiority. One need not force the true revelation of God upon an audience. Since it truly comes from God, it carries with it its own persuasive powers. But to try to sell some man-made theory is to take upon one's shoulders the entire burden of persuasion. The Holy Spirit is not in the business of helping the demagogue brainwash the public. That is why such teachers become fanatics. God's word needs only to be expounded. Man's theoretical concoctions must be argued. One cannot teach the commands of God and the traditions of men at the same time. This is clear from

Verse 8 - "For laying aside the commandment of God, ye hold the tradition of men, as the washing of pots and cups; and many other such like things ye do."

ἀφέντες τὴν ἐντολὴν τοῦ θεοῦ κρατεῖτε τὴν παράδοσιν τῶν ἀνθρώπων.

ἀφέντες (2d.aor.act.part.nom.pl.masc.of ἀφίημι, adverbial, temporal) 319.
τὴν (acc.sing.fem.of the article in agreement with ἐντολὴν) 9.
ἐντολὴν (acc.sing.fem.of ἐντολή, direct object of ἀφέντες) 472.
τοῦ (gen.sing.masc.of the article in agreement with θεοῦ) 9.
θεοῦ (gen.sing.masc.of θεός, definition) 124.
κρατεῖτε (2d.per.pl.pres.act.ind.of κρατέω, customary) 828.
τὴν (acc.sing.fem.of the article in agreement with παράδοσιν) 9.
παράδοσιν (acc.pl.fem.of παράδοσις, direct object of κρατεῖτε) 1140.
τῶν (gen.pl.masc.of the article in agreement with ἀνθρώπων) 9.
ἀνθρώπων (gen.pl.masc.of ἄνθρωπος, description) 341.

Translation - "Forsaking the divine commandment you are always propagating the human tradition."

Comment: The basic meaning of ἀφίημι (#319) and κρατέω (#828) is crystal clear here. Compare the two meanings. The Pharisees and Scribes customarily had forsaken the commandment of God (τὴν ἐντολὴν τοῦ θεοῦ) and stoutly defended or guarded the human tradition. The figure is that of a battle with the two standards raised in opposition to each other, like battle flags. Jesus is saying that it is apparent upon which side the Pharisees and Scribes were fighting. He procedes to spell it out in more detail in vss. 9-13.

Verse 9 - "And he said unto them, Full well ye reject the commandment of God, that ye may keep your own tradition."

Καὶ ἔλεγεν αὐτοῖς, Καλῶς ἀθετεῖτε τὴν ἐντολὴν τοῦ θεοῦ, ἵνα τὴν παράδοσιν ὑμῶν στήσητε.

Καὶ (continuative conjunction) 14.
ἔλεγεν (3d.per.sing.imp.act.ind.of λέγω, progressive duration) 66.

αὐτοῖς (dat.pl.masc.of αὐτός, indirect object of ἔλεγεν) 16.

Καλῶς (adverbial) 977.

ἀθετεῖτε (2d.per.pl.pres.act.ind.of ἀθετέω, customary) 2164.

τὴν (acc.sing.fem.of the article in agreement with ἐντολὴν) 9.

τοῦ (gen.sing.masc.of the article in agreement with θεοῦ) 9.

θεοῦ (gen.sing.masc.of θεός, definition) 124.

ἵνα (final conjunction introducing a purpose clause) 114.

τὴν (acc.sing.fem.of the article in agreement with παράδοσιν) 9.

παράδοσιν (acc.sing.fem.of παράδοσις, direct object of στήσητε) 1140.

ὑμῶν (gen.pl.masc.of σύ, possession) 104.

στήσητε (3d.per.pl.aor.act.subj.of ἵστημι, purpose) 180.

Translation - "He went on, 'It is logical that you reject the commandment of God in order to establish your own tradition.' "

Comment: Καλῶς is sarcasm, since normally it is an adverb of approbation (#977). How then can Jesus use it to describe the rejection of the commandment of God? However unethical, immoral and philosophically shortsighted it may be to replace divine commands with human tradition, it is at least logical and consistent with one's purpose to do so if the teacher is an empire builder, since the two systems of thought are in diametric opposition. An attempt to hold both at the same time is illogical and stupid. To install man's system one must first reject God's. Which is not saying much for the sophistication of some who cannot see the difference between ἡ ἐντολὴ τοῦ θεοῦ and ἡ παράδοσις τῶν ἀνθρώπων. The deacon who rejects the Holy Spirit's leadership as issuing from a God-called pastor, in order to run the church "on a business basis" is a fool and a knave to assert that his ideas necessarily coincide with God's, since God's Word clearly says that the pastor is the head of the church.

But, however foolish and wicked such assumption of authority may be, if he openly asserts with pride that there is a difference between his plans and God's, at least he is logical and merits the sarcastic observation involved in καλῶς in our passage. Goodspeed catches the essence of the passage with his translation: "How skillful you are . . . in nullifying what God has commanded in order to observe what has been handed down to you."

Cf.#2164 and notice especially John 12:48 where θετέω and μὴ λαμβάνων are adjoined as heads and tails of the same coin. ἀθετέω involves violation of contract in business (Gal.3:15) or in social relations, even when the sanctity of one's pledged word involves one in murder (Mk.6:26). The Pharisees and Scribes cared nothing for that. When one is convinced that he knows more than God, ethics and morals become unimportant.

To say that God's commands are opposite to man's traditions and that to adopt the latter necessitates rejection of the former is to assert something that must be proved. Hence the inferential argument of verses 10 and 11.

Verse 10 - "For Moses said, 'Honor thy father and thy mother; and, Whoso curseth father or mother, let him die the death."

Μωϋσῆς γὰρ εἶπεν Τίμα τὸν πατέρα σου καὶ τὴν μητέρα σου, καί Ὁ κακολογῶν πατέρα ἢ μητέρα θανάτῳ τελευτάτω.

Μωϋσῆς (nom.sing.masc.of Μωϋσῆς, subject of εἶπεν) 715.
γὰρ (causal conjunction) 105.
εἶπεν (3d.per.sing.aor.act.ind.of εἶπον, constative) 155.
Τίμα (2d.per.sing.pres.act.impv.of τιμάω, command) 1142.
τὸν (acc.sing.masc.of the article in agreement with πατέρα) 9.
πατέρα (acc.sing.masc.of πατήρ, direct object of τίμα) 238.
σου (gen.sing.masc.of σύ, relationship) 104.
καὶ (adjunctive conjunction joining nouns) 14.
τὴν (acc.sing.fem.of the article in agreement with μητέρα) 9.
μητέρα (acc.sing.fem.of μήτηρ, direct object of τίμα) 76.
σου (gen.sing.masc.of σύ, relationship) 104.
καί (continuative conjunction) 14.
Ὁ (nom.sing.masc.of the article in agreement with κακολογῶν) 9.
κακολογῶν (pres.act.part.nom.sing.masc.of κακολογέω, subject of τελευτάτω) 1143.
πατέρα (acc.sing.masc.of πατήρ, direct object of κακολογῶν) 238.
ἢ (disjunctive particle) 465.
μητέρα (acc.sing.fem.of μήτηρ, direct object of κακολογῶν) 76.
θανάτῳ (instru.sing.masc.of θάνατος, means) 381.
τελευτάτω (3d.per.sing.pres.act.impv.of τελευτάω, command) 231.

Translation - "Because Moses said, 'Honor your father and your mother.' And the one who is speaking ill of father or mother shall be put to death."

Comment: The burden of proof is upon Jesus. He had just said that the commandment of God is contrary to the tradition of the fathers which the Pharisees and Scribes were trying to hard to uphold. He now points out the contrariety between the two.

Moses said two things about the relation between children and their parents, *viz.*, Τίμα . . . σου and ὁ κακολογῶν . . . τελ. The citations are from Exodus 20:12 and Exodus 21:17. *Cf.*#1142 for the meaning of τιμάω. "Put a high value upon your parents and thus take good care of them." This includes old age security in a financial sense. If all men obeyed Moses' order today the state would need no social security program except for the superannuate who had no children. The former command is positive and is the only one of the commandments with a promise attached. The latter is negative with a threat in connection. Long life is promised to those who obey. The sentence of death rests upon those who disobey. θανάτῳ τελευτάτω - "Let him die by means of death imposed" or "Let him be put to death." One is reminded of the judge who decrees that a criminal shall be hanged by the neck until he is "dead, dead, dead."

Note how Jesus interchanges τοῦ θεοῦ of verse 9 with Μωϋσῆς of verse 10. The Pharisees dared not challenge this since the difference is only that of direct and indirect agency.

So much for what God, through Moses, said. What were the Pharisees saying?

Verse 11 - "*But ye say, If a man shall say to his father or mother, It is Corban, that is to say, a gift, by whatsoever thou mightest be profited by me, he shall be free.*"

ὑμεῖς δὲ λέγετε, Ἐὰν εἴπῃ ἄνθρωπος τῷ πατρὶ ἢ μητρί, Κορβᾶν, ὅ ἐστιν, Δῶρον, ὅ ἐὰν ἐξ ἐμοῦ ὀφεληθῇς,

ὑμεῖς (nom.pl.masc.of σύ, subject of λέγετε) 104.

δὲ (adversative conjunction) 11.

λέγετε (2d.per.pl.pres.act.ind.of λέγω, customary) 66.

Ἐὰν (conditional particle in a third-class condition) 363.

εἴπῃ (3d.per.sing.aor.act.subj.of εἶπον, constative, third-class condition) 155.

ἄνθρωπος (nom.sing.masc.of ἄνθρωπος, subject of εἴπῃ) 341.

τῷ (dat.sing.masc.of the article in agreement with πατρὶ) 9.

πατρὶ (dat.sing.masc.of πατήρ, indirect object of εἴπῃ) 238.

ἢ (disjunctive particle) 465.

τῇ (dat.sing.fem.of the article in agreement with μητρί) 9.

μητρί (dat.sing.fem.of μήτηρ, indirect object of εἴπῃ) 76.

Κορβᾶν (nom.sing.neut.of κορβᾶν, appellation) 1618.

ὅ (nom.sing.neut.of ὅς, relative pronoun, subject of ἐστιν, apposition) 65.

ἐστιν (3d.per.sing.pres.ind.of εἰμί, aoristic) 86.

Δῶρον (nom.sing.neut.of δῶρον, predicate nominative) 191.

ὅ (nom.sing.neut.of ὅς, subject of the verb understood) 65.

ἐὰν (conditional particle in a broken third-class condition, aposiopesis) 363.

ἐξ (preposition with the ablative of source) 19.

ἐμοῦ (abl.sing.masc.of ἐμός, source) 1267.

ὠφεληθῇς (2d.per.sing.aor.pass.subj.of ὠφελέω, in a third-class elliptical condition) 1144.

Translation - "*But you are saying, 'If a man say to his father or to his mother, Korban, which means* **Gift**, *by which if given you would receive benefit from me. . .*"

Comment: I have been very literal with the translation of Mark's fractured Greek. The apodosis of the first third-class condition is in verse 12. The second third-class condition is elliptical, as the apodosis is missing. Goodspeed has transmitted the sense of the passage faithfully with a free translation - "But you say, 'If a man says to his father or mother, "Anything of mine that might have been of use to you is Korban," that is, consecrated to God, you let him off from doing anything more for his father or mother. . . κ.τ.λ.".

Money, if given by a son to his parents, would help them greatly in their time of need. Such money, so given, would be in obedience to God's law with reference to a son's obligation to his parents. But let us suppose that the son tells his parents that the money has already been pledged to God? It is Korban, which means a gift to be given at the temple. In that case the money which rightfully belonged to his parents is given into the temple treasury and the parents are powerless to object. Jesus was describing the subterfuge by which the Pharisees evaded their obligation to their parents and made it look like an act of pious worship. A man might approach his poverty stricken parents whom Moses had ordered him to support and say, "I have here some money which, if I gave it to you, would help you out, but I cannot. It is Korban, *i.e.* a gift already pledged to the temple." Thus the temple demands (human tradition) prevented obedience to divine demands, as set forth by Moses.

Jesus is not blaming the poor man who is caught in the dilemma of spreading scarce resources between the legitimate needs of the temple and those legitimate needs of his parents. He is blaming the Pharisees for instituting and maintaining the Korban tradition. There is a modern application. How many Christians today can afford to give an offering above his tithe to the church (which modern Pharisees suggest) and also take care of aged parents? Mt.25:33-40 imposes further financial obligations upon the Christian who wishes to be obedient to all of the scripture. Someone gets left out and in many cases it is the parents. So the secular state, through the welfare program, takes care of the aged and needy, while the church drains off the money, calling it Korban (tithes and offerings) and spends it upon institutional promotion which may or may not be demanded by the Word of God.

The sentence goes on, supplying the apodosis of the third-class condition in

Verse 12 - "And ye suffer him no more to do ought for his father or his mother."

οὐκέτι ἀφίετε αὐτὸν οὐδὲν ποιῆσαι τῷ πατρὶ ἢ τῇ μητρί,

οὐκέτι (adverb of denial) 1289.
ἀφίετε (2d.per.pl.pres.act.ind.of ἀφίημι, customary) 319.
αὐτὸν (acc.sing.masc.of αὐτός, direct object of ἀφίετε) 16.
οὐδὲν (acc.sing.neut.of οὐδείς, direct object of ποιῆσαι) 446.
ποιῆσαι (aor.act.inf.of ποιέω, complementary) 127.
τῷ (dat.sing.masc.of the article in agreement with πατρὶ) 9.
πατρὶ (dat.sing.masc.of πατήρ, personal advantage) 238.
ἢ (disjunctive particle) 465.
τῇ (dat.sing.fem.of the article in agreement with μητρί) 9.
μητρί (dat.sing.fem.of μήτηρ, personal advantage) 76.

Translation - ". . . you no longer allow him to do anything for his father or mother,"

Comment: *Cf.*#319. ἀφίημι means to "stand away from," "let alone," "*laissez faire*," "decontrol," or "give freedom to." The Pharisees were not doing that any more. Once they did and presumably the Jews, free from the galling restrictions of Korban, obeyed Moses and provided for their parents, ". . . that their days might be long in the land . . . κ.τ.λ." (Exodus 20:12). No more. No longer do the religious dictators stand aside. On the contrary they confront - "stand up to" the Jew with the strident demand for the Korban and the sly suggestion that if Korban is pledged, parental care obligations can be avoided. Hence the Jew does nothing for his parents and justifies his failure on the ground of his financial devotion to the temple.

When Christians stand before the judgment seat of Christ (II Cor.5:10) there may be some who will plead extenuation for their lack of obedience on the grounds of Korban. There is an added reason why Korban is a good idea for those who wish to evade Christian responsibility in financial matters. Under current law the gift into the temple treasury provides an income tax dodge. Thanks to Korban there are some wealthy Pharisees whose contributions on Sunday morning cost them nothing.

Jesus goes on in verse 13 to say that the Korban tradition is one concrete example of the way the Pharisees and Scribes had substituted the traditions of their fathers for the Word of God.

Verse 13 - "Making the word of God of none effect through your tradition, which ye have delivered: and many such like things do ye."

ἀκυροῦντες τὸν λόγον τοῦ θεοῦ τῇ παραδόσει ὑμῶν ᾗ παρεδώκατε, καὶ παρόμοια τοιαῦτα πολλὰ ποιεῖτε.

ἀκυροῦντες (pres.act.part.nom.pl.masc.of ἀκυρόω, adverbial, telic) 1145.
τὸν (acc.sing.masc.of the article in agreement with λόγον) 9.
λόγον (acc.sing.masc.of λόγος, direct object of ἀκυροῦντες) 510.
τοῦ (gen.sing.masc.of the article in agreement with θεοῦ) 9.
θεοῦ (gen.sing.masc.of θεός, description) 124.
τῇ (instru.sing.fem.of the article in agreement with παραδόσει) 9.
παραδόσει (instru.sing.fem.of παράδοσις, means) 1140.
ὑμῶν (gen.pl.masc.of σύ, possession) 104.
ᾗ (instru.sing.fem.of ὅς, attracted in case to παραδόσει, subject of παρεδώκατε) 65.
παρεδώκατε (2d.per.pl.perf.act.ind.of παραδίδωμι, consummative) 368.
καὶ (continuative conjunction) 14.

#2301 παρόμοια (acc.pl.neut.of παρόμοιος, direct object of ποιεῖτε).

like things - Mk.7:13.

Meaning: παρά (#154) plus ὅμοιος (#923). Hence, along side or like. In this particular context "parallel in similarity" - the same principle involved but with differing details.

τοιαῦτα (acc.pl.neut.of τοιοῦτος, in agreement with παρόμοια) 785.
πολλὰ (acc.pl.neut.of πολύς, in agreement with παρόμοια) 228.
ποιεῖτε (2d.per.pl.pres.act.ind.of ποιέω, customary) 127.

Translation - "... in order that you may denude the Word of God of its authority by means of your tradition which, having propagated, you continue to enforce. Moreover many such parallel practices you continue to carry out."

Comment: Cf.#1145 for the basic meaning of ἀκυρόω. τῇ παραδόσει - "by means of your tradition." ᾗ - an example of a relative pronoun attracted in case to its antecedent, παραδόσει. The perfect tense in παρεδώκατε is interesting. It speaks of a present condition as a result of a past action. Once, in the past, they instituted Korban and it had become traditional by their continual maintenance of it, which had extended to the moment of their encounter with Jesus. The fact that traditions are old and consistently maintained is no evidence that they are wise. Whether an ancient principle is wise or not depends upon the source. "Honor thy father and mother" began in the eternal wisdom of God and was handed down to Moses upon tablets of stone. Obedience to the command is implicit in its wisdom and thus its ripple effects for good throughout society. The Korban principle was born in the scheming brain of some unknown innovator in opposition to Moses' command. It had been maintained by demagogues.

Not only in the matter of Korban but also in many other similar practices they were guilty of supplanting the Word of God. παρόμοια (#2301) - parallel instances, where details are different but where the principle, *viz.*,withholding obedience to God's law by substituting human tradition, is the same. Jesus did not specify the other cases which He had in mind, but He does insist that examples would not be hard to find.

All of the material in vss.6-13 is parenthetical to the main line of thought in the context. This argument started when the Pharisees and Scribes noticed that Jesus' disciples ate their lunch without first washing their hands. In their protest they mentioned the traditions of their forefathers, which triggered Jesus' attack upon traditional Jewish religion as opposed to genuine worship. Now in verse 14*ff* Jesus takes up the question of whether it is wrong to eat with dirt on the hands. In doing so, He addresses a wider audience.

Verse 14 - "And when he had called all the people unto him, he said unto them, Hearken unto me, everyone of you, and understand."

Καὶ προσκαλεσάμενος πάλιν τὸν ὄχλον ἔλεγεν αὐτοῖς, 'Ακούσατέ μου πάντες καὶ σύνετε.

Καὶ (continuative conjunction) 14.
προσκαλεσάμενος (aor.mid.part.nom.sing.masc.of προσκαλέω, adverbial, temporal) 842.
πάλιν (adverbial) 355.
τὸν (acc.sing.masc.of the article in agreement with ὄχλον) 9.
ὄχλον (acc.sing.masc.of ὄχλος, direct object of προσκαλεσάμενος) 418.
ἔλεγεν (3d.per.sing.imp.act.ind.of λέγω, inceptive) 66.
αὐτοῖς (dat.pl.masc.of αὐτός, indirect object of ἔλεγεν) 16.
'Ακούσατε (2d.per.pl.aor.act.impv.of ἀκούω, command) 148.
μου (gen.sing.masc.of ἐγώ, after ἀκούω) 123.
πάντες (voc.pl.masc.of πᾶς, address) 67.
καὶ (adjunctive conjunction joining verbs) 14.
σύνετε (2d.per.pl.aor.act.impv.of συνίημι, command) 1039.

Translation - "And when He had again summoned the crowd to gather about Him, He began to speak to them, saying, 'Hear me, all of you, and understand."

Comment: πάλιν connects Jesus' action with Mk.6:55,56 which describes the scene before Jesus was so rudely interrupted by the bigots. Now that He has disposed of them He is ready to resume His teaching and healing ministry.

Note ἀκούσατέ μου - the genitive after ἀκούω. Remember Broadus' rule, "With verbs the genitive means this and no other, while the accusative with verbs means this and no more," (Robertson, *Short Grammar*, 230). "Hear me and no other." (*cf.* John 6:60). Hear with rapport - audibly and perceptively. Hear with respect. Jesus could have added, "Pay no attention to the Pharisees." *Cf.*#1039 for the meaning. "Stand with it." Understand it, perceive it, grasp its meaning, accept it." The hippies say, "Get with it" or "Dig it."

Now that the Pharisees have raised the question about cleanliness and its connections with morals and religious observance, Jesus may as well speak to the subject as He does in

Verse 15 - "There is nothing from without a man that entering into him, can defile him: but the things which come out of him, those are they that defile the man."

οὐδέν ἐστιν ἔξωθεν τοῦ ἀνθρώπου εἰσπορευόμενον εἰς αὐτὸν ὃ δύναται κοινῶσαι αὐτόν, ἀλλὰ τὰ ἐκ τοῦ ἀνθρώπου ἐκπορευόμενά ἐστιν τὰ κοινοῦντα τὸν ἄνθρωπον.

οὐδέν (nom.sing.neut.of οὐδείς, subject of ἐστιν) 446.

ἐστιν (3d.per.sing.pres.ind.of εἰμί, aoristic) 86.

ἔξωθεν (adverbial) 1455.

τοῦ (abl.sing.masc.of the article in agreement with ἀνθρώπου) 9.

ἀνθρώπου (abl.sing.masc.of ἄνθρωπος, separation) 341.

εἰσπορευόμενον (pres.part.nom.sing.neut.of εἰσπορεύομαι, adjectival, restrictive, modifies οὐδέν) 1161.

εἰς (preposition with the accusative of extent) 140.

αὐτὸν (acc.sing.masc.of αὐτός, extent) 16.

ὃ (nom.sing.neut.of ὅς, subject of δύναται) 65.

δύναται (3d.per.sing.pres.ind.of δύναμαι, customary) 289.

κοινῶσαι (aor.act.inf.of κοινόω, complementary) 1152.

αὐτόν (acc.sing.masc.of αὐτός, direct object of κοινῶσαι) 16.

ἀλλὰ (adversative alternative conjunction) 342.

τὰ (nom.pl.neut.of the article in agreement with ἐκπορευόμενα) 9.

ἐκ (preposition with the ablative of separation) 19.

τοῦ (abl.sing.masc.of the article in agreement with ἀνθρώπου) 9.

ἀνθρώπου (abl.sing.masc.of ἄνθρωπος, separation) 341.

ἐκπορευόμενα (nom.pl.neut.of ἐκπορεύομαι, substantival, subject of ἐστιν) 270.

ἐστιν (3d.per.sing.pres.ind.of εἰμί, aoristic) 86.

τὰ (nom.pl.neut.of the article in agreement with κοινοῦντα) 9.

κοινοῦντα (pres.act.part.nom.pl.neut.of κοινόω, substantival, predicate nominative) 1152.

τὸν (acc.sing.masc.of the article in agreement with ἄνθρωπον) 9.

ἄνθρωπον (acc.sing.masc.of ἄνθρωπος, direct object of κοινοῦντα) 341.

Translation - "*There is not one thing outside the man entering into him which is able to defile him, but the things that come out of the man are the things that defile the man.*"

Comment: οὐδέν here used as a substantive, the subject of ἐστιν. *Cf.*#446 for other examples. It is emphatic - "Not one thing . . " ἔξωθεν τοῦ ἀνθρώπου in the light of verse 19 means "outside the human body." The things outside the body that enter in are referred to in the relative clause. They are unable to defile the man.

To deny this statement is to assert that there is something which God created which works to defile God's crowning achievement in creation - the man. Everything else in creation was designed by the Creator to serve man, who alone was created "in the image of God." If "the earth is the Lord's and the fullness thereof" (Ps.24:1); if God saw that all that He created was "good" (Gen.1:31), and if God gave man dominion over everything else He created (Gen.1:28), then Jesus' statement in our verse must follow. Nothing in the universe, if taken internally by man can harm him *if taken in small enough quantities.* Chemists know that everything is food; nothing is food. Everything is toxic; nothing is toxic. Pure water is poisonous if taken in sufficient quantity. Physicians know about hydrotoxia, which is "water poisoning." Strychnine is food if taken in small enough doses. It acts to thin the blood stream when it is needed. People with too much cholesterol in their blood take "rat poison" as a remedy. The dosage is very small. When we feed it to the rats for extermination purposes the dosage is much heavier and they bleed to death internally. Nitroglycerin will blow up a bridge or forestall a heart attack. Hence the Christian position on what he should take into his body through his mouth is answered by the word "Everything" in temperate quantities. There are no exceptions because God created it all and it is good. Alcohol is not bad but the scriptures warn against intemperance. Nicotine is good for something. Perhaps we have not yet found its proper place in the ecological scheme which the Creator had in mind. The same is true with the drugs, which wreak such havoc when we misuse them. Destruction results and therefore the sin occurs because of intemperance.

Should we eat dirt? This was the question that the Pharisees were asking. The answer is contingent upon another question - "How much?" Jesus did not deny that ordinary care to wash one's hands before eating is proper, but the Pharisees practised it with the fanaticism described in verse 3 (*q.v.*, both translation and comment). They were therefore saying, "We must eat no dirt." This ban on dirt is an impossibility. If it were bad little children would die before reaching their first birthday. What is wrong with dirt? The chemist finds in "dirt" the same elements we find in "food." So "dirt" and "poison" are only words of opprobium, used by demagogues who wish to darken counsel with words without knowledge - the linguistic device of the fanatic. Teetotalism or total abstinence is not taught in Scripture as a virtue. Why not? Because our bodies possess such marvelous chemical qualities that the reaction in the alimentary canal purges everything we ingest, uses what we need and excretes what we cannot use. This is by the design of our Creator Who made our bodies "fearfully and wonderfully" (Ps.139:14).

More on this in comment upon verses 18 and 19.

The last half of the verse is introduced by the strong adversative ἀλλά. The new subject is τά . . . ἐκπορευόμενον - "the things which go out of the man." The context is in terms of the human body. The "going out things" are the one that are also the "defiling things." What these "going out things" are and from whence they come, Jesus expounds in verses 20-23. The source of "dirt" and "poison" is God. God made "dirt." Every farmer rejoices! What would a Nebraska wheat farmer do without dirt? God made "poison" and explosives and all things else, which, when used in excess by ignorant man brings about his destruction. But the source of those items mentioned in verses 22 and 23 is the depraved human heart. The Pharisees had their source analysis confused. They were banning that which God produced in order to nurture what their own wicked hearts produced. They were calling good, evil and evil good. "Woe unto them. . . " (Isa. 5:20).

Note the aorist infinitive κοινῶσαι. They cannot defile him *once* or *at all*. But, in contrast, the present tense in κοινοῦντα - they keep on defiling him! Thus our Lord reveals a deep insight into the psychology which we attribute to the disciples of Freud.

Verse 16 - "If any man have ears to hear, let him hear."

This verse is not found in the Westcott/Hort text. "This verse, though present in the majority of witnesses is absent from important Alexandrian witnesses (Sinaiticus B L Δ* al). It appears to be a scribal gloss (derived perhaps from 4.9 or 4.23, introduced as an appropriate sequel to ver.14." (Metzger, *A Textual Commentary on the Greek New Testament*, 94,95). For an exposition of the expression *cf.* comment on Mark 4:9 or any other passage listed appropriately under #887.

Verse 17 - "And when he was entered into the house from the people, his disciples asked him concerning the parable."

Καὶ ὅτε εἰσῆλθεν εἰς οἶκον ἀπὸ τοῦ ὄχλου, ἐπηρώτων αὐτὸν οἱ μαθηταὶ αὐτοῦ τὴν παραβολήν.

Καὶ (continuative conjunction) 14.
ὅτε (conjunction introducing a definite temporal clause) 703.
εἰσῆλθεν (3d.per.sing.aor.act.ind.of εἰσέρχομαι, culminative) 234.
εἰς (preposition with the accusative of extent) 140.
οἶκον (acc.sing.masc.of οἶκος, extent) 784.
ἀπὸ (preposition with the ablative of separation) 70.
τοῦ (abl.sing.masc.of the article in agreement with ὄχλου) 9.
ὄχλου (abl.sing.masc.of ὄχλος, separation) 418.
ἐπηρώτων (3d.per.pl.imp.act.ind.of ἐπερωτάω, inceptive) 973.
αὐτὸν (acc.sing.masc.of αὐτός, direct object of ἐπηρώτων) 16.
οἱ (nom.pl.masc.of the article in agreement with μαθηταὶ) 9.,
μαθηταὶ (nom.pl.masc.of μαθητής, subject of ἐπηρώτων) 421.
αὐτοῦ (gen.sing.masc.of αὐτός, relationship) 16.

τὴν (acc.sing.fem.of the article in agreement with παραβολήν) 9.
παραβολήν (acc.sing.fem.of παραβολή, general reference) 1027.

Translation - "And when He came into a house, away from the people, His disciples began to ask Him about the parable."

Comment: Mark uses ὅτε and the indicative in a definite temporal clause. A more sophisticated Greek literary author might have used a genitive absolute in the aorist tense.

The parallel account in Mt.15:12-14 tells us that Jesus' disciples came to Him and asked Him if He knew that His remark of Mk.7:15 had offended the Pharisees. Jesus replied to the effect that the Pharisees were plants (weeds) which the Father had not planted and that they were destined to be uprooted. He then counselled the disciples to let the Pharisees alone, because they were blind guides, destined along with those whom they misled to fall into the ditch. Matthew also records that it was Peter who asked Jesus for an explanation of the parable (Mt.15:15). Note that Mark uses the older Classical "catch-all" use of the accusative of general reference in τὴν παραβολήν, following the verb ἐπηρώτων. Later Greek usage would have used περί and the genitive of reference. The meaning is the same. They wanted Him to talk about His statement about what does and what does not defile man. The confusion of the disciples may indicate that they also believed in and practised the traditional hand-washing ceremony, at least on some occasions, though they had neglected to do so on this occasion, and that they felt that the Pharisees were somewhat justified in their criticism of their behavior, which Jesus seemed to defend.

It is important to remember therefore that Jesus' reply in vss.18-23 was for the disciples' ears only - not for general public consumption.

Verse 18 - "And he saith unto them, Are ye so without understanding also? Do ye not perceive that whatsoever thing from without entereth into the man, it cannot defile him."

καὶ λέγει αὐτοῖς, Οὕτως καὶ ὑμεῖς ἀσύνετοί ἐστε; οὐ νοεῖτε ὅτι πᾶν τὸ ἔξωθεν εἰσπορευόμενον εἰς τὸν ἄνθρωπον οὐ δύναται αὐτὸν κοινῶσαι,

καὶ (inferential conjunction) 14.
λέγει (3d.per.sing.pres.act.ind.of λέγω, historical) 66.
αὐτοῖς (dat.pl.masc.of αὐτός, indirect object of λέγει) 16.
Οὕτως (demonstrative adverb) 74.
καὶ (adjunctive conjunction) 14.
ὑμεῖς (nom.pl.masc.of σύ, subject of ἐστε) 104.
ἀσύνετοί (nom.pl.masc.of ἀσύνετος, predicate adjective) 1159.
ἐστε (2d.per.pl.pres.ind.of εἰμί, aoristic) 86.
οὐ (summary negative conjunction in rhetorical question) 130.
νοεῖτε (2d.per.pl.pres.act.ind.of νοέω, aoristic) 1160.
ὅτι (conjunction introducing an object clause) 211.
πᾶν (nom.sing.neut.of πᾶς, in agreement with εἰσπορευόμενον) 67.

τό (nom.sing.neut.of the article subject of δύναται) 9.

ἔξωθεν (adverbial) 1455.

εἰσπορευόμενον (pres.part.nom.sing.neut.of εἰσπορεύομαι, adverbial, temporal) 1161.

εἰς (preposition with the accusative of extent) 140.

τὸν (acc.sing.masc.of the article in agreement with ἄνθρωπον) 9.

ἄνθρωπον (acc.sing.masc.of ἄνθρωπος, extent) 341.

οὐ (summary negative conjunction with the indicative) 130.

δύναται (3d.per.sing.pres.ind.of δύναμαι, customary) 289.

αὐτὸν (acc.sing.masc.of αὐτός, direct object of κοινῶσαι) 16.

κοινῶσαι (aor.act.inf.of κοινόω, complementary) 1152.

Translation - "Therefore He said to them, 'You also are confused about this? Do you not think that all that which is without, when it enters into the man is not able to defile him?"

Comment: We sacrifice rhetorical smoothness when we translate literally. This I have chosen to do out of deference to the dignity of the divine text. A smoother way to say it is, with Goodspeed, "Do you not see that nothing that goes into a man from outside can pollute him . . . ?"

Jesus' passion as revealed in this outburst is better understood when we examine the intervening information supplied by Mt.15:12-14, *q.v. en loc.* He had just pronounced eventual doom upon the Rabbinical system as then currently represented by the Pharisees and their bigotry. He blames the "blind guides" (Mt.15:14) more than those who are guided though He adds that both guides and those guided will fall into the abyss. The disciples had been undiplomatic enough to suggest that Jesus might better look to His public relations with the Jerusalem party by their anxious inquiry of Mt.15:12, and were rewarded by His stern order that they disassociate themselves completely from the Pharisees in view of the contemptible ignorance of the Establishment leaders.

To all of this the disciples had said nothing until they were alone with Jesus (Mk.7:17) when Peter (Mt.15:15) and the other disciples (Mk.7:17) asked Him for an explanation. Verse 18 states what we have already said in comment upon verse 15. Go back and reread it.

οὕτως in the sense of "with respect to the foregoing." καὶ can be taken either as adjunctive, as we have, or ascensive. "*Even* you are confused?!" This was spoken in the spirit of Julius Caesar's "*Et tu, Brute?*"

We must keep in mind that the disciples had been divinely called and enabled to think God's thoughts and to understand the Father's message. They had come to Christ because the desire had been given to them by the Father. See for support for all this our comments on John 6:27-71. Yet they did not grasp Jesus' point. In fact they seemed almost as obtuse as the Pharisees! Which may demonstrate that there is a difference between effectual call to salvation and the spiritual and intellectual enlightenment which comes for the believer after he is saved - a curriculum which we call Christian education or "growth in grace" (II Pet.3:18).

An ordinary chemist who understands the chemical function of the alimentary canal should understand what Jesus sets forth in verses 18 and 19, though the disciples knew little about zoology and biology. But Jesus knew it of course. Unitarians who reject plenary divine inspiration of the Word of God must explain how Jesus, a Nazarene carpenter who had never been to medical school, knew so much about the digestive function of the human body. Trinitarians have a simple answer. Our Lord is the God who created the alimentary canal and ordained all of the laws of chemistry and biophysics which govern it.

Jesus distinguishes between the physical body and the "heart", by which He means, not the cardiovascular system, but, speaking metaphorically, the spiritual and intellectual part of man. If there is nothing outside the body, taken into the mouth which can damage it, why not? Jesus explains with His anatomical description in

Verse 19 - "Because it entereth not into his heart, but into the belly, and goeth out into the draught, purging all meats."

ὅτι οὐκ εἰσπορεύεται αὐτοῦ εἰς τὴν καρδίαν ἀλλ' εἰς τὴν κοιλίαν, καὶ εἰς τὸν ἀφεδρῶμα ἐκπορεύεται; —καθαρίζων πάντα τὰ βρώματα.

ὅτι (causal conjunction) 211.

οὐκ (summary negative conjunction with the indicative) 130.

εἰσπορεύεται (3d.per.sing.pres.ind.of εἰσπορεύομαι, customary) 1161.

αὐτοῦ (gen.sing.masc.of αὐτός, possession) 16.

εἰς (preposition with the accusative of extent) 140.

τὴν (acc.sing.fem.of the article in agreement with καρδίαν) 9.

καρδίαν (acc.sing.fem.of καρδία, extent) 432.

ἀλλ' (alternative conjunction) 342.

εἰς (preposition with the accusative of extent) 140.

τὴν (acc.sing.fem.of the article in agreement with κοιλίαν) 9.

κοιλίαν (acc.sing.fem.of κοιλία, extent) 1008.

καὶ (adjunctive conjunction joining verbs) 14.

εἰς (preposition with the accusative of extent) 140.

τὸν (acc.sing.masc.of the article in agreement with ἀφεδρῶνα) 9.

ἀφεδρῶμα (acc.sing.masc.of ἀφεδρών, extent) 1163.

ἐκπορεύεται (3d.per.sing.pres.ind.of ἐκπορεύομαι, customary) 270.

καθαρίζων (pres.act.part.nom.sing.masc.of καθαρίζω, adverbial, telic) 709.

πάντα (acc.pl.neut.of πᾶς, in agreement with βρώματα) 67.

τὰ (acc.pl.neut.of the article in agreement with βρώματα) 9.

βρώματα (acc.pl.neut.of βρῶμα, direct object of καθαρίζων) 1118.

Translation - "Because it does not enter into his heart, but into his stomach and and is voided - all food is cleansed in the process."

Comment: ὅτι introduces a causal clause as Jesus explains in verse 19 what He said in verse 18. There is no direct connection between the mouth and gullet and the heart, but (alternative ἀλλά) there is such a connection between the mouth and the stomach, so that whatever is taken into the mouth passes through the gullet into the stomach, then through the intestinal tract into the ἀφεδρῶμα. *Cf.*#1163 for this word. In this process all food (#1118 for βρῶμα does not mean "meat" exclusively, but "food") is purified and the body is protected from chemical damage. Impurities which otherwise would harm the body are eliminated through the excretory system, while the nourishment in the food is picked up by the circulatory system and delivered to all parts of the body. The body, by the design of its Creator is equipped to thus guard itself from pollution from τὰ ἔξωθεν - "things without." So why all of the Pharisaic concern about the "dirt" we might swallow if we eat without first washing our hands?

Robertson (*Grammar*, 438) calls ". . . Mark's explanatory *addendum* a real anacoluthon." This "somewhat more complicated kind of anacoluthon is where a digression is caused by an intervening sentence or explanatory clause." (*Ibid.*,437) ". . . the free use of the participle in long sentences (*cf.* Paul) renders it peculiarly subject to anacoluthon." (*Ibid.*,439). The difficulty arises when we try to use a participle when a new sentence with a verb would do as well. It is possible to say that the last phrase, καθαρίζων πάντα τὰ βρώματα is joined to λέγει (vs.18) at the beginning of the sentence and therefore that it means that Jesus, by saying this, pronounced all food clean. So Montgomery, "By these words he pronounced all foods clean." And Goodspeed, "So he declared all food clean." Moffatt, "(thus he pronounced all food clean)." ASV, "This he said, making all meats clean." But καθαρίζω (#709) does not mean "to declare clean" but "to cleanse." I have taken καθαρίζων as an adverbial telic participle. If so the sense is that the ingestive, digestive and elimination processes function as they do *in order that* (purpose) all foods are clean.

A problem arises when we remember that Moses, in the dietary regulations of Leviticus (Lev.11) forbade certain foods as "unclean." Is there a contradiction? Jesus promised not to contradict Moses (Mt.5:17). The point is that, while the digestive system is equipped by divine creation to take care of whatever we put into our mouths, if not taken in such excess as to overtax the protective capacity of the alimentary canal (which is Jesus' point), it is nevertheless true that some food is better for us than other. Food supplies normally are in great enough supply that we can choose between foods of differing qualities and choose the better. Hence Moses laid down dietary regulations which *under normal circumstances* are wise to follow. Beef is better for us than pork, even in modern times, when pork is produced and processed under sanitary conditions equal to that of beef. Moses is not saying that pork will kill and, conversely, Jesus is not saying that pork is as healthful as beef. Moses was seeking to protect Israel's health at the beginning of a long trek (38 years) through a desert where food was scarce, and Jesus is saying that real defilement is not dirt in the stomach but moral filth, philosophical paganism and intellectual nonesense in the heart of fallen man. What comes from man defiles - not what goes in. This He says in

Verse 20 - "And he said, That which cometh out of the man, that defileth the man."

ἔλεγεν δὲ ὅτι Τὸ ἐκ τοῦ ἀνθρώπου ἐκπορευόμενον ἐκεῖνο κοινοῖ τὸν ἄνθρωπον.

ἔλεγεν (3d.per.sing.imp.act.ind.of λέγω, inceptive) 66.
δὲ (adversative conjunction) 11.
ὅτι (recitative) 211.
Τὸ (nom.sing.neut.of the article in agreement with ἐκπορευόμενον) 9.
ἐκ (preposition with the ablative of separation) 19.
τοῦ (abl.sing.masc.of the article in agreement with ἀνθρώπου) 9.
ἀνθρώπου (abl.sing.masc.of ἄνθρωπος, separation) 341.
ἐκπορευόμενον (pres.part.nom.sing.neut.of ἐκπορεύομαι, substantival, subject of κοινοῖ) 270.
ἐκεῖνο (nom.sing.neut.of ἐκεῖνος, deictic, in agreement with τὸ ἐκπορευόμενον) 246.
κοινοῖ (3d.per.sing.pres.act.ind.of κοινόω, customary) 1152.
τὸν (acc.sing.masc.of the article in agreement with ἄνθρωπον) 9.
ἄνθρωπον (acc.sing.masc.of ἄνθρωπος, direct object of κοινοῖ) 341.

Translation - "But He went on to say, 'That which comes out of the man - that pollutes the man.' "

Comment: δὲ is adversative as Jesus, having denied the Pharisees' position in verse 18, now states the true position in verse 20.

If we did not have verses 21-23 to guide us what Jesus says in verse 19 could refer to fetal matter - the excreted nitrogenous waste material in what we eat, which the digestive system, finding it unacceptable, and in defense of the body, rejects and expels. However γὰρ in verse 21 is clearly illative and introduces Jesus' exposition of what He means by τὸ ἐκπορευόμενον. He speaks of what comes out of the heart of man, not out of his bowels, and specifies the catalogue of sins, physical and spiritual. Chemical impurities are excreted and hence do not defile us. Spiritual impurities, which originate in the heart of man, emerge from the mouth. They are defiling. What a sly way for Jesus to suggest that the Pharisees were regurgitating spiritual and intellectual filth!

Verse 21 - "For from within, out of the heart of men, proceed evil thoughts, adulteries, fornications, murders . . . "

ἔσωθεν γὰρ ἐκ τῆς καρδίας τῶν ἀνθρώπων οἱ διαλογισμοὶ οἱ κακοὶ ἐκπορεύονται, πορνεῖαι, κλοπαί, φόνοι.

ἔσωθεν (adverbial) 672.
γὰρ (illative) 105.
ἐκ (preposition with the ablative of source) 19.
τῆς (abl.sing.fem.of the article in agreement with καρδίας) 9.
καρδίας (abl.sing.fem.of καρδία, source) 432.
τῶν (gen.pl.masc.of the article in agreement with ἀνθρώπων) 9.
ἀνθρώπων (gen.pl.masc.of ἄνθρωπος, definition) 341.
οἱ (nom.pl.masc.of the article in agreement with διαλογισμοὶ) 9.
διαλογισμοὶ (nom.pl.masc.of διαλογισμός, subject of ἐκπορεύονται) 1165.
οἱ (nom.pl.masc.of the article in agreement with κακοὶ) 9.
κακοὶ (nom.pl.masc.of κακός, in agreement with διαλογισμοὶ) 1388.

ἐκπορεύονται (3d.per.pl.pres.ind.of ἐκπορεύομαι, customary) 270.
πορνεῖαι (nom.pl.fem.of πορνεία, subject of ἐκπορεύονται) 511.
κλοπταί (nom.pl.fem.of κλοπτή, subject of ἐκπορεύονται) 1168.
φόνοι (nom.pl.masc.of φόνος, subject of ἐκπορεύονται) 1166.

Translation - "For within, out of the heart of men wicked arguments go forth - fornications, thefts, murders . . . "

Comment: γάρ is illative as Jesus explains what He had just said, *viz.*, that what comes out of men, not what goes in, defiles him. He procedes to list some specific defiling items which originate inside. ἔσωθεν, taken alone could refer to κοιλία or some other physical organ, but Jesus adds ἐκ τῆς καρδίας τῶν ἀνθρώπων" - "out of the heart of men." This is an ablative of source. Thus Jesus indicates that His thought is on the psychological, not on the physical level. Nothing physically corrupt flows from the human heart. But He uses καρδία to refer, not anatomically, but metaphorically, to the seat of the human personality. Intellect, will and emotion are involved. Thus Jesus is saying that the human will, intellect and emotional nature of man is the source of the list beginning with οἱ διαλογισμοὶ οἱ κακοί (vs.21) and ending with ἀφροσύνη (vs.22), and adds in verse 23 that all of these things are evil.

Note that the first of the list is an intellectual sin. Not all διαλογισμοί are κακοί, but some are and they trigger the physical sins which follow - immorality, thefts and murders. This was Jesus' thought in Mt.5:21,22,27,28. Note the emphatic attributive position of the adjective οἱ κακοί, after διαλογισμοί, which is the Greek's strongest way to emphasize how evil our wicked thoughts are.

Saints also have "inner thoughts" (II Cor.7:5; 4:16) where ἔσωθεν applies to believers, who, of course are also capable of originating from within οἱ διαλογισμοὶ οἱ κακοί. Jesus is teaching that the thought precedes the act, whether they be good or evil. No one ever committed sin without thinking about it first, either consciously or subconsciously. How necessary therefore for us to bring ". . . into captivity every thought to the obedience of Christ" (II Cor.10:5).

The list is completed in verse 22. All substantives are in the nominative case, subjects of ἐκπορεύονται of verse 21.

The KJV has the order of the items confused. In the Greek text κλοπταί comes before φόνοι.

Verse 22 - "Thefts, covetousness, wickedness, deceit, lasciviousness, an evil eye, blasphemy, pride, foolishness."

μοιχεῖαι, πλεονεξίαι, πονηρίαι, δόλος, ἀσέλγεια, ὀφθαλμὸς πονηρός, βλασφημία, ὑπερηφανία, ἀφροσύνη.

μοιχεῖαι (nom.pl.fem.of μοιχεία, subject of ἐκπορεύονται) 1167.
#2302 πλεονεξίαι (nom.pl.fem.of πλεονεξία, subject of ἐκπορεύονται).

covetousness - Mk.7:22; Lk.12:15; Rom.1:29; II Cor.9:5; Eph.5:3; Col.3:5; I Thess.2:5; II Pet.2:3.
covetous practice - II Pet.2:14.

greediness - Eph.4:19.

Meaning: πλέον ("more") plus ἔχω (#82). *Cf.* also πλεονάζω (#3907), πλεονεκτέω (#4276) and πλεονέκτης (#4141). Hence "the desire to have more." Greed, avarice, cupidity. Identified with εἰδωλολατρία in Col.3:5; contributory to ἀκαθαρσίας πάσης in Eph.4:19. Generally elsewhere.

πονηρίαι (nom.pl.fem.of πονηρία, subject of ἐκπορεύονται) 1419.

δόλος (nom.sing.masc.of δόλος, subject of ἐκπορεύονται) 1557.

#2303 ἀσέλγεια (nom.sing.fem.of ἀσέλγεια, subject of ἐκπορεύονται).

lasciviousness - Mk.7:22; II Cor.12:21; Gal.5:19; Eph.4:19; I Pet.4:3; Jude 4.
pernicious ways - II Pet.2:2.
wantonness - Rom.13:13; II Pet.2:18.
filthy - II Pet.2:7.

Meaning: The behavior of one who is ἀσελγής. It is believed by some that it comes from α privative plus Σέλγη, a city in Pisidia famous for its strict morals. Hence, non-Selgian or "immoral" generally. Others suggest α intensive plus σαλαγεῖν - "to raise a disturbance," "create mayhem." Others (Thayer says a majority) tie it to α privative plus θέλγω, which means "to persuade" (θέλω #88 plus ἄγω #876), seduce, entice with pleasant words. Hence ἀθέλγω would mean to coerce, force, put unpleasant pressure on. In this connection *cf.* Eph.4:19 where we have ἀσέλγεια εἰς ἐργασίαν ἀκαθαρσίας πάσης ἐν πλεονεξίᾳ, which, if we accept the definition of coercion, would translate "coercion which results in all uncleannesss by means of convetousness (desire for more).

Moulton & Milligan cite BGU IV.1024 v.17 a "badly-spelt document of iv/v AD" which seems to contain the word, spelt ἀθελγία, as some evidence that popular etymology associated the word with θέλγω But M.&M.conclude that ". . . it is dubious at best, and the history of the word is really unknown." *Cf.* Lightfoot's comment on Gal.5:19. The idea of "undue pressure to commit sin is not present in the list, if not in ἀσέλγεία. Jude 4 may give us a hint which, if so. supports the idea of "undue pressure" - μετατιθέντες εἰς ἀσέλγειαν τὴν τοῦ θεοῦ ὑμῶν χάριτα - "twisting to the point of coercion the grace of our God." Is this a reference to antinomianism? Seduction is promoted by antinomianism, the view that sin always glorifies God because it gives Him an opportunity to forgive, which brings glory to His name. Paul states it as "We ought to continue in sin that grace may abound" (Rom.6:1) - to which Paul responds with "God forbid." ἀσέλγεια is a means by which the sins of the flesh are induced (II Pet.2:2,18) but this does not necessarily mean coercion. At what point does applied force become seduction as the victim slowly arrives at the point of submission, acquiescence and finally enthusiastic participation?

ὀφθαλμὸς (nom.sing.masc.of ὀφθαλμός, subject of ἐκπορεύονται) 501.

πονηρός (nom.sing.masc.of πονηρός, in agreement with ὀφθαλμὸς) 438.

βλασφημία (nom.sing.fem.of βλασφημία, subject of ἐκπορεύονται) 1001.

#2304 ὑπερηφανία (nom.sing.fem.of ὑπερηφανία, subject of ἐκπορεύονται).

pride - Mk.7:22.

Meaning: Cf. ὑπερήφανος (#1830). ὑπέρ (#545) plus φαίνω (#100) - hence, "to appear to be superior." Pride, haughty attitude, sense of superiority.

#2305 ἀφροσύνη (nom.sing.fem.of ἀφροσύνη, subject of ἐκπορεύονται).

folly - II Cor.11:1.
foolishness - Mk.7:22.
foolishly - II Cor.11:17,21.

Meaning: Cf. ἄφρων (#2462). α privative plus φρήν (#4235). Hence, without understanding. Foolish, reckless behavior. Paul recognized it as such in II Cor.11:1, 17,21. Generally in Mk.7:22.

Translation - ". . . *adulteries, evidences of greed, acts of wickedness, trickery, coercion, an evil eye, blasphemy, pride, stupidity. . .* "

Comment: Evil dialogue - οἱ διαλογισμοὶ οἱ κακοί - produces twelve evil fruits listed in vss.21,22. There are twelve fruits on the tree of life, the leaves of which, are for the healing of the nations (Rev.22:2). In contrast to the tree of life in heaven, the heart of man produces twelve kinds of death. The first six are listed as plural; the last six as singular. Acts of fornication, theft, murder, adultery, covetousness and wickedness are repeated again and again. Deceit, coercion or inducement to evil, the perverted outlook, blasphemy, pride and folly are continuous stages of being and attitude. A study of each of these words, listed under their appropriate numbers, reveals much about the wickedness of the human heart. Man is a fallen, sinful, depraved creature. The outward fruit is an outgrowth of an inner rebellion against God and His law. For the unregenerate, who makes no pretense of religion, his animal nature unblushingly produces his animal behavior. He is possessed with pig sty morals and he behaves like a pig. For the unregenerate religionist, of whom the Pharisees and Scribes were typical, his animal nature expresses itself, but only with a sugar-coating of devious rationalization of devotion to man-made religious tradition as superior to and therefore a legitimate substitute for the commands of God. This is the entire thrust of the passage of Mk.7:1-23. A little "clean dirt" on your hands when you eat is not going to kill you. Your body is equipped to sort it out and reject what it cannot use. A little evil thought in your heart opens Pandora's box of hellish behavior which damns you and ruins society.

Verse 23 - "*All these evil things come from within and defile the man.*"

πάντα ταῦτα τὰ πονηρὰ ἔσωθεν ἐκπορεύεται καὶ κοινοῖ τὸν ἄνθρωπον.

πάντα (nom.pl.neut.of πᾶς, in agreement with πονηρὰ) 67.
ταῦτα (nom.pl.neut.of οὗτος, in agreement with πονηρὰ) 93.
τὰ (nom.pl.neut.of the article in agreement with πονηρὰ) 9.

πονηρὰ (nom.pl.neut.of πονηρός, subject of ἐκπορεύεται) 438.
ἔσωθεν (adverbial) 672.
ἐκπορεύεται (3d.per.sing.pres.ind.of ἐκπορεύομαι, customary) 270.
καὶ (continuative conjunction) 14.
κοινοῖ (3d.per.sing.pres.act.ind.of κοινόω, customary) 1152.
τὸν (acc.sing.masc.of the article in agreement with ἄνθρωπον) 9.
ἄνθρωπον (acc.sing.masc.of ἄνθρωπος, direct object of κοινοῖ) 341.

Translation - "All these evil things come from within and they pollute the man."

Comment: Note the present tenses in the two verbs with their linear action. It is customary for all of the evil things mentioned in verses 21 and 22 to constantly come out of man and as they come out they defile him. This is Jesus' summation of the passage.

This completes Period II, Part V, which comprises the material from the choosing of the Twelve to the withdrawal into northern Galilee, AD 28-29, a time period of about one year. Period III, which covers six months, extends from the withdrawal into northern Galilee to the final departure for Jerusalem. The year is AD 29. These events are the last that the Galileans saw of Jesus. They are recorded from Mark 7:24 to Mark 9:50; Matthew 15:21 to Matthew 18:35; Luke 9:18-50 and John 7:1-9. Thus we shall see only nine verses in John's gospel in this section. The synoptics carry the story.

(1) In Various Regions

(Mk.7:24-30; Mt.15:21-28)

Mark 7:24 - "And from thence he arose, and went into the borders of Tyre and Sidon, and entered into an house and would have no man know it, but he could not be hid."

Ἐκεῖθεν δὲ ἀναστὰς ἀπῆλθεν εἰς τὰ ὅρια Τύρου καὶ εἰσελθὼν εἰς οἰκίαν οὐδένα ἤθελεν γνῶναι, καὶ οὐκ ἠδυνήθη λαθεῖν.

Ἐκεῖθεν (adverbial) 396.
δὲ (continuative conjunction) 11.
ἀναστὰς (aor.act.part.nom.sing.masc.of ἀνίστημι, adverbial, temporal) 789.
ἀπῆλθεν (3d.per.sing.aor.ind.of ἀπέρχομαι, constative) 239.
εἰς (preposition with the accusative of extent) 140.
τὰ (acc.pl.neut.of the article in agreement with ὅρια,extent) 218.
ὅρια (acc.pl.neut.of ὅριον, extent) 218.
Τύρου (gen.sing.masc.of Τύρος, definition) 939.
καὶ (continuative conjunction) 14.
εἰσελθὼν (aor.part.nom.sing.masc.of εἰσέρχομαι, adverbial, temporal) 234.
εἰς (preposition with the accusative of extent) 140.
οἰκίαν (acc.sing.masc.of οἰκία, extent) 186.
οὐδένα (acc.sing.masc.of οὐδείς, general reference in an object clause) 446.
ἤθελεν (3d.per.sing.imp.act.ind.of ἐθέλω, variant spelling for θέλω, progressive description) 88.
γνῶναι (2d.aor.act.inf.of γινώσκω, complementary) 131.

καὶ (adversative conjunction) 14.
οὐκ (summary negative conjunction with the indicative) 130.
ἠδυνήθη (3d.per.sing.1st.aor.ind.Attic, of δύναμαι, constative) 289.
λαθεῖν (2d.aor.inf.of λάνθανω, complementary) 2247.

Translation - "And He arose and went away from there into Tyre country and when He had entered into a house He wanted no one to know, but He was unable to hide."

Comment: "The words καὶ Σιδῶνος seem to be an assimilation to Mt.15.21 and Mk.7.31. If they had been present originally, there is no reason why they should have been deleted. The witnesses in support of the shorter text include representatives of the Western and Caesarean types of text." (Metzger, *A Textual Commentary on the Greek New Testament*, 95). No damage is done by the omission since Tyre and Sidon are in the same general vicinity and τὰ ὅρια Τύρου are also τὰ ὅρια Σιδῶνος. Despite His desire to remain incognito Jesus was unable to hide. His point of departure had been Capernaum, where He had engaged the Pharisees and Scribes in controversy over the "unwashed hands" incident. It was about forty miles northwest to Tyre and another twenty five to Sidon. Both are seaports on the Mediterranean. Jesus entered τὰ ὅρια - "the surrounding regions" not necessarily the cities. *Cf.*the parallel passage in Mt.15:21 where Matthew uses ἀναχωρέω (#200) and μέρος (#240). His wish to remain alone with the disciples was as vain in Gentile territory as it had been in Galilee, as we see in

Verse 25 - "For a certain woman, whose young daughter had an unclean spirit, heard of him, and came and fell at his feet."

ἀλλ' εὐθὺς ἀκούσασα γυνὴ περὶ αὐτοῦ, ἧς εἶχεν τὸ θυγάτριον αὐτῆς πνεῦμα ἀκάθαρτον, ἐλθοῦσα προσέπεσεν πρὸς τοὺς πόδας αὐτοῦ.

ἀλλ' (adversative conjunction) 342.
εὐθὺς (adverbial) 258.
ἀκούσασα (aor.act.part.nom.sing.fem.of ἀκούω, adjectival, ascriptive) 148.
γυνὴ (nom.sing.fem.of γυνή, subject of προσέπεσεν) 103.
περὶ (preposition with the genitive of reference) 173.
αὐτοῦ (gen.sing.masc.of αὐτός, reference) 16.
ἧς (gen.sing.fem.of ὅς, relationship) 65.
εἶχεν (3d.per.sing.imp.act.ind.of ἔχω, progressive description) 82.
τὸ (nom.sing.neut.of the article in agreement with θυγάτριον) 9.
θυγάτριον (nom.sing.neut.of θυγάτριον, subject of εἶχεν) 2234.
αὐτῆς (gen.sing.fem.of αὐτός, relationship, redundant) 16.
πνεῦμα (acc.sing.neut.of πνεῦμα, direct object of εἶχεν) 83.
ἀκάθαρτον (acc.sing.neut.of ἀκάθαρτος, in agreement with πνεῦμα) 843.
ἐλθοῦσα (aor.part.nom.sing.fem.of ἔρχομαι, adverbial, temporal) 146.
προσέπεσεν (3d.per.sing.aor.act.ind.of προσπίπτω, constative) 699.
πρὸς (preposition with the accusative of extent) 197.

πρὸς (preposition with the accusative of extent) 197.
τοὺς (acc.pl.masc.of the article in agreement with πόδας) 9.
πόδας (acc.pl.masc.of πούς, extent) 353.

Translation - "On the contrary immediately a woman, the little daughter of whom had been troubled with an unclean spirit, heard about Him and came and fell down at His feet."

Comment: Jesus was unable to remain in solitude (vs.24). The participle ἀκούσασα is adjectival, ascribing to the woman a certain characteristic. She was the "having heard about Him woman." She is also identified by the relative clause ἧς εἶχεν τὸ θυγάτριον αὐτῆς πνεῦμα ἀκάθαρτον. She was the woman who had a little daughter who for some time (imperfect tense in εἶχεν) had been afflicted. Demon possession was common then as now.

Jesus' fame had gone before Him. The poor woman was desperate for help for her little daughter. Nothing could stop or dissuade her, as we shall see.

αὐτῆς is redundant after ἧς. "This was also a Hebrew idiom, but the vernacular κοινή shows similar examples. . . . Cf.also the redundant personal pronoun with the relative like the Hebrew idiom . . . οὖ — αὐτοῦ (Mt.3:12), ἧς — αὐτῆς (Mk.7:25), οὕς — αὐτούς (Ac.15:17), οἷς — αὐτοῖς (Rev. 7:2). But this idiom appeared also in the older Greek and is not merely Semitic. (Winer-Thayer, *A Grammar of the Idiom of the New Testament*, 148, as cited in Robertson, *Grammar*, 683). Robertson adds that "It occurs in Xenophon and Sophocles."

Verse 26 - "The woman was a Greek, a Syrophenician by nation; and she besought him that he would cast forth the devil out of her daughter."

ἡ δὲ γυνὴ ἦν Ἑλληνίς, Συροφοινίκισσα τῷ γένει, καὶ ἠρώτα αὐτὸν ἵνα τὸ δαιμόνιον ἐκβάλῃ ἐκ τῆς θυγατρὸς αὐτῆς.

ἡ (nom.sing.fem.of the article in agreement with γυνή) 9.
δὲ (adversative conjunction) 11.
γυνὴ (nom.sing.fem.of γυνή, subject of ἦν) 86.
ἦν (3d.per.sing.imp.ind.of ἰμί, progressive description) 86.

#2306 Ἑλληνίς (nom.sing.fem.of ἑλληνίς, predicate nominative).

Greek - Mk.7:26; Acts 17:12.

Meaning: A Greek. With reference to the Syrophenician woman of Mk.7:26; to the Bereans - Acts 17:12. *Cf.*#2373.

#2307 Συροφοινίκισσα (nom.sing.fem.of Συροφοινίκισσα, apposition).

Syrophenician - Mk.7:26.

Meaning: A resident of the Syrian portion of Phoenicia - Mk.7:26.

τῷ (dat.sing.neut.of the article in agreement with γένει) 9.

γένει (dat.sing.neut.of γένος, reference) 1090.
καὶ (concessive conjunction) 14.
ἠρώτα (3d.per.sing.imp.act.ind.of ἐρωτάω, inceptive) 1ː72.
αὐτὸν (acc.sing.masc.of αὐτός, direct object of ἠρώτα) 16.
ἵνα (final conjunction introducing a purpose clause) 114.
τὸ (acc.sing.neut.of the article in agreement with δαιμόνιον) 9.
δαιμόνιον (acc.sing.neut.of δαιμόνιον, direct object of ἐκβάλῃ) 686.
ἐκβάλῃ (3d.per.sing.aor.act.subj.of ἐκβάλλω, purpose) 649.
ἐκ (preposition with the ablative of separation) 19.
τῆς (abl.sing.fem.of the article in agreement with θυγατρὸς) 9.
θυγατρὸς (abl.sing.fem.of θυγάτηρ, separation) 817.
αὐτῆς (gen.sing.fem.of αὐτός, relationship) 16.

Translation - "But the woman was a Greek, a Syrophoenician by birth. Yet she began to beg him that He would cast out the demon from her daughter."

Comment: Adversative δὲ and concessive καὶ at the beginning of the second clause both indicate that there was something highly improper about the woman's behavior. It was against all Jewish mores for this Gentile to even approach a Jew, much less beg Him for His help. Matthew's account of her approach (Mt.15:22-24) reveals her insight into who Jesus was (vs.22) and the disciples' reaction to her behavior (vs.23). Thus in our passage δὲ is adversative and καὶ is concessive. "Though only a Greek" (concessive καὶ) she began to beg for His help (inceptive imperfect in ἠρώτα). Jesus, in order to test her faith and to teach His disciples a valuable lesson, ignored her (Mt.15:23) and His disciples asked Him to send her away because she was annoying them (Mt.15:23). He then told her that His mission was to Israel, not to the Greeks (Mt.15:23). She continued to worship Him with her plea, "Lord, help me." A further test of her faith comes in

Verse 27 - "But Jesus said unto her, Let the children first be filled; for it is not meet to take the children's bread, and to cast it unto the dogs."

καὶ ἔλεγεν αὐτῇ, Ἄφες πρῶτον χορτασθῆναι τὰ τέκνα, οὐ γάρ ἐστιν καλὸν λαβεῖν τὸν ἄρτον τῶν τέκνων καὶ τοῖς κυναρίοις βαλεῖν.

καὶ (adversative conjunction) 14.
ἔλεγεν (3d.per.sing.imp.act.ind.of λέγω, inceptive) 66.
αὐτῇ (dat.sing.fem.of αὐτός, indirect object of ἔλεγεν) 16.
Ἄφες (2d.per.sing.aor.act.impv.of ἀφίημι, command) 319.
πρῶτον (acc.sing.neut.of πρῶτος, temporal adverb) 487.
χορτασθῆναι (aor.pass.inf.of χορτάζω, epexegetical) 428.
τὰ (acc.pl.neut.of the article in agreement with τέκνα) 9.
τέκνα (acc.pl.neut.of τέκνον, general reference) 229.
οὐ (summary negative conjunction with the indicative) 130.
γάρ (causal conjunction) 105.
ἐστιν (3d.per.sing.pres.ind.of εἰμί, aoristic) 86.
καλὸν (acc.sing.neut.of καλός, predicate adjective) 296.

λαβεῖν (aor.act.inf.of λαμβάνω, substantival, subject of ἐστιν) 533.
τὸν (acc.sing.masc.of the article in agreement with ἄρτον) 9.
ἄρτον (acc.sing.masc.of ἄρτος, object of λαβεῖν) 338.
τῶν (gen.pl.neut.of the article in agreement with τέκνων) 9.
τέκνων (gen.pl.neut.of τέκνον, possession) 229.
καὶ (adjunctive conjunction joining infinitives) 14.
τοῖς (dat.pl.neut.of the article in agreement with κυναρίοις) 9.
κυναρίοις (dat.pl.neut.of κυνάριον, indirect object of βαλεῖν) 1174.
βαλεῖν (aor.act.inf.of βάλλω, substantival, subject of ἐστιν) 299.

Translation - "But Jesus began to say to her, 'First let the children be filled, because it is not proper to take the bread of the children and throw it to the little dogs.' "

Comment: Jesus did not say that He would not attend to her request - only that she would have to wait her turn (Rom.1:16). All of the blessings that Jesus had to bestow would be poured out first upon Israel until she had all she wanted. *Cf.*#428 for the meaning of χορτάζω. But Jesus had already offered Himself to Israel and had been rejected out of hand. *Cf.* John 6:26. οὐ γὰρ . . . βαλεῖν. It is improper to upset the chronologican order. The child/little dog figure was used (a) to point up the fact that, despite her unbelief, Israel is God's chosen nation while Gentiles are outcasts, comparatively speaking and (b) to awaken in the woman, whose request, of course, He knew He would grant, a proper sense of humility. He had used similar tactics in dealing with Nicodemus (John 3:10) and the Samaritan woman (John 4:16-18). If this Greek could stay on her knees before Jesus, pleading for her child, after He had called her a little dog (τὸ κυνάριον), it would indicate her true humility and the intensity of her desire to have His healing for her child. The Pharisees under similar treatment would have picked up stones to stone Him.

　　Once again we stress the importance of coordinating Mark's account with that given in Mt.15:21-28, in order to get a full orbed picture of what happened.

　　Note Mark's use of the infinitives as subjects of ἐστιν, in the last clause in which the predicate comes before the double subject - "To take the bread of the children and to cast it to the little dogs is not proper."

　　Jesus was not trying to argue with the woman, but had He done so He would have lost the argument as we see in

Verse 28 - "And she answered and said unto him, Yes, Lord; yet the dogs under the table eat of the children's crumbs."

ἡ δὲ ἀπεκρίθη καὶ λέγει αὐτῷ, Κύριε, καὶ τὰ κυνάρια ὑποκάτω τῆς τραπέζης ἐσθίουσιν ἀπὸ τῶν φιχίων τῶν παιδίων.

ἡ (nom.sing.fem.of the article, subject of ἀπεκρίθη and λέγει) 9.
δὲ (adversative conjunction) 11.
ἀπεκρίθη (3d.per.sing.aor.ind.of ἀποκρίνομαι, constative) 318.
καὶ (adjunctive conjunction joining verbs) 14.

λέγει (3d.per.sing.pres.act.ind.of λέγω, historical) 66.

αὐτῷ (dat.sing.masc.of αὐτός, indirect object of λέγει) 16.

Κύριε (voc.sing.masc.of κύριος, address) 97.

καὶ (concessive conjunction) 14.

τὰ (nom.pl.neut.of the article in agreement with κυνάρια) 9.

κυνάρια (nom.pl.neut.of κυνάριον, subject of ἐσθίουσιν) 1174.

ὑποκάτω (improper preposition with the ablative of separation) 1429.

τῆς (abl.sing.fem.of the article in agreement with τραπέζης) 9.

τραπέζης (abl.sing.fem.of τράπεζα, separation) 1176.

ἐσθίουσιν (3d.per.pl.pres.act.ind.of ἐσθίω, customary) 610.

ἀπό (preposition with the ablative of source) 70.

τῶν (abl.pl.neut.of the article in agreement with φιχίων) 9.

φιχίων (abl.pl.neut.of φιχίον, source) 1175.

τῶν (gen.pl.neut.of the article in agreement with παιδίων) 9.

παιδίων (gen.pl.neut.of παιδίον, possession) 174.

Translation - "But she answered and said to Him, 'Despite this, Sir, the little dogs under the table eat of the scraps which the little children leave."

Comment: δὲ is adversative as the argument continues. Had she had less faith - a faith born of desperation, she would have withdrawn without another word. Κύριε - the term of highest respect. She had called Him the "Son of David" before (Mt.15:22). She won her argument by agreeing with Jesus insofar as He had gone, but pointing out that His analysis was not all that could be said. There was a distinction, to be sure, between τὰ τεκνα (Jews) and κυνάρια (Greeks Gentiles, Syrophoenicians) and she was willing to take her place, not at the table with the children, but under the table with the little dogs. The privilege of sitting on the floor under the table where the Son of God presides is not to be despised. The crumbs that fall unheeded from such a table are priceless.

Even κυνάρια have their place and the rights associated with it.

Note the diminutives - "Little dogs, little crumbs, little children." Where is the lowly place for these lowly people? ὑποκάτω τῆς τραπέζης. What are the rights of those who occupy such a place? ἐσθίουσιν ἀπό φιχίων τῶν παιδίων. Note that even the crumbs belong to the little children though they are disc.rded and only then do the dogs get a chance to eat.

The second καὶ is concessive. By conceding Jesus' point and going further with His thought she won the argument. Note Mark's grammatical error as he used the plural verb ἐσθίουσιν with the neuter plural subject τὰ κυνάρια. He should have written ἐσθίει as Matthew did (Mt.15:27).

Matthew points out that the table belongs to the Lord, while the crumbs belong to the children at the table, though eaten by the little dogs under the Lord's table.

Jesus, of course, really wanted her to win the point in this delightful *tete-a-tete*, which reveals the woman's great humility and hence great faith - faith that few Jews were willing to display.

Verse 29 - "And he said unto her, For this saying go thy way; the devil is gone out of thy daughter."

καὶ εἶπεν αὐτῇ, Διὰ τοῦτον τὸν λόγον ὕπαγε, ἐξελήλυθεν ἐκ τῆς θυγατρός σου τὸ διαμόνιον.

καὶ (inferential conjunction) 14.

εἶπεν (3d.per.sing.aor.act.ind.of εἶπον, constative) 155.

αὐτῇ (dat.sing.fem.of αὐτός, indirect object of εἶπεν) 16.

Διὰ (preposition with the accusative, cause) 118.

τοῦτον (acc.sing.masc.of οὗτος, in agreement with λόγον) 93.

τὸν (acc.sing.masc.of the article in agreement with λόγον) 9.

λόγον (acc.sing.masc.of λόγος, cause) 510.

ὕπαγε (2d.per.sing.pres.act.impv.of ὑπάγω, command) 364.

ἐξελήλυθεν (3d.per.sing.perf.ind.of ἐξέρχομαι, consummative) 161.

ἐκ (preposition with the ablative of separation) 19.

τῆς (abl.sing.fem.of the article in agreement with θυγατρός) 9.

θυγατρός (abl.sing.fem.of θυγάτηρ, separation) 817.

σου (gen.sing.fem.of σύ, relationship) 104.

τὸ (nom.sing.neut.of the article in agreement with δαιμόνιον) 9.

δαιμόνιον (nom.sing.neut.of δαιμόνιον, subject of ἐξελήλυθεν) 686.

Translation - *"Therefore He said to her, 'Because of this remark, go away. The demon has left your daughter."*

Comment: καὶ now becomes inferential. The argument is over and the woman has won it. Διὰ τοῦτον τὸν λόγον is a causal construction. *Cf.*#118 for other examples. The perfect tense in ἐξελήλυθεν is consummative - a present condition as a result of a past completed action. When Jesus said this the demon had already left the child. The departure of the demon was contingent upon the statement by the woman, which in turn had been motivated by her heart felt faith. Romans 10:9,10 gives us the order - (a) believe in the heart, (b) confess with the mouth, (c) salvation. Some argue, without scriptural basis, that since we are truly Christian we need not talk about it. The rebuttal is that those who are truly Christian cannot keep quiet about it. This does not mean that Christians must demonstrate their faith in the uproarious manner of those often seen in a "holy roller meeting." But ". . . with the heart man believes unto righteousness, and *with the mouth confession is made unto salvation."* Jesus clearly says that it was *because* of the woman's last brilliant speech which revealed her willingness to take her place as a *little dog* under her Lord's table, that the cure was effected. We may be sure that as soon as she met the conditions, our Lord granted her wish. Mt.15:28 gives us the clue that her faith brought about the desired result.

The faith of this Gentile woman is on a par with that of the Roman soldier of Mt.8:8-10. She got results just as the Centurion did (Mt.8:13).

Verse 30 - *"And when she was come to her house, she found the devil gone out, and her daughter laid upon the bed."*

καὶ ἀπελθοῦσα εἰς τὸν οἶκον αὐτῆς εὗρεν τὸ παιδίον βεβλημένον ἐπὶ τὴν κλίνην καὶ τὸ δαιμόνιον ἐξεληλυθός.

καὶ (continuative conjunction) 14.

ἀπελθοῦσα (aor.part.nom.sing.fem.of ἀπέρχομαι, adverbial, temporal) 239.
εἰς (preposition with the accusative of extent) 140.
τὸν (acc.sing.masc.of the article in agreement with οἶκον) 9.
οἶκον (acc.sing.masc.of οἶκος, extent) 784.
αὐτῆς (gen.sing.fem.of αὐτός, possession) 16.
εὗρεν (3d.per.sing.aor.act.ind.of εὑρίσκω, constative) 79.
τὸ (acc.sing.neut.of the article in agreement with παιδίον) 9.
παιδίον (acc.sing.neut.of παιδίον, direct object of εὗρεν) 174.
βεβλημένον (perf.pass.part.acc.sing.neut.of βάλλω, adverbial, circumstantial) 299.
ἐπὶ (preposition with the accusative of extent, indicating place where) 47.
τὴν (acc.sing.fem.of the article in agreement with κλίνην) 9.
κλίνην (acc.sing.fem.of κλίνη, extent, place where) 779.
καὶ (adjunctive conjunction joining nouns) 14.
τὸ (acc.sing.neut.of the article in agreement with δαιμόνιον) 9.
δαιμόνιον (acc.sing.neut.of δαιμόνιον, direct object of εὗρεν) 686.
ἐξεληλυθός (perf.pass.part.acc.sing.neut.of ἐξέρχομαι, adverbial, circumstantial) 161.

Translation - "And when she had gone away unto her home she found the little girl lying upon the pallet and the demon gone."

Comment: Note the two perfect passive participles, each used circumstantially. When the woman arrived at her home she found her daughter lying on the pallet, having been cast there, perhaps by the demon, but she also found that the demon had been forced to leave. Mt.15:28 says that the healing was simultaneous with the woman's statement of faith and Jesus' commendation. Thus our Lord bestowed His blessing upon an outcast alien from the Commonwealth of Israel. It is not the first time that we have seen that God's grace, in response to saving faith, knows no national boundary lines. *Cf.* John 4:1-42; Mt.8:5-13.

Healing of a Deaf Mute in the Regions of Decapolis

(Mk.7:31-37; Mt.15:29-31)

Mark 7:31 - "And again departing from the coasts of Tyre and Sidon, he came unto the Sea of Galilee, through the midst of the coasts of Decapolis."

Καὶ πάλιν ἐξελθὼν ἐκ τῶν ὁρίων Τύρου ἦλθεν διὰ Σιδῶνος εἰς τὴν θαλασσαν τῆς Γαλιλαίας ἀνὰ μέσον τῶν ὁρίων Δεκαπόλεως.

Καὶ (continuative conjunction) 14.
πάλιν (adverbial) 355.
ἐξελθὼν (aor.part.nom.sing.masc.of ἐξέρχομαι, adverbial, temporal) 161.
ἐκ (preposition with the ablative of separation) 19.
τῶν (abl.pl.neut.of the article in agreement with ὁρίων) 9.
ὁρίων (abl.pl.neut.of ὅριον, separation) 218.
Τύρου (gen.sing.masc.of Τύρος, definition) 939.

ἦλθεν (3d.per.sing.aor.ind.of ἔρχομαι, constative) 146.

διὰ (preposition with the genitive, "through" in a spatial sense) 118.

Σιδῶνος (gen.sing.masc.of Σιδών, "through" in a spatial sense) 940.

εἰς (preposition with the accusative of extent) 140.

τὴν (acc.sing.fem.of the article in agreement with θάλασσαν) 9.

θάλασσαν (acc.sing.fem.of θάλασσα, extent) 374.

τῆς (gen.sing.fem.of the article in agreement with Γαλιλαίας) 9.

Γαλιλαίας (gen.sing.fem.of Γαλιλαία, definition) 241.

ἀνὰ (preposition with the accusative of extent) 1059.

μέσον (acc.sing.neut.of μέσος, extent) 873.

τῶν (gen.pl.neut.of the article in agreement with ὁρίων) 9.

ὁρίων (gen.pl.neut.of ὅριον, definition) 218.

Δεκαπόλεως (gen.sing.of Δεκαπόλεως, definition) 419.

Translation - "And again He left the territory of Tyre and came through Sidon to the Sea of Galilee and up into the midst of Decapolis country."

Comment: His path led out of Tyre country, by way of Sidon to the Sea of Galilee, across the Jordan River eastward into the heart of the territory of Decapolis. Thus He travelled up the coast north of Tyre to Sidon before He turned back to the southeast to the northern tip of Galilee, after which He continued south and east into Decapolis - a total distance of approximately 75 miles.

Verse 32 - "And they bring unto him one that was deaf, and had an impediment in his speech; and they beseech him to put his hand upon him."

καὶ φέρουσιν αὐτῷ κωφὸν καὶ μογιλάλον, καὶ παρακαλοῦσιν αὐτὸν ἵνα ἐπιθῇ αὐτῷ τὴν χεῖρα.

καὶ (continuative conjunction) 14.

φέρουσιν (3d.per.pl.pres.act.ind.of φέρω, historical) 683.

αὐτῷ (dat.sing.masc.of αὐτός, indirect object of φέρουσιν) 16.

κωφὸν (acc.sing.masc.of κωφός, direct object of φέρουσιν) 833.

καὶ (adjunctive conjunction joining substantives) 14.

#2308 μογιλάλον (acc.sing.masc.of μογιλάλος, direct object of φέρουσιν).

having an impediment in one's speech - Mk.7:32.

Meaning: - μόις (#2342) plus λαλέω (#815). Hence, hardly able to speak - Mk.7:32.

καὶ (continuative conjunction) 14.

παρακαλοῦσιν (3d.per.pl.pres.act.ind.of παρακαλέω, historical) 230.

αὐτὸν (acc.sing.masc.of αὐτός, direct object of παρακαλοῦσιν) 16.

ἵνα (final conjunction introducing a purpose clause) 114.

ἐπιθῇ (3d.per.sing.aor.act.subj.of ἐπιτίθημι, purpose) 818.

αὐτῷ (loc.sing.masc.of αὐτός, place where) 16.

τὴν (acc.sing.fem.of the article in agreement with χεῖρα) 9.

χεῖρα (acc.sing.fem.of χείρ, direct object of ἐπιϑῇ) 308.

Translation - "And they brought to Him a deaf man who also was hardly able to speak and they begged Him to lay His hand on him."

Comment: *Cf.*#833 for the meaning of κωφός. It is the context that tells us that this particular affliction was deafness. κωφός does not in itself mean "deaf." He also had an impediment in his speech. We need not translate φέρω as "bear" or "carry" since the man could walk. Those who brought him to Jesus spoke for him since he was unable to speak clearly for himself.

The healing ministry of Jesus was effective, whether the patient was present or absent, whether it was carried out by a word or a touch, whether the patient was ill physically or mentally, whether he was Jew, Gentile, black or white and was always available to those who could believe. Mark here centers his attention upon a specific case. Matthew describes our Lord's healing in behalf of many patients, with differing ailments, who needed Jesus' help (Mt.15:30). In the case before us Jesus was neither unwilling nor unable to deliver the man from his malady.

Verse 33 - "And he took him aside from the multitude, and put his fingers into his ears, and he spit, and touched his tongue. . . "

καὶ ἀπολαβόμενος αὐτὸν ἀπὸ τοῦ ὄχλου κατ' ἰδίαν ἔβαλεν τοὺς δακτύλους αὐτοῦ εἰς τὰ ὦτα αὐτοῦ καὶ πτύσας ἥψατο τῆς γλώσσης αὐτοῦ,

καὶ (continuative conjunction) 14.
ἀπολαβόμενος (aor.mid.part.nom.sing.masc.of ἀπολαμβάνω, adverbial, temporal) 2131.
αὐτὸν (acc.sing.masc.of αὐτός, direct object of ἀπολαβόμενος) 16.
ἀπὸ (preposition with the ablative of separation) 70.
τοῦ (abl.sing.masc.of the article in agreement with ὄχλου) 9.
ὄχλου (abl.sing.masc.of ὄχλος, separation) 418.
κατ' (preposition with the accusative, adverbial) 98.
ἰδίαν (acc.sing.fem.of ἴδιος, general reference, adverbial) 778.
ἔβαλεν (3d.per.sing.aor.act.ind.of βάλλω, constative) 299.
τοὺς (acc.pl.masc.of the article in agreement with δακτύλους) 9.
δακτύλους (acc.pl.masc.of δάκτυλος, direct object of ἔβαλεν) 1434.
αὐτοῦ (gen.sing.masc.of αὐτός, possession) 16.
εἰς (preposition with the accusative of extent) 140.
τὰ (acc.pl.neut.of the article in agreement with ὦτα) 9.
ὦτα (acc.pl.neut.of ὠτίον, extent) 1595.
αὐτοῦ (gen.sing.masc.of αὐτός, possession) 16.
καὶ (adjunctive conjunction joining verbs) 14.

#2309 πτύσας (aor.act.part.nom.sing.masc.of πτύω, adverbial, temporal).

spit - Mk.7:33; 8:23; John 9:6.

Meaning: To spit; expectorate. With reference to Jesus' healing ministry ᐟ

Meaning: To spit; expectorate. With reference to Jesus' healing ministry - speech impediment - Mk.7:33; blindness - Mk.8:23; John 9:6.

ἥψατο (3d.per.sing.aor.mid.ind.of ἅπτω, constative) 711.
τῆς (gen.sing.fem.of the article in agreement with γλώσσης) 9.
γλώσσης (gen.sing.fem.of γλῶσσα, definition) 1846.
αὐτοῦ (gen.sing.masc.of αὐτός, possession) 16.

Translation - "And having taken him aside from the crowd, by himself, He put His fingers into His ears, spat and touched His tongue."

Comment: The idiom κατ' ἰδίαν is really redundant, since ἀπολαβόμενος ... ἀπὸ τοῦ ὄχλου means "having taken him away from (separate from) the crowd. "By himself" (κατ' ἰδίαν) is therefore not necessary. But that is the way Mark wrote it and that is how we translate it. The text does not tell us why Jesus isolated the man before He healed him. Perhaps it was because of the unusual manner in which the healing was effected. The Greek does not make clear that Jesus spat upon the man's tongue or placed saliva upon it with His finger. The precise manner in which the healing was carried out is not important. The important thing is that Jesus healed him. The time of action of ἔβαλεν is not necessarily simultaneous with that of ἥψατο, though πτύσας is prior to ἥψατο. Jesus could have (a) placed His fingers into the patient's ears; (b) then withdrawn them; (c) then spat, and (d) touched the man's tongue, either with His fingers or with saliva. Montgomery translates " . . . put his finger in the man's ears and moistened his tongue with saliva . . . ". Goodspeed's rendering is similar - ". . . touched his tongue with saliva." These translations are possible by inference only. If that is what Mark intended to convey he had at his disposal the Greek grammar and syntax to make it clear. δακτύλους is plural, a point that Montgomery misses and πτύσμα ("spittle") in John 9:6, does not occur in the passage, though Montgomery and Goodspeed translate as though it were. There is nothing to say that the saliva came in contact with the man's tongue. Since Jesus had both His fingers in the man's ears, He could not have applied spittle to the man's tongue with His finger, without first withdrawing one of them. The grammar allows this but Mark could have made it clear by writing βαλλούσας (aor.act.part.of βάλλω) instead of ἔβαλεν (aor.act.ind.) It is a small point but it is better to translate what is there and only what is there and leave the exact procedure unrevealed.

In view of the contentious nature of some church congregations this passage could become the grounds for a denominational separation with names like "The spit (or no spit) Church." If congregations split over a piano, a tuning fork or whether the Lord served wine or grape juice, why not over a bit of saliva?!
*Cf.*Meyer, *en loc.,* for a classic example of eisegesis!!

Verse 34 - "And looking up to heaven, he sighed, and saith unto him Ephphatha, that is, Be opened."

καὶ ἀναβλέψας εἰς τὸν οὐρανὸν ἐστέναξεν, καὶ λέγει αὐτῷ, Εφφαθα, ὅ ἐστιν, Διανοίχθητι.

καὶ (continuative conjunction) 14.
ἀναβλέψας (aor.act.part.nom.sing.masc.of ἀναβλέπω, adverbial, circumstantial) 907.
εἰς (preposition with the accusative of extent) 140.
τὸν (acc.sing.masc.of the article in agreement with οὐρανὸν) 9.
οὐρανὸν (acc.sing.masc.of οὐρανός, extent) 254.

#2310 ἐστέναξεν (3d.per.sing.aor.act.ind.of στενάζω, constative).

> groan - Rom.8:23; II Cor.5:2,4.
> grudge - Jam.5:9.
> sigh - Mk.7:34.
> with grief - Heb.13:17.

Meaning: To sigh; not to groan necessarily, as a result of suffering physical pain. The expression of discontent or displeasure. An expression of desire to be relieved of some unpleasantness. With reference to the Christian who is wearied with the fight against the flesh, who longs for glorification with its release from temptation - Rom.8:23; II Cor.5:2 (where it is associated with βαρούμενοι - #1589); of one Christian's impatient complaint against another - James 5:9. The opposite of μετὰ χαρᾶς in Heb.13:17, *i.e.* with discontented resignation. With reference to Jesus, Who was physically tired and wanted rest - Mk.7:34.

καὶ (adjunctive conjunction) 14.
λέγει (3d.per.sing.pres.act.ind.of λέγω, historical) 66.
αὐτῷ (dat.sing.masc.of αὐτός, indirect object of λέγει) 16.

#2311 Εφφαθα.

Ephphatha - Mk.7:34.

Meaning: An Aramaic word, the ethpaal imperative of the Hebrew verb "to open." "Be opened." With reference to the ears of the deaf man - Mk.7:34.

ὅ (nom.sing.neut.of ὅς, subject of ἐστιν) 65.
ἐστιν (3d.per.sing.pres.ind.of εἰμί, aoristic) 86.
Διαωοίχθητι (2d.per.sing.aor.act.impv.of διανοίγω, command) 1888.

Translation - "*And having looked up into the sky He sighed and said to him, 'Ephphtha' which translates 'Be opened.'* "

Comment: *Cf.*#2310. "Groan" is too strong. Some expression of discontent or resignation to the rigor's of one's position is what is in view. Jesus was expressing in an anthropomorphic way His physical fatigue. He needed physical rest and for the most part sought it unsuccessfully as the events of verse 32 indicate. He was often vexed at the visible results of sin, in this case the patient's pitiable condition. *Cf.*#831 in John 11:38.

Verse 35 - "And straightway his ears were opened, and the string of his tongue was loosed, and he spake plain."

καὶ (ευθέως) ἠνοίγησαν αὐτοῦ αἱ ἀκοαί, καὶ ἐλύθη ὁ δεσμὸς τῆς γλώσσης αὐτοῦ, καὶ ἐλάλει ὀρθῶς.

καὶ (continuative conjunction) 14.
(εὐθέως) (adverbial) 392.
ἠνοίγησαν (3d.per.pl.2d.aor.pass.ind.of ἀνοίγω, culminative) 188.
αὐτοῦ (gen.sing.masc.of αὐτός, possession) 16.
αἱ (nom.pl.fem.of the article in agreement with ἀκοαί) 9.
ἀκοαί (nom.pl.fem.of ἀκοή, subject of ἠνοίγησαν) 409.
καὶ (continuative conjunction) 14.
ἐλύθη (3d.per.sing.aor.pass.ind.of λύω, culminative) 471.
ὁ (nom.sing.masc.of the article in agreement with δεσμὸς) 9.
δεσμὸς (nom.sing.masc.of δεσμός, subject of ἐλύθη) 2229.
τῆς (gen.sing.fem.of the article in agreement with γλώσσης) 9.
γλώσσης (gen.sing.fem.of γλῶσσα, description) 1846.
αὐτοῦ (gen.sing.masc.of αὐτός, possession) 16.
καὶ (continuative conjunction) 14.
ἐλάλει (3d.per.sing.imp.act.ind.of λαλέω, inceptive) 815.
ὀρθῶς (adverbial) 2174.

Translation - "And his ears were opened and that which bound his tongue was broken and he began to enunciate correctly."

Comment: Ears opened and tongue set free. Whatever held his ability to articulate in check, whether it was anatomical or psychological, lost its power. *Cf.*#2229. The word means "that which binds." Modern speech therapists should not take the KJV's "string of his tongue" as a serious translation of the Greek. δεσμός does not mean "string" or anything else necessarily physical. The verb ἐλύθη means "broken" or "loosed." The man was totally healed. Hearing was restored and his speech impediment, of whatever source, lost its power to annoy and impede him further. The result that he began (incpeptive imperfect) to chatter like a magpie, but with a correct enunciation. *Cf.*#1888 for Jesus' ability to open what should be opened but it closed - hearts, minds, ears, understanding.

Verse 36 - "And he charged them that they should tell no man; but the more he charged them, so much the more a great deal they published it."

καὶ διεστείλατο αὐτοῖς ἵνα μηδενὶ λέγωσιν, ὅσον δὲ αὐτοῖς διεστέλλετο, αὐτοὶ μᾶλλον περισσότερον ἐκήρυσσον.

καὶ (continuative conjunction) 14.
διεστέλλετο (3d.per.sing.imp.ind.of διαστέλλομαι, progressive duration)
αὐτοῖς (dat.pl.masc.of αὐτός, indirect object of διεστείλατο) 16.

ἵνα (final conjunction introducing a purpose clause) 114.
μηδενὶ (dat.sing.masc.of μηδείς, indirect object of λέγωσιν) 713.
λέγωσιν (3d.per.pl.pres.act.subj.of λέγω, purpose) 66.
ὅσον (acc.sing.neut.of ὅσος, indefinite relative pronoun, degree) 660.
δὲ (adversative conjunction) 11.
αὐτοῖς (dat.pl.masc.of αὐτός, indirect object of διεστέλλετο) 16.
αὐτοὶ (nom.pl.masc.of αὐτός, subject of ἐκήρυσσον) 16.
μᾶλλον (comparative adverb) 619.
περισσότερον (acc.sing.neut.comparative of περισσός) 525.
ἐκήρυσσον (3d.per.pl.imp.act.ind.of κηρύσσω, progressive duration) 249.

Translation - "And He began to admonish them that they tell no one, but the more He continued His remonstrance the more they reported it."

Comment: Jesus began to forbid the people to tell about the miracle (ingressive aorist), but they disobeyed. He continued to demand that they remain silent, but it was to no avail. The more He pleaded with them the more they published it far and wide. Who is they, since the healing had been effected in private? (vs.33). Obviously when the patient returned to society, hearing distinctly and speaking perfectly the healing became apparent to all.

Note ὅσον with μᾶλλον - "the more . . . even more" modified by the comparative περισσότερον. It is awkward Greek, in Mark's fashion, but we know what he means.

Why did Jesus try to avoid the publicity? The text does not tell us but the context indicates that He needed physical and mental rest. One recalls ἐστέναξεν in verse 34. On ὅσον . . . μᾶλλον περισσότερον, Meyer says, "They exceeded the degree of the prohibition by the *yet* far greater degree in which they made it known. So transported were they by the miracle, that the prohibition only heightened their zeal and they prosecuted the κηρύσσειν with still greater energy than if He had not interdicted it to them." περισσότερον intensifies μᾶλλον.

The measure of their enthusiasm is explained in

Verse 37 - "And were beyond measure astonished saying, He hath done all things well: he maketh both the deaf to hear and the dumb to speak."

καὶ ὑπερπερισσῶς ἐξεπλήσσοντο λέγοντες, Καλῶς πάντα πεποίηκεν, καὶ τοὺς κωφοὺς ποιεῖ ἀκούειν καὶ (τοὺς) ἀλάλους λαλεῖν.

καὶ (causal conjunction) 14.

#2312 ὑπερπερισσῶς (adverbial).

beyond measure - Mk.7:37.

Meaning: A combination of ὑπέρ (#545) and περισσός (#525). Hence a doubly strengthened superlative. As modern parlance has it, "Out of sight!"

ἐξεπλήσσοντο (3d.per.pl.imp.ind.of ἐκπλήσσομαι, progressive description) 705.

λέγοντες (pres.act.part.nom.pl.masc.of λέγω, adverbial, temporal) 66.
Καλῶς (adverbial) 977.
πάντα (acc.pl.neut.of πᾶς, direct object of πεποίηκεν) 67.
πεποίηκεν (3d.per.sing.perf.act.ind.of ποιέω, consummative) 127.
καὶ (adjunctive conjunction) 14.
τοὺς (acc.pl.masc.of the article in agreement with κωφούς) 9.
κωφοὺς (acc.pl.masc.of κωφός, general reference) 833.
ποιεῖ (3d.per.sing.pres.act.ind.of ποιέω, static) 127.
ἀκούειν (pres.act.inf.of ἀκούω, substantival, direct object of ποιεῖ) 148.
καὶ (adjunctive conjunction) 14.

#2313 ἀλάλους (acc.pl.masc.of ἄλαλος, general reference).

dumb - Mk.7:37; 9:17,25.

Meaning: α privative plus λαλέω (#815). Hence dumb; unable to speak.
Speechless. As a noun in Mk.7:37; as an adjective with πνεῦμα in Mk.9:17,25.

λαλεῖν (pres.act.inf.of λαλέω, substantival, object of ποιεῖ) 815.

Translation - "And they were amazed beyond measure as they repeated over and over, 'He has done everything well. He makes both the deaf to hear and the dumb to speak.' "

Comment: It is difficult to translate the literal Greek into smooth English, so we have left the precise meaning to the Comment. They continued (progressive duration in the imperfect ἐξεπλήσσοντο) in an unusually high state of excitement, so much so that they continued to repeat (present tense in λέγοντες) what is recorded. Their amazement was "beyond measure." This is the only place in the New Testament where ὑπερπερισσῶς occurs. Note the consummative force of the perfect πεποίηκεν. "Everything He attempts is done with a continuous consistency of excellent performance."

There are three grammatical principles not often seen in the New Testament. Note the καὶ . . . καὶ sequence, in an adjunctive sense. - "both . . . and." Also note the static present tense in ποιεῖ. "The present tense may be used to represent a condition which is assumed as perpetually existing, or to be ever taken for granted as a fact." (Mantey, *Manual*, 186). II Pet.3:4; John 15:27 and I John 3:8 are other examples. Note also the noun use of the two infinitives as objects of the finite verb ποιεῖ with κωφούς and ἀλάλους adjoined as accusatives of general reference.

Thus the people in Decapolis sang His praises! *Cf.* Mt.15:31. The speechless speak, the deaf hear, the lame walk. The God of Israel was present. When we compare Mk.5:17 we note that the people in the region have had a change of attitude toward Jesus. This time they did not lose their pigs.

The Feeding of the Four Thousand

(Mt.15:32-39; Mk.8:1-10)

Mark 8:1 - "In those days the multitude being very great, and having nothing to eat, Jesus called his disciples unto him, and saith unto them. . . "

Ἐν ἐκείνας ταῖς ἡμέραις πάλιν πολλοῦ ὄχλου ὄντος καὶ μὴ ἐχόντων τί φάγωσιν, προσκαλεσάμενος τοὺς μαθητὰς λέγει αὐτοῖς.

Ἐν (preposition with the locative of time point) 80.

ἐκείναις (loc.pl.fem.of ἐκεῖνος, in agreement with ἡμέραις) 246.

ταῖς (loc.pl.fem.of the article in agreement with ἡμέραις) 9.

ἡμέραις (loc.pl.fem.of ἡμέρα, time point) 135.

πάλιν (adverbial) 355.

πολλοῦ (gen.sing.masc.of πολύς, in agreement with ὄχλου) 228.

ὄχλου (gen.sing.masc.of ὄχλος, genitive absolute) 418.

ὄντος (pres.part.gen.sing.masc.of εἰμί, genitive absolute) 86.

καὶ (adjunctive conjunction joining participles) 14.

μὴ (qualified negative conjunction with the participle) 87.

ἐχόντων (pres.act.part.gen.pl.masc.of ἔχω, genitive absolute) 82.

τί (acc.sing.neut.of τίς, direct object of φάγωσιν) 281.

φάγωσιν (3d.per.pl.aor.act.subj.of ἐσθίω, deliberative subjunctive) 610.

προσκαλεσάμενος (aor.mid.part.nom.sing.masc.of προσκαλέω, adverbial, temporal) 842.

τοὺς (acc.pl.masc.of the article in agreement with μαθητὰς) 9.

μαθητὰς (acc.pl.masc.of μαθητής, direct object of προσκαλεσάμενος) 421.

λέγει (3d.per.sing.pres.act.ind.of λέγω, historical) 66.

αὐτοῖς (dat.pl.masc.of αὐτός, indirect object of λέγει) 16.

Translation - "During those days when a great crowd was present who had nothing to eat, He called the disciples and said to them . . . "

Comment: ἐν . . . ἡμέραις - a locative of time. Cf.#80 for other examples of which there are many. Cf.#135 for ἡμέρα in this sense, rather than meaning a twelve or twenty-four hour period. We have a double genitive absolute joined by adjunctive καὶ - πολλοῦ ὄχλου ὄντος and μὴ ἐχόντων. Note the deliberative subjunctive in φάγωσιν, joined with τί, the interrogative pronoun used like a relative. "Just as ὅς and ὅστις came to be used as interrogatives, so τίς drifted occasionally to a mere relative. We have seen (I Tim.1:7) how the relative and the interrogative come to be used side by side. 'In English, the originally interrogative pronouns 'who' and 'which' have encroached largely on the use of the primitive relative 'that.' " (Simcox, Language of the New Testament, 67, as cited in Robertson, Grammar, 737). Moulton's sketch of the facts makes it clear that in the N.T. τίς may be relative if the exigencies call for it. Moulton finds it only in the illiterate papyri, but the usage is supported by inscriptions. (Dieterich, Untersuchungen zur Geschichte der Sprache von der hellen. Zeit bis zum 10, Jaharh, 200, as cited in Ibid.). The modern Pontic dialect supports it. Robertson adds that "The plainest New Testament example of τίς as ὅς appears to be Mk.14:36." Other examples are Mt.26:39, Mt.15:32; Mk.8:1; Mk.6:36.

πάλιν suggests that the situation is not new. Cf. John 6. Jesus' popularity at this point assured that a large crowd would assemble wherever He went, although this was no longer true in Capernaum.

*Verse 2 - "I have compassion on the multitude because they have now been with
me three days, and have nothing to eat."*

Σπλαγχνίζομαι ἐπὶ τὸν ὄχλον ὅτι ἤδη ἡμέραι τρεῖς προσμένουσίν μοι καὶ
οὐκ ἔχουσιν τί φάγωσιν.

Σπλαγχνίζομαι (1st.per.sing.pres.mid.ind.of σπλαγχνίζομαι, aoristic) 835.

ἐπὶ (preposition with the accusative to express emotion) 47.

τὸν (acc.sing.masc.of the article in agreement with ὄχλον) 9.

ὄχλον (acc.sing.masc.of ὄχλος, emotion expression) 418.

ὅτι (conjunction introducing a subordinate causal clause) 211.

ἤδη (adverbial) 291.

ἡμέραι (nom.pl.fem.of ἡμέρα, parenthetic nominative) 135.

τρεῖς (numeral) 1010.

προσμένουσιν (3d.per.pl.pres.act.ind.of προσμένω, progressive) 1179.

μοι (dat.sing.masc.of ἐγώ, personal interest) 123.

καὶ (adversative conjunction) 14.

οὐκ (summary negative conjunction with the indicative) 130.

ἔχουσιν (3d.per.pl.pres.act.ind.of ἔχω, aoristic) 82.

τί (acc.sing.neut.of τίς, direct object of ἔχουσιν) 281.

φάγωσιν (3d.per.pl.aor.act.subj.of ἐσθίω, purpose) 610.

*Translation - "I am sorry for the people because they have remained with me for
three days already, but they do not have anything to eat."*

Comment: ἐπὶ with the accusative is used to express emotion. *Cf.*#47. The
subordinate causal clause is introduced by ὅτι. ἤδη here as indicating a condition
which existed simultaneous with the time of the Jesus' remark. "The time spent
with me is now three days." The margin has ἡμέραις τρισίν, but the parenthetic
nominative will do *Cf.* Mt.15:32 where Matthew reports in the same terms.
προσμένουσίν μοι - "near to me" in a physical sense. *Cf.*#1179 and note Acts
11:23 and I Tim.5:5 in a spiritual sense. καὶ is adversative. It is uplifting,
intellectually and spiritually to be near Jesus, *but* the people had no food and
they were hungry. The drawing power of Jesus is thus revealed. When four
thousand people so far forget their stomachs for three days in order to remain
near to Jesus, He is no ordinary man. Note that Jesus realized their problem and
spoke of it before they did. Note the participial μὴ ἐχόντων τί φάγωσιν of verse
1 and οὐκ ἔχουσιν τί φάγωσιν of verse 2.

*Verse 3 - "And if I send them away fasting to their own houses, they will faint by
the way: for divers of them came from far."*

καὶ ἐὰν ἀπολύσω αὐτοὺς νήστεις εἰς οἶκον αὐτῶν, ἐκλυθήσονται ἐν τῇ ὁδῷ,
καί τινες αὐτῶν ἀπὸ μακρόθεν ἥκασιν.

καὶ (continuative conjunction) 14.

ἐὰν (conditional particle in a third-class condition) 363.

ἀπολύσω (1st.per.sing.aor.act.subj.of ἀπολύω, third-class condition) 92.

αὐτοὺς (acc.pl.masc.of αὐτός, direct object of ἀπολύσω) 16.
νήστεις (acc.pl.masc.of νῆστις, in agreement with αὐτοὺς) 1180.
εἰς (preposition with the accusative of extent) 140.
οἶκον (acc.sing.masc.of οἶκος, extent) 784.
αὐτῶν (gen.pl.masc.of αὐτός, possession) 16.
ἐκλυθήσονται (3d.per.pl.fut.pass.ind.of ἐκλύω, predictive) 1181.
ἐν (preposition with the locative of place where) 80.
τῇ (loc.sing.fem.of the article in agreement with ὁδῷ) 9.
ὁδῷ (loc.sing.fem.of ὁδός, place where) 199.
καί (emphatic conjunction) 14.
τινες (nom.pl.masc.of τίς, subject of ἥκασιν) 486.
αὐτοῦ (gen.sing.masc.of αὐτός, relationship) 16.
ἀπὸ (preposition with the ablative of separation) 70.
μακρόθεν (adverbial) 1600.
ἥκασιν (3d.per.pl.perf.act.ind.of ἥκω, consummative) 730.

Translation - *"And if I send them away hungry unto their homes they will collapse on the road. In fact some of them have come a long distance."*

Comment: Jesus is putting together His observation of the facts of the case with the possibility of further trouble for the people. He is sorry for them because they have been there three days and food supplies are exhausted, with the result that the people are very hungry. Furthermore, if He dismisses them, they will try to get home, only to faint from weakness along the homeward path, due to lack of food. The third-class condition has His prediction in the apodosis. Not the subjunctive contrary to fact in the protasis. Jesus is speaking hypothetically. He is not going to send them away on empty stomachs. He is only predicting what would happen if He did. The final καὶ can be taken as emphatic, as we have done, or as causal. *Cf.*#1181 for the basic meaning. Goodspeed translates "give out."

Thus Jesus poses the dilemma, not that He does not know what to do about it, but to test the disciples' faith. Keep in mind that the disciples had seen Jesus meet this type of crisis before (Mk.6:30-44). Their response in verse 4 is therefore quite amazing.

Verse 4 - *"And his disciples answered him, From whence can a man satisfy these men with bread here in the wilderness?"*

καὶ ἀπεκρίθησαν αὐτῷ οἱ μαθηταὶ αὐτοῦ ὅτι Πόθεν τούτους δυνήσεταί τις ὧδε χορτάσαι ἄρτων ἐπ᾽ ἐρημίας;

καὶ (inferential conjunction) 14.
ἀπεκρίθησαν (3d.per.pl.aor.ind.of ἀποκρίνομαι, constative) 318.
αὐτῷ (dat.sing.masc.of αὐτός, indirect object of ἀπεκρίθησαν) 16.
οἱ (nom.pl.masc.of the article in agreement with μαθηταὶ) 9.
μαθηταὶ (nom.pl.masc.of μαθητής, subject of ἀπεκρίθησαν) 421.
aÿ to§ (gen.sing.masc.of αὐτός, relationship) 16.
ὅτι (recitative) 211.

Πόθεν (interrogative conjunction) 1061.

τούτους (acc.pl.masc.of οὗτος, direct object of χορτάσαι) 93.

δυνήσεται (3d.per.sing.fut.ind.of δύναμαι, deliberative) 289.

τις (nom.sing.masc.of τις, subject of δυνήσεται) 486.

ὧδε (an adverb of place) 766.

χορτάσαι (aor.act.inf.of χορτάζω, complementary) 428.

ἄρτων (gen.pl.masc.of ἄρτος, definition) 338.

ἐπ' (preposition with the genitive, place description) 47.

ἐρημίας (gen.sing.fem.of ἐρημία, place description) 1182.

Translation - "And in reply His disciples said, "How could anybody feed these people with bread here in the wilderness?' "

Comment: The question of the disciples is deliberative future. It is really a rhetorical question. The answer seems obivous. Nobody would be able to feed that many people until they were satisfied. ἐπὶ with the genitive often indicates place where. *Cf.*#47. *Cf.* Mt.15:33 and Mt.14:17 where the disciples were perplexed with the same problem on a previous occasion.

Some commentators think that the writers have given us two separate accounts of the same event. But the details are different, and Jesus Himself recognized two separate incidents of miraculous feeding (Mk.8:19-21). In the former case (Mk.6:36) there was food available for purchase within walking distance. Such was not the case here. "The rejection of the historicity of Ch.8:1-9 requires the assignment of Ch.8:14-21 to the limbo of creative redaction or false tradition. . . Mark clearly understood that there were two occasions when Jesus miraculously fed a multitude." (William L. Lane, *The Gospel According to Mark,* 272, *The New International Commentary on the New Testament*).

Verse 5 - "And he asked them, How many loaves have ye? And they said, Seven."

καὶ ἠρώτα αὐτούς, Πόσους ἔχετε ἄρτους; οἱ δὲ εἶπαν, Ἑπτά.

καὶ (continuative conjunction) 14.

ἠρώτα (3d.per.sing.imp.act.ind.of ἐρωτάω) 1172.

αὐτούς (acc.pl.masc.of αὐτός, direct object of ἠρώτα) 16.

Πόσους (acc.pl.masc.of πόσος, in agreement with ἄρτους) 603.

ἔχετε (2d.per.pl.pres.act.ind.of ἔχω, direct question) 82.

ἄρτους (acc.pl.masc.of ἄρτος, direct object of ἔχετε) 338.

οἱ (nom.pl.masc.of the article, subject of εἶπαν) 9.

δὲ (continuative conjunction) 11.

εἶπαν (3d.per.pl.aor.act.ind.of εἶπον, constative) 155.

Ἑπτά (numeral) 1024.

Translation - "And He asked them, 'How many loaves do you have?' And they said, 'Seven.' "

Comment: Matthew 15:34 adds καὶ ὀλίγα ἰχθύδια. The number seven clearly distinguishes this incident from the preceding one (Mk.6:30-46; Mt.14:13-21) in which five loaves and two fish were involved.

Verse 6 - "And he commanded the people to sit down on the ground: and he took the seven loaves, and gave thanks, and brake and gave to his disciples to set before them; and they did set them before the people."

καὶ παραγγέλλει τῷ ὄχλῳ ἀναπεσεῖν ἐπὶ τῆς γῆς, καὶ λαβὼν τοὺς ἑπτὰ ἄρτους εὐχαριστήσας ἔκλασεν καὶ ἐδίδου τοῖς μαθηταῖς αὐτοῦ ἵνα παρατιθῶσιν καὶ παρέθηκαν τῷ ὄχλῳ.

καὶ (continuative conjunction) 14.

παραγγέλλει (3d.per.sing.pres.act.ind.of παραγγέλλω, historical) 855.

τῷ (dat.sing.masc.of the article in agreement with ὄχλῳ) 9.

ὄχλῳ (dat.sing.masc.of ὄχλος, indirect object of παραγγέλλει) 418.

ἀναπεσεῖν (aor.act.inf.of ἀναπίπτω, complementary) 1184.

ἐπὶ (preposition with the genitive, place where) 47.

τῆς (gen.sing.fem.of the article in agreement with γῆς) 9.

γῆς (gen.sing.fem.of γῆ, place where) 157.

καὶ (continuative conjunction) 14.

λαβὼν (aor.act.part.nom.sing.masc.of λαμβάνω, adverbial, temporal) 533.

τοὺς (acc.pl.masc.of the article in agreement with ἄρτους) 9.

ἑπτὰ (numeral) 1024.

ἄρτους (acc.pl.masc.of ἄρτος, direct object of λαβὼν) 338.

εὐχαριστήσας (aor.act.part.nom.sing.masc.of εὐχαριστέω, adverbial, temporal) 1185.

ἔκλασεν (3d.per.sing.aor.act.ind.of κλάω, ingressive) 1121.

καὶ (adjunctive conjunction joining verbs) 14.

ἐδίδου (3d.per.sing.imp.act.ind.of δίδωμι, inceptive) 362.

τοῖς (dat.pl.masc.of the article in agreement with μαθηταῖς) 9.

μαθηταῖς (dat.pl.masc.of μαθητής, indirect object of ἐδίδου) 421.

αὐτοῦ (gen.sing.masc.of αὐτός, relationship) 16.

ἵνα (final conjunction introducing a purpose clause) 114.

παρατιθῶσιν (3d.per.pl.pres.act.subj.of παρατίθημι, purpose) 1055.

καὶ (continuative conjunction) 14.

παρέθηκαν (3d.per.pl.aor.act.ind.of παρατίθημι, ingressive) 1055.

τῷ (dat.sing.masc.of the article in agreement with ὄχλῳ) 9.

ὄχλῳ (dat.sing.masc.of ὄχλος, indirect object of παρέθηκαν) 418.

Translation - "And He commanded the people to recline upon the ground, and after He had taken the seven loaves and had given thanks, He began to break and to give to His disciples so that they might serve it and they began to set it before the people."

Comment: It takes a while to get 4000 people to sit down. Jesus may have walked about through the assembly, suggesting to all that they assume the position upon the ground that they normally assumed before their tables at home. *Cf.*#1184. The temporal participles λαβὼν and εὐχαρίστησας, being aorist, indicate action prior to that of the ingressive aorist ἔκλασεν and the inceptive imperfect ἐδίδου. This, of course, is the normal order of things. We point it out only to show how precise the Greek grammar is. First Jesus took the bread into His hands; then He gave thanks to God for it after which He *began* (ingressive aorist) to break it into small portions and *began* (inceptive imperfect) to parcel it out to His disciples. Why? The purpose clause follows with ἵνα and the subjunctive in παρατίθωσιν - "in order that they might serve it to the people." Finally the disciples *began* (ingressive aorist) to set the food before the people. *Cf.* our comments on Mt.14:19.

The miracle of continuous production of more and more bread to twelve men who continued to place it before the people is explained only on the grounds of direct, special creation by the Creator incarnate in human flesh. No other explanation explains! It has been our experience that those who wish to explain away this miracle are the same people who try to rob Christianity of any and all supernatural elements. Thus they seek to reduce the Christian system and the institution that propagates it to the level of human sociology and psychology. The leap of faith comes when we decide who Jesus is. Once we recognize Him as God incarnate, there is no further difficulty in accepting at face value the accounts of what He did, however impossible such feats would be if attempted by us. If Mark had written that you, my reader, fed 4000 people with seven loaves of bread, I would not believe it, any more than I would expect you to believe it if Mark had said that I did it. Either the story is true as recorded or Mark lied about it. Spiritual interpretations or metaphorical applications do violence to the text, although the spiritual lessons which followed in Jesus' teachings are valid.

*Cf.*comment on Mt.15:35,36. Note that Matthew uses ἐπὶ τὴν γῆν instead of ἐπὶ τῆς γῆς as in Mark. Both accusative and genitive cases, following ἐπί can mean place where. We call this to attention to show that the dictation theory of divine inspiration cannot be sustained in the light of the facts. If there had been any danger that exegetes would have misunderstood the passage because of the differing cases following ἐπί, the Holy Spirit would have guarded against it. Otherwise He allowed Matthew and Mark to write it as they were inclined to do. It is not the *words* (ῥῆμα, #343) that are supernaturally directed in inspiration, but the *word* (# λόγος, #510). We have a supernatural Bible that we can trust because the total message that our Lord wishes for us to understand is adequately revealed.

The menu was not confined to bread. A balanced diet was provided since they also had a few small fish, as we see in

Verse 7 - "And they had a few small fishes: and he blessed, and commanded to set them also before them."

καὶ εἶχον ἰχθύδια ὀλίγα, καὶ εὐλογήσας αὐτὰ εἶπεν καὶ ταῦτα παρατιθέναι.

καὶ (continuative conjunction) 14.

εἶχον (3d.per.pl.imp.act.ind. of ἔχω, progressive description) 82.

ἰχθύδια (acc.pl.neut.of ἰχθύδιον, direct object of εἶχον) 1183.
ὀλίγα (acc.pl.neut.of ὀλίγος, in agreement with ἰχθύδια) 669.
καὶ (continuative conjunction) 14.
εὐλογήσας (aor.act.part.nom.sing.masc.of εὐλογέω, adverbial, temporal) 1120.
αὐτὰ (acc.pl.neut.of αὐτός, direct object of εὐλογήσας) 16.
εἶπεν (3d.per.sing.aor.act.ind.of εἶπον, constative) 155.
καὶ (adjunctive conjunction, joining nouns) 14.
ταῦτα (acc.pl.neut.of οὗτος, direct object of παρατιθέναι) 93.
παρατιθέναι (pres.act.inf.of παρατίθημι, complementary) 1055.

Translation - "And they had a few little fish: and He blessed them and told them also to serve these."

Comment: Note the present infinitive - "continue to serve the fish until all are fed."

Our Lord adds His miraculous blessing and amplification only when we give Him *all* that we have, however insignificant it may be. He will increase 100% to infinity. He will not expand 99% at all! Which is better - an infinite augmentation of a little, which is nevertheless all we have, or no expansion of a lot which is less than all we have?

Verse 8 - "So they did eat, and were filled: and they took up of the broken meat that was left seven baskets."

καὶ ἔφαγον καὶ ἐχορτάσθησαν, καὶ ἦραν περισσεύματα κλασμάτων ἑπτὰ σπυρίδας.

καὶ (continuative conjunction) 14.
ἔφαγον (3d.per.pl.aor.act.ind.of ἐσθίω, constative) 610.
καὶ (adjunctive conjunction joining verbs) 14.
ἐχορτάσθησαν (3d.per.pl.aor.pass.ind.of χορτάζω, culminative) 428.
καὶ (continuative conjunction) 14.
ἦραν (3d.per.pl.aor.act.ind.of αἴρω, culminative) 350.
περισσεύματα (acc.pl.neut.of περίσσευμα, direct object of ἦραν) 1003.
κλασμάτων (gen.pl.neut.of κλάσμα, partitive genitive) 1122.
ἑπτὰ (numeral) 1024.
σπυρίδας (acc.pl.fem.of σπυρίς, measure) 1186.

Translation - "And they ate until they were filled; and they picked up seven baskets full of remaining fragments."

Comment: They ate all that they could hold. The bits and pieces that remained were picked up. The excess production filled seven baskets. In the previous miraculous feeding (John 6:12) the disciples did this work. It is reasonable to assume that here also, those who served the food also rescued the remains.

Verse 9 - "And they that had eaten were about four thousand: and he sent them away."

ἦσαν δὲ ὡς τετρακισχίλιοι. καὶ ἀπέλυσεν αὐτούς.

ἦσαν (3d.per.pl.aor.ind.of εἰμί, aoristic) 86.
δὲ (explanatory conjunction) 11.
ὡς (comparative adverb) 128.
τετρακισχίλιοι (nom.pl.masc.of τετρακισχίλιος, predicate nominative) 1187.
καὶ (continuative conjunction) 14.
ἀπέλυσεν (3d.per.sing.aor.act.ind.of ἀπολύω, constative) 92.
αὐτούς (acc.pl.masc.of αὐτός, direct object of ἀπέλυσεν) 16.

Translation - "Now there were about four thousand present; and He sent them away."

Comment: δὲ is explanatory. ὡς in the sense of "approximately." *Cf*.#128 for other such uses. Mark ends his account abruptly. Jesus had seen and met the needs of the people and now He must hasten on to others who also needed His help.

Verse 10 - "And straightway he entered into a ship with his disciples, and came into the parts of Dalmanutha."

Καὶ εὐθὺς ἐμβὰς εἰς τὸ πλοῖον μετὰ τῶν μαθητῶν αὐτοῦ ἦλθεν εἰς τὰ μέρη Δαλμανουθά.

Καὶ (continuative conjunction) 14.
εὐθὺς (adverbial) 258.
ἐμβὰς (aor.act.part.nom.sing.masc.of ἐμβαίνω, adverbial, temporal) 750.
εἰς (preposition with the accusative of extent) 140.
τὸ (acc.sing.neut.of the article in agreement with πλοῖον) 9.
πλοῖον (acc.sing.neut.of πλοῖον, extent) 400.
μετὰ (preposition with the genitive of accompaniment) 50.
τῶν (gen.pl.masc.of the article in agreement with μαθητῶν) 9.
μαθητῶν (gen.pl.masc.of μαθητής, accompaniment) 421.
αὐτοῦ (gen.sing.masc.of αὐτός, relationship) 16.
ἦλθεν (3d.per.sing.aor.ind.of ἔρχομαι, constative) 146.
εἰς (preposition with the accusative of extent) 140.
τὰ (acc.pl.neut.of the article in agreement with μέρη) 9.
μέρη (acc.pl.neut.of μέρος, extent) 240.

#2314 Δαλμανουθά (indeclin., description).

Dalmanutha - Mk.10:10.

Meaning: A little village near Magdala, on the west side of the Sea of Galilee, south of Capernaum.

Translation - "And forthwith He boarded the ship with His disciples and went to the vicinity of Dalmanutha."

Comment: Contrast Mt.14:22,23. After Jesus had fed the 5000, He sent His disciples across the Sea of Galilee while He went up into the mountain to pray. In the story before us He boarded the ship with His disciples and went, not to Capernaum, but to Dalmanutha, south of Capernaum. Clearly we have two miracles of feeding the people, not one, as some suppose. *Cf.* Mt.15:39 - Magada or Magdala, is the larger area. Dalmanutha is a small village within the larger jurisdiction. No conflict.

The Pharisees and Sadducees Seek a Sign

(Mark 8:11-13; Matthew 15:39-16:4)

(The student should review the comments in Matthew)

Mark 8:11 - "And the Pharisees came forth, and began to question with him, seeking of him a sign from heaven, tempting him."

Καὶ ἐξῆλθον οἱ Φαρισαῖοι καὶ ἤρξαντο συζητεῖν αὐτῷ, ζητοῦντες παρ' αὐτοῦ σημεῖον ἀπὸ τοῦ οὐρανοῦ, πειράζοντες αὐτόν.

Καὶ (continuative conjunction) 14.
ἐξῆλθον (3d.per.pl.aor.ind.of ἐξέρχομαι, constative) 161.
οἱ (nom.pl.masc.of the article in agreement with Φαρισαῖοι) 9.
Φαρισαῖοι (nom.pl.masc.of Φαρισαῖος, subject of ἐξῆλθον and ἤρξαντο) 276.
καὶ (adjunctive conjunction joining verbs) 14.
ἤρξαντο (3d.per.pl.aor.mid.ind.of ἄρχω, ingressive) 383.
συζητεῖν (pres.act.inf.of συζητέω, complementary) 2060.
αὐτῷ (dat.sing.masc.of αὐτός, indirect object of συζητεῖν) 16.
ζητοῦντες (pres.act.part.nom.pl.masc.of ζητέω, adverbial, telic) 207.
παρ' (preposition with the ablative of source) 154.
αὐτοῦ (abl.sing.masc.of αὐτός, source) 16.
σημεῖον (acc.sing.neut.of σημεῖον, direct object of ζητοῦντες) 1005.
ἀπὸ (preposition with the ablative of source) 70.
τοῦ (abl.sing.masc.of the article in agreement with οὐρανοῦ) 9.
οὐρανοῦ (abl.sing.masc.of οὐρανός, source) 254.
πειράζοντες (pres.act.part.nom.pl.masc.of πειράζω, adverbial, telic) 330.
αὐτόν (acc.sing.masc.of αὐτός, direct object of πειράζοντες) 16.

Translation - "And the Pharisees emerged and began to argue with Him, seeking from Him a sign from the heaven, in order to tempt Him."

Comment: Jesus and the disciples landed somewhere near Dalmanutha in the Magdala area, on the west coast of the Sea of Galilee, south of Capernaum. Here came the Pharisees out of town into the countryside to meet Him. They started an argument. Specifically they were challenging Him to perform a miracle in substantiation of His claim to deity. We recall John 6:30. Their real motive was to induce Him to evil by indulging in a vulgar display of His miraculous power. Satan had attempted the same in Mt.4:6,7. We can take the participles ζητοῦντες and πειράζοντες as telic or modal. The purpose of the argument which the Pharisees started was that they might induce Jesus to prove by some miracle that He was God, and thus their purpose of tempting Him would be realized. They wished to see Him degrade Himself to their low level of controversy.

Jesus' miracles were always performed in order to help someone who was thirsty, hungry, demented, blind, deaf, speechless, about to drown, poverty stricken or grief stricken. Would a miracle on this occasion in response to their challenge have helped the Pharisees? No! Why? Because they had already seen enough evidence of His miraculous power to have converted them a thousand times over had they been intellectually honest enough to really want to know. Another miracle, however astounding, would only have forced them to a greater rationalization to explain it away.

Christians have not accepted Jesus as Lord because we saw His tricks and miracles. We came to Him because we were drawn to Him by the Father. This was His clear teaching in John 6:27-71, *q.v.* More evidence for a dishonest man merely means more intellectual dishonesty. The Pharisees would have provided for themselves a satisfactory explanation for whatever Jesus might have done. "He casteth out demons by Beelzebub, the Prince of demons." How utterly illogical, but it satisfied one who was already determined to hate Jesus. To have accommadated the Pharisees would have become guilty of "casting genuine pearls before genuine swine." *Cf.*other examples of arguments under #2060. Also *cf.*#1005 (2), for instances where miracles were requested for nefarious reasons. This was not the only time that Jesus was challenged to show evidence of His deity.

The point at issue here explains the opposite approaches of the two schools of Christian Apologetics. Presuppositionalists would never try to convince the unsaved by demonstrable "proofs" that the Christian system is valid. Empiricists, on the other hand, in the Pharisaic tradition, see value in such demonstrations. The legalistic Judaizers who gave Paul so much trouble, were joined later by Pelagius, Thomas Aquinas, Arminius, Erasmus and modern legalists in the view that Adam's fall left his intellect uncorrupted and that sinners can reason their way to God. Outside of Christ, Adam's fallen race is dead, not sick, and totally unable correctly to evaluate empirical evidence and to follow its argument to a logical conclusion. The evangelist who understands why Jesus did not rise to meet the challenge of the Pharisees, will never try to convince an audience by intellectual arguments that they should come to Christ. What he does is to proclaim the gospel in the power of the Holy Spirit and depend upon the Spirit to draw to Christ all those whom God has given to His Son. Good preaching *dares* the skeptic to take the leap of faith and accept *a priori* the truth of the incarnation of Jesus Christ.

Jesus develops this thought in

Verse 12 - "And he sighed deeply in his spirit and saith, Why doth this generation seek after a sign? Verily, I say unto you, There shall no sign be given unto this generation."

καὶ ἀναστενάξας τῷ πνεύματι αὐτοῦ λέγει, Τί ἡ γενεὰ αὕτη ζητεῖ σημεῖον;
ἀμὴν λέγω ὑμῖν, εἰ δοθήσεται τῇ γενεᾷ ταύτῃ σημεῖον.

καὶ (inferential conjunction) 14.

#2315 ἀναστενάξας (aor.act.part.nom.sing.masc.of ἀναστενάζω, adverbial,
temporal).

sigh deeply - Mk.8:12.

Meaning: A combination of ἀνά (#1059) and στενάζω (#2310). To give audible
evidence of boredom, resignation, disgust. A stronger word than #2310, which
may refer to internal feeling of disgust but without outward evidence. In
Mk.8:12 it is joined by τῷ πνεύματι αὐτοῦ - "in His spirit."

τῷ (loc.sing.neut.of the article in agreement with πνεύματι) 9.
πνεύματι (loc.sing.neut.of πνεῦμα, sphere) 83.
αὐτοῦ (gen.sing.masc.of αὐτός, possession) 16.
λέγει (3d.per.sing.pres.act.ind.of λέγω, historical) 66.
Τί (acc.sing.neut.of τίς, interrogative pronoun, cause) 281.
ἡ (nom.sing.fem.of the article in agreement with γενεά) 9.
γενεά (nom.sing.fem.of γενεά, subject of ζητεῖ) 922.
αὕτη (nom.sing.fem.of οὗτος, in agreement with γενεά) 93.
ζητεῖ (3d.per.sing.pres.act.ind.of ζητέω, aoristic) 207.
σημεῖον (acc.sing.neut.of σημεῖον, direct object of ζητεῖ) 1005.
ἀμὴν (explicative) 466.
λέγω (1st.per.sing.pres.act.ind.of λέγω, aoristic) 66.
ὑμῖν (dat.pl.masc.of σύ, indirect object of λέγω) 104.
εἰ (conditional particle in a first-class elliptical condition) 337.
δοθήσεται (3d.per.sing.fut.pass.ind.of δίδωμι, first-class condition) 362.
τῇ (dat.sing.fem.of the article in agreement with γενεᾷ) 9.
ταύτῃ (dat.sing.fem.of οὗτος, in agreement with γενεᾷ) 93.
σημεῖον (acc.sing.neut.of σημεῖον, direct object of δοθήσεται) 1005.

Translation - "*Therefore He heaved a deep sigh in His spirit and said, 'Why is
this generation always looking for a sign? Truly I am telling you that no sign will
be given to this generation.*"

Comment: *Cf.*#2315 for the meaning, as distinct from #2310. Jesus heaved a
deep sigh of disgust and weary resignation that came from the depths of His
human spirit. The humanity of our Lord is showing. *Cf.* Mk.2:8; 8:12; Lk.23:46;
John 11:33; 13:21; 19:30 for the other instances of πνεῦμα in the sense of the
human spirit of Jesus. Always divine, Jesus was also truly human in His nature
after the incarnation. These evidences that He reacted emotionally as we might
react show that we have a High Priest who can be touched with the feeling of our
infirmities (Heb.4:15). His question is rhetorical. Note that Mark omits διά with
the interrogative Τί - "On account of what?" "Why is this crowd always asking
for a sign?!" Jesus did not need an answer. He already had the answer. He was

aware of the tactics of the Pharisees. They wanted an argument, so that they could trap Him into an unguarded remark that they could use against Him. He refused to lower His dignity by playing their game.

The last clause εἰ δοθήσεται τῇ γενεᾷ ταύτῃ σημεῖον, is the protasis of a first-class elliptical condition. The apodosis is missing. This is a case of aposiopesis. "In the same way (suppression of apodosis) is to be explained the use of εἰ . . . in the sense of 'not,' in solemn oaths or questions. The apodosis is wanting. . . So Heb.3:11; 4:3,5. . . It is an apparent imitation of the Hebrew idiom, though not un-Greek in itself. Radermacher (*N. T. Gr.*, p.184) treats this idiom in Mk.8:12 as due to translation from the Hebrew (Aramaic)." (Robertson, *Grammar, 1023, 1024).* Meyer calls the construction a Hebraism. It is strongly negative. It is as though Jesus broke off the sentence in disgust and left it unfinished. "If a sign were given to this generation . . . " we might finish perhaps with ". . . they would not believe it in any case." *Cf.* Mt.16:1-12. The material in Mt.16:2-4 was spoken on this occasion. *Cf.* also Mt.12:38-40. Mark records only the abbreviated form as Jesus broke off in disgust. What's the use?! The enlightened Christian who has often been bored with the boorish thickness of spiritual blindness among unbelievers is heartened to note that Jesus also felt the same way upon occasion. *Cf.* Heb.4:3,5 for other examples of a suppressed apodosis.

Jesus did give to the world one sign - the sign of the prophet Jonah, but that was not a sign in the sense in which the Pharisees were asking.

Spectacular evangelism, with its "dog and pony show" glamour is not the evangelism of the Holy Spirit. A rich man in Hades suggested to Abraham that if Lazarus rose from the dead and returned to earth to warn his brothers of their coming fate, they would be so impressed that they would repent. Abraham suggested that they read their Bibles, and added that if they would not believe Moses and the prophets, they would not believe even if one arose from the dead (Lk.16:27-31). It would be hard even for Hollywood to stage a revival meeting with as great appeal to the public as would be generated by the return from Paradise of a saint like the beggar Lazarus. Yet such appeals to the flesh do not induce repentance and faith. (I Cor.12:3; John 6:44).

Jesus wasted no time with the Pharisees as we see in

Verse 13 - "And he left them and entering into the ship again departed to the other side."

καὶ ἀφεὶς αὐτοὺς πάλιν ἐμβὰς ἀπῆλθεν εἰς τὸ πέραν.

καὶ (continuative conjunction) 14.

ἀφεὶς (aor.act.part.nom.sing.masc.of ἀφίημι, adverbial, temporal) 319.

αὐτοὺς (acc.pl.masc.of αὐτός, direct object of ἀφεὶς) 16.

πάλιν (adverbial) 355.

ἐμβὰς (aor.act.part.nom.sing.masc.of ἐμβαίνω, adverbial, temporal) 750.

ἀπῆλθεν (3d.per.sing.aor.act.ind.of ἀπέρχομαι, constative) 239.

εἰς (preposition with the accusative of extent) 140.

τὸ (acc.sing.neut.of the article, joined with the improper preposition and used adverbially) 9.

πέραν (improper preposition used adverbially, extent) 375.

Translation - "And Jesus, having walked away from them, went·on board and again crossed to the other side."

Comment: Jesus had no chance to help anyone during His short stay in Dalmanutha. As soon as He arrived the Pharisees tried to start an argument and Jesus walked out on them in disgust.

The Disciples' Perplexity About Leaven and Jesus' Explanation

(Mt.16:5-12; Mk.8:14-21)

(The student should review Mt.16:5-12)

Mk.8:14 - "Now the disciples had forgotten to take bread, neither had they in the ship with them more than one loaf."

Καὶ ἐπελάθοντο λαβεῖν ἄρτους, καὶ εἰ μὴ ἕνα ἄρτον οὐκ εἶχον μεθ' ἑαυτῶν ἐν τῷ πλοίῳ.

Καὶ (explanatory conjunction) 14.
ἐπελάθοντο (3d.per.pl.2d.aor.ind.of ἐπιλανθάνομαι, culminative) 1196.
λαβεῖν (aor.act.inf.of λαμβάνω, complementary) 533.
ἄρτους (acc.pl.masc.of ἄρτος, direct object of λαβεῖν) 338.
καὶ (emphatic conjunction) 14.
εἰ (conditional particle in an elliptical condition) 337.
μὴ (qualified negative conjunction in an elliptical condition) 87.
ἕνα (acc.sing.masc.of εἷς, in agreement with ἄρτον) 469.
ἄρτον (acc.sing.masc.of ἄρτος, direct object of εἶχον understood) 338.
οὐκ (summary negative conjunction with the indicative) 130.
εἶχον (3d.per.pl.imp.act.ind.of ἔχω, progressive description) 82.
μεθ' (preposition with the genitive of accompaniment) 50.
ἑαυτῶν (gen.pl.masc.of ἑαυτός, accompaniment) 288.
ἐν (preposition with the locative of place where) 80.
τῷ (loc.sing.neut.of the article in agreement with πλοίῳ) 9.
πλοίῳ (loc.sing.neut.of πλοῖον, place where) 400.

Translation - "Now they had forgotten to take bread. In fact, except for one loaf, they had none with them in the ship."

Comment: Their stay in Dalmanutha was cut short by the abrupt departure of Jesus, who terminated the discussion with the Pharisees and ordered immediate departure. The disciples had no time to think about provisions for the future. Note the emphatic use of καὶ - "In fact . . . κ.τ.λ." Mark uses an elliptical condition to say that they had only one loaf of bread on board. Literally, "If they had not had one loaf on board, they would have had none." Mark's syntactical peculiarity is evident here in εἰ μὴ ἕνα ἄρτον οὐκ εἶχον, but the meaning is not obscure. The oversight gave Jesus an opportunity to teach by a parable, as in verse 15 He said,

Verse 15 - "And he charged them saying, Take heed, beware of the leaven of the Pharisees and of the leaven of Herod."

καὶ διεστέλλετο αὐτοῖς λέγων, Ὁρᾶτε, βλέπετε ἀπὸ τῆς ζύμης τῶν Φαρισαίων καὶ τῆς ζύμης Ἡρώδου.

καὶ (continuative conjunction) 14.
διεστέλλετο (3d.per.sing.imp.act.ind.of διαστέλλομαι, inceptive) 2244.
αὐτοῖς (dat.pl.masc.of αὐτός, indirect object of διεστέλλετο) 16.
λέγων (pres.act.part.nom.sing.masc.of λέγω, recitative) 66.
Ὁρᾶτε (2d.per.pl.pres.act.impv.of ὁράω, command) 144.
βλέπετε (2d.per.pl.pres.act.impv.of βλέπω, command) 499.
ἀπὸ (preposition with the ablative, cause) 70.
τῆς (abl.sing.fem.of the article in agreement with ζύμης) 9.
ζύμης (abl.sing.fem.of ζύμη, cause) 1072.
τῶν (gen.pl.masc.of the article in agreement with Φαρισαίων) 9.
Φαρισαίων (gen.pl.masc.of Φαρισαῖος, definition) 276.
καὶ (adjunctive conjunction joining nouns) 14.
τῆς (abl.sing.fem.of the article in agreement with ζύμης) 9.
ζύμης (abl.sing.fem.of ζύμη, cause) 1072.
Ἡρώδου (gen.sing.masc.of Ἡρώδης, definition) 136.

Translation - "And He began to admonish them, saying, 'Now look here, Be on your guard against the leaven of the Pharisees and the leaven of Herod.'"

Comment: Jesus listened, perhaps with some amusement, to the frantic discussion of the disciples when they discovered that they had only one loaf of bread on board. This was due to somebody's oversight. Our Lord saw a chance to turn the bread shortage to good account with His parable. So He began (inceptive imperfect in διεστέλλετο) to admonish them. First He had to get their attention, since their thoughts were occupied with their failure to go to the market and replenish the food supply. This Jesus did with Ὁρᾶτε. It was the practice of tutors to begin the day's lecture with "Attention!" ἀπὸ with the ablative sometimes indicates cause. *Cf.*#70 for the list. *Cf.*#499 for other instances of βλέπετε followed by ἀπό and the ablative, meaning, "Beware of... " *Cf.* also #708. ζύμη is used here in an evil sense. *Cf.*#1072. The basic idea is that of mingling with and permeating that with which it comes in contact. Leaven invades and pervades. It conquers. To fellowship with it is to be enslaved by it. When the yeast is good its action to permeate the system is fortunate. When the yeast is evil, as in the case before us, to be imbued with it is to be contaminated by it - something against which Jesus was warning His disciples.

This advice, immediately following Jesus' most recent encounter with the Pharisees suggests that He had reference to their vulgar request for a sign from heaven on the basis of which they were willing to consider accepting Him. If so, the leaven here means the philosophy that evidence must precede commitment. This is the inductive method often associated with scientific research, although basic research uses some presuppositions. The Pharisees had been insincere.

They made their request in order to tempt Jesus (Mk.8:11). Thus they revealed their malignant and sly effort to induce Him to evil. Comment on Mk.8:11-12 has already made clear that the Pharisees would not have accepted Jesus even if He had shown them evidence.

Mark does not give us Jesus' explanation of the leaven - only His admonition to them to beware of it. But the Matthew account (Mt.16:12) makes clear that Jesus meant the teachings of the Pharisees and Sadducees. This covers a great deal of ground - all of it heretical. Jesus may have felt that some of His disciples saw in His refusal to comply with the request of His detractors an admission that He could not always perform miracles; hence they needed the admonition to beware of such heresy. He reminded them that He had been abundantly competent to perform miracles when there was a good reason to do so.

Just what specifically He meant by the leaven of Herod, as distinct from that of the Pharisees and Sadducees is not revealed in the text. Herod later revealed the same vulgar curiosity when he sought a command performance, as did the Pharisees and Sadducees in Dalmanutha. *Cf.* Lk.23:8. This man is Herod Antipas, the son of Herod the Great who ordered the slaughter of the children in Bethlehem in Matthew 2.

The disciples missed the point of His allusion to leaven and thought only of their lack of bread.

Verse 16 - *"And they reasoned among themselves, saying, It is because we have no bread."*

καὶ διελογίζοντο πρὸς ἀλλήλους ὅτι Ἄρτους οὐκ ἔχουσιν.

καὶ (inferential conjunction) 14.
διελογίζοντο (3d.per.pl.imp.mid.ind.of διαλογίζομαι, inceptive) 1197.
πρὸς (preposition with the accusative after a verb of speaking) 197.
ἀλλήλους (acc.pl.masc.of ἀλλήλων, after a verb of speaking) 1487.
ὅτι (recitative) 211.
Ἄρτους (acc.pl.masc.of ἄρτος, direct object of ἔχομεν) 338.
οὐκ (summary negative conjunction with the indicative) 130.
ἔχομεν (1st.per.pl.pres.act.ind.of ἔχω, aoristic) 82.

Translation - *"Therefore they began a discussion with one another (saying) 'We have no bread.' "*

Comment: The disciples failed to understand Jesus' remark about leaven. It precipitated a discussion in which they assumed that Jesus' reference to ζυμή was to the fact that they had no bread on board. ὅτι is recitative, introducing the direct discourse. Why should they, the disciples, who had recently seen Jesus on two occasions feed thousands of people by direct creation, be worried about food when Jesus was on board? They should have looked for a metaphorical meaning in His reference to leaven.

These were the same men who had heard Jesus' discourse on the Bread of Life (John 6) and had chosen to remain at His side after others deserted Him. Peter, speaking for the group had said, "You have the words of eternal life; and we believe and know that you are the Holy One of God" (John 6:68-69). When we remember that the disciples, though regenerated, were not yet filled with the Holy Spirit, we must admit that they were no more obtuse than most of us are now. In fact Peter and his colleagues had a better excuse than we, because they were living before Pentecost. They also had no New Testament to read as we have now.

Verse 17 - "And when Jesus knew it, he saith unto them, Why reason ye because ye have no bread? Perceive ye not yet, neither understand? Have ye your heart yet hardened?"

καὶ γνοὺς λέγει αὐτοῖς, Τί διαλογίζεσθε ὅτι ἄρτους οὐκ ἔχετε; οὔπω νοεῖτε οὐδὲ συνίετε; πεπωρωμένην ἔχετε τὴν καρδίαν ὑμῶν;

καὶ (inferential conjunction) 14.

γνοὺς (aor.act.part.nom.sing.masc.of γινώσκω, adverbial, causal) 131.

λέγει (3d.per.sing.pres.act.ind.of λέγω, historical) 66.

αὐτοῖς (dat.pl.masc.of αὐτός, indirect object of λέγει) 16.

Τί (acc.sing.neut.of τίς, interrogative pronoun, cause) 281.

διαλογίζεσθε (2d.per.pl.pres.mid.ind.of διαλογίζομαι, direct question) 1197.

ὅτι (causal conjunction) 211.

ἄρτους (acc.pl.masc.of ἄρτος, direct object of ἔχετε) 338.

οὐκ (summary negative conjunction with the indicative) 130.

ἔχετε (2d.per.pl.pres.act.ind.of ἔχω, aoristic) 82.

οὔπω (adverbial) 1198.

νοεῖτε (2d.per.pl.pres.act.ind.of νοέω, direct question) 1160.

οὐδὲ (disjunctive particle) 452.

συνίετε (2d.per.pl.pres.act.ind.of συνίημι, direct question) 1039.

πεπωρωμένην (perf.pass.part.acc.sing.fem.of πωρόω, perfect periphrastic, with ἔχετε, predicate adjective) 2282.

ἔχετε (2d.per.pl.pres.act.ind.of ἔχω, perfect periphrastic) 82.

τὴν (acc.sing.fem.of the article in agreement with καρδίαν) 9.

καρδίαν (acc.sing.fem.of καρδία, direct object of ἔχετε) 432.

ὑμῶν (gen.pl.masc.of σύ, possession) 104.

Translation - "Therefore because He noticed it He said to them, 'Why are you arguing because you have no bread? Do you not yet perceive nor understand? Do you now have your hearts hardened?'"

Comment: Although Jesus was not involved in the discussion He knew of course that it was going on. Therefore (causal γνοὺς) He spoke to them. "Why the ruckus over such an insignificant matter?" Notice that Jesus did not say ". . . ὅτι ἄρτους οὐκ ἔχομεν - because *we* have no bread." He is in the same boat with them but the fact that they forgot to buy bread is their problem, since apparently they do not expect Jesus to do anything about it. One would think that by this time, having seen two miraculous provisions of food sufficient to feed 9000 people out of only 12 loaves and a few little fish, the disciples would not give their food shortages another thought! Since their dispute is based upon their assumption that Jesus is only an ordinary mortal, Jesus lays the bread problem on their doorstep. It is as though He were saying, "You fellows are out of bread. I am not. I not only *have* bread, *I A M* the bread of life." Why could they not see it? This is what Jesus wants to know. He had had a hard day. He was tired and disgusted. Not only did the Pharisees seek a sign, but now His own disciples are so blind as not to realize that Jesus can indeed produce a sign, if it is necessary *to meet a human need.* The Pharisees had sought a sign from wrong motives. The Twelve had not even thought to ask for a sign when the question of motives was not sinfully involved. "When are you going to learn?" asks Jesus.

οὔπω. . . οὐδὲ - "not yet . . . nor?" Perception and the mental ability to put it all together - this is what is involved in νοεῖτε and συνίετε. *Cf.#*'s 1160 and 1039. We have here an unusual perfect periphrastic in πεπωρωμένην ἔχετε. "The use of ἔχω (so common in later Greek and finally triumphant in modern Greek) has a few parallels in the N.T. (*Cf.*Jannaris, *A Historical Greek Grammar,*438, as cited in Robertson, *Grammar*, 902). *Cf.* ἔχε με παρῃτημένον (Lu.14:19) with Latin idiom "I have him beaten." *Cf.* ἔχω κείμενα (Lu.12:19, pres.part.used as perf), ἐξηραμμένην ἔχων τὴν χεῖρα (Mk.3:1), *Cf.* Mk.8:17; Heb.5:14; John 17:13, ἔχωσιν — πεπληρωμένην. Here the perfect part. is, of course, predicate, but the idiom grew out of such examples. The modern Greek uses not only ἔχω δεμένο, but also δεμένα, but, if a conjunctive pron. precedes, the part. agrees in gender and number (*cf.* French). So τὴν ἔχω ἰδωμένη, 'I have seen her' (Thumb, *Handb.*, p.162). Passive is εἶμαι δεμένος.(*Ibid.*).

The participle is also adjectival in the predicate, modifying καρδίαν - "You now have your hearts (consummative present in the periphrastic perfect) . . . " - in what condition? ". . . already hardened?" Of course it is a rhetorical question. The hearts of the disciples, hardened in the past, by too much reasoning at the human level, and unmixed with faith, were now (at the time that Jesus said this) hardened. They were not thinking like enlightened disciples of the Messiah/ Saviour. And, unfortunately, as they were thinking, so were they speaking. In verse 18 Jesus applies to His regenerated followers the same scripture quotation that is elsewhere applied to the unsaved. *Cf.* Mk.4:12; Acts 28:26; Mt.13:14,15.

Verse 18 - "Having eyes, see ye not? And having ears, hear ye not? And do ye not remember?"

ὀφθαλμοὺς ἔχοντες οὐ βλέπετε καὶ ὦτα ἔχοντες οὐκ ἀκούετε; καὶ οὐ μνημονεύετε,

ὀφθαλμοὺς (acc.pl.masc.of ὀφθαλμός, direct object of ἔχοντες) 501.

ἔχοντες (pres.act.part.nom.pl.masc.of ἔχω, adverbial, concessive) 82.

οὐ (summary negative conjunction with the indicative in rhetorical question) 130.

βλέπετε (2d.per.pl.pres.act.ind.of βλέπω, rhetorical question) 499.

καὶ (continuative conjunction) 14.

ὦτα (acc.pl.neut.of ὠτίον, direct object of ἔχοντες) 1595.
ἔχοντες (pres.act.part.nom.pl.masc.of ἔχω, concessive) 82.
οὐκ (summary negative conjunction with the indicative) 130.
ἀκούετε (2d.per.pl.pres.act.ind.of ἀκούω, rhetorical question) 148.
καὶ (ascensive conjunction) 14.
οὐ (summary negative conjunction with the indicative) 130.
μνημονεύετε (2d.per.pl.pres.act.ind.of μνημονεύω, aoristic) 1199.

Translation - "Although you have eyes you do not see and although your have ears you do not hear? You do not even remember!"

Comment: The participle ἔχοντες in both clauses is concessive. The questions are rhetorical. "Despite the fact that you have eyes and ears, you do not see nor hear, do you?" Jesus expected a negative reply. Then, with ascensive καὶ He adds, "You do not even remember." The reference is to Jer.5:21. *Cf.* also Ezek.12:2. Jesus had used the same scripture against the people in Mk.4:12, but at that time He told His disciples that this was not true of them (Mk.4:11). Now He is chiding the Twelve, to whom has been given the ability to understand, in the same way He commented about less enlightened people. The backslidden, defeated Christian, who is dominated by the flesh, is as blind to the subtle nuances of the Christian revelation as are the unsaved. The writer to the Hebrews encountered this obtuse stupidity in Heb.5:11ff.

Since obviously the disciples did not see what Jesus meant, He tried to help them in verses 19-21.

Verse 19 - "When I broke the five loaves among five thousand, how many baskets full of fragments took ye up? They say unto him, Twelve."

ὅτε τοὺς πέντε ἄρτους ἔκλασα εἰς τοὺς πεντακισχιλίους, πόσους κοφίνους κλασμάτων πλήρεις ἤρατε; λέγουσιν αὐτῷ, Δώδεκα.

ὅτε (conjunction introducing a definite temporal clause) 703.
τοὺς (acc.pl.masc.of the article in agreement with ἄρτους) 9.
πέντε (numeral) 1119.
ἄρτους (acc.pl.masc.of ἄρτος, direct object of ἔκλασα) 338.
ἔκλασα (1st.per.sing.aor.act.ind.of κλάω, constative) 1121.
εἰς (preposition with the accusative for the dative of personal advantage) 140.
τοὺς (acc.pl.masc.of the article in agreement with πεντακισχιλίους) 9.
πεντακισχιλίους (acc.pl.masc.of πεντακισχίλιος, personal advantage. *Cf.* comment *infra*) 1125.
πόσους (acc.pl.masc.of πόσος, in agreement with κοφίνους) 603.
κοφίνους (acc.pl.masc.of κόφινος, direct object of ἤρατε) 1123.
κλασμάτων (gen.pl.neut.of κλάσμα, description) 1122.
πλήρεις (acc.pl.masc.of πλήρης, in agreement with κοφίνους) 1124.
ἤρατε (2d.per.pl.1st.aor.act.ind.of αἴρω, direct question) 350.
λέγουσιν (3d.per.pl.pres.act.ind.of λέγω, historical) 66.
αὐτῷ (dat.sing.masc.of αὐτός, indirect object of λέγουσιν) 16.

Δώδεκα (numeral) 820.

Translation - "When I broke the five loaves for the five thousand, how many baskets full of fragments did you pick up? They said to Him, 'Twelve.' "

Comment: ὅτε introduces the definite temporal clause. The time is definite by virtue of the indicative mode in ἔκλασα. Lawyers in court often say to a witness, "I call your attention to the time when ..." We have in εἰς τοὺς πεντακισχιλίους an example of what Robertson calls the decay of the dative. Another example is found in Rom.8:18. In each of these passages εἰς with the accusative is used for the concept of personal advantage - an idea usually conveyed by the dative case. Cf.#140 (IV) for a list of passages where εἰς is used with the accusative as the dative normally is used. On that occasion Jesus performed a notable miracle, attesting fully to the fact that He is the Creator of the universe. But in keeping with His policy He was acting in behalf of a needy group of people. He broke the bread εἰς τοὺς πεντακισχιλίους - "for the benefit of five thousand people." Now that the disciples know what Jesus is talking about, He asks if it were not true that His power to create food for such a large number was greater than the need? On both occasions when Jesus fed the multitudes He demonstrated Eph.3:20. Faced with the question the disciples immediately responded with the correct answer. They had picked up fragments to fill twelve baskets. Jesus could have added, "And yet you are sitting in this boat worrying about food?" No wonder Jesus was disgusted. Then, like a relentless cross examiner, Jesus pursues the point in

Verse 20 - "And when the seven among four thousand, how many baskets full of fragments took ye up? And they said, Seven."

Ὅτε τοὺς ἑπτὰ εἰς τοὺς τετρακισχιλίους, πόσων σπυρίδων πληρώματα κλασμάτων ἤρατε; καὶ λέγουσιν (αὐτῷ) Ἑπτά.

Ὅτε (conjunction introducing a definite temporal clause) 703.
τοὺς (acc.pl.masc.of the article in agreement with ἄρτους, understood) 9.
ἑπτά (numeral) 1024.
εἰς (preposition with the accusative for the dative of personal advantage) 140.
τοὺς (acc.pl.masc.of the article in agreement with τετρακισχιλίους) 9.
τετρακισχιλίους (acc.pl.masc.of τετρακισχίλιοι, personal advantage) 1187.
πόσων (gen.pl.fem.of πόσος, in agreement with σπυρίδων) 603.
σπυρίδων (gen.pl.fem.of σπυρίς, description) 1186.
πληρώματα (acc.pl.neut.of πλήρωμα, extent) 805.
κλασμάτων (gen.pl.neut.of κλάσμα, description) 1122.
ἤρατε (2d.per.pl.aor.act.ind.of αἴρω, constative) 350.
καὶ (continuative conjunction) 14.
λέγουσιν (3d.per.pl.pres.act.ind.of λέγω, historical) 66.
αὐτῷ (dat.sing.masc.of αὐτός, indirect object of λέγουσιν) 16.
Ἑπτά (numeral) 1024.

Translation - "On the occasion of the seven loaves for the four thousand, how

many baskets full of fragments did you pick up? And they said to Him, 'Seven.'"

Comment: Mark omits the verb and its object, since he had used them in the previous formulation in verse 19. Note his faithfulness in reporting the second feeding. He uses σπυρίδων in keeping with Mk.8:8, rather than κοφίνος, which conforms to John 6:13 and Mk.6:43. Two different events; two different situations; two different amounts of food; two different sizes of crowds of hungry people. Schenkel, of course, must deny all that Jesus says here which clearly distinguishes two separate miracles, rather than two confused accounts of the same event, as he charges. Indeed! Once we start questioning the text we find it more and more necessary and easier and easier to deny it again. One wonders why the higher critics study it at all?

That the results of the German school of higher criticism should be the end of any serious exegesis of the Bible, evident among the followers of this method, is evident in the dearth of such study and the resultant ignorance of the laity of Biblical matters. The presuppositional prejudice against the inerrancy of an inspired because Holy Spirit supervised text conditions these critics to search with diligence for every opportunity to show the text in error. What they look for so assiduously they delude themselves into believing that they have found. The fruit of this kind of unbelief may be seen in the fact that only a few German christians had sufficient christian conviction to withstand the rise of Adolf Hitler and his Third Reich which brought Germany down in ruins at the cost of millions of lives throughout the world. William L. Shirer reports that "The German Christians," who "had some three thousand out of a total of seventeen thousand pastors," gave ardent support to the Nazi doctrines of race and the leadership principle espoused by the little Austrian corporal. They wanted a Reich Church ". . . which would bring all Protestants into one all-embracing body." The "German Christians" were opposed by another small group called the "Confessional Church." This group had about as many pastors as the German Christians and was eventually led by Niemoeller. It opposed the "Nazification of the Protestant churches, rejected the Nazi racial theories and denounced the anti-Christian doctrines of Rosenberg and other Nazi leaders." Thus there were two minority groups of christians, the one which gave full support to the Nazis and the other which opposed them at great personal cost. Shirer adds, "In between lay the majority of Protestants, who seemed too timid to join either of the two warring groups, who sat on the fence and eventually, for the most part, landed in the arms of Hitler, accepting his authority to intervene in church affairs and obeying his commands without open protest." Shirer adds that "It is difficult to understand the behavior of most German Protestants in the first Nazi years unless one is aware of two things: their history and the influence of Martin Luther." He then recalls that Luther was "a passionate anti-Semite and a ferocious believer in absolute obedience to political authority."

One can legitimately doubt that the acquiesence of the German church to Hitler was altogether the fault of Martin Luther. Indeed we must doubt it, in all fairness to the Great Reformer, since he is not present to defend himself. It is true that Luther did not like the Jews, but a good Lutheran should know that anti-

Semitism is wrong. This should be apparent to any child of God who made only a minimal effort to study his Bible. He should also know that no first century Christian yielded "absolute obedience" to Imperial Rome. But it is not likely that many German christians knew very much about a Bible that had been attacked by the higher critics for more than a century before Adolf Hitler was born. No busy intellectual is likely to give unremitting attention to a book with as much error in it as the higher critics allege. It is true that Karl Barth opposed the Nazis, despite the fact that Barth himself contributed greatly to German indifference to Bible study, since he seemed unwilling to allow the Bible to teach precisely what it says.

Thus the German Protestants rolled over and played dead at a time when a vigorous protest against Hitler would have forestalled his rise to power. "During the Reichstag elections one could not help but notice that the Protestant clergy — Niemoeller was typical — quite openly supported the Nationalist and even the Nazi enemies of the Republic. Like Niemoeller, most of the pastors welcomed the advent of Adolf Hitler to the chancellorship in 1933." (William L. Shirer, *The Rise and Fall of the Third Reich*, 235 - 237, *et passim*).

There were forty-five million Protestant church members, most of whom belonged to the twenty-eight Lutheran and Reformed bodies, in Germany in 1933. Out of a total population of more than eighty million people, Adolf Hitler and his Nazis were never able to gain the support of a majority of the voters in any election prior to his appointment to the Chancellorship in 1933. "At the crest of their popular strength, in July 1932, the National Socialists had attained but 37 per cent of the vote. But the 63 per cent of the German people who expressed their opposition to Hitler were much too divided and shortsighted to combine against a common danger which they must have known would overwhelm them unless they united, however temporarily, to stamp it out." (*Ibid.*, 185).

One wonders how concerned American Christians in 1979 are about the evidences of Nazi terrorism in the United States. The riots in Skokie, Illinois, where the population is largely Jewish, and the activities of the Ku Klux Klan are cases in point. The drive to study the Bible with the degree of consistency that results in our grasping its ethical message, derives from a profound faith in the proposition that it is a supernatural revelation of God's truth which cannot be found elsewhere. Take from the laity that faith in plenary divine inspiration and the result will follow: he will devote himself, if he reads anything at all, to the sports page or the latest sex novel. Such a church member is not likely to protest the rise of a demagogue, especially if to do so is going to cost him anything.

Jesus had made His point with the disciples. He "(stirred) up (their) pure minds by way of remembrance," (II Pet.3:1). They gave Him two right answers - "Twelve" and "Seven." They could no longer attribute their confusion about bread to their lack of awareness of the two events to which Jesus alluded. They even remembered the precise details, once they were reminded. With all of that factual data why could they not put it all together? This is the question Jesus asks in

Verse 21 - "And he said unto them, How is it that ye do not understand?"

καὶ ἔλεγεν αὐτοῖς, Οὔπω συνίετε;

καὶ (continuative conjunction) 14.
ἔλεγεν (3d.per.sing.imp.act.ind.of λέγω, progressive duration) 66.
αὐτοῖς (dat.pl.masc.of αὐτός, indirect object of ἔλεγεν) 16.
Οὔπω (adverbial) 1198.
συνίετε (2d.per.pl.pres.act.ind.of συνίημι, aoristic) 1039.

Translation - *"And He repeated to them again and again, 'You do not understand yet . . . you do not understand yet. . . you do not understand yet. . ."*

Comment: The imperfect tense in ἔλεγεν indicates that Jesus repeated it over and over, perhaps half unto Himself, as though He could hardly believe it.

Mark gives us no further information, but *cf.* Mt.16:11,12. He was warning the Twelve against the teachings of the Pharisees and Sadducees. Though all of their religious teachings were false, the previous experience with them in Dalmanutha (Mk.8:10-13) seems to be immediately in view. They had demanded from Jesus further supernatural evidence in terms of signs and wonders from heaven, on the basis of their evaluation of which, they could then decide whether or not to accept Him. This is an ancient heresy which denies the total depravity of man. According to this view the intellectual powers of man are not affected by Adam's fall. On the contrary the Pharisees believed that they were quite able to reason their way to truth. It was as though they said to Jesus, "I will evaluate your worth on the basis of the empirical evidence once I have seen you perform. Show me a sign from heaven."

If man came to Christ on this basis then he would be on an intellectual level with God. The reasoning continues like this: "I will accept only what I understand. Nothing must be mysterious. I must understand it all clearly. God with His grace may come in to save, but only when I open the door, and I will decide to open the door solely upon the evidence which I observe and evaluate."

Roman theology, based on Thomism and Arminian theology says that God can only make salvation possible. He cannot actually save us unless we want to be saved. They forget to ask why, how and by whom the sinner is brought to the place in his thinking where he wants to be saved. Many otherwise orthodox evangelists are demonstrating the leaven of the Pharisees when they attempt to *prove* with intellectual argumentation the truths of the Christian gospel on the theory that, spiritually speaking, the way to a man's heart is through his head. Christian Evidences is a discipline to be studied only after regeneration has taken place. Jesus never performed feats of supernatural power in order to convince the gainsayers. On the contrary He regarded such behavior as casting genuine pearls before genuine swine. Presuppositional apologetics is a proper subject to discuss with the unsaved. We are told to be ready to give to the world the philosophical basis for our faith. Once the sinner is saved and in need of growth in grace and knowledge (II Pet.3:18) he can be given the scientific evidences that Christianity is indeed true.

The final region during this time period where Jesus paused to heal was in Bethsaida where He met a blind man.

Mk.8:22 - *"And he cometh to Bethsaida; and they bring a blind man unto him, and besought him to touch him."*

Καὶ ἔρχονται εἰς Βηθσαϊδάν. καὶ φέρουσιν αὐτῷ τυφλὸν καὶ παρακαλοῦσιν αὐτὸν ἵνα αὐτοῦ ἅψηται.

Καὶ (continuative conjunction) 14.
ἔρχονται (3d.per.pl.pres.ind.of ἔρχομαι, historical) 146.
εἰς (preposition with the accusative of extent) 140.
Βηθσαϊδάν (acc.sing.of Βηθσαϊδά, extent) 938.
καὶ (continuative conjunction) 14.
φέρουσιν (3d.per.pl.pres.act.ind.of φέρω, historical) 683.
αὐτῷ (dat.sing.masc.of αὐτός, personal interest) 16.
τυφλὸν (acc.sing.masc.of τυφλός, direct object of φέρουσιν) 830.
καὶ (adjunctive conjunction joining verbs) 14.
παρακαλοῦσιν (3d.per.pl.pres.act.ind.of παρακαλέω, historical) 230.
αὐτὸν (acc.sing.masc.of αὐτός, direct object of παρακαλοῦσιν) 16.
ἵνα (final conjunction introducing a purpose clause) 114.
αὐτοῦ (gen.sing.masc.of αὐτός, designation) 16.
ἅψηται (3d.per.sing.aor.mid.subj.of ἅπτω, purpose) 711.

Translation - *"And they came to Bethsaida. And they brought to Him a blind man and were begging Him to touch him."*

Comment: Mark likes the historical present tense. This usage occurs when action in the past is described as going on at the time of writing. "The present tense is thus employed when a past event is viewed with the vividness of a present occurrence." (Mantey, *Manual*, 185).Note the genitive in αὐτοῦ with a verb, which designates the blind man as the sole object of Jesus' healing touch. "With verbs the genitive means this and no other, while the accusative with verbs means this and no more." (Broadus, as cited in Robertson, *Short Grammar*, 230).

Verse 23 - *"And he took the blind man by the hand and led him out of the town; and when he had spit on his eyes and put his hands upon him, he asked him if he saw ought."*

καὶ ἐπιλαβόμενος τῆς χειρὸς τοῦ τυφλοῦ ἐξήνεγκεν αὐτὸν ἔξω τῆς κώμης, καὶ πτύσας εἰς τὰ ὄμματα αὐτοῦ, ἐπιθεὶς τὰς χεῖρας αὐτῷ, ἐπηρώτα αὐτόν, Εἴ τι βλέπεις;

καὶ (continuative conjunction) 14.
ἐπιλαβόμενος (aor.mid.part.nom.sing.masc.of ἐπιλαμβάνω, adverbial, temporal) 1133.
τῆς (gen.sing.fem.of the article in agreement with χειρὸς) 9.
χειρὸς (gen.sing.fem.of χείρ, designation) 308.
τοῦ (gen.sing.masc.of the article in agreement with τυφλοῦ) 9.
τυφλοῦ (gen.sing.masc.of τυφλός, possession) 830.

#2316 ἐξήνεγκεν (3d.per.sing.aor.act.ind.of ἐξάγω, constative).

bring forth - Acts 5:19.
bring out - Acts 7:36,40; 12:17; 13:17; 16:39.
fetch out - Acts 16:37.
lead out - Mk.8:23; 15:20; Lk.24:50; John 10:3; Acts 21:38; Heb.8:9.

Meaning: A combination of ἐκ (#19) and ἄγω (#876). Hence, to lead or bring out. Once illustratively in John 10:3. In all other uses physical conduct of person or persons out of one place to another. Peter, John and the other apostles out of jail - Acts 5:19; Israel out of Egypt - Acts 7:36,40; 13:17; 21:38; Heb.8:9; Peter out of prison - Acts 12:17; Paul and Silas out of prison - Acts 16:37,39; Jesus led the blind man out of town to heal him - Mk.8:23. Jesus led the disciples out to the ascension site - Lk.24:50; Jesus was led out to be crucified - Mk.15:20.

αὐτὸν (acc.sing.masc.of αὐτός, direct object of ἐξήνεγκεν) 16.
ἔξω (improper preposition used adverbially with the ablative of separation) 449.
τῆς (abl.sing.fem.of the article in agreement with κώμης) 9.
κώμης (abl.sing.fem.of κώμη, separation) 834.
καὶ (adjunctive conjunction joining verbs) 14.
πτύσας (aor.act.part.nom.sing.masc.of πτύω, adverbial, temporal) 2309.
εἰς (preposition with the accusative of extent) 140.
τὰ (acc.pl.neut.of the article in agreement with ὄμματα) 9.
ὄμματα (acc.pl.neut.of ὄμμα, extent) 1339.
αὐτοῦ (gen.sing.masc.of αὐτός, possession) 16.
ἐπιθεὶς (aor.act.part.nom.sing.masc.of ἐπιτίθημι, adverbial, temporal) 818.
τὰς (acc.pl.fem.of the article in agreement with χεῖρας) 9.
χεῖρας (acc.pl.fem.of χείρ, direct object of ἐπιθεὶς) 308.
αὐτῷ (loc.sing.masc.of αὐτός, place where) 16.
ἐπηρώτα (3d.per.sing.imp.act.ind.of ἐπερωτάω, inceptive) 973.
αὐτόν (acc.sing.masc.of αὐτός, direct object of ἐπηρώτα) 16.
Εἴ (conditional particle in a first-class elliptical condition) 337.
τι (acc.sing.neut.of τις, direct object of βλέπεις) 486.
βλέπεις (2d.per.sing.pres.act.ind.of βλέπω, aoristic, in direct question) 499.

Translation - "*And He took the blind man by the hand and led him out of the village, and having spit into his eyes, He laid hands on him and began to ask him, 'Do you see anything?'* "

Comment: Note the aorist middle participle ἐπιλαβόμενος followed by the genitive of designation. Jesus laid His hand (middle voice) upon the hand of the blind man. In this case the Greek says that Jesus spat into the man's eyes. It is εἰς - "into" rather than ἐπί - "upon," which would have indicated his eyelids. Jesus placed His hands αὐτῷ - "upon him." Perhaps upon his eyes, though the text does not say so. Jesus *began* to ask him the question. This inceptive imperfect is a little strange here. The constative aorist would have done as well. The elliptical condition Εἰ τι βλέπεις is direct question. We have the protasis but not the apodosis. "The use of εἰ in a question is elliptical. It is really a condition with the conclusion not expressed or it is an indirect question (cf. Mk.15:44; Lu.23:6; Ph.3:12). It is used in the N.T., as in the LXX quite often (Gen.17:17, etc.). This construction with a direct question is unclassical and may be due to the Septuagint rendering of the Hebrew word by εἰ as well as by μή (Cf.Blass, *Grammar of New Testament Greek*, 260, as cited in Robertson, *Grammar*, 916). Cf.Mt.12:10, where we have Εἰ ἔξεστιν τοῖς σάββασιν θεραπεῦσαι; see also Mt.19:3; Mk.8:23; Lu.13:23; 22:49; Ac.1:6; 7:1; 19:2; 21:37; 22:25. Note the frequency in Luke. In Mk.10:2 (parallel to Mt.19:3) the question is indirect. The idiom, though singular, has "attained to all the rights of a direct interrogative" (Winer-Thayer, 509) by this time. The idiom may be illustrated by the Latin *an* which in later writers was used in direct questions. So *si,* used in the Vulgate to translate this εἰ, became in late Latin a direct interrogative particle. A similar ellipsis appears in the use of εἰ (cf. Heb.3:11) in the negative sense of a strong oath (from the LXX also) (Robertson, *Short Grammar, 179, as cited in Ibid*). Cf. our comments on Mk.8:12 (*Renaissance New Testament*, 5, 573).It will help the student to understand this idiom if he imagines what the apodosis would be if the conditional sentence were complete. In Mk.8:12 "If a sign is given to this generation — — — they would not believe it." In Mk.8:23 "If you see anything — — — tell me."

Note our comment on Mk.7:33,34. Since Jesus did spit into the blind man's eyes it is possible that He spat upon the dumb man's tongue, though we repeat that Mk.7:33 does not make it clear. Any explanation as to why Jesus took the deaf mute and the blind man aside to effect the respective healings would be completely fanciful, since the text does not tell us why in either case.

In reply to Jesus' question the man said,

Verse 24 - "And he looked up and said, I see men as trees, walking."

καὶ ἀναβλέψας ἔλεγεν, Βλέπω τοὺς ἀνθρώπους, ὅτι ὡς δένδρα ὁρῶ περιπατοῦντας.

καὶ (inferential conjunction) 14.

ἀναβλέψας (aor.act.part.nom.sing.masc.of ἀναβλέπω, adverbial, temporal) 907.

ἔλεγεν (3d.per.sing.imp.act.ind.of λέγω, inceptive) 66.

Βλέπω (1st.per.sing.pres.act.ind.of βλέπω, progressive) 499.

τοὺς (acc.pl.masc.of the article in agreement with ἀνθρώπους) 9.

ἀνθρώπους (acc.pl.masc.of ἄνθρωπος, direct object of βλέπω) 341.

ὅτι (declarative conjunction introducing indirect discourse with the participle) 211.

ὡς (adverb introducing a comparative clause) 128.

δένδρα (acc.pl.neut.of δένδρον, direct object of ὁρῶ) 294.

ὁρῶ (1st.per.sing.pres.act.ind.of ὁράω, progressive) 144.

περιπατοῦντας (pres.act.part.acc.pl.masc.of περιπατέω, adverbial, circumstantial) 384.

Translation - *"Therefore he looked up and said, 'I see the men as though I see trees walking around.' "*

Comment: We could translate, ". . . but they look to me like trees walking about," or "I see the men as trees." The imperfect in ἔλεγεν indicates the man's excitement. In reply to Jesus' question he began to speak and repeated it again and again, "I see. . . I see. . . I see. . . " Meyer interprets ὅτι as causal - thus, "I see the men because as trees I see them walking around." Goodspeed reads into ὅτι both a causal and an adversative idea, with "I can see the people, *for* (because/but, *our parenthesis*) they look to me like trees, *only* (but, except that *our parenthesis*) they are moving about." All of these translations are close enough to the original so as not to confuse the reader. The patient was helped but not yet cured.

Verse 25 - *"After that he put his hands again upon his eyes, and made him look up: and he was restored, and saw every man clearly."*

εἶτα πάλιν ἐπέθηκεν τὰς χεῖρας ἐπὶ τοὺς ὀφθαλμοὺς αὐτοῦ, καὶ διέβλεψεν, καὶ ἀπεκατέστη, καὶ ἐνέβλεπεν τηλαυγῶς ἅπαντα.

εἶτα (temporal conjunction) 2185.
πάλιν (adverbial) 355.
ἔθηκεν (3d.per.sing.aor.act.ind.of τίθημι, constative) 455.
τὰς (acc.pl.fem.of the article in agreement with χεῖρας) 9.
χεῖρας (acc.pl.fem.of χείρ, direct object of ἔθηκεν) 308.
ἐπὶ (preposition with the accusative, extent) 47.
τοὺς (acc.pl.masc.of the article in agreement with ὀφθαλμούς) 9.
ὀφθαλμοὺς (acc.pl.masc.of ὀφθαλμός, extent, place where) 501.
αὐτοῦ (gen.sing.masc.of αὐτός, possession) 16.
διέβλεψεν (3d.per.sing.aor.act.ind.of διαβλέπω, ingressive) 650.
καὶ (adjunctive conjunction joining verbs) 14.
ἀπεκατέστη (3d.per.sing.aor.pass.ind.of ἀποκαθίστημι, culminative) 978.
καὶ (adjunctive conjunction joining verbs) 14.
ἐνέβλεπεν (3d.per.sing.imp.act.ind.of ἐμβλέπω, inceptive) 614.

#2317 τηλαυγῶς (adverbial).

clearly - Mk.8:25.

Meaning: From τῆλε "from afar" plus αὐγή "radiance." Hence, at a distance and clearly. "The force of the word is well brought out in a magical formula, P Oxy VI.886 (iii/A.D.), which, after various directions for obtaining an omen, ends χρημαθισθήσῃ (*l.*χρηματισθήσῃ) τηλαυγῶς, "you will obtain an illuminating answer" (Edd.). (Moulton and Milligan, *The Vocabulary of the Greek New Testament,* 633).

ἅπαντα (acc.pl.neut.of ἅπας, direct object of ἐνέβλεπεν) 639.

Translation - "*Then again He put His hands upon his eyes, and he began to see with penetrating vision, and his sight was restored, and he began to look with clarity at everything in the distance.*"

Comment: εἶτα - "then" in the sense of "after that."In πάλιν we have the evidence that Jesus did, in fact, lay His hands upon the man's eyes before (vs.23), although Mark did not then say so. The tenses of the verbs which follow are revealing. The patient began to see clearly, with no obstruction (ingressive aorist in διέβλεφεν). His sight was completely restored (culminative aorist in ἀπεκατέστη). And he began (inceptive imperfect in ἐνέβλεπεν) to test the cure by looking at everything (ἅπας) at a distance, all of which he saw clearly (τηλαυγῶς). Note that Mark uses the intensive ἅπας (#639) rather than πᾶς (#67).

A careful study of all of the significant words in this story will provide many insights into spiritual matters. The student should run the references on #'s 830, 2316, 978, 650 and 614. Because Jesus was destined to be led out to Calvary to die for our sins, He was able to lead the blind man out of the village in order to restore his sight. He heals spiritual as well as physical blindness. The child of God sees with penetration and is fully restored in Christ to the position for which God created him.

Verse 26 - "*And he sent him away to his house, saying, Neither go into the town, nor tell it to any in the town.*"

καὶ ἀπέστειλεν αὐτὸν εἰς οἶκον αὐτοῦ λέγων, Μηδὲ εἰς τὴν κώμην εἰσέλθῃς.

καὶ (continuative conjunction) 14.
ἀπέστειλεν (3d.per.sing.aor.act.ind.of ἀποστέλλω, constative) 215.
αὐτὸν (acc.sing.masc.of αὐτός, direct object of ἀπέστειλεν) 16.
εἰς (preposition with the accusative of extent) 140.
οἶκον (acc.sing.masc.of οἶκος, extent) 784.
αὐτοῦ (gen.sing.masc.of αὐτός, possession) 16.
λέγων (pres.act.part.nom.sing.masc.of λέγω, adverbial, modal) 66.
Μηδὲ (disjunctive particle) 612.
εἰς (preposition with the accusative of extent) 140.
τὴν (acc.sing.fem.of the article in agreement with κώμην) 9.
κώμην (acc.sing.fem.of κώμη, extent) 834.
εἰσέλθῃς (2d.per.sing.2d.aor.subj.of εἰσέρχομαι, prohibition) 234.

Translation - "*And He sent him away unto his home, saying, 'But do not go into the village.'* "

Comment: Jesus ordered the man to go home and added that he should not go back to the village on the way. Note the subjunctive of prohibition instead of the imperative. Had the man gone back to Bethsaida he would have created a sensation, something which Jesus apparently wished to avoid.

The second section of Part III contains a series of episodes with Jesus and the

Twelve, the first of which involves His question in Caesarea Philippi - Mk.8:27-30; Mt.16:13-20; Lk.9:18-21. Review Mt.16:13-20. We shall now examine Mk.8:27-30.

Mk.8:27 - "And Jesus went out and his disciples into the towns of Caesarea Philippi: and by the way he asked his disciples saying unto them, Whom do men say that I am?"

Καὶ ἐξῆλθεν ὁ Ἰησοῦς καὶ οἱ μαθηταὶ αὐτοῦ εἰς τὰς κώμας Καισαρείας τῆς Φιλίππου, καὶ ἐν τῇ ὁδῷ ἐπηρώτα τοὺς μαθητὰς αὐτοῦ λέγων αὐτοῖς, Τίνα με λέγουσιν οἱ ἄνθρωποι εἶναι;

Καὶ (continuative conjunction) 14.

ἐξῆλθεν (3d.per.sing.aor.ind.of ἐξέρχομαι, constative) 161.

ὁ (nom.sing.masc.of the article in agreement with Ἰησοῦς) 9.

Ἰησοῦς (nom.sing.masc.of Ἰησοῦς, subject of ἐξῆλθεν) 3.

καὶ (adjunctive conjunction joining nouns) 14.

οἱ (nom.pl.masc.of the article in agreement with μαθηταὶ) 9.

μαθηταὶ (nom.pl.masc.of μαθητής, subject of ἐξῆλθεν) 421.

αὐτοῦ (gen.sing.masc.of αὐτός, relationship) 16.

εἰς (preposition with the accusative of extent) 140.

τὰς (acc.pl.fem.of the article in agreement with κώμας) 9.

κώμας (acc.pl.fem.of κώμη, extent) 834.

Καισαρείας (gen.sing.fem.of Καισαρείας, description) 1200.

τῆς (gen.sing.fem.of the article in agreement with Καισαρείας) 9.

Φιλίππου (gen.sing.masc.of Φίλιππος, description) 1108.

καὶ (continuative conjunction) 14.

ἐν (preposition with the locative of time point) 80.

τῇ (loc.sing.fem.of the article in agreement with ὁδῷ) 9.

ὁδῷ (loc.sing.fem.of ὁδός, time point) 199.

ἐπηρώτα (3d.per.sing.imp.act.ind.of ἐπερωτάω, inceptive) 973.

τοὺς (acc.pl.masc.of the article in agreement with μαθητὰς) 9.

μαθητὰς (acc.pl.masc.of μαθητής, direct object of ἐπηρώτα) 421.

αὐτοῦ (gen.sing.masc.of αὐτός, relationship) 16.

λέγων (pres.act.part.nom.sing.masc.of λέγω, adverbial, modal) 66.

αὐτοῖς (dat.pl.masc.of αὐτός, indirect object of λέγων) 16.

Τίνα (acc.sing.masc.of τίς, direct object of λέγουσιν, indirect question) 281.

με (acc.sing.masc.of ἐγώ, general reference) 123.

λέγουσιν (3d.per.pl.pres.act.ind.of λέγω, aoristic) 66.

οἱ (nom.pl.masc.of the article in agreement with ἄνθρωποι) 9.

ἄνθρωποι (nom.pl.masc.of ἄνθρωπος, subject of λέγουσιν) 341.

εἶναι (pres.act.inf.of εἰμί, indirect discourse) 86.

Translation - "And Jesus and His disciples went out into the villages of Caesarea Philippi; and as they went He began to ask His disciples, saying to them, 'Who do the people say that I am?' "

Comment: It was time that Jesus force upon His disciples a commitment. They had followed Him now for a little more than two years. They had seen His miracles - feats of miraculous performance which could be explained only with the assumption that God walked on earth incarnate in human flesh (John 3:1-3). They had heard His teachings, as He taught with an authority which the Scribes could not command. They had witnessed His bouts with Israel's best gainsayers and had seen them leave the battlefield speechless, crestfallen and burning with the insane hatred born only of frustration. They had heard Him say that saving faith is a gift of the Father, given to whom He has chosen and not contingent upon human reason and/or merit (John 6:27-71.

It was not that the disciples had been totally devoid of spiritual perception. When Jesus lost His crowds at the close of His statement of John 6:27-65 and turned to Peter and his colleagues suggesting that perhaps they too would like to join the deserters, Peter's statement was a thrilling confession of the faith of those uneducated Galileans. The big fisherman had asked, "Lord, to whom shall we go? You have the words of eternal life, and we believe and are convinced that you are the Holy One from God" (John 6:68,69). Yet there were times when the disciples had failed to display the spiritual perceptivity which He had some reason, by this time, to expect (Mk.8:14-21, *e.g.*).

Our Lord was about to reveal the future to them, but He must get from them a firm confession that He was indeed the Messiah, since what He was about to tell them was, from their limited point of view, totally inconsistent with the role that they understood the Messiah was to play. Jesus' description of the shape of things soon to come was replete with shocking, terrifying and yet glorious events. His death, burial, bodily resurrection and second coming was to be revealed to them in only a few more days, but not until they indicated clearly that they knew who He is. It was time to put them on record.

A good teacher looks ahead and tries to anticipate the reaction of his students to new material which he is about to reveal. Preliminary breaking of the mental ground is necessary if the student is to avoid the trauma that otherwise may result from the revelation of what to the student is inconsistent with the pattern which he has been constructing. This is a concession to the gestalt psychology, known perfectly, of course by Him in Whom are hid all the treasures of wisdom and knowledge (Col.2:3), although only recently discovered by His inept creations.

Jesus' approach was oblique. Had His motive been evil we would be justified in calling it devious or underhanded. But His motives were never evil and His pedagogy here is superb. It was easy for the disciples to tell Him what other men said about Him. Such reporting involved no personal commitment. So they replied to His first question, which He pressed upon them again and again (inceptive imperfect) with alacrity. Will they be so eager to reply when He puts them on the spot? Note the present infinitive εἶναι in indirect discourse, which conforms to the tense used in direct discourse. Directly men were saying, "Jesus *is* . . . . κ.τ.λ." Thus the infinitive is in the present tense.

Verse 28 - "And they answered, John the Baptist: but some say, Elias; and others,

One of the prophets."

οἱ δὲ εἶπαν αὐτῷ λέγοντες (ὅτι) Ἰωάννην τὸν βαπτιστήν, καὶ ἄλλοι, Ἡλίαν, ἄλλοι δὲ ὅτι εἷς τῶν προφητῶν.

οἱ (nom.pl.masc.of the article in agreement with λέγοντες) 9.

δὲ (continuative conjunction) 11.

εἶπαν (3d.per.pl.aor.act.ind.of εἶπον, constative) 155.

αὐτῷ (dat.sing.masc.of αὐτός, indirect object of εἶπαν) 16.

λέγοντες (pres.act.part.nom.pl.masc.of λέγω, substantival, subject of εἶπαν) 66.

(ὅτι) (recitative) 211.

Ἰωάννην (acc.sing.masc.of Ἰωάννης, predicate accusative) 247.

τὸν (acc.sing.masc.of the article in agreement with βαπτιστήν) 9.

βαπτιστήν (acc.sing.masc.of βαπτιστής, apposition) 248.

καὶ (adversative conjunction) 14.

ἄλλοι (nom.pl.masc.of ἄλλος, subject of λέγουσιν, understood) 198.

Ἡλίαν (acc.sing.masc.of Ἡλίας, predicate accusative) 921.

ἄλλοι (nom.pl.masc.of ἄλλος, subject of λέγουσιν, understood) 198.

δὲ (adversative conjunction) 11.

ὅτι (conjunction introducing an object clause in indirect discourse) 211.

εἷς (nom.sing.masc.of εἷς, predicate nominative) 469.

τῶν (gen.pl.masc.of the article in agreement with προφητῶν) 9.

προφητῶν (gen.pl.masc.of προφήτης, partitive genitive) 119.

Translation - "And those who replied said, 'John the Baptist,' but others said, 'Elias,' but still others say that you are one of the prophets."

Comment: Not all of the disciples responded to Jesus' question. Those who did (οἱ λέγοντες) said (εἶπαν) what is reported. They reported accurately what the people were saying, although what was being said was incorrect. It was when in verse 29, Jesus asked them for their opinion that Peter gave the right response.

Public opinion was mixed with reference to the question. All agreed that Jesus who had appeared on the horizon of human history was no ordinary individual, whether they attributed His powers to Satan or to God. His miracles, His teaching, His personality - everything about Him suggested the supernatural, be He deity or demoniac. That Israel should fail to see Him as their Messiah is strange. But at least they attributed to Him a supernatural origin and a great many believed that it was heavenly, not hellish.

Perhaps John the Baptist had returned from the grave to haunt Herod, Salome and Herodias (Mt.14:2). Perhaps He was Elijah in fulfillment of Mal.4:5,6. Others suggested one of the prophets. The use of the article makes it definite to indicate that they meant some one from the particular roster of prophets, whose writings comprised the Old Testament - Jeremiah, Isaiah, Amos, etc., etc - not a hitherto unknown prophet, come to terminate the long reign of silence following Malachi.

Jesus' enemies had called Him Beelzeboul (#883, Mt.10:25). It is significant that the common people, while not recognizing Jesus as Messiah, at least considered Him a messenger from God. At a later time they will call Him "The Son of David" as the Syrophoenician woman, a pagan, already had done. *Cf.* comment on Mt.16:14.

Verse 29 - "And he saith unto them, But whom say ye that I am? And Peter answereth and saith unto him, Thou art the Christ."

καὶ αὐτὸς ἐπηρώτα αὐτοῖς, Ὑμεῖς δὲ τίνα με λέγετε εἶναι; ἀποκριθεὶς ὁ Πέτρος λέγει αὐτῷ, Σὺ εἶ ὁ Χριστός.

καὶ (continuative conjunction) 14.

αὐτὸς (nom.sing.masc.of αὐτός, subject of ἐπηρώτα) 16.

ἐπηρώτα (3d.per.sing.imp.act.ind.of ἐπερωτάω, inceptive) 973.

αὐτούς (acc.pl.masc.of αὐτός, direct object of ἐπηρώτα) 16.

Ὑμεῖς (nom.pl.masc.of σύ, subject of λέγετε, emphatic) 104.

δὲ (adversative conjunction) 11.

τίνα (acc.sing.masc.of τίς, direct object of λέγετε, indirect discourse) 281.

με (acc.sing.masc.of ἐγώ, general reference) 123.

λέγετε (2d.per.pl.pres.act.ind.of λέγω, indirect discourse) 66.

εἶναι (pres.inf.of εἰμί, indirect discourse) 86.

ἀποκριθεὶς (aor.part.nom.sing.masc.of ἀποκρίνομαι, adverbial, modal) 318.

ὁ (nom.sing.masc.of the article in agreement with Πέτρος) 9.

Πέτρος (nom.sing.masc.of Πέτρος, subject of λέγει) 387.

λέγει (3d.per.sing.pres.act.ind.of λέγω, historical) 66.

αὐτῷ (dat.sing.masc.of αὐτός, indirect object of λέγει) 16.

Σὺ (nom.sing.masc.of σύ, subject of εἶ, emphatic) 104.

εἶ (2d.per.sing.pres.ind.of εἰμί, aoristic) 86.

ὁ (nom.sing.masc.of the article in agreement with Χριστός) 9.

Χριστός (nom.sing.masc.of Χριστός, predicate nominative) 4.

Translation - "But He began to press them with the question, 'But you - who do you say that I am?' In reply Peter said to Him, 'You - you are the Messiah.' "

Comment: Comes now the moment of truth. Jesus pressed them with His question (inceptive imperfect in ἐπηρώτα). δὲ is adversative, as though Jesus were saying, "I know what the people are saying about me, *but* what about *you*?" Note that Ὑμεῖς is also emphatic. "Never mind what others are saying. What is *your* opinion? You know me better than anyone else. Yours has been the closest and most intimate relationship with me. You have had the best opportunity to evaluate both my person and my work." His question may be thought of in the same light as His challenge to the Pharisees, "Which of you convinces me of sin?" (John 8:46). Certainly if the disciples had seen the slightest evidence of sin in Jesus' behavior Peter would not have replied as he did, since moral guilt, however small, was totally out of character with their conception of the Messiah. And yet Peter answered simply and without a moment's hesitation. Σὺ εἶ ὁ Χριστός. Matthew's report adds ὁ υἱὸς τοῦ θεοῦ τοῦ ζῶντος - "the son of the living God" (Mt.16:16). Peter had made a previous confession in John 6:68,69.

Note Mt.16:17 where Jesus denies that Peter's confession is the result of his having observed and weighed evidence, but rather of his having had revealed unto him the truth by the Father. This is in line with what Jesus had said prior to Peter's confession in John 6:44,65,68,69. To content that on the basis of pragmatic observation Peter had reasoned his way to faith in Christ, is to partake of the leaven of the Pharisees who were willing to consider evidence on their own terms if Jesus would supply it. This is to reason in the tradition of Thomas Aquinas who argued that man's reasoning process is not fallen, but rather a sure guide to truth. Roman Catholic theologians since, with the exception of Blaise Pascal and his Jansenist followers, should be embarrassed by Jesus' disclaimer of Mt.16:17. Arminians, in the tradition of Pelagius, also reveal some toleration for this idea, when they say that the salvation equation rests upon God's will and man's decision arrived at by his uninfluenced intellect.

At this point Mark and Luke prepare to close the incident while Matthew adds the material in Mt.16:17-19, *q.v.*

Verse 30 - "And he charged them that they should tell no man of him."

καὶ ἐπετίμησεν αὐτοῖς ἵνα μηδενὶ λέγωσιν περὶ αὐτοῦ.

καὶ (continuative conjunction) 14.
ἐπετίμησεν (3d.per.sing.aor.act.ind.of ἐπιτιμάω, constative) 757.
αὐτοῖς (dat.pl.masc.of αὐτός, indirect object of ἐπετίμησεν) 16.
ἵνα (final conjunction introducing a purpose clause) 114.
μηδενὶ (dat.sing.masc.of μηδείς, indirect object of λέγωσιν) 713.
λέγωσιν (3d.per.pl.pres.act.subj.of λέγω, purpose) 66.
περὶ (preposition with the genitive of reference) 173.
αὐτοῦ (gen.sing.masc.of αὐτός, reference) 16.

Translation - "And He sternly ordered them not to talk to anyone about Him."

Comment: Matthew, Mark and Luke all use ἐπιτιμάω here. *Cf.* Mt.16:20 and Luke 9:21. He give them strict orders not to tell anyone what they knew about Him. "Threaten" is to strong, but Jesus may have had an edge on His voice. The purpose clause with ἵνα follows. Why not? The text does not tell us why Jesus made this demand. *The Expositors' Greek Testament* says, "The prohibition might have a double reference: to the people, to prevent the spread of crude ideas as to the Messiahship of Jesus; to the disciples that they might keep the new faith to themselves till it took deep root in their own souls. Recall Carlyle's counsel to young men: if thou hast an idea keep it to thyself for as soon as thou hast spoken it it is dead to thee" - "Stump Orator in Latter Day Pamphlets" (*Expositors' Greek Testament*, I, 397).

Luke 9:18 - "And it came to pass, as he was alone praying, his disciples were with him: and he asked them, saying, Whom say the people that I am?"

Καὶ ἐγένετο ἐν τῷ εἶναι αὐτὸν προσευχόμενον κατὰ μόνας συνῆσαν αὐτῷ οἱ μαθηταί, καὶ ἐπηρώτησεν αὐτοὺς λέγων, Τίνα με λέγουσιν οἱ ὄχλοι εἶναι;

Καὶ (continuative conjunction) 14.

ἐγένετο (3d.per.sing.aor.ind.of γίνομαι, constative) 113.

ἐν (preposition introducing a temporal clause with the articular infinitive) 80.

τῷ (loc.sing.masc.of the article, time point) 9.

εἶναι (pres.inf.of εἰμί, loc.of time point) 86.

αὐτὸν (acc.sing.masc.of αὐτός, general reference) 16.

προσευχόμενον (pres.part.acc.sing.masc.of προσεύχομαι, adverbial, circumstantial) 544.

κατὰ (preposition with the accusative, adverbial, general reference) 98.

μόνας (acc.pl.masc.of μόνος, general reference, with κατὰ) 339.

συνῆσαν (3d.per.pl.imp.act.ind.of σύνειμι, progressive duration) 2194.

αὐτῷ (instrumental of association after σύν, in composition) 16.

οἱ (nom.pl.masc.of the article in agreement with μαθηταὶ) 9.

μαθηταὶ (nom.pl.masc.of μαθητής, subject of συνῆσαν) 421.

καὶ (continuative conjunction) 14.

ἐπηρώτησεν (3d.per.sing.aor.act.ind.of ἐπερωτάω, ingressive) 973.

αὐτοὺς (acc.pl.masc.of αὐτός, direct object of ἐπηρώτησεν) 16.

λέγων (pres.act.part.nom.sing.masc.of λέγω, recitative) 66.

Τίνα (acc.sing.masc.of τίς, direct object of λέγουσιν) 281.

με (acc.sing.masc.of ἐγώ, general reference) 123.

οἱ (nom.pl.masc.of the article in agreement with ὄχλοι) 9.

ὄχλοι (nom.pl.masc.of ὄχλος, subject of λέγουσιν) 418.

λέγουσιν (3d.per.pl.pres.act.ind.of λέγω, progressive) 66.

εἶναι (pres.inf.of εἰμί, indirect discourse) 86.

Translation - *"And it so happened that while He was alone in prayer (the disciples were with Him) He began to ask them, 'Who do the people say that I am?' "*

Comment: The temporal clause here is introduced by ἐν with the articular infinitive in the locative case, indicating a point in time. It was while He was praying. The participle is circumstantial. He was alone. *Cf.* Mk.4:10 for κατὰ μόνας as an adverbial idiom. Luke adds in an aside that the disciples were with Him, a fact that is in keeping with Matthew and Mark. *Cf.* Mt.16:13; Mk.8:27. Though accompanied by His disciples Jesus was temporarily free from the endless crowds of people who normally surrounded Him. He asked the disciples the direct question introduced by λέγων. Note the infinitive εἶναι is indirect discourse. We can be certain that ἐπηρώτησεν (Lk.9:18) is ingressive, since we have the inceptive imperfect forms in the parallel accounts in Mt.16:13 and Mk.6:27. Note that in Mark and Luke we have με, while Matthew has τὸν υἱὸν τοῦ ἀνθρώπου.

Luke does not report on any of the events reported from Mk.6:45 to Mk.8:26, although Matthew, who probably had the Markan document before him, parallels Mark's story. We can only conjecture as to the reason for this hiatus.

There is no gap in the revelation since Mark and Matthew record the intervening history in detail. Lk.9:17 records the feeding of the five thousand, while Lk.9:18 picks up the story after the healing of the blind man in Bethsaida.

Verse 19 - "They answering said, John the Baptist; but some say, Elias; and others say that one of the old prophets is risen again."

οἱ δὲ ἀποκριθέντες εἶπαν, Ἰωάννην τὸν βαπτιστήν, ἄλλοι δὲ Ἡλίαν, ἄλλοι δὲ ὅτι προφήτης τις ἀρχαίων ἀνέστη.

οἱ (nom.pl.masc.of the article, subject of εἶπαν) 9.
δὲ (continuative conjunction) 11.
ἀποκριθέντες (aor.part.nom.pl.masc.of ἀποκρίνομαι, adverbial, modal) 318.
εἶπαν (3d.per.pl.aor.act.ind.of εἶπον, constative) 155.
Ἰωάννην (acc.sing.masc.of Ἰωάννης, predicate accusative) 247.
τὸν (acc.sing.masc.of the article in agreement with βαπτιστήν) 9.
βαπτιστήν (acc.sing.masc.of βαπτιστής, apposition) 248.
ἄλλοι (nom.pl.masc.of ἄλλος, subject of λέγουσιν, understood) 198.
δὲ (adversative conjunction) 11.
Ἡλίαν (acc.sing.masc.of Ἡλίας, predicate accusative) 921.
ἄλλοι (nom.pl.masc.of ἄλλος, subject of λέγουσιν understood) 198.
δὲ (adversative conjunction) 11.
ὅτι (conjunction introducing an object clause in indirect discourse) 211.
προφήτης (nom.sing.masc.of προφήτης , subject of ἀνέστη) 119.
τις (nom.sing.masc.of τις, indefinite pronoun, in agreement with προφήτης) 486.
τῶν (gen.pl.masc.of the article in agreement with ἀρχαίων) 9.
ἀρχαίων (gen.pl.masc.of ἀρχαῖος, partitive genitive) 475.
ἀνέστη (3d.per.sing.aor.act.ind.of ἀνίστημι, culminative) 789.

Translation - "And in reply they said, 'John the Baptist; but others say Elias and still others that a certain of the old prophets has arisen.' "

Comment: "A certain prophet of the old school" as it would be expressed in some sections of the United States. Note the strong active voice which Luke uses in ἀνέστη. Mark's language in Mk.8:28 left us in doubt as to whether the people meant one of the old prophets who had died and been resurrected, or a new one who claimed a divine commission. Luke leaves no doubt that they meant it in the former sense. Thus we have the advantage of the correlative accounts. *Cf.* comments on Mt.16:14 and Mk.8:28.

Verse 20 - "He said unto them, But whom say ye that I am? Peter answering said, The Christ of God."

εἶπεν δὲ αὐτοῖς, Ὑμεῖς δὲ τίνα με λέγετε εἶναι; Πέτρος δὲ ἀποκριθεὶς εἶπεν, Τὸν Χριστὸν τοῦ θεοῦ.

εἶπεν (3d.per.sing.aor.act.ind.of εἶπον, constative) 155.
δὲ (adversative conjunction) 11.

αὐτοῖς (dat.pl.masc.of αὐτός, indirect object of εἶπεν) 16.
Ὑμεῖς (nom.sing.masc.of σύ, subject of λέγετε, emphatic) 104.
δὲ (adversative conjunction) 11.
τίνα (acc.sing.masc.of τίς, direct object of λέγετε, indirect discourse) 281.
με (acc.sing.masc.of ἐγώ, general reference) 123.
λέγετε (2d.per.pl.pres.act.ind.of λέγω, aoristic) 66.
εἶναι (pres.infinitive of εἰμί, indirect discourse) 86.
Πέτρος (nom.sing.masc.of Πέτρος, subject of εἶπεν) 387.
δὲ (continuative conjunction) 11.
ἀποκριθεὶς (aor.part.nom.sing.masc.of ἀποκρίνομαι, adverbial, modal) 318.
εἶπεν (3d.per.sing.aor.act.ind.of εἶπον, constative) 155.
Τὸν (acc.sing.masc.of the article in agreement with Χριστὸν) 9.
Χριστὸν (acc.sing.masc.of Χριστός, predicate accusative) 4.
τοῦ (abl.sing.masc.of the article in agreement with θεοῦ) 9.
θεοῦ (abl.sing.masc.of θεός, source) 124.

Translation - "But He said to them, 'But you - whom do you say that I am?' Peter said in reply, 'The Anointed One from God.' "

Comment: We may take δὲ as adversative, as Jesus contrasts what others were saying about Him with what the disciples might say. Matthew and Mark report Jesus' question in identical formulation with Luke's account. Peter, the spokesman for the disciples replied. Luke shortens Mark's version while Matthew gives the full statement. *Cf.* comment on the parallel accounts in Mt.16:16 and Mk.8:29.

Verse 21 - "And he straitly charged them, and commanded them to tell no man that thing."

Ὁ δὲ ἐπιτιμήσας αὐτοῖς παρήγγειλεν μηδενὶ λέγειν τοῦτο,

Ὁ (nom.sing.masc.of the article, subject of παρήγγειλεν) 9.
δὲ (continuative conjunction) 11.
ἐπιτιμήσας (aor.act.part.nom.sing.masc.of ἐπιτιμάω, adverbial, modal) 757.
αὐτοῖς (dat.pl.masc.of αὐτός,indirect object of ἐπιτιμήσας) 16.
παρήγγειλεν (3d.per.sing.aor.act.ind.of παραγγέλλω, constative) 855.
μηδενὶ (dat.sing.masc.of μηδείς, indirect object of λέγειν) 713.
λέγειν (pres.act.inf.of λέγω, complementary) 66.
τοῦτο (acc.sing.neut.of οὗτος, direct object of λέγειν) 93.

Translation - "And He inexorably ordered them to tell this to no one."

Comment: It would be natural to suppose that Jesus would wish the disciples to go about preaching the good news that Messiah, long anticipated by a suffering people, had at last arrived. On the contrary He sternly demanded total silence on the point. The reason is clear in verse 22. The participle ἐπιτιμήσας carried with it a degree of emphasis that amounts almost to severity. τοῦτο in Luke is defined in Mk.8:30 as περὶ αὐτοῦ and in Mt.16:20 as ὅτι αὐτός ἐστιν ὁ Χριστός.

Christ Foretells His Death and Resurrection and Rebukes Peter

(Lk.9:22-25; Mt.16:21-26; Mk.8:31-37)

(Review Mt.16:21-26)

Lk.9:22 - "... *saying, The Son of Man must suffer many things, and be rejected of the elders and chief priests and scribes, and be slain, and be raised the third day.*"

εἰπὼν ὅτι Δεῖ τὸν υἱὸν τοῦ ἀνθρώπου πολλὰ παθεῖν καὶ ἀποδοκιμασθῆναι ἀπὸ τῶν πρεσβυτέρων καὶ ἀρχιερέων καὶ γραμματέων καὶ ἀποκτανθῆναι καὶ τῇ τρίτῃ ἡμέρᾳ ἐγερθῆναι.

εἰπὼν (aor.act.part.nom.sing.masc.of εἶπον, adverbial, causal) 155.
ὅτι (recitative) 211.
Δεῖ (3d.per.sing.impersonal, present of δέω, aoristic) 1207.
τὸν (acc.sing.masc.of the article in agreement with υἱὸν) 9.
υἱὸν (acc.sing.masc.of υἱός, general reference) 5.
τοῦ (gen.sing.masc.of the article in agreement with ἀνθρώπου) 9.
ἀνθρώπου (gen.sing.masc.of ἄνθρωπος, definition) 341.
πολλὰ (acc.pl.neut.of πολύς, direct object of παθεῖν) 228.
παθεῖν (aor.act.inf.of πάσχω, epexegetical) 1208.
καὶ (adjunctive conjunction joining infinitives) 14.
ἀποδοκιμασθῆναι (1st.aor.pass.inf.of ἀποδοκιμάζω, epexegetical) 1390.
ἀπὸ (preposition with the ablative of agent) 70.
τῶν (abl.pl.masc.of the article in agreement with πρεσβυτέρων) 9.
πρεσβυτέρων (abl.pl.masc.of πρεσβύτερος, agency) 1141.
καὶ (adjunctive conjunction joining nouns) 14.
ἀρχιερέων (abl.pl.masc.of ἀρχιερεύς, agency) 151.
καὶ (adjunctive conjunction joining nouns) 14.
γραμματέων (abl.pl.masc.of γραμματεύς, agency) 152.
καὶ (adjunctive conjunction joining infinitives) 14.
ἀποκτανθῆναι (1st.aor.pass.inf.of ἀποκτείνω, epexegetical) 889.
καὶ (adjunctive conjunction joining infinitives) 14.
τῇ (loc.sing.fem.of the article in agreement with ἡμέρᾳ) 9.
τρίτῃ (loc.sing.fem.of τρίτος, in agreement with ἡμέρᾳ) 1209.
ἡμέρᾳ (loc.sing.fem.of ἡμέρα, time point) 135.
ἐγερθῆναι (1st.aor.pass.inf.of ἐγείρω, epexegetical) 125.

Translation - "... *because He went on to say, 'It is necessary for the Son of Man to endure much suffering and to be repudiated by the elders and priests and scribes and to be killed and on the third day to be raised from the dead.'* "

Comment: εἰπὼν, the causal participle, tells us why Jesus ordered the disciples not to announce Him as the Messiah. They were correct about His person, but were only partially informed about His work (Mt.16:17,23). ὅτι introduces Jesus' statement in direct discourse. Δεῖ - "It is in God's plan and therefore necessary." *Cf.*#1207, 5 for other uses of δεῖ in this sense. Whatever God has decreed is "necessary" *i.e.* it *must* happen. There is a good series of sermons in these examples of Divine Necessity. *Cf.*Mt.26:54; Lk.4:43; Mt.16:21; 17:10; Lk.2:49; John 3:14; Lk.9:22. Δεῖ is completed and explained by the epexegetical infinitives ἀποκτανθῆναι, ἀποδοκιμασθῆναι, ἐγερθῆναι and παθεῖν. He must suffer, be rejected, murdered, but raised again. *Cf.*#1390 for the meaning of ἀποδοκιμάζω. I Pet.2:4,7; Mt.21:42; Mk.12:10; Lk.20:17; Mk.8:31; Lk.9:22; 17:25; Heb.12:17. In all cases except Heb.12:17 the words refers to Christ. Esau in Heb.12:17. Our Lord's death was necessary for our salvation. The designation ῾Ο υἱὸς τοῦ ἀνθρώπου - "The Son of Man" marks Him as Messiah, to be sure, but Messiah cannot reign over a perfect society of perfected people until He has paid the sin debt for those people.

The humiliation of repudiation by the petty elders, priests and scribes was an affront to which Jesus was compelled to submit. It was a part of His *kenosis* - *cf.*#388 (Phil.2:7). No one except Him, in whom are hid all of the treasures of wisdom and knowledge (Col.2:3) could know the frustration of being snubbed by the petty generation - a haughty but utterly superficial lot of religious bigots in Israel. But *it had to be.* (Δεῖ). ἀποκτανθῆναι - "murdered" is not too strong a word for translation, since from the Jewish legal viewpoint, there was no ground in either Jewish or Roman law for His execution. The final καὶ can be taken as gloriously adversative! He suffered, He was humiliated, He was murdered, **BUT** there is resurrection. How many obscenities and indecencies, how much ribaldry and smut, how dreadful the scurrility and lewdness and how excruciating the agony involved in πολλὰ no one but the Son of God knows!

It is clear now why Jesus told the disciples not to tell anyone that He was the Messiah. Messiah, indeed, but in His first coming He must suffer and die. This is the part of God's plan that Israel did not understand. "Blindness in part hath happened to Israel" (Rom.11:25). Had the disciples proclaimed Him King and then added that the King must be rejected by His own subjects, confusion would have resulted. It was a problem in pedagogy. A good teacher does not force feed his students.

Meyer points out that Messiah's right to David's throne is authenticated by His resurrection (Rom.1:4). Resurrection occurs only among "crucified" Messiahs. The announcement that Jesus was King Messiah awaited His bodily resurrection. It was only after the resurrection that the Apostles openly proclaimed Him King of the Jews.

Matthew at this point reports Peter's remonstrance against Jesus' death and our Lord's response. *Cf.* Mt.16:22,23. If even Peter did not understand, how could we expect the Jewish public to understand? The delightful news that Messiah had arrived , that Peter was one of Messiah's chosen ones and that the golden age was imminent died hard for Peter and the other disciples. They saw a part of God's plan, but only a part. The most important part, upon which all else depends, was still obscure to all - even to the disciples. Suffering for the King means suffering also for His subjects. This is the thought in the next four verses.

Verse 23 - "And he said to them all, If any man will come after me, let him deny himself, and take up his cross daily, and follow me."

Ἔλεγεν δὲ πρὸς πάντας, Εἴ τις θέλει ὀπίσω μου ἔρχεσθαι, ἀρνησάσθω
ἑαυτὸν καὶ ἀράτω τὸν σταυρὸν αὐτοῦ καθ' ἡμέραν, καὶ ἀκολουθείτω μοι.

Ἔλεγεν (3d.per.sing.imp.act.ind.of λέγω,inceptive) 66.

δὲ (emphatic conjunction) 11.

πρὸς (preposition with the accusative, after a verb of speaking) 197.

πάντας (acc.pl.masc.of πᾶς, extent after a verb of speaking) 67.

Εἴ (conditional particle in a first-class condition) 337.

τις (nom.sing.masc.of τις, indefinite pronoun, subject of θέλει) 486.

θέλει (3d.per.sing.pres.act.ind.of θέλω aoristic) 88.

ὀπίσω (improper preposition with the ablative of separation, adverbial) 302.

μου (abl.sing.masc.of ἐγώ, separation) 123.

ἔρχεσθαι (pres.inf.of ἔρχομαι, complementary) 146.

ἀρνησάσθω (3d.per.sing.1st.aor.mid.impv.of ἀρνέομαι, command) 895.

ἑαυτὸν (acc.sing.masc.of ἑαυτός, direct object of ἀρνησάσθω) 288.

καὶ (adjunctive conjunction joining verbs) 14.

ἀράτω (3d.per.sing.1st.aor.act.impv.of αἴρω, command) 350.

τὸν (acc.sing.masc.of the article in agreement with σταυρὸν) 9.

σταυρὸν (acc.sing.masc.of σταυρός, direct object of ἀράτω) 899.

αὐτοῦ (gen.sing.masc.of αὐτός, possession) 16.

καθ' (preposition with the accusative, adverbial, general reference) 98.

ἡμέραν (acc.sing.fem.of ἡμέρα, adverbial) 135.

καὶ (adjunctive conjunction joining verbs) 14.

ἀκολουθείτω (3d.per.sing.pres.act.impv.of ἀκολουθέω, command) 394.

μοι (dat.sing.masc.of ἐγώ, personal advantage) 123.

Translation - "In fact He continued to say to all, 'If anyone wishes to come after me, let him deny himself and let him take up his cross day by day, and let him follow me.' "

Comment: What is said in verse 23 is pursuant to Jesus' statement of verse 22. Note emphatic δὲ and our translation. There is more suffering in the Kingdom of God than that to be endured by the King Himself. If Jesus must suffer then all who wish to be identified with Him must also suffer. Jesus insisted upon it (imperfect tense in ἔλεγεν). πρὸς πάντας - "to all of them", because He had just been speaking to Peter only (Mt.16:23). We have a first-class condition with εἰ and the indicative θέλει in the protasis, and three imperatives in the apodosis. Jesus assumes in the first-class condition that some will in fact wish to follow Him. As a matter of fact He was aware of the terms of the covenant of redemption between Him and the Father and He knew the personnel of His bride for whom He would die. But He accommodates His statement to our thinking. "If you want to come along these are the terms of discipleship." Self denial, daily cross bearing (which means more than wearing a gold trinket on one's lapel) and followship are the costs and privileges of discipleship. If some think that the price is too high, let him consider Whom he is following and the long-range benefits. In the light of eternity the price our Lord asks is insignificant.

Cf.#302 for ὀπίσω in a metaphorical sense. ἀρνέομαι (#895) is used here in this sense, *i.e.* in the sense of personal sacrifice. Note the metaphorical use of σταυρός (#899). It is interesting that ἀράτω is an aorist imperative, denoting a once-for-all action, and yet disciples of our Lord must make the irreversible decision every day (καθ᾽ ἡμέραν). "All day today and day by day, without exception (ἀράτω) I will carry my cross. Tomorrow and every other day (καθ᾽ ἡμέραν) I will make the same irreversible decision." In this connection note also that ἀκολουθείτω is the present tense imperative - "be always following me." Jesus presents an interesting paradox in

Verse 24 - "For whosoever will save his life, shall lose it: but whosoever will lose his life for my sake, the same shall save it."

ὃς γὰρ ἂν θέλῃ τὴν ψυχὴν αὐτοῦ σῶσαι, ἀπολέσει αὐτήν, ὃς δ᾽ ἂν ἀπολέσῃ τὴν ψυχὴν αὐτοῦ ἕνεκεν ἐμοῦ, οὗτος σώσει αὐτήν.

ὃς (nom.sing.masc.of the relative ὅς, subject of θέλῃ) 65.
γὰρ (causal conjunction) 105.
ἂν (particle in a third-class condition) 205.
θέλῃ (3d.per.sing.pres.act.subj.of θέλω, third-class condition) 88.
τὴν (acc.sing.fem.of the article in agreement with ψυχὴν) 9.
ψυχὴν (acc.sing.fem.of ψυχή, direct object of σῶσαι) 233.
αὐτοῦ (gen.sing.masc.of αὐτός, possession) 16.
σῶσαι (aor.act.inf.of σώζω, complementary) 109.
ἀπολέσει (3d.per.sing.fut.act.ind.of ἀπόλλυμι, predictive) 208.
αὐτήν (acc.sing.fem.of αὐτός, direct object of ἀπολέσει) 16.
ὃς (nom.sing.masc.of the relative pronoun ὅς, subject of ἀπολέσῃ) 65.
δ᾽ (adversative conjunction) 11.
ἂν (particle in a third-class condition) 205.
ἀπολέσῃ (3d.per.sing.1st.aor.act.subj.of ἀπόλλυμι, third-class condition) 208.
τὴν (acc.sing.fem.of the article in agreement with ψυχὴν) 9.
ψυχὴν (acc.sing.fem.of ψυχή, direct object of ἀπολέσῃ) 233.
αὐτοῦ (gen.sing.masc.of αὐτός, possession) 16.
ἕνεκεν (improper preposition with the genitive - "for my sake") 435.
ἐμοῦ (gen.sing.masc.of ἐμός, reference) 1267.
οὗτος (nom.sing.masc.of οὗτος, deictic, subject of σώσει) 93.
σώσει (3d.per.sing.fut.act.ind.of σώζω, predictive) 109.
αὐτήν (acc.sing.fem.of αὐτός, direct object of σώσει) 16.

Translation - "Because whoever may wish to save his life will lose it, but whoever should lose his life in my behalf, that one will save it."

Comment: ψυχή (#233) means self-consciousness - the part of us that makes us aware of ourselves as distinct entities and separate entities. It involves physical life (βίος - #2202), but it means more than biological life, something which plants and trees have. To say, "body, soul and spirit" is to distinguish between βίος, ψυχή and πνεῦμα. Plants have the former; animals, birds and fish have the first two; only man has all three. The final πνεῦμα gives to man God-consciousness. Here the word is ψυχή and can be translated both body and soul. Jesus has just prophesied (verse 22) that he would be murdered. His disciples are told to follow Him to the cross. It is human nature to seek to preserve life. Hence, the natural man will reject Christ in order to save his ψυχήν (physical life) but in the end he will lose his ψυχήν (soul). The first αὐτήν has the first ψυχήν as its antecedent, being in agreement with both gender (fem.) and number (sing.). To save one's life by repudiating Christ as did the elders, priests and scribes (vs.22) is to join the Jewish religious leaders who hated Jesus and murdered Him. This is the pathway to physical safety but it leads to the loss of one's soul.

The second half of the verse reverses the idea. To follow Christ is to obey verse 23 and this path leads to Calvary, where the disciple is very likely to lose his life ἕνεκεν ἐμοῦ - "for my sake." But this path leads to the salvation of the soul. The last αὐτήν has the second ψυχήν as its antecedent. So - save your life and lose your soul; lose your life for Jesus' sake and save your soul.

Syntactically the verse consists of two third-class conditional sentences with the subjunctive and ἄν in the protasis and the future indicative in the apodosis. σῶσαι, the aorist infinitive completes θέλῃ. Jesus is not specifying the identity of any individual in either group. He is not saying that anyone will or will not choose to follow Him. He is only stating the results which are sure to follow when either course is followed.

The passage makes clear that there is warfare between God and the world. Jesus is the Messiah Who has come from God (vs.20). In the world He will be repudiated and slain (vs.22). His disciples must follow Him to death (vs.23) but, though murdered, Christ will be raised from the dead (vs.22). Therefore prospective disciples are placed in a dilemma. They have two choices: (1) They can repudiate Jesus , join His enemies, save their lives in the short run and lose their bodies, souls and spirits in the long run, or (2) they can follow Christ, lose their physical lives in the short run, but save their bodies, souls and spirits in the long run (vs.24). We cannot have it both ways. We must choose between short run gain and eternal loss of all and short-run loss of physical life and eternal gain with no loss, either of body, soul or spirit.

Whatever Jesus is, world leaders regard Him as a threat and an enemy, but in the final analysis, He shall judge and reign over the world. This is so because He rose from the dead. The grave was not the final chapter in the life of the Son of God. This kind of eschatology is the basis for Christian discipleship. Without it there is no long run gain to compensate for the Christian's short run loss. Jesus, speaking like an economist, poses the axiological question in

Verse 25 - "For what is a man advantaged, if he gain the whole world, and lose himself, or be cast away?"

τί γὰρ ὠφελεῖται ἄνθρωπος κερδήσας τὸν κόσμον ὅλον ἑαυτὸν δὲ ἀπολέσας ἤ ζημιωθείς;

τί (acc.sing.neut.of τίς, direct object of ὠφελεῖται) 281.

γὰρ (illative conjunction) 105.

ὠφελεῖται (3d.per.sing.pres.mid.ind.of ὠφελέω, customary) 1144.

ἄνθρωπος (nom.sing.masc.of ἄνθρωπος, subject of ὠφελεῖται) 341.

κερδήσας (aor.act.part.nom.sing.masc.of κερδαίνω, adverbial, temporal) 1214.

τὸν (acc.sing.masc.of the article in agreement with κόσμον) 9.

κόσμον (acc.sing.masc.of κόσμος, direct object of κερδήσας) 360.

ὅλον (acc.sing.masc.of ὅλος, in agreement with κόσμον) 112.

ἑαυτὸν (acc.sing.masc.of ἑαυτός, direct object of ἀπολέσας and ζημιωθείς) 288.

δὲ (adversative conjunction) 11.

ἀπολέσας (aor.act.part.nom.sing.masc.of ἀπόλλυμι, adverbial, temporal) 208.

ἢ (disjunctive particle) 465.

ζνμιωθείς (aor.pass.part.nom.sing.masc.of ζημιόω, adverbial, temporal) 1215.

Translation - "Therefore how much profit does a man make for himself after he has cornered the entire world market but has lost himself or has been been rejected.?"

Comment: The conjunction γὰρ is illative, as Jesus builds a conclusion on His statement of verse 24. Suppose that a man saves his life by repudiating Christ (vs.24), then, having secured his position in the world's favor, he cashes his social, economic and political advantage, until he has literally gained control of the entire world market? However in the process of rising to the economic, social and political heights in the world, he has destroyed himself and at the judgment bar of the Christ Whom he has rejected (John 5:22) is condemned to eternal loss? Our Lord's question is τί ὠφελεῖται? - "What profit is there? Where is the profit? How much net gain? Profits increase net worth. Net worth equals assets minus liabilities, but in this case there are no liabilities, since the man in question owns the entire world. Hence, Jesus is asking for a comparison of weights. Gain the entire world and call it profit. Lose yourself and be excluded from Christ's everlasting kingdom and you lose all to Him because when Messiah comes again "the kingdoms of this world (will) become the kingdoms of our Lord and of His Christ, and He shall reign into the ages of the ages" (Rev.11:15). Thus all previous gain is now loss. Jesus is calling for the last audit. After our Lord returns is there a net gain for the Christ rejector? Can the temporal profit absorb the eternal loss and show the books still in the black? Or does the loss which must be endured into the ages of the ages absorb the profit and more? The entire question is contingent upon whether or not Jesus Christ will arise from the dead and ultimately rule the world. All men regret loss and are pleased with gain. That is normal and proper, but the wise man wants to secure his gain in a society over which the Lord Jesus Christ will exercise jurisdiction.

If Jesus died and remained dead, contrary to His prediction, then give me the world for there is nothing else. I can enjoy it at least for a short season. But since

He is alive and therefore very much in everyone's future, He must be reckoned with. And when we confront Him there is no chance that our wishes will prevail in the event that they are out of harmony with His, because after He arose from the dead, in the same body in which He suffered, He said, "All power is given unto me in heaven and in earth" (Mt.28:18).

That a proper exegesis of Jesus' thought in this passage must be based upon His resurrection from the grave and coming jurisdiction over the world, is clear when we examine what He added in

Verse 26 - "For whosoever shall be ashamed of me and of my words, of him shall the Son of Man be ashamed, when he shall come in his own glory, and in his Father's, and of the holy angels."

ὅς γὰρ ἂν ἐπαισχυνθῇ με καὶ τοὺς ἐμοὺς λόγους, τοῦτον ὁ υἱὸς τοῦ ἀνθρώπου ἐπαισχυνθήσεται, ὅταν ἔλθῃ ἐν τῇ δόξῃ αὐτοῦ καὶ τοῦ πατρὸς καὶ τῶν ἁγίων ἀγγέλων.

ὅς (nom.sing.masc.of the relative pronoun ὅς, subject of ἐπαισχυνθῇ) 65.

γὰρ (causal conjunction) 105.

ἂν (conditional particle in a third-class conditional sentence) 205.

#2318 ἐπαισχυνθῇ (3d.per.sing.1st.aor.subj.of ἐπαισχύνομαι, third-class condition).

    be ashamed - Mk.8:38,38; Lk.9:26,26.
    be ashamed of - Rom.1:16; 6:21; II Tim.1:8,12,16; Heb.2:11; 11:16.

Meaning: A combination of ἐπί (#47) and αἰσχύνομαι (#2563). *Cf.* also αἰσχύνη (#2523). To be ashamed. Of Christ, His words and His works - Mk.8:38a; Lk.9:26a; of the gospel of Christ - Rom.1:16; II Tim.1:18. Of sufferings and persecution brought about by Christian witnessing - II Tim.1:12,16. Of former sins, committed before regeneration - Rom.6:21. Christ is not ashamed to call us "Brethren" - Heb.2:11; nor to be known as our God - Heb.11:16. But Christ will be ashamed of some at His coming - Mk.8:38b; Lk.9:26b.

    με (acc.sing.masc.of ἐγώ, general reference) 123.

    καὶ (adjunctive conjunction joining a pronoun with a noun) 14.

    τοὺς (acc.pl.masc.of the article in agreement with λόγους) 9.

    ἐμοὺς (acc.pl.masc.of ἐμός, in agreement with λόγους) 1267.

    λόγους (acc.pl.masc.of λόγος, general reference) 510.

    τοῦτον (acc.sing.masc.of οὗτος, general reference) 93.

    ὁ (nom.sing.masc.of the article in agreement with υἱὸς) 9.

    υἱὸς (nom.sing.masc.of υἱός, subject of ἐπαισχυνθήσεται) 5.

    τοῦ (gen.sing.masc.of the article in agreement with ἀνθρώπου) 9.

    ἀνθρώπου (gen.sing.masc.of ἄνθρωπος, designation) 341.

    ἐπαισχυνθήσεται (3d.per.sing.fut.pass.ind.of ἐπαισχύνομαι, predictive) 2318.

    ὅταν (temporal conjunction introducing an indefinite temporal clause) 436.

ἔλθῃ (3d.per.sing.aor.subj.of ἔρχομαι, indefinite temporal clause) 146.
ἐν (preposition with the instrumental of accompanying circumstance) 80.
τῇ (instru.sing.fem.of the article in agreement with δόξῃ) 9.
δόξῃ (instru.sing.fem.of δόξα, accompanying circumstance) 361.
αὐτοῦ (gen.sing.masc.of αὐτός, possession) 16.
καὶ (adjunctive conjunction joining a pronoun with a noun) 14.
τοῦ (gen.sing.masc.of the article in agreement with πατρὸς) 9.
πατρὸς (gen.sing.masc.of πατήρ, possession) 238.
καὶ (adjunctive conjunction joining nouns) 14.
τῶν (gen.pl.masc.of the article in agreement with ἀγγέλων) 9.
ἁγίων (gen.pl.masc.of ἅγιος, in agreement with ἀγγέλων) 84.
ἀγγέλων (gen.pl.masc.of ἄγγελος, possession) 96.

Translation - "Because whoever shall be ashamed of me and of my words, of that one shall the Son of Man be ashamed, when He shall come in His glory and in that of the Father and of the holy angels."

Comment: γὰρ is causal as Jesus continues to support His statement of verse 25, in which He raised the question of possible long term profits for the unbeliever. There is no profit for those who reject Him. Why? "Because . . . κ.τ.λ." The verse consists of an indefinite relative clause, like a third-class condition, with the subjunctive in the protasis and the future indicative in the apodosis. Then we have an indefinite temporal clause to tell us when the prophecy of the first clause will be fulfilled. Jesus is not saying that anyone specifically will be ashamed of Him and of His message, but He is implying that there will be some and He is saying definitely that whoever is so ashamed will face a terrible judgment, when He comes. Again, Jesus does not specify the precise date of His coming. The temporal clause with ὅταν and the subjunctive is indefinite, but though the time of His coming is not definite, the fact of His coming is most definite. Cf.#2318 for a study of the new word. Should there be one who cannot endure the offense of the cross, of him will Christ be ashamed at His second coming.

Jesus associates His person inextricably with His message. Some wish to make a division between the Man and His message, saying that they very much admire the man but cannot accept His message. This bifurcation cannot be made. The reason why men hated Jesus Christ and clamored for His blood was that His message offended them. So modernists today damn Jesus with faint praise as they extol His character but hasten to say that they have too much sophistication to accept what He had to say. Others circumvent the problem by saying that a man of Jesus' superb character could not possibly have said the things that are attributed to Him in the New Testament.

This is a curious rationalization indeed. Apparently those who assume this posture view the New Testament as a book to be trusted when it describes Jesus as they like to think of Him, but totally unworthy of their trust when it tells them what Jesus said. One recalls the Catholic nun who wore a bathrobe when she took a shower bath. Bertrand Russell relates that when she was asked why, since no one could see her, she said, "Oh, but you forget the sovereign God!" Russell adds that apparently she perceived the Deity as a universal Peeping Tom whose omnipotence permitted Him to see through a brick wall only to be foiled by a bathrobe. This kind of logic is mind boggling, but no more so than that of him who says that the same book that reveals Jesus in all of His glory is the book that falsifies His message. The lawyer who depends upon a witness to establish a vital point in his case does not procede in cross examination to demonstrate that the same witness is known for his mendacity. If the report of Jesus' message in the New Testament is unworthy of our trust, how can we believe the description of His character, which comes from the same New Testament? Thus the intellectual poverty of unbelief is demonstrated. The latest and best research in the field of textual criticism is all upon the side of evangelical Christian theology. Jesus is indeed all that the New Testament says He is, and He did indeed preach what the New Testament says He preached. We must accept the Man and His message or we must reject both Him and what He is alleged to have said.

To accept Jesus and to love Him is to follow Him and to believe and propagate all that He said.

There is no doubt about whom Jesus will be ashamed when He comes again. τοῦτον is out of place in the last clause and thus deictic and emphatic. " . . . *of him* shall the Son of Man be ashamed. . . κ.τ.λ.*"

When will the unbeliever feel the scorn of the Son of God? In verse 22 Jesus predicted His bodily resurrection. "Christ being raised from the dead, dieth no more. Death hath no more dominion over Him. For in that He died, He died unto sin once; but in that He liveth, He liveth unto God" (Rom.6:9,10). He is the only one who ever conquered death. He will die no more. This means that the world will never be rid of Him. It is therefore logical to expect Him to say something about His future role in the affairs of men and nations. His second coming to judge the world and to demonstrate His ability to administer the perfect society upon earth is a corollary of His victory over death. Who else is qualified to rule the world?

He came once, but not with the accompanying glorious circumstances which will characterize His second coming. The angels attended His birth (Heb.1:6) but kings did not. The only king who heard about it tried to kill Him. Born in a manger his birth was attended only by a few barnyard animals and a poverty stricken carpenter and a few shepherds. But when He comes again His glory will be reavealed " . . . in flaming fire taking vengeance on them that know not God, and that obey not the gospel of our Lord Jesus Christ, Who shall be punished with everlasting destruction from the presence of the Lord, and from the glory of His power, when He shall come to be glorified in His saints, and to be admired in all them that believe (because our testimony among you was believed) in that day" (II Thess.1:8-10). Alight with His own glory as Creator (Rev.4:11) and Redeemer (Rev.5:9,10) His coming will be accompanied also by the glory of His Father and of the holy angels (Rev.19:11-16).

Thus His prophecy of suffering and death (vs.22) is balanced by His prophecy of resurrection (vs.22), and His call for us to follow Him to Calvary, always bearing our cross, thus to lose our lives in the short run (vss.23,24), is balanced by His promise of reward at His glorious return. We are assured from the first that ours is the winning team, because He is the "Captain of our salvation" (Heb.2:10), and that glory awaits us at the end.

Notice His definite promise of reward in the parallel passage in Mt.16:27.

The idea that Messiah had come to die was a hard lesson for the disciples. That He should actually arise from the dead, ascend into heaven and finally return to earth seemed too good to be true. Jesus, of course, was aware of this - which is why He promised them a preview of His coming glory in

Verse 27 - "But I tell you of a truth, there be some standing here which shall not taste of death, till they see the kingdom of God."

λέγω δὲ ὑμῖν ἀληθῶς, εἰσίν τινες τῶν αὐτοῦ ἑστηκότων οἳ οὐ μὴ γεύσωνται θανάτου ἕως ἂν ἴδωσιν τὴν βασιλείαν τοῦ θεοῦ.

λέγω (1st.per.sing.pres.act.ind.of λέγω, aoristic) 66.

δὲ (emphatic conjunction) 11.

ὑμῖν (dat.pl.masc.of σύ, indirect object of λέγω) 104.

ἀληθῶς (adverbial) 1136.

εἰσίν (3d.per.pl.pres.ind.of εἰμί, aoristic) 86.

τινες (nom.pl.masc.of τις, subject of εἰσίν) 486.

τῶν (gen.pl.masc.of the article in agreement with ἑστηκότων) 9.

αὐτοῦ (gen.sing.masc.of αὐτός, pronominal adverb) 16.

ἑστηκότων (perf.act.part.gen.pl.masc.of ἵστημι, consummative) 180.

οἳ (nom.pl.masc.of ὅς, relative pronoun, subject of γεύσωνται) 65.

οὐ (summary negative conjunction, with μή) 130.

μὴ (qualified negative conjunction with οὐ and the subjunctive) 87.

γεύσωνται (3d.per.pl.1st.aor.subj.of γεύομαι, emphatic negation) 1219.

θανάτου (gen.sing.masc.of θάνατος, definition) 381.

ἕως (improper preposition in an indefinite temporal clause) 71.

ἂν (particle with the subjunctive in an indefinite temporal clause) 205.

ἴδωσιν (3d.per.pl.aor.act.subj.of ὁράω, indefinite temporal clause) 144.

τὴν (acc.sing.fem.of the article in agreement with βασιλείαν) 9.

βασιλείαν (acc.sing.fem.of βασιλεία, direct object of ἴδωσιν) 253.

τοῦ (gen.sing.masc.of the article in agreement with θεοῦ) 9.

θεοῦ (gen.sing.masc.of θεός, description) 124.

Translation - "In fact I am telling you truthfully that there are some of those standing here who shall never taste death until they shall see the kingdom of God."

Comment: δὲ is emphatic. Jesus had just made a statement that was hard for the disciples to believe. He had spoken of His death, but then said that after that He would come to earth in glory. Now, to bolster their sagging faith He adds, "As a matter of fact, I am going to give some of you who are standing here with me now a preview of that glorious end time event.

The promise was not to the entire group. τινες - only *some* of them. The partitive genitive in τῶν ἑστηκότων limits His selection to those who had been standing (perfect tense) there and were still there. Note the pronominal adverb αὐτοῦ. Others in the New Testament are οὕτως, ὡσαύτως, ποτέ, τότε, ὧδε. *Cf.*#16 for other examples of αὐτός as an adverb. Here it is used like ὧδε. Note the direct attraction of the relative pronoun οἵ to its antecedent, the indefinite pronoun τινες.

Eight days later Jesus kept this promise for Peter, James and John on the Mount of Transfiguration. This event (Mt.17:1-9; Mk.9:2-13; Lk.9:28-36), planned, as are all of God's plans, from eternity, was designed to stimulate and nourish the faith of the disciples, so that they could face the future sufferings and death of Christ with the full assurance that it would be followed by resurrection and ultimate triumph. We must remember that we read of the death of Jesus but react to it in the light of our knowledge of what followed. This knowledge, contained in the New Testament, was not available to the early Christians, except as it was given to them by Jesus' personal promise.

Before we examine the story of the Transfiguration we must look at Mark's account of Jesus' prediction of death in Mark 8:31 - 9:1.

Mk.8:31 - "And he began to teach them that the Son of Man must suffer many things, and be rejected of the elders, and of the chief priests, and scribes, and be killed, and after three days rise again."

Καὶ ἤρξατο διδάσκειν αὐτοὺς ὅτι δεῖ τὸν υἱὸν τοῦ ἀνθρώπου πολλὰ παθεῖν καὶ ἀποδοκιμασθῆναι ὑπὸ τῶν πρεσβυτέρων καὶ τῶν ἀρχιερέων καὶ τῶν γραμματέων καὶ ἀποκτανθῆναι καὶ μετὰ τρεῖς ἡμέρας ἀναστῆναι.

Καὶ (continuative conjunction) 14.
ἤρξατο (3d.per.sing.aor.mid.ind.of ἄρχω, ingressive) 383.
διδάσκειν (pres.act.inf.of διδάσκω, complementary) 403.
αὐτοὺς (acc.pl.masc.of αὐτός, direct object of διδάσκειν) 16.
ὅτι (conjunction introducing an object clause in indirect discourse) 211.
δεῖ (3d.per.sing.pres.ind.impersonal, of δέω, aoristic) 1207.
τὸν (acc.sing.masc.of the article in agreement with υἱὸν) 9.
υἱὸν (acc.sing.masc.of υἱός, general reference) 5.
τοῦ (gen.sing.masc.of the article in agreement with ἀνθρώπου) 9.
ἀνθρώπου (gen.sing.masc.of ἄνθρωπος, definition) 341.
πολλὰ (acc.pl.neut.of πολύς, direct object of παθεῖν) 228.
παθεῖν (aor.act.inf.of πάσχω, complementary) 1208.
καὶ (adjunctive conjunction joining infinitives) 14.
ἀποδοκιμασθῆναι (aor.pass.inf.of ἀποδοκιμάζω, complementary) 1390.
ὑπὸ (preposition with the ablative of agency) 117/
τῶν (abl.pl.masc.of the article in agreement with πρεσβυτέρων) 9.
πρεσβυτέρων (abl.pl.masc.of πρεσβύτερος, agency) 1141.
καὶ (adjunctive conjunction joining nouns) 14.
τῶν (abl.pl.masc.of the article in agreement with ἀρχιερέων) 9.
ἀρχιερέων (abl.pl.masc.of ἀρχιερεύς, agent) 151.
καὶ (adjunctive conjunction joining nouns) 14.
τῶν (abl.pl.masc.of the article in agreement with γραμματέων) 9.
γραμματέων (abl.pl.masc.of γραμματεύς, agent) 152.

καὶ (adjunctive conjunction joining infinitives) 14.
ἀποκτανθῆναι (aor.pass.inf.of ἀποκτείνω, complementary) 889.
καὶ (adjunctive conjunction joining infinitives) 14.
μετὰ (preposition with the accusative of time extent) 50.
τρεῖς (numeral) 1010.
ἡμέρας (acc.pl.fem.of ἡμέρα, time extent) 135.
ἀναστῆναι (2d.aor.act.inf.of ἀνίστημι, complementary) 789.

Translation - *"And He began to teach them that it was necessary for the Son of Man to suffer much and be repudiated by the elders and the priests and the scribes and be murdered and after three days to rise."*

Comment: *Cf.*comment on the parallel passages in Mt.16:21 and Lk.9:22. Matthew says that all of this will take place in Jerusalem. Mark uses the active ἀναστῆναι while Matthew and Luke use the passive infinitive, ἐγερτῆναι.

Verse 32 - *"And he spake that saying openly. And Peter took him, and began to rebuke him."*

καὶ παρρησίᾳ τὸν λόγον ἐλάλει. καὶ προσλαβόμενος οἱ Πέτρος αὐτὸν ἤρξατο ἐπιτιμᾶν αὐτῷ.

καὶ (explanatory conjunction) 14.

#2319 παρρησίᾳ (instrumental sing.fem.of παρρησία, manner).

boldness - Acts 4:13,29,31; Eph.3:12; Phil.1:20; I Tim.3:13; Heb.10:19; I John 4:17.
boldness of speech - II Cor.7:4.
confidence - Acts 28:31; Heb.3:6; 10:35; I John 2:28; 3:21; 5:14.
plainness of speech - II Cor.3:12.
boldly - John 7:26.
openly - Mark 8:32; John 7:4,13; 11:54; 18:20.
plainly - John 10:24; 11:14; 16:25,29.
boldly - Eph.6:19; Heb.4:16.
freely - Acts 2:29.
be bold - Philemon 8.

Meaning: A combination of πᾶς (#67) and ῥῆσις - "saying, speech." The willingness to say everything available on a subject, without reserve or reticence. The opposite of ἀῤῥησία - "silence." *Cf.* κατάῤῥησις - "accusation." προῤῥησις - prediction. Thus the words mean "complete speech," "no speech," "speech against" and "speech before." παρρησία - the state of being willing to tell all despite consequences. Hence, boldness, if telling it all involves personal danger. Speech without reserve. Openness, frankness. Acts 4:13,29,31; Phil.1:20; II Cor.7:4; Acts 28:31; II Cor.3:12; John 7:26; Mk.8:32; John 7:4,13; 18:20; 10:24; 11:14; 16:25,29; Eph.6:19; Acts 2:29; Philemon 8. Complete confidence which grows out of great faith - Eph.3:12; I Tim.3:13; Heb.10:19; I John 4:17; Heb.3:6; 10:35; I John 2:28; 3:21; 5:14; Heb.4:16. *Cf.* also John 11:54 - "in open sight of all."

τὸν (acc.sing.masc.of the article in agreement with λόγον) 9.

λόγον (acc.sing.masc.of λόγος, direct object of ἐλάλει) 510.

ἐλάλει (3d.per.sing.imp.act.ind.of λαλέω, progressive description) 815.

καὶ (inferential conjunction) 14.

προσλαβόμενος (aor.act.part.nom.sing.masc.of προσλαμβάνω, adverbial, temporal) 1210.

ὁ (nom.sing.masc.of the article in agreement with Πέτρος) 9.

Πέτρος (nom.sing.masc.of Πέτρος, subject of ἤρξατο) 387.

αὐτὸν (acc.sing.masc.of αὐτός, direct object of ἐπιτιμᾶν) 16.

ἤρξατο (3d.per.sing.aor.mid.ind.of ἄρχω, ingressive) 383.

ἐπιτιμᾶν (pres.act.inf.of ἐπιτιμάω, complementary) 757.

αὐτῷ (dat.sing.masc.of αὐτός, indirect object of ἐπιτιμᾶν) 16.

Translation - "Now He was speaking the message completely. Therefore Peter took Him aside and began to rebuke Him."

Comment: Mark's addition to Matthew's account (Mt.16:22) is that Jesus' statement was without reservation. παρρησίᾳ is a new word. #2319. Jesus had now revealed the entire divine plan of redemption. He had withheld nothing from His disciples. The Son of Man is Messiah. There could be no doubt of that. This much the Jewish people had been taught to expect. It satisfied their hopes for national sovereignty. But what they did not understand was that Messiah was to have two comings. In His first He was to suffer, die, be buried and resurrected. This part of the revelation was new to the disciples and to the nation as a whole. A suffering Messiah who would carry out redemption's plan by His vicarious sacrifice on a cross was a foreign concept to them. Hence Peter's reaction, for comment upon which *cf.* Mt.16:22.

Peter, whose motives were pure insofar as he understood them, was nevertheless mouthing the philosophy of Satan, whose prime interest it was to keep Jesus off the cross, since it was to be there, in His death, that our Lord would "destroy him that has the power of death, that is the devil" (Heb.2:14; John 12:31, upon which *cf.* comment). It is evident that Peter's remonstrance displeased Jesus as we see in

Verse 33 - "But when he had turned about and looked on his disciples, he rebuked Peter saying, Get thee behind me, Satan; for thou savourest not the things that be of God, but the things that be of men."

ὁ δὲ ἐπιστραφεὶς καὶ ἰδὼν τοὺς μαθητὰς αὐτοῦ ἐπετίμησεν Πέτρον καὶ λέγει,Ὕπαγε ὀπίσω μου, Σατανᾶ, ὅτι οὐ φρονεῖς τὰ τοῦ θεοῦ ἀλλὰ τὰ τῶν ἀνθρώπων.

ὁ (nom.sing.masc.of the article, subject of ἐπετίμησεν) 9.

δὲ (adversative conjunction) 11.

ἐπιστραφεὶς (aor.act.part.nom.sing.masc.of ἐπιστρέφω, adverbial, temporal) 866.

καὶ (adjunctive conjunction joining participles) 14.

ἰδὼν (aor.act.part.nom.sing.masc.of ὁράω, adverbial, temporal) 144.

τοὺς (acc.pl.masc.of the article in agreement with μαθητὰς) 9.

μαθητὰς (acc.pl.masc.of μαθητής, direct object of ἰδὼν) 421.

αὐτοῦ (gen.sing.masc.of αὐτός, relationship) 16.

ἐπετίμησεν (3d.per.sing.aor.act.ind.of ἐπιτιμάω, ingressive) 757.

Πέτρον (acc.sing.masc.of Πέτρος, direct object of ἐπετίμησεν) 387.

καὶ (ascensive conjunction) 14.

λέγει (3d.per.sing.pres.act.ind.of λέγω, historical) 66.

Ὕπαγε (2d.per.sing.pres.act.impv.of ὑπάγω, command) 364.

ὀπίσω (improper preposition with the ablative of separation) 302.

μου (abl.sing.masc.of ἐγώ, separation) 123.

Σατανᾶ (voc.sing.masc.of Σατανᾶ, address) 365.

ὅτι (causal conjunction) 211.

οὐ (summary negative conjunction with the indicative) 130.

φρονεῖς (2d.per.sing.pres.act.ind.of φρονέω, customary) 1212.

τὰ (acc.pl.neut.of the article, direct object of φρονεῖς) 9.

τοῦ (abl.sing.masc.of the article in agreement with θεοῦ) 9.

θεοῦ (abl.sing.masc.of θεός, source) 124.

ἀλλὰ (alternative conjunction) 342.

τὰ (acc.pl.neut.of the article, direct object of φρονεῖς) 9.

τῶν (abl.pl.masc.of the article in agreement with ἀνθρώπων) 9.

ἀνθρώπων (abl.pl.masc.of ἄνθρωπος, source) 341.

Translation - "But when He had turned around and seen His disciples, He began to rebuke Peter. He even said, 'Get behind me, Satan, because you never reflect upon the philosophy that comes from God, but you are always entertaining ideas that come from men."

Comment: This conversation between Peter and Jesus was being conducted apart from the other disciples. Jesus' desire was that His disciples should understand the divine plan and thus be prepared for what was to come. Peter (vs.22) reacted with antagonism and found that Jesus was not prepared to take his advice. Jesus turned to look at the other disciples to see if they had heard Peter's remark, and if so, what their reaction to it was. Would they agree with Peter and join him in trying to persuade Jesus to avoid the cross? Apparently what Jesus observed in the faces of all of them made it necessary to rebuke Peter with strong language which they would overhear. There had been a great deal of stern talk on this occasion as seen in the use of ἐπιτιμάω in verses 30,32 and 33. First Jesus used a severe tone when He ordered the disciples to refrain from telling the people what He had just told them (vs.30). Following His shocking announcement of His death, Peter countered with his own harsh rebuke, only to receive our Lord's unsparing retort (vs.33).

Why all the disputation? When the subject of the essential deity of Jesus of Nazareth, His death, burial and resurrection is before us, it is no time to be gentle. Stern measures are needed. Diplomacy generally results in promoting the devil's philosophy. The gospel is to be preached definitely. Sinners, portrayed here by Peter and his diabolic nonesense, are adamant and pandemonic in their opposition, but that is to be expected since they are under the control of the "god of this world" who "has blinded "their minds lest the glorious light of the gospel of the glory of Christ" should shine upon them (II Cor.4:4). But Jesus was getting opposition from Peter, to whom He had said only a moment before that he had been the recipient of a revelation which could not have come from flesh and blood (Mt.16:17). Matthew reports that Jesus said to Peter σκάνδαλον εἶ ἐμοῦ - ". . . you are an offence to me." He even went so far as to call Peter, "Satan." This is why we have taken καὶ here as ascensive. The statement recalls ὕπαγε Σατανᾶ in Mt.4:10 where the one spoken to was actually Satan. Here in Peter's rebuke of Mk.8:32 we see Satan's philosophy spoken by Peter's lips. Jesus is not actually saying that Peter is identified with Satan, but He is suggesting that it is Satan, in Peter, who is speaking against Calvary. For other comments *cf.* Mt.16:23.

Verse 34 - "And when he had called the people unto him with his disciples also, he said unto them, Whosoever will come after me, let him deny himself, and take up his cross, and follow me."

Καὶ προσκαλεσάμενος τὸν ὄχλον σὺν τοῖς μαθηταῖς αὐτοῦ εἶπεν αὐτοῖς, Εἴ τις θέλει ὀπίσω μου ἐλθεῖν, ἀπαρνησάσθω ἑαυτὸν καὶ ἀράτω τὸν σταυρὸν αὐτοῦ καὶ ἀκολουθείτω μοι.

Καὶ (continuative conjunction) 14.

προσκαλεσάμενος (aor.act.part.nom.sing.masc.of προσκαλέω, adverbial, temporal) 842.

τὸν (acc.sing.masc.of the article in agreement with ὄχλον) 9.

ὄχλον (acc.sing.masc.of ὄχλος, direct object of προσκαλεσάμενος) 418.

σὺν (preposition with the instrumental of association) 1542.

τοῖς (instru.pl.masc.of the article in agreement with μαθηταῖς) 9.

μαθηταῖς (instru.pl.masc.of μαθητής, association) 421.

αὐτοῦ (gen.sing.masc.of αὐτός, relationship) 16.

εἶπεν (3d.per.sing.aor.act.ind.of εἶπον, constative) 155.

αὐτοῖς (dat.pl.masc.of αὐτός, indirect object of εἶπεν) 16.

Εἴ (conditional particle introducing a first-class condition) 337.

τις (nom.sing.masc.of τις, the indefinite pronoun, subject of θέλει) 486.

θέλει (3d.per.sing.pres.act.ind.of θέλω, aoristic, in a first-class condition) 88.

ὀπίσω (improper preposition used adverbially with the ablative of separation) 302.

μου (abl.sing.masc.of ἐγώ, separation) 123.

ἐλθεῖν (aor.inf.of ἔρχομαι, complementary) 146.

ἀπαρνησάσθω (3d.per.sing.aor.mid.impv.of ἀπαρνέομαι, entreaty) 1213.

ἑαυτὸν (acc.sing.masc.of ἑαυτός, direct object of ἀπαρνησάσθω) 288.

καὶ (adjunctive conjunction joining verbs) 14.

ἀράτω (3d.per.sing.aor.act.impv.of αἴρω, entreaty) 350.

τὸν (acc.sing.masc.of the article in agreement with σταυρὸν) 9.

σταυρὸν (acc.sing.masc.of σταυρός, direct object of ἀράτω) 899.

αὐτοῦ (gen.sing.masc.of αὐτός, possession) 16.

καὶ (adjunctive conjunction joining verbs) 14.

ἀκολουθείτω (3d.per.sing.pres.act.impv.of ἀκολουθέω, entreaty) 394.

μοι (dat.sing.masc.of ἐγώ, personal advantage) 123.

Translation - *"And He called the people to Him, along with His disciples and said to them, 'If anybody wishes to come after me, let him deny himself and let him pick up his cross and let him follow me.' "*

Comment: Mark says that Jesus addressed this comment to the people (τὸν ὄχλον) and to His disciples. Lk.9:23 says that He said it to all (ἔλεγεν δὲ πρὸς πάντας). Matthew mentions only the disciples. *Cf.* Mt.16:24 and Lk.9:23 for comment on this great challenge by our Lord. It is more evidence that Jesus was speaking παρρησίᾳ (Mk.8:32). After the statement, no man should have any illusions about the cost of discipleship in a gainsaying society. Too often it is preached that it is easy, profitable and glorious to follow Christ. In the long run, it is profitable and glorious, but, as Lord Keynes was fond of saying, "In the long run we are all dead." Indeed eternity will pay infinite dividends in terms of profit and glory to those who have invested themselves in Christ, but in the temporal short run, it is not easy.

　　The student should not miss the first-class condition with Εἰ and the indicative in θέλει . Here is a case where we cannot force the rule that the first-class condition assumes as true the statement in the protasis. The indefinite pronoun τις, makes it clear that Jesus was not speaking of any specific individual. He knew specifically who wished to follow Him and who did not. Had He named someone (John, for example) we could translate "Since John wishes to follow me . . . κ.τ.λ." Jesus was sure that those whom the Father had given to Him (John 17:2,6,7,9,20,24) would eventually wish to come to Him. But He does not say that here. In a general way He is laying down the principle that the decision to follow Christ involves self-denial, cross bearing and constant followship. To follow Christ in this way is to incur the wrath of the unsaved slaves of Satan who are participating in the world's rat race (John 16:33; 17:14; Mt.5:10,11; I Pet.4:12,13).

Verse 35 - *"For whosoever will save his life shall lose it; but whosoever shall lose his life for my sake and the gospel's the same shall save it."*

ὃς γὰρ ἐὰν θέλῃ τὴν ψυχὴν αὐτοῦ σῶσαι ἀπολέσει αὐτήν, ὃς δ' ἂν ἀπολέσει τὴν ψυχὴν αὐτοῦ ἕνεκεν (ἐμοῦ καὶ) τοῦ εὐαγγελίου σώσει αὐτήν.

ὃς (nom.sing.masc.of the relative pronoun ὅς, subject of θέλει) 65.

γὰρ (inferential conjunction) 105.

ἐὰν (conditional particle with the subjunctive in a third-class condition) 363.

θέλῃ (3d.per.sing.pres.act.subj.of θέλω, third-class condition) 88.

τὴν (acc.sing.fem.of the article in agreement with ψυχὴν) 9.

ψυχὴν (acc.sing.fem.of ψυχή, direct object of σῶσαι) 233.

αὐτοῦ (gen.sing.masc.of αὐτός, possession) 16.

σῶσαι (aor.act.inf.of σώζω, complementary) 109.

ἀπολέσει (3d.per.sing.fut.act.ind.of ἀπόλλυμι, predictive) 208.

αὐτήν (acc.sing.fem.of αὐτός, direct object of ἀπολέσει) 16.

ὅς (nom.sing.masc.of ὅς, subject of ἀπολέσει) 65.

δ' (adversative conjunction) 11.

ἄν (conditional particle with the future indicative in an indefinite relative clause) 205.

ἀπολέσει (3d.per.sing.fut.act.ind.of ἀπόλλυμι, indefinite relative clause) 208.

τήν (acc.sing.fem.of the article in agreement with ψυχήν) 9.

ψυχήν (acc.sing.fem.of ψυχή, direct object of ἀπολύσει) 233.

αὐτοῦ (gen.sing.masc.of αὐτός, possession) 16.

ἕνεκεν (improper preposition with the genitive) 435.

(ἐμοῦ) (gen.sing.masc.of ἐμός, "for my sake") 1267.

(καὶ) (adjunctive conjunction, joining a possessive pronoun and a noun) 14.

τοῦ (gen.sing.neut.of the article in agreement with εὐαγγελίου) 9.

εὐαγγελίου (gen.sing.neut.of εὐαγγέλιον, "for the sake of") 405.

σώσει (3d.per.sing.fut.act.ind.of σώζω, predictive) 109.

αὐτήν (acc.sing.fem.of αὐτός, direct object of σώσει) 16.

Translation - *"Therefore whoever may wish to save his life will lose it, but whoever is going to lose his life for my sake and for the sake of the gospel will save it."*

Comment: Mt.16:25 and Lk.9:24 write this passage with third-class conditions in both clauses relative clauses. Mark has ἐὰν θέλῃ in the first clause but ἄν with the future indicative in the second. There is no doubt as to meaning. For further comment *cf.* Lk.9:24 and Mt.16:25.

Verse 36 - *"For what shall it profit a man, if he shall gainthe whole world, and lose his own soul?"*

τί γὰρ ὠφελεῖ ἄνθρωπον κερδῆσαι τὸν κόσομον ὅλον καὶ ζη μιωθῆναι τὴν ψυχὴν αὐτοῦ;

τί (nom.sing.neut.of τίς, subject of ὠφελεῖ) 281.

γὰρ (inferential conjunction) 105.

ὠφελεῖ (3d.per.sing.pres.act.ind.of ὠφελέω, aoristic) 1144.

ἄνθρωπον (acc.sing.masc.of ἄνθρωπος, general reference) 341.

κερδῆσαι (aor.act.inf.of κερδαίνω, used like the protasis of a conditional clause) 1214.

τὸν (acc.sing.masc.of the article in agreement with κόσμον) 9.

κόσμον (acc.sing.masc.of κόσμος, direct object of κερδῆσαι) 360.

ὅλον (acc.sing.masc.of ὅλος, in agreement with κόσμον) 112.

καὶ (adversative conjunction) 14.

ζημιωθῆναι (aor.pass.inf.of ζημιόω, used like a conditional clause) 1215.

τὴν (acc.sing.fem.of the article in agreement with ψυχήν) 9.

ψυχὴν (acc.sing.fem.of ψυχή, direct object of ζημιωθῆναι) 233.

αὐτοῦ (gen.sing.masc.of αὐτός, possession) 16.

Translation - "Therefore to what extent does a man profit if he gains the entire world but loses his soul?"

Comment: The two infinitives serve in the same way that third-class conditional protases would serve, in which case we would translate, "If a man should gain the whole world but lose his soul, to what extent would he profit?"

To gain one object is to lose the other. The short run gain would be the entire world. The long run loss would be his soul. To gain the world, even if one could gain it all, would be to enjoy its benefits only until death. To gain one's soul is to enjoy it forever. In fact those who gain their souls will also have their bodies and the physical world as bonus in eternity. For there will be a new heaven and a new earth, wherein dwells righteousness.

Cf. ὠφελέω in John 6:63 - "the flesh has no profit." Neither has even the Word of God unless it is mixed with faith (Heb.4:2). Thus faith seems to be the catalyst. Only by faith could the people believe that Jesus was truly the Messiah, after He announced that He was scheduled to die for the sins of the world and be raised again. False religion is fleshly, and hence unprofitable, even when the true message of the Word of God is preached, but unmixed by faith.

With reference to Mark's use of ἄν and the future indicative in verse 35, Burton says, "In addition to the relative clause having the Subjunctive with ἄν, which is the regular form both in classical and New Testament Greek," other forms may occur "in the New Testament to express a future supposition with more probability." (Burton, *New Testament Moods and Tenses,* 122). He then lists the Future Indicative with or without ἄν, the Subjunctive without ἄν and the Present Indicative with or without ἄν. Examples of the future indicative with or without ἄν, as we have it in Mk.8:35 are Mt.5:41; 10:32; 18:4; 23:12; Mk.8:35; Lk.12:8,10; 17:31; Acts 7:7; Rev.4:9 (*Ibid.,* 123).

Verse 37 - "Or what shall a man give in exchange for his soul?"

τί γὰρ δοῖ ἄνθρωπος ἀντάλλαγμα τῆς ψυχῆς αὐτοῦ;

τί (acc.sing.neut.of τίς, in agreement with ἀντάλλαγμα) 281.
γὰρ (inferential conjunction) 105.
δοῖ (3d.per.sing.2d.aor.act.subj.of δίδωμι, deliberative subjunctive) 362.
ἄνθρωπος (nom.sing.masc.of ἄνθρωπος, subject of δοῖ) 341.
ἀντάλλαγμα (acc.sing.neut.of ἀντάλλαγμα, direct object of δοῖ) 1216.
τῆς (gen.sing.fem.of the article in agreement with ψυχῆς) 9.
ψυχῆς (gen.sing.fem.of ψυχή, designation) 233.
αὐτοῦ (gen.sing.masc.of αὐτός, possession) 16.

Translation - "Therefore what will a man give up in exchange for his soul?"

Comment: This is only another way of stating the proposition of verse 36. The salvation question is one of values and their respective weights when viewed in relation to time and eternity. One is well advised to keep eternity's values in view. This concept is admirably expressed in II Cor.4:17,18, *q.v.*

Verse 38 - "Whosoever therefore shall be ashamed of me and of my words in this adulterous and sinful generation, of him also shall the Son of Man be ashamed when he cometh in the glory of his Father with the holy angels."

ὃς γὰρ ἐὰν ἐπαισχυνθῇ με καὶ τοὺς λόγους ἐν τῇ γενεᾷ ταύτῃ μοιχαλίδι καὶ ἁμαρτωλῷ, καὶ ὁ υἱὸς τοῦ ἀνθρώπου ἐπαισχυνθήσεται αὐτὸν ὅταν ἔλθῃ ἐν τῇ δόξῃ τού πατρὸς αὐτοῦ μετὰ τῶν ἀγγέλων τῶν ἁγίων.

ὃς (nom.sing.masc.of the relative pronoun ὅς, subject of ἐπαισχυνθῇ in a conditional relative clause) 65.

γὰρ (inferential conjunction) 105.

ἐὰν (conditional particle with the subjunctive in a conditional relative clause) 363.

ἐπαισχυνθῇ (3d.per.sing.1st.aor.mid.ind.of ἐπαισχύνομαι, conditional relative clause) 2318.

με (acc.sing.masc.of ἐγώ, general reference) 123.

καὶ (adjunctive conjunction joining a pronoun with a noun) 14.

τοὺς (acc.pl.masc.of the article in agreement with λόγους) 9.

ἐμοὺς (acc.pl.masc.of ἐμός, in agreement with λόγους) 1267.

λόγους (acc.pl.masc.of λόγος, general reference) 510.

ἐν (preposition with the locative with plural/collective nouns/pronouns - "in the midst of" or "among") 80.

τῇ (loc.sing.fem.of the article in agreement with γενεᾷ) 9.

γενεᾷ (loc.sing.fem.of γενεά, "in the midst of") 922.

ταύτῃ (loc.sing.fem.of οὗτος, in agreement with γενεᾷ) 93.

τῇ (loc.sing.fem.of the article in agreement with γενεᾷ) 9.

μοιχαλίδι (loc.sing.fem.of μοιχάλις, in agreement with γενεᾷ) 1006.

καὶ (adjunctive conjunction joining adjectives) 14.

ἁμαρτωλῷ (loc.sing.fem.of ἁμαρτωλός, in agreement with γενεᾷ) 791.

καὶ (adjunctive conjunction joining a relative pronoun with a noun) 14.

ὁ (nom.sing.masc.of the article in agreement with υἱὸς) 9.

υἱὸς (nom.sing.masc.of υἱός, subject of ἐπαισχυνθήσεται) 5.

τοῦ (gen.sing.masc.of the article in agreement with ἀνθρώπου) 9.

ἀνθρώπου (gen.sing.masc.of ἄνθρωπος, designation) 341.

ἐπαισχυνθήσεται (3d.per.sing.fut.mid.ind.of ἐπαισχύνομαι, predictive) 2318.

αὐτὸν (acc.sing.masc.of αὐτός, general reference) 16.

ὅταν (temporal conjunction introducing an indefinite temporal clause) 436.

ἔλθῃ (3d.per.sing.aor.act.subj.of ἔρχομαι, indefinite temporal clause) 146.

ἐν (preposition with the instrumental of accompanying circumstance) 80.

τῇ (instru.sing.fem.of the article in agreement with δόξῃ) 9.

δόξῃ (instru.sing.fem.of δόξα, accompanying circumstance) 361.

τοῦ (gen.sing.masc.of the article in agreement with πατρὸς) 9.

πατρὸς (gen.sing.masc.of πατήρ, possession) 238.

αὐτοῦ (gen.sing.masc.of αὐτός, relationship) 16.

μετά (preposition with the genitive of accompaniment) 50.

τῶν (gen.pl.masc.of the article in agreement with ἀγγέλων) 9.

ἀγγέλων (gen.pl.masc.of ἄγγελος, accompaniment) 96.

τῶν (gen.pl.masc.of the article in agreement with ἁγίων) 9.

ἁγίων (gen.pl.masc.of ἅγιος, in agreement with ἀγγέλων) 84.

Translation - "Therefore whoever shall be ashamed of me and of my messages in this adulterous and sinful generation - also shall the Son of Man be ashamed of him when He shall come in the glory of His Father with the holy angels."

Comment: Review with care the comments on the parallel passage in Mt.16:27, where we are concerned with another analysis.

The Christian should not be embarrassed because of Jesus and/or His teachings. If there should be such a person (note the third-class condition with ἐάν and the subjunctive in ἐπαισχυνθῇ, to express some doubt) - humiliated by the scorn and contempt of his unsaved associates, whom Jesus describes as μοιχαλίδι and ἁμαρτωλῷ ("adulterous and sinful"), then Jesus will reciprocate when he comes.

The date of His second coming is left in doubt - ὅταν ἔλθῃ is an indefinite temporal clause), but not the fact. Our Lord will surely come, surrounded by all of the glory of His Father and escorted by the holy angels of heaven. To contemplate the fact that on that day the King will be ashamed of us, is sufficient motivation for us now to "endure the cross, and despise the shame" (Heb.12:2) as Jesus once did. It is natural to wish to avoid the shame of Calvary, heaped upon us by our unbelieving contemporaries. It is supernatural to despise it. Let us despise it.

Mark 9:1 - "And he said unto them, Verily I say unto you, That there be some of these that stand here, which shall not taste of death, till they have seen the kingdom of God come with power."

Καὶ ἔλεγεν αὐτοῖς, Ἀμὴν λέγω ὑμῖν ὅτι εἰσίν τινες ὧδε τῶν ἑστηκότων οἵτινες οὐ μὴ γεύσωνται θανάτου ἕως ἂν ἴδωσιν τὴν βασιλείαν τοῦ θεοῦ ἐληλυθυῖαν ἐν δυνάμει.

Καὶ (emphatic conjunction) 14.

ἔλεγεν (3d.per.sing.imp.act.ind.of λέγω, inceptive) 66.

αὐτοῖς (dat.pl.masc.of αὐτός, indirect object of ἔλεγεν) 16.

Ἀμὴν (explicative) 466.

λέγω (1st.per.sing.pres.act.ind.of λέγω, aoristic) 66.

ὑμῖν (dat.pl.masc.of σύ, indirect object of λέγω) 104.

ὅτι (conjunction introducing an object clause in indirect discourse) 211.

εἰσίν (3d.per.pl.pres.ind.of εἰμί, progressive) 86.

τινες (nom.pl.masc.of τις, subject of εἰσίν) 486.

ὧδε (adverbial) 766.

τῶν (gen.pl.masc.of the article in agreement with ἑστηκότων) 9.

ἑστηκότων (perf.part.gen.pl.masc.of ἵστημι, substantival, partitive genitive) 180.

οἵτινες (nom.pl.masc.of ὅστις, subject of γεύσωνται) 163.

οὐ (summary negative conjunction with μή and the subjunctive) 130.

μή (qualified negative conjunction, with οὐ and the subjunctive) 87.

γεύσωνται (3d.per.pl.aor.subj.of γεύομαι, emphatic negation) 1219.

θανάτου (gen.sing.masc.of θάνατος, description) 381.

ἕως (temporal conjunction introducing an indefinite temporal clause) 71.

ἄν (particle with the subjunctive in an indefinite temporal clause) 205.

ἴδωσιν (3d.per.pl.aor.subj.of ὁράω, indefinite temporal clause) 144.

τήν (acc.sing.fem.of the article in agreement with βασιλείαν) 9.

βασιλείαν (acc.sing.fem.of βασιλεία, direct object of ἴδωσιν) 253.

τοῦ (gen.sing.masc.of the article in agreement with θεοῦ) 9.

θεοῦ (gen.sing.masc.of θεου, description) 124.

ἐληλυθυῖαν (2d.perf.part.acc.sing.fem.of ἔρχομαι, adverbial, circumstantial) 146.

ἐν (preposition with the instrumental of means) 80.

δυνάμει (instru.sing.fem.of δύναμις, means) 687.

Translation - "And He began to say to them, 'Truly I am telling you that there are some of those standing here who will never taste death until they see the kingdom of God having come by power.' "

Comment: The object clause is indirect discourse introduced by ὅτι. The partitive genitive in τῶν ἑστηκότων makes it clear that not all of the disciples, but only some (indefinite relative pronoun) of those who had been and still were standing there, were included in Jesus' promise. They were Peter, James and John as the next verse reveals. They were to have a preview of the glory which all will see when He comes. Note the emphatic negation with the double negative οὐ μή and the subjunctive γεύσωνται.

In Luke 9:27 we pointed to Luke's use of the third personal pronoun αὐτοῦ as a pronominal adverb, equivalent to ὧδε which Mark uses.

The temporal clause introduced by ἕως is indefinite since it has ἄν ἴδωσιν, the subjunctive construction. Jesus promised that they would see Him in transfiguration some time before they died, but He did not specify the date. Actually it occurred about a week later.

The second perfect participle ἐληλυθυίαν speaks of a present linear condition as a result of a past completed (perfected) action. When the kingdom of God is fully established it will be in full and permanent operation. Consistent with this is the perfect εἴληφας in Rev.11:16 which will occur at the time of the seventh (last) trumpet (I Cor.15:52). The heavenly chorus at that time will sing, "We give thanks to you, Lord God the Almighty One, Who is and who has been, because *you have taken your great power* and you have *begun* to reign." The consummative perfect and the ingressive aorist tell the same story that Jesus tells us in Mk.9:1 when He says ἕως ἄν ἴδωσιν τὴν βασιλείαν τοῦ θεοῦ ἐληλυθυίαν ἐν δυνάμει - ". . . until such time as you see the Kingdom of God *having already come* (and therefore permanently established) with power."

Thus did Jesus move to give support to the faltering faith of the disciples who had no doubts that Jesus was the Messiah, but who were now being asked to believe also that His current incarnation was for purposes of sacrificial death, burial and resurrection; further, that it was to be distinguished from His second coming at which time the Messianic expectation of Israel was to be fulfilled. This faith tonic which Jesus promised recalls John 6:62 q.v. Cf.#1219 for a study of γεύομαι, where several good sermon ideas lie hidden!

Note the parallel passages in Mt.16:28 and Lk.9:27.

The Transfiguration Near Caesarea Philippi

(Mk.9:2-8; Mt.17:1-8; Lk.9:28-36)

Mk.9:2 - "And after six days Jesus taketh with him Peter and James and John, and leadeth them up into an high mountain apart by themselves; and he was transfigured before them."

Καὶ μετὰ ἡμέρας ἒξ παραλαμβάνει ὁ Ἰησοῦς τὸν Πέτρον καὶ τὸν Ἰάκωβον καὶ τὸν Ἰωάννην, καὶ ἀναφέρει αὐτοὺς εἰς ὄρος ὑψηλὸν κατ᾽ ἰδίαν μόνους, καὶ μετεμορφώθη ἔμπροσθεν αὐτῶν.

Καὶ (continuative conjunction) 14.

μετὰ (preposition with the accusative of time extent) 50.

ἡμέρας (acc.pl.fem.of ἡμέρα, time extent) 135.

ἒξ (numeral) 1220.

παραλαμβάνει (3d.per.sing.pres.act.ind.of παραλαμβάνω, historical) 102.

ὁ (nom.sing.masc.of the article in agreement with Ἰησοῦς) 9.

Ἰησοῦς (nom.sing.masc.of Ἰησοῦς, subject of παραλαμβάνει) 3.

τὸν (acc.sing.masc.of the article in agreement with Πέτρον) 9.

Πέτρον (acc.sing.masc.of Πέτρος, direct object of παραλαμβάνει) 387.

καὶ (adjunctive conjunction joining nouns) 14.

τὸν (acc.sing.masc.of the article in agreement with Ἰάκωβον) 9.

Ἰάκωβον (acc.sing.masc.of Ἰάκωβον, direct object of παραλαμβάνει) 397.

καὶ (adjunctive conjunction joining nouns) 14.

Ἰωάννην (acc.sing.masc.of Ἰωάννης, direct object of παραλαμβάνει) 399.

καὶ (adjunctive conjunction joining verbs) 14.

ἀναφέρει (3d.per.sing.pres.act.ind.of ἀναφέρω, historical) 1221.

αὐτοὺς (acc.pl.masc.of αὐτός, direct object of ἀναφέρει) 16.

εἰς (preposition with the accusative of extent) 140.

ὄρος (acc.sing.neut.of ὄρος, extent) 357.

ὑψηλὸν (acc.sing.neut.of ὑψηλός, in agreement with ὄρος) 358.

κατ᾽ (preposition with the accusative, adverbial, general reference) 98.

ἰδίαν (acc.sing.fem.of ἴδιος, general reference, adverbial) 778.

μόνους (acc.pl.masc.of μόνος, in agreement with αὐτοὺς) 339.

καὶ (adjunctive conjunction joining verbs) 14.

μετεμορφώθη (3d.per.sing.aor.pass.ind.of μεταμορφόω, constative) 1222.

ἔμπροσθεν (improper preposition with the ablative of separation) 459.
αὐτῶν (abl.pl.masc.of αὐτός, separation) 16.

Translation - "And six days later Jesus took Peter and James and John and led them up into a high mountain by themselves; and He was transfigured in their presence."

Comment: Note our comment on Mt.17:1. At this point it seems that my opinion when I wrote on Mt.17:1 was a bit too fanciful. It is true that παραλαμβάνω refers to the rapture in Mt.24:40,41 and John 14:3 and that ἀναφέρω applies to Jesus' rapture in Lk.24:51. It is possible that Jesus took Peter, James and John aside, near to Him, to a point separate from the other nine and then supernaturally lifted them (ἀναφέρω) up into the high mountain. I now suggest that ἀναφέρω can mean "to lead up" in an ordinary natural sense. φέρω does not mean "lead" however, but "lift." He "lifted" them up, according to Matthew and Mark. Luke 9:28 uses ἀναβαίνω (#323) which carries no idea of rapture in the supernatural sense. It is an interesting question, but whichever way we decide it, the result does not alter the main thrust of the passage. I tend now to lean toward the notion that He led them up the mountain rather than having "raptured" them to the higher altitude. He was abundantly capable of either method. "We shall understand it better by and by."

μετὰ with the accusative of time extent, translated "after," is followed by εἰς with the accusative of space extent. *Cf.*#'s 98 and 778 for other examples of κατ' ἰδίαν with μόνους. Note also the improper preposition (called improper because ἔμπροσθεν is never found in composition with a verb) with the ablative of separation meaning "before them," "in their presence," or "within their view."

Cf.#1222. What happened to Jesus can and should happen to the saints (Rom.12:2; II Cor.3:18).

Verse 3 - "And his raiment became shining, exceeding white as snow; so as no fuller on earth can white them."

καὶ τὰ ἱμάτια αὐτοῦ ἐγένετο στίλβοντα λευκὰ λίαν οἷα γναφεὺς ἐπὶ τῆς γῆς οὐ δύναται οὕτως λευκᾶναι.

καὶ (continuative conjunction) 14.
τὰ (nom.pl.neut.of the article in agreement with ἱμάτια) 9.
ἱμάτια (nom.pl.neut.of ἱμάτιον, subject of ἐγένετο) 534.
αὐτοῦ (gen.sing.masc.of αὐτός, possession) 16.
ἐγένετο (3d.per.sing.aor.ind.of γίνομαι, culminative) 113.

#2320 στίλβοντα (pres.act.part.nom.pl.neut.of στίλβω, adjectival, ascriptive, predicate adjective).

shine - Mk.9:3.

Meaning: To shine; to glisten. In connection with Jesus' garments in transfiguration - Mk.9:3.

λευκά (nom.pl.neut.of λευκός, predicate adjective, in agreement with ἱμάτια) 522.

λίαν (adverbial) 214.

οἷα (nom.pl.neut.of οἷος, in agreement with ἱμάτια) 1496.

#2321 γναφεύς (nom.sing.masc.of γναφεύς, subject of δύναται).

fuller - Mk.9:3.

Meaning: from γνάπτω - "to card," *i.e.* to dress wool by combing out tangles with a card or currycomb. Hence γναφεύς is a dresser of wool fabric, who prepares the woolen fiber for spinning.

ἐπί (preposition with the genitive of place description) 47.
τῆς (gen.sing.fem.of the article in agreement with γῆς) 9.
γῆς (gen.sing.fem.of γῆ, place description) 157.
οὐ (summary negative conjunction with the indicative) 130.
δύναται (3d.per.sing.pres.ind.of δύναμαι, aoristic) 289.
οὕτως (demonstrative adverb) 74.

#2322 λευκᾶναι (pres.act.inf.of λευκαίνω, complementary).

make white - Rev.7:14.
white - Mk.9:3.

Meaning: Cf.#522. Hence, to whiten; make white. With reference to the garments of Jesus in transfiguration - Mk.9:3. Metaphorically, of the cleansing of the garments of the saints in the blood of the Lamb - Rev.7:14.

Translation - "And His clothing began to glisten with a dazzling whiteness like unto which no bleacher upon the earth is able to whiten."

Comment: Matthew describes the transfigured appearance of our Lord by saying ἐγένετο λευκά ὡς φῶς - "it came to be as white as light." That was precisely what it was. The Shekinah glory of God, such as Moses saw at the bush (Exodus 3:2), because of which the bush appeared to be on fire and on the mountain where he was protected in the cleft of the rock and saw the "afterglow" of God (Exodus 33:23). The whiteness of earth (ἐπί τῆς γῆς) is not to be compared with that of heaven. *Cf.* Mt.17:2. What Peter, James and John saw was the glory of God surrounding Jesus, as He had promised in Mk.8:38.

Verse 4 - "And there appeared unto them Elias with Moses: and they were talking with Jesus."

καὶ ὤφθη αὐτοῖς Ἡλίας σὺν Μωϋσεῖ, καὶ ἦσαν συλλαλοῦντες τῷ Ἰησοῦ.

καί (continuative conjunction) 14.
ὤφθη (3d.per.sing.1st.aor.pass.ind.of ὁράω, constative) 144.
αὐτοῖς (dat.pl.masc.of αὐτός, personal interest) 16.
Ἡλίας (nom.sing.masc.of Ἡλίας, subject of ὤφθη) 921.
σύν (preposition with the instrumental of association) 1542.

Μωϋσεῖ (instru.sing.masc.of Μωϋσῆς, association) 715.
καὶ (continuative conjunction) 14.
ἦσαν (3d.per.pl.imp.ind.of εἰμί, imperfect periphrastic) 86.
συλλαλοῦντες (pres.act.part.nom.pl.masc.of συλλαλέω, imperfect periphrastic) 1223.
τῷ (dat.sing.masc.of the article in agreement with Ἰησοῦ) 9.
Ἰησοῦ (dat.sing.masc.of Ἰησοῦς, personal advantage) 3.

Translation - "And Elias appeared to them with Moses and they were talking with Jesus."

Comment: The imperfect periphrastic is decidedly durative, and is used to show with what intense concentration the conversation was going on. Ordinary linear action in the past can be shown with the progressive duration of the imperfect. But Elias and Moses were engaged in a conversation with Jesus that invited no outside interruptions. How the three disciples must have been thunderstruck, although Peter was not unduly impressed to remain silent! *Cf.* comment on Mt.17:3 and Lk.9:30. It would be natural to assume that the glorious aspect of the phenomenon - the glistening radiance of the Shekinah, Jesus' radiant face, the appearance in glory of Elijah and Moses, two notables in Jewish history - these should have produced an awesome silence in the disciples. For James and John, it did. Not for the irrepressible Peter, whose impertinence becomes hellish when we learn from Luke's account what Jesus, Moses and Elijah were talking about.

Verse 5 - "And Peter answered and said to Jesus, Master, it is good for us to be here: and let us make three tabernacles; one for thee, and one for Moses, and one for Elias."

καὶ ἀποκριθεὶς ὁ Πέτρος λέγει τῷ Ἰησοῦ, Ῥαββί, καλόν ἐστιν ἡμᾶς ὧδε εἶναι, καὶ ποιήσωμεν τρεῖς σκηνάς, σοὶ μίαν καὶ Μωϋσεῖ μίαν καὶ Ἡλίᾳ μίαν.

καὶ (continuative conjunction) 14.
ἀποκριθεὶς (aor.part.nom.sing.masc.of ἀποκρίνομαι, adverbial, temporal) 318.
ὁ (nom.sing.masc.of the article in agreement with Πέτρος) 9.
Πέτρος (nom.sing.masc.of Πέτρος, subject of λέγει) 387.
τῷ (dat.sing.masc.of the article in agreement with Ἰησοῦ) 9.
Ἰησοῦ (dat.sing.masc.of Ἰησοῦς, indirect object of λέγει) 3.
Ῥαββί (voc.sing.masc.of Ῥαββί, address) 1443.
καλόν (acc.sing.neut.of καλός, predicate accusative) 296.
ἐστιν (3d.per.sing.pres.ind.of εἰμί, aoristic) 86.
ἡμᾶς (acc.pl.masc.of ἐγω, general reference) 123.
ὧδε (adverbial) 766.
εἶναι (pres.inf.of εἰμί, noun use, subject of ἐστιν) 86.
καὶ (inferential conjunction) 14.
ποιήσωμεν (1st.per.pl.aor.act.subj.of ποιέω, hortatory) 127.

τρεῖς (numeral) 1010.

σκηνάς (acc.pl.fem.of σκηνή, direct object of ποιήσωμεν) 1224.

σοὶ (dat.sing.masc.of σύ, personal advantage) 104.

μίαν (acc.sing.fem.of εἷς, in agreement with σκηνήν, understood) 469.

καὶ (adjunctive conjunction joining phrases) 14.

Μωϋσεῖ (dat.sing.masc.of Μωϋσῆς, personal advantage) 715.

μίαν (acc.sing.fem.of εἷς, in agreement with σκηνήν, understood) 469.

καὶ (adjunctive conjunction joining phrases) 14.

Ἠλίᾳ (dat.sing.masc.of Ἠλίας, personal advantage) 921.

μίαν (acc.sing.fem.of εἷς, in agreement with σκηνήν, understood) 469.

Translation - *"And in response Peter said to Jesus, 'Rabbi, to be here is good for us. Therefore let us build three tabernacles: - for you one and for Moses one, and for Elias one.' "*

Comment: *Cf.*Mt.17:4 and Lk.9:28-36 for further comment. We will be a little more inclined to forgive Peter for this innane outburst when we read Mark's explanation for it in the next verse. Note that Mark says that Peter's remark was in reply (ἀποκριθείς) to something. And yet there is no record that anyone had spoken to him! Peter was the type who "replied" even when he was not a participant in the discussion. Perhaps he was reacting, not to what anyone said to him, but to what was going on in his terrified mind.

Verse 6 - *"For he wist not what to say; for they were sore afraid."*

οὐ γὰρ ᾔδει τί ἀποκριθῇ, ἔκφοβοι γὰρ ἐγένοντο.

οὐ (summary negative conjunction with the indicative) 130.

γὰρ (causal conjunction) 105.

ᾔδει (3d.per.sing.pluperfect act.ind.of οἶδα,intensive) 144.

τί (acc.sing.neut.of τίς, direct object of ᾔδει) 281.

ἀποκριθῇ (3d.per.sing.aor.subj.of ἀποκρίνομαι, deliberative subjunctive in indirect question) 318.

#2323 ἔκφοβοι (nom.pl.masc.of ἔκφοβος, predicate adjective).

sore afraid - Mk.9:6; Heb.12:21.

Meaning: A combination of ἐκ (#19) and φοβέομαι (#101). *Cf.* ἐκφοβέω (#4363). The prepositional prefix intensifies the degree of fear. To be filled with consternation. With reference to the disciples at the transfiguration - Mk.9:6. Of Moses at Sinai - Heb.12:21.

γὰρ (causal conjunction) 105.

ἐγένοντο (3d.per.pl.aor.mid.ind.of γίνομαι, progressive description) 113.

Translation - *"Because he had not known what to say, because they were terrified."*

Comment: Mark apologizes for Peter's stupid, wicked and totally inappropriate suggestion of verse 5. He said it because (causal γάρ) he had not known (pluperfect in ᾔδει) what to say. Note the deliberative subjunctive in indirect question after a secondary tense. *Cf.*Mk.6:36; Lk.5:19; 12:36. Mark tells us why Peter was confused. It was because of fear.

It did not occur to Peter, as perhaps it did to James and John, that when one knows not what to say, he should say nothing. This was not in Peter's nature. We shall discuss this further in our comments on Luke's account which is soon to follow.

Verse 7 - "And there was a cloud that overshadowed them: and a voice came out of the cloud, saying, This is my beloved Son: hear him."

καὶ ἐγένετο νεφέλη ἐπισκιάζουσα αὐτοῖς, καὶ ἐγένετο φωνὴ ἐκ τῆς νεφέλης, Οὗτος ἐστιν ὁ υἱός μου ὁ ἀγαπητός, ἀκούετε αὐτοῦ.

καὶ (continuative conjunction) 14.

ἐγένετο (3d.per.sing.aor.ind.of γίνομαι, constative) 113.

νεφέλη (nom.sing.fem.of νεφέλη, subject of ἐγένετο) 1225.

ἐπισκιάζουσα (pres.act.part.nom.sing.fem.of ἐπισκιάζω, adverbial, circumstantial) 1226.

αὐτοῖς (loc.pl.masc.of αὐτός, "upon," in a spatial sense, after ἐπί in composition) 16.

καὶ (continuative conjunction) 14.

ἐγένετο (3d.per.sing.aor.ind.of γίνομαι, constative) 113.

φωνὴ (nom.sing.fem.of φωνή, subject of ἐγένετο) 222.

ἐκ (preposition with the ablative of source) 19.

τῆς (abl.sing.fem.of the article in agreement with νεφέλης) 9.

νεφέλης (abl.sing.fem.of νεφέλη, source) 1225.

Οὗτος (nom.sing.masc.of οὗτος, subject of ἐστιν, deictic) 93.

ἐστιν (3d.per.sing.pres.ind.of εἰμί, aoristic) 86.

ὁ (nom.sing.masc.of the article in agreement with υἱός) 9.

υἱός (nom.sing.masc.of υἱός, predicate nominative) 5.

μου (gen.sing.masc.of ἐγώ, relationship) 123.

ὁ (nom.sing.masc.of the article in agreement with ἀγαπητός) 9.

ἀγαπητός (nom.sing.masc.of ἀγαπητός, apposition) 327.

ἀκούετε (2d.per.pl.pres.act.impv.of ἀκούω, command) 148.

αὐτοῦ (gen.sing.masc.of αὐτός, designation) 16.

Translation - "And there came a cloud overshadowing them, and there came a voice out of the cloud, 'This man is my Son, the Beloved. Hear only Him.' "

Comment: Heaven's answer to Peter's nonesense was an overshadowing cloud and a voice speaking from it. *Cf.*#'s 1225 and 1226 for the uses of νεφέλη and ἐπισκιάζω elsewhere. Note the direct discourse with neither ὅτι nor λέγων in introduction. Οὗτος is deictic - sternly so. God wants all attention directed toward His Son. Emphasis is also found in the emphatic attributive position of ἀγαπητός, and in the genitive in αὐτοῦ after a verb of hearing. "**This** is my Son, **The Beloved One. Hear only Him.**" With verbs the genitive means "this and no other." Thus the emphasis on Οὗτος is reinforced. Thus also a warning to Moses and Elijah (who did not need to be warned) and to James and John (who may have needed the warning) to pay no attention to Peter and his immature remarks.

At this high moment of exaltation, when Jesus, temporarily tenting among men (John 1:14) in a voluntary κένόσις (Phil.2:7), returns briefly for demonstration purposes for three faltering disciples, to His eternal glory, one of the disciples for whose benefit the extravaganza is being staged, seeks to upstage the star with a stupid suggestion that they appoint a building committee and hire an architect and a crew of carpenters! Οὗτος focuses attention upon Jesus. Moses was God's law giver and Elijah was His prophet, but Jesus is His Beloved Son. God's advice was to ignore this red-necked fisherman. If anyone talks let it be Jesus. But He was not saying a word. Insecurity breeds loquacity, while a serene confidence in one's standing is often demonstrated by dignified silence. Jesus considered equality with God something that He did not need to seek (Phil.2:6).

Verse 8 - "And suddenly when they had looked around about, they saw no man any more, save Jesus only with themselves."

καὶ ἐξάπινα περιβλεφάμενοι οὐκέτι οὐδένα εἶδον ἀλλὰ τὸν Ἰησοῦν μόνον μεθ' ἑαυτῶν.

καὶ (continuative conjunction) 14.

#2324 ἐξάπινα (adverbial).

suddenly - Mk.9:8.

Meaning: A rare later Greek form for ἐξαπίνης. Suddenly. *Cf.*#1879.

περιβλεφάμενοι (aor.mid.part.nom.pl.masc.of περιβλέπομαι, adverbial, temporal) 2107.
οὐκέτι (adverbial) 1289.
οὐδένα (acc.sing.masc.of οὐδείς, direct object of εἶδον) 446.
εἶδον (3d.per.pl.aor.ind.of ὁράω, constative) 144.
μεθ' (preposition with the genitive of accompaniment) 50.
ἑαυτῶν (gen.pl.masc.of ἑαυτός, accompaniment) 288.
ἀλλὰ (alternative conjunction) 342.
τὸν (acc.sing.masc.of the article in agreement with Ἰησοῦν) 9.
Ἰησοῦν (acc.sing.masc.of Ἰησοῦς, direct object of εἶδον) 3.
μόνον (acc.sing.masc.of μόνος, in agreement with Ἰησοῦν) 339.

Translation - "And suddenly, when they had looked around, they saw no man any longer with them but Jesus alone."

Comment: Moses and Elijah suddenly vanished, shocked and annoyed no doubt by Peter's suggestion. Peter, James and John looked all about them. They surveyed the scene. Their search revealed no man. Not any longer. But Jesus was standing with them. The Father ordered the disciples to hear Jesus only. There was no further need for the presence of Moses and Elijah. They had completed their mission, the nature of which we shall discuss in comment on Lk.9:31. Horrified by Peter's suggestion and his rude attempt to steal the show, they had no desire to do so. They went back to the glory, leaving Jesus in sole command of the situation.

We now examine Luke's account of the Transfiguration in Luke 9:28-36.

Lk.9:28 - "And it came to pass about an eight days after these sayings, he took Peter and John and James, and went up into a mountain to pray."

Ἐγένετο δὲ μετὰ τοὺς λόγους τούτους ὡσεὶ ἡμέραι ὀκτὼ (καὶ) παραλαβὼν Πέτρον καὶ Ἰωάννην καὶ Ἰάκωβον ἀνέβη εἰς τὸ ὄρος προσεύξασθαι.

Ἐγένετο (3d.per.sing.aor.ind.of γίνομαι, constative) 113.

δὲ (continuative conjunction) 11.

μετὰ (preposition with the accusative in a time expression) 50.

τοὺς (acc.pl.masc.of the article in agreement with λόγους) 9.

λόγους (acc.pl.masc.of λόγος, time expression, after μετὰ) 510.

τούτους (acc.pl.masc.of οὗτος, in agreement with λόγους) 93.

ὡσεὶ (adverbial) 325.

ἡμέραι (nom.pl.fem.of ἡμέρα, subject of a verb understood) 135.

ὀκτὼ (numeral) 1886.

παραλαβὼν (aor.act.part.nom.sing.masc.of παραλαμβάνω, adverbial, temporal) 102.

Πέτρον (acc.sing.masc.of Πέτρος, direct object of παραλαβὼν) 387.

καὶ (adjunctive conjunction joining nouns) 14.

Ἰωάννην (acc.sing.masc.of Ἰωάννης, direct object of παραλαβὼν) 399.

καὶ (adjunctive conjunction joining nouns) 14.

Ἰάκωβον (acc.sing.masc.of Ἰάκωβον, direct object of παραλαβὼν) 397.

ἀνέβη (3d.per.sing.aor.act.ind.of ἀναβαίνω, constative) 323.

εἰς (preposition with the accusative of extent) 140.

τὸ (acc.sing.neut.of the article in agreement with ὄρος) 9.

ὄρος (acc.sing.neut.of o3row, extent) 357.

προσεύξασθαι (aor.mid.inf.of προσεύχομαι, purpose) 544.

Translation - "And it happened that about eight days after this conversation when He had taken Peter and John and James aside He went up into the mountain to pray."

Comment: Jesus led the three disciples aside for the trip up Mount Horeb. *Cf.*#323 and note that ἀναβαίνω is used in John 3:13; 6:62; Eph.4:8,9,10; Rev.4:1; 11:12; John 1:51; 20:17; Acts 2:34; Rom.10:6 of an ascent into heaven. The case is not conclusive, but the idea that Jesus may have supernaturally transported the three disciples into the mountain, rather than leading them upon a burdensome trek to the higher altitudes, is fairly found within the meaning of παραλαμβάνω and ἀναφέρω in Matthew and Luke, as well as in ἀναβαίνω in

Luke. προσεύξασθαι is an infinitive of purpose. Luke alone tells us that Jesus was going up the mountain to pray and that it was during His prayer that the transfiguration experience occurred.

The time question is interesting. Mark says that it was *after* six days. Luke says that it was *about* eight days after Jesus' remarks recorded in Lk.9:27; Mt.16:28 and Mk.9:1. There is no contradiction. Anything that is *about* eight days after an event is also *after* six days. The difference between the texts only proves that the‍ Holy Spirit was not interested in telling us the precise time.

Verse 29 - *"And as he prayed, the fashion of his countenance was altered, and his raiment was white and glistering."*

καὶ ἐγένετο ἐν τῷ προσεύχεσθαι αὐτὸν τὸ εἶδος τοῦ προσώπου αὐτοῦ ἕτερον καὶ ὁ ἱματισμὸς αὐτοῦ λευκὸς ἐξαστράπτων.

καὶ (continuative conjunction) 14.

ἐγένετο (3d.per.sing.aor.ind.of γίνομαι, constative) 113.

ἐν (preposition with the locative of time point) 80

τῷ (loc.sing.neut.of the article in agreement with προσεύχεσθαι) 9.

προσεύχεσθαι (pres.inf.of προσεύχομαι, articular infinitive, time point) 544.

αὐτὸν (acc.sing.masc.of αὐτός, general reference) 16.

τὸ (nom.sing.neut.of the article in agreement with εἶδος) 9.

εἶδος (nom.sing.neut.of εἶδος, subject of ἐγένετο, understood) 1950.

τοῦ (gen.sing.neut.of the article in agreement with προσώπου) 9.

προσώπου (gen.sing.neut.of πρόσωπον, definition) 588.

αὐτοῦ (gen.sing.masc.of αὐτός, possession) 16.

ἕτερον (nom.sing.neut.of ἕτερος, predicate adjective) 605.

καὶ (continuative conjunction) 14.

ὁ (nom.sing.masc.of the article in agreement with ἱματισμὸς) 9.

ἱματισμὸς (nom.sing.masc.of ἱματισμός, subject of ἐγένετο understood) 2159.

αὐτοῦ (gen.sing.masc.of αὐτός, possession) 16.

λευκὸς (nom.sing.masc.of λευκός, predicate adjective) 522.

#2325 ἐξαστράπων (pres.act.part.nom.sing.masc.of ἐξαστράπτω, adjectival, ascriptive).

Meaning: A combination of ἐκ (#19) and ἀστήρ (#145). *Cf.* also ἀστραπή (#1502) and ἀστράπτω (#2617). Hence, to shine out as from lightning or as from a star. To dazzle with brilliant white light. To glisten. With reference to Jesus' garments and person in transfiguration - Lk.9:29.

Translation - *"And while He was praying the appearance of His face changed and His garment became dazzlingly white."*

Comment: The articular infinitive introduced by ἐν in ἐν τῷ προσεύχεσθαι αὐτὸν is in the locative case indicating time point. It was while Jesus was praying that the transformation of His face and clothing occurred. Heaven's glory bathed Him in its brilliant whiteness. Note a similar word in Lk.24:4 (ἀστράπτω #2617). The same garments that shone here with the effulgence of the light of heaven were the stakes in a game of dice in which a mob of drunken Roman soldiers were engaged at the foot of His cross (John 19:24).

Verse 30 - "And behold, there talked with Him two men, which were Moses and Elias."

καὶ ἰδοὺ ἄνδρες δύο συνελάλουν αὐτῷ, οἵτινες ἦσαν Μωϋσῆς καὶ Ἠλίας.

καὶ (continuative conjunction) 14.
ἰδοὺ (exclamation) 95.
ἄνδρες (nom.pl.masc.of ἀνήρ, subject of συνελάλουν) 63.
δύο (numeral) 385.
συνελάλουν (3d.per.pl.imp.act.ind.of συλλαλέω, inceptive) 1223.
αὐτῷ (dat.sing.masc.of αὐτός, indirect object of συνελάλουν) 16.
οἵτινες (nom.pl.masc.of ὅστις, subject of ἦσαν) 163.
ἦσαν (3d.per.pl.imp.ind.of εἰμί, progressive description) 86.
Μωϋσῆς (nom.sing.masc.of Μωϋσῆς, predicate nominative) 715.
καὶ (adjunctive conjunction joining nouns) 14.
Ἠλίας (nom.sing.masc.of Ἠλίας, predicate nominative) 921.

Translation - "And Look! Two men began to talk with Him, who were Moses and Elias."

Comment: *Cf.* comment on Mt.17:3 and Mk.9:4.

Verse 31 - "Who appeared in glory, and spoke of his decease which he should accomplish at Jerusalem."

οἱ ὀφθέντες ἐν δόξῃ ἔλεγον τὴν ἔξοδον αὐτοῦ ἣν ἤμελλεν πληροῦν ἐν Ἰερουσαλήμ.

οἱ (nom.pl.masc.of ὅς, subject of ἔλεγον) 65.
ὀφθέντες (1st.aor.pass.part.nom.pl.masc.of ὁράω, adverbial, temporal) 144.
ἐν (preposition with the instrumental of manner) 80.
δόξῃ (instru.sing.fem.of δόξα, manner) 361.
ἔλεγον (3d.per.pl.imp.act.ind.of λέγω, inceptive) 66.
τὴν (acc.sing.fem.of the article in agreement with ἔξοδον) 9.

#2326 ἔξοδον (acc.sing.fem.of ἔξοδος, direct object of ἔλεγον).

decease - Lk.9:31; II Pet.1:15.
departing - Heb.11:22.

Meaning: A combination of ἐκ (#19) and ὁδός (#199). Hence, the way out; a departure. With reference to the exit of the chidlren of Israel from Egypt - Heb.11:22. Of the death of Peter - II Pet.1:15. Of Jesus' death on the cross - Lk.9:31.

αὐτοῦ (gen.sing.masc.of αὐτός, possession) 16.

ἥν (acc.sing.fem.of ὅς, attracted in case to its antecendent ἔξοδον) 65.
ἤμελλεν (3d.per.sing.imp.act.ind.of μέλλω, inceptive) 206.
πληροῦν (pres.act.inf.of πληρόω, complementary) 115.
ἐν (preposition with the locative of place where) 80.
Ἰερουσαλήμ (loc.sing.neut.of Ἰερουσαλήμ, place where) 141.

Translation - "Who having made a glorious entrance began to discuss with Him His exodus which He was in the process of completing in Jerusalem."

Comment: "Having appeared gloriously - " The participle is adverbially temporal and the manner of the dramatic entrance of Moses and Elijah is expressed with the instrumental phrase ἐν δόξῃ. "in glory" is a possible translation if we designate "glory" as a place of glory, like heaven itself, or a high mountain top where the Shekinah glory rested. *Cf.*#361, (11). Moses and Elijah wasted no time. As soon as they appeared they began to talk with Jesus (inceptive imperfect in ἔλεγον).

Luke is the only writer who tells us what they talked about. *Cf.*#2326. The Exodus recalls the visit of the death angel in Egypt as the tenth plague was visited upon the oppressors of God's elect nation. It was then that the Paschal Lamb was slain and the blood was applied to the door posts. Only if this were done could the first born escape death. Moses and Elijah understood this well. They called Jesus' death His Exodus. He is the Lamb of God (John 1:29; I Pet.1:19; I Cor.5:7). He must be perfect - ". . . without spot of blemishd (Heb.9:14; I Pet.1:19). He must be the First Born (Mt.3:15). He must die (Lk.9:20-22) and be raised again. Note that Moses and Elijah spoke of His death as something in process of being accomplished. The inceptive imperfect in ἤμελλεν indicates this. Jesus was to descend from Mount Horeb and set His face with grim resolution toward Jerusalem (Lk.9:51). He had announced to His disciples a week before that His Exodus was a part of His mission (Mt.16:21; Mk.9:1; Lk.9:22). He was now in the process of carrying out His redemptive mission. A week later He was still engaged in the ministry which culminated in His death. It was called, not a defeat, but a fulfillment - an accomplishment. The infinitive πληροῦν (#115) indicates this. What Jesus was about to do at Jerusalem fulfilled (completed, finished, finalized) an eternal plan.

Moses and Elijah had each attempted a reformation in Israel and had failed. Moses succeeded in leading Israel out of bondage but failed to introduce them to the heavenly appointed Canaan (Exodus 14; 34:4,5) land which God had given in covenant promise to Abraham. Elijah too tried and failed. He beheaded 450 false prophets of Baal (I Kings 18) only to flee for his life from Jezebel, who had not pursued him, collapse under a juniper tree and ask God to take his life (I Kings 19:4). Now, both having failed, they appear on Mount Horeb and admonish Jesus not to fail. He was the fulfillment of both the legal standards of Moses and the prophetic hopes of Elijah (Rom.3:21). Moses with his tablet of stone and Elijah with his fiery denunciations hurled into the teeth of Ahab had witnessed of a higher righteousness than either of them could produce. But they pointed forward to Jesus Who fulfilled the law of Moses (Mt.5:17) and will usher in a political kingdom characterized by peace and prosperity beyond the wildest expectations of Elijah. Now that Jesus is transfigured in glory atop Horeb they are called from glory to discuss it with Him. What happens to Him soon in Jerusalem is not a tragedy as Peter supposed (Mt.16:22,23; Mk.8:32,33) but an accomplishment.

Peter should have been reminded with shame of his attempt to talk Jesus out of the cross a week before. But he was not. He was about to make another stupid suggestion, which if followed, would have by-passed Golgotha and defeated God's eternal purpose. *Cf.* comment on Mt.17:1-5.

Verse 32 - "But Peter and they that were with him were heavy with sleep: and when they were awake, they saw his glory, and the two men that stood with him."

ὁ δὲ Πέτρος καὶ οἱ σὺν αὐτῷ ἦσαν βεβαρημένοι ὕπνῳ. διαγρηγορήσαντες δὲ εἶδον τὴν δόξαν αὐτοῦ καὶ τοὺς δύο ἄνδρες τοὺς συνεστῶτας αὐτῷ.

ὁ (nom.sing.masc.of the article in agreement with Πέτρος) 9.

δὲ (adversative conjunction) 11.

Πέτρος (nom.sing.masc.of Πέτρος, subject of ἦσαν) 387.

καὶ (adjunctive conjunction joining substantives) 14.

οἱ (nom.pl.masc.of the article, subject of ἦσαν) 9.

σὺν (preposition with the instrumental of association) 1542.

αὐτῷ (instru.sing.masc.of αὐτός, association) 16.

ἦσαν (3d.per.pl.imp.ind.of εἰμί, pluperfect periphrastic) 86.

βεβαρημένοι (perf.pass.part.nom.pl.masc.of βαρέομαι, pluperfect periphrastic) 1589.

ὕπνῳ (instru.sing.masc.of ὕπνος, means) 126.

#2327 διαγρηγορήσαντες (aor.act.part.nom.pl.masc.of διαγρηγορέω, pluperfect periphrastic).

be awake - Lk.9:32.

Meaning: A combination of διά (#118) and γρηγορέω (#1520). Hence, to be thoroughly watchful; wide awake; alert. With reference to the disciples who were awakened from sleep on the Mount of Transfiguration - Lk.9:32.

δὲ (adversative conjunction) 11.

εἶδον (3d.per.pl.aor.act.ind.of ὁράω, constative) 144.

τὴν (acc.sing.fem.of the article in agreement with δόξαν) 9.

δόξαν (acc.sing.fem.of δόξα, direct object of εἶδον) 361.

αὐτοῦ (gen.sing.masc.of αὐτός, possession) 16.

καὶ (adjunctive conjunction joining substantives) 14.

τοὺς (acc.pl.masc.of the article in agreement with ἄνδρας) 9.

δύο (numeral) 385.

ἄνδρας (acc.pl.masc.of ἀνήρ, direct object of εἶδον) 63.

τοὺς (acc.pl.masc.of the article in agreement with συνεστῶτας) 9.

#2328 συνεστῶτας (perf.pact.part.acc.pl.masc.of συνίστημι, adjectival, restrictive).

approve - II Cor.6:4; 7:11.
commend - Rom.3:5; 5:8; 16:1; II Cor.3:1; 4:2; 5:12; 10:12,18,18; 12:11.
consist - Col.1:17.
make - Gal.2:18.
stand - II Pet.3:5.
stand with - Lk.9:32.

Meaning: A combination of σύν (#1542) and ἵστημι (#180). Hence, literally to stand or to hang together. To cleave to. Demonstrate physical consistency. With reference to the land masses, in and out of the seas - II Pet.3:5; of all things, physically, logically, philosophically, etc., being consistent - Col.1:17. In Lk.9:32 of three persons standing together in one place. In the sense of demonstrating a consistent way of life: Paul, consistent with the claims of the gospel - II Cor.3:1; 4:2; 5:12; 6:4; 12:11. Of the Corinthian saints - II Cor.7:11; of any act or attitude being consistent - Rom.3:5. Of false teachers who attempt to "sell" themselves, *i.e.* prove themselves to be genuine - II Cor.10:12,18a. Paul says that if he returned to his old unregenerate life style he would be standing consistently with a transgressor - Gal.2:18. Only God can conclusively demonstrate that a preacher is commendable - II Cor.10:18b. Paul recommended Phoebe to the Romans, *i.e.* he built up their confidence in her as a christian - Rom.16:1. Finally God proved His love to us by providing Christ as our sacrificial substitute - Rom.5:8. In all of these passages, the idea of consistency, physical, philosophical or psychological is present.

αὐτῷ (instru.sing.masc.of αὐτός, association) 16.

Translation - "But Peter and the men with him had been overwhelmed by sleep; however when they awakened they saw His glory and the two men who had been standing with Him.

Comment: The Shekinah appeared while Jesus was praying. Moses and Elijah also came at that time and began to talk with Jesus about the Exodus (vss.29-31). We learn now that Peter, James and John had gone to sleep while Jesus was praying and did not witness the beginning of the transfiguration nor hear the conversation about the ἔξοδος. This is clear from the pluperfect periphrastic ἦσαν βεβαρημένοι - "having been overcome with sleep" - a past complete event - "they were still sleeping" - a present condition as its result. But now they were awake and saw the shining light and Moses and Elijah standing beside Jesus. The fact that Peter missed the conversation relieves him of some of the opprobrium attached to his ill advised suggestion about building the three tabernacles, and demands that I soften somewhat my comments about him in Mt.17:4. What Peter said was out of place. What he might have said or whether or not he would have said anything if he had been awake and had heard the converstion between Jesus, Moses and Elijah is conjectural. *Cf.* also comment on Mk.9:5,6.

Verse 33 - "And it came to pass, as they departed from him, Peter said unto Jesus, Master, it is good for us to be here: and let us make three tabernacles; one for thee, and one for Moses, and one for Elias: not knowing what he said."

καὶ ἐγένετο ἐν τῷ διαχωρίζεσθαι αὐτοὺς ἀπ' αὐτοῦ εἶπεν ὁ Πέτρος πρὸς τὸν Ἰησοῦν, Ἐπιστάτα, καλόν ἐστιν ἡμᾶς ὧδε εἶναι, καὶ ποιήσωμεν σκηνὰς τρεῖς, μίαν σοὶ καὶ μίαν Μωϋσεῖ καὶ μίαν Ἡλίᾳ, μὴ εἰδὼς ὃ λέγει.

καὶ (continuative conjunction) 14.

ἐγένετο (3d.per.sing.aor.ind.of γίνομαι, constative) 113.

ἐν (preposition with the locative of time point) 80.

τῷ (loc.sing.neut.of the article, time point, in an articular infinitive) 9.

#2329 διαχωρίζεσθαι (pres.mid.inf.of διαχωρίζομαι, time point).

depart - Lk.9:33.

Meaning: A combination of διά (#118) and χωρίζω (#1291). To depart. Intensified by the prepositional prefix διά. In the middle voice, to take one's leave. With reference to Moses and Elijah - Lk.9:33.

αὐτοὺς (acc.pl.masc.of αὐτός, general reference) 16.

ἀπ' (preposition with the ablative of separation) 70.

αὐτοῦ (abl.sing.masc.of αὐτός, separation) 16.

εἶπεν (3d.per.sing.aor.act.ind.of εἶπον, constative) 155.

ὁ (nom.sing.masc.of the article in agreement with Πέτρος) 9.

Πέτρος (nom.sing.masc.of Πέτρος, subject of εἶπεν) 387.

πρὸς (preposition with the accusative of extent, after a verb of speaking) 197.

τὸν (acc.sing.masc.of the article in agreement with Ἰησοῦν) 9.

Ἰησοῦν (acc.sing.masc.of Ἰησοῦς, extent after a verb of speaking) 3.

Ἐπιστάτα (voc.sing.masc.of ἐπιστάτης, address) 2047.

καλόν (acc.sing.neut.of καλός, predicate accusative adjective) 296.

ἐστιν (3d.per.sing.pres.ind.of εἰμί, aoristic) 86.

ἡμᾶς (acc.pl.masc.of ἐγώ, general reference) 123.

εἶναι (pres.inf.of εἰμί, noun use, subject of ἐστιν) 86.

καὶ (emphatic conjunction) 14.

ποιήσωμεν (1st.per.pl.aor.act.subj.of ποιέω, hortatory) 127.

σκηνὰς (acc.pl.fem.of σκηνή, direct object of ποιήσωμεν) 1224.

τρεῖς (numeral) 1010.

μίαν (acc.sing.fem.of εἷς, in agreement with σκηνή, understood) 469.

σοὶ (dat.sing.masc.of σύ, personal advantage) 104.

καὶ (adjunctive conjunction joining phrases) 14.

μίαν (acc.sing.fem.of εἷς, in agreement with σκηνή, understood) 469.

Μωϋσεῖ (dat.sing. masc.of Μωϋσῆς personal advantage) 715,

καὶ (adjunctive conjunction joining phrases) 14.

μίαν (acc.sing.fem.of εἷς, in agreement with σκηνή, understood) 469.

Ἡλίᾳ (dat.sing.masc.of Ἡλίας, personal advantage) 921.

μὴ (qualified negative conjunction with the participle) 87.

εἰδὼς (pres.part.nom.sing.masc.of οἶδα, adverbial, circumstantial) 144.

δ (nom.sing.neut.of ὅς, subject of λέγει) 65.
λέγει (3d.per.sing.pres.act.ind.of λέγω, historical) 66.

Translation - "And it happened that while they were taking their leave of Him, Peter said to Jesus, 'Master, it is good for us to be here. In fact, let us build three tabernacles - one for you and one for Moses and one for Elijah,' not realizing what he was saying."

Comment: The articular infinitive is in the locative case, indicating time point. As Moses and Elijah were leaving, Peter, who until only a moment before had been asleep, although now thoroughly awake, not knowing what to say, but feeling compelled to say something, made his irrational suggestion. It was indeed good for them to be there. If it had not been, Jesus never would have brought them. But his suggestion, with ποιήσωμεν, the hortatory subjunctive, had at least three fallacies in it: (1) although it was good for them to be there, it was not good for them to remain there. Christians, especially those who enjoy emotional worship, are loath to leave the mountain top experiences and descend the mountain side to face the rough and tumble encounter with the devil's world system. The theological gospel, although basic to Christianity, must produce a practical application of the blessings of the social gospel to others who were not fortunate enough to be with Jesus on the mountain in the moments of His transfiguration. (2) Peter also implied that Jesus, Moses and Elijah were coordinates in the economy of God and ought, therefore, to be treated alike. This is the error of Unitarianism. Many are willing to grant that Jesus was indeed a great teacher and a jealous humanitarian who went about doing good. But so were Moses, Elijah, St. Thomas Aquinas, St. Francis of Assisi, Albert Einstein and a host of others who rated a page in the history books. Moses and Elijah were the first to repudiate the idea and demonstrated their objection to it by hastening to depart. (3) Had Peter's suggestion been followed, Christ would never have gone to Calvary and Peter's remonstrance of a week before would have been successful (Mt.16:22).

Cf.#1224. Note especially those references where σκηνή relate to God's true tabernacle which the saints shall enjoy, *e.g.* Heb.8:2; 9:11; Rev.13:6; 15:5; 21:3; Acts 15:16. If Jesus had permitted Peter to build his tabernacles on Mt. Horeb, God's true tabernacle would never have been built. The destruction of Jesus' bodily tabernacle was necessary if God was ever to possess a tabernacle with men. Note that in John 1:14 the verb ἐσκήνωσεν is used, and *cf.* comment thereon. This glorious consummation of the eternal plan of redemption was what Peter was attempting to forestall, although he did not realize it, just as he had argued against the death of Christ a week before (Mt.16:22 and the parallel passage in Mk.8:32). No doubt, had Moses and Elijah not already been on their way out when Peter spoke, they would speedily have left to prevent the Big Fisherman from carrying out his suggestion.

Verse 34 - "While he thus spoke, there came a cloud and overshadowed them, and they feared as they entered into the cloud."

ταῦτα δὲ αὐτοῦ λέγοντος ἐγένετο νεφέλη καὶ ἐπεσκίαζεν αὐτούς.

ἐφοβήθησαν δὲ ἐν τῷ εἰσελθεῖν αὐτοὺς εἰς τὴν νεφέλην.

ταῦτα (acc.pl.neut.of οὗτος, direct object of λέγοντος) 93.
δὲ (adversative conjunction) 11.
αὐτοῦ (gen.sing.masc.of αὐτός, genitive absolute) 16.
λέγοντος (pres.act.part.gen.sing.masc.of λέγω, genitive absolute) 66.
ἐγένετο (3d.per.sing.aor.ind.of γίνομαι, constative) 113.
νεφέλη (nom.sing.fem.of νεφέλη, subject of ἐγένετο) 1225.
καὶ (adjunctive conjunction joining verbs) 14.
ἐπεσκίαζεν (3d.per.sing.imp.act.ind.of ἐπεσκιάζω, inceptive) 1226.
αὐτούς (acc.pl.masc.of αὐτός, direct object of ἐπεσκίαζεν) 16.
ἐφοβήθησαν (3d.per.pl.aor.mid.ind.of φοβέομαι, ingressive) 101.
δὲ (continuative conjunction) 11.
ἐν (preposition with the locative of time point) 80.
τῷ (loc.sing.neut.of the article in agreement with εἰσελθεῖν) 9.
εἰσελθεῖν (aor.inf.of εἰσέρχομαι, time point, articular infinitive) 234.
αὐτοὺς (acc.pl.masc.of αὐτός, general reference) 16.
εἰς (preposition with the accusative of extent) 140.
τὴν (acc.sing.fem.of the article in agreement with νεφέλην) 9.
νεφέλην (acc.sing.fem.of νεφέλη, extent) 1225.

Translation - "*But as he was saying these things a cloud gathered and began to overshadow them. And they were seized with fear as they entered into the cloud.*"

Comment: The intensity of adversity in the first δὲ comes not from the word itself, but from the context. Peter's suggestion was so outrageous that God moved quickly to silence him. As though to bring him to silence, the overwhelming cloud appeared while he was speaking. This is the force of the genitive absolute ταῦτα . . αὐτοῦ λέγοντος, in the present tense, denoting contemporaneity of its action with that of the main verbs ἐγένετο and ἐπεσκίαζεν. The appearance of the cloud interrupted Peter. Otherwise he might have preached forty minutes and given an invitation!

It is interesting that #1226 reveals that Peter's own shadow later fell upon the sick to heal them (Acts 5:15).

As they entered into the cloud they were *seized with fear* (ingressive aorist in ἐφοβήθησαν). *Cf.* John 11:35 - "Jesus burst into tears." The time of action in the verbs involved is important. As Moses and Elijah withdrew Peter began to speak (vs.33); while he was speaking the cloud appeared (vs.34). Thus the exit of Moses and Elijah, Peter's remark and the appearance of the cloud were all simultaneous events. One more event took place at the same time as we see in

Verse 35 - "*And there came a voice out of the cloud, saying, This is my beloved Son: hear Him.*"

καὶ φωνὴ ἐγένετο ἐκ τῆς νεφέλης λέγουσα, Οὗτός ἐστιν ὁ υἱός μου ὁ ἐκλελεγμένος, αὐτοῦ ἀκούετε.

καί (continuative conjunction) 14.

φωνή (nom.sing.fem.of φωνή, subject of ἐγένετο) 222.

ἐγένετο (3d.per.sing.aor.ind.of γίνομαι, constative) 113.

ἐκ (preposition with the ablative of source) 19.

τῆς (abl.sing.fem.of the article in agreement with νεφέλης) 9.

νεφέλης (abl.sing.fem.of νεφέλη, source) 1225.

λέγουσα (pres.act.part.nom.sing.fem.of λέγω, adverbial, recitative) 66.

Οὗτός (nom.sing.masc.of οὗτος, predicate nominative) 93.

ἐστιν (3d.per.sing.pres.ind.of εἰμί, aoristic) 86.

ὁ (nom.sing.masc.of the article in agreement with υἱός) 9.

υἱός (nom.sing.masc.of υἱός, subject of ἐστιν) 5.

μου (gen.sing.masc.of ἐγώ, relationship) 123.

ὁ (nom.sing.masc.of the article in agreement with ἐκλελεγμένος) 9.

ἐκλελεγμένος (perf.pass.part.nom.sing.masc.of ἐκλέγω, adjectival, restrictive) 2119.

αὐτοῦ (gen.sing.masc.of αὐτός, designation) 16.

ἀκούετε (2d.per.pl.pres.act.impv.of ἀκούω, command) 148.

Translation - "And a voice spoke from the cloud, saying, 'This man is my Son, the Chosen One. Listen to no one but Him.'"

Comment: We have emphatic Οὗτός at the beginning of the heavenly statement, and exclusive αὐτοῦ at the end. Οὗτός is the predicate nominative, since it is without the article and ὁ υἱός μου is the subject of ἐστιν. But Οὗτος, which is the predicate nominative outranks the subject in position. Hence the emphasis. "*THIS MAN* is my Son, *the ONLY ONE CHOSEN*, hear *HIM.*" There is also emphasis in the middle of the statement. The participle ἐκλελεγμένος is an adjective and it is restrictive. It can apply only to Οὗτος. Note also that the participle, being in the perfect tense, speaks of a finished decision in the past, which results in a present and ever prevailing status. Having, in eternity past, been elected to the position, Jesus forever in the present and future enjoys His status as the Son of God. Of course the grammar seeks to accommodate divine thinking to human perception. With God there is no past, present or future. These are only temporal modes with which we poor mortals try to communicate. Remember that the genitive with verbs means "this and only this." Thus the exclusivity of αὐτοῦ. It is as though God was warning James and John not to pay any attention to what Peter might yet say.

Note the force of the divine rebuke to Peter. The disappearance of Moses and Elijah, the overshadowing cloud, the voice of God from it, the emotional impact upon the disciples and the emphatic statement of the preeminence of Jesus Christ, in Greek grammar and syntax as strong as its structure will permit. Poor Simon Peter! But we shall see that he finally learned to respect this Almighty and Altogether Lovely Jesus! The tribute of the Father to His Son is magnificant. *Cf.*#2119. Whom and what else has God chosen? Note James 2:5 and I Cor.1:27,27,28 especially. What God calls good and what the world calls good is quite opposite. Christ on a Roman cross - His ἔξοδος - the shame, agony, disgrace and apparent defeat! But Golgotha was the scene of God's mightiest victory, around which all of human history moves.

Verse 36 - "And when the voice was past, Jesus was found alone. And they kept it close and told no man in those days any of these things which they had seen."

καὶ ἐν τῷ γενέσθαι τὴν φωνὴν εὑρέθη Ἰησοῦς μόνος. καὶ αὐτοὶ ἐσίγησαν καὶ οὐδενὶ ἀπήγγειλαν ἐν ἐκείναις ταῖς ἡμέραις οὐδὲν ὧν ἑώρακαν.

καὶ (continuative conjunction) 14.
ἐν (preposition with the locative of time point) 80.
τῷ (loc.sing.neut.of the article in an articular infinitive, time point) 9.
γενέσθαι (aor.inf.of γίνομαι, temporal articular infinitive) 113.
τὴν (acc.sing.fem.of the article in agreement with φωνήν) 9.
φωνὴν (acc.sing.fem.of φωνή, general reference) 222.
εὑρέθη (3d.per.sing.aor.pass.ind.of εὑρίσκω constative) 79.
Ἰησοῦς (nom.sing.masc.of Ἰησοῦς, subject of εὑρέθη) 3.
μόνος (nom.sing.masc.of μόνος, predicate adjective) 339.
καὶ (adversative conjunction) 14.
αὐτοὶ (nom.pl.masc.of αὐτός, subject of ἐσίγησαν) 16.

#2330 ἐσίγησαν (3d.per.pl.aor.act.ind.of σιγάω, constative).

hold one's peace - Lk.18:39; 20:26; Acts 12:17; 15:13; I Cor.14:30.
keep close - Lk.9:36.
keep secret - Rom.16:25.
keep silence - Acts 15:12; I Cor.14:28,34.

Meaning: To remain silent. To say nothing. With reference to those in controversy who have nothing to say in rebuttal - Lk.20:26; to cease speaking - Acts 12:17; 15:13. Of a multitude that becomes silent - Acts 15:12; In the imperative mode, an order to one with the gift of tongues or of prophecy to refrain - I Cor.14:28 (tongues); 14:30 (prophecy). With reference to women in the church assembly - I Cor.14:34. In the passive voice of God's mysteries which have been kept secret - Rom.16:25. Of Peter, James and John who said nothing about the transfiguration - Lk.9:36. Of the blind man at Jericho - Lk.18:39.

καὶ (emphatic conjunction) 14.
οὐδενὶ (dat.sing.masc.of οὐδείς, indirect object of ἀπήγγειλαν) 446.
ἀπήγγειλαν (3d.per.pl.aor.act.ind.of ἀπαγγέλλω, constative) 176.
ἐν (preposition with the locative of time point) 80.
ἐκείναις (loc.pl.fem.of ἐκεῖνος, in agreement with ἡμέραις) 246.
ἡμέραις (loc.pl.fem.of ἡμέρα, time point) 135.
οὐδὲν (acc.sing.neut.of οὐδείς, direct object of ἀπήγγειλαν) 446.
ὧν (gen.pl.neut.of ὅς, partitive genitive) 65.
ἑώρακαν (3d.per.pl.perf.act.ind.of ὁράω, consummative) 144.

Translation - "And when the voice ceased, Jesus was found alone. And these remained silent. In fact in those days they did not tell to a single person one part of that which they had experienced."

Comment: Here we have the articular infinitive in the aorist tense in a temporal clause. The voice from the cloud fell silent, but not until the disciples, cowering in abject fear, had understood clearly what the Lord had said. And when they looked about they found Jesus standing there alone with them. Moses was gone, because ". . . the law made nothing perfect, but the bringing in of a better hope did, by which we draw night to God" (Heb.7:19). And the God Who brought the hope that was better than that which legalism could inspire, by Whose sacrifice we can draw nigh to the Father, stood before them. Elijah was also gone, because when the Fulfillment is present the prophecy that predicts Him is no longer needed.

Mt.17:9 and Mk.9:9 reveal that the disciples were under orders not to tell about it. Accordingly they were not talking about it. Luke's statement is strong. "They became silent and said not one thing in those days to not one person about any of that which they had seen." Note the perfect tense in ἑώρακαν. It was a real experience in the past. Now it was complete. But the present benefit would remain theirs into eternity. Never could Peter, James and John forget it.

After the resurrection of our Lord the story was no longer off the record and we may be sure that the three disciples told the story many times. Peter included it in his second epistle (II Pet.1:16-18).

With this we close the book on Volume 5 of *The Renaissance new Testament*. Volume 6 will find us following Jesus, Peter, James and John down the slopes of Mount Horeb on His last earthly journey to the city which He loved and where its citizens would put Him to death.

According to His prophecy (Mt.23:37-38; 24:1-2) Titus and his Roman soldiers squared the divine accounts with a vengeance that was not spent as long as one stone remained fastened to another. Today the city is in the eye of the hurricane of international tension that will bring Antichrist to the world stage to play out his little part.

Then He shall come again. Not on a jackass, nor bearing a cross, but with His holy angels, surrounded by the same glory that shone about the high peaks of Horeb two thousand years ago. And when He comes Plato's dream will be realized. A Philosopher will be King. *"And it shall come to pass in the last days that the mountain of the Lord's house shall be established in the top of the mountains, and shall be exalted above the hills, and all nations shall flow unto it. And many people shall go and say, Come ye, and let us go up to the mountain of the Lord, to the house of the God of Jacob; and he will teach us of his ways, and we will walk in his paths: for out of Zion shall go forth the law, and the word of the Lord from Jerusalem. And he shall judge among the nations, and shall rebuke many people: and they shall beat their swords into plowshares, and their spears into pruninghooks: national shall not lift up sword against nation, neither shall they learn war any more. O house of Jacob, come ye, and let us walk in the light of the Lord"* (Isaiah 2:2-5; Micah 4:1-3).

Then, when we have united notions we shall have a viable United Nations.

INDEX

END OF VOLUME FOUR

INDEX TO VOLUME FIVE

END OF VOLUME FIVE